Presented to

The Official Guide to American Historic Inns

Rated "Outstanding" by Morgan Rand.

Winner of Benjamin Franklin Award - Best Travel Guide
Winner of Travel Publishing News - Best Travel Reference
Winner of Benjamin Franklin Award - Best Directory

Comments from print media:

" ... helps you find the very best hideaways (many of the book's listings appear in the National Register of Historic Places.)" **Country Living.**

"I love your book!" Lydia Moss, Travel Editor, **McCall's.**

"Delightful, succinct, detailed and well-organized. Easy to follow style ... " Don Wudke, **Los Angeles Times.**

"This is one of the best guidebooks of its kind. It's easy to use, accurate and the thumbnail sketches give the readers enough description to choose among the more than 1,000 properties detailed and thousands others listed." **Dallas Morning News.**

" ... thoughtfully organized and look-ups are hassle-free ... well-researched and accurate ... put together by people who know the field. There is no other publication available that covers this particular segment of the bed & breakfast industry — a segment that has been gaining popularity among travelers by leaps and bounds. The information included is valuable and well thought out." **Morgan Directory Reviews.**

"Readers will find this book easy to use and handy to have. The Sakachs have conveyed their love of historic inns and have shared that feeling and information in an attractive and inviting guide. An excellent, well-organized and comprehensive reference for inngoers and innkeepers alike." **Inn Review**, Kankakee, Illinois.

"This guide has become the favorite choice of travelers and specializes only in professionally operated inns and B&Bs rather than homestays (lodging in spare bedrooms)." **Laguna Magazine.**

"This is the best bed and breakfast book out. It outshines them all!" Maggie Balitas, **Rodale Book Clubs.**

"Most of us military families have lived all over the world, so it takes an unusual book, service or trip to excite us! As I began to look through ***The Official Guide to American Historic Inns*** *by Tim and Deborah Sakach, my heart beat faster as I envisioned what a good time our readers could have visiting some of these very special historic bed and breakfast properties."* Ann Crawford, **Military Living.**

Comments from radio:

"Absolutely beautiful!" KQIL talk show radio.

"This is a great book. It makes you want to card everything." KBRT Los Angeles radio talk show.

"All our lines were tied up! We received calls from every one of our 40 stations." Business Radio Network, regarding talk show about **The Official Guide to American Historic Inns.**

Comments from innkeepers:

"Your book is wonderful. I have been reading it as one does a novel." Olallieberry Inn, Cambria, California.

"Congratulation! You did it again. Another superb B&B publication!" Host Homes, Boston, Mass.

"We've just received the new edition of ***The Official Guide to American Historic Inns.*** *Congratulations on this magnificent book. You've done it again!"* Gilbert House, Charlestown, West Virginia.

"I appreciate the wonderful clientele your book brought me in California and hope that you will consider including me in your next publication." Inn of the Animal Tracks, Santa Fe, New Mexico.

"As per your request I'm sending you copies of newspaper articles. We hope these are sufficient to again be included in your marvelous book. We appreciate the care and thoughtfulness that have gone into each edition and are looking forward to being included in the Third Edition." California innkeeper.

"We want to tell you how much we love your book. We have it out for guests to use. They love it; each featured inn stands out so well. Thank you for the privilege of being in your book." Fairhaven Inn, Bath, Maine.

"What a wonderful book! We love it and have been very pleased with the guests who have made reservations using your book." Vermont innkeeper.

"You're doing a great job in helping our small, country inn business compete with the chains for the attention of the traveling public. Please keep it up." Inn at Long Trail, Killington, Vermont.

"We have had fantastic response. Thanks!" Liberty Rose Colonial B&B, Williamsburg, Virginia.

"We love your guidebook. It has brought us more reservations than any of the others." The Shield House, Clinton, North Carolina.

"American Historic Inns is wonderful! We are proud and delighted to be included. Thank you for creating such a special guidebook." The Heirloom, Ione, California.

"Your new edition of ***The Official Guide to American Historic Inns*** *has maintained the fine quality of previous editions and we are very pleased to be included."* The Victoriana 1898, Traverse City, Michigan.

"Thanks so much for all your hard work. We receive the largest number of guidebook referrals from ***The Official Guide to American Historic Inns."*** Saddle Rock Ranch, Sedona, Arizona.

"Your book brings the most response of any book listing we have, except the telephone yellow pages. Thank you for your fine publication." The Pollyanna, Oneida, New York.

"Your book has been invaluable to us." Ellis River House, Jackson, New Hampshire.

"Your guide has high praises from guests who use it." The Inn on South Street, Kennebunkport, Maine.

"Thank you for all the time and work you put into this guidebook. We have had many guests find our inn because of you." Kaleidoscope Inn, Nipomo, California.

"We are thrilled with your book. We appreciate your incredible traveling spirit captured in these pages!" Thorwood, Hastings, Minn.

"This is a wonderful book. We love it!" Rich Obermeyer, Vice President, Wisconsin B&B Homes and Historic Inns Association, Historic Bennett House, Wisconsin Dells, Wis.

Recommended by:

McCall's, Changing Times, Women's Day, USA Today, Library Journal, Publishers Weekly, Book-of-the-Month Club News, Los Angeles Times

BED & BREAKFASTS AND COUNTRY INNS

The Official Guide to American Historic Inns

Bed & Breakfasts and Country Inns

The Official Guide to American Historic Inns

by Tim & Deborah Sakach

Published by
American Historic Inns, Inc.
Association of American Historic Inns
Dana Point, California

Published by
American Historic Inns, Inc.
PO Box 336
Dana Point, California 92629

Every effort has been made to produce a dependable reference based on information gathered from innkeepers and from the authors' personal observations. We recommend that you contact each inn and B&B to verify information herein prior to making reservations. Information included in this publication has been checked for accuracy prior to publication. Since changes do occur, the publishers cannot be responsible for any variations from the information printed.

Front cover: Rhett House Inn, Beaufort, SC.
Front and back photos by Tim Sakach. Maine Stay Inn photo provided by innkeeper.

Editorial assistants: Lynette Weigand, Tiffany Crosswy and Carol Ziehm.
Database manager: Sandy Imre.
Public relations: Kris Windes.
Some of the drawings in this book were done by artist Claire Read of San Juan Capistrano, California.

Publisher's Cataloging in Publication Data
Sakach, Timothy J. & Deborah Edwards

American Historic Inns, Inc.
Association of American Historic Inns
Bed & Breakfasts and Country Inns
The Official Guide to American Historic Inns
1. Bed & Breakfast Accommodations — United States, Directories, Guide Books.
2. Travel Directories, Guide Books.
3. Bed & Breakfast Accommodations — Directories, Guide Books.
4. Hotel Accommodations — Bed & Breakfast Inns, Directories, Guide Books.
5. Hotel Accommodations — United States, Inns, Directories, Guide Books.
I Title. II Author. III Bed & Breakfast, Bed & Breakfasts and Country Inns / The Official Guide to American Historic Inns

ISBN: 0-9615481-4-2
Softcover
Library of Congress: ISSN 1043-1195, 87-71501
647'.947

Printed in the United States of America

Contents

HOW TO USE THIS BOOK

You hold in your hands the most comprehensive collection of America's best Bed & Breakfasts and Country Inns. Only historic Country Inns and historic B&B inns are included here. Most were built in the 17th, 18th and 19th centuries. There are also many from the early 20th century. We use the US Park Service (National Register of Historic Places) limit for historic buildings — must have been constructed prior to 1940.

When you stay in a historic inn, not only are you taking delight in a pleasant getaway, you are promoting and supporting the preservation of America's architectural and cultural heritage. The majority of these homes are privately owned and have been restored with the private funds of individual families. They are maintained and improved by revenues collected from B&B guests.

With few exceptions, we omitted homestays (B&Bs with only one or two rooms operated casually or as a hobby.) However, most of these can be reached through the reservation services listed in the appendix of this book.

MAP COORDINATES

Each town or city in the main body of the book has two map coordinates which mark the location of that city or town on **Rand McNally** state road maps.

The first coordinate goes with **Rand McNally** products using large maps. The second coordinate goes with the compact maps.

CITY	Large Map/*Compact map*
CLEVELAND	NG19/*C5*

Note: Some very small towns may not appear on your map. If so, the coordinates will point you to the general vicinity.

Rand McNally products using the **large** maps (first coordinate):

- **Road Atlas**
- **Road Atlas and Vacation Guide**
- **Business Travelers Road Atlas**
- **Motor Carriers Road Atlas**

Rand McNally products using the **compact** maps (second coordinate):

- **The Best Bed & Breakfast and Country Inns - West
South
Northeast
Midwest (all four by Tim & Deborah Sakach).**
- **Compact Road Atlas**
- **Deluxe Road Atlas and Travel Guide**
- **Interstate Road Atlas**
- **Road Atlas and Trip Planner**

These books are available from your local book store or from other stores where **Rand McNally** products are sold.

CROSS REFERENCE CITIES

Some inns desired to be listed under a nearby city or town. This is helpful to travelers who may not be familiar with the proximity of a lesser-known town. Most cross-referenced cities are located within a 30-minute drive of the better known city.

CODES

We have kept the use of codes to a minimum and have used them only to refer to those things with which we are all very familiar:

CREDIT CARDS

MC: MasterCard
VISA
DC: Diner's Club
CB: Carte Blanche
AX: American Express
DS: Discover

MEALS

Continental breakfast: coffee, juice, toast or pastry.

Continental-plus breakfast: A continental breakfast plus a variety of breads cheeses and fruit.

Full breakfast: coffee, juice, breads, fruit and an entree.

B&B: A full or continental breakfast included in the price of the room. (Some inns serve a continental breakfast during the week and a full breakfast on the weekend while others serve a full breakfast off season and a continental breakfast during the summer or vice versa.)

AP: American Plan. All three meals are included in the price of the room. Check to see if the rate quoted is for two people or per person.

MAP: Modified American Plan. Breakfast and dinner are included in the price of the room.

EP: European Plan. No meals are included. We have included only a few historic hotels that operate on an EP plan.

RATES

Unless indicated with a "pp" (per person), all rates are quoted double occupancy — for two people. Those marked with "❀" have made special offers to the readers of this book that may be found in the discount certificate section of the appendix.

This symbol "✻" identifies inns that can be booked through a reservation service or travel agent. If your travel agent is unfamiliar with the inn, show him or her a copy of *The Official Guide to American Historic Inns.*

All rates are listed as ranges. The range covers both off-season low rates and busy season high rates. When making reservations you should verify rates. Although rates were accurate at the time the book was compiled, they are always subject to change.

SMOKING

The majority of Country Inns and B&Bs in historic buildings prohibit smoking; therefore, if you are a smoker we advise you to call and specifically check with each inn to see if and how they accommodate smokers.

"SEEN IN:"

We required that each inn provide copies of magazine or newspaper articles written by travel writers about their establishments. If they were featured on radio or TV shows we have also indicated that in the listing. Only a few exceptions were made. (If an inn has opened recently or is in a remote area, it may not have attracted press attention.) Articles written about the inns may be available either from the source as a reprint or through libraries or from the inn itself.

COMMENTS FROM INN GUESTS

Over the years, we have collected reams of guest comments about our favorite inns. Our files are jammed with thousands of documented comments. At the end of each inn description, we include a guest comment received about that inn.

Travelers have been talking about their accommodations for centuries. The oldest guest comment in this book was by a French duke, who stayed at Woodstock Hall Tavern in Charlottesville, Virginia. He wrote, *"Mr Woods' Inn is so good and cleanly ... I cannot forbear mentioning those circumstances with pleasure."*

"INNSPECTIONS"

This book contains more than 1,400 major listings of historic inns plus a comprehensive directory of more than 6,000 historic B&Bs and inns. Each year we travel across the country visiting hundreds of inns. Since 1981 we have had a happy informal team of inn travelers who report to us about new bed and breakfast discoveries and repeat visits to favorite inns.

However, inspecting inns is not the major focus of our travels. We visit as many as possible, photograph them and get acquainted with innkeepers. Some inns are grand mansions filled with classic museum-quality antiques. Others are rustic, such as a reassembled log cabin. We have enjoyed them all and cherish our memories of each establishment — pristine or rustic. Only rarely have we come across a "bad" inn — poorly kept or poorly managed. These usually do not survive because an inn's success depends upon repeat business and word of mouth referrals from satisfied guests.

Travel is an adventure into the unknown, full of surprises and rewards. A seasoned traveler learns that even after elaborate preparations and careful planning, travel provides the new and unexpected. The traveler learns to live with uncertainty and considers it part of the adventure.

To the tourist, whether accidental or otherwise, new experiences are disconcerting. Tourists want no surprises. They expect things to be exactly as they had envisioned them. To tourists we recommend staying in a hotel or motel chain where the same formula is followed from one locale to another.

Experienced inn goers are travelers at heart. They relish the differences in America's intimate historic inns. This is the magic that makes traveling from inn to inn the delightful experience it is.

HOW TO NOMINATE YOUR FAVORITE INN

We've always enjoyed hearing from our readers and have carefully cataloged all letters and recommendations.

If you wish to participate in evaluating your inn experiences, use the Inn Evaluation Form in the back of this book. You might want to make copies of this form prior to departing on your journey. The authors read each evaluation form.

MINIMUM STAY REQUIREMENTS.

When traveling during peak seasons, expect two-night minimum stay requirements, particularly on weekends.

ADVANCE RESERVATIONS REQUIRED

On weekends and in resort areas during peak seasons, it is not unusual for popular inns to have all rooms reserved 12 or more weeks in advance. We recommend reservations be made well in advance of such periods.

WHAT TO DO IF THE INN YOU CALL IS FULL

Ask the innkeeper for recommendations. They may know of an inn that has recently opened or one nearby but off the beaten path.

Call a reservation service for that area. See Reservation Services in the appendix.

Call the local Chamber of Commerce in the town you hope to visit. They may know of inns that have recently opened.

Call or write to the state tourism bureau. See the State Tourism Information section.

ALABAMA

ANNISTON G12/C4

The Noble McCaa Butler House

1025 Fairmont
Anniston AL 36201
(205) 236-1791

Circa 1887. This was once the home of the Nobles, Anniston's founding family. In the National Register, the three-story red and white Victorian boasts a

graceful veranda and gazebo overlooking the front garden with its Victorian plants and flowers. The Victorian-Revival decor includes authentic period antiques, English reproduction papers and Persian carpets. A full southern breakfast is served.

Rates: $85-$145. C. Robert & Prudence Johnson.
6 R. 3 PB. Phone available. TV in room. Beds: QDT. Full breakfast. FAX. CCs: MC VISA AE CB.
Seen in: *NBC, CBS, Birmingham News.*

"We're spoiled for life. No other place compares! Excellent hosts, superb breakfast!"

FAIRHOPE U4/H1

Mershon Court

203 Fairhope Ave
Fairhope AL 36532
(205) 928-7398

Circa 1900. This happy blue Victorian house is trimmed in white with pink blossoms hugging the white picket fence. Dolly Parton has stayed at the inn. (Susie was Dolly's secretary for a decade.) Linger awhile on the porch swing and enjoy the scents of honeysuckle mingled with the salt air. Mobile Bay is within two blocks.

Rates: $45-$69. Susie Glickman.
4 R. 2 PB. Phone available. TV available. Beds: DT. Swimming pool. CCs: MC VISA. Fishing, golf.
Seen in: *Los Angeles Times, Southern Living, New Orleans Times, Memphis Magazine.*

"Thanks again for being a superb hostess."

MENTONE C12/A4

Mentone Inn

Highway 117, PO Box 284
Mentone AL 35984
(205) 634-4836

Circa 1927. Mentone is a refreshing stop for those looking for the cool breezes and natural air-conditioning of the mountains. Here antique treasures mingle with modern-day conveniences. A sun deck and spa complete the experience. Sequoyah Caverns, Little River Canyon and DeSoto Falls are moments away. The inn has its own hiking trails.

Location: On Lookout Mountain in northeast Alabama.
*Rates: $35-$70. Season: April - November 1. Amelia Kirk.
12 R. 12 PB. Phone available. TV available. Beds: QDT. Full breakfast. Conference room. Wedding receptions, lunches and dinners are available with prior arrangements.
Seen in: *Birmingham News.*

MOBILE T3/H1

Vincent-Doan Home

1664 Springhill Ave
Mobile AL 36604
(205) 433-7121

Circa 1827. This is not only the oldest house in Mobile but also the last remaining example of French Creole architecture. The house has been restored and retains its original roof line, galleries and facade. Each bedroom has a fireplace and provides direct access to the gallery overlooking the garden.

Rates: $50-$70. Betty Doan.
3 R. 3 PB. Phone in room. TV in room. Beds: DT. Full breakfast. CCs: MC VISA.
Seen in: *Mobile Press Register.*

"Your breakfast is better than Brennans in New Orleans!"

ALASKA

FAIRBANKS E6/*B3*

Alaska's 7 Gables

4312 Birch Ln, PO Box 80488
Fairbanks AK 99708
(907) 479-0751

This Tudor-style inn features stained glass throughout the house. Located near the river, guests may have use of a canoe for a 50-minute trip to the best restaurant in town. There is a flower-filled solarium and a spa. Bicycles may be borrowed for cycling to and from the university nearby. The innkeepers received the Fairbanks Golden Heart Award for their excellent hospitality.

Rates: $35-$55. Paul & Leicha Welton.
9 R. 4 PB. Phone in room. TV in room. Beds: QDT. Full breakfast. CCs: MC VISA. Swimming, hiking, fishing, dog mushing, skiing. View the Northern Lights.
Seen in: *Fairbanks Daily News-Miner, Anchorage Times.*

"Beautiful home and the most hospitable of hosts."

GUSTAVUS H10/*C5*

Gustavus Inn

PO Box 31
Gustavus AK 99826
(907) 697-3311

Circa 1928. This New England-style country inn was first established by the owner's grandmother. The innkeepers offer expert guidance to help

their guests experience the best of Glacier Bay National Park. Included in the rate is transportation to the inn and to Bartlett Cove in the park, fishing poles, bikes and an afternoon guided nature walk. Homemade sourdough pancakes and rhubarb sauce are house specialties. Direct flights are available from Seattle.

Rates: $160. David & JoAnn Lesh.
14 R. 7 PB. Beds: QD. Full breakfast. Restaurant. FAX. CCs: MC VISA AE. Fishing charters, sightseeing boat tours.
Seen in: *New York Times, Self, Travel-Holiday.*

HOMER H5/*C3*

Driftwood Inn

135-T W Bunnell Ave
Homer AK 99603
(907) 235-8019

Circa 1920. Clean, comfortable and unpretentious, the Driftwood Inn is in a historic building on the shores of Kachemak Bay. The inn caters to families and sportsmen and all-you-can-eat breakfasts are a special feature. There are spectacular mountain and water views.

Location: On the beach with views of mountains, glaciers and the bay.
Rates: $45-$75. Shonie Cordes.
8 R. 7 PB. Phone available. TV available. Full breakfast. Sauna. Moose watching, wildflower photography.

ARIZONA

AJO N5/F3

The Mine Manager's House

One Greenway Dr, PO Box 486
Ajo AZ 85321
(602) 387-6505

Circa 1919. Overlooking the southwestern Arizona desert and a mile-wide copper mine pit, the Mine Manager's is a large Craftsman home situated on three acres. Built by the local copper mining industry, it has 10-inch thick walls. There is a library, coin laundry and gift shop on the premises. The Greenway Suite features a marble tub and shower and two other suites boast two queen size beds each. A full breakfast is served in the formal dining room.

Rates: $59-$99. Martin & Faith Jeffries.
5 R. 5 PB. Phone available. TV available. Beds: Q. Full breakfast. Handicap access. CCs: MC VISA.
Seen in: *Arizona Daily Star, Tucson Citizen, The Catalina-Oracle, Arizona Sun.*

"The hospitality is what makes this place so inviting!"

BISBEE P11/G5

Park Place B&B

200 E Vista
Bisbee AZ 85603
(602) 432-5516 (602)990-0682

Circa 1919. Grant McGregor was a civil engineer and designed mines and mills throughout the world. One of Bisbee's pioneer homes, the McGregor house incorporates several styles including Spanish-Mediterranean, Greek Revival and Italian Villa. Graceful old sycamores and evergreens provide shady spaces, while peach, fig, pomegranate, and plum trees add seasonal splashes of color. Owners of a local bakery and a restaurant, Innkeepers Bob & Janet Watkins, serve a full breakfast on the terrace, or in the library.

*Rates: $50-$70. Bob & Janet Watkins.
4 R. 2 PB. 2 FP. Phone available. TV available. Beds: QDT. B&B. Conference room. CCs: MC VISA. Tennis, golf, underground mine tour.

FLAGSTAFF G7/C4

Birch Tree Inn

824 W Birch Ave
Flagstaff AZ 86001
(602) 774-1042 (602) 774-8156

Circa 1917. This bungalow is surrounded by a wraparound veranda supported with Corinthian columns. Southwestern and antique decor is

featured including shaker pine and white wicker. Nature lovers and ski enthusiasts will appreciate the Ponderosa Pine Forest nearby. Adjacent to the inn, cross-country ski trails are especially popular. In summer an afternoon tea is served.

Rates: $60-$75. Donna & Rodger Pettinger, Sandy & Ed Znetko.
5 R. 3 PB. Phone available. TV available. Beds: KQT. Full breakfast. Game room. CCs: MC VISA. Horseback riding, cross-country & downhill skiing, telescope viewing.
Seen in: *Phoenix Gazette.*

"Charming hosts and wonderful food."

Comfi Cottages

1612 N Aztec
Flagstaff AZ 86001
(602) 779-2236 (602) 779-1008

Circa 1920. Located in the heart of historic downtown Flagstaff, these three cottages are freshly decorated and simply furnished with antiques and southwestern pieces. Each two-bedroom unit sleeps six people and features polished wood floors, a wood stove and a washer and dryer. The kitchens are stocked with cooking utensils and breakfast foods. Fenced yards afford the convenience of picnic tables, lawn chairs and a barbeque grill. Guests may borrow bicycles to explore historic Flagstaff.

*Rates: $80-$100. Pat & Ed Wiebe.
5 R. 1 PB. Phone in room. TV in room. Beds: QTC. Full breakfast. CCs: MC VISA. Tennis, downhill & cross-country skiing.

"Beautiful and relaxing. A port in the storm."

PHOENIX K6/E3

Maricopa Manor

15 W Pasadena Ave
Phoenix AZ 85013
(602) 274-6302 (602) 266-3904

Circa 1928. The secluded Maricopa Manor stands amid palm trees on an acre of land. The Spanish-styled house features four graceful columns in the entry hall, an elegant living room with a marble mantel and a music room with a grand piano and an Irish harp. The spacious suites are decorated with satins, lace, antiques and leather-bound books. Guests may relax on the deck, on the patio or in the gazebo spa.

Rates: $69-$99. Season: Sept. - May. Mary Ellen & Paul Kelley.
5 R. 5 PB. 2 FP. Phone in room. TV in room. Beds: KQDT. Continental-plus breakfast. Spa. Game room. Conference room. FAX. Golf, tennis, horseback riding, hiking.
Seen in: *Arizona Business Journal.*

"I've stayed 200+ nights at B&Bs around the world, yet have never before experienced the warmth and sincere friendliness of Maricopa Manor.

Westways "Private" Resort Inn

PO Box 41624
Phoenix AZ 85080
(602) 582-3868

Circa 1939. The contemporary tone of this Spanish Mediterranean house

refects the South. The inn is on an acre landscaped with plants from the various regions of Arizona. There are palm, grapefruit and orange trees,

mountain pines and desert cactus. The focal point of the courtyard is a tranquil Mexican fountain. A gratuity is charged.
Location: Northwest Phoenix, adjacent to Arrowhead Country Club.
*❀Rates: $49-$102. Darrell Trapp & Brian Curran.
7 R. 6 PB. Phone in room. TV in room. Beds: QD. B&B. Spa. Handicap access. Swimming pool. Conference room. CCs: MC VISA AE.
Seen in: *Los Angeles Times, TravelAge West, The Arizona Republic.*
"Personalized service made our stay memorable."

PRESCOTT I5/D3

Marks House Inn
203 E Union
Prescott AZ 86303
(602) 778-4632
Circa 1894. In the 1890s four prominent residences dominated Nob Hill. One of them was the Marks

house. Built by Jake Marks, cattle rancher and mine owner it's now in the National Historic Register. This Victorian mansion provides a special setting in which to enjoy rare antiques, gracious breakfasts, and majestic sunsets. Fireplaces are in the living and dining rooms.
Location: Ninety miles north of Phoenix. One block from Courthouse Square.
*Rates: $75-$110. Anita & Kristin Fetterly.
4 R. 4 PB. Phone available. Beds: KQD. B&B. Conference room. CCs: MC VISA. Hiking, art fairs, antiquing. May Territorial Days. World's oldest rodeo, July.
Seen in: *Member of B&B in Arizona.*
"Exceptional!"

Prescott Pines Inn
901 White Spar Rd
Prescott AZ 86303
(602) 445-7270 (800)541-5374 US only
Circa 1902. A white picket fence beckons guests to the veranda of this comfortably elegant country Victorian inn, originally the Haymore Dairy. There are masses of fragrant pink roses, lavender and delphiniums, and stately ponderosa pines tower above the inn's four renovated cottages, which were once shelter for farmhands. The acre of grounds in-

cludes a garden fountain and romantic tree swing.
Location: One-and-a-third miles south of Courthouse Plaza.
❀Rates: $44-$69-$145. Jean Wu and Michael Acton.
13 R. 13 PB. 4 FP. Phone in room. TV in room. Beds: KQC. Full breakfast. Gourmet meals. Conference room. CCs: MC VISA. Horseback riding, hiking, golf, tennis.
Seen in: *Sunset Magazine*
"The ONLY place to stay in Prescott! Tremendous attention to detail."

SEDONA H7/C4

Garland's Oak Creek Lodge
PO Box 152, Hwy 89A
Sedona AZ 86336
(602) 282-3343
Circa 1930. Orchards of peach, apple, pear, apricot, plum and cherry surround the original homestead, and there are rustic log cabins overlooking Oak Creek (a stocked fishing stream) or the gardens. Some cabins are tucked into the apple orchard while others have views of red cliff walls. A massive stone fireplace dominates the dining room, and gourmet country cooking includes organically grown vegetables. There are day trips to the Painted Desert, Petrified Forest, Indian reservations and ghost towns.
Location: Eight miles north of Sedona.
Rates: $134-$154 Season: April-Nov. 18. Gary & Mary Garland.
15 R. 15 PB. 12 FP. Phone available. Beds: KQDC. MAP. CCs: MC VISA. Nearby horseback riding, golf, hiking, fishing, tennis, creek swimming. Clay tennis court.
Seen in: *Scottsdale Scene, Tempe Daily News, Food & Wine, Bon Appetit.*
"Felt as if this were home."

Saddle Rock Ranch
PO Box 10095
Sedona AZ 86336
(602) 282-7640
Circa 1926. If you want an authentic Old West experience, stay at the Saddle Rock Ranch. Nipper, the RCA Victor dog, greets visitors at the front door. The house is constructed of native red rock, beamed ceilings and wood and flagstone floors. Guest suites feature fieldstone fireplaces and panoramic vistas of the surrounding red rocks. The house has often been featured in motion pictures depicting the Old West.

Location: On three acres of hillside, one mile from the center of town.
❀Rates: $65-$108. Fran & Dan Bruno.
3 R. 3 PB. 2 FP. Phone available. TV available. Beds: KQT. Continental-plus breakfast. Spa. Swimming pool. Conference room. Horseback riding, hiking, fishing, golf, tennis, archaeological and backcountry jeep expeditions.
Seen in: *Sedona Red Rock News.*
"Thank you for sharing your ranch with us. It has been the highlight of our trip."

TUCSON N8/F4

La Posada Del Valle
1640 N Campbell Ave
Tucson AZ 85719
(602) 795-3840
Circa 1929. The 18-inch thick walls of this southwest adobe wrap around to form a courtyard. Ornamental orange trees surround the property, which is across the street from the University Medical Center. All the rooms have outside entrances and open to the patio or overlook the courtyard and fountain. Twenties decor includes a fainting couch. Afternoon tea is served.
Location: Walking distance to the University of Arizona.
*Rates: $60-$110. Charles & Debbi Bryant.
5 R. 5 PB. Phone in room. TV available. Beds: KQT. B&B. CCs: MC VISA. Gourmet breakfast, individual heating and cooling in each room. Turn-down service.
Seen in: *Gourmet.*
"Thank you so much for such a beautiful home, romantic room and warm hospitality."

The Peppertrees B&B
724 E University
Tucson AZ 85719
(602) 622-7167
Circa 1900. Two ancient peppertrees shade the front of this red brick territorial house, near the University of Arizona. Inside you will find English antiques inherited from the innkeeper's family. There is a patio filled with flowers and a fountain. Each of two newly built southwest-style guesthouses feature two bedrooms and two bathrooms, a kitchen, laundry

and a private patio. Blue-corn pecan pancakes and Scottish shortbread are house specialties. Peppertrees is within walking distance to the university, shops, theatres, museums and restaurants.
✻❀Rates: $45-$125. Marjorie G. Martin.
5 R. Phone available. TV available. Beds: QT. EP. Gourmet meals. CCs: MC VISA. Shops, theaters, museums.
Seen in: *Tucson Guide, Travel Age West.*
"We have not yet stopped telling our friends what a wonderful experience we shared at your lovely home."

ARKANSAS

BRINKLEY G9/C5

The Great Southern Hotel

127 W Cedar

Brinkley AR 72021

(501) 734-4955

Circa 1913. The Victorian-style Great Southern Hotel was built at the crossroads of seven railroads. Now only one remains. The hotel is across

from the Rock Island railroad tracks and adjacent to the Union passenger depot. Both the hotel and depot are in a National Historic District. Recently restored, the inn has an elegant and serene atmosphere. There are two balconies and a wraparound veranda.

Location: Midway between Memphis and Little Rock.

*Rates: $38-$40. Stanley & Dorcas Prince.

4 R. 4 PB. Phone available. TV in room. Beds: QD. Full breakfast. Restaurant. Sauna. Exercise room. Conference room. CCs: MC VISA AE DC CB DS. Fishing, duck and quail hunting.

Seen in: *Southern Living, Arkansas Times, Arkansas Gazette.*

"Absolutely terrific! Beautiful."

"A lovely, quaint place."

EUREKA SPRINGS B3/A2

Dairy Hollow House

515 Spring St

Eureka Springs AR 72632

(501) 253-7444 (800) 562-8650

Circa 1888. Dairy Hollow House, the first of Eureka Springs' bed and breakfast inns, consists of a restored Ozark vernacular farmhouse and a 1940s bungalow-style cottage, both in a national historic district. Stenciled walls set off a collection of Eastlake Victorian furnishings. Outstanding *"Nouveau 'zarks"* cuisine is available by reservation. The innkeeper is the author of several books, including the award-winning *Dairy Hollow House Cookbook.*

Location: At the junction of Spring & Dairy Hollow Road.

*Rates: $95-$155. Ned Shank & Crescent Dragonwagon.

6 R. 6 PB. 6 FP. Phone in room. Beds: QDC. Full breakfast. Restaurant. Spa. Conference room. CCs: MC VISA AE DC DS. Hiking, fishing, rafting.

Seen in: *Innsider, Christian Science Monitor, Los Angeles Times.*

"The height of unpretentious luxury."

Heart of the Hills Inn

5 Summit

Eureka Springs AR 72632

(501) 253-7468

Circa 1883. Three suites and a Victorian cottage comprise this antique-furnished homestead located just four blocks from downtown. The Victorian Room is furnished with a white iron bed, dresser, antique lamp and antique pedestal sink. Evening dessert is served. The village trolly stops at the inn.

Rates: $55-$70 Season: Feb - Dec. Jan Jacobs Weber.

5 R. 5 PB. Phone available. TV in room. Beds: KQDTC. Full breakfast. CCs: MC VISA. Horseback riding, water skiing, fishing.

Seen in: *The Carroll County Tribune's Peddler.*

"It was delightful-the bed so comfortable, room gorgeous, food delicious and ohhh those chocolates."

The Heartstone Inn & Cottages

35 King's Hwy

Eureka Springs AR 72632

(501) 253-8916

Circa 1903. Described as a "pink and white confection," this handsome restored Victorian with its wraparound verandas is located in the historic district. The award winning inn is filled with antiques and artwork from the innkeeper's native England. Live music is featured, May fine arts festival and September jazz festival. Afternoon refreshments are available on the sunny deck overlooking a wooded ravine. Pink roses line the picket fence surrounding the inviting garden.

Location: Northwest Arkansas. Ozarks.

❀Rates: $55-$92. Iris & Bill Simantel.

12 R. 12 PB. 1 FP. Phone available. TV in room. Beds: KQDC. B&B. Conference room. CCs: MC VISA AE. Horseback riding, water sports, golf, country music shows, museums, galleries. Private cottages available. "The Great Passion Play".

Seen in: *Innsider Magazine, Arkansas Times, The New York Times, Arkansas Gazette, Southern Living, Country Home.*

"Extraordinary! Best breakfasts anywhere!"

Palace Hotel & Bath House

135 Spring St

Eureka Springs AR 72632

(501) 253-7474

Circa 1901. The Palace Hotel and Bath House has been extensively renovated. The lobby and guest rooms are furnished in Victorian antiques recalling opulent turn-of-the-century beginnings. Each guest room has a double-sized water-jet tub and a wet bar. Built on the edge of a cliff, the hotel features a lower mineral-bath level. The bath house is equipped with original six-foot-long clawfoot tubs (whirlpool machines have been added), and the Victorian-era Eucalyptus steam barrels are still in service. Each tub is situated in a private alcove.

*Rates: $85-$110. Steve & Francie Miller.
8 R. 8 PB. Phone in room. TV in room. Beds: K. Continental-plus breakfast. Spa. CCs: MC VISA AE DS. Fishing, canoeing, water & jet ski, golf, horseback riding, hiking, shopping. Coffee maker, secretarial services, conference areas available.
Seen in: *Country Home, Southern Living, Ladies Home Journal, The New York Times, USA Weekend, Washington Post.*
"We absolutely loved the turn-down service, the comfort and the romantic atmosphere!"

The Piedmont House
165 Spring St
Eureka Springs AR 72632
(501) 253-9258

Circa 1880. An original guest book from the inn's days as a tourist home is a cherished item here. The Piedmont offers the best views in town and is in the National Register.
Rates: $65-$75. Rose & Larry Olivet.
8 R. 8 PB. Phone available. TV available. Beds: DT. Full breakfast. CCs: MC VISA AE. Walking distance to downtown shops and restaurants. Presently offer "Stress Management Workshop."
Seen in: *Arkansas Times.*
"Wonderful atmosphere and your personalities are exactly in sync with the surroundings."

Singleton House B&B
11 Singleton
Eureka Springs AR 72632
(501) 253-9111

Circa 1895. This pink Queen Anne Victorian is highlighted with blue and burgundy brackets. Guest rooms are whimsically decorated with an eclec-

tic collection of folk art and country furnishings. Breakfast is served on the balcony overlooking a wildflower garden, goldfish pond, a curious birdhouse collection and serene wooded view. Created by a local artist, the garden features paths that wind through arches and arbors. Guests may stroll one block down a wooded footpath to shops and restaurants and ride the trolley through town.
Rates: $55-$65. Barbara Gavron.
5 R. 3 PB. Phone available. TV available. Beds: DT. Full breakfast. CCs: MC VISA AE.
"An old-fashioned place with a touch of magic."

HELENA H10/D6

Edwardian Inn
317 S Biscoe
Helena AR 72342
(501) 338-9155

Circa 1904. Mark Twain wrote in *Life on the Mississippi*, "Helena occupies one of the prettiest situations on the

river." William Short, cotton broker and speculator, agreed and built his stately home here. The Edwardian Inn boasts a large rotunda and two verandas wrapping around both sides of the house. Inside are wood carpets and floor designs imported from Germany that are composed of 36 pieces of different woods arranged in octagon shapes. Polished-oak paneling and woodwork are set off with a Victorian-era decor.
Rates: $50-$59. Mrs. Jerri Steed.
12 R. 12 PB. Phone in room. TV in room. Beds: KD. Continental-plus breakfast. Handicap access. Conference room. CCs: MC VISA AE. Golf, tennis, fishing, duck hunting.
Seen in: *Arkansas Times Magazine, The Dallas Morning News.*
"The Edwardian Inn envelops you with wonderful feelings, smells and thoughts of the Victorian era."

HOT SPRINGS H4/D3

Williams House Inn
420 Quapaw St
Hot Springs AR 71901
(501) 624-4275

Circa 1890. Williams House is a brownstone and brick Victorian nestled among towering oaks and a 40-foot tulip tree. Light and airy

rooms are filled with antiques and plants. The carriage house, hitching posts and mounting blocks are still on the property, and the inn is listed in the National Register of Historic Places. Eggs Benedict is popular for breakfast.
Location: Fifty miles southwest of Little Rock, three blocks off Hwy 7.
Rates: $50-$80. Mary & Gary Riley.
6 R. 4 PB. Phone available. TV available. Beds: QDT. Full breakfast. CCs: MC VISA AE.
Seen in: *Los Angeles Times, USA Today, Arkansas Times.*

MOUNTAIN VIEW D7/B4

The Commercial Hotel
A Vintage Guest House
Washington at Peabody St,
PO Box 72
Mountain View AR 72560
(501) 269-4383

Circa 1920. The inn's wraparound porches are a gathering place for local musicians who often play old-time music. If you rock long enough you're

likely to see an impromptu hootenanny in the Courthouse Square across the street. Since there are no priceless antiques, children are welcome. However, you may have to watch them (and yourself) because there's a tempting first-floor bakery that's always "fixin' up" divinity cookies, macaroons and hot breads.
Location: In the Ozarks.
❀Rates: $35-$50. Todd & Andrea Budy.
8 R. 3 PB. Phone available. Beds: DTC. B&B. CCs: AE. White-water rafting, horseback riding, caverns. Gourmet bakery on site.
Seen in: *Midwest Living, The New York Times, Dan Rather & CBS.*
"It's the kind of place you'll look forward to returning to."

CALIFORNIA

ALAMEDA NP7/E1

Garratt Mansion

900 Union St
Alameda CA 94501
(415) 521-4779

Circa 1893. This handsome, 27-room Colonial Revival mansion was built for industrialist W.T. Garratt. It features walnut and oak paneling, crystal windows and ornate mantled fireplaces. The staircase rises three stories with hundreds of gleaming Jacobean turned balusters. A set of stained-glass windows encircles a bay at the stairwell landing. The elegance of the mansion is matched by the warmth of its proprietress, Betty Gladden. On weekends an authentic English tea is often presented.

Rates: $65-$120. Royce & Betty Gladden.
6 R. 3 PB. 1 FP. Phone in room. TV available. Beds: QDT. B&B. Conference room. CCs: AE. Tennis, golf, wind surfing, bicycling, jogging, beach.
Seen in: *Alameda Times Star, The Denver Post.*
"I'm delighted that you haven't commercialized."

ALBION NK3/D1

Albion River Inn

PO Box 100
Albion CA 95410
(707) 937-1919

Circa 1919. The Albion River Inn is located on ten acres along a spectacular bluffside. Most guest rooms are distinguished by a dramatic view of the ocean and Albion Cove. The dining room is among the finest on the Northern California coast.

Rates: $75-$190. Flurry Healy & Peter Wells.
20 R. 20 PB. 14 FP. Beds: KQ. Full breakfast. Spa.
Seen in: *California Magazine, San Francisco Chronicle.*
"Warm hospitality and wonderful cuisine."

Fensalden Inn

PO Box 99
Albion CA 95410
(707) 937-4042

Circa 1860. Originally a stagecoach station, Fensalden looks out over the Pacific Ocean as it has for more than 100 years. The Tavern Room has wit-

nessed many a rowdy scene. If you look closely you can see bullet holes in the original redwood ceilings. The inn provides 20 acres for walks, whale-watching, viewing deer and bicycling.

Location: Seven miles south of Mendocino on Hwy 1.
❀Rates: $75-$125. Scott & Frances Brazil.
7 R. 7 PB. Phone available. Beds: KQ. Full breakfast. CCs: MC VISA.
"Closest feeling to Heaven on Earth."

ALTADENA SK14/J4

Eye Openers

PO Box 694
Altadena CA 91003
(818) 797-2055 (213) 684-4428

Circa 1926. Eye Openers is a reservation service representing homes and inns throughout Southern California.

One of their listings, a Normandy-style house, was built as a summer home for a railroad industrialist, and has a two-story living room. The former owner, an opera singer, sang to her guests from the half-balcony on the upper level.

Rates: $35-$135.
Seen in: *Los Angeles Times, Pasadena Star News.*
"Our hostess was delightful and gracious in sharing her home with us."

ANAHEIM SM14/J4

Anaheim Country Inn

856 S Walnut St
Anaheim CA 92802
(714) 778-0150

Circa 1910. An elegant Craftsman farmhouse built by Mayor John Cook, the inn with its circular porch, is sur-

rounded by nearly an acre of lawns, gardens and avocado trees. Detailed woodwork graces the entry and staircase, and beveled and leaded windows cast rainbows in the parlor and dining room. A gazebo and spa are just steps from the honeymoon suite.

Location: One mile from Disneyland.
✻Rates: $65-$90. Lois Ramont & Marilyn Watson.
9 R. 6 PB. Phone available. TV available. Beds: QDT. Full breakfast. Spa. Conference room. CCs: MC VISA AE DS.
"My husband is still telling anyone who'll listen how good the breakfasts were."

ANGELS CAMP NO12/F3

Cooper House

1184 Church St, PO Box 1388
Angels Camp CA 95222
(209) 736-2145

Circa 1911. This Craftsman bungalow was built by Dr. George Cooper. A magnificent greenstone fireplace is the

focal point of the living room, while a spacious veranda overlooks the garden path as it winds down to a gazebo. Many of the inn's furnishings were once owned by the well-known Archie Stevenot, "Mr. Mother Lode," and guests can visit the nearby Stevenot Winery. Angels Camp is the home of Mark Twain's celebrated Jumping Frog of Calaveras County.
Rates: $78-$85. Chris Sears.
3 R. 3 PB. Phone available. Beds: KQD. Full breakfast. CCs: MC VISA. Tennis, swimming, skiing, water sports, bicycling, backpacking on foot or horseback, gold panning.
Seen in: *The Calaveras Enterprise, The Times, Sunset Magazine.*
"The house is lovely, your breakfast was great and your hospitality unsurpassed!"

APTOS SB3/F2

Apple Lane Inn
6265 Soquel Dr
Aptos CA 95003
(408) 475-6868
Circa 1872. Ancient apple trees border the lane that leads to this Victorian farmhouse set on two acres of gardens

and fields. Built by the Porter brothers, founding fathers of Aptos, the inn is decorated with Victorian wallpapers and hardwood floors. The original wine cellar still exists, as well as the old barn and apple-drying shed used for storage after harvesting the orchard. Miles of beaches are within walking distance. The Grooms were married at the inn and later purchased it.
Rates: $70-$125. Douglas & Diana Groom.
5 R. 3 PB. Phone available. TV available. Beds: QD. Full breakfast. CCs: MC VISA. Darts and horseshoes. Close to beaches, golfing, fishing, hiking.
Seen in: *Santa Barbara Times, 1001 Decorating Ideas, New York Times.*
"Our room was spotless and beautifully decorated."

Bayview Hotel B&B Inn
8041 Soquel Dr
Aptos CA 95003
(408) 688-8654
Circa 1878. This Victorian hotel was built by Joseph Arano, a French immigrant who married the youngest daughter of General Rafael Castro,

owner of the 6,680-acre Rancho de Aptos. Lillian Russell and King Kalakaua were among famous guests in the past. Newly renovated, there is a restaurant on the first floor, lodging on the second and third. The hosts come from a family of British innkeepers.
*❀Rates: $80-$100. Katya & James Duncan.
8 R. 8 PB. Beds: D. B&B. Restaurant. CCs: MC VISA. Hiking, bicycling, tennis, golf, fishing, boating, beaches.
Seen in: *Mid-County Post, Santa Cruz Sentinel.*
"Thank you so much for all of your tender loving care and great hospitality."

Mangels House
570 Aptos Creek Rd, PO Box 302
Aptos CA 95001
(408) 688-7982
Circa 1886. Like the Spreckels family, Claus Mangels made his fortune in sugar beets, and built this house in the style of a southern mansion. The

inn, with its encircling veranda, stands on four acres of lawns and orchards. It is bounded by the Forest of Nisene Marks, 10,000 acres of redwood trees, creeks, and trails. Monterey Bay is three-quarters of a mile away.
Location: Central Coast.
*Rates: $89-$115. Jacqueline & Ron Fisher.
5 R. 3 PB. 1 FP. Phone available. Beds: QDT. B&B. Game room. Conference room. CCs: MC VISA. Horseback riding, golf, tennis, water sports, hiking.
Seen in: *Inn Serv, Innviews.*
"Compliments on the lovely atmosphere. We look forward to sharing our discovery with friends and returning with them."

ARCATA NE3/B1

Plough & the Stars Country Inn
1800 27th St
Arcata CA 95521
(707) 822-8236
Circa 1860. After losing his ranch and all his possessions to the 1862 Indian raids, Isaac Minor, businessman and

rancher, built this farm. It's surrounded on three sides by 100 acres of lillies. The house, of post & beam construction, supports ground floor joists of 12"x12" hand-hewn redwood beams. The Courtia Worth suite has an elegant Victorian atmosphere and features a woodstove. Guests are welcome to invite friends over for hors d'oeuvres or late evening snacks, for an additional charge.
Rates: $75-$105. Season: Feb. 15-Dec. 15 Bill & Melissa Hans.
5 R. 3 PB. 1 FP. Phone available. Beds: QDT. B&B. Spa. Handicap access. Hiking, bicycling, canoeing, bird watching, golf, tennis, swimming, croquet & lawn bowling.
Seen in: *Sunset, New York Times, Los Angeles Times, US Croquet Association Gazette.*
"When we'd been here for an hour it felt like we'd been on a vacation for a week."

ARROYO GRANDE SH7/H2

Guest House
120 Hart Ln
Arroyo Grande CA 93420
(805) 481-9304
Circa 1850. Set among old-fashioned gardens, this New England Colonial was built by an eastern sea captain. The flavor of that period is kept alive with many family heirlooms and a colorful garden terrace. It is located 17 miles south of San Luis Obispo.

Location: In the village.
Rates: $60. Mark V. Miller.
3 R. Phone available. Beds: QD. Wineries,

beaches, Hearst Castle and antique shops nearby.
Seen in: *Five Cities Times.*
"The charm of the home is only exceeded by that of the hosts."

Rose Victorian Inn
789 Valley Rd
Arroyo Grande CA 93420
(805) 481-5566
Circa 1885. Once the homestead for a large walnut farm, this picturesque Victorian inn features a tower that rises four stories, providing a view of meadows, sand dunes and the ocean. Surrounded by a white picket fence, the inn is decorated with authentic Victorian furnishings. A 30-foot-long rose arbor leads to a gazebo in the garden, a favorite setting for weddings. Rates include dinner at the inn's restaurant.
Location: Halfway between Los Angeles and San Francisco.
*Rates: $130-$165. Ross & Diana Cox.
11 R. 7 PB. Phone available. TV available. Beds: KQ. MAP. Restaurant. Handicap access. Conference room. CCs: MC VISA AE.
Seen in: *Los Angeles Times, Daughters of Painted Ladies, Sunset Magazine.*

AUBURN NL10/*E3*

Power's Mansion Inn
164 Cleveland Ave
Auburn CA 95603
(916) 885-1166
Circa 1885. This elegant Victorian mansion was built by Harold Power with the proceeds from his gold mine. Many prominent people, including engineer Herbert Hoover, visited here, and the second floor halls contain notes and memorabilia concerning its history. The luxury of the inn is typified by the honeymoon suite, which has a heart-shaped tub and a fireplace at the foot of the brass bed.
Location: In the heart of downtown.
*❀Rates: $70-$160. Arno & Jean Lejnieks, Anthony Verhaart.
13 R. 13 PB. 2 FP. Phone in room. TV available. Beds: Q. B&B. Gourmet meals. Spa. Conference room. CCs: MC VISA AE. Water rafting, cross-country skiing, horseback riding, antiquing.
Seen in: *Sierra Heritage Magazine.*
"The rooms are so relaxing and the breakfast is fantastic."

AVALON SN13/*K3*

The Inn on Mt. Ada
Box 2560, 207 Wrigley Rd
Avalon CA 90704
(213) 510-2030 (213) 510-2311
Circa 1921. This Georgian mansion was built by the famous Wrigley family. Wrigley brought the Chicago Cubs to Avalon for spring training and watched them from his house. Once the summer White House for Presidents Coolidge and Harding, the inn's breathtaking ocean and bay views are framed by a multitude of wide windows and terraces. Weekends are booked six months ahead.
Location: Catalina Island.
Rates: $170-$490. Susie Griffin & Marlene Mc Adam.
6 R. 6 PB. 4 FP. Phone available. TV available. Beds: QD. Full breakfast. Restaurant. Gourmet meals. Conference room. CCs: MC VISA AE. Scuba diving, fishing, golf, tennis, horseback riding, charter boats, tours. Private parties.
Seen in: *Los Angeles Times, Chicago Tribune, Los Angeles Magazine.*
"Mere words cannot describe this place! The breath-taking views, beautifully appointed rooms and marvelous cuisine surpass any I have enjoyed anywhere!"

BENICIA NO7/*E2*

The Union Hotel
401 First St
Benicia CA 94510
(707) 746-0100
Circa 1882. Once a famed bordello, this clapboard hotel has been refurbished with whitewash, polished brass and stained glass. The inn is set

in a picturesque town that served as the capital of California for one year. Extra comfort is provided by whirlpool tubs available in all guest rooms. Some rooms feature water views of Carquinez Strait.
*Rates: $75-$125. Stephen Lipworth.
12 R. 12 PB. Phone in room. TV in room. Beds: KQ. Continental breakfast. Restaurant. Gourmet meals. Spa. Handicap access. Conference room. FAX. CCs: MC VISA AE DC DS. Marine World & Wine Country nearby. Sunday brunch, entertainment five nights a week, bar.
Seen in: *PG&E Progress, Marin Independent Journal.*
"Spent a wonderful night. Hope to be back."

BERKELEY NO7/*E1*

Gramma's Inn
2740 Telegraph
Berkeley CA 94705
(415) 549-2145
Circa 1898. Four buildings comprise Gramma's, including a half-timbered Tudor mansion and a Tudor cottage. All rooms are decorated with Victorian antiques and feature handmade quilts. The Fay House boasts views of the bay from its third floor rooms. Cookies and milk and wine and cheese are served in the evening. The University of California campus is five minutes away.
*Rates: $85-$175. Barry Cleveland.
30 R. 28 PB. 14 FP. Phone in room. TV in room. Beds: KQDTC. Full breakfast. Gourmet meals. Handicap access. Conference room. CCs: MC VISA AE. Museums, shops, parks, restaurants. Wine and cheese.
Seen in: *Sunset, The Independent & Gazette, Travel & Leisure.*
"Everything was superlative! Great service. All your people were terrific!"

BIG BEAR LAKE SK17/*J5*

Knickerbocker Mansion
869 S Knickerbocker, PO 3661
Big Bear Lake CA 92315
(714) 866-8221 (714) 866-5332
Circa 1917. The inn is one of the few vertically designed log structures in the area. Built of local lumber by Bill Knickerbocker, the first damkeeper of Big Bear, the mansion is set against a

backdrop of trees. Spacious front lawns provide seating for the annual summer "Astronomy Weekends" led by a Griffith Park Observatory astronomer.
Location: One-quarter mile south of Big Bear Village.
*Rates: $85-$150. Phyllis Knight.
10 R. 6 PB. Phone available. Beds: KQT. Full breakfast. Conference room. CCs: MC VISA. Horseback riding, skiing, parasailing, water slide. One suite with spa. Weddings.
Seen in: *Los Angeles Magazine, Yellow Brick Road.*
"Best breakfast I ever had. We especially enjoyed the hot tub with its terrific view."

BIG SUR SD3/G1

Deetjen's Big Sur Inn
Highway One
Big Sur CA 93920
(408) 667-2377
Circa 1938. Norwegians Helmut and Helen Deetjen built these casual, rustic rooms on several acres of a redwood canyon. Today they are

managed by a non-profit corporation and provide employment for local residents. Two rooms overlook a bubbling stream. Some have fireplaces and down comforters. The inn's restaurant is open daily. The adventurous will appreciate the setting and the whimsy, but the rustic nature of the accommodations may not be for everyone.
Location: Twenty-eight miles south of Carmel.
Rates: $50-$100. Bettie Walters.
19 R. 14 PB. Beds: QDT. EP. Handicap access. Hiking trails and beaches nearby.
Seen in: *New York Times, California Magazine.*
"Like stepping back in time, so unique and charming."

BISHOP NQ18/G5

Chalfant House
213 Academy St
Bishop CA 93514
(619) 872-1790
Circa 1898. "It has been Earth's nearest touch of heaven above," wrote P.A. Chalfant of his Victorian home. As founder of the area's first newspaper, Mr. Chalfant enjoyed its village setting in full view of the surrounding mountains. For a time the house served as a hotel for area Tungsten miners, and in the 1920s was managed by Big Bertha. Now restored and decorated with antiques, collectibles, and quilts, each guest room has been named after Chalfant family members.
*❀Rates: $60-$75. Fred & Sally Manecke.
5 R. 5 PB. 2 FP. Phone available. TV available. Beds: QDT. Full breakfast. Gourmet meals. CCs: AE. Biking, fishing, boating, back packing, museums.
Seen in: *Inyo County Resister.*
"You set the standards for hospitality and quality in the B&B industry."

CALISTOGA NM6/E2

Brannan Cottage Inn
109 Wapoo Ave
Calistoga CA 94515
(707) 942-4200
Circa 1860. This Greek Revival cottage was built as a guest house for the old Calistoga Hot Springs Resort. Behind

a white picket fence towers the original palm tree planted by Sam Brannan and noted by Robert Louis Stevenson in his "Silverado Squatters." Five graceful arches, an intricate gingerbread gableboard, and unusual scalloped ridge cresting make this a charming holiday house. Hand-painted flower stencils of sweet peas, wild iris, violets, morning glories and wild roses are part of the fresh country Victorian decor.
Location: Napa Valley.
*Rates: $110-$145. Jack & Pamela Osborn.
6 R. 6 PB. Phone available. Beds: QT. Full breakfast. Handicap access. CCs: MC VISA AE. Ballooning, spas, hiking, biking, tennis, golf, hot springs, gliding, wine tasting, petrified forest.
Seen in: *New York Herald Tribune, Los Angeles Herald Examiner, Chicago Tribune, Orange County Register.*
"I think of you as the caretakers of romance in our busy world."

Foothill House
3037 Foothill Blvd
Calistoga CA 94515
(707) 942-6933
Circa 1887. This country farmhouse overlooks the western foothills of Mt. St. Helena. Graceful old California oaks and pockets of flowers greet guests. Each room features a four-poster bed adorned with Sue's handmade quilts and a fireplace. Breakfast is served in the sun room or is delivered personally to your room in a basket. Two rooms offer private jacuzzi tubs.
Location: Napa Valley.
❀Rates: $95-$225. Susan & Michael Clow.
3 R. 3 PB. 3 FP. Phone available. TV available. Beds: KQT. Continental-plus breakfast. Conference room. CCs: MC VISA. Hiking, bicycling, gliders, balloons.
Seen in: *The Herald Examiner.*
"The most restful weekend we've had in months - your hospitality was perfect."

Scarlett's Country Inn
3918 Silverado Trail N
Calistoga CA 94515
(707) 942-6669
Circa 1890. Formerly a winter campground of the Wappo Indians, the property now includes a restored farmhouse. There are green lawns and country vistas of woodland and vineyards. Each room has a private entrance and is air conditioned. Breakfast is often served beneath the apple trees or poolside.

Location: Napa Valley wine country.
*❀Rates: $85-$125. Scarlett & Derek Dwyer.
3 R. 3 PB. 1 FP. Phone in room. TV available. Beds: Q. Continental-plus breakfast. Swimming pool. Hiking, biking, fishing, water skiing, ballooning, gliding, mud baths.
"Wonderful, peaceful, serene."

Trailside Inn
4201 Silverado Tr
Calistoga CA 94515
(707) 942-4106
Circa 1930. This secluded valley farmhouse overlooks Three Palms Vineyard and the distant Sterling Winery. Each accommodation is a tastefully decorated suite with its own porch, private entrance, small kitchen and fireplace. Furnished with country antiques and old quilts, two suites have an extra bedroom to accommodate a family of four. House specialties are banana and blueberry breads, freshly baked and brought to your room. A neighbor's donkey and Nubian goats provide wakeup calls.
Location: Napa Valley.
Rates: $85-$110. Randy & Lani Gray.
3 R. 3 PB. 3 FP. Phone available. Beds: QDTC. Continental breakfast. Hiking, golf, biking, wineries, glider & hot air balloon rides.
Seen in: *San Francisco Examiner, Wine Country Review.*
"Thank you so much for your warmth and hospitality. Don't change a thing!"

CAMBRIA SG5/H2

Olallieberry Inn
2476 Main St
Cambria CA 93428
(805) 927-3222

Circa 1873. This Greek Revival house originally was built by a German pharmacist, but has been influenced by other owners, including dairy

farmers and a Morro Bay fisherman. Restored and recently refurbished, the rose and beige lace honeymoon suite features a canopied bed and sunken tub. The cheery breakfast room faces a well-groomed lawn with a small fountain. Hearst Castle is seven miles up the coast.

*Rates: $85-$106. Linda Boyers & Faye Janni.
6 R. 6 PB. Phone available. Beds: KQD. Continental-plus breakfast. Handicap access. CCs: MC VISA. Private tennis, pool, bicycles available. Fishing, hiking, beaches, wineries, Hearst Castle.
Seen in: *Los Angeles Times, Elmer Dills Radio Show.*
"Our retreat turned into relaxation, romance and pure Victorian delight."

CAPITOLA-BY-THE-SEA SB3/F2

The Inn at Depot Hill
250 Monterey Ave
Capitola-by-the-Sea CA 95010
(408) 462-3376

Circa 1901. Situated in a quaint Monterey Bay beach town that is reminiscent of a mediterranean fishing village, the Inn at Depot Hill is a converted Southern Pacific Railroad depot. The depot's Round Room still retains the old ticket window and there are 14-foot-high ceilings in the living and dining rooms. Guest rooms are named after railroad stations of the world and decorated accordingly (Stratford on Avon is Country English and Statione de Milano has an Italian theme). The Railroad Barn Room resembles a plush, private pullman car. Spas and featherbeds are features of some rooms.

*Rates: $115-$185. Suzanne Lankes.
8 R. 8 PB. 8 FP. Phone in room. TV in room. Beds: KQ. Continental-plus breakfast. Handicap access. FAX. CCs: MC VISA AE DC DS. Beaches, state parks.
Seen in: *Santa Cruz Sentinel.*
"The highlight of our honeymoon. Five stars in our book!"

CARMEL SC3/G1

Gatehouse Inn
See: Pacific Grove, CA

Happy Landing Inn
Monte Verde between 5th & 6th
Carmel CA 93921
(408) 624-7917

Circa 1925. Built as a family retreat, this early Comstock-design inn has evolved into one of Carmel's most

romantic places to stay. The Hansel-and-Gretel look is accentuated with a central garden and gazebo, pond and flagstone paths. There are cathedral ceilings and the rooms are filled with antiques.

Rates: $100-$115. Robert & Carol Ballard.
7 R. 7 PB. 3 FP. Phone available. TV in room. Beds: KQD. Continental-plus breakfast. Handicap access. CCs: MC VISA. Golf.
Seen in: *San Francisco Chronicle.*
"Just what the doctor ordered!"

Vagabond's House Inn
Box 2747
Carmel CA 93921
(408) 624-7738 (800) 262-1262 Outside CA

Shaded by the intertwined branches of two California live oaks, the stone-paved courtyard of the Vagabond's House sets the tone of this romantic retreat. The inn is comprised of a cluster of white stucco cottages built into a slope. Some include kitchens, but all feature a fireplace and an antique clock. In the morning continental breakfast is delivered to you near the camellias or in the privacy of your room.

Location: 4th & Dolores.
*Rates: $79-$135. Honey Jones & Dennis Levett.
11 R. 11 PB. 11 FP. Phone in room. TV in room. Beds: KQD. Continental breakfast. CCs: MC VISA AE. Golf, tennis, bicycling, hiking, fishing, kayaking.
Seen in: *Diversion, Cat Fancy.*
"Charming & excellent accommodations and service. Very much in keeping with the character and ambience of Carmel's historic setting."

CARMEL VALLEY SD4/G2

Stonepine
150 E Carmel Valley Rd
Carmel Valley CA 93921
(408) 659-2245

Circa 1929. Once the country estate of the Crocker family (of Crocker Bank fame), this Italian-villa style manor sits on 330 acres. Stonepine trees imported from Italy surround the inn's lawns. Like the gracious country homes of the English gentry, Stonepine welcomes house guests with lavishly decorated rooms and refined hospitality. In the walnut paneled dining room, the table is resplendent with china and crystal ready for an elegant dinner. (Make dinner reservations at the same time you make room reservations.)

Rates: $160-$550. Dirk Oldenburg.
12 R. 12 PB. Full breakfast. CCs: MC VISA AE. Stonepine is an equestrian center.
Seen in: *Gourmet, Los Angeles Times.*

CLIO NI12/D3

White Sulphur Springs Ranch
PO Box 136, Hwy 89 S
Clio CA 96106
(916) 836-2387

Circa 1852. Originally built by partners in the Jamison mine, this stage coach stop serviced the Truckee to Quincy stage. The inn has passed

from relative to relative to friend and has not been sold since 1867 when it was purchased by George McLear. Elegantly restored, the rooms still retain many of the original furnishings, now embellished with colorful wallpapers and fabrics. The Marble Room features a moss green velvet fainting couch, marble topped antiques and a splendid view of the Mohawk Valley. Breakfast is served in the dining room. Mineral waters from five 85-degree springs fill the inn's swimming pool.

*Rates: $70-$120. Don & Karen Miller, Tom & Linda Vanella.
6 R. 1 PB. Phone available. Beds: KQDT. Full breakfast. Swimming pool. Conference room. CCs: MC VISA DS. Horseback riding, fishing, hiking, skiing, golf.
Seen in: *The Sacramento Union, Plumas-Sierra.*
"White Sulphur Springs is alive with its past and its present."

CLOVERDALE NL5/D1

Vintage Towers Inn
302 N Main St
Cloverdale CA 95425
(707) 894-4535

Circa 1900. This gracious Queen Anne Victorian mansion boasts three towers

- square, round and octagonal. Guests may try a different tower room each visit, and each one features an antique bedstead and memorabilia. Bicycles are available to ride to nearby vineyards.

Location: Six blocks from Russian River.
*Rates: $70-$110. James Mees & Garrett Hall.
7 R. 5 PB. Phone available. TV available. Beds: KQD. Full breakfast. Conference room. CCs: MC VISA AE DS. Wineries, white water rafting, horseback riding, fishing.
Seen in: *The Healdsburg Tribune.*
"Your inn is magical and magnetic."

COLUMBIA NO12/F3

City Hotel
PO Box 1870, Main St
Columbia CA 95310
(209) 532-1479 (209) 532-1486

Circa 1856. Closed to auto traffic, only pedestrians and horses may pass the

City Hotel fronting the wooden staircase of Main Street. This National Historic District celebrates the days when $87 million in gold was mined in Columbia. The two-story brick hotel has been preserved and filled with museum furnishings which include massive mahogany beds and marble-topped dressers. The inn's dining room is of note. Nearby shops maintained by the Park Service include a working blacksmith shop, a courthouse, and a carpenter shop. The old saloon still pours sarsaparilla, and the Matelot Gulch Mining Store still sells gold panning equipment.

*Rates: $65-$85. Tom Bender.
9 R. 9 PB. Phone available. Beds: QDT. Continental-plus breakfast. Restaurant. Gourmet meals. Conference room. CCs: MC VISA AE. Horseback riding, swimming, fishing, tennis, gold panning.
Seen in: *Innsider, Bon Appetit, New York Times, Country Inn, Sunset.*
"Excellent, by any standard."

Fallon Hotel
PO Box 1870, Washington St
Columbia CA 95310
(209) 532-1470 (209) 532-1479

Circa 1855. The Fallon Hotel, restored and operated by the State of California Parks and Recreation Department, still boasts the main-floor theater where productions are featured year-round. Original furnishings from the hotel's gold-rush days have been repaired, polished and reupholstered, including a fine Turkish loveseat in the parlor. Bradbury & Bradbury redesigned the nine wallpaper patterns featured. The best rooms are upstairs with balconies overlooking the town's four blocks of saloons, cash stores, an ice cream parlor, blacksmith shop and the stage coach that periodically rambles through town.

Rates: $50-$80. Tom Bender.
14 R. 14 PB. Phone available. Beds: DC. Continental-plus breakfast. Handicap access. Conference room. CCs: MC VISA AE. Swimming, tennis, gold panning, skiing, horseback riding.
Seen in: *Home & Garden, Innsider.*
"Excellent food and service."

COULTERVILLE NP13/F3

Hotel Jeffery
PO Box 440
Coulterville CA 95311
(209) 878-3471 (209) 878-3473

Circa 1851. This Gold Rush hotel was once a stagecoach inn for miners and passengers on their way to Yosemite. The historic Magnolia Saloon with its bat-wing entrance doors still provides an Old West flavor. Dancing and live weekend music may be heard in the guest rooms upstairs so it may be noisy for early sleepers but great fun for others.

Rates: $55-$68. Skip Carnigie.
20 R. 5 PB. Phone available. TV available. Beds: QDT. Continental breakfast. Restaurant. Conference room. CCs: MC VISA. Water sports, fishing, Yosemite. Conference-banquet room will seat 120.
Seen in: *Los Angeles Times, Motorland.*
"Extremely friendly, excellent food."

CROWLEY LAKE NP17/F4

Rainbow Tarns
PO Box 1097, Rt 1
Crowley Lake CA 93546
(619) 935-4556

Circa 1920. Just south of Mammoth Lakes, at an altitude of 7,000 feet, you'll find this secluded retreat amid

three acres of hot springs, ponds, open meadows and the High Sierra Mountains. Country-style here includes luxury touches, such as a double spa and a skylight for stargazing. In the Thirties, ponds on the property served as a "U-Catch-Em;" folks rented fishing poles and paid 10 cents an inch for the fish they caught. Nearby Crowley Lake is still one of the best trout-fishing areas in California. Corrals are provided should you bring your horses for unlimited riding trails. A small charge is levied for feed.

Location: Eight-tenths of a mile north of Tom's Place off Crowley Lake Drive on Rainbow Tarns Road.
Rates: $85-$125. Lois Miles.
3 R. 1 PB. 1 FP. Phone available. TV available. Beds: QDT. Full breakfast. Spa. Handicap access. Skiing, horseback riding, backpacking, fishing, hunting, hiking, bird watching, biking.
Seen in: *Mammoth-Sierra Magazine, Eastside Journal, Eastern Sierra Fishing Guide, Mammoth-June Ski Preview.*
"I love it! I'd rather stay here than go on to Tahoe!"

DAVENPORT SB2/F1

New Davenport B&B
31 Davenport Ave
Davenport CA 95017
(408) 425-1818 (408) 426-4122

Circa 1902. Captain John Davenport came here to harvest the gray whales that pass close to shore during migration. The oldest building remaining originally was used as a public bath. It later became a bar, restaurant and

dance hall before conversion into a private home. Completely renovated, it now houses four of the inn's rooms.
Location: Halfway between Carmel and San Francisco on the coast.
*Rates: $60-$105. Bruce & Marcia McDougal.
12 R. 12 PB. 1 FP. Phone in room. Beds: KQD. Full breakfast. Restaurant. Handicap access. CCs: MC VISA AE. Whale watching, wind surfing, hiking, elephant seal viewing, beach access.
Seen in: *Monterey Life, Travel & Leisure, Sacramento Bee, Peninsula Time Tribune.*
"I cannot express the wonderful thrill at the first glimpse of our room with its lovely country appeal and garden."

DULZURA SQ18/*L5*

Brookside Farm

1373 Marron Valley Rd
Dulzura CA 92017
(619) 468-3043

Circa 1928. Ancient oaks shade terraces leading from the farmhouse to a murmuring brook. Behind a nearby stone barn there is a grape arbor and

beneath it, a spa. Each room in the inn and its two cottages is furnished with vintage pieces and handmade quilts. Adventurous hikers can explore mines nearby, which date from the gold rush of 1908. Innkeeper Edd Guishard is a former award-winning restaurant owner.
Location: Thirty-five minutes southeast of San Diego.
*Rates: $45-$65. Edd Guishard.
9 R. 6 PB. Phone available. Beds: Q. Full breakfast. Spa. Handicap access. Conference room.
Seen in: *California Magazine, San Diego Home & Garden.*
"Our stay at the farm was the most relaxing weekend we've had in a year."

ELK NK3/*D1*

Elk Cove Inn

PO Box 367
Elk CA 95432
(707) 877-3321

Circa 1883. This mansard-style Victorian home was built as a guest house for lumber baron L. E. White. Operated as a full-service country inn for over 21 years, Elk Cove Inn commands a majestic view from atop a

scenic bluff. Two cabins and an addition to the house feature large bay windows, skylights, and Victorian fireplaces. Antiques, hand-embroidered linens, and sun-dried sheets add to the amenities. Below the inn is an expansive driftwood-strewn beach. French and German specialities are served in the ocean-view dining rooms.
Location: 6300 S Hwy 1, 15 miles south of Mendocino.
Rates: $98-$138. Hildrun-Uta Triebess.
6 R. 6 PB. Phone available. Beds: Q. AP. Handicap access. Ocean kayaking, beachcombing, tennis, golf, wineries nearby through the redwoods.
Seen in: *AAA & Mobil guidebooks.*
"Quiet, peaceful, romantic, spiritual. This room, the Inn, and the food are all what the doctor ordered."

Harbor House Inn by the Sea

5600 S Hwy 1
Elk CA 95432
(707) 877-3203

Circa 1916. Built by a lumber company for executives visiting from the East, the inn is constructed entirely of redwood. The parlor's vaulted, carved ceiling and redwood paneling were sealed by hot beeswax and hand

rubbed. Edwardian decor adds elegance to the guest rooms. Views of the ocean and arches carved in the massive rocks that jut from the sea may be seen from the blufftop cottages. Benches nestle along a path edged with wildflowers that winds down the bluff to the sea.
Rates: $145-$210.MAP Dean & Helen Turner.
10 R. 10 PB. 9 FP. Phone available. MAP. Private beach. Garden fresh cuisine served in ocean view dining room.
Seen in: *California Visitor's Review.*
"A window of love, beauty and the sea."

EUREKA NE2/*B1*

An Elegant Victorian Mansion

14th & C Sts
Eureka CA 95501
(707) 444-3144 (707) 443-6512

Circa 1888. Made of 1,000-year-old virgin redwood, this inn was built by

one of Eureka's leading timber barons.
*❀Rates: $85-$105. Doug & Lily Vieyra.
4 R. 2 PB. Phone available. TV available. Beds: QD. Full breakfast. Spa. Sauna. Exercise room. Game room. CCs: MC VISA. Horseback riding, cross-country skiing, water sports, tennis, fishing, hiking, rafting, hunting.
Seen in: *Sunset, Westcoast Victorians.*
"A magnificent masterpiece, both in architecture and service."

Carter House

1033 Third St
Eureka CA 95501
(707) 445-1390 (707) 444-8062

Circa 1884. The Carters found a pattern book in an antique shop and built this inn according to the architectural plans for an 1890 San Fran-

cisco Victorian. (The architect, Joseph Newsom, also designed the Carson House across the street.) Three open parlors with bay windows and marble fireplaces provide an elegant backdrop for relaxing. Guests are free to

visit the kitchen in quest of coffee and views of the bay. The inn is famous for its three-course breakfast, including an Apple Almond Tart featured in *Gourmet* magazine.
Location: Corner of Third & L streets in Old Town.
*Rates: $79-$299. Mark & Christi Carter.
7 R. 4 PB. 1 FP. Phone available. TV available. Beds: QD. B&B. Gourmet meals. Spa. Handicap access. Conference room. CCs: MC VISA AE. Carriage rides.
Seen in: *Sunset Magazine, U.S. News & World Report.*
"We've traveled extensively throughout the U.S. and stayed in the finest hotels. You've got them all beat!!"

Gingerbread Mansion
See: Ferndale, CA

Old Town B&B Inn
1521 Third St
Eureka CA 95501
(707) 445-3951
Circa 1871. This early Victorian/Greek Revival was the original family home of Lumber Baron William Carson. It

was constructed of virgin redwood and Douglas fir. (Redwood from the Carson's mill was used to build a significant portion of San Francisco.) Try and time your stay on a day when the Timber Beast breakfast menu is served, and be sure to take home a copy of the inn's cookbook.
*Rates: $60-$95. Leigh & Diane Benson.
5 R. 3 PB. Phone available. Beds: KQDT. B&B. CCs: MC VISA AE. Sport fishing, whale watching, hiking, beaches, mountains, museums, redwood forests.
Seen in: *The Times-Standard, Country.*
"You set the standard by which other B&B's should be measured. Absolutely top drawer!

FERNDALE NF2/B1

Gingerbread Mansion
400 Berding St
Ferndale CA 95536
(707) 786-4000
Circa 1899. Built for Dr. H.J. Ring, the Gingerbread Mansion is now the most photographed of Northern California's inns. Near Eureka, it is in the fairy-tale Victorian village of Ferndale (a California Historical Landmark). Outside the inn are for-

mal English gardens. Gingerbread Mansion is a unique combination of Queen Anne and Eastlake styles with elaborate gingerbread trim. Inside are spacious and elegant rooms including two suites with "his" and "her" bathtubs. There are four parlors. Bicycles are available for riding through town and the surrounding countryside.
*Rates: $85-$175. Wendy Hatfield & Ken Torbert.
9 R. 9 PB. 3 FP. Phone available. Beds: QT. Continental-plus breakfast. CCs: MC VISA. Bicycling, fishing, beaches, wilderness park.
Seen in: *Los Angeles Times, The New York Times, Innsider, San Francisco Examiner.*
"Absolutely the most charming, friendly and delightful place we have ever stayed at."

Shaw House Inn
PO Box 1125, 703 Main St
Ferndale CA 95536
(707) 786-9958
Circa 1854. The Shaw House is thought to be one of the oldest inns in California. It is an attractive Gothic house with gables, bays and balconies set back on an acre of garden. An old buckeye tree frames the front gate, and in the back a secluded deck overlooks a creek. Nestled under the wallpapered gables are several guest rooms filled with antiques and fresh flowers.

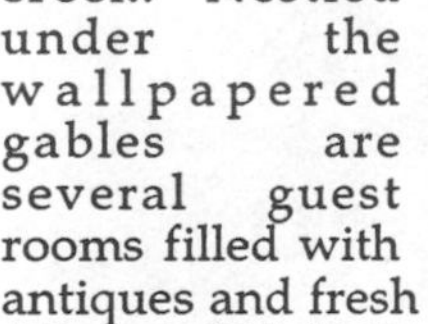

*Rates: $65-$115. Norma & Ken Bessingpas.
5 R. 2 PB. 2 FP. Phone available. Beds: KQDT. Continental-plus breakfast. Conference room. CCs: MC VISA AE. Bikes available, hiking, sleeping, reading.
Seen in: *Travel & Leisure.*
"Lovely place and lovely people." Willard Scott.

FORT BRAGG NJ3/C1

Avalon House
561 Stewart St
Fort Bragg CA 95437
(707) 964-5555
Circa 1905. This redwood California Craftsman house was extensively remodeled in 1988, and furnished with a mixture of antiques and willow furniture. There are fireplaces, whirlpool tubs, down comforters and pillows. The inn is in a quiet residential area, three blocks from the Pacific Ocean, one block from Hwy. 1, and two blocks from the Skunk Train depot.
*Rates: $70-$115. Anne Sorrells.
6 R. 6 PB. 3 FP. Phone available. TV available. Beds: QDT. B&B. Spa. CCs: MC VISA AE. Hiking, fishing, biking, horseback riding, whale watching, Skunk Train. Can arrange and cater small weddings or other events.
Seen in: *Advocate News.*
"Elegant, private and extremely comfortable. We will never stay in a motel again."

Country Inn
632 N Main St
Fort Bragg CA 95437
(707) 964-3737
Circa 1890. The Union Lumber Company once owned this two-story townhouse built of native redwood. It features rooms with slanted and

peaked ceilings, and several rooms have fireplaces. Camellia trees, flower boxes, and a white picket fence accent the landscaping, while two blocks away a railroad carries visitors on excursions through the redwoods.
Rates: $70-$115. Don & Helen Miller.
8 R. 8 PB. Phone available. Beds: KQ. Continental-plus breakfast. Handicap access. CCs: MC VISA.
Seen in: *The Santa Rosa Press Democrat.*
"Each room is so charming, how do you choose one?"

DeHaven Valley Farm
See: Westport, CA

Grey Whale Inn
615 N Main St
Fort Bragg CA 95437
(707) 964-0640 (800) 382-7244 CA only
Circa 1915. Built with weathered, old-growth redwood, this stately four-story inn has been skillfully

renovated. Airy and spacious guest

rooms include some with ocean views and cozy spaces from which to spot whales during the annual December-toMarch migration. Other rooms feature amenities such as a fireplace, whirlpool tub, or private deck.
Location: Two blocks from downtown in historic North Fort Bragg.
*Rates: $65-$140. Colette & John Bailey.
14 R. 14 PB. 2 FP. Phone available. TV available. Beds: KQDT. B&B. Spa. Handicap access. Game room. Conference room. CCs: MC VISA AE. Tennis, golf, fishing, party boats, Skunk Train, bicycling, horseback riding, beachcombing, art gallery & antiquing. Whale watching December to March. Fireside lounge.
Seen in: *San Francisco Examiner, Travel.*
"Just spent the loveliest week in our traveling history. The inn surpassed any Hyatt Regency in service and attitude. The accommodations were superb."

Noyo River Lodge
500 Casa Del Noyo Dr
Fort Bragg CA 95437
(707) 964-8045 (800) 628-1126
Circa 1868. Located on a two-and-one-half acre pinnacle of wooded land overlooking the Noyo River, harbor and fishing village, the lodge is a

mansion once owned by the local lumber baron. Garden pathways lead to romantic picnic spots under the redwoods. Guest rooms are furnished with antiques. A newly constructed building features five luxury suites with ocean views, balconies, fireplaces, and two-person soaking tubs. The lodge's restaurant provides fireside dining and picturesque views of the river.
Rates: $75-$125. Joe Patton & Ellie Sinsel.
13 R. 7 PB. 5 FP. Phone available. Beds: KQ. Continental breakfast. Restaurant. CCs: MC VISA. Horseback riding on beach, whale watching trips, steam train ride. State and national parks.
Seen in: *San Francisco Examiner.*

"Such beauty and serenity words cannot describe. We left the city in search of peace and tranquility and discovered it here."

Pudding Creek Inn
700 N Main St
Fort Bragg CA 95437
(707) 964-9529
Circa 1884. Originally constructed by a Russian count, the inn comprises two picturesque Victorian homes. In the front garden, mounds of begonias,

fuchsias and ferns are framed by a white picket fence. The Count's Room, in royal cranberry velvets, features inlaid redwood paneling, a stone fireplace, and a brass bed. Piping hot, homemade coffee cakes are served at breakfast.
Location: Corner of Bush and North Main.
*Rates: $55-$90. Season: Feb.-Dec. Marilyn & Gene Gundersen.
10 R. 10 PB. 2 FP. Phone available. TV available. Beds: KQD. Full breakfast. CCs: MC VISA AE. Tennis, horseback riding, bicycling, hiking, beachcombing.
Seen in: *Evening Outlook, North Shore Shopper.*
"Best stop on our trip!"

FREESTONE NN5/*E1*

Green Apple Inn
520 Bohemian Hwy
Freestone CA 95472
(707) 874-2526
Circa 1862. Located on five acres of redwood trees and meadows, this inn was built by Trowbridge Wells, squire,

pundit, grocer and postman for Freestone, the county's first designated historic district. Freestone was once the site of a Russian experimental farm (to grow wheat for Sitka, Alaska in 1814), a stagecoach stop en route to the coast and a key station on the bootleg Underground Railway. Freestone itself has only one street, and that one is crooked.
Location: Near Bodega Bay.
*Rates: $78. Rogers & Rosemary Hoffman.
4 R. 4 PB. Phone available. Beds: QD. Full breakfast. Handicap access. CCs: MC VISA. Horseback riding nearby, deep-sea fishing, canoes, biking. Enzyme baths nearby.
Seen in: *Sonoma Monthly, San Francisco Chronicle.*
"The Green Apple is a cozy inn. Not rushed but you can take your time." Emma, age 6.

GARBERVILLE NM3/*C1*

Benbow Inn
445 Lake Benbow Dr
Garberville CA 95440
(707) 923-2125
Circa 1926. The Benbow family commissioned famous architect Albert Far to design this Tudor-style inn. An im-

posing sight, it is set among Japanese maple trees and an English rose garden. Each summer the park service builds a dam to form a lake, creating a sandy beach and backdrop for Shakespeare plays performed in July and August. The lobby and main rooms of the inn are filled with fine paintings, antiques, old clocks and books. The dining room overlooks green lawns leading down to the banks of the Eel River.
Location: On the Eel River, two miles south of Garberville.
*Rates: $78-$220. Patsy & Chuck Watts.
55 R. 55 PB. Phone available. TV available. Beds: KQDT. EP. Spa. CCs: MC VISA. Lake swimming, hiking, biking. Afternoon tea & scones, wine.
Seen in: *New York Times.*
"An astonishing place with charm by the ton!! This is our fifth visit."

GEORGETOWN NL11/*E3*

American River Inn
Orleans St, PO Box 43
Georgetown CA 95634

(916) 333-4499 (916) 333-9253
Circa 1853. Just a few miles from where gold was discovered in Coloma stands this completely restored boarding house. Mining cars dating back to

the original Woodside Mine Camp are visible. The lode still runs under the inn, although no one knows exactly where. Maybe you can find a nugget as large as the one that weighed in at 126 ounces! Swimmers will enjoy a spring-fed pool on the property.
*Rates: $74-$98. Maria & Will Collin & Helene Linney.
27 R. 15 PB. 2 FP. Phone available. Beds: KQ. Full breakfast. Spa. Handicap access. Swimming pool. Conference room. FAX. CCs: MC VISA AE. Fishing, hiking, skiing, golf, rafting, ballooning. White water rafting on the American River.
Seen in: *Los Angeles Times, Sunset.*
"Our home away from home. We fell in love here in all its beauty and will be back for our fourth visit in April, another honeymoon for six days."

GILROY SB4/*F2*

Country Rose Inn A Bed & Breakfast

PO Box 1804
Gilroy CA 95021-1804
(408) 842-0441
Circa 1920. Amidst five heavily wooded acres a half-hour's drive south of San Jose, sits the aptly named Country Rose Inn, a roomy Dutch Colonial manor, once a farmhouse on the Lucky Hereford Ranch. Every room features a rose theme, including wallpaper and quilted bedspreads. Each window offers a relaxing view of sheep grazing on rolling hills, fertile fields, or the tranquil grounds, which boast magnificent 100-year old oak trees.
Location: Masten Avenue exit off Hwy 101 in San Martin, north of Gilroy.
Rates: $85-$149. Rose Hernandez.
5 R. 5 PB. 2 FP. Phone available. Beds: KQDT. Full breakfast. Conference room. CCs: MC VISA AE. Golf, hot air ballooning, hiking, bicycling, wineries. Honeymoon suite.
Seen in: *San Jose Mercury News, Houston Chronicle, San Jose Magazine.*
"The quiet, serene country setting made our anniversary very special. Rose is a delightful, gracious hostess and cook."

GRASS VALLEY NK10/*D3*

Swan-Levine House

328 S Church St
Grass Valley CA 95945
(916) 272-1873
Circa 1880. Originally built by a local merchant, this Queen Anne Victorian was converted into a hospital by Dr. John Jones and it served the area as a medical center until 1968. Innkeepers/artists Howard and Margaret Levine renovated the house including a printmaking studio and guesthouse. The old surgery is now a guest room, with rose-painted walls and octagonal white floor tiles, providing a grand view from the wicker-furnished turret.
Rates: $55-$85. Howard & Peggy Levine.
4 R. 4 PB. Phone available. TV available. Beds: KQT. Full breakfast. Swimming pool. CCs: MC VISA. Swimming, badminton and nearby skiing, hiking, fishing. Etching instruction at the inn.
Seen in: *Country Living Magazine.*
"You made us feel at home. An atmosphere of open-hearted friendship is rather rare these days."

GROVELAND NP13/*F3*

The Groveland Hotel

18767 Main St, PO Box 481
Groveland CA 95321
(209) 962-4000
Circa 1849. Located 25 miles from Yosemite National Park, the newly restored hotel features an 1849 adobe building with 18-inch-thick walls constructed during the Gold Rush and a

1914 building erected to house workers for the Hetch Hetchy Dam. Both feature two-story balconies. There is a Victorian parlor, an exercise room, a restaurant and a Western saloon. Guest rooms feature European antiques and down comforters.
*Rates: $65-$125. Peggy & Grover Mosley.
19 R. 19 PB. 1 FP. Phone in room. TV available. Beds: QT. MAP. Restaurant. Gourmet meals. Spa. Handicap access. Exercise room. Conference room. FAX. CCs: MC VISA AE DC CB. Golf, water sports. Yosemite packages, golf tours.
Seen in: *The Union Democrat.*
"Hospitality is outstanding."

GUALALA NL4/*D1*

The Old Milano Hotel & Restaurant

38300 Hwy 1
Gualala CA 95445
(707) 884-3256
Circa 1905. This three-acre oceanfront estate overlooking Castle Rock is surrounded by lush English gardens. Built by Bert Lucchinetti and named after his birthplace, Milan, the Old Milano was called "Big Bert's" by local residents. Most rooms offer views of the ocean, and The Caboose, a fanciful cottage, is tucked among the cedars for privacy. Situated atop the bluff is a hot tub overlooking a spectacular view of the Pacific Ocean.
Rates: $75-$160. Leslie L. Linscheid.
9 R. 3 PB. 2 FP. Phone available. Beds: QD. B&B. Restaurant. Gourmet meals. Spa. CCs: MC VISA AE. Horseback riding, hiking, whale watching, beach.
Seen in: *LA Magazine, Nursing Weekly.*

GUERNEVILLE NM5/*E1*

Ridenhour Ranch

12850 River Rd
Guerneville CA 95446
(707) 887-1033
Circa 1906. Located on a hill overlooking the Russian River, this ranch house is shaded by redwoods, oaks and laurels. There are seven guest rooms and a cottage, overlooking the rose garden. The innkeepers are former restauranteurs from Southern California and provide a changing dinner menu for their guests. The Korbel Champagne cellars are nearby and it's a five-minute walk to the river.
Location: Russian River.
*Rates: $65-$115. Diane & Fritz Rechberger.
8 R. 5 PB. 3 FP. Phone available. TV available. Beds: QD. Full breakfast. Gourmet meals. CCs: MC VISA. Hiking, biking, horseback riding, canoeing.
Seen in: *Los Angeles Times, The Orange County Register.*
"Your hospitality and food will ensure our return!"

HALF MOON BAY NQ7/*F1*

Mill Rose Inn

615 Mill St
Half Moon Bay CA 94019
(415) 726-9794
Circa 1903. This Victorian country inn is part of the original Miramontes

land grant, and played an important part in local coastal history. English country gardens bloom year-round

under the magical hand of innkeeper and landscape designer Terry Baldwin. Canopy beds, claw-foot tubs, hand-painted fireplaces, and an inside garden spa create an opulent setting in which to relax.
*Rates: $145-$225. Eve & Terry Baldwin.
6 R. 6 PB. 5 FP. Phone in room. TV in room. Beds: KQ. Full breakfast. Spa. Conference room. CCs: MC VISA. Horseback riding, beach, wineries, whale watching. Musicians and masseuses on call, VCR and movies.
Seen in: *New York Times, LA Times, Dallas Morning News.*
"One of the loveliest retreats this side of the Cotswolds." San Diego Union.

Old Thyme Inn
779 Main St
Half Moon Bay CA 94019
(415) 726-1616
Circa 1897. Redwood harvested from nearby forests and dragged by oxen was used to construct this Queen Anne Victorian on historic Main

Street. Decorated in a distinctly English style, the inn boasts fireplaces and four-poster and canopy beds. The skylight in the Garden Suite, above a double whirlpool tub, treats bathers to a view of the night sky. Innkeeper Anne Lowings has cultivated 80 varieties of herbs in her garden, and serious herbalists are provided with a cutting kit to take samples back home.
*❀Rates: $65-$190. Anne & Simon Lowings.
7 R. 7 PB. 3 FP. Phone available. Beds: QDT. B&B. Spa. CCs: MC VISA AE. Golf, tennis, tidepools, horseback riding, fishing, whale watching, beaches.
Seen in: *California Weekends, Los Angeles Magazine.*
"Furnishings, rooms and garden were absolutely wonderful."

Zaballa House
324 Main St
Half Moon Bay CA 94019
(415) 726-9123 (800) 77BNB4U
Circa 1859. The Zaballa House is the oldest building still standing in Half Moon Bay. The inn features an elegant reception room, a breakfast nook and a parlor with comfortable Victorian-style chairs. Windows, some dating back to the house's construction, have been restored. Guest rooms have such

amenities as 10-foot ceilings, vaulted ceilings, fireplaces, claw-foot tubs and garden views.
*❀Rates: $75-$120. Patricia Lee.
9 R. 9 PB. 4 FP. Phone available. Beds: QD Continental-plus breakfast. Spa. CCs: MC VISA AE. Horseback riding, golf, tennis, fishing, whale watching, biking.
Seen in: *Half Moon Bay Review.*
"The hospitality extended to us made us feel very welcome."

HEALDSBURG NM6/*D1*

Camellia Inn
211 North St
Healdsburg CA 95448
(707) 433-8182
Circa 1869. An elegant Italianate Victorian town house, the Camellia Inn has twin marble parlor fireplaces and an ornate mahogany dining room fireplace. Antiques fill the guest rooms, complementing Palladian windows and classic interior moldings. The award-winning grounds feature 30 varieties of camellias and are accentuated with a pool.
Location: Heart of the Sonoma Wine Country.
*Rates: $65-$115. Ray & Del Lewand.
9 R. 7 PB. 4 FP. Phone available. Beds: QT. Full breakfast. Handicap access. Swimming pool. CCs: MC VISA DS. Three rooms have double whirlpool tubs.
Seen in: *San Fernando Valley Daily News, San Diego Union, Sacramento Bee, Healdsburg Tribune.*
"A bit of paradise for city folks."

Haydon House
321 Haydon St
Healdsburg CA 95448
(707) 433-5228
Circa 1912. Architectural buffs will have fun naming the several architectural styles found in the Haydon House. It has the curving porch and

general shape of a Queen Anne Victorian, the expansive areas of siding and unadorned columns of the Bungalow style, and the exposed roof rafters of the Craftsman.
Location: Western Sonoma County, heart of the wine country.
*Rates: $75-$135. Richard & Joanne Claus.
8 R. 5 PB. 1 FP. Phone available. TV available. Beds: QT. Full breakfast. Conference room. CCs: MC VISA.
Seen in: *Los Angeles Magazine.*
"Adjectives like class, warmth, beauty, thoughtfulness with the right amount of privacy, attention to details relating to comfort, all come to mind. Thank you for the care and elegance."

Healdsburg Inn On The Plaza
110-116 Matheson St, PO Box 1196
Healdsburg CA 95448
(707) 433-6991
Circa 1900. A former Wells Fargo building, the inn is a renovated brick gingerbread overlooking the plaza in historic downtown Healdsburg. Ornate bay windows, embossed wood paneling and broad, paneled stairs present a welcome entrance. There are fireplaces and the halls are filled with sunlight from vaulted glass skylights. A roof garden-solarium is the setting for breakfast and afternoon tea. A large covered porch extends along the entire rear of the building. Shops on the premises sell gifts, toys, quilts and fabric. A bakery and art gallery can be found there as well.
❀Rates: $65-$145. Genny Jenkins, Dyanne Celi.
9 R. 9 PB. 4 FP. TV in room. Beds: Q. Full breakfast. CCs: MC VISA DS. Bicycles, canoes, river rafts, sailing, balloon rides, wineries, local art.
Seen in: *Healdsburg Tribune, Los Angeles Daily News, New York Times.*
"The first thing in the morning juice and coffee was much appreciated."

Madrona Manor A Country Inn
PO Box 818 1001 Westside Rd
Healdsburg CA 95448
(707) 433-4231 (707) 433-4433
Circa 1881. The inn is comprised of four historic structures in a National

Historic District. Surrounded by eight

acres of manicured lawns and terraced flower and vegetable gardens, the stately mansion was built for John Paxton, a San Francisco businessman. Embellished with turrets, bay windows, porches, and a mansard roof, it provides a breathtaking view of surrounding vineyards. Elegant antique furnishings and a noteworthy restaurant add to the genuine country inn atmosphere. The Gothic-style Carriage House offers more casual lodging.

Location: In the heart of the wine country, Sonoma County.

*❀Rates: $100-$185. John & Carol Muir.

21 R. 21 PB. 18 FP. Phone available. Beds: KQDTC. EP. Restaurant. Gourmet meals. Handicap access. Swimming pool. Conference room. FAX. CCs: MC VISA AE DC. Canoeing, wine tasting, picnics, bicycles, antique shopping. Golf and tennis nearby.

Seen in: *San Francisco Examiner, Northern California Home & Garden, Gourmet, Country Inns, Woman's Day Home Decorating Ideas, Conde Nast Traveler.*

"Our fourth visit and better every time."

HOPE VALLEY NL14/*F4*

Sorensen's Resort

Hwy 88

Hope Valley CA 96120

(916) 694-2203 (800) 423-9949

Circa 1876. Where Danish sheepherders settled in this 7,000-foot-high mountain valley, the Sorensen family

built a cluster of fishing cabins. Thus began a century-old tradition of valley hospitality. The focal point of Sorensen's is a "stave" cabin - a reproduction of a 13th-century Nordic house. Now developed as a Nordic ski resort, a portion of the Mormon-Emigrant Trail and Pony Express Route pass near the inn's 165 acres. In the summer, river rafting, fishing, pony express re-rides, and llama treks are popular Sierra pastimes. Lake Tahoe lies 20 miles to the north.

*Rates: $50-$190. John & Patty Brissenden.

27 R. 25 PB. 14 FP. Phone available. Beds: QDC. B&B. Restaurant. Sauna. Conference room. CCs: MC VISA. Horseback & llama pack riding, hiking, rafting, fishing, biking, skiing.

Seen in: *Sunset Magazine, San Francisco Chronicle, Los Angeles Times.*

"We had a great time and really appreciate your wonderful hospitality."

IDYLLWILD SM18/*K5*

Wilkum Inn

26770 Hwy 243, PO Box 1115

Idyllwild CA 92349

(714) 659-4087 (714) 659-3321

Circa 1939. The inn is noted for its Old World charm, and the original knotty pine reflects Idyllwild's history of lumbering and sawmills. The pine-crafted stair-rails, unique to the area's construction in the Thirties, were milled locally.

Location: Three-fourths of a mile south of village center.

*Rates: $55-$75. Annamae Chambers & Barbara Jones.

5 R. 2 PB. Beds: QDT. Continental-plus breakfast. Handicap access. Visual and performing arts, quaint shops, hiking. Afternoon snacks.

Seen in: *Los Angeles Times.*

"Your inn really defines the concept of country coziness and hospitality."

INVERNESS NO6/*E1*

Ten Inverness Way

10 Inverness Way

Inverness CA 94937

(415) 669-1648

Circa 1904. Shingled in redwood, this bed and breakfast features a stone fireplace, good books, player piano

and access to a great hiking area. The view from the breakfast room invites you to include a nature walk in your day's plans. According to local folklore a ghost used to call Ten Inverness Way his home. However, since the innkeepers had each room blessed, he seems to have disappeared. The inn is now known for its peace and refreshment.

Location: Near Point Reyes National Seashore.

*Rates: $100-$120. Mary Davies.

4 R. Phone available. Beds: Q. B&B. Spa. CCs: MC VISA. Birdwatching, horseback-ing, hiking.

Seen in: *Los Angeles Times, New York Times, Travel & Leisure, Sunset, Gourmet.*

IONE NN11/*E3*

The Heirloom

214 Shakeley Ln, PO Box 322

Ione CA 95640

(209) 274-4468

Circa 1863. A two-story Colonial with columns, balconies, and a private English garden, the antebellum Heirloom is true to its name. It has many

family heirlooms and a square grand piano once owned by Lola Montez. The building was dedicated by the Native Sons of the Golden West as a historic site.

Location: California Gold Country.

*❀Rates: $50-$85. Melisande Hubbs & Patricia Cross.

6 R. 4 PB. 3 FP. Phone available. Beds: KQDT. Full breakfast. FAX. Swings, bicycles, croquet.

Seen in: *San Francisco Chronicle, Country Living.*

"Hospitality was amazing. Truly we've never had such a great time."

JACKSON NN11/*E3*

Court Street Inn

215 Court St

Jackson CA 95642

(209) 223-0416

Circa 1876. This cheery yellow and white Victorian era house is accentuated with green shutters and a porch stretching across the entire

front. Behind the house, a two-story brick structure that once served as a Wells Fargo office and a museum for Indian artifacts now houses guests. Hors d'oeuvres and wine are served in the dining room under a pressed, carved tin ceiling. Guests relax in front of a marble fireplace in the parlor topped by a gilded mirror. Guest rooms are decorated in antiques. Downtown is only two blocks away.

*❀Rates: $75-$125. Janet & Lee Hammond & Gia & Scott Anderson.

7 R. 3 PB. 3 FP. Phone available. TV in room. Beds: QD. Full breakfast. Spa. Handicap access. Conference room. CCs: MC VISA. Gold panning, swimming, biking, skiing, fishing, wineries.
Seen in: *Amador Dispatch, Sunset.*
"Warm hospitality, great breakfasts, and genuine family atmosphere. All our friends will only hear wonderful thoughts about the Court Street Inn."

JAMESTOWN NO12/*F3*

Historic National Hotel B&B

Main Street, PO Box 502
Jamestown CA 95327
(209) 984-3446

Circa 1859. One of the oldest continuously operating hotels in California, the inn maintains its original redwood bar where thousands of dol-

lars in gold dust were spent. Ten years ago electricity and plumbing were added for the first time when the inn was restored. It is decorated with gold rush period antiques, brass beds and handmade quilts. The restaurant is considered to be one of the finest in the Mother Lode.
Location: Center of town.
✻❀Rates: $45-$75. Stephen Willey.
11 R. 5 PB. Phone available. TV available. Beds: QT. AP. Restaurant. Gourmet meals. Handicap access. Conference room. CCs: MC VISA. Gold panning, water sports, horseback riding, snow skiing, Yosemite, Columbia National and Big Trees state parks.
Seen in: *Bon Appetit.*
"Excellent, wonderful place!"

JULIAN SO18/*K5*

Julian Gold Rush Hotel

2032 Main St, PO Box 1856
Julian CA 92036
(619) 765-0201

Circa 1897. The dream of a former slave and his wife lives today in this sole surviving hotel in Southern California's "Mother Lode of Gold

Mining." This Victorian charmer is listed in the National Register of Historic Places and is a designated State of California Point of Historic Interest (#SDI-09). Guests enjoy the feeling of a visit to grandma's and a tradition of genteel hospitality.
Location: Center of town.
✻❀Rates: $64-$145. Steve & Gig Ballinger.
18 R. 5 PB. 1 FP. Phone available. Beds: QDT. EP. Conference room. CCs: MC VISA AE. Horseback riding, fishing, hiking, historic gold mining town.
Seen in: *San Diego Union, PSA.*
"Any thoughts you have about the 20th century will leave you when you walk into the lobby of this grand hotel..." Westways Magazine.

KYBURZ NL13/*E3*

Strawberry Lodge

Hwy 50
Kyburz CA 95720
(916) 659-7030

Circa 1935. Nestled in the Sierra Nevada Mountains high above Lake Tahoe, Strawberry Lodge was named for Ira Fuller Berry. (It was said that he was so tight-fisted that he passed off straw for hay to teamsters driving their wagons up to the lodge. When they arrived, they would yell, "Got any more of that straw, Berry?") The lodge features brass beds and hand-painted furniture. Nearby, golden eagles nest on the high cliffs of Lover's Leap.
Location: 15 miles west of Lake Tahoe.
✻Rates: $35-$100. Richard Mitchell.
39 R. 34 PB. Phone available. TV available. Beds: KQT. EP. Swimming pool. Conference room. CCs: MC VISA. German brown and rainbow trout fishing, swimming, tennis. Dancing in the dance room.
Seen in: *San Francisco Examiner, City Sports.*

LA JOLLA SP16/*L4*

The B&B Inn at La Jolla

7753 Draper Ave
La Jolla CA 92037
(619) 456-2066

Circa 1913. The architect Irving Gill, father of tilt slab construction, built this home once occupied by John Philip Sousa and his family. All the guest rooms are beautifully designed, many with garden and ocean views. Honeymooners will be charmed by the room with the white canopy bed, fireplace and white sofa. Each room has one of Innkeeper Ardath Albee's fresh floral arrangements.
Location: One block to the ocean.
✻Rates: $75-$200. Ardath Albee.
16 R. 15 PB. Phone available. TV available. Beds: QT. Continental breakfast. Handicap access. CCs: MC VISA. Tennis across the street. Swimming, surfing, sunning.
Seen in: *Innsider, Country Inns.*
"Perfection, elegance, style! May I buy this room?"

LAGUNA BEACH SN15/*K4*

Carriage House

1322 Catalina St
Laguna Beach CA 92651
(714) 494-8945

Circa 1920. A Laguna Beach historical landmark, this inn has a Cape clapboard exterior. It housed an art gallery and a bakery before it was converted

into apartments with large rooms and kitchens. Now as a cozy inn, each room has a private parlor. Outside, the courtyard fountain is shaded by a large carrotwood tree with hanging moss.
Location: Two & one-half blocks from the ocean.
✻Rates: $95-$150. Dee & Vernon Taylor.
6 R. 6 PB. Phone available. TV available. Beds: KQDT. Continental-plus breakfast. Swimming, shopping.
"A true home away from home with all the extra touches added in."

Casa Laguna

2510 S Coast Hwy
Laguna Beach CA 92651
(714) 494-2996 (800) 233-0449

Circa 1930. A romantic combination of California Mission and Spanish Revival architecture, the Mission House and cottages were built in the

early Thirties. The casitas were added in the Forties. The hillside setting of secluded gardens, winding paths, and flower-splashed patios invites guests to linger and enjoy ocean views. Be sure to arrive in time to watch the sunset from the Bell Tower high above the inn.
Location: On an oceanview hillside.
✻❀Rates: $90-$205. Larry & Joline Terry.
20 R. 20 PB. 1 FP. Phone in room. TV in room. Beds: KQTC. Continental-plus breakfast. Swimming pool. Game room. Conference room. CCs: MC VISA AE DC CB DS.

Seen in: *Los Angeles Magazine, Houston Post.*
"What a fantastic place. Who needs a casa in Spain?"

Eiler's Inn
741 S Coast Hwy
Laguna Beach CA 92651
(714) 494-3004

This New Orleans-style inn surrounds a lush courtyard and fountain. The rooms are decorated with antiques and wallpapers. Wine and cheese is served during the evening in front of the fireplace. Named after Eiler Larsen, famous town greeter of Laguna, the inn is just a stone's throw from the beach on the ocean side of Pacific Coast Highway.
Location: In the heart of the village.
*Rates: $100-$170. Henk & Annette Wirtz.
12 R. 12 PB. 2 FP. Phone available. TV available. Beds: KQDT. B&B. CCs: MC VISA AE. Swimming, sunning.
Seen in: *Home & Garden.*
"Who could find a paradise more relaxing than an old-fashioned bed and breakfast with Mozart and Vivaldi, a charming fountain, wonderful fresh baked bread, ocean air, and Henk's conversational wit?"

LAKE ARROWHEAD SK17/J5

Storybook Inn
See: Skyforest, CA

LITTLE RIVER NJ3/D1

Glendeven
8221 N Hwy 1
Little River CA 95456
(707) 937-0083

Circa 1867. Lumber merchant Isaiah Stevens built this farmhouse on a two-acre headland meadow with the bay of Little River in the distance.

Gray clapboard siding and high-pitched roof lines reflect the architecture of Stevens' native Maine. Stevenscroft is a recent addition of four rooms, each with its own fireplace, views of the bay and breakfast in your room. One can often hear the sound of waves rolling onto the beach.
Location: One-and-a-half miles to Mendocino.
Rates: $70-$150. Jan & Janet deVries.
11 R. 10 PB. Beds: QDT. Continental-plus breakfast. Spa. CCs: MC VISA. Tennis, golf, horseback riding nearby. Wonderful hiking. Fine arts gallery on the property.
Seen in: *Arizona Republic, Contra Costa Times, Los Angeles Times, Country Inns.*
"Thank you for letting us be among those special people who experience the wonderment and joy of Eastlin at Glendeven."

The Victorian Farmhouse
7001 N Hwy 1, PO Box 357
Little River CA 95456
(707) 937-0697

Circa 1877. Built as a private residence, this Victorian farmhouse is located on two-and-a-half acres in Lit-

tle River. Two miles south of the historic village of Mendocino, the inn offers a relaxed country setting with deer, quail, flower gardens, an apple orchard and a running creek (School House Creek). A short walk will take you to the shoreline.
Rates: $80-$100. George & Carole Molnar.
10 R. 10 PB. Phone available. Beds: KQ. Continental-plus breakfast. Handicap access. Conference room. CCs: MC VISA. Horseback riding, canoeing, fishing, golf and hiking nearby. Garden weddings are popular.
"This morning when we woke up at home we really missed having George deliver breakfast. You have a lovely inn and you do a super job."

LONG BEACH SM14/J4

Lord Mayor's B&B Inn
435 Cedar Ave
Long Beach CA 90802
(213) 436-0324

Circa 1904. Charles Windham, first mayor of Long Beach, built this Edwardian-style home with granite pillars flanking the veranda. Bay windows and a decorative pediment top the second story. A grand piano occupies the foyer and often is used to play the wedding march for area weddings. Decorated in antiques such as a carved oak Hawaiian bedstead, all guest rooms have access to a sun deck. The Convention Center is within walking distance.
*Rates: $75-$85. Laura & Reuben Brasser.
5 R. 5 PB. Phone available. TV available. Beds: QDT. Full breakfast. Conference room. CCs: MC VISA AE. Queen Mary, Spruce Goose.
Seen in: *KCET Magazine, Daily News Los Angeles, Press Telegram.*
"Your hospitality and beautiful room were respites for the spirit and body after our long trip."

LOS ALAMOS SJ8/I2

Union Hotel & Victorian Annex
PO Box 616, 362 Bell St
Los Alamos CA 93440
(805) 344-2744 (805)489-9113

Circa 1864. The casual board and batten facade of the Union Hotel is in sharp contrast with its intensely decorated interiors. Richly

upholstered and carved furnishings, Egyptian burial urns, and an enormous Tiffany grandfather clock furnish the parlor. Fantasy guest rooms in the Victorian annex include the Egyptian room, entered through a one-ton stone door. An enormous pillared bed is draped in white, and there is a private soaking tub, fireplace and King Tut statue.
Location: Santa Barbara County.
*Rates: $80-$200. Dick Langdon.
20 R. 9 PB. 7 FP. Phone in room. TV in room. Beds: KQDT. Full breakfast. Restaurant. Spa. Swimming pool. Game room. Conference room. CCs: MC VISA. Missions, wineries, shopping.
Seen in: *Los Angeles Times, The Good Life, Pacific Coast.*
"The entire weekend was a fairy tale turned into a reality by you and the rest of your staff."

LOS ANGELES SL14/J4

Channel Road Inn
See: Santa Monica, CA

Eastlake Victorian Inn
1442 Kellam Ave
Los Angeles CA 90026
(213) 250-1620

Circa 1887. Faithfully restored, decorated and furnished, the Eastlake Victorian Inn is situated in Los Angeles' first historic preservation zone. Private tours of two National

Register Victorian homes are available, as well as old-fashioned hot-air ballooning and other nearby attractions.
Location: Near downtown and the Music Center.
**Rates: $49-$150. Murray Burns & Planaria Price.
9 R. 6 PB. Phone available. TV available. Beds: Q. B&B. Conference room. CCs: MC VISA AE. Museums and shopping.
Seen in: *USA Today, Travel & Leisure, Travel Holiday, Sunset.*
"Incomparably romantic!" Los Angeles Times.

Salisbury House
2273 W 20th St
Los Angeles CA 90018
(213) 737-7817 (800) 373-1778
Circa 1909. Located in Arlington Heights, the inn is part of the old West Adams area of Los Angeles. It features original stained and leaded-

glass windows, wood-beamed ceilings, and an abundance of wood paneling. Used as a location for movies and commercials, Salisbury House is known for its gourmet breakfasts and old-fashioned graciousness.
*Rates: $70-$90. Sue & Jay German.
5 R. 3 PB. 1 FP. Phone available. TV available. Beds: KQT. Full breakfast. CCs: MC VISA AE.
Seen in: *Sunset Magazine, Southern California Magazine, Los Angeles Magazine.*
"The finest bed and breakfast we've seen. Not only is the house exquisite but the hospitality is unmatched!"

Terrace Manor
1353 Alvarado Terrace
Los Angeles CA 90006
(213) 381-1478 (213) 388-6674
Circa 1902. This three-story Tudor is a National Register Landmark house. Tastefully decorated, the inn displays extraordinary stained-glass windows installed by the builder who owned a stained glass factory at the turn of the century.
*Rates: $70-$100. Sandy & Shirley Spillman.
5 R. 5 PB. Phone available. TV available. Beds: KQDT. Full breakfast. Conference room. CCs: MC VISA AE DC CB. Entrance to Magic Castle.
Seen in: *Victorian Homes.*
"Lovely! Sandy does magic in the parlor; Shirley in the kitchen!"

West Adams B&B Inn
1650 Westmoreland Blvd
Los Angeles CA 90006
(213) 737-5041
Circa 1913. The Rosenblum brothers built this splendid Craftsman home, and added a German-lodge style log fireplace. Natural mahogany wood-

work and elegant Arts and Crafts light fixtures are among the home's special touches. Built-in furnishings include a rare hideaway bed that has an arched cover which rolls toward the room creating a sleeping porch.
*Rates: $75-$80. Jon Rake & Jeffrey Stvrtecky.
3 R. 2 PB. 1 FP. Phone available. TV available. Beds: KQD. Full breakfast. Conference room. CCs: MC VISA. Convention Center, Los Angeles Music Center, art museums, Exposition Park.
Seen in: *Los Angeles Conservancy Newspaper, The Art of Living in L.A.*
"You really made us feel at home and treated us as special guests."

MAMMOTH LAKES NP16/F4

Rainbow Tarns
See: Crowley Lake, CA

MCCLOUD ND8/B3

McCloud Guest House
606 W Colombero Dr
McCloud CA 96057
(916) 964-3160
Circa 1907. The deep verandas that wrap around this massive Craftsman-style house extend a warm greeting to guests. For 50 years it served as a guest house for the McCloud River Lumber Company, accommodating the company's VIPs and executives. Luminaries such as Herbert Hoover and the Hearst family have stayed here. Elegantly restored, the inn includes an acclaimed restaurant enhanced by wood-beam ceilings, leaded-glass windows and handsome chandeliers.
Rates: $70-$90. Bill & Patti Leigh & Dennis & Pat Abreu.
5 R. 5 PB. 1 FP. Phone available. Beds: D. Continental breakfast. Restaurant. Game room. CCs: MC VISA. Downhill & cross-country skiing, golf, trout fishing.
Seen in: *Ski Country Magazine, Siskiyou County Scene.*

MENDOCINO NJ4/C1

Agate Cove Inn
PO Box 1150
Mendocino CA 95460
(707) 937-0551
Circa 1860. Perched on a blufftop overlooking the Pacific Ocean, the Agate Cove Inn was constructed by Mathias Brinzing, owner of the first beer brewery in Mendocino. Cottages are lovingly decorated, and some have stunning white water views. Jake, a former New York City ad agency executive, reigns supreme in the breakfast room, while multi-paned windows highlight the view. (On his first foray to a country fair, he entered his inn-baked bread and won a blue ribbon.)
Rates: $69-$155. Sallie McConnell & Jake Zahavi.
10 R. 10 PB. 9 FP. Phone available. TV in room. Beds: KQ. Full breakfast. CCs: MC VISA AE. River canoeing, hiking, fishing, horseback riding, tennis, golf.
Seen in: *Travel & Leisure, San Francisco Magazine, San Francisco Examiner.*
"Warmest hospitality, charming rooms, best breakfast and view in Mendocino."

DeHaven Valley Farm
See: Westport, CA

Glendeven
See: Little River, CA

The Headlands Inn
PO Box 132, Howard & Albion Sts
Mendocino CA 95460
(707) 937-4431
Circa 1868. Originally a small barbershop on Main Street, the building later became the elegant "Oyster and Coffee Saloon" in 1884. Finally, horses

pulled the house over log rollers to its present location. The new setting provides a spectacular view of the

ocean, the rugged coastline, and breathtaking sunsets. Antiques, paintings, and fireplaces warm each guest room. There is a romantic honeymoon cottage, an English-style garden, and two parlors. Full gourmet breakfast is served directly to your room.
Location: Two blocks from the village center.
Rates: $95-$138. Pat & Rod Stofle.
5 R. 5 PB. 6 FP. Phone available. Beds: KQ. B&B. Handicap access. Hiking in state parks, redwood groves, wineries, little theater, shops/galleries. No smoking or pets.
Seen in: *Los Angeles Times, Innsider, The Oakland Tribune, Orange County Register, Contra Costa Times.*
"If a Nobel Prize were given for breakfasts, you would win hands down. A singularly joyous experience!!"

John Dougherty House

571 Ukiah St, PO Box 817
Mendocino CA 95460
(707) 937-5266

Circa 1867. Early American furnishings and country-style stenciling provide the decor for this newly opened inn. Four rooms have outstanding

water views, including the Captain's Room. The water tower room has an 18-foot ceiling and wood-burning stove.
Location: Historic District.
*❀Rates: $85-$125. Dave & Marion Wells.
6 R. 6 PB. 3 FP. Phone available. TV in room. Beds: Q. Continental-plus breakfast. Conference room. CCs: MC VISA AE DS. Hiking, ocean sports, whale watching, shopping, restaurants. Garden weddings.
Seen in: *Mendocino Beacon.*
"The inn is beautiful and very comfortable."

Joshua Grindle Inn

44800 Little Lake Rd, PO Box 647
Mendocino CA 95460
(707) 937-4143

Circa 1879. The town banker, Joshua Grindle, built this New England-style home on two acres. The decor is light and airy, with Early American antiques, clocks and quilts. In addition to lodging in the house, there are rooms in the water tower and in an adjacent cottage. Six of the guest

rooms have fireplaces. Some have views over the town to the ocean.
Location: On the Pacific Ocean at the edge of the village.
Rates: $65-$100. Arlene & Jim Moorehead.
10 R. 10 PB. Phone available. Beds: QDT. Full breakfast. Handicap access. CCs: MC VISA DS. Hiking, golf, deep sea fishing, bicycling, art galleries.
Seen in: *Peninsula, Copley News Service.*
"We are basking in the memories of our stay. We loved every moment."

MacCallum House Inn

45020 Albion St
Mendocino CA 95460
(707) 937-0289

Circa 1882. Built by William H. Kelley for his newly wed daughter Daisy MacCallum, the MacCallum House Inn is a splendid example of New England architecture in the Victorian village of Mendocino. Besides the main house, accommodations include the barn, carriage house, greenhouse, gazebo and water tower rooms.
Location: North Coast.
*Rates: $45-$135. Melanie & Joe Reding.
20 R. 7 PB. Phone available. Beds: KQTC. Continental breakfast. Handicap access. CCs: MC VISA.
Seen in: *California Visitors Review.*

Mendocino Hotel

PO Box 587, 45080 Main St
Mendocino CA 95460
(707) 937-0511 (800) 548-0513

Circa 1878. Rising prominently on the blufftop, the Mendocino Hotel was originally established as a temperance hotel for lumbermen. An Old-West

facade was added. The historic Heeser House, home of Mendocino's first settler, was annexed by the hotel along with its acre of gardens. Many of the guest rooms and suites boast tall four-poster and canopy beds or fireplaces and coastal views. The hotel has several dining rooms.
*Rates: $65-$275. Mark Bowery.
51 R. 39 PB. 20 FP. Phone in room. TV in room. Beds: KQDT. Restaurant. Handicap access. Conference room. CCs: MC VISA AE. Whale watching, canoeing, river & ocean fishing, golf, tennis, horseback riding, hiking. Wedding and reception facilities.
Seen in: *Los Angeles Times, The Tribune.*
"The hotel itself is magnificent, but more importantly, your staff is truly incredible."

Mendocino Village Inn

44860 Main St, PO Box 626
Mendocino CA 95460
(707) 937-0246

Circa 1882. Originally the home of physician Dr. William McCornack, this graceful Victorian has been beautifully restored. One of the ar-

chitectural gems of Mendocino, the inn has a variety of rooms with both Victorian and country decor. Seven of the rooms have fireplaces with neatly stacked wood beside them. The ocean and the pleasures of the North Coast lie just beyond the house's white picket fence.
Location: Walking distance to everything in the village.
Rates: $55-$120. Sue & Tom Allen.
12 R. 10 PB. 7 FP. Phone available. Beds: Q. Full breakfast. CCs: MC VISA.
Seen in: *Wine Country Review.*
"Thanks for making our visit very special! We enjoyed the ambience you provided - Vivaldi, Diamond Lil, homemade breakfast and of course, Mendocino charm!"

The Stanford Inn by the Sea

PO Box 487
Mendocino CA 95460
(707) 937-5615 (707) 937-5026

Circa 1898. Tucked against a forested hillside, the Stanford Inn, a new building, affords every guest a view

of the ocean. Its 10 acres include an expansive lawn studded with flower

gardens that slopes down to a duck pond and redwood barn where the inn's llamas and horses graze. Each room has a four-poster bed, a wood-burning fireplace and watercolors and paintings by local artists. A Thirties cottage is on the premises and there is a turn of the century homestead. Complimentary red and white Mendocino wines are offered.
Rates: $145-$250. Joan & Jeff Stanford.
26 R. 26 PB. 26 FP. Phone in room. TV in room. Beds: KQ. Continental-plus breakfast. Spa. Sauna. Handicap access. Swimming pool. Conference room. CCs: VISA AE DC CB DS. Canoeing, ocean kayaking, horseback riding, mountain bikes & bike racks to lend, shopping.
Seen in: *The Oakland Tribune, Bride's, Contra Costa Times.*
"As working parents with young children, our weekends away are so terribly few in number, that every one must be precious. Thanks to you, our weekend in Mendocino was the finest of all."

Whitegate Inn
PO Box 150, 499 Howard St
Mendocino CA 95460
(707) 937-4892
Circa 1883. When it was first built, the local newspaper called Whitegate Inn "one of the most elegant and best ap-

pointed residences in town." It is resplendent with bay windows, a steep gabled roof, redwood siding and fishscale shingles. The house's original wallpaper adorns one of the double parlors. There, an antique 1827 piano, at one time part of Alexander Graham Bell's collection, and inlaid pocket doors take you back to a simpler time. The silver, Baccarat crystal and Rosenthal china used at breakfast add a crowning touch to the inn's elegant hospitality.
Rates: $65-105. Patricia Patton.
5 R. 5 PB. 4 FP. Phone available. Beds: KQDT. B&B. Conference room. Horseback riding, canoeing, Pacific Ocean.
Seen in: *Innsider, Country Inns.*
"Made our honeymoon a dream come true."

MILL VALLEY NO6/*E1*

Mountain Home Inn
810 Panoramic Hwy
Mill Valley CA 94941
(415) 381-9000
Circa 1912. At one time the only way to get to Mountain Home was by taking the train up Mount Tamalpais. With 22 trestles and 281 curves, it was called "the crookedest railroad in the world." Now accessible by auto, the trip still provides a spectacular view of San Francisco Bay. Each guest room has a view of the mountain, valley or bay.
Location: Mt. Tamalpais.
*Rates: $112-$178. Ed & Susan Cunningham.
10 R. 10 PB. 3 FP. TV available. Beds: KQ. B&B. Spa. Handicap access. Conference room. CCs: MC VISA. Ocean beach 10 minutes away. Above giant redwoods of Muir Woods.
Seen in: *San Francisco Examiner, California Magazine.*
"A luxurious retreat. Echoes the grand style and rustic feeling of national park lodges." Ben Davidson, *Travel and Leisure.*

MONTARA NH18/*F1*

The Goose & Turrets Bed & Breakfast
PO Box 937
Montara CA 94037-0937
(415) 728-5451
Circa 1908. This Northern Italian villa-style house has served as an art gallery, veterans hall, nursing home, church and nudist colony. It is now an

antique-filled bed and breakfast. The Hummingbird Room with its wood-burning stove and sitting area, includes an English towel warmer, goose-down comforter and desk. Southwest corn-pepper pancakes with salsa and sour cream are often served at breakfast along with Emily's entertaining stories about the old house. A water fountain, rose garden and herb garden are surrounded by a 20-foot-tall cypress hedge. The inn's white China geese are favorites of guests.
Rates: $80-$90. Raymond & Emily Hoche-Mong.
5 R. 1 PB. 1 FP. Phone available. Beds: KQDT. Full breakfast. CCs: MC VISA AE DS.
Seen in: *Half Moon Bay Review, Peninsula Times Tribune, San Mateo Times, The Los Angeles Times.*
"Lots of special touches. Great Southern hospitality — we'll be back."

MONTEREY SC3/*G1*

Gatehouse Inn
See: Pacific Grove, CA

The Jabberwock
598 Laine St
Monterey CA 93940
(408) 372-4777
Circa 1911. Set in a half-acre of gardens, this Victorian inn provides a fabulous view of Monterey Bay and its famous barking seals. When you're

ready to settle in for the evening, you'll find huge Victorian beds complete with lace-edged sheets and goose-down comforters. Early evening hors d'oeuvres and aperitifs are served in an enclosed veranda.
Location: Four blocks above Cannery Row, the beach and Monterey Bay Aquarium.
Rates: $95-$170. Jim & Barbara Allen.
7 R. 3 PB. 1 FP. Phone available. Beds: KQ. Full breakfast. Conference room. Biking, boating, horseback riding. Fisherman's Wharf, Seventeen-Mile Drive.
Seen in: *Sacramento Bee, San Francisco Examiner, Los Angeles Times.*
"Not only were the accommodations delightful but the people were equally so."

Old Monterey Inn
500 Martin St
Monterey CA 93940
(408) 375-8284
Circa 1929. Built in the Tudor style with half-timbers, the ivy-covered Old Monterey Inn looks and feels like an English country house. Brick pathways and a comfortable hammock beckon guests outside to the garden. Redwood, pine and old oak trees shelter an acre of pansies, roses, peonies and rhododendrons. Most of the guest rooms have wood-burning fireplaces, skylights and stained-glass windows. Smoking is permitted in the garden.
Location: Five minutes from Monterey Bay Aquarium.
Rates: $150-$210. Ann & Gene Swett.

10 R. 10 PB. 8 FP. Phone available. Beds: KQT. B&B. Designer robes in each closet, executive retreats.
Seen in: *Los Angeles Times, PSA Magazine, San Francisco Focus, Country Inns, Travel & Leisure, Glamour.*
"Bed and Breakfast Inn of the Year." Hideaway Report.

MURPHYS NN12/E3

Dunbar House, 1880
271 Jones St, PO Box 1375
Murphys CA 95247
(209) 728-2897

Circa 1880. A picket fence frames this Italianate home, built by Willis Dunbar for his bride. Later, distinguished

sons who served in the state assembly and ran the Dunbar Lumber Company lived here. On the porch, rocking chairs overlook century-old gardens. Inside are antiques, lace, quilts and claw-foot tubs. Breakfast is delivered to your room in a picnic basket, or you may join others by the fireplace in the dining room.
Location: Two blocks from the center of town.
*Rates: $95-$135. Bob & Barbara Costa.
4 R. 4 PB. 4 FP. Phone available. TV available. Beds: Q. Full breakfast. CCs: MC VISA. Tennis, swimming, jacuzzi, sauna, exercise room, game room and fishing nearby. Skiing 39 miles. Winery and gold panning tours.
Seen in: *Los Angeles Times, Gourmet Magazine, Victorian Homes.*
"Your beautiful gardens and gracious hospitality combine for a super bed and breakfast."

NAPA NM7/E2

Beazley House
1910 First St
Napa CA 94559
(707) 257-1649

Circa 1902. Nestled in green lawns and gardens, this graceful shingled mansion is frosted with white trim on its bays and balustrades. Stained-glass windows and polished wood floors set the atmosphere in the parlor. There are five rooms in the main house and the carriage house features five more, many with fireplaces and whirlpool tubs. The venerable Beazley House was Napa's first bed and breakfast inn.
*Rates: $100-$175. Jim & Carol Beazley.

10 R. 10 PB. 6 FP. Phone available. Beds: KQ. B&B. Spa. Handicap access. CCs: MC VISA DS. Horseback riding, water sports, wineries.
Seen in: *Los Angeles Times, USA Today.*
"It has everything: history, style, romance."

The Candlelight Inn
1045 Easum Dr
Napa CA 94558
(707) 257-3717

Circa 1929. This graceful English Tudor-style house is situated on an acre of lawns and gardens a few blocks from the center of town. Hardwood floors shine under the light of the fireplace in the parlor. Each guest accommodation is a suite, and the Candlelight Suite boasts a canopy bed and a private sauna. The inn's dining room features French doors and windows overlooking the garden. A candlelight breakfast is served here.
Rates: $125-$140. Joe & Carol Farace.
3 R. 3 PB. Beds: D. Continental-plus breakfast. Handicap access. CCs: MC VISA. River boat cruises, hot air ballooning, wine train tour, bicycle tours, glider rides, golf.
"We still haven't stopped talking about the great food, wonderful accommodations and gracious hospitality."

Churchill Manor
485 Brown St
Napa CA 94559
(707) 253-7733

Circa 1889. This historic Second Empire mansion, one of Napa's stateliest, features 2,500 square feet of verandas supported by Greek columns. Inside are handsome antiques and luxurious touches such as a 24-carat, gold-trimmed claw-foot tub, carved bedsteads, a gold-laced fireplace and a red and black spa. Guests can borrow the tandem bike or play croquet in the side garden of this two-acre estate.
Rates: $75-$145. Joanna Guidotti.
8 R. 8 PB. 3 FP. Phone in room. Beds: KQ. Continental-plus breakfast. Gourmet meals. Spa. Game room. Conference room. CCs: MC VISA AE. Balloon rides, golf, horseback riding, bicycling, mud baths, wineries. Weddings, conferences, complimentary evening wine.
Seen in: *Napa County Record, The Food & Beverage Journal.*
"We have told many of our friends about your house, the rooms and the warm atmosphere."

Coombs Residence Inn on the Park
720 Seminary St
Napa CA 94559
(707) 257-0789

Circa 1852. Nathan Coombs, who laid out the city of Napa, and who was ambassador to Japan during President Harrison's term, built this two-story Victorian home for his son Frank. The inn is decorated with European and American antiques. Across the street is historic Fuller Park.
Location: One hour from San Francisco.
*Rates: $80-$100. Dave & Pearl Campbell.
4 R. 1 PB. Phone available. TV available. Beds: KQD. Continental breakfast. Spa. Swimming pool. CCs: MC VISA.
"We feel like we are back in Europe! Your hospitality is unmatched! Simple elegance with warm friendly atmosphere. Our favorite B&B, a house with its own personality."

Country Garden Inn
1815 Silverado Trail
Napa CA 94558
(707) 255-1197

Circa 1860. This historic carriage house is situated on the Napa River and one-and-a-half acres of woodland. A circular rose garden with a lily pond and fountain add to the natural beauty of the location. Many of the guest rooms have spas, canopy beds, fireplaces, or private decks looking out over the water. English innkeepers serve hors d'oeuvres in the early evening and desserts later.
Location: South end of Napa Valley.
*Rates: $100-$150. Lisa & George Smith.
10 R. 10 PB. 4 FP. Phone available. Beds: KQ. B&B. Spa. Handicap access. CCs: MC VISA AE. Wine tasting, hiking, golf, horseback riding.
Seen in: *Los Angeles Times, San Francisco Examiner.*

The Hennessey House B&B
1727 Main St
Napa CA 94559
(707) 226-3774

Circa 1889. This gracious Queen Anne Eastlake Victorian was once home to Dr. Edwin Hennessey, a Napa County physician. Pristinely renovated, the inn features stained-glass windows and a curving wraparound porch. A handsome hand-painted, stamped-tin ceiling graces the dining room. All rooms are furnishied in antiques. The four guest rooms in the carriage

house boast whirlpool baths and fireplaces.
Location: One hour from San Francisco.
Rates: $80-$155. Lauriann Zemann & Andrea Weinstein.
10 R. 10 PB. 4 FP. Beds: Q. Continental-plus breakfast. Spa. Sauna. CCs: MC VISA AE. Bike rental, health club, wine train, golf.
Seen in: *AM-PM Magazine.*

Napa Inn
1137 Warren St
Napa CA 94559
(707) 257-1444
Circa 1898. Herb and flower gardens frame this Queen Anne Victorian, nestled in the heart of a serene wine country neighborhood. Furnished

with antiques, the inn has a sitting room with a fireplace. Breakfast is brought to each room. Shaded parks, gourmet and family restaurants are a short stroll from the inn.
Location: In the historic district.
❀Rates: $90-$135. Doug & Carol Morales.
4 R. 4 PB. 1 FP. Phone available. Beds: KQ. Full breakfast. CCs: MC VISA. Horseback riding, wine touring, balloon rides.
Seen in: *San Francisco Examiner.*

Old World Inn
1301 Jefferson
Napa CA 94559
(707) 257-0112
Circa 1906. In 1981 Macy's Department Store chose the Old World Inn to showcase a new line of fabrics inspired by the work of Scandinavian artist Carl Larsson. French pinks, blues and peaches were chosen for the canopy beds and stenciled wall designs all happily blended with Victorian antiques and polished hardwood floors. Wine and cheese are served in the afternoon and a dessert buffet is provided in the evening.
Rates: $77-$132. Diane M. Dumaine.
8 R. 8 PB. Phone available. Beds: QD. Continental-plus breakfast. Spa. Conference room. CCs: MC VISA AE. Hot air ballooning, hiking, biking, horseback riding, golf, mud baths, wine train.
Seen in: *Napa Valley Traveller.*
"Excellent is an understatement. We'll return."

NEVADA CITY NK11/*D3*

Downey House
517 W Broad St
Nevada City CA 95959
(916) 265-2815
Circa 1869. This Eastlake Victorian house is one of Nevada City's noted Nabob Hill Victorians. There are six sound-proofed guest rooms, a curved

veranda, and in the garden, a pond and restored red barn. One can stroll downtown where the evening streets are lit by the warm glow of gas lights.

Location: On Nabob Hill close to the Historic District.
✻Rates: $70-$90. Miriam Wright.
6 R. 6 PB. Phone available. TV available. Beds: QD. B&B. CCs: MC VISA. Tennis, fishing, gold panning, boating, watersports, wineries, horseback riding, skiing. Horse-drawn carriages, trolley.
Seen in: *San Francisco Examiner, Country Living.*
"The best in Northern California."

Grandmere's Inn
449 Broad St
Nevada City CA 95959
(916) 265-4660
Circa 1856. Arron Sargent, U.S. Congressman, senator, and author of the women's suffrage bill, was the first owner of this white Colonial Revival house. He and his wife often received Susan B. Anthony here. Shaker pine furnishings and white wooden shutters predominate the interior design. Lavish creature comforts include six pillows to a bed and cut crystal water glasses in the bathrooms. Huge country breakfasts may include Dutch baby pancakes, baked brie in sherry, potatoes with cheddar and the inn's

trademark, bread pudding. A half acre of terraced gardens cascade behind the inn to the block below.
Rates: $95-$135.
7 R. 7 PB. Phone available. TV available. Beds: Q. B&B. CCs: MC VISA. Horseback riding, cross-country & downhill skiing nearby.
Seen in: *Country Living, Gourmet, Sierra Heritage, California Inns.*
"Thanks for making me feel at home - no, better than home!"

National Hotel
211 Broad St
Nevada City CA 95959
(916) 265-4551
Circa 1852. The National Hotel is said to be California's oldest continually operating hotel. Antiques from the Gold Rush era are featured in the inn and some guest rooms have canopy and four-poster beds. A Victorian dining room is available for breakfast, lunch or dinner. Ask for a quiet room during weekends when live entertainment is featured.
Rates: $43-$105. Thomas A. Coleman.
42 R. 30 PB. 1 FP. Phone in room. TV in room. Beds: KQDT. EP. Restaurant. Handicap access. Swimming pool. Conference room. CCs: MC VISA AE.
Seen in: *Early American Life, Mobil Travel Guide.*
"Your hotel is No. 1 in my book!"

The Red Castle Inn
109 Prospect St
Nevada City CA 95959
(916) 265-5135
Circa 1857. The Smithsonian has lauded the restoration of this four-story brick Gothic Revival known as "The Castle" by townsfolk. Its roof is

laced with wooden icicles and the bal-

conies are festooned with gingerbread. Within, there are intricate moldings, antiques, Victorian wallpapers, canopy beds and woodstoves. Verandas provide views of the historic city through cedar, chestnut and walnut trees, and of terraced gardens with a fountain pond.
Location: Within the historic district overlooking the town.
*Rates: $70-$110. Conley & Mary Louise Weaver.
8 R. 6 PB. Phone available. Beds: QD. Full breakfast. CCs: MC VISA. Cross-country skiing, swimming, tennis, golf, whitewater rafting. Horse-drawn carriage rides to town.
Seen in: *Sunset, Gourmet, Northern California Home and Garden, Sacramento Bee.*
"The Red Castle Inn would top my list of places to stay. Nothing else quite compares with it." Gourmet.

NICE NK6/D1

Featherbed Railroad Company B&B
2870 Lakeshore Blvd
Nice CA 95464
(707) 274-8378 (707) BRGuest
Located on five acres on Clear Lake, this unusual inn features guest rooms in five luxuriously renovated, painted, and papered cabooses. Each has its own featherbed and private bath. The Southern Pacific cabooses have a bay window alcove while those from the Santa Fe feature small cupolas. Bicycles, canopied patio boats and jet skis are available for rent.
Rates: $75-$108. Lorraine & Len Bassignani.
5 R. 5 PB. TV in room. Beds: DT. Continental-plus breakfast. Spa. Swimming pool. CCs: MC VISA AE.
Seen in: *Santa Rosa Press Democrat, Fairfield Daily Republic.*

NIPOMO SI7/F2

The Kaleidoscope Inn
Box 1297, 130 E Dana St
Nipomo CA 93444
(805) 929-5444
Circa 1887. A picket fence framed by pink Shasta daisies sets off this Victorian farmhouse. Inside are antique sofas, an old wooden trunk of the owner's great grandmother and vintage photographs. Breakfast is served in the dining room. Sunlight filtering through the stained-glass windows creates a kaleidoscope effect.
Location: Twenty miles south of San Luis Obispo, near Pismo Beach.
**Rates: $65-$70. Patty & Bill Linane.
3 R. 2 PB. 1 FP. Phone available. TV available. Beds: KQ. Continental-plus breakfast. Spa. CCs: MC VISA. Golfing, horseback riding, mineral springs, wind surfing,

water skiing. Dinner & theater reservations.
Seen in: *Santa Maria Times, Los Angeles Times.*
"Beautiful room, chocolates, huge bathroom, fresh flowers, peaceful night's rest, great breakfast."

NIPTON SG22/I7

Hotel Nipton
HCI, Box 357
Nipton CA 92364
(619) 856-2335
Circa 1904. This southwestern-style adobe hotel with its wide verandas once housed gold miners and Clara Bow, wife of movie star Rex Bell. It is

decorated in period furnishings and historic photos of the area. A 1920s rock and cactus garden blooms and an outdoor spa provides the perfect setting for watching a flaming sunset over Ivanpah Valley, the New York Mountains, and Castle Peaks. Later, a magnificent star-studded sky appears undimmed by city lights.
Location: East Mojave National scenic area.
*Rates: $48.15. Jerry & Roxanne Freeman.
4 R. Beds: DT. Continental-plus breakfast. Spa. CCs: MC VISA. Mining tours, Cottonwood Cove.

OJAI SK11/I3

Ojai Manor Hotel
210 E Matilija
Ojai CA 93023
(805) 646-0961
Circa 1874. Once a schoolhouse, this is Ojai's oldest building. Turn-of-the-century furnishings are combined with modern prints and sculpture for an original decor. In the parlor are blue velvet couches and a big willow chair next to an old pot-bellied stove where sherry is served in the evening. Several good restaurants are nearby.
Location: One block from Main Street.
Rates: $90. Mary Nelson.
6 R. Continental-plus breakfast. CCs: MC VISA. Walk to shops & restaurants. Drive to hot springs.
Seen in: *Country Inns.*
"Best hotel we've ever stayed in and best breakfast we've ever had."

ORLAND N18/D3

The Inn at Shallow Creek Farm
Rt 3, Box 3176
Orland CA 95963
(916) 865-4093
Circa 1900. This vine-covered farmhouse was once the center of a well-known orchard and sheep ranch. The old barn, adjacent to the farmhouse, was a livery stop. The citrus orchard, now restored, blooms with 165 trees. Apples, pears, peaches, apricots, persimmons, walnuts, figs, and pomegranates are also grown here. Guests can meander to examine the Polish crested chickens, silver guinea fowl, Muscovy ducks, and African geese. The old caretaker's house is now a four-room guest cottage. Hundreds of narcissus grow along the creek that flows through the property.
Location: Northern California, 3 miles off Interstate 5.
*Rates: $45-$75. Mary & Kurt Glaeseman.
4 R. 2 PB. 1 FP. Phone in room. TV available. Beds: QT. B&B. River boating, fishing, hiking, birding.
Seen in: *Adventure Road, Orland Press Register.*
"Now that we've discovered your country oasis, we hope to return as soon as possible."

PACIFIC GROVE SC3/G1

Gatehouse Inn
225 Central Ave
Pacific Grove CA 93950
(408) 649-8436 (408) 649-1881
Circa 1884. This Italianate Victorian seaside inn is just a block from the ocean and Monterey Bay. The inn is decorated with Victorian and 20th-century antiques and touches of Art Deco. Guest rooms feature fireplaces, claw-foot tubs and down comforters. Some rooms have ocean views. The dining room boasts opulent Bradbury & Bradbury Victorian wallpapers as do some of the guest rooms. Afternoon hors d'oeuvres, sherry, wine and tea are served. The refrigerator is stocked for snacking.
Rates: $95-$175. Ann Young.

8 R. 8 PB. 3 FP. Phone in room. Beds: Q. Continental-plus breakfast. Handicap access. CCs: MC VISA AE. Sport fishing, golf, tennis, polo, horseback riding, scuba diving, surfing.
Seen in: *San Francisco Chronicle, Monterey Herald, Time, Newsweek, Country Inns.*
"Thank you for spoiling us."

Gosby House Inn

643 Lighthouse Ave
Pacific Grove CA 93950
(408) 375-1287

Circa 1887. Built as an upscale Victorian inn for those visiting the old Methodist retreat, this sunny yellow

mansion features an abundance of gables, turrets and bays. During renovation the innkeeper slept in all the rooms to determine just what antiques were needed and how the beds should be situated. Gosby House is in the National Register.
Location: Six blocks from the ocean.
*Rates: $85-$130. Shelley Claudel.
22 R. 20 PB. Phone in room. Beds: QC. Full breakfast. Conference room. CCs: MC VISA AE. Afternoon tea & hors d'oeuvres.
Seen in: *Los Angeles Times, Travel & Leisure.*

Green Gables Inn

104 5th St
Pacific Grove CA 93950
(408) 375-2095

Circa 1888. This half-timbered Queen Anne Victorian appears as a fantasy of gables overlooking spectacular Monterey Bay. The parlor has stained-glass panels framing the fireplace and bay windows looking out to sea. A favorite focal point is an antique carousel horse. Most of the guest

rooms have panoramic views of the ocean, fireplaces, gleaming woodwork, soft quilts, and flowers.
Location: On Monterey Bay four blocks from Monterey Bay Aquarium.
*Rates: $95-$150. Roger & Sally Post with Claudia Long.
11 R. 7 PB. Phone available. TV available. Beds: QD. Full breakfast. Conference room. CCs: MC VISA DS. Picnicking, scuba diving, swimming, golfing. Honeymoon packages.
Seen in: *Travel & Leisure, Country Living.*

Roserox Country Inn By-The-Sea

557 Ocean View Blvd
Pacific Grove CA 93950
(408) 373-7673

Circa 1904. Roserox was designed and built by Dr. Julia Platt, first woman mayor of Pacific Grove, doctor of

zoology and world-renowned scientist. This is a warm and intimate four-story inn, enhanced by original patterned-oak floors and 10-foot-high redwood beamed ceilings. All rooms are oceanfront with sounds of the surf to lull you to sleep.
Location: Oceanfront.
Rates: $125-$205. The Browncroft family.
8 R. 4 PB. Phone available. Beds: QT. Full breakfast. Walk to Monterey Bay Aquarium. Golf, swimming beach, bike rentals, Cannery Row. An oceanfront six-mile jog and bicycle trail starts in front of the inn. Full country-style breakfast, complimentary wine and cheese hour, special gifts for guests.
Seen in: *This Month's Magazine, The Monterey Peninsula Guide, Stanford Journal.*
"I have never tasted anything so delicious as Dawn's German streusel coffee cake."

Seven Gables Inn

555 Ocean View Blvd
Pacific Grove CA 93950
(408) 372-4341

Circa 1886. At the turn of the century, Lucie Chase, a wealthy widow and civic leader from the East Coast, em-

bellished this Victorian with gables and verandas, taking full advantage of its spectacular setting on Monterey Bay. All guest rooms feature ocean views, and there are elegant antiques, intricate Persian carpets, chandeliers and beveled-glass armoires throughout. Sea otters, harbor seals and whales often can be seen from the inn.
Rates: $95-$175. The Flatley Family.
14 R. 14 PB. Phone available. TV available. Beds: Q. B&B. CCs: MC VISA. Golf, hiking, biking, beaches, whale watching.
Seen in: *Travel & Leisure Magazine.*
"We could not have spent the last two nights at a more charming home."

PALM SPRINGS SM18/*K5*

Casa Cody Country Inn

175 S Cahuilla
Palm Springs CA 92262
(619) 320-9346

Circa 1933. Casa Cody, built by a relative of Wild Bill Cody and situated in the heart of Palm Springs, is the town's second oldest operating inn. The San Jacinto Mountains provide a

scenic background for the tree-shaded spa, the pink bouganvillaea and the blue waters of the inn's swimming pool. Each suite has a small kitchenette and features a soft-pink and turquoise Southwestern decor. There are Mexican pavers, French doors and private patios.
Rates: $35-$160. Therese Hayes, Frank Tysen.
17 R. 17 PB. 6 FP. Phone in room. TV in room. Beds: KQTC. Continental breakfast. Spa. Handicap access. Swimming pool. Conference room. CCs: MC VISA AE. Hiking, horseback riding, tennis, golf,

water sports, polo, ballooning, cross-country skiing. Weddings.
Seen in: *Palm Springs Life, The Desert Sun, KCET Magazine, New York Times, San Diego Magazine.*
"Your kindness and hospitality made us feel so relaxed."

PALO ALTO NQ7/F1

The Victorian On Lytton
555 Lytton Ave
Palo Alto CA 94301
(415) 322-8555
Circa 1895. This Queen Anne home was built for Hannah Clapp, a descendant of Massachusetts Bay colonist Roger Clapp. The house has been gra-

ciously restored and each guest room features its own sitting area. Most rooms boast a canopy or four-poster bed. Stanford University is within walking distance.
Rates: $90-135. Susan & Maxwell Hall.
10 R. 10 PB. TV available. Beds: KQ. Continental breakfast. CCs: MC VISA AE.
Seen in: *USA Today.*
"A beautiful inn! My favorite."

POINT RICHMOND NO7/E1

East Brother Light Station Inc
117 Park Pt
Point Richmond CA 94801
(415) 233-2385
Circa 1873. Managed by a non-profit organization, this lighthouse inn is located on an acre of island. Guest quarters, furnished simply, are situated in the outbuildings and on the second story of the innkeeper's Victorian house. The light has been automated since 1969.
Location: Ten minutes from dock.
Rates: $250 MAP. Linda & Leigh Hurley.
4 R. 2 PB. Continental-plus breakfast.
Seen in: *Uncommon Lodgings.*

QUINCY NH11/D3

The Feather Bed
542 Jackson St, PO Box 3200
Quincy CA 95971
(916) 283-0102
Circa 1893. Englishman Edward Huskinson built this charming Queen Anne house shortly after he began his mining and real estate ventures. Ask for the secluded cottage with its own deck and claw-foot tub. Other rooms in the main house overlook downtown Quincy or the mountains. Check out a bicycle to explore the countryside.
Location: In the heart of Plumas National Forest.
*Rates: $60-$90. Chuck & Dianna Goubert.
7 R. 7 PB. Phone in room. TV available. Beds: QD. Full breakfast. Conference room. CCs: MC VISA AE. Horseback riding, water sports, cross country skiing, hiking. Bicycles available.
Seen in: *Focus, Reno Gazette, SF Chronicle.*
"After living and traveling in Europe where innkeepers are famous, we have found The Feather Bed to be one of the most charming in the U.S. and Europe!"

RANCHO CUCAMONGA SL15/J4

Christmas House B&B Inn
9240 Archibald Ave
Rancho Cucamonga CA 91730
(714) 980-6450
Circa 1904. This Queen Anne Victorian has been renovated in period elegance, emphasizing its intricate wood carvings and red and green stained-glass windows. Once sur-

rounded by 80 acres of citrus groves and vineyards, the home, with its wide, sweeping veranda, is still a favorite place for taking in beautiful lawns and palm trees. The elegant atmosphere attracts the business traveler, romance-seeker and vacationer.
Location: East of downtown Los Angeles, three miles from Ontario Airport.
*Rates: $55-$125. Jay & Janice Ilsley.
7 R. 4 PB. 4 FP. Phone available. TV available. Beds: QD. B&B. Gourmet meals. Spa. Conference room. Snow skiing.
Seen in: *Los Angeles Times, Elan Magazine.*
"Coming to Christmas House is like stepping through a magic door into an enchanted land. Many words come to mind warmth, serenity, peacefulness."

RED BLUFF NG7/C2

Buttons & Bows B&B Inn
427 Washington St
Red Bluff CA 96080
(916) 527-6405
Circa 1882. This charming Victorian house is framed by a white picket fence. Near the Sacramento River, it provides a welcome spot to recuperate from hours on the Interstate 5. Gleaming wood floors and white walls set off the guest rooms, each with colorful bows and a jar of buttons from Betty's extensive collection. Marvin is a retired Lutheran pastor and enjoys helping with the weddings that are popular here.
Rates: $50-$65. Betty & Marvin Johnson.
3 R. 1 FP. Phone available. Beds: DT. Full breakfast. Spa. Fishing, golf, boating.
Seen in: *The Daily News, Red Bluff.*
"Beautiful rooms, wonderful town, great breakfast."

Faulkner House
1029 Jefferson St
Red Bluff CA 96080
(916) 529-0520
Circa 1890. This Queen Anne Victorian stands on a quiet, tree-lined street of vintage homes. The house has original stained-glass windows, ornate molding, and eight-foot pocket

doors separating the front and back parlors. Church bells nearby chime the hour as you relax on the porch.
*Rates: $55-$80. Harvey & Mary Klingler.
4 R. 1 PB. Phone available. Beds: QD. Full breakfast. Conference room. Lassen National Park. Fishing, hiking, skiing, golf.
Seen in: *Red Bluff Daily News.*
"Enjoyed our stay at your beautiful home."

REDLANDS SL17/J5

Georgianna Manor
816 East High Ave
Redlands CA 92374
(714) 793-0423
Circa 1888. This yellow and white Victorian was once at the center of a 70-acre orange grove. Gables, stained glass, a turret with 360-degree views and an encircling veranda create a fantasy that is carried out in the interiors. The Hopalong Cassidy room features a seven-piece mahogany bedroom suite that was purchased from the estate of Hopalong Cassidy. There are tin ceilings, oiled redwood

and an enormous collection of Victorian antiques.
❀Rates: $80-$110. Ione Hansen.
3 R. 1 FP. Beds: QD. Skiing.
Seen in: *Redlands Daily Facts.*
"Wonderful accommodations, 'Southern' California hospitality."

SACRAMENTO NN10/*E2*

Amber House
1315 22nd St
Sacramento CA 95816
(916) 444-8085
Circa 1905. This Craftsman-style bungalow on the city's Historic Preservation Register is in a neighborhood of

fine old homes eight blocks from the capitol. Each room is named for a famous poet and features stained glass, English antiques, selected volumes of poetry and fresh flowers. Ask for the Lord Byron Room where you can soak by candlelight in the whirlpool tub.
Location: Eight blocks to the capitol.
*Rates: $70-$135. Michael & Jane Richardson.
5 R. 5 PB. Phone in room. TV available. Beds: QD. Full breakfast. Conference room. CCs: MC VISA AE. Near Old Town, Convention Center. River rafting. Bicycles available.
Seen in: *Travel & Leisure, The Village Crier.*
"Your cordial hospitality, the relaxing atmosphere and delicious breakfast made our brief business/pleasure trip so much more enjoyable."

Driver Mansion Inn
2019 21st St
Sacramento CA 95818
(916) 455-5243
Circa 1899. This 6,500 square-foot, white Colonial Revival is graced with a Victorian tower, massive bays and an impressive columned entrance suitable for its former owner, turn-of-the century attorney Philip Driver. Crisp white walls and woodwork frame antique furnishings upholstered in rose, blue and soft pink. A Victorian gazebo in the back garden is a favorite spot for photographs.
Rates: $85-$225. Richard & Sandy Kann.
9 R. 9 PB. 3 FP. Phone in room. TV in room. Beds: KQ. Full breakfast. Spa. Conference room. CCs: MC VISA AE DC. Close to state capitol.
Seen in: *The Sacramento Bee.*
"Room and breakfast were exquisite! A wonderful place to stay."

Sterling Hotel
1300 H St
Sacramento CA 95814
(916) 448-1300
Circa 1894. The gables and bays, turrets and verandas of this 15,000 square-foot Queen Anne Victorian home testify to the affluence of its

former owners, the Carter-Hawley Hale family, of Weinstocks department store fame. The foyer and drawing room boast black marble fireplaces and marble floors, while guest rooms feature writing desks, designer furnishings, private spas and marble baths. A reproduction Victorian glass conservatory houses one of the dining rooms of the inn's four star restaurant, Chanterelle.
*Rates: $95-$225. Richard Kann.
12 R. 12 PB. Phone in room. TV in room. Beds: KQ. Restaurant. Spa. Conference room. FAX. CCs: MC VISA AE DC.
Seen in: *Sacramento Magazine.*
"Fabulous. Looking forward to my return."

SAINT HELENA NM7/*E2*

Cinnamon Bear B&B
1407 Kearney St
Saint Helena CA 94574
(707) 963-4653
Circa 1904. This Craftsman bungalow has broad wraparound porches with inviting bent-willow furniture and braided rugs. The country decor includes teddy bears everywhere - in the chairs and sofas, on corners and in bathrooms. Guests who stay for more than one night are often surprised to see a huge bear on their bed, dressed in the guest's pajamas.
Location: Two blocks from town.
Rates: $65-$140. Genny Jenkins & Brenda Cream.
4 R. 4 PB. Phone available. TV available. Beds: Q. Full breakfast. CCs: MC VISA DS. Biking, shopping, wine train, river boat.
Seen in: *Napa Register.*
"Just like home, only better."

Deer Run B&B
3995 Spring Mtn Rd
Saint Helena CA 94574
(707) 963-3794
Circa 1929. This secluded mountain home is located on four forested acres just up the road from the house used for the television show "Falcon Crest." A pine tree shaded deck provides a quiet spot for breakfast while watching birds and deer pass by. Your host, Tom, was born on Spring Mountain and knows the winery area well.
Location: Napa Valley.
Rates: $77-$98. Tom & Carol Wilson.
3 R. 3 PB. 1 FP. Phone available. TV in room. Beds: KQ. Continental-plus breakfast. Swimming pool. Golf, tennis, ballooning, glider rides, wineries.
Seen in: *Chicago Tribune, Napa Record.*
"Very beautiful rooms, serene and comfortable."

Ink House
1575 St Helena Hwy
Saint Helena CA 94574
(707) 963-3890
Circa 1884. Theron H. Ink, owner of thousands of acres in Marin, Napa

and Sonoma counties, was an investor in livestock, wineries and mining. He built his Italianate Victorian with a glass-walled observatory on top, and from this room, visitors can enjoy 360-degree views of the Napa Valley and surrounding vineyards.
Location: In the heart of Napa Valley wine country.
*Rates: $95-$150. Lois & George Clark.
4 R. 4 PB. Phone available. Beds: QD. Continental breakfast. Nearby wine tours, spas & mud baths, soaring, ballooning.
Seen in: *Canadian Living.*
"Your hospitality made us feel so much at home. This is a place and a time we will long remember."

Shady Oaks Country Inn
399 Zinfandel
Saint Helena CA 94574
(707) 963-1190

Circa 1880. This country inn is secluded on two acres, among the finest wineries in the Napa Valley. There are two buildings, a 1920s

home and a winery. The winery features original stone walls and is now a luxurious guest suite. Rooms in the main house boast original wallpaper, antiques, a private deck or a view of the gardens and vineyards. Wine and cheese are served fireside each evening in the parlor or on the Roman-pillared patio. A full champagne breakfast is the subject of rave reviews by guests and may include Eggs Benedict or Belgian waffles. Picnic baskets are available.

Location: Two miles south of town.
*Rates: $50-$120. Lisa Wild-Runnells & Jon Runnells.
4 R. 4 PB. Phone available. Beds: KQ. Full breakfast. Handicap access. CCs: MC VISA. Near restaurants, biking, ballooning. Hammock, croquet, bicycles.
"Can't decide which is the most outstanding, the rooms, the breakfast or the sensational hospitality." Rocky Mountain News.

SAN ANDREAS NN12/E3

Robin's Nest
PO Box 1408, 247 W St Charles
San Andreas CA 95249
(209) 754-1076

Circa 1895. This three-story Queen Anne Victorian features a bay window, veranda, and double gables. Guest rooms are decorated with turn-of-the-century modes of transportation. The Buggy Room, for instance, boasts an antique buggy seat and an expansive view of the city. Guests are welcome to raid the refrigerator.

Rates: $55-$95. Greta Cannon.
9 R. 7 PB. TV available. Beds: QT. Full breakfast. Tennis, swimming, cross-country skiing, wineries.
Seen in: *The Stockton Record, In Flight.*
"An excellent job of making guests feel at home."

SAN DIEGO SN19/L4

Britt House
406 Maple St
San Diego CA 92103
(619) 234-2926

Circa 1887. This lavish Queen Anne Victorian house once belonged to the Scripps family of publishing fame. They created a chain of 35

newspapers, including the San Diego Sun. The house is noted for an unusual two-story rose and blue stained-glass window depicting morning, noon and night. Other features of the inn include carved oak fretwork, a golden-oak staircase, turrets and formal English gardens.

*Rates: $95-$110. Elizabeth Lord.
10 R. 1 PB. Phone available. Beds: Q. Full breakfast. Picnics and special dinners by arrangement.
Seen in: *LA Magazine, California Magazine, Toronto Sun, San Diego Home & Gardens.*
"The 'Gold Standard' for California B&B's."

Heritage Park B&B Inn
2470 Heritage Park Row
San Diego CA 92110
(619) 295-7088

Circa 1889. Situated on a seven-acre Victorian park in the heart of Old Town, this inn is one of seven preserved classic structures. Built for

Hartfield and Myrtle Christian, it was featured in *The Golden Era* as an "outstandingly beautiful home of Southern California." It has a variety of chimneys, shingles, a two-story corner tower, and a wraparound porch.

Location: In historic Old Town.
*Rates: $80-$120. Don & Angela Thiess.
9 R. 5 PB. Phone available. Beds: QD. Full breakfast. Handicap access. Conference room. CCs: MC VISA. Walking distance to golf and tennis. Sportfishing charters located five miles away. Candlelight dinners in room.
Seen in: *Los Angeles Herald Examiner, Insider, Los Angeles Times, Orange County Register, San Diego Union, In-Flight Magazine.*
"A beautiful step back in time. Peaceful and gracious."

SAN FRANCISCO ND21/E1

Archbishop's Mansion
1000 Fulton St
San Francisco CA 94117
(415) 563-7872 (800) 543-5820

Circa 1904. This French Empire-style manor was built for the Archbishop of San Francisco. It is designated as a San Francisco historic landmark. The grand stairway features redwood paneling, Corinthian columns and a stained-glass dome. The parlor has a hand-painted ceiling. Each of the guest rooms is named for an opera and decorated to reflect its spirit. Rooms have antiques, Victorian window treatments, fresh flowers, and embroidered linens. Breakfast is served in French picnic baskets.

*Rates: $100-$285. Kathleen Austin.
15 R. 15 PB. 11 FP. Phone in room. TV in room. Beds: KQ. Continental-plus breakfast. Spa. Conference room. CCs: MC VISA AE. Fisherman's Wharf, museums, art galleries, The Opera House.
Seen in: *Travel-Holiday, Travel & Leisure.*
"The ultimate, romantic honeymoon spot."

Art Center/Wamsley Gallery/B&B
1902 Filbert St
San Francisco CA 94123
(415) 567-1526

Circa 1857. The Art Center Bed & Breakfast was built during the Louisiana movement to San Francisco during the Gold Rush. It was the only permanent structure on the path between the Presido and Yerba Buena village. There are four guest apartments here, convenient to much of San Francisco. The building is next to what was reputedly Washer Woman's Cove, a freshwater lagoon at the foot of Laguna Street that served as the village laundry.

Location: Two blocks south of Lombard (Rt 101) on the corner of Laguna.
*❀Rates: $65-$115. George & Helvi Wamsley.

4 R. 4 PB. 3 FP. Phone available. TV in room. Beds: QT. Continental-plus breakfast. Spa. CCs: MC VISA AE DC CB DS. Whale watching, fishing, golf, tennis, boat cruises.
Seen in: *Richmond News, American Artist Magazine.*

Beazley House
See: Napa, CA

The Chateau Tivoli
1057 Steiner St
San Francisco CA 94115
(415) 776-5462 (800)228-1647

Circa 1892. Built for lumber magnate Daniel Jackson, this 10,000-square-foot mansion is painted in 22 colors with

highlights of glimmering gold leaf accentuating its turrets and towers. It has been named "The Greatest Painted Lady in the World" by Elizabeth Pomada and Michael Larson, authors of the Painted Ladies series. Antiques and art from the estates of Cornelius Vanderbilt, Charles de Gaulle and J. Paul Getty are featured throughout. Canopy beds, marble baths, fireplaces and balconies are all reminiscent of San Francisco's Golden Age of Opulence. Chateau Tivoli holds an award from the California Heritage Council for best restoration of a Victorian house in California, 1989.
*Rates: $100-$300. Rodney Karr & Willard Gersbach.
7 R. 4 PB. 2 FP. Phone in room. TV available. Beds: QD. Continental-plus breakfast. Conference room. FAX. CCs: VISA. Parks, museums, Fisherman's Wharf.
Seen in: *Bay City Guide, Elle Decor Magazine, Northern California Jewish Bulletin.*
"The romance and charm has made Chateau Tivoli the place to stay whenever we are in San Francisco."

Golden Gate Hotel
775 Bush St
San Francisco CA 94108
(415) 392-3702

Circa 1913. News travels far when there's a bargain. Half of the guests visiting this four-story Edwardian hotel at the foot of Nob Hill are from abroad. Great bay windows on each floor provide many of the rooms with gracious spaces at humble prices. An original bird cage elevator kept in working order floats between floors. Antiques, fresh flowers, and afternoon tea further add to the atmosphere. Union Square is two-and-a-half blocks from the hotel.

*❀Rates: $55-$89. John & Renate Kenaston.
23 R. 14 PB. Phone available. TV in room. Beds: QDT. B&B. CCs: MC VISA AE DC CB. Cable car, theatre, shopping.
Seen in: *Los Angeles Times, Travel Tips.*
"Stayed here by chance, will return by choice!"

Moffatt House
431 Hugo St
San Francisco CA 94122
(415) 661-6210

Circa 1910. A simple two-story Edwardian home, the Moffatt House has a vivid stained-glass window that contrasts with its light, neutral interior. Guest rooms are artfully decorated and several face Mt. Sutra's fog-veiled heights. Guests take in the neighborhood shops, bakeries and cafes. The Haight-Ashbury district and Golden Gate Park are nearby.
Location: One block from Golden Gate Park.
Rates: $39-$54. Ruth Moffatt.
4 R. Phone available. Beds: QTC. Continental-plus breakfast. CCs: MC VISA.
"It was neat and clean...excellent breakfast. I would return."

The Nolan House
A Bed & Breakfast Inn
1071 Page St
San Francisco CA 94117
(415) 863-0384 (800) 736-6526

Circa 1889. This fanciful Victorian features a four-story bay and distinctively painted elements, decorative moldings, dentil designs and shingles. A double parlor inside boasts two marble fireplaces. The dining room overlooks a subtropical garden. French Victorian furnishings, feather beds and marble fireplaces add to a luxurious San Francisco experience. There is a deck and carriage house on the property and Golden Gate Park is two blocks away.

*❀Rates: $85-$115. Timothy W. Beaver & Timothy F. Sockett.
4 R. 3 FP. Phone available. TV available. Beds: Q. B&B. Conference room. CCs: MC VISA. Horseback riding, bicycling, tennis.
Seen in: *Sentinel.*
"A wonderful home with a lot of character and your breakfast was superb. The best we've had at any B&B!"

Petite Auberge
863 Bush St
San Francisco CA 94108
(415) 928-6000

Circa 1919. This five-story hotel features an ornate baroque design with curved bay windows. Now transformed to a French country inn, there are antiques, fresh flowers, and country accessories. Most rooms also have working fireplaces. It's a short walk to the Powell Street cable car.
Location: Two-and-a-half blocks from Union Square.
*Rates: $105-$195. Richard Revas.
26 R. 26 PB. Full breakfast. CCs: MC VISA. Shopping, theater.
Seen in: *Los Angeles Times, Brides.*
"Breakfast was great, and even better in bed!"

Spencer House
1080 Haight St
San Francisco CA 94117
(415) 626-9205

Circa 1887. This opulent mansion, which sits on three city lots, is one of San Francisco's finest examples of Queen Anne Victorian architecture. Ornate parquet floors, original

wallpapers, gaslights, and antique linens are featured. Breakfast is served with crystal and silver in the elegantly paneled dining room.
Location: Ten minutes from the wharf.
*Rates: $95-$155. Barbara & Jack Chambers.
6 R. 6 PB. Phone available. TV available. Beds: KQD. Full breakfast.
Seen in: *Painted Ladies Guide to Victorian California.*

Stanyan Park Hotel

750 Stanyan St
San Francisco CA 94117
(415) 751-1000

Circa 1905. Many of the guest rooms of this restored Victorian inn overlook Golden Gate Park. The turret suites and bay suites are popular, but all

rooms are decorated in a variety of antiques and color schemes. Museums, horseback riding and biking are available in the park, as well as the Japanese Tea Garden.
*Rates: $73-$89. Brad Bihlmeyer.
36 R. 36 PB. Phone in room. TV in room. Beds: QTC. Continental breakfast. Handicap access. Conference room. FAX. CCs: MC VISA AE DS. Aquarium, planetarium, museums.
Seen in: *Metropolitan Home, New York Times.*

Victorian Inn On The Park

301 Lyon St
San Francisco CA 94117
(415) 931-1830

Circa 1897. This grand three-story Queen Anne inn, built by William Curlett, has an open belvedere turret with a teahouse roof and Victorian railings. Silk-screened wallpapers, created especially for the inn, are accentuated by intricate mahogany and redwood paneling. The opulent Belvedere Suite features French doors opening to a Roman tub for two. Overlooking Golden Gate Park, the inn is 10 minutes from downtown.
*❀Rates: $84-$280. Lisa & William Benau.
12 R. 12 PB. 4 FP. Phone in room. TV in room. Beds: QDT. B&B. FAX. CCs: MC VISA AE. Golf, walking trails, Japanese Tea Gardens.
Seen in: *Innsider Magazine, Country Inns, Good Housekeeping.*

"The excitement you have about your building comes from the care you have taken in restoring and maintaining your historic structure."

White Swan Inn

845 Bush St
San Francisco CA 94108
(415) 775-1755

Circa 1908. This four-story inn is near Union Square and the Powell Street cable car. Beveled glass doors open to a reception area with granite floors, an antique carousel horse and English artworks. Bay windows and a rear deck contribute to the feeling of an English garden inn.

The guest rooms are decorated with softly colored English wallpapers and prints. All rooms have fireplaces. Turn-down service is provided.
Location: In the heart of downtown.
*Rates: $145-$250. Rich Revaz.
26 R. 26 PB. Phone in room. Beds: KQT. Full breakfast. Conference room. CCs: MC VISA. Afternoon tea and hors d'oeuvres.
Seen in: *Victoria Magazine.*

SAN LEANDRO NP7/F2

Best House

1315 Clarke St
San Leandro CA 94577
(415) 351-0911

Circa 1867. This beautifully detailed farmhouse was once home to Daniel Best, inventor of the Caterpillar tractor. Recently renovated, its Victorian embellishments are detailed in mauve, highlighting the yellow and white

paint scheme. A gazebo and fountain grace the back garden along with a myriad of colorful blooms. Antiques and reproductions are featured throughout the inn. The Parlor Bridal Suite is perfect for a special anniversary. A Bart station nearby is convenient for seeing San Francisco's attractions.
Rates: $75-$85. Donna Lawrence & Deborah Tafua.
5 R. 5 PB. Phone available. TV in room. Beds: QT. Full breakfast. CCs: MC VISA AE DC. Weddings, receptions, anniversaries.
Seen in: *Oakland Tribune, Daily Review.*
"Just wonderful! It touches the heart!"

SAN LUIS OBISPO SG8/H2

Garden Street Inn

1212 Garden Street
San Luis Obispo CA 93401
(805) 545-9802

Circa 1887. Innkeepers Dan and Kathy Smith recently restored this elegant home, paying meticulous attention to

detail. Each room has a special theme. The Field of Dreams room dedicated to Kathy Smith's father, includes memorabilia from his sports reporting days, toy figures from various baseball teams and framed pictures of antique baseball cards. The Cocoon room diplays dozens of beautiful butterfly knickknacks. Situated downtown, the inn is within walking distance of shops and restaurants and

the San Luis Obispo Mission. Pismo Beach and Hearst Castle are also neaby attractions.
Rates: $80-$160 Dan and Kathy Smith
13 R. 13 PB. 5 FP. Phone available. Beds: KQ. Full breakfast. Spa. Handicap access. CCs: MC VISA AE. Horseback riding, golf, tennis, wine tasting. Wine country tours.
Seen in: *Telegram-Tribune, Pacific Coast.*
"We appreciate your warmth and care."

SAN RAFAEL NO6/E1

Casa Soldavini

531 "C" St
San Rafael CA 94901
(415) 454-3140

Circa 1932. The first Italian settlers in San Rafael built this home. Their grandchildren now own it, and proudly hang pictures of their family. Grandfather Joseph, a wine maker, who planned and planted what are now the lush gardens surrounding the home. The many Italian antiques throughout the house complement the Italian-style decor. Pets are welcome.
Location: Fifteen minutes north of Golden Gate Bridge.
*Rates: $60-$80. Linda Soldavini-Cassidy & Dan Cassidy.
3 R. 2 PB. Phone available. TV available. Beds: QT. Continental-plus breakfast. Within 30-45 minutes of woods, beaches, horses, wineries.
"Scrumptious breakfast, quiet and charming."

SANTA BARBARA SJ9/I3

Bath Street Inn

1720 Bath St
Santa Barbara CA 93101
(805) 682-9680

Circa 1873. Overlooking the Victorian front veranda, a semi-circular "eyelid" balcony on the second floor seems to wink, beckoning guests to come in for an old-fashioned taste of hospitality provided by innkeeper Susan Brown. Originally the home of a merchant tailor, the inn is within a few blocks of the heart of Old Santa Barbara. Guest chambers upstairs have polished hardwood floors, floral wallpapers and antiques. The back garden deck, filled with wicker, or the summer house surrounded by wisteria and blossoming orange trees, are among the four locations available for enjoying breakfast.
*Rates: $70-$125. Susan Brown & Joanne Thorne.
7 R. 7 PB. Phone available. TV in room. Beds: KQT. Full breakfast. CCs: MC VISA AE. Ocean nearby, all water sports, polo, bicycles. Evening refreshments.
Seen in: *Sunset Magazine.*
"Like going to the home of a favorite aunt." Country Inns Magazine.

Blue Quail Inn

1908 Bath St
Santa Barbara CA 93101
(805) 687-2300

Circa 1915. The main house and adjacent cottages are decorated in American and English Country style. The Hummingbird is a cottage guest room featuring a chaise lounge, queen-size white iron bed, and a private brick patio. Wine and light hors d'oeuvres are served in the late afternoon, and hot apple cider is served each evening.
Location: Quiet residential area near town and the beach.
*Rates: $75-$100. Jeanise Suding Eaton.
8 R. 6 PB. 1 FP. Phone available. TV available. Beds: KQT. Full breakfast. CCs: MC VISA. Bicycles, sailing, horseback riding, golf tennis. Nearby gliding, wine tasting.
Seen in: *Los Angeles Times, Santa Barbara Magazine.*
"Mahvolous, simply maaahvolous! Loved everything. And just think, I'm here on a business trip - boy, love this job! I'll be back for sure - business of course."

Cheshire Cat Inn

36 W Valerio
Santa Barbara CA 93101
(805) 569-1610

Circa 1892. The Eberle family built two graceful houses side by side, one a Queen Anne, the other a Colonial Revival. President McKinley was entertained here on a visit to Santa Barbara. There is a pagoda-like porch, a square and a curved bay, and rose gardens, grassy lawns and a gazebo. Laura Ashley wallpapers are featured here and in the owner's other inn, a 12th century manor in Scotland.
Location: Downtown.
*Rates: $99-$179. Christine Dunstan, Midge Goeden.
11 R. 11 PB. Phone in room. Beds: KQT. Continental-plus breakfast. Spa. Conference room. Bicycling. Liqueurs and chocolates. Outdoor spa.
Seen in: *Two on the Town, KABC, Los Angeles Times, Santa Barbara Magazine.*
"Romantic and quaint."

Harbour Carriage House

420 W Montecito St
Santa Barbara CA 93101
(805) 962-8447 (800)594-4633

Circa 1895. The Harbour Carriage House, set behind a white picket fence, consists of two historic homes adorned with fish-scale shingles and gabled roofs. Guest rooms, named for wild flowers, are decorated with a combination of French and English country antiques. Try Forget-Me-Not and enjoy a private spa, a fireplace and a view of the mountains from the canopied, king-size bed.
Location: Two blocks to the beach, close to downtown.
*Rates: $85-$175. Vida-Marie McIsaac.
9 R. 9 PB. 6 FP. Phone in room. TV available. Beds: KQ. Full breakfast. Spa. Handicap access. CCs: MC VISA. Biking, horseback riding, sailing, wine tasting, gliding.
Seen in: *Los Angeles Times.*
"Thank you for a lovely weekend. If it wouldn't be any trouble could we have your recipes for the delicious breakfast?"

The Old Yacht Club Inn

431 Corona Del Mar
Santa Barbara CA 93103
(805) 962-1277 (805) 962-2629

Circa 1912. This California Craftsman house was the home of the Santa Barbara Yacht Club during the Roaring Twenties. It was opened as Santa

Barbara's first B&B and has become renowned for its gourmet food and superb hospitality. Innkeeper Nancy Donaldson is the author of *The Old Yacht Club Inn Cookbook.*
Location: East Beach.
*Rates: $70-$130. Nancy Donaldson, Sandy Hunt & Lu Caruso.
9 R. 9 PB. Phone in room. TV available. Beds: KQD. Full breakfast. Gourmet meals. Spa. Conference room. CCs: MC VISA AE DS. Water sports, bicycling, golf, horseback riding, boating, fishing, tennis.
Seen in: *Los Angeles Magazine, Valley Magazine.*
"Donaldson is one of Santa Barbara's better-kept culinary secrets."

Simpson House Inn

121 E Arrellaga St
Santa Barbara CA 93101
(805) 963-7067

Circa 1874. If you were one of the Simpson family's first visitors, you would have arrived in Santa Barbara

by stagecoach or by ship. The railroad was not completed for another 14

years. A stately Italianate Victorian house, the inn is situated on an acre of lawns and gardens hidden behind a 20-foot-tall eugenia hedge. Mint juleps are often served in the early evening, and are particularly enjoyable under the shade of the magnolia trees.
Location: Five-minute walk to downtown Santa Barbara and the historic district.
*❀Rates: $75-$150. Gillean Wilson, Linda & Glyn Davies.
6 R. 5 PB. 1 FP. Beds: KQD. Full breakfast. Handicap access. Conference room. CCs: MC VISA. English croquet, chickens and ducks. Complimentary bicycles.
Seen in: *Country Inns Magazine, Santa Barbara Magazine, Glamour.*
"Perfectly restored and impeccably furnished. Your hospitality is warm and heartfelt and the food is delectable."

SANTA CLARA NQ9/F2

Madison Street Inn
1390 Madison St
Santa Clara CA 95050
(408) 249-5541
Circa 1890. This Queen Anne Victorian inn still boasts its original doors and locks, and "No Peddlers or Agents" is engraved in the cement of

the original carriageway. Guests, however, always receive a warm and gracious welcome to high-ceilinged rooms furnished in antiques, oriental rugs, and Victorian wallpaper.
Location: Ten minutes from San Jose.
❀Rates: $60-$85. Ralph & Teresa Wigginton.
5 R. 3 PB. Phone in room. TV available. Beds: QT. B&B. Spa. Sauna. Swimming pool. CCs: MC VISA AE DC.
Seen in: *Discovery Magazine.*
"We spend many nights in hotels that look and feel exactly alike whether they are in Houston or Boston. Your inn was delightful. It was wonderful to bask in your warm and gracious hospitality."

SANTA CRUZ SA2/F1

Babbling Brook B&B Inn
1025 Laurel St
Santa Cruz CA 95060
(408) 427-2437
Circa 1909. This inn was built on the foundations of an 1870 tannery and a 1790 grist mill. Secluded, yet within

the city, the inn features a cascading waterfall and meandering creek on one acre of gardens and redwoods. Country French decor, cozy fireplaces, and deep soaking whirlpool tubs are luxurious amenities of the Babbling Brook.
Location: North end of Monterey Bay.
*Rates: $85-$125. Helen King.
12 R. 12 PB. 10 FP. Phone in room. TV available. Beds: KQ. Full breakfast. Handicap access. FAX. CCs: MC VISA AE DC CB DS. Tennis and the ocean are within walking distance. Romantic garden gazebo for weddings. Inn-to-inn tour package.
"We were impressed with the genuine warmth of the inn. The best breakfast we've had outside our own home!"

Bayview Hotel B&B Inn
See: Aptos, CA

Chateau Victorian
118 First St
Santa Cruz CA 95060
(408) 458-9458
Circa 1890. This elegant Victorian was built by a prosperous young sea captain from the East Coast. A favorite choice of guests is the Ocean View Room, which has a marble fireplace and a claw-foot tub as well as views of Monterey Bay. Breakfast may be enjoyed on the rooftop terrace, the dining area or the secluded deck. The waterfront is a block away.
Location: One block from the beach near the boardwalk and wharf.
Rates: $90-$120. Franz & Alice-June Benjamin.
7 R. 7 PB. 7 FP. Phone available. Beds: Q. Continental-plus breakfast. CCs: MC VISA. Golfing, fishing, sailing, ballooning, whale watching.
Seen in: *Times Tribune, Santa Cruz Sentinel, Good Times.*
"Certainly enjoyed our most recent stay and have appreciated all of our visits."

Cliff Crest
407 Cliff St
Santa Cruz CA 95060
(408) 427-2609
Circa 1887. Warmth, friendliness and comfort characterize this elegantly restored Queen Anne Victorian house. An octagonal solarium, tall stained-glass windows, and a belvedere overlook Monterey Bay and the Santa Cruz Mountains. The mood is airy and romantic. The spacious gardens were designed by John McLaren, landscape architect for Golden Gate Park. Antiques and fresh flowers fill the rooms, once home to William Jeter, lieutenant governor of California.
Location: One-and-a-half blocks from the beach and boardwalk.
*Rates: $80-$125. Sharon & Bruce Taylor.
5 R. 5 PB. 1 FP. Phone available. Beds: KQ. Full breakfast. CCs: MC VISA. Theater, wineries, train ride. Hammock.
Seen in: *Los Angeles Times.*
"Delightful place, excellent food and comfortable bed."

SANTA MONICA SL13/J4

Channel Road Inn
219 W Channel Rd
Santa Monica CA 90402
(213) 459-1920 (213) 454-7577
Circa 1910. This shingle-clad building is a variation of the Colonial Revival Period, one of the few remaining in

Los Angeles. The abandoned home was saved from the city's wrecking crew by Susan Zolla, with the encouragement of the local historical society. Amenities for business guests and beach visitors are available, and there is a spectacular cliffside spa.
Location: One block from the ocean.
*Rates: $85-$175. Susan Zolla & Kathy Jensen.
14 R. 14 PB. Phone in room. TV available. Beds: KQDT. B&B. Spa. Handicap access. Conference room. FAX. CCs: MC VISA. Bicycles provided for beach bike path.
Seen in: *Los Angeles Magazine, Brides Magazine.*
"One of the most romantic hotels in Los Angeles."

SANTA ROSA NM6/E1

The Gables
4257 Petaluma Hill Rd
Santa Rosa CA 95404
(707) 585-7777
Circa 1877. Fifteen gables accentuate this striking Gothic Revival house with a French influence situated on three-and-a-half acres in the historic district. It was built by William Roberts for his high-school

sweetheart, after he returned from the gold mines. Inside, there are 12-foot ceilings, a winding staircase with ornately carved balustrades, and three marble fireplaces. The Brookside Suite overlooks Taylor Creek and is decorated in an Edwardian theme. Other rooms feature views of the sequoias, meadows and the barn.
✻Rates: $95-$115. Michael & Judy Ogne.
6 R. 6 PB. 2 FP. Phone in room. TV in room. Beds: KQD. B&B. Gourmet meals. Handicap access. Conference room. CCs: MC VISA AE. Golf, horseback riding, wineries.
Seen in: *Press Democrat.*
"You all have a warmth about you that makes it home here."

Melitta Station Inn
5850 Melita Rd
Santa Rosa CA 95409
(707) 538-7712
Circa 1880. Originally built as a stagecoach stop, this rambling structure became a freight station for the little town of Melitta's depot. Basalt stone quarried from nearby hills was sent by rail to San Francisco where it was used to pave the cobblestone streets. Still located down a country lane, the station has been charmingly renovated. Oiled-wood floors, a rough-beam cathedral ceiling and French doors opening to a balcony are features of the sitting room. Wineries and vineyards stretch from the station to the town of Sonoma.
✻❀Rates: $80-$90. Season: Nov. - April. Diane & Vic.
6 R. 4 PB. Phone available. Beds: QD. Full breakfast. Conference room. CCs: MC VISA. Horseback riding, biking, hiking, swimming, fishing, sailing.
Seen in: *Los Angeles Times, The New York Times, Press Democrat.*
"Warm welcome and great food."

SAUSALITO — NL19/*E1*

Casa Madrona Hotel
801 Bridgeway
Sausalito CA 94965
(415) 332-0502
Circa 1885. This Victorian mansion was first used as a lumber baron's mansion. As time went on, additional buildings were added, giving it a European look. A registered Sausalito Historical Landmark, it is the oldest building in town. Each room has a unique name, such as "Lord Ashley's Lookout" or "Kathmandu," and the appointments are as varied as the names. The inn faces San Francisco Bay, enabling guests to enjoy the barking seals, the evening fog and the arousing sunsets.
Location: Downtown Sausalito.
Rates: $95-$185. John W. Mays.
34 R. 34 PB. 21 FP. Phone in room. Spa. Conference room. Checks not accepted.
Seen in: *Los Angeles Times, The Register.*
"Had to pinch myself several times to be sure it was real! Is this heaven? With this view it sure feels like it."

Sausalito Hotel
16 El Portal
Sausalito CA 94965
(415) 332-4155
Circa 1900. Built in the Mission Revival style, this hotel is nestled near the ferry landing at the water's edge. It has witnessed the transformation of a once sleepy Portuguese fishing village into a Prohibition headquarters, an artist colony and a world-class resort. The collection of massive Victorian pieces includes a magnificently carved mahogany bed once belonging to Ulysses S. Grant. Each of the inn's guest chambers displays a view of San Francisco Bay or Vina del Mar Park.
Location: Adjacent to the ferry landing in the heart of Sausalito.
Rates: $75-$160. Manager Liz MacDonald, owner Gene Hiller.
15 R. 8 PB. 1 FP. Phone in room. TV in room. Beds: KDTC. Continental breakfast. FAX. CCs: MC VISA AE DC CB. Windsurfing, sailing, golf, tennis, hiking. All water sports nearby.
Seen in: *Country Inns.*
"One of our favorite hobbies is to B&B hop. Yours is truly one of our favorites!"

SEAL BEACH — L11/*J4*

The Seal Beach Inn & Gardens
212 5th St
Seal Beach CA 90740
(213) 493-2416
Circa 1924. This is an exquisitely restored inn with fine antiques and historical pieces. Outside, the gardens blaze with color and there are Napoleonic *jardinieres* filled with flowers. A 300-year-old French fountain sits in the pool area and an an-

tique Parisian fence surrounds the property. In the neighboring historic area, you'll find a Red Car on Electric Street. It's a reminder of the time when the Hollywood crowd came to Seal Beach on the trolley to gamble and drink rum.
Location: 300 yards from the ocean, five minutes from Long Beach.
✻Rates: $98-$155. Marjorie Bettenhausen.
22 R. 22 PB. 1 FP. Phone in room. TV in room. Beds: KQDTC. B&B. Gourmet meals. Swimming pool. Conference room. CCs: MC VISA AE DC. Swimming, tennis, golf. Gondola & honeymoon packages.
Seen in: *Brides Magazine, Country Inns.*
"The closest thing to Europe since I left there."

SIERRA CITY — NJ12/*D3*

Busch & Heringlake Country Inn
PO Box 68
Sierra City CA 96125
(916) 862-1501
Circa 1871. This weathered old stone and brick building once housed the Wells Fargo Express, a telegraph office and a general store. Window boxes filled with petunias offer an invitation to enter through the two-foot thick walls. The reconstructed interiors feature wide-plank floors, country style furnishings and the original old Wells Fargo sign. A favorite choice is The Phoenix Room with its own fireplace and spa.
Rates: $75-$100. Carlo Giuffre.
4 R. 4 PB. 1 FP. TV available. Beds: QT. Continental-plus breakfast. Spa. CCs: MC VISA. Horseback riding, skiing, water sports, hiking, white water rafting, fishing, gold panning. Cafe on ground floor.
Seen in: *South Valley Times.*

SKY FOREST — SK17/*J5*

Storybook Inn
PO Box 362, 28717 Hwy 18
Sky Forest CA 92385
(714) 336-1483
Circa 1939. Formerly known as the Fouch Estate, this 9,000-square-foot home illustrates Mr. Fouch's romantic flair. Its abundant mahogany paneling was bleached to match the color of his bride's hair! Two massive brick fireplaces dominate the main lobby. The three-story inn has enclosed

solariums and porches. A hot tub nestled under ancient oaks provides a view of snow-capped mountains, forests and on clear days, the Pacific Ocean.
✲❀Rates: $95-$175. Kathleen & John Wooley.
9 R. 9 PB. Phone available. TV available. Beds: KQD. Full breakfast. Spa. Handicap access. Conference room. CCs: MC VISA. Horseback riding, snow & water skiing, hiking, fishing, picnicking.
Seen in: *Los Angeles Times, Los Angeles Magazine, California Magazine.*

SONOMA NM5/*E2*

The Hidden Oak
214 E Napa St
Sonoma CA 95476
(707) 996-9863
Circa 1913. This shingled California craftsman bungalow features a gabled roof and front porch with stone pillars. Located a block and a half from the historic Sonoma Plaza, the inn once served as the rectory for the Episcopal Church. Rooms are furnished with antiques and wicker. Nearby wineries may be toured by hopping on one of innkeeper Catherine Cotchett's bicycles.
✲Rates: $85-$130. Catherine S. Cotchett.
3 R. 3 PB. 1 FP. Phone available. Beds: Q. B&B. CCs: AE. Bicycles, wineries, festivals.
"The room was delightful and breakfast was excellent."

Sonoma Hotel
110 W Spain St
Sonoma CA 95476
(707) 996-2996
Circa 1879. Originally built as a two-story adobe, a third story was added in the Twenties and it became the Plaza Hotel. The first floor now boasts an award-winning restaurant. The top two floors contain antique-filled guest rooms. The Vallejo Room is furnished with a massive carved rosewood bedroom suite, previously owned by General Vallejo's family. In room 21, Maya Angelou wrote "Gather Together in My Name." A short walk from the tree-lined plaza are several wineries.
✲Rates: $62-$105. Dorene Musilli.
17 R. 5 PB. Phone available. Beds: DT. B&B. Restaurant. Gourmet meals. CCs: MC VISA AE. Ballooning, horseback riding, wineries, art galleries.
Seen in: *Americana, House Beautiful.*
"Great food and service!"

Victorian Garden Inn
316 E Napa St
Sonoma CA 95476
(707) 996-5339
Circa 1870. Authentic Victorian gardens cover more than an acre of grounds surrounding this Greek Revival farmhouse. Pathways wind

around to secret gardens, and guests can walk to world-famous wineries and historical sites. All rooms are decorated with the romantic flair of the innkeeper, an interior designer. Ask to stay in the renovated water tower.
✲Rates: $69-$135. Donna Lewis.
4 R. 3 PB. 1 FP. Beds: QT. Full breakfast. Swimming pool. Conference room. CCs: MC VISA AE. Winery tours, swimming, nearby golf, tennis, bicycles. Full concierge services.
Seen in: *Denver Post, Los Angeles Times.*

SONORA NO12/*F3*

City Hotel
See: Columbia, CA

Lulu Belle's
85 Gold St
Sonora CA 95370
(209) 533-3455
Circa 1886. This sturdy home with its spacious lawns, rambling porches and free form picket fence was built for John Rother, a local builder. "There

was always music at the Rother home - early and late you could hear the piano going," wrote Ora Morgan in an early Sonora newspaper. Now the music room is enjoyed by guests for after-dinner entertainment. The house is filled with Victorian antiques. The historic village dotted with 1850's store fronts housing gourmet restaurants and antique shops is two blocks away.
Rates: $60-$90. Janet & Chris Miller.
5 R. 5 PB. 1 FP. Phone available. TV available. Beds: KQDTC. Full breakfast. Conference room. Horseback riding, water sports, snow skiing, gold panning, antiquing.
Seen in: *California Magazine, Union Democrat-Gadabout.*
"Hospitality and friendliness matched only by the beautiful accommodations! We'll be back for sure."

The Ryan House B&B
153 S Shepherd St
Sonora CA 95370
(209) 533-3445
Circa 1855. This restored homestead is set well back from the street in a quiet residential area. Green lawns and gar-

dens with 35 varieties of roses surround the house. Each room is individually decorated with handsome antiques and there is a wood-burning stove in the parlor. An antique-style cookstove sets the mood for a country breakfast served in the dining room.
Location: Two blocks from the heart of historic Sonora.
✲Rates: $75-$80. Nancy & Guy Hoffman.
3 R. 3 PB. Phone in room. TV available. Beds: QT. B&B. CCs: MC VISA DC. Golf, gold panning, hiking. Washstands in the rooms.
Seen in: *Home and Garden, Union Democrat, California Magazine.*
"Everything our friends said it would be: warm, comfortable and great breakfasts. You made us feel like long-lost friends the moment we arrived."

TAHOE CITY NK13/*E4*

Mayfield House
236 Grove St, PO Box 5999
Tahoe City CA 95730
(916) 583-1001
Circa 1932. Norman Mayfield, Lake Tahoe's pioneer contractor, built this house of wood and stone, and Julia

Morgan, architect of Hearst Castle, was a frequent guest. Dark-stained

pine paneling, a beamed ceiling, and a large stone fireplace make an inviting living room. Many rooms have mountain, woods, or golf course views.
Location: Downtown on Highway 28.
✻❀Rates: $70-$105. Cynthia & Bruce Knauss.
5 R. Phone available. TV available. Beds: KQT. Full breakfast. CCs: MC VISA. Horseback riding, skiing, water sports, bicycles, hiking, golf.
Seen in: *Sierra Heritage, Tahoe Today.*
"The place is charming beyond words, complete with down comforters and wine upon checking in. The breakfast is superb."

TEMPLETON SG6/*H2*

Country House Inn
91 Main St
Templeton CA 93465
(805) 434-1598
Circa 1886. This Victorian home, built by the founder of Templeton, is set off by rose-bordered gardens. It was

designated as a historic site in San Luis Obispo County. All of the rooms are decorated with antiques and fresh flowers. Hearst Castle and six wineries are nearby.
Location: Twenty miles north of San Luis Obispo on Hwy 101.
✻Rates: $65-$80. Dianne Garth.
7 R. 3 PB. Phone available. Beds: KQ. Full breakfast. CCs: MC VISA. Horseback riding, tennis, waterskiing, wine tasting.
"A feast for all the senses, an esthetic delight."

TRUCKEE NI13/*D4*

White Sulphur Springs Ranch
See: Clio, CA

UKIAH NK5/*D1*

Vichy Hot Springs Resort & Inn
2605 Vichy Springs Rd
Ukiah CA 95482
(707) 462-9515 (707) 462-9516
Circa 1854. This famous spa once attracted guests such as Jack London, Mark Twain and Teddy Roosevelt. Twelve rooms and two redwood cottages have been renovated for bed and breakfast, while the concrete 1860s baths remain unchanged. A magical waterfall is a 30-minute walk along a year-round stream.
✻❀Rates: $95-$135. Gilbert & Marjorie Ashoff.
14 R. 14 PB. 2 FP. Phone in room. TV available. Beds: QT. Continental-plus breakfast. Gourmet meals. Spa. Sauna. Handicap access. Swimming pool. Conference room. FAX. CCs: MC VISA AE DC CB. Horseback riding, water sports, tennis, fishing, health club membership. Historic Skunk Train.
Seen in: *Sunset, Mendocino Grapevine, Sacramento Bee, San Jose Mercury News, Gulliver.*
"Very beautiful grounds and comfortable accommodations."

VENTURA SJ11/*J3*

Bella Maggiore Inn
67 S California St
Ventura CA 93001
(805) 652-0277 (800) 523-8479 CA
Circa 1926. Albert C. Martin, the architect of the former Grauman's Chinese Theater, designed and built this Spanish Colonial Revival-style hotel. Located three blocks from the beach, it is noted for its richly-carved caste-stone entrance and frieze. An Italian chandelier and a grand piano dominate the parlor. Rooms surround a courtyard with a fountain. Miles of coastal bike paths are nearby, as well as restaurants and antique shops.
✻Rates: $60-$150. Thomas Wood.
30 R. 30 PB. 6 FP. Phone in room. TV in room. Beds: KQD. Full breakfast. Spa. Handicap access. Conference room. FAX. CCs: MC VISA AE DC DS. Water sports, bicycling, beach.
Seen in: *Ventura County & Coast Reporter, Sunset.*
"Very friendly and attentive without being overly attentive."

La Mer
411 Poli St
Ventura CA 93001
(805) 643-3600
Circa 1890. This three-story Cape Cod Victorian overlooks the heart of historic San Buenaventura and the spectacular California coastline. Each room is decorated to capture the feel-

ing of a specific European country. French, German, Austrian, Norwegian and English-style accommodations are available. Gisela, your hostess, is a native of Siegerland, Germany. Midweek specials include a Western Package, complete with barbeque, stagecoach ride and wild west show at a nearby dude ranch.
Location: Second house north of City Hall.
✻Rates: $98-$140. Gisela Baida.
5 R. 5 PB. 1 FP. Phone available. TV available. Beds: KQDT. Full breakfast. CCs: MC VISA. Swimming, tennis, golf, biking or walking to the beach a few blocks away. Goosedown feather beds.
Seen in: *Los Angeles Times, California Bride, Los Angeles Magazine.*
"Where to begin? The exquisite surroundings, the scrumptious meals, the warm feeling from your generous hospitality! What an unforgettable weekend in your heavenly home."

WESTPORT NI13/*C1*

DeHaven Valley Farm
39247 N Highway One
Westport CA 95488
(707) 961-1660
Circa 1875. This farmhouse was built by Alexander Gordon, a prosperous sawmill owner and rancher. A double-tiered porch wraps around the front

and side of the house and extends across the wing, offering vistas of the inn's 20 acres of meadows, woodland and coastal hills. A hilltop hot tub

provides a panoramic view of the ocean. Stroll around the farm and feed the horses, sheep, geese, rabbits, chickens, llamas and even the donkeys. Guest rooms are in the main house and in cottages. The DeHaven Cottage features cabbage rose prints, a Franklin stove and a king-size bed. Dinner is served Wednesday through Saturday in the farm's dining room by prior arrangement.
Rates: $85-$125. Jim & Kathy Tobin.
8 R. 6 PB. 5 FP. Phone available. Beds: KQD. B&B. Restaurant. Spa. FAX. CCs: MC VISA AE. Horseback riding, redwoods, Skunk Train, ocean fishing, diving (renowned abalone beds).
"We've talked about it so much that convoys of Southern California folks might be heading your way this very minute!"

Howard Creek Ranch

40501 N Hwy, PO Box 121
Westport CA 95488
(707) 964-6725

Circa 1871. First settled as a land grant of thousands of acres, Howard Creek Ranch is now a 20-acre farm with sweeping views of the Pacific

Ocean, sandy beaches and rolling mountains. A 75-foot bridge spans a creek that flows past barns and outbuildings to the beach 200 yards away. The farmhouse is surrounded by green lawns, an award-winning flower garden, and grazing cows and horses. This rustic rural location is highlighted with antiques and collectibles.
Location: Mendocino Coast on the ocean.
Rates: $50-$95. Charles & Sally Grigg.
7 R. 3 PB. 3 FP. Phone available. Beds: KQD. Spa. Sauna. Swimming pool. CCs: MC VISA. Horseback riding, whale watching.
Seen in: *California Magazine.*
"Of the dozen or so inns on the West Coast we have visited, this is easily the most enchanting one."

YOUNTVILLE NM7/E2

Magnolia Hotel

PO Box M, 6529 Yount St
Yountville CA 94599
(707) 944-2056

Circa 1873. This handsome vine-covered brick and fieldstone hotel was formerly a bordello and bootlegging center during prohibition. Its current character and elegance is enhanced by cozy fireplaces, balconies and private gardens. A redwood deck, draped in jasmine, houses a secluded spa. The brick walled dining room is the gathering place for a hearty breakfast.
Location: Napa Valley.
Rates: $89-$169. Bruce & Bonnie Locken.
12 R. 12 PB. 5 FP. Phone available. Beds: KQD. Full breakfast. Spa. Swimming pool. Golf, tennis, hot air balloons, gliders.
Seen in: *Country Inns of America.*

YUBA CITY NK9/D2

The Wicks

560 Cooper Ave
Yuba City CA 95991
(916) 674-7951

Circa 1920. A hedge of pink roses surrounds this Craftsman bungalow. In the dining room, hand-carved white pine tables in the French country style provide the setting for the inn's highly regarded English teas. Royal Albert china, lace table runners, and crystal goblets add to the elegance, while guest rooms feature Victorian decor.
Rates: $80. Linda, Glenn & Shirley Renwick.
2 R. 2 PB. Phone available. TV available. Beds: QDC. Full breakfast. Gourmet meals. Conference room. CCs: MC VISA AE DC CB. Water sports, parks, bike trails. Weddings, receptions, Victorian teas.
Seen in: *Home & Garden, The Yuba-Sutter Appeal-Democrat.*
"You were the most gracious host & hostess - we relaxed!"

COLORADO

ALAMOSA N11/F4

Cottonwood Inn

123 San Juan
Alamosa CO 81101
(719) 589-3882

Circa 1912. This refurbished Colorado bungalow is filled with antiques and paintings by local artists. The dining

room set once belonged to Billy Adams, a Colorado governor in the 1920s. Blue-corn blueberry pancakes or flaming Grand Marnier omelets are the inn's specialties. A favorite day trip is riding the Cumbres -Toltec Scenic Railroad over the La Magna Pass, site of an Indiana Jones movie.

❀Rates: $42-$54. Julie Mordecai.
5 R. 2 PB. Phone available. TV available. Beds: KQDC. Full breakfast. CCs: MC VISA. Cross-country skiing, bird watching.
Seen in: *Rocky Mountain News, The Pueblo Chieftain.*

"My husband wants to come over every morning for blueberry pancakes and strawberry rhubarb sauce."

ASPEN H8/D3

Sardy House

128 E Main St
Aspen CO 81611
(303) 920-2525

Circa 1892. This Queen Anne Victorian was built by J. William Atkinson, an owner of the Little Annie Mine and Aspen's first freight company. The mansion is built with thick brick walls, sandstone detailing, and wood ornamental trim. A Colorado blue spruce on the grounds is more than 90 feet tall, the tallest in Aspen. There are deluxe guest rooms and six suites. Dinner is available nightly. At the Sardy House guests enjoy the ul-

timate in pampered luxury.

*❀Rates: $120-$575. Season: Closed May. Jayne Poss.
20 R. 20 PB. Phone in room. TV in room. Beds: KQT. Full breakfast. Restaurant. Spa. Sauna. Conference room. Tennis, rafting, horses, gliding, ballooning, water skiing, bar, heated swimming pool. Open mid-Nov. to mid-April and mid-June to mid-Oct.
Seen in: *Country Inns.*

"I was overwhelmed by your attention to details. A job well done!"

BOULDER E12/C4

Pearl Street Inn

1820 Pearl St
Boulder CO 80302
(303) 444-5584

Circa 1895. Located in downtown Boulder, the Pearl Street Inn is composed of a restored Victorian brick house and a new contemporary style

addition. The guest rooms overlook a tree-shaded courtyard garden where a gourmet continental breakfast is served. Antiques, cathedral ceilings, bleached oak floors and fireplaces are featured in all rooms.

Rates: $65-$95. Yossi Shem-Avi & Cathy Surratt.
7 R. 7 PB. 7 FP. Phone in room. TV in room. Beds: QDT. Continental-plus breakfast. Gourmet meals. Conference room. CCs: MC VISA AE DC CB. Hiking, bicycling, golf, tennis, swimming, skiing.
Seen in: *Bon Appetit, Rocky Mountain News/Travel.*

"Enter the front door and find the sort of place where you catch your breath in awe."

COLORADO SPRINGS J13/D5

Hearthstone Inn

506 N Cascade Ave
Colorado Springs CO 80903
(719) 473-4413 (800) 521-1885

Circa 1885. This elegant Queen Anne is actually two houses joined by an old carriage house. It has been res-

tored as a period showplace with six working fireplaces, carved oak staircases, and magnificent antiques throughout. A lush lawn, suitable for croquet, surrounds the house, and flower beds match the Victorian colors of the exterior.

Location: A resort town at the base of Pikes Peak.
*Rates: $68-$105. Dot Williams & Ruth Williams.
23 R. 23 PB. 3 FP. Phone available. Beds: KQDTC. Full breakfast. Gourmet meals. Conference room. CCs: MC VISA AE. Jogging, tennis, swimming. Skiing nearby. Working fireplaces, private porches, banquets for groups of 20-48, gourmet breakfast a specialty.
Seen in: *Rocky Mountain News.*

"We try to get away and come to the Hearthstone at least twice a year because people really care about you!"

Holden House-1902 B&B

1102 W Pikes Peak Ave
Colorado Springs CO 80904
(719) 471-3980

Circa 1902. This Victorian home and carriage house were built by Isabel Holden. The Holdens owned mining interests in Colorado towns for which the Aspen, Cripple Creek, Silverton, Leadville and Goldfield guestrooms

are named. The Aspen suite boasts an open turret and now has an 80-gallon "tub for two." Guests enjoy scenic mountain views from the wide veranda. "Mingtoy", the resident cat, is the official greeter.
Location: Near the historic district, "Old Colorado City."
*❀Rates: $57-$85. Sallie & Welling Clark.
3 R. 3 PB. Phone available. TV available. Beds: Q. Full breakfast. CCs: MC VISA AE. Horseback riding, skiing, golf, hiking, tennis nearby. Honeymoon package. Smoke-free home.
Seen in: *Rocky Mountain News, Victorian Homes, Pikes Peak Journal.*
"Your love of this house and nostalgia makes a very delightful experience."

Outlook Lodge
See: Green Mountain Falls, CO

CRIPPLE CREEK J12/*D4*

Imperial Hotel
123 N Third St
Cripple Creek CO 80813
(719) 689-2922
Circa 1896. This is the only original Cripple Creek hotel still standing. There is a collection of Gay Nineties memorabilia and the inn is known for its excellent cuisine. A cabaret-style melodrama is performed twice daily. Breakfast is available but not included in the rates.
*Rates: $40-$45. Season: Mid-May to October. Stephen & Bonnie Mackin.
26 R. 12 PB. Phone available. Beds: QDT. Conference room.
Seen in: *Rocky Mountain News.*
"This was truly an experience of days gone by - we loved our stay!"

DENVER F13/*C5*

Castle Marne
1572 Race St
Denver CO 80206
(303) 331-0621 (800) 92MARNE
Circa 1890. This 6,000 square-foot fantasy was designed by William Lang, and is in the National Register. It is constructed of hand-hewn rhyolite stone. Inside, polished oak, maple and black ash woodwork enhance the ornate fireplaces, period antiques and opulent Victorian decor. For special occasions ask for the Presidential Suite with its fireplace, tower sitting room, king-size tester bed and whirlpool tub in the solarium.
Rates: $74-$135. Jim & Diane Peiker.
9 R. 9 PB. 3 FP. Phone in room. Beds: KQDT. Full breakfast. Game room. CCs: MC VISA AE. Museums, restaurants, shopping.
Seen in: *Denver Post, Innsider, Rocky Mountain News.*
"Aside from the beautiful surroundings, your kindness, caring and attentiveness to our needs made three weary travelers feel the warmth of home."

Queen Anne Inn
2147 Tremont Place
Denver CO 80205
(303) 296-6666
Circa 1879. Recipient of the Outstanding Achievement Award by the Association of American Historic Inns, this Queen Anne Victorian was

designed by Colorado's most famous architect, Frank Edbrooke. Furnishings, including pillared canopy beds, music, art and vintage books add to the Victorian experience. In an area of meticulously restored homes and flower gardens, the inn is four blocks from the center of the central business district.
*❀Rates: $54-$121. Ann & Charles Hillestad.
10 R. 10 PB. Phone in room. Beds: KQDT. Continental-plus breakfast. Conference room. CCs: MC VISA AE.
Seen in: *New York Times, USA Today, Travel Holiday, New Woman, Bon Appetit, Conde Nast Traveler.*

DURANGO O5/*F2*

Blue Lake Ranch
16919 Hwy 140
Durango CO 81326
(303) 385-4537
Circa 1900. Built by Swedish immigrants, this renovated Victorian farmhouse is surrounded by spectacular flower gardens. The inn is filled with comforts such as down quilts, vases of fresh flowers and family antiques. The property is designated as a wildlife refuge and there is a cabin overlooking trout-filled Blue Lake. In the evening, guests enjoy soaking in the spa under star-studded skies, and in the morning dining on Tia's gourmet breakfasts.
Location: Twenty minutes from Durango.
*Rates: $70-$125. Season: May to October. David & Tia Alford.
4 R. 4 PB. Phone available. TV in room. Beds: Q. Restaurant. Spa. Handicap access. Conference room. Fishing, swimming, hiking.
Seen in: *Colorado Home & Lifestyles, Durango Herald.*
"What a paradise you have created - we would love to return!!"

ELDORA F11/*C4*

Goldminer Hotel
601 Klondyke Ave
Eldora CO 80466
(303) 258-7770 (800)422-4629
Circa 1897. With its rough-hewn log exterior, this alpine lodge has served continuously as a hotel since 1897.

Situated near Indian Peaks wilderness, the scenic old mining town of Eldora is on the banks of Middle Boulder Creek. Except for the rental cabin behind the inn, all guest rooms are on the second floor. The decor is country antiques supplemented with mountain crafts and art work. A stone fireplace set in the log walls of the lobby provide the focal point of the inn. Alpine trout fishing and scenic Rocky Mountain National Park is nearby.
*❀Rates: $30-$85. Carol Rinderknecht & Scott Bruntjen.
5 R. 3 PB. 1 FP. Phone in room. TV available. Beds: DTC. Full breakfast. Spa. Handicap access. Conference room. FAX. CCs: MC VISA. Downhill skiing, trout fishing.
Seen in: *Daily Camera.*

ESTES PARK D11/*B4*

The Baldpate Inn
PO Box 4445RM
Estes Park CO 80517
(303) 586-6151 (303)586-5397
Circa 1917. Tucked 9,000 feet high in the Twin Sisters Peaks and adjacent to Rocky Mountain National Park is this handsome mountain lodge with a

wide porch that provides spectacular views. Guest rooms and private cabins feature a country-and-western decor that includes calico dust ruffles and handmade quilts. More than 10,000 keys from the inn's famous collection are displayed from the ceiling and walls of the Key Room. Egg and cheese pie with hash browns is one hearty item of the inn's breakfast repertoire.

Rates: $60-$100. Season: Memorial Day-Oct. 1. Mike, Lois, Jenn & MacKenzie Smith.

13 R. 2 PB. Phone available. TV available. Beds: KDTC. Full breakfast. Restaurant. Gourmet meals. Conference room. CCs: MC VISA. Hiking, horseback riding, fishing, boating, golf, swimming, shopping.

Seen in: *The Manhattan Mercury, Rocky Mountain News, Country Inns.*

"This place unlocked my heart!"

GOLDEN F12/*C4*

The Dove Inn

711 14th St
Golden CO 80401
(303) 278-2209

Circa 1878. This Victorian house has a two-story bay window that overlooks giant blue spruce and the foothills of

the Rockies. Breakfast is served before the 100-year-old fireplace. In the same neighborhood are beautiful old homes that once housed Colorado's political leaders. The Colorado School of Mines and Coors Brewery are a short walk away. The innkeepers prefer married couples.

Rates: $41-$59. Sue & Guy Beals.

6 R. 6 PB. Phone in room. TV in room. Beds: KQ. Continental breakfast. CCs: MC VISA AE DC CB. Cross-country skiing at 8,000 feet. Seen in: *Rocky Mountain News.*

"Our first experience at a bed and breakfast was delightful, thanks to your hospitality at The Dove Inn."

GREEN MOUNTAIN FALLS I13/*D4*

Outlook Lodge

Box 5
Green Mountain Falls CO 80819
(719) 684-2303

Circa 1889. Outlook Lodge was originally the parsonage for the historic Little Church in the Wildwood. Hand-carved balustrades surround a

veranda that frames the alpine village view, and inside are many original parsonage furnishings. Iron bedsteads topped with patchwork quilts add warmth to the homey environment. This secluded mountain village is nestled at the foot of Pikes Peak.

Rates: $40-$65. Season: March to Oct. 30. Tom & Ilka Fremin.

8 R. 6 PB. 1 FP. Phone available. TV available. Beds: QDTC. B&B. Handicap access. Swimming pool. Conference room. CCs: MC VISA. Swimming, fishing, volleyball, tennis, riding stables, hiking. Melodramas, concerts.

Seen in: *Colorado Springs Gazette.*

"Thoroughly enjoyed our stay."

LEADVILLE H9/*C3*

The Leadville Country Inn

127 E Eighth St
Leadville CO 80461
(719) 486-2354 (800)748-2354

Circa 1893. Built by a mining executive, this large Queen Anne Victorian boasts a shingled turret and a rounded porch. Upholstered walls, pull-chain toilets, an intricately carved fireplace mantle and a copper-lined wooded bathtub are some of the unique items found in the inn. The innkeepers can arrange a carriage or sleigh ride for guests.

Rates: $52-$77. Sid & Judy Clemmer.

9 R. 9 PB. Phone available. TV available. Beds: KQDT. Full breakfast. Gourmet meals. Spa. CCs: MC VISA AE DC CB DS. Skiing, fishing, hiking, snowmobiling, music festivals. Horsedrawn sleigh rides with private candlelight dinner.

Seen in: *Rocky Mountain News, The Herald Democrat.*

"Everything was wonderful; the room, the romantic sleighride, dinner and most of all, the people."

MINTURN G9/*C3*

Eagle River Inn

PO Box 100, 145 N Main St
Minturn CO 81645
(303) 827-5761 (800) 344-1750

Circa 1894. Ten miles west of Vail, the Eagle River Inn appeals to those who enjoy the sounds of rushing water. All new interiors and exteriors belie its old-fashioned roots. Decorated in a Southwestern theme, the inn features Mayan and Aztec stenciling. Each room has its own handmade headboard, and a view of Lion's Head Mountain or the river. Decks and willow trees draw guests to the back garden.

Location: Vail Valley.

Rates: $79-$155. Beverly Rude.

12 R. 12 PB. Phone available. TV in room. Beds: KT. Full breakfast. Spa. CCs: MC VISA AE. Downhill & cross-country skiing, snowmobiling, fishing, golf, tennis, hiking, bicycling, white water rafting.

Seen in: *Rocky Mountain News, Country Accents, Travel Holiday, Resorts Magazine, Vail Valley Magazine.*

"We love this place and have decided to make it a yearly tradition!"

OURAY L5/*E2*

St. Elmo Hotel

426 Main St, PO Box 667
Ouray CO 81427
(303) 325-4951

Circa 1898. The inn was built by Kitty Heit, with views of the amphitheater, Twin Peaks and Mt. Abrams, and has operated as a hotel for most of its life. Rosewood sofas and chairs covered in red and green velvet, and a player piano furnish the parlor. The Bon Ton Restaurant occupies the stone-walled basement, and it's only a short walk to the hot springs.

*Rates: $68-$78. Dan & Sandy Lingenfelter.

9 R. 9 PB. Phone available. TV available. Beds: KQDC. Full breakfast. Restaurant. Spa. Sauna. CCs: MC VISA. Fishing, hiking, swimming, horseback riding, cross-country skiing.

Seen in: *Colorado Homes & Lifestyles.*

"Another enjoyable stay. A treat we look forward to yearly."

PUEBLO L14/*E5*

Abriendo Inn

300 W Abriendo Ave
Pueblo CO 81004
(719) 544-2703

Circa 1906. This three-story, 7,000 square-foot foursquare-style mansion is embellished with dentil work and wide porches supported by Ionic columns. Elegantly paneled and carved oak walls and woodwork provide a gracious setting for king-size brass beds, antique armoires and oriental rugs. Breakfast specialties include raspberry muffins, Italian strada and nut breads. Ask for the music room with its own fireplace and bay window.

Rates: $48-$85. Kerrelyn & Chuck Trent.
7 R. 5 PB. 2 FP. Phone in room. TV in room. Beds: KQ. Full breakfast. CCs: MC VISA DC. Golf, water activities, shops, galleries. Weddings, "slumber" party showers, seminars, catered large parties.
Seen in: *The Pueblo Chieftain, Rocky Mountain News.*
"Thank you for warm hospitality, cozy environments and fine cuisine!"

SALIDA K10/*D4*

Poor Farm Country Inn
8495 Co Rd 160
Salida CO 81201
(719) 539-3818

Circa 1892. This modest brick house, a National Register building, is located on the banks of the Arkansas River, a mile from town. It was once the poor farm, for folks down on their luck who were willing to work in exchange for food and lodging. The house has been renovated and decorated in a country-eclectic style featuring oak antiques, with generously-sized guest rooms enhanced by views of the mountains. The location appeals to fishermen and families planning a river-rafting excursion. A dormitory in the attic has 12 bunk beds, popular with young skiers and rafters. Belgian waffles are a breakfast specialty and the innkeeper will pan fry your morning catch.

Rates: $39-$49. Herb & Dottie Hostetler.
5 R. 2 PB. Phone available. TV available. Beds: KQTC. Full breakfast. CCs: MC VISA. Skiing, hunting, white water rafting, hot springs pool, mountain bike riding, hiking, jeep trails. Weddings, special on honeymoons, family reunions.
Seen in: *Denver Magazine, Rocky Mountain News, Colorado Country Life.*
"We will always remember your generous hospitality in your beautiful home."

TELLURIDE M5/*E2*

Johnstone Inn
PO Box 546
Telluride CO 81435
(303) 728-3316 (800)752-1901

Circa 1891. This Victorian farmhouse is located on Telluride's main street, in view of the San Juan Mountain ski slopes. Guest rooms all have new bathrooms with marble floors and showers. Brass beds are painted with pink and white flowers and topped with fluffy comforters. Hot chocolate is served in the evening. Laundry and light kitchen use is available. Ski lifts are a short walk away.

Rates: $30-$75. Bill Schiffbauer.
8 R. 8 PB. Phone in room. Beds: Q. Full breakfast. Spa. CCs: MC VISA AE. Skiing, fishing, hiking, music & film festivals.
Seen in: *Rocky Mountain News.*
"Cannot say enough good things, had a great time."

San Sophia
330 W Pacific Ave, PO Box 1825
Telluride CO 81435
(303) 728-3001 (800) 537-4781

An observation tower rises gingerly from the inn's gabled roofline, providing 360-degree views from the valley

floor to the 13,000-foot peaks of the Saint Sophia Ridge. Rooms are decorated with antiques, brass beds and wallpapers, and feature soaking tubs and bay windows or balconies. The two-story windows of the dining room reveal views of waterfalls plunging from the peaks on one side and ski slopes on the other.

✻❀Rates: $70-$175. Dianne & Gary Eschman.
16 R. 16 PB. Phone in room. TV in room. Beds: KQD. Full breakfast. Spa. Conference room. FAX. CCs: MC VISA AE. Skiing, outside dining, observatory.
Seen in: *Rocky Mountain News, Snow Country, Country Inns.*
"Telluride is a great town and your bed and breakfast is part of the charm and beauty of the entire area."

CONNECTICUT

BOLTON E13/E4

Jared Cone House

25 Hebron Rd
Bolton CT 06043
(203) 643-8538

Circa 1775. Once the town post office and library, this is a lavishly embellished Georgian post-and-beam house. There are seven fireplaces and a

dramatic Palladian window on the second floor. A pond at the rear of the property provides ice skating for both townsfolk and guests, and in spring, sugar maples surrounding the house are tapped for the inn's breakfasts.

Location: Ten miles east of Hartford via I-384 & Exit #5.

Rates: $60-$70. Jeff & Cinde Smith.

3 R. 1 PB. Phone available. TV available. Beds: QTC. Full breakfast. Conference room. Sleigh rides, hay rides, cross-country skiing, canoeing, bicycling, hiking, antiquing. Canoe to lend.

Seen in: *Manchester Herald, Weekend Plus.*

"Beautiful colonial home, delightful breakfasts."

BRISTOL F9/E3

Chimney Crest Manor

5 Founders Dr
Bristol CT 06010
(203) 582-4219

Circa 1930. This 32-room Tudor mansion possesses an unusual castle-like arcade and a 45-foot living room with a stone fireplace at each end. Many of the rooms are embellished with oak paneling and ornate plaster ceilings. The inn is located in the Federal Hill District, an area of large colonial homes.

*Rates: $70-$95. Dan & Cynthia Cimadamore.

4 R. 4 PB. 2 FP. Phone available. TV in

room. Beds: Q. B&B. Swimming pool. Conference room. CCs: MC VISA. Ballooning, cross-country & downhill skiing, sleigh rides, tubing. Honeymoon and anniversary weekends.

Seen in: *Record-Journal.*

"Great getaway - unbelievable structure. They are just not made like this mansion anymore."

BROOKLYN E18/E5

Tannerbrook

329 Pomfret Rd
Brooklyn CT 06234
(203) 774-4822

Circa 1750. Built by the earliest settlers of Brooklyn, Connecticut, Tannerbrook is an 18th-century landmark. Amid towering maples, the inn overlooks lovely gardens and a private spring-fed lake. It features antique furnishings.

Rates: $65. Jean & Wendell Burgess.

2 R. 2 PB. 2 FP. Phone available. TV in room. Beds: DT. Full breakfast. CCs: MC VISA. Fishing, nature hiking. Weddings, receptions, honeymoons.

Seen in: *Fairpress, Gannett News.*

"Four star hospitality. Thank you."

CLINTON K13/G4

Captain Dibbell House

21 Commerce St
Clinton CT 06413
(203) 669-1646

Circa 1865. Built by a sea captain, this graceful Victorian house is only two blocks from the harbor where innkeeper Ellis Adams sails his own vessel. A ledger of household accounts dating from the mid-1800s is on display, and there are fresh flowers and fruit baskets in each guest room.

Location: Exit 63 & I-95, south on Rt. 81, east for 1 block, right on Commerce.

❀Rates: $50-$75. Season: Closed January. Ellis & Helen Adams.

3 R. 3 PB. Phone available. TV available. Beds: KQT. Continental-plus breakfast. CCs: MC VISA. Boating, swimming, fishing, hiking, bicycling.

Seen in: *Clinton Recorder.*

"This was our first experience with B&B and frankly, we didn't know what to expect. It was GREAT!"

COVENTRY E15/E4

Maple Hill Farm B&B

365 Goose Ln
Coventry CT 06238
(203) 742-0635

Circa 1731. This historic farmhouse still possesses its original kitchen cupboards and a flour bin used for

generations. Family heirlooms and the history of the former home owners are shared with guests. There is a three-seat outhouse behind the inn. Visitors, of course, are provided with modern plumbing, as well as a

screened porch and greenhouse in which to relax.
*Rates: $50-$60. Tony & Mary Beth Felice.
4 R. Beds: TDC. Full breakfast. Swimming pool. Swimming, golf, biking, horseback riding, volleyball.
Seen in: *Journal Inquirer, The Coventry Journal.*
"Comfortable rooms and delightful country ambience."

DEEP RIVER J13/F4

Riverwind
209 Main St
Deep River CT 06417
(203) 526-2014

Circa 1832. Chosen "most romantic inn in Connecticut" by *Discerning Traveler Newsletter*, this inn features a

wraparound gingerbread porch filled with gleaming white wicker furniture. A happy, informal country decor includes antiques from Barbara's Virginia home. There are fireplaces everywhere including a 12-foot cooking fireplace in the keeping room.
Rates: $85-$145. Barbara & Bob.
8 R. 8 PB. Phone available. Beds: QD. Full breakfast. CCs: MC VISA AE. Badminton, croquet, theater, swimming, golf.
Seen in: *The Hartford Courant, New Haven Register, Country Living Magazine, Country Inns, Country Decorating.*
"If we felt any more welcome we'd have our Time *subscription sent here."*

EAST HADDAM I13/F4

Bishopsgate Inn
7 Norwich Rd, PO Box 290
East Haddam CT 06423
(203) 873-1677

Circa 1818. This center chimney colonial house is appointed with antiques of the Empire period. There's a working beehive oven where Molly often bakes bread and simmers a warm wintry soup. In the suite, guests can order a candlelight dinner in front of the fireplace. (There's a deck and sauna, also.) Vintage musicals are performed at the Goodspeed Opera House, a block away.
Rates: $75-$100. Molly & Dan Swartz.
6 R. 6 PB. 4 FP. Phone available. Beds: QD. MAP. Gourmet meals. Sauna. CCs: MC VISA. State parks, opera.
Seen in: *The Discerning Traveler, Adventure Road, The Manhattan Cooperator.*
"Outstanding! The very best. Thank you for the wonderful hospitality."

EAST WINDSOR D12/E4

The Stephen Potwine House
84 Scantic Rd
East Windsor CT 06088
(203) 623-8722

Circa 1831. Acres of farmland surround this old homestead. In keeping with its rural setting a country decor has been chosen, and rooms look out

over a pond shaded by graceful willow trees and a barn completes the picture. The hosts' special interests are highlighted in seminars on stress management, music imagery and other renewal experiences. Sturbridge Village is 30 miles away.
Rates: $55-$75. Season: March to Dec. Bob & Vangy Cathcart.
4 R. 1 PB. Beds: QTD. Full breakfast. Spa. Swimming, tennis, skiing, ice skating, bicycling, canoeing, jogging.
Seen in: *The Hartford Woman, Boston Globe, Journal Inquirer.*
"...a charming mix of antique, Vangies' artwork & stenciling, fresh flowers, and aura of peace."

ESSEX J14/F4

Griswold Inn
36 Main St
Essex CT 06426
(203) 767-1776

Circa 1776. The main building of the colonial Griswold Inn is said to be the first three-story frame structure built

in Connecticut. The Tap Room, just behind the inn, has been called the most handsome barroom in America. Built by Lucius Beebe, the inn is famous for its English Hunt Breakfast served at the request of the British after they invaded the harbor at Essex during the war of 1812. Fried chicken, scrambled eggs, lamb kidneys with sauteed mushrooms, corn bread and creamed ham are some of the items still available on Sunday mornings. Ask for a quiet room at the back of the inn unless you'd enjoy a Fife & Drum corps marching by under your window on Main Street.
Rates: $80-$165. William & Victoria Winterer.
23 R. 23 PB. 4 FP. Phone in room. TV available. Beds: DTC. Continental breakfast. Conference room. FAX. CCs: MC VISA AE.
Seen in: *Yankee Magazine, House Beautiful.*
"A man in search of the best Inn in New England has a candidate in the quiet, unchanged town of Essex, Connecticut," Country Journal.

GLASTONBURY F12/E4

Butternut Farm
1654 Main St
Glastonbury CT 06033
(203) 633-7197

Circa 1720. This Colonial house sits on two acres of landscaped grounds amidst trees and herb gardens. Prize-

winning goats, pigeons, and chickens are housed in the old barn on the property. Eighteenth-century Connecticut antiques including a cherry highboy and cherry pencil-post canopy bed, are placed throughout the inn, enhancing the natural beauty of the pumpkin-pine floors and brick fireplaces.
Location: South of Glastonbury Center, 1 1/2 miles, 10 minutes to Hartford.
Rates: $65-$83. Don Reid.
4 R. 2 PB. 2 FP. TV in room. Beds: DT. Full breakfast. CCs: MC VISA AE.
Seen in: *New York Times, House Beautiful.*

GREENWICH N3/H1

Stanton House Inn
76 Maple Ave
Greenwich CT 06830
(203) 869-2110

Circa 1881. It took 150 years for one of the Saketts to finally build on the land given them in 1717. The manor they built was remodeled on a grand scale at the turn-of-the-century under ar-

chitect Sanford White. In the Thirties the house became a tourist home and received visitors for many years. Renovated recently, it now offers spacious rooms decorated in a colonial style.
Rates: $70 & up. Tog & Doreen Pearson.
24 R. 20 PB. 5 FP. Phone in room. TV in room. Beds: KQDT. Continental breakfast. Conference room. CCs: MC VISA AE. Jogging, YMCA, golf, tennis, beach rights.
Seen in: *Foster's Business Review.*
"For a day, or a month or more, this is a special place."

HARTFORD D11/*E3*

The Old Mill Inn
See: Somersville, CT

IVORYTON J14/*F4*

Copper Beech Inn
46 Main St
Ivoryton CT 06442
(203) 767-0330
Circa 1890. The Copper Beech Inn was once the home of ivory importer A.W. Comstock, one of the early owners of the Comstock Cheney Company,

producer of ivory products and pianos. The village took its name from the ivory trade centered here. An enormous copper beech tree shades the property. Each room in the renovated Carriage House boasts a spa and French doors opening onto a deck. The inn's restaurant has received numerous accolades.
Location: Lower Connecticut River valley.
Rates: $95-$155. Eldon & Sally Senner.
13 R. 13 PB. 2 FP. Phone available. TV in room. Beds: KQDT. B&B. Restaurant. Gourmet meals. Spa. Conference room. CCs: MC VISA AE DC CB. Water sports, antique shops.
Seen in: *Los Angeles Times.*
"The grounds are beautiful...just breathtaking...accommodations are wonderful."

Ivoryton Inn
115 Main St
Ivoryton CT 06442
(203) 767-0422 (203) 767-0318
Circa 1840. Once a school for young ladies, the main building was moved here from Deep River. It became a boarding house for workers in the ivory factory where piano keys were made. The large inn has a dining room and nightly entertainment.
Rates: $85-$125. George E., Birte M. Bant.
30 R. 28 PB. Phone in room. TV available. Beds: KQDT. Full breakfast. Restaurant. Gourmet meals. Handicap access. Conference room. CCs: MC VISA AE.
Seen in: *Main Street News.*

LAKEVILLE C4/*D1*

Wake Robin Inn
Rt 41
Lakeville CT 06039
(203) 435-2515
Circa 1898. Once the Taconic School for Girls, this inn is located on 15 acres of landscaped grounds in the Connecticut Berkshires. A library has been added as well as antique furnishings. The recently renovated property also includes a few private cottages. Award winning restaurant on premises.
❀Rates: $75-$200. H.J.P. Manassero.
40 R. 40 PB. Beds: KQT. Restaurant. Spa. Sauna. Conference room. CCs: MC VISA. Swimming, cycling, horseback riding.
"A new sophistication has arrived in Lakeville, Connecticut with the restoration of the Wake Robin Inn."

LEDYARD I17/*F5*

Applewood Farms Inn
528 Col Ledyard Hwy
Ledyard CT 06339
(203) 536-2022
Circa 1826. Five generations of the Gallup family worked this farm near Mystic. The classic center chimney colonial, furnished with antiques and

early-American pieces, is situated on 33 acres of fields and meadows. Stone fences meander through the property and many of the original outbuildings remain. It is in the National Register, cited as one of the best surviving examples of a 19th-century farm in Connecticut.
Rates: $65-$95. Frankie & Tom Betz.
6 R. 3 PB. 4 FP. Phone available. TV available. Beds: KD. Full breakfast. CCs: MC VISA AE. Horseback riding, water sports, hiking, bird watching, surrey rides.
Seen in: *Country, New Woman.*
"This bed & breakfast is a real discovery."

LITCHFIELD G5/*E2*

Tollgate Hill Inn
Rt 202 and Tollgate Rd
Litchfield CT 06759
(203) 567-4545
Circa 1745. Formerly known as the Captain Bull Tavern, the inn underwent extensive renovations in 1983. Listed in the National Register, features include Indian shutters, wide pine-paneled walls, a Dutch door fireplace, and an upstairs ballroom. Next door is a historic schoolhouse that contains four of the inn's guestrooms.
Rates: $110-$175. Frederick Zivic.
20 R. 20 PB. 8 FP. Phone in room. TV in room. Beds: QDT. MAP. Restaurant. Conference room. CCs: MC VISA AE DC. Horseback riding, skiing, water sports, golf, tennis.
Seen in: *Food & Wine, Travel & Leisure, The New York Times, Bon Appetit.*

MADISON K12/*G4*

Madison Beach Hotel
94 W Wharf Rd, Box 546
Madison CT 06443
(203) 245-1404
Circa 1800. Since most of Connecticut's shoreline is privately owned, the Madison is one of the few waterfront lodgings available. It was originally constructed as a stagecoach stop and later became a popular vacation spot for those who stayed for a month at a time with maids and chauffeurs. Art Carney is said to have driven a Madison Beach Hotel bus here when his brother was the manager. Rooms are furnished in a variety of antiques and wallpapers and many have splendid views of the lawn and the Long Island Sound from private porches.
Rates: $60-$195. Season: March 1 to Jan. 1. Henry & Betty Cooney, Robin & Kathy Bagdasarian.
35 R. 35 PB. Phone in room. TV in room. Beds: QT. EP. Restaurant. Handicap access. Conference room. CCs: MC VISA AE DC. Tennis, water sports. Weddings.
Seen in: *New England Travel.*
"The accommodations were wonderful and the service was truly exceptional."

MIDDLEBURY H7/*F2*

Tucker Hill Inn
96 Tucker Hill Rd
Middlebury CT 06762
(203) 758-8334
Circa 1923. There's a cut-out heart in the gate that opens to this handsome three-story estate framed by an old stone wall. The spacious Colonial-style house is shaded by tall trees. Guests enjoy a parlor with fireplace

and an inviting formal dining room. Guest rooms are furnished with a flourish of English country or romantic Victorian decor.
Location: New England.
Rates: $55-$75. Susan & Richard Cebelenski.
4 R. 2 PB. Phone available. Beds: QT. Full breakfast. CCs: MC VISA. Horseback riding, skiing, water sports, golf, tennis, fishing, hiking. Complimentary champagne for special occasions.
Seen in: *Star, Waterbury American Republican.*
"Thanks for a special visit. Your kindness never went unnoticed."

MYSTIC J18/F5

The Inn at Mystic
Jct Rt 1 & 27
Mystic CT 06355
(203) 536-9604 (800) 237-2415
Circa 1904. This is a Colonial Revival mansion built by Katherine Haley, widow of one of the owners of the old Fulton Fish Market. A columned Victorian veranda overlooks the harbor and sound. All the rooms are individually decorated and may include a canopy bed, whirlpool tub or a wood-burning fireplace. There is also a motor inn on the property so be sure to request rooms in the original house. Old Mistick Village, Mystic Seaport Museum and the Aquarium are all nearby.
*Rates: $95-$195. Jody Dyer.
68 R. 68 PB. 25 FP. Phone in room. TV in room. Beds: KQDTC. EP. Restaurant. Spa. Handicap access. Swimming pool. Conference room. FAX. CCs: MC VISA AE DC DS. Sailing, rowing, canoeing, swimming, walking trails, tennis.
Seen in: *Travel & Leisure.*

Queen Anne Inn & Antique Gallery
See: New London, CT

Red Brook Inn
PO Box 237
Mystic CT 06372
(203) 572-0349
Circa 1740. Situated on a bluff surrounded by seven acres of woodland, the inn has been recently restored and has a traditional center chimney. All rooms are furnished with period antiques such as canopy beds and many rooms have working fireplaces. Breakfast is served in the large keeping room of the Haley Tavern in front of a great hearth.
Rates: $85-$149. Ruth Keyes.
10 R. 10 PB. 7 FP. Phone available. TV available. Beds: QDT. B&B. Game room. CCs: MC VISA. Horseback riding, water skiing, boating, fishing. Whirlpools, parlors, picnic area. Mystic seaport.
Seen in: *Travel & Leisure, Yankee Magazine, New York Magazine, Country Decorating.*

NEW HARTFORD D8/D3

Cobble Hill Farm
Steele Rd
New Hartford CT 06057
(203) 379-0057
Circa 1796. This rambling Colonial inn was selected by *Country Living Magazine* as one of their favorite ten

inns in the country. It is located in Litchfield Hills on 40 acres of gardens, meadows, woodlands, and wildlife. Signs of deer and wild turkey can be seen while you are strolling along the dirt road. A spring-fed pond is filled with tadpoles and trout, and the barn houses horses, chickens, and pigs.
Location: Foothills of the Berkshires.
*Rates: $95. Season: April 1 - Jan 1 Jo & Don McCurdy.
4 R. 3 PB. Phone available. TV available. Beds: KQDC. Full breakfast. Hay & sleigh rides, horseback riding, tubing on river, swimming.
Seen in: *New York Post, Country Living.*
"Do you know what it's like to relive one's happy childhood except in technicolor? We loved it. The accommodations and food were excellent, too."

NEW HAVEN K9/Q3

The Inn at Chapel West
1201 Chapel St
New Haven CT 06511
(203) 777-1201 fax (203) 776-7363
Circa 1847. This green-and-white Victorian has recently undergone a $2 million renovation. Its lavish appoint-

ments include items such as a Bavarian canopy bed, mahogany and French country furnishings, and a musical doll collection. Maple woodwork, parquet floors and seven fireplaces adorn the inn. There are crystal glasses in the bathrooms and Laura Ashley prints on the walls.
Location: Downtown, one block from the Yale campus.
*Rates: $125-$175. Steven Schneider.
10 R. 10 PB. 3 FP. Phone in room. TV in room. Beds: KQTC. Continental-plus breakfast. Handicap access. Conference room. FAX. CCs: MC VISA AE DC CB. Tours, theater.
Seen in: *New York Times, Business Digest of Greater New Haven.*

NEW LONDON J17/F5

Queen Anne Inn & Antique Gallery
265 Williams St
New London CT 06320
(203) 447-2600 (800) 347-8818
Circa 1903. Several photographers for historic house books have been attracted to the classic good looks of the

recently renovated and freshly painted Queen Anne Inn. The traditional tower, wrap around verandas, and elaborate frieze invite the traveler to explore the interior with its richly polished oak walls and intricately carved alcoves. Double stained glass windows curve around the circular staircase landing. Period furnishings include brass beds and many rooms have their own fireplace. Afternoon tea is served.
*Rates: $75-$149. Ray & Julie Rutledge.
10 R. 8 PB. 2 FP. Phone in room. TV in room. Beds: KQDT. B&B. Spa. Conference room. FAX. CCs: MC VISA AE DC CB DS. Antiquing, theater, concerts. Victorian-style afternoon tea.
Seen in: *New London Day Features, New York Times.*
"Absolutely terrific - relaxing, warm, gracious - beautiful rooms and delectable food."

NEW MILFORD G4/F2

Homestead Inn
5 Elm St
New Milford CT 06776
(203) 354-4080
Circa 1853. Built by the first of three generations of John Prime Treadwells, the inn was established 80 years later. Victorian architecture includes high

ceilings, spacious rooms and large verandas. There is a small motel adjacent to the inn. Marilyn Monroe and Arthur Miller were among the Homestead's famous guests.
Location: North of Danbury, 15 miles.
*Rates: $65-$85. Rolf & Peggy Hammer.
14 R. 14 PB. 2 FP. Phone in room. TV in room. Beds: KQDTC. Continental-plus breakfast. CCs: MC VISA AE DS. Golf, hiking, downhill and cross-country skiing. Massage therapist on staff.
Seen in: *The Litchfield County Times, ABC Home Show.*
"One of the homiest inns in the U.S.A. with most hospitable hosts. A rare bargain to boot."

NEW PRESTON F5/E2

Boulders Inn
Rt 45
New Preston CT 06777
(203) 868-0541 (203) 868-7918
Circa 1895. Outstanding views of Lake Waramaug and its wooded shores can be seen from the living room and many of the guest rooms and cottages of this country inn. The terrace is open in the summer for cocktails and dinner and sunsets over the lake. Antique furnishings, a basement game room, a beach house with a hanging wicker swing and a tennis court are all part of Boulders Inn.
Location: Lake Waramaug.
Rates: $200-$225. Kees & Ulla Adema.
17 R. 17 PB. 11 FP. Phone in room. TV available. Beds: KQDT. MAP. Game room. Conference room. CCs: MC VISA AE. Tennis, hiking, sailing, canoeing, paddleboats, swimming.
Seen in: *The New York Times, Travel & Leisure, Country Inns.*
"Thank you for a welcome respite from the daily hurly-burly."

NORFOLK B6/D2

Blackberry River Inn
Rt 44
Norfolk CT 06058
(203) 542-5100
Circa 1763. The Blackberry River Inn is nestled in the foothills of the Berkshires on 17 scenic acres. Listed in the National Register of Historic Places, the inn has a tavern, three sitting rooms with fireplaces and a restaurant for leisurely candlelight dining.
Rates: $80-$150. Kim & Bob Zuckerman.
19 R. 12 PB. 4 FP. Phone available. TV available. Beds: KQDTWC. Continental-plus breakfast. Restaurant. Gourmet meals. Spa. Swimming pool. Conference room. CCs: MC VISA AE DC CB. Horseback riding, skiing, hiking, fishing, canoeing, theaters, antiquing. Weddings & honeymoons.
Seen in: *Innsider, The New York Times.*
"Eric and I had the most wonderful time at your inn. You made us feel so welcome!"

Manor House
Maple Ave, PO Box 447
Norfolk CT 06058
(203) 542-5690 (800) 488-5690
Circa 1898. Charles Spofford, designer of London's subway, built this home with many gables, exquisite cherry paneling, and grand staircase. There

are Moorish arches and Tiffany windows. Guests can enjoy hot mulled cider after a sleigh ride, hay ride, or horse-and-carriage drive along the country lanes nearby. The inn was named by *Discerning Traveler* as Connecticut's most romantic hideaway.
❀Rates: $70-$150. Hank & Diane Tremblay.
9 R. 7 PB. 2 FP. Phone available. TV available. Beds: KQDT. B&B. Conference room. CCs: MC VISA AE. Cross-country skiing, hiking, biking, riding stables, swimming, boating.
Seen in: *Boston Globe, The Journal, Philadelphia Inquirer.*
"Queen Victoria, eat your heart out."

NORWALK M4/G2

Silvermine Tavern
194 Perry Aves
Norwalk CT 06850
(203) 847-4558
Circa 1786. The Silvermine consists of the Old Mill, the Country Store, the Coach House, and the Tavern itself. Primitive paintings and furnishings, as well as family heirlooms, decorate the inn. Guest rooms and dining rooms overlook the Old Mill, the waterfall, and swans gliding across the millpond.
Rates: $74-$80. Frank Whitman, Jr.
10 R. 10 PB. B&B. Restaurant.

OLD LYME K14/G4

Old Lyme Inn
85 Lyme St
Old Lyme CT 06371
(203) 434-2600
Circa 1850. This elegantly restored mansion features original wall paintings in its front hall, portraying his-

toric Old Lyme buildings and the scenic countryside. Elegance is reflected throughout the inn with marble fireplaces, antique mirrors, and Victorian and Empire furnishings.
*❀Rates: $95-$125. Season: Jan. 15- Dec. 31. Diana Field Atwood.
13 R. 13 PB. 3 FP. Phone in room. TV available. Beds: QT. Continental-plus breakfast. Restaurant. Handicap access. Conference room. CCs: MC VISA AE DC CB DS. Tennis, golf, cross-country skiing, water sports, bicycling.
Seen in: *Gourmet Getaways, New York Times.*
"Gracious and romantic rooms with exquisite dining. Our favorite inn!"

RIDGEFIELD K4/G1

West Lane Inn
22 West Ln
Ridgefield CT 06877
(203) 438-7323
Circa 1880. This National Register Victorian mansion on two acres features an enormous front veranda filled with white bamboo chairs and tables overlooking a manicured lawn. A polished oak staircase rises to a third-floor landing and lounge. Chandeliers, wall sconces and floral wallpapers help to establish an intimate atmosphere. Although the rooms do not have antiques, they feature amenities such as heated towel racks, extra thick towels, air-conditioning and desks. The inn holds a four diamond award.
Rates: $120-$160. Maureen Mayer.
20 R. 20 PB. 2 FP. Phone in room. TV in room. Beds: Q. Continental breakfast. Handicap access. CCs: MC VISA AE DC. Skiing, swimming, golf, tennis, ice skating, fishing.
Seen in: *Stanford-Advocate, Greenwich Times, Home & Away Connecticut.*
"Thank you for the hospitality you showed us. The rooms are comfortable and quiet. I haven't slept this soundly in weeks."

SALISBURY B4/D2

Under Mountain Inn

482 Undermountain Rd
Salisbury CT 06068
(203) 435-0242

Circa 1740. Situated on three acres, this was originally the home of iron magnate Jonathan Scoville. A thorned locust tree, believed to be the oldest in

Connecticut, shades the inn. Paneling that now adorns the pub was discovered hidden between the ceiling and attic floorboards. The boards were probably placed there in violation of a colonial law requiring all wide lumber to be given to the king of England. British-born Peter was happy to reclaim it in the name of the Crown.

*❀Rates: $75.MAP pp. Peter & Marged Higginson.

7 R. 7 PB. Phone available. Beds: KQDT. MAP. Restaurant. Gourmet meals. CCs: MC VISA AE DS. Golf, tennis, horseback riding, boating, hiking, swimming, bikes.

Seen in: *Travel & Leisure, Country Inns Magazine, Yankee, New England GetAways.*

"You're terrific!"

Yesterday's Yankee B&B

Rt 44 E
Salisbury CT 06068
(203) 435-9539

Circa 1744. Shaded by ancient towering maples, this lovely home is unusual because in 1744 the individual Cape Cod design was limited to the

Cape, 250 miles away. Its original Colonial atmosphere is retained by low ceilings, wide board floors, small paned windows, whitewashed walls, and period furnishings. Breakfast is served in the keeping room near the fireplace.

*❀Rates: $65-$80. Doris & Dick Alexander.

3 R. Phone available. TV available. Beds: KQT. B&B. CCs: MC VISA AE. Water sports, hiking, summer theater, music centers, antiquing, winter sports, horseback riding, skiing, sports car racing, golf.

Seen in: *New England Getaways, New England Magazine.*

"Lovely house & hosts, great breakfasts - 5 star!"

SOMERSVILLE B12/D4

The Old Mill Inn

63 Maple St
Somersville CT 06072
(203) 763-1473

Circa 1850. Owners of the old woolen mill bought this home at the turn-of-the-century, and it was occupied by the storekeeper of the Somersville general store. The dining room walls are painted with flowering shrubs and trees in keeping with the inn's landscaping.

Location: Five miles east of Exit 47 on I-91, 1 block south of Rt. 190.

*Rates: $45-$50. Ralph & Phyllis Lumb.

4 R. 2 PB. 1 FP. Phone available. TV available. Beds: DTW. Continental-plus breakfast. Golf, museums, historic homes.

"We loved staying here! You are both delightful. P.S. We slept like a log."

SOUTH WOODSTOCK C18/D5

The Inn at Woodstock Hill

94 Plaine Hill Rd, PO Box 98
South Woodstock CT 06267
(203) 928-0528

Circa 1816. This classic Georgian house with its black shutters and

white clapboard exterior reigns over 14 acres of rolling farmland. Inside are several parlors, pegged-wood floors, English country wallpapers, floral chintzes and a fireplace for each room.

*Rates: $55-$140. Sheila Becks & Richard Naumann.

19 R. 19 PB. Phone available. TV available. Beds: QT. Continental-plus breakfast. Restaurant. Conference room. CCs: MC VISA. Horseback riding, skiing, hiking, flower garden tours.

Seen in: *The Hartford Courant, Worcester Telegram, Connecticut Magazine.*

"Where the world is the way it's meant to be."

TOLLAND D14/E4

Tolland Inn

63 Tolland Green, PO Box 717
Tolland CT 06084
(203) 872-0800

Circa 1800. This white clapboard house on the village green originally provided lodging for travelers on the old Post Road between New York and Boston. After extensive renovation,

the Tolland Inn has been opened once again and has been refurbished with antiques and many furnishings made by the innkeeper. Nearby is the town hall and the Old Jail Museum.

Location: On the village green, 1/2 mile to exit 68 & I-84.

Rates: $50-$60. Susan & Stephen Beeching.

5 R. 3 PB. Phone available. Beds: DT. B&B. CCs: MC VISA AE. Antiquing, Caprilands herb farm, University of Connecticut, Old Sturbridge Village.

Seen in: *Journal Inquirer, Hartford Courant, Tolland County Times.*

"The rooms are very clean, the bed very comfortable, the food consistently excellent and the innkeepers very courteous."

DELAWARE

DOVER F23/B7

The Inn at Meeting House Square

305 S Governors Ave
Dover DE 19901
(302) 678-1242

Circa 1849. An arched front porch accentuates this two-and-a-half-story house located across the street from

the Delaware State Museum, formerly the 1790 Presbyterian Church. A traditional-style decor features memorabilia collected on family travels. An old-fashioned swing is a favorite place to relax on the brick-walled sun porch. Walnut bread, French toast and sticky buns are house favorites. Enjoy breakfast on the patio addition.

Rates: $42-$58. Sherry & Carolyn DeZwarte.
4 R. 4 PB. Phone in room. TV in room. Beds: KQDT. B&B. CCs: MC VISA. Water sports, wildlife refuge, museums.

"Thank you for making us so comfortable and keeping us so well-fed."

LAUREL J23/D7

Spring Garden

Rt 1 Box 283-A
Laurel DE 19956
(302) 875-7015

Circa 1780. This gracious white brick and clapboard plantation was built in a Federal-style with Georgian overtones. It features outstandingly preserved 18th-century heart-pine paneling, four fireplaces and wide-planked floors. Lawns and meadows bloom with lilies and lilacs. A stream meanders through the forest on the

property. Spring Garden was awarded first place for "Excellence in Hospitality" by the Delaware Tourism Bureau.

Location: Fourteen miles north of Salisbury, MD, 30 minutes to Atlantic Ocean beaches and Chesapeake Bay.
*Rates: $55-$75. Gwen North.
6 R. 2 PB. Phone available. TV available. Beds: DT. Full breakfast. Handicap access. Conference room. Bicycling, horseback riding, badminton, tennis, swimming, fishing, antiquing, wilderness canoe trails.
Seen in: *The Sun, Newsday.*

"The warmest, most gracious hostess on the Eastern shore. We rated all the inns we stayed in on a scale of one to 10. You got the 10."

NEW CASTLE C23/A7

The Jefferson House B&B

5 The Strand at the Wharf
New Castle DE 19720
(302) 323-0999 (302) 322-8944

Circa 1800. Overlooking the Strand and the Delaware River, The Jefferson

House served as a hotel, a rooming house and a shipping-company office during colonial times. On the side lawn is a "William Penn landed here" sign. The inn features heavy paneled doors, black marble mantels over the fireplaces and a fanlight on the third floor. There is private access to the river, and a spa beckons guests after a long day of sightseeing. Cobblestone streets add to the quaintness of the first capital city of the colonies.

Location: Mid-Atlantic region.
*❀Rates: $65-$85. Chris Bechstein.
3 R. 3 PB. 1 FP. Phone available. TV in room. Beds: D. B&B. Restaurant. Spa. CCs: MC VISA. Kayaking, walking, bicycling.
Seen in: *Roll Call.*

"I loved sleeping on an old brass bed, in a room filled with antiques and charm, just feet from where William Penn landed in New Castle."

William Penn Guest House

206 Delaware St
New Castle DE 19720
(302) 328-7736

Circa 1682. William Penn slept here. In fact, his host Arnoldus de LaGrange witnessed the ceremony in which Penn gained possession of the Three Lower Colonies. Mrs. Burwell, who lived next door to the historic house "gained possession" of it one day about 44 years ago while her husband was away. After recovering from his wife's surprise purchase, Mr. Burwell rolled up his sleeves and began restoring the house. Guests may stay in the very room slept in by Penn.

Rates: $40. Irma & Richard Burwell.
4 R. Phone available. TV in room. Beds: DT. Continental breakfast. CCs: MC VISA.
Seen in: *Asbury Press.*

"An enjoyable stay, as usual. We'll return in the spring."

FLORIDA

AMELIA ISLAND C12/A4

The 1735 House
584 S Fletcher Ave
Amelia Island FL 32034
(904) 261-4148 (800) 872-8531
Circa 1928. Perched at the edge of the Atlantic, the inn is just 15 steps across the sand to the ocean (any closer and

it would be below the tide line). All rooms in this New England clapboard-style inn are actually suites. Antiques, wicker and rattan add to the decor and comfort. A lighthouse-type building is popular with families. Breakfast is delivered to your door in a picnic hamper.
Location: Oceanfront.
*Rates: $75-$105. Gary & Emily Grable.
6 R. 6 PB. Phone available. TV in room. Beds: KQDT. B&B. CCs: MC VISA AE. Tennis, golf, horseback riding.
Seen in: *The Palm Beach Post, Traveler.*
"It was a delightful surprise to find a typical old New England inn in Florida with the charm of Cape Cod and warm ocean breezes and waves lapping at the door."

Florida House Inn
PO Box 688
Amelia Island FL 32034
(904) 261-3300
Circa 1857. Located in the heart of a 50-block National Historic Register area, the Florida House Inn is thought to be the oldest continuously operating tourist hotel in Florida. Recently renovated, the inn features a small pub, a guest parlor, a library and a New Orleans-style courtyard in which guests may enjoy the shade of 200-year-old oaks. Rooms are decorated with country pine and oak antiques, cheerful handmade rugs and quilts.

The Carnegies and Rockefellers have been guests.
*Rates: $55-$120. Bob & Karen Warner.
12 R. 12 PB. 6 FP. Phone in room. TV in room. Beds: KQTC. Full breakfast. Restaurant. Spa. Handicap access. FAX. CCs: MC VISA AE. Golf, tennis, fishing, boating, horseback riding, beach.
Seen in: *Amelia Now, The Tampa Tribune, Miami Herald.*

BRADENTON O8/E3

Harrington House B&B
See: Holmes Beach, FL

FERNANDINA BEACH C12/A4

Bailey House
PO Box 805
Fernandina Beach FL 32034
(904) 261-5390
Circa 1895. This elegant Queen Anne Victorian was a wedding present that

steamship agent Effingham W. Bailey gave to his bride. He shocked the locals by spending the enormous sum of $10,000 to build the house with all its towers, turrets, gables and verandas. The parlor and dining room open to a fireplace in a reception hall with the inscription "Hearth Hall - Welcome All." A spirit of hospitality has reigned in this home from its beginning.
Location: In Historic District on Amelia Island.
*Rates: $65-$95. Tom & Diane Hay.
4 R. 4 PB. 2 FP. Phone available. TV in room. Beds: QDT. B&B. CCs: AE. Beach, horseback riding, tennis & golf in the vicinity. Bicycles for guests.
Seen in: *Innsider Magazine, Southern Living, Victorian Homes, St. Petersburg Times.*
"Well, here we are back at Mickey Mouse land. I think we prefer the lovely Bailey House!"

HOLMES BEACH O8/E3

Harrington House B&B
5626 Gulf Dr
Holmes Beach FL 34217
(813) 778-5444 (813) 778-6335
Circa 1925. A mere 40 feet from the water, this gracious home is set among pine trees and palms. Con-

structed of 14-inch-thick coquina blocks, the house features a living room with a 20-foot-high beamed ceiling, fireplace, Twenties wallpaper and French doors. All the guest rooms have four-poster beds, antique wicker furnishings and French doors opening onto a deck overlooking the swimming pool and water.
*Rates: $85-$115. Walt & Betty Spangler.
7 R. 7 PB. Phone available. TV in room. Beds: KQDT. Full breakfast. Swimming pool. CCs: MC VISA. Tennis, deep-sea fishing, diving, shelling, water sports, sailboat/jetski rental. Kayak and bicycles available.
Seen in: *Sarasota Herald Tribune, Island Sun,*

Islander Press.
"Elegant house and hospitality."

JACKSONVILLE D11/B4

Florida House Inn
See: Amelia Island, FL

House on Cherry St
1844 Cherry St
Jacksonville FL 32205
(904) 384-1999

Circa 1909. Seasonal blooms fill the pots that line the circular entry stairs to this Federal-style house on tree-lined Cherry Street. It was moved in two pieces to its present site on St. Johns River in the historic Riverside area. Traditionally decorated rooms include antiques, collections of hand-carved decoy ducks and old clocks that chime and tick. Most rooms overlook the river. Your hosts are a social worker and family doctor.
Location: Historic Avondale.
*Rates: $65-$80. Carol & Merrill Anderson.
4 R. 4 PB. Phone available. TV in room. Beds: QDT. Full breakfast. CCs: MC VISA. Tennis, water sports, jogging.
Seen in: *Florida Wayfarer, Tampa Tribune.*

KEY WEST Z11/H4

Colours Key West The Guest Mansion
410 Fleming St
Key West FL 33040
(305) 294-6977

Circa 1889. Completely renovated, this Victorian mansion has maintained all the original architectural detail, in-

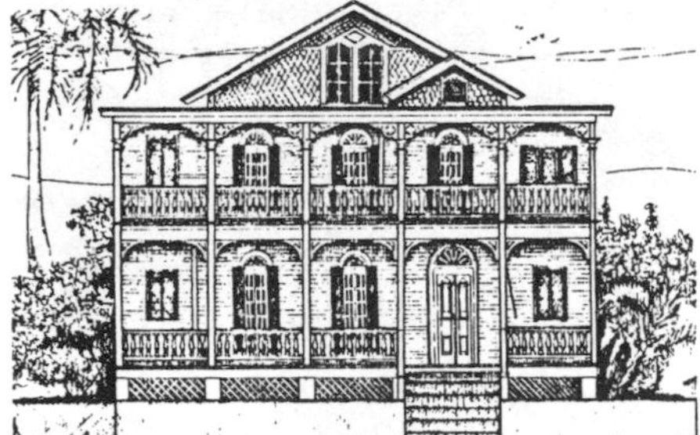

cluding 14-foot ceilings, chandeliers, polished wood floors and graceful verandas. The house is said to be haunted by Hetty, a ghost who has been seen by many folks over the years. The innkeeper says that the inn is for the liberal-minded adult only.
Location: Historic Old Town District.
*Rates: $55-$150. James Remes.
12 R. 10 PB. Phone in room. Beds: KD. Continental-plus breakfast. Swimming pool. FAX. CCs: MC VISA. Water skiing, snorkeling, scuba diving, boating. Turndown service, cocktails.
Seen in: *Sunshine News, Sun Sentinel, Key West Citizen.*
"I have stayed at several guest houses in Key West - none compare. Constant clean towels and the freshness of everything is impressive."

Duval House
815 Duval St
Key West FL 33040
(305) 294-1666

Circa 1890. The Duval House's two Victorian houses surround a garden and a swimming pool. French doors open onto the tropical gardens. Guests may relax on the balconies. Breakfast is served in the pool lounge. Rooms have wicker and antique furniture and Bahamian fans.
Rates: $59-$150. Richard Kamradt.
28 R. 25 PB. Phone available. TV available. Beds: QD. Continental-plus breakfast. Swimming pool. CCs: MC VISA AE. Beaches, water skiing, snorkeling, conch train tours. Weddings.
Seen in: *Cleveland Plain-Dealer, Roanoke Times.*
"You certainly will see us again."

Eden House
1015 Fleming
Key West FL 33040
(305) 296-6868 (800) 533-5397

Circa 1924. This simply furnished hotel is located in the historic district. French doors open from the lobby

onto the pool area, where a handsome new gazebo has been constructed around the base of a palm tree. Painted iron bedsteads, ceiling fans and verandas add to the tropical ambience.
*Rates: $45-$145. Season: December to April. Mike Eden.
38 R. 20 PB. Phone in room. TV in room. Beds: QDT. Restaurant. Swimming pool. CCs: MC VISA AE. Sailing, snorkeling, scuba diving, para-sailing.
Seen in: *Glamour, Cosmopolitan, Woman's Day.*
"We feel lucky to have found such a relaxing place, and we look forward to returning."

Heron House
512 Simonton St
Key West FL 33040
(305) 294-9227

Circa 1856. One of the oldest homes remaining in Key West, this house is an early pre-1860 example of Conch architecture. Bougainvillea, jasmine and orchids bloom in the tropical gar-

dens. Light and airy rooms with wicker furnishings have a tropical feeling.
Location: One block from Duval St. in center of Historic District.
*Rates: $55-$195. Fred Geibelt.
19 R. 19 PB. Phone available. Beds: QD. Continental-plus breakfast. Swimming pool. CCs: MC VISA AE.
Seen in: *Sun Sentinel.*
"The common pool and garden area gave us the feeling that we were in a tropical paradise."

The Popular House, Key West B&B
415 William St
Key West FL 33040
(305) 296-7274 (305) 294-3630

Circa 1890. This pink and white Victorian sits elegantly behind a white picket fence. It was constructed by shipbuilders with sturdy heart-pine walls and 13-foot ceilings. With two stories of porches, the inn is located in the center of the Historic District.
Location: Two blocks from the Gulf.
*Rates: $55-$135. Jody Carlson.
7 R. 2 PB. Phone available. Beds: KQDT. Continental-plus breakfast. Spa. Sauna. Conference room. CCs: MC VISA AE. Fishing, shopping, all water sports, dining.
Seen in: *Palm Beach Life.*
"The essence of charming."

The Watson House
525 Simonton
Key West FL 33040
(305) 294-6712 (305) 294-6210

Circa 1860. Purchased by an Ohio couple during the Civil War, this home was remodeled as a Bahamian-style home, ideal for its sub-tropical

climate. In 1986, after two years of restoration, the house became the recipient of the Excellence in

Rehabilitation award granted by the Historic Florida Keys Preservation Board.
*Rates: $85-$295. Joe Beres & Ed Czaplicki.
3 R. 3 PB. Phone in room. TV in room. Beds: QD. AP. Spa. Swimming pool. FAX. CCs: MC VISA AE. All suites with kitchens.
Seen in: *Florida Wayfarer.*
"Your home is absolutely beautiful. It was truly a delightful treat."

Whispers B&B Inn at Gideon Lowe House

409 William St
Key West FL 33040
(305) 294-5969

Circa 1846. This columned Greek Revival-style house, listed in the National Register, shows the architectural influence of the Victorian period with ornamental fretwork on the porch railings. Bahamian tropical additions include shuttered windows, ceiling scuttles and double-decked porches. Air-conditioned rooms are furnished in antiques. Ceiling fans and lush gardens add to the atmosphere. In the center of the historic district, the house is in view of the Gulf harbor.
Location: Heart of Old Town Key West.
*Rates: $69-$105. Marilyn & Les Tipton.
6 R. Phone available. TV in room. Full breakfast. Gourmet meals. CCs: MC VISA. Reef diving, fishing, tennis, bicycles, biplane rides, sunset cruises, beaches.
Seen in: *Physicians Lifestyle Magazine.*

LAKE WALES M11/D4

Chalet Suzanne

US 27 & 17A, Drawer AC
Lake Wales FL 33859-9003
(813) 676-6011 (800)288-6011

Circa 1921. Carl & Vita Hinshaw are carrying on the traditions begun by Carl's mother, Bertha, who was known as a world-traveler, gourmet

cook and antique-collector. Following the stock market crash and her husband's death, she turned her home into an inn and dining room. The whimsical architecture includes gabled roofs, balconies, spires and steeples. The restaurant received the Craig Claiborne award as one of the 121 best restaurants in the world.
Location: Four miles north of Lake Wales. Twenty minutes south of I-4.
*Rates: $95-$165. Carl & Vita Hinshaw.
30 R. 30 PB. Phone in room. TV in room. Beds: KDTC. EP. Restaurant. Handicap access. Swimming pool. Conference room. FAX. CCs: MC VISA AE DC CB DS. Lawn games, golf and tennis nearby. Private airstrip and lake. Murder-mystery weekends.
Seen in: *USA Today, The New York Times, Country Magazine, Innsider.*
"I now know why everyone always says, 'Wow!' when they come up from dinner. Please don't change a thing."

MICANOPY G9/C3

Herlong Mansion

Cholakka Blvd, PO Box 667
Micanopy FL 32667
(904) 466-3322

Circa 1875. This mid-Victorian mansion features four two-story carved-wood Roman Corinthian columns on its veranda. The mansion is surrounded by a garden with statuesque old oak and pecan trees. Herlong Mansion features leaded-glass windows, mahogany inlaid oak floors, 12-foot ceilings and floor-to-ceiling windows in the dining room. Guest rooms have fireplaces and are furnished with antiques.
Rates: $80-$110. H.C. (Sonny) Howard, Jr.
6 R. 6 PB. 6 FP. Phone available. TV available. Beds: KQD. Continental-plus breakfast. CCs: MC VISA. Antiquing. Weddings.
Seen in: *Florida Trend.*

MONTICELLO C4/A2

Peppermill B&B

625 E Washington St
Monticello FL 32344
(904) 997-4600

Circa 1888. This Classic Revival frame house with graceful white Doric columns is listed in the National Register of Historic Places. Polished oak and pine floors are complimented by 12-foot-ceilings. The inn features a sun porch paneled in magnolia wood. A porch provides views of a camellia garden amd there's a balcony that overlooks the picturesque street of old houses. Afternoon tea is often served in the upstairs foyer.
Rates: $60-$85. Dick & Cheryl Lepanen.
5 R. 1 PB. 1 FP. Phone available. TV available. Beds: QDTWC. Full breakfast. Restaurant. Conference room. CCs: MC VISA. Tennis, golf, swimming. Weddings, honeymoon specials.
Seen in: *The Tampa Tribune, Monticello News.*
"Thank you for your hospitality and comfortable accommodations."

OCALA H10/C3

Seven Sisters Inn

820 SE Fort King St
Ocala FL 32671
(904) 867-1170

Circa 1888. This Queen Anne-style Victorian house is located in the heart of the historic district. Guests may relax on the large covered porches or visit with other guests in the Club Room. One of the innkeepers, Norma Johnson, is the eldest of seven sisters. Each room, named for one of the sisters, has a childhood picture of its namesake and is decorated in her favorite colors. The rooms feature king-size beds, sitting rooms, fireplaces and luxury linens. A gourmet breakfast includes caviar, homemade muffins and fresh fruits.
Rates: $75-$125. Jerry & Norma Johnson.
7 R. 7 PB. TV available. Beds: K. Full breakfast. Gourmet meals. CCs: MC VISA. Horse farms.

ORLANDO K12/D4

The Courtyard at Lake Lucerne

211 N Lucerne Circle E
Orlando FL 32801
(407) 648-5188

Circa 1883. The Courtyard at Lake Lucerne consists of three buildings: the Wellborn, an Art Deco building furnished in period style; the I.W. Phillips house, an antebellum-style manor with authentic Belle Epoque fittings and wraparound porches; and the Norment-Parry Inn, a Victorian-style house with English and American antiques. The Norment-Parry Inn is the oldest documented house still standing in Orlando and overlooks Lake Lucerne. The complex includes an elaborate turn-of-the-century fountain and lush gardens.
*Rates: $85-$150. Charles E., Sam & Paula Meiner.
22 R. 22 PB. 2 FP. Phone in room. TV in room. Beds: KQDTC. Continental-plus breakfast. Spa. Sauna. Handicap access. CCs: MC VISA AE. Amusement parks nearby. Weddings, honeymoon & anniversary specials.
Seen in: *Florida Historic Homes, Country Inns.*
"Best kept secret in Orlando."

SAINT AUGUSTINE F12/B4

Carriage Way B&B

70 Cuna St
Saint Augustine FL 32084
(904) 829-2467

Circa 1883. A two-story veranda dominates the facade of this square Victorian. Painted creamy white with blue trim, the house is located in the heart of the historic district. It's within a four-block walk to restaurants and shops and the Intracoastal Waterway. Guest rooms reflect the charm of a light Victorian touch, with brass, canopy and four-poster beds. Many furnishings have been in the house for 60 years. On Saturday evenings the dining-room table is laden with scrumptious desserts and coffee. A buffet breakfast is provided in the morning.

*❀Rates: $49-$97. Karen Burkley-Kovacik & Frank Kovacik.

7 R. 7 PB. Phone available. TV available. Beds: QDC. B&B. Gourmet meals. CCs: MC VISA. Beach, tennis, bicycles.

Seen in: *Miami Herald, Florida Times Union, Palm Beach Post.*

"Charming in every detail."

Casa de la Paz

22 Avenida Menendez
Saint Augustine FL 32084
(904) 829-2915

Circa 1915. Overlooking Matanzas Bay, Casa de la Paz was built after the devastating 1914 fire leveled much of the old city. An ornate stucco Mediter-

ranean Revival house, it features clay barrel tile roofing, bracketed eaves, verandas and a lush walled courtyard. Guest rooms offer ceiling fans, central air, hardwood floors, antiques and chocolates.

*Rates: $75-$135. Kramer & Sandy Upchurch.

5 R. 5 PB. Phone available. TV in room. Beds: KQDT. Continental-plus breakfast. CCs: MC VISA AE. Boat rides, beach, golf, tennis, biking.

Seen in: *Innsider.*

"We will always recommend your beautifully restored, elegant home."

Kenwood Inn

38 Marine St
Saint Augustine FL 32084
(904) 824-2116

Circa 1865. Originally built as a summer home, the Kenwood Inn has taken in guests for more than 100

years. Early records show that it was advertised as a private boarding house as early as 1886. Rooms are decorated in periods ranging from the simple Shaker decor to more formal colonial and Victorian styles.

Location: One block from the bay front.

Rates: $55-$125. Mark, Kerrianne & Caitlin Constant.

12 R. 12 PB. 1 FP. Phone available. TV available. Beds: KQD. Continental breakfast. Swimming pool. Game room. CCs: MC VISA DS. Boating, beaches, golf. Courtyard with fish pond.

Seen in: *Palm Beach Post.*

"It's one of my favorite spots for a few days of relaxation and recuperation."

St. Francis Inn

279 St George St
Saint Augustine FL 32084
(904) 824-6068

Circa 1791. Long noted for its hospitality, the St. Francis Inn is near

the oldest house in town. A classic example of Old World architecture, it was built by Gaspar Garcia who received a Spanish grant to the plot of land. Coquina, was the main building material. Saint Augustine was founded in 1565.

Location: In the St. Augustine Historic District, the nation's oldest city.

*Rates: $45-$104. Marie Register.

14 R. 14 PB. 7 FP. TV in room. Beds: KQTC. Continental breakfast. Swimming pool. CCs: MC VISA. Bicycles.

Seen in: *Orlando Sentinel.*

"We have stayed at many nice hotels but nothing like this. We are really enjoying it."

SAINT PETERSBURG N8/*E3*

Bayboro House on Old Tampa Bay

1719 Beach Dr, SE
Saint Petersburg FL 33701
(813) 823-4955

Circa 1904. The Bayboro has a Victorian flavor and was built by one of the founding fathers of the city, C. A. Harvey. He was the first real-estate developer and the first to have the vision to construct the port. Across from Lassing Park, the house has an unobstructed view of Old Tampa Bay. The Bayboro House also has a seasonal apartment available at a weekly rate.

Location: Off exit 9 (I-275), downtown St. Petersburg.

*❀Rates: $65. Gordon & Antonia Powers.

4 R. 4 PB. 1 FP. Phone available. TV in room. Beds: QT. Continental-plus breakfast. CCs: MC VISA. Sailing, tennis, shuffleboard.

Seen in: *Miami Herald, Sun Sentinal.*

"Special touches from the fine linen, pretty quilts, plants, shells and lovely antique furniture made my brief stay enjoyable."

Harrington House B&B

See: Holmes Beach, FL

SARASOTA O8/*E3*

Harrington House B&B

See: Holmes Beach, FL

TALLAHASSEE D3/*A1*

The Riedel House

1412 Fairway Dr
Tallahassee FL 32301
(904) 222-8569

Circa 1937. This white brick Georgian-style house is situated on an acre of

woodland. It was built by Cary Landis, an attorney general. (Landis Hall on the Florida State University campus is named for him.) The focal point of the large entrance foyer is a handsome spiral staircase, which reaches to an art gallery displaying watercolors by innkeeper Carolyn Riedel. Breakfast is served in the dining room with views of terraced gardens.

*Rates: $65. Carolyn Riedel.

3 R. 3 PB. Phone available. TV in room. Beds: QDTW. Continental-plus breakfast. Gourmet meals. Conference room. Jogging, golf.

Seen in: *Tallahassee Magazine.*

"Lovely. We thoroughly enjoyed ourselves!"

TAMPA M9/*D3*

Harrington House B&B

See: Holmes Beach, FL

TARPON SPRINGS L8/D3

Spring Bayou Inn

32 W Tarpon Ave
Tarpon Springs FL 34689
(813) 938-9333

Circa 1905. The massive two-story rotunda of this Victorian house is surrounded by a veranda and a balcony. Inside, glowing curly pine paneling adorns the staircase and fireplace. In addition to Victorian furnishings, a variety of miniature collections are gathered in polished cabinets throughout the inn. The butler's pantry, not to be left undecorated, features a dressmaker's form attired in an 1800s black lace frock. A scenic bayou surrounded by high green banks and huge oak trees is only a block from the inn. The sponge docks, made famous by Greek sponge divers, are within walking distance.

Rates: $50-$75. Season: Oct. 1 to Aug 15.
Ron & Cher Morrick
5 R. 4 PB. 1 FP. Phone available. TV available. Beds: QDT. B&B. Golf, tennis, parks, beaches, fishing.
Seen in: *Florida Home & Garden Magazine, Sunshine Magazine, Miami Today, Palm Beach Post.*

"Lots to do in the area, and the decor was very nice."

WEST PALM BEACH Q17/F5

Hibiscus House

PO Box 2612
West Palm Beach FL 33402
(407) 863-5633

Circa 1922. Built for John Dunkle, once the mayor of West Palm Beach, the Hibiscus House has period furniture, hand-loomed rugs, glossy pine floors, arched doorways and a marble hearth. Guests may relax in a gazebo draped with bougainvillea, on a second-floor terrace or in a quaint courtyard beside a small swimming pool. Airy guest rooms feature brass fans, armoires and potted palms. Fresh-picked fruit is served at the inn.

Rates: $55-$75. Raleigh Hill.
5 R. 5 PB. Phone in room. TV in room. Beds: Q. Full breakfast. Beach.
Seen in: *Ft. Lauderdale-Sun Sentinel.*

"You have such a warm and beautiful home. We have told everyone of our stay there."

GEORGIA

ATLANTA G5/C2

Beverly Hills Inn

65 Sheridan Dr NE
Atlanta GA 30305
(404) 233-8520

Circa 1929. Period furniture and polished wood floors decorate this inn located in the Buckhead neighborhood. There are private balconies, kitchens and a library with a collection of newspapers and books. The governor's mansion, Saks, Neiman-Marcus and Lord & Taylor are five minutes away.

Location: North on Peachtree 15 minutes then 1/2 block off Peachtree.
*❀Rates: $74-$90. Mit & Hima Amin.
18 R. 18 PB. Phone in room. TV in room. Beds: QDC. Continental breakfast. Handicap access. Conference room. CCs: MC VISA AE. Health club. Honeymoon & anniversaries.
Seen in: *Country Inns.*
"Our only regret is that we had so little time. Next stay we will plan to be here longer."

Shellmont B&B Lodge

821 Piedmont NE
Atlanta GA 30308
(404) 872-9290

Circa 1891. This grand Victorian showplace derives its name from two distinctions: the shell motif embossed on the exterior bay and portico and its prominent location on Piedmont Avenue. Architect W.T. Downing further carried out the shell theme with carved wooden shells, bows and garlands. Five panels of stained glass two-stories high accentuate the foyer and are thought to have been designed by Tiffany & Co. Victorian wallpapers and appropriate antiques add to the inn's romantic ambience. It is in the National Register and is a City of Atlanta Landmark building.

*Rates: $75-$90. Ed & Debbie McCord.
4 R. 4 PB. 3 FP. Phone available. TV available. Beds: D. B&B. CCs: MC VISA AE. Tennis, jogging, theater, Botanical Gardens.
Seen in: *Southern Homes, Georgia Trend.*
"Thanks for the warm welcome and good cheer."

The Woodruff B&B Inn

223 Ponce de Leon Ave
Atlanta GA 30302
(404) 875-9449

Circa 1915. A gigantic oak shades the porches of this beautifully renovated white brick mansion. Polished heart-of-pine floors are found throughout, and there's a staircase with heart shapes cut out of the banisters. Bright and airy rooms feature high ceilings, beveled mirrors and antique bedsteads. Favored southern breakfasts are served in the dining room or by prior arrangement in your room. In the evening, fireside chats often include entertaining stories of Miss Bessie, a former owner of the house. Some of Atlanta's best restaurants are within a block of the inn.

Rates: $75-$125. Doug & Joan Jones, Dan & Sandy Jones.
12 R. 12 PB. Phone in room. TV available. Beds: D. Full breakfast. Spa. CCs: MC VISA AE.
Seen in: *CNN TV, Athens Magazine, Atlanta Business Chronicle, Atlanta Journal—Constitution.*
"They really show you what is meant by southern hospitality."

AUGUSTA H13/C5

Oglethorpe Inn

836 Greene St
Augusta GA 30901
(404) 724-9774 (404) 722-2222

Circa 1888. The Oglethorpe, named after General James Oglethorpe, Augusta's founder, is actually two

Victorian-era houses and a carriage house. Shaded by 100-year-old magnolias, the inn is located in the heart of the central business district near Riverwalk, Civic Center and the federal courts. There are whirlpool tubs and fireplaces in many of the rooms, as well as original antique furnishings. An outdoor hot tub is available as well.
*Rates: $85-$125. Danielle Horne.
20 R. 20 PB. 12 FP. Phone in room. TV in room. Beds: KQDTC. B&B. Gourmet meals. Spa. Conference room. FAX. CCs: MC VISA AE DC. Water sports, horse events, river events.
Seen in: *Southern Homes, Augusta Magazine.*
"Thanks for giving us a break from the world."

BRUNSWICK Q15/F6

Brunswick Manor

825 Egmont St
Brunswick GA 31520
(912) 265-6889

Circa 1886. Nestled in the heart of historic Old Town Brunswick, this Victorian inn features the original carved oak staircase, high ceilings, Victorian mantels with beveled glass mirrors, antiques and period reproductions. Guests may relax on the rockers or wicker swing on the columned porch and enjoy the moss-draped oaks and tall palm trees. A stroll through the gardens leads to the greenhouse, fish pond and fountain.

*Rates: $65-$85. Claudia & Harry Tzucanow.

5 R. 5 PB. 2 FP. Phone available. TV available. Beds: Q. Full breakfast. Gourmet meals. Conference room. Golf, tennis, fishing, boating, beaches. Honeymoon packages.

Seen in: *Southern Homes, Bon Appetit.*

"Your great charm and warm hospitality is your legacy."

CLARKESVILLE D8/A3

Glen-Ella Springs Hotel

Rt 3, Bear Gap Rd
Clarkesville GA 30523
(404) 754-7295 (800) 552-3479

Circa 1875. This renovated hotel adjacent to the Chattahoochee National Forest is an outstanding example of early 19th and 20th-century inns that

dotted the Georgia countryside. The luxury of private baths and a plethora of porches have been added. A great stone fireplace is the focal point of the parlor, decorated in bright chintzes. Local hand-crafted pieces and antiques furnish the guest rooms. Two suites feature whirlpool baths. Bordered by Panther Creek, the property includes 17 acres of meadows, flower and herb gardens and original mineral springs.

*Rates: $65-$130. Barrie & Bobby Aycock.

16 R. 16 PB. 2 FP. Phone in room. Beds: KQDTC. EP. Restaurant. Gourmet meals. Spa. Handicap access. Swimming pool. Conference room. CCs: MC VISA AE. Horseback riding, hiking, white-water rafting, golf, boating, tennis, large swimming pool with sun deck. Complete facilities for small conference groups.

Seen in: *Atlanta Magazine, Southern Homes, The Telegraph.*

"Quality is much talked about and too seldom found. With you folks it's a given."

DAHLONEGA D6/B2

Smith House

202 S Chestatee St
Dahlonega GA 30533
(404) 864-3566 (800) 852-9577

Circa 1885. This inn in the Blue Ridge Mountains stands on a vein of gold. (In 1884 the landowner tried, without success, to get permission from city officials to set up a mining operation.) The inn features original woodwork, dry-rock fireplaces and a large wraparound porch with rocking chairs. Some guest rooms have porches. Family-style dining is offered.

Location: One block south of town square.

Rates: $45-$60. Freddy & Shirley Welch.

16 R. 16 PB. TV in room. Beds: KQD. Continental breakfast. Restaurant. Handicap access. Swimming pool. CCs: MC VISA AE DS. Gold panning, canoeing, tubing, shopping.

Seen in: *Gainesville Times, Atlanta Constitution, Atlanta Magazine.*

FORT OGLETHORPE C2/A1

Captain's Quarters B&B Inn

13 Barnhardt Circle
Fort Oglethorpe GA 30742
(404) 858-0624

Circa 1902. This delightfully renovated gray and white cypress clapboard house was once the predominant home in an elite Army post. Now the porches are filled with wicker furnishings, and there's a valentine-red entrance door. Brightly upholstered Ethan Allen furnishings are featured inside as well as lace curtains, period wallpaper and floral bed covers with heart-shaped pillows. A special guest snack room has a microwave, fridge, tv and piles of homemade cookies.

Rates: $45-$75. Pam Humphrey & Ann Gilbert.

3 R. 3 PB. Phone available. TV in room. Beds: KQDT. Full breakfast. CCs: MC VISA AE. Lookout Mountain, Ruby Falls. Craft shows.

Seen in: *The Catoosa County News, The Chattanooga Times.*

"Your hospitality and beautiful home was a very pleasurable experience. Thank you both for being so gracious."

MACON K8/D3

1842 Inn

353 College St
Macon GA 31201
(912) 741-1842

Circa 1842. Judge John J. Gresham, cotton merchant and founder of the Bibb Manufacturing Company, built this antebellum Greek Revival house. It features graceful columns, elaborate mantels, crystal chandeliers and oak

parquet floors inlaid with mahogany. Guest rooms boast cable television discreetly tucked into antique armoires. There are whirlpool baths available in the main house and in an adjoining Victorian cottage.

*Rates: $60-$90. Aileen P. Hatcher

22 R. 22 PB. 8 FP. Beds: KQTC. Full breakfast. Spa. Handicap access. Conference room. CCs: MC VISA.

Seen in: *The Christian Science Monitor, Southern Living, Daily News.*

"The best B&B we've seen! Deserves all four stars!"

The Carriage Stop Inn

1129 Georgia Ave
Macon GA 31201
(912) 743-9740

Circa 1840. Pictured in the Library of Congress as an excellent example of Greek Revival architecture, this three-

story house was built for Judge Thaddeus Holt. Eleven fluted Doric columns rise from the portico across the front and side of the inn. At one time the wrought-iron handrails flanking the double horseshoe stairs had newels topped with solid silver balls. High ceilings, chandeliers, paneled doors and heart of pine floors echo a gracious lifestyle. Original gold-framed mantel mirrors are hung over the dining and drawing-room fireplaces. Guest rooms are furnished with a collection of English and European antiques.

Rates: $85-$105. Vic & Judy Wilkinson.

4 R. 4 PB. 3 FP. Phone in room. TV in room. Beds: QT. B&B. Swimming pool. Conference room. CCs: MC VISA AE. Tours of historic downtown.

Seen in: *Daily News, Macon Telegraph and News, Southern Homes.*

"We loved every minute and look forward with eagerness to a return visit."

MOUNTAIN CITY C8/A3

The York House

PO Box 126

Mountain City GA 30562

(404) 746-2068

Circa 1896. Bill and Mollie York opened The York House as an inn in 1896, and it has operated continuously ever since. Two stories of shaded

verandas overlook tall hemlocks, Norwegian spruce, lawns and mountains. Adjacent to the Old Spring House is a stand of pines that provides a romantic setting for weddings. Breakfast is carried to the room each morning on a silver tray, and each room is plumbed with natural spring water.

*Rates: $50-$75. Phyllis & Jimmy Smith.

13 R. 13 PB. Phone available. Beds: DC. Continental breakfast. Handicap access. Conference room. CCs: MC VISA. Skiing, horseback riding, hiking, swimming.

Seen in: *Blue Ridge Country, Mountain Review.*

SAUTEE D7/A3

Stovall House

Rt 1 Box 1476

Sautee GA 30571

(404) 878-3355

Circa 1837. This house, built by Moses Harshaw and restored in 1983 by Ham Schwartz, has received two state awards for its restoration. The hand-

some farmhouse has an extensive wraparound porch providing vistas of 28 acres of cow pasture, meadows and creeks. High ceilings, polished walnut woodwork and decorative stenciling provide a pleasant backdrop for the inn's collection of antiques. Victorian bathroom fixtures include pull-chain toilets and pedestal sinks. The inn has its own restaurant.

Rates: $70. Ham Schwartz.

5 R. 5 PB. 1 FP. Phone available. Beds: KDC. Continental breakfast. Restaurant. CCs: MC VISA. Horseback riding, rafting, hiking.

Seen in: *The Atlanta Journal.*

"Great to be home again."

SAVANNAH N16/E6

417 The Haslam-Fort House

417 East Charlton St

Savannah GA 31401

(912) 233-6380

Circa 1872. This is a free-standing, three-story brick town house built in an Italianate style with a colorful side

garden. Located on a quiet square, the two-bedroom suite has a living room with fireplace, full bath and country kitchen. The inn's attractive decor has been featured in many national magazines and newspapers.

Location: In the heart of Savannah's Historic District.

Rates: $65-$150. Alan Fort & Richard McClellan.

2 R. 1 PB. Beds: KQC. Continental-plus breakfast. Handicap access.

"Alan is by far the most qualified host I've met. He gives 'home away from home' a brand new meaning."

Ballastone Inn

14 E Oglethorpe Ave

Savannah GA 31401

(912) 236-1484 (800) 822-4553

Circa 1853. The inn is located in the heart of the largest historic district in the nation (two-and-a-half-square

miles). Four stories of luxurious furnishings are accentuated with authentic Savannah colors and Scalamandre fabrics. Each guest room is furnished with period antiques and some have fireplaces and spas. Turn-down service features chocolates and brandy.

*Rates: $90-$175. Richard Carlson & Tim Hargus.

18 R. 18 PB. Phone in room. TV in room. Beds: KQD. B&B. Handicap access. CCs: MC VISA AE. Carriage rides. Ocean is 17 miles away for boating, swimming. Elevator, courtyard, full-service bar, breakfast in bed.

Seen in: *The New York Times, Bride's Magazine, Glamour Magazine.*

"To a fabulous inn - magnificent!" Patricia Neal.

Bed & Breakfast Inn

117 W Gordon St at Chatham Sq

Savannah GA 31401

(912) 238-0518

Circa 1853. This bed and breakfast offers an economic choice in the historic district across from Chatham Square. Two townhouses are joined with a back balcony. There are three apartments and 10 guest rooms, all decorated pleasantly with original art work and some four-poster beds. Guests enjoy sipping their morning coffee in the garden amidst beds of azeleas and bougainvilla and hybiscus. In January a Japanese plum tree blooms. Breakfast is served in the sunny dining room. All rooms are air conditioned.

*Rates: $38-$65. Robert McAlister & Pamela Gray.

13 R. 31 PB. 9 FP. Phone in room. TV in room. Beds: QTC. Continental-plus breakfast. Conference room. CCs: MC VISA AE DS. Museums, restaurants.

Seen in: *New York Times, Chicago Tribune, Atlanta Constitution.*

"Enjoyed it tremendously. Food was good and service gracious."

Foley House Inn

14 W Hull St

Savannah GA 31401

(912) 232-6622

Circa 1896. Fine craftsmen have faithfully restored the inn, and there is a fireplace in each room. Antiques, sil-

ver, china, Oriental rugs and hand-colored engravings come from around the world. Churches, museums, galleries and the waterfront are within

walking distance.
*Rates: $100-$190. Susan Steinhauser.
20 R. 20 PB. Beds: KDTC. Continental-plus breakfast. Spa. CCs: MC VISA.
"I'll send all my romantic friends here."

The Forsyth Park Inn

102 W Hall St
Savannah GA 31401
(912) 233-6800

Circa 1893. This graceful yellow and white three-story Victorian features bay windows and a large veranda overlooking Forsyth Park. Sixteen-foot

ceilings, polished parquet floors of oak and maple, and a handsome oak stairway provide an elegant background for the guest rooms. There are several whirlpool tubs, marble baths and four-poster beds.
Location: Savannah's historic district, opposite Forsyth Park.
Rates: $75-$145. Hal & Virginia Sullivan.
10 R. 10 PB. 9 FP. Phone available. TV in room. Beds: KQT. Continental breakfast. Spa. CCs: MC VISA. Tennis, jogging. Honeymoon package.
Seen in: *Savannah Morning News.*
"Breathtaking, exceeded my wildest dreams."

Jesse Mount House

209 W Jones St
Savannah GA 31401
(912) 236-1774

Circa 1854. A Greek Revival town house, Jesse Mount has two spacious, luxurious three-bedroom suites complete with gas-burning fireplaces. There is a Savannah-style walled garden. Exceptional antiques include gilded harps, a grand piano and a coach used by Tom Thumb to meet Queen Victoria. The hostess is an internationally known concert harpist. A pre-Revolutionary London clock chimes gently to urge you to step from your historic lodgings into the compelling charm of Old Savannah.
Location: In historic district of Savannah.
*Rates: $90. Howard Crawford & Lois Bannerman.
2 R. 2 PB. Phone in room. Beds: QC. Full breakfast. Seen in: *New York Times, Atlanta Constitution, Savannah Morning News, Early American Life.*
"Marvelous. We enjoyed your gracious hospitality, delicious breakfast, and elegant surroundings."

Liberty Inn 1834

128 W Liberty St
Savannah GA 31401
(912) 233-1007

Circa 1834. In 1949, the innkeepers met for their first date at the Liberty Cafe. Many years later, they purchased it and converted it to an inn. A

National Register Landmark, it was constructed of clapboard over brick and has survived many Savannah fires. The builder, Colonel Williams, was a publisher, bookseller, and six-time mayor of the city. Period pieces, original fireplaces, and exposed interior brick walls are featured.
Location: Northeast corner of Liberty & Barnard Streets.
Rates: $95-$165. Frank & Janie Harris.
5 R. 7 PB. Beds: Q. Continental breakfast. Spa. CCs: MC VISA. River harbor cruises.
Seen in: *The Orlando Sentinel, Savannah Morning News.*
"Incredibly beautiful. Perfectly charming."

Magnolia Place Inn

503 Whitaker St
Savannah GA 31401
(912) 236-7674 (800) 238-7674

Circa 1878. This southern Victorian features a two-story ornately styled veranda that stretches across the entire facade of the house, providing views of Forsyth Park Square. It was built for a descendant of the Declaration of Independence signer Thomas W. Hayward. Romantic four-poster or canopy beds are complemented by antiques and fireplaces. Some rooms have a whirlpool tub. Turn-down service is provided.
*Rates: $85-$165. Season: Mid-Feb. to Mid-Jan. Ron J. Strahan.
13 R. 13 PB. 11 FP. Phone in room. TV in room. Beds: KQ. Continental-plus breakfast. Spa. CCs: MC VISA AE. Tennis nearby, golf in area.
Seen in: *Esquire, New York Magazine.*
"Absolutely quintessential Southern excess."

Olde Harbour Inn

508 E Factors Walk
Savannah GA 31401
(912) 234-4100 (800) 553-6533

Circa 1892. Located in the historic district, this building once housed the offices, warehouse and shipping center of the Tidewater Oil Company and in 1930, the Alexander Blue Jean Manufactory. Now converted to condos, the suites are richly decorated in a traditional style and all boast river views. Within walking distance are some of the South's finest restaurants.
**Rates: $95-$135. Pamela Barnes.
24 R. 24 PB. Phone available. TV available. Beds: QDTC. Continental-plus breakfast. CCs: MC VISA AE. Riverfront vacation package.
"Wonderful time. Loved the river view."

Presidents' Quarters

225 E President St
Savannah GA 31401
(912) 233-1600 (800) 233-1776

Circa 1855. Situated in the heart of the largest urban historic landmark district in America is the President's Quarters. The facade of this inn was used in the television version of Alex Haley's *Roots*. Each of the nine rooms and seven suites is named for a United States president who visited Savannah. The decor varies from mahogany period reproductions to white pine rustic, but each room carries out the presidential theme by displaying memorabilia (such as authentic campaign posters) of the life of a president. Room service, a pool, in-room spas and stocked refrigerators are among this inn's amenities.
*Rates: $97-$147. Muril L. Broy.
16 R. 16 PB. 16 FP. Phone in room. TV in room. Beds: KQDC. Continental-plus breakfast. Spa. Handicap access. Conference room. CCs: MC VISA AE DC DS. Beach nearby.
Seen in: *Country Inn Magazine, Southern Homes.*
*"Presidents' Quarters was truly a home away from home,"*Karl Malden.

Pulaski Square Inn

203 W Charlton
Savannah GA 31401
(800) 227-0650 (912) 232-8055

Circa 1853. The Pulaski Square Inn is in the heart of historic Savannah. The inn features a garden courtyard, 12-foot ceilings, polished heart-pine floors, Oriental rugs, antiques, 11-foot gold leaf peer mirrors, fireplaces, old English brass and irons and marble mantels.
Rates: $48-$88. Hilda Smith.
8 R. 4 PB. 6 FP. Phone in room. TV in room. Beds: KQDTC. Continental-plus breakfast. CCs: MC VISA AE.
Seen in: *Atlanta Journal, Charlotte Observer, Southern Living.*

Remshart-Brooks House
106 W Jones St
Savannah GA 31401
(912) 234-6928

Circa 1853. Remshart-Brooks House is in the center of the historic district. Guests enjoy a terrace-garden suite with bedroom, living room, bath and kitchen. Home-baked delicacies enhance the continental breakfast.

Location: Center of historic district.
Rates: $65. Anne Barnett.
1 R. 1 PB. 2 FP. Phone in room. Beds: Q. Continental-plus breakfast.

RSVP Savannah B&B Reservation Service
417 E Charlton St
Savannah GA 31401
(912) 232-7787 (800) 729-7787

Circa 1848. This service specializes in the traveler seeking history and beauty, from South Carolina's Low Country to Georgia's Sea Islands. Accommodations are available in elegantly restored inns, guest houses, private homes or villas on the water. Areas include Savannah, Tybee, St. Simons Islands, Macon, Darien and Brunswick in Georgia; Beaufort and Charleston in South Carolina; and St. Augustine, Florida.

Rates: $60-$175. Alan Fort.
250 R. 250 PB. Beds: KQTC. Continental breakfast. Restaurant. Spa. Handicap access. Swimming pool. CCs: MC VISA. Golf, tennis, sailing, deep-sea fishing, water sports.
Seen in: *National Geographic Traveler, Innsider, Antique Monthly.*

SENOIA I5/C2

Culpepper House
PO Box 462
Senoia GA 30276
(404) 599-8182

Circa 1871. This Queen Anne Victorian was built by a Confederate veteran and later occupied for 50 years by Dr. Culpepper. With original moldings, stained-glass windows and mantelpieces, the house is decorated in cozy Victorian clutter and comfortable whimsy. The inn offers guests Southern hospitality at its finest.
Rates: $50-$60. Mary Brown.
3 R. 1 PB. Phone available. TV available. Beds: QDT. B&B.
Seen in: *The Newman Times-Herald.*
"Thank you for your generous hospitality."

The Veranda - Hollberg Hotel
252 Seavy St, Box 177
Senoia GA 30276-0177
(404) 599-3905

Circa 1907. Doric columns adorn the verandas of this 9,000-square-foot neo-classical hotel. William Jennings Bryan stayed here, and it is said that Margaret Mitchell *(Gone With the Wind)* came here to interview Georgia veterans of the Civil War who held their annual reunion at the hotel. Furnishings include walnut bookcases owned by President William McKinley and a rare Wurlitzer player piano-pipe organ. There are Victorian collections of hair combs, walking canes, books and one of the largest assortments of kaleidoscopes in the Southeast.

Location: Thirty miles south of Atlanta airport.
*Rates: $65-$95. Jan & Bobby Boal.
9 R. 9 PB. Phone available. Beds: QT. B&B. Gourmet meals. Handicap access. Conference room. CCs: MC VISA AE. Golf (with prior arrangements), tennis, fishing.
Seen in: *The Newnan Times Herald, Georgia Trend, Atlanta Magazine.*
"The mystique and reality of The Veranda are that you're being elaborately entertained by friends in their private home."

THOMASVILLE S7/G2

Susina Plantation Inn
Rt 3 Box 1010
Thomasville GA 31792
(912) 377-9644

Circa 1841. Four towering columns support the enormous portico of this Greek Revival plantation home designed by John Wind. Its commanding position provides a view of 115 acres of lawns, woodlands and ancient oak and magnolia trees. The dining room, drawing rooms and verandas are graciously furnished with fine antiques. A deep well on the property is noted for its superb drinking water. Fishing the stocked pond is a popular plantation activity.
Rates: $150. Anne-Marie Walker.
8 R. 8 PB. Phone available. Beds: KQDT. MAP. Restaurant. Gourmet meals. Swimming pool. Conference room. Golf.
Seen in: *The Palm Beach Post.*
"We saved the best for last!"

HAWAII

HAIKU, MAUI E9/F4

Haikuleana B&B Inn

69 Haiku Rd
Haiku, Maui HI 96708
(808) 575-2890

Circa 1850. A true plantation house, the Haikuleana sits in the midst of pineapple fields and Norfolk pine trees. With high ceilings and a tropical decor the inn has all of the flavor of Hawaiian country life. The porch looks out over exotic gardens. Beaches and waterfalls are nearby.
Location: Twelve miles east of Kahului.
*Rates: $65. Denise & Clark Champton.
2 R. Phone available. TV available. Beds: KQTC. B&B. Windsurfing, golf, tennis.
Seen in: *Neighbor Island Feature.*
"Great, great, extra great! Maui is paradise thanks to your daily guidance, directions and helpful hints."

HONOLULU, OAHU C6/H3

The Manoa Valley Inn

2001 Vancouver Dr
Honolulu, Oahu HI 96822
(808) 947-6019 (800) 634-5115

Circa 1915. An Iowa lumber executive built this mansion situated on a half-acre of lush greenery. Gables sup-

ported by fanciful buttresses add unique detail to the inn, now in the National Register. Lanais furnished with white wicker overlook Diamond Head. The guest rooms are filled with carefully chosen antiques, reproduction wallpaper and cozy comforters.
Location: On the island of Oahu.
Rates: $85-$155. Timothy McDonough.
8 R. 5 PB. Beds: KQD. Continental-plus breakfast. Parlor piano, pool table, croquet.
Seen in: *Travel & Leisure, LA Style.*
"A wonderful place!! Stepping back to a time of luxury!"

KOLOA, KAUAI B2/E1

Poipu B&B Inn

2720 Hoonani Rd, Poipu Beach
Koloa, Kauai HI 96756
(808) 742-1146 (800) 552-0095

Circa 1933. The sounds of the ocean and a nearby stream can be heard from this restored plantation house, one block from the beach. Hand-

crafted wood interiors, traditional lanais, carousel horses, pine antiques and white wicker decorate the inn. In addition to rooms in the main house, oceanfront cottages are available.
Location: Poipu Beach.
*Rates: $90-$150. Dotti Cichon.
7 R. 7 PB. Phone available. TV in room. Beds: KQTC. Continental-plus breakfast. Spa. Handicap access. Swimming pool. CCs: MC VISA AE DC CB. Swimming, scuba, snorkeling, surfing, boating, horseback riding, golf, tennis. Honeymoon champagne. Afternoon tea.
Seen in: *Travel & Leisure, Travel-Holiday.*
"Thank you for sharing your home as well as yourself with us. I'll never forget this place, it's the best B&B we've stayed at."

LAHAINA, MAUI E8/F4

The Lahaina Hotel

127 Lahainaluna Rd
Lahaina, Maui HI 96761
(808) 661-0577

After a fire in 1963, the hotel was rebuilt in a frontier storefront style. Recently renovated by Rick Ralston, founder of Crazy Shirts, the inn has been appointed in furnishings chosen from Ralston's warehouse of 12,000 antiques. All rooms have balconies and some have ocean views.
*Rates: $110-$170. Ken Eisley.
13 R. 13 PB. Beds: KQD. Restaurant. FAX. CCs: MC VISA AE.
Seen in: *Tour & Travel News.*
"Just what Hawaii needs."

VOLCANO H11/H5

My Island B&B

Box 100
Volcano HI 96785
(808) 967-7216 (808) 967-7110

Circa 1886. Once home to the Lyman family of missionaries, this three story shiplap house was built in the style of a Connecticut farmhouse. It is located amid flower gardens atop one of the world's most active volcanoes. Furnishings include family heirlooms and koa pieces. The Morses operated Hawaii Island Safaries for 23 years and have an extensive collection of volcano books and maps. The speciality of the house is all the macadamia nuts you can eat.
Rates: $45-$50. Gordon & Joann Morse.
5 R. 3 PB. 1 FP. Phone in room. TV in room. Beds: QT. Full breakfast. Handicap access. Hiking, golf. Volcano National Park, helicopter tours.
Seen in: *Good Housekeeping, Sunset.*
"Wonderful hospitality, hearty breakfast. I'll be back."

IDAHO

BOISE L4/*F1*

Idaho Heritage Inn

109 W Idaho St
Boise ID 83702
(208) 342-8066

Circa 1904. This Colonial Revival home, set back on a tree-lined street near downtown, was once the home of Senator Frank Church and is in the National Register. Because of its location in the historic Warm Springs district, geothermal water is used for heating and bathing. Period furnishings and wall coverings are found throughout. Bicycles are available for enjoying the nearby greenbelt which winds along the Boise River.

Location: Six blocks from downtown.
Rates: $45-$75. Tom & Phyllis Lupher.
5 R. 3 PB. Phone available. TV available. Beds: QD. Continental-plus breakfast. Conference room. CCs: MC VISA AE. Water sports, skiing, camping, fishing, hiking, river rafting. Honeymoon special.
Seen in: *The Idaho Statesman, The American West, The Idaho Business Review.*
"Thanks so much for the hospitality and warmth."

COEUR D'ALENE D2/*B1*

Greenbriar B&B Inn

315 Wallace
Coeur d'Alene ID 83814
(208) 667-9660

Circa 1908. Winding mahogany staircases, woodwork and window seats are features of Greenbriar, now in the National Register. Antiques, imported Irish down comforters with linen covers, sheer curtains, and gabled ceilings decorate the guest rooms. The inn is four blocks from Lake Coeur d'Alene, one of the most beautiful lakes in the country.

❀Rates: $35-$70. Kris McIlvenna.
9 R. 5 PB. Phone available. Beds: KQTC. Full breakfast. Restaurant. CCs: MC VISA. Canoeing, bicycling, skiing, snowmobiling. Dinner, bed and breakfast packages available.
Seen in: *Spokesman Review Chronicle, Downwind.*
"It made our wedding celebration so special. You're a real professional."

STANLEY L5/*F2*

Idaho Rocky Mountain Ranch

HC 64 Box 9934
Stanley ID 83278
(208) 774-3544

Circa 1930. This large cattle ranch is situated at the 6,600-foot level in the Sawtooth Valley. A rustic lodge dining

room overlooks the Salmon River, a mile away, to the spectacular ragged ridges of the Sawtooth Mountains. Near the edge of the river the owners have constructed a pool from a natural hot springs. Homey accommodations in lodgepole pine cabins feature handmade log furniture and fieldstone fireplaces.

Location: Fifty miles north of Sun Valley.
Rates: $48. Season: June-Oct., Dec.-May. Bill & Jeana Leavell.
21 R. 21 PB. 17 FP. Phone available. Beds: QDT. Full breakfast. Restaurant. Gourmet meals. Spa. Swimming pool. Conference room. FAX. CCs: MC VISA. White water rafting, horseback riding, rock climbing, hiking, fishing, mountain bicycling, cross-country skiing. Hayride and barbeque two nights a week. Live, western entertainment four nights a week.
Seen in: *The Washington Post.*
"We had such a great time! The kids loved it! Can't you adopt us so we can stay longer?"

ILLINOIS

CHICAGO D15/B5

Bed & Breakfast/Chicago

PO Box 14088
Chicago IL 60614-0088
(312) 951-0085

The 70 listings of this reservation service include guest rooms in private family homes and self-contained apartments located throughout the Greater Chicago area. If you'd like to stay in the Gold Coast, just north of Magnificent Mile, a popular choice is a converted historic mansion one block from Lake Shore Drive. It offers apartments with wood-burning fireplaces and antique furnishings. Or you may prefer a high-rise condo with a panoramic city view or a handsome guest room with a four-poster bed in a charming Old Town house where the host is a local reporter.

Rates: $50-$80.
75 R. Phone in room. TV in room. Beds: QDT. Continental breakfast. CCs: MC VISA AE. Theaters, restaurants, universities, museums.

COLLINSVILLE R7/F2

Maggie's B&B

2102 N Keebler Rd
Collinsville IL 62234
(618) 344-8283

Circa 1900. A rustic two-acre wooded area surrounds this friendly Victorian inn, once a boarding house. Rooms with 14-foot ceilings are furnished with exquisite antiques and art objects collected on worldwide travels. Downtown St. Louis, the Gateway Arch and the Mississippi riverfront are just 10 minutes away.

Rates: $35-$50. Maggie Leyda.
5 R. 1 PB. Phone available. TV available. Beds: QDTC. Full breakfast. Spa. Handicap access. Game room. Conference room. Shopping.
Seen in: *Collinsville Herald Journal, Innsider, Belleville News.*
"We enjoyed a delightful stay. You've thought of everything. What fun!"

ELSAH Q6/F2

Green Tree Inn

15 Mill St, PO Box 96
Elsah IL 62028
(618) 374-2821

Circa 1850. Located in a New England-style village, this red clapboard inn is just a short walk from the Mississippi River. Opening onto a large front porch, the first floor provides an 1850s country store with Victorian linens and lace, hand-blown glass, dried flowers, herbs and teas for sale. Each room is decorated in a period style and features a private porch. Monthly seminars offer insight into 19th-century perennial and herb gardening. Bicycles are provided so guests may enjoy the 16-mile Vadalabene bike trail that winds along the river and offers views of sailboats and the Delta Queen, and in winter, an occasional bald eagle.

Rates: $65-$90. Mary Ann Pitchford.
9 R. 9 PB. 1 FP. Phone available. TV available. Beds: QDT. Full breakfast. Game room. Conference room. CCs: MC VISA. Horseback riding, skiing, water sports, biking, antiquing.
Seen in: *Midwest Living, Chicago Tribune, Good Morning America.*
"Thank you for the wonderful stay at your inn."

GALENA B6/A2

Aldrich Guest House

900 Third St
Galena IL 61036
(815) 777-3323

Circa 1845. This elegant brick Greek Revival-style house was built by an Illinois state representative. Victorian

antiques are set against a background of white woodwork and Victorian mauves and greens. The parlor features a grand Steinway piano. The McClellan Room features a bay window and carved antique bedstead. Most of the bathrooms have pull-chain commodes and claw-foot tubs. Breakfast is served in the formal dining room or on the porch overlooking the croquet lawn where Civil War troops were drilled by General Grant.

Rates: $65-$95. Judy Green.
5 R. 3 PB. Beds: QT. Full breakfast. CCs: MC VISA AE DS. Horseback riding, pool, golf, skiing, shopping, all nearby.
Seen in: *Chicago Tribune, Telegraph Herald.*
"Thank you for the 'personal touch' you give to your guests."

Avery Guest House

606 S Prospect St
Galena IL 61036
(815) 777-3883

Circa 1848. Avery Guest House is named for Major George Avery who served in the Civil War and later led parades through Galena each year.

The house was originally owned by a steamboat captain and later by a wagon-maker. There is a porch swing for leisurely evenings. Breakfast is served in the sunny dining room with bay windows overlooking the Galena River Valley. It's an easy walk to the historic downtown area.

Rates: $45-$60. Flo & Roger Jensen.
4 R. Phone available. TV available. Beds: QTC. Continental-plus breakfast. Handicap access. CCs: MC VISA AE. Horseback riding, swimming, skiing, hiking, bicycling.
Seen in: *The Galena Gazette, Chicago Tribune.*
"We've stayed in several B&Bs, and this one is the most pleasant and friendly."

Belle Aire Mansion

11410 Rt 20 W
Galena IL 61036
(815) 777-0893

Circa 1834. Situated on 16 acres with a barn and windmill, the Belle Aire Mansion was originally a log cabin. Remodeled in 1879, the charming

white Federal-style house features a two-story columned porch looking out over lawns and a circular drive. Original logs and flooring, as well as a fieldstone basement remain. Decor is early American and country. With two small children of their own, the hosts welcome children of all ages.

Location: Thirteen miles east of Dubuque, Iowa.

❀Rates: $60-$80. Jan & Lorraine Svec.
4 R. 2 PB. Phone available. TV available. Beds: KDC. B&B. Downhill and cross-country skiing, golf, horseback riding, hiking. Mississippi riverboat gambling.
Seen in: *Chicago Sun-Times.*
"Loved the house and the hospitality!"

DeSoto House Hotel

230 S Main St
Galena IL 61036
(815) 777-0090 (800) 343-6562

Circa 1855. Abraham Lincoln, Theodore Roosevelt and Mark Twain are among the DeSoto's famous guests. An original winding staircase still graces the lobby, and a ballroom with floor-to-ceiling windows is used for banquets. The renovated hotel features comfortable rooms, two restaurants, lounge and five shops.

Rates: $65-$125.
55 R. 55 PB. Phone in room. TV in room. Beds: KD. Continental-plus breakfast. CCs: MC VISA AE DS.

Hellman Guest House

318 Hill St
Galena IL 61036
(815) 777-3638

Circa 1895. A corner tower and an observatory turret rise above the gabled roof line of this Queen Anne house built of Galena brick. The house was constructed from designs drawn by Schoppel of New York. An antique telescope in the parlor is a favorite of guests who wish to view the town. Stained glass, pocket doors and antique furnishings add to the inn's charms. The Tower Room with its brass bed and village views is recommended.

Rates: $65-$95. Merilyn Tommaro.
4 R. 4 PB. Phone available. Beds: QD. B&B. CCs: MC VISA AE. Horseback riding, golf, swimming, cycling, cross-country & downhill skiing.
Seen in: *Innsider, Midwest Living, Chicago Tribune.*
"We found your home a treasure, the breakfast delicious and your company superb."

Ryan Mansion Inn

Rt 20 W
Galena IL 61036
(815) 777-2043

Circa 1867. This stately Italianate mansion sits on 120 acres of natural parkland. Beautiful period furnishings highlight the inn's interior, which also

features parquet flooring, marble fireplaces and crystal chandeliers. There is a motel on the property so be sure and request a room in the mansion.

Rates: $74-$105. Ken & Linda Pluyon.
5 R. 5 PB. 4 FP. Phone available. TV in room. Beds: QD. Continental breakfast. Spa. Swimming pool. Game room. Conference room. CCs: MC VISA AE. Golf, tennis, fishing, hayride, horseback riding, antiquing, dog track.
Seen in: *Chicago Tribune.*

Spring Street Guest House

418 Spring St
Galena IL 61036
(815) 777-0354

Circa 1876. This stone and brick building was originally an icehouse for a brewery. The inn's king-size beds were designed and built by one of the innkeepers, artist Charles Fach. The bedposts feature handcast bronze sculptures. The inn has rare 1940s Lightolier chandeliers. The suite with a hunt motif features a wood-burning stove and tiles with bas relief faces of hunting dogs. Doors and trim are made of locally grown and milled red

oak.

Rates: $65-$87. Charles & Sandra Fach.
2 R. 2 PB. 1 FP. TV in room. Beds: K. Full breakfast. CCs: MC VISA AE DC CB DS. Swimming, golf, skiing, horseback riding.
Seen in: *Innsider, Home.*
"The guest house is lovely; however, it was the personal attention I received from the two of you that really made my visit."

Stillman's Country Inn

513 Bouthillier
Galena IL 61036
(815) 777-0557

Circa 1858. This grand Victorian mansion, built by merchant Nelson Stillman, is just up the hill from Ulysses S. Grant's house. In fact, Grant

and his wife dined here often. Original working fireplaces and handsome antiques grace the guest rooms.

Location: Across from General Grant's house.

Rates: $65-$95. Pam & Bill Lozeau.
5 R. 5 PB. 3 FP. Phone available. TV in room. Beds: Q. Continental breakfast. Restaurant. Spa. Conference room. CCs: MC VISA AE DS.
Seen in: *National Geographic Traveler, Midwest Living.*

LANARK

C8/A3

Standish House

540 W Carroll St
Lanark IL 61046
(815) 493-2307

Circa 1892. Four generations of Standishes are associated with this Queen Anne Victorian house. The current owner is Norman Standish, descendant of Captain Myles Standish. Furnishings include English antiques

from the 17th and 18th centuries. The inn is closed during Thanksgiving week as the innkeepers sponsor a series of lectures on early American history and Myles Standish for school groups.
Location: One hundred twenty miles west of Chicago on route 64.
Rates: $50-$65. Maggie Aschenbrenner.
5 R. 1 PB. Phone available. TV available. Beds: Q. B&B. CCs: MC VISA. Skiing, fishing, hunting, hiking. Pilgrim history lectures.
Seen in: *Prairie Advocate, Northwestern Illinois Dispatch, Freeport Journal Standard.*
"Absolutely beautiful! Immaculate, enjoyable, comfortable, very refreshing."

MOSSVILLE I9/C3

Old Church House Inn B&B

1416 E Mossville Rd
Mossville IL 61552
(309) 579-2300

Circa 1869. Nestled in this quaint old river village, this inn was originally a Colonial-style Presbyterian Church. It is listed in the National Historic American Building Survey. The inn features 18-foot ceilings, arched windows, antiques and an elevated library with ornate railing above the entryway. Guests are served afternoon tea in the dining room or in warmer weather, lemonade in the garden. Guest rooms have antiques, handmade quilts, and one room has a carved walnut bedstead from the 1860s. The inn offers turn-down service, including a fine Swiss chocolate.
Rates: $65-$85. Dean & Holly Ramseyer.
3 R. 1 PB. Full breakfast. CCs: VISA DS.
Seen in: *The Chillicothe Bulletin, Journal Star.*
"Your hospitality, thoughtfulness, the cleanliness, beauty, I should just say everything was the best."

OREGON C9/A3

Pinehill B&B

400 Mix St
Oregon IL 61061
(815) 732-2061

Circa 1874. This Italianate country villa, in the National Register, was constructed by local artisans from a sketch found in a Chicago home sketch shop. Special features include a three-story cupola, 10-foot windows, arched doorways and seven marble fireplaces. Mural wallpaper along the stairway was silk-screened in Paris in 1919 especially for the house.

Somerset Maugham was a frequent visitor in the Thirties.
*Rates: $75-$110. Lois & George Fischer
5 R. 3 PB. 3 FP. Phone available. TV available. Beds: D. Continental-plus breakfast. Spa. Conference room. FAX. CCs: MC VISA. Golf, state parks. Afternoon tea.
Seen in: *Oregon Republican Reporter, Freeport Journal, The Winnetka Paper.*

ROCKFORD B10/A3

Victoria's B&B

201 N 6th St
Rockford IL 61107
(815) 963-3232

Circa 1901. This turn-of-the-century mansion features a parlor with eight different hand-painted wallpapers. Guests may relax on the front-porch swing, the outside benches or in the Victorian parlor by a cozy fire. Breakfast is served in the second-floor parlor.
Rates: $69-$169. Bette Coulter.
4 R. 4 PB. Phone in room. TV in room. Beds: KQD. Continental breakfast. Spa. Conference room. CCs: MC VISA DS. Bike path, shopping. Honeymoon & wedding specials.
Seen in: *Midwest Living.*
"The house is magnificent from canaries to creaks in the floor!"

SYCAMORE D12/A4

Stratford Inn

355 W State
Sycamore IL 60178
(815) 895-6789

Circa 1926. The Stratford Inn was once the site for a stagecoach shop and a mansion for the town's first mayor. The inn features a lobby with oak wainscoting and fabric wall coverings, solid oak and brass decor, ceramic tile floors and antiques. Guest rooms have deep-pile carpet and fluffy comforters.
Rates: $46-$59. Ernest Herrmann.
39 R. 39 PB. Phone in room. TV in room. Beds: KQDC. Restaurant. Spa. Conference room. CCs: MC VISA AE DC CB. Golf, biking, state park. Weddings, banquets, conferences.
Seen in: *The Rochelle News-Leader.*
"The very best."

WINNETKA C15/A5

Chateau des Fleurs

552 Ridge Rd
Winnetka IL 60093
(708) 256-7272

Circa 1936. This is an authentic French-style country home near Lake Michigan. The lawn and terraced English gardens are shaded by cotton-

wood, willow and apple trees. A Steinway baby grand piano is in the living room, and there is a library available to guests. The Northwestern Train to the Chicago Loop is four blocks away.
Location: Thirty minutes to the Chicago Loop.
Rates: $80. Sally Ward.
3 R. 3 PB. Phone in room. TV available. Beds: KQT. Continental-plus breakfast. Spa. Swimming pool. Conference room. CCs: MC VISA. Jogging, golf, croquet.
Seen in: *Pioneer Press.*
"We will always remember your wonderful hospitality and your delightful gardens."

INDIANA

CHESTERTON B6/A2

The Gray Goose

350 Indian Boundary Road
Chesterton IN 46304
(219) 926-5781

Circa 1939. This English country house is situated on one hundred acres of towering pine and oak trees overlooking a private lake where gray geese nest year-round and Canadian geese stop by. Guest rooms are handsomely decorated in an English country theme, and some have fireplaces. The master suite features a splendid four-poster canopy bed. Breakfast is served by candlelight in the dining room.

Rates: $72-$85. Tim Wilk & Charles Ramsey.

5 R. 5 PB. 2 FP. Phone available. TV available. Beds: KQD. Full breakfast. Gourmet meals. Conference room. CCs: MC VISA AE DS. Swimming, golf, hiking, cross-country & downhill skiing, paddle boats, row boats, bikes. Wedding packages, gourmet dinners available.

Seen in: *Innsider, The Post-Tribune, The Vidette-Messenger.*

"Extremely gracious!"

COLUMBUS Q11/F4

The Columbus Inn

445 Fifth St
Columbus IN 47501
(812) 378-4289

Circa 1895. Dances, basketball games and poultry shows once convened in the auditorium of the old Columbus City Hall during its years as the focal point of town.

The original terra-cotta floors, enormous brass chandeliers and hand-carved oak woodwork now welcome overnight guests. Lavishly decorated rooms feature reproduction antiques such as cherry sleigh beds. Twelve-foot-high windows and 21-foot ceilings grace the Charles Sparrell Suite with its separate sleeping level. A horse and buggy stops at the inn's front door. Awarded AAA four-diamond rating.

Rates: $80-$245. Paul A. Staublin.

34 R. 34 PB. Phone in room. TV in room. Beds: QDC. B&B. Restaurant. Gourmet meals. Handicap access. Game room. Conference room. FAX. CCs: MC VISA AE DC CB DS. Horse and buggy rides, fishing, canoeing.

Seen in: *Chicago Sun-Times, Country Inns, Home & Away, The Cincinnati Enquirer, Glamour, Innsider, InnReview.*

"A delicious and beautifully served breakfast was the crowning glory of our stay."

HAGERSTOWN M15/D5

Teetor House

300 W Main St
Hagerstown IN 47346
(317) 489-4422

Circa 1936. Inventor Ralph Teetor (cruise control) built this luxurious mansion on acres of rolling lawns. The house's gracious stairway is a

replica of the Waldorf Astoria's stairways, and the house also boasts cherry paneling and a two-story leaded and stained-glass window. A Steinway grand piano has been converted to an electric player piano in the inn's parlor, and there are hundreds of old piano rolls. Among Mr. Teetor's early guests were Lowell Thomas, Wendell Wilkie and his friend Charles Kittering.

Location: Five miles N of I70 in east-central Indiana, 1 hour from Dayton, Ohio and Indianapolis, Indiana.

Rates: $75-$85. Jack & Joanne Warmoth.

4 R. 4 PB. Phone available. TV in room. Beds: KT. B&B. Conference room. FAX. CCs: MC VISA. Golf, swimming, health recreation center.

Seen in: *Palladium-Item, Midwest Living, Home & Away.*

"Everyone should live like this."

INDIANAPOLIS N10/E3

Renaissance Tower Historic Inn

230 E 9th St
Indianapolis IN 46204
(317) 631-2328 (800) 676-7786

Circa 1929. Nestled in the heart of one of Indianapolis' most historic areas, this historic hotel is listed in the Na-

tional Register of Historic Places. The hotel features flamboyant construction details. Guest rooms have solid cherry four-poster beds, Queen Anne solid cherry furniture and elegant sitting rooms.

*❀Rates: $49.95. Betty Hereth.

81 R. 81 PB. Phone in room. TV in room. Beds: D. Continental breakfast. CCs: MC VISA AE. Zoo, museums.

Seen in: *Indianapolis Business Journal.*

"As always, your kindness is appreciated."

KNIGHTSTOWN M13/D4

Lavendar Lady

130 W Main St
Knightstown IN 46148
(317) 345-5400

Circa 1890. This lavender-painted Victorian home is situated in the heart of a historic town in the National Register. There is a wraparound porch overlooking a side garden of lavender and herbs nestled around a small pond. The parlor features plum, blue and gold paisley wallpapers, original oak woodwork and carefully gathered antiques. Ask for the Violet Room and enjoy deep-purple walls, white lace curtains, a fireplace and a bed piled

high with crisp white linens and a paisley comforter. High tea is served on Wednesdays and Thursdays.
Location: On Rte. 40, 30 miles east of Indianapolis.
Rates: $60. Judie & Clyde Larrew.
3 R. 3 PB. Phone available. Beds: QT. Full breakfast. Seen in: *Greenfield Daily Reporter.*
"Artfully and tastefully restored. A fine addition to the B&B industry."

Old Hoosier House

Rt 2 Box 299-I
Knightstown IN 46148
(317) 345-2969

Circa 1836. The Old Hoosier House was owned by the Elisha Scovell family, who were friends of President Martin Van Buren. They named their child

after him. Features of this early Victorian house include tall, arched windows and a gabled entrance. Rooms are air-conditioned and decorated with antiques and lace curtains. Only real Hoosier breakfasts are served here.
Location: Greensboro Pike & Rd. 750 S.
*Rates: $58. Season: May to Nov. Jean & Tom Lewis.
4 R. 3 PB. 1 FP. Phone in room. TV available. Beds: KQTC. B&B. Golf, fishing, hiking, bicycling, tennis.
Seen in: *Indianapolis Star News.*
"We had such a wonderful time at your house. Very many thanks."

MADISON T14/G5

Main Street B&B

739 W Main St
Madison IN 47250
(812) 265-3539 (800) 362-6246

Circa 1843. This white brick Greek Revival house, bordered by a black wrought-iron fence, and yellow tulips in spring, has a stately portico entrance with columns and molding. Gleaming hardwood floors, original Classic Revival fireplace mantels and cherry and mahogany reproductions create an elegant setting. In the formal dining room, breakfast often includes raspberry cheesecake or peach-and-cinnamon coffeecake served with Sally's Hoosier Peach jam presented on Royal Albert china. Quilts by the innkeeper and her grandmother are displayed throughout the inn.
Location: Downtown historic Madison.
Rates: $50-$73. Sally & Ken McWilliams.
3 R. 3 PB. Phone available. Beds: QDT. Continental-plus breakfast. CCs: MC VISA. Riverboat cruises, antique shopping.
Seen in: *Innsider, Colonial Homes, Indianapolis Star.*
"You can't know what a difference it makes to have a nice, quiet, comfortable home away from home to catch your breath."

METAMORA O15/E5

The Thorpe House

Clayborne St, PO Box 36
Metamora IN 47030
(317) 647-5425 (317) 932-2365

Circa 1840. One block from the canal is The Thorpe House. Guests arriving by the Whitewater Valley Railroad can be met by a horse-drawn carriage. The inn has ornate cast hinges on the front door, original pine and poplar floors, antiques and country accessories. Guest rooms feature stenciling and views of the picturesque canal town. The inn serves homemade biscuits, soups and pies.
Rates: $50-$60. Season: April to Christmas. Mike & Jean Owens.
6 R. 4 PB. Phone available. TV available. Beds: DTC. Full breakfast. Restaurant. CCs: MC VISA. Water sports, golf, canoeing, bicycle trails.
Seen in: *The Cincinnati Enquirer, Electric Consumer, Indiana Business, Countryside Connection.*
"Thanks to all of you for your kindness and hospitality during our stay."

MIDDLEBURY B12/A4

Varns Guest House

PO 125, 205 S Main St
Middlebury IN 46540
(219) 825-9666

Circa 1898. Built by the innkeepers great-grandparents, this home has been in the family for over 90 years. Recently restored, it is located on the town's tree-shaded main street.

Guests enjoy gliding on the front porch swing while they watch Amish horses and buggies clip-clop past the inn. The Kinder Room features a whirlpool tub.
Rates: $60. Carl & Diane Eash.
5 R. 5 PB. Phone available. TV available. Beds: QT. Continental-plus breakfast. CCs: MC VISA. Golf, Amish tours.
Seen in: *Heritage Country Magazine.*
"In terms of style, decor, cleanliness and hospitality, there is none finer!"

MISHAWAKA B10/A3

The Beiger Mansion Inn

317 Lincoln Way E
Mishawaka IN 46544
(219) 256-0365 (219) 255-9191

Circa 1907. This neo-classical limestone mansion was built to satisfy Susie Beiger's wish to copy a friend's Newport, Rhode Island estate. Palatial rooms that were once a gathering

place for local society now welcome guests who seek gracious accommodations. Notre Dame, St. Mary's and Indiana University in South Bend are nearby.
Location: Northern Indiana.
*Rates: $65-$125. Ron Montandon & Phil Robinson.
10 R. 5 PB. 2 FP. Phone in room. TV in room. Beds: D. B&B. Restaurant. Gourmet meals. Conference room. FAX. CCs: MC VISA AE DC CB DS. Seen in: *Tribune.*
"Can't wait until we return to Mishawaka to stay with you again!"

NASHVILLE Q10/F3

Story Inn

PO Box 64
Nashville IN 47448
(812) 988-2273

Circa 1916. Marking the center of town, this rustic "Dodge City"-style general store, with its weathered tin facade, is flanked by two illuminated Red and Gold Crown gas pumps set on the front porch. There's a first-floor restaurant that draws guests from hours away for its fancy desserts and delicious farm-fresh meals. Upstairs, where Studebaker buggies were previously assembled, attractive guest rooms now feature antique four-poster beds, quilts and down pillows.
Rates: $65. Benjamin & Cynthia Schultz.
13 R. 12 PB. Phone available. TV available. Beds: QDTC. Full breakfast. Restaurant. Gourmet meals. CCs: MC VISA AE. Pool, tennis, horseback riding, hiking. Air conditioned.
Seen in: *The New York Times, Chicago Tribune, Los Angeles Times, Midwest Living.*
"I never wanted to leave."

PAOLI U9/G3

Braxtan House Inn B&B

210 N Gospel St
Paoli IN 47454
(812) 723-4677

Circa 1893. Thomas Braxtan, son of original Quaker settlers, was a business owner and stock trader who built

this Victorian house. With 21 rooms, the inn became a hotel when nearby mineral springs lured guests to Paoli. Oak, cherry, chestnut and maple woodwork are featured. The inn is furnished in antiques and highlighted with stained and leaded glass.

Location: Downtown Paoli on state road 37N.

*Rates: $35-$70. Terry & Brenda Cornwell.
6 R. 6 PB. Phone available. TV available. Beds: QDT. Full breakfast. Conference room. CCs: MC VISA. Skiing, swimming, fishing, golf, tennis, hiking. Ski packages.
Seen in: *Paoli News-Republican, Bloomington Herald Times.*

"Wonderful. Lovely hospitality."

SOUTH BEND B10/A3

Beiger Mansion Inn

See: Mishawaka, IN

WARSAW E12/B4

White Hill Manor

2513 E Center
Warsaw IN 46580
(219) 269-6933

Circa 1934. This elegantly crafted 4,500-square-foot English Tudor was constructed during the Depression when fine artisans were available at low cost. Handsome arched

entryways and ceilings, crown molding and mullioned windows create a gracious intimate atmosphere. The mansion has been carefully renovated and decorated with a combination of traditional furnishings and contemporary English fabrics.

Rates: $70-$105. Michael & Donna Saldivar.
8 R. 8 PB. Phone in room. TV in room. Beds: KQC. Full breakfast. Spa. Handicap access. Conference room. CCs: MC VISA AE. Theater.
Seen in: *Indiana Business, USA Today.*

"It's the perfect place for an at-home getaway."

WASHINGTON T5/G2

Mimi's House

101 W Maple
Washington IN 47501
(812) 254-5562

Circa 1913. This Prairie-style home features oak and mahogany woodwork, fireplaces with oak and tile mantelpieces, French windows, three large murals, two tapestries and early 20th-century furniture. There is an open brick porch and an enclosed porch with mosaic tile floors. The inn is in the National Register of Historic Places.

Rates: $50-$75. David & Stuart Graham.
6 R. 4 PB. Phone available. TV available. Beds: DT. Continental-plus breakfast. Game room. Fishing, nearby Amish community.
Seen in: *Evansville Courier.*

"The good Lord provided fantastic weather and gorgeous scenery, and you supplied true southern hospitality."

IOWA

ANAMOSA H21/C7

The Shaw House

509 S Oak
Anamosa IA 52205
(319) 462-4485

Circa 1872. Framed by pine and large oak trees, this three-story Italianate mansion was built in the style of a Maine sea captain's house. Bordered by sweeping lawns and situated hillside on 45 acres, the inn provides views of graceful pastureland from the front porch swing and the tower. Polished oak, walnut and pine floors highlight the carved woodwork and antique furnishings.

Rates: $45-$65. Connie & Andy McKean.
5 R. 3 PB. 1 FP. Phone available. TV available. Beds: QDTC. Full breakfast. Conference room. Canoeing, golf, museums, antiquing. Honeymoon/anniversary specials, local tours.
Seen in: *Cedar Rapids Gazette, Anamosa Journal-Eureka.*

ATLANTIC L7/D2

Chestnut Charm B&B

1409 Chestnut St
Atlantic IA 50022
(712) 243-5652

Circa 1898. This Victorian manor features a sunroom, a fountained patio, natural hardwood floors and ornate woodwork. The inn is decorated in the style of the Twenties and Thirties. A stained-glass window on the stairway overlooks the courtyard, which features a wading pool and bird bath.

Rates: $55-$75. Bruce & Barbara Stensvad.
5 R. 2 PB. Phone available. TV available. Beds: KQD. Full breakfast. Gourmet meals. CCs: MC VISA. Golf, fishing, hunting, parks, shopping.
Seen in: *Atlantic News Telegraph.*

AVOCA L6/D2

Victorian B&B Inn

425 Walnut St
Avoca IA 51521
(712) 343-6336 (800) 397-3914

Circa 1904. This Victorian home was built by Fred Thiessen, a local contractor and builder. The house is noted for its fish-scale shingling and golden pine woodwork. Detailed columns enhance the parlor and dining rooms.

Midwestern antiques and locally made quilts decorate the guest rooms. Guests may arrange to have dinner at the inn, either down-home Iowa cooking or gourmet selections, all served on fine china, crystal and sterling.

*Rates: $50-$55. Jan & Gene Kuehn.
4 R. 1 PB. Phone available. TV available. Beds: QD. B&B. Gourmet meals. CCs: MC VISA. Seen in: *Kansas City Star, Des Moines Register.*

"Your hospitality was exceptional. We'll be back...with our friends!"

CALMAR C18/A6

Calmar Guesthouse

RR 1 Box 206
Calmar IA 52132
(319) 562-3851

Circa 1890. This beautifully restored Victorian was built by John Kay, lawyer and poet. Stained-glass windows, carved moldings, an oak-and-walnut staircase and gleaming woodwork highlight the gracious interior. A grandfather clock ticks in the living room and in the foyer, a friendship yellow rose is incorporated into the stained-glass window pane. Breakfast is served in the formal dining room. The Laura Ingalls Wilder Museum is nearby in Burr Oak. Smoking is not permitted.

Rates: $40-$45. Art & Lucille Kruse.
5 R. Phone available. TV available. Beds: Q. Full breakfast. CCs: MC VISA. Skiing, canoeing, golfing, fishing, hunting.
Seen in: *Calmar Courier, Minneapolis Star-Tribune.*

"What a delight it was to stay here. No one could have made our stay more welcome or enjoyable."

DUBUQUE F23/B8

Redstone Inn

504 Bluff St
Dubuque IA 52001
(319) 582-1894

Circa 1894. The Redstone Inn, a 23-room duplex, was built by pioneer industrialist A. A. Cooper as a wedding gift for his daughter Nell. The side occupied by Nell's family is of grand Victorian decor, generously embellished with turrets and porches.

Maple and oak woodwork, beveled, leaded and stained-glass windows and marble and tile fireplaces are elegant features. Dubuque conservationists and business people converted the mansion into a luxurious antique-filled inn.

*Rates: $65-$165. Mary Moody, manager.
15 R. 15 PB. Phone available. TV in room. Beds: QD. Full breakfast. Spa. Conference room. CCs: MC VISA AE DC. River ride and ski packages. Dickens Christmas and ski packages.
Seen in: *Country Inns, Journal Star, Midwest Living.*

"Very nice!"

The Richards House

1492 Locust St
Dubuque IA 52001
(319) 557-1492 (319) 557-1002

Circa 1883. Innkeeper David Stuart estimates that it will take several years to remove the concrete-based brown paint applied by a bridge painter in the Sixties to cover the 7,000-square-foot Stick-Style Victorian house. The interior, however, only needed a tad of polish. The varnished cherry and bird's-eye maple woodwork is set aglow under electrified gaslights. Ninety stained-glass windows, eight

pocket doors with stained glass and a magnificent entry way reward those who pass through.

*❀Rates: $35-$75. Michelle Delaney, manager.

5 R. 3 PB. 7 FP. Phone in room. TV in room. Beds: Q. Full breakfast. CCs: MC VISA AE. Riverboat cruises, antique shops, cable car & trolley rides. Weddings.

Seen in: *Collectors Journal, Telegraph Herald.*

"Although the guide at the door had warned us that the interior was incredible, we were still flabbergasted when we stepped into the foyer of this house."

Stout House

1105 Locust

Dubuque IA 52001

(319) 582-1890

Circa 1890. This Richardsonian-Romanesque mansion was built by Frank D. Stout for $300,000. The intricate wood carvings were a showcase

for the finest skilled craftsmen of the day, working in rosewood, maple, oak and sycamore. One of the 10 wealthiest men in Chicago, Stout entertained Dubuque's upper crust elegantly in his rough-hewn sandstone house.

*Rates: $55-$100. Jodi & Roland Emond.

6 R. 6 PB. Phone in room. TV in room. Beds: QD. Restaurant. Spa. Conference room. CCs: MC VISA AE DC.

Seen in: *Telegraph Herald, Country Inns, Innkeeping.*

"The surroundings were exquisite."

HOMESTEAD J19/C6

Die Heimat Country Inn

Main St, Amana Colonies

Homestead IA 52236

(319) 622-3937

Circa 1854. The Amana Colonies is a German settlement listed in the National Register. This two-story clapboard inn houses a collection of handcrafted Amana furnishings of walnut and cherry. Country-style quilts and curtains add personality to

each guest room. Nearby, you'll find museums, wineries and a woolen mill that imports wool from around the world.

Location: South of Cedar Rapids, west of Iowa City.

❀Rates: $35-$60. Don & Sheila Janda.

19 R. 19 PB. Phone available. TV in room. Beds: QDC. Continental-plus breakfast. CCs: MC VISA DS. Nature trail, golf, cross-country skiing, biking. Hayrack tour package.

"Staying at Die Heimat has been one of our life's highlights. We loved the clean rooms, comfortable beds and history."

NEWTON K14/C5

La Corsette Maison Inn

629 First Ave E

Newton IA 50208

(515) 792-6833

Circa 1909. This unusual Mission-style building has an Arts and Crafts interior. All the woodwork is of quarter-sawn oak, and the dining-

room furniture was designed by Limbert. Stained and beveled glass is found throughout. French bedchambers feature reproduction and antique furnishings. The inn's restaurant has received four and one half stars from the *Des Moines Register's* Grumpy Gourmet.

*Rates: $55-$175. Kay Owen.

4 R. 4 PB. 1 FP. Phone available. TV available. Beds: KQD. Full breakfast. Gourmet meals. Conference room. CCs: MC VISA.

Seen in: *Cedar Rapids Gazette.*

"We felt so welcome, and your hospitality was sincerely warm and loving."

SPENCER C7/A2

The Hannah Marie Country Inn

Rt 1, Hwy 71 S

Spencer IA 51301

(712) 262-1286 (712)332-7719

Circa 1910. This beautifully restored farmhouse is Northwest Iowa's first country inn. Guest rooms are decorated with down comforters, Iowa-made quilts, antiques and lace curtains. The Sweetheart Room has an in-room claw-foot tub with pillows. Lunches and afternoon teas include

Queen Victoria's Chocolate Tea or Tea with the Mad Hatter, all served in costume to the public in the Carl Gustav Dining Rooms. Green lawns, croquet and golden fields of corn surround the inn. Guests are given walking sticks and parasols for strolling to the old creek. Picnic baskets are available for sale.

Location: Six miles south of Spencer.

*❀Rates: $50-$60. Season: April - mid-Dec. Mary & Dave Nichols.

3 R. 3 PB. Phone in room. Beds: QD. Full breakfast. Gourmet meals. CCs: MC VISA. Croquet, museums, antique shops. Afternoon tea & chocolate truffles. Rooms are air-conditioned.

Seen in: *Innsider, Midwest Living, Country Woman, Brides Magazine.*

"Best bed & breakfast in Iowa," Des Moines Register.

WEBSTER CITY G12/B4

Centennial Farm

1091 220th St

Webster City IA 50595

(515) 832-3050

Circa 1869. Parts of the original homestead and barns have been incorporated into this new air-conditioned farmhouse situated among fields of corn and soybeans. Tom and Shirley Yungclas are fourth-generation farmers here, and Tom was born in the downstairs bedroom. Guests can gather eggs for breakfast and poke about to view the 1929 Model A Ford and see the farm operation.

Rates: $35. Tom & Shirley Yungclas.

2 R. Phone available. TV available. Beds: D. Full breakfast. Handicap access. Canoeing, golf, swimming, antiquing.

Seen in: *Fort Dodge Messenger, Freeman Journal.*

"The accommodations were excellent along with the great breakfasts."

KANSAS

COUNCIL GROVE F19/C6

The Cottage House Hotel

25 N Neosho
Council Grove KS 66846
(316) 767-6828 (800) 888-8162

Circa 1872. The inn is located in Council Grove, the birthplace of the Santa Fe Trail. The building grew

from a boarding house to an elegant home before it became the hotel of a local banker. Listed in the National Register of Historic Places, the inn has been completely renovated and is a beautiful example of Victorian architecture in a prairie town.

Location: Northeast Kansas, intersection of 56 & 177.

*Rates: $37-$70. Connie Essington.

26 R. 26 PB. Phone in room. TV in room. Beds: KQDWC. Continental breakfast. Spa. Sauna. Handicap access. Conference room. CCs: MC VISA AE DS. Historic sites, golf in town, lake nearby, fishing, skiing. Dinner package, group tours.

Seen in: *Manhattan Mercury, The Gazette, Globe and Mail, Kansas City Star, Wichita Eagle.*

"A walk back into Kansas history; preserved charm and friendliness."

KANSAS CITY E24/B8

Halcyon House

See: Lawrence, KS

LAWRENCE E22/C8

Halcyon House

1000 Ohio
Lawrence KS 66044
(913) 841-0314

Circa 1886. This remodeled Victorian house is located within three blocks of the University of Kansas. Polished oak floors in the parlor lead to an expansive kitchen featuring a vaulted ceiling, brick floor and floor-to-ceiling window walls. Guest rooms are

brightly painted with an eclectic mix of cheerful furnishings. The master suite features a circular bathtub and skylights.

Location: Twenty-five miles west of Kansas City.

Rates: $40-$70. Esther Wolfe & Gail Towle.

8 R. 3 PB. 1 FP. Phone in room. TV available. Beds: KQDT. Full breakfast. CCs: MC VISA AE. Honeymoons, special events.

Seen in: *University Daily Kansan, Midwest Living, Kansas Business News.*

TOPEKA E21/B7

Halcyon House

See: Lawrence, KS

Heritage House

3535 SW 6th St
Topeka KS 66606
(913) 233-3800

Circa 1900. This was the original Midwestern farm home of the Menninger Clinic. A wide porch that wraps around the front is filled with wicker furnishings. Each room was decorated by a different design firm when the inn appeared as a designer showcase home. Dr. Karl's Study is popular with its luminous paneling and desk. The bridal suite boasts a four-poster bed and whirlpool.

Rates: $55-$125. Marilyn Kappler.

13 R. 13 PB. Phone in room. TV in room. Beds: KQDTC. Full breakfast. Gourmet meals. Conference room. FAX. CCs: MC VISA AE DC DS.

Seen in: *Adventure Road.*

"The meal served, the service and the setting were second to none."

WICHITA J16/D5

Max Paul Inn

3910 E Kellogg
Wichita KS 67218
(316) 689-8101

Circa 1930. Max Paul Inn consists of three converted English Tudor cottages. Guest rooms feature such amenities as European antiques, feather beds, vaulted ceilings, wood-burning fireplaces, skylights, bay windows, antique tapestries, stained-glass windows and balconies. Most rooms overlook the inn's garden with its arbor, pond and deck. On weekends, guests may have breakfast served in their rooms or in the garden.

Rates: $65-$115. Jill & Roberta Eaton.

14 R. 14 PB. 4 FP. Phone in room. TV in room. Beds: KQDT. Continental-plus breakfast. Spa. Exercise room. Conference room. CCs: MC VISA AE DC CB DS. Tennis, basketball courts, golf.

Seen in: *Houston Chronicle, Wichita Business Journal, Kansas, Midwest Living.*

"Your inn is very special. The rooms are enchanting and very comfortable."

The Inn at the Park

3751 E Douglas
Wichita KS 67208
(316) 652-0500

Circa 1910. Cyrus Beachy, of Steffen Ice & Ice Cream Company built this massive three-story brick house with a two-level wraparound porch, in the best part of town. A Symphony Showcase house, the inn was decorated by 27 designers. French Country, Oriental, Neoclassic and Art Nouveau are among the themes carried out in the 12 guest rooms. The carriage house suites feature extra amenities such as a hot tub and a private courtyard.

*Rates: $85-$135. Gregg Johnson & Kevin Daves, Cindy Cline.

12 R. 12 PB. 8 FP. Phone in room. TV in room. Beds: KQ. Continental breakfast. Spa. Conference room. FAX. CCs: MC VISA AE. Carriage rides.

Seen in: *Wichita Business Journal.*

"This is truly a distinctive hotel. Your attention to detail is surpassed only by your devotion to excellent service."

KENTUCKY

BARDSTOWN K12/C7

Bruntwood 1802
714 N 3 St
Bardstown KY 40004
(502) 348-8218

Circa 1830. This antebellum mansion is listed in the National Register of Historic Places. The inn features elegantly carved woodwork, stained glass, ash floors, a grand entrance foyer and spiral staircase. There is a lookout on top of the house. The inn is furnished with antiques.

Rates: $55-$75. Susan & Zyg Danielak.
8 R. 7 PB. 7 FP. Phone available. TV available. Beds: QDTC. Full breakfast. CCs: MC VISA. Outdoor drama, dinner train, home tours. Honeymoon & wedding specials.
Seen in: *Kentucky Travel Guide.*

Jailer's Inn
111 W Stephen Foster Ave
Bardstown KY 40004
(502) 348-5551

Circa 1819. This old jail was constructed of native limestone. There were two cells and an upstairs dungeon to house prisoners. The back building, sometimes referred to as the new jail, is completely surrounded by a stone wall. Jailer's Inn was a residence for many years before becoming a bed and breakfast.

Location: South of Louisville 35 miles.
Rates: $55-$75. Season: March to Dec. Challen & Fran McCoy.
4 R. Phone available. TV available. Continental breakfast. CCs: VISA. Dinner train and drama package.
"One of the oldest and most picturesque houses in Bardstown, a city noted for its fine homes," Joe Creason, *Courier Journal.*

Kenmore Farms
1050 Bloomfield Rd, US 62E
Bardstown KY 40004
(502) 348-8023

Circa 1860. This Victorian-style home on 170 acres features antique furniture, Oriental rugs, poplar floors and a cherry banister. The bed linens are authentic period pieces decorated with lace. The inn serves a full Kentucky country breakfast. The champion saddle horse, Beau Brummel, lived at the farm for ten years.

Rates: $65. Dorothy & Bernie Keene.
3 R. 3 PB. Phone available. TV available. Beds: DT. Full breakfast. Golf, tennis, state park. Honeymoon and anniversary specials.
Seen in: *The Kentucky Standard, Nelson County Record.*
"Thanks for your hospitality, your comfortable home and the exceptional meals."

BEREA L17/C9

Boone Tavern Hotel
Main St CPO 2345
Berea KY 40403
(606) 986-9358

Circa 1909. This white three-story Georgian hotel is run by a non-profit organization for the benefit of Berea College. The school is famous for a

work-study program that makes a college education available to motivated students from the Kentucky mountains. To enjoy an example of Kentucky's finest dining, make reservations and be sure to arrive on time, since there is only one seating.

Location: Center of Berea College campus.
Rates: $52-72. Robert Stewart.
59 R. 59 PB. Phone in room. TV in room. Beds: QDTC. Restaurant. Handicap access. Conference room. CCs: MC VISA AE DC CB DS. Tennis, gym, hiking. Alumni packages.
Seen in: *Country Folk Art Magazine.*

COVINGTON D16/A8

Amos Shinkle Townhouse
215 Garrard St
Covington KY 41011
(606) 431-2118

Circa 1854. This restored mansion has won several preservation awards. It features a Greco-Italianate facade with a cast-iron filigree porch. Inside there are lavish crown moldings and Italianate mantels on the fireplaces. Sixteen-foot ceilings and Rococo Revival chandeliers add to the formal elegance. Guest rooms boast four-poster or massive Victorian-style beds

and period furnishings. Here, southern hospitality is at its finest.

Location: Fifteen-minute walk to downtown Cincinnati.
*Rates: $65-$105. Bernie Moorman.
7 R. 7 PB. 3 FP. Phone available. TV available. Beds: D. Full breakfast. Spa. Conference room. CCs: MC VISA AE DC DS.
Seen in: *Executive Lifestyles, Bluegrass Magazine, Cincinnati Magazine, Cincinnati Post, Lexington Herald-Leader.*
"It's like coming home to family and friends."

GEORGETOWN I15/B8

Log Cabin B&B
350 N Broadway
Georgetown KY 40324
(502) 863-3514

Circa 1809. This rustic Kentucky log cabin, with its shake-shingle roof and chinked logs, was restored by the McKnight family. The huge fieldstone fireplace often holds a roaring fire, and there is a kitchen and an additional bedroom upstairs. Country decor and collections fill the house. Art Linkletter and Alex Haley enjoyed visits here.

Location: Two miles off I-75, 10 miles from Lexington.
Rates: $64. Clay & Janis McKnight.
1 FP.
Seen in: *Lexington Herald Leader.*
"What a wonderful, cozy house. Wish I could stay longer."

HARRODSBURG K14/C8

Beaumont Inn

638 Beaumont Dr
Harrodsburg KY 40330
(606) 734-3381

Circa 1845. The Beaumont Inn, managed by fourth-generation innkeeper Chuck Dedman, is comprised of several historic buildings. Six Ionic columns mark the entryway to the main building constructed in 1845 as a college for young women. Here guests find common rooms filled with paintings and antiques collected for generations, a gift shop and a restaurant. Greystone House, built in 1929 for a niece of Eli Lilly, is a Colonial Revival and contains four guest rooms. Well-groomed lawns of Kentucky bluegrass are studded with more than 30 varieties of trees, including magnolias and oaks.

Location: 32 miles southwest of Lexington.
Rates: $65-$95. Season: Mid March - mid Dec. Chuck & Helen Dedman.
33 R. 33 PB. Phone in room. TV in room. Beds: KQDTC. EP. Restaurant. Swimming pool. CCs: MC VISA AE. Tennis.
Seen in: *Country Inns, Innsider, Bon Appetit, Victoria, The Kentucky Advocate.*
"You will feel like you've stepped back in time at this gracious old antique-filled inn," Susan Miller, *Community.*

Canaan Land Farm B&B

4355 Lexington Rd
Harrodsburg KY 40330
(606) 734-3984

Circa 1795. This National Register farmhouse, one of the oldest brick houses in Kentucky, was built of Flemish bond brick set over a

fieldstone foundation. The innkeepers' have border collies and Italian Anatolian and Shar Planinetz sheep dogs for their white Polypay and black Border Leicester sheep. There are 168 acres of woodland and rolling pastureland. Guests particulary enjoy seeing new lambs born in December and in the spring. Nubian dairy goats are also raised. A clapboard addition houses two of the guest rooms and the Wool Room where the innkeeper spins and weaves. Antiques, quilts and featherbeds add to the ambience.

Location: Two miles from Shakertown.
Rates: $45-$55. Fred & Theo Bee.
3 R. Phone available. Beds: DT. Full breakfast. Swimming pool. Golf, crafts, riverboat rides, village tours.
Seen in: *Danville Advocate.*
"You truly have a gift for genuine hospitality."

Shakertown At Pleasant Hill

3500 Lexington Rd
Harrodsburg KY 40330
(606) 734-5411

Circa 1805. A non-profit organization preserves this 19th-century Shaker village set atop a pleasant meadow. Guest rooms are in 15 restored buildings. The old road running through the village is a National Landmark and is restricted to foot traffic. Reproductions of authentic Shaker furnishings fill the guest rooms. Air conditioning is hidden, and there are no closets. Instead, clothes (and sometimes chairs and lamps) are hung on Shaker pegs spaced one foot apart on all four walls. Costumed interpreters in the craft buildings describe Shaker culture and craft.

Location: Twenty-five miles southwest of Lexington on US Hwy 68.
Rates: $45-$85. Ann Voris.
81 R. 81 PB. Phone in room. TV in room. Beds: DTC. EP. Restaurant. Gourmet meals. Conference room. FAX. Horse farms.
Seen in: *Southern Living, Traveler, Richmond Times-Dispatch.*
"We can't wait to return! We treasure our memories here of peaceful, pleasant days."

HENDERSON J4/C5

McCullagh House

304 S Main St
Henderson KY 42420
(502) 826-0943

Circa 1847. This Italianate-style house was once a women's academy. Guest rooms are spacious and furnished with antiques. The inn serves fresh

pastries, seasonal fruits and freshly perked imported coffees.

Rates: $55-$65. Season: March 15 - Dec. 15. Pamela & Michael Wolf.
4 R. 4 PB. 6 FP. Phone in room. TV in room. Beds: KDTC. Continental-plus breakfast. Handicap access. Exercise room. Conference room. CCs: MC VISA. Golf, tennis, biking, horse races. Honeymoon & anniversary specials, home tours.
Seen in: *The Evansville Press, Country Inns.*
"Once again, thanks so much for your kindness."

MURRAY P1/E4

The Diuguid House

603 Main St
Murray KY 42071
(502) 753-5470

Circa 1895. This Victorian house features 8-foot wide hallways and a golden oak staircase with stained-glass window. There is a sitting area

adjoining the portico. Guest rooms are generous in size. Thick brick walls make the house soundproof.

Location: Downtown Murray.
*Rates: $40. George & Karen Chapman.
3 R. Phone available. TV available. Beds: QT. Full breakfast. Conference room. CCs: MC VISA. Horseback riding, tennis, boating within 15 miles.
Seen in: *The Murray State News.*
"We enjoyed our visit in your beautiful home, and your hospitality was outstanding."

SPRINGFIELD K13/07

Maple Hill Manor

Perryville Rd
Springfield KY 40508
(606) 336-3075

Circa 1851. This brick Revival home with Italianate detail is a Kentucky Landmark home and is listed in the National Register of Historic Places. It features 13-1/2-foot ceilings, 10-foot doors, 9-foot windows, a cherry spiral staircase, stenciling in the foyer, a large parlor with a fireplace, hardwood floors and period furnishings. The library has floor-to-ceiling mahogany bookcases. The large patio area is set among old maple trees.

Rates: $55-$75. Bob & Kay Carroll.
7 R. 7 PB. Phone available. Beds: DT. Full breakfast. Spa. CCs: MC VISA. Honeymoon and anniversary specials.
Seen in: *The Springfield Sun, Eastside Weekend.*
"Thank you again for you friendly and comfortable hospitality."

LOUISIANA

MONROE C6/A3

Boscobel Cottage
185 Cordell Ln
Monroe LA 71202
(318) 325-1550

Circa 1820. The Boscobel Cottage is in the heart of cotton country on the Ouachita River. The cottage, surrounded by century-old pecan trees, is in the National Register of Historic Places. Guest rooms are on the grounds of the cottage. A quaint chapel was once the plantation overseer's office. It features a Victorian bed, down pillows and European-style bedding and quilts. The garconniere is a bachelor's apartment with a balcony overlooking a New Orleans-style courtyard. Breakfast is served in your room, on the front porch or under the gazebo.
Rates: $75. Kay & Cliff LaFrance.
2 R. 2 PB. Phone available. TV available. Beds: Q. Full breakfast. CCs: MC VISA. Walking & bird-watching. Champagne for honeymooners.
Seen in: *New Orleans Times.*
"Words like exquisite just don't convey enough of the gratitude I feel for being allowed to visit here."

NAPOLEONVILLE J9/E5

Madewood Plantation
4250 Hwy 308
Napoleonville LA 70390
(504) 369-7151 (504) 524-1988

Circa 1846. Six massive Ionic columns support the central portico of this striking Greek Revival mansion. Framed by live oaks and ancient mag-

nolias, Madewood, on 20 impeccably groomed acres, overlooks Bayou Lafourche. It was designed by Henry Howard, a noted architect from Cork, Ireland. Elegant double parlors, a ballroom, library, music room and dining room are open to guests. Breakfast and dinner are included.
Location: Seventy-five miles from New Orleans.
*Rates: $89-$159. Keith & Millie Marshall.
9 R. 9 PB. 1 FP. Phone available. TV available. Beds: QDT. MAP. Conference room. CCs: MC VISA AE. Swamp and plantation tours.
Seen in: *Travel & Leisure, The New York Times, Southern Living, Los Angeles Magazine.*
"We have stayed in many hotels, other plantations and English manor houses, and Madewood has surpassed them all in charm, hospitality and food."

NEW ORLEANS J11/E6

B&B at The Chimes
1360 Moss St, PO Box 52257
New Orleans LA 70152-2257
(504) 525-4640 (800) 749-4640

Circa 1876. The Bed and Breakfast at The Chimes features quaint guest cottage/suites that sit behind an 1876 Uptown home. The cottages have stained and leaded-glass windows, French doors, cypress staircases and a brick courtyard.
Rates: $60-$125. Jill & Charles Abbyad.
3 R. 3 PB. Phone in room. TV in room. Beds: QT. Continental-plus breakfast. River boats, antiquing, jazz, Cajun dancing, sightseeing. Honeymoon specials.
Seen in: *The Times-Picayune.*
"Why did we wait so long to taste this wonderful approach to out-of-town accommodations?"

Columns Hotel
3811 St Charles Ave
New Orleans LA 70115
(504) 899-9308

Circa 1883. The Columns was built by Simon Hernsheim, a tobacco merchant, who was the wealthiest philanthropist in New Orleans. The floors are three layers deep made of oak, mahogany and pine. The two-story columned gallery and portico provide a grand entrance into this restored mansion. The estate was selected by Paramount Studios for the site of the movie *Pretty Baby* with Brook Shields. The hotel is in the National Register of Historic Places.
*Rates: $50-$125. Claire & Jacques Creppel.
19 R. 9 PB. Phone in room. Beds: KDTW. Continental breakfast. Restaurant. Gourmet meals. Conference room. CCs: MC VISA AE. Audubon Zoo, shopping.
Seen in: *Good Housekeeping, New York Times, Vogue, Good Morning America.*
"...like experiencing life of the Old South, maybe more like living in a museum."

Dauzat House
337 Burgandy St
New Orleans LA 70130
(504) 524-2075

Circa 1788. Nestled in the French Quarter, the Dauzat House is a private compound with a lush courtyard and pool. Guest rooms have antiques, original artwork, wood-burning fireplaces and fresh flowers. There's a two-bedroom suite with sunken tub off the courtyard. Two renovated slave quarters feature balconies, fireplaces and kitchenettes. The inn offers freshly ground coffee and homemade amaretto, and evening room service is available. Breakfast is available at nearby restaurants.
Rates: $75-$500. Richard Nicolais & Donald Dauzat.
4 R. 5 PB. 3 FP. Phone in room. TV in room. Beds: D. EP. Swimming pool. CCs: AE.
Seen in: *Esquire Magazine, Playboy Magazine.*

Grenoble House
329 Dauphine
New Orleans LA 70112
(504) 522-1331

Circa 1854. Grenoble House is really several renovated historic buildings in the French Quarter. The suites all include kitchens. A spa and pool are available.
Location: In the heart of the French Quarter.
*Rates: $95-$195. Peggy Martin.
17 R. 17 PB. Phone available. TV available. Beds: KQ. EP. Spa. Swimming pool. CCs: MC VISA.
Seen in: *Los Angeles Times, Travel & Leisure.*
"Absolutely wonderful. Would never stay anywhere else!"

Hotel Maison de Ville

727 Rue Toulouse
New Orleans LA 70130
(504) 561-5858

The original part of this pink stucco inn dates from the Spanish period. Antoine Peychaud, a pharmacist, built the house. Some rooms are tiny, while others feature Victorian four-poster beds, grand armoires and sitting areas. A bricked garden leads to Audubon Cottages, seven private suites with individual courtyards and full kitchens. A continental breakfast is served in the courtyard or parlor or you may have it brought to your room. The Bistro at Maison de Ville, one of New Orleans most highly acclaimed restaurants, is adjacent to the inn.

Location: In the heart of the French Quarter between Bourbon and Royal.
Rates: $115-$195. Al Danner.
16 R. 16 PB. Phone in room. TV in room. Beds: QDT. Continental breakfast. Swimming pool. CCs: MC VISA DC. Complimentary shoe shine service, anniversary and birthday champagne.
Seen in: *Southern Accent, New York Times.*
"The service and the atmosphere remain top notch," Carolyn Thornton & Allan Nation, *Innsider.*

Hotel Ste. Helene

508 Rue Chartres St
New Orleans LA 70130
(504) 522-5014

Circa 1835. This elegantly refurbished hotel once housed Hart's Pharmaceuticals. The company was known throughout the country for Harts Elixirs. With its 20% alcohol content, it was guaranteed to "cure what ails you." The inn is decorated in a European style. Guests gravitate to the hotel's courtyard for breakfast, or for a dip in the pool. Within a one-block radius are Jackson Square and St. Louis Cathedral, Bourbon Street, as well as world-famous Brennan's and Antoines restaurants.

*Rates: $65-$115. Ian Hardcastle, Barbara Coffey.
16 R. 16 PB. Phone in room. TV in room. Beds: KDT. B&B. Swimming pool. FAX. CCs: MC VISA AE. Horseback riding, water sports, riverboat cruises, zoo.
Seen in: *Los Angeles Times.*
"Our memories of our stay is promoting a desire to return in the near future."

Jensen's B&B

1631 Seventh St
New Orleans LA 70115
(504) 897-1895

Circa 1897. This is a simple Victorian house embellished with a two-story bay, a front porch and balcony. Eclectically appointed, there are antiques and modern furnishings and art. Rooms are spacious with 12-foot-high coved ceilings. St. Charles Avenue and the street car are one block away.

Rates: $55. Shirley, Bruce & Joni Jensen.
5 R. TV in room. Beds: KQDT. Continental breakfast. Sightseeing.
Seen in: *The Times-Picayune.*
"Your house is beautiful, breakfast yummy and hospitality superb!"

Lafitte Guest House

1003 Bourbon St
New Orleans LA 70116
(504) 581-2678 (800) 331-7971

Circa 1849. This elegant French manor house has been meticulously restored. The house is filled with fine antiques and paintings collected from around

the world. Located in the heart of the French Quarter, the inn is near world-famous restaurants, museums, antique shops and rows of Creole and Spanish cottages. Wine and hors d'oeuvres are served.

*Rates: $69-$155. John Maher.
14 R. 14 PB. 8 FP. Phone in room. TV available. Beds: KQDTC. Continental breakfast. CCs: MC VISA AE DS.
Seen in: *Glamour, Antique Monthly.*
"This old building offers the finest lodgings we have found in the city," McCall's Magazine.

Lamothe House

621 Esplanade Ave
New Orleans LA 70116
(504) 947-1161

Circa 1840. A carriageway that formerly cut through the center of many French Quarter buildings was enclosed at the Lamothe House in 1866, and is now the foyer. Splendid Victorian furnishings enhance moldings, high ceilings, and hand-turned mahogany stairway railings. Gilded opulence goes unchecked in the Mallard and Layfayette suites. Registration takes place in the second-story salon above the courtyard.

*Rates: $75-$205. Carol Chauppette.
20 R. 20 PB. Beds: TD. Continental breakfast. Conference room. CCs: MC VISA.

Seen in: *Houston Post, Travel & Leisure.*

Prytania Inn

1415 Prytania St
New Orleans LA 70130
(504) 566-1515

Circa 1852. The Prytania received the Historic District Landmark Commission's 1984 award for its restoration. Eleven-foot ceilings, old plaster moldings and hand-carved cornices set a pleasant background for the inn's collection of white wicker. A double parlor boasts two black marble mantels over the fireplaces. Eggs Benedict is a popular choice for breakfast and is served on china. Tables have fresh flowers. Petunias and hibiscus bloom in the inn's courtyard.

**Rates: $45-$65. Sally & Peter Schreiber.
18 R. 18 PB. Phone available. TV available. Beds: KQDTW. B&B. CCs: MC VISA AE DS. One block to St. Charles Streetcar, five minutes to French Quarter, sightseeing.
Seen in: *Times Picayune.*

Soniat House

1133 Chartres St
New Orleans LA 70116
(504) 522-0570 (800) 544-8808

Circa 1830. Located in one of the French Quarter's quiet byways, the Soniat House combines Creole style with classic Greek Revival detail. The courtyard features a fountain, magnolia trees, hibiscus and wisteria vines that climb the ancient walls. The inn is furnished with fine English, French and Louisiana antiques, antique Oriental rugs and paintings on loan from the New Orleans Museum of Art. Guests may enjoy homemade preserves and rich Creole coffee. Soniat House was chosen as one of the 10 best small hotels in the United States by "Conde Nast Travel".

Rates: $135-$185. Rodney & Frances Smith.
24 R. 24 PB. Phone in room. TV in room. Beds: KQDT. Continental breakfast. Spa. Handicap access. Conference room. CCs: MC VISA AE DC.
Seen in: *Travel & Leisure, New York Magazine, Vis a Vis.*
"Beautiful, peaceful and relaxing."

Terrell House Mansion

1441 Magazine St
New Orleans LA 70130
(504) 524-9859 (800) 878-9859

Circa 1858. Cotton broker Richard Terrell built his Classical Revival mansion with floor-to-ceiling windows, balconies and galleries. It's located in the Lower Garden District, the oldest purely residential neighborhood outside the French Quarter. A collection of Prudent Mallard furnishings made by the famous New Orleans craftsman in the 1840s is featured in rooms one and three. Other heirlooms and antiques are accentuated with a collection of gaslighting fixtures, Oriental rugs, paintings and gold leaf mirrors.

*Rates: $65-$90. Harry Lucas.
9 R. 9 PB. 12 FP. Phone in room. TV in room. Beds: KQDT. Continental breakfast. CCs: MC VISA AE.
Seen in: *San Francisco Examiner.*
"You really added to my already positive feeling about the folks who operate B&Bs."

SAINT FRANCISVILLE H8/D4

Barrow House

524 Royal St, PO Box 1461
Saint Francisville LA 70775
(504) 635-4791

Circa 1809. This saltbox with a Greek Revival addition was built during Spanish colonial times. Antiques dating from 1840-1860 include a Mississippi plantation bed with full canopy and a massive rosewood armoire crafted by the famous New Orleans cabinetmaker Mallard. One room has a Spanish-moss mattress, traditional Louisiana bedding material used for more than 200 years. Six nearby plantations are open for tours.
Rates: $65-$75. Shirley Dittloff
4 R. 4 PB. 3 FP. Beds: KQD. Continental breakfast. Gourmet meals. Golf.
Seen in: *Louisiana Life.*
"This was the icing on the cake."

Myrtles Plantation

US Hwy 61N, PO Box 1100
Saint Francisville LA 70775
(504) 635-6277

Circa 1796. Sitting high on the rolling hills of St. Francisville, the Myrtles Plantation is elegantly appointed with many original pieces of artwork and furniture. Its entrance hall features a French chandelier of Baccarat crystal and hand-painted and etched stained glass that is original to the mansion. Two parlors have chandeliers, Carrara marble mantles and French gilded mirrors. Garden cottages are also available.
Rates: $75-$250. Mark Sowers & David Saling.
10 R. 10 PB. Phone available. Beds: QD. Continental breakfast. Gourmet meals. CCs: MC VISA. Golf, shops.
Seen in: *Innsider, Wall Street Journal.*

SHREVEPORT C2/A1

Fairfield Place

2221 Fairfield Ave
Shreveport LA 71104
(318) 222-0048

Circa 1890. This blue Victorian structure is located in the Highland Restoration District, a neighborhood of gracious mansions framed by stately oaks. French hand-printed Victorian reproduction wallpaper adorns the foyer. Bradbury papers provide the background for the French, English, German and Scandinavian antiques in the guest rooms. Two rooms feature upholstered walls of English floral chintz. Guests enjoy the secluded New Orleans-type courtyard, porches and gardens that bloom year-round.
Rates: $85-$95. Janie Lipscomb.
6 R. 6 PB. Phone in room. TV in room. Beds: KQ. B&B. CCs: MC VISA AE. Horse races, lakes. Smoking in courtyard and gardens only.
Seen in: *Dallas Herald, Verandah Magazine.*
"We have been here many times and love it more each time we come."

WHITE CASTLE J8/E4

Nottoway Plantation Inn & Restaurant

Mississippi River Rd, PO Box 160
White Castle LA 70788
(504) 545-2730

Circa 1859. Virginian John Hampden Randolph built the South's largest plantation home. Twenty-two columns support the exterior structure, a combination of Greek Revival and Italianate architecture. Listed in the National Register, the mansion is more than 53,000 square feet. The White Ballroom is the most famous of Nottoway's 64 rooms.

*Rates: $120-$250. Cindy Hidalgo & Faye Russell.
13 R. 13 PB. Phone in room. TV in room. Beds: QD. Continental breakfast. Restaurant. Handicap access. Swimming pool. Conference room. CCs: MC VISA AE DS. Tennis nearby. Weddings, special functions.
Seen in: *Woman's Day, Dallas Morning News, Parenting Magazine.*
"Southern hospitality at its finest. Your restaurant has got to be Louisiana's best-kept secret."

MAINE

BAR HARBOR G9/F4

Black Friar Inn

10 Summer St
Bar Harbor ME 04609
(207) 288-5091

Circa 1910. When this three-story house was renovated in 1981, the owners added mantles, handcrafted woodwork and windows gleaned

from old Bar Harbor mansions that had been torn down. Victorian and country furnishings are accentuated with fresh flowers and soft carpets. Breakfast is presented in the greenhouse, a room that boasts cypress panelling and embossed tin recycled from an old country church.

Rates: $80-$95. Season: May to November. Barbara & Jim Kelly.
6 R. 6 PB. Phone available. TV available. Beds: Q. Full breakfast. CCs: MC VISA. Hiking, bird watching, horseback riding, scenic boat trips. Special salmon fishing trips.

"A great place and great innkeepers!"

The Inn at Canoe Point

Rt 3 Box 216R - Hull's Cove
Bar Harbor ME 04644
(207) 288-9511

Circa 1889. This oceanfront inn has served as a summer residence for several generations of families escaping city heat. Guests are treated to the gracious hospitality of the past, surrounded by the ocean and pine forests. They can relax on the deck overlooking Frenchman's Bay, or pursue outdoor activities in the National Park.

Rates: $55-$175. Don Johnson & Esther Cavagnaro.

5 R. 5 PB. 1 FP. Phone available. TV available. Beds: KQT. B&B. Conference room. Ocean.
Seen in: *The New York Times, Travel-Holiday Magazine.*

Canterbury Cottage

12 Roberts Ave
Bar Harbor ME 04609
(207) 288-2112

Circa 1901. This house is one of three year-round cottages designed by architect Fred Savage. It was built for station master Frank Whitmore of the Maine Central Railroad Ferry service, which operated from the Bar Harbor Pier and brought all the visitors to the island. The inn is furnished with antiques and accessories of the Victorian period. A wholesome breakfast is served.

Rates: $65-$85. Season: June - Oct. Michele & Richard Suydam.
4 R. 2 PB. Beds: QD. Horseback riding, hiking, bicycling, swimming, boating, wind surfing, fishing, tennis, golf.

"Thank you for your gracious hospitality."

Cottage Inns of Bar Harbor

16 Roberts Ave
Bar Harbor ME 04609
(207) 288-3443

Circa 1900. Two gabled Victorian cottages, the Ridgeway and the Maples, were built on quiet residential streets to house summer visitors to Bar Harbor. Recently refurbished, guest chambers include comfortable rooms and suites. The Wingwood Suite, for instance, features a queen-size four-poster bed and a working fireplace tucked in the corner. Shops, restaurants and the scenic harbor are within walking distance.

Rates: $45-$110. Katy Wood.
12 R. 10 PB. 2 FP. Phone available. Beds: KQDT. B&B. Conference room. CCs: MC VISA. Acadia National Park.
Seen in: *New England Guide.*

Graycote Inn

40 Holland Ave
Bar Harbor ME 04609
(207) 288-3044 (800) GRA-COTE

Circa 1881. On an acre of land in town, this summer house was built for Christopher Leffingwell, the Episcopal Bishop of Maine. It has served

as a guest house since 1929 and was recently restored. King-size canopy beds, antiques, and fireplaces provide luxury. The ocean, harbor and shops are a four-block stroll from the inn.

Rates: $75-$110. Season: April - Nov. William & Darlene DeMao.
10 R. 10 PB. 3 FP. Phone available. Beds: KQ. Full breakfast. CCs: MC VISA. Hiking, bicycling, horseback riding, canoe and kayak rentals.

"We appreciated your hospitality. Your inn is by far our favorite."

The Hearthside

7 High St

Bar Harbor ME 04609

(207) 288-4533

Circa 1907. Originally built for a doctor, this three-story shingled house sits on a quiet street in town. Guests enjoy four working fireplaces and a porch. The parlor includes a library and fireplace. Acadia National Park is five minutes away.

Rates: $65-$95. Susan & Barry Schwartz.

9 R. 7 PB. 3 FP. Phone available. Beds: Q. B&B. CCs: MC VISA. Near skiing, hiking, whale watching, boating, swimming.

Seen in: *Philadelphia Jewish Exponent.*

"I have only one word to describe this place, Wow! My wife and I are astonished at the splendor, the warmth of your care and the beauty of the surroundings."

Holbrook House

74 Mount Desert St

Bar Harbor ME 04609

(207) 288-4970

Circa 1876. A local merchant built this Victorian inn in the Bar Harbor double-bracket style, for vacationers who came to enjoy the beauty of Mt.

Desert Island. The inn is located in the town's historic corridor. There is a library, sunroom, and parlor.

Location: Mt. Desert Island.

Rates: $85-$110. Season: June 15-Oct. 15. Dorothy & Mike Chester.

10 R. 10 PB. Phone available. TV available. Beds: QDT. B&B. CCs: MC VISA. Tennis, golf, swimming, hiking, biking (with secured bicycle storage), canoeing, horseback riding, sailing. Acadia National Park entrance one mile.

Seen in: *The Discerning Traveler.*

"When I selected Holbrook House all my dreams of finding the perfect little country inn came true."

Ledgelawn Inn

66 Mount Desert

Bar Harbor ME 04609

(207) 288-4596

Circa 1904. Gables, bays, columns and verandas are features of this rambling three-story summer house located on an acre of wooded land within walk-

ing distance to the waterfront. The red clapboard structure sports black shutters and a mansard roof. Filled with antiques and fireplaces the inn features a sitting room and library.

*Rates: $85-$185. Season: April-Nov. Nancy & Mike Cloud.

35 R. 35 PB. 10 FP. Phone in room. TV in room. Beds: KQD. EP. Spa. Sauna. Swimming pool. Conference room. FAX. CCs: MC VISA AE. Bike riding, canoeing, water sports, sailing.

Seen in: *New York Times.*

"A lovely place to relax and enjoy oneself. The area is unsurpassed in beauty and the people friendly."

Manor House Inn

104 West St

Bar Harbor ME 04609

(207) 288-3759

Circa 1887. Colonel James Foster built this 22-room Victorian mansion, now in the National Register. It is an ex-

ample of the tradition of gracious summer living for which Bar Harbor was and is famous. In addition to the main house, there are several charming cottages situated in the extensive gardens on the property.

Location: Close to Acadia National Park.

Rates: $79-$149. Season: April 15 - November. Mac Noyes, Jim Dennison.

14 R. 14 PB. Phone available. TV available. Beds: KQDT. Continental-plus breakfast. CCs: MC VISA AE. Horseback riding, bicycling, hiking, canoeing, tennis, swimming, boating.

Seen in: *Discerning Traveler.*

"Wonderful honeymoon spot!"

Mira Monte Inn

69 Mt Desert St

Bar Harbor ME 04609

(207) 288-4263

Circa 1864. A gracious 18-room Victorian mansion, the Mira Monte has been newly renovated in the style of early Bar Harbor. It features period furnishings, pleasant common rooms, a library and wraparound porches. Situated on estate grounds, there are sweeping lawns, paved terraces, and many gardens. The inn was one of the earliest of Bar Harbor's famous summer cottages.

Location: Five-minute walk from the waterfront, shops and restaurants.

*Rates: $75-$135. Season: May - late October. Marian Burns.

11 R. 11 PB. Beds: KQT. Continental-plus breakfast. CCs: MC VISA AE. Outdoor games.

Seen in: *Los Angeles Times.*

"On our third year at your wonderful inn in beautiful Bar Harbor. I think I enjoy it more each year. A perfect place to stay in a perfect environment."

BATH 14/G2

Elizabeth's B&B

360 Front St

Bath ME 04530

(207) 443-1146

Circa 1820. This early Federal house was built by a family of shipbuilders. From its location on the Kennebec River, Elizabeth's provides a relaxing atmosphere with country antiques and "Mr. T," the resident cat. The dining room features stenciled walls and flagstone and brick floors. Choose the Captain's Quarters for a king-size bed, wide pine flooring, window seat and river view.

Rates: $40-$60. Season: April 15 - Dec. 31. Elizabeth A. Lindsay.

5 R. 2 FP. Phone available. TV available. Beds: KDT. Continental-plus breakfast. Tennis, beaches, boating, hiking.

Seen in: *The Times Record.*

"It was truly a warming experience to feel so at home, away from home."

Fairhaven Inn

RR 2 PO Box 85, N Bath Rd

Bath ME 04530

(207) 443-4391

Circa 1790. With its view of the Kennebec River, this site was so attractive that Pimbleton Edgecomb built his Colonial house where a log cabin had previously stood. His descendants occupied it for the next 125 years. Antiques and country furniture fill the inn. Meadows and lawns, and woods of hemlock, birch and pine cover the inn's 27 acres.

Rates: $50-$70. George & Sallie Pollard.

6 R. 4 PB. Phone available. TV available. Beds: QT. Full breakfast. Conference room. CCs: MC VISA. Cross-country skiing, snowshoeing, beaches nearby. Winter weekend candlelight dinners available.

Seen in: *The State, Coastal Journal.*

"The Fairhaven is now marked in our book with a red star, definitely a place to remember and visit again."

Packard House

45 Pearl St
Bath ME 04530
(207) 443-6069

Circa 1790. This elegant Georgian house once belonged to shipbuilder Benjamin F. Packard, and a book "Portrait of a Ship-The Benjamin F. Packard" has recently been written about one of his clipper ships. The house has been renovated and authentic historical colors are featured. Period furnishings and shipbuilding memorabilia recapture the romantic past of Bath. The Kennebec River is just a block away.

Location: Historic district.
Rates: $60-$75. Vincent & Elizabeth Messler.
3 R. 1 PB. Phone available. Beds: QT. Full breakfast. CCs: MC VISA. Beaches, boating, golf, tennis, fishing, museums, theaters.
Seen in: *The Times Record, Maine Sunday Telegram, Coastal Journal.*
"Thanks for being wonderful hosts."

BELFAST G7/F3

The Jeweled Turret Inn

16 Pearl St
Belfast ME 04915
(207) 338-2304

Circa 1898. This grand Victorian is named for the staircase that winds up the turret, lighted by stained and leaded-glass panels and jewel-like em-

bellishments. It was built for attorney James Harriman. Dark pine beams adorn the ceiling of the den, and the fireplace is constructed of bark and rocks from every state in the Union. Elegant antiques furnish the guest rooms of this National Register home.

Rates: $50-$75. Carl & Cathy Heffentrager.
7 R. 7 PB. Phone available. TV available. Beds: QDT. Full breakfast. Swimming, horseback riding, golf, tennis, deep-sea fishing. Afternoon tea.
Seen in: *The Republican Journal, Waterville Sentinel.*
"This was the most fun we had in all of the places we've seen all week."

Penobscot Meadows

Rt 1
Belfast ME 04915
(207) 338-5320

Circa 1900. This three-story country house with its gambrel roof and large enclosed porch overlook Penobscot Bay. Inside, polished woodwork, antiques and quilts add to the country feeling. A stone fireplace is a favorite spot in the living room. Dining is four-star rated and especially pleasant in summer when sitting on the open porch facing the ocean. Guests enjoy views from the deck and strolling along the seashore.

Location: Mid-coast Maine, on Penobscot Bay.
Rates: $39-$89. Dini & Bernie Chapnick.
7 R. 7 PB. Phone available. TV available. Beds: KQDT. Continental-plus breakfast. Restaurant. Gourmet meals. CCs: MC VISA DS. Skiing, boating, hiking, swimming, tennis.
Seen in: *Maine Times, Bangor Daily News.*

BETHEL G2/F1

Hammons House

Broad St
Bethel ME 04217
(207) 824-3170

Circa 1859. Built by Congressman David Hammons, this is an elegant Greek Revival with a side-hall plan. The adjacent barn was converted to a

small summer theater in the early 1920s and is now used as an antique shop June through October. Every day a full country breakfast is served. The inn is surrounded by porches, a patio, and beautiful perennial gardens.

Location: Centrally located on the village common.
Rates: $65-$75. Sally Rollinson.
4 R. Phone available. TV available. Beds: DT. Full breakfast. Conference room. CCs: MC VISA. Downhill & cross-country ski areas nearby.
Seen in: *Lewiston Sunday newspaper.*
"The charm of your home was a highlight of our New England tour."

BOOTHBAY I5/G2

Kenniston Hill Inn

Rt 27
Boothbay ME 04537
(207) 633-2159

Circa 1786. Six fireplaces warm this white clapboard, center-chimney Colonial set amidst four acres of gardens and woodlands. It was built by David Kenniston, a prominent shipbuilder and landowner, and was occupied by the Kennistons for more than 100 years. The parlor has a huge, open hearth fireplace. For several years the inn was used as a country club and later as a restaurant.

*Rates: $60-$80. David & Susan Straight.
10 R. 10 PB. 4 FP. Phone available. Beds: KQD. Full breakfast. CCs: MC VISA. Golf, deep-sea fishing, horseback riding, bicycling, sailing, antiquing.
"England may be the home of the original bed and breakfast, but Kenniston Hill Inn is where it has been perfected!"

BOOTHBAY HARBOR I5/G2

Admiral's Quarters Inn

105 Commercial St
Boothbay Harbor ME 04538
(207) 633-2474

Circa 1830. Set on a rise looking out to the sea, this handsome sea captain's house commands a splendid harbor

view. The inn is decorated with white wicker and antiques and each accommodation features French doors or sliding glass doors that open to a private deck or terrace to take advantage of the view of the harbor. Guests may walk a short distance to the wharf.

Location: On the point of Commercial, facing up the harbor.
Rates: $70-$90. Season: April - October 31. Jean & George Duffy.
10 R. 10 PB. Phone in room. TV in room. Beds: Q. Continental breakfast. CCs: MC VISA. Boating, cruises, shopping.
Seen in: *Franklin Business Review.*
"Unbelievable views. Jean, please book us for next year."

BRIDGTON H2/G1

Noble House

PO Box 180
Bridgton ME 04009
(207) 647-3733

Circa 1903. This inn is tucked among three acres of old oaks and a grove of pine trees, providing an estate-like

view from all guest rooms. The elegant parlor contains a library, grand piano and hearth. Bed chambers are furnished with antiques, wicker and quilts. A hammock placed at the water's edge provides a view of the lake and Mt. Washington. The inn's lake frontage also allows for canoeing at sunset and swimming.

Location: Forty miles northwest of Portland.

Rates: $75-$130. Season: June to Oct. 15. The Starets Family.

9 R. 6 PB. Phone available. TV available. Beds: QDT. Full breakfast. Spa. CCs: MC VISA AE. Golf, tennis, horseback riding, fishing, hiking, boating.

Seen in: *The Bridgton News.*

"It's my favorite inn."

Tarry-a-While Resort

Box A, Highland Ridge Rd
Bridgton ME 04009
(207) 647-2522

Circa 1900. The Tarry-a-While Resort brings the charm of Switzerland to the western hills of Maine with the help of innkeeper Hans, who was born in Switzerland. The dining room features weathered barnboard paneling, pine tables, Swiss cowbells, a giant alpenhorn and a picture window looking down Highland Lake and across the White Mountains. Guests dine on gourmet Swiss cooking. The resort consists of a Victorian mansion, cottages and a social hall. Rooms have quaint old-world furnishings, including furniture hand-made by Hans and painted with colorful flowers by Barbara.

Rates: $100-$120. Season: June to September. Hans & Barbara Jenni.

36 R. 26 PB. 2 FP. Beds: KQDT. Continental-plus breakfast. Canoeing, pedal boats, tennis, bicycles, ping-pong, shuffle board, putting green.

Seen in: *Down East, Yankee Magazine.*

"The views, space, personal attention and laid-back ambience is just what we needed on our precious vacation time."

BRUNSWICK I4/G2

Brunswick B&B

165 Park Row
Brunswick ME 04011
(207) 729-4914

Circa 1860. This completely restored Greek Revival home overlooks the park in the Brunswick Historic District. The inn features twin front parlors with park views. A tasteful collection of antiques fill the rooms. In 1987 the inn was a Christmas show house for American University Women. Bowdoin College is two blocks away. L.L. Bean and Freeport are within a 10-minute drive.

Rates: $60-$70. Travis B. & Nancy Keltner.

5 R. 3 PB. 3 FP. Phone available. TV available. Beds: DT. Full breakfast. Water sports, golf, cross-country skiing.

Seen in: *Times Record, Coastal Journal.*

"Just as wonderful as we remembered!"

BUCKSPORT F7/F3

The Old Parsonage Inn

PO Box 1577, 190 Franklin St
Bucksport ME 04416
(207) 469-6477

Circa 1800. The inn was built as a federal style, double house with front entrances on the gable ends. The rooms and winding staircases on

either side are mirror images. The third floor was originally a meeting hall. The bowed ceiling and built-in benches remain. The local Masonic lodge held their first meeting here in 1809. Eight fireplaces, two with beehive ovens, remain, along with wide board wainscotting, pine floors and cornices.

Rates: $35-$50. Brian & Judith Clough.

3 R. 1 PB. Phone available. TV available. Beds: DT. Full breakfast. CCs: MC VISA. Boating, fishing, Acadia National Park, Penobscot Bay.

Seen in: *Maine Times, Bucksport Free Press.*

"Your kindness, great food, and beautiful location gave us a favorable opinion of bed and breakfasts in general."

CAMDEN H7/F3

Blackberry Inn

82 Elm St
Camden ME 04843
(207) 236-6060

Circa 1860. The exterior of this elaborate Italianate Victorian-style home is highlighted by contrasting shades of Blackberry Purple outlining its bays and friezes. The interiors are lavished with elaborate plaster ceiling designs, polished parquet floors, finely crafted fireplace mantels, and original tin ceilings. A collection of antique Bar Harbor wicker fills the Morning Parlor, once enjoyed by Bette Davis when she visited the inn when it was known as Broadlawn. Most guest rooms have views of Mt. Battie.

Rates: $50-$100. Vicki & Ed Doudera.

4 R. 4 PB. 3 FP. Phone available. Beds: QDT. Full breakfast. CCs: MC VISA. Horseback riding, golf, cross-country & downhill skiing, sailing, swimming, shopping.

Seen in: *The Miami Herald, Daughters of Painted Ladies, Yankee.*

"Charming. An authentic reflection of a grander time."

Blue Harbor House

67 Elm St, Rt 1
Camden ME 04843
(207) 236-3196 (800) 248-3196

Circa 1835. James Richards, Camden's first settler, built this Cape house on a 1768 homesite. (The King granted him

the land as the first person to fulfill all the conditions of a settler.) An 1806 carriage house has been refurbished to offer private suites. The bustling harbor is a five-minute walk away.

Location: Camden Village.

❀Rates: $50-$110. Jody Schmoll & Dennis Hayden.

8 R. 6 PB. Phone available. TV available. Beds: QDT. Full breakfast. Spa. Conference room. CCs: MC VISA. Water sports, sailing, fishing, swimming, hiking, horseback riding, golf, bikes.

The Camden Maine Stay Inn

22 High St
Camden ME 04843
(207) 236-9636

Circa 1802. Listed in the National Register of Historic Places, this treasured colonial is one of the oldest of the 66 houses which comprise High Street Historic District. The inn's antiques include interesting pieces from the 17th, 18th and 19th centuries. It is

a short five-minute walk down High Street to the center of the village and the Camden Harbor. The innkeeper is known for his down-east stories told in a heavy down-east accent.
Rates: $74-$86. Peter & Donny Smith and Diana Robson.
8 R. 2 PB. 4 FP. Phone available. TV available. Beds: QDT. B&B. CCs: MC VISA. Sailing, windsurfing, skiing, tennis, golf, hiking, swimming, biking, whale watching.
Seen in: *The Miami Herald, Lewiston Sun-Journal, Waterville Sentinel, Haverhill Gazette, Country Inns.*
"We've travelled the East Coast from Martha's Vineyard to Bar Harbor and this is the only place we know we must return to."

Edgecombe-Coles House
64 High St, HCR 60 Box 3010
Camden ME 04843
(207) 236-2336
Circa 1830. Admiring the view of Penobscot Bay, Chicago lawyer Chauncey Keep built this house on the foundation of a sea captain's

house. By 1900, his 22-room cottage was too small and he built a 50-room mansion up the hill, retaining this as a guest house. Country antiques set the tone and many rooms command a spectacular ocean view.
Location: North of Camden Harbor on Highway 1.
Rates: $75-$145. Terry & Louise Price.
6 R. 6 PB. 1 FP. Phone available. Beds: KQDT. Full breakfast. CCs: MC VISA DC. Skiing, mountain climbing, fishing, sailing, hiking, tennis, golf.
Seen in: *Uncommon Lodgings.*
"A beautiful view, beautiful decor and a lovely hostess make this a very special place," Shelby Hodge, *Houston Post.*

The Elms B&B
84 Elm St, Rt 1
Camden ME 04843
(207) 236-6250
Circa 1806. Captain Calvin Curtis built this Colonial a few minutes stroll from the picturesque harbor. Candlelight shimmers year round from the inn's windows. A sitting room, library, and parlour are open for guests and tastefully appointed bed chambers scattered with antiques are available in both the main house and the carriage house.
Rates: $50-$90. Joan A. James.
6 R. 3 PB. 2 FP. Phone available. Beds: D. Full breakfast. CCs: MC VISA. Sailing, skiing, hiking, tennis, golf.
"The warmth of your home is only exceeded by the warmth of yourself."

Hartstone Inn
41 Elm St
Camden ME 04843
(207) 236-4259
Circa 1835. A third story, mansard roof and large bay windows were added to this house at the turn-of-the-century, changing it to a stately Victorian. Both the parlor and dining room feature fireplaces. A carriage house with barn beams, kitchen, skylights and sleeping loft is available as well as the comfortable rooms in the main house. Located in the village, the inn is a block away from the harbor with its fleet of windjammers.
Rates: $60-$90. Sunny & Peter Simmons.
7 R. 7 PB. 2 FP. Phone available. TV available. Beds: QDTC. Full breakfast. Gourmet meals. CCs: MC VISA AE. Sailing, golf, swimming, hiking, tennis, skiing.
Seen in: *Bangor Daily News, Newsday.*
"When can I move in?"

Hawthorn Inn
9 High St
Camden ME 04843
(207) 236-8842
Circa 1894. This handsome yellow and white turreted Victorian, in the National Register, sits on a large sloping lawn in view of the harbor. It features a grand three-story staircase and original stained glass windows. A carriage house boasts additional rooms with private decks, spas and apartments. The English hostess serves afternoon tea and biscuits in the drawing room. Ask for a room with a harbor view or the Turret Room with its view of Mt. Battie.
*Rates: $75-$135. Pauline & Bradford Staub.
11 R. 9 PB. 2 FP. Phone available. Beds: KQDT. B&B. Restaurant. Spa. Conference room. CCs: MC VISA. Hiking, swimming, sailing, skiing, kyaking, volleyball, childrens play set. Wedding packages during the off season.

Seen in: *Glamour, Country Inns.*
"Heavenly accommodations, delightful hospitality. Thanks."

Hosmer House
Four Pleasant St
Camden ME 04843
(207) 236-4012
Circa 1806. Located near the center of the village, this Greek Revival house offers spacious rooms simply decorated with small print wallpapers, painted floors and comforters. A country-style breakfast is served by candlelight in the dining room. Within a two-block walk are the public landing and the waterfall at Camden Harbor.
Rates: $50-$135. Richard & Dodie Schmidgall.
3 R. 3 PB. Phone available. Beds: KQDTC. Full breakfast. Handicap access. Horseback riding, swimming, kayaking, sailing, sail boarding, hiking. Ferry service to downhill & cross-country skiing, white water rafting, antiquing. Holiday & concert packages. Seen in: *Camden Herald.*
"Great hospitality and a sumptuous breakfast."

CENTER LOVELL H1/*F1*

Center Lovell Inn
Rt 5
Center Lovell ME 04016
(207) 925-1575
Circa 1805. A wraparound porch connects the original farmhouse with a Cape-style annex added in 1830. Governor of Florida, Eckley Stearns, transformed this house into its present Mississippi steamboat style

with the addition of a mansard roof and third floor. Acclaimed by *Architectural Digest*, the inn overlooks Kezar Lake Valley with a panoramic view of the White Mountains.
Location: Western Maine mountains along the New Hampshire border.
*Rates: $42-$160. Season: May - October. Bil & Susie Mosca.
11 R. 7 PB. Phone available. TV available. Beds: DT. EP. Spa. Swimming pool. Conference room. CCs: MC VISA. Horseback riding, golf, hiking, canoeing, kayaking.
Seen in: *New York Magazine, Architectural Digest.*
"Finest food I have ever eaten in 40 states and 30 countries, located in one of the most beautiful areas anywhere."

CHEBEAGUE ISLAND J3/G2

Chebeague Island Inn

PO Box 492-MBB

Chebeague Island ME 04107

(207) 846-5155 (207) 774-5891

Circa 1926. This three-story inn overlooks rolling lawns and Casco Bay. The wraparound porch is a popular place to rock and immerse yourself in the view. A huge stone fireplace dominates the great room. The inn caters to weddings and lunch and dinner can be taken on the inn's porch. Bicycles are available and a scenic golf course is adjacent to the inn. White sandy beaches abound.

Rates: $65-$98. Season: May to October. Wendy & Kevin Bowden.

21 R. 15 PB. Phone available. TV available. Beds: DTC. Continental-plus breakfast. Restaurant. Gourmet meals. Game room. Conference room. CCs: MC VISA AE DC CB DS. Golf, tennis, ocean beaches, bicycling, volleyball. Honeymoon, wedding, family reunions, lobster bakes.

Seen in: *Harbus News, Yankee Magazine, Maine Times.*

CLARK ISLAND I6/G3

Craignair Inn

Clark Island Rd

Clark Island ME 04859

(207) 594-7644

Circa 1930. Craignair originally was built to house stonecutters working in nearby granite quarries. Overlooking the docks of the Clark Island Quarry,

where granite schooners once were loaded, this roomy, three-story inn is tastefully decorated with local antiques.

Rates: $42-$87. Season: March - December. Norman & Terry Smith.

16 R. 5 PB. Phone available. Beds: DTC. Full breakfast. Restaurant. Handicap access. CCs: MC VISA DS. Tennis, horseback riding, sailing, skiing, water sports, boating, fishing.

Seen in: *Boston Globe, Free Press.*

"We thoroughly enjoyed our stay with you. Your location is lovely and private. Your dining room and service and food were all 5 star!"

DAMARISCOTTA I5/G2

Brannon-Bunker Inn

PO Box 045, HCR 64

Damariscotta ME 04543

(207) 563-5941

Circa 1820. This Cape-style house has been a home to many generations of Maine residents, one of whom was captain of a ship that sailed to the

Arctic. During the Twenties, the barn served as a dance hall. Later, it was converted into comfortable guest rooms. Victorian and American antiques are featured and there are collections of military and political memorabilia.

*Rates: $45-$65. Joe & Jeanne Hovance.

8 R. 5 PB. Phone available. TV available. Beds: QDTC. B&B. CCs: MC VISA. Bicycling, fishing, golf, hiking, hay rides, hunting, fishing, sailing, cross-country skiing, sleigh rides, tennis.

Seen in: *The Times-Beacon Newspaper.*

"Wonderful beds, your gracious hospitality and the very best muffins anywhere made our stay a memorable one."

Crown 'N' Anchor Inn

See: Newcastle, ME

DEER ISLE VILLAGE H8/F3

Laphroaig B&B

Rte 15, PO Box 67

Deer Isle Village ME 04627

(207) 348-6088

Circa 1854. Laphroaig (la froyg) is Celtic for "the beautiful hollow by the broad bay," which describes the inn's

location overlooking Penobscot Bay. The inn is appointed with antiques and collections such as glass slippers, miniature pitchers and dolls. Guests often borrow books from the library and head to the porch swing or a secluded garden bench. Situated on over an acre, there are shaded lawns, perennial gardens and a plot of vegetables. Laphroaig is particularly popular with Canadians but all guests enjoy the homebaked breads, handmade afghans and lavish clumps of old-fashioned roses.

❀Rates: $60-$70. John & Andrea Maberry.

2 R. 2 PB. Phone available. TV in room. Beds: QD. Full breakfast. Cross-country skiing, golf, tennis, swimming, hiking, sailing.

Seen in: *The Ellsworth American.*

"An unexpected delight, good rest, delicious food and genuine hospitality — to a Southern boy, that means a lot."

DENNYSVILLE E12/E5

Lincoln House Country Inn

Rts 1 & 86

Dennysville ME 04628

(207) 726-3953

Circa 1787. Theodore Lincoln, ancestor of Abraham Lincoln and son of Benjamin Lincoln, who accepted the sword of surrender from Cornwallis

after the American Revolution, built this house. The four-square colonial looks out to the Dennys River and its salmon pools. John James Audubon stayed here on his way to Labrador. He loved the house and family so much that he named the Lincoln Sparrow in their honor.

Rates: $58-$140. Season: May - October. Mary & Jerry Haggerty.

6 R. 2 FP. Phone available. Beds: QDT. MAP. Restaurant. Conference room. CCs: MC VISA. Bird watching, hiking, fishing, boating, cross-country skiing. Reservations required.

Seen in: *Good Housekeeping, Washington Post.*

"The food was delicious, the ambience special."

EASTPORT E13/E5

Todd House

Todd's Head

Eastport ME 04631

(207) 853-2328

Circa 1775. Todd House is a typical full Cape with a huge center chimney. In 1801, Eastern Lodge No. 7 of the Masonic Order was chartered here. It became a temporary barracks when Todd's Head was fortified. Guests may use barbecue facilities overlooking Passamaquoddy Bay.

Rates: $35-$75. Ruth McInnis.

6 R. 2 PB. 3 FP. Phone available. TV in room. Beds: QDT. Continental-plus break-

fast. Handicap access. Boat rides, whale watching.
Seen in: *Portland Press Herald.*
"Your house and hospitality were real memory makers of our vacation."

Weston House
26 Boynton St
Eastport ME 04631
(207) 853-2907
Circa 1810. Jonathan Weston, an 1802 Harvard graduate, built this Federal-style house on a hill overlooking Pas-

samaquoddy Bay. John Audubon stayed here as a guest of the Westons while awaiting passage to Labrador in 1833.
Rates: $40-$60. Jett & John Peterson.
5 R. Phone available. Beds: KQT. Full breakfast. Conference room. Fishing, golf, hiking, bicycling, boating.
Seen in: *Downeast Magazine, Los Angeles Times.*
"The most memorable bed and breakfast experience we have ever had."

ELIOT L2/H1

High Meadows B&B
Rt 101
Eliot ME 03903
(207) 439-0590
Circa 1736. A ship's captain built this house, now filled with remembrances of colonial days. At one point, it was

raised and a floor added underneath, so the upstairs is older than the downstairs. It is conveniently located to factory outlets in Kittery, Maine, and great dining and historic museums in Portsmouth, New Hampshire. Smoking is permitted on the porch and terrace.
Rates: $50-$60. Season: April - Oct. Elaine Raymond.
5 R. 3 PB. Phone available. TV available. Beds: QDTW. Full breakfast. Conference room. Golf, tennis, whale watching.
Seen in: *Portsmouth Herald, York County Focus.*
"High Meadows was the highlight of our trip."

FREEPORT I4/G2

The Bagley House
RR 3 Box 269C
Freeport ME 04032
(207) 865-6566 (800) 765-1772
Circa 1772. Six acres of fields and woods surround the Bagley House, once an inn, a store, and a schoolhouse. Guest rooms are decorated

with colonial furnishings and hand-sewn Maine quilts. For breakfast, guests gather in the country kitchen in front of a huge brick fireplace and beehive oven.
Location: Route 136, Durham.
*Rates: $80-$100. Sigurd A. Knudsen, Jr.
5 R. 5 PB. 1 FP. Phone available. Beds: QDF. B&B. Conference room. CCs: MC VISA AE. Cross-country skiing, hiking, croquet.
Seen in: *Los Angeles Times, New England Getaways.*
"I had the good fortune to stumble on the Bagley House. The rooms are well appointed and the innkeeper is as charming a host as you'll find."

Captain Josiah Mitchell House
188 Main St
Freeport ME 04032
(207) 865-3289
Circa 1779. Captain Josiah Mitchell was commander of the clipper ship Hornet, which sailed in the 1800s. In 1865, en route from New York to San Francisco it caught fire, burned and was lost. The passengers and crew survived in three longboats, drifting for 45 days. It is the longest recorded survival at sea in an open boat. When the boats finally drifted into one of the South Pacific Islands, Mark Twain was there. He befriended the Captain and both sailed back to the Mainland together. The diary of Captain Mitchell parallels episodes of *Mutiny on the Bounty*. Flower gardens and a porch swing on the veranda now welcome guests to Freeport and the Captain's House.
*Rates: $68 & up. Alan & Loretta Bradley.
7 R. 7 PB. Phone available. TV in room. Beds: DT. Full breakfast. Spa. CCs: MC VISA.
Seen in: *Famous Boats and Harbors.*
"Your wonderful stories brought us all together. You have created a special place that nurtures and brings happiness and love. This has been a dream!"

Harraseeket Inn
162 Main St
Freeport ME 04032
(207) 865-9377 (800) 342-6423
Circa 1850. The tavern and drawing room of this inn are decorated in the Federal style. Guest rooms are fur-

nished with antiques and half-canopied beds. Some have whirlpools and fireplaces. The L.L. Bean store is just two blocks away, with other outlet stores nearby, such as Ralph Lauren, Laura Ashley and Anne Klein.
*Rates: $85-$165. Paul & Nancy Gray.
54 R. 54 PB. 16 FP. Phone in room. TV in room. Beds: KQD. EP. Restaurant. Gourmet meals. Spa. Handicap access. Conference room. FAX. CCs: MC VISA AE DC DS. Boating, fishing, golf, tennis, hiking, skiing.
Seen in: *Village Bed & Breakfast.*

Isaac Randall House
5 Independence Dr
Freeport ME 04032
(207) 865-9295
Circa 1823. Isaac Randall's Federal style farmhouse was once a dairy farm and a stop on the Underground Railway for slaves escaping into Canada. Randall was a descendant of John Alden and Priscilla Mullins of the *Mayflower*. Longfellow immortalized their romance in *The Courtship of Miles Standish*. The inn is located on six wooded acres with a pond. Guest rooms are air conditioned.
❀Rates: $50-$100. Season: July - Oct. 31. Jim & Glyn Friedlander.
8 R. 6 PB. Phone available. Beds: KQC. Full breakfast. Spa. Handicap access. Conference room. Cross-country skiing, hiking.
"Enchanted to find ourselves surrounded by all your charming antiques and beautiful furnishings."

GREENVILLE C5/D2

Greenville Inn
Norris St, PO Box 1194
Greenville ME 04441
(207) 695-2206
Circa 1895. The Greenville Inn sits on

a hill, one block from town. It's also one block from the shore line of Moosehead Lake, the largest lake

completely contained in any one state. A wealthy lumber family built the house. Ten years were needed to complete the cherry and mahogany paneling. There are six fireplaces with carved mantels and mosaics. From the dining room, guests have an excellent water view.
Location: Moosehead Lake.
Rates: $65-$85. The Schnetzers.
9 R. 7 PB. 2 FP. Phone available. TV available. Beds: KQDT. EP. Restaurant. Game room. Conference room. CCs: MC VISA DS. Horseback riding, golf, tennis, steamship excursions, hiking. Seen in: *Maine Times, Portland Monthly Magazine, Bangor Daily News.*
"The fanciest place in town."

ISLE AU HAUT H8/G3

The Keeper's House
PO Box 26
Isle Au Haut ME 04645
(207) 367-2261
Circa 1907. Designed and built by the U.S. Lighthouse Service, the handsome 48-foot high Robinson Point Light guided vessels into this once

bustling island fishing village. Guests arrive on the mailboat. Innkeeper Judi Burke, whose father was a keeper at the Highland lighthouse on Cape Cod, provides picnic lunches so guests may explore the scenic island trails. Dinner is served in the keeper's dining room. The lighthouse is adjacent to the most remote section of Acadia National Park. It's not uncommon to hear the cry of an osprey, see deer approach the inn, or seals and porpoises cavorting off the point. Guest rooms are comfortable and serene, with stunning views of the island's ragged shore line, forests and Duck Harbor.
❀Rates: $205. Season: May - Oct. 31. Jeff & Judi Burke.
6 R. Beds: D. AP. Hiking. Three rooms feature woodstoves.
Seen in: *New York Times, USA Today, Los Angeles Times, Ladies Home Journal.*
"Simply one of the unique places on Earth."

KENNEBUNK BEACH K2/H1

Sundial Inn
PO Box 1147, 48 Beach Ave
Kennebunk Beach ME 04043
(207) 967-3850
Circa 1891. This yellow and white clapboard house faces the ocean and Kennebunk Beach. The inn is decorated with country Victorian an-

tiques, and some rooms have a whirlpool bath. An elevator makes for easy access. Beachcombing for sand dollars, sea shells and sea urchins is a popular pastime, along with enjoying splendid views from the porch rockers and guest rooms.
Location: Beach Avenue #48.
Rates: $60-$170. Pat & Larry Kenny.
34 R. 34 PB. Phone in room. TV in room. Beds: KQT. B&B. Spa. Handicap access. Conference room. CCs: MC VISA AE DC CB. Seen in: *New England Travel.*
"My time on your porch watching the sea was the best part of my vacation. Whenever I am stressed I wander back in my mind to a day at the Sundial where I found such inner peace."

KENNEBUNKPORT K2/H1

1802 House
Box 646A Locke St
Kennebunkport ME 04046
(207) 967-5632
Circa 1802. Many of the guest rooms in the 1802 House possess private fireplaces. All are decorated with colonial wallpaper and antiques, such as four-poster beds. The ringing of a ship's bell announces breakfast. Guests dine overlooking a golf course next to the inn. Water sports, fall foliage, cross-country skiing and the Seashore Trolley Museum are all popular attractions.
❀❀Rates: $80-$115. Pat Ledda.
6 R. 6 PB. 2 FP. TV available. Beds: QTD. EP. CCs: MC VISA AE. Golf, tennis, cross-country skiing, hiking, boating.

Captain Lord Mansion
Pleasant & Green, PO Box 800
Kennebunkport ME 04046
(207) 967-3141 (800) 522-3141
Circa 1812. In the National Register, the Captain Lord Mansion was built during the War of 1812, and is one of the finest examples of Federal ar-

chitecture on the coast of Maine. A four-story spiral staircase winds up to the cupola where one can view the town and the Kennebunk River and Yacht Club. The inn is furnished with elegant antiques. Many bed chambers have working fireplaces and there's a cottage with a fireplace in the bathroom. A family-style breakfast is served in the country kitchen.
Rates: $115-$175. Bev Davis & Rick Litchfield.
16 R. 16 PB. Beds: KQ. Full breakfast. Spa. Conference room. CCs: MC VISA DS. Cross country skiing, cruises, sailing, beaches, tennis, golf, discount shopping.
Seen in: *Andrew Harper's Hideaway Report, Colonial Homes, Yankee, New England Get Aways.*
"A showcase of elegant architecture. Meticulously clean and splendidly appointed. It's a shame to have to leave."

The Inn at Harbor Head
Pier Rd, RFD 2 Box 1180
Kennebunkport ME 04046
(207) 967-5564 (207) 967-4873
Circa 1890. This shingled saltwater farmhouse is located directly on the water in historic Cape Porpoise — a

fishing village where lobstermen have worked for generations. Sounds of sea gulls and bellbuoys blend with the foghorn from the lighthouse nearby and there are outstanding views of the harbor, ocean and islands. Guest rooms feature antiques, paddle fans and down comforters. A gourmet breakfast is served in the stenciled dining room amidst collections of pewter and crystal.
Location: On the rocky shore of Cape Porpoise Harbor.
Rates: $95-$160. Joan & David Sutter.
4 R. 4 PB. Phone available. Beds: KQT. Full

breakfast. Spa. CCs: MC VISA. Swimming, beach, horseback riding, golf, cross-country skiing, whale watching, boat cruises all nearby. Winter packages available.
Seen in: *The Boston Globe, Country Inns, Los Angeles Times.*
"Your lovely home is our image of what a New England B&B should be. Unbelievably perfect! So glad we found you."

Harbor Inn

Ocean Ave, PO Box 538A
Kennebunkport ME 04046
(207) 967-2074

Circa 1903. Tucked behind a white iron Victorian fence is the Harbor Inn. A yellow canopy covers the stairs leading to the veranda. There, you can hear the quiet purring of fishing boats

or smell the fresh, sea air. Guest rooms are furnished with canopied or four-poster beds, period lighting, Oriental rugs, and antique coverlets. The inn's kitchen has blue iris stained-glass windows and an old wood stove set on a brick hearth. Just past the inn, where the Kennebunk River runs to the sea, are Spouting Rock and Blowing Cave.
Rates: $90-$145. Season: May 15-Nov. 1. Charlotte & Bill Massmann.
8 R. 8 PB. Phone available. TV available. Beds: QDT. Full breakfast. Horseback riding, golf, tennis, biking, boating, fishing, water sports.
Seen in: *Country Inns, Yankee Travel Guide.*
"Everything is beautifully done. It's the best we've ever been to."

Kennebunkport Inn

Box 111, Dock Sq
Kennebunkport ME 04046
(207) 967-2621

Circa 1899. The Kennebunkport Inn offers relaxation with its main lounge furnished with velvet loveseats and chintz sofas. Bedrooms are furnished with mahogany queen-sized beds, wing chairs and Queen Anne writing desks.
Rates: $62-$145. Rick & Martha Griffin.
34 R. 34 PB. 1 FP. Phone available. TV in room. Beds: QDT. MAP. Restaurant. Gourmet meals. Swimming pool. CCs: MC VISA. Deep-sea fishing, sailing, whale watching, canoeing, horseback riding, bicycling.
Seen in: *Getaways for Gourmets, Coast Guide.*
"From check in, to check out, from breakfast through dinner, we were treated like royalty."

Kylemere House 1818

South St, PO Box 1333
Kennebunkport ME 04046
(207) 967-2780

Circa 1818. Located in Maine's largest historic district, this Federal-style house was built by Daniel Walker, a descendant of an original Kennebunkport family. Later, Maine artist and architect Abbot Graves purchased the property and named it Crosstrees for its maple trees. The inn features New England antiques and brilliant flowering gardens in view of the formal dining room in spring and summer. A full breakfast is provided. Art galleries, beaches, antiquing and golf are nearby.
Rates: $60-$85. Season: May - December. Mary & Bill Kyle.
5 R. 3 PB. 1 FP. Phone available. Beds: KQT. Full breakfast. CCs: AE. Water sports, fishing, boating, bicycling, beaches, shopping.
Seen in: *Boston Globe, Glamour Magazine, Regis and Kathie Lee Show.*
"Beautiful inn. Outstanding hospitality. Thanks for drying our sneakers, fixing our bikes. You are all a lot of fun!"

Maine Stay Inn & Cottages

Maine St, PO Box 500A
Kennebunkport ME 04046
(207) 967-9117

Circa 1860. In the National Register, this is a square-block Italianate contoured in a low hip-roof design. Later

additions of the Queen Anne period include a suspended spiral staircase, crystal windows, ornately carved mantels and moldings, bay windows and porches. A sea captain built the handsome cupola that became a favorite spot for making taffy. In the Twenties, the cupola was a place from which to spot offshore rumrunners. Guests enjoy afternoon tea with stories of the Maine Stay's heritage.
Location: In the Kennebunkport National Historic District.
*Rates: $85-$150. Lindsay & Carol Copeland.
17 R. 17 PB. 1 FP. Phone available. TV in room. Beds: QDTC. B&B. Handicap access. Conference room. CCs: MC VISA AE. Beaches, golf.
"We have travelled the east coast from Martha's Vineyard to Bar Harbor, and this is the only place we know we must return to."

Old Fort Inn

Old Fort Ave, PO Box M 24
Kennebunkport ME 04046
(207) 967-5353 (800) 828-3678

Circa 1880. The Old Fort Inn is a luxurious mini-resort nestled in a secluded setting with an English gar-

den. It has a tennis court, fresh-water swimming pool and shuffleboard. Bikes are also available. Country furniture, primitives, and china are featured in an antique shop on the property. The ocean is just a block away.
*Rates: $98-$225. Season: Mid April-Mid Dec. Sheila & David Aldrich.
16 R. 16 PB. Phone in room. TV in room. Beds: KQT. Full breakfast. Spa. Conference room. FAX. CCs: MC VISA DS. Bicycling, swimming, golf, tennis.
Seen in: *Country Inns.*
"My husband and I have been spending the last two weeks in August at the Old Fort Inn for years. It combines for us a rich variety of what we feel a relaxing vacation should be."

The Inn on South Street

PO Box 478A, South St
Kennebunkport ME 04046
(207) 967-5151 (207) 967-4639

Circa 1806. Built in the Greek Revival style, the inn stands on a quiet side street in the historic area. In 1901, it

was towed by oxen from its original location after a wealthy citizen complained that it was cutting off her river view. The inn boasts a handsome 'good-morning' staircase, original pine-plank floors and an old-

fashioned herb garden. Breakfast, served in the country kitchen on the second floor, includes enjoying river views and Professor Downs' German pancakes.
*Rates: $75-$110. Jack & Eva Downs.
4 R. 4 PB. 2 FP. Phone in room. Beds: QT. B&B. Spa. Conference room. CCs: AE. Water sports, hiking, bicycling, walking.
Seen in: *Summertime, Country Inns.*
"Superb hospitality. We were delighted by the atmosphere and your thoughtfulness."

The White Barn Inn
Beach St, RR 3 Box 387
Kennebunkport ME 04046
(207) 967-2321
Circa 1810. Over the past 150 years, various owners have added onto this farmhouse and its signature white barn. Each addition to the rambling

grey structure has been distinctive. Stately Queen Anne furnishings, soft down sofas, bright floral prints and country tweeds decorate the suites. There are four-posters and whirlpool tubs in some rooms. Candlelight dining is popular in the three-story barn.
Location: South of Portland ½ hour, I-95 1½ hour north of Boston.
*Rates: $85-$220. Laurie Bongiorno & Carole Hackett.
25 R. 25 PB. 7 FP. Phone in room. TV in room. Beds: KQDT. MAP. Restaurant. Gourmet meals. Spa. Conference room. FAX. CCs: MC VISA AE. Golf, tennis, cross-country & downhill skiing, beach, sailing, fishing.
Seen in: *Colonial Homes, USA Today, Relais & Chateaux, AAA four-diamond rating.*
"It is clear you are in the business of very fine hospitality and we appreciated the warm welcome we received from you and your staff."

KINGFIELD E4/*E2*

The Inn on Winter's Hill
RR 1 Box 1272
Kingfield ME 04947
(207) 265-5421
Circa 1898. The twin Stanley brothers (Stanley Steamer) designed this house on a lazy summer afternoon. Their creative genius resulted in an exciting example of Georgian Revival architecture, now restored to its original beauty. Today, it houses Julia's Restaurant which specializes in New England cuisine. There is a lighted

skating rink and shuttle service to and from Sugarloaf USA.
Rates: $120+. Diane Winnick.
15 R. 15 PB. Phone in room. TV in room. Beds: QDC. EP. Restaurant. Spa. Handicap access. Swimming pool. Conference room. CCs: MC VISA AE DS. Golf, white water rafting, canoeing, downhill & cross-country skiing, ice skating.
Seen in: *The Franklin Journal.*

LUBEC E13/*E5*

Peacock House
27 Summer St
Lubec ME 04652
(207) 733-2403
Circa 1860. This three-story Victorian house overlooks the Bay of Fundy, two blocks away. Four generations of the Peacock family lived here, and the

R.J. Peacock Canning Co. is the only remaining sardine packing plant in the area. Innkeepers Veda and her daughter Debbie offer a full breakfast. For those who enjoy sleeping in, there is also a continental breakfast open till 10 a.m. Lunch baskets are popular and may be ordered the night before. Don't miss the afternoon tea with homemade scones and English biscuits.
Rates: $65-$75. Season: May 30-Oct. 30. Chet & Veda Childs.
4 R. 2 PB. Phone available. TV in room. Beds: QD. Full breakfast. CCs: MC VISA. Golf, sailing, whale watching.
Seen in: *Quoddy Tides, Downeast Coastal Press.*
"A perfect B&B — great beds, fantastic breakfast and a hospitable family."

NAPLES I2/*G1*

The Augustus Bove House
RR 1 Box 501
Naples ME 04055
(207) 693-6365
Circa 1856. A long front lawn nestles up against the stone foundation and veranda of this house, once known as

the Hotel Naples, one of the area's summer hotels in the 1800s. The guest rooms are decorated in a colonial style with antiques and wallpapers. Many rooms provide a view of Long Lake. A fancy country breakfast is provided.
Rates: $49-$75. David & Arlene Stetson.
12 R. 5 PB. 1 FP. Phone available. TV available. Beds: KQDTC. EP. CCs: MC VISA AE. Hiking, canoeing, fishing, cycling, swimming, golf, horseback riding, theaters, boating, cross-country & downhill skiing, ice fishing, skating, sliding.
Seen in: *Brighton Times.*
"Beautiful place, rooms, and people."

The Inn at Long Lake
Lake House Rd, PO Box 806
Naples ME 04055
(207) 693-6226
Circa 1906. This recently reopened inn housed the overflow guests from the Lake House Resort 80 years ago. Guests traveled to the resort via the

Oxford-Cumberland Canal. Each room is named for a historic canal boat and is decorated to match.
Rates: $59-$75. Maynard & Irene Hincks.
16 R. 16 PB. 1 FP. Phone available. TV in room. Beds: QDT. Continental-plus breakfast. CCs: MC VISA AE. Golf, water skiing, boating, bicycling, cross-country skiing.
Seen in: *The Bridgton News.*
"Convenient location, tastefully done and the prettiest inn I've ever stayed in."

NEW HARBOR I5/*G2*

Gosnold Arms
Northside Rd, Rt 32
New Harbor ME 04554
(207) 677-3727
Circa 1870. Located on the historic Pemaquid penninsula, the Gosnold

Arms includes a remodeled, saltwater farmhouse situated on a rise above

the harbor. There are several cottages and many accommodations with views. A cozy lounge offers two large stone fireplaces and a glassed-in dining porch overlooking the water.
Rates: $75-$115. Season: May - November. The Phinney family.
26 R. 26 PB. Phone available. Beds: QDTC. Full breakfast. CCs: MC VISA. Dinner and Sunday Brunch is served. Known in area for its fine food.
Seen in: *New York Magazine, Down East.*

NEWCASTLE I5/*G2*

Crown 'N' Anchor Inn

River Rd, PO Box 17
Newcastle ME 04553
(207) 563-8954

Circa 1790. This Greek Revival house features both Victorian baroque and colonial antiques. A collection of British coronation memorabilia dis-

played throughout the inn includes 200 items. Guests gather in the Victorian parlor or the formal library. The innkeepers, two college librarians and an academic book seller, lined the shelves with several thousand volumes, including extensive Civil War and British royal family collections and travel, theater and nautical books. The floor-to-ceiling windows of the Eliza Hitchcock Room overlook the Damariscotta River. Royal Dalton china, crystal and fresh flowers create a festive breakfast setting.
*Rates: $40-$65. John Barclay, Jim & Martha Forester.
4 R. 1 PB. Phone available. TV in room. Beds: DT. Full breakfast. CCs: MC VISA. Water sports, nature preserves, whale watching, island tours.
Seen in: *Lincoln County News, Yankee Magazine.*
"Absolute hospitality and helpfulness."

The Newcastle Inn

RR 2 Box 24, River RD
Newcastle ME 04553
(207) 563-5685

Circa 1860. The Newcastle Inn is a Federal-style colonial picturesquely situated on a lawn that slopes down to the Damariscotta River. Most rooms

feature antique beds and water views. Honeymooners like the room with the old-fashioned canopy bed. Breakfast consists of four courses and may include eggs with caviar on puff pastry, or brioche with lemon curd. A five-course dinner is available.
Location: Tidal Damariscotta River.
Rates: $85-$95. Ted & Chris Sprague.
15 R. 15 PB. Phone available. Beds: KQT. MAP. Gourmet meals. CCs: MC VISA. Cross-country skiing, golf, bicycling, swimming, fishing.
Seen in: *Yankee Magazine, Downeast Magazine, Romantic Hideaways.*
"To eat and stay here is to know life to the fullest."

NORTH WATERFORD H2/*F1*

Olde Rowley Inn

Rt 35 N
North Waterford ME 04267
(207) 583-4143

Circa 1790. Two hundred years ago, settlers from Rowley, Massachusetts

who had served together in the French Revolution moved here. This farm belonged to one of those families. It later became a stagecoach stop and inn, and for over 100 years the Rice family served here as innkeepers. Recently restored, the inn offers pleasant and spacious guest rooms. The dining rooms are in the carriage house and barn.
Rates: $50-$65. Brian & Meredith Thomas.
6 R. 3 PB. Phone available. Beds: D. Full breakfast. Restaurant. CCs: MC VISA AE. Skiing, horse-drawn sleigh and hay rides.
Seen in: *The Bridgton News, Sunday River Times.*
"Our accommodations were clean and neat. With your hospitality we felt very welcomed and at home."

NORTHEAST HARBOR H9/*F4*

Harbourside Inn

Northeast Harbor ME 04662
(207) 276-3272

Circa 1888. This rambling country inn is an appealing version of the rustic shingle style. Situated on three wooded acres, it is adjacent to Acadia National Park. Glimpses of the harbor may be seen through the woods. Guest rooms are clean and bright and there are several suites with private porches. Some kitchenettes are available.
Rates: $90. Season: June - September. The Sweet Family.
14 R. 14 PB. 10 FP. Phone available. Beds: KQDT. Continental breakfast. Hiking, boating, swimming, sailing, golf, tennis, bicycling, canoeing.
Seen in: *The New York Times.*
"We so much appreciate your long hours of work mostly unseen by us except for the spotless results."

OGUNQUIT L2/*H1*

Hartwell House

118 Shore Rd, PO Box 393
Ogunquit ME 03907
(207) 646-7210

Circa 1714. Hartwell House offers suites and guest rooms furnished with distinctive Early American and English antiques. Many rooms are available with French doors opening to private balconies overlooking sculpted flower gardens. Breakfast may be enjoyed in the dining room, on the patio or in one's guest room.
Rates: $65-$175. Jim & Trisha Hartwell.
16 R. 16 PB. 1 FP. Phone available. TV available. Beds: QT. Continental-plus breakfast. CCs: MC VISA AE. Golf, swimming, fishing, sailing, museums, antiques, theaters. Honeymoon & anniversary specials, weddings.
Seen in: *Innsider.*
"This engaging country inn will be reserved for my special clients." Travel agent.

Morning Dove B&B

30 Bourne Ln, PO Box 1940
Ogunquit ME 03907
(207) 646-3891

Circa 1860. The Moses Littlefields lived in this three-story farmhouse for over 100 years and the family still retains the adjacent property. Renovated by Pete and Eeta Sachon, it is filled with carefully collected antiques and paintings by local artists. A Palladian window spreads sunlight around Grandma's Attic, a favorite room. Surrounded by bright and blooming gardens, the inn is a short stroll to beaches, restaurants and galleries.

❄❀Rates: $55-$110. Peter & Eeta Sachon.

6 R. 4 PB. Phone available. Beds: KQDT. B&B. CCs: MC VISA AE. Bird watching, art and antique galleries, outlet malls. Golf and tennis nearby.

PEMAQUID I5/G2

Little River Inn

Rt 130

Pemaquid ME 04558

(207) 677-2845

Circa 1840. Located beside the Pemaquid River, this Cape-style farmhouse is located on four acres of meadow and woodland. Most bedrooms are upstairs in the rustic gallery and feature paneling and views and sounds of the river. The downstairs room has floral stenciling and an antique bedstead.

Rates: $50-$65. Kristina De Khan.

4 R. 1 PB. Beds: D. Full breakfast. CCs: MC VISA. Horseback riding, water sports, beach, canoe rentals, hiking.

"Wonderful! Three nights aren't long enough."

PORTLAND J3/G2

Pomegranate Inn

49 Neal St

Portland ME 04102

(207) 772-1006 (800)356-0408

Circa 1884. This three-story inn is furnished with a mix of contemporary art and antiques. *Faux*-finished wood-

work painted by the innkeeper's daughter includes mouldings, fireplace mantels and columns. Another local artist handpainted the guest room walls. Two bathrooms contain Grecian marble.

Rates: $95. Alan & Isabel Smiles.

6 R. 6 PB. Phone in room. TV in room. Beds: QDT Continental-plus breakfast. Conference room. FAX. CCs: MC VISA AE.

Seen in: *Portland Monthly Magazine, Portland Press Herald.*

*"The most wonderful inn I have ever been in!"*Irish visitor.

SEARSPORT G7/F3

McGilvery House

PO Box 588

Searsport ME 04974

(207) 548-6289

Circa 1860. A prominent sea captain, William McGilvery, built this handsome estate in the mansard domestic style, with a soaring center-gambrel

gable. Guest rooms provide an excellent view of Penobscot Bay, and some feature ornate marble fireplaces.

❄Rates: $55. Sue Omness.

3 R. 3 PB. Phone available. Beds: Q. Continental breakfast. Golf, hiking, boating, museums, antiquing.

Seen in: *The Courier-Gazette.*

"It was a thrill being in your lovely home. Your personal touches are evident everywhere. The breakfasts are tops. We'll be back."

SOUTHPORT I5/G2

Albonegon Inn

Capitol Island

Southport ME 04538

(207) 633-2521

Circa 1876. Built on a rocky ledge, this old lodge provides each guest room with a splendid view of either the harbor, islands or beach. Floral chintz curtains and homey furnishings keep the old-fashioned feel of the original inn. Although there is live theater, boating and hiking and tennis, some guests are known to spend all their days rocking on the wraparound veranda.

Rates: $62-$100. Season: June-Oct. 15. Bob & Kim Peckham.

15 R. 3 PB. Beds: QDT. Continental breakfast. Tennis, beaches, boating.

Seen in: *The Boston Herald.*

"In all my travel, this is the place I feel the happiest."

SOUTHWEST HARBOR H9/F4

The Island House

PO Box 1006

Southwest Harbor ME 04679

(207) 244-5180

Circa 1830. The first guests arrived at Deacon Clark's door as early as 1832 when steamboat service from Boston

began in the 1850s. The Island House became a popular summer hotel. Among the guests was Ralph Waldo Emerson. In 1912, the hotel was taken down and rebuilt as two separate homes using much of the woodwork from the original building.

Location: Mount Desert Island (Acadia National Park).

Rates: $50-$60. Season: May 1 - Oct. 31. Ann R. Gill.

4 R. 1 PB. Phone available. TV available. Beds: QW. Full breakfast. Horseback riding, swimming, canoeing, sailing, cycling. Piano.

Seen in: *Bangor Daily News.*

"Island House is a delight from the moment one enters the door! We loved the thoughtful extras. You've made our vacation very special!"

Lindenwood Inn

PO Box 1328

Southwest Harbor ME 04679

(207) 244-5335

Circa 1906. Sea Captain Mills named his home "The Lindens" after stately linden trees that line the front lawn. The cypress paneling retains its original finish and adorns the entrance and dining room. Gull's Nest and Casablanca are among the rooms overlooking the harbor.

Location: Mt. Desert Island.

Rates: $50-$115. T. Gardiner, Marilyn & Matthew Brower.

7 R. 3 PB. Phone available. TV available. Beds: QD. Full breakfast. Harpsichord to play, hiking, biking, sailing, lake across the street.

Seen in: *Maine.*

"We had a lovely stay at your inn. Breakfast, room and hospitality were all first rate. You made us feel like a special friend instead of a paying guest."

WATERFORD H2/F1

Lake House

Rts 35 & 37
Waterford ME 04088
(207) 583-4182

Circa 1797. Situated on the common, the Lake House was first a hotel and stagecoach stop. In 1817, granite baths

were constructed below the first floor. The inn opened as "Dr. Shattuck's Maine Hygienic Institute for Ladies." It continued as a popular health spa until the 1890s. Now noted for excellent country cuisine, there are two dining rooms for non-smokers. Four guest rooms are upstairs. The spacious Grand Ballroom Suite features curved ceilings, a sitting room and a canopy bed. Views of Lake Keoka are enjoyed from the inn's veranda.

Rates: $69-$89. Suzanne & Michael Uhl-Myers

4 R. 4 PB. Phone available. Beds: DT. Full breakfast. Restaurant. CCs: MC VISA. Hiking, lake across the street.

Seen in: *Country Inns.*

"Your hospitality was matched only by the quality of dinner that we were served."

WISCASSET I5/G2

The Squire Tarbox Inn

RR 2 Box 620
Wiscasset ME 04578
(207) 882-7693

Circa 1825. North of Bath, deep into the country and woods, Squire Tarbox built his rambling farmhouse around

a building originally constructed in 1763. Today, the rooms are warm and comfortable in the inn and in the remodeled hayloft. The innkeepers raise Nubian goats, all photogenic, that have become part of the entertainment (milking and goat cheese). A house-party atmosphere pervades the inn.

Location: Route 144, 8½ miles on Westport Island.

*Rates: $110-$170.MAP. Season: May - October. Bill & Karen Mitman.

11 R. 11 PB. 4 FP. Phone available. Beds: KQTD. Continental breakfast. CCs: MC VISA. Sailing, fishing, sand dunes, ocean, antiquing.

Seen in: *Washington Post.*

"Your hospitality was warm, friendly, well-managed and quite genuine. That's a rarity, and it's just the kind we feel best with."

YORK L2/H1

Dockside Guest Quarters

PO Box 205, Harris Island
York ME 03909
(207) 363-2868

Circa 1885. This inn is located on Harris Island, a private peninsula in York Harbor. The "Maine House" is typical

of large, cottage-style New England summer homes. Splendid water views encompass the ocean and harbor. Museum quality antiques may be found. Guest rooms in the inn and cottages are cheerfully but simply appointed with painted furnishings and small print wallpapers or paneling. Waterfront dining is available at the inn's restaurant.

Location: Harris Island, Maine Rt. 103

*Rates: $48-$117. Season: May - October. The David Lusty family.

21 R. 19 PB. 1 FP. Phone available. TV available. Beds: KQDTC. EP. Restaurant. Handicap access. Conference room. CCs: MC VISA. Deep sea fishing, tennis, golf, beaches, shopping.

Seen in: *Boston Globe.*

"We've been back many years. It's a paradise for us, the scenery, location, maintenance, living quarters."

YORK HARBOR L2/H1

York Harbor Inn

PO Box 573, Rt 1A
York Harbor ME 03911
(207) 363-5119 (800) 343-3869

Circa 1637. The core building of the York Harbor Inn is a small log cabin constructed on the Isles of Shoals. Moved and reassembled at this dramatic location overlooking the entrance to York Harbor, the cabin is now a gathering room with a handsome stone fireplace. There is an English-style pub in the cellar with booths made from horse stalls.

Location: York Harbor's historic district.

*❀Rates: $45-$125. Joe, Jean, Garry & Nancy Dominguez.

32 R. 27 PB. 3 FP. Phone in room. TV available. Beds: D. Continental-plus breakfast. Restaurant. Gourmet meals. Spa. Handicap access. Conference room. FAX. CCs: MC VISA AE. Beach, golf, tennis, boating, fishing, cross-country skiing, swimming. Outlet shopping nearby.

Seen in: *New York Times, Down East.*

"It's hard to decide where to stay when you're paging through a book of country inns. This time we chose well."

MARYLAND

ANNAPOLIS G18/C6

Gibson's Lodgings

110 Prince George St
Annapolis MD 21401
(301) 268-5555

Circa 1786. This Georgian house in the heart of the Annapolis Historic District was built on the site of the Old Courthouse, circa 1680. Two his-

toric houses make up the inn and there is an annex built in 1988. All the rooms, old and new, are furnished with antiques. Only a few yards away is the City Dock Harbor and within two blocks is the Naval Academy visitor's gate. Parking on premises.
*Rates: $58-$120. Jeanne & Claude Schrift.
20 R. 7 PB. Beds: QT. Continental breakfast. Conference room. CCs: MC VISA.
Seen in: *Mid Atlantic Country.*

Historic Inns of Annapolis

16 Church Circle
Annapolis MD 21401
(301) 263-2641

Circa 1700. Five beautifully restored historic inns comprise Paul Pearson's Historic Inns of Annapolis: Robert Johnson House, State House, Maryland Inn, Reynolds Tavern and the Governor Calvert House. The Tavern, for instance, took seven years to restore. During that time, workers confirmed local legends that the tavern was once a center for smuggling and included a network of tunnels extending to the Annapolis waterfront. Architectural styles include Victorian, Georgian and Colonial with furnishings of the same period. (The Maryland Inn has been in continuous operation for over 200 years.) There is also a new hotel attached to the State House.

*Rates: $85-$175. William Burrurs, Jr.
141 R. 141 PB. Phone in room. TV in room. Beds: KQDTC. EP. Restaurant. Spa. Handicap access. Conference room. FAX. CCs: MC VISA AE DC. Swimming, sailing, power boat, all water sports.
Seen in: *Washingtonian, Historic Preservation, Boating.*

Prince George Inn

232 Prince George St
Annapolis MD 21401
(301) 263-6418

Circa 1884. The Prince George Inn is a three-story brick town house comfortably furnished with an emphasis on Victorian decor. The guest parlor, breakfast room, porch and courtyard offer areas for relaxing. In the heart of the colonial city, the inn is near restaurants, museums, shops and the City Dock. The Naval Academy is two blocks away.

Location: Historic District of Annapolis.
*Rates: $75. Bill & Norma Grovermann.
4 R. Phone available. TV available. Beds: QDT. Continental-plus breakfast. CCs: MC VISA. Sailing, walking tours, golf, tennis.
Seen in: *WMAR TV, Country Inns, Annapolitan Magazine.*
"Thoroughly enjoyed our six days in your lovely home!"

Shaw's Fancy B&B

161 Green St
Annapolis MD 21401
(301) 268-9750 (301) 263-0320

Circa 1902. This three-story house boasts a large parlor in the front bay, tiger-oak woodwork and tiled fireplaces. The innkeepers have decorated it in a light Victorian style and all the rooms boast both a queen-sized brass bed and a double daybed. The largest accommodation has an eight-poster bed, separate sitting room and claw-foot tub. Guests may walk one minute to shops and restaurants and just a little longer to the state Capitol building.
❀Rates: $70-$125. Jack House & Lilith Ren.
4 R. 2 PB. Phone available. TV available. Beds: Q. Continental-plus breakfast. Spa. Sailing, hiking, biking, antiquing, health-club privileges.
"You've spoiled us completely. Keep the joy going."

BALTIMORE E17/B6

Admiral Fell Inn

888 S Broadway
Baltimore MD 21231
(301) 522-7377 (800) 292-INNS

Circa 1790. This inn consists of four contiguous buildings, the oldest of which is a tan brick, three-story storefront structure with Victorian

moldings. At one time the complex served as a boarding house for sailors, and a vinegar-bottling plant, as well as home of the first mayor of Baltimore. Each room is tastefully furnished with fine antiques and period pieces.
Location: Fell's Point, next to downtown Baltimore.
*Rates: $94-$145. Dominik Eckenstein.
38 R. 38 PB. Phone in room. TV in room. Beds: KDTC. Continental breakfast. Restaurant. Gourmet meals. Spa. Handicap access. Game room. Conference room. FAX. CCs: MC VISA AE. Boating, sailing, shopping.
Seen in: *The New York Times, Cover of Mid-Atlantic Country.*
"Beautiful rooms, excellent services."

Betsy's B&B

1428 Park Ave
Baltimore MD 21217
(301) 383-1274 (301) 225-0001

Circa 1870. This four-story town house with 13-foot ceilings features many elegant architectural touches.

The hallway floor is laid in alternating strips of oak and walnut, and there are six carved marble fireplaces. The most elaborate, carved in fruit designs, is in the dining room. The inn is decorated with handsome brass rubbings made by the owner during a stay in England.

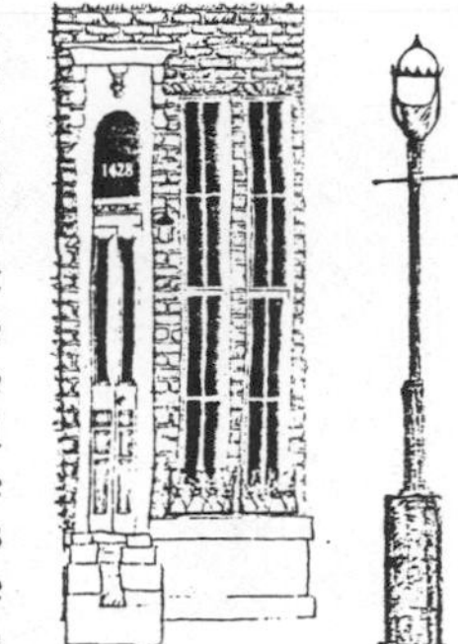

Location: Inner Harbor, about 1.5 miles north.
*Rates: $60-$65. Betsy Grater.
3 R. 1 PB. Phone in room. TV in room. Beds: KQT. Continental-plus breakfast. Spa. Swimming pool. FAX. CCs: MC VISA AE. Cycling.
Seen in: *Peabody Reflector, Baltimore/Washington Business Journal, Nation's Business, Times Herald.*
"What hotel room could ever compare to a large room in a 115-year-old house with 12-foot ceilings and a marble fireplace with hosts that could become dear longtime friends?"

The Shirley-Madison Inn

205 W Madison St
Baltimore MD 21201
(301) 728-6550

Circa 1880. An elegant Victorian mansion located in a downtown historic neighborhood, The Shirley-Madison Inn has an English stairway of polished ash that winds up four stories. The original 100-year-old lift still carries no more than three guests. The inn is decorated with Victorian and Edwardian antiques and turn-of-the-century artwork. The Inner Harbor, business district and cultural centers are a short walk away.
Location: Ten blocks from the Inner Harbor.
*Rates: $65-$95. Stanley Gondzer.
25 R. 25 PB. Phone in room. TV in room. Beds: KQDTC. Continental breakfast. Conference room. CCs: MC VISA AE DC. Boating, museums.
Seen in: *Mid-Atlantic Country, New York Magazine.*
"Charming, comfortable rooms, reasonable rates and friendly staff."

Society Hill Government House

1125 N Calvert St
Baltimore MD 21202
(301) 752-7722

Circa 1897. This is the official guest house for Baltimore's visiting dignitaries, as well as the general public. Three town houses comprise the inn, located in the Mt. Vernon historic district. Features include chandeliers, ornate wallpapers, and Victorian antiques. Each bedchamber has its own view.
Rates: $100-$120. Linda Cooley.
18 R. 18 PB. Beds: KQDC. Continental breakfast. Handicap access. Conference room. CCs: MC VISA AE.

Society Hill Hopkins

3404 St Paul St
Baltimore MD 21218
(301) 235-8600

Circa 1920. The embassy-like atmosphere of this inn makes it popular for small meetings as well as romantic getaways. Antiques and original art

fill the rooms, decorated in a variety of period styles. Breakfast may be taken in the guest room or dining room.
Rates: $65-$135. Joanne Fritz & Douglas Pence.
26 R. 26 PB. Phone in room. TV in room. Beds: QC. Continental-plus breakfast. Conference room. FAX. CCs: MC VISA AE DC CB. Museum of Art.
Seen in: *Baltimore Business Journal, New York Times, Weekend Getaways.*
"...most friendly and comfortable and very efficiently run."

Twin Gates

308 Morris Ave
Baltimore MD 21093
(800) 635-0370 (301)252-3131

Circa 1857. While renovating Twin Gates, the innkeepers discovered two secret rooms used to hide runaway slaves heading north by means of the

Underground Railroad. One of them is a small, half-height room that, prior to renovation, was accessed through a trap-door from the room below. All the public rooms have 12-foot ceilings and are decorated with antiques.
Location: Lutherville, a Victorian village north of Baltimore.
*Rates: $85. Gwen & Bob Vaughan.
7 R. 3 PB. Phone available. TV available. Beds: Q. Full breakfast. Winery tours. National Aquarium.
Seen in: *The Towson Flier, Baltimore Magazine.*

BETTERTON E20/*B7*

Lantern Inn

115 Ericsson Ave, PO Box 29
Betterton MD 21610
(301) 348-5809

Circa 1904. Framed by a picket fence and a wide front porch, this four-story country inn is located one block from Betterton beach, a boating and fishing area. Simply furnished rooms are comfortable and air-conditioned. A hearty hunter's breakfast is served each morning. The surrounding area is world-famous for its hunting of Canadian geese and snow geese from the arctic tundra.
Rates: $60-$75. Ken & Ann Washburn.
7 R. 2 PB. Phone available. TV available. Beds: KQDT. Full breakfast. CCs: MC VISA. Swimming, boating, bicycling, tennis.
Seen in: *Richland Times-Dispatch, North Carolina Outdoorsman.*
"Thanks for your warm hospitality."

BUCKEYSTOWN E13/*B4*

The Inn at Buckeystown

3521 Buckeystown Pike Gen Del
Buckeystown MD 21717
(301) 874-5755 (800) 272-1190

Circa 1897. Gables, bay windows and a wraparound porch are features of this grand Victorian mansion located on two-and-a-half acres of lawns and gardens (and an ancient cemetery). Nearby St. John's Reformed Church, built in 1884, has been refurbished as a cottage. The inn features a polished staircase, antiques and elegantly decorated guest rooms. Ask for the Fireplace Room, which boasts a lavish canopy bed with draperies. At dinner, cream of lemon soup, German duck and West Virginia black walnut apple cake are house specialties. The village of Buckeystown is in the National Register.
*Rates: $125-$225. Daniel Pelz & Chase Barnett.
10 R. 5 PB. 2 FP. Phone available. Beds: QDT. MAP. Spa. Conference room. CCs: MC VISA AE. Hiking, biking, fishing, swimming.
Seen in: *The Washingtonian.*
"The courtesy of you and your staff were the glue that bound the whole experience together."

CAMBRIDGE J20/D7

Glasgow Inn
1500 Hambrooks Blvd
Cambridge MD 21613
(301) 221-0297 (301) 228-0575

Circa 1760. Located along the Choptank River on seven acres, this brick colonial is reached by way of a long tree-lined driveway. The house was built by Dr. William Murray whose son was a friend to Thomas Jefferson and John Quincy Adams. (According to local legend, part of the U.S. Constitution was written here.) The inn is decorated with country colonial antiques and reproductions, enhanced by high ceilings, a mahogany staircase and deep-window seats.

Rates: $80-$100. Louise Lee Roche & Martha Ann Rayne.

6 R. 3 PB. 6 FP. Phone available. TV available. Beds: KQC. Full breakfast. CCs: MC VISA. Sailing, biking, fishing, crabbing, bird-watching. Quilt conferences.

Seen in: *Mid-Atlantic Country, Tidewater Times.*

CASCADE B12/A4

Bluebird On The Mountain
14700 Eyler Ave
Cascade MD 21719
(301) 241-4161 (301) 241-4150

Circa 1900. In the mountain village of Cascade, this gracious shuttered Georgian manor is situated on two acres of

trees and wildflowers. All the accommodations are suites with whirlpool tubs. The Rose Garden Room features a fireplace and a private porch overlooking the back garden. The inn is appointed with antiques, white linens, lace and white wicker.

Rates: $85-$105. Edie Smith-Eley.

4 R. 4 PB. 2 FP. Phone available. TV in room. Beds: KQ. Continental-plus breakfast. Spa. CCs: MC VISA. Hiking, horseback riding, skiing, sightseeing.

Seen in: *Warm Welcomes Magazine.*

"A wonderful balance of luxury and at-home comfort."

CHESTERTOWN F20/B7

Brampton
RR2, Box 107
Chestertown MD 21620
(301) 778-1860

Circa 1860. Situated on 35 acres of Maryland's Eastern Shore between the Chester River and Chesapeake Bay, Brampton is a three-story brick, Greek Italianate Revival house. A massive walnut staircase winds to the second and third floor. Swiss innkeeper Danielle Hanscom selected family antiques to furnish the parlor and dining room. Upstairs the spacious rooms feature canopied beds, antiques and reproductions. A full country breakfast is served.

Rates: $85-$95. Michael & Danielle Hanscom.

6 R. 6 PB. 4 FP. Phone available. TV available. Beds: QDTC. EP. Conference room. CCs: MC VISA. Hunting, crabbing, fishing, cycling, antiquing.

Seen in: *The Washington Post.*

"A stately beauty that exudes peace and tranquility."

White Swan Tavern
231 High St
Chestertown MD 21620
(301) 778-2300

Circa 1730. During the 1978 restoration of this inn, an archeological dig made an interesting discovery. Before 1733, the site was a tannery operated by the Shoemaker of Chestertown. His one-room dwelling is now a converted guest room. After additions to the building, it became a tavern in 1793 and was described as *"situated in the center of business...with every attention given to render comfort and pleasure to such as favor it with their patronage."*

Location: Eastern shore of Maryland. Downtown historic district.

Rates: $75-$125. Mary Susan Maisel.

6 R. 6 PB. Phone available. TV available. Beds: QDTC. Full breakfast. Conference room.

"You could not find a more authentic, atmospheric sleeping room in Colonial Williamsburg," Michael W. Robbins, *New York.*

FREDERICK D13/B4

Bluebird On The Mountain
See: Cascade, MD

Spring Bank - A B&B Inn
7945 Worman's Mill Rd
Frederick MD 21701
(301) 694-0440

Circa 1880. Both Gothic Revival and Italianate architectural details are featured in this brick Victorian in the National Register. High ceilings accommodate 10-foot arched windows. The original interior shutters remain. The parlor has a marbleized slate fireplace, and there is original

hand-stenciling in the billiards room. Victorian and Chippendale furnishings have been collected from the family's antique shop. Black birch, pine, maple and poplar trees dot the inn's 10 acres.

Location: Two and a half miles north of Frederick Historic District.

❀Rates: $70-$85. Beverly & Ray Compton.

6 R. 1 PB. Phone available. Beds: DT. Continental-plus breakfast. CCs: MC VISA AE. Fishing, bicycling, canoeing, cross-country skiing.

Seen in: *The Washington Post, Los Angeles Times, Cleveland Plain Dealer.*

"From two B&B frequenters - this one wins the blue ribbon."

HAGERSTOWN C11/A4

Lewrene Farm B&B
RD 3 Box 150, Downsville Pike
Hagerstown MD 21740
(301) 582-1735

Circa 1900. This attractive white colonial farmhouse is headquarters for the Lehmans' 125 acres of sweet corn, alfalfa and hay. The Rose Retreat

Room looks out over cornfields and includes a four-poster bed and whirlpool tub. Guests may assist in gathering blue eggs from the farm's Oriental chickens, buy fresh sweet corn from the roadside stand out front or watch the peacocks strut about. A country breakfast is served.

Rates: $45-$70. Lewis & Irene Lehman.

6 R. 3 PB. Phone available. Beds: QDTC. Full breakfast. Horseback riding.

Seen in: *Hagerstown Journal, Country, Maryland Farmer.*

"Thank you so much for your lovely hospitality. We thoroughly enjoyed staying here."

HAVRE DE GRACE C20/B6

The Spencer Silver Mansion

200 S Union Ave
Havre De Grace MD 21078
(301) 939-1097

Circa 1896. This elegant granite Victorian mansion is graced with bays, gables, balconies, a turret and a gazebo veranda. The Victorian decor, with antiques and Oriental rugs, complements the house's carved-oak woodwork, fireplace mantels and parquet floors. The Concord Point Lighthouse (oldest continuously operated lighthouse in America) is only a walk away.

❀Rates: $50-$75. Jim & Carol Nemeth.
4 R. 1 PB. 1 FP. Phone available. TV available. Beds: D. Full breakfast. Boating, hiking, fishing, duck hunting. Weddings.
Seen in: *Mid-Atlantic Country.*
"We were lucky to find such a gem of a place."

NEW MARKET E14/B5

National Pike Inn

9 W Main St, PO Box 299
New Market MD 21774
(301) 865-5055

Circa 1796. This red shuttered brick Federal house is one of the few inns remaining on the National Pike, the old East West route between Bal-

timore and points west. The inn's colonial decor includes wingback chairs, Oriental rugs and four-poster beds. There's a private courtyard and fountain bordered by azalea gardens.

Rates: $60-$100. Tom & Terry Rimel.
4 R. 3 PB. 2 FP. Phone available. Beds: QD. Full breakfast. CCs: MC VISA. Tennis, golf, hiking, antiquing. Excellent dining a few steps away.
Seen in: *Mid-Atlantic Country.*
"A total joy! A relaxed, charming and romantic setting."

OXFORD J20/C6

1876 House

110 N Morris St
Oxford MD 21654
(301) 226-5496

Circa 1876. This early Victorian house has a welcoming front porch, ten-foot ceilings and wide-planked pine floors. A queen-size four-poster bed is in the master suite, which looks out over North Morris Street. A continental breakfast is served in the formal dining room.

Rates: $81-$92. Season: Closed Christmas. Eleanor & Jerry Clark.
3 R. 1 PB. Phone available. Beds: QDT. Continental-plus breakfast.

The Robert Morris Inn

On The Tred Avon, PO Box 70
Oxford MD 21654
(301) 226-5111

Circa 1710. Once the home of Robert Morris Sr., a representative of an English trading company, the house was constructed by ship carpenters with wooden-pegged paneling, ship's nails and hand-hewn beams. Bricks brought to Oxford as ballast in trading ships were used to build the fireplaces. Robert Morris Jr., a partner in a Philadelphia law firm, used his entire savings to help finance the Continental Army. He signed The Declaration of Independence, The Articles of Confederation and The United States Constitution.

Rates: $70-$160. Jay Gibson, Wendy & Ken Gibson.
33 R. 33 PB. Phone available. TV available. Beds: KQDT. FP. CCs: MC VISA AE. Golf, tennis, antiquing, sailing, goose hunting (seasonal), private beach.
Seen in: *Southern Accents, The Evening Sun.*
"Impressed!"

SAINT MICHAELS I19/C6

Kemp House Inn

412 S Talbot St, PO Box 638
Saint Michaels MD 21663
(301) 745-2243

Circa 1805. This two-story Georgian house was built by Colonel Joseph Kemp, a shipwright and one of the town forefathers. The inn is appointed in period furnishings accentuated by candlelight. Guest rooms include patchwork quilts, a collection of four-poster rope beds and old-fashioned nightshirts. There are several working fireplaces. Robert E. Lee is said to have been a guest.

❀Rates: $55-$95. Stephen & Diane Cooper.
8 R. 3 PB. Beds: QD. Continental breakfast. CCs: MC VISA. Waterskiing, hunting, boating, fishing, bicycling, crabbing. Walking distance to shops, antiques, restaurants and Chesapeake Maritime Museum, in a historic waterside village.

Parsonage Inn

210 N Talbot St
Saint Michaels MD 21663
(301) 745-5519

Circa 1883. A striking Victorian steeple rises next to the wide bay of this brick residence, once the home of Henry Clay Dodson, state senator,

pharmacist and brickyard owner. The house features brick detail in a variety of patterns and inlays, perhaps a design statement for brick customers. Porches are decorated with filigree and spindled columns. Laura Ashley linens, late Victorian-era furnishings, fireplaces and decks add to the creature comforts. Four 12-speed bikes await guests who wish to ride to Tilghman Island or to the ferry that goes to Oxford.

✻❀Rates: $72-$94+ tax. Sharon & Dave Proctor.
7 R. 7 PB. 4 FP. Phone available. TV available. Beds: KQDC. Continental-plus breakfast. Handicap access. Conference room. CCs: MC VISA. Chesapeake Bay Maritime Museum.
Seen in: *Wilmington, Delaware News Journal.*
"Striking. Extensively renovated."

SCOTLAND N19/E6

St Michael's Manor B&B

Scotland MD 20687
(301) 872-4025

Circa 1805. Twice featured on the Maryland House and Garden Tour, St. Michael's is located on Long Neck Creek, a half mile from Chesapeake

Bay. The original hand-crafted woodwork provides a handsome backdrop for the inn's antique collection. A three-acre vineyard is on the property.

Rates: $55. Joe & Nancy Dick.
3 R. 1 PB. Phone available. TV available. Beds: DT. Full breakfast. Swimming pool. Bicycles and canoe to use.
"You made our stay the most unforget-

table B&B experience we've had to date."

SHARPSBURG D11/*B4*

The Inn at Antietam

PO Box 119
Sharpsburg MD 21782
(301) 432-6601

Circa 1908. Eight acres of meadows surround this gracious white Vic-

torian framed by English walnut trees. A columned veranda provides a view of the countryside, the town with its old stone churches and the Blue Mountains. Gleaming floors accentuate romantically designed Victorian guest rooms. An inviting smokehouse features beamed ceilings, a wide brick fireplace and handsome upholstered chairs.

Rates: $75-$95. Season: Jan. 5 to Dec. 20. Betty N. Fairbourn.

5 R. 5 PB. 1 FP. Phone available. Beds: QDT. EP. Conference room. CCs: AE. Hiking, bicycling, cross-country skiing, golf, tennis. Civil War battlefield tours.

Seen in: *Country Inns.*

"A romantic setting and a most enjoyable experience."

WESTMINSTER C15/*B5*

The Winchester Country Inn

430 S Bishop St
Westminster MD 21157
(301) 876-7373 (301) 848-9343

Circa 1760. William Winchester, the founder of Westminster, built this unusual English-style house. It has a steeply slanted roof similar to those found in the Tidewater area. A central fireplace opens to both the parlor and the central hall. Colonial period furnishings prevail, with some items loaned by the local historic society. Community volunteers, historians, craftsmen and designers helped restore the inn. A non-profit agency provides some of the housekeeping and gardening staff from its developmentally disabled program.

Rates: $60-$65. Estella Williams.

5 R. 3 PB. Phone available. TV available. Beds: QDT. B&B. CCs: MC VISA. Horseback riding, museums.

Seen in: *Country Living, Evening Sun, The Towson Flier.*

"We give your inn an A+. Our stay was perfect."

MASSACHUSETTS

AMHERST F8/C4

The Wildwood Inn
See: Ware, MA

ASHFIELD D6/B3

Ashfield Inn
Main St, PO Box 129
Ashfield MA 01330
(413) 628-4571
Circa 1919. This handsome Georgian mansion was built as a summer home for Milo Belding. Enormous porches overlook spectacular perennials and

herb gardens, and there are views of the lake, hills and countryside. Nestled in the gardens are several tree swings. The romantic interior includes a reception hall and a grand stairway.
*Rates: $75-$95. Craig & Colette Christian. 8 R. 3 PB. Phone available. TV available. Beds: QDTC. Continental-plus breakfast. Gourmet meals. Conference room. CCs: MC VISA AE. Golf, skiing, hiking, swimming, tennis.
"Privacy, elegance, fabulous food, amenities (like terry robes, flowers and fruit) that made me feel pampered. Wonderful hospitality in a spectacular romantic setting."

AUBURN H12/C6

Captain Samuel Eddy House Inn
609 Oxford St S
Auburn MA 01501
(508) 832-5282
Circa 1765. This beautiful 18th-century farmhouse has been painstakingly restored by the innkeepers. The south parlor is decorated with colonial furniture, while the north parlor has modern furnishings and a TV. Innkeeper Carilyn O'Toole often cooks over the hearth and sometimes dresses in a colonial frock to present

breakfast. An herb garden and flock of geese are behind the inn.
*Rates: $60-$85. Jack & Carilyn O'Toole. 5 R. 5 PB. Phone available. TV available. Beds: KQDTC. MAP. Restaurant. Gourmet meals. Swimming pool. Game room. Conference room. CCs: MC VISA. Hiking, skating, fishing.
Seen in: *The Boston Herald, Auburn News, New York Times.*
"Like stepping back in time."

BARNSTABLE L23/E9

Ashley Manor Inn
3660 Olde Kings Hwy PO Box 856
Barnstable MA 02630
(508) 362-8044
Circa 1699. An addition to this house was built in 1750, the first of a succession of expansions through the years.

The inn, thought to be a hiding place for Tories during the Revolutionary War, features huge, open-hearth fireplaces with beehive ovens and a secret passageway connecting the upstairs and downstairs suites. Reminiscent of a gracious English country house, the inn is filled with Oriental rugs and antiques. The two acres of manicured lawns include a full regulation-size tennis court. Cherry and apple trees dot the grounds.
Location: In the heart of Cape Cod's historic district.
*Rates: $100-$165. Donald & Fay Bain. 6 R. 6 PB. 5 FP. Phone available. Beds: KQD. Full breakfast. CCs: MC VISA AE. Croquet and bicycles on the premises. New tennis court. Walk to beach village, whale watching, sportfishing, boating, golf, museums.
Seen in: *Chicago Tribune, Boston Globe, Bon Appetit, Tennis.*
"This is absolutely perfect! So many very special, lovely touches."

The Inn at Fernbrook
See: Centerville, MA

Honeysuckle Hill
See: West Barnstable, MA

Thomas Huckins House
2701 Main St, Rt 6A
Barnstable MA 02630
(508) 362-6379
Circa 1705. Merchants and shippers, the Huckins family settled in Barnstable in 1639. Thomas built this Cape half-house across from Calves

Pasture Lane — common grazing land used by the colonists. There is a 10-foot walk-in fireplace in the keeping room, original paneling and windows and authentic stenciling. American antique furnishings with canopy beds add to the gracious colonial feeling. Bouquets of fresh flowers from the inn's perennial gardens find their way to guest's bedchambers.
Location: Cape Cod.
Rates: $75-$95. Burt & Eleanor Eddy. 4 R. 4 PB. 2 FP. Phone available. TV available. Beds: QD. Full breakfast. CCs: MC VISA.
Seen in: *Early American Life.*
"Your home is even warmer and more

charming in person than the lovely pictures in Early American Life.*"*

BARNSTABLE VILLAGE L23/E9

Beechwood Inn

2839 Main St
Barnstable Village MA 02630
(508) 362-6618

Circa 1853. Beechwood is a carefully restored Queen Anne house offering period furnishings, fireplaces and ocean views. Its warmth and elegance

make it a favorite hideaway for couples looking for a peaceful return to the Victorian era. The inn is named for rare old beech trees that shade the veranda.

Location: Cape Cod's historic North Shore.
Rates: $95-$135. Anne & Bob Livermore.
6 R. 6 PB. 2 FP. Phone available. Beds: KQD. Full breakfast. CCs: MC VISA AE. Golf, beaches, whale watching, bicycles.
Seen in: *National Trust Calendar.*

"Your inn is pristine in every detail. We concluded that the innkeepers, who are most hospitable, are the best part of Beechwood."

BOSTON F18/C7

Beacon Hill B&B

27 Brimmer St
Boston MA 02108
(617) 523-7376

Circa 1869. This six-story Victorian rowhouse overlooks the Charles River in a quiet residential area of downtown Boston. Rooms are spacious and each has a fireplace. Two guest rooms and the dining room have views of the river. There's an elevator for toting luggage. The Boston Common and Freedom Trail, Quincy Market, conference hotels and the Back Bay are all within walking distance.

Rates: $90-$100. Susan Butterworth.
3 R. 3 PB. 3 FP. Phone available. TV available. Beds: QD. Full breakfast. Shopping.

"Enjoyed your lovely home, your cooking, your friendliness and the vibrant, alive decor."

Black Friar Brook Farm

See: Duxbury, MA

The Emma James House

47 Ocean St
Boston MA 02124
(617) 288-8867 (617) 282-5350

Circa 1894. This lovely old Victorian, in a neighborhood of similar houses, features a wide front porch, bay windows, balconies, stained glass, polished woodwork and a double parlor. A fireplace warms the foyer. Breakfast is self-catered but the innkeepers are on hand for advice and information. It is a five-minute walk downhill to the Ashmont Station on the Red Line.

Rates: $50-$70. Vicki & Bob Rugo, Moo Bishop & Michael Stella.
6 R. 2 PB. Phone available. TV available. Beds: QDTC. Continental-plus breakfast. Kennedy Library, downtown Boston.
Seen in: *Yankee Magazine, The Boston Globe.*

"It was everything I could ask for and more!"

Host Homes of Boston

PO Box 117, Waban Branch
Boston MA 02168
(617) 244-1308

Circa 1864. One of the host homes is a stately town house on Commonwealth Avenue in Boston's chic Back Bay area, less than one block away from the Boston Common, and a short walk to Copley Square. The house was built for the Robbins family, prominent clockmakers of the period. Since 1890, it has served as a private professional club providing cultural and intellectual programs. Overnight lodging is now offered for B&B guests as well as for members.

Location: Additional homes in Beacon Hill, Back Bay, Cambridge, Greater Boston.
Rates: $57-$125. Marcia Whittington.
7 R. 4 PB. Beds: DT. Continental breakfast. Handicap access. CCs: MC VISA AE.
Seen in: *Changing Times, USA Today.*

"Very special."

The Salem Inn

See: Salem, MA

Spray Cliff on the Ocean

See: Marblehead, MA

BREWSTER K25/E10

Isaiah Clark House

1187 Old King's Hwy
Brewster MA 02631
(508) 896-2223 (508) 896-2138

Circa 1780. This Cape-Cod-style house rambles across the lawn, shaded by a giant spruce tree brought as a seedling from Norway by Captain Clark. The original wide-board floors remain, setting off antique furnishings and canopy or four-poster beds. Fruit trees and patches of wild berries flourish on the inn's five acres. A hearty New England breakfast is served on the deck or in the old keeping room.

Rates: $68-$105. Charles Phillipe Di Cesare.
12 R. 8 PB. 5 FP. Phone in room. TV in room. Beds: KQDTC. Full breakfast. Conference room. CCs: MC VISA AE DS. Horseback riding, swimming, tennis, canoeing, fishing, biking.
Seen in: *Milwaukee Journal, Orange County Register, Houston Chronicle.*

"The room exploded with comfort and breakfast was our palates' delight!"

Old Manse Inn

1861 Main St, PO Box 839
Brewster MA 02631
(508) 896-3149

Circa 1800. This old sea captain's house is tucked behind tall trees and has a gracious mansard roof. It was built by Captain William Lewis Knowles, and served as a link in the Underground Railroad during the Civil War. The rooms are decorated with old-fashioned print wallpapers, original paintings and antiques.

Location: Cape Cod.
Rates: $65-$88. Season: March 15 - Jan. 1. Sugar & Doug Manchester.
9 R. 9 PB. Phone available. Beds: QTD. Full breakfast. Restaurant. Handicap access. CCs: MC VISA AE. Tennis, golf, swimming, bicycling, fishing, walk to beach and antique shops. Gourmet restaurant in season, cocktails, beer and wine.
Seen in: *Travel & Leisure, Boston Herald.*

"Our stays at the Old Manse Inn have always been delightful. The innkeepers are gracious, the decor charming and the dining room has a character all its own."

Old Sea Pines Inn

2553 Main St, PO Box 1026
Brewster MA 02631
(508) 896-6114

Circa 1900. This turn-of-the-century mansion on three-and-one-half acres of lawns and trees was formerly the

Sea Pines School of Charm and Personality for Young Women, established in 1907. Recently renovated, the inn displays elegant wallpapers and a grand sweeping stairway. It is located near beaches and bike paths, as well as village shops and restaurants.

Location: Cape Cod.
*Rates: $40-$90. Stephen & Michele Rowan.
21 R. 16 PB. 3 FP. Phone available. TV in room. Beds: QDT. Full breakfast. Restaurant. Handicap access. Conference

room. CCs: MC VISA AE DC CB. Beaches, tennis, golf.
Seen in: *New York Times, Boston, For Women First.*
"The loving care applied by Steve, Michele and staff is deeply appreciated."

BROOKLINE F18/C7

Host Homes of Boston
See: Boston, MA

BUCKLAND D6/B3

1797 House
Charlemont Rd
Buckland MA 01338
(413) 625-2975
Circa 1797. This house was built by Zenas Graham who married the same year and went on to have 12 children. The Graham family retained the

house well into the 1940s. At one time, it served as the Winter School for Young Ladies, run by Mary Lyon, founder of Mount Holyoke College. Features include 12-over-12 windows, four fireplaces, and a peaceful screened porch. Comfort is everywhere and very enticing after a day of sightseeing at historic Deerfield or many other local attractions.
Location: Three miles south of Mohawk Trail.
Rates: $65. Season: Jan. 15 - Oct. Janet Turley.
3 R. 3 PB. Phone available. TV available. Beds: DT. Full breakfast. Conference room. Hiking, downhill & cross-country skiing, tennis, swimming.
"The most restful nights ever spent away from home. When I become stressed I send my mind to your porch."

CAMBRIDGE F18/C7

A Cambridge House B&B Inn
2218 Massachusetts Ave
Cambridge MA 02140
(617) 491-6300 (800) 232-9989
Circa 1892. Listed in the National Register, A Cambridge House has been restored to its turn-of-the-century elegance. A remarkable carved cherry fireplace dominates the den, and some rooms have four-poster canopy beds and fireplaces. The

library is often the setting for mulled cider, wine or tea served fireside on brisk afternoons. Parking is available and the subway is four blocks away.
Location: Minutes from downtown Boston.
*Rates: $79-$165. Ellen Riley & Tony Femmino.
10 R. 1 PB. 2 FP. Phone in room. TV in room. Beds: QDT. Full breakfast. CCs: MC VISA AE. Museums.
Seen in: *Evening Magazine, Glamour Magazine, Los Angeles Times, Entrepreneur.*
"I'm afraid you spoiled us quite badly! Your home is elegant, charming and comfortable. Breakfasts were delicious and beautifully served."

CAPE COD

For Cape Cod see: Barnstable, Barnstable Village, Brewster, Centerville, Chatham, Dennis, East Orleans, East Sandwich, Eastham, Falmouth, Hyannis, North Eastham, Provincetown, Sandwich, West Barnstable, West Dennis, West Harwich, West Hyannisport, Woods Hole, Yarmouth Port.

CENTERVILLE M23/E9

Copper Beech Inn
497 Main St
Centerville MA 02632
(508) 771-5488
Circa 1830. Shaded by a massive European beech tree is this white clapboard house, in the National Register. It was built by Captain

Hillman Crosby a name long associated with boat builders and fast sailing ships. Preserved and restored, the inn is a walk away to Craigville Beach, considered one of the 10 best beaches in the United States. Summer theater and fine restaurants are also nearby.
Rates: $75-$80. Joyce & Clark Diehl.
3 R. 3 PB. Phone available. TV available. Beds: KD. Full breakfast. CCs: MC VISA AE. Bicycling, ocean beach.
Seen in: *Innsider, Cape Cod Life, Cape Cod Times, Country Magazine.*
"Everything we were looking for, clean and private, but best of all were our wonderful hosts."

The Inn at Fernbrook
481 Main St
Centerville MA 02632
(508) 775-4334
Circa 1881. Stay at this romantic Queen Anne Victorian mansion for a truly elegant experience on Cape Cod. The house boasts a massive tower and

turret, verandas and gables. Lavish gardens, originally created by Frederick Olmstead who designed Central Park in New York, include the heart-shaped Sweetheart Rose Garden and many exotic trees. A rare weeping beech shades one of the duck ponds. The house was designed over a century ago so that no two guest rooms share the same wall. Carefully selected antiques, soft wallpapers and oriental carpets are set against handsome floors of cherry, maple and oak.
*Rates: $105-$185. Brian Gallo/Sal DiFlorio.
7 R. 7 PB. 2 FP. Phone available. Beds: KQD. Full breakfast. Conference room. CCs: MC VISA AE. Swimming, deep-sea fishing, sailing, boating, horseback riding, golf, tennis, whale watching.
Seen in: *Los Angeles Times, Bon Appetit, Country Inns, Travel & Leisure, GetAways.*
"Our hosts were warm and helpful, always searching for ways to make our stay a wonderful experience."

CHATHAM L26/E10

Chatham Town House Inn
11 Library Ln
Chatham MA 02633
(508) 945-2180 (508) 945-3990 (FAX)
Circa 1881. This three-story sea captain's house was built by Daniel Webster Nickerson, a descendant of William Nickerson who came over on the *Mayflower*. Resting on two acres in the village, the inn is surrounded with charming gardens. Victorian wallpapers, hand stenciling and canopy beds are features of most

guest rooms and there are two cottages with fireplaces. Hospitality is provided by an international staff and Scandinavian hosts.
*Rates: $115-$175. Season: Closed Jan. Russell & Svea Marita Peterson.
22 R. 22 PB. 2 FP. Phone in room. TV in room. Beds: KQDC. EP. Spa. Handicap access. Swimming pool. Conference room. FAX. CCs: MC VISA AE DC CB DS. Horseback riding, water skiing, sport fishing, swimming, surf sailing. Full-service restaurant with Swedish chef.
Seen in: *Cape Cod Times, New York Times, Yankee Magazine.*

The Cranberry Inn at Chatham
359 Main St
Chatham MA 02633
(508) 945-9232 (800) 332-4667
Circa 1830. Continuously operating for over 150 years, this inn was originally called the Traveler's Lodge, then the Monomoyic after a local Indian tribe. A cranberry bog adjacent to the property inspired the current name. Recently restored, the inn is located in the heart of the historic district. It's within walking distance of the lighthouse, beaches, shops and restaurants. Guest rooms feature four-poster beds, wide planked floors and coordinated fabrics. A tap room is on the premises.
*Rates: $85-$135. Season: March - Mid Dec. Richard Morris & Peggy DeHan.
14 R. 14 PB. Phone in room. TV in room. Beds: QDT. Continental-plus breakfast. CCs: MC VISA AE. Swimming, water sports, golf, tennis (all nearby).
Seen in: *Cape Cod Chronicle, Goodtimes.*

Moses Nickerson House
364 Old Harbor Rd
Chatham MA 02633
(508) 945-5859 (800) 628-6972
Circa 1839. Framed by a white picket fence, this rambling sea captain's house has been lovingly renovated by the new innkeepers. There are wide pine floors, three staircases and windowseats here and there. Furnished in Oriental rugs and antiques, most of the rooms feature English floral wallpapers. The Emily Dickinson room is a favorite with honeymooners and boasts a lavish four-poster bed, French doors and a fireplace. A new solarium houses the breakfast room.
Rates: $70-$135. Season: Feb. 15-Dec. 20. Carl & Elsie Piccola.
7 R. 7 PB. 3 FP. Phone available. Beds: Q. Continental-plus breakfast. CCs: MC VISA AE. Horseback riding, swimming, beach, tennis, biking, golf, bird watching. Honeymoons, romantic getaways.
Seen in: *Cape Cod Life, The Discerning Traveler.*
"Thank you so much for all the special touches."

CONCORD E16/*B7*

Anderson-Wheeler Homestead
154 Fitchburg Turnpike
Concord MA 01742
(508) 369-3756
Circa 1890. When Route 117 was the main road between Boston and Fitchburg, the Lee family operated a stagecoach stop here. They provided room and board, a change of horses, and a leather and blacksmith shop. The building burned in 1890, and a Victorian house was built by Frank Wheeler, developer of rust-free asparagus. The property has remained in the family, and the veranda overlooks an extensive lawn and the Sudbury River.
*Rates: $70-$85. David & Charlotte Anderson.
5 R. 2 PB. 2 FP. Phone available. TV in room. Beds: KDTC. Continental-plus breakfast. Conference room. CCs: MC VISA AE DC CB. Bird-watching, cross-country skiing, canoeing.
Seen in: *New England Getaways, Concord Journal.*
"The five nights spent with you were the most comfortable and most congenial of the whole cross-country trip."

Colonel Roger Brown House
1694 Main St
Concord MA 01742
(508) 369-9119
Circa 1775. The oldest house in West Concord was the home of Minuteman Roger Brown who fought at the Old North Bridge. The frame for this center-chimney colonial was raised April 19, the day the battle took place. Other parts of the house were built in 1708. Next door is the Damon Mill, now developed as an office complex with a fitness club available to guests.

Rates: $65-$75. Kate Williams.
5 R. 5 PB. 1 FP. Phone in room. TV in room. Beds: QDT. Continental-plus breakfast. Spa. Sauna. Swimming pool. FAX. CCs: MC VISA AE DC. Golf, canoeing, skiing, tennis. Health club.
Seen in: *Middlesex News.*
"My boss won't stay anywhere else!" Secretary.

Hawthorne Inn
462 Lexington Rd
Concord MA 01742
(508) 369-5610
Circa 1870. The Hawthorne Inn is situated on land that once belonged to Ralph Waldo Emerson, the Alcotts and Nathaniel Hawthorne. It was here

that Bronson Alcott planted his fruit trees, made pathways to the Mill Brook, and erected his Bath House. Hawthorne purchased the land and repaired a path leading to his home with trees planted on either side. Two of these trees still stand. Across the road is Hawthorne's House, The Wayside. Next to it is the Alcott's Orchard House, and Grapevine Cottage where the Concord grape was developed. Nearby is Sleepy Hollow Cemetery where Emerson, the Alcotts, the Thoreaus, and Hawthorne were laid to rest.
*Rates: $110-$150. G. Burch & M. Mudry.
7 R. 7 PB. Phone available. Beds: TCD. Continental-plus breakfast. Cross-country skiing, swimming.
Seen in: *New York Times, Boston Globe, Yankee Magazine.*
"Surely there couldn't be a better or more valuable location for a comfortable, old-fashioned country inn."

DEERFIELD D7/*B4*

Deerfield Inn
The Street
Deerfield MA 01342
(413) 774-5587
Circa 1885. Deerfield was settled in 1670. Farmers in the area still unearth bones and ax heads from an ancient Indian massacre. Now 50 beautifully

restored colonial and Federal homes line mile-long The Street, considered by many to be the loveliest street in New England. Twelve of these houses

are museums open to the public. The inn is situated at the center of this peaceful village and is filled with antiques from historic Deerfield's remarkable collection. The village has been designated a National Historic Landmark.
Location: Middle of historic village.
Rates: $115-$125. Karl & Jane Sabo.
23 R. 23 PB. TV available. Beds: KQT. Full breakfast. Restaurant. Handicap access. Conference room. CCs: MC VISA DC. Golf, downhill & cross-country skiing, buggy rides.
Seen in: *Travel Today, Country Accents, Colonial Homes.*
"We've stayed at many New England inns, but the Deerfield Inn ranks among the best."

DENNIS L24/*E10*

Four Chimneys Inn
946 Main St, Rt 6A
Dennis MA 02638
(508) 385-6317
Circa 1881. This spacious Victorian stands across from Lake Scargo. Legend says the lake was created at the command of an Indian chief whose daughter needed a larger fishbowl for her goldfish. The village maidens dug the lake with clam shells and all the fish happily multiplied. The inn has eight-foot windows, high ceilings, a cozy library and parlor, and a gracious summer porch from which to view the "fishbowl."
Location: Cape Cod.
Rates: $45-$90. Christina Jervant & Diane Robinson.
9 R. 7 PB. Phone available. Beds: QDT. Continental-plus breakfast. Conference room. CCs: MC VISA AE DS. Bicycling, tennis, golf, fishing, swimming, theater.
Seen in: *The Littleton Independent.*

Isaiah Hall B&B Inn
152 Whig St
Dennis MA 02638
(508) 385-9928 (800) 736-0160
Circa 1857. Adjacent to the Cape's oldest cranberry bog is this Greek Revival farmhouse built by Isaiah Hall, a cooper. His brother was the

first cultivator of cranberries in America and Isaiah designed and patented the original barrel for shipping cranberries. In 1948, Dorothy Gripp, an artist, established the inn. Many examples of her artwork remain.
Location: Cape Cod.
*Rates: $48-$85. Season: Mid-March-End Oct. Marie & Dick Brophy.
11 R. 10 PB. 1 FP. Phone available. TV available. Beds: QDT. Full breakfast. Conference room. CCs: MC VISA AE. Swimming, golf, tennis, bike trails.
Seen in: *Cape Cod Life, New York Times.*

DUXBURY I21/*D8*

Black Friar Brook Farm
636 Union St
Duxbury MA 02332
(617) 834-8528
Circa 1708. Josiah Soule, grandson of pilgrim George Soule, built this saltbox house on 11 acres of farmland. Part of an original land grant of 150 acres, the house has gun-stock beams and colonial antiques. The private guest suite includes a bedroom, sitting room and dining area. The hostess runs a reservation service for other New England homestays.
Location: Close to Historic Plymouth with easy access to both Boston and Cape Cod.
Rates: $45-$55. Season: March - Nov. Ann & Walter Kopke.
2 R. 2 PB. Phone available. Beds: DT. Full breakfast. Beach.
Seen in: *Detroit Free Press.*

EAST ORLEANS K26/*E10*

The Nauset House Inn
PO Box 774
East Orleans MA 02643
(508) 255-2195
Circa 1810. Located a short distance from the water, the Nauset House is a renovated farmhouse set on three acres which include an old apple or-

chard. A Victorian conservatory was purchased from a Connecticut estate and reassembled here, then filled with wicker furnishings, Cape flowers and stained glass. Hand-stenciling, handmade quilts, antiques and more bouquets of flowers decorate the rooms. The breakfast room features a fireplace, brick floor and beamed ceiling. Afternoon tea and hors d'oeuvres are served at 5:30 p.m.
Rates: $55-$95. Season: April - Oct. Diane & Al Johnson.
14 R. 8 PB. 2 FP. Phone available. Beds: KQDT. Continental breakfast. CCs: MC VISA. Horseback riding, swimming, bicycling, hiking, whale & seal watching.
Seen in: *Country Living, Glamour, West Hartford News, Travel & Leisure.*
"The inn provided a quiet, serene, comforting atmosphere."

The Parsonage
202 Main St, PO Box 1016
East Orleans MA 02643
(508) 255-8217
Circa 1770. This 18th-century parsonage is a full Cape-style house, complete with ancient wavy glass in the windows and antique furnishings

throughout. In addition to the five old Cape Cod rooms, an efficiency and a private cottage are available. "Breakfast in a basket" is served in the courtyard or in guest rooms. Main Street, the road to Nauset Beach, is lined with the old homes of sea captains and other early settlers.
Rates: $60-$110. Chris & Lloyd Shand.
5 R. 5 PB. Phone available. Beds: QD. Continental-plus breakfast. CCs: MC VISA. Beaches, tennis, bicycling.
Seen in: *Miami Herald.*
"Your hospitality was as wonderful as your home. Your home was as beautiful as Cape Cod. Thank you!!"

Ships Knee's Inn
186 Beach Rd, PO Box 756
East Orleans MA 02643
(508) 255-1312
Circa 1817. This restored sea captain's house is located just a short walk from the ocean and Nauset Beach. Guest rooms feature beamed ceilings,

four-poster beds piled with quilts, and a special colonial color scheme. Heated cottages and efficiencies overlook Orleans Cove.
Location: One-and-a-half hours from Boston.
*Rates: $38-$98. Nancy & Carl Wideberg.
22 R. 9 PB. Phone available. Beds: KQDTC. Continental breakfast. Swimming pool & tennis on the premises.

"Warm, homey and very friendly atmosphere. Very impressed with the beamed ceilings."

EAST SANDWICH L22/E9

Wingscorton Farm Inn

11 Wing Blvd

East Sandwich MA 02537

(508) 888-0534

Circa 1757. Wingscorton is a working farm on seven acres of lawns, gardens and orchards. It adjoins a short walk to a private ocean beach. This Cape Cod manse, built by a Quaker family, is a historical landmark on what was once known as the King's Highway, the oldest historical district in the United States. All the rooms are furnished with working fireplaces (one with a secret compartment where runaway slaves hid), as well as fully restored antiques. Breakfast features fresh produce with eggs, meats and vegetables from the farm's livestock and gardens.

Location: North Side of Cape Cod, off Route 6A.

Rates: $115-$150. Dick Loring & Sheila Weyers.

7 R. 7 PB. 7 FP. Phone available. TV available. Beds: QTC. EP. Gourmet meals. Spa. CCs: MC VISA AE. Boating, fishing, whale watching.

Seen in: *The Boston Globe, The New York Times.*

"Absolutely wonderful. We will always remember the wonderful time."

EASTHAM K26/E10

Over Look Inn

3085 County Rd, PO Box 771

Eastham MA 02642

(508) 255-1886 (800) 356-1121

Circa 1869. Schooner Captain Barnabus Chipman built this three-story home for his wife. In 1920 it opened as an inn and was frequented by author and naturalist Henry Beston as he wrote "The Outermost House." Located on one-and-a-half acres of grounds, the inn is furnished with Victorian antiques and reproductions. A collection of Winston Churchill books fills the inn's library. The Aitchisons, from Edinburgh are known for their warm Scottish charm and occasional bagpipe serenades.

*Rates: $70-$90. Ian & Nan Aitchison.

10 R. 10 PB. Phone available. Beds: QDT. Full breakfast. Conference room. CCs: MC VISA AE. Afternoon tea, billiard room, library.

Seen in: *Conde Nast Traveler, Victorian Homes.*

*"A delightful experience,"*Max Nichols, *Oklahoma City Journal Record.*

Whalewalk Inn

220 Bridge Rd

Eastham MA 02642

(508) 255-0617

Circa 1839. Three acres of meadow and lawn surround the Whalewalk, originally a whaling captain's house. An old picket fence frames the elegant house and there is a widow's walk. In addition to the main house, suites are available in a separate guest house, a renovated barn and a studio cottage.

Rates: $90-$150. Season: April to Dec. 15. Carolyn & Dick Smith.

12 R. 12 PB. 3 FP. Phone available. TV available. Beds: KQDT. Full breakfast. Bike trails, ocean beaches, bay beaches, horseback riding, hiking trails, antiquing.

"Your hospitality will long be remembered."

EDGARTOWN O22/F9

The Arbor

222 Upper Main St

Edgartown MA 02539

(508) 627-8137

Circa 1890. Originally built on the adjoining island of Chappaquidick, this house was moved over to Edgartown

on a barge at the turn of the century. Located on the bicycle path, it is within walking distance from downtown and the harbor. Guests may relax in the hammock, have tea on the porch, or walk the unspoiled island beaches of Martha's Vineyard.

Location: Martha's Vineyard.

*Rates: $50-$110. Season: May - Oct. Peggy Hall.

10 R. 8 PB. Phone available. Beds: QDWT. Continental breakfast. CCs: MC. Beaches, bike trails, sailing, fishing, nature.

"Thank you so much for your wonderful hospitality! You are a superb hostess. If I ever decide to do my own B&B your example would be my guide."

Captain Dexter House of Edgartown

35 Pease's Point Way

Edgartown MA 02539

(508) 627-7289

Circa 1840. Located just three blocks from Edgartown's harbor and historic district, this black-shuttered sea merchant's house has a graceful lawn and terraced flower gardens. A gentle colonial atmosphere is enhanced by original wooden beams, exposed floor boards, working fireplaces, old-fashioned dormers, and a collection of period antiques. Luxurious canopy beds are featured.

Location: On a tree-lined residential street in downtown Edgartown.

*Rates: $65-$175. Michael Maultz.

11 R. 11 PB. 4 FP. Phone available. TV available. Beds: QD. Continental breakfast. CCs: MC VISA AE. Horseback riding, boating, tennis, golf, bird watching, bicycling, fishing, hiking.

Seen in: *Island Getaways, Vineyard Gazette.*

"It was a perfect stay!"

Chadwick Inn

67 Winter St

Edgartown MA 02539

(508) 627-4435 (508) 627-5656

Circa 1840. The winding staircase in this Greek Revival house was crafted by the carpenter who built the Edgar-

town Old Whaling Church tower. You may wish to stay in the original house with its high ceilings, fireplaces, terraces, antiques, and canopy beds, or in the newer Garden Wing. Guests enjoy the veranda, with views of the spacious lawn and blooming flower beds. Numerous shops and galleries are just down the block.

Location: Martha's Vineyard Island.

*Rates: $75-$260. Peter & Jurate Antioco.

21 R. 21 PB. 12 FP. Phone available. TV available. Beds: KQDT. Continental-plus breakfast. Handicap access. Conference room. FAX. CCs: MC VISA AE. Swimming, horseback riding, bicycling.

Seen in: *Cape Cod Life.*

"Wonderful hospitality. I hated to leave, it's such a comfortable, caring inn."

Colonial Inn of Martha's Vineyard

38 N Water St, PO Box 68

Edgartown MA 02539

(508) 627-4711

Circa 1911. The Colonial Inn is a huge sprawling affair, recently renovated, with picket fences and rose bushes here and there. Although larger than the standard bed and breakfast inn, rooms are light and airy and have air conditioning and TV. Frequent package weekends include April cycling with bikes to borrow, a Christmas gift package and Halloween face painting.

Rates: $45-$195. Season: April - Dec. 10. Linda Malcouronne.

42 R. 42 PB. Phone available. TV in room. Beds: QDTC. Continental-plus breakfast. Handicap access. Conference room. CCs: MC VISA AE. Horseback riding, water

sports, fishing, golf, tennis, health club. Seen in: *New England Travel.*
"Everyone very friendly and very efficient."

Edgartown Inn
56 N Water
Edgartown MA 02539
(508) 627-4794

Circa 1798. The Edgartown Inn was originally built as a home for whaling Captain Thomas Worth. (Fort Worth, Texas, was later named for his son.) The house was converted to an inn around 1820, when Daniel Webster was a guest. The innkeeper admonished his children not to "sop the platter" in Webster's presence, that is, not to dip their bread into the gravy. To the delight of the children, Webster himself "sopped the platter." Later, Nathaniel Hawthorne stayed here and proposed to the innkeeper's daughter Eliza Gibbs (who turned him down).
Location: Martha's Vineyard.
Rates: $55-$145. Season: April - Nov. 1. Liliane & Earle Radford.
21 R. 13 PB. Phone available. TV available. Beds: KDT. Full breakfast. Tennis, golf, sailing.
Seen in: *Vineyard Gazette.*
"Breakfast in the garden is unbeatable and your staff couldn't be friendlier."

Point Way Inn
104 Main St, PO Box 128
Edgartown MA 02539
(508) 627-8633 (508) 627-8579

Circa 1840. The reception area of Point Way Inn is papered with navigational charts from a 4,000-mile cruise the

innkeepers made with their two daughters. After the voyage, they discovered this old sea captain's house. They completely renovated it, filling it with New England antiques, period wallpapers, and canopied beds. There are working fireplaces and French doors opening onto private balconies.
Location: Martha's Vineyard.
*Rates: $75-$210. Ben & Linda Smith.
15 R. 15 PB. Phone available. TV available. Beds: KQDTC. Continental-plus breakfast. Conference room. CCs: MC VISA. Croquet, golf, horseback riding, bicycling. Complimentary car available.
Seen in: *Boston Herald American.*
"One of the most pleasant old New England inns around," The Boston Monthly.

ESSEX C20/B8

George Fuller House
148 Main St (Rte 133)
Essex MA 01929
(508) 768-7766

Circa 1830. This three-story Federal-style home is situated on a lawn that reaches to the salt marsh adjoining the Essex River. Original Indian shutters and Queen Anne baseboards remain. All the guest accommodations boast Boston rockers, and some feature canopy beds and fireplaces. For a view of the water, ask for the Andrews Suite. Belgian waffles and cranberry muffins are a house specialty. Your host offers sailing lessons on the Essex River aboard his 30-foot sailboat, the "Glass Jewel." Many of the town's 50 antique shops are within walking distance of the inn.
Rates: $70-$98. Cindy & Bob Cameron.
5 R. 5 PB. 2 Fireplaces. Phone available. TV in room. Beds: KQD. Full breakfast. CCs: MC VISA AE. Seen in: Gloucester Times.
"Thank you for the wonderful time we had at your place. We give you a 5-star rating!"

FAIRHAVEN M19/E8

Edgewater B&B
2 Oxford St
Fairhaven MA 02719
(508) 997-5512

Circa 1760. On the historic Moby Dick Trail, Edgewater overlooks the harbor from the grassy slopes of Poverty

Point. The inn is in the charming, rambling, eclectic-style of the area. Its lawns and porches provide water views. Across the harbor in New Bedford, is Herman Melville's "dearest place in all New England". There, visitors immerse themselves in the history and lore of whaling. Near the inn is the Gothic Revival-style Unitarian Church with stained glass by Tiffany.
*Rates: $45-$65. Kathy Reed.
5 R. 5 PB. Phone available. TV in room. Beds: KQDT. Continental breakfast. CCs: MC VISA AE. Beach, tennis, golf, factory outlet shopping. Seen in: *The Standard Times, Fairhaven Advocate.*

FALMOUTH M21/F9

Captain Tom Lawrence House
75 Locust St
Falmouth MA 02540
(508) 540-1445

Circa 1861. After completing five whaling trips around the world, each four years in length, Captain Lawrence retired at 40 and built this

house. There is a Steinway piano here now, and elegantly furnished guest rooms, some with canopied beds. The house is near the beach, bikeway, ferries and train station. Freshly ground organic grain is used to make Belgian waffles with warm strawberry sauce, crepes Gisela and pancakes. German is spoken here.
Location: Cape Cod.
❀Rates: $65-$95. Barbara Sabo-Feller.
6 R. 6 PB. Phone available. Beds: KQT. Full breakfast. CCs: MC VISA. Golf, tennis, bicycling. Seen in: *Country Inns, Honda Acura Magazine.*
"This is our first B&B experience. Better than some of the 4-star hotels!! We loved it here."

The Marlborough
See: Woods Hole, MA

Mostly Hall B&B Inn
27 Main St
Falmouth MA 02540
(508) 548-3786

Circa 1849. Albert Nye built this Southern plantation house with wide verandas and a cupola to observe shipping in Vineyard Sound. It was a

wedding gift for his New Orleans bride. Because of the seemingly endless halls on every floor (some 30 feet

long) it was whimsically called Mostly Hall. All rooms have queen-size canopy beds.
Location: In the historic district across from the village green.
Rates: $75-$105. Season: Feb. 15-Dec. 31. Caroline & Jim Lloyd.
6 R. 6 PB. Phone available. TV available. Beds: Q. Full breakfast. Bicycling, tennis, golf, swimming, boating, theater.
Seen in: *Bon Appetit.*
"Of all the inns we stayed at during our trip, we enjoyed Mostly Hall the most. Imagine, Southern hospitality on Cape Cod!!"

Palmer House Inn

81 Palmer Ave
Falmouth MA 02540
(508) 548-1230

Circa 1901. It's just a short walk to the village common from this turn-of-the-century Victorian. The original stained-glass windows and rich

woodwork are typical of the gracious homes in the historic district of Falmouth.
Rates: $65-$110. Season: Feb. 1 to Dec 31. Ken & Joanne Baker.
8 R. 8 PB. 1 FP. Phone available. TV available. Beds: QDT. Full breakfast. Gourmet meals. CCs: MC VISA AE. Horseback riding, water sports, tennis, golf, bicycling, beaches. Honeymoon packages, mystery weekends.
Seen in: *Country Inns.*
"Exactly what a New England inn should be!"

Peacock's "Inn on the Sound"

313 Grand Ave, PO Box 201
Falmouth MA 02541
(508) 457-9666

Circa 1880. Located in Falmouth Heights on a bluff overlooking the Vineyard Sound, this inn is decorated in country cottage comfort. Guests may relax in the common area by a huge stone fireplace and enjoy a view of the ocean. The front porch also overlooks the ocean. Guest rooms feature fireplaces, hardwood floors, ocean views, comforters and baskets of flowers.
Rates: $50-$98. Phillis & Bud Peacock.
10 R. 10 PB. 2 FP. Phone available. TV available. Beds: Q. B&B. CCs: MC VISA. Swimming, wind surfing, golf, tennis, biking, museums. Honeymoon special.
Seen in: *Falmouth Enterprise.*
"Our stay was enhanced by your warm hospitality and your wonderfully delicious breakfasts."

Village Green Inn

40 W Main St
Falmouth MA 02540
(508) 548-5621

Circa 1804. The inn was originally built in the Federal style for Braddock Dimmick, son of Revolutionary War General Joseph Dimmick. Later, cran-

berry king John Crocker, moved the house onto a granite slab foundation, remodeling it in the Victorian style. There are inlaid floors, large porches and gingerbread trim.
Location: Falmouth's historic village green.
Rates: $70-$100. Linda & Don Long.
5 R. 5 PB. 5 FP. Phone available. TV available. Beds: QT. Full breakfast. CCs: MC VISA AE. Bicycling, beach, boating, sailing, fishing, water skiing, tennis, horses, golf, swimming. Seen in: *Country Inns.*
"Like we've always said, it's the innkeepers that make the inn!"

GREAT BARRINGTON G2/C2

Round Hill Farm

17 Round Hill Rd
Great Barrington MA 01230
(413) 528-3366

Circa 1907. On 300 acres of rolling meadows, this hilltop inn offers panoramic views of the Berkshire Hills. An 1850s dairy barn hayloft has

been transformed into two handsome suites with cathedral ceilings and antiques. Guest rooms in the farmhouse with its wraparound porches feature private entrances. This bed and breakfast inn caters exclusively to non-smokers.
*Rates: $65-$140. Dr. & Mrs. Thomas J. Whitfield.
8 R. 3 PB. Phone in room. Beds: QDT. B&B. CCs: MC VISA AE.
Seen in: *Berkshire Eagle, Boston Globe.*

Seekonk Pines Inn

142 Seekonk Cross Rd
Great Barrington MA 01230
(413) 528-4192

Circa 1832. Known as the Crippen Farm from 1835-1879, Seekonk Pines Inn now includes both the original farmhouse and a Dutch Colonial

wing. Green lawns, gardens and meadows surround the inn. The name *Seekonk* was the local Indian name for the Canadian geese which migrate through this part of the Berkshires. The inn is an easy drive to Tanglewood.
Location: Near Tanglewood.
Rates: $60-$87. Linda & Chris Best.
6 R. 4 PB. 1 FP. Phone available. TV available. Beds: QTDC. Full breakfast. Swimming pool. CCs: MC VISA. Cross-country & downhill skiing, theater.
Seen in: *Los Angeles Times, The Boston Sunday Globe.*
"Of all the B&Bs we trekked through, yours was our first and most memorable!"

Windflower Inn

Egremont Star Rt, Box 25 Rt 23
Great Barrington MA 01230
(413) 528-2720

Circa 1850. This country manor is situated on 10 acres shaded by giant oaks and maples. Early American and English antiques fill the spacious guest rooms. There is a piano room with shelves of books, and a clock collection is featured throughout. The inn's dinners have received excellent reviews and feature herbs, vegetables and berries from the garden. Guests may cross the street for tennis and golf at the country club.
Rates: $160-$190.MAP Barbara & Gerald Liebert, Claudia & John Ryan.
13 R. 13 PB. 6 FP. Phone available. TV in room. Beds: KQDTC. Full breakfast. Restaurant. Gourmet meals. Swimming pool. Downhill & cross-country skiing, museums, antique shops.
Seen in: *The Los Angeles Times, Boulevard Magazine.*
"Every creative comfort imaginable, great for heart, soul and stomach."

HOLYOKE G7/C4

Yankee Pedlar Inn

1866 Northampton St
Holyoke MA 01040
(413) 532-9494

Circa 1875. Five buildings comprise this Connecticut River Valley inn. There is a tavern and dining room decorated with brass lamps, Blue

Onion china, copper pieces and Currier & Ives prints. The kitchen has no doors, an invitation to guests to visit and watch their dinner being prepared. All the rooms are decorated in an Early American style and some include canopy beds.

*Rates: $58-$80. The Banks family.
47 R. 47 PB. Phone in room. TV in room. Beds: KQDTC. EP. Conference room. CCs: MC VISA DC. Ten minutes to skiing Mt. Tom.

HYANNIS L24/E9

The Inn at Fernbrook

See: Centerville, MA

Palmer House Inn

See: Falmouth, MA

The Inn on Sea Street

358 Sea St
Hyannis MA 02601
(508) 775-8030

Circa 1849. This elegant two-story Victorian inn is listed on the town's register of historic houses. Its charms include colonial portraits, fine Persian rugs and a grand curved staircase. Furnishings in the guest rooms include four-poster beds with lace canopies. A former sun room has been transformed into a guest room with its own entrance. Guests may enjoy home-baked breads and muffins with their breakfasts on the antique tables covered with lace cloths and set with sterling silver, crystal and flowers from the garden.

Rates: $55-$85. Season: April to November. Lois M. Nelson/J.B. Whitehead.
6 R. 3 PB. Phone available. Beds: QDT. Full breakfast. CCs: MC VISA AE. Water sports, golf, bicycling, tennis.
Seen in: *The Journal.*

"A lot of people really don't know how much they are missing, until they visit you."

The Whalewalk Inn

See: Eastham, MA

LENOX F2/C2

Blantyre

Rt 20
Lenox MA 01240
(413) 637-3556 (413)298-3806 winter

Circa 1900. Situated on manicured lawns near Tanglewood, this Tudor manor is entered through a massive portico. Grandly-sized rooms include

the Great Hall and an elegantly paneled dining room. Breakfast is graciously served in the conservatory. Formal grounds offer four tennis courts, two championship croquet courts, a pool and carriage house.

*Rates: $150-$500. Season: May - Nov. Roderick Anderson.
23 R. 23 PB. 7 FP. Phone in room. TV in room. Beds: KQDT. Continental-plus breakfast. Restaurant. Gourmet meals. Spa. Sauna. Swimming pool. Conference room. FAX. CCs: MC VISA AE DC CB DS. Riding.
Seen in: *The Hideaway Report.*

"There was not a single aspect of our stay with you that was not worked out to total perfection."

Brook Farm Inn

15 Hawthorne St
Lenox MA 01240
(413) 637-3013

Circa 1890. Brook Farm Inn is named after the original Brook Farm, a literary commune that sought to combine thinker and worker through a society of intelligent, cultivated members. In keeping with that theme, this gracious Victorian inn offers poetry and writing seminars and has a 650-volume poetry library. Canopy beds and Mozart tend to the spirit.

Rates: $55-$145. Bob & Betty Jacob.
12 R. 12 PB. 5 FP. Phone available. Beds: QTF. Full breakfast. Swimming pool. CCs: MC VISA. Hiking, swimming.
Seen in: *Berkshire Eagle.*

"We loved everything about your inn, especially the friendliness and warmth of both of you. The only bad thing about your inn is leaving it!"

East Country Berry Farm

830 East St
Lenox MA 01240
(413) 442-2057

Circa 1798. At the time of the French and Indian War, this land was given to the widow and children of Captain

Stevens. Later, the farm was owned by the Sears family for approximately 150 years. Now, two historic, restored farmhouses combine to create the inn which is located on 23 acres of lawn, fields, trees and flowers.

*Rates: $55-$145. Rita F. Miller.
6 R. 4 PB. Beds: KQTC. Continental-plus breakfast. Downhill & cross-country skiing, horseback riding, golf & tennis nearby. Ten minutes to Tanglewood, summer music and theater festivals.
Seen in: *Boston Globe.*

"You have all the cultural advantages and all the country setting."

The Gables Inn

103 Walker St, Rt 183
Lenox MA 01240
(413) 637-3416

Circa 1885. At one time, this was the home of Pulitzer Prize-winning novelist Edith Wharton. The Queen Anne-style Berkshire cottage features a handsome eight-sided library and Mrs. Wharton's own four-poster bed. An unusual indoor swimming pool with spa is available in warm weather. The inn also features tennis courts.

Location: Within walking distance to Tanglewood, summer home of the Boston Symphony Orchestra.
Rates: $60-$140. Mary & Frank Newton.
14 R. 14 PB. 5 FP. Phone available. TV available. Beds: QDT. Continental-plus breakfast. Restaurant. Spa. CCs: MC VISA. Skiing, hiking, golf.
Seen in: *P.M. Magazine, New York Times.*

"You made us feel like old friends and that good feeling enhanced our pleasure. In essence it was the best part of our trip."

Garden Gables Inn

141 Main St
Lenox MA 01240
(413) 637-0193

Circa 1770. Several distinctive gables adorn this home set on five wooded acres. Deer occasionally wander into the garden to help themselves to fallen apples. Breakfast is served in the dining room which overlooks tall maples, flower gardens and fruit

trees. The swimming pool was the first built in the county, and is still the longest.
*Rates: $60-$140. Mario & Lynn Mekinda.
11 R. 11 PB. Phone available. Beds: KQDT. Full breakfast. Spa. Skiing, hiking, tennis, golf, horseback riding.
Seen in: *Berkshire Eagle.*
"Charming and thoughtful hospitality. You restored a portion of my sanity and I'm very grateful."

Underledge Inn
76 Cliffwood St
Lenox MA 01240
(413) 637-0236
Circa 1876. Drive along Cliffwood Street under an archway of greenery, then up Underledge's winding drive to a peaceful setting overlooking the

Berkshire Hills. The inn sits resplendently atop four acres, providing rooms with sunset views. In the foyer you'll find an exquisite oak staircase and floor-to-ceiling oak fireplace. A solarium is the setting for breakfast. Just down the street are quaint shops and fine restaurants.
Rates: $75-$160. Marcie & Cheryl Lanoue.
9 R. 9 PB. Phone available. TV available. Beds: KQT. Continental breakfast. CCs: VISA. Golf, tennis, swimming.
"We were received like a guest in a luxurious private house. We now think of Underledge as our summer home."

Village Inn
16 Church St
Lenox MA 01240
(413) 637-0020
Circa 1771. Four years after the Whitlocks built this Federal-style house they converted it and two adjoining barns for lodging. Since 1775, it has operated as an inn. Recently renovated, there are stenciled wallpapers, maple floors and four-poster canopied beds. Rates do not include breakfast. An afternoon tea including scones and clotted cream, is

available from $5.50.
Location: In the heart of the Berkshires.
*Rates: $40-$140. Clifford Rudisill & Ray Wilson.
29 R. 27 PB. 5 FP. Phone available. TV available. Beds: KQDT. MAP. Restaurant. Gourmet meals. Spa. Handicap access. Game room. Conference room. CCs: MC VISA AE DC CB. Hiking, cross-country & downhill skiing, tennis, golf, horseback riding, fishing, boating.
Seen in: *The London Independent.*
"Kathy and I stayed at your beautiful inn in early October. It was the highlight of our trip to New England."

Walker House
74 Walker St
Lenox MA 01240
(413) 637-1271
Circa 1804. This beautiful Federal-style house sits in the center of the village on three acres of graceful woods

and restored gardens. Guest rooms have fireplaces and private baths. Each is named for a favorite composer such as Beethoven, Mozart, or Handel. The innkeepers' musical backgrounds include associations with the San Francisco Opera, the New York City Opera, and the Los Angeles Philharmonic. Walker House concerts are scheduled from time to time.
Location: Route 183 & 7A.
Rates: $50-$140. Richard & Peggy Houdek.
8 R. 8 PB. Phone available. TV available. Beds: KQT. Continental-plus breakfast. Handicap access. Conference room. Bicycles, croquet, badminton, skiing, hiking.
Seen in: *Boston Globe, PBS, Los Angeles Times.*
"We had a grand time staying with fellow music and opera lovers! Breakfasts were lovely."

Whistler's Inn
5 Greenwood St
Lenox MA 01240
(413) 637-0975 (413) 637-2190
Circa 1820. Whistler's Inn is an English Tudor home surrounded by eight acres of woodland and gardens. Inside, elegance is abundant. In the impressive Louis XVI music room you'll find a Steinway piano, chandeliers, and gilt palace furniture. There is an English library with chintz-covered sofas, hundreds of volumes of books, and a fireplace of black marble. Here, guests have sherry or tea and perhaps engage in conversation with their well-traveled hosts, both authors. A baronial dining room features a Baroque candelabrum.
*Rates: $80-$180. Richard & Joan Mears.
11 R. 11 PB. 8 FP. Phone available. Beds: KQDTC. Continental-plus breakfast. Conference room. CCs: MC VISA AE. Skiing, hiking, horseback riding 100 yards away.
Seen in: *The Berkshire Book.*

LYNN E19/*B8*

Caron House
142 Ocean St
Lynn MA 01902
(617) 599-4470 (800) 666-3076
Circa 1911. This 22-room Georgian house was built for shoe manufacturer P.J. Harney-Lynn. The Charles Pinkham family (son of Lydia Pinkham - health tonic producer) later purchased it. Many of the original fixtures and wall coverings remain. There are several views of the ocean from the house, but the porch is the most popular spot for sea gazing. Breakfast is brought to your room, the dining room or porch.
*Rates: $80. Sandra & Jerry Caron.
5 R. 4 PB. Phone in room. TV in room. Beds: DT. Continental-plus breakfast. Conference room. FAX. CCs: MC VISA AE. Swimming, jogging, biking.
"The room was spectacular and breakfast was served beautifully."

MARBLEHEAD D20/*B8*

Harbor Light Inn
58 Washington St
Marblehead MA 01945
(617) 631-2186
Circa 1712. This handsomely restored Federal home has been filled with antique mahogany furnishings, Oriental

carpets and expertly framed etchings to enhance its 18th-century architecture. Chandeliers and brasswork add to the decor. There are two suites with

their own spas. A roof-top walk provides a view of the Marblehead light and the harbor. Sam, an enormous marmalade colored cat, is the inn's mascot.
Rates: $75-$175. Marie Trott.
12 R. 12 PB. 6 FP. Phone in room. TV in room. Continental breakfast. Spa.
Seen in: *Los Angeles Times, New England Get Aways.*
"This is fabulous. Beautifully decorated and delightful in every way. One of the finest places I have visited."

Spray Cliff on the Ocean

25 Spray Ave
Marblehead MA 01945
(508) 741-0680 (800) 446-2995

Circa 1910. Panoramic views stretch out in grand proportions from this English Tudor mansion set high above the Atlantic. The inn provides a spacious and elegant atmosphere inside.

The grounds of the inn include a brick terrace surrounded by lush flower gardens where eider ducks, black cormorants and seagulls abound.
Location: Fifteen miles north of Boston.
*Rates: $95-$200. Richard & Diane Pabich.
6 R. 6 PB. 3 FP. Phone available. Beds: KQD. Continental-plus breakfast. CCs: MC VISA DC. Ocean views.
"I prefer this atmosphere to a modern motel. It's more relaxed and love is everywhere!"

MARTHA'S VINEYARD 021/F9

Captain Dexter House of Vineyard Haven

100 Main St, PO Box 2457
Martha's Vineyard MA 02568
(508) 693-6564

Circa 1843. Captain Dexter House was the home of sea captain Rodolphus Dexter. Authentic 18th-century antiques, early-American oil paintings and oriental rugs are among the inn's appointments. There are Count Rumford fireplaces and hand-stenciled walls in several rooms. Located on a street of fine historic homes, the inn is a short stroll to the beach.
Location: Martha's Vineyard.
*Rates: $65-$160. Alisa Lengel.
8 R. 8 PB. 2 FP. Phone available. TV available. Beds: QD. Continental breakfast. Conference room. CCs: MC VISA AE.

Horseback riding, wind surfing, bicycling, tennis, boating, golf.
Seen in: *Martha's Vineyard Times.*
"The house is sensational. Your hospitality was all one could expect. You've made us permanent bed and breakfast fans."

Thorncroft Inn

278 Main St, PO Box 1022
Martha's Vineyard MA 02568
(508) 693-3333

Circa 1918. The Thorncroft Estate is a classic craftsman bungalow with a dominant roof and neo-colonial details. It was built by Chicago grain merchant John Herbert Ware as the guest house of a large oceanfront estate.

Guests experience an authentic turn-of-the-century ambience with canopied beds, walnut Victorian suites, and balconies, situated on three and one-half acres of lawns and woodlands. The inn received AAA 4 diamond rating.
Location: Martha's Vineyard Island.
*Rates: $105-$225. Karl & Lynn Buder.
19 R. 19 PB. 9 FP. Phone in room. TV available. Beds: QD. B&B. Gourmet meals. Spa. FAX. CCs: MC VISA AE. Beaches, bicycles. Now serving dinner, full menu.
Seen in: *Cape Cod Life, New England Travel, Glamour Magazine.*
"It's the type of place where we find ourselves falling in love all over again."

NANTUCKET P25/G10

The Carlisle House Inn

26 N Water St
Nantucket MA 02554
(508) 228-0720

Circa 1765. For over 100 years, the Carlisle House has served as a notable Nantucket lodging establishment. Three floors of picture-perfect rooms provide accommodations from the simple to the deluxe. Hand stenciling, polished wide-board floors, handsome color schemes and carpets fill each room. Special candelight dinners are

occasionally served at a harvest table in the kitchen. The ferry is a five-minute walk.
Rates: $65-$135. Peter & Suzanne Conway.
14 R. 10 PB. 4 FP. Phone available. TV available. Beds: QDT. B&B. CCs: AE. Swimming, tennis, golf, fishing.
Seen in: *Cape Cod Life, Boston Globe, Los Angeles Times.*

Century House

10 Cliff Rd, PO Box 603
Nantucket MA 02554
(508) 228-0530

Circa 1833. Captain Calder built this Federal-style house and supplemented his income by taking in guests when the whaling industry slowed down.

This is the oldest continually operating inn on the island. It is surrounded by other large homes on a knoll in the historic district. Museums, beaches and restaurants are a short walk away. The inn's motto for the last 100 years has been, "An inn of distinction on an island of charm." Ask about the inn's secluded rose-covered cottage.
*Rates: $75-$145. Jean Heron & Gerry Connick.
14 R. 12 PB. Phone available. Beds: KQDTW. Continental-plus breakfast. Surfing, wind surfing, sandcastle building, biking.
Seen in: *Palm Beach Daily News.*
"Thanks so much for the warmth hospitality. Century House is beautiful!"

Cobblestone Inn

5 Ash St
Nantucket MA 02554
(508) 228-1987

Circa 1725. Located on a cobbled side street, the Cobblestone Inn boasts four fireplaces, wide floorboards, curved corner support posts from the frame of a ship and an airy sunporch with white wicker furniture. Guest rooms have period decorations; some have fireplaces and canopy beds. A third-

floor room offers a good view of the boats sailing in the harbor.
*Rates: $50-$130. Robin & Keith Yankow.
5 R. 5 PB. 2 FP. Phone available. TV available. Beds: KQTC. Continental-plus breakfast. FAX. Biking, water sports, beaches, tennis, golf. Honeymoons, reunions, anniversaries.
Seen in: *Yankee Magazine.*
"Your warmth and hospitality made our stay all the more pleasureful!"

Corner House
49 Centre St, PO Box 1828
Nantucket Island MA 02554
(508) 228-1530

Circa 1723. The Corner House is a charming 18th-century inn. Architectural details such as the original pine floors, paneling and fireplaces have

been preserved. A screened porch overlooks the English perennial garden, where guests often take afternoon tea. Many of the romantically appointed bed chambers feature canopy beds.
*Rates: $55-$130. Season: Feb. 15-Jan. 3. Sandy & John Knox-Johnston.
16 R. 16 PB. 3 FP. Phone available. TV available. Beds: KQDT. Continental-plus breakfast. Gourmet meals. Conference room. CCs: MC VISA.
Seen in: *Detroit Free Press, The Atlanta Journal, Newsday.*
"The most beautiful place we've ever been to and the most comfortable!!"

The Folger Hotel & Cottages
Easton St
Nantucket MA 02554
(508) 228-0313 (800) FOL-GERI

Circa 1891. This large Victorian hotel was built for turn-of-the-century vacationers who usually stayed a month at a time and brought the whole family. Its weathered, brown-shingled exterior is brightened with white trim, balustraded porches, white lawn furniture and a rose-covered picket fence. Several cottages are available and a restaurant adjoins the hotel.
*Rates: $103. Season: June - Oct. 12. Bob & Barb Bowman.
60 R. 40 PB. Phone in room. TV available. Beds: KQDTC. Full breakfast. Restaurant. CCs: MC VISA AE DC DS. Horseback riding, sailing, water sports, tennis, bicycling.
Seen in: *Boston Globe.*
"A busy and fun hotel."

Four Chimneys
38 Orange St
Nantucket Island MA 02554
(508) 228-1912

Circa 1855. The Four Chimneys is located on famous Orange Street where 126 sea captains built mansions. Cap-

tain Frederick Gardner built this Greek Revival, one of the largest houses on Nantucket Island. The Publick Room is a double parlor with twin fireplaces. Porches stretch across three levels of the house providing views of the harbor and beyond.
Rates: $98-$155. Season: April - Dec. Bernadette Mannix.
10 R. 10 PB. 5 FP. Phone available. TV available. Beds: Q. Continental-plus breakfast. Conference room. FAX. CCs: MC VISA AE. Golf, boating, fishing, swimming, tennis.
Seen in: *Country Home, Gourmet.*

Jared Coffin House
29 Broad St
Nantucket MA 02554
(508) 228-2400

Circa 1845. Jared Coffin was one of the island's wealthiest shipowners and the first to build a three-story mansion. The house's brick walls and

slate roof resisted the Great Fire of 1846 and, in 1847, it was purchased by the Nantucket Steamship Company for use as a hotel. Additions were made and a century later, the Nantucket Historical Trust purchased and restored the house. Today, the inn consists of five historic houses and a 1964 building. The oldest is the Swain House.
*Rates: $100-$175. Phil and Peg Read.
60 R. 60 PB. Phone in room. TV in room. Beds: QDT. EP. Restaurant. Gourmet meals. Conference room. FAX. CCs: MC VISA AE DC CB. Swimming, sailing, tennis, golf, charter fishing nearby.
Seen in: *Coast & Country.*
"The dining was superb, the atmosphere was gracious and the rooms were charming and spotless."

Quaker House
5 Chestnut St
Nantucket MA 02554
(508) 228-0400

Circa 1847. The recently renovated Quaker House is situated in the Nantucket Historic District on a quiet side street once known as Petticoat Lane because during the whaling era women operated most of the businesses here. Guest rooms are furnished with Oriental rugs and period antiques that include brass, iron and carved wood. Its restaurant is recommended for reasonable rates and outstanding breakfasts.
Rates: $75-$110. Season: May - September. Caroline & Bob Taylor.
9 R. 9 PB. Phone available. Beds: Q. EP. Restaurant. CCs: MC VISA. Beaches, sailing, surfing, fishing, tennis, golf, whale watching.
Seen in: *Boston Magazine.*
"From two Quakers, it was enlightening and grand."

Stumble Inne
109 Orange St
Nantucket MA 02554
(508) 228-4482

Circa 1704. This Nantucket Island inn is appointed with fine antiques. Six of the inn's rooms are across the street from the Stumble Inne at the Starbuck House, an early 19th-century Nantucket "half-house." Rooms feature wide pine floors and antique beds with handstitched quilts.
Rates: $45-$115. Mary Kay & Mal Condon.
13 R. 11 PB. Phone available. TV in room. Beds: QDC. Continental-plus breakfast. CCs: MC VISA AE. Bicycling, sailing, fishing, tennis.
Seen in: *Innsider.*
"We realize much of our happiness was due to the warm hospitality that was a part of every day."

The Woodbox Inn
29 Fair St
Nantucket MA 02554
(508) 228-0587 (407) 471-1999 winter

Circa 1709. Nantucket's oldest inn was built by Captain Bunker. In 1711, the Captain constructed an adjoining house. Eventually the two houses were made into one by cutting into

the sides of both. Guest rooms are furnished with period antiques. The inn's gourmet dining room features an Early American atmosphere with low-beamed ceilings and pine-paneled walls.
Rates: $110-$180. Season: June - Mid Oct. Dexter Tutein.
9 R. 9 PB. 6 FP. Phone available. Beds: KQDT. EP. Restaurant. Handicap access. Conference room. Swimming, tennis, bicycling.
Seen in: *Wharton Alumni Magazine.*
"Best breakfast on the island," Yesterday's Island.

NEW BEDFORD M19/*E8*

Durant Sail Loft Inn
1 Merrill's Wharf
New Bedford MA 02740
(508) 999-2700

Circa 1848. This massive granite block structure, once the Bourne Counting House, was owned by whaling mer-

chant Jonathan Bourne. Located on the waterfront at Merrills Wharf, it offers an authentic Portugese/Spanish cafe, and a port-side restaurant serving continental and Northern Italian cuisine.
*Rates: $58-$88. Michael DeLacey.
18 R. 18 PB. Phone in room. TV in room. Beds: KQTC. Restaurant. Conference room. CCs: MC VISA AE. Beach, museums.
Seen in: *The Standard-Times, Money.*
"We had always assumed inns lacked privacy and were too expensive. What a wonderful surprise!"

Edgewater B&B
See: Fairhaven, MA

Salt Marsh Farm
See: South Dartmouth, MA

NEWBURYPORT B19/*A8*

Garrison Inn
On Brown Square
Newburyport MA 01950
(617) 465-0910 (617) 327-6929

Circa 1809. This recently renovated four-story townhouse is located near Newburyport's restored downtown and waterfront areas. Originally built as a residence, the house served as a doctor's office, boarding house, and embroidery business. At the turn of the century it became an inn. Exposed brick walls, hewn beams and furnishings that reflect the colonial era add character to the guest rooms. There is elevator service to all levels. The Moses Brown Pub boasts vaulted brick arches, a wood-burning stove and granite walls.
*Rates: $75-$135. Roy Hamond.
24 R. 24 PB. 12 FP. Phone in room. TV in room. Beds: KQDTC. Restaurant. Handicap access. Conference room. CCs: MC VISA AE DC CB. Beaches, golf, skiing, boating, fishing.
Seen in: *Yankee Travel Guide, New England Getaways.*

Windsor House
38 Federal St
Newburyport MA 01950
(508) 462-3778

Circa 1786. This brick Federal-style mansion was designed as a combination home and chandelry (a ship's outfitter and brokerage company for cargo). The basement served as a warehouse and the Merchant Suite was once the main office. This suite features a 14-foot ceiling with hand-hewn, beveled beams. It is appointed with a wing-back chair from the Old Boston Opera, a sleigh bed and an antique hope chest and has a private entrance. The English innkeeper serves a hearty English country breakfast and a full English tea in the afternoon. Children are welcome.
Rates: $85-$115. Judith Alison & John Royston Harris.
6 R. 3 PB. Phone available. TV available. Beds: KQDTC. Full breakfast. Gourmet meals. CCs: MC VISA. Swimming, hiking, bird watching, whale watching.
Seen in: *The New York Times.*
"You will find what you look for and be met by the unexpected too. A good time!"

NEWTON F17/*C7*

Host Homes of Boston
See: Boston, MA

NORTH EASTHAM J26/*D10*

The Penny House
Rt 6, PO Box 238
North Eastham MA 02651
(508) 255-6632

Circa 1751. Captain Isaiah Horton built this house with a shipbuilder's bow roof. Traditional wide-planked floors and 200-year-old beams buttress the ceiling of the public room. The Captain's Quarters, the largest guest room with its own fireplace, bears the motto: *Coil up your ropes and anchor here, Til better weather doth appear.*
Location: One mile from National seashore. Route 6, Cape Cod.
*Rates: $65-$100. Bill & Margaret Keith.
12 R. 7 PB. Phone available. Beds: KQT. Full breakfast. CCs: MC VISA AE. Bicycling, fishing.
"Enjoyed my stay tremendously. My mouth waters thinking of your delicious breakfast."

OAK BLUFFS N22/*F9*

The Oak House
PO Box 299AA Seaview Ave
Oak Bluffs MA 02557
(508) 693-4187

Circa 1872. Massachusetts Gov. William Claflin purchased this gingerbread cottage because of its fine location and splendid view of the ocean. He imported oak timbers and employed ship's carpenters to carve oak ceilings, wall panels and interior pillars. A servants' wing, an additional floor, and a wide veranda were added, all for the purpose of entertaining important Massachusetts leaders. As a bed and breakfast, the Oak House maintains the grand style with authentic Victorian furnishings and refined hospitality.
*❀Rates: $85-$190. Betsi Convery-Luce.
10 R. 10 PB. Phone available. TV available. Beds: KQ. Continental-plus breakfast. CCs: MC VISA. Fishing, golf, biking, riding, tennis. Afternoon Victorian tea.
Seen in: *Vineyard Gazette.*
"I feel like a guest in a friend's home."

PETERSHAM E10/*B5*

Winterwood at Petersham
N Main St
Petersham MA 01366
(508) 724-8885

Circa 1842. The town of Petersham is often referred to as a museum of Greek Revival architecture. One of the grand houses facing the common is

Winterwood. It boasts fireplaces in almost every room and the two-room suite has twin fireplaces. Private dining is available for small groups.
*Rates: $80-$100. Jean & Robert Day.
5 R. 5 PB. 4 FP. Phone available. Beds: TF. Continental-plus breakfast. Conference room. CCs: MC VISA AE. Hiking, cross-country skiing, museums.
Seen in: *Boston Globe.*
"Between your physical facilities and

Jean's cooking, our return to normal has been made even more difficult. Your hospitality was just a fantastic extra to our total experience."

PROVINCETOWN I24/D10

Bradford Gardens Inn

178 Bradford St
Provincetown MA 02657
(508) 487-1616

Circa 1820. Framed by a split-rail fence, this Cape Cod house is conveniently located within a mile of all of Provincetown. Behind the inn is the

Loft Lodge with cathedral ceilings, a kitchen, and its own fireplace. An informal New England decor with period furnishings is enhanced by a collection of original paintings. If your visit is in the spring, request the Cherry Tree Room and enjoy the delicate blossoms from your window.
*Rates: $69-$118. Season: Apr. - Dec. Susan Culligan.
12 R. 12 PB. 10 FP. Phone available. TV in room. Beds: QD. EP. CCs: MC VISA AE.
Seen in: *Country Inns.*
"We return year after year for the gourmet breakfasts, incredibly beautiful gardens and the warm atmosphere."

Land's End Inn

22 Commercial St
Provincetown MA 02657
(508) 487-0706

Circa 1907. Built as a shingle-style summer cottage for Boston merchant Charles Higgins, Land's End stands high on a hill overlooking Provincetown and all of Cape Cod Bay. Part of the Higgins' collection of oriental wood carvings and stained glass is housed at the inn. Furnished lavishly in a Victorian style, the inn offers a comforting atmosphere for relaxation and beauty.
Rates: $70-$170. David Schoolman.
15 R. 11 PB. Phone available. Beds: DT. Full breakfast. Swimming, bicycling.
Seen in: *Travel Magazine, Cape Cod Review.*

Rose And Crown Guest House

158 Commercial St
Provincetown MA 02657
(508) 487-3332

Circa 1787. Located in Massachusett's second largest historic district, this Georgian "shingled square rigger", framed by an ornate iron fence, was named after the many inns in Britain.

Above the paneled entrance, a ship's figurehead of Jane Elizabeth is posed. Victorian antiques and art work fill the inn. A cottage and an apartment are available in addition to the six rooms in the main house.
*Rates: $65-$150. Preston Babbitt, Jr.
8 R. 5 PB. Phone available. TV in room. Beds: KQDT. Continental breakfast. CCs: AE. Water sports, golf, bicycling, horseback riding.
Seen in: *Hotels.*
"We had a great time due to your hospitality."

Watership Inn

7 Winthrop St
Provincetown MA 02657
(508) 487-0094

Circa 1820. George Miller built this home, used as a private residence until 1948. Over the past 10 years it has been renovated and the beamed

ceilings and polished plank floors provide a background for the inn's antiques. Rooms are light and airy. Guests enjoy the inn's sun decks.
Location: One half block from Provincetown Harbor.
*❀Rates: $29-$80. James F. Foss.
15 R. 13 PB. Phone available. TV in room. Beds: D. Continental breakfast. CCs: MC VISA AE. Horseback riding, wind surfing, whale watching, boat rentals, sailing, bicycle trains, beaches.
"We found your hospitality and charming inn perfect for our brief yet wonderful escape from Boston."

REHOBOTH K17/E7

Perryville Inn

157 Perryville Rd
Rehoboth MA 02769
(508) 252-9239

Circa 1824. The Perryville Inn was a dairy farm for more than 140 years. During that time, in 1897, the original two-story colonial was remodeled into a handsome three-story Victorian. (The house was raised and an additional floor added underneath.) The pasture is now a public golf course, but the icehouse remains. There are old stone walls, a mill pond, trout stream and wooded paths. Inside the inn, cozy rooms are decorated with comfortable antiques.
*Rates: $40-$75. Tom & Betsy Charnecki.
5 R. 3 PB. Phone available. Beds: QTD. Continental-plus breakfast. Conference room. CCs: MC VISA. Hay & sleigh rides, cross-country skiing, golf, tennis, bicycles, hot air balloon rides.
Seen in: *The Providence Journal-Bulletin, Evening Magazine.*
"The family voted the Perryville the best place we stayed on our entire trip, without hesitation!"

ROCKPORT C21/B8

Addison Choate Inn

49 Broadway
Rockport MA 01966
(508) 546-7543

Circa 1851. Addison Choate built his home on the site of a blueberry bog. He became the talk of the town when he installed the first bathtub of the

area in his kitchen. A long petunia-filled porch wraps around the inn. Inside are pumpkin pine floors, polished woodwork and a delightful assortment of guest rooms. If Addison returned to the house today, surely he would choose the ocean-view suite with a bathtub under a stained glass ceiling and skylight. Other guest rooms feature canopied or brass beds and are decorated with a personal collection of antiques.
Rates: $83-$110. Peter & Chris Kelleher.
10 R. 10 PB. Phone available. Beds: KQDT. Full breakfast. Swimming pool. Golf, tennis, boating, horseback riding, cross-country skiing, whale watching.
Seen in: *Los Angeles Times, Detroit Free Press, Gloucaster Daily Times.*
"Lovely! Charming and quaint."

The Inn on Cove Hill

37 Mt Pleasant St
Rockport MA 01966
(508) 546-2701

Circa 1791. Pirate gold found at Gully Point paid for this Federal-style house. An exquisitely-crafted spiral staircase, random-width, pumpkin-pine floors, and hand-forged hinges display the artisan's handiwork. A picket fence

and granite walkway welcome guests.
Rates: $48-$91. Season: April - October. John & Marjorie Pratt.
11 R. 9 PB. Phone available. TV in room. Beds: QDT. Continental breakfast. Ocean swimming, whale watching, bicycling.
Seen in: *The Boston Globe, Yankee Magazine.*
"Everything was superb. Love your restorations, your muffins and your china."

Old Farm Inn
291 Granite St
Rockport MA 01966
(508) 546-3237
Circa 1799. This old red farmhouse remains a charming example of period country style. Rustic beams, paneling, wide-pine flooring and six fireplaces are original. The initials of James, grandson of the earliest owner, are chiseled on the old granite gatepost along with the date, 1799. *The Yankee Bodleys*, a novel by Naomi Babson, is based on the lives of people who lived on the farm in the 1830s.
Location: At Halibut Point on Cape Ann.
*Rates: $78-$98. Season: April to Dec. The Balzarini family.
9 R. 9 PB. Phone available. TV in room. Beds: KQTDC. Continental-plus breakfast. CCs: MC VISA AE. Tennis, fishing, golf, bicycling, sailing, whale watching.
Seen in: *New York Times, San Francisco Examiner.*
"We had a wonderful time, the room was so cozy. A fantastic stay with wonderful hosts!"

Rocky Shores Inn
Eden Rd
Rockport MA 01966
(508) 546-2823
Circa 1905. This grand country mansion was built on wooded land selected to provide maximum views

of Thacher Island and the open sea. There are seven unique fireplaces, handsome woodwork, and a graceful stairway. Guest rooms are in the main house, or in several cottages nestled among the trees. Lawns flow from the mansion down to the picturesque shoreline.
Location: On a knoll overlooking the ocean.
*Rates: $76-$93. Season: March 30 - Oct. 27. Gunter & Renate Kostka.
10 R. 10 PB. 7 FP. Phone available. TV in room. Beds: QDT. Continental-plus breakfast. Conference room. CCs: MC VISA. Nearby whale watching, sailing, fishing, diving, tennis, golf.
Seen in: *Yankee Magazine, The Hartford Courant.*
"Fabulous! You and your inn are a five-star rating as far as we are concerned."

Yankee Clipper Inn
Box 2399, 96 Granite St
Rockport MA 01966
(508) 546-3407 (800) 545-3699
Circa 1840. This white clapboard oceanfront mansion features sweeping views of the sea and the rocky shoreline. Gleaming mahogany woodwork and fireplaces combined with fine antiques create an old-fashioned, elegant ambience in the main building. Some accommodations offer canopy beds and balconies. The Bulfinch House, a Greek Revival building housing extra guest rooms, is situated away from the water uphill from the main inn. A heated salt-water pool is in view of the ocean.
Rates: $47-$102. Bob & Barbara Ellis.
27 R. 27 PB. Phone in room. TV available. Beds: KQDT. MAP. Restaurant. Gourmet meals. Swimming pool. Conference room. CCs: MC VISA AE DS. Whale watching, boating, fishing, golf, tennis, ocean beach swimming. Weddings.
Seen in: *Gloucester Daily Times, Los Angeles Times, North Shore Life.*
"The rooms were comfortable, the views breathtaking from most rooms, and the breakfasts delicious, with prompt and courteous service."

SALEM D19/*B8*

Amelia Payson Guest House
16 Winter St
Salem MA 01970
(508) 744-8304
Circa 1845. This elegantly restored two-story wooden house is a prime example of Greek Revival architecture. Located in the heart of the Salem Historic District, it is a short walk to shops, museums and the wharf.

Train service to Boston is four blocks away.
Location: Thirteen miles north of Boston.
❀Rates: $65-$85. Ada & Donald Roberts.
4 R. 2 PB. Phone available. TV available. Beds: QDT. Continental-plus breakfast. CCs: MC VISA AE. Whale watching.
"Your hospitality has been a part of my wonderful experience."

Coach House Inn
284 Lafayette St
Salem MA 01970
(508) 744-4092
Circa 1879. Captain Augustus Emmerton was one of the last Salem natives to earn his living from maritime com-

merce. He was master of the barkentine *Sophronia* and the ship *Neptune's Daughter* that sailed to Zanzibar and the Orient. Emmerton's house is an imposing example of Second Empire architecture situated two blocks from the harbor. The House of Seven Gables and the Salem Witch Museum are nearby.
Rates: $69-$85.
11 R. 9 PB. 7 FP. Phone available. TV in room. Beds: DT. B&B. CCs: MC VISA. Museums.
Seen in: *The North Shore.*

The Salem Inn
7 Summer St
Salem MA 01970
(508) 741-0680 (800) 446-2995
Circa 1834. Captain Nathaniel West, first owner of this historic building, believed that at all times his home

should be maintained in readiness for his return from sea. Today that same philosophy is practiced for guests of the Salem Inn. The guest rooms are uniquely decorated with homey touches and there are two-room suites with kitchens for families.
Location: Historic downtown.

*Rates: $80-$100. Richard & Diane Pabich. 21 R. 21 PB. 10 FP. Beds: KQT. Continental-plus breakfast.
Seen in: *New York Times, Boston Sunday Globe.*
"Delightful, charming. Our cup of tea."

Stephen Daniels House
1 Daniels St
Salem MA 01970
(508) 744-5709

Circa 1667. This lovely 300-year-old captain's house is one of the few three-story homes of this vintage still intact. Two large walk-in fireplaces grace the common rooms and each guest room includes antique furnishings, a canopy bed, and a wood-burning fireplace. A pleasant English garden is filled with colorful blooms. Children and well-behaved pets are welcome.
*Rates: $60-$85. Catherine Gill.
5 R. 3 PB. 4 FP. TV available. Beds: DT. Continental breakfast. Conference room.
Seen in: *Country Living.*
"Like going back to earlier times."

SANDISFIELD H4/D2

New Boston Inn
Jct Rt 8 & 57
Sandisfield MA 01255-0120
(413) 258-4477

Circa 1737. Said to be the oldest inn in the Berkshires, this Federal-style hostelry was operated as an inn for more than 200 years. The oldest section houses an English-style pub with floors and walls of 24-inch-wide planks. Guest rooms feature stenciling, antiques or wallpapers and there is a ballroom sometimes used for rehearsal dinners. On the inn's three acres are gardens, a fish pond and space for playing horseshoe. Across the road is the West branch of the Farmington River.
Location: Berkshire Mountains.
Rates: $95-$110. Anne & Bill McCarthy.
8 R. 8 PB. Phone available. TV available. Beds: QDT. MAP. Restaurant. Handicap access. Conference room. CCs: MC VISA AE. Riding, skiing, canoeing, sailing, hiking, blueberry picking.
Seen in: *Springfield Union News, Yankee Magazine.*
"We appreciate all you did to make us feel special."

SANDWICH L22/E9

Captain Ezra Nye House
152 Main St
Sandwich MA 02563
(800) 388-2278 (508) 888-6142

Circa 1829. Captain Ezra Nye built this house after a record-shattering Halifax to Boston run, and the stately Federal-style house reflects the

opulence and romance of the clipper ship era. Hand-stenciled walls and museum-quality antiques decorate the interior. Within walking distance are the Doll Museum, the Glass Museum, restaurants, shops, the famous Heritage Plantation, and the beach and marina.
*Rates: $55-$80. Elaine & Harry Dickson.
6 R. 4 PB. 1 FP. Phone available. TV available. Beds: KQDT. Continental-plus breakfast. Conference room. CCs: MC VISA AE. Beaches, tennis, bike trails, piano.
Seen in: *Sandwich, A Cape Cod Town.*
"The prettiest room and most beautiful home we have been to. We had a wonderful time."

The Dan'l Webster Inn
149 Main St
Sandwich MA 02563
(508) 888-3622

Circa 1692. Originally built as a parsonage, this property became Patriot headquarters when it later served as

the Fessenden Tavern. Daniel Webster came here to hunt and fish in the 1850s and to complain when the new glass factory workers began to discover his favorite hunting spots. The inn was destroyed by a devastating fire in 1970 and was rebuilt. The 1826 Fessenden House next door was added to the property a few years later. The inn holds a Travel-Holiday Distinctive Dining Award.
*Rates: $65-$165. Steve Catania, Paul Rumul.
46 R. 47 PB. 7 FP. Phone in room. TV in room. Beds: KQDT. MAP. Restaurant. Gourmet meals. Spa. Handicap access. Swimming pool. Conference room. FAX. CCs: MC VISA AE DC CB. Golf, tennis, horse & carriage tours, charter fishing, whale-watching, beaches.
Seen in: *Bon Appetit, New York Times, Great Weekends.*
"Excellent accommodations and great food."

Isaiah Jones Homestead
165 Main St
Sandwich MA 02563
(508) 888-9115 (800) 526-1625

Circa 1849. This fully restored Victorian homestead is situated on Main Street in the village. Eleven-foot ceil-

ings and two bay windows are features of the Gathering Room. Guest rooms contain antique Victorian bedsteads such as the half-canopy bed of burled birch in the Deming Jarves Room where there is an over-sized whirlpool tub. Candlelight breakfasts are highlighted with the house speciality, freshly baked cornbread, inspired by nearby Sandwich Grist Mill.
*❀Rates: $65-$110. Steve & Kathy Catania.
4 R. 4 PB. Phone available. Beds: Q. B&B. CCs: MC VISA AE DS. Bike paths, tennis, beach, museums. Antique shops and auctions.
Seen in: *Cape Cod Life, New England Travel.*
"Excellent! The room was a delight, the food wonderful, the hospitality warm & friendly. One of the few times the reality exceeded the expectation."

The Summer House
158 Main St
Sandwich MA 02563
(508) 888-4991

Circa 1835. The Summer House is a handsome Greek Revival in a setting of historic homes and public buildings. (Hiram Dillaway, one of the

owners, was a famous mold maker for the Boston & Sandwich Glass Company.) The house is fully restored and decorated with antiques and hand-stitched quilts. Four of the guest rooms have black marble fireplaces. The porch overlooks an old-fashioned perennial gardens, antique rose bushes, and a 70-year-old rhododendron hedge.
Location: Center of village, Cape Cod.
*❀Rates: $50-$70. David & Kay Merrell.
5 R. 1 PB. 4 FP. Phone available. Beds: KQDT. Continental-plus breakfast. CCs: MC VISA AE. Beach, museums.
Seen in: *Country Living Magazine.*

"This is just full of charm. As beautiful as a fairy world."

SHEFFIELD H2/D2

Ivanhoe Country House

Rt 41
Sheffield MA 01257
(413) 229-2143 (413) 229-3405

Circa 1780. Vast reaches of manicured lawns provide the setting for this country house on 25 acres, adjacent to the Appalachian Trail. The Chestnut Room is a popular gathering area with its fireplace, library and games. Antiques and comfortable country furnishings are found throughout the inn. Breakfast is brought to each guest bedroom. Genteely raised pets are welcome, though requirements are stringent.

Rates: $65-$99. Carole & Dick Maghery.
9 R. 9 PB. Phone available. TV available. Beds: DTC. Continental breakfast. Swimming pool. Game room. Hiking, boating, golf, tennis, antiquing.
"Everything was terrific, especially the blueberry muffins."

Staveleigh House

PO 608, S Main St
Sheffield MA 01257
(413) 229-2129

Circa 1821. The Reverend Bradford, minister of Old Parish Congregational Church, the oldest church in the Berkshires, built this home for his family. Afternoon tea is served and the inn is especially favored for its four-course breakfasts and gracious hospitality. Located next to the town green, the house is in a historic district in the midst of several fine antique shops.

❀Rates: $70-$85. Dorothy Marosy & Marion Whitman.
5 R. 2 PB. Phone available. Beds: KQTD. B&B. Skiing, horseback riding, hiking, bicycling, canoeing, golf.
Seen in: *Los Angeles Times.*
"Exceptionally good."

SOUTH DARTMOUTH M19/F8

Salt Marsh Farm

322 Smith Neck Rd
South Dartmouth MA 02748
(508) 992-0980

Circa 1775. In 1665, John Smith traded his house in Plymouth for this land in Dartmouth so he could escape the overcrowding in Plymouth. The land was called Smith's Neck. Later, Isaac Howland built this two-story hip-roofed colonial house. The farm has 90 acres of salt meadows, tidal marshes, hay fields and woodlands. The innkeeper is a descendant of John Smith and enjoys sharing local history.

Location: Southeastern Massachusetts.
Rates: $65-$75. Larry & Sally Brownell.
2 R. 2 PB. Phone available. Beds: DT. Full breakfast. CCs: MC VISA. Tandem bicycle, nature trails.
Seen in: *The Standard-Times, The Chronicle.*
"A peaceful setting for the refreshment of both body & spirit."

SOUTH EGREMONT H2/C2

Egremont Inn

Old Sheffield Rd
South Egremont MA 01258
(413) 528-2111 (413) 528-2113

Circa 1780. This three-story inn is adjacent to a quiet, tree-lined stream where guests have spent many a summer day. There are private tennis courts on the premises. A wraparound porch is decorated with white wicker and guest rooms are furnished with antiques. There is a tavern and a dining room.

Rates: $90-$155. John Black.
22 R. 22 PB. Phone available. TV available. Beds: DTC. MAP. Restaurant. Swimming pool. Conference room. CCs: MC VISA AE. Tennis, golf, hiking, riding, skiing.
"To say our stay at the Egremont Inn was unforgettable would be understating the case."

Weathervane Inn

Rt 23, Main St
South Egremont MA 01258
(413) 528-9580

Circa 1785. Nine years were spent restoring this rambling old house that was formerly a kennel, store, and dance studio. Long ago, it was also an inn. Today high ceilings, handsome moldings, and a beehive oven are featured attractions.

Location: Main Street, Route 23.
Vincent & Anne Murphy and Robert & Olena Murphy.
10 R. 10 PB. Phone available. TV available. Beds: KQT. Full breakfast. Restaurant. Handicap access. Conference room. CCs: MC VISA. Downhill & cross-country skiing, fishing, tennis, golf.
Seen in: *New York Times, Berkshire Eagle, Boston Herald.*
"...the Murphy family exemplifies the best tradition of New England hospitality," Berkshire Business Journal.

SOUTH LANCASTER E14/B6

Deershorn Manor B&B

357 Sterling Rd, PO Box 805
South Lancaster MA 01561
(508) 365-9022

Circa 1886. This 20-room mansion is located on three acres emcompassing a rose garden with gazebo, fountains, aviary and formal plantings. Intricately carved Victorian antiques are combined with crystal chandeliers, Oriental rugs and velvet drapes to create a lavish yet elegant decor. The bridal suite offers a lace canopy bed, fireplace, windowseat and a bathroom with its own fireplace. An 800-square-foot library is adjacent to the solarium and music room.

Rates: $45-$125. Sylvia Lamb.
6 R. 3 PB. 4 FP. Phone available. TV in room. Beds: KQDT. Continental-plus breakfast. Gourmet meals. Game room. Conference room. Horseback riding, skiing, golf, antiquing. Weddings.
Seen in: *Clinton Daily Item, Journal Express.*
"A wonderful, peaceful place. Great hospitality."

SOUTH LEE G3/C2

Merrell Tavern Inn

Rt 102 Main St
South Lee MA 01260
(413) 243-1794

Circa 1794. This elegant stagecoach inn was carefully preserved under supervision of the Society for the Preservation of New England Antiquities. Architectural drawings of Merrell Tavern have been preserved by the Library of Congress. Eight fireplaces in the inn include two with original beehive and warming ovens. An antique circular birdcage bar serves as a check-in desk. Comfortable rooms feature canopy and four-poster beds with Hepplewhite and Sheraton-style antiques.

❀Rates: $65-$130. Charles & Faith Reynolds.
10 R. 10 PB. Phone available. Beds: QDT. Full breakfast. CCs: MC VISA AE. Downhill & cross-country skiing.
"One of the most authentic period inns on the East Coast," The Discerning Traveler.

SPRINGFIELD H7/*D4*

The Old Mill Inn
See: Somersville, CT 06072

STERLING E13/*B6*

Sterling Orchards B&B
60 Kendall Hill Rd, Box 455
Sterling MA 01564
(508) 422-6595 (508) 422-6170

Circa 1740. The orchards planted in 1920 by Robert Smiley's father provide a suitable setting to frame the 250-year-old farmhouse that has been thoroughly renovated. Original Indian shutters are still in place. A hiding place in the 12-square-foot center chimney, originally built by settlers, can still be found. The largest guest room (20x30) served as the town ballroom at the 1881 centennial. Afternoon tea is available in the Appleseed Tea Room, the inn's dining room.
Rates: $65. Season: April - Dec. Robert & Shirley P. Smiley.
2 R. 2 PB. Phone in room. TV in room. Beds: QT. Full breakfast. Swimming pool. Conference room. Wineries. Mt. Wauchusett ski area is eight miles away (day and night skiing).
Seen in: *Boston Globe, Worcester Telegram.*
"It's like stepping back in time with every modern convenience."

STOCKBRIDGE G2/*C2*

Merrell Tavern Inn
See: South Lee, MA

The Inn at Stockbridge
Rt 7 Box 618
Stockbridge MA 01262
(413) 298-3337

Circa 1906. Giant maples shade the drive leading to this Southern-style Georgian Colonial with its impressive pillared entrance. Located on 12 acres, the grounds include a reflecting pool, a fountain, meadows and woodland as well as wide vistas of the rolling hillsides. The guest rooms feature antiques and handsome 18th-century reproductions. Breakfast is graciously presented with fine china, silver and linens.
Rates: $80-$200. Lee & Don Weitz.
7 R. 7 PB. 2 FP. Phone available. Beds: KQD. Full breakfast. Swimming pool. CCs: MC VISA AE. Golf, tennis, canoeing, horseback riding all nearby. Honeymoon, birthday and wedding specials.
Seen in: *Vogue, New York Magazine, New York Daily News.*
"Classy & comfortable."

STURBRIDGE H11/*D5*

Commonwealth Inn
11 Summit Ave
Sturbridge MA 01566
(508) 347-7603

Circa 1890. This 16-room Victorian house overlooks the Quinebaug River just a few minutes from Old Sturbridge Village. Two parlors, each

with a marble fireplace, are available to guests. The inn is decorated in a country style. The veranda has two gazebos, one on each end.
Rates: $40-$55. Kevin MacConnell.
8 R. 5 PB. Phone available. Full breakfast. Spa. Fishing, boating, tennis, golf, cross-country skiing, hiking.

Sturbridge Country Inn
530 Main St
Sturbridge MA 01566
(508) 347-5503

Circa 1840. Shaded by an old silver maple, this classic Greek Revival house boasts a two-story columned entrance. The attached carriage house now serves as the lobby and displays the original post-and-beam construction and exposed rafters. All guestrooms have individual fireplaces and whirlpool tubs. They are gracefully appointed in reproduction colonial furnishings, including queen-size four posters. A patio and gazebo are favorite summertime retreats.
❀Rates: $69-$110. Kevin MacConnell.
9 R. 9 PB. 9 FP. Phone in room. TV in room. Beds: KQDT. Continental breakfast. CCs: MC VISA AE. Fishing, boating, tennis, golf, cross-country skiing, hiking.
Seen in: *Southbridge Evening News, Worcester Telegram & Gazette.*
"Best lodging I've ever seen."

The Wildwood Inn
See: Ware, MA

TYRINGHAM G3/*C2*

The Golden Goose
Main Rd, PO Box 336
Tyringham MA 01264
(413) 243-3008

Circa 1800. This white colonial house rests on six acres. The innkeeper has gathered antiques for the inn from her shopkeeping days in Manhattan where she sold Victorian oak pieces. Cheery wallpapers and wide plank floors create a fresh country decor. From the dining room, beveled French doors lead to a deck that overlooks the back grounds. Across the road is Hop Brook, a trout fishing spot.
Location: In the Berkshires.
Rates: $60-$110. Lilja & Joseph Rizzo.
7 R. 5 PB. Phone available. Beds: KQDT. Continental-plus breakfast. Hiking, skiing, swimming, biking, golf, tennis.
Seen in: *Boston Sunday Globe, Travel & Leisure.*
"The classical music puts the final touch on a classic inn and two classic hosts!"

VINEYARD HAVEN N21/*F9*

Lothrop Merry House
Owen Park, PO Box 1939
Vineyard Haven MA 02568
(508) 693-1646

Circa 1790. Eight yoke of oxen moved this house to its present beach-front location. A wedding gift from father to daughter, the house has a classic

center chimney and six fireplaces. Breakfast is served in season on the flower-bedecked patio overlooking stunning harbor views. A private beach beckons at the end of a sloping lawn.
Location: Martha's Vineyard.
Rates: $68-$155. John & Mary Clarke.
7 R. 4 PB. Phone available. Beds: QTC. Continental breakfast. CCs: MC VISA. Golf, tennis, bicycling, sailing, canoeing.
Seen in: *Cape Cod Life.*
"It is the nicest place we've ever stayed."

WARE G10/*C5*

The Wildwood Inn
121 Church St
Ware MA 01082
(413) 967-7798

Circa 1880. This yellow Victorian has a wraparound porch and a beveled-glass front door. American primitive antiques include a collection of New England cradles, a cobbler's bench, and a spinning wheel. The inn's two

acres are dotted with maple, chestnut and apple trees. Through the woods you'll find a river.
❀Rates: $38-$75. Fraidell Fenster, Richard Watson.
5 R. Phone available. Beds: QTD. Full breakfast. CCs: AE. Tennis, canoeing, swimming, hiking, cross-country skiing.
Seen in: *The Boston Globe.*
"Excellent accommodations, not only in rooms, but in the kind and thoughtful way you treat your guests. We'll be back!"

WEST BARNSTABLE L23/E9

Honeysuckle Hill
591 Main St
West Barnstable MA 02668
(508) 362-8418 (508) 362-4914
Circa 1810. This Queen Anne Victorian built by Josiah Goodspeed is in the National Register. Guest rooms are

decorated with Victorian sofas, Peter Rabbit memorabilia, and St. Louis antiques. Feather beds, Laura Ashley linens and fluffy pillows are among the other amenities.
Location: Cape Cod.
*Rates: $90-$105. Barbara & Bob Rosenthal.
3 R. 3 PB. 1 FP. Phone available. TV available. Beds: KQ. Full breakfast. Game room. Conference room. CCs: MC VISA AE DS. Bicycling, beach.
"The charm, beauty, service and warmth shown to guests are impressive, but the food overwhelms. Breakfasts were divine!" Judy Kaplan, *St. Louis Journal.*

WEST BOYLSTON F13/C6

The Rose Cottage
24 Worcester St, Rts 12 & 40
West Boylston MA 01583
(508) 835-4034
Circa 1850. Overlooking the placid water of Wachusett Reservoir, this yellow Gothic Revival house features dormers and a gabled roof trimmed with gingerbread. Inside, wide-board floors, floor-to-ceiling windows and marble fireplaces remain. Guest rooms are decorated with small print wallpapers, quilts and antiques. There is an antique shop in the barn.
Rates: $65 & up. Michael & Loretta Kittredge.
5 R. 1 PB. 3 FP. Phone available. TV available. Beds: DTC. Full breakfast. Gourmet meals. Conference room. Tennis, golf, bike rentals, skiing, swimming, museums. Seminars, receptions, retreats.
Seen in: *The Evening Gazette.*
"Your concern, your caring, your friendliness made me feel at home!"

WEST DENNIS L24/E10

The Lighthouse Inn
Lighthouse Rd
West Dennis MA 02670
(508) 398-2244
Circa 1855. This old-fashioned waterfront inn is operated by third-generation Stones, grandchildren of the original creator of the resort. Historic Bass River lighthouse, part of the main building, has recently received approval for a new light. The inn features rooms in the main building and several cottages. Old-fashioned furnishings haven't yet acquired the decorator touch. There's a small swimming beach.
Rates: $54-$186. Robert Stone.
Full breakfast.

WEST HARWICH L25/E10

Lion's Head Inn
186 Belmont Rd PO Box 444
West Harwich MA 02671
(508) 432-7766 (800) 321-3155
Circa 1804. This Cape Cod half-house was built by Captain Thomas Snow. Recently renovated, the inn has retained its colonial feeling and includes the Captain's Staircase, a steep stairway original to the house. The inn is decorated in antiques and traditional furnishings. Several old maps hang in the Map Room, once used as a study for Captain Snow.
*Rates: $55-$125. Fred, Deborah & Ricky Denton.
6 R. 6 PB. Phone available. TV available. Beds: KQT. Full breakfast. Swimming pool. CCs: MC VISA. Badminton, beach, fishing, boating, golf.
Seen in: *Harwich Oracle, Suburban Spotlight.*
"The best innkeepers we have met on the Cape!"

Sunny Pines B&B Inn
77 Main St, PO Box 667
West Harwich MA 02671
(508) 432-9628
Circa 1900. Caleb Chase of Chase and Sanbourne coffee fame built this house as a parsonage for the local Baptist Church. It later became the

town library and in the Forties, a guest house. The inn has a Victorian atmosphere. A big Irish breakfast is served on bone china with crystal and candlelight. The innkeeper was an oceanographer for 20 years.
*Rates: $80. Jack & Eileen Connell.
6 R. 6 PB. 1 FP. Phone in room. TV in room. Beds: KQT. B&B. Gourmet meals. Spa. Swimming pool. CCs: MC VISA AE. Hiking, bicycling, water sports, tennis, golf, croquet, horseshoes, darts, barbecue.
Seen in: *Innsider.*
"Your bed and breakfast is number one!"

WEST HYANNISPORT M23/E9

B&B Cape Cod
PO Box 341
West Hyannisport MA 02672
(508) 775-2772
Circa 1709. This reservation service represents many exquisitely restored historic houses in almost every nook and cranny on the Cape, Nantucket and Martha's Vineyard. Many are in the National Register. One of the oldest, an Early American home, is two blocks from Cape Cod Bay. Furnished in an early 1700s decor, the home has four-poster beds and period antiques. A hearty country breakfast is served. All 70 host homes have been inspected for cleanliness and comfort by the agency.
Rates: $45-$177. General manager Clark Diehl.
Phone available. CCs: MC VISA AE.
Seen in: *Innsider Magazine.*
"Clean, orderly and comfortable."

WILLIAMSTOWN C3/A2

The Sedgwick Inn
See: Berlin, NY

WOODS HOLE N21/F8

The Marlborough
320 Woods Hole
Woods Hole MA 02543
(508) 548-6218
Circa 1939. This is a faithful reproduction of a Cape-style cottage complete with picket fence and rambling roses,

set on spacious grounds. Although the inn is beautifully decorated with antiques, designer sheets and wall coverings, children are welcome. In winter, a proper high tea with finger sandwiches, pate and scones with clotted cream is served. An English paddle-tennis court, a swimming pool and a gazebo are popular spots in summer.
Rates: $85. Patricia Morris.
6 R. 6 PB. 1 FP. Phone available. TV available. Beds: QDTC. B&B. Swimming pool. Private beach.
Seen in: *Cape Cod Life.*
"Our stay at the Marlborough was a little bit of heaven."

WORCESTER-RUTLAND F12/C5

The General Rufus Putnam House
344 Main St
Worcester-Rutland MA 01543
(508) 886-4256
Circa 1750. This restored Federal house, listed in the National Register, was the home of General Rufus Putnam, founder of Marietta, Ohio. A memorial tablet on the house states that "to him it is owing...that the United States is not now a great slaveholding empire." Surrounded by tall maples and a rambling stone fence, the inn rests on seven acres of woodlands and meadows. There are eight fireplaces, blue Delft tiles and a beehive oven. Afternoon tea and breakfast are served fireside in the

keeping room.
Location: Rural/Central Massachusetts.
Rates: $75-$90. Gordon & Marcia Hickory.
3 R. 1 PB. Phone available. TV available. Beds: DTC. Full breakfast. Swimming pool. Golf, fishing, concerts.
Seen in: *Sunday Telegram, The Land Mark, Washusett People.*
"We were thrilled with the beauty and luxury of this B&B and especially the wonderful hospitality."

YARMOUTH PORT L24/E10

Colonial House Inn
Rt 6A, 277 Main St
Yarmouth Port MA 02675
(508) 362-4348 (800) 999-3416
Circa 1730. Although the original structure was built in pre-revolutionary times, a third floor was later added and another section was

shipped in from Europe. The innkeepers renovated the carriage house, creating 10 new rooms. Dining areas include the Colonial Room with hand-stenciled walls and a fireplace, and the Common Room, a recent glass-enclosed addition with a view of the veranda and town green. A traditional Thanksgiving dinner is served every year, and guests may enjoy other specialities, including murder-mystery, Las Vegas and wine-tasting weekends.
*Rates: $60-$95. Malcolm Perna.
21 R. 21 PB. 4 FP. Phone available. TV in room. Beds: KQDTC. MAP. Restaurant. Gourmet meals. Spa. Handicap access. Exercise room. Swimming pool. Conference room. CCs: MC VISA AE DS. Horseback riding, skiing, water sports, golf, tennis.
Seen in: *The New York Times, Yankee Magazine.*
"The nicest place I've ever stayed."

Crook' Jaw Inn
186 Main St, Rt 6A
Yarmouth Port MA 02675
(508) 362-6111
Circa 1790. This Georgian full-cape was named Crook Jaw after the notorious whale hunted in the 1700s by Yarmouth sea captains. The inn is situated on two-and-a-half acres (much of it English country gardens), in the center of Yarmouth Port. The area is called Captains' Row, named for the sea captains who lived there. The innkeepers provides a full breakfast and choice of dinner menu in the price of the room.
❀Rates: $90-$105. Don Spagnolia & Ed Shedlock.
7 R. 7 PB. 8 FP. Phone available. TV available. Beds: KD. Full breakfast. CCs: MC VISA AE. Golf, tennis, swimming, cross-country skiing. Picnic baskets available for day trips. Wedding specials.
Seen in: *Cape Cod Times, Cape Cod Life Magazine.*
"Hospitality is fantastic, food superb, atmosphere delightful."

Liberty Hill Inn
77 Main St, Rt 6A
Yarmouth Port MA 02675
(508) 362-3976
Circa 1825. This Greek Revival mansion is located on the site of the original Liberty Pole dating from Revolutionary times. To benefit the

Cape Cod Conservatory of Music several local decorators restored the rooms. There are outstanding English gardens and the inn's setting on the hill affords views of Cape Cod Bay. On historic Old King's Highway, it's a brief walk to antique shops, auctions and restaurants.
*Rates: $75-$100. Beth & Jack Flanagan.
5 R. 5 PB. Phone available. TV available. Beds: KQT. B&B. Gourmet meals. Conference room. Beaches, nature trails, golf. Tennis on grounds.
Seen in: *Cape Cod Life, Frommer's New England.*
"Your homey hospitality makes us want to return."

MICHIGAN

ALLEGAN V6/G2

DeLano Inn

302 Cutler St
Allegan MI 49010
(616) 673-2609

Circa 1863. This Italian Provincial mansion, surrounded by a wrought-iron fence, is listed in the National Register of Historic Places. The inn offers cozy sitting rooms and a summer porch. There are stenciled floors, lace curtains, marble fireplaces, crystal chandeliers, a spiral staircase, antique furnishings and European feather beds.

Rates: $45-$85. Bob & Jean Ashley.
6 R. Phone available. TV available. Beds: QDT. Continental-plus breakfast. Conference room. CCs: MC VISA. Horseback riding, downhill & cross-country skiing, snowmobiling, canoeing, all water sports. Ski, wedding & honeymoon packages.
Seen in: *Allegan County News & Gazette.*
"The world would be a much more peaceful place if we all celebrated hospitality the way you folks do."

Winchester Inn

524 Marshall St
Allegan MI 49010
(616) 673-3621

Circa 1863. This neo-Italian Renaissance mansion was built of double-layer brick and has been restored to its original beauty. Surrounded by a

unique hand-poured iron fence, the inn is decorated with period antiques and romantically furnished bedchambers. Depending on your wishes, you can have breakfast in the elegant dining room or in bed.

*Rates: $45-$95. Dave & Denise Ferber.
5 R. 5 PB. Phone available. TV available. Beds: QT. Full breakfast. Handicap access. Conference room. CCs: MC VISA. Skiing, boating, horseback riding, fishing. Murder-mystery weekends.
Seen in: *Architectural Digest.*
"This is one of Michigan's loveliest country inns."

BAY CITY Q12/F4

Stonehedge Inn

924 Center Ave
Bay City MI 48708
(517) 894-4342

Circa 1889. This massive English Tudor home was once a lumber baron's home. The inn has hardwood flooring and a magnificent oak staircase. German artisans were brought to Bay City to hand-carve the home's woodwork. The marble fireplaces and ornate brass light fixtures original to the home were imported from Italy. The speaking tubes and the dumb waiter are still operable.

Rates: $65-$85. Ruth Koerber & John Kleekamp.
7 R. Phone in room. TV available. Beds: QDT. Continental-plus breakfast. Conference room. CCs: MC VISA AE DS. Riverwalk, parks, boating, fishing, bowling, golfing. Wedding, showers and reception specials.
Seen in: *Bay City Times.*
"Your facilities provided a unique and warm atmosphere, and your friendly hospitality added a very personal touch."

BEULAH M5/D2

Brookside Inn

115 N Michigan, PO Box 506
Beulah MI 49617
(616) 882-9688

Circa 1939. By Crystal Lake, the Brookside Inn is furnished with Victorian and country furniture. Guest rooms feature mirrored canopied waterbeds, private Polynesian hot tubs and a log stove. Guests may dine alfresco beside the creek behind the inn. Across a log bridge is the inn's herb garden.

Rates: $180-$240. Pam & Kirk Lorenz.
19 R. 19 PB. 19 FP. Beds: KW. MAP. Restaurant. Spa. Sauna. Handicap access. Conference room. CCs: MC VISA AE. Horseback riding, skiing, water sports, golf. Honeymoon & anniversary specials. Local tour guide service.
Seen in: *Detroit Free Press.*
"Michigan's romantic retreat...works a spell," Rick Sylvain, *Detroit Free Press.*

BIG BAY D1/A1

The Big Bay Point Lighthouse B&B

3 Lighthouse Rd
Big Bay MI 49808
(906) 345-9957

Circa 1896. With 4,500 feet of frontage on Lake Superior, this landmark lighthouse commands 534 acres of forests and a five-acre lawn. The interior of the lighthouse features a brick fireplace. Several guest rooms look out to the water. The tower room on the top floor boasts truly unforgettable views. Breakfast is light so pack some extra food.

Location: Four miles northeast of Big Bay.
*Rates: $90-$115. Buck & Marilyn Gotschall.
6 R. 4 PB. 1 FP. Phone available. Beds: DT. Continental-plus breakfast. Sauna. Exercise room. Conference room. Hiking, bicycling, skiing.
Seen in: *Los Angeles Times, USA Today.*
"The fact that anyone who has ever met Buck Gotschall or stayed at the Lighthouse will tell everyone they know that they have to go there, in my opinion, makes Buck Gotschall the ambassador of the year," Vic Krause, state representative.

BLISSFIELD Y13/H4

Hiram D. Ellis Inn

415 W Adrian St (US 223)
Blissfield MI 49228
(517) 486-3155 (517) 486-2141

Circa 1883. This red brick Italianate house is part of a collection of six Victorian houses being restored by the Weebers. It is directly across from the 1851 Hathaway House, an elegant historic restaurant. Rooms at the Hiram D. Ellis Inn feature handsome antique bedsteads, armoires and floral wallpapers. Amenities include cable TV and air conditioning. Breakfast is served in the inn's common room. Bicycles are available for riding around town.

Rates: $50-$65. Donalta DeSoto.
4 R. 4 PB. Phone in room. TV in room.

Beds: QDC. Continental-plus breakfast. Conference room. CCs: MC VISA. Bicycling, museums.
Seen in: *Ann Arbor News, Michigan Living.*
"I have now experienced what it is truly like to have been treated like a queen."

COLDWATER X9/*H3*

Chicago Pike Inn

215 E Chicago St
Coldwater MI 49036
(517) 279-8744

Circa 1903. This exquisite colonial mansion was built by an architect who designed many of the homes on Mackinac Island. Furnished with

period antiques, the inn features chandeliers, stained glass, parquet flooring and a stunning cherry staircase that add to a feeling of Victorian elegance. The inn derives its name from Coldwater's midway location on the old Detroit-Chicago turnpike. Guests will enjoy exploring Coldwater's historic buildings or perhaps a visit to the Victorian-style Tibbits Opera House built in 1882.
Rates: $75-$130. Rebecca Schultz.
6 R. 6 PB. 1 FP. Phone in room. TV in room. Beds: QT. Full breakfast. Gourmet meals. CCs: MC VISA AE. Cross-country skiing, bicycles.
Seen in: *Innsider, Flint Journal, The Daily Reporter.*
"Your warmth and hospitality added so much to the time we spent with you."

DETROIT W15/*G5*

The Blanche House Inn

506 Parkview Dr
Detroit MI 48214
(313) 822-7090

Circa 1905. This massive "White House"-style Victorian mansion has two-story columns supporting a rotunda entrance. Located on the Stanton Canal a block from the Detroit River, the inn provides an expansive view of Detroit's waterways. Polished wood floors, etched glass, Pewabic tile, gleaming woodwork and antiques fill the inn's 10,000 square feet. The home was built by Marvin Stanton, former overall manufacturer and Detroit lighting commissioner. In the Twenties this house and adjoining "Castle" served as a private boys' school where Henry Ford II attended.
Location: Three miles east of downtown on the canal.
Rates: $60-$120. Mary Jean & Sean Shannon.
13 R. 13 PB. Phone in room. TV in room. Beds: QT Continental-plus breakfast. Conference room. CCs: MC VISA AE. Near the theater district.
Seen in: *Detroit Monthly, Crain's Detroit Business.*

FENNVILLE V5/*G2*

Crane House

6051 124th Ave
Fennville MI 49408
(616) 561-6931

Circa 1870. A restored Victorian farmhouse in a quiet rural setting, this inn is located on the grounds of a working fruit farm. Beautiful antique furnishings, most from the owner's collection, are featured in each guest room and throughout the house. Handmade quilts and feather beds add to the country feeling and the backyard even sports an old-fashioned outhouse. Holland, famous for its annual Tulip Festival, is a short drive away.
*Rates: $60-$80. Nancy Crane McFarland.
5 R. 3 PB. Phone available. TV available. Beds: DT. Full breakfast. Handicap access. CCs: MC VISA DS. Beaches, water sports, fishing.
Seen in: *Kalamazoo Gazette, The Holland Sentinel.*
"I'd been fretting for such a heavenly weekend all winter. Many thanks again."

The Kingsley House

626 W Main St
Fennville MI 49408
(616) 561-6425

Circa 1886. Construction of this Queen Anne Victorian, with a three-story turret, was paid for in silver bricks by the Kingsley family. Mr.

Kingsley is noted for having introduced the apple tree to the area. In recognition of him, guest rooms are named Dutchess, Golden Delicious and Granny Smith, McIntosh and Jonathan. The Northern Spy, complete with hot tub, is nestled in the third-floor suite. A winding oak staircase leads to the antique-filled guest chambers. Family heirlooms and other period pieces add to the inn's elegance.
*Rates: $65-$125. David & Shirley Witt.
5 R. 5 PB. Phone available. TV available. Beds: QDT. Full breakfast. Conference room. CCs: MC VISA. Walking trails, bicycling, cross-country skiing, Lake Michigan nearby.
Seen in: *Innsider, Battle Creek Enquirer, The Fennville Herald, The Commercial Record.*
"It was truly enjoyable. You have a lovely home and a gracious way of entertaining."

HOLLAND U5/*G2*

Crane House

See: Fennville, MI

Dutch Colonial Inn

560 Central Ave
Holland MI 49423
(616) 396-3664

Circa 1928. Romantic rooms at this Dutch-inspired home include the Hideaway Room with a Brattenberg lace coverlet and whirlpool for two.

Another choice is the Jenny Lind Room with a king canopy bed and raspberry and creme decor. A few prized family heirlooms from the Netherlands are featured. A sun porch overlooks part of the inn's lawns.
Rates: $60-$80. Bob & Pat Elenbaas.
5 R. 5 PB. 1 FP. Phone in room. TV available. Beds: KQD. Full breakfast. CCs: MC VISA. Beaches, bike paths, cross-country ski trails.
Seen in: *Shoreline Living.*
"Thank you again for your generous hospitality and excellent breakfasts."

The Old Holland Inn

133 W 11th St
Holland MI 49423
(616) 396-6601

Circa 1895. Innkeeper Dave Plaggemars is a descendant of one of Holland's 10 original founding families. The entrance hall to his National Register Victorian home opens to an oak staircase. Grecian columns support an elaborate fireplace with brass inlays and an 1895 heat-reflecting insert. The oak pocket doors were crafted by first-generation Dutch woodworkers. Now, family collections and period antiques are scattered

throughout the spacious guest rooms. A pear hedge on the property provided the inspiration for Dave Plaggemars' poached pears in cranberry sauce.

Rates: $45-$75. Dave & Fran Plaggemars.
5 R. 2 PB. TV available. Beds: DT. Continental-plus breakfast. Conference room. CCs: VISA DS. Tennis, trout fishing, Lake Michigan.
Seen in: *The Ann Arbor News, Holland Evening Sentinel, Country Inn Cookbook.*
"We enjoyed the touches of live flowers, a selection of books and the wonderful deck."

HUDSON Y11/H4

The Sutton-Weed Farm

18736 Quaker Rd
Hudson MI 49247
(517) 547-6302 (517) 339-1492

Circa 1874. This farm with its 170 acres has been in the same family since it was purchased by Albert Clin-

ton-Weed in 1873. The seven-gabled Victorian house features furnishings collected from five generations. There is a secretary made without nails, with poured-glass windows. A rope bed, a spinning wheel and antique chests are featured. Corn, soy beans or wheat are planted. In the woods, where maple syrup is still collected are ancient sugar maples once "tapped" by the Potowatami Indians.

*Rates: $55. Jack & Barb Sutton.
13 R. Phone available. TV available. Beds: QDTC. Continental-plus breakfast. CCs: MC VISA. Golf, cross-country skiing, lakes all nearby.
Seen in: *Hudson Post Gazette.*
"Just like going home to Grandma's—complete with homemade maple syrup at the breakfast table."

KALAMAZOO W7/G2

Hall House

106 Thompson St
Kalamazoo MI 49007
(616) 343-2500

Circa 1923. This Georgian Colonial Revival-style house was constructed by builder H.L. Vander Horst as his private residence. During the Depres-

sion when the construction slowed, Mr. Vander Horst busied himself painting the vaulted ceiling with a Dutch landscape now much admired. Other special features of the house include a 10-head shower, an early intercom system and secret drawers. The hillside campus of Kalamazoo College and the city center are nearby.

Rates: $75. Pam & Terry O'Connor.
4 R. 4 PB. 1 FP. Phone available. TV in room. Beds: Q. Continental-plus breakfast. CCs: MC VISA AE DS. Fishing, winery tours, museums.
Seen in: *Canton Observer, Encore Magazine.*
"A step into the grace, charm and elegance of the 19th century but with all the amenities of the 20th century right at hand."

LAKESIDE Y4/H1

The Pebble House

15093 Lakeshore Rd
Lakeside MI 49116
(616) 469-1416

Circa 1912. Across the street from a private beach on Lake Michigan, this was the main house of a summer cottage colony for Orthodox Jews. It is named for the local stones collected to construct the fireplace, some of the exterior walls and fence posts. There are three guest buildings connected by wooden walks and pergolas. Rooms feature antique and wicker furnishings. The hosts give seminars on the Arts & Crafts Movement.

Rates: $90-$130. Jean & Ed Lawrence.
7 R. 7 PB. Phone available. Beds: KQ. Full breakfast. Handicap access. CCs: MC VISA. Tennis, cross-country skiing, beach, nature centers.
Seen in: *Chicago Sun-Times.*
"Beautiful place, wonderful hospitality, cute cats."

LUDINGTON P4/E2

The Inn at Ludington

701 E Ludington Ave
Ludington MI 49431
(616) 845-7055

Circa 1889. This Victorian mansion features English country furniture and collectibles. Guest rooms offer four-poster and brass beds, handmade quilts and fresh flowers. The inn serves homemade muffins.

Rates: $45-$85. Diane Shields
6 R. 4 PB. 2 FP. Phone available. Beds: QDT. Full breakfast. CCs: MC VISA. Swimming, fishing, hiking, cross-country skiing. Special weekend packages.
Seen in: *Ludington Daily News.*
"Loved the room and everything else about the house."

MACKINAC ISLAND H10/C3

Haan's 1830 Inn

PO Box 123
Mackinac Island MI 49757
(906) 847-6244 (414)248-9244

Circa 1830. The clip-clopping of horses is still heard from the front porch of this inn as carriages and wagons transport visitors around the island. Said to be the oldest Greek Revival-style house in the Northwest Territory, Haan's 1830 Inn is behind a picket fence and just across the street from the bay. Victorian antiques include a writing desk used by Colonel Preston, an officer at Fort Mackinac at the turn of the century. A cannonball bed built in 1790 still sports a horsehair mattress.

Rates: $75-$95. Season: May 25 - Oct. 15. Joyce & Vernon and Nicholas & Nancy Haan.
7 R. 5 PB. Phone available. Beds: QDTC. B&B. Golf, horseback riding, carriage trips & tours.
Seen in: *Detroit Free Press, Chicago Tribune, Innsider Magazine.*
"The ambience, service and everything else was just what we needed."

MARQUETTE E2/B1

Michigamme Lake Lodge

2403 US-41W
Marquette MI 49855
(906) 225-1393 (906) 339-4400

Circa 1934. Listed in the State Register of Historic Sites, this lodge is on the shore of Lake Michigamme, atop a bluff surrounded by ancient birch trees. It features native white-pine log walls, pegged oak floors, a cedar chandelier, original woolen area rugs from Europe, original handmade furniture and hand-hewn stairways that

lead to twin balconies. The massive stone fireplace stretches to the 33-foot-high vaulted ceiling. A sun porch overlooks the lake.
Rates: $100-$125. Season: May 1 to November 1. Linda & Frank Stabile.
9 R. 3 PB. Phone available. Beds: QDT. Continental-plus breakfast. CCs: MC VISA. Hiking, biking, canoeing, fishing, boating, beach.
Seen in: *Midwest Living, Livonia Observer, The Mining Journal.*
"... secluded lodge recaptures grandeur of an earlier era," Greats Lakes Getaway.

MENDON X7/H3

The Mendon Country Inn
440 W Main St
Mendon MI 49072
(616) 496-8132
Circa 1873. This two-story inn was constructed with St. Joseph River clay bricks fired on the property. There are 8-foot windows, high ceilings and a walnut staircase. Country antiques are accentuated with rag rugs, collectibles and bright quilts. The Indian Room has a fireplace. A creek runs by the property, and a romantic courting canoe is available to guests. Depending on the season, guests may also borrow a tandem bike or arrange for an Amish sleigh ride.
Location: Halfway between Chicago and Detroit.
*Rates: $45-$125. Dick & Dolly Buerkle.
18 R. 18 PB. Phone available. TV available. Beds: QD. Continental breakfast. Spa. Handicap access. Conference room. CCs: MC VISA DS. Fishing, tennis, golf, bicycles, swimming, cross-country skiing.
Seen in: *Innsider, Country Home.*
"A great experience. Good food and great hosts. Thank you."

NILES Y5/H2

Yesterday's Inn
518 N 4th St
Niles MI 49120
(616) 683-6079
Circa 1875. Nearly every style of architecture can be found on 4th Street in the historic district. This distinctive Italianate house has a graceful porch and tall shuttered windows. The walls are 12 inches thick with the interior plaster applied directly onto the brick. A favorite breakfast treat is Dutch Babies, an apple pancake.
Location: Eight miles north of South Bend.
❀Rates: $55. Elizabeth Baker.
5 R. 3 PB. Full breakfast. Spa. CCs: MC VISA.
"A lovely experience. Great hospitality."

NORTHPORT K7/D2

Old Mill Pond Inn
202 W Third St
Northport MI 49670
(616) 386-7341
Circa 1895. This three-story summer cottage nestled among tall trees is surrounded by extensive gardens including a Roman garden with fountain

and statues. Inside the house is an unusual collection of memorabilia from around the world. Breakfast is served by the fireside or on the screened porch with its white wicker furnishings. Shops and restaurants are within two blocks, and the beach is a quarter of a mile away.
Rates: $65. David Chrobak.
6 R. Phone available. TV available. Beds: QT. Full breakfast. CCs: MC VISA. Sailing, fishing, swimming.
Seen in: *Great Lakes Getaway.*
"You made the visit extra special."

NORTHVILLE V14/G4

The Atchison House
501 W Dunlap
Northville MI 48167
(313) 349-3340
Circa 1882. Located in the middle of Northville's historic district, this Italianate inn features pedestal sinks, a claw-foot tub, a natural wood-vaulted ceiling and many period antiques. The 5,000-square-foot inn is surrounded by dozens of elegant Victorian homes, and much of its furnishings are of that style. Two rooms feature Murphy beds if additional accommodations are needed. The town's business district, with gazebos, ice cream parlors and restaurants, is a few blocks away. A library and conference room are popular with executive guests. Nearby attractions include Dearborn's Greenfield Village and Henry Ford Museum.
Location: Heart of the historic district.
Rates: $70-$125. Don Mroz & Susan Lapine.
5 R. 5 PB. Phone in room. TV available. Beds: QD. Continental-plus breakfast. Spa. Conference room. CCs: MC VISA AE. Cross-country skiing, biking, horseback riding, state park.
Seen in: *Crain's Detroit Business.*
"Like pages out of a book except for the hospitality, which is like another era, when people were treated as something special!"

PETOSKEY J9/C3

Bear & The Bay
421 Charlevoix Ave
Petoskey MI 49770
(616) 347-6077
Circa 1890. Once the home of a local lumber baron, this inn is nestled in a setting of evergreens and black walnut trees. Beautiful woodwork is found throughout, including ash, carved oak and a bird's-eye maple staircase. Petoskey stone shops and the city's famous Gaslight District are just minutes away. The Bear River runs through the inn's grounds, and some of Michigan's best skiing spots are within easy driving distance. Nina's formal breakfasts feature her considerable culinary skill. (Her father was a chef, and she was once in the catering business).
Rates: $65. Lyle & Nina Ankrapps.
4 R. Phone available. TV available. Beds: QDT. Full breakfast. CCs: MC VISA. Horseback riding, downhill & cross-country skiing, boating, fishing, golf, sailing, snowmobiling.
Seen in: *Great Lakes Getaway.*

PORT HURON T17/G5

Victorian Inn
1229 Seventh St
Port Huron MI 48060
(313) 984-1437
Circa 1896. This finely renovated Queen Anne Victorian house has both an inn and restaurant. Gleaming carved-oak woodwork, leaded-glass windows and fireplaces in almost every room reflect the home's gracious air. Authentic wallpapers and draperies provide a background for carefully selected antiques. Victorian-inspired menus include such entrees as partridge with pears and filet of beef Africane, all served on antique china.
Rates: $45-$60. Sheila Marinez.
4 R. 2 PB. Phone available. TV available. Beds: QDT. Continental breakfast. Restaurant. CCs: MC VISA AE DS. Water sports, golf, tennis, museums of art & history.
Seen in: *Detroit Free Press.*
"In all of my trips, business or pleasure, I have never experienced such a warm and courteous staff."

PORT SANILAC R17/F5

Raymond House Inn

M-25, 111 S Ridge St
Port Sanilac MI 48469
(313) 622-8800

Circa 1871. Uri Raymond, owner of Michigan's first hardware store, built this Victorian house with its gingerbread facade and white icicle

trim dripping from the eaves. The inn is filled with antiques and features classic moldings, high ceilings and a winding staircase. The innkeeper is a sculptor who works as a restoration artist at the U.S. Capitol. Be sure to visit the historic lighthouse nearby.

Location: I-94 to Port Huron, then 30 miles on M-25.

*Rates: $45-$60. Season: April to Nov. Shirley Denison.

7 R. 7 PB. Phone available. TV available. Beds: Q. Continental-plus breakfast. CCs: MC VISA. Sport fishing, swimming, sailing, golf, bicycling, scuba diving.

Seen in: *Adventure Magazine.*

"A warm, friendly, relaxed, homey atmosphere like visiting friends and family."

SAGINAW R12/F4

Brockway House

1631 Brockway
Saginaw MI 48602
(517) 792-0746

Circa 1864. Located on one acre, the Brockway House features a Corinthian-columned front porch. Antiques include an old-fashioned tin tub with walnut trim in the Bliss Room. Another guest room boasts a log cabin quilt atop a king-size brass bed. Children are welcome.

Rates: $65-$85. Richard & Danice Zuehlke.

4 R. 2 PB. Phone available. TV available. Beds: KQT. Full breakfast. Conference room. CCs: MC VISA AE. Frankenmuth German Village.

Seen in: *The Saginaw News.*

"I could not have chosen a more perfect place."

SALINE W13/H4

The Homestead B&B

9279 Macon Rd
Saline MI 48176
(313) 429-9625

Circa 1851. The Homestead is a two-story brick farmhouse situated on 50 acres of fields, woods and river. The

house has 15-inch-thick walls and is furnished with Victorian antiques and family heirlooms. This was a favorite camping spot for Indians while they salted their fish, and many arrowheads have been found on the farm. Activities include long walks through meadows of wildflowers and cross-country skiing in season. It is 40 minutes from Detroit and Toledo and five minutes from Ann Arbor.

Location: Southeastern Michigan, within six miles of I-94 & US 23.

*Rates: $50-$65. Shirley Grossman.

6 R. 1 PB. Phone available. TV available. Beds: D. Full breakfast. Conference room. CCs: MC VISA DC CB. Golf, tennis, downhill & cross-country skiing. Honeymoon and anniversary specials.

Seen in: *Ann Arbor News, Country Focus, Saline Reporter.*

"One of the nicest B&Bs we've ever stayed in."

SAUGATUCK U5/G2

Crane House

See: Fennville, MI

Kemah Guest House

633 Pleasant St
Saugatuck MI 49453
(616) 857-2919

Circa 1906. Stained-glass windows, beamed ceilings, and stone and tile fireplaces are trademarks of this house. There is a billiard room, and a

Bavarian rathskeller has German inscriptions on the wall and original wine kegs. Deco Dormer, a guest room with a mahogany bedroom suite, was featured in a 1926 *Architectural Digest.* That same year, a Frank Lloyd Wright-style solarium with its own waterfall was added to the house. Kemah is situated on two hilltop acres with a view of the water. Spelunkers will want to explore the cave found on the property.

*Rates: $50-$95. Cindi & Terry Tatsch.

7 R. 3 FP. Phone available. TV available. Beds: DT. Continental-plus breakfast. Game room. Conference room. CCs: MC VISA. Golf, sailing, cross-country skiing.

Seen in: *Innsider, West Michigan Magazine, Grand Rapids Press, Buildings of Michigan.*

"What a wonderful time we had at Kemah. Thank you for a delightful stay. Your home is very special."

The Kirby House

294 W Center St, PO Box 1174
Saugatuck MI 49453
(616) 857-2904

Circa 1890. This impressive Victorian home sits behind a picket fence. It's framed by tall trees and a veranda

that wraps around three sides. The inn has four fireplaces and a grand staircase.

Location: Near Lake Michigan.

Rates: $85-$100. Marsha & Loren Kontio.

10 R. 6 PB. Phone available. Beds: QDT. Full breakfast. Spa. Swimming pool. CCs: MC VISA. Beachcombing, hiking, swimming. Seen in: *Michigan Today Magazine, Lansing State Journal.*

"Living only a few miles away from your inn, we never had a reason to remain overnight - until now. Thanks for your hospitality."

The Park House

888 Holland St
Saugatuck MI 49453
(616) 857-4535

Circa 1857. This Greek Revival-style home is the oldest residence in Saugatuck and was constructed for the first mayor. Susan B. Anthony was a guest here for two weeks in the

1870s, and the local Women's Christian Temperance League was established in the parlor. A country theme pervades the inn, with antiques, old

woodwork and pine floors.
**Rates: $65-$85. Lynda & Joe Petty.
8 R. 8 PB. Phone available. TV available. Beds: Q. Continental-plus breakfast. Handicap access. Conference room. CCs: MC VISA DS. Cross-country skiing, swimming, hiking. Seen in: *Detroit News, Insider, Gazette, South Bend Tribune.*
"Thanks again for your kindness and hospitality during our weekend."

SOUTH HAVEN W5/G2

Yelton Manor
140 N Shore Dr
South Haven MI 49090
(616) 637-5220
Circa 1872. The Yelton Manor is on the shoreline of Lake Michigan. The inn is decorated in country Victorian-style with stained-glass windows, antiques, oak furnishings made by Amish craftsmen and decorative Amish quilts. Common rooms include a sun porch, TV room, third-floor library and second-floor "widow's watch" with a view of Lake Michigan.
Rates: $85-$140. Jenny, Jay & Joyce Yelton.
11 R. 11 PB. 1 FP. Phone available. TV in room. Beds: KQDT. Full breakfast. Spa. Conference room. CCs: MC VISA AE. Beach, boating, golfing, biking. Seen in: *Great Lakes Getaway, Adventure Roads.*
"All the good things we were told about your place were true and still didn't explain the feeling of staying here."

SUTTONS BAY L7/D2

The Cottage B&B
503 St Joseph Ave, PO Box 653
Suttons Bay MI 49682
(616) 271-6348
Circa 1920. The Cottage B&B offers comfortable furnishings with antique accents. The inn has a common living room/library and cozy guest rooms.
Rates: $70. Alice & Phil Krupa.
3 R. 3 PB. Phone available. TV in room. Beds: DT. Full breakfast. Water sports, hiking, skiing, horseback riding.
Seen in: *The Detroit News.*
"Thank you very much for making our stay here in your home a very pleasant experience."

TRAVERSE CITY M7/D2

Cherry Knoll Farm
2856 Hammond Rd East
Traverse City MI 49684
(616) 947-9806
Circa 1870. Located on 115 acres, this renovated farmhouse boasts an old-fashioned front porch. The inn features country furnishings and decor with plaid wallpaper, brick fireplace in the den and patchwork quilts and crocheted bed spreads in the air-conditioned bedrooms. A Traverse City

specialty, cherry sausage, often is served at breakfast. (Dorothy caters to any special dietary needs as well.) There are 1,200 cherry trees in the summer and guests are invited to pick all the cherries they can eat.
Rates: $60. Dorothy & Percy Cump.
3 R. 1 FP. Phone available. TV available. Beds: D. Full breakfast. CCs: MC VISA. Boating, canoeing, tubing, beach, water sports, skiing, horseback riding. Cherry picking, mushroom hunting.
Seen in: *Great Lakes Getaway, Preview Community Weekly.*
"The weekend was everything we had hoped for, and I will always remember your hospitality and the efficiency with which your B&B is run."

The Victoriana
622 Washington St
Traverse City MI 49684
(616) 929-1009
Circa 1898. Egbert Ferris, a partner in the European Horse Hotel, built this Italianate Victorian manor and a two-story carriage house. Later, the bell

tower from the old Central School was moved onto the property and now serves as a handsome Greek Revival gazebo. The house has three parlors, all framed in fretwork. Etched and stained glass is found throughout. Guest rooms are furnished with family heirlooms. The house speciality is Belgian waffles topped with homemade cherry sauce.
*Rates: $55-$75. Flo & Bob Schermerhorn.
3 R. 3 PB. 2 FP. Phone available. TV available. Beds: KQDT. Full breakfast. CCs: MC VISA. Bicycling, water sports, downhill & cross-country skiing, wineries, theater.
Seen in: *Midwest Living.*
"We will long remember your beautiful home, those delectable breakfast creations and our pleasant chats."

Warwickshire Inn
5037 Barney Rd
Traverse City MI 49684
(616) 946-7176
Circa 1902. The Warwickshire is located in a tree-shaded country setting. Gleaming oak woodwork and pocket doors add to the early-20th-century

atmosphere. The inn features antique furnishings throughout. A full breakfast is served family-style on fine English china.
Location: Two miles west of City Center.
*Rates: $65-$75. Dan & Pat Warwick.
2 R. 2 PB. Phone available. TV available. Beds: QDT. Full breakfast. CCs: MC VISA. Bicycling, water sports, downhill & cross-country skiing, golf.
"House of character - out of this world! And the hosts were just as beautiful and gracious."

UNION PIER Y4/H1

The Inn at Union Pier
9708 Berrien, PO Box 222
Union Pier MI 49129
(616) 469-4700
Circa 1915. Set on a shady acre across a country road from Lake Michigan, this inn features unique Swedish ceramic fireplaces, a hot tub and sauna, a veranda ringing the house and a large common room with comfortable overstuffed furniture and a grand piano. Rooms offer such amenities as private balconies and porches, whirlpools, views of the English garden and furniture dating from the early 1900s. Breakfast includes fresh fruit and homemade jams made of fruit from local farms.
Rates: $85-$125. Libby Johnston, Madeleine & Bill Reinke.
15 R. 15 PB. 11 FP. Phone available. TV available. Beds: KQT. Full breakfast. Gourmet meals. Spa. Sauna. Handicap access. Conference room. CCs: MC VISA. Horseback riding, water sports, cross-country skiing, golf, tennis, winery tours, antiquing, galleries. Family & friend reunion weekends. Seen in: *Chicago Tribune, USA Today, The Detroit News.*
"The food, the atmosphere, the accommodations, and of course, the entire staff made this the most relaxing weekend ever."

MINNESOTA

CHASKA T10/G3

Bluff Creek Inn

1161 Bluff Creek Dr
Chaska MN 55318
(612) 445-2735

Circa 1864. This two-story brick Victorian folk home was built on land granted by Abe Lincoln to one of the earliest settlers in the area. It boasts a wide veranda and three summer porches. Family antiques are accentuated by Laura Ashley and Merrimekko quilts and linens. A three-course breakfast is served in the country dining room with Bavarian crystal and old English china.

Rates: $65-$85. Anne Karels.

4 R. 1 PB. Phone available. Beds: QD. Full breakfast. CCs: MC VISA. Bike trails, cross-country skiing, walking paths.

Seen in: *Sailor.*

"Thank you for your wonderful hospitality and extra special considerations."

GRAND MARAIS C14/A5

Cascade Lodge

PO Box 693
Grand Marais MN 55604
(218) 387-1112 (800) 322-9543 (MN only)

Circa 1938. A main lodge and several vintage cabins (1920s) comprise Cascade Lodge tucked away in the midst of Cascade River State Park overlooking Lake Superior. Cascade Creek meanders between the cabins toward the lake. The lodge has a natural-stone fireplace and lounge areas decorated with hunting trophies of moose, coyote, wolves and bear. Canoeing, hiking to Lookout Mountain, walking along Wild Flower Trail and watching the sunset from the lawn swing are favorite summer activities. Skiing, snowshoeing, photography and fireside conversations are popular in winter.

Location: Highway 61.

✻❀Rates: $50-$115. Gene & Laurene Glader.

27 R. 27 PB. 9 FP. Phone in room. TV in room. Beds: QDTC. AP. Restaurant. Spa. Game room. Conference room. CCs: MC VISA AE.

Seen in: *Country Inns.*

"We needed to get away and recharge ourselves. This was the perfect place."

HASTINGS U12/G4

The River Rose

620 Ramsey
Hastings MN 55033
(612) 437-3297

Circa 1880. This romantic Queen Anne Victorian has several verandas and porches. Grained cherry woodwork and nine fireplaces add elegance to the inn. Most rooms in The River Rose have fireplaces. In the Mississippi Under the Stars Room, a skylight shines down on the whirlpool tub. This 1,200-square-foot suite features a baby grand piano, tapestries, paisleys and a copper soaking tub as well as a round shower.

Rates: $75-$200. Dick & Pam Thorsen.

6 R. Beds: QD. Full breakfast. Restaurant. CCs: MC VISA. Limousine & dinner package.

Seen in: *Travel Holiday.*

Thorwood

315 Pine St
Hastings MN 55033
(612) 437-3297 (612) 437-8093

Circa 1880. This three-story Victorian mansion, built by lumberman William Thompson, is in the National Register. It has been carefully preserved and restored and lavishly decorated. The inn's best view is from Sara's Suite, a romantic three-level room with 15-foot ceilings, a skylight and double whirlpool tub. Another room boasts a see-through fireplace visible from both bed and bath. Hat-box suppers featuring Cornish game hens and deluxe desserts are available to be delivered to your room, and picnic lunches may be taken to nearby rivers and lakes or the Vermillion waterfall. Hastings is a Mississippi River town with third and fourth-generation shopkeepers selling arts and crafts and antiques from restored store fronts.

Rates: $75-$200. Dick & Pam Thorsen.

15 R. 15 PB. 9 FP. Phone available. TV available. Beds: QDT. Full breakfast. Gourmet meals. Spa. Handicap access. Conference room. CCs: MC VISA AE DS. Canoeing, downhill & cross-country skiing, golf, swimming, tennis, bicycling.

Seen in: *Business Ink, St. Paul Pioneer Press Dispatch, Midwest Living.*

"A special place. The service was warm, the food great and the whole atmosphere excellent."

LAKE CITY V14/G5

Red Gables Inn

403 N High St
Lake City MN 55041
(612) 345-2605

Circa 1865. This red Victorian features a Greek Revival center section with Italianate styling and a veranda that wraps around two sides of the house. Lace curtains and floral wallpapers provide a background for antiques, Oriental rugs and the inn's handsome black walnut staircase. Guest rooms are named for the old riverboats of the area and are furnished with iron and brass beds and antique armoires. Breakfast is served in the formal dining room or on the screened-in porch. Hors d'oeuvres are served in the parlor at twilight. Bicycles are available.

Rates: $68. Mary & Doug De Roos.

4 R. 2 PB. Phone available. Beds: KQD. Full breakfast. Gourmet meals. CCs: MC VISA. Boating, fishing, water skiing, swimming, bird-watching, biking, snowmobiling, snow skiing. Group or club luncheons, picnic baskets.

Seen in: *Red Wing Eagle, Chicago Sun-Times, San Francisco Examiner, Star-Tribune.*

"You made it very personal and special by doing small things, and those things are what count!"

LANESBORO Y15/H5

Carrolton Country Inn

RR 2 Box 139
Lanesboro MN 55949
(507) 467-2257

Circa 1880. This inn is nestled among hills overlooking the Root River and Trail. It features hardwood floors, yellow pine woodwork, original milk paint on woodwork, an open staircase, antiques and a dumbwaiter in the butler's pantry. The original homestead, a three-story log cabin

built in 1856, is within walking distance.
Rates: $55-$80. Charles & Gloria Ruen.
4 R. 2 PB. Phone in room. TV available. Beds: QDT. Full breakfast. CCs: MC VISA. Horseback riding, cross-country skiing, hiking, biking, fishing, canoeing, tennis, swimming. Honeymoon specials, local Amish tours.
Seen in: *Rochester Post-Bulletin, Winona Daily News.*
"Enjoyed every aspect of our stay here, especially the solitude and scenery."

Mrs. B's Historic Lanesboro Inn
101 Pkwy
Lanesboro MN 55949
(507) 467-2154

Circa 1872. Steep bluffs surround Lanesboro on three sides with hundreds of forested acres providing spectacular fall colors. Mrs. B's is an old limestone building that was once a furniture store and funeral parlor. Now handsomely renovated and furnished, the inn has a baby grand piano and a well-stocked library in the downstairs lobby. Four-poster and half-canopied beds in the upstairs guest rooms are topped with quilts. Weekend dinner packages are tasty and highly recommended. (Ask for the baked trout with pilaf or fillet of beef tenderloin with Yorkshire pudding.) The inn has a resident storyteller.
Rates: $48-$90. Nancy & Jack Bratrud.
9 R. 9 PB. 2 FP. Phone in room. TV in room. Beds: QT. Full breakfast. Gourmet meals. Handicap access. Conference room. Cross-country skiing, biking, canoeing, tennis, golf, trout fishing.
Seen in: *Travel & Leisure, Minneapolis Star-Tribune.*
"Each time I come, I feel more and more at peace with myself."

Scanlan House
708 Park Ave S
Lanesboro MN 55949
(507) 467-2158

Circa 1889. This gracious Victorian, a National Register house, was built by the Scanlans, successful merchants and bankers. Since then, more recent owners have added window boxes and garden areas. There are stained-glass windows throughout, and carved-oak woodwork adorns the dining room and staircase.

*Rates: $65-$90. Mary, Gene & Kirsten Mensing.
5 R. 1 PB. 1 FP. Phone available. TV in room. Beds: QD. Full breakfast. Spa. CCs: MC VISA AE. Horseback riding, cross-country skiing, bicycles, golf, tennis, tubing, canoeing, sailing, snowmobiling.
Seen in: *Post-Bulletin, Lacrosse Tribune.*
"We were refreshed and inspired and when the sun was out, wanted not to budge from the balcony."

PARK RAPIDS L6/D2

Dorset Schoolhouse
PO Box 201
Park Rapids MN 56470
(218) 732-1377

Circa 1920. In this former schoolhouse there are miniature chalkboard signs designating the guest rooms as grades one through six. Each guest room has a wooden school desk and a patio door leading to the deck, where guests may enjoy the morning sun, the afternoon shade or the evening stars. The inn features antiques, country furnishings and folk art. The enlarged cloak room offers a place to relax or read. The nurse's office and library are now three large baths.
Rates: $40-$60. Tom & Denise Hafner.
6 R. Phone available. Continental breakfast. CCs: MC VISA.
Seen in: *The Forum, Park Rapid Enterprise.*
"This is a great place to stay. You get an A+ in our book!"

RED WING U13/G4

Pratt-Taber Inn
706 W Fourth
Red Wing MN 55066
(612) 388-5945 (612) 388-0166

Circa 1876. City treasurer A. W. Pratt built this Italianate house during the town's centennial. He added star-studded porch detailing to the gingerbread trim to celebrate the event. Feather-painted slate fireplaces and gleaming butternut woodwork provide a backdrop for early Renaissance Revival and country Victorian furnishings. There is a Murphy bed hidden in the library buffet. Other library items include 1,000 stereopticon slides and a Victrola. Secret bureau drawers, authentic Victorian

wallpapers, dress-up clothes and hand-stenciling add to the atmosphere.
Location: Fifty-five miles south of the Twin Cities.
*Rates: $69-$89. Jane Walker, Jan McDermott, Darrell Molander.
6 R. 2 PB. 1 FP. Phone available. TV available. Beds: KQD. Continental-plus breakfast. Spa. Handicap access. Conference room. CCs: MC VISA. Golf, hiking, bicycling, boating, dinner cruises.
Seen in: *Better Homes & Gardens, Midwest Living.*
"When I need a peaceful moment I dream of the Pratt-Taber and the big screened-in porch with church bells chiming a favorite tune."

SAINT PAUL T12/G4

Chatsworth B&B
984 Ashland
Saint Paul MN 55104
(612) 227-4288

Circa 1902. This three-story red Victorian is framed by maple and basswood trees. Guest rooms are decorated in an international theme

except for the Four Poster Room. It features a canopy bed, whirlpool bath, mirrored armoire and a rose-print wallpaper that covers both the ceiling and the walls. Vegetarian breakfasts are available. Don't forget to ask the innkeeper for her famous cranberry bread.
Rates: $45-$90. Donna & Earl Gustafson.
5 R. 3 PB. Phone available. TV available. Beds: KQDT. B&B. Conference room. Jogging, biking, museums.

Seen in: *St. Paul Pioneer Press and Dispatch.*
"Wonderful and romantic surroundings everywhere. So beautifully kept, fresh and clean. Tremendous service."

University Club of St. Paul

420 Summit Ave
Saint Paul MN 55102
(612) 222-1751

Circa 1912. Established to enhance literary, cultural and social activities for the well-educated, this Tudor

Revival club is modeled after the Cambridge and Oxford Clubs in London. Fine English antiques and oil paintings of English landscapes decorate the interiors. In the Grill Bar, F. Scott Fitzgerald's initials can be found carved beside those of other club members. There is a library, dining room, Fireside Room and a fitness center.

Rates: $45-$85. John Rupp.
5 R. 5 PB. TV available. Beds: QT. Restaurant. Sauna. Swimming pool. Conference room. CCs: MC VISA DC. Tennis, exercise room, playground.
Seen in: *Minnesota USA Magazine, Corporate Report.*

SPICER S7/F2

Spicer Castle

11600 Indian Beach Rd
Spicer MN 56288
(612) 796-5870 (612) 796-5243

Circa 1893. This English Tudor-style house is situated on five wooded acres on the southeast shore of Green Lake with 600 feet of waterfront. In the National Register, the house was the summer home of John Spicer, the innkeeper's grandfather. Many furnishings are original to the house. Breakfast is served on the porch overlooking the lake in the summer or beside the dining-room fireplace in winter. Two private cottages are also available. Afternoon tea is served.

Rates: $60-$90. Ginger & Renee Hanson.
6 R. 6 PB. 2 FP. Beds: Q. Full breakfast. Gourmet meals. Conference room. CCs: MC VISA AE. Cross-country skiing, lake activities.
Seen in: *West Central Tribune, Midwest Flyer.*
"What a wonderfully hospitable place!"

STILLWATER S13/F4

Lowell Inn

102 N Second St
Stillwater MN 55082
(612) 439-1102

Circa 1930. The Palmer family has operated this Williamsburg-style hotel since Christmas Day 1930, collecting

antiques and fine tableware all this time. The George Washington Room is a parlor containing collections of Dresden china, a Charles III Sheffield silver service, Williamsburg ladder-back chairs and colonial draperies. A natural spring bubbles in the Garden Room. Guest rooms include four suites with jacuzzi baths.

Rates: $89-$239. Arthur & Maureen Palmer.
21 R. 21 PB. Beds: KQC. AP. Restaurant. Spa. Conference room. CCs: MC VISA. Downhill & cross-country skiing, hiking, canoeing, biking, swimming.
Seen in: *The New York Times.*

Rivertown Inn

306 W Olive St
Stillwater MN 55082
(612) 430-2955 (800)562-3632

Circa 1882. This three-story Victorian was built by lumbermill owner John O'Brien. Framed by an iron fence, the home has a wraparound veranda.

Each guest room has been decorated with care, but we suggest the honeymoon suite or Patricia's Room with its giant whirlpool and tall oak bedstead. A burl-wood buffet in the dining room is laden each morning with home-baked breads and cakes. The St. Croix River is a short walk away.

❀Rates: $49-$139. Chuck & Judy Dougherty.
9 R. 9 PB. 3 FP. Phone available. Beds: D. B&B. Spa. Conference room. CCs: MC VISA. Golf, biking, skiing, canoeing, swimming, river excursions.
Seen in: *Country Magazine.*
"Fantastic place for a romantic getaway!"

WALKER L8/D3

Chase On The Lake Lodge & Motor Inn

PO Box 206
Walker MN 56484
(218) 547-1531 (800) 533-2083

Circa 1921. Located on the shoreline of Leech Lake, this Tudor-style hotel in the National Register was renovated in 1987. A Twenties-style

predominates. The hotel has a private sandy swimming beach. The city docks are a block away, and Main Street is two blocks away.

Rates: $52-$72. Jim & Barb Aletto.
30 R. 30 PB. Phone in room. TV in room. Beds: QDTC. B&B. Restaurant. Conference room. CCs: MC VISA AE DS. Golf, water slide, movie theater, shopping, tennis, boating, launch fishing.
Seen in: *Minneapolis Star-Tribune, Fargo Forum.*
"We thoroughly enjoyed ourselves with the wonderful view, excellent menu and friendly service."

MISSISSIPPI

BILOXI P10/H4

Red Creek Colonial Inn

See: Long Beach, MS

FAYETTE K5/F2

Historic Springfield Plantation

Hwy 553
Fayette MS 39069
(601) 786-3802

Circa 1791. Historic Springfield Plantation is the oldest mansion in Mississippi. The mansion was the site of Andrew Jackson's wedding. It contains the original Georgian-Adams-Federal woodwork and mantels hand-carved in Virginia in the 18th century. From the upstairs gallery, visitors may view 1,000 acres of the working plantation.

Rates: $55-$75. Historic Springfield Foundation.

3 R. 3 FP. Phone available. TV available. Beds: DT. Continental breakfast. Conference room. Hiking, fishing.

Seen in: *Mississippi Magazine, The Clarion-Ledger, Natchez Democrat.*

JACKSON J7/E3

Millsaps-Buie House

628 N State St
Jackson MS 39202
(601) 352-0221

Circa 1888. Major Millsaps, founder of Millsaps College, built this stately mansion 100 years ago. Today the house remains in the family. A handsome, columned entrance, bays and gables are features of the house decorated by Berle Smith, designer for Mississippi's governor's mansion. The parlor features a French dating bench and a grand piano. The guest rooms are appointed in antiques and canopied beds.

*Rates: $75-$130. Judy Fenter, Dottie Stewart & Nancy Fleming.

11 R. 11 PB. Phone in room. TV in room. Beds: KQT. Full breakfast. Handicap access. Conference room. FAX. CCs: MC VISA AE DC DS. Art museums, theater, dance, symphony, opera. Honeymoons, weddings, receptions, small parties.

Seen in: *The New York Times, Jackson Daily News, Mississippi.*

LONG BEACH P10/H4

Red Creek Colonial Inn

7416 Red Creek Rd
Long Beach MS 39560
(601) 452-3080 (800) 729-9670

Circa 1899. This inn was built in the raised French cottage-style by a retired Italian sea captain who wished

to entice his bride to move from her parents' home in New Orleans. There are two swings on the 64-foot front porch and one swing that hangs from a 300-year-old oak tree. Magnolias and ancient live oaks, some registered with the Live Oak Society of the Louisiana Garden Club, dot 11 acres. The inn features a parlor, six fireplaces, ceiling fans and antiques, including a Victorian organ and wooden radios.

**Rates: $39-$69. Mike & Miki Pavloff.

7 R. 5 PB. 3 FP. Phone available. TV available. Beds: D. Continental-plus breakfast. Gourmet meals. CCs: MC VISA DC CB. Golf, croquet, river rafting, deep-sea fishing.

Seen in: *Innviews.*

"We loved waking up here on these misty spring mornings. The Old South is here."

LORMAN K5/E2

Rosswood Plantation

Hwy 552
Lorman MS 39096
(601) 437-4215

Circa 1857. Rosswood is a stately, columned mansion in an original plantation setting. Here, guests may find antiques, buried treasure, ghosts, history of a slave revolt, a Civil War battleground, the first owner's diary and genuine southern hospitality.

Voted the "prettiest place in the country" by *Farm & Ranch Living*, the manor is a Mississippi Landmark and is in the National Register.

*Rates: $90. Jean & Walt Hylander.

4 R. 4 PB. 4 FP. Phone in room. TV in room. Beds: QDTC. Full breakfast. Conference room. CCs: MC VISA. Fishing.

Seen in: *Southern Living, The New York Times, Mississippi Magazine.*

"The plantation to see if you can only see one."

MERIDIAN I11/E4

Lincoln, Ltd. B&B

PO Box 3479
Meridian MS 39303
(601) 482-5483 (800) 633-MISS

Circa 1830. Lincoln, Ltd. Bed & Breakfast is a Mississippi reservation service representing more than 50 historic inns and private homes throughout the state and western Alabama, eastern Louisiana and Tennessee. More than 225 rooms are available. Listings include antebellum mansions and historic log homes.

Rates: $40-$150. May White & Kathy Tanner.

Phone in room. TV in room. Beds: QDTC. Continental breakfast. Spa. Swimming pool. CCs: MC VISA.

Seen in: *The Meridian Star, Country Inns, Woman's Day.*

"I would have missed 99 percent of Mississippi's charm had I not stayed in your B&Bs. Thank you."

NATCHEZ L4/F1

The Burn

712 N Union St
Natchez MS 39120
(601) 442-1344 (800) 654-8859

Circa 1834. White Doric columns support the front portico of this Greek Revival gem set in four blossoming acres of dogwoods, magnolias and

camellias. An extensive antique collection graces the inn with gaslight chandeliers, Belgian draperies and finely carved woodwork adding to the genteel setting. The lavish Pink Room features an exquisite antique four-poster bed built by master craftsman Prudent Mallard and canopied with swagged damask draperies. Further pampering is provided with a plantation breakfast served at a polished mahogany dining table set with crystal and silver. The innkeeper served for 20 years as mayor of Natchez.

*Rates: $75-$125. Loveta & Tony Byrne.
6 R. 6 PB. 4 FP. Phone available. TV in room. Beds: QDT. B&B. Swimming pool. Conference room. FAX. CCs: MC VISA AE DC CB DS. Golf, tennis, water sports, fishing. Gourmet meals for groups are served.
Seen in: *Country Inns, Bon Appetit.*
"We are still basking in the pleasures we found at The Burn."

PORT GIBSON K5/E2

Oak Square Plantation

1207 Church St
Port Gibson MS 39150
(601) 437-4350 (800) 729-0240

Circa 1850. Six 22-foot-tall fluted Corinthian columns support the front gallery of this 30-room Greek Revival plantation. The owners furnished the mansion with Mississippi heirloom antiques, some as old as 200 years. The parlor holds a carved rosewood Victorian suite, original family documents and a collection of Civil War memorabilia. Enormous oaks and magnolia trees grace the grounds. The inn holds a four-diamond award.
Location: US 61 between Natchez & Vicksburg.
*Rates: $65-$85. Mr. & Mrs. William D. Lum.
10 R. 10 PB. Phone in room. TV in room.

Beds: QDT. Full breakfast. CCs: MC VISA AE DS. Parks, museums, historical sites.
Seen in: *Quad-City Times, The Dallas Morning News.*
"We just cannot say enough about the wonderful ambience of Oak Square...except it is even better than four stars."

VICKSBURG J5/E2

Anchuca Clarion Carriage House Inn

1010 First E
Vicksburg MS 39180
(601) 636-4931 (800) 262-4822

Circa 1830. This early Greek Revival mansion rises resplendently above the brick-paved streets of Vicksburg. It houses magnificent period antiques and artifacts and features gas-burning chandeliers. Confederate President Jefferson Davis once addressed the townspeople from the balcony while his brother was living in the home during the Civil War. The former slave quarters and a more recent 1900s cottage house have been transformed into enchanting hideaways with formal decor and four poster beds.
Location: Historic District.
*❀Rates: $75-$115. May C. Burns.
9 R. 9 PB. 2 FP. Phone in room. TV in room. Beds: QDTC. Full breakfast. Spa. Swimming pool. CCs: MC VISA AE DS. Tennis, golf.
Seen in: *The Times Herald, Southern Living, Innsider, West County Journal.*
"The 'Southern Hospitality' will not be forgotten."

Cedar Grove Mansion Inn

2300 Washington St
Vicksburg MS 39180
(800) 862-1300

Circa 1840. It's easy to relive *Gone With the Wind* at this grand antebellum estate built by John Klein as a wedding present for his bride. Visitors sip mint juleps and watch gas chandeliers flicker in the finely appointed parlors. The children's rooms and master bedroom contain their original furnishings. Although Cedar Grove survived the Civil War, a Union cannonball is still lodged in the parlor wall. There is a magnificent view of the Misissippi from the terraces and front galleries. Four acres of gardens include fountains and gazebos.

*Rates: $75-$140. Estelle Mackey.
18 R. 18 PB. 5 FP. Phone in room. TV in room. Beds: KQD. Full breakfast. Spa. Handicap access. Swimming pool. Conference room. CCs: MC VISA AE.
Seen in: *Vicksburg Post, Southern Living.*
"Love at first sight would be the best way to describe my feelings for your home and the staff."

The Corners Inn

601 Klein St
Vicksburg MS 39180
(800) 444-7421 (601) 636-7421

Circa 1872. Listed in the National Register, The Corners was built as a wedding present. It is an interesting combination of architectural styles, in-

cluding Steamboat Gothic, Louisiana Raised Cottage, Italianate, Greek Revival and Vicksburg Pierced Columns. Lovely antiques and canopy beds fill the mansion. It's the only inn in Vicksburg with original parterre gardens, and it has a view of the Mississippi River from the front gallery. Breakfast is a real southern experience.

*❀Rates: $65-$95. Cliff & Bettye Whitney.
7 R. 7 PB. 3 FP. Phone in room. TV in room. Beds: QDT. B&B. Gourmet meals. Handicap access. Conference room. CCs: MC VISA AE. Golf, boating, museums.
Seen in: *Travel-Holiday, Better Homes & Gardens, Verandah Magazine, Vicksburg Post.*
"The highlight of our trip was the night we spent in Vicksburg with you. It was just great!"

MISSOURI

BONNE TERRE K20/D6

1909 Depot

Oak & Allen St
Bonne Terre MO 63628
(314) 731-5003

Circa 1909. Completely restored in 1987, the Depot features a Queen Anne Victorian tower and a long veranda. The inn and restaurant are in

the National Register. Victorian-furnished guest rooms are on the second and third floors above the restaurant and Whistle Stop Bar. Cocktails are served in the caboose, and the restaurant is in the dining car. Rail lamps and old train memorabilia are part of the decor.

Rates: $80. Catherine & Douglas Goergens.
7 R. 7 PB. Phone available. TV in room. Beds: KDT. Continental breakfast. Restaurant. Conference room. CCs: MC VISA AE DS. Horseback riding, carriage rides, scuba diving, nature trails, fishing.
Seen in: *People Magazine, St. Louis Post-Dispatch.*
"Our accommodations were no less than superb!"

The Lamplight Inn B&B

207 E School St
Bonne Terre MO 63628
(314) 358-4222

Circa 1880. Built by the St. Joe Lead Mining Company, the main house of the inn is an imposing blue Victorian featuring an enormous wraparound veranda. Floral wall coverings accentuate handsomely decorated rooms that are filled with antiques, needlework and homemade quilts. Second-generation innkeeper and Cordon Bleu graduate Krista Wibskov organizes gourmet weekends that feature private cooking classes in the Fireside Room.

Rates: $55-$75. Krista & Jorgen Wibskov.
4 R. 3 PB. Phone available. TV available. Beds: D. Full breakfast. Restaurant. Gourmet meals. Conference room. CCs: MC VISA AE. Golf, swimming, tennis, racquetball. Gourmet weekends, weddings, honeymoons.
Seen in: *St. Louis Post-Dispatch.*
"You have lovely accommodations and peace and quiet!"

Mansion Hill Country Inn

Mansion Hill Dr
Bonne Terre MO 63628
(314) 358-5311 (314) 731-5003

Circa 1909. This massive 32-room house is situated on a wooded hilltop, part of a 132-acre estate overlooking the foothills of the Ozarks. The inn-

keepers have collected antiques and nautical memorabilia for Mansion Hill. The inn's owners operate the West End Diving Centers in St. Louis and the Bonne Terre Mine Billion Gallon Lake, said to be the world's largest man-made caverns.

Rates: $80. Catherine & Douglas Goergens.
6 R. 2 PB. Phone available. TV available. Beds: DT. Continental breakfast. Restaurant. CCs: MC VISA AE DS. Horseback riding, carriage rides, scuba diving, nature trails, fishing.
Seen in: *St. Louis Post-Dispatch, People Magazine, Suburban Journals.*
"Great weekend getaway! Plenty of activities to do as well as quiet nature trails for those peaceful times."

BRANSON P13/F3

Branson House

120 4th St
Branson MO 65616
(417) 334-0959

Circa 1923. A landscape architect for the Missouri State Park system, A. L. Drumeller, built this bungalow house, surrounding it with rock walls, gardens and orchards. Exposed-beam ceilings, built-in glass cabinets and pine woodwork add to the house's charm. From its hillside location, the veranda overlooks the town and Lake Taneycomo. Sherry is served in the

late afternoon. In the evening, cookies and milk are set out for the guests.

Location: Downtown.
Rates: $50-$65. Season: March - Dec. Opal Kelly.
7 R. 7 PB. Phone available. TV available. Beds: TW. Full breakfast. Fishing, boating, water sports.
"Thank you so much for your warm hospitality. It really made our trip special."

CAPE GIRARDEAU M23/E7

Trisha's B&B

See: Jackson, MO

CARTHAGE N9/E2

Brewer's Maple Lane Farms B&B

RR 1 Box 203
Carthage MO 64836
(417) 358-6312

Circa 1900. This three-story Carthage stone mansion features a red-tiled roof. In the National Register of Historic Places, the house is located on a 1,000-acre wheat and alfalfa farm. The parlor boasts a carved-oak fireplace, and there is an antique pipe organ. An ornately carved Austrian bedroom set is featured in the twin-bedded room. Peacocks roam the grounds, and Archie and Renee keep a llama, miniature horses, Sicilian donkeys, eight types of ducks and the family collie.

Rates: $50. Arch & Renee Brewer.
6 R. 1 PB. 2 FP. TV available. Beds: DTC.

Continental-plus breakfast. Game room. Golf, tennis, fishing. Church retreats, local tour guide service.
Seen in: *Missouri Farm.*
"Warm hospitality and beautiful home."

FULTON H16/*C4*

Loganberry Inn
310 W 7th St
Fulton MO 65251
(314) 642-9229

Circa 1899. The Loganberry Inn is decorated in berry shades and has antique furnishings in the English country-style. Upstairs are pegged doors from the 1850s that predate the house. Guests may relax in the parlor by the fireplace. The inn serves homemade bread and apple butter.
Rates: $50-$55. Bob & Deb Logan.
5 R. 3 PB. 2 FP. Phone available. TV available. Beds: QDTC. Full breakfast. CCs: MC VISA. Famous sites, antique shops. Wedding receptions.
Seen in: *The Fulton Sun.*
"Thank you for sharing your lovely home and gracious hospitality with us."

HANNIBAL E18/*B5*

Fifth Street Mansion B&B
213 S Fifth St
Hannibal MO 63401
(314) 221-0445

Circa 1858. This 20-room Italianate house displays the typical extended eaves and heavy brackets, tall windows and decorated lintels. A cupola

affords a view of the town. Mark Twain was invited to dinner here by the Garth family and joined Laura Frazer (his Becky Thatcher) for the evening. An enormous stained-glass window lights the stairwell. The library stained-glass window holds the family crest. The library also features hand-grained walnut paneling.
Location: North of St. Louis 100 miles.
*Rates: $50-$70. Donalene & Mike Andreotti.
7 R. 7 PB. Phone available. TV available. Beds: QDTC. B&B. Conference room. CCs: MC VISA. Water sports, fishing, Mississippi River cruises.
Seen in: *Innsider.*
"We thoroughly enjoyed our visit. Terrific food and hospitality!"

Garth Woodside Mansion
RR 1
Hannibal MO 63401
(314) 221-2789

Circa 1871. This Italian Renaissance mansion is set on 39 acres of meadow and woodland. Authentic Victorian antiques fill the house. An unusual

flying staircase with no visible means of support vaults three stories. Best of all, is the Samuel Clemens Room where Mark Twain slept in a "button bed." An elegant afternoon tea is served, and there are night shirts tucked away in your room.
Location: Just off highway 61.
*❀Rates: $55-$75. Irv & Diane Feinberg.
8 R. 6 PB. 8 FP. Phone available. TV available. Beds: QD. Full breakfast. Conference room. CCs: MC VISA. Riverboat rides.
Seen in: *Country Inns, Chicago Sun-Times.*
"So beautiful and romantic and relaxing, we forgot we were here to work," Jeannie and Bob Ransom, *Innsider.*

JACKSON M23/*E7*

Trisha's B&B
203 Bellevue
Jackson MO 63755
(314) 243-7427

Circa 1905. This inn offers a sitting room, library and spacious guest rooms. Some rooms have bay windows and are furnished with antiques

and family heirlooms. Trisha provides fresh flowers and serves hand-picked fruits and homemade baked goods.
Rates: $40-$55. Gus & Trisha Wischmann.
4 R. 1 PB. Phone available. Beds: KQD. Full breakfast. Gourmet meals. State parks, steam-powered train, antiquing. Honeymoon & anniversary specials.
Seen in: *Cape Girardeau News Guardian, Cash-Book Journal.*
"You have created a beautiful home so naturally. Your B&B is filled with love and care - a really special place."

JOPLIN N9/*E2*

Visages
327 N Jackson
Joplin MO 64801
(417) 624-1397

Circa 1898. This handsome two-story Dutch colonial house faced the wrecking crews a few years ago before Marge and Bill Meeker set about to

rescue it. A Grecian statue graces the front garden of the house. Upstairs guest rooms boast polished pine floors and turn-of-the-century antiques. The inn is named Visages after the character faces Bill created and installed in the stone wall surrounding the house. Several watercolors featured in the inn were also painted by Bill.
Rates: $30-$50. Bill & Marge Meeker.
3 R. 1 PB. Phone available. TV available. Beds: QDTC. Full breakfast. CCs: MC VISA AE. Flea markets.
Seen in: *The Joplin Globe.*
"Your home is truly a masterpiece."

KANSAS CITY G9/*B2*

Southmoreland on the Plaza
116 E 46th St
Kansas City MO 64112
(816) 531-7979

Circa 1913. Located inside the illustrious Country Club Plaza, this Colonial Revival mansion features a carriage house and three courtyards. Paired glass doors flank the foyer and original stair designs and fireplaces have been restored. Guests can explore the elegant shops that line the Plaza or visit Crown Center, an elaborate enclosed area featuring specialty shops and gourmet restaurants. A drive to nearby Mission Hills displays beautiful tudor-style mansions, including that of candymaker Russel Stover and the Hall family, owners of Hallmark corporation.
Rates: $100-$135. Susan Moehl & Penni

Johnson.
12 R. 12 PB. 2 FP. Phone in room. TV available. Beds: KQDT. B&B. Gourmet meals. Spa. Handicap access. Conference room. FAX. CCs: MC VISA AE. Museums, shops.
Seen in: *Inn Business Review.*
"Southmoreland on the Plaza goes beyond just setting new standards for an emergent class of inns in the European tradition. It is a uniquely Kansas City interpretation of an ancient form of roadside respite," Lawrence Goldblatt, *Kansas City Business Journal.*

MARSHFIELD M14/E3

The Dickey House B&B Inn
331 S Clay St
Marshfield MO 65706
(417) 468-3000

Circa 1910. Opened in the spring of 1991, this Colonial Revival mansion is framed by ancient oak trees and boasts eight two-story Ionic columns. Burled woodwork, beveled glass and polished hardwood floors accentuate the gracious rooms. Interior columns soar in the parlor, creating a suitably elegant setting for the innkeeper's outstanding collection of antiques. A queen-size canopy bed, fireplace and balcony are featured in the Heritage Room.
Rates: $45-$65. William & Dorothy Buesgen.
4 R. 4 PB. 1 FP. Phone available. TV available. Beds: QD. Full breakfast. Conference room. CCs: MC VISA. Wild-animal park, fishing. Evening desserts, chocolates in the rooms.

PLATTE CITY F8/B2

Basswood Country Inn B&B
15880 Interurban Rd
Platte City MO 64079
(816) 431-5556

Circa 1935. Once the country estate of A.J. Stephens, this unusual B&B combines an RV resort with a country inn. However, with more than 73 wooded acres, there's plenty of room for both. The setting is pristine with seven spring-fed fishing lakes stocked with bass, crappie and carp. We recommend the original red cottage situated at the water's edge. It features a large stone fireplace and a brass bed with bucolic views of water and woodland. The motel-like main building also has a lake view.
Rates: $59-$89. Don & Betty Soper.
5 R. 5 PB. 1 FP. Phone in room. TV in room. Beds: KQD. Continental-plus breakfast. Swimming pool. Conference room. CCs: MC VISA. Golf, skiing, antiquing. Weddings, reunions, retreats.
Seen in: *The Landmark, Platte Dispatch-Tribune, Electric Farmer.*
"From the moment we walked into our cabin to the moment we left (although we didn't want to!), we experienced one of the most relaxing, enjoyable weekends we've had in years."

ROCHEPORT G15/C4

School House B&B
Third & Clark St
Rocheport MO 65279
(314) 698-2022

Circa 1914. This three-story brick building was once a schoolhouse. Now luxuriously appointed as a country inn, it features 13-foot-high

ceilings, small print wallpapers and a bridal suite with Victorian furnishings and a private spa. The basement houses an antique and craft shop. Nearby is a winery and a trail along the river providing many scenic miles for cyclists and hikers.
Rates: $60-$95. John & Vicki Ott.
8 R. 5 PB. Phone available. TV available. Beds: Q. Full breakfast. Spa. Handicap access. CCs: MC VISA. Theater, antique shopping, vineyards.
Seen in: *Midwest Motorist, Missouri Wein Press, Successful Farming.*

SAINT CHARLES H21/C6

Boone's Lick Trail Inn
1000 S Main St
Saint Charles MO 63301
(314) 947-7000

Circa 1840. This Greek Revival brick and limestone house overlooks the Missouri River State Trail and the Lewis and Clark Trail. From the gal-

lery porch guests may watch the Missouri River flow by Frontier Park. The inn is furnished with antiques, lace curtains and old quilts.
Location: 10 minutes from St. Louis airport.
Rates: $58-$75. V'Anne Mydler.
6 R. 4 PB. Phone available. TV available. Beds: QD. Full breakfast. CCs: MC VISA DS. Art museums, the ferry, historic district. Missouri River, Louis & Clark launching site.
Seen in: *St. Louis Post-Dispatch, Midwest Motorist, Midwest Living.*
"Makes your trip back in time complete."

SAINT LOUIS I21/C6

The Coachlight B&B
PO Box 8095
Saint Louis MO 63156
(314) 367-5870

Circa 1904. This three-story brick house is in an exclusive district of elegant homes. These homes were once considered "private places" where home owners even owned the streets. The neighborhood has been beautifully maintained and is near St. Louis and Washington Universities. The parlor features Queen Anne furnishings with Laura Ashley prints.

Location: Central west end.
✻❀Rates: $65 & up.
3 R. 3 PB. Phone in room. TV in room. Beds: KQDT. Full breakfast. Conference room. CCs: MC VISA AE. Golf, handball, zoo, art museums.
Seen in: *St. Louis Sun, Santa Cruz Sentinel.*
"Your B&B is more beautiful and luxurious than any hotel I have ever visited. In every corner you find such delightful surprises."

Geandaugh House
3835-37 S Broadway
Saint Louis MO 63118
(314) 771-5447

Circa 1790. The old limestone "Prairie House" section of Geandaugh House located in South St. Louis, is one of

the oldest structures in the state. A brick Federal-style house was added in the 1800s. Antiques and collections fill the inn, revealing Gea & Wayne's love for history. Lady Elizabeth's

Room boasts high ceilings, walnut furnishings and Irish lace curtains. There is a craft shop on the premises.
❀Rates: $45-$55. Gea & Wayne Popp.
4 R. 1 PB. 4 FP. Phone available. TV available. Beds: DT. Continental-plus breakfast. Handicap access. Horseback riding, riverboats, museums. Afternoon tea.
Seen in: *South Side Journal, St. Louis Post-Dispatch.*
"Thank you for making us feel so welcome and comfortable in your home."

Lafayette House
2156 Lafayette Ave
Saint Louis MO 63104
(314) 772-4429
Circa 1876. Captain James Eads, designer and builder of the first trussed bridge across the Mississippi River, built this Queen Anne mansion

as a wedding present for his daughter Margaret. The rooms are furnished in antiques, and there is a suite with a kitchen on the third floor. The house overlooks Lafayette Park.
Location: In the center of St. Louis.
*Rates: $40-$70. Sarah & Jack Milligan.
5 R. 2 PB. Phone available. TV available. Beds: DTC. Full breakfast.
"We had a wonderful stay at your house and enjoyed the furnishings, delicious breakfasts and friendly pets."

The Winter House
3522 Arsenal
Saint Louis MO 63118
(314) 664-4399
Circa 1897. This three-story brick house was built with a decorative balcony above the entrance. A turret in the dining room rises to the second level. Embossed French panels, three fireplaces and pressed-tin ceilings are featured. There is an unusual 20-foot-long underground garage. Tennis courts are nearby in Tower Grove Park adjacent to the Missouri Botanical Garden.
Rates: $48. Kendall & Sarah Winter.
2 R. 1 PB. Phone available. TV available. Beds: DT. Continental-plus breakfast. CCs: MC VISA. Tennis, fitness trail, bike path, swimming pool at local YMCA. Tea & piano on weekends.
Seen in: *Innsider.*
"A delightful house with spotless, beautifully appointed rooms, charming hosts. Highly recommended."

SAINTE GENEVIEVE K22/*D6*

The Southern Hotel
146 S Third St
Sainte Genevieve MO 63670
(314) 883-3493 (800) 275-1412
Circa 1800. This Federal building is the largest and oldest brick home west of the Mississippi. It features a long front porch, large parlors and a spacious dining room. Highlights of the guest rooms include cedar bedposts carved in the shape of Old Man River, a hand-painted headboard and a delicately carved Victorian bed. The claw-foot tubs are hand-painted. Guests are invited to add their names to a quilt-in-progress, which is set out in the parlor.
Rates: $55-$90. Mike & Barbara Hankins.
8 R. 8 PB. 4 FP. Phone available. Beds: KD. Full breakfast. Game room. Conference room. CCs: MC VISA. Wineries, antiquing, parks.
Seen in: *Innsider, St. Louis Gourmet, River Heritage Gazette.*
"I can't imagine ever staying in a motel again! It was so nice to be greeted by someone who expected us. We felt right at home."

SPRINGFIELD N12/*E3*

The Mansion at Elfindale
1701 S Fort
Springfield MO 65807
(417) 831-5400 (417)831-7242
Circa 1800. The Mansion at Elfindale once served as the St. de Chantel Academy for girls. The gray stone structure features a turret observation room, ornate fireplaces, stained-glass windows, vaulted ceilings, marble-finish furnishings, wicker furniture and antiques. Breakfast includes foods from around the world.
Rates: $50-$125. Kitty White.
13 R. 13 PB. Phone available. TV available. Beds: KQDT. Full breakfast. Handicap access. Conference room. CCs: MC VISA AE. Water sports. Wedding specials, local tour-guide service.
"Many thanks for your warm hospitality."

WASHINGTON I19/*C5*

Schwegmann House
438 West Front Street
Washington MO 63090
(314) 239-5025
Circa 1853. John F. Schwegmann, a native of Germany, built a flour mill on the Missouri riverfront. His stately three-story home was constructed to provide extra lodging for overnight customers who traveled long hours to town. Today, guests enjoy the formal gardens and patios overlooking the river, as well as gracious rooms

decorated with antiques and handmade quilts.
Location: One hour west of St. Louis.
*Rates: $50-$70. George Bocklage.
9 R. 7 PB. 2 FP. Phone available. Beds: DT. Continental-plus breakfast. Handicap access. CCs: MC VISA. Wineries, antique shopping. Central air-conditioning.
Seen in: *St. Louis Post-Dispatch, West County Journal.*
"Like Grandma's house many years ago."

MONTANA

BIG TIMBER K13/*D4*

Lazy K Bar Ranch
Box 550 HI
Big Timber MT 59011
(406) 537-4404

Circa 1922. This Montana ranch is situated at 6,000 feet in a high valley beneath Crazy Mountain. Operated by fifth- and sixth-generation owners, the 20,000-acre ranch was established 110 years ago by Paul Van Cleve. Cabins are made of hand-hewn logs and each has its own stone fireplace. Western decor includes Navajo rugs and antelope heads. Although riding is the main activity, great eating and fishing run a close second. A minimum stay of one week is required.

Location: In a mountain canyon in south-central Montana.
Rates: $445. Season: June 23 - Labor Day. The Van Cleve Family.
19 R. 19 PB. 18 FP. Beds: TC. AP. Swimming pool. Riding, hiking, fishing on 42,000 private acres, billiards, piano. Store, library.
Seen in: *Saturday Evening Post, USA Today, Milwaukee Journal, Town & Country.*
"We loved all the wonderful meals and fellowship."

BOZEMAN K11/*D4*

The Torch & Toes B&B
309 S Third Ave
Bozeman MT 59715
(406) 586-7285

Circa 1906. This Colonial Revival home, three blocks from the center of town, boasts an old-fashioned front porch and a carriage house. Antique furnishings in the parlor feature a Victrola. A pillared and carved oak fireplace and bay window seat adorn the dining room. Ron is a professor of architecture at nearby Montana State University.

Rates: $42-$50. Ronald & Judy Hess.
4 R. 2 PB. 1 FP. Phone available. TV available. Beds: QT. Full breakfast. CCs: MC VISA. Skiing, hiking, rafting, horseback riding. Honeymoon, champagne and flowers.
Seen in: *Bozeman Chronicle, San Francisco Peninsula Parent.*
"Thanks for your warm hospitality."

Voss Inn
319 S Willson
Bozeman MT 59715
(406) 587-0982

Circa 1883. The Voss Inn is a restored two-story house with a large front porch and a Victorian parlor. Old-

fashioned furnishings include an upright piano and chandelier. A full breakfast is served, with fresh baked rolls kept in a unique warmer that's built into an ornate 1880s radiator.

Location: Four blocks south of downtown.
*Rates: $50-$70. Bruce & Frankee Muller.
6 R. 6 PB. Phone available. TV available. Beds: KQ. Full breakfast. CCs: MC VISA DC. Skiing, hiking, fishing, hunting, biking, horseback riding. Day trips to Yellowstone Park.
Seen in: *Sunset Magazine, Cosmopolitan.*
"First class all the way."

ESSEX D6/*B2*

Izaak Walton Inn
PO Box 653
Essex MT 59916
(406) 888-5700

Circa 1939. The Izaak Walton Inn was built as an overnight lodging for Great Northern Railway workers. It is located now on the Burlington-North-

ern Mainline and is served twice daily by Amtrak. The inn is in a strategic location for enjoying Glacier National Park. You can take trails and rivers into the Rocky Mountain forests and meadows.

*❀Rates: $55-$74. Larry & Lynda Vielleux.
30 R. 10 PB. Phone available. Beds: DT. Restaurant. Sauna. Game room. Conference room. CCs: MC VISA. Hiking, fishing, rafting, horseback riding, cross-country skiing, guided backcountry ski tours.
Seen in: *Outdoor America-Summer, Seattle Times.*
"The coziest cross-country ski resort in the Rockies."

GALLATIN GATEWAY L11/*D3*

Gallatin Gateway
Hwy 191, PO Box 376
Gallatin Gateway MT 59730
(406) 763-4672

Circa 1927. This was originally one of the great railroad hotels of the Rocky Mountains and the old railroad clock continues to tick in the massive lobby. Recently restored, the original hand-hewn beams, Paladian windows and mahogany woodwork grace the common rooms. The inn has its own casting pond and a famous fly-fishing school is hosted here.

Rates: $45-$100. Catherine Wrather.
20 R. 16 PB. Phone in room. TV in room. Beds: KQT. Continental breakfast. Spa. Conference room. CCs: MC VISA AE DS.
Seen in: *Travel & Leisure, Dallas Morning News, New York Times, Country Living, House & Garden, Historic Preservation.*

GREAT FALLS F11/*B4*

Three Pheasant Inn
626 5th Ave N
Great Falls MT 59401
(406) 453-0519

Circa 1914. This Victorian house, in the historic area, was built for A. T. Belzer. It was converted to a boarding house during the Depression and remained until the mid-1980s. The house was restored in 1987 and became the Three Pheasant Inn. Its common rooms include glassed-in sun porches, a parlor and library. Guest rooms are filled with Victorian-style antiques. A 100-year-old fountain and

a gazebo grace the garden.
Rates: $40-$60. B.J. Morse.
5 R. 2 PB. Phone in room. TV available. Beds: QDT. Full breakfast. Walk to museums, shops and businesses. Golf, walking trails, fishing, hunting and skiing nearby. Golf, walking trails, fishing, hunting and skiing nearby.
"Have stayed at many B&Bs in England, Scotland and Ireland, but yours has been the nicest."

HELENA I9/C3

The Sanders - Helena's Bed & Breakfast

328 N Ewing
Helena MT 59601
(406) 442-3309

Circa 1875. This historic inn is filled with elegantly carved furnishings, paintings and collections that are original to the house. William Sanders, an attorney and a Montana senator, built his house near the Governor's Mansion, in the heart of Helena. The three-story house features a front and side porch, and balconies and bay windows that provide views of the mountains and downtown Helena. Sourdough pancakes are a specialty.
Rates: $50-$70. Bobbi Uecker & Rock Ringling.
7 R. 7 PB. 1 FP. Phone in room. TV in room. Beds: QDT. Full breakfast. Gourmet meals. Conference room. CCs: MC VISA DS. Hiking, fishing, biking, snow and water skiing, boating. Catering.
Seen in: *The Independent Record, The Washington Post, The New York Times, The Boston Globe.*
"Food is marvelous, the room is wonderful and your hostessing and hosting is the best we have experienced."

RED LODGE M15/E5

Willows Inn

224 S Platt Ave, PO Box 886
Red Lodge MT 59068
(406) 446-3913

Circa 1903. This shuttered three-story Victorian, framed by spruce trees and a white picket fence, was once a boarding house for Finnish mine workers. Rooms feature four-poster, brass and iron beds. Some have mountain views. Charles Kuralt called the Beartooth Highway that runs through Red Lodge "the most beautiful drive in America." Rock Creek, noted for its trout fishing, is a block from the inn.
**❀Rates: $45-$65. Elven Boggio.
6 R. 4 PB. Phone available. TV available. Beds: KQT. Continental-plus breakfast. CCs: MC VISA. Cross-country and downhill skiing, hiking, fishing, hunting, golf, biking, Yellowstone Park.
Seen in: *The Billings Gazette, Innsider.*
"It was heavenly. The bed was comfortable and we loved the decor."

NEBRASKA

ELGIN I18/GB6

Plantation House

Rt 2 Box 17
Elgin NE 68636
(402) 843-2287

Circa 1880. This 28-room colonial mansion, once a gambling club, is situated on five acres dotted with pine and spruce, apple, pear and plum

trees. The exterior Greek Ionic columns are duplicated in the interior columns. The innkeepers' hour-long tours of the estate are available to guests. Outside is a turn-of-the-century band-stand style gazebo. A country breakfast with homemade jams and jellies is served. Across the street is a city park.

Rates: $35-$45. Merland & Barbara Clark.
5 R. 2 PB. Phone available. Beds: QTW. Full breakfast. Wedding and meetings.
Seen in: *Omaha World Herald, Norfolk Daily News, Home & Away Magazine.*
"Gorgeous house! Relaxing atmosphere. Just like going to Mom's house."

GRAND ISLAND M17/D6

Kirschke House B&B

1124 W 3rd St
Grand Island NE 68801
(308) 381-6851

Circa 1902. A steeply sloping roofline and a two-story tower mark this distinctive, vine-covered brick Victorian house. Meticulously restored, there are polished wood floors, fresh wallpapers and carefully chosen antiques. The Roses Roses Room is a spacious accommodation with a canopy bed, rocking chair and decorating accents of roses and vines. In the old brick wash house is a wooden hot tub. In winter and spring, the area is popular for viewing the migration of sandhill cranes and whooping cranes.

Rates: $45. Lois Hank.
4 R. Phone available. TV available. Beds: DT. Full breakfast. CCs: MC VISA.
Seen in: *Grand Island Daily Independent.*
"We have been to many B&Bs in England, Canada and America. The Kirschke House ranks with the finest we've stayed in."

LINCOLN N22/D7

Rogers House

2145 B St
Lincoln NE 68502
(402) 476-6961

Circa 1914. Ivy covers one wing of the three-story Jacobean Revival Rogers House. In the Hillsdale National Historic District, the house is a few blocks from the University of Nebraska and the Capitol building. A ballroom on the third floor has been converted to three guest rooms, but the original built-in ballroom benches remain. Mahogany paneling, cross-beamed ceilings, fireplaces and antique bedsteads are featured.

Rates: $45-$55. Nora Houstma.
8 R. 8 PB. Beds: QDT.
Seen in: *Innsider.*
"Here I am in Egypt enjoying travel on the Nile in luxury almost up to the Rogers House standards," Guest's postcard.

OMAHA L24/C8

Offutt House

140 N 39th St
Omaha NE 68131
(402) 553-0951

Circa 1894. This two-and-a-half story 14-room house is built like a chateau with a steep roof and tall windows.

During the 1913 tornado, although almost every house in the neighborhood was leveled, the Offutt house stood firm. It is said that a decanter of sherry was blown from the dining room to the living room without anything spilling. The large parlor features a handsome fireplace, a wall of books and an inviting sofa. A bridal suite is tucked under the gables of the third floor.

Location: One block from downtown.
*Rates: $45-$75. Jeannie K. Swoboda.
7 R. 3 PB. Beds: KDT. Continental breakfast. Conference room. CCs: MC VISA. Sightseeing, walking.
Seen in: *Midwest Living, Innsider.*
"Hospitable, comfortable, lovely. A wonderful place to stay and great central location."

NEVADA

GENOA H2/D1

Wild Rose Inn

2332 Main St, PO Box 256
Genoa NV 89411
(702) 782-5697 (408) 739-7461

Located 15 miles from Lake Tahoe in Nevada's oldest settlement, this newly built Victorian is resplendent with gables, porches and a two-story turret. The Garden Gate room is housed in the tower and features five windows overlooking the valley and the Sierras. Among the antiques is a collection of old toys and oak telephones. Freshly baked pecan rolls are often prepared for breakfast.

Rates: $85-$105. Sandi & Joe Antonucci.
4 R. 4 PB. Beds: Q. Full breakfast. Swimming, biking are nearby.
Seen in: *The Sacramento Bee.*

"We enjoyed our stay so much. The room was great!"

RENO G2/C1

White Sulphur Springs Ranch

See: Clio, CA

UNIONVILLE E5/B2

Old Pioneer Garden Guest Ranch

HC-64, Box 79
Unionville NV 89418
(702) 538-7585

Circa 1861. Once a bustling silver mining town, Unionville now has only a handful of citizens, and Old Pioneer Garden Guest Ranch is just down the road from town. Accommodations are in a renovated blacksmith's house, a farmhouse and across the meadow in the Hadley House. A Swedish-style gazebo rests beside a bubbling stream, and there are orchards, grape arbors, vegetable gardens, sheep and goats. A country supper is available.

Location: 139 miles east of Reno.
Rates: $45-$55. Mitzi & Lew Jones.
10 R. 2 PB. 1 FP. Beds: D. Full breakfast. Gourmet meals. Handicap access. Game room. Conference room. Fishing, lake swimming, hiking, mountain climbing. Weddings, honeymoon & anniversary catering.
Seen in: *Denver Post.*

"An array of charm that warms the heart and delights the soul."

VIRGINIA CITY G2/D1

Edith Palmer's Country Inn

South B Street, PO Box 756
Virginia City NV 89440
(702) 847-0707

Circa 1862. This white clapboard two-story country house has a wine cellar with walls two feet thick. The addition of a skylight makes this a romantic setting for dining and for weddings. Furnishings are country antiques, and the inn is within easy walking distance of the historic district of Virginia City.

Location: One hour from Lake Tahoe.
Rates: $65-$80. Earlene Brown.
5 R. 3 PB. Phone available. TV available. Beds: KDT. Full breakfast. Conference room. Weddings, receptions.
Seen in: *San Francisco Chronicle, Great Getaways.*

"Everything, including the hostess, was charming."

NEW HAMPSHIRE

ANDOVER M8/E4

The English House

PO Box 162
Andover NH 03216
(603) 735-5987

Circa 1906. An unsuspecting guest probably could not imagine the amount of work put into this house by innkeepers Ken and Gillian Smith, formerly of Andover, Hampshire in England. Now in Andover, New Hampshire, they restored this old building, making it a place of comfort, rest and relaxation. The Smiths continue their efforts by offering quilting and craft lessons to guests. Gillian brings to potential quilters her wealth of experience and talent gleaned from design school and from teaching the craft in England. However, true to tradition, all work stops and guests gather round for English tea at mid-afternoon.

Rates: $70. Ken & Gillian Smith.
7 R. 7 PB. Phone available. TV available. Beds: QT. Full breakfast. CCs: MC VISA. Downhill & cross-country skiing, golf, sailing, fishing, tennis, hiking. Afternoon tea.
Seen in: *Manchester Union Leader.*

"We have found the accommodations to be superb, the food delicious and our hosts wonderful."

ASHLAND K9/E4

Glynn House Victorian Inn

43 Highland St, PO Box 819
Ashland NH 03217-0819
(603) 968-3775

Circa 1895. A three-story turret, gables and verandas frosted with Queen Anne gingerbread come together in an appealing mass of Victoriana in the Glynn House. Carved oak woodwork and pocket doors accentuate the foyer. Period furnishings and ornate Oriental wall coverings decorate the parlor. The village of Ashland is a few minutes from "On Golden Pond" (Squam Lake) and the White Mountains.

Rates: $65-$80. Karol & Betsy Paterman.
4 R. 4 PB. 2 FP. Phone available. TV available. Beds: QDT. Full breakfast. Gourmet meals. Spa. Conference room. FAX. Skiing, boating, hiking, swimming.

"The best place we've ever been. It's homey and relaxing. Super hosts. Expect lots of our friends!"

BARTLETT I10/D5

The Country Inn at Bartlett

Rt 302 Box 327
Bartlett NH 03812
(603) 374-2353

Circa 1885. This New England farmhouse, built as a summer home by a Portland sea captain, rests in a stand of tall pines adjacent to national

forest land. For the last 50 years it has provided a homey atmosphere for families and friends coming to the White Mountains. Accommodations are in the house or in cottage rooms. An outdoor hot tub takes advantage of the crisp, pine-scented air.

✻❀Rates: $64-$72. Mark Dindorf.
17 R. 11 PB. 2 FP. Phone available. TV available. Beds: DT. B&B. Spa. CCs: MC VISA AE. Hiking, downhill & cross-country skiing. A hearty family-style dinner is served with prior arrangements.

"Walking through your door felt like stepping back in time."

BETHLEHEM H8/C4

The Bells

Strawberry Hill, PO Box 276
Bethlehem NH 03574
(603) 869-2647

Circa 1892. This unusual Queen Anne house is a wonderful example of Victorian ingenuity. Basically square with

wraparound porches, the oriental roof makes the house look like a pagoda. Eighty hand-carved wooden bells hang under the second floor eaves and eight large tin bells hang from the upper corners of the roofs. The inn is appointed with family heirlooms, lace and wicker and interesting collections such as chiming mantle clocks. Ask for the splendid Cupola Room with its view of mountains. All the rooms are suites with sitting rooms.

Location: In town. Just off Rt. 302 in the White Mountains.
Rates: $60-$70. Bill & Louise Sims.
4 R. 4 PB. Phone available. TV available. Beds: TD. Full breakfast. CCs: MC VISA. Golf, tennis, hiking, skiing, antiquing. All White Mountain attractions nearby.
Seen in: *Charlotte Observer, New England GetAways.*

"It was so nice to be fussed over, not to mention being treated like old friends. Everything was superb and we went bananas over the decor!"

The Mulburn Inn

Main St
Bethlehem NH 03574
(603) 869-3389

Circa 1913. This summer cottage was

known as the Ivie Estate. Mrs. Ivie and Mrs. Frank Woolworth of 'Five and Dime' fame were sisters. Many of

the Ivie and Woolworth family members vacationed here in summer. Cary Grant and Barbara Hutton spent their honeymoon at the mansion. Polished oak staircases and stained glass windows add to the atmosphere.

*Rates: $55-$80. Linda & Moe Mulkigian, Bob & Cheryl Burns.

7 R. 7 PB. 3 FP. Phone available. TV available. Beds: KQTD. Full breakfast. CCs: MC VISA AE DS. Hiking, bicycling, swimming, fishing, tennis, skiing.

Seen in: *The Record.*

"You have put a lot of thought, charm, beauty and warmth into the inn. Your breakfasts were oh, so delicious!!"

BRADFORD N7/F4

The Bradford Inn

RFD 1 Box 40, Main St

Bradford NH 03221

(603) 938-5309 (800) 669-5309

Circa 1898. The Bradford Hotel was the most elaborate lodging in town when it first boasted of electricity, a coal furnace and a large dining room.

Now restored and polished to its original turn-of-the-century charm, guests can once again enjoy the grand staircase, the wide halls, parlors, high ceilings and sunny rooms.

Location: Rural country village.

*❀Rates: $80-$104.MAP. Connie & Tom Mazol.

12 R. 12 PB. Phone available. TV available. Beds: DTC. B&B. Restaurant. Handicap access. Conference room. CCs: MC VISA AE DC CB DS. Lake cruises, hiking, skiing, antiques, auctions.

Seen in: *New York Times, Granite State Vacationer.*

"We enjoyed excellent breakfasts and dinners as well as a clean and spacious suite and a most pleasant host and hostess."

Mountain Lake Inn

Rt 114

Bradford NH 03221

(603) 938-2136 (800) 662-6005

Circa 1760. This white colonial house is situated on 167 acres, 17 of which are lakefront. A sandy beach on Lake

Massasecum is inviting for sunning, but guests often prefer to take out the canoe and the rowboat. The Pine Room has floor-to-ceiling windows that look out to the garden. A 75-year-old Brunswick pool table is in the lounge, along with a wood-burning fireplace.

*Rates: $80. Carol & Phil Fullerton.

9 R. 9 PB. Phone available. TV available. Beds: KQDT. Full breakfast. Gourmet meals. Conference room. CCs: MC VISA DS. Swimming, skiing, snowshoeing packages, boating, fishing, country cooking weekend.

Seen in: *Country Inns, Boston Globe.*

"We loved your place! From the moment I entered the door that afternoon and caught the aroma of a country dinner I was hooked. You give the inn such personal warmth."

CAMPTON J8/D4

Mountain Fare Inn

Mad River Rd

Campton NH 03223

(603) 726-4283

Circa 1850. This white farm house is surrounded by flower gardens in the summer and unparalleled foliage in the fall. Ski teams, family reunions

and other groups often enjoy the outdoors here with Mountain Fare as a base. In the winter everyone seems to be a skier, and in the summer there are boaters and hikers. The inn is decorated in a casual New Hampshire-style country decor. A garden-fresh dinner is available upon request.

Location: Two hours from Boston in the White Mountains.

❀Rates: $48-$70. Susan & Nick Preston.

8 R. 5 PB. 1 FP. Phone available. TV available. Beds: DTC. AP. Golf, hiking, canoeing, biking, downhill & cross-country skiing, tennis, fishing, skating. Specialize in family reunions and small gatherings. Guided hiking weekends.

Seen in: *Ski, Skiing, Snow Country.*

"Charming and casual. Truly country."

CENTRE HARBOR K9/E5

Red Hill Inn

RD 1 Box 99M

Centre Harbor NH 03226

(603) 279-7001

Circa 1904. The mansion was once the centerpiece of a 1,000-acre estate. It was called "keewaydin" for the strong

north wind that blows across Sunset Hill. When the Depression was over, the inn was sold. New owners included European royalty escaping from Nazi Germany. Now the mansion is a lovely restored country inn with spectacular views of the area's lakes and mountains. From your room you can see the site of the filming of "On Golden Pond."

Location: Central New Hampshire in the Lakes Region.

*Rates: $75-$135. Don Leavitt & Rick Miller.

23 R. 23 PB. 19 FP. Phone in room. TV available. Beds: DTC. EP. Restaurant. Spa. Conference room. CCs: MC VISA AE DC CB. Cross-country skiing on groomed trails. Rental equipment available.

Seen in: *New England Getaways.*

"Our stay was very enjoyable."

CHOCORUA J11/D5

Staffords-in-the-Field

PO Box 270

Chocorua NH 03817

(603) 323-7766

Circa 1778. The main building of Stafford's, home to a prosperous farm family for over 150 years, is Federal style. It became a guest house in the 1890s. An old apple orchard and sugarhouse remain and there's a kitchen garden and a nine-hole golf course on the inn's 12 acres. A rocky brook still winds through the rolling fields and in the adjacent woods, there's a natural swimming hole. Guest rooms are lovingly furnished in antiques. A canoe on nearby Chocorua is available to guests.

Location: White Mountains.

Rates: $60-$95. Season: May - April. Fred

& Ramona Stafford.
12 R. 6 PB. 1 FP. Phone available. TV available. Beds: KQDTC. MAP. Restaurant. Gourmet meals. CCs: MC VISA AE. Hiking, climbing, skiing, horseback riding, swimming, boating, golf, tennis.
Seen in: *Esquire, Boston Globe, Seattle Times, Los Angeles Times.*
"Delicious food, delightful humor!"

CLAREMONT M6/F3

Goddard Mansion B&B
25 Hillstead Rd
Claremont NH 03743
(603) 543-0603
Circa 1905. This mansion with its gazebo is set amid acres of lawn. The living room has a large fireplace and there is a baby grand piano and a

1939 Wurlitzer jukebox with 78s. Many of the guest rooms have panoramic views of mountains in New Hampshire and Vermont. The airy French Country Room and the surreal Cloud Room are favorites. Homemade muffins are served with preserves made from fruit grown on the property.
*Rates: $55-$95. Frank & Debbie Albee.
8 R. 2 PB. Phone available. TV available. Beds: DTW. Full breakfast. Conference room. CCs: MC VISA DS. Horseback riding, skiing, water sports, canoeing.
Seen in: *Eagle Times.*
"Our trip would not have been as enjoyable without having stayed at your inn."

CONWAY J11/D5

The Darby Field Inn
Bald Hill, PO Box D
Conway NH 03818
(603) 447-2181 (800) 426-4147 (in NH)
Circa 1826. This rambling, blue clapboard farmhouse has a huge fieldstone fireplace, stone patio and outstanding views of the Mt. Washington Valley and the Presidential Mountains. For many years it was called the Bald Hill Grand View lodge but was renamed to honor the first man to climb Mt. Washington, Darby Field.
Location: Half a mile south of Conway.
Rates: $65-$90pp.MAP. Marc & Maria Donaldson.
16 R. 14 PB. TV available. Beds: KQDT.

Swimming pool. CCs: MC VISA AE. Swimming, private cross-country ski trails.
"If an inn is a place for a weary traveler to relax, recover and feel the hospitality and warmth of the innkeeper, then the Darby Field Inn is one of the finest."

Mountain Valley Manner
148 Washington St
Conway NH 03818
(603) 447-3988
Circa 1885. Built on the Revolutionary era mustering grounds of the Conway volunteer militia, this Victorian is lo-

cated within 200 yards of two historic kissing bridges. The inn is appointed with many antiques and three of the guest rooms overlook the 1889 Swift River covered bridge and Mt. Washington. In addition to a full breakfast, afternoon beverages and snacks are served.
*Rates: $58-$72. Bob, Lynn & Amy Lein.
4 R. 2 PB. Phone available. TV available. Beds: KQDW. B&B. Swimming pool. CCs: MC VISA AE. Golf, hiking, skiing, tubing, fishing. Tennis, pool & skating rink nearby. Air conditioned.
"Accommodations excellent, hospitality better than the Ritz, surroundings very nice, meals way above expectation."

CORNISH L6/E3

Home Hill Country Inn
RFD 23
Cornish NH 03745
(603) 675-6165
Circa 1812. Tall maples shade this massive white brick Federal house located on the banks of the Connecticut River. Its 25 acres of grounds include a large white horse barn, acres of fields bordered by whitewashed fences, a tennis court, swimming pool, pool house, ski trails and riding paths. Guest rooms are furnished with country French and American antiques and appealing wallpapers. A notable French restaurant fills three fireplaced dining rooms.
Rates: $$95-$120. Roger Nicolas.
9 R. 9 PB. Phone available. Beds: KQD. Continental breakfast. Swimming pool. CCs: MC VISA AE. Golf, canoeing, fishing, hiking, biking, tennis, cross-country skiing.
Seen in: *Country Living, Bon Appetit, Discerning Traveller.*
"What a wonderful memory maker."

DURHAM N12/F6

Maple Lodge B&B
See: Stratham, NH

EAST HEBRON K8/E4

Six Chimneys
Star Rt Box 114
East Hebron NH 03232
(603) 744-2029
Circa 1791. This was once a stagecoach stop where 20 fresh horses were kept for changes. Beds and a drink of rum were 10 cents. Located

on five acres, at the head of Newfound Lake, the home retains wide pine boards, pine paneling, and old beams.
Location: Newfound Lake between Bristol and Plymouth.
*Rates: $55-$60. Peter & Lee Fortescue.
4 R. 4 PB. Phone available. TV available. Beds: KQDT. B&B. CCs: MC VISA. Skiing, hiking. Tennis & golf nearby.
Seen in: *Bristol Enterprise.*
"The welcome you gave us, the stimulating nightly conversations in the den, and those fabulous breakfasts stand out above all the rest."

EATON CENTER J11/D5

The Inn at Crystal Lake
Rt 153
Eaton Center NH 03832
(603) 447-2120 (800) 343-7336
Circa 1884. A Greek Revival house with Victorian touches, this cozy inn is located a few steps from Crystal Lake. Victorian decor predominates with canopy beds and antique dressers. An inn since 1884, there are balconies and porches on all three floors to capture the scenic views. Evening meals are served in the dining room with its fireplace and

crystal. Walter is a former geology professor-metal sculptor turned chef who trained at a French restaurant after purchasing the inn. His specialties include Hungarian goulash, shrimp steamed in Vermouth and chicken in brie sauce.
Rates: $60-$68.MAP. Walter & Jacqueline Spink.
11 R. 11 PB. Phone available. TV available. Beds: QDC. Full breakfast. Restaurant. Gourmet meals. CCs: MC VISA AE. Canoeing, sailing, fishing, swimming, hiking, skiing, ice skating, relaxing. Honeymoon specials.
Seen in: *The Boston Globe, Bon Appetit, Carroll County Independent.*
"Thanks for a terrific time, good weather, fabulous food and equally fabulous company."

Rockhouse Mountain Farm-Inn

Eaton Center NH 03832
(603) 447-2880

Circa 1890. This handsome old house is framed by maple trees on 400 acres of forests, streams, fields and wildflowers. Milking cows, pigs, geese, peacocks and llamas provide entertainment for city youngsters of all ages. Three generations of the Edges have operated this inn and some guests have been coming all 44 years it has been open. A 200-year-old barn at times bulges with new-mown hay, and there is a nearby beach for water sports.
Rates: $96-$116.MAP. Season: June 15 to Nov. 1. The Edge Family.
15 R. 7 PB. 1 FP. Phone available. TV available. Beds: DT. Handicap access. Hiking.
Seen in: *Family Circle, Womans Day, Boston Globe, Country Vacations.*
"We have seen many lovely places, but Rockhouse remains the real high spot, the one to which we most want to return."

ETNA K6/E3

Moose Mountain Lodge

Moose Mountain Rd
Etna NH 03750
(603) 643-3529

Circa 1938. This old log lodge is perched high on the western side of Moose Mountain providing views of the Connecticut River Valley and the Green Mountains. The inn's land connects with the Appalachian Trail for extended hikes and ski tours. In the summer the lodge participates in "inn to inn canoeing" on the Connecticut River. Bountiful gardens provide fresh vegetables for lunch and dinner.
Location: Part of town of Hanover.
Rates: $100-$140. Season: Jan-March,June-Oct Peter & Kay Shumway.
12 R. Phone available. Beds: QTD. AP. Restaurant. Gourmet meals. Game room. Conference room. CCs: MC VISA. Cross-

country skiing, bicycling, hiking, swimming.
"Moose Mountain is just like some of the old European ski lodges, relaxed, warm, friendly, and very comfortable."

EXETER 011/G6

Exeter Inn

90 Front St
Exeter NH 03833
(603) 772-5901 (800) 782-8444

Circa 1932. Built by the Phillips Exeter Academy, this brick Georgian inn has served families and visiting alumni of the school for decades. Business people and tourists who happen upon the inn are pleased with the fine food and handsome accommodations. Reproduction and antique furnishings are highlighted by traditional wallpapers.
*Rates: $70-$95. J.H. Hodgins.
50 R. 50 PB. 4 FP. Phone in room. TV in room. Beds: KQDTC. EP. Restaurant. Gourmet meals. Sauna. Exercise room. Conference room. FAX. CCs: MC VISA AE DC CB DS. Horseback riding, golf, canoeing, tennis, squash. Limited cross-country skiing.
Seen in: *Business Digest, Exeter News, Foster's Daily Democrat.*
"An experience in hospitality."

Maple Lodge B&B

See: Stratham, NH

FITZWILLIAM P6/G3

Amos Parker House

PO Box 202
Fitzwilliam NH 03447
(603) 585-6540

Circa 1780. An antique liberty pole is attached to the original part of this appealing Federal house. (Liberty poles were used to identify meeting places for Revolutionaries.) Situated on three acres, with mountain views, the house is bordered by green lawns and perfect flower beds. Antiques, Spode china, beautiful stenciling and Oriental carpet collections add grace and style to the rooms. Freda, a former travel agent from Chicago, exudes enthusiasm for all New

Hampshire's sights and is an expert on the area. Hopefully, your arrival will coincide with a breakfast menu of spinach souffle' with mushroom Newburg sauce or "Praline French Toast."
Rates: $55-$80. Freda B. Houpt.
5 R. 4 PB. 6 FP. Phone available. TV available. Beds: KQDT. B&B. Cross-country skiing, biking, water sports, mountain climbing.
Seen in: *The New York Times, Washington Post, The Tampa Tribune-Times, Boston Globe, Christian Science Monitor.*
"Care and solicitation is what makes staying here more the experience of visiting a wealthy and hospitable relative in the country than simply staying at an inn or hotel."

Fitzwilliam Inn

Fitzwilliam NH 03447
(603) 585-9000

Circa 1796. For almost 200 years this old New England inn has offered food, lodging and grog. Over the parlor presides a portrait of the Earl of

Fitzwilliam, the 18th century nobleman for whom the town is named. In the rustic pub the innkeeper still provides his own special grog.
Rates: $35-$55. John Wallace.
28 R. 14 PB. Phone available. TV available. Beds: QDTC. EP. Restaurant. Handicap access. Swimming pool. Conference room. CCs: MC VISA AE DC. Cross-country skiing, hiking, fishing. Gift shop on premises.
Seen in: *Boston Globe.*
"Like a dream, no, it was a dream come true!"

The Hannah Davis House
186 Depot Rd
Fitzwilliam NH 03447
(603) 585-3344

Circa 1820. In the heart of the Monadnock region is this restored Federal-style home. The Hannah Davis House features antiques, high beds, braided rugs, simple country quilts and crisp antique linens. There is a screened porch where guests may relax and enjoy breakfast which includes homemade breads and freshly ground coffee.

Rates: $65-$70. Michael & Kathleen Terpstra.

3 R. Full breakfast. Swimming, skiing.

"We loved Mike and Kate's congeniality and generosity and that silver platter of chocolate toast cookies."

FRANCONIA H8/C4

Bungay Jar B&B
PO Box 15
Franconia NH 03580
(603) 823-7775

An 18th-century barn was taken down and moved piece by piece to Easton Valley six miles from Franconia. A post-and-beam barn-style-home was constructed, nestled onto eight wooded acres with a stream nearby and the White Mountains in view. The two-story living room, reminiscent of a hay loft, is decorated with antique country furnishings, as are all the guest rooms. Your host, a landscape architect, has planted herb and perennial gardens.

❀❀Rates: $60-$100. Kate Kerivan, Lee Strimbeck.

6 R. 4 PB. 1 FP. Phone available. Beds: KDT. B&B. Sauna. CCs: MC VISA AE. Skiing, hiking, bird-watching, antiquing. Afternoon tea.

Seen in: *Newsday.*

"Such a perfect spot with such a great view."

Franconia Inn
Easton Rd
Franconia NH 03580
(603) 823-5542 (800) TREADWAY

Circa 1936. This inn was originally built in 1868 when most of the area's farmers took in summer boarders. Each farmer had a wagon marked

with his farm's name and would pick up guests at the train station in Littleton. In the 30s, fire destroyed the old house and it was rebuilt as an inn. A basement rathskeller is well known by the ski-touring circuit. There is also an oak-paneled library upstairs.

Location: Exit 38 off I-93, two-and-a-half miles south on Route 116.

❀Rates: $65-$110. Season: May 20-April. Alec & Richard Morris.

35 R. 35 PB. 3 FP. Phone available. TV available. Beds: KQDTC. MAP. Restaurant. Gourmet meals. Spa. Swimming pool. Game room. Conference room. CCs: MC VISA AE. Croquet, bicycles, pool, soaring, swimming, cross-country skiing, tennis, horseback riding, bicycles, hiking, horse-drawn sleigh rides, ice skating - all on the premises.

Seen in: *The Philadelphia Inquirer, Boston Globe.*

"The piece de resistance of the Franconia Notch is the Franconia Inn," Philadelphia Inquirer.

Lovett's Inn
Rt 18, Profile Rd
Franconia NH 03580
(603) 823-7761 (800) 356-3802

Circa 1784. This is a rambling Cape-style house in the National Register. Rooms are in the main house and in

woodland and poolside cottages with fireplaces. The inn's candlelit dining room is managed by four-star chef Peter Tavino. Trout streams, hiking and cross-country trails dot the inn's 90 acres at the base of Cannon Mountain.

Rates: $50-$216. Anthony & Sharon Avrutine.

30 R. 19 PB. Phone available. TV available. Beds: QDTC. AP. Handicap access. Swimming pool. Conference room. Gliding, horseback riding, golf nearby. Ski trails on premises.

"Room very pleasant, comfortable and clean. Delicious dinner. We appreciated being made to feel welcome and at home."

GREENFIELD O8/G4

The Greenfield B&B Inn
PO Box 400
Greenfield NH 03047
(603) 547-6327 (603) 547-2418

Circa 1817. In the 1850s this inn was purchased by Henry Dunklee, innkeeper of the old Mayfield Inn across the street. When there was an overflow of guests at his tavern, Mr. Dunklee accommodated them here. This totally renovated Victorian mansion features veranda views of Crotched, Temple and Monadnock Mountains. The comfortable interiors and gracious innkeepers have been enjoyed by many well-traveled guests including Dolores and Bob Hope.

Location: Southern New Hampshire, 90 minutes from Boston.

❀Rates: $45-$60. Barbara & Vic.

9 R. 5 PB. Phone in room. Beds: KDT. B&B. Conference room. CCs: MC VISA. Mountain climbing, skiing, bicycling, swimming, fishing, golf, antique shops.

Seen in: *New England Getaways, Manchester Union Leader, Innsider Magazine.*

"I'm coming back for more of this New Hampshire therapy," Bob Hope.

HAMPSTEAD P10/G5

Stillmeadow B&B at Hampstead
545 Main St, PO Box 565
Hampstead NH 03841
(603) 329-8381

Circa 1850. The old Ordway home rests on several acres on the Main Street of Hampstead, just across a meadow from the Hampstead Cro-

quet Associations' grass courts. The Dawn Suite features a fireplace, and a sitting area with a trundle bed, while the Tulip Suite has two queen beds and a double bathroom. Private stairs lead from this room to a playroom. The cookie jar at Stillmeadow is said to be always full.

Rates: $55-$80. Lori & Randy Offord.

4 R. 4 PB. 2 FP. Phone available. TV in room. Beds: QDTWC. Continental-plus breakfast. Conference room. CCs: AE. Skiing, tennis, croquet, fenced-in children's playground.

Seen in: *Lawrence Eagle Tribune, New Hampshire Profiles.*

"No less than monumental."

HAMPTON O12/G6

The Inn at Elmwood Corners
252 Winnacunnet Rd
Hampton NH 03842
(603) 929-0443

Circa 1870. This old sea captain's house boasts a wide wrap-around porch, filled with wicker in the summer. The inn is decorated with stencilled walls, braided rugs and collections such as antique teddy bears and dolls. Mary has stitched the

quilts that top the beds. The library is jammed and guests may borrow a book and finish reading it at home. A favorite breakfast is John's poached brook trout or Eggs Benedict.
Rates: $50-$90. John & Mary Hornberger.
7 R. 2 PB. Phone available. TV available. Beds: QT. Full breakfast. Game room. CCs: MC VISA. Swimming, tennis, golf, cross-country skiing, shopping.
Seen in: *The Portsmouth Herald, The Hampton Union, The Boston Globe.*
"Very hospitable, can't think of a thing you need to add."

HANCOCK O7/G4

John Hancock Inn
Main St
Hancock NH 03449
(603) 525-3318
Circa 1789. Travelers have enjoyed this old inn, now in the National Register of Historic Places, since the days it served as a stagecoach stop over 200 years ago. Canopied beds are found in some rooms and there are hooked rugs, wing-back chairs and rockers. The Mural Room boasts a pastoral mural painted in 1825. The Carriage Room lounge features tables of old bellows, seats from early buggies and a blazing hearth.
Rates: $73. Glynn & Pat Wells.
10 R. 10 PB. Phone available. TV available. Beds: KDTC. EP. Restaurant. Conference room. CCs: MC VISA. Swimming, tennis, golf, fishing, boating, skiing, hiking, horseback riding. Weddings.
Seen in: *Country Inns, The Boston Globe, The Keene Sentinel, Yankee Homes.*
"The warmth you extended was the most meaningful part of our visit."

HANOVER K6/E3

The Trumbull House
PO Box C29
Hanover NH 03755
(603) 643-1400
Circa 1919. This handsome two-story farmhouse was concocted and built by Walter Trumbull from materials he gathered from old Dartmouth College buildings and fraternity houses. Presiding over 16 acres with stands of maple and pine, and a meandering brook, the inn offers a cozy refuge for all, including cross-country skiers and Dartmouth College alumni and parents. The parlor features Country English chairs, sofas and lace curtains.
Rates: $110-$130. Ann C. Fuller.
5 R. 5 PB. Phone available. TV available. Beds: QT. B&B. Alpine & cross-country skiing, golf, swimming, riding, sailing, canoeing, biking, hiking.
Seen in: *Boston Globe, Upper Valley News.*
"From the beautiful setting outdoors through every elegant and thoughtful detail indoors, including your exquisite sunlit breakfast, we were in heaven!"

HAVERHILL I7/D4

Haverhill Inn
Box 95
Haverhill NH 03765
(603) 989-5961
Circa 1810. This handsome Federal house commands sweeping views of the Upper Connecticut River Valley and the Vermont hills. Indian shutters,

a fireplace in every room, and an old kitchen hearth and bake oven add to the charm. Cross-country trails start at the back door and in summer, guests often canoe inn-to-inn.
Location: On Route 10.
Rates: $75. Stephen Campbell.
4 R. 4 PB. 4 FP. Phone available. Beds: QT. Full breakfast. Hiking, cross-country skiing, canoeing.
Seen in: *Sunday Boston Globe.*

HENNIKER N8/F4

The Meeting House Inn & Restaurant
35 Flanders Rd
Henniker NH 03242
(603) 428-3228
Circa 1850. Just up the road from this rural country farmstead is the site of the first meeting house in Henniker.

Hearty New England cooking is served in the 200-year-old barn/restaurant. Wide pine floors, brass beds and antique accessories decorate guest rooms in the main house.
Location: Off 114S, 2 miles from Henniker Center.
Rates: $63-$93. June & Bill Davis, Peter & Cheryl Bakke.
6 R. 6 PB. Phone available. TV available. Beds: QDT. Full breakfast. Restaurant. Spa. Sauna. Conference room. CCs: MC VISA AE. Downhill & cross-country skiing, golf, swimming, hiking, horseback riding, water sports, bicycling.
Seen in: *Boston Globe.*
"Thank you for giving us a honeymoon worth waiting eleven years for."

HOLDERNESS K9/E4

The Inn on Golden Pond
Rt 3 Box 680
Holderness NH 03245
(603) 968-7269
Circa 1879. Framed by meandering stone walls and split-rail fences more than 100 years old, this inn is situated on 55 acres of woodlands. Most rooms overlook picturesque countryside and nearby is Squam Lake, setting for the film "On Golden Pond." An inviting, 60-foot screened porch provides a place to relax during the summer.
Location: Four miles from Exit 24, I-93.
*Rates: $75-$85. Bill & Bonnie Webb.
9 R. 7 PB. Phone available. TV available. Beds: QT. Full breakfast. CCs: MC VISA. Skiing, boating, fishing, swimming.
Seen in: *The Boston Globe, The Baltimore Sun, Los Angeles Times.*

INTERVALE I11/D5

New England Inn
Rt 16A Box 428
Intervale NH 03845
(603) 356-5541 (800) 82-NEINN
Circa 1809. Surrounded by the magnificent White Mountains, the New England Inn offers the main inn, cozy fireplaced single-room cottages and cottage suites. The inn provides homey touches: stenciled walls, an antique spinning wheel, quilted wall hangings, a Shaker grandfather clock, braided rugs and oil lamps. The Intervale Tavern provides local entertainment. Guests may also enjoy sleigh rides.
Rates: $57-$96.MAP Kathy Whitbeck.
38 R. 38 PB. 13 FP. Phone in room. TV in room. Beds: KQDTC. EP. Restaurant. Swimming pool. Conference room. CCs: MC VISA AE. Cross-country & downhill skiing, shopping, theaters. Weddings & receptions.
Seen in: *The Irregular.*
"Even grandmother was impressed (and this is hard to do)."

JACKSON I10/D5

Ellis River House

Rt 16 Box 656
Jackson NH 03846
(603) 383-9339

Circa 1890. Andrew Harriman built this colonial farmhouse, as well as the village town hall and three-room schoolhouse where the innkeepers' child attends school. Classic antiques fill the guest rooms and cottage and each window reveals views of magnificent mountains, the vineyard, or spectacular Ellis River. As a working farm, the Ellis River House includes a population of chickens, geese, ducks, pigs, a pony and a milk cow.

Location: White Mountain area.
❀Rates: $40-$120. Barry & Barbara Lubao.
6 R. 1 PB. Phone available. TV available. Beds: QT. AP. Spa. CCs: MC VISA. World class cross-country skiing, horseback riding, tennis, golf, biking, hiking in White Mountains National Forest. Gather your own farm fresh eggs. Homemade breads baked daily.
Seen in: *The Mountain Ear.*
"We have stayed at many B&Bs all over the world and are in agreement that the beauty and hospitality of Ellis River House is that of a world-class bed & breakfast."

The Inn at Jackson

PO Box H
Jackson NH 03846
(603) 383-4321 (800)289-8600

Circa 1890. Architect Stanford White built this inn overlooking the village and White Mountains. The atmosphere is comfortable and inviting, and breakfast is served in a glassed-in porch which provides a panoramic view. In winter, sleigh rides can be arranged and in summer, hay rides and horseback riding.

*Rates: $70-$80. Lori & Steve Tradewell.
6 R. 6 PB. 3 FP. Phone available. TV available. Beds: DT. B&B. CCs: MC VISA AE. Golf, skiing, tennis, hiking.
Seen in: *Country Inns.*
"We had a terrific time and found the inn warm and cozy and most of all relaxing."

The Inn at Thorn Hill

PO Box A, Thorn Hill Rd
Jackson NH 03846
(603) 383-4242

Circa 1895. Follow a romantic drive through the Honeymoon Covered Bridge to Thorn Hill Road where this country Victorian stands, built by architect Stanford White. Its 10 acres are adjacent to the Jackson Ski Touring trails. Inside, the decor is Victorian and a collection of antique light fixtures accentuates the guest rooms, pub, drawing room, and parlor.
*Rates: $55-$96. Season: May to March. Peter & Linda LaRose.
20 R. 18 PB. Phone available. TV available. Beds: KQDT. MAP. Restaurant. Gourmet meals. Swimming pool. Conference room. CCs: MC VISA AE DS. Cross-country skiing, golf, tennis, horseback riding, hiking, shopping.
Seen in: *Mature Outlook, The Reporter, New England GetAways, Bon Appetit.*
"Magnificent, start to finish! The food was excellent but the mountain air must have shrunk my clothes!"

Village House

Rt 16A Box 359
Jackson NH 03846
(603) 383-6666

Circa 1860. Village House was built as an annex to the larger Hawthorne Inn which eventually burned. It is a colonial building, with a porch winding around three sides. The Wildcat River flows by the inn's seven acres, and there is a swimming pool, clay tennis court and shuffleboard set in view of the White Mountains.

Rates: $40-$100. Robin Crocker.
10 R. 8 PB. Phone available. TV available. Beds: TW. EP. Swimming pool. CCs: MC VISA. Clay tennis courts, hiking, downhill & cross-country skiing, golf, ice skating, horses, hay & sleigh rides.
Seen in: *The Foxboro Reporter.*
"Your hospitality and warmth made us feel right at home. The little extras, such as turn-down service, flowers and baked goods are all greatly appreciated."

JAFFREY P7/G4

The Benjamin Prescott Inn

Rt 124 E
Jaffrey NH 03452
(603) 532-6637

Circa 1853. Colonel Prescott arrived on foot in Jaffrey in 1775, with an ax in his hand and a bag of beans on his back. The family built this classic Greek Revival many years later. Now, candles light the windows, seen from the stonewall-lined lane adjacent to the inn. Each room bears the name of a Prescott family member and is furnished with antiques.

*Rates: $60-$130. Barry & Jan Miller.
10 R. 10 PB. Phone available. TV in room. Beds: KQDT. B&B. CCs: MC VISA. Hiking, climbing, cross-country skiing, sleigh rides, bicycling, antiquing.
"The coffee and breakfasts were delicious and the hospitality overwhelming."

JEFFERSON G9/C5

Jefferson Inn

Rt 2
Jefferson NH 03583
(603) 586-7998

Circa 1896. This rambling Victorian house features a turret, gables, and verandas. English antiques fill the inn and afternoon tea is served.

*❀Rates: $40-$65. Season: Dec-March,May-Oct. Greg Brown & Bertie Koelewijn.
10 R. 5 PB. Phone available. TV available. Beds: QDT. B&B. Handicap access. Conference room. CCs: MC VISA AE. Skiing, hiking, swimming, golf, tennis, cycling, horseback riding.
"Marvelous breakfast and a warm, comfortable atmosphere."

LITTLETON H8/C4

Beal House Inn

247 West Main St
Littleton NH 03561
(603) 444-2661

Circa 1833. This Federal Renaissance farmhouse has been an inn for 54 years. The original barn still stands, now covered with white clapboard and converted to an antique shop. The inn is furnished with antiques, that are for sale. Beal House is a Main Street landmark as well as the area's first bed and breakfast inn.

*Rates: $45-$85. Jim & Ann Carver & son John.
14 R. 12 PB. Phone available. Beds: KQDT. B&B. CCs: MC VISA AE DC. Downhill & cross-country skiing, hiking, golf, canoeing.
Seen in: *Country Inn, Glamour Magazine.*

"These innkeepers know and understand people, their needs and wants. Attention to cleanliness and amenities, from check-in to check-out is a treasure."

Thayers Inn

136 Main St
Littleton NH 03561
(603) 444-6469

Circa 1843. Ulysses Grant is said to have spoken from the inn's balcony during a federal court hearing. In those days, fresh firewood and candles were delivered to guest rooms each day as well as a personal thunderjug. The handsome facade features four 30-foot, hand-carved pillars and a cupola with views of the surrounding mountains.

Rates: $40-$70. Don & Carolyn Lambert.
40 R. 36 PB. Phone in room. TV in room. Beds: KDT. AP. Restaurant. FAX. CCs: MC VISA AE DS. Skiing, hiking, natural wonders.
Seen in: *Business Life, Vacationer, Bon Appetit.*

"This Thanksgiving Russ and I spent a lot of time thinking about the things that are most important to us. It seemed appropriate that we should write to thank you for your warm hospitality as innkeepers."

LYME K6/D3

Lyme Inn

Route 10
Lyme NH 03768
(603) 795-2222 (603) 795-4404

Circa 1809. This four-story country inn, standing at the village common has served guests for almost 200 years. Early American decor includes maple hutches, antique clocks, tester beds, quilts and hooked rugs. A favorite room features Eastlake-style painted "cottage" furnishings. In winter, a wood-burning stove warms the lobby with its old wing-back chairs, exposed beams and wideboard floors. Townsfolk mingle with guests on the porch or in the inn's tavern and restaurant.

Rates: $66-$150. Fred & Judy Siemons.
14 R. 12 PB. 6 FP. Phone available. TV available. Beds: DT. MAP. Restaurant. CCs: MC VISA AE. Horseback riding, skiing, water sports, fishing, canoeing, antiquing, hiking, ice skating. Weddings.
Seen in: *House Beautiful, Colonial Homes, Sky, Delta Air.*

"The food was delicious, the facilities perfect and you did everything possible to make us feel comfortable."

MANCHESTER O9/G5

Stillmeadow B&B at Hampstead

See: Hampstead, NH

MEREDITH K9/E5

New Hampshire Bed & Breakfast

RFD 4, Box 88
Meredith NH 03253
(603) 279-8348

This bed and breakfast travel service makes reservations for over 60 inns and homestays throughout the granite state. There are ocean front inns, cozy mountain hideaways, country retreats, lakeside homes or historic houses in downtown locations. Properties include a 1785 tavern in Tamworth Village, an inn with a private beach on Lake Winnipesaukee at Center Harbor and a restored 1765 colonial in Northwood. The director also operates the Tuckernuck Inn.

Rates: 50-$150. Director Ernie Taddei.
Full breakfast. CCs: MC VISA.

NEW LONDON M7/F4

New London Inn

Box 8, Main St
New London NH 03257
(603) 526-2791 (800) 526-2791

Circa 1792. This classic New England inn is situated right on Main Street and features a two-story veranda. Inside are bed chambers decorated in colonial furnishings. Guests may dine beside the fire at the inn's restaurant. Colby-Sawyer College is nearby.

*Rates: $75-$90. Maureen & John Follansbee.
30 R. 30 PB. Phone in room. TV available. Beds: KQDT. MAP. Restaurant. Gourmet meals. Conference room. FAX. CCs: MC VISA AE. Skiing, water sports, golf, tennis, theater, museums, antiquing.
Seen in: *Boston Globe, New Hampshire Profiles.*

NEWPORT M4/F3

The Inn at Coit Mountain

HCR 63, PO 3 Rt 10
Newport NH 03773
(603) 863-3583 (800)367-2364

Circa 1790. This gracious Georgian was once the home of Rene Cheronette-Champollion a descendant of the famous Egyptologist who deciphered the Rosetta stone. A 35-foot, two-story library adds elegance with its oak paneling and massive granite fireplace. Lake Sunapee is nearby.

Location: Lake Sunapee Region, 8 miles south from Exit 13 on Route 10.
Rates: $85-$150. Dick & Judi Tatem.
5 R. 1 PB. 2 FP. Phone available. Beds: KQDTC. B&B. Gourmet meals. Handicap access. Conference room. CCs: MC VISA. Skiing, swimming, boating, fishing, snowmobiling, sleigh rides.
Seen in: *The Advisor.*

"We stopped at many B&Bs on our trip. Yours is the loveliest by far!"

NORTH CONWAY I11/D5

The 1785 Inn

Rt 16 at The Scenic Vista
North Conway NH 03860
(603) 356-9025 (800) 421-1785

Circa 1785. The main section of this center-chimney house was built by Captain Elijah Dinsmore of the New Hampshire Rangers. He was granted the land for service in the American Revolution. Original hand-hewn beams, corner posts, fireplaces, and a brick oven are still visible and operating.

*Rates: $60 $115. Charlie & Becky Mallar.
17 R. 12 PB. Phone available. TV available. Beds: KC. AP. Swimming pool. Conference room. Canoeing, golf, tennis, mountain biking, hiking, walking, cross-country & downhill skiing.
Seen in: *New England Getaways, The Valley Visitor, Bon Appetit.*

"Occasionally in our lifetimes is a moment so unexpectedly perfect that we use it as our measure for our unforgettable moments. We just had such an experience at The 1785 Inn."

The Buttonwood Inn

Mt Surprise Rd, PO Box 1817
North Conway NH 03860
(603) 356-2625 (800)882-9928

Circa 1820. This center-chimney, New England-style inn was once a working

farm of more than 100 acres on the mountain. Of the original outbuildings only the granite barn foundation remains. Through the years the house has been extended to 20 rooms.
Location: Tucked away on Mt. Surprise, two miles from town.
*Rates: $40-$170. Ann & Hugh Begley & Family.
9 R. 2 PB. Phone available. TV available. Beds: KQDTC. AP. Swimming pool. CCs: MC VISA AE. Swimming, downhill skiing, 60K of groomed cross-country trails from the doorstep, golfing, hiking, hunting.
Seen in: *Northeast Bound, Skiing, Boston Globe, Yankee Travel.*
"The very moment we spotted your lovely inn nestled midway on the mountainside in the moonlight, we knew we had found a winner."

Cranmore Mt Lodge

Kearsarge Rd, PO Box 1194
North Conway NH 03860
(603) 356-2044 (800)356-3596

Circa 1850. Babe Ruth was a frequent guest at this old New England farmhouse when his daughter was the owner. There are many rare Babe Ruth photos displayed in the inn and one guest room is still decorated with his furnishings. The barn on the property is held together with wooden pegs and contains dorm rooms.
Location: Village of Kearsarge.
❀Rates: $56-$95. Dennis & Judy Helfand.
20 R. 5 PB. 2 FP. Phone available. TV in room. Beds: DTC. MAP. Spa. Handicap access. Swimming pool. Game room. CCs: MC VISA AE DS. Tennis, fishing, hiking, bicycling, basketball, cross-country skiing, tobogganing.
Seen in: *New England Getaways, Ski Magazine.*
"Your accommodations are lovely, your breakfasts delicious."

Nereledge Inn & White Horse Pub

River Rd Off Main St, PO Box 547
North Conway NH 03860
(603) 356-2831

Circa 1787. This big white house is decorated simply in a New England style, featuring cozy English eiderdowns and rocking chairs in the guest

rooms. A woodstove warms the sitting room and there is an English-style pub, usually open on weekends, featuring darts, backgammon and draft beer. For breakfast you may be served apple crumble with ice cream as a dessert after the main course. Dave Halpin grew up in Burnley, England where his family ran a bed and breakfast.
Location: In the heart of Mt. Washington Valley.
Rates: $59-$75. Valerie & Dave Halpin.
9 R. 4 PB. Phone available. TV available. Beds: QDT. Full breakfast. CCs: MC VISA AE. Downhill & cross-country skiing, fishing, hiking, rock & ice climbing, cycling.
Seen in: *New England Getaways, Outside.*
"It is the kind of place you can really look forward to for a wonderful time."

Peacock Inn

PO Box 1012
North Conway NH 03860
(603) 356-9041

Circa 1773. The guest book at this inn dates from 1875. Since that time the inn has been renovated and placed on the federal map as a national

landmark. Some of the rooms have skylights as well as brass beds or canopy beds and antique rockers. Breakfast is served fireside. Across the street flows a babbling brook.
Location: Kearsarge Road, 1 mile from Mt. Cranmore.
*❀Rates: $39-$59. Claire & Larry Jackson.
18 R. 16 PB. 1 FP. Phone available. TV available. Beds: KQTC. Full breakfast. Sauna. Swimming pool. Conference room. CCs: MC VISA AE DS. Swimming, hiking.
Seen in: *The Standard-Times, The Irregular, Fosters Business Review, Granite State News.*
"Although I expected this to be a nice, cozy place, I was not prepared for the royal treatment my family and I received. We cast our vote for Larry and Claire as innkeepers of the year."

Stonehurst Manor

Rt 16
North Conway NH 03860
(603) 356-3113 (800) 525-9100

Circa 1876. This English-style manor stands on lush, landscaped lawns and 30 acres of pine trees. It was built as the summer home for the Bigelow family, founder of the Bigelow Carpet Company. Inside the tremendous front door is an elegant display of leaded and stained-glass windows, rich oak woodwork, a winding stair-

case and a massive, hand-carved oak fireplace.
Rates: $50-$135. Peter Rattay.
24 R. 22 PB. Phone available. Beds: QTD. AP. Restaurant. Spa. Handicap access. Swimming pool. Conference room. CCs: MC VISA. Swimming, canoeing, hiking.
Seen in: *The Boston Globe, New York Daily News, Bon Appetit.*
"An architecturally preserved replica of an English country house, a perfect retreat for the nostalgic-at-heart," Phil Berthiaume, *Country Almanac.*

NORTH SUTTON M7/*F4*

Follansbee Inn

PO Box 92, Keyser St
North Sutton NH 03260
(603) 927-4221

Circa 1840. This New England farmhouse was enlarged in 1929, becoming an inn, no doubt because of its attractive location on the edge of

Kezar Lake. It has a comfortable porch, sitting rooms with fireplaces, and antique-furnished bedrooms. Enjoy the best of the past while nestled in a small country village. Cross-country skiing starts at the doorstep. The inn is popular for small seminars.
❀Rates: $70-$90. Sandy & Dick Reilein.
23 R. 11 PB. Phone available. Beds: KDT. Full breakfast. CCs: MC VISA. Skiing, golf, tennis nearby. Boating, fishing, swimming, rowboat, sail board, canoe & paddle boat. Bicycle-built-for-two available for guests. Non-smoking.
Seen in: *Country Inns.*
"Bravo! A great inn experience. Super food."

PLYMOUTH K8/*E4*

Colonel Spencer Inn

Rt 3S, RFD 1 Box 206
Plymouth NH 03264
(603) 536-3438 (603) 536-1944

Circa 1764. This pre-revolutionary colonial boasts Indian shutters, gleam-

ing plank floors and secret passageways. Benjamin Baker, one of the house's early owners, fought at Bunker Hill and with General Washington at Cambridge. Within view of the river and the mountains, the inn is now a cozy retreat with a cheery country colonial decor. Afternoon tea and evening coffee and dessert are served. A suite with kitchen is also available. Occasional evening meals may be arranged by reservation.
Rates: $45-$65. Carolyn & Alan Hill.
6 R. 6 PB. 2 FP. Phone available. TV available. Beds: DTC. Full breakfast. Cross-country & downhill skiing, skating, horseback riding, hiking, swimming, boating, mountain climbing, biking.
"You have something very special here and we very much enjoyed a little piece of it!"

Crab Apple Inn
RR 4 Box 1955
Plymouth NH 03264
(603) 536-4476
Circa 1835. Behind an immaculate, white picket fence is a brick Federal house beside a small brook at the foot

of Tenney Mountain. There are fireplaces on the second floor and panoramic vistas from the third floor. Rooms are furnished with canopy beds and claw-foot tubs. The grounds include an English garden and meandering wooded paths.
Location: Gateway to White Mountains in the Baker River Valley.
Rates: $70-$85. Bill & Carolyn Crenson.
5 R. 5 PB. Phone available. Beds: QDT. B&B. CCs: MC VISA. Skiing, hiking, horseback riding, golf.
Seen in: *Bon Appetit.*
"We are still excited about our trip. The Crab Apple Inn was the unanimous choice for our favorite place to stay."

PORTSMOUTH 012/F6

Garrison Inn
See: Newburyport, MA

Leighton Inn
69 Richards Ave
Portsmouth NH 03801
(603) 433-2188
Circa 1809. Immediately after cabinetmaker Samuel Wyatt built this fashionable clapboard Federal house, the *Portsmouth Oracle* advertised it for auction in their December 23, 1809 edition. An impressive entranceway and Empire antiques accentuate the gracious atmosphere of this handsome home.
Location: North of Boston 55 miles.
Rates: $55-$75. Catherine Stone.
5 R. 4 PB. Phone available. TV available. Beds: QDT. Full breakfast. CCs: MC VISA. Tennis, swimming, sailing.
Seen in: *Country Inns, Portsmouth Herald.*
"Your hospitality, charm and friendliness was greatly appreciated. You're a terrific cook."

Maple Lodge B&B
See: Stratham, NH

Martin Hill Inn
404 Islington St
Portsmouth NH 03801
(603) 436-2287
Circa 1820. Lieutenant-Governor George Vaughan sold this land in 1710 for 50 British pounds. The Main House, a colonial, contains three guest rooms and the Guest House has four. All bedrooms are decorated in elegant antiques including canopy and four-poster beds, writing tables and sofas or sitting areas. Amenities include air-conditioning.
❀Rates: $75-$90. Jane & Paul Harnden.
7 R. 7 PB. Phone available. Beds: QDT. Full breakfast. CCs: MC VISA.
Seen in: *New Hampshire Profiles, Country Inn Magazine.*
"Beautifully furnished with antiques. Delicious gourmet breakfasts served on exquisite china."

The Inn at Strawbery Banke
314 Court St
Portsmouth NH 03801
(603) 436-7242
Circa 1800. A few blocks from the waterfront and Strawbery Banke's restored village and living museums is this house built by Captain Holbrook. Cozy rooms reflect the charm of those bygone days with polished pine floors and homey furnishings. Strawberry butter is a speciality here and in spring, guests can pick their own breakfast from the strawberry patch out back.
Location: Historic downtown Old Portsmouth.
✻Rates: $60-$85. Sarah Glover O'Donnell.
7 R. 7 PB. 1 FP. Phone available. Beds: QDT. Full breakfast. Handicap access. Conference room. CCs: MC VISA AE. Downhill & cross-country skiing, swimming, antiquing, shopping.
"Excellent! Most welcoming and kind. We'll be back."

SNOWVILLE J11/D5

Snowvillage Inn
Box 176 AAHI
Snowville NH 03849
(603) 447-2818
Circa 1900. Frank Simonds, noted World War I historian and government consultant, called his retreat here "Blighty." The beams in the main

house are hand-hewn and were taken from the original 1850 farmhouse. The inn has a spectacular sweeping view of Mt. Washington, and resembles a European mountain home with an Austrian flavor. (The hostess was born in Austria.)
Location: In White Mountains.
Rates: $40-$80. Peter, Trudy & Frank Cutrone.
18 R. 18 PB. 6 FP. Phone available. Beds: KQDT. MAP. Restaurant. Sauna. Conference room. CCs: MC VISA. Cross-country skiing, hiking, tennis, volleyball, swimming, majestic view.
Seen in: *New England GetAways, Los Angeles Times, The Boston Globe.*
"A jewel of a country inn with gourmet food."

STRATHAM 012/F6

Maple Lodge B&B
68 Depot Rd
Stratham NH 03885
(603) 778-9833
Circa 1900. Built by an old sea captain, the living room of Maple Lodge overlooks Great Bay. An enormous stone fireplace is a favored place for guests in winter, while the screened veranda is popular in summer. Guest rooms are spacious with comfy beds and floral wallpapers. A hearty breakfast is served in keeping with the country setting.
Rates: $65. John & Natalie Fortin.
3 R. 1 FP. Phone available. Beds: DT. B&B. CCs: MC VISA DS. Beaches, whale watches.
"The personal, caring touch given to every small detail captured our satisfaction to the fullest."

SUGAR HILL H8/C4

The Hilltop Inn

Main Street, PO Box 9
Sugar Hill NH 03585
(603) 823-5695

Circa 1895. This rambling Victorian guest house is located on the quiet main street of town. The rooms are decorated with antiques and there are several cozy common rooms for relaxing after a day of canoeing, horseback riding, or skiing. A spacious deck provides views of the surrounding gardens.
Location: White Mountain National Forest area.
Rates: $50-$85. Meri & Mike Hern.
6 R. 2 PB. Phone available. TV available. Beds: QDTC. Full breakfast. CCs: MC VISA AE. Skiing, hiking, swimming, tennis, golf, horseback riding.
Seen in: *Boston Globe, Littleton Courier.*
"Relaxing and comforting, better than being home!"

Ledgeland Inn & Cottages

RR 1, Box 94
Sugar Hill NH 03585
(603) 823-5341

Circa 1926. The main house of this inn is open from June to October but the private cottages on the surrounding

acreage are available all year. Furnishings are comfortable country pieces collected during the inn's 43 years of operation. There are wood-burning fireplaces and kitchens in the cottages.
Rates: $60-$110. The Whipples and Johnstons.
23 R. 23 PB. 12 FP. Phone available. TV available. Beds: KDTC. Continental-plus breakfast. Alpine skiing, cross-country skiing, hiking, fishing, tennis, swimming.
"We loved it at Ledgeland. Your place offered the kind of peace and beauty we desperately needed."

TAMWORTH J10/D5

Tamworth Inn

Main St
Tamworth NH 03886
(603) 323-7721 (800) 933-3902

Circa 1833. Thoroughbred horses frolic in the pasture that borders the inn's three acres. Originally a stagecoach stop, Tamworth Inn is furnished with many antiques and handmade quilts. There's a sparkling trout stream adjacent to the property and across the street is the Barnstormer's

Theater, one of the country's oldest summer stock theaters. The library has a cozy fireplace.
Rates: $80-$130. Phil & Kathy Bender.
14 R. 14 PB. 1 FP. Phone available. TV available. Beds: KQDT. EP. Restaurant. Gourmet meals. Swimming pool. Conference room. CCs: MC VISA. Swimming, fishing, cross-country & downhill skiing, hiking.
Seen in: *Boston Globe.*
"It was great spending the day touring and returning to the quiet village of Tamworth and your wonderful inn."

WAKEFIELD M11/E6

Wakefield Inn

Mountain Laurel Rd, Rt 1 Box 2185
Wakefield NH 03872
(603) 522-8272

Circa 1803. Early travelers pulled up to the front door of the Wakefield Inn by stagecoach and while they disem-

barked, their luggage was handed up to the second floor. It was brought in through the door which is still visible over the porch roof. A spiral staircase, ruffled curtains, wallpapers and a wraparound porch all create the romantic ambience of days gone by. In the dining room an original three-sided fireplace casts a warm glow on dining guests as it did 186 years ago.
Location: Historic district.
Rates: $65. Harry & Lou Sisson.
6 R. 6 PB. Phone available. TV available. Beds: DT. Full breakfast. Restaurant. CCs: MC VISA AE. Cross-country & downhill skiing, horseback riding, snowmobiling, hiking, biking, golf.
Seen in: *New England GetAways.*
"Comfortable accommodations, excellent food and exquisite decor highlighted by your quilts."

WEST FRANKLIN M8/F4

Maria Atwood Inn

RFD 2, Rt 3a
West Franklin NH 03235
(603) 934-3666

Circa 1830. This brick colonial was constructed with double-course brick made on the property by builder

Henry Greenleaf. Original Indian shutters, Count Rumford fireplaces, wide-plank wood floors and original paneling remain. The innkeepers filled the rooms with their antique collection and maintain an antique shop.
✻❀Rates: $65. Phil & Irene Fournier.
7 R. 7 PB. 4 FP. Phone available. TV available. Beds: QDT. Full breakfast. CCs: MC VISA AE DC. Horseback riding, canoeing, fishing, boating, downhill & cross-country skiing, biking, historic sightseeing.
Seen in: *Concord Newspaper, Alumni Magazine.*
"Wouldn't stay anywhere else."

WOLFEBORO L10/E5

Tuc'Me Inn

PO 657
Wolfeboro NH 03894
(603) 569-5702

Circa 1880. Wolfeboro, on the shores of New Hampshire's largest lake, Lake Winnipesaukee, is said to be the oldest summer resort in the United

States. This colonial inn is two blocks from the lakefront. A library and two screened porches offer relaxation.
Rates: $50-$90. Irma Limberger.
7 R. 3 PB. Phone available. TV available. Beds: QT. Full breakfast. CCs: MC VISA. Skiing, swimming.
Seen in: *Granite State News.*
"This is the most delightful place I have ever stayed."

NEW JERSEY

BAY HEAD N14/E5

Conover's Bay Head Inn

646 Main Ave
Bay Head NJ 08742
(908) 892-4664

Circa 1905. This shingle-style house is one of many similar summer cottages in Bay Head. (Most of these are still owned by the original families who came from Princeton.) Downstairs rooms feature tones of lavender and mauve surrounding antique photographs and furnishings. Guest rooms are decorated with antiques and Laura Ashley and Ralph Lauren fabrics. Views of the ocean, bay and marina may be seen.

Rates: $70-$140. Carl & Beverly Conover and son Timothy.
12 R. 12 PB. 1 FP. Phone available. Beds: QDT. Continental-plus breakfast. Gourmet meals. Spa. CCs: MC VISA AE. Horseback riding, water sports, sailing, windsurfing, tennis.
Seen in: *New Jersey Monthly, Good Housekeeping.*
"If you want action look elsewhere; this is a place to go to relax," Great Getaways.

CAPE MAY Z7/H2

The Abbey

Columbia Ave & Gurney St
Cape May NJ 08204
(609) 884-4506

Circa 1869. This inn consists of two bluidings, one a seaside Gothic Revival villa with a 60-foot tower, Gothic arched windows and shaded verandas. Furnishings include floor-to-ceiling mirrors, an ornate gas chandelier, marble-topped dressers and beds of carved walnut, wrought iron, brass or wicker. The cottage adjacent to the villa is a Second Empire-style home with a mansard roof. A full breakfast is served in spring and fall, a continental-plus buffet in the summer.

Rates: $80-$150. Season: April to December. Jay & Marianne Schatz.
14 R. 14 PB. Phone available. Beds: KQD. Conference room. CCs: MC VISA AE. Sailing, hiking, swimming, horseback riding, surfing, nature trails, birding. Wedding and conference specials.
Seen in: *The Richmond Times-Dispatch, New York Times, Glamour.*
"Staying with you folks really makes the difference between a 'nice' vacation and a great one!"

Abigail Adams B&B

12 Jackson St
Cape May NJ 08204
(609) 884-1371

Circa 1888. The front porch of this Victorian, one of the Seven Sisters, is only 100 feet from the ocean. There is a free-standing circular staircase, and original fireplaces and woodwork throughout. The decor is highlighted with flowered chintz and antiques, and the dining room is hand-stenciled.

Rates: $65-$120. Kate Emerson.
5 R. 3 PB. 2 FP. Phone available. Beds: QD. Full breakfast. CCs: MC VISA AE. Biking, beaches.
"What a wonderful time. Comfortable & homey."

Albert G. Stevens Inn

127 Myrtle Ave
Cape May NJ 08204
(609) 884-4717

Circa 1889. If you feel right at home, even before you reach the front door, it may be because you've seen this Queen Anne Free Classic Victorian house on local postcards. Next door to the Wilbrahan Mansion, it features a wraparound veranda, a tower, Victorian antiques and carved woodwork. A full country breakfast is served and during fall and winter dinners are included. The beach is three blocks away. Beach tags are available.

Rates: $70-$105. Curt & Diane Rangen.
8 R. 8 PB. Phone available. TV in room. Beds: QD. Full breakfast. CCs: MC VISA. Beach, golf, tennis, swimming, cycling, bird watching, horseback riding. Anniversary, honeymoon, birthday specials.
Seen in: *The Jersey Shore.*

Angel Of The Sea

5 Trenton Ave
Cape May NJ 08204
(800) 848-3369 (609) 884-3369

Circa 1850. This recently renovated Second Empire-style mansion features a mansard roof, a tower and views of the ocean from almost every room. A double-tiered oceanfront veranda stretches across the house. Each room boasts handsome antique beds and sounds of the sea. Victorian hospitality shines with a special changing room available for guests who wish to stay past check-out, afternoon refreshments and beach chairs, umbrellas, towels and bikes to borrow.

Rates: $63-$230. John & Barbara Girton.
27 R. 27 PB. 10 FP. Phone available. TV in room. Beds: QD. Full breakfast. Gourmet meals. Conference room. CCs: MC VISA AE. Beach, surfing, boating, fishing, bicycling, carriage rides, museums. Honeymoons, anniversaries, weddings & receptions.
Seen in: *Washingtonian, Mid Atlantic Country, Philadelphia Inquirer, Boston Sun, The New York Times.*
"We've travelled bed and breakfasts for years and this is by far the best."

Barnard-Good House

238 Perry St
Cape May NJ 08204
(609) 884-5381

Circa 1865. The Barnard-Good House is a Second Empire Victorian with a mansard roof and original shingles. A wraparound veranda adds to the charm of this lavender, blue and tan cottage along with the original picket fence and a concrete-formed flower garden. The inn was selected by *New Jersey Magazine* as the No. 1 spot for breakfast in New Jersey.

Rates: $85-$113. Season: March 15 - Nov. 15. Nan & Tom Hawkins.

5 R. 5 PB. Phone available. Beds: KD. Full breakfast. CCs: MC VISA. Water sports, tennis, historic tours.
Seen in: *The New York Times.*

"Even the cozy bed can't hold you down when the smell of Nan's breakfast makes its way upstairs."

Captain Mey's Inn

202 Ocean St
Cape May NJ 08204
(609) 884-7793 (609) 884-9637

Circa 1881. Named after a Dutch West India captain who named the area, the inn displays its Dutch heritage with table-top Persian rugs, Delft china and

imported Dutch lace curtains. The dining room features chestnut and oak Eastlake paneling. Breakfast is served by candlelight.

❀Rates: $65-$125. Milly LaCanfora & Carin Feddermann.
9 R. 3 PB. Phone available. Beds: QDT. Full breakfast. Conference room. CCs: MC VISA. Swimming, tennis, horse & buggy rides. Seen in: *Americana Magazine, Country Living, New Jersey Monthly.*

"The innkeepers pamper you so much you wish you could stay forever."

The Carroll Villa B&B

19 Jackson St
Cape May NJ 08204
(609) 884-9619 (609) 884-5970

Circa 1881. This national landmark is in the heart of Cape May's historic district. The inn features antique furnishings, Victorian wallpaper and overhead fans. Guests may relax in the wicker-filled living room, garden terrace and panoramic cupola. Breakfast includes fresh-squeezed juices

and homemade fruit breads. Guests may dine on the garden terrace, skylit dining room or front porch.

*Rates: $38-$94. Season: March to December. Mark Kulkowitz & Pamela Ann Huber.
23 R. 17 PB. Phone available. TV available. Beds: QDT. Continental breakfast. Restaurant. Gourmet meals. Conference room. CCs: MC VISA. Horseback riding, ocean swimming, nature trails. Lighthouse & Victorian house tours.
Seen in: *Atlantic City Press, Asbury Press.*

"Mr. Kulkowitz is a superb host. He strives to accommodate the diverse needs of guests."

The Chalfonte

301 Howard St
Cape May NJ 08204
(609) 884-8409

Circa 1876. This 103-room hotel has a rambling veranda. Rooms are simple and the cooking is southern. Cook Helen Dickerson, now in her eighties,

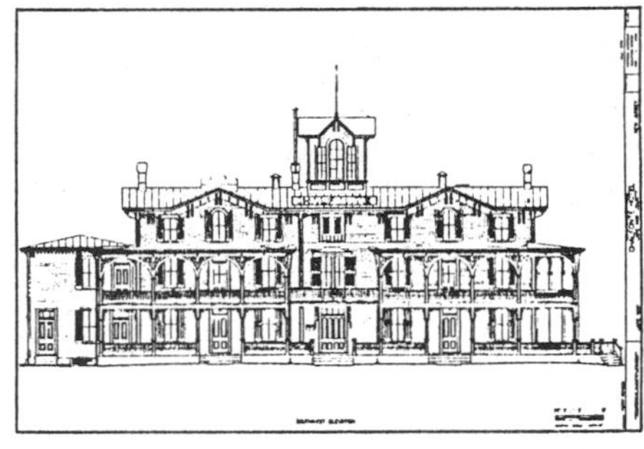

has been with the hotel since her mother brought her here at the age of four. Children of all ages are welcome and there is a children's dining room, library and special children's programs.

Location: Centrally located in the historic district, two blocks from beaches.
*Rates: $60-$140. Season: May to October. Anne LeDuc & Judy Bartella.
103 R. 11 PB. Phone available. TV available. Beds: KQDTC. MAP. Restaurant. Game room. Conference room. CCs: MC VISA. Swimming, sailing, tennis, golf, bicycling, bird watching, nature trails. Special workshops. Classical & folk music. Bar. Seen in: *Travel & Leisure, Philadelphia Inquirer.*

"The well-loved building, enthusiastic innkeepers, great food and friendly atmosphere made the weekend a success."

COLVMNS by the Sea

1513 Beach Dr
Cape May NJ 08204
(609) 884-2228

Circa 1905. Dr. Davis, the Philadelphia physician who created calamine lotion, built this oceanfront house in the

days when a summer cottage might have 20 rooms, 12-foot ceilings, three-story staircases and hand-carved ceilings. Large, airy rooms provide magnificent views of the ocean. The innkeepers supply beach tags and towels as well as bikes. Afternoon tea is served.

Rates: $95-$135. Season: 4/27-12/25. Barry & Cathy Rein.
11 R. 11 PB. 2 FP. Phone available. TV available. Beds: KQDT. B&B. Conference room. CCs: MC VISA.
Seen in: *New York Times.*

"We relaxed surrounded by terrific food, a warm atmosphere and elegance."

Dormer House, International

800 Columbia Ave
Cape May NJ 08204
(609) 884-7446

Circa 1899. This Colonial Revival estate is three blocks from the ocean and the historic walking mall. It was built by marble-dealer John Jacoby

and retains much of the original marble and furniture. Several years ago the inn was converted into guest suites with kitchens.

Location: Corner of Franklin & Columbia in the historic district.
Rates: $Call. Ruth & Stephen Fellin.
8 R. 8 PB. 1 FP. Phone available. TV available. Beds: DT. EP. CCs: MC VISA. Beach, water sports, tennis, golf.
Seen in: *Cape May Star & Wave.*

"Our 7th year here. We love it."

Duke of Windsor Inn

817 Washington St

Cape May NJ 08204

(609) 884-1355

Circa 1896. This Queen Anne Victorian was built by Delaware River boat pilot Harry Hazelhurst and his wife Florence. They were both six feet

tall, so the house was built with large open rooms and doorways, and extra-wide stairs. The inn has a carved, natural oak open staircase with stained-glass windows at top and bottom. Five antique chandeliers grace the dining room. Beach tags and parking on premises.

Rates: $60-$108. Season: February to Dec. Bruce, Fran & Barbara Prichard.

9 R. 8 PB. Phone available. Beds: DT. B&B. CCs: MC VISA. Tennis, beach. Christmas grand tour in December.

Seen in: *Philadelphia Inquirer, Innsider.*

"Tom and I loved staying in your home! We certainly appreciate all the hard work you put into renovating the house."

Gingerbread House

28 Gurney St

Cape May NJ 08204

(609) 884-0211

Circa 1869. The Gingerbread is one of eight original Stockton Row Cottages, summer retreats built for families from Philadelphia and Virginia. It is a half-block from the ocean and breezes waft over the wicker-filled porch. The inn is decorated with period antiques and a fine collection of paintings.

Location: Historic District, one-half block from the beach.

Rates: $72-$125. Fred & Joan Echevarria.

6 R. 3 PB. 1 FP. Phone available. Beds: D.

"The elegance, charm and authenticity of historic Cape May, but more than that, it appeals to us as 'home'."

Humphrey Hughes House

29 Ocean St

Cape May NJ 08204

(609) 884-4428

Circa 1903. Stained-glass windows mark each landing of the staircase, and intricately carved American chestnut columns add to the atmosphere in this 30-room mansion. The land was purchased by the Captain

Humphrey Hughes family in the early 1700s and remained in the family till 1980. Dr. Harold Hughes' majestic grandfather clock remains as one of many late-Victorian antiques.

Rates: $85-$120. Lorraine & Terry Schmidt.

10 R. 10 PB. Phone available. Beds: KQ. Full breakfast. Handicap access. Biking, golf, beach. Seen in: *New York Times.*

"Thoroughly enjoyed our stay."

Mainstay Inn & Cottage

635 Columbia Ave

Cape May NJ 08204

(609) 884-8690

Circa 1872. This was once the elegant and exclusive Jackson's Clubhouse popular with gamblers. Many of the guest rooms and the grand parlor look much as they did in the 1840s.

Fourteen-foot-high ceilings, elaborate chandeliers, a sweeping veranda and a cupola add to the atmosphere. Tom and Sue Carroll received the annual American Historic Inns award in 1988 for their preservation efforts.

❀Rates: $85-$140. Season: March 15-Dec. 15. Tom & Sue Carroll.

12 R. 12 PB. Phone available. Beds: KQDT. Full breakfast. Conference room. Beach, tennis, bicycling, croquet, bird watching.

Seen in: *The Washington Post, Good Housekeeping, The New York Times.*

"By far the most lavishly and faithfully restored guesthouse...run by two arch-preservationists." Travel and Leisure.

The Mason Cottage

625 Columbia Ave

Cape May NJ 08204

(609) 884-3358

Circa 1871. Since 1940, this house has been open to guests. The curved mansard wood-shingle roof was built by local shipyard carpenters. Much of the original furniture remains in the

house, and it has endured both hurricanes and the 1878 Cape May fire.

❀Rates: $75-$135. Season: May to Nov. Dave & Joan Mason.

5 R. 4 PB. Phone available. Beds: D. Continental-plus breakfast. CCs: MC VISA. Trolley tours, carriage rides, walking tours. Honeymoon packages.

"We look forward so much to coming back each summer and enjoying your hospitality and very special inn."

Poor Richard's Inn

17 Jackson St

Cape May NJ 08204

(609) 884-3536

Circa 1882. The unusual design of this Second Empire house has been accentuated with five colors of paint. - Arched gingerbread porches tie

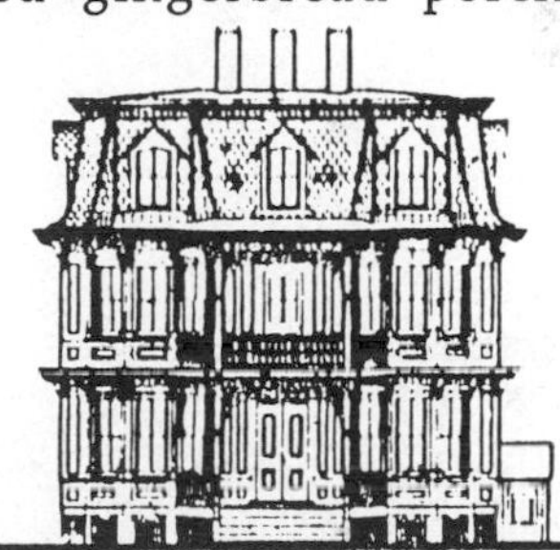

together the distinctive bays of the house's facade. The combination of exterior friezes, ballustrades and fretwork has earned the inn an individual listing in the National Register. Some rooms sport an eclectic country Victorian decor with patchwork quilts and pine furniture, while others tend toward a more traditional turn-of-the-century ambience. Many rooms are air-conditioned. A few apartment suites are available.

Rates: $35-$92. Season: Feb. 14 - Dec. 31. Harriett & Richard Samuelson.

9 R. 4 PB. Phone available. TV available. Beds: DC. Continental breakfast. CCs: MC VISA. Riding, golf, fishing, bird watching, historic tours, ocean.

Seen in: *Washington Post, New York Times, National Geographic.*

"Hold our spot on the porch. We'll be back before you know it."

The Prince Edward

38 Jackson St

Cape May NJ 08204

(609) 884-2131

Circa 1896. This classic Queen Anne seaside cottage is on the oldest street in Historic Cape May and is listed in the Cape May survey for the National

Register of Historic Places. The inn has a shady wraparound veranda, a sunny upper deck, original chestnut woodwork, 9 and 10-foot ceilings, stenciled walls and 12 stained-glass windows. Guest rooms feature 19th century antiques, crocheted spreads, quilts, lace curtains, Oriental rugs and high ceilings with ceiling fans.
*Rates: $60-$135. Season: Closed Jan.2-Feb.28. Pat & Ed Lightcap.
3 R. 3 PB. 1 FP. Phone available. TV in room. Beds: QDT. Conference room. Ocean, fishing, boating, birding, tennis, golf, horseback riding.
Seen in: *Trentonian, Workshop News, Gazette Leader, Atlantic City Press.*

The Queen Victoria

102 Ocean St
Cape May NJ 08204
(609) 884-8702
Circa 1881. The Sherwin-Williams Company used this restored seaside villa to illustrate its line of Victorian paints, and *Victorian Homes* featured 23 color photographs of it. Amenities

include afternoon tea and mixers, a fleet of bicycles, and evening turn-down service. Suites feature a whirlpool tub, fireplace or private porch.
Location: In the heart of the historic district, one block from the beach.
Rates: $55-$218. Dane & Joan Wells.
24 R. 20 PB. 2 FP. Phone available. TV in room. Beds: KQTDC. B&B. Spa. Handicap access. Conference room. CCs: MC VISA. Bicycling, beach, nature trails, bird watching.
"Everything was perfect in a beautiful surrounding."

Sand Castle Guest House

829 Stockton Ave
Cape May NJ 08204
(609) 884-5451
Circa 1873. This Carpenter Gothic was built by John Bullitt, a wealthy Philadelphia lawyer and a key figure in the development of Cape May in the mid-19th century. The inn is one block from the ocean and the two-

mile-long promenade. The decor is a light blend of country and Victorian with lace, oak, quilts and chintz.
❀Rates: $65-$125. Peg Barradale.
10 R. 7 PB. Phone available. Beds: QDTC. Continental-plus breakfast. CCs: MC VISA. Beach. Afternoon tea.
"Your friendly atmosphere and decor can't be beat. Thanks for making a needed vacation such a pleasant one."

Seventh Sister Guesthouse

10 Jackson St
Cape May NJ 08204
(609) 884-2280
Circa 1888. Most of the Seventh Sister's guest rooms have ocean views. The inn is in the National Register. Extensive wicker and original art collections are featured and three floors are joined by a spectacular central circular staircase. The center of town is one block away.
Rates: $60-$75. Bob & Jo-Anne Myers.
6 R. Phone available. Beds: D. Bicycling, beach.
Seen in: *New York Times, 1001 Decorating Ideas.*

Springside

18 Jackson St
Cape May NJ 08204
(609) 884-2654
Circa 1891. This Renaissance Revival cottage with three bright and airy stories is one of the Seven Sister houses built by architect Stephen Decatur Button. Most rooms have a partial ocean view and the front porch provides rocking chair views of the water, half a block away. The inn is furnished with mahogany pieces built in the thirties. A large doll house and

collections of art and sculpture are featured. Smoking is not permitted.
Rates: $50-$65. Meryl & Bill Nelson.
4 R. Phone available. Beds: K. EP. CCs: MC VISA. Beach.
"A unique combination of historic atmosphere and creature comforts."

Windward House

24 Jackson St
Cape May NJ 08204
(609) 884-3368
Circa 1905. All three stories of this blue Edwardian-style cottage contain antique-filled guest rooms. Beveled and stained glass cast rainbows of flickering light from the windows and

French doors, while gleaming chestnut and oak paneling set off a collection of museum-quality antiques and mannequins adorned in Victorian dress. The Eastlake and Empire rooms feature ocean views. All rooms have ceiling fans and air conditioning.
Rates: $85-$115. Owen & Sandy Miller.
8 R. 8 PB. Phone available. Beds: QD. B&B. CCs: MC VISA. Bicycles. Beaches and shopping one half block away. World-class collection of German bisque bathing beauty figurines.
Seen in: *New Jersey Monthly, Delaware Today, Mid Atlantic Country, Country Inns, Victorian Homes.*
"The loveliest and most authentically decorated of all the houses we visited."

The Wooden Rabbit

609 Hughes St
Cape May NJ 08204
(609) 884-7293
Circa 1838. Robert E. Lee brought his wife to stay at this sea captain's house to ease her arthritis. The house was also part of the Underground Railroad. Throughout the inn are whimsi-

cal touches such as the "rabbit hutch" in the living room which holds a collection of Beatrix Potter figures. The decor is country, with folk art and collectables that can accommodate hands-on exploration. Children are welcome.
Rates: $65-$145. Greg & Debby Burow.
3 R. 3 PB. Beds: KQT. Full breakfast. CCs: MC VISA. Swimming, bicycling, tennis, golf.
Seen in: *The Sandpaper.*
"The room was perfect, our breakfast delicious. We will be back."

Woodleigh House

808 Washington St
Cape May NJ 08204
(609) 884-7123

Circa 1866. Woodleigh House is a country Victorian built by sea captain Isaac Smith. Collections of glass and Royal Copenhagen are found

throughout along with Victorian-era furnishings. The front porch sports rocking chairs and wicker furniture. There is a secluded brick courtyard and back garden. The Woods, both educators, attend to guests' needs and are happy to make beach bikes available.
*Rates: $75-$100. Buddy & Jan Wood.
8 R. 8 PB. Phone available. TV available. Beds: DT. B&B. CCs: MC VISA. Beach, biking.
Seen in: *The Shopper's Guide-N.*
"What a warm and friendly home..."

FRENCHTOWN J6/C2

Old Hunterdon House

12 Bridge St
Frenchtown NJ 08825
(201) 996-3632

Circa 1865. Framed by an antique wrought iron fence, this Italianate Victorian is crowned with a handsome cupola that provides views of the

Delaware River, a block away, and rolling green hills beyond. Empire and Victorian antiques include massive burled four-poster beds. Frenchtown is noted for a number of fine restaurants.
Rates: $80-$100. Tony & Gloria Cappiello.
7 R. 7 PB. 1 FP. Phone available. Beds: QDT. B&B. CCs: MC VISA. Horseback riding, cycling, hiking, ballooning & gliding, river activities.
Seen in: *Innsider, New York Times.*
"We are so fortunate to have the luxury of a retreat like this, and it definitely recharges the batteries."

LYNDHURST G13/B4

The Jeremiah J. Yereance House

410 Riverside
Lyndhurst NJ 07071
(201) 438-9457

Circa 1841. In the National Register, this tiny house was built by a ship joiner who worked at the shipyards on the Passaic River. The inn is adjacent to a one-room schoolhouse built in 1804 which is now a museum of local history. There are cobblestone walks and a wisteria arbor. It is across from a riverside park.
*Rates: $55-$75. Evelyn & Frank Pezzolla.
4 R. 1 PB. 2 FP. Phone available. TV available. Beds: DT. Continental breakfast. CCs: AE. Tennis, bicycling, walking trails.
Seen in: *The Record.*
"A perfect setting to start our honeymoon!"

OCEAN CITY V10/G3

BarnaGate B&B

637 Wesley Ave
Ocean City NJ 08226
(609) 391-9366

Circa 1895. Three-and-a-half blocks from the ocean, the BarnaGate B&B offers Victorian-style guest rooms with paddle fans and country quilts. The top floor of the four-story inn features a private sitting room. Guests enjoy fresh fruit and homemade breads at breakfast.
Rates: $50-$70. Lois & Frank Barna.
5 R. 1 PB. Phone available. TV available. Beds: DT. Continental-plus breakfast. Gourmet meals. CCs: MC VISA. Swimming, boating, water slide, wineries, antique trails.
Seen in: *The Star-Ledger, The Intelligencer-Record, The Press of Atlantic City.*
"You two must have invented the meaning of the word 'hospitality'."

Top O'The Waves

5447 Central Ave
Ocean City NJ 08226
(609) 399-0477 (609) 391-1541

Circa 1912. If you are looking for "on-the-beach" in New Jersey, then your best bet might not be in Cape May but rather in Ocean City. Located right on the beach, this B&B encourages guests to become members of the Cedar Shores Innkeepers Guild for a small fee and be entitled to discounts at member inns.
Rates: $72-$155. Des & Dolly Nunan.
6 R. 6 PB. Phone in room. TV in room. Beds: QD. Continental-plus breakfast. Restaurant. Handicap access. CCs: MC VISA AE. Fishing, sailing, boating, tennis, golf. Casinos nearby. Honeymoons & anniversary specials.
Seen in: *The Morning Call, The Intelligencer/Record, The Sentinel-Ledger.*
"We all had a terrific time. The accommodations and your hospitality were top notch."

OCEAN GROVE M14/D5

The Cordova

26 Webb Ave
Ocean Grove NJ 07756
(908) 774-3084 (212)751-9577

Circa 1886. Founded as a Methodist retreat, ocean-bathing and cars were not allowed here until a few years ago, so there are no souvenir shops

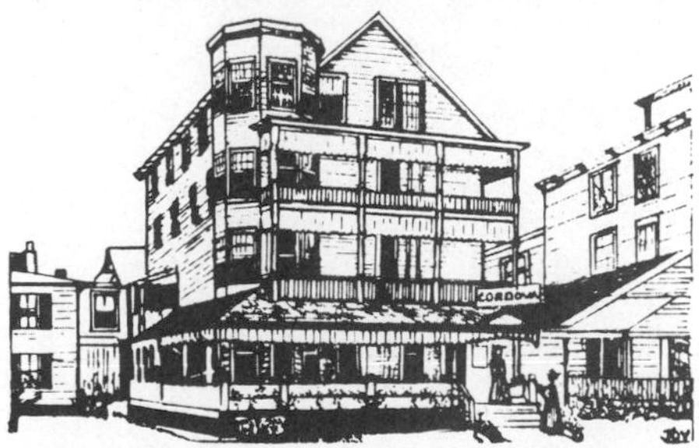

along the white sandy beach and wooden boardwalk. The inn has hosted Presidents Wilson, Cleveland and Roosevelt who were also speakers at the Great Auditorium with its 7,000 seats. Guests here feel like family and have the use of kitchen, lounge and barbecue.
*Rates: $30-$90. Season: May to Sept. Doris & Vlad Chernik.

17 R. 3 PB. Phone available. TV available. Beds: TDC. B&B. Swimming, tennis, volleyball, bicycling, jogging, fishing.
Seen in: *New Jersey Magazine, Asbury Park Press.*
"Warm, helpful and inviting, homey and lived-in atmosphere."

Pine Tree Inn
10 Main Ave
Ocean Grove NJ 07756
(908) 775-3264

Circa 1880. This small Victorian hotel is operated by long-standing residents of the area. Guestrooms are decorated in antiques and all the rooms are equipped with sinks. Bicycles are available as well as beach towels.
Rates: $30-$85. Karen Mason & Francis Goger.
13 R. 3 PB. Phone available. Beds: KQT. Full breakfast. CCs: MC VISA. Swimming, bicycling, jogging.
Seen in: *Country Living.*

PRINCETON K9/D3

The Stockton Inn, Colligan's
See: Stockton, NJ 08559

SALEM S3/F1

Brown's Historic Home B&B
41-43 Market St
Salem NJ 08079
(609) 935-8595

Circa 1738. Brown's Historic Home was originally built as a Colonial house. About 1845 the house was modernized to the Victorian era. The

inn is furnished with antiques and heirlooms, including a handmade chess set and quilt. The fireplaces are made of King of Prussia marble. The backyard garden features a lily pond, wildflowers and a waterfall.
Rates: $55. Bill & Marle Brown.
6 R. 3 PB. 2 FP. Phone available. TV available. Beds: DT. Full breakfast. CCs: MC VISA.
Seen in: *Mid Atlantic Country, Early American Life, Today's Sunbeam.*

SEA GIRT N14/E5

Holly Harbor Guest House
112 Baltimore Blvd
Sea Girt NJ 08750
(908) 449-9731

Circa 1905. Holly trees border the lawn of this three-story shingled cottage located eight houses away from the beach. A wide front porch is framed by a border of peonies. In the summer, a full buffet breakfast is served.
Rates: $75-$100. Bill & Kim Walsh.
12 R. Phone available. Beds: KQDT. Full breakfast. CCs: MC VISA AE. Water sports, biking, sailing, deep-sea fishing, walking.
Seen in: *New Jersey Monthly.*
"Your hospitality and warmth is unequaled."

SPRING LAKE M14/D5

Chateau
500 Warren Ave
Spring Lake NJ 07762
(908) 974-2000

Circa 1888. In addition to the lake, this village has a two-mile boardwalk along the ocean. The Chateau is a Vic-

torian-era inn with many rooms providing scenic vistas of the park, lake and gazebo. Borders of flowers surround the white pillared verandas and there are brick patios, sun-filled balconies and private porches. The Spring Lake Trolley departs every half hour from the front door.
*Rates: $49-$132. Season: April to November. Scott Smith.
40 R. 40 PB. 4 FP. Phone in room. TV in room. Beds: KQDTC. B&B. Handicap access. Conference room. FAX. CCs: MC VISA AE. Swimming, surfing, boating, fishing, tennis, golf, bicycling.
Seen in: *Great Water Escapes.*
"One of the top five inns in New Jersey." Mobil Travel Guide.

The Normandy Inn
21 Tuttle Ave
Spring Lake NJ 07762
(908) 449-7172

Circa 1888. An Italianate villa with Queen Anne influences, the Normandy Inn features sunburst designs and neoclassical interiors. Victorian antiques are accentuated by Victorian colors documented and researched by

Roger Moss. The house was moved onto the present site around 1910.
Location: One half block from the ocean.
❀Rates: $89-$125. Michael & Susan Ingino.
19 R. 19 PB. Phone available. TV available. Beds: KQDTC. Full breakfast. Conference room. Bicycling.
Seen in: *New York Times, Country, New Jersey Magazine.*
"The cozy and delicious accommodations of your inn were beyond expectations."

Sea Crest by the Sea
19 Tuttle Ave
Spring Lake NJ 07762
(908) 449-9031

Circa 1885. You can hear the surf from most rooms in this Victorian mansion. Guests will be pampered with Egyptian cotton and Belgian lace linens, queen size beds, fresh flowers and

classical music. Tunes from a player piano announce afternoon tea at 4 p.m. — a good time to ask if John's freshly baked scones will be on the menu in the morning. Family china, crystal and silver add to the ambience of breakfast. Bicycles are available and the beach is a half-block away.
*Rates: $90-$120. John & Carol Kirby.
12 R. 12 PB. 2 FP. Phone available. TV in room. Beds: Q. Continental-plus breakfast. CCs: VISA. Golf, tennis, sailing, deep sea fishing, water sports, horse racing, arts center. Afternoon tea.
Seen in: *Shore Holiday News, CBS.*
"This romantic storybook atmosphere is delightful! A visual feast."

Stone Post Inn
115 Washington Ave
Spring Lake NJ 07762
(908) 449-1212

Circa 1882. Originally built as a lodging establishment, this Victorian inn was known as the Rest-A-While and

then The Washington House. It is located in a quiet residential area surrounded by tree-shaded lawns and gardens, much enjoyed by guests rockering on the inn's beflowered wraparound porch. Popular for weddings, there are French and English antiques and the parlor offers a baby grand piano. There are two dining rooms. The ocean and the village are within one block of the inn.
Location: One block from the ocean and the village.
*Rates: $50-$100. Julia Paris & daughters Janine & Connie.
20 R. 9 PB. Phone available. TV available. Beds: KT. Continental-plus breakfast. Conference room. CCs: MC VISA AE. Tennis, horseback riding, golf, fishing.
Seen in: *New Jersey Focus.*
"The joy of our weekend at your charming inn lingers on and on. I'm still filled with warmth and a sense of peaceful excitement."

STANHOPE F9/*B3*

Whistling Swan Inn
Box 791, 110 Main Street
Stanhope NJ 07874
(201) 347-6369
Circa 1900. This Queen Anne Victorian has a limestone wraparound veranda and a tall steep-roofed turret. Family antiques fill the rooms and highlight the polished ornate woodwork, pocket doors and winding staircase. It is a little over a mile from Waterloo Village and the International Trade Zone.
Rates: $60-$80. Paula Williams & Joe Mulay.
10 R. 10 PB. Beds: Q. Full breakfast. Conference room. FAX. CCs: MC VISA AE. Skiing, boating, golf, horseback riding, hunting, fishing.
Seen in: *Sunday Herald.*

STOCKTON K7/*D2*

The Stockton Inn, Colligan's
1 Main St, PO Box C
Stockton NJ 08559
(609) 397-1250
Circa 1710. Colligan's has operated as an inn since 1796. It received national

prominence when Richard Rogers & Lorenz Hart included reference to it in a song from musical comedy — "There is a small hotel with a wishing well". (The Broadway show was "On Your Toes".) Band leader Paul Whiteman later signed off his radio and television shows announcing he was going to dinner at "Ma Colligan's". Guest rooms are scattered throughout the inn's four buildings and feature fireplaces, balconies or canopy beds. The restaurant serves innovative American/Continental cuisine and there is a full service bar.
Rates: $60-$130. Andrew McDermott.
11 R. 11 PB. 8 FP. Phone available. TV in room. Beds: QDT. B&B. Restaurant. Conference room. CCs: MC VISA AE. Horseback riding, skiing, ballooning, canoeing, hiking, antiquing.
Seen in: *New York Times, Colonial Homes, New York Magazine.*
"My well-traveled parents say this is their favorite restaurant."

Woolverton Inn
6 Woolverton Rd
Stockton NJ 08559
(609) 397-0802
Circa 1793. This charming mansard-roofed inn was built by John Prall, a merchant who owned the Prallsville Mills nearby. The stone manor house

is set among formal gardens. Each room is decorated in a different era and named after one of the previous owners or noted people of the area.
Rates: $66-$110. Louise Warsaw.
12 R. 2 PB. Phone available. Beds: KTD. Handicap access. CCs: MC VISA. Horse back riding, tennis, swimming, cross-country skiing.
Seen in: *New York Magazine, Colonial Homes.*
"Thank you for providing a perfect setting and relaxed atmosphere for our group. You're terrific."

WOODBINE W8/*H3*

Henry Ludlam Inn
124 S Delsea Dr, RD 3 Box 298
Woodbine NJ 08270
(609) 861-5847
Circa 1760. Each of the guest rooms has a fireplace and view of Ludlam Lake. Canoeing and fishing are

popular activities and the innkeepers make sure you enjoy these at your peak by providing you with a full country breakfast.
Location: Cape May County.
*Rates: $65-$90. Ann & Marty Thurlow.
5 R. 3 PB. 3 FP. Phone available. TV available. Beds: DT. Full breakfast. Gourmet meals. Conference room. CCs: MC VISA. Cross-country skiing, hiking, biking, fishing, canoeing, ice skating.
Seen in: *Atlantic City Press, Herald Dispatch.*
"A place to escape to - to get away from our hectic lifestyles!"

NEW MEXICO

ALBUQUERQUE F5/C3

Casas de Suenos

310 Rio Grande SW
Albuquerque NM 87104
(505) 247-4560

Circa 1930. Graceful cottonwoods shade the extensive gardens, courtyards and patios of the 10 adobe casitas that form the exterior walls of Casas de Suenos. A 1977 modern addition, designed by world famous architect Bart Prince, provides a stunning entry building, once the home of the late artist J.R. Willis. Pink climbing roses and concord grape vines drape lusciously over walkways. White adobe walls and *viga* ceilings are accentuated with a continental breakfast served from 7 a.m. A full breakfast starts at 9 a.m.

Rates: $65-$200. Paul J. Guschewsky.
10 R. 10 PB. 4 FP. Phone in room. TV in room. Beds: KQDTC. Continental-plus breakfast. Spa. Handicap access. Exercise room. Conference room. CCs: MC VISA. Croquet, museums, theatre, zoo.
Seen in: *Albuquerque Living, The Albuquerque Tribune.*
"Your warm hospitality and adobe accommodations are truly magnificent."

Casita Chamisa

850 Chamisal Rd NW
Albuquerque NM 87107
(505) 897-4644

Circa 1850. Beneath her old adobe, Kit, an archaeologist, discovered a deeply stratified Indian village attributed to the Pueblo IV Period, 1300-1650 A.D. After a two-year excavation, a viewing site was created. There is an indoor swimming pool and bicycles are available. An aerial tram and hot-air ballooning is nearby.

Location: Fifteen minutes from town.
Rates: $60. Season: Closed Jan. & Feb. Kit & Arnold Sargeant.
3 R. 2 PB. Beds: KQT. Continental-plus breakfast. Swimming pool. CCs: MC VISA.

W.E. Mauger Estate

701 Roma Ave NW
Albuquerque NM 87102
(505) 242-8755

Circa 1897. This former boarding house is now an elegantly restored Victorian in the National Register. Third floor rooms are done in Art

Deco with views of downtown Albuquerque and the Sandia Mountains beyond. The second floor is decorated with antiques and lace. The inn is located in an area undergoing renovation, six blocks from the Convention Center.

Location: Central Albuquerque.
*Rates: $60-$95 Richard & Uta Carleno.
6 R. 6 PB. Phone available. Beds: QD. Continental-plus breakfast. Conference room. CCs: MC VISA AE DC CB DS. Water skiing, horseback riding, fishing. Daily Indian dances. Organized tours of Indian Pueblos & petroglyphs.
Seen in: *Albuquerque Journal.*
"Because of your hospitality, kindness and warmth, we will always compare the quality of our experience by the W.E. Mauger Estate."

CHIMAYO D6/B4

La Posada De Chimayo

Box 463
Chimayo NM 87522
(505) 351-4605

The rustic charm of this adobe inn is matched only by the enthusiasm of innkeeper Sue Farrington, who built the two-room guest house herself. Sturdy oak vigas, brick floors and a Navajo fireplace offer guests an authentic New Mexico experience while the furnishings feature a distinct Mexican flavor. The natural, no-frills, setting of the inn is a treat for those weary of city life, and many guests make frequent return visits to relax and partake of the generous and delicious meals. Historic weaving and woodworking shops are nearby.

Location: Rural Chimayo, off the main road.
Rates: $75-$85. Sue Farrington.
2 R. 2 PB. 2 FP. Phone available. Beds: D. Full breakfast. CCs: MC VISA. Hiking, shopping, Indian pueblos, Bandelier National Monument.
Seen in: *Chicago Tribune, Sage Magazine, St. Louis Post-Dispatch, Albuquerque Journal.*
"Thank you for this retreat and your thoughtfulness in all details."

CIMARRON C8/A5

Casa del Gavilan

PO Box 518
Cimarron NM 87714
(505) 376-2246

Circa 1908. Situated against the base of Tooth of Time Peak, in the foothills of the Sangre de Cristo Mountains, Casa del Gavilan's 18-inch-thick adobe walls have provided the setting for decades of superb hospitality. Will James and Zane Grey knew the house well, and Grey used it as the setting for his *Knights of the Range.* The pueblo-style house, part of the UU Bar Ranch, features 12-foot ceilings and museum-quality southwestern antiques.

Rates: $65-$100. Bettye Knox & Harriett Faudree.
7 R. 6 PB. 2 FP. Phone available. TV available. Beds: DTW. Full breakfast. Gourmet meals. CCs: MC VISA AE. Horseback riding, skiing, back-packing, hiking, hunting, fishing, bird watching.
Seen in: *The Santa Fe Trail Revisited.*
"We cannot let a day go by without remembering something wonderful about our stay with you."

CLOUDCROFT K7/E4

The Lodge at Cloudcroft

PO Box 497
Cloudcroft NM 88317
(505) 682-2566 (800) 842-4216

Circa 1899. This Bavarian-style lodge building, topped with an enormous cupola, is situated at 9,200 feet in the Southern Rockies. Eleven of the rooms are located in The Pavillion - the lodge's bed and breakfast inn. These rooms have stone fireplaces, knotty pine walls and down comforters. The four-story high copper-domed observatory contains a sitting room and has views that stretch 150 miles towards White Sands, the San Andres Mountains and the Black Range. Past guests were Pancho Villa, Judy Garland and Clark Gable. The country's highest golf course is here.

*Rates: $59-$150. Mike Coy.
59 R. 47 PB. 3 FP. Phone in room. TV in room. Beds: KQDTC. B&B. Restaurant. Gourmet meals. Spa. Sauna. Handicap access. Swimming pool. Conference room. FAX. CCs: MC VISA AE DC DS. Biking, golf, tennis, cross-country skiing, fishing, snowmobiling, hunting, hiking, ice skating.
Seen in: *New Mexico Architecture, The Golf Traveler.*

GALISTEO F7/C4

Galisteo Inn

Box 4
Galisteo NM 87540
(505) 982-1506

Circa 1750. In the historic Spanish village of Galisteo, this adobe hacienda is surrounded by giant cottonwoods. The inn features a comfortable southwestern decor, a library, and eight fireplaces. Located on eight acres, there is a duck pond and a creek (the Galisteo River) forms the boundary of the property. Sophisticated cuisine includes dishes such as Brie Quesadilla with Pineapple Salsa. Blue corn waffles are favorites for breakfast.
Location: Twenty-three miles southeast of Santa Fe, 1 block east of Hwy 41.
Rates: $60-$150. Joanna Kaufman & Wayne Aarniokoski.
11 R. 7 PB. 4 FP. Phone available. Beds: KQDT. Continental-plus breakfast. Restaurant. Spa. Sauna. Handicap access. Swimming pool. CCs: MC VISA. Horseback riding, hiking, massage, ghost towns, 8 miles to petroglyphs. At the beginning of Turquoise Trail.
Seen in: *Physicians Lifestyle Magazine, Innsider.*

LINCOLN J8/E4

Casa de Patron

PO Box 27
Lincoln NM 88338
(505) 653-4676

Circa 1860. This historic adobe once was used to imprison Billy the Kid and played an integral part in the colorful frontier days of Lincoln County. A shaded courtyard and walled garden add to the authentic Old West atmosphere, and the comfortable rooms are supplemented by two casitas. Cleis plays the inn's organ and arranges soapmaking and Apache basket weaving workshops for guests. Salon evenings feature ragtime jazz and cafe cookery. Dinner is available by advance reservation.

Rates: $55-$90. Season: Closed February. Jeremy & Cleis Jordan.
3 R. 2 PB. Phone available. TV available. Beds: QT. Full breakfast. Gourmet meals. FAX. CCs: MC VISA. Hiking, fishing, horseback riding, skiing.
Seen in: *Preservation News, The Roswell Daily Record, Sunset.*
"The two of you and your perfect home were just a perfect combination."

SANTA FE E6/B4

Alexander's Inn

529 E Palace Ave
Santa Fe NM 87501
(505) 986-1431

Circa 1903. This Craftsman-style brick and wood home features twin gables and a massive front porch. An eclectic decor includes antiques that add a light Victorian touch.
❀Rates: $65-$125. Mary Jo Schneider.
4 R. Continental-plus breakfast.
Seen in: *The New Mexican.*
"Thanks to the kindness and thoughtfulness of the staff, our three days in Santa Fe were magical."

Canyon Road Casitas

652 Canyon Rd
Santa Fe NM 87501
(505) 988-5888 (800) 279-0755

Circa 1887. This territorial adobe is located in the Eastside Historic District. The five guest rooms include a suite with a dining room, kitchen and two beds. Each accommodation enjoys puffy featherbeds, fireplaces, and a private entrance through a walled garden. Canyon Road is considered the oldest continuously used road in the United States.
*❀Rates: $85-$165. Trisha Ambrose.
2 R. 2 PB. 2 FP. Phone in room. TV available. Beds: Q. Continental breakfast. CCs: MC VISA AE DC CB DS. Museums, shops, galleries, restaurants.
Seen in: *Radiance.*
Awarded "most spectacular inn in New Mexico" by Rocky Mountain Bed and Breakfast Association.

El Paradero

220 W Manhattan
Santa Fe NM 87501
(505) 988-1177

Circa 1820. This was originally a two-bedroom Spanish farmhouse that doubled in size to a Territorial style in 1860, was remodeled as a Victorian in 1912, and became a Pueblo Revival in 1920. All styles are present and provide a walk through many years of history.
Location: Downtown.
*Rates: $45-$125. Ouida MacGregor & Thom Allen.
14 R. 10 PB. 5 FP. Phone in room. TV in room. Beds: QT. EP. Gourmet meals. Conference room. Hiking, horseback riding, white water rafting, Indian ruins & pueblos. Tea is served from 5:00 to 6:30 p.m.
Seen in: *Innsider, Country Inns.*
"I'd like to LIVE here."

Grant Corner Inn

122 Grant Ave
Santa Fe NM 87501
(505) 983-6678 (505) 984-9001

Circa 1905. Judge Robinson and his family lived here for 30 years and many couples were married in the parlor. Still a romantic setting, the inn is secluded by a garden with willow trees, and there is a white picket fence. Rooms are appointed with antique furnishings and the personal art collections of the Walter family.

*Rates: $50-$125. Season: Feb. to Dec. Louise Stewart & Martin Walter.
13 R. 7 PB. 1 FP. Phone in room. TV in room. Beds: KQDTC. B&B. Gourmet meals. Handicap access. Conference room. CCs: MC VISA. Downhill & cross-country skiing, hiking, fishing, horseback riding.
Seen in: *New England Bride, Galveston Daily News.*
"The very best of everything - comfort, hospitality, food and T.L.C."

Inn of the Animal Tracks

707 Paseo de Peralta
Santa Fe NM 87501
(505) 988-1546

Circa 1902. Los Andadas is the Spanish phrase that may be translated "animal tracks" or "end of the trail." Each guest room of this turn-of-the-

century house carries an animal theme. The Soaring Eagle room has an inviting fireplace and six large windows with views of apple, pear and honey locust trees in the garden. The vibrant Santa Fe colors selected for Loyal Wolf reflect the impressive sunsets visible from the windows. Lilac trees and fragrant junipers are just outside. Breakfast and afternoon tea are all made from scratch and reflect the ten years Daun spent as proprietor of one of California's first bed & breakfast inns.

*Rates: $85-$95. Daun Martin.

5 R. 5 PB. 2 FP. Phone in room. TV available. Beds: Q. B&B. Handicap access. CCs: MC VISA AE. Horseback riding, swimming, wind surfing, hiking, skiing.

Seen in: *The Dallas Morning News, The New Mexican.*

We feel most fortunate to have been able to stay with you and enjoy your hospitality and delicious food."

TAOS C7/B4

Casa de las Chimeneas

Box 5303
Taos NM 87571
(505) 758-4777

Circa 1930. An adobe wall encompasses the hacienda, formal gardens and fountains of Casa de las Chimeneas, located two blocks from the Taos Plaza. Shaded by large cottonwoods, each room has a private entrance and amenities such as kiva fireplaces, bathrooms with skylights, hand-carved beds and regional paintings and watercolors. Huevos rancheros and green chile, blue corn pancakes are specialties.

Rates: $98-$128. Susan Vernon & Ron Rencher.

3 R. 3 PB. 3 FP. Phone available. TV available. Beds: KQTC. Full breakfast. Spa. CCs: MC VISA. Horseback riding, skiing, hiking, fishing.

Seen in: *Los Angeles Times, The Denver Post, Glamour Magazine, Bon Appetit.*

Hacienda del Sol

109 Mabel Dodge Ln, Box 177
Taos NM 87571
(505) 758-0287

Circa 1800. Mabel Dodge, patron of the arts, purchased this old hacienda as a hideaway for her Indian husband Tony Luhan. The spacious adobe sits among huge cottonwoods, blue spruce, and ponderosa pines, with an uninterrupted view of the mountains across 95,000 acres of Indian lands. Among Dodge's famous guests were Georgia O'Keefe, who painted here, and D. H. Lawrence. The mood is tranquil and on moonlit nights guests can hear Indian drums and the howl of coyotes.

Location: North of Santa Fe at the base of Sangre de Cristo Mountains.

*Rates: $45-$100. Mari & Jim Ulmer.

7 R. 5 PB. 5 FP. Phone available. TV available. Beds: KQDTC. Continental-plus breakfast. Spa. CCs: MC VISA. Downhill & cross-country skiing, hiking, fishing, hunting, white water rafting.

Seen in: *Phoenix Gazette, Rocky Mountain News.*

"Your warm friendliness and gracious hospitality have made this week an experience we will never forget!"

La Posada De Taos

309 Juanita Ln, PO Box 1118
Taos NM 87571
(505) 758-8164

Circa 1900. Located within the historic district in a secluded residential area, La Posada is built in the adobe vernacular of the Southwest. Log-beamed ceilings (*vigas*), polished floors, Mexican headboards, handwoven spreads, and whitewashed walls hung with local paintings contribute to the southwestern decor. French doors open onto a garden with views of the mountains. There are four guest rooms and a honeymoon cottage.

Rates: $55-$85. Sue Smoot.

5 R. 5 PB. TV available. Beds: KQT. B&B. Handicap access. Horseback riding, skiing, biking, fishing.

Seen in: *New York Times, Bon Appetit, Country Inns.*

"Since we left your inn we have talked of our time there often. We look forward to coming again."

The Taos Inn

125 Paseo del Pueblo Norte
Taos NM 87571
(505) 758-2233 (800)826-7466

Circa 1660. Circa 1800. The Taos Inn is a historic landmark with sections dating back to the 1600s. It is a rustic wood and adobe setting with wood-burning fireplaces, vigas, and wrought iron. The exotic tri-cultural heritage of Spanish, Anglo, and Indian is displayed in hand-loomed Indian bedspreads, antique armoires,

Taos furniture, and Pueblo Indian fireplaces.

Location: A quarter-block north of historic Taos Plaza.

*Rates: $80-$125. Carolyn Haddock, Scott Sanger, Douglas Smith.

39 R. 39 PB. 31 FP. Phone in room. TV in room. Beds: KQDTC. EP. Restaurant. Spa. Handicap access. Swimming pool. CCs: MC VISA AE DC CB. Horseback riding, skiing, water sports, golf, museums.

Seen in: *Bon Appetit, The Toronto Sun, The Naples Daily News, New York Times.*

"It is charming, warm, friendly and authentic in decor with a real sense of history."

NEW YORK

ALBANY EN15/E9

Mansion Hill Inn & Restaurant

115 Philip St at Park Ave
Albany NY 12202
(518) 465-2038 (518) 434-2313

Circa 1865. This old Victorian store houses guest rooms and apartment suites on the top two floors and a res-

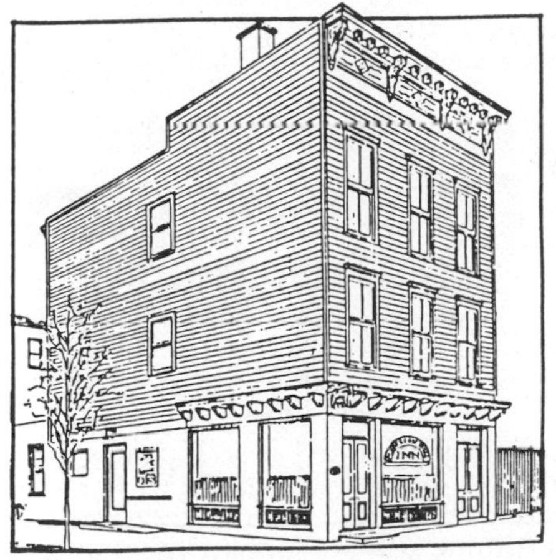

taurant on the street level. Originally the home of brush maker Daniel Brown, it later served as a bulk grocery store. It is located in the historic district just around the corner from the Governor's Executive Mansion in the Mansion Neighborhood. It is a few minutes walk to the State Capitol and the downtown Albany business district.

Rates: $95-$135. Maryellen & Steve Stofelano, Jr.
12 R. 12 PB. Phone in room. TV in room. Beds: QDC. Full breakfast. Restaurant. Gourmet meals. Handicap access. Conference room. FAX. CCs: MC VISA AE DC. Use of swimming pool and private health club can be arranged.
Seen in: *The Albany Review.*
"Rooms were beautiful and comfortable down to the shower curtain."

The Westchester House

See: Saratoga Springs, NY

ALFRED WI17/F4

Angelica Inn

See: Angelica, NY 14709

AMENIA ES16/G9

Troutbeck

Box 26, Leedsville Rd
Amenia NY 12501
(914) 373-9681

Circa 1918. This English country estate on 422 wooded acres enjoyed its heyday in the Twenties. The NAACP was conceived here and the literati

and liberals of the period, including Teddy Roosevelt, were overnight guests. Weekend room rates include six meals on weekends and an open bar as well as luxurious accommodations for a couple. During the week the inn is a corporate retreat and has been awarded Executive Retreat of the Year.

Location: Foothills of the Berkshires.
*Rates: $575-$790. James Flaherty & Bob Skibsted.
34 R. 29 PB. 6 FP. Phone available. TV available. Beds: QTDC. AP. Restaurant. Gourmet meals. Spa. Sauna. Exercise room. Swimming pool. Game room. Conference room. FAX. CCs: AE. Horseback riding, downhill & cross-country skiing, fishing. Tennis courts.
Seen in: *Good Housekeeping, New York Magazine.*
"Connoisseurs of country inns rummage fruitlessly through their memories to summon up an establishment that satisfies their expectations as completely as Troutbeck." Travel & Leisure.

ANGELICA WH16/F4

Angelica Inn

64 W Main St
Angelica NY 14709
(716) 466-3295

Circa 1886. Located in the Allegany foothills, the Angelica Inn features stained glass, crystal chandeliers, par-

quet floors, an oak staircase, carved woodwork, antique furnishings and scented rooms. Guest rooms offer such amenities as fireplaces, a porch and a breakfast alcove area.

*Rates: $55-$65. John & Fleuretta Pelletier.
5 R. 5 PB. 9 FP. Phone available. Beds: QDTC. Full breakfast. Conference room. CCs: MC VISA DS. Hunting, golf, skiing, hiking, bicycling, fishing.
"Victorian at its best!"

AVERILL PARK EN15/E9

The Gregory House

PO Box 401
Averill Park NY 12018
(518) 674-3774

Circa 1837. This colonial house was built in the center of the village by stockbroker Elias Gregory. It became a restaurant in 1984. The historic section of the building now holds the restaurant while a new portion accommodates overnight guests. It is decorated with Early American braided rugs and four-poster beds.

Location: Minutes from Albany.
*Rates: $65-$80. Bette & Bob Jewell.
12 R. 12 PB. Phone available. TV available. Beds: QT. EP. Restaurant. Swimming pool. CCs: MC VISA DC CB.
Seen in: *The Courier, The Sunday Record.*
"We experienced privacy and quiet, lovely surroundings indoors and out, excellent service, and as much friendliness as we were comfortable with, but no more."

BERLIN EN16/E10

The Sedgwick Inn
Route 22, Box 250
Berlin NY 12022
(518) 658-2334 (518) 658-3998

Circa 1791. The Sedgwick Inn sits on 12 acres in the Taconic Valley in the Berkshire Mountains. The main house features guest rooms, the low-ceil-

inged Coach Room Tavern and a glass-enclosed dining porch facing an English garden. A colonial-style motel behind the main house sits beside a rushing brook. The Gourmet Shop, once a Civil War recruiting station, is designed in the neo-classic style of the early 19th century. A converted carriage house with a hardwood dance floor and hand-hewn beams serves as a gift shop with prints, paintings and sculptures.

Location: Berkshire Mountains.

*Rates: $60-$100. Robert & Edith Evans.

11 R. 11 PB. Phone in room. TV in room. Beds: KQD. Full breakfast. Handicap access. Conference room. CCs: MC VISA AE DC. Skiing, swimming, museums, theaters.

Seen in: *Berkshire Eagle, Hudson Valley Magazine, Albany Times Union.*

"We were absolutely enchanted. We found this to be a charming place, a rare and wonderful treat."

BROOKLYN WP11/H1

Bed & Breakfast on the Park
113 Prospect Park W
Brooklyn NY 11215
(718) 499-6115 (718) 499-8961

Circa 1895. This four-story Park Slope brownstone brims with Victorian finery — canopied beds, feather comforters, flowing chintz curtains and handcrafted rugs. Original oil paintings hang on the walls. Guests may enjoy city and park views through the stained-glass windows swathed in old lace. A "convenience flat" on the garden level with a separate entrance is available. The aroma of freshly baked bread draws guests to the dining room where tables are set with Irish tablecloths, period china and flatware.

Location: Two miles from downtown Manhattan.

Rates: $100-$135. Liana Paolella.

6 R. 4 PB. 8 FP. Phone in room. TV in room. Beds: DT. Full breakfast. Handicap access. FAX. CCs: MC VISA. Brooklyn museum, botanical gardens, shopping.

Seen in: *The Brooklyn Paper, Kings Courier.*

"Wonderful breakfasts, beds, rooms, conversation!"

BUFFALO WE12/E2

Asa Ransom House
See: Clarence, NY

BURDETT WH21/F5

The Red House Country Inn
Finger Lks Nat'l Forest, Picnic Rd
Burdett NY 14818
(607) 546-8566

Circa 1844. Nestled within the 13,000-acre Finger Lakes National Forest, this old farmstead has a large veranda

overlooking groomed lawns, flower gardens and picnic areas. Pet Samoyeds and goats share the seven acres. Next to the property are acres of wild blueberry patches and stocked fishing ponds. The Red House is near Seneca Lake, world-famous Glen Gorge, and Cornell University.

Location: Finger Lakes National Forest, near Watkins Glen.

*❀Rates: $55-$85. Sandy Schmanke & Joan Martin.

6 R. 1 FP. Phone available. TV available. Beds: QDT. Full breakfast. Handicap access. Swimming pool. CCs: MC VISA AE. Cross-country skiing, hiking, 36 wineries. Dinners available November through April with advance notice. Seen in: *New York Alive, The Discerning Traveler.*

"Delightful. Beautifully located for hiking, cross-country skiing. Guest rooms are charming."

CAZENOVIA EM6/E6

Brae Loch Inn
5 Albany St, US Rt 20
Cazenovia NY 13035
(315) 655-3431

Circa 1805. The innkeeper here wears a kilt to highlight the Scottish theme. Four of the oldest rooms have fireplaces. There are Stickley furnishings, and the Princess Diana Room has a canopy of white eyelet. Guest rooms are on the second and third floors above the restaurant.

Location: U.S. Route 20.

*Rates: $59-$125. H. Grey Barr & Doris L. Barr.

14 R. 12 PB. Phone in room. Beds: KQDC. Continental-plus breakfast. Restaurant. Conference room. CCs: MC VISA AE DC. Horseback riding, cross-country skiing, golf, hiking.

Seen in: *The Globe and Mail, Traveler Magazine.*

"Everything was just perfect."

Lincklaen House
79 Albany St, Box 36
Cazenovia NY 13035
(315) 655-3461

Circa 1835. A fine example of Federal architecture, the Lincklaen House boasts high ceilings, classical carved

moldings, painted wood panels and Williamsburg chandeliers. Each guest room is stenciled with its own design. Summer guests may dine on the courtyard under maple trees. Seven Stone Steps, the house's tavern, has Merrill Bailey oil paintings. One of the dining rooms features grand Delft chandeliers, white brick walls and terra cotta floors. The white signpost in front was erected in 1835 and served as a hitching post for stagecoach teams.

Location: Finger Lake Region.

*Rates: $70-$130. Howard M. Kaler.

21 R. 21 PB. Phone in room. TV in room. Beds: KQDTC. Continental-plus breakfast. Restaurant. Conference room. FAX. CCs: MC VISA. Downhill & cross-country skiing, zoo, park, university.

Seen in: *The Colgate Maroon.*

"Delightful! A most hospitable place."

CLARENCE WE14/E3

Asa Ransom House
10529 Main St
Clarence NY 14031
(716) 759-2315

Circa 1853. Set on spacious lawns, behind a white picket fence, the Asa Ransom House rests on the site of the first grist mill built in Erie County. Sil-

versmith Asa Ransom, constructed an inn and grist mill here in response to the Holland Land Company's offering of free land to anyone who would start and operate a tavern. A specialty of the dining room is "Chicken & Leek Pie" and "Pistachio Banana Muffins."
*Rates: $90-$110. Season: Feb. to Dec. 31. Bob & Judy Lenz.
4 R. 4 PB. 3 FP. Phone available. TV in room. Beds: KQD. EP. Restaurant. Gourmet meals. Conference room. CCs: MC VISA DS. Antiquing.
Seen in: *Country Living Magazine.*
"Popular spot keeps getting better."

COOPERSTOWN EN10/*E8*

The Inn at Cooperstown
16 Chestnut St
Cooperstown NY 13326
(607) 547-5756

Circa 1874. In 1986, New York state awarded the Certificate of Achievement in Historic Preservation for the restoration of this three-story, Second

Empire hotel. A block from Otsego Lake, the inn is within walking distance of most of Cooperstown's attractions.
*Rates: $75-$90. Michael Jerome.
17 R. 17 PB. Phone available. TV available. Beds: QT. B&B. Handicap access. Conference room. CCs: MC VISA AE DC DS. Swimming, cross-country skiing, horseback riding, snow tubing, golf, tennis, hang gliding, boating.
Seen in: *The Plain Dealer, The New York Times, The Atlanta Journal.*
"In the evenings, a quiet soothes the soul like brandy in a portly gentleman." Travel-Holiday.

CORNING WI20/*F5*

Rosewood Inn
134 E First St
Corning NY 14830
(607) 962-3253

Circa 1855. Rosewood Inn was originally built as a Greek Revival house. In 1917, the interior and exterior were remodeled in an English Tudor style. Original black walnut and oak woodwork grace the interior, decorated with authentic wallpapers, period draperies and fine antiques. It is within walking distance to historic, restored Market Street and museums.
Location: Off U.S. Route 17.
Rates: $70-$110. Winnie & Dick Peer.
6 R. 4 PB. 1 FP. TV available. Beds: QTDC. Full breakfast. CCs: MC VISA DC.
Seen in: *Syracuse Herald-Journal.*
"Rosewood Inn is food for the soul! You both made us feel like friends instead of guests. We'll be back!"

CROTON-ON-HUDSON EV14/*H9*

Alexander Hamilton House
49 Van Wyck St
Croton-on-Hudson NY 10520
(914) 271-6737

Circa 1889. Nestled on a cliff above the Hudson River, the Alexander Hamilton House offers a large living room with a stone fireplace, a formal dining room and a 35-foot sunporch that overlooks the Hudson in the winter and the small apple orchard in the summer. The house is decorated with Victorian antiques and handicrafts. Also available is a furnished first-floor apartment with a private bath and kitchen.
Rates: $55-$125. Barbara Notarius.
6 R. 2 PB. 1 FP. Phone available. TV available. Beds: KQDTC. Full breakfast. Swimming pool. Conference room. CCs: MC VISA AE. Sailing, hiking, antiquing.
Seen in: *Heart Beat, USA Today.*
"I've been back four times. It feels like coming home."

DAVENPORT EP10/*F8*

The Davenport Inn
Main St
Davenport NY 13750
(607) 278-5068

Circa 1819. In 1799, a tavern was built on this lot, part of an original land grant of John Jacob Astor. The inn has

always catered to working folk and was a gathering place for townsfolk. Grazing cattle and meadows studded with farmhouses may be seen from guest rooms. Fine and hearty family-style meals are served on weekends.
Rates: $34-$46. Stewart Wohlrab, Bill Hodge.
5 R. 4 PB. Phone available. TV in room. Beds: QDT. Continental-plus breakfast. Restaurant. Gourmet meals. Conference room. CCs: MC VISA. Horseback riding, swimming, golf, tennis.
Seen in: *Oneonta Daily Star.*
"The operators of the Davenport Inn with their innate hospitality, graciousness, comfort and gourmet meals make it a place worth stopping and staying."

DRYDEN E04/*F6*

Sarah's Dream
49 W Main St, PO Box 1087
Dryden NY 13053
(607) 844-4321

Circa 1828. This graceful Greek Revival was built for physician Daniel Page, who originated the Bunker Hill

apple, working with a small orchard on the property. Antique-filled guest chambers include one with a fringed canopy bed and an old trunk. Upon arrival, guests are greeted with refreshments. In the morning a lavish breakfast is presented with a table set with antique dinnerware and silver.
*Rates: $50-$120. Judi Williams & Ken Morusty.
7 R. 7 PB. 1 FP. Phone available. TV available. Beds: KQDT. B&B. Conference room. CCs: MC VISA. Downhill skiing, golf, sailing, wind surfing, antiquing.
Seen in: *Ithaca Times, The Grapevine.*
"Gracious hosts. Tastefully decorated. Blockbuster breakfast."

EAST WINDHAM EP13/*F9*

Point Lookout Mountain Inn
Rt 23, PO Box 33
East Windham NY 12439
(518) 734-3381

Circa 1929. This mountainside retreat offers a panoramic view encompassing five states. Guest rooms feature spectacular views of the sunrise. The inn has a lounge with fireplace, outdoor decks and the Sunset Room, where guests enjoy meals and a sweeping view of the colorful sunsets over the northern Catskill Mountains. The inn will accommodate those who seek low-cholesterol, sugar-free or vegetarian meals.

Rates: $55-$120. Rosemary Jensen, Mariana Di Toro.
14 R. 14 PB. Phone available. TV in room. Beds: D. Continental-plus breakfast. Restaurant. Gourmet meals. Conference room. CCs: MC VISA AE DC CB DS. Horseback riding, skiing, hiking, fishing, swimming, golf.
Seen in: *Catskill Country.*
"Just wanted to thank you, once again, for a great time."

FORESTBURG ET11/G8

The Inn at Lake Joseph
PO Box 81
Forestburg NY 12777
(914) 791-9506

Circa 1879. This Queen Anne Victorian, with a massive screened veranda is set on 20 acres and was once the vacation home of Cardinal Hayes and Cardinal Spellman. The inn is surrounded by rolling lawns and woodlands and a small swimming beach is located within a short walk. It is in the National Register.
Rates: $118-$218. Ivan Weinger & Meri Kramer.
9 R. 4 PB. 2 FP. Phone available. TV available. Beds: KQD. MAP. Gourmet meals. Game room. Conference room. CCs: MC VISA AE. Golf, horseback riding, skiing, snowmobiling, rafting, ballooning, hunting, tennis, boating, fishing.
Seen in: *New York Times, Kaatskill Life Magazine.*
"This is a secluded spot where every detail is attended to, making it one of the country's best inns."

FREDONIA WH10/F2

The White Inn
52 E Main St
Fredonia NY 14063
(716) 672-2103

Circa 1868. Built on the homesite of the county's first physcian, this elegant mansion features a 100-foot-long veranda where refreshments are served. Period antiques and reproductions are found in every bedroom. Guests enjoy gourmet meals at this inn, a charter member of the Duncan Hines "Family of Fine Restaurants". Local wineries offer tours and wine tasting. Specialty and antique shops are nearby. Chautaugua Institute is a short drive from the Inn, and guests can arrange Chautaugua-White Inn packages. Fredonia is also the summer home of the Buffalo Bills. Lake Erie provides relaxation and an opportunity to enjoy a sail aboard the inn's 37-foot sloop.
Rates: $59-$159. David & Nancy Palmer & David Bryant.
23 R. 23 PB. Beds: KQDT. Full breakfast. Restaurant. CCs: MC VISA AE.
Seen in: *Country Living, Innsider.*

"Thanks again for another wonderful stay."

FULTON EK4/D6

Battle Island Inn
RD 1 Box 176
Fulton NY 13069
(315) 593-3699

Circa 1840. Topped with a gothic cupola, this family farmhouse overlooks the Oswego River and a golf course. There are three antique-filled

parlors. Guest accommodations are furnished in a variety of styles including Victorian and Renaissance Revival. There are four wooded acres with lawns and gardens. Guests are often found relaxing on one of the inn's four porches, enjoying the views.
Location: Seven miles south of Oswego on Lake Ontario.
❀Rates: $55-$95. Richard & Joyce Rice.
6 R. 6 PB. Phone in room. TV in room. Beds: QDT. Full breakfast. Conference room. CCs: MC VISA. Golf, cross-country skiing, fishing, museums.
Seen in: *Lake Effect.*
"We will certainly never forget our wonderful weeks at Battle Island Inn."

GARRISON EV14/H9

Bird & Bottle Inn
Rt 9, Old Post Rd
Garrison NY 10524
(914) 424-3000

Circa 1761. Built as Warren's Tavern, this three-story yellow farmhouse served as a lodging and dining spot on the old New York-to-Albany Post

Road, now a national historic landmark. George Washington, Hamilton, Lafayette and many other historic figures frequently passed by. The inn's four acres include secluded lawns, a bubbling stream and Hudson Valley woodlands. Timbered ceilings, old paneling and fireplace mantels in the inn's notable restaurant, maintain a Revolutionary War era ambience. Second floor guest rooms have canopied or four-poster beds and each is warmed by its own fireplace.
*Rates: $195-$215. Ira Boyar.
4 R. 4 PB. 4 FP. Phone available. Beds: QD. MAP. Restaurant. Gourmet meals. FAX. CCs: MC VISA AE DC. Cross-country skiing, golf, horseback riding, hiking, swimming, boating.
Seen in: *Colonial Homes, Hudson Valley, Westchester Spotlight.*

GENESEO WF17/E4

American House
39 Main St
Geneseo NY 14454
(716) 243-5483

Circa 1897. The American House was a tavern and stagecoach stop in the early 1800s. When it burned, a private home was built and it is now in the National Register. Centrally located in the village, it's a short walk to the campus of the State University of New York. The second oldest active fox hunt in the country is the Genesee Valley Hunt.
Location: Thirty miles south of Rochester, 60 miles east of Buffalo.
*Rates: $50-$65. Harry & Helen Wadsworth.
6 R. 2 PB. 2 FP. Phone available. TV available. Beds: QTD. B&B. Cross-country skiing, horseback riding, swimming, boating.
"You certainly set the tone for Jodi's wedding day. Many thanks from a grandmother who enjoyed every moment of that memorable stay."

GENEVA WE20/E5

Geneva On The Lake
1001 Lochland Rd, Rt 14 S
Geneva NY 14456
(315) 789-7190 (800) 343-6382

Circa 1911. This opulent world-class inn is a replica of the Rennaissance-era Lancellotti Villa in Frascati, Italy. It is listed in the National Register. Although originally built as a residence, it became a monastery for Capuchin monks. It rejected these to find its true calling as one of the finest resorts in the U.S. Meticulously restored in 1980-1982 under the direction of award-winning designer William Schickel, all rooms have kitchens and there are two-bedroom suites — some with views of the lake. Here, you may have an experience as fine as Europe can offer, without leaving the states. Some compare it to the Grand Hotel du Cap-Ferrat on the French Riviera.
Rates: $149-$322. Norbert H. Schickel, Jr.
29 R. 29 PB. 3 FP. Phone in room. TV in room. Beds: QDTC. Continental breakfast.

Restaurant. Handicap access. Swimming pool. Conference room. CCs: MC VISA AE DS. Golf, tennis, skiing.
Seen in: *Country Inns, Innsider, Bride's, The Catholic Register, Pittsford-Brighton Post.*
"The food was superb and the service impeccable."

GREENVILLE F14/G2

Greenville Arms
South St, Box 2 (Greene County)
Greenville NY 12083
(518) 966-5219
Circa 1889. William Vanderbilt had this graceful Victorian built with Queen Anne gables and cupolas. Seven acres of lush lawns are dotted

with gardens of daffodils, tulips and lilacs. There are floor-to-ceiling fireplaces, chestnut woodwork and wainscoting, and Victorian bead work over the doorways. Painting workshops are held in summer and fall.
Location: On SR 32, 2 1/2 hours from New York City.
*Rates: $75-$110. Eliot & Letitia Dalton.
20 R. 14 PB. Phone available. TV available. Beds: QDT. Full breakfast. Restaurant. Gourmet meals. Swimming pool. Conference room. CCs: MC VISA AE. Golf, fishing, tennis, horseback riding, hiking, bicycling, skiing. Weddings, conferences and gourmet dining by arrangement.
Seen in: *Victorian Homes, New York Magazine, Yankee.*
"Just a note of appreciation for all your generous hospitality, and wonderful display of attention and affection!"

ITHACA EP3/F6

Peregrine House
140 College Ave
Ithaca NY 14850
(607) 272-0919
Circa 1874. This eight-bedroom brick Victorian was built by an Englishman who came to town to work on Ezra Cornell's house. It is three blocks from the edge of Cornell campus and a block away from several ethnic restaurants.
*Rates: $79-$99. Nancy Falconer & Susan Vance.
8 R. 5 PB. Beds: QTD. Full breakfast. CCs: MC VISA. Boating, swimming, ice skating, cross-country skiing.
Seen in: *Ithaca Daily Journal, Cornell Daily Sun.*
"Elegant, warm, first rate. One is made to feel comfortable and relaxed."

Rose Inn
Rt 34 N, Box 6576
Ithaca NY 14851-6576
(607) 533-7905
Circa 1851. This classic Italianate mansion has long been famous for its circular staircase of Honduran mahogany. It is owned by Sherry

Rosemann, a noted interior designer specializing in mid-19th-century architecture and furniture, and her husband Charles, a hotelier from Germany. On 20 landscaped acres, it is 10 minutes from Cornell University. The inn has been the recipient of many awards for its lodging and dining.
*Rates: $95-$225. Sherry & Charles Rosemann.
15 R. 15 PB. 2 FP. Phone available. TV available. Beds: KQDT. Full breakfast. Spa. Handicap access. Conference room. CCs: MC VISA AE CB. Downhill & cross-country skiing, sailing, windsurfing.
Seen in: *Country Inn Magazine, New York Times, Ithaca Times, New Woman Magazine.*
"The blending of two outstanding talents, which when combined with your warmth, produce the ultimate experience in being away from home. Like staying with friends in their beautiful home."

KEENE EF14/B9

The Bark Eater
Alstead Mill Rd
Keene NY 12942
(518) 576-2221
Circa 1830. Originally a stagecoach stop on the old road to Lake Placid, The Bark Eater (English for the Indian

word Adirondacks) has been in almost continuous operation since the 1800s. Then it was a full day's journey over rugged, mountainous terrain with two teams of horses. The inn features wide-board floors, fireplaces and rooms filled with antiques.
Location: One mile from town.
*Rates: $75 to $110. Joe Pete Wilson.
12 R. 6 PB. Phone available. TV available. Beds: KQTC. AP. Handicap access. Conference room. CCs: AE. All summer & winter sports, horseback riding, cross country skiing. Adironacks high peaks climbing.
"Staying at a country inn is an old tradition in Europe, and is rapidly catching on in the United States... A stay here is a pleasant surprise for anyone who travels." William Lederer, *Ugly American.*

KINGSTON ER14/G9

Margaretville Mountain Inn
See: Margaretville, NY

Village Victorian Inn
See: Rhinebeck, NY

LAKE GEORGE EJ15/D9

The Westchester House
See: Saratoga Springs, NY

LAKE LUZERNE EK14/D9

Lamplight Inn
PO Box 70, 2129 Lake Ave (9N)
Lake Luzerne NY 12846
(518) 696-5294
Circa 1890. Howard Conkling, a wealthy lumberman, built this Victorian Gothic estate on land that had been the site of the Warren County Fair.

The home was designed for entertaining since Conkling was a very eligible bachelor. It has 12-foot beamed ceilings, chestnut wainscoting and moldings and a chestnut keyhole staircase crafted in England.
*Rates: $65-$125. Gene & Linda Merlino.
10 R. 10 PB. 5 FP. Phone available. TV available. Beds: QD. Full breakfast. Conference room. CCs: AE. Horseback riding, swimming, cross-country & downhill skiing, boating, white water rafting.
Seen in: *Getaways for Gourmets.*
"Rooms are immaculately kept and clean. The owners are the nicest, warmest, funniest and most hospitable innkeepers I have ever met."

LAKE PLACID EE13/B9

Highland House Inn

3 Highland Pl
Lake Placid NY 12946
(518) 523-2377

Circa 1910. This inn is situated on the hill in the village, a five-minute walk to Main Street and the Olympic Center. The rooms are decorated in a charming country style. A separate cottage on the property has all the comforts of home, including a fireplace.

Location: Above Main Street in the village.
*Rates: $50-$85. Teddy & Cathy Blazer.
8 R. 8 PB. Phone available. TV available. Beds: DT. Full breakfast. Conference room. CCs: MC VISA. Lakes, beaches, skiing.
Seen in: *Weekender.*
"You have the perfect place to rest and relax."

The Stagecoach Inn

370 Old Military Rd
Lake Placid NY 12946
(518) 523-9474

Circa 1833. This old inn was once a stagecoach stop and post office on the Elizabethtown-Saranac Lake route. The long wraparound porch and window sills of hand-hewn timbers add authenticity to the experience. Rooms are not luxurious but comfortable, old-fashioned tourist rooms.
Location: Adirondack Mountains.
Rates: $70. Lynn White.
9 R. 6 PB. 3 FP. Phone available. TV available. Beds: DT. Full breakfast. Hiking, skiing, boating, fishing, swimming.
Seen in: *New York Times, Country Inns.*
"This inn is really special."

LIVINGSTON MANOR ES10/G8

Lanza's Country Inn

RD 2 Box 446, Shandelee Rd
Livingston Manor NY 12758
(914) 439-5070

Circa 1901. Located on seven acres, the inn has a country taproom with a fireplace. It is furnished with antiques and there is a separate cottage on the property for groups of four.
Rates: $62-$84. Dick Lanza.

8 R. 8 PB. Phone available. TV available. Beds: KQDT. B&B. Restaurant. CCs: MC VISA AE. Horseback riding, water sports, golf, tennis. Stream fishing nearby.
Seen in: *Hudson Valley Magazine.*
"We were treated like family. Excellent food."

MANHATTAN EH13/C9

Bed & Breakfast on the Park

See: Brooklyn, NY 11215

MARGARETVILLE EQ11/F8

Margaretville Mountain Inn

Margaretville Mountain Rd
Margaretville NY 12455
(914) 586-3933

Circa 1886. Reminiscent of the Victorian era, this home rests on the site of the nation's first cauliflower farm.

The owners have restored the slate roof, elaborate exterior woodwork and decorative interior woodwork. A full breakfast is served in the formal dining room on English china, or guests can enjoy the morning meal on the veranda which overlooks the Catskills Mountains. The surrounding area offers a variety of activities including antique shopping, ice-skating and hiking.
*Rates: $69-$99. Carol & Peter Molnar.
8 R. 6 PB. Phone available. TV available. Full breakfast. Conference room. FAX. CCs: MC VISA AE. Horseback riding, skiing, water sports, fishing, hunting, ice skating, downhill & cross-country skiing. Weekend romance package.
"Thanks for the wonderful stay and hospitality."

MAYVILLE WI10/F2

Plumbush B&B at Chautauqua

Chautauqua - Stedman Rd, Box 332
Mayville NY 14757
(716) 789-5309

Circa 1865. Situated on 125 acres of meadows and woodlands, Plumbush is a mauve and pale pink, Italianate Victorian shaded by towering maples.

Eleven-foot ceilings accommodate the nine-foot tall arched windows. There is a music room, and a staircase winds up to the three-story turret.
*Rates: $55-$85. George & Sandy Green.
4 R. 4 PB. Phone available. TV available. Beds: QDT. Continental-plus breakfast. CCs: MC VISA. Hiking, cross-country ski trails, bicycles. One mile to Chautauqua Institute.
Seen in: *Buffalo News, Mayville Sentinel, Innsider.*
"A wonderful piece of heaven."

MOUNT TREMPER ER13/F8

Mt. Tremper Inn

Rt 212 & Wittenberg Rd
Mount Tremper NY 12457
(914) 688-5329

Circa 1850. Nettie & Charles Lamson built this Victorian inn to accommodate guests who would stay all summer with husbands and fathers

commuting by rail from New York City on the weekends. Now with Hunter Mountain skiing 16 miles away, the inn is popular all year. Romantic classical music wafts through the Victorian parlor decorated with velvet Empire sofas, burgundy velvet walls, Oriental car-

pets and museum quality antiques. A large blue stone fireplace warms guests who gather for nighttime chats. Each bedchamber has Victorian wallpapers, French lace curtains, luxury linens and antique bedsteads.
Location: Corner of Route 212 and Wittenberg Road.
Rates: $60-$90. Lou Caselli & Peter LaScala.
12 R. 2 PB. Phone available. Beds: DT. B&B. CCs: MC VISA. Horseback riding, hiking, swimming, fishing, cross-country skiing.
Seen in: *The New York Times, Mature Outlook, New York Magazine, Victorian Homes Magazine, Ski Magazine.*
"Two fantastic hosts, thank you! Great place, great people!"

NEW YORK EY14/*H1*

Sea Crest by the Sea
See: Spring Lake, NJ 07762

NORTH RIVER EH13/*C9*

Highwinds Inn
Barton Mines Rd
North River NY 12856
(518) 251-3760
Circa 1933. This mountain retreat offers panoramic views of the Siamese wilderness area and the Adirondacks. Every room has a view of the mountains. The inn offers a garnet stone fireplace and a view of the sunset on the dining porch.
Rates: $70-$150. Season: Closed November. Kimberly A. Repscha.
4 R. 1 PB. 1 FP. Phone available. TV available. Beds: KD. MAP. Restaurant. Gourmet meals. CCs: MC VISA. Cross-country skiing on premises. Mountain bikes, canoeing, hiking, tennis.
Seen in: *The Post Star.*

OLEAN WJ14/*F3*

Angelica Inn
See: Angelica, NY 14709

The Old Library Inn
120 S Union St
Olean NY 14760
(716) 373-9804 (716) 373-9805
Circa 1895. Olean's first B&B inn, located next to The Old Library Restaurant (also owned by Louis and Mary Marra), was once the home of a local oil producer and community doctor. The house has 27 rooms including a large ballroom that was discovered in the attic. Parquet flooring with original designs for each room was discovered during renovation. The stairway and entryway receives light through Tiffany-style stained glass windows.
Rates: $60-$125. Louis & Mary B. Marra.
7 R. 6 PB. 2 FP. Phone in room. TV in room. Beds: KQC. Full breakfast. Exercise room. Conference room. FAX. CCs: MC VISA AE DC. Total use of YMCA next door. Wedding receptions, honeymoon suites.
Seen in: *Olean Times Herald.*
"Very lovely atmosphere, excellent hospitality!"

ONEIDA EL7/*D7*

The Pollyanna
302 Main St
Oneida NY 13421
(315) 363-0524
Circa 1862. Roses and iris grace the gardens of this Italian villa. Inside are special collections, antiques and three

Italian-marble fireplaces. Of the two crystal chandeliers, one is still piped for original gas. A hand-crafted white wool and mohair rug runs up the staircase to the rooms where guests are pampered with bed warmers and down quilts. The innkeeper teaches spinning, felting, bobbin lace and other crafts.
Location: Route 46, 5 miles from Thruway 90, exit off route 5.
*Rates: $50-$70. Doloria & Ken Chapin.
6 R. 5 PB. Phone available. TV available. Beds: QDT. Full breakfast. Gourmet meals. Spa. Conference room. CCs: MC VISA AE. Water skiing, hiking.
Seen in: *Oneida Daily Dispatch.*
"Great hospitality and super breakfast. We really enjoyed all the interesting things."

PITTSFORD WD18/*D4*

Oliver Loud's Inn
1474 Marsh Rd
Pittsford NY 14534
(716) 248-5200
Circa 1812. This buttercup-yellow Federal and Greek Revival-style inn is tucked into a grove of tall trees. The lawn reaches to the banks of the Erie Canal. Antique rockers line the porch. The inn is decorated with 19th-century paintings and antiques. Guest rooms have views of the water or the trees and boast Stickley reproductions and Early American furnishings.

Richardson's Canal House, the oldest Erie Canal Tavern, is across the lawn and features French and American country cooking.
Rates: $135. Vivienne Tellier.
8 R. 8 PB. Phone in room. TV available. B&B. Hot-air ballooning, museums.
Seen in: *Country Inns, Bon Appetit, The Philadelphia Inquirer, Times-Union, Country Living.*
"Excellent in every way. I have never stayed at a finer place in my 35 years as a rover."

POUGHKEEPSIE ET14/*G9*

Village Victorian Inn
See: Rhinebeck, NY

QUEENSBURG EL14/*D9*

The Crislip's B&B
RD 1 Box 57, Ridge Rd
Queensburg NY 12804
(518) 793-6869
Circa 1820. This Federal-style house was built by Quakers. It was owned by the area's first doctor who used it as a training center for young interns. There are historic stone walls on the property.
Location: Lake George, Saratoga area.
Rates: $55-$75. Ned & Joyce Crislip.
3 R. 3 PB. Phone available. Beds: KD. CCs: MC VISA.

RHINEBECK ER14/*G9*

The Jacob Kip River House B&B
Long Dock Rd
Rhinebeck NY 12572
(914) 876-8330
Circa 1708. Nestled into a hillside overlooking the Hudson River 100 yards away is this stone house built by Hendrick Kip for his brother Jacob. They purchased the land from Sapasco Indians in 1686. The house served as a tavern for travelers taking the ferry service to Kingston. During a recent restoration, a hidden chamber thought to have been used on the Underground Railroad, was found beneath the dining room. George Washington slept here in 1783 during his triumphal tour following the Revolutionary War.
*Rates: $65-$95. Katherine Mansfield & Norman Shatkin.

4 R. 1 PB. Phone available. TV available. Beds: KDT. B&B. CCs: MC VISA. Tennis, swimming, cross-country skiing, bird-watching.

Village Victorian Inn

31 Center St
Rhinebeck NY 12572
(914) 876-8345

Circa 1860. A white picket fence surrounds this appealing yellow-and-white Victorian. It is furnished with French Victorian fabrics, floral wallpapers, local antiques and canopy or brass beds. Cheese blintzes or eggs Benedict are often the choices for breakfast, which is served in the dining room.

*Rates: $135-$195. Judy & Rich Kohler.
7 R. 7 PB. 2 FP. Phone available. TV available. Beds: KQ. B&B. Gourmet meals. Conference room. CCs: MC VISA AE. Sailing, cross-country skiing, antiquing.
Seen in: *Travel & Leisure Magazine, Weekend Trader.*
"Thank you for all your hospitality and for making our stay so wonderful. Breakfast was delicious."

ROCHESTER WD18/D4

Strawberry Castle B&B

1883 Penfield Rd, Rt 441
Rochester NY 14526
(716) 385-3266

Circa 1875. A rosy brick Italianate villa, Strawberry Castle was once known for the grapes and strawberries grown on the property. Ornate

plaster ceilings and original inside shutters are special features. There are six roof levels, carved ornamental brackets, and columned porches topped by a white cupola.

Location: East of Rochester on Route 441.
Rates: $60-$75. Charles & Cynthia Whited.
3 R. Phone available. TV available. Continental-plus breakfast. Swimming pool. Conference room. CCs: MC VISA. Swimming.
Seen in: *Upstate Magazine.*
"You have a most unusual place. We applaud your restoration efforts and are thankful you've made it available to travelers."

SARANAC LAKE EE13/B9

The Point

Star Route
Saranac Lake NY 12983
(518) 891-5674

Circa 1930. Designed by renowned architect William Distin and built for William Rockefeller, this Adirondack Great Camp has hosted fashionable

house parties for the Vanderbilts, Whitneys and Morgans. No expense was spared to create the elegant, rustic lakefront estate with its walk-in-fieldstone fireplaces, rare Adirondack antiques and massive hand-hewn beams. Each day a cord of wood is needed to fuel all the fireplaces. This lavish camp welcomes those who prefer to rough it with style.

*Rates: $525-$675. Bill & Claudia McNamee.
11 R. 11 PB. 11 FP. Phone available. TV available. Beds: K. AP. Game room. Conference room. FAX. CCs: AE. Swimming, canoeing, water-skiing, horseback riding. Snow picnics, snow skiing. Old mahogany runabouts.
Seen in: *New York Magazine, House & Garden, Country Inns, Washingtonian, Brides, Connoisseur.*
"Simply the most attractive private home in America." Irene Miki Rawlings, *New York Times.*

SARATOGA SPRINGS EL14/D9

Adelphi Hotel

365 Broadway
Saratoga Springs NY 12866
(518) 587-4688

Circa 1877. This Victorian hotel is one of two hotels still remaining from Saratoga's opulent spa era. A piazza overlooking Broadway features three-story columns topped with Victorian fretwork. Recently refurbished with lavish turn-of-the-century decor, rooms are filled with antique furnishings and opulent draperies and wall coverings, highlighting the inn's high ceilings and ornate woodwork. Breakfast is delivered to each room in the morning.

Rates: $65-$280. Season: May - October. Gregg Siefher & Sheila Parkert.
34 R. 34 PB. Phone in room. TV in room. Beds: QTDC. B&B. Restaurant. CCs: MC VISA AE. Horseback riding, skiing, racetracks, boating, water skiing, sailing.
Seen in: *New York Times.*

The Inn on Bacon Hill

200 Wall St
Saratoga Springs NY 12871
(518) 695-3693 (518) 695-3502

Circa 1865. State legislator Alexander Baucus built his mid-Victorian mansion in the country a few miles from

Saratoga Springs. A guest parlor, marble fireplaces, a carved staircase and original moldings add to the gracious country gentleman lifestyle. Antique beds are piled with flowered quilts in the guest rooms.

*Rates: $60-$125. Andrea Collins-Breslin.
4 R. 2 PB. Phone available. Beds: DT. Full breakfast. CCs: MC VISA. Tennis, golf, swimming, cross-country skiing, ballet & opera. Three-day extended weekend inn-keeping course (November - April).
Seen in: *Boston Globe, The Saratogian, Early American Life, Americana.*
"We'll long remember the warmth and pleasures of sharing a little piece of summer with you."

The Inn on Bacon Hill

See: Schuylerville, NY

The Six Sisters B&B

149 Union Ave
Saratoga Springs NY 12866
(518) 583-1173

Circa 1880. This Victorian features a two-story porch filled with rocking chairs, a half block from the Racing Museum. Rooms are spacious and comfortably decorated with furnishings such as wing chairs and brass beds. Guests often cross the street early in the morning to watch the horses being put through their paces, then return to the inn for a hearty breakfast.

Location: Capitol District.
Rates: $60-$75. Kate Benton & Steve Ramirez.
4 R. 4 PB. Phone available. TV in room. Beds: KQD. Full breakfast. Handicap access. Tennis, swimming, golf, skiing, antiquing.
Seen in: *The Saratogian.*
"The mineral bath and massage at the spa the day we left really put 'the icing on the cake'."

The Westchester House

102 Lincoln Ave, PO Box 944
Saratoga Springs NY 12866
(518) 587-7613

Circa 1880. This gracious Queen Anne Victorian has been welcoming vacationers for more than 100 years. Antiques from four generations of the

Melvin's family grace the high-ceilinged rooms. Oriental rugs top gleaming wood floors, while antique clocks and lace curtains set a graceful tone. Guests gather on the wraparound porch, in the parlors or gardens for an afternoon refreshment of old-fashioned lemonade. Racing season rates are quoted separately.

Location: Thirty miles north of Albany in the Adirondack foothills.

❀Rates: $70-$100. Season: Feb.-Dec. Bob & Stephanie Melvin.

7 R. 7 PB. Phone available. Beds: KDT. Continental-plus breakfast. Conference room. CCs: MC VISA AE. Golf, tennis, swimming, cross-country skiing, ice skating, mineral spas, Philadelphia Orchestra. Porches and gardens. NYC Ballet & Opera at the Arts Center, Thoroughbred Race Track.

Seen in: *Getaways for Gourmets, The Albany Times Union, The Saratogian, Capital, Country Inns, New York Daily News, WNYT.*

"I adored your B&B and have raved about it to all. One of the most beautiful and welcoming places we've ever visited."

SKANEATELES EM4/E6

Sherwood Inn

26 W Genesee St
Skaneateles NY 13152
(315) 685-3405

Circa 1807. During the Knickerbocker Tours of the 1820s, stagecoaches making the rounds between New

York and Niagara Falls chose Isaac Sherwood's tavern as their favorite stopping place. Many of the rooms face scenic Skaneateles Lake. The inn is noted for its continental and American menu.

*Rates: $70-$100. Ellen Seymour.

17 R. 17 PB. Phone in room. TV available. Beds: DT. Continental breakfast. Restaurant. Conference room. CCs: MC VISA AE DC. Boating, swimming, tennis, skiing, horseback riding, golf, polo.

Seen in: *Glamour, Travel & Leisure.*

SODUS POINT WC20/D5

Carriage House Inn

8375 Wickham Blvd
Sodus Point NY 14555
(315) 483-2100

Circa 1870. Located on four acres in a quiet residential area, the Carriage House Inn overlooks Lake Ontario and a historic lighthouse. The main house is an old wooden farmhouse and there's an interesting Victorian stone house and a barn. The inn caters to fishermen and couples looking for a cozy getaway.

❀Rates: $60. James Den Decker.

8 R. 8 PB. Phone available. TV available. Beds: TK. Full breakfast. Handicap access. CCs: MC VISA. Beach access, golf, charter fishing, water sports, skiing, swimming.

Seen in: *Finger Lakes Times, Democrat and Chronicle.*

"My wife and I have been telling everyone about the beautiful room we had and your courtesy."

SOUTHOLD WL22/G4

Goose Creek Guesthouse

1475 Waterview Dr
Southold NY 11971
(516) 765-3356

Circa 1860. Grover Pease left for the Civil War from this house, and after his death his widow Harriet ran a summer boarding house here. The

basement actually dates from the 1780s and is constructed of large rocks. The present house was moved here and put on the older foundation. Southold has many old historic homes and a guidebook is provided for visitors.

Rates: $60-$70. Mary J. Mooney-Getoff.

4 R. Phone available. TV available. Beds: KQT. Full breakfast. Tennis, golf, horseback riding, beaches, museums, antique shops.

Seen in: *New York Times, Newsday.*

"We will be repeat guests. Count on it!!"

STONY BROOK WN17/G3

Three Village Inn

150 Main St
Stony Brook NY 11790
(516) 751-0555

Circa 1751. Since 1751, generations of innkeepers, including Captain Jonas Smith, the Melvilles and the Roberts have managed this Long Island

colonial inn. The original part of the inn is a tavern room, the Sandbar. Good food, twilight walks by the marina and Laura Ashley decorated guest rooms make for a refreshing getaway.

Rates: $85-$110. Jimmy & Lou Miaritis.

32 R. Beds: KQDT. Restaurant. Handicap access. CCs: MC VISA AE. Horse-drawn carriage rides, nature walks, fishing, swimming, golf, tennis, biking, antiquing, apple picking.

Seen in: *Five One Six Magazine.*

"It was perfectly lovely and comfortable."

SYRACUSE EL5/D6

Lincklaen House

See: Cazenovia, NY 13035

WATERLOO WE21/E5

The Historic James R. Webster Mansion

115 E Main St - Rts 5 & 20
Waterloo NY 13165
(315) 539-3032

Circa 1845. James Russell Webster, relative of Noah Webster and friend of Abraham Lincoln, built this Greek Revival mansion with a classical pil-

lared Greek temple front. In addition to elegant 17th, 18th and 19th century European and Asian furnishings, museum quality collections include rare European clocks and cat figurines. Richly crafted woodwork is found throughout. Two palacial suites (one a 2,000-square-feet villa with 14-foot ceilings) cater to couples celebrating honeymoons, anniversaries and birthdays. Barbara's fine cuisine was recently acknowledged by membership in the Master Chefs Institute of America. There is an extra charge for breakfast.
Location: Routes 5 & 20 between Geneva and Seneca Falls, Exit 41 off I-90.
*Rates: $330. Leonard & Barbara N. Cohen.
2 R. 2 PB. 2 FP. Phone available. Beds: D. Continental-plus breakfast. Restaurant. Gourmet meals. Conference room. CCs: MC VISA DC CB. Winery trails, Women's Hall of Fame, Women's National Historic Park, turn-of-the-century "Street of Shops Mall".
Seen in: *New York Alive, Syracuse New Times, ABC TV.*
"Thank you for making our honeymoon a fabulous fairy tale. Wonderful antiques. Absolutely gourmet meals. We think you have reached perfection."

WESTFIELD WH10/F1

Westfield House
E Main Rd, PO Box 505
Westfield NY 14787
(716) 326-6262
Circa 1840. Westfield was part of the Granger Homestead. Benjamin Hopson, a local ice merchant, built a mag-

nificent Gothic Revival addition in 1860. His daughter Lucy used the living room with its large crystal windows as a tea room. The Gothic detailed interiors include a winding staircase to the six upstairs bed chambers.
Location: Southwestern New York state.
❀Rates: $55 to $85. Betty & Jud Wilson
6 R. 6 PB. Phone available. Beds: KQ. B&B. Handicap access. Conference room. CCs: MC VISA. Cross-country skiing, water sports. Complimentary boat rides on Chautauqua Lake.
Seen in: *Buffalo News, Innsider.*
"Your accommodations and hospitality are wonderful! Simply outstanding. The living room changes its character by the hour."

The William Seward Inn
RD 2, S Portage Rd, Rt 394
Westfield NY 14787
(716) 326-4151
Circa 1821. This two-story Greek Revival estate stands on a knoll overlooking the forest and Lake Erie. Seward was a Holland Land Com-

pany agent before becoming governor of New York. He later served as Lincoln's Secretary of State and is known for the Alaska Purchase. George Patterson bought Seward's home and also became governor of New York. Most of the mansion's furnishings are dated 1790 to 1870 from the Sheraton-Victorian period.
Location: Three hours from Cleveland, Pittsburgh and Toronto.
Rates: $63-$92. Peter & Joyce Wood.
10 R. 10 PB. 1 FP. Phone available. TV available. Beds: KQT. Full breakfast. Gourmet meals. Conference room. FAX. CCs: MC VISA. Downhill & cross-country skiing, lakes, Chautauqua Institution.
Seen in: *New York Times, Pittsburgh Post-Gazette, Toronto Globe & Mail.*
"The breakfasts are delicious. The solitude and your hospitality are what the doctor ordered."

WESTHAMPTON BEACH WO20/H4

1880 Seafield House
2 Seafield Ln
Westhampton Beach NY 11978
(516) 288-1559 (800)346-3290
Circa 1880. On Westhampton Beach's exclusive Seafield Lane, this country estate includes a pool and tennis court, and it is just a short walk to the ocean beach. The inn is decorated with Victorian antiques, Shaker benches, and Chinese porcelain creating a casual, country inn atmosphere.
Location: Ninety minutes from Manhattan.
*Rates: $75. Elsie Collins.
2 R. 2 PB. Phone available. TV in room. Beds: D. B&B. Swimming pool. Tennis.
"From the moment we stepped inside your charming home we felt all the warmth you sent our way which made our stay so comfortable and memorable."

NORTH CAROLINA

ASHEVILLE F1/C3

Aberdeen Inn

64 Linden Ave
Asheville NC 28801
(704) 254-9336

Circa 1909. Twelve white pillars and a large veranda filled with rocking chairs greet visitors to this colonial house. There are five fireplaces, and on cool evenings guests often enjoy wine in front of a cozy fire. The house sits on an acre of park-like grounds with giant maple, oak, pine and dogwood trees. It's a six-block walk to town. Breakfast is served on the wraparound porch or in the plant-filled solarium.

*Rates: $55-$75. Linda & Ross Willard.
9 R. 9 PB. 5 FP. Phone available. TV in room. Beds: K. B&B. CCs: MC VISA. Swimming, skiing, hiking, tennis.

"It was the highlight of our trip!"

Albemarle Inn

86 Edgemont Rd
Asheville NC 28801
(704) 255-0027

Circa 1907. Tall Grecian columns mark the majestic entrance to Albemarle. A wide veranda, shaded by mountain pines, welcomes guests. Inside, a carved-oak staircase and massive oak-paneled doors are polished to a high gleam. Guest rooms feature 11-foot ceilings and claw-foot tubs. The Hungarian composer Bela Bartok is said to have written his third concerto for piano while in residence at the inn.

*Rates: $58-$74. John & Rosina Mellin.
12 R. 12 PB. 2 FP. Phone in room. TV in room. Beds: KQD. Full breakfast. Swimming pool. CCs: MC VISA. Tennis, white-water rafting, hiking.

"Reminds me of my grandmother's house. Most outstanding breakfast I've ever had."

Applewood Manor

62 Cumberland Circle
Asheville NC 28801
(704) 254-2244

Circa 1906. This is a spacious Colonial Revival house furnished comfortably with antiques. Raspberry-cream cheese French toast is a frequent item on the breakfast menu, while cold peach soup and Italian cookies are favorites at afternoon tea.

Location: Montford Historic District.
❀Rates: $70-$100. Jim & Linda Lo Presti.
5 R. 5 PB. 3 FP. Phone available. Beds: Q. Full breakfast. CCs: MC VISA AE. Horseback riding, white-water rafting, hiking. Small weddings, honeymoons.
Seen in: *Rutledge Hill Press, Innsider.*

"You've got a great, wonderful, special thing going here."

Cedar Crest Victorian Inn

674 Biltmore Ave
Asheville NC 28803
(704) 252-1389

Circa 1891. This Queen Anne mansion is one of the largest and most opulent residences surviving Asheville's 1890s

boom. A captain's walk, projecting turrets and expansive verandas welcome guests to lavish interior woodwork and stained glass. All rooms are furnished in antiques with satin and lace trappings.

Rates: $70-$100. Barbara & Jack McEwan.
13 R. 10 PB. 1 FP. Phone in room. TV available. Beds: QDT. B&B. CCs: MC VISA AE DS. Tennis, skiing, rafting all nearby. Afternoon beverage, evening hot chocolate & tea.
Seen in: *New Woman, Southern Living, Good Housekeeping, House Beautiful.*

"Cedar Crest is a real beauty and will hold a special place in our hearts."

Cornerstone Inn

230 Pearson Dr
Asheville NC 28801
(704) 253-5644

Circa 1924. This Dutch Tudor house was built by Dr. Charles Cocke. Standing in the heart of the Montford Historic District, it is surrounded by other homes of distinctive architecture, in an active restoration area. The inn is filled with antiques the Wyatts gleaned from their southern families and collected from 10 years of living and traveling in Europe. Local wildflowers grown within a rock-walled garden provide a summertime breakfast setting.

*Rates: $60-$65. Lonnie & Evelyn Wyatt.
4 R. 4 PB. Phone available. TV in room. Beds: D. B&B. CCs: MC VISA. Hiking, horseback riding, festivals, botanical gardens.
Seen in: *Asheville Citizen-Times.*

"We had a lovely stay in a very hospitable home."

Dry Ridge Inn

See: Weaverville, NC

Flint Street Inn

100 & 116 Flint St
Asheville NC 28801
(704) 253-6723

Circa 1915. Side by side, these two lovely old family homes are located in Asheville's oldest neighborhood and are within comfortable walking distance of downtown. A lovely breakfast room invites guests to linger, and 200-year-old oaks, old-fashioned gardens, and a fish pond add to the atmosphere. Rooms are air-conditioned.

Location: Montford Historic District.
*Rates: $75. Rick, Lynne & Marion Vogel.
8 R. 8 PB. 3 FP. Phone available. Beds: D. CCs: MC VISA AE DS.
Seen in: *Country Inns, Mid-Atlantic Country, The Charlotte Observer.*

"Our home away from home."

The Old Reynolds Mansion

100 Reynolds Hgts
Asheville NC 28804
(704) 254-0496

Circa 1855. This handsome three-story brick, antebellum mansion listed in the National Register is furnished with antiques. Guests enjoy mountain views from all rooms, wood-burning fireplaces, a two-story wraparound veranda and a swimming pool. It is situated on a four-acre knoll of Reynolds Mountain.

Location: Ten minutes north of downtown Asheville.
Rates: $40-$75. Fred & Helen Faber.
10 R. 8 PB. 4 FP. Phone available. Beds: QDT. B&B.
Seen in: *Greensboro News & Record, Blue Ridge Country.*
"This was one of the nicest places we have ever stayed. We spent every sundown on the porch waiting for the fox's daily visit."

Pine Crest Inn
See: Tryon, NC

Reed House B&B
119 Dodge St
Asheville NC 28803
(704) 274-1604

Circa 1892. This yellow and white Queen Anne Victorian, in the National Register, sports a handsome, three-story tower. During renovation, the owners discovered a secret passageway from the top of the tower down between the walls to an exit in the crawl space under the house. Inside the house, rose-colored cherubs decorate the fireplace tile. Rockers and a porch swing occupy the veranda.
Location: South of Asheville.
Rates: $50-$60. Season: May to Nov. Marge Turcot.
4 R. 1 PB. 4 FP. Phone available. TV available. Beds: DTC. B&B. CCs: MC VISA. Golfing, fishing, hiking, rafting.
Seen in: *Old House Journal, CBS Morning Show.*
"Thanks for the memories."

Richmond Hill Inn & Conference Center
87 Richmond Hill Dr
Asheville NC 28806
(704) 252-7313 (800) 545-9238

Circa 1889. This newly renovated Victorian mansion was designed for the Pearson family by James G. Hill, ar-

chitect of the U. S. Treasury Buildings. Richmond Pearson was a renowned statesman, congressman and friend of Theodore Roosevelt. This elegant estate features a grand entry hall, two parlors, a ballroom and 10 master fireplaces with neoclassical revival mantels.
*Rates: $90-$185. Susan Michel.
12 R. 12 PB. 4 FP. Phone in room. TV in room. Beds: QDTC. MAP. Gourmet meals. Spa. Handicap access. Conference room. FAX. CCs: MC VISA AE. Fishing, rafting, downhill skiing.
Seen in: *Winston-Salem Journal, The Atlanta Journal and Constitution, Asheville Citizen-Times, The Courier-Tribune.*
"A great adventure into history."

The Waverly Inn
See: Hendersonville, NC

BALSAM 05/C2

Balsam Mountain Inn
PO Box 40
Balsam NC 28707
(704) 456-9298

Circa 1906. This mountain inn with neoclassical architecture overlooks the scenic hamlet of Balsam. The inn is listed in the National Register of His-

toric Places and is designated a Jackson County, North Carolina Historic Site. It features a mansard roof and wraparound porches with mountain views.
*Rates: $60-$150. Merrily Teasley.
30 R. 30 PB. Phone available. TV available. Beds: KDTC. EP. Restaurant. Game room. Conference room. FAX. CCs: MC VISA. Hiking, fishing, white water rafting, Smokey Mountain National Park.
Seen in: *Knoxville News Sentinel, Country Inns.*

BANNER ELK D4/B4

Archers Inn
Rt 2 Box 56-A
Banner Elk NC 28604
(704) 898-9004

Perched on the side of Beech Mountain, the Archers Inn offers spectacular views of the Elk River Valley and the Sugar and Grandfather Mountains. Rooms offer such amenities as stone fireplaces with love seats, a sunken tub and private decks. The living room features a huge fieldstone fireplace and a piano. A country-style breakfast is served with homemade jams and homemade biscuits.
Rates: $45-$95. Joe & Bonny Archer.
14 R. 14 PB. 14 FP. Phone available. TV available. Beds: QD. Full breakfast. CCs: MC VISA. Skiing, horseback riding, swimming, golf, hiking, carriage rides. Weddings.
Seen in: *Blue Ridge Country.*
"There have been few times in my life when I have encountered such warmth and friendliness."

BEAUFORT J22/D9

Captains' Quarters Bed & Biscuit
315 Ann St
Beaufort NC 28516
(919) 728-7711

Circa 1902. This two-story, balloon-frame house has a welcoming, wraparound front porch. It has been home to both a 19th-century whaler

and now, a 20th-century aviator. Built of heart pine, the home is furnished with antiques and family heirlooms. Ruby is famous for her yummy "riz" biscuits.
Location: Corner of Ann & Turner Streets in the heart of historical district.
*Rates: $50-$100. Ruby & Captain Dick Collins.
3 R. 3 PB. Phone available. TV available. Beds: DT. Continental-plus breakfast. Conference room. FAX. CCs: MC VISA AE. Fishing, golf, tennis, beaches, boating, biking and antiquing.
Seen in: *The News-Times, Innsider.*
"Captain Dick Collins greets his visitors with a toast to the sunset on his expansive front porch. A retired commercial airline pilot (and Navy), he is long on sea tales and full of information about the history of Beaufort," Virginia Myers Kelly, *The Journal.*

Cedars at Beaufort
305 Front St
Beaufort NC 28516
(919) 728-7036

Circa 1768. Cedars at Beaufort stands amid old cedars above the harbor of the historic port town. The inn features antiques, rocking chair porches and grounds with geometric-patterned plantings and an herb garden that serves the restaurant. The inn of-

fers fresh flowers, fresh fruit, chocolate on guests' pillows, home-baked breads and pastries and freshly ground coffee.
Rates: $55-$125. William & Patricia Kwaak.
11 R. 11 PB. 4 FP. Phone available. TV available. Beds: KQDT. Full breakfast. Restaurant. Gourmet meals. Conference room. CCs: MC VISA AE. Water sports, golf, tennis. Honeymoon & anniversary specials, weddings, tour-guide service.
Seen in: *The Washington Post, Greensboro News & Record.*

BELHAVEN F22/C9

River Forest Manor
600 E Main St
Belhaven NC 28710
(919) 943-2151

Circa 1898. Both Twiggy and Walter Cronkite have passed through the two-story, pillared rotunda entrance of this white mansion located on the

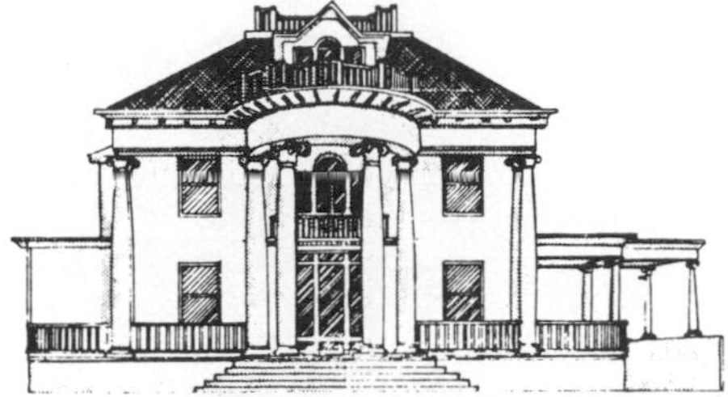

Atlantic Intercoastal Waterway. Ornate, carved ceilings, cut and leaded-glass windows and crystal chandeliers grace the inn. Antiques are found throughout. Each evening a smorgasbord buffet features more than 65 items from the inn's kitchen.
Rates: $60-$75. Melba G. Smith.
12 R. 12 PB. 5 FP. Phone in room. TV in room. Beds: KQDW. Full breakfast. Restaurant. Spa. Swimming pool. FAX. CCs: MC VISA. Tennis, fishing, water sports.
Seen in: *Southern Living, National Geographic.*

BLOWING ROCK D4/B4

Ragged Garden B&B
PO Box 1927
Blowing Rock NC 28605
(704) 295-9703

Circa 1900. Surrounded by rhododendron and majestic trees, this inn features guest rooms decorated with early 1900s furniture. Stone for the fireplaces and stairs was quarried from nearby Grandfather Mountain. The inn's Northern Italian cuisine features homemade pasta. Guests may enjoy breakfast in their rooms, in one of the three dining rooms or on an outside portico.
❀Rates: $45-$110. Season: March - Jan. Joyce & Joe Villani.
9 R. 9 PB. 3 FP. Phone available. TV available. Beds: KQDT. Full breakfast. Restaurant. Gourmet meals. Spa. CCs: MC VISA AE. Golf, white-water rafting, tennis, caverns, shops.
Seen in: *The Blowing Rocket, Lenois News-Topic.*
"I've never felt more welcome anywhere!"

BREVARD P7/C2

Red House Inn
412 W Probart St
Brevard NC 28712
(704) 884-9349

Circa 1851. Originally built as a trading post, this inn was also the county's first post office and railroad station. It survived the Civil War and years of neglect. Recently renovated, it is furnished with Victorian antiques. The center of town is four blocks away.
*Rates: $47-$59. Season: April to December. Lynn Ong.
6 R. 1 PB. 4 FP. TV available. Beds: DT. Full breakfast. Hiking.
Seen in: *The Transylvania Times.*
"Lovely place to stay - clean and bright."

BRYSON CITY O4/C2

Folkestone Inn
767 W Deep Creek Rd
Bryson City NC 28713
(704) 488-2730

Circa 1926. This farmhouse is constructed of local stone and rock. Pressed-tin ceilings, stained-glass windows and claw-foot tubs remain. The

dining room, where breakfast is served, features floor-to-ceiling windows on all sides with views of the mountains. There is a stream with a rock bridge on the property, and you can walk 10 minutes to waterfall views in the Smoky Mountain National Park.
*❀Rates: $59-$79. Norma & Peter Joyce.
9 R. 9 PB. Phone available. Beds: D. Full breakfast. Hiking, horseback riding, fishing, tubing, rafting.
Seen in: *Asheville Citizen Times.*
"Thanks to you we were able to stop and smell the flowers last weekend! You have a lovely place."

Fryemont Inn
PO Box 459
Bryson City NC 28713
(704) 488-2159

Circa 1923. Captain Amos Frye, a lumber baron, built this rough-sawn hilltop lodge with the choicest chestnut, walnut, oak and cherry woods found in the region. A wide cedar porch overlooks the Tuckaseigee Valley and the Great Smoky Mountains National Park. Massive fireplaces were crafted of stone — one large enough to burn 8-foot logs. All bedrooms are paneled in chestnut, and some are furnished with antiques, including hand-hewn furniture original to the lodge. Meals in the dining room feature fresh mountain trout and prime rib.
❀Rates: $75-$160. Sue & George Brown.
40 R. 40 PB. 5 FP. Phone available. TV in room. Beds: KDTC. MAP. Restaurant. Gourmet meals. Swimming pool. Conference room. CCs: MC VISA. Horseback riding, train ride, white-water rafting, tennis.
Seen in: *Bon Appetit.*
"The inn is so comfortable, the scenery breathtaking and the food and service outstanding."

Randolph House
PO Box 816
Bryson City NC 28713
(704) 488-3472 (404) 938-2268

Circa 1895. Randolph House is a mountain estate tucked among pine trees and dogwoods, near the entrance of Great Smoky Mountain National Park. The house provides an unforgettable experience, not the least of which is the gourmet dining provided on the terrace or in the dining room.
Rates: $55-$75. Season: April - Nov. 1 Bill & Ruth Randolph Adams.
6 R. 3 PB. Phone available. TV available. Beds: DT. MAP. Restaurant. Gourmet meals. Handicap access. Conference room. CCs: MC VISA AE. White-water activities, horseback riding, hiking, trout streams. Honeymoon and anniversary specials.
Seen in: *Tourist News.*
"Very enjoyable, great food."

CHARLOTTE H7/C5

The Homeplace B&B
5901 Sardis Rd
Charlotte NC 28226
(704) 365-1936

Circa 1902. This country Victorian house sits on two and one-half wooded acres and has a wraparound porch and a garden gazebo. The foyer features a handcrafted staircase, 10-foot beaded ceilings and heart-of-pine floors. Paintings by Peggy's father, John Gentry, who painted from age 79 to 90, join collections of antiques and other family treasures found in the inn.
*Rates: $63-$68. Frank & Peggy Dearien.

3 R. 3 PB. Phone available. TV available. Beds: Q. Full breakfast. CCs: MC VISA AE. Antiques. Garden gazebo.
Seen in: *Charlotte Observer, Charlotte Magazine, Birmingham News.*
"Everything was perfect. The room was superb, the food excellent!"

Morehead Inn

1122 E Morehead St
Charlotte NC 28204
(704) 376-3357

Circa 1917. This old-fashioned southern house is set on a huge corner lot dotted with oaks and azaleas. Guests gather in the great room, library and dining room, all furnished with English and American antiques. Balconies, canopy and four-poster beds and whirlpool tubs are among the amenities offered in some of the rooms. The Solarium Suite is a favorite choice. A two-bedroom carriage house with a stone fireplace is available for families or two couples traveling together.
Rates: $91-$101. Shirley Kelley.
11 R. 11 PB. Phone in room. TV in room. Beds: KQDC. Continental breakfast. Spa. Conference room. FAX. CCs: MC VISA AE DC. YMCA nearby. Honeymoon and anniversary specials.
Seen in: *Business Journal.*
"Thank you for your gracious attentiveness and hospitality."

Still Waters

6221 Amos Smith Rd
Charlotte NC 28214
(704) 399-6299

Circa 1928. This log house was built as a summer retreat on Lake Wylie. A sawmill was set up on the site and the

rocks for the great-room fireplace were gathered from the yard. Each room boasts a view of the lake. The Canopy Room features a king-size canopy waterbed while the Family Suite has the feeling of a private cabin with its separate entrance. The Charlotte airport is ten minutes away.
*Rates: $65-$85. Janet & Rob Dyer.
3 R. 3 PB. 1 FP. Phone available. Beds: KQW. Full breakfast. CCs: MC VISA. Boat ramp, slips and dock. Near Carrowinds Amusement Park.
"Your location on Lake Wiley was unbelievable. I could not imagine such a pretty, wooded and quiet place could be so close to a city. I give you a 10 on the Tom Peter's scale for Passion for Customers."

CLINTON I16/D7

The Shield House

216 Sampson St
Clinton NC 28328
(919) 592-2634 (800) 462-9817

Circa 1916. This house was built for businessman Robert Herring. The facade is dominated by four colossal fluted columns rising 22 feet to sup-

port a portico. The veranda, with 12 Ionic columns, wraps around three sides. Intricately designed leaded glass highlights the entrance, and inside are walnut and mahogany antiques. A 22-foot-long mural of Orton Plantation can be seen in the dining room. The innkeepers are twin sisters who are also nurses.
*Rates: $45-$60. Anita Green & Juanita G. McLamb.
6 R. 6 PB. 7 FP. Phone in room. TV in room. Beds: QDTC. Full breakfast. Conference room. CCs: MC VISA DS. Tennis and golf nearby.
Seen in: *The Sampson Independent, Country.*
"I have never been pampered so much. A beautiful home and a beautiful spirit."

DURHAM E14/B7

Arrowhead Inn

106 Mason Rd
Durham NC 27712
(919) 477-8430

Circa 1775. The Lipscombe family and later owners made additions to the original white colonial manor house,

but none destroyed the handsome fanlight, moldings, wainscoting, mantelpieces and heart-of-pine floors. Past its doors, Catawba and Waxhaw Indians traveled the Great Path to Virginia. A stone arrowhead and marker at the inn's front door designate the path. Current visitors enjoy a long tradition of hospitality. From time to time, the hosts conduct classes for prospective innkeepers.
*Rates: $59-$95. Jerry & Barbara Ryan.
9 R. 5 PB. 5 FP. Phone available. TV available. Beds: QDT. Full breakfast. Conference room. CCs: MC VISA AE. Golf, tennis, horseback riding, croquet, horseshoes, fishing nearby.
Seen in: *USA Today, Food & Wine, House & Garden.*
"Thanks a million for your hospitality."

EDENTON D22/B9

The Lords Proprietors' Inn

300 N Broad St
Edenton NC 27932
(919) 482-3641

Circa 1787. On Albemarle Sound, Edenton was one of the colonial capitals of North Carolina. The inn con-

sists of three houses providing elegant accommodations in Edenton's Historic District. A guided walking tour from the Visitor's Center provides an opportunity to see museum homes.
Location: Main street of town.
Rates: $48-$70. Arch & Jane Edwards.
20 R. 20 PB. Phone in room. TV in room. Beds: KQTC. Continental-plus breakfast. Gourmet meals. Handicap access. Swimming pool. Conference room. Guided walking tours.
Seen in: *Southern Living, Mid-Atlantic Country, House Beautiful, Washington Post.*
"One of the friendliest and best-managed inns I have ever visited."

FAYETTEVILLE I14/D7

The Shield House

See: Clinton, NC

GREENSBORO D11/B6

Colonel Ludlow Inn

See: Winston-Salem, NC

Greenwood B&B

205 N Park Dr
Greensboro NC 27401
(919) 274-6350

Circa 1905. Greenwood is a fully renovated, stick-style chalet on the park in the historic district. President Hayes was once a guest here. The inn is decorated with wood carvings and art from around the world. There are

two living rooms, each with a fireplace. Air conditioning and a swimming pool in the backyard are among the amenities.
Location: Central Greensboro in the historic district.
✻❀Rates: $50-$75. JoAnne Green.
5 R. 3 PB. Phone in room. TV available. Beds: KQT. B&B. Game room. CCs: MC VISA AE. Tennis, hiking, golf.
Seen in: *Triad Style.*
"Marvelous renovation. Courteous, helpful, knowledgeable hostess and perfectly appointed room and bath. Interesting fine-art interior decorating."

HENDERSON C16/*B7*

La Grange Plantation Inn
Rt 3 Box 610
Henderson NC 27536
(919) 438-2421
Circa 1770. This restored plantation, in the National Register, is a simple Greek Revival-style house with 10-foot-high windows and heart-of-pine floors. The foyer, furnished with antique prints and an Oriental rug, features a 15-foot-high ceiling. Mrs. Cornell is English and has decorated the inn with antiques and reproductions to resemble an English country house. A short path through the woods leads to Kerr Lake.
Rates: $85. Jean & Dick Cornell.
5 R. 5 PB. 5 FP. Phone available. Beds: QDT. Full breakfast. Swimming pool. CCs: MC VISA. Fishing, boating, hiking, horseback riding, golf, antiquing.
Seen in: *Henderson Daily Dispatch, Spectator, Historic Preservation.*
"I love your inn...and you!"

HENDERSONVILLE G1/*C3*

Claddagh Inn at Hendersonville
755 N Main St
Hendersonville NC 28792
(800) 225-4700 (704)697-7778
Circa 1898. Claddagh has been host for more than 90 years to visitors staying in Hendersonville. The wide, wraparound veranda is filled with inviting rocking chairs, while the library is filled with inviting books. Many of North Carolina's finest craft and antique shops are just two blocks from the inn. Carl Sandburg's house and the Biltmore Estate are nearby, and

within a short drive are spectacular sights in the Great Smoky Mountains and the Blue Ridge Parkway.
Location: One-half block north from 7th Avenue (US 64 W) on Main St (US 25).
✻❀Rates: $49-$69. Marie & Fred Carberry.
14 R. 14 PB. 4 FP. Phone in room. TV available. Beds: KQDTC. Full breakfast. Conference room. FAX. CCs: MC VISA AE DS. Horseback riding, swimming, tennis, golf, fishing, racquetball, boating. Air conditioning.
Seen in: *New York Times, New Yorker Magazine, Innsider Magazine.*
"Excellent food, clean, home atmosphere."

The Waverly Inn
783 N Main St
Hendersonville NC 28792
(800) 537-8195 (704)692-1090
Circa 1898. In the National Register, this three-story Victorian and Colonial Revival house has a two-tiered sawn

work trimmed porch and widow's walk. A beautifully carved Eastlake staircase and an original registration desk grace the inn. There are four-poster canopy beds and claw-foot tubs. Breakfast is served in the handsome dining room. The Waverly is the oldest surviving inn in Hendersonville.
Location: Corner of 8th Avenue & Main Street (Rt. 25 North)
✻Rates: $58-$78. Season: June to October 31. John & Diane Sheiry.
16 R. 16 PB. Phone available. TV available. Beds: KQTDC. B&B. CCs: MC VISA AE DS. Horseback riding, tennis, golf, murder-mystery weekends, fishing, hiking. Biltmore Estates, Flatrock Playhouse, Blue Ridge Parkway.
Seen in: *The New York Times, Country Magazine, Blue Ridge Country Magazine.*
"Our main topic of conversation while driving back was what a great time we had at your place."

HERTFORD C22/*B9*

Gingerbread Inn
103 S Church St
Hertford NC 27944
(919) 426-5809
Circa 1904. In a Colonial Revival-style this yellow and white house has a wraparound porch with paired columns and turned balusters. There

are gables and leaded-glass windows, and the spacious rooms are furnished comfortably. The hallmark of the inn is freshly baked gingerbread.
Rates: $45. Jenny Harnisch
3 R. 3 PB. Phone available. TV in room. Beds: KQT. Full breakfast. CCs: MC VISA. On the historic walking tour. Fishing nearby.
Seen in: *The Daily Advance, The Raleigh Times, Coastal Cruising.*

HILLSBOROUGH D13/*B6*

Hillsborough House Inn
209 E Tryon St, PO Box 880
Hillsborough NC 27278
(919) 644-1600 (919) 644-0325.
Circa 1790. This Italianate-style house, on seven wooded acres, sits back on a spacious, well-tended lawn, the site for croquet, hide-and-seek games and picnics for the Webb family for more than 140 years. In the Hillsborough Historic District, the inn boasts an 80-foot-long veranda and an 1850 addition. The decor is both elegant and eclectic, such as the 10-foot-high papier-mache cactus that rests next to an English sideboard from the 1800s. A favorite guest room features a high queen bed draped from the ceiling with yards of white voile. Your hostess is an artist and has her studio here.
Rates: $85-$135. Bev & Katherine Webb.
5 R. 5 PB. Phone available. TV available. Beds: QT. Continental-plus breakfast. Spa. Swimming pool. Conference room. CCs: MC VISA. Weddings, receptions, business meetings.
Seen in: *Durham Morning Herald, The News of Orange County.*

"What a marvelous discovery! Creative genius everywhere."

The Inn at Teardrop

175 W King St
Hillsborough NC 27278
(919) 732-1120

Circa 1768. The Inn at Teardrop offers several cozy places for guests to relax, including secluded gardens, a back veranda and a parlor with a baby grand piano. The inn is furnished with antiques and reproductions made by a local craftsman. Bright rugs cover the wooden floors. A collection of teddy bears sits in chairs and sofa corners on the first floor.

Rates: $50-$95. Tom Roberts.
6 R. 4 PB. 6 FP. Phone available. TV available. Beds: QDTC. Full breakfast. Game room. Conference room. CCs: MC VISA. Antique & craft shops. Weddings.
Seen in: *The Bridal Guide, The Chapel Hill News, Durham Morning Herald, Orange County News.*
"Excellent (everything)."

KILL DEVIL HILLS D25/*B10*

Ye Olde Cherokee Inn

500 N Virginia Dare Trail
Kill Devil Hills NC 27948
(919) 441-6127

Circa 1940. Originally a hunting and fishing lodge, this large pink beach house is just across the road from the ocean. Guest rooms are paneled in knotty cypress creating a rustic cabin atmosphere. Behind the inn is the Wright Brothers Memorial and nearby, the spot where they made their first flight.

Location: Outer Banks.
*Rates: $55-$75. Season: April to Oct. Phyllis & Robert Combs.
6 R. 6 PB. Phone available. TV in room. Beds: D. MAP. CCs: MC VISA AE. Swimming, fishing, sailing, golf, tennis, hang gliding. Seen in: *The North Carolina Independent, This Week.*
"Thanks for another wonderful visit! It gets harder to leave each time we come."

LAKE JUNALUSKA N6/*C2*

Providence Lodge

1 Atkins Loop
Lake Junaluska NC 28745
(704) 456-6486 (704) 452-9588

Circa 1915. This is a simple and very rustic lodge in the Blue Ridge Mountains 26 miles from Asheville. Dinner is available and the inn is noted for its dining.

Rates: $70. Season: June - Sept. 1. Ben & Wilma Cato.
16 R. 10 PB. Phone available. Beds: DTC. MAP. Handicap access. Swimming pool. Boating, tennis and golf nearby.
"Food, fellowship, etc. was superb as usual."

MARSHALL M7/*B3*

Marshall House

5 Hill St, PO Box 865
Marshall NC 28753
(704) 649-9205 (800)562-9258

Circa 1903. Richard Sharp Smith, a resident architect for the Biltmore Estates, designed this house with a large veranda to maximize the view of the French Broad River and Appalacian Mountains. Pebble-dash, a type of masonry brought to the area by George Vanderbilt, was applied to the exterior. The 5,200-square-foot house has a bountiful supply of antiques to complement the original pocket doors, wavy glass and wood floors.

*Rates: $35-$50. James & Ruth Boylan.
8 R. 2 PB. 4 FP. Phone available. TV available. Beds: DT. B&B. Handicap access. Conference room. CCs: MC VISA AE DC CB DS. Horseback riding, skiing, white-water rafting, fishing, golf, hiking.
Seen in: *Asheville Citizen Times, Blue Ridge Business.*
"Thank you for your hospitality. We felt right at home."

MILTON B13/*A6*

Woodside Inn

PO Box 197
Milton NC 28305
(919) 234-8646 (919) 694-4450

Circa 1838, Sheltered by locust trees, this National Register house is in the Greek-Revival style. It was in a dilapidated state and had never had indoor plumbing till the McPhersons' renovation in 1985. Now guests enjoy the beautifully crafted mahogany newel post, arched doors, fireplaces and heart-pine flooring. Late Federal and American Empire furnishings include canopy beds, dry sinks, sideboards, pier tables and plantation hunt boards. The garden has been refashioned with perennials and old-time roses.

*Rates: $59-$69. Tom & Lib McPherson.
4 R. 4 PB. Phone available. TV in room. Beds: QD. Full breakfast. Restaurant. Conference room. CCs: MC VISA AE. Fishing, boating, swimming, water skiing, biking. Murder-mystery evenings, weddings, honeymoons, family reunions.
Seen in: *Raleigh News and Observer, Winston-Salem Journal, Burlington Daily Times.*
"You were more than mere innkeepers; you were very congenial hosts."

MOUNT AIRY B8/*A5*

Pine Ridge Inn

2893 W Pine St
Mount Airy NC 27030
(919) 789-5034

Pine Ridge is a grand English-style mansion set on eight acres at the foot of the Blue Ridge Mountains. This

10,000-square-foot country inn prides itself on providing many of the amenities found in large hotels such as its wood-paneled library, Nautilus-equipped exercise room and hot tub. An old barn remains on the property.

Rates: $60-$100. Ellen & Manford Haxton.
5 R. 5 PB. Phone in room. TV in room. Beds: QDTC. Continental breakfast. Restaurant. Handicap access. Swimming pool. Game room. Conference room. CCs: MC VISA AE. Golf, skiing, white-water rafting.
"The Haxtons have updated all the facilities without destroying its grandeur. Their attitude is one of warmth and charm, openness and pleasantness."

NEW BERN H21/*C9*

The Aerie

509 Pollock St
New Bern NC 28560
(919) 636-5553

Circa 1882. This late Victorian home was built by Samuel Street, proprietor of the Old Gaston House Hotel, as his

private residence. An appealing three-sided bay houses the downstairs parlor and an upstairs guest chamber. Fine antiques add to the gracious atmosphere of the inn and include an old mahogany player piano tuned and waiting for guests. Tryon Palace is a one block walk from the inn.

*Rates: $80. Rick & Lois Cleveland.
7 R. 7 PB. 5 FP. Phone in room. TV in room. Beds: QTC. B&B. CCs: MC VISA

AE. Swimming, camping, hiking.

Harmony House Inn

215 Pollock St

New Bern NC 28560

(919) 636-3810

Circa 1850. Long ago, this two-story Greek Revival was sawed in half and

modate new hallways, additional rooms and a staircase. A wall was then built to divide the house into two sections. The rooms are decorated with antiques, family heirlooms and collectibles. Offshore breezes sway blossoms in the lush garden. Cross the street to an excellent restaurant or take a picnic to the shore.

Location: Walk to Tryon Palace.
Rates: $70. Diane & A.E. Hansen.
9 R. 9 PB. 9 FP. Beds: QTC. Full breakfast. Conference room. CCs: MC VISA. Complimentary juices and sodas.
Seen in: *Americana.*
"We feel nourished even now, six months after our visit to Harmony House."

King's Arms Inn

212 Pollock St

New Bern NC 28560

(919) 638-4409

Circa 1848. Four blocks from the Tryon Palace, in the heart of the New Bern Historic District, this colonial-

style inn features a mansard roof and touches of Victorian architecture. Two doors down from the inn is the federal-style Henderson House, the town's most notable restaurant. Guest rooms are decorated with antiques, canopy and four-poster beds and fireplaces. An old tavern in town was the inspiration for the name of the inn.

*Rates: $55-$75. David & Diana Parks.
9 R. 9 PB. 8 FP. Phone available. TV in room. Beds: QDTC. Continental-plus breakfast. CCs: MC VISA AE. Tennis, golf, windsurfing, sailing, biking, hiking, canoeing.
Seen in: *Washington Post, Southern Living.*
"Delightful."

OCRACOKE H24/C10

The Berkley Center Country Inn

PO Box 220

Ocracoke NC 27960

(919) 928-5911

Circa 1860. Once a harbor for the pirate Blackbeard, Ocracoke is a fishing village on a small island in the middle of Hattaras National Seashore,

accessible only by ferry or private boat. Located on three acres in the village, the inn is framed by red and white myrtles. The weathered shingled main house boasts an enormous square tower rising from a second-story gable. The walls of the tower room are lined with windows looking out to Pamlico Sound and the Atlantic. With cedar paneling and wooden ceilings, the inn has a lodge-like atmosphere and is filled with comfortable furnishings.

*Rates: $65-$85. Season: March 15-Nov. 15. Ruth & Wes Egan.
9 R. 7 PB. Phone available. TV available. Beds: D. Continental breakfast. Handicap access. Conference room. Swimming, fishing, hiking, biking.
Seen in: *Mid-Atlantic Country, The New York Times, The Washington Post.*
"Outstanding hospitality, unsurpassed!"

PITTSBORO F13/C6

The Fearrington House

2000 Fearrington Village Ctr

Pittsboro NC 27312

(919) 542-2121 (919)542-4000

Circa 1927. The Fearrington is an old dairy farm. Several of the original outbuildings, including the silo and barn, have been converted into a village with a potter's shop, bookstore, jewelry shop, and a southern garden shop. The original homestead houses an award-winning restaurant. The inn itself was built three years ago.

Rates: $125-$185. Richard & Debbie Delany.

14 R. 14 PB. TV available. Beds: Q. Continental breakfast. Handicap access. Swimming pool. Conference room. FAX. CCs: MC VISA. Swimming, bicycling, golf and tennis nearby.
"There is an aura of warmth and caring that makes your guests feel like royalty in a regal setting!"

RALEIGH E15/B7

The Oakwood Inn

411 N Bloodworth St

Raleigh NC 27604

(919) 832-9712

Circa 1871. Presiding over Raleigh's Oakwood Historic District, this lavender and gray Victorian beauty is in the National Register. A formal parlor is graced by rosewood and red velvet, while guest rooms exude an atmosphere of vintage Victoriana.

*Rates: $75-$95. Terri Jones/Diana Newton.
6 R. 6 PB. 6 FP. Phone available. TV available. Beds: QD. Full breakfast. Conference room. CCs: MC VISA AE DS. Canoeing, paddle & row boats, skiing, swimming (nearby), tennis, walking tours.
Seen in: *Business Digest, Connoisseur.*
"Resplendent and filled with museum-quality antique furnishings." Kim Devins, *Spectator.*

SALISBURY F8/C5

The 1868 Stewart-Marsh House

220 S Ellis St

Salisbury NC 28144

(704) 633-6841

Circa 1868. This Federal-style home is in the West Square Historic District. The inn features a cozy, pine-paneled library, an elegant parlor, a shaded, screened porch with wicker furniture, antiques, heirlooms and collectibles. Most of the window glass is original. Guest rooms have heart pine floors.

*Rates: $45-$50. Gerry Webster.
2 R. 2 PB. Phone available. TV available. Beds: QT. Continental-plus breakfast. CCs: MC VISA. Golf, tennis, fishing. Guided tours of historic district.
Seen in: *Salisbury Post.*
"Being here was like an extension of our home. Your hospitality was warm and welcome."

Rowan Oak House

208 S Fulton St
Salisbury NC 28144
(704) 633-2086

Circa 1901. This Queen Anne house, in the middle of the Salisbury Historic District, features a carved-oak front door, leaded and stained glass, meticulously carved mantles and the original ornate electric and gaslights. Guests may enjoy afternoon tea, wine or sherry and homemade cookies and candies in the Victorian parlor, on the columned wraparound porch or on an upstairs porch overlooking a garden. Guest rooms have antiques, historic wallpaper and down comforters.

Rates: $65-$85. Bill & Ruth Ann Coffey.
3 R. 3 PB. 2 FP. Phone in room. TV available. Beds: DT. Full breakfast. Spa. Game room. CCs: MC VISA. Golf, fishing, boating, walking. Champagne for honeymooners, anniversaries.
Seen in: *The Salisbury Post, The Daily Independent.*

"A stay at the Rowan Oak House is the quintessential B&B experience. Their home is as interesting as it is beautiful, and they are the most gracious host and hostess you can imagine."

SYLVA O5/C2

Mountain Brook

Rt 2 Box 301
Sylva NC 28779
(704) 586-4329

Circa 1930. Located in the Great Smokies, Mountain Brook consists of 12 cottages on a hillside amid rhododendron, elm, maple and oak trees. The resort's 200-acre terrain is crisscrossed with brooks and waterfalls and contains a trout-stocked pond. Two cottages are constructed with logs from the property while nine are made from native stone. They feature fireplaces and porch swings. and have brass, four-poster and canopy beds, quilts and rocking chairs.

Rates: $70-$120. Gus & Michele McMahon.
12 R. 12 PB. 12 FP. Phone available. Beds: KDC. Spa. Sauna. Handicap access. Game room. White-water rafting, train riding, horseback riding, hot-air balloons, gem mining. Honeymoon, anniversaries, romantic weekend packages.
Seen in: *Brides Magazine, Today, The Hudspeth Report.*

"The cottage was delightfully cozy, and our privacy was not interrupted even once."

TRYON H2/C3

Pine Crest Inn

PO Box 1030, 200 Pine Crest Ln
Tryon NC 28982
(704) 859-9135 (800) 633-3001

Circa 1906. Carter Brown purchased this former sanitarium on a wooded knoll close to the center of town and in 1917 opened a small resort. Each of the cabins he added to the complex were given a secluded porch, a terrace, a fireplace and a private bath. The inn's dining room has rough-hewn decor reminiscent of a colonial tavern. Mr. Brown initiated the fox hunts, steeplechase racing and horse shows that have made Tryon a popular equine center.

*Rates: $50-$135. Jennifer & Jeremy Wainwright.
29 R. 29 PB. 24 FP. Phone in room. TV in room. Beds: KQDTC. Full breakfast. Restaurant. Gourmet meals. Handicap access. Conference room. FAX. CCs: MC VISA. Golf, tennis, hiking, fox hunting.
Seen in: *Southern Living.*

"We felt pampered and at home in your lovely refurbished Pine Crest Inn."

VALLE CRUCIS D4/B4

Mast Farm Inn

PO Box 704
Valle Crucis NC 28691
(704) 963-5857

Circa 1885. Listed in the National Register of Historic Places, this 18-acre farmstead includes a main house and seven outbuildings. The inn features a wraparound porch with rocking chairs, swings and a view of the mountain valley. The inn features homemade breads and vegetables fresh from the garden. Rooms are furnished with antiques, quilts and mountain crafts.

Rates: $75-$135 MAP. Season: 12/27-3/4,4/27-11/5. Sibyl & Francis Pressly.
12 R. 10 PB. 1 FP. Phone available. Beds: KQDT. MAP. Handicap access. CCs: MC VISA. Fishing, hiking, skiing, golf, canoeing, white-water rafting. Weddings.
Seen in: *Southern Bride, The News and Observer, Blue Ridge Country.*

"Your warm hospitality is a rare find and one that we will remember for a long time."

WASHINGTON F20/C9

Pamlico House

400 E Main St
Washington NC 27889
(919) 946-7184

Circa 1906. This gracious Colonial Revival home once served as the rectory for St. Peter's Episcopal Church. A veranda wraps around the house in a graceful curve. Furnished in Victorian antiques, the inn has the modern convenience of air conditioning. Nearby is the city's quaint waterfront. Washington is on the Historic Albemarle Tour Route and within easy driving distance to the Outer Banks.

Location: Eastern North Carolina.
Rates: $45-$65. Jeanne & Lawrence Hervey.
4 R. 4 PB. Phone in room. Beds: KQDT. Full breakfast. CCs: MC VISA. Air conditioning. Tennis, fishing, sailing.

WAYNESVILLE N6/C2

Grandview Lodge

809 Valley View Cir Rd
Waynesville NC 28786
(704) 456-5212 (800)255-7826

Circa 1900. Grandview Lodge is located on two-and-a-half acres in the Smoky Mountains. The land surrounding the lodge has an apple orchard, rhubarb patch, grape arbor and vegetable garden for the inn's kitchen. Rooms are available in the main lodge and in a newer addition. The inn's dining room is known throughout the region and Linda, a home economist, has written "Recipes from Grandview Lodge."

**Rates: $75-$85. Stan & Linda Arnold.
15 R. 15 PB. 3 FP. Phone available. TV in room. Beds: QDT. MAP. Restaurant. Gourmet meals. Handicap access. Horseback riding, golf, hiking, tennis, swimming. Recreation room.
Seen in: *Asheville Citizen, Winston-Salem Journal, Raleigh News and Observer.*

"It's easy to see why family and friends have been enjoying trips to Grandview."

Hallcrest Inn

299 Halltop Cir
Waynesville NC 28786
(704) 456-6457 (800) 334-6457

Circa 1880. This simple white frame farmhouse was the home of the owner of the first commercial apple orchard in western North Carolina. Atop Hall

Mountain, it commands a breathtaking view of Waynesville and Balsam Mountain Range. A gathering room, a

dining room, and eight guest rooms are furnished with family antiques. The side porch features four rooms with balconies. Family-style dining is offered around Lazy-Susan tables.
Location: US 276N from Waynesville, left on Mauney Cove Road.
*Rates: $50-$70. Season: Late May to October. Russell & Margaret Burson.
12 R. 12 PB. 5 FP. Phone available. TV available. Beds: D. MAP. Restaurant. CCs: MC VISA. Golf, hiking, horseback riding, white-water rafting.
Seen in: *Asheville Citizen.*
"Country charm with a touch of class."

The Palmer House B&B

108 Pigeon St
Waynesville NC 28786
(704) 456-7521
Circa 1885. This rambling old inn reflects the small-town charm so often found in the mountains. The hosts are

book-lovers as evidenced by the stocked library at the rear of the inn. The inn is known for delicious food, great service and a relaxing atmosphere. Nearby activities include hiking, golfing and skiing.
Rates: $50. Kris Gillet & Jeff Minick.
7 R. 7 PB. Phone available. Continental-plus breakfast.
Seen in: *Creative Loafing, The Mountaineer.*
"Each guest room has its own particular charm."

The Swag

Rt 2 Box 280-A
Waynesville NC 28786
(704) 926-0430
The Swag is composed of six hand-hewn log buildings, one dating to 1795. They were moved to the site

and restored. An old church was reassembled and became the cathedral-ceilinged common room. The fireplace in this room was constructed of river stones with no mortar to maintain authenticity. The inn's 250 acres feature a nature trail, a spring-fed pond with gazebo and hammock and thick forests. A two-and-a-half mile gravel road winds through a heavily wooded hillside to the inn. In the evening, dinner is served on pewter ware at long walnut tables. Listening to folk music and mountain storytelling afterwards is popular.
Location: On edge of Great Smoky Mountain National Park.
Rates: $128-$198. Season: May to October 31. Deener Matthews.
12 R. 12 PB. 7 FP. Phone available. TV available. Beds: KQDTC. AP. Restaurant. Spa. Sauna. Handicap access. Conference room. CCs: MC VISA. Riding, rafting, hiking, racquet ball, croquet, badminton.
Seen in: *The Atlanta Journal, Mid-Atlantic Country.*
"The Swag gives us both a chance to relax our bodies and revitalize our brains."

WEAVERVILLE M7/C3

Dry Ridge Inn

26 Brown St
Weaverville NC 28787
(704) 658-3899
Circa 1849. This house was built as the parsonage for the Salem Campground, an old religious revival camping area. Because of the high al-

titude and pleasant weather, it was used as a camp hospital for Confederate soldiers suffering from pneumonia during the Civil War. The area was called Dry Ridge by the Cherokee Indians before the campground was established.
Location: Ten minutes North of Asheville.
Rates: $50-$55. John & Karen VanderElzen.
6 R. 6 PB. Phone available. Beds: DC. B&B. CCs: MC VISA. Bicycling, hiking, golf, skiing, rafting, fishing.
Seen in: *Asheville Citizen Times, Marshall News Record.*
"Best family vacation ever spent."

WILMINGTON L17/E8

Anderson Guest House

520 Orange St
Wilmington NC 28401
(919) 343-8128
Circa 1851. The main house, a brick Italianate, features cherry woodwork, stained glass and gaslights that still work. The guest house, built from the remnants of a children's playhouse and shed, has its own fireplace and overlooks the lawn and garden. Breakfast is served in the main house.
Location: Wilmington's Historic District.
Rates: $65. Landon & Connie Anderson.
2 R. 2 PB. 2 FP. Phone available. TV available. Beds: Q. EP. Golfing, water skiing.
Seen in: *Star-News.*
"The most gracious hostess in the state."

Catherine's Inn on Orange

N 410 Orange
Wilmington NC 28401
(919) 251-0863 (800) 476-0723
Circa 1875. This Italianate-style house is in the heart of Wilmington's Historic District. The inn offers a large mural painting in the foyer and an enclosed porch with a view of the landscaped garden. The parlor features a fireplace, high ceilings and an heirloom baby grand piano. The inn is furnished with antiques and reproductions.
Rates: $60. Catherine & Walter Ackiss.
3 R. 3 PB. 3 FP. Phone in room. TV in room. Beds: KDT. Full breakfast. Swimming pool. CCs: MC VISA AE. Golf, tennis, water sports. Honeymoon, anniversary, wedding specials.
Seen in: *This Week, Country Inns.*
"This is the best!"

James Place B&B

9 S Fourth St
Wilmington NC 28401
(919) 251-0999
Circa 1909. On a tree-lined street of two-story, turn-of-the-century houses, this neatly painted taupe home has gleaming white trim highlighting the porch and shutters. Each room features air conditioning and ceiling fans. Fresh coffee is brought to guest rooms in the morning, and later, a full breakfast is served downstairs. The downtown waterfront is a short stroll away.
Rates: $55-$65. J.W. Smith.
3 R. 2 PB. Phone available. TV available. Beds: KQDW. B&B. CCs: MC VISA. Boating, fishing, golf, tennis, ocean beaches.
Seen in: *Encore Magazine.*
"An ideal setting for rejuvenation! Thanks so much for the southern hospitality."

Worth House
A Victorian Inn

412 S Third St
Wilmington NC 28401
(919) 762-8562
Circa 1893. This handsome Queen Anne Victorian boasts two turrets and a wide double veranda, all framed by a white iron fence. The paneled front

hall, crystal chandelier and spindled staircase welcome guests to a retreat of quiet elegance. There is a player piano and a Victrola, and all rooms feature wood-burning fireplaces, fine linens and antiques. A gourmet breakfast is served in the dining room, in bed or on the veranda.
Location: Historic District.
Rates: $70-$85. Kate Walsh & Terry Meyer.
4 R. 4 PB. 4 FP. Phone available. Beds: KQD. B&B. Golf, paddle boats, horse-drawn carriages, dinner cruises, ocean.
Seen in: *The News and Observer.*

WILSON F17/C8

Miss Betty's B&B Inn
600 W Nash St
Wilson NC 27893
(919) 243-4447
Circa 1858. This Italianate house is on Nash Street, which was once described as one of the 10 most beautiful streets in the world. It was

built by the grandson of the state's first printer. The inn provides a touch of Victorian elegance and comfort with Victorian wallpapers, antiques and furnishings featured throughout.
Location: Central North Carolina, near I-95 highway.
Rates: $65-$75. Betty & Fred Spitz.
8 R. 8 PB. 7 FP. Phone in room. TV in room. Beds: KDT. Full breakfast. Handicap access. Conference room. CCs: MC VISA AE DS. Bicycling.
Seen in: *Wilson Daily Times, Triangle East.*

WINSTON-SALEM D9/B5

Colonel Ludlow Inn
Summit & W 5th
Winston-Salem NC 27101
(919) 777-1887
Circa 1887. This Queen Anne house features graceful wrap-around porches and a hipped gable roof. There is an ornate entrance and several stained-glass windows bordering the stairway. The dining room has a gold-plated chandelier and reproduction wallpaper. The guest rooms feature antique beds and more stained-glass windows, and some have two-person whirlpool tubs.
Location: Off highway I-40.
*Rates: $58-$114. Ken Land.
9 R. 9 PB. 3 FP. Phone in room. TV in room. Beds: KQD. B&B. Spa. Conference room. FAX. CCs: MC VISA AE DS. Parks, swimming, tennis, fine arts.
Seen in: *Charlotte Observer, Mid-Atlantic Country.*
"I have never seen anything like the meticulous and thorough attention to detail," Dannye Romine, *The Charlotte Observer.*

NORTH DAKOTA

CARRINGTON E11/C6

Kirkland Bed and Breakfast

RR 2 Box 18
Carrington ND 58421
(701) 652-2775

Circa 1910. Major Ralph and Mary Hall, great grandparents of the Harmon family, founded this farm. Designated a North Dakota Centennial

Farm and in the National Register of Historic Places, the farmhouse is a colonial-plantation style with a columned two-story wraparound porch. There is a library with antique books and a collection of farm items originally used by Major Hall when he was a territorial sheriff and Indian agent. Breakfast specialities include deer sausage, blueberry pancakes and fresh garden produce in season.

Rates: $45-$80. The Harmon family.
2 R. Beds: QD. Full breakfast.
Seen in: *Horizon Magazine, Foster County Independent, The Jamestown Sun.*
Need guest comment:

FESSENDEN E10/C5

Beiseker Mansion

1001 Second St NE
Fessenden ND 58438
(701) 547-3313

Circa 1899. Situated on nearly a city block, this 15-room Queen Anne Victorian is bordered by an old-fashioned wrought iron fence. Features include a splendid wraparound veranda and two turrets. The original golden oak woodwork is seen in the staircase, fireplace and dining room wainscoting. The turret room, with its king-size sleigh bed and marble-topped dresser, is a favorite choice. A third floor library, open to guests, contains 3,000 volumes. The house is in the National Register of Historic Places.

Rates: $45. Paula & Jerry Tweton.
6 R. 2 PB. Phone available. TV in room. Beds: KQDTC. Full breakfast. Gourmet meals. Conference room. CCs: MC VISA. Horseback riding, golf, swimming, fishing, hunting, cross-country skiing. Honeymoon and anniversary specials, weddings, receptions, educational seminars and business retreats.
Seen in: *Grand Forks Herald, Fessenden Herald Press.*
"What a beautiful house! The food and atmosphere were lovely."

LUVERNE F14/C7

Volden Farm

RR2 Box 50
Luverne ND 58056
(701) 769-2275

Circa 1926. Perennial gardens and a hedge of lilacs surround this redwood house with its newer addition. A favorite room is the North Room with

a lace canopy bed, an old pie safe and a Texas Star quilt made by the host's grandmother. Guests enjoy soaking in the claw-foot tub while looking out to the apple and plum orchard. There is a library, music room and game room. A stream, bordered by old oaks and formed by a natural spring, meanders through the property. The chickens here lay green and blue eggs. Supper is available by advance arrangement. Your host family were in the Air Force for 27 years.

Location: 80 miles northwest of Fargo.
Rates: $40-$50. Jim & Joanne Wold.
2 R. 1 PB. 1 FP. Phone available. Beds: D. Full breakfast.
Seen in: *Fargo Forum, Horizons Magazine, Grand Forks Herald.*
"Very pleasant indeed! Jim & Joanne make you feel good. There's so much to do, and the hospitality is amazing!"

MEDORA G3/D1

The Rough Riders

Medora ND 58645
(701) 623-4444

Circa 1865. This old hotel has the branding marks of Teddy Roosevelt's cattle ranch as well as other brands stamped into the rough-board facade out front. A wooden sidewalk helps to maintain the turn-of-the-century cow-town feeling. Rustic guest rooms are above the restaurant and are furnished with homesteader antiques original to the area. In the summer an outdoor pageant is held complete with stagecoach and horses. In October deer hunters are accommodated. The hotel along with two motels is managed by the non-profit Theodore Roosevelt Medora Foundation.

Rates: $55. Season: May to September.
9 R. 9 PB. Continental breakfast. CCs: MC VISA.

REGENT H5/E2

The Old West B&B

Box 211
Regent ND 58650
(701) 563-4542

This reservation service represents 12 bed and breakfast homes located throughout North Dakota. Included in the collection is a Scandanavian log house located near Bismark. Another home is close to the Fort Berthold Indian Reservation where rodeos and Indian powwows are held in summer. These are all small private homestays with one or two bedrooms available in each house.

Rates: $25-$60. Marlis Prince, director.
Beds: QDT. Full breakfast.
Seen in: *Bismarck Tribune.*
"This was my first bed and breakfast in this country. The host was genial and friendly and the accommodations were very comfortable. I'm spoiled rotten!" Visitor from Great Britain.

OHIO

CINCINNATI SH3/H1

Prospect Hill B&B
408 Boal St
Cincinnati OH 45210
(513) 421-4408

Circa 1867. Nestled in a wooded hillside in the Prospect Hill Historic District, this Italianate townhouse offers spectacular views of downtown Cincinnati. The inn has original woodwork, doors and light fixtures. Each guest room is decorated in a particular historical period. Guests may relax under a shade tree or on the side porch and enjoy the view.

*Rates: $65-$75. Gary Hackney.
4 R. 2 PB. 3 FP. Phone available. TV available. Beds: QD. Continental-plus breakfast. CCs: MC VISA. Zoo, beer brewery tours, amusement park.
Seen in: *Cincinnati Downtowner, Cincinnati Enquirer.*
"Over and over we had a wonderful time. Thanks to you and your great hospitality."

CIRCLEVILLE SD12/G4

Castle Inn
610 S Court St
Circleville OH 43113
(614) 477-3986

Circa 1900. Arches, battlements, towers and stained glass bedeck this medieval castle-like house constructed over a two-year period by Chicago builders engaged by Samuel Ruggles. Affording romantic anniversaries and honeymoons, the Round Tower Room boasts an ornate Victorian bedstead and a pink marble bathroom. Breakfast is served on English china in a handsome dining room overlooking the Shakespeare Garden, which displays only flowers and herbs featured in Shakespeare's plays. Weekends often include imaginative packages such as an "Elizabethan House Party" or a "Dickens Theatre Party."

*Rates: $55-$75. Jim & Sue Maxwell.
4 R. 4 PB. 3 FP. Phone in room. TV in room. Beds: D. Full breakfast. CCs: MC VISA. Walking distance to good restaurants, antique shops and more.
Seen in: *Circleville Herald, The Packet, Southeast Ohio Magazine.*
"The atmosphere is romantic, the food excellent, the hospitality super!"

CLEVELAND NG19/C5

The Coach House Inn B&B
See: Milan, OH

Glidden House
1901 Ford Dr
Cleveland OH 44106
(216) 231-8900

Circa 1910. This eclectic French Gothic mansion is listed in the National Register of Historic Places. The inn features elaborate stone carvings, carved oak paneling, Adamesque molded ceilings, lace curtains and fireplaces with carved wood or stone mantel pieces. Guest rooms are decorated in an early-American motif.
Rates: $89-$125. Paul Eddington.
60 R. 60 PB. 1 FP. Phone in room. TV in room. Beds: QDC. Continental-plus breakfast. Handicap access. Conference room. CCs: MC VISA AE DC CB DS. Museums, antiques.
Seen in: *The Plain Dealer, The Vindicator, The Detroit News.*
"A great place to stay and the only one we'll use in Cleveland."

COLUMBUS SB12/F4

Castle Inn
See: Circleville, OH

Central House
See: Pickerington, OH

The Coach House Inn B&B
See: Milan, OH

COSHOCTON NP18/F6

1890 B&B
663 N Whitewoman St
Coshocton OH 43812
(614) 622-1890

Circa 1878. This Victorian house is located in the restored canal village of Roscoe, next to the old towpath of the Ohio & Erie Canal. The village is operated as a Williamsburg-style living museum where potters, candlemakers, weavers and spinners live and work, often in period dress. The inn, furnished with turn-of-the-century antiques, has its own Victorian linen, lace and gift shop on the first floor.
Location: Historic Roscoe Village.
Rates: $50-$70. Curt & Debbi Crouso.
4 R. 2 PB. Phone available. TV available. Beds: DT. Continental-plus breakfast. CCs: MC VISA AE DS. Canal boat rides, swimming, museums.
Seen in: *The Columbus Dispatch, The Plain Dealer, Plane Talk.*
"Very charming."

DANVILLE NN16/E5

The White Oak Inn
29683 Walhonding Rd (SR 715)
Danville OH 43014
(614) 599-6107

Circa 1915. Begonias hang from the wide front porch of this three-story

farmhouse situated on 13 green acres. It is located on the former Indian trail

and pioneer road that runs along the Kokosing River, and an Indian mound has been discovered on the property. The inn's woodwork is all original white oak, and guest rooms are furnished in antiques. Visitors often shop for maple syrup, cheese and handicrafts at nearby Amish farms.
Location: North central Ohio.
*Rates: $70-$100. Joyce & Jim Acton.
10 R. 1 PB. 3 FP. Phone available. Beds: QD. Full breakfast. Conference room. CCs: MC VISA. Fishing, hunting, hiking, canoeing, cross-country skiing, bicycles.
Seen in: *Ladies Home Journal, Columbus Monthly, News Journal-Mansfield, Cleveland Plain Dealer.*
"We are moving, but we would go well out of our way to stay with the Actons. It was lovely."

DELLROY NM22/*E7*

Pleasant Journey Inn
4247 Roswell Rd SW
Dellroy OH 44620
(216) 735-2987
Circa 1868. This 14-room Victorian mansion is situated on 12 acres of woodland, stream and garden near the Atwood Lake area. Four years were spent building the house, but the depression that followed the Civil War prevented the original family from moving in. Seven marble fireplaces, a curved staircase of gleaming walnut, an oil chandelier and antiques and crafts collected locally add to the inn's gracious atmosphere. A favored fishing spot is a short walk out the back door.
Rates: $46-$60. Jim & Marie Etterman.
4 R. 1 PB. Phone available. TV available. Beds: DT. Continental-plus breakfast. CCs: MC VISA. Horseback riding, boating, golf, tennis, hiking, swimming, skiing.
Seen in: *Western Reserve, Free Press Standard.*
"The atmosphere at the inn is so serene and relaxing."

KELLEYS ISLAND NF13/*C4*

The Beatty House
South Shore Dr, PO Box 402
Kelleys Island OH 43438
(419) 746-2379
Circa 1861. In the National Register, this 14-room limestone house was built by Ludwig Bette, a Russian immigrant who became a grape-grower and winemaker. Large, cave-like wine cellars beneath the house stored more than 75,000 gallons of wine. Antiques include those of the original owner and the innkeepers. Guest rooms and parlors have both the views and breezes of Lake Erie. Breakfast is also served on the porch facing the lake. Vineyards, a winery and a state park are on this 3-by-5-mile island.

Location: Twenty-minute ferry ride from Marblehead.
Rates: $50-$60. Season: May to Nov. Martha & Jim Seaman.
3 R. 1 FP. Phone available. TV available. Beds: DC. B&B. Hiking, biking, fishing, cruise boats.
Seen in: *Sandusky Register, Toledo Metropolitan Magazine.*

Sweet Valley Inn
Division St, PO Box 733
Kelleys Island OH 43438
(419) 746-2750
Circa 1892. Graceful old maples shade this pretty yellow Victorian with gables festooned in white gingerbread. Porches and a bay window look out over rolling lawns. Named after the Sweet Valley Wine Company, the inn has been renovated to display cherry and cedar woodwork. Four working fireplaces, Oriental rugs, quilts, antiques and wallpapers create an old-time atmosphere.

Rates: $65. Bev & Paul Johnson.
4 R. 1 FP. Phone available. TV available. Beds: D. Full breakfast. CCs: MC VISA. Swimming, fishing, hiking, biking, horse & buggy rides.
"Relaxing and peaceful."

LEBANON SF5/*G2*

Burl Manor
230 S Mechanic St
Lebanon OH 45231
(513) 932-1266
Circa 1837. This handsome Greek Revival mansion was originally built for William Denney, an early editor and publisher for Ohio's oldest weekly newspaper, the Western Star. An outstanding collection of antiques made from cherry, mahogany and walnut burl woods are featured in the inn. There are Oriental rugs, period wallpapers and carved fireplaces. Guests can ride a bike along the paved trails beside the Little Miami River or rent a canoe from one of the many canoe liveries in town. In the evening, take a short walk to the Golden Lamb for dinner.

Rates: $50-$60. Ruth Ann & John Ware.
3 R. 3 PB. 5 FP. Phone available. TV available. Beds: D. Continental-plus breakfast. Amusement park, museum.
Seen in: *Hyde Park Living, Community Publications.*
"The host and hostess were most gracious."

Golden Lamb
27 South Broadway
Lebanon OH 45036
(513) 932-5065
Circa 1803. Jonas Seaman obtained a license to operate a house of public entertainment and created the Golden Lamb. Most of the furnishings are Shaker, and the collection is so large that two museum-style rooms on the fourth floor are set aside to house it. Eleven presidents and Charles Dickens stayed at the Golden Lamb.
Rates: $60. Jackson Reynolds.
18 R. 18 PB. Phone available. EP.
Seen in: *Antique Review.*

LEXINGTON NM14/*E5*

The White Fence Inn
8842 Denman Rd
Lexington OH 44904
(419) 884-2356
Circa 1900. This picturesque Ohio farm is set on 73 acres of pasture and farmland. The inn is decorated in a country-style, and each guest room has a theme such as the Victorian Room, the Amish Room and the Primitive Room. Giant willow trees hang from a small vineyard and over a creek that meanders through the property. The innkeepers harvest Con-

cord grapes to make grape juice for their guests. Tom Sawyer-style bamboo fishing poles are available for those who want to angle bass or blue gill from the fish pond. Sleigh and hay rides are available.
Rates: $53-$85. Bill & Ellen Hiser.
6 R. 4 PB. 1 FP. Phone available. TV available. Beds: KQDTC. Full breakfast. Handicap access. Horseback riding, downhill & cross-country skiing, canoeing, hiking, museums. Wedding night or anniversary baskets.
Seen in: *Adventure Road, Mainstream, Mansfield News Journal.*
"I feel very lucky to have found a little corner of heaven in Lexington."

LOGAN SE15/*G5*

The Inn at Cedar Falls

21190 State Rt 374
Logan OH 43138
(614) 385-7489

Circa 1840. This barn-style inn was constructed in 1987 on 80 acres adjacent to Hocking State Park and a half mile from the waterfalls. The kitchen and dining room is in a 19-century log house with a wood-burning stove, plank floor and 18-inch-wide logs. Accommodations in the new barn building are simple and comfortable, each furnished with antiques. Verandas provide sweeping views of woodland and meadow. The grounds include gardens for the inn's gourmet dinners, and there are mink, weasel, red fox, wild turkey and whitetail deer.
Rates: $57-$75. A. Castle, E. Grinsteider, D. Coyan, K. Nesbitt.
9 R. 9 PB. Phone available. Beds: DT. Full breakfast. Restaurant. Gourmet meals. Handicap access. Conference room. CCs: MC VISA. Horseback riding, hiking, skiing, swimming.
Seen in: *The Post.*
"Very peaceful, relaxing and friendly. Couldn't be nicer."

LUCAS NL15/*E5*

Pleasant Valley Lodge

1983 Pleasant Valley Rd
Lucas OH 44843
(419) 892-2443

Circa 1903. Located on 40 acres near Malabar Farm State Park, this rambling old house is built on a hillside. The brick and aluminum siding exterior is soon forgotten once inside. There are handsome Victorian sofas, a massive English cherry wardrobe, slate floors, beamed ceilings and stained-glass windows throughout. A gazebo on the hill provides views of the surrounding countryside. Antique linens, quilts and china add to the gracious atmosphere. An old barn on the property is filled with antiques

available for sale. Curried egg strata is a speciality.
Rates: $70. Ron & Susan Randall.
4 R. 4 PB. 1 FP. Phone available. TV available. Beds: QT. Full breakfast. Conference room. Biking, hiking, swimming, boating, horseback riding, canoeing.
Seen in: *The Plain Dealer, News Journal.*
"We are still basking in the glow from our wonderful refreshing weekend. You really have the gift of hospitality."

MARBLEHEAD NF13/*C4*

Old Stone House Inn

133 Clemons St
Marblehead OH 43440
(419) 798-5922

Circa 1861. Built by Alexander Clemons, owner of the first stone quarry in the area, the Stone House overlooks Lake Erie. Now a guest

room, the enclosed Captain's Tower features a 15-foot ceiling, spindled railings around the staircase and the best view of the lake and shoreline. The inn's green lawns and gardens slope to the shore, where guests may fish from the rocks or swim.
Location: Marblehead Peninsula.
Rates: $55-$85. Dorothy Bright & Pat Whiteford Parks.
12 R. Phone available. TV available. Beds: DT. Continental-plus breakfast. Conference room. CCs: MC VISA DS. Island tours, summer & winter charter fishing, cross-country skiing, lake swimming.
Seen in: *Marion Star, Cleveland Plain Dealer, The Midweek Plus.*
"Thank you so much!! Everything was wonderful!"

MARIETTA SF21/*G7*

House Of Seven Porches

331 Fifth St
Marietta OH 45750
(614) 373-1767

Circa 1835. Situated on a tree-lined street of historic houses, this bed and breakfast is an appealing Greek Revival home. In the 1830s, a Marietta College professor from Charleston chose the house's design, copied from a plantation house that still stands in Charleston. The porches, jib doors (a combination door and window) and foot-thick walls reflect the southern influence. The back porch has a Concord grapevine that provides homemade juice served at breakfast. Your hostess is an expert on the history of Marietta.
Rates: $40-$50. Jeane Kelso.
3 R. 2 PB. Phone available. Beds: DTC. Continental breakfast. Horseback riding, water skiing, swimming, tennis, biking, carriage rides.
Seen in: *Marietta Times, Country Living, The Pittsburgh Press.*
"Your home is magnificent! Your hospitality warm and friendly."

Larchmont B&B

524 Second St
Marietta OH 45750
(614) 373-5907

Circa 1824. Towering cypress trees shade this magnificent Greek Revival mansion overlooking the Muskingum River. The inn's elegant interiors are

appointed with fine antiques and Oriental rugs. It features a handsomely crafted hanging stairway, 14 and 15-foot ceilings and a grand ballroom. Breakfast is served with fine china, crystal and linens and includes specialties such as apple raspberry crumb cake. Because of the series of secret passageways and an outside tunnel, Larchmont is thought to have sheltered runaway slaves. The house once served as a school and later as a tourist home in the Thirties.
Rates: $68-$88. Janet J. Grams.
3 R. 3 PB. 1 FP. Phone available. TV available. Beds: DT. Full breakfast. Conference room. CCs: MC VISA. Horse & buggy

rides, paddle wheel boat rides, museums. Weddings.
Seen in: *The Marietta Times, The Parkersburg News.*
"You made us feel warm and welcome in your home."

MILAN NH14/C5

The Coach House Inn B&B

304 SR 113 W, PO Box 537
Milan OH 44846
(419) 499-2435 (800) 843-2624

Circa 1841. This graceful Greek Revival home was built by a clippership builder when the Milan Canal was at its peak. Handsomely situated on 15 acres of walnut, oak and maple trees, the inn overlooks the Huron River and the village of Milan. Antique furnishings, wood floors and fresh flowers add to the ambience. The innkeepers will lend you a picnic basket and a canoe for leisurely river excursions.
*Rates: $65. Tom & Sandy Susko.
3 R. 1 PB. 1 FP. Phone available. TV in room. Beds: Q. Full breakfast. Handicap access. Exercise room. CCs: MC VISA. Canoeing, biking, hiking, Cedar Point.
Seen in: *The Reporter/Voice, Norwalk Reflector.*
"Everything was perfect — the house, the bed, the food and especially the innkeepers!"

MORROW SF5/G2

Country Manor B&B

6315 Zoar Rd
Morrow OH 45152
(513) 899-2440

Circa 1863. This historic house boasts a bucolic setting on 55 acres of woodland and ponds. The home features hardwood floors and high ceilings. Traditional furnishings include a baby grand piano in the living room. Each guest room has a homey eclectic decor and provides a sitting area. The suite features a canopy bed and a crystal chandelier in the bathroom. A front porch swing and a pond off the back veranda entice guests to relax in warm weather. There is an indoor training stable, and stalls are available should you bring your horse. Bobby keeps Belgian draft horses.
Rates: $50-$60. Rhea Hughes.
3 R. 1 PB. Phone available. TV in room. Beds: DT. Full breakfast. Lakes, amusement parks, sports center and a 13-mile paved trail along the river.
Seen in: *Country Magazine.*
"Everything was just perfect, especially the wonderful breakfasts."

MOUNT VERNON NO14/E5

The Russell-Cooper House

115 E Gambier St
Mount Vernon OH 43050
(614) 397-8638

Circa 1829. Dr. John Russell and his son-in-law Colonel Cooper modeled a simple brick Federal house into a unique Victorian. Its sister structure is the

Wedding Cake House of Kennebunk, Maine. There is a hand-painted plaster ceiling in the ballroom and a collection of Civil War items and antique medical devices. Woodwork is of cherry, maple and walnut, and there are etched and stained-glass windows. Hal Holbrook called the town America's Hometown.
Rates: $45-$68. Tim & Maureen Tyler.
6 R. 6 PB. Phone available. Beds: QDT. Full breakfast. Conference room. CCs: MC VISA. Downhill & cross-country skiing, fishing, canoeing, golf. Mystery weekends.
Seen in: *Ohio Business.*
"A salute to the preservation of American history and culture. Most hospitable owners!"

PAINESVILLE NE21/B7

Rider's 1812 Inn

792 Mentor Ave
Painesville OH 44077
(216) 354-8200 (216) 942-2742

Circa 1812. Although originally an inn and tavern serving the frontier Western Reserve, Rider's became a private family home when lake

steamers and the railroad began to replace oxcarts and wagons as the preferred modes of travel. The Gathering Room features an original fireplace and wavy window panes, and most of the inn's floors are rare long-needle pine. A passageway in the cellar is said to have been part of the underground railroad. An English-pub-style restaurant is on the premises.
Rates: $70-$85. Elaine Crane & Courtney Sherman.
7 R. 6 PB. 1 FP. Phone in room. TV available. Beds: QDTC. Continental-plus breakfast. Handicap access. Conference room. CCs: MC VISA AE. Horseback riding, sailing, swimming, fishing, cross-country skiing. English pubs, mystery weekends, honeymoon suite.
Seen in: *Business Review, The News-Herald.*
"The hospitality of yourself and your employees is unbeatable, so personal yet professional."

PICKERINGTON SB13/F4

Central House

27 W Columbus St, Old Village
Pickerington OH 43147
(614) 837-0932

Circa 1860. The restoration of the old Central House began after the possums, honeybees and other wildlife were evicted. It required extensive

reconstruction because the log foundations had rotted away. The house had to be jacked up, straightened and a new foundation poured underneath. Now, all gussied up, its Victorian atmosphere makes guests feel as though they had been to Grandma's. The inn is famous for its giant cinnamon rolls.

Rates: $45-$55. Jim & Sue Maxwell, Mary Lou Boyd.
4 R. 4 PB. Phone available. TV available. Beds: D. B&B. Restaurant. Handicap access. CCs: MC VISA. Tennis. Golf nearby.
Seen in: *Lancaster Eagle Gazette, Fairfield North, NeighborNews East, Southeast Messenger, Country Living.*
"Pleasant, charming, comfortable, relaxing and wonderful hostesses."

PIQUA NP4/F2

Pickwinn B&B

707 N Downing St
Piqua OH 45356
(513) 773-8877 (513) 773-6137

Circa 1883. This Empire-style brick house is in the Caldwell Historic District. It boasts a graceful wraparound

front porch. Appointments are reminiscent of English country decor with English pine and English oak pieces. Floral prints, hunting pictures and hardwood floors add to the atmosphere. A country breakfast is featured.
Rates: $50-$60. Season: March through Oct. Paul & Rosemary Gutmann.
4 R. 1 PB. Phone available. TV in room. Beds: QDT. Full breakfast. Museum, canal boat ride. Weddings.
Seen in: *Miami Valley Sunday News, The Cincinnati Post, The Sidney News.*
"Your inn is fantastic! It could not be more perfect."

POLAND NJ25/*D8*

The Inn at the Green
500 S Main St
Poland OH 44514
(216) 758-4688
Circa 1876. Main Street in Poland has a parade of historic houses including Connecticut Western Reserve colonials, Federal and Greek Revival houses. The Inn at the Green is a Victorian Baltimore townhouse. All the common rooms including a greeting room, parlor and sitting room library have working marble fireplaces. Interiors evoke an authentic 19th-century atmosphere with antiques and oriental rugs that enhance the moldings, 12-foot ceilings and poplar floors.
Location: Seven miles southeast of Youngstown, Ohio.
Rates: $50. Ginny & Steve Meloy.
4 R. 4 PB. 3 FP. Phone available. TV in room. Beds: DT. Continental breakfast. Conference room. CCs: MC VISA. Cross-country skiing, golf, tennis, fly fishing, canoeing, sailing
Seen in: *The Vindicator.*
"Thank you for a comfortable and perfect stay in your beautiful Victorian home."

POMEROY SI17/*H6*

Holly Hill Inn
114 Butternut Ave
Pomeroy OH 45769
(614) 992-5657 (800)445-8525
Circa 1836. This gracious clapboard inn with its many shuttered windows is shaded by giant holly trees. Original window panes of blown glass remain, as well as wide-board floors, mantels and fireplaces. The family's antique collection includes a crocheted canopy bed in the Honeymoon Room overlooking a working fireplace. Dozens of antique quilts are displayed and for sale. Guests are invited to borrow an antique bike to ride through the countryside.
Rates: $55-$69. John & Marilyn Fultz, Marc & Ellen Fultz.
4 R. 2 FP. Phone available. TV available. Beds: DTC. Full breakfast. Conference room. CCs: MC VISA DS. Horseback riding, canoeing, boating, outdoor plays.
Seen in: *The Sunday Times-Sentinel.*
"Your inn is so beautiful, and it has so much historic charm."

RIPLEY SK7/*I4*

The Signal House
234 N Front St
Ripley OH 45167
(513) 392-1640
Circa 1830. This Greek Italiante home is said to have been used to aid the Underground Railroad. A light in the attic told Rev. John Rankin, a dedicated abolitionist, that it was safe to bring slaves across the waterfront to freedom. Located within a 55-acre historical district, guests can take a glance back in time, exploring museums and antique shops. Twelve-foot ceilings with ornate plaster-work grace the parlor, and guests can sit on any of three porches watching paddlewheelers traverse the Ohio River.
Rates: $58-68. Vic and Betsy Billingsley.
2 R. 2 PB. Continental breakfast. Annual tobacco festival, sternwheel regattas, historical district

SAGAMORE HILLS NH20/*C7*

The Inn at Brandywine Falls
8230 Brandywine Rd
Sagamore Hills OH 44067
(216) 467-1812 (216) 650-4965
Circa 1848. Overlooking Brandywine Falls and situated snuggly on national parkland, this National Register Greek Revival house has recently been

renovated. Antiques made in Ohio are featured in the Greek Revival-style rooms and include sleigh and four-poster beds. The kitchen has been designed to allow guests to chat with the innkeepers while sipping coffee in front of a crackling fireplace and watching breakfast preparations. Choose the Simon Perkins Room (he was the founder of Akron) for views of the waterfall. George and Katie give scheduled tours of the inn, the Falls and the park aided by Lolly the trolly.
Location: The Cuyahoga Valley National Park.
Rates: $75-$140. Katie & George Hoy.
6 R. 6 PB. 1 FP. Phone in room. TV in room. Beds: KDT. B&B. Gourmet meals. Spa. Handicap access. CCs: MC VISA. Hiking, bicycling, cross-country and downhill skiing, golf, sledding. Refrigerator and microwave in room.
Seen in: *The Plain Dealer, The Vindicator, Western Reserve Magazine, Innsider, Dayton Daily News.*
"A beauty amidst beauty."

SANDUSKY NG13/*C4*

The Coach House Inn B&B
See: Milan, OH

Old Stone House on the Lake
See: Marblehead, OH

Wagner's 1844 Inn
230 E Washington St
Sandusky OH 44870
(419) 626-1726
Circa 1844. This inn was originally constructed as a log cabin. Additions and renovations were made, and the house evolved into an Italianate-style accented with brackets under the eaves and black shutters on the second-story windows. A wrought-iron fence frames the house, and there are ornate wrought-iron porch rails. A billiard room and screened-in porch are available to guests. The ferry to Cedar Point and Kellys Island is within walking distance.
❀Rates: $50-$75. Walt & Barbara Wagner.
3 R. 3 PB. 4 FP. Phone available. TV available. Beds: QD. B&B. FAX. CCs: MC VISA. Cedar Point Amusement Park, lakes, history.
Seen in: *Lorain Journal.*

TIPP CITY SB5/*F2*

Willow Tree Inn
1900 W State, Rt 571
Tipp City OH 45371
(513) 667-2957
Circa 1830. This Federal-style mansion is a copy of a similar house in North Carolina, former home of the builders. Antique period furnishings and polished wood floors add to the atmosphere of this rambling homestead.
❀Rates: $69. Tom & Peggy Nordquist.
4 R. 1 PB. Phone available. TV in room. Beds: DC. Full breakfast. Conference room. CCs: MC VISA. Swimming, golf, tennis, museums, antiquing all nearby. Weddings/receptions on premises.
Seen in: *Troy Daily News, Dayton News.*
"Very quiet place to stay. The grounds are beautiful, service excellent!"

TOLEDO NE9/*C3*

The Coach House Inn B&B
See: Milan, OH

Mansion View
2035 Collingwood Blvd
Toledo OH 43620
(419) 244-5676
Circa 1887. This corbeled brick Queen Anne house in the National Register was built for Fred Reynolds, a wealthy grain merchant. A Vermont slate roof tops the gabled roof. The Italian marble entry leads to an ornately carved grand hall. A few antiques original to the house remain, and others have been collected to fill the guest rooms. The owners plan to add six more guest rooms and a restaurant.
*Rates: $75. Tam Gagen, Matt Jasin, Tim Oller.
4 R. 4 PB. 2 FP. Phone in room. TV in room. Beds: D. Full breakfast. Conference room. FAX. CCs: MC VISA.
"Thank you for a beautiful alternative to the pre-fab, broken neon hotels we had on our honeymoon. We'll remember it always and be back for our anniversaries."

TROY NQ5/F2

H.W. Allen Villa B&B
434 S Market St
Troy OH 45373
(513) 335-1181
Circa 1874. Constructed for the president of the local First National Bank, this Italianate Victorian is three stories

high and has 14 rooms in its 7,000 square feet. Restored and refurbished with Victorian-era antiques, the inn features natural woodwork and a winding walnut staircase to the third floor. Elegant plaster ceiling crown molding and duplicated stenciling are the finishing touches. Private baths are inroom.
*Rates: $40-$60. Robert W. & F. June Smith.
6 R. 4 PB. 4 FP. Phone in room. TV in room. Beds: DT. Full breakfast. Conference room. CCs: MC VISA AE. Trapshoot, tennis, golf, swimming, ice skating, bicycling, nature walks, wineries. Snack bar with refrigerator, ice maker, microwave, coffee maker and snacks.
Seen in: *Miami Valley Sunday News.*
"Such a beautiful place to stay and such a congenial greeting."

VERMILION NG15/C5

Village Square Annex B&B
720 Main St
Vermilion OH 44089
(216) 967-1950 (216) 967-1688
Circa 1900. This former parsonage in the National Register has been transformed into a tea room (the Parson's Parlor), antique shops and a bed-and-breakfast inn. Polished cherry and oak woodwork is underscored with floral wallpapers and antiques. Located three blocks from the water, it is convenient to restored captains' homes and area shops.
Rates: $50-$75. Ron & Elizabeth Millett.
4 R. Phone available. TV available. Beds: QD. Full breakfast. CCs: MC VISA DS. Fishing, swimming, museums.
Seen in: *Lake Front News, The Journal, Buckeye Marketeer.*
"The realization was even better than the expectation."

WOODSFIELD SC23/F7

The Black Walnut Inn & Magnolia Manor
203 W Marietta St
Woodsfield OH 43793
(614) 472-0002 (800) 422-4233
Circa 1890. The Black Walnut Inn is a Dutch colonial house that was built in the Roaring Twenties with more than

5,000 square feet. It boasts 6 fireplaces, a library and estate grounds with a clay tennis court. Nearby is Magnolia Manor, a Victorian house with high ceilings, bay windows and stained glass. Afternoon tea is served, and there is a gift shop called Victoria's Garden. Accommodation is also available in the Country Cottage with its own swimming pool.
Rates: $32-$55. Todd & Joanne Willman, Margaret Bauer.
11 R. 3 PB. 10 FP. Phone available. TV in room. Beds: QDT. Continental breakfast. Swimming pool. Conference room. CCs: MC VISA AE. Bicycle tours, golf, antiquing. Honeymoon & anniversary packages. Gift shop.

Seen in: *Monroe County Beacon.*
"What a pretty place."

YOUNGSTOWN NI25/D8

The Inn at the Green
See: Poland, OH

ZOAR NM20/E7

Cobbler Shop Inn
Corner of 2nd & Main St
Zoar OH 44697
(216) 874-2600
Circa 1828. The original structure, a cobbler shop, was enlarged to twice its size in 1860. It is in the center of the historic district, where a Christian

communal society had been established in 1817. A favorite at the inn is the waist-high rope bed spread with an 1835 coverlet.
Rates: $65. Marian "Sandy" Worley.
5 R. 1 PB. Phone available. TV available. Beds: DT. Full breakfast. CCs: MC VISA AE. Water skiing, golf, swimming, museums, shops.
Seen in: *Cleveland Plain Dealer, Record Courier.*
"Your kindness and generosity were outstanding. I gained 10 pounds, but what the heck!"

Cowger House #9
9 Fourth St
Zoar OH 44697
(216) 874-3542
Circa 1817. German Separatists built this log house located in the restored village. Guest rooms include a bridal suite with spa and fireplace. Polished plank flooring, a hand-cut stone fireplace and rag rugs set the tone for the dining room. The innkeepers provide a delightful 19th-century dinner theater situation where Ed, a history teacher, plays a Civil War soldier to Mary's German immigrant role. Menu for each evening is set by the first guest who reserves that day.
Rates: $50-$125. Ed & Mary Cowger.
6 R. 3 PB. 7 FP. Phone available. Beds: KQD. Full breakfast. Restaurant. Spa. CCs: MC VISA. Horseback riding, canoeing, boating. Honeymoon & wedding specials, local tours. Seen in: *Beacon Journal.*
"Such a wonderful time, and the breakfast feast was fabulous!"

OKLAHOMA

ALINE D14/A5

Heritage Manor

RR1 Box 33
Aline OK 73716
(405) 463-2563

Circa 1903. A wonderful way to experience Oklahoma history is to stay at the Heritage Manor, two turn-of-the century restored homes. One is an American Four Square house and the other, a glorified Arts-and-Crafts-style home. Antiques were gathered from area pioneer homes and include an Edison Victrola Morning Glory Horn and a cathedral pump organ. Antique sofas and English leather chairs fill the sitting room. Mannequins dressed in pioneer clothing add to the decor. There are several fireplaces, and a widow's walk tops the main house.
Rates: $50. A.J. & Carolyn Rexroat.
4 R. Beds: D. Full breakfast. Alabaster Caverns, the Great Salt Plains Lake, Glass Mountain State Park.
Seen in: *Country Magazine, Enid Morning News, the Daily Oklahoman.*

GUTHRIE F17/B6

Harrison House

124 W Harrison
Guthrie OK 73044
(405) 282-1000 (800) 375-1001 (OK only)

Circa 1902. This is the old Guthrie Savings Bank. Totally restored, Harrison House is Oklahoma's first bed-

and-breakfast inn. The rooms are named after famous citizens such as Tom Mix, a Guthrie bartender who became a Hollywood cowboy star. The original vault is still in the inn, now completely furnished with Victorian antiques. Patchwork quilts, lace curtains and antique washstands are featured in each room. Guthrie, the original capital of Oklahoma, has a turn-of-the-century downtown.
Location: Thirty minutes north of Oklahoma.
*❀Rates: $60-$80. Phyllis Murray.
23 R. 23 PB. Phone in room. TV available. Beds: KDT. B&B. CCs: MC VISA AE DC CB DS. Horseback riding, fishing. Pollard Theater, Lazy E Ranch nearby.
Seen in: *Country Inns, Glamour, Historic Preservation, Country, Tulsa Tribune, Houston Chronicle.*
"I'd been in 10 different hotels in 10 days and couldn't remember a thing about the other nine or where they were. Harrison House I'll remember forever."

Stone Lion Inn

1016 W Warner
Guthrie OK 73044
(405) 282-0012

Circa 1907. This inn is named for the two stone lions guarding the front door. The inn has original oak floors, replica wallpaper, leaded-glass doors, original light fixtures and two formal parlors. The main parlor features an 1861 square grand piano, Oriental rugs and 200-year-old grand hall lion's head chairs from Spain. Some guest rooms offer private sitting rooms and claw-foot tubs.
Rates: $50-$95. Becky L. Luker.
6 R. 6 PB. 1 FP. Phone available. TV available. Beds: KD. Full breakfast. Restaurant. Gourmet meals. Conference room. CCs: MC VISA. Golf, fishing, lake, water skiing, swimming. Murder-mystery weekends, weddings, anniversaries.
Seen in: *Oklahoma Today, The Daily Oklahoman, News Press Weekender.*
"You do everything in such a special way that we all felt wonderfully catered to and spoiled!"

OKLAHOMA CITY G17/B6

The Grandison

1841 NW 15th
Oklahoma City OK 73106
(405) 521-0011

Circa 1896. This brick and shingled three-story house is situated on lawns and gardens shaded by pecan, apple and fig trees. You'll also find a pond and gazebo. Original Belgian stained

glass remains and the decor is an airy country Victorian. The bridal suite includes a working fireplace, white lace curtains and a claw-foot tub.
Rates: $40-$90. Bob & Claudia Wright.
5 R. 5 PB. 3 FP. Phone in room. TV available. Beds: QD. B&B. Gourmet meals. CCs: MC VISA AE.
Seen in: *The Daily Oklahoman, Oklahoma Pride.*
"Like going home to Grandma's!"

TULSA E21/B7

Holloway House

PO Box 52423
Tulsa OK 74152-0423
(918) 582-8607 (800) 657-6040

Circa 1924. Located in historic Riverparks, this cozy clapboard house offers a touch of New England. Elegantly decorated rooms include

Victorian and Art Deco themes. The Williamsburg Room boasts a canopy bed and private spa as a handsome fireplace. There is a baby grand piano and fireplace in the parlor. Gourmet breakfasts are often served on the morning terrace.
Location: Riverparks Historic District.
Rates: $90-$110. Mary Claire Holloway.
3 R. 2 PB. 1 FP. TV in room. Beds: QD. Full breakfast. Spa. Sauna. CCs: MC VISA AE.
Seen in: *Oklahoma Life Style, ABC.*
"What a wonderful experience walking into your paradise today."

OREGON

ASHLAND P6/F2

Buckhorn Springs

2200 Buckhorn Springs Rd
Ashland OR 97520
(503) 488-2200

Circa 1864. Located on 120 secluded acres in a mountain valley 12 miles east of Ashland, Buckhorn Springs is a newly renovated resort. In the National Register, it was once a sacred healing site for Modoc, Takilma, Rogue and Klamath Indians. At the turn of the century it became a health spa popular for its mineral spring waters. Four restored cabins are located beside a bubbling stream, Emigrant Creek. Each guest room in the lodge is decorated in a different era important to the history of Buckhorn and each has a claw foot tub outfitted with a third spigot which pipes in hot mineral bath waters.

Rates: $55-$125. Season: April - Dec. Bruce & Leslie Sargent, Chris Fowler.
12 R. 8 PB. Phone available. Beds: KQDTC. Full breakfast. Restaurant. Gourmet meals. Spa. Conference room. CCs: MC VISA. Horseback riding, hiking. Weddings, family reunions, retreats.
Seen in: *Ashland Daily Tidings, Medford Mail Tribune, Sunset.*
"A tremendous addition to the useable historic sites in this area."

Chanticleer B&B Inn

120 Gresham St
Ashland OR 97520
(503) 482-1919

Circa 1920. This gray clapboard, Craftsman-style house has been totally renovated and several rooms added. The inn is light and airy and decorated with antiques. Special features include the open hearth fireplace and bricked patio garden.

Rates: $79-$160. Jim & Nancy Beaver
7 R. 7 PB. 1 FP. Phone in room. TV available. Beds: QT. Full breakfast. Gourmet meals. CCs: MC VISA. Ashland Shakespeare Festival.
Seen in: *Country Home, Pacific Northwest.*
"Chanticleer has set the standard by which all others will be judged."

Cowslip's Belle

159 N Main St
Ashland OR 97520
(503) 488-2901

Circa 1913. Cowslip's Belle is a Craftsman bungalow, the simple design a rebellion against the ornate and often over-decorated Victorian.

The inn is named for a flower mentioned in *A Midsummer Night's Dream*, each of the guest rooms is named for one of Shakespeare's favorite flowers, and each room has a private entrance.

Rates: $58-$92. Jon & Carmen Reinhardt.
4 R. 4 PB. Phone available. Beds: QT. Full breakfast. CCs: VISA DS. Snow skiing, water sports, water skiing, wind surfing, wineries.
Seen in: *The Daily Tidings, San Francisco Chronicle, Los Angeles Times.*
"The atmosphere was delightful, the decor charming, the food delicious and the company grand. Tony says he's spoiled forever."

Edinburgh Lodge B&B

586 E Main St
Ashland OR 97520
(503) 488-1050

Circa 1908. The Edinburgh, built by a miner, became the J. T. Currie Boarding House for teachers and railroad workers. Handmade quilts and period

furnishings adorn each guest room and afternoon tea is served at 5:00 p.m. The country garden features hollyhocks and delphiniums.

Rates: $49-$65. Ann Rivera.
6 R. 6 PB. Phone available. Beds: QT. Full breakfast. CCs: MC VISA.
"The rooms are so warm and quaint... like visiting family. Breakfast was delicious. I'm sure there's an Edinburgh Cookbook on its way. I want a copy!"

Hersey House

451 N Main St
Ashland OR 97520
(503) 482-4563

Circa 1904. A saltbox Victorian built with leaded-glass windows, the inn also features an L-shaped staircase.

James Hersey, Ashland city councilman, was the first of five generations of Herseys to occupy the house.

*Rates: $70-$85. Season: May - Nov. Gail E. Orell & K. Lynn Savage.
4 R. 4 PB. Phone available. Beds: QT. Full breakfast. Bicycling, tennis, horseback riding, fishing, swimming.
Seen in: *San Francisco Examiner, Pacific Northwest Magazine, Mature Outlook, Organic Gardening.*
"Delicious breakfasts and thoughtful social hour. We couldn't have asked for anything more. Your house and gardens are beautiful."

Morical House

688 N Main St
Ashland OR 97520
(503) 482-2254

Circa 1880. The Morical House is a mile away from the Shakespeare festival, and blooming rose gardens frame this exquisitely restored Victorian farmhouse in summer. All guest rooms are furnished with period antiques and handmade com-

forters, and each has a view of the Cascade Mountains. The inn's acre of grounds provides a putting green and croquet lawn.
Rates: $90-$95. Season: Closed Jan. 15-31. Patricia (Pat) & Peter Dahl.
5 R. 5 PB. Phone available. TV available. Beds: QDT. Full breakfast. CCs: MC VISA. Fishing, white water rafting, skiing, mineral baths.
Seen in: *Pacific Northwest Magazine.*
"Gracious hosts who spoiled us with such attention to detail and unparalleled warm hospitality."

Reames House
See: Jacksonville

RoyAl Carter House
514 Siskiyou Blvd
Ashland OR 97520
(503) 482-5623
Circa 1909. Listed in the National Register, the RoyAl (Roy and ALyce are the hosts) Carter House is sur-

rounded by tall trees and lovely gardens. The inn has a secluded deck. The four guest rooms are spacious and decorated in a homey style.
Location: Four blocks from the Shakespeare theater.
Rates: $54-$70. Roy & Alyce Levy.
Phone available. TV in room. Beds: KQDT. Horseback riding, skiing, water sports.
"Thank you! I really feel special here!"

The Woods House B&B
333 N Main St
Ashland OR 97520
(503) 488-1598
Built and occupied for almost 40 years by a prominent Ashland physican, each room of this lovely inn boasts special detail. Many guest rooms offer canopy beds, and the Courtyard Room features a queen-sized poster bed. Guests can enjoy a full gourmet breakfast with culinary delights such as pumpkin pancakes with honey pecan syrup or mushroom tarragon quiche. After breakfast, take a stroll through the reconstructed English rose garden. Local activites include exploring nearby caves or taking a tour of Oregon wineries.
Rates: $70-93. Ted and Michele Lockwood.
6 R. 6 PB. Beds: KQT. Full breakfast. CCs: MC VISA.
"Classiest B&B in the Northwest. Loved the lace in the carriage house."

ASTORIA A4/A1

Grandview B&B
1574 Grand Ave
Astoria OR 97103
(800) 488-3250
Circa 1900. To fully enjoy its views of the Columbia River, this Victorian house sports both a tower and a tur-

ret. Antiques and white wicker furnishings contribute to the inn's casual, homey feeling. The Meadow Room is particularly appealing to bird lovers with its bird call recordings, bird books and bird wallpaper. Breakfast, served in the main floor turret, frequently includes smoked salmon with bagels and cream cheese.
Rates: $38-$75. Charleen C. Maxwell.
6 R. 6 PB. 1 FP. Phone available. Beds: QT. Continental-plus breakfast. CCs: MC VISA DS. Tennis, charter fishing, hiking, beaches.
Seen in: *Pacific Northwest, Northwest Discoveries.*
"We're still talking about our visit and the wonderful breakfast you served."

CLOVERDALE E3/B1

Sandlake Country Inn
8505 Galloway Rd
Cloverdale OR 97112
(503) 965-6745
Circa 1894. This two-story farmhouse was built of 3 x 12 bridge timbers from a Norwegian sailing vessel. It shipwrecked on the beach south of Cape Lookout on Christmas Day 1890. On two acres adjacent to the Suislaw National Forest, the inn's garden is occasionally host to deer and other wildlife. Guest rooms feature canopied beds, down comforters and fresh flowers. A creekside country cottage is popular with honeymooners.
Location: On the Oregon coast.
*Rates: $65-$85. Margo Underwood.

3 R. 3 PB. Phone available. TV in room. Beds: Q. B&B. Spa. Hiking, fishing, hang gliding, clamming, crabbing, creek-side hammock, croquet, horseback riding on beach nearby. Bicycles. Private garden spa.
Seen in: *Headlight Herald, The Bridal Connection of Oregon.*
"A wonderful pampered retreat, revitalizing!"

EUGENE I5/C2

Campus Cottage
1136 E 19th Ave
Eugene OR 97403
(503) 342-5346
Circa 1922. The three guest rooms of Campus Cottage are appointed in a country French decor with antiques,

cozy comforters and fresh flowers. "The Cottage Room," for instance, has a queen-size oak bed and a day bed, plus a vaulted ceiling, bay window and private entrance. Bicycles are available for traveling around the University of Oregon, located two blocks from the inn.
Rates: $78-$93. Ursula Bates.
3 R. 3 PB. Beds: QT. Full breakfast.
Seen in: *New York Times, PM Magazine, Los Angeles Times.*

House in the Woods
814 Lorane Hwy
Eugene OR 97405
(503) 343-3234
Circa 1910. This handsome Craftsman house on two landscaped acres was built by a Minnesota lawyer. It was originally accessible by streetcar. Antiques include a square grand piano of rosewood, and a collection of antique wedding photos. The house is attractively furnished and surrounded by flower gardens.
*Rates: $55-$60. Eunice & George Kjaer.
2 R. 1 PB. Phone available. TV available. Beds: QTDC. Full breakfast. Conference room. Golf, tennis, hiking, bicycling, swimming, fishing.
Seen in: *The Register-Guard, The Oregonian.*
"Lovely ambiance and greatest sleep ever.

Delicious and beautiful food presentation."

GRANTS PASS 04/E2

Ahlf House
762 NW 6th St
Grants Pass OR 97526
(503) 474-1374 (503) 474-1381

Circa 1902. This four-story Queen Anne Victorian stands on a hill, framed by tulip, pine and cedar trees. With 5,500 square feet, it is the largest historic house in Grants Pass. Delicately painted in three shades of blue, the house boasts a double-tiered veranda and bay with fish-scale siding. A gracious Victorian home feeling is carried out in antique decor and a parlor with classical or popular music by Rosemary, and desserts by Betty. A breakfast dish popular with guests is Fluffy French Fingers with Orange Sauce.

Rates: $65. Herbert & Betty Buskirk/Rosemary Althaus.
2 R. Phone available. TV available. Beds: DT. Full breakfast. Conference room. Rafting, Rogue River. Weddings, yearly Christmas open house.
Seen in: *Daily Courier, Horizon Air Magazine.*
"We felt very pampered and relaxed. The atmosphere is much more than money can buy."

Lawnridge House
1304 NW Lawnridge
Grants Pass OR 97526
(503) 476-8518

Circa 1909. This graceful, gabled clapboard house is shaded by 200-year-old oak trees. The inn features two bridal suites, each with a canopy bed.

Breakfast often includes quiche or baked salmon and croissants. Nearby, the Rogue River provides kayaking, river rafting and salmon and steelhead fishing.

*Rates: $45-$70. Barbara Head.
3 R. 2 PB. Beds: KQ. Full breakfast. Tennis, golf, horseback riding, hiking, skiing. Air conditioning.
Seen in: *CBS TV, Grants Pass Courier, This Week.*
"Thank you for your incredible friendliness, warmth, and energy expended on our behalf! I've never felt so nestled in the lap of luxury - what a pleasure!"

HALFWAY F21/B7

Birch Leaf Farm
Route 1 Box 91
Halfway OR 97834
(503) 742-2990

Circa 1896. Nestled in the middle of a 42-acre farm, this inn boasts original woodwork and hardwood floors. Each guest room has a view of the Wallowa Mountains. A country-style breakfast is served complete with locally made jams and honey. Nearby activities include whitewater rafting, jet-boat trips and pack trips through local mountains. Plane rides in Hells Canyon National Recreation Area can be arranged.

*Rates: $50-60. Dave and Maryellen Olson.
5 R. 1 PB. Phone available. TV available. Beds: KQDT. Full breakfast. CCs: MC VISA. Horseback riding, skiing, gold mine tours.
Seen in: *Hells Canyon Journal.*
"I will always remember the warmth and quiet comfort of your place."

HOOD RIVER C9/A3

State Street Inn
1005 State St
Hood River OR 97031
(503) 386-1899

Circa 1932. This traditionally styled English house with gabled roof and leaded-glass windows overlooks the Columbia River and Mt. Adams. Each of the four guest rooms is decorated in a different style Colorado Old West, Massachusetts Colonial, California Sunshine and Southern Maryland. Guests may sample Oregon wines at nearby wineries, or take a scenic train ride through local orchards.

Location: Heart of the scenic Columbia River Gorge.
Rates: $50-$70. Mac Lee & Amy Goodbar.
4 R. Phone available. Beds: QD. Full breakfast. Conference room. CCs: MC VISA. Fishing, windsurfing, white water rafting, wineries, antiquing.
Seen in: *Northwest Best Places, Bicycling.*
"The quality B&B we hoped to find."

JACKSONVILLE 05/F2

Livingston Mansion
4132 Livingston Rd, PO Box 1476
Jacksonville OR 97530
(503) 899-7107

Circa 1915. This stately shingled manor was built for Charles Connor, an orchardist. The inn features spacious rooms, including a suite with a fireplace. The town of Jacksonville was founded in 1851, following the discovery of gold in Rich Gulch, and is now a National Historic Landmark.

Rates: $90-$100. Bob & Elaine Grathwol & Wallace Lossing.
3 R. 3 PB. 1 FP. Phone available. TV available. Beds: KQT. Full breakfast. Handicap access. CCs: MC VISA AE. White water rafting, downhill skiing, hiking, festivals.
Seen in: *San Francisco Focus.*
"We truly enjoyed our stay. What a treat!"

McCully House Inn
240 E California
Jacksonville OR 97530
(503) 899-1942

Circa 1860. This Classical Revival house is in the National Register, and many furnishings are original to the house, incuding a square grand piano and a black walnut Renaissance Revival bedroom set. Both were shipped around the Horn. Paintings throughout the inn are by Jon Cruson, a leading Oregon artist. A well-respected restaurant on the premises serves dinner outside on the garden patio in summer.

❀Rates: $65-$75. Season: March - Jan. Patricia Grody & Philip Accetia.
3 R. 3 PB. 1 FP. Phone available. Beds: KDTC. Full breakfast. Restaurant. CCs: MC VISA AE. Rafting, horseback riding, hiking. Honeymoon and wedding specials.
Seen in: *The Mail Tribune, Jackson County Business Review.*
"Great people and food!"

Reames House
540 E California St, PO Box 128
Jacksonville OR 97530
(503) 899-1868

Circa 1868. This white frame house, in the National Register of Historic Places, was built for Thomas Reames, Wells Fargo banker and town sheriff.

Perennial gardens bloom throughout the yard and climbing roses frame the front veranda. The plant filled, white wicker sitting room is brightened by hand stenciled pink roses. The Colonial Room features a canopy bed while The Victoria boasts a carved walnut bed and clawfoot tub. In spring and summer guests enjoy boarding the horse-drawn wagon that passes nearby and meanders through

Jacksonville. Bicycles, tennis rackets and gold panning equipment may be borrowed.
*Rates: $70-$90. George & Charlotte Harrington-Winsley.
4 R. 2 PB. Phone available. Beds: QDT. Full breakfast. River rafting, fishing, hiking, skiing, bicycling, shopping.
Seen in: *Oregonian.*
"Such a beautiful house and location."

JUNCTION CITY H5/C2

Black Bart Bed & Breakfast
94125 Love Lake Rd
Junction City OR 97448
(503) 998-1904
Circa 1880. Graceful maples and tall redwood trees dot the 13 acres that are home to Black Bart, a National Grand Champion mammoth donkey. The old farmhouse has been renovated with a sunroom overlooking gardens of tulips and rhododendrons. Ruffled curtains and Early American pieces highlight the country decor. Guests are sometimes invited to take a ride on an antique buggy pulled around the farm by Black Bart.
❀Rates: $45-$60. Irma & Don Mode.
2 R. 2 PB. Phone in room. TV available. Beds: KT. Full breakfast. CCs: MC VISA. Biking, jogging, golfing, boating, swimming, tennis.
Seen in: *Northwest Discoveries, Spring Home Improvement Guide.*
"Loved it!"

MEDFORD O6/E2

Reames House
See: Jacksonville

PORTLAND D6/B2

John Palmer House
4314 N Mississippi Ave, Ste AA
Portland OR 97217
(503) 284-5893 Ext. 400
Circa 1890. Located in a redevelopment area, this Queen Anne house features five gables, elaborate spool and spindle work, and roof cresting. It

was once the Multnomah Conservatory of Music, and the former owners, Oskar and Lotta Hoch, were founders of the Portland Symphony. Inside, a total of 37 splendid silk-screened and gold-leafed Victorian wallpapers adorn the walls and ceilings, often with five papers to a room. Polished woodwork and lavish antiques add to an opulence not easily forgotten.
Location: City Center.
*Rates: $30-$95. Mary & Richard Sauter.
7 R. 2 PB. Phone available. TV available. Beds: DT. Full breakfast. Restaurant. Gourmet meals. Spa. Handicap access. Conference room. CCs: MC VISA. Horse-drawn carriage tours. One hour to skiing, wine country, wind surfing, Pacific Ocean.
Seen in: *The Oregonian.*
"We stayed a whole week, a wonderful week! Can't believe breakfast could be so fantastic each day."

Mumford Manor
1130 SW King
Portland OR 97205
(503) 243-2443
Circa 1885. Flowering trees and mounds of azaleas frame this Queen Anne Tudor home in the National Register. Graceful bay windows and a porch gazebo take advantage of views of the historic neighborhood. Classic Victorian pieces are found throughout the inn. Guestrooms include a spacious suite with fireplace and twin fainting couches. Goosedown comforters and fresh flowers are additional touches. Portland's famous Rose Test Garden is a walk away.
Rates: $70-$125. Janis & Courtland Mumford.
5 R. 4 PB. 4 FP. Phone available. TV available. Beds: KQDT. Full breakfast. CCs: MC VISA AE. Windsurfing, skiing, shopping.
Seen in: *Northwest Palate, Pacific Northwest.*
"If the mothers of the world opened a B&B, this would be it!"

SALEM F5/B2

State House B&B
2146 State St
Salem OR 97301
(503) 588-1340
Circa 1920. This three-story house sits on the banks of Mill Creek where ducks and geese meander past a huge old red maple down to the water. (A baby was abandoned here because the house looked "just right" and "surely had nice people there." The 12-year-old boy who found the baby on the side porch grew up to become a supreme court judge and legal counsel to Governor Mark Hatfield.) The inn is close to everything in Salem.
Location: One mile from the I-5 Santiam turn-off.
Rates: $45-$65. Mike Winsett & Judy Uselman.
6 R. 5 PB. 1 FP. Phone in room. TV available. Beds: QD. B&B. Spa. CCs: MC VISA DS.
Seen in: *Statesman-Journal.*
"You do a wonderful job making people feel welcome and relaxed."

SEASIDE B3/A1

The Gilbert Inn, B&B
341 Beach Dr
Seaside OR 97138
(503) 738-9770
Circa 1892. This yellow Victorian with its turret and third-story garret is framed with a white picket fence and gardens of lilies, roses and tulips. There are down quilts, antiques, and fresh country fabrics in the guest rooms. A house specialty is stuffed French toast topped with apricot sauce. The ocean and the historic promenade, which stretches for a mile and a half along the sand, are a block away.
Rates: $65-$80. Carole & Dick Rees.
10 R. 10 PB. Phone available. TV in room. Beds: QT. Full breakfast. CCs: MC VISA DS. Bicycles, skates, surreys, kites, bumper cars, aquarium, beach.

THE DALLES D10/B4

Williams House Inn
608 W 6th St
The Dalles OR 97058
(503) 296-2889
Circa 1899. This handsome, green-and-white gingerbread Victorian possesses a veranda, gazebo and belvedere. Lush green lawns, trees and shrubs slope down to Mill Creek. The popular Harriet's Room overlooks Klickitat Hills and the Columbia River, and has a canopied four-poster bed, chaise lounge and period writing desk. Each summer the hosts harvest their 25-acre cherry orchard. They are active in the historic preservation of the area.
*Rates: $55-$75. Don & Barbara Williams.
3 R. 1 PB. Phone in room. TV in room. Beds: D. Full breakfast. CCs: MC VISA AE DC. Hiking, surfing, skiing, rafting, self-guided sight-seeing tours.
Seen in: *Oregonian, New York Times, Glamour Magazine.*
"A fantasy come true, including the most gracious, delightful company in conversation, Barb and Don Williams!"

PENNSYLVANIA

ADAMSTOWN ER10/*F10*

The Adamstown Inn B&B

62 W Main St, PO Box 938
Adamstown PA 19501
(215) 484-0800 (800) 594-4808

Circa 1830. With 2,500 antique dealers in the area, Adamstown has been called the antique capital of the world. Catering to antiquers, this

square brick house features an Oriental rug and an 1850s pump organ in the large parlor. Local folk art, some family heirlooms and Victorian wallpapers decorate the rooms along with handmade quilts and lace curtains. Before breakfast, coffee, tea or hot chocolate is brought to your room.

Rates: $50-$95. Tom & Wanda Berman.

4 R. 2 PB. 1 FP. Phone available. TV available. Beds: KQD. Continental-plus breakfast. Spa. Swimming pool. CCs: MC VISA. Shopping. Weddings, honeymoon special, Amish dinners arranged.

Seen in: *Lancaster Intelligencer, Reading Eagle.*

"Your warm hospitality and lovely home left us with such pleasant memories."

AIRVILLE EV8/*G9*

Spring House

Muddy Creek Forks
Airville PA 17302
(717) 927-6906

Circa 1798. Spring House, always the prominent home in this pre-Revolutionary War village, was constructed of massive stones over a spring that supplies water to most of the village. The walls are either whitewashed or retain their original stenciling. Furnished with country antiques, quilts, Oriental rugs, and paintings, the guest

rooms are cozy with featherbeds in winter. There is a library and grand piano.

*Rates: $60-$85. Ray Constance Hearne.

5 R. 3 PB. 4 FP. Phone available. Beds. Q. Full breakfast. Fishing, bicycling, horseback riding, scenic railroads, wineries, antiquing, exploring Amish country.

Seen in: *Woman's Day, Country Decorating, Innsider Magazine.*

"What a slice of history! Thank you for your hospitality. We couldn't have imagined a more picturesque setting."

BEAR CREEK EK11/*C10*

Bischwind

Box 7, One Coach Rd
Bear Creek PA 18602
(717) 472-3820

Circa 1881. This spacious Tudor estate was built on prime acreage above the waterfall in Bear Creek Village by lumber and ice baron Albert Lewis. Dr. & Mrs. A.H. Von Dran have spent many years restoring the mansion. Filled with antiques, some rooms boast furnishings original to the house. An elegant breakfast with silver, crystal and fine linens is served by a maid in French uniform. Horses are raised on the property.

Location: In a village in the Pocono mountains.

Rates: $150-$200. Barbara Von Dran.

3 R. 3 PB. 3 FP. Phone in room. TV in room. Beds: QD. Full breakfast. Swimming pool. Cross-country & downhill skiing, horse races, golf, white-water rafting, walking trails.

Seen in: *People's Press.*

"Beautiful home, scrumptuous breakfast."

BIRD-IN-HAND ET9/*F9*

Greystone Manor B&B

2658 Old Philadelphia Pike
Bird-in-hand PA 17505
(717) 393-4233 (800)430-1453

Circa 1860. This Victorian mansion and carriage house is in the heart of Pennsylvania Dutch country, amid two acres of natural beauty. The Greystone Manor recaptures another era with its stained-glass windows, cut crystal doors, antique bath fixtures, tiled fireplaces and moulded plaster ceilings. The guest rooms are decorated in country themes in the Carriage House and in Victorian finery in the mansion.

*Rates: $46-$84. Sally & Ed Davis.

13 R. 13 PB. Phone available. TV in room. Beds: KQDC. Continental breakfast. Conference room. CCs: MC VISA. Golf, tennis, hiking, biking.

Seen in: *Valley News Ledger.*

"Your blueberry muffins and humor were the perfect start every morning."

BLOOMSBURG EM7/*D9*

The Inn at Turkey Hill

991 Central Rd
Bloomsburg PA 17815
(717) 387-1500

Circa 1839. Turkey Hill is an elegant, white brick farmhouse. All the guest rooms are furnished with handcrafted reproductions from Habersham Plantation in Georgia, and all have views of the duck pond and the gazebo. In the dining room are hand-painted scenes of the rolling Pennsylvania countryside.

Location: Two miles north of Bloomsburg at Exit 35 on I-80.

*Rates: $68-$140. Babs & Andrew B. Pruden.

18 R. 18 PB. 2 FP. Phone in room. TV in room. Beds: KQC. B&B. Restaurant. Spa. Handicap access. Conference room. CCs: MC VISA AE DC CB DS. Golf, tennis, fishing, hunting.

Seen in: *The Baltimore Sun, Tempo Magazine, Philadelphia Inquirer.*

"How nice to find an enclave of good taste and class, a special place that seems to care about such old-fashioned virtues as quality and the little details that mean so much," Art Carey, *Philadelphia Inquirer.*

CANADENSIS EK14/C11

Brookview Manor B&B Inn

RR #1 Box 365
Canadensis PA 18325
(717) 595-2451

Circa 1911. By the side of the road, hanging from a tall evergreen, is the welcoming sign to this forest retreat.

There are brightly decorated common rooms and four fireplaces. The carriage house has three bedrooms and is suitable for small groups. The innkeepers like to share a "secret waterfall" within a 20-minute walk from the inn.

Location: On scenic route 447, Pocono Mountains.
Rates: $50-$90. David & Patty DeMaria.
8 R. 6 PB. Phone available. TV available. Beds: QTD. Full breakfast. CCs: MC VISA. Cross-country skiing, fishing, hiking, golf, tennis, antiquing. Fine dining nearby.
Seen in: *Mid-Atlantic Country.*
"Thanks for a great wedding weekend. Everything was perfect."

CHURCHTOWN ES10/F10

Churchtown Inn

2100 Main St
Churchtown PA 17555
(215) 445-7794

Circa 1735. This handsome, stone Federal house with its panoramic views was once known as the Edward Davies Mansion, but was also once a

tinsmith shop and rectory. It has heard the marching feet of Revolutionary troops and seen the Union Army during the Civil War. Tastefully furnished with antiques and collectables, the inn features canopy, pencil-post and sleigh beds. Breakfast is served in a lovely new glass garden room. There is music everywhere, as the innkeeper directed choruses appearing at Carnegie Hall and the Lincoln Center. By prior arrangement, guests may dine in an Amish home.

Location: Five miles from Pennsylvania Turnpike.
Rates: $49-$95. Hermine & Stuart Smith, Jim Kent.
8 R. 6 PB. Phone available. TV in room. Beds: QT. Full breakfast. Conference room. CCs: MC VISA. Swimming, hiking, bicycling. Amish meals arranged.
Seen in: *Bon Appetit, The Boston Globe, Intelligencer Journal, Innsider, Chicago Star.*
"Magnificent atmosphere. Outstanding breakfasts. Our favorite B&B."

The Foreman House B&B

2129 Main St, Rt 23
Churchtown PA 17555
(215) 445-6713

Circa 1919. A prominent local farmer, Peter Foreman, built this house and then forbade all seven of his children

to marry or they would lose their inheritance. Six obeyed. Surrounded by Amish farmlands, the inn provides views of horsedrawn carriages. A selection of the most sought after quilts in the country may be purchased in the parlors of farm ladies nearby.

Location: Lancaster County on Route 23.
Rates: $55. Jacqueline & Stephen Mitrani.
2 R. Phone available. Beds: DT. Full breakfast. Golf, boating.
Seen in: *Lancaster Daily Newspaper.*
"We couldn't have been happier staying anywhere else! You have a lovely home."

The Inn at Twin Linden

2092 Main St
Churchtown PA 17555
(215) 445-7619

Circa 1840. Named for two 100-foot-tall linden trees planted in front of it, this beautiful Greek Revival-style home stands across from a church where George Washington once worshipped. Four rooms feature canopy beds, and the Cottage Room houses an antique claw-foot tub. Elaborate breakfasts include local country sausage and freshly ground coffee, and special gourmet meals are available, prepared by Innkeeper Donna Leahy. Parlors, wicker-filled porches and beautifully landscaped grounds add extra ambience to the inn, which features afternoon tea and evening turn-down service.

Rates: $70-$90. Donna & Bob Leahy.
6 R. 6 PB. 1 FP. Phone available. TV available. Beds: QDT. Full breakfast. Restaurant. Gourmet meals. Spa. Conference room. CCs: MC VISA AE. Cross-country skiing, biking, buggy rides.
Seen in: *Lancaster News, Reading Eagle, Country Folk Art.*
"Your inn exceeds all others."

CLARK WK2/C1

Tara

Box 475, 3665 Valley View
Clark PA 16113
(412) 962-3535

Circa 1854. After many years of abandonment, this Greek Revival mansion was renovated. Innkeepers Donna and

Jim Winner patterned every detail to match Scarlett O'Hara's country manor. Rooms feature names such as Rhett Butler and Miss Melanie. All guest quarters boast fireplaces and sitting rooms. Many include extravagances such as sunken tubs, canopy beds or an antique sleigh bed. Guests may enjoy lunch at Stonewall's, an 1850s-style tavern complete with bar maids, stone walls and beam ceilings, or they may feast on a seven-course gourmet meal at Ashley's.

Rates: $75-$198. Donna and Jim Winner.
27 R. 27 PB. 27 FP. Phone in room. TV in room. Beds: KQDT. MAP. Restaurant. Gourmet meals. Sauna. Exercise room. Swimming pool. Conference room. FAX. CCs: MC VISA DS.

COLUMBIA ET7/F9

The Columbian

360 Chestnut St
Columbia PA 17512
(717) 684-5869 (800) 422-5869

Circa 1898. This stately three-story mansion is a fine example of Colonial Revival architecture. Antique beds, a stained-glass window and home-baked breads are among its charms. Guests may relax on the wraparound sun porches.

Rates: $55-$70. Linda & John Straitiff.
5 R. 5 PB. Phone available. TV in room. Beds: QT. Full breakfast. CCs: MC VISA. Shopping.
Seen in: *Philadelphia Inquirer, Lancaster Intelligencer Journal, Columbia News.*
"In a word, extraordinary!"

DOYLESTOWN ER15/F11

The Inn at Fordhook Farm

105 New Britain Rd
Doylestown PA 18901
(215) 345-1766

Circa 1760. Three generations of Burpees (Burpee Seed Company) have dispensed hospitality on this 60-acre farm. Guest rooms are in the family's

18th-century fieldstone house and Victorian carriage house. The inn is filled with family heirlooms and guests can sit at the famous horticulturist's desk in the secluded study where Mr. Burpee wrote his first seed catalogs.

Location: Bucks County.
Rates: $94-$175. Elizabeth Romanella & Blanche Burpee Dohan.
7 R. 4 PB. 2 FP. Phone available. TV available. Beds: KQD. B&B. Conference room. CCs: MC VISA AE. Cross-country skiing, hiking.
Seen in: *Bon Appetit, Mid-Atlantic Country, Gourmet.*

"The inn is absolutely exquisite. If I had only one night to spend in Bucks County, I'd do it all over again at Fordhook Farms!"

EAST BERLIN EU5/G8

The Bechtel Mansion Inn

400 W King St
East Berlin PA 17316
(717) 259-7760

Circa 1897. The town of East Berlin, near Lancaster and Gettysburg, was settled by Pennsylvania Germans prior to the American Revolution.

William Leas, a wealthy banker, built this many-gabled romantic Queen Anne mansion, now listed in the National Register. The inn is furnished with an abundance of museum quality antiques and collections. Mennonite quilts top many of the handsome bedsteads.

*Rates: $75-$130. Ruth Spangler.
8 R. 8 PB. Phone available. TV available. Beds: QTD. Continental-plus breakfast. Conference room. CCs: MC VISA AE DS. Skiing.
Seen in: *The Washington Post.*

"Ruth was a most gracious hostess and took time to describe the history of your handsome museum-quality antiques and the special architectural details."

ELIZABETHVILLE EP5/F9

The Inn at Elizabethville

30 W Main St
Elizabethville PA 17023
(717) 362-3476

Circa 1865. This comfortable, two-story house was owned by a Civil War veteran and founder of a local wagon company. The innkeepers decided to buy and fix up the house to help support their other business, renovating old houses. The conference room features an unusual fireplace with cabinets and painted decorations. Rooms are filled with antiques and Mission oak-style furniture. County auctions, local craft fairs and outdoor activities entice guests. Comfortable living rooms, porches and a sun parlor are available for relaxation.

*Rates: $60. Beth & Jim Facinelli.
5 R. 5 PB. 1 FP. Phone available. TV available. Beds: DT. Continental breakfast. Conference room. FAX. CCs: MC VISA. Hiking, hunting, fishing, canoeing, golf.
Seen in: *Harrisburg Patriot-News, Upper Dauphin Sentinel.*

EPHRATA ES9/F9

Covered Bridge Inn

990 Rettew Mill Rd
Ephrata PA 17522
(717) 733-1592

Circa 1814. This Federal-style limestone farm house features original hand-carved woodwork, rare Indian doors, corner cupboard floorboards, and old glass panes. Three herb gardens and views of the covered bridge, old mill, and barn all add to the rustic setting guests enjoy from the summer porch.

Rates: $55-$58. Betty Lee Maxcy.
4 R. Phone available. TV available. Beds: QD. Full breakfast. Badminton, croquet.
Seen in: *Los Angeles Times, The Post.*

"We've been to quite a few B&Bs and by far yours out ranks them all. You both are as special as the inn is. We loved the place so much we're not sure we want to share it with anyone else!"

Gerhart House B&B

287 Duke St
Ephrata PA 17522
(717) 733-0263

Circa 1926. Originally built as a combination home, office and detached butcher shop, the house is unique in its use of hardwoods for inlaid floor designs and its chestnut trim work. Sunny, stenciled guest rooms include one with a queen-size canopy bed covered with a Mennonite quilt. Ephrata Cloister is seven blocks away.

Rates: $50-$75. Richard & Judith Lawson.
5 R. 3 PB. Phone available. Beds: QDTC. Full breakfast. CCs: MC VISA. Fishing, community pool.

"We are still taking about all our fun as your guests."

The King's Cottage

See: Lancaster, PA

Smithton Inn

900 W Main St
Ephrata PA 17522
(717) 733-6094

Circa 1763. Henry Miller opened this inn and tavern on a hill overlooking the Ephrata Cloister, a religious society he belonged to, known as

Seventh Day Baptists. Several of their medieval-style German buildings are now a museum. This is a warm and welcoming inn with canopy beds or four posters, candlelight, fireplaces and nightshirts provided for each guest. If you're not allergic, ask for a lavish feather bed to be put in your room.

Location: Lancaster County.
Rates: $55-$105. Dorothy Graybill.
8 R. 8 PB. 7 FP. Phone available. Beds: KQDTC. AP. Spa. Handicap access. CCs: MC VISA AE. Touring Amish farms, historic sites, crafts, antiques.
Seen in: *New York Magazine, Country Living, Early American Life.*

"After visiting over 50 inns in four countries Smithton has to be one of the most romantic picturesque inns in America. I have never seen its equal!"

ERWINNA EP15/E12

Evermay-on-the-Delaware

River Rd
Erwinna PA 18920
(215) 294-9100

Circa 1740. Twenty-five acres of Bucks County at its best — rolling green meadows, lawns, stately maples and the silvery Delaware River, surround this three-story manor. Serving as an inn since 1871, it has hosted such guests as the Barrymore family. Rich walnut wainscotting, a grandfather clock and twin fireplaces warm the parlor, scented by vases of roses or gladiolus. Antique-filled guest rooms overlook the river or gardens.

*Rates: $70-$125. Ron Strouse & Fred Cresson.
16 R. 16 PB. Phone in room. Beds: KQD. Continental-plus breakfast. Gourmet meals. Handicap access. Conference room. FAX. CCs: MC VISA. Rafting, canoeing, sailing, horseback riding, ballooning, hiking, cross-country skiing.
Seen in: *New York Times, Philadelphia Magazine, Travel and Leisure, Food and Wine.*
"It was pure perfection. Everything from the flowers to the wonderful food."

Golden Pheasant Inn

River Rd
Erwinna PA 18920
(215) 294-9595

Circa 1857. Originally built to serve the mule barge workers and travelers, the Golden Pheasant is located be-

tween the Pennsylvania Canal and the Delaware River. Features of the inn include fieldstone walls, exposed beams, and hardwood floors. There is a greenhouse dining room with views of the historic canal, lit in the evenings with spotlights. The cuisine here is highly rated.

Location: Bucks County.
Rates: $95-$125. Barbara & Michel Faure.
6 R. 1 PB. Phone available. Beds: QT. Restaurant. Conference room. CCs: MC VISA. Horseback riding, hiking, swimming, bicycling, cross-country skiing, canoeing.
Seen in: *The Philadelphia Inquirer.*
"A more stunningly romantic spot is hard to imagine. A taste of France on the banks of the Delaware."

EVERETT WT13/G5

Newry Manor

Rt 1 Box 475
Everett PA 15537
(814) 623-1250

Circa 1805. Newry Manor and the adjacent stone woolen mill are both listed in the National Register. Four generations of the Lutz family lived in and expanded the house into its current blend of stone, brick and log. The inn is filled with family heirlooms and antiques. A beautiful Prussian blue fireplace mantel is in the keeping room. On quiet days, guests can hear the trickle of the Raystown Branch of the Juniata River flowing past the old mill.

Location: Lutzville Road, 1 mile south of U.S. Route 30, near Everett.
Rates: $30-$60. Season: April - Nov. Rosie & Carl Mulert.
3 R. 3 PB. 2 FP. Phone available. TV available. Beds: QT. Continental-plus breakfast. Canoeing.
Seen in: *Bedford Gazette, Bedford County Shoppers Guide.*
"You are wonderful people. We will always remember this as our honeymoon home!"

GARDNERS ET3/G7

Goose Chase

200 Blueberry Rd
Gardners PA 17324
(717) 528-8877

Circa 1762. Originally a settler's log cabin, Goose Chase was enlarged in 1810 and 1988 with stone additions. Troops en route to the Gettysburg Bat-

tlefield once passed by. Comfortable interiors include original wide board floors, stenciled walls and 18th-century antiques. Located on 25 secluded acres, this home is one of the oldest in the Gettysburg area and offers a peaceful respite from the 20th century.

Location: Twelve miles north of Gettysburg.
Rates: $59-$89. Marsha & Rich Lucidi.
5 R. 3 PB. 5 FP. TV available. Beds: KQDT. Full breakfast. Gourmet meals. Swimming pool. CCs: MC VISA. Cross-country & downhill skiing, bicycling, fishing, golf, horseback riding. Walking trails. Afternoon refreshments.
Seen in: *The Gettysburg Times.*
"Everything was perfect. We were amazed at your fine decor."

GETTYSBURG EU3/G7

Bluebird On The Mountain

See: Cascase, MD

The Brafferton Inn

44 York St
Gettysburg PA 17325
(717) 337-3423

Circa 1786. The earliest deeded house in Gettysburg, the inn was designed by James Gettys, and is listed in the National Register of Historic Places.

The walls of this huge brownstone range from 18 inches to two-and-one-half-feet thick. There are skylights in all the guest rooms and a primitive mural of famous scenes in the area painted on the four dining room walls.

Location: Ninety miles north of Washington, D.C.
*❀Rates: $60-$80. Mimi & Jim Agard.
10 R. 6 PB. Phone available. Beds: DT. EP. Handicap access. CCs: MC VISA. Horseback riding, skiing, hiking, biking, swimming, golf.
Seen in: *Early American Life, Country Living.*
"Your house is so beautiful - every corner of it - and your friendliness is icing on the cake. It was fabulous!"

The Doubleday Inn

104 Doubleday Ave
Gettysburg PA 17325
(717) 334-9119

Circa 1929. Located directly on the Gettysburg Battlefield and bordered by original stone breastworks, this restored colonial home is furnished

with Victorian sofas and period antiques. Available to guests is one of the largest known Civil War libraries with over 500 volumes devoted exclusively to the Battle of Gettysburg. On selected evenings, guests can par-

ticipate in discussions with a Civil War historian who brings the battle alive with accurate accounts and authentic memorabilia and weaponry.
Location: On the Gettysburg Battlefield.
*❀Rates: $65-$100. Joan & Sal Chandon with Olga Krossick.
9 R. 5 PB. Phone available. Beds: DT. B&B. CCs: MC VISA. Horseback riding, skiing, golfing, battlefield touring. Afternoon tea, hor d'oeuvres.
Seen in: *Innsider Magazine, New York Magazine.*
"What you're doing for students of Gettysburg & the Civil War in general is tremendous! Our stay was wonderful!!"

Keystone Inn B&B
231 Hanover St
Gettysburg PA 17325
(717) 337-3888
Circa 1913. Furniture-maker Clayton Reaser constructed this three-story brick Victorian with a wide-columned porch hugging the north and west

sides. Cut stone graces every door and windowsill, each with a keystone. A chestnut staircase ascends the full three stories, and the interior is decorated with comfortable furnishings, ruffles and lace.
Location: Route 116 East of Gettysburg.
❀Rates: $60-$70. Wilmer & Doris Martin.
4 R. 2 PB. Beds: KQDT. Full breakfast. CCs: MC VISA. Tennis, bicycling.
Seen in: *Gettysburg Times, Hanover Sun.*
"We slept like lambs. This home has a warmth that is soothing."

The Old Appleford Inn
218 Carlisle St
Gettysburg PA 17325
(717) 337-1711
Circa 1867. Located in the historic district, this Federal-style brick mansion offers a taste of 19th-century charm and comfort. Among its inviting features are a plant-filled sunroom and a parlor with a baby grand piano.
Rates: $78-$98. Maribeth & Frank Skradski.
12 R. 12 PB. 2 FP. Phone available. Beds: QD. Full breakfast. Conference room. CCs: MC VISA AE. Golf, horseback on battlefield, skiing, antiquing.
Seen in: *The Gettysburg Times.*
"Everything in your place invites us back."

GORDONVILLE ET10/G9

The Osceola Mill House
313 Osceola Mill Rd
Gordonville PA 17529
(717) 768-3758
Circa 1766. This handsome limestone mill house rests on the banks of Pequea Creek in a quaint historic setting adjacent to a 1757 mill and a miller's

cottage. There are deep-set windows and wide-pine floors. Working fireplaces in the keeping room and in the bedrooms add to the warmth and charm. Amish neighbors farm the picturesque fields adjoining the inn and their horse and buggies clip-clop past the mill house often.
Location: Lancaster County, 15 miles east of Lancaster.
Rates: $85. Sterling & Robin Schoen.
3 R. 2 FP. Phone available. TV available. Beds: Q. Full breakfast. Gourmet meals. Amish tours, biking, museums.
Seen in: *The Journal, Country Living, Washington Times.*
"We had a thoroughly delightful stay at your inn. Probably the most comfortable overnight stay we've ever had."

HALIFAX EQ5/E8

The Inn at Elizabethville
See: Elizabethville, PA

HANOVER EV5/G8

Beechmont Inn
315 Broadway
Hanover PA 17331
(717) 632-3013
Circa 1834. This gracious Georgian inn was a witness to the Civil War's first major battle on free soil, the Battle of Hanover. Decorated in Federal period antiques, several guest rooms are named for the battle's commanders. The romantic Diller Suite contains a marble fireplace and queen canopy bed. The inn is noted for elegant breakfasts, often served by candlelight.
❀Rates: $70-$95. Terry & Monna Hormel.
7 R. 7 PB. 1 FP. Phone available. TV available. Beds: QD. Full breakfast. CCs: MC

VISA. Boating, horseback riding, wineries, swimming. Gettysburg National Park, Amish farmland and great antiquing nearby. Dutch Days, Gettysburg National Park.
Seen in: *The Evening Sun, York Daily Record.*
"I had a marvelous time at your charming, lovely inn."

HAWLEY EI14/C11

Academy Street B&B
528 Academy St
Hawley PA 18428
(717) 226-3430 (201) 316-8148
Circa 1863. This restored Civil War Victorian home boasts a mahogany front door with the original glass paneling, two large fireplaces, one in mosaic, the other in fine polished marble, and a living room with oak sideboard, polished marble mantle and yellow pine floor. The airy guest rooms have canopied brass beds. Guests are welcome to afternoon tea, which includes an array of cakes and pastries.
Rates: $75. Season: May to October. Judith & Sheldon Lazan.
7 R. 4 PB. TV in room. Beds: QDT. Full breakfast. CCs: MC VISA. Hiking, rafting, swimming, boating, horseback riding, golf, blueberry picking, picnicking.
Seen in: *The Wayne Independent, Citizens' Voice.*
"Truly wonderful everything!"

Settlers Inn
4 Main Ave
Hawley PA 18428
(717) 226-2993 (800) 833-8527
Circa 1927. When the Wallenpaupack Creek was dammed up to form the lake, the community hired architect Louis Welch and built this Grand

Tudor Revival-style hotel featuring chestnut beams, leaded-glass windows and an enormous stone fireplace. The dining room, the main focus of the inn, is decorated with hand-made quilts, hanging plants and chairs that once graced a Philadelphia cathedral. If you're looking for trout you can try your luck fishing the Lackawaxen River which runs behind the inn.

Rates: $60-$80. Jeanne & Grant Genzlinger.

18 R. 18 PB. Phone available. TV available. Beds: D. Full breakfast. Restaurant. Gourmet meals. Conference room. CCs: MC VISA AE. Swimming, boating, hiking, tennis, museums, fishing. Air conditioning in all rooms.

Seen in: *Travel Holiday Magazine, New Jersey Monthly.*

"Country cozy with food and service fit for royalty."

HOLICONG EQ16/*F12*

Ash Mill Farm

PO Box 202
Holicong PA 18928
(215) 794-5373

Circa 1790. This estate includes a Federal addition completed in 1830. The finish on the house is 18th-century plaster over stone. The original

section has a five-foot walk-in fireplace with a beehive oven and original cooking crane. Breakfast is served here, and afternoon tea is also available. Grazing sheep dot the farm pastures.

Location: Four miles south of New Hope on Route 202.

*Rates: $75-$125. Patricia & Jim Auslander.

6 R. 4 PB. 2 FP. Phone available. Beds: Q. EP. CCs: MC VISA. Horseback riding, canoeing, biking, hiking, golf, tennis.

"The home's appointments are lovely and the quaint characteristics of the house itself a pleasure to look at."

INTERCOURSE ET9/*F10*

The King's Cottage

See: Lancaster, PA

JIM THORPE EN11/*D10*

Harry Packer Mansion

Packer Hill
Jim Thorpe PA 18229
(717) 325-8566

Circa 1874. This extravagant Second Empire mansion was constructed of New England sandstone, and local brick and stone trimmed in cast iron.

Past ornately carved columns on the front veranda, guests enter 400-pound, solid walnut doors. The opulent interior includes marble mantels, hand-painted ceilings, and elegant antiques.

Location: Six miles south of Exit 34.

*Rates: $75-$110. Robert & Patricia Handwerk.

13 R. 8 PB. Phone available. Beds: QD. Full breakfast. Conference room. CCs: MC VISA. Horseback riding, downhill & cross-country skiing, swimming, white water rafting, fishing. Murder mystery weekends.

Seen in: *Philadelphia Inquirer, New York Magazine, Victorian Homes.*

"The best B&B we have ever stayed at! We'll be back."

KANE WH11/*B4*

Kane Manor Country Inn

230 Clay St
Kane PA 16735
(814) 837-6522

Circa 1896. This Georgian Revival inn, on 250 acres of woods and trails, was built for Dr. Elizabeth Kane, the first

female doctor to practice in the area. Many of the family's possessions dating back to the American Revolution and the Civil War remain. (Ask to see the attic.) Decor is a mixture of old family items in an unpretentious country style. There is a pub, popular with locals, on the premises.

Rates: $69-$89. Laurie Anne.

10 R. 6 PB. Phone available. Beds: DT. Full breakfast. CCs: MC VISA AE. Cross-country skiing, fishing, hunting, swimming, bicycling, golf, tennis. Afternoon tea and famous peanut butter cream pie.

Seen in: *The Pittsburg Press, News Herald.*

"It's a place I want to return to often for rest and relaxation."

KENNETT SQUARE EU12/*G10*

Meadow Spring Farm

201 E St Rd
Kennett Square PA 19348
(215) 444-3903

Circa 1836. This working, 245-acre dairy farm has more than 300 holsteins grazing in pastures beside the old red barn. The two-story,

white-brick house is decorated with old family pieces and collections of whimsical animals and antique wedding gowns. A Victorian doll collection fills one room. Breakfast is hearty country style. Afterwards, guests may see the milking operation, gather eggs or pick vegetables from the garden.

Location: Forty-five minutes from Philadelphia, 2 hours from New York.

*Rates: $45-$75. Anne Hicks.

6 R. 3 PB. 1 FP. Phone available. TV in room. Beds: QT. Full breakfast. Gourmet meals. Spa. Swimming pool. Game room. Hiking and fishing on premises.

Seen in: *Weekend GetAways, The Washington Post.*

LAHASKA EQ15/*F12*

Golden Plough Inn

Rt 202, Box 218
Lahaska PA 18931
(215) 794-4004 (215) 794-4003

Circa 1750. This Early American inn features French Colonial influences including a mansard roof. It is located in Peddler's Village, a reproduction 18th-century colonial village. Nearby are high-quality specialty shops, the Pearl Buck house, Bucks County Playhouse and Dinner Theater. The inn is five miles from New Hope and the Delaware River.

Location: Peddler's Village, Route 202.

*Rates: $85-$200. Earl Jamison.
45 R. 45 PB. 14 FP. Phone in room. TV in room. Beds: KQTC. Continental breakfast. Restaurant. Gourmet meals. Spa. Handicap access. Conference room. FAX. CCs: MC VISA AE DC CB. Horseback riding, hot air balloon, boating, tubing.
Seen in: *The Washington Post, New York Times, Bon Appetit, Mid-Atlantic Country.*
"We were very pleased with everything. It was great being within walking distance of the shops and restaurants."

LAMPETER ET9/G9

Walkabout Inn B&B
837 Village Rd
Lampeter PA 17537
(717) 464-0707
Circa 1925. The Walkabout Inn offers hospitality Australian-style thanks to Australian Richard Mason, one of the

innkeepers. Tea is imported from down under and breakfasts are prepared from Australian recipes. From the wrap-around porch, guests can watch Amish buggies pass by. Bed chambers have antique furniture, Pennsylvania Dutch quilts and hand-painted wall stencilings. Each room is named from the image stenciled on its walls.
*❀Rates: $55. Richard & Margaret Mason.
5 R. 3 PB. Phone in room. TV in room. Beds: DTC. Full breakfast. Gourmet meals. Game room. Conference room. CCs: MC VISA AE. Horseback riding, golf, tennis, swimming pool.
Seen in: *The New York Post, Intelligencer Journal.*
"You anticipated our every need and that is not done in too many places."

LANCASTER ET8/F9

The Adamstown Inn B&B
See: Adamstown, PA

Cameron Estate Inn
See: Mount Joy, PA

Foreman House B&B
See: Churchtown, PA

Greystone Manor B&B
See: Bird-in-hand, PA

The King's Cottage
1049 E King St
Lancaster PA 17602
(717) 397-1017 (800) 747-8717
Circa 1913. This Mission Revival house features a red-tile roof and stucco walls, common in many stately turn-of-the century houses in Califor-

nia and New Mexico. Its elegant interiors include a sweeping staircase, a library with marble fireplace, stained-glass windows, and a solarium. The inn is appointed with Oriental rugs and antiques and fine 18th-century English reproductions. The formal dining room provides the location for gourmet morning meals.
*❀Rates: $75-$105. Karen & Jim Owens.
7 R. 7 PB. Phone available. TV available. Beds: KQ. Full breakfast. Game room. Conference room. CCs: MC VISA. Biking, hiking, tennis, swimming, golf. Amish tours, dinner with Amish family, afternoon tea, cordials.
Seen in: *Country, USA Weekend, Bon Appetit, Intelligencer Journal, The Times.*
"I appreciate your attention to all our needs and look forward to recommending your inn to friends."

The Osceola Mill House
See: Gordonville, PA

The Inn at Twin Linden
See: Churchtown, PA

Walkabout Inn
See: Lampeter, PA

Witmer's Tavern - Historic 1725 Inn
2014 Old Philadelphia Pike
Lancaster PA 17602
(717) 299-5305
Circa 1725. This pre-Revolutionary War inn opened 265 years ago, and is the sole survivor of 62 inns that once lined the old Lancaster-to-Philadel-

phia turnpike. Conestoga wagon trains were loaded here for western and southern journeys. Designated a National Landmark property, a painstaking restoration is in progress. Therefore, this inn is not for those who want absolute perfection. There are sagging wide board floors and antiques with original finish. On the other hand, history buffs will enjoy seeing signs of a secret tunnel and knowning President John Adams once stayed here. Guest rooms feature antiques, old quilts, and freshly-cut flowers.
Location: One mile east of Lancaster on Route 340.
*Rates: $55-$75. Brant Hartung & his sister Pamela Hartung.
5 R. Beds: D. Continental breakfast. Canoeing, hiking, biking, flying, antiquing.
Seen in: *Stuart News.*
"Your personal attention and enthusiastic knowledge of the area and Witmer's history made it come alive and gave us the good feelings we came looking for."

LITITZ E8/F0

The Alden House
62 E Main St
Lititz PA 17543
(717) 627-3363
Circa 1850. For over 200 years, breezes have carried the sound of church bells to the stately brick homes lining Main Street. The Alden House is a town house in the center of this historic district, and within walking distance of the Pretzel House (first in the country) and the chocolate factory. A favorite room choice is the suite with a sleeping loft, appealing to families traveling with youngsters. A breakfast buffet is served, often carried to one of the inn's three porches.
Rates: $65-$95. Gloria Adams.
7 R. 5 PB. Phone available. TV available. Beds: QDT. Continental-plus breakfast. CCs: MC VISA.
Seen in: *Early American Life, Travel.*
"Truly represents what bed & breakfast hospitality is all about."

LUMBERVILLE EQ15/E12

Black Bass Hotel

River Rd
Lumberville PA 18933
(215) 297-5770

Circa 1745. The Black Bass Hotel is located on the River Road north of New Hope. In its early days, the innkeepers were of Tory persuasion and attracted a Loyalist clientele. Today, the hotel is noted for its excellent cuisine. Electrified oil and tin lamps and railroader's lanterns are displayed, along with a collection of British Royal Family memorabilia. Guest rooms are furnished with 18th and 19th-century antiques. Some rooms have private balconies overlooking the Delaware River.

Rates: $55-$175. Herbert E. Ward.
10 R. 3 PB. Beds: DT. Continental breakfast. Restaurant. Conference room. CCs: MC VISA AE DC CB. Horseback riding, water sports, river swimming.
Seen in: *The New York Times, Country Living Magazine.*
"...like the European country hotel."

LYKENS EP6/E8

The Inn at Elizabethville

See: Elizabethville, PA

MANHEIM ES8/F9

Herr Farmhouse Inn

2256 Huber Dr
Manheim PA 17545
(717) 653-9852

Circa 1738. One of the earliest structures built in Lancaster County, this fully restored stone farmhouse sits on

26 acres of scenic farmland. All woodwork, including moldings, doors, cabinets and pine flooring is original. Lancaster quilts enhance the inn's colonial decor. Six working fireplaces add warmth in the winter while air conditioning cools in summer.

Location: Nine miles west of Lancaster off Route 283 (Mt. Joy 230 exit).
Rates: $65-$85. Barry Herr.
4 R. 2 PB. 2 FP. Phone available. TV available. Beds: DT. Continental-plus breakfast. CCs: MC VISA.
"Your home is lovely — a beautiful job of restoring and remodeling."

MERCER WK3/C2

The Magoffin Inn

129 S Pitt St
Mercer PA 16137
(412) 662-4611

Circa 1884. Dr. Magoffin built this house for his Pittsburgh bride, Henrietta Bouvard. The Queen Anne style is characterized by patterned brick

masonry, gable detailing, bay windows and a wraparound porch. The technique of marbelizing was used on six of the nine fireplaces. Magoffin Muffins are featured each morning. Lunch is available Monday through Saturday, and dinner, Tuesday through Saturday.

Location: Near I-79 and I-80.
Rates: $50-$90. Jacque McClelland, Gene Slagle.
9 R. 7 PB. Beds: QDC. Full breakfast. Conference room. CCs: MC VISA. Swimming, golf, tennis, fishing.
Seen in: *Western Reserve Magazine, Youngstown Vindicator.*
"While in Arizona we met a family from Africa who had stopped at the Magoffin House. After crossing the United States they said the Magoffin House was quite the nicest place they had stayed."

MERCERSBURG WU16/G6

The Mercersburg Inn

405 S Main St
Mercersburg PA 17236
(717) 328-5231

Circa 1910. Situated on a hill overlooking the Blue Ridge Mountains, the valley and village, this 20,000 square-

foot Georgian Revival mansion was built for industrialist Harry Byron. Six massive columns mark the entrance, which opens to a majestic hall featuring chestnut wainscoting and an elegant double stairway and rare scagliola (marbelized) columns. All the rooms are furnished with antiques and reproductions. A local craftsman built the inn's four-poster, canopied king-size beds. Many of the rooms have their own balconies and a few have fireplaces. The inn's chef is noted for his elegant six-course dinners, but the menu also includes a'la carte choices.

Rates: $70-$155. Fran Wolfe.
15 R. 15 PB. 6 FP. Phone in room. TV available. Beds: KQDT. Continental breakfast. Restaurant. Gourmet meals. Game room. Conference room. CCs: MC VISA AE. Horseback riding nearby, rafting, boating, tennis, skiing.
Seen in: *Mid-Atlantic Country, Washington Post, The Herald-Mail, Richmond News Leader, Washingtonian, Philadelphia Inquirer.*
"Elegance personified! Outstanding ambience and warm hospitality."

MERTZTOWN EP12/E10

Longswamp B&B

RD 2 PO Box 26
Mertztown PA 19539
(215) 682-6197

Circa 1789. Country gentleman Colonel Trexler added a mansard roof to this stately Federal mansion in 1860. Inside is a magnificent walnut staircase and pegged wood floors. As the story goes, the colonel discovered his unmarried daughter having an affair and shot her lover. He escaped hanging, but it was said that after his death his ghost could be seen in the upstairs bedroom watching the road. In 1905, an exorcism was reported to have sent his spirit to a nearby mountaintop.

Rates: $60-$65. Elsa Dimick.
9 R. 5 PB. 2 FP. Phone available. TV available. Beds: QC. B&B. Gourmet meals. CCs: MC VISA. Horseback riding, biking, boccie, horseshoes.
Seen in: *Washingtonian, Weekend Travel, The Sun.*
"The warm country atmosphere turns strangers into friends."

MILLERSBURG EP5/E8

The Inn at Elizabethville

See: Elizabethville, PA

MONTOURSVILLE EK5/C8

The Carriage House at Stonegate

RD 1 Box 11A
Montoursville PA 17754
(717) 433-4340

Circa 1830. President Herbert Hoover was a descendant of the original settlers of this old homestead in the

Loyalsock Creek Valley. Indians burned the original house, but the present farmhouse and numerous outbuildings date from the early 1800s. The Carriage House is set next to a lovely brook.

Location: Six miles off I-180, north of Montoursville.

Rates: $45-$70. Harold & Dena Mesaris.

4 R. 2 PB. TV available. Beds: QTC. Continental-plus breakfast. Conference room. Hiking, golf, cross-country skiing, canoeing.

"A very fine B&B - the best that can be found. Gracious hosts."

MONTROSE EG10/*B10*

The Montrose House

26 S Main St
Montrose PA 18801
(717) 278-1124

Circa 1806. Located above a tavern and banquet room, the inn features hardwood floors and antiques creating a homey, old-fashioned atmosphere. Innkeeper Rick Rose, a graduate from the Culinary Institute of America, prepares scrumptious country-style breakfasts and candle-lit dinners. An observatory and planetarium are nearby, and guests will find local auctions, antique shopping and an annual blueberry festival enjoyable.

Rates: $35-$60. Rick & Candace Rose.

12 R. 8 PB. Phone in room. TV available. Full breakfast. Restaurant. CCs: MC VISA AE DC DS. Golf, swimming, hiking, cross-country & downhill skiing, museums.

Seen in: *The Susquehanna County Independent, Profiles of the Twin Tiers.*

MOUNT JOY ES7/*F9*

Cameron Estate Inn

RD 1 Box 305
Mount Joy PA 17552
(717) 653-1773

Circa 1805. Simon Cameron, Abraham Lincoln's first Secretary of War, entertained his guests in this Federal-period estate situated on 15 acres of towering oaks with an old stone bridge and two trout streams. There are Oriental rugs, antiques, and working fireplaces. Groff's Farm Restaurant is near the inn.

*Rates: $60-$105. Janice Rote, innkeeper, Abe & Betty Groff, owners.

18 R. 16 PB. 7 FP. Phone available. TV available. Beds: KQDT. Continental breakfast. Restaurant. Conference room. FAX. CCs: MC VISA AE DC. Tennis, swimming, cross-country skiing, golf, hiking, biking, sky diving, ballooning, yard games.

Seen in: *Chicago Sun-Times, San Francisco Examiner, Mid-Atlantic Country.*

"Betty runs from pillar to post, filled with joy!" Stephanie Edwards, Los Angeles talk show host.

Cedar Hill Farm

305 Longenecker Rd
Mount Joy PA 17552
(717) 653-4655

Circa 1817. Situated on 51 acres overlooking Chiques Creek, this stone farmhouse boasts a two-tiered front veranda affording pastoral views of

the surrounding fields. The host was born in the house and is the third generation to have lived here since the Swarr family first purchased it in 1878. Family heirlooms and antiques include an elaborately carved walnut bedstead, a marble-topped washstand and a "tumbling block" quilt. In the kitchen a copper kettle, bread paddle and baskets of dried herbs accentuate the walk-in fireplace, where guests often linger over breakfast. Cedar Hill is a working poultry farm.

Rates: $55. Russel & Gladys Swarr.

4 R. 4 PB. Phone available. TV available. Beds: QDTC. Continental-plus breakfast. CCs: MC VISA AE.

Seen in: *Women's World, Lancaster Farming.*

"Dorothy can have Kansas, Scarlett can take Tara, Rick can keep Paris — I've stayed at Cedar Hill Farm."

MYERSTOWN EQ8/*F9*

Tulpehocken Manor Inn & Plantation

650 W Lincoln Ave
Myerstown PA 17067
(717) 866-4926 (717) 392-2311

Circa 1700. George Washington slept here, and it is documented. Listed in the National Register of Historic Places, there are five buildings on a 150-acre working cattle farm. Among the buildings is a three-story Victorian stone house. Other structures are rare examples of Germanic Swiss Bank houses, constructed over a central arch. Rooms are appointed with handmade quilts, period furniture and Oriental rugs. Apartments are also available for rent on the plantation.

Rates: $69-$79. James Henry & Esther Nissly.

6 R. 1 PB. TV available. Beds: DT. Full breakfast.

Seen in: *Sunday Patriot-News, Reading Eagle.*

NEW HOPE EQ16/*F12*

Ash Mill Farm

See: Holicong, PA

Backstreet Inn of New Hope

144 Old York Rd
New Hope PA 18939
(215) 862-9571

Circa 1750. Tucked away on a quiet street, this inn sits on three acres of park-like lawns that include a stream,

an old wishing well, and a gurgling brook. Several rooms reveal the stone walls of the house and are decorated with antiques. A favorite is the Anne Frank Room down a small hallway hidden by a sliding bookcase.

Rates: $89-$125. Bob Puccio.

7 R. 5 PB. Phone available. TV available. Beds: D. Full breakfast. Gourmet meals. Swimming pool. CCs: MC VISA. Horse and carriage rides.

Seen in: *Treutonian Press, Newark Star Ledger.*

"Just felt like taking my shoes off and being right at home, most relaxing."

Golden Plough Inn

See: Lahaska, PA

Hotel Du Village

N River Rd
New Hope PA 18938
(215) 862-9911

Circa 1907. Once part of a William Penn land grant, the Hotel du Village features 10 acres of trees, lawns and a creek. The Tudor-style hotel once served as a boarding school for girls, while the restaurant is part of the old White Oaks estate. Chestnut panelling, Persian carpets and three working fireplaces provide a backdrop to chef Omar Arbani's French cuisine.

Rates: $80-$95. Barbara & Omar Arbani.

20 R. 20 PB. Phone available. Beds: KQDT. B&B. Restaurant. Handicap access. Swimming pool. Conference room. CCs: AE. Horseback riding nearby, tennis.

Seen in: *Trenton Times, The Burlington County Times.*

"The food is wonderful - fireplaces burning makes everything so romantic!"

Logan Inn
Main & Ferry Sts
New Hope PA 18938
(215) 862-2300

Circa 1722. Said to be one of the five oldest inns in America, the Logan was originally known as the Ferry Tavern,

established by John Wells, founder of New Hope. The oldest section of the inn contains the tavern (open until 2 a.m.), with a colonial fireplace, murals and antique woodwork. Original art, antiques, and four-poster canopy beds are featured in each guest room. A private stone-walled cottage has its own fireplace. Under new ownership, the inn's dining rooms are becoming known for their excellent cuisine and gracious service.

Rates: $95-$125. Gwen Davis.

16 R. 16 PB. Phone in room. TV in room. Beds: KQDTC. B&B. Restaurant. Conference room. CCs: MC VISA AE DC CB. Horse-drawn carriage tours, ghost tours, boats, bicycles, canoeing, balloon rides, children's amusement park, museums.

Seen in: *The Philadelphia Inquirer, The Home News.*

"...the food was PERFECTION and served in a gracious and extremely courteous manner...our intentions had been to explore different restaurants, but there was no reason to explore, we had found what we wanted."

The Wedgwood Inn
111 W Bridge
New Hope PA 18938
(215) 862-2570

Circa 1870. A Victorian and a Classic Revival house sit side by side and compose the Wedgwood Inn. Twenty-six-inch walls are in the stone house. Lofty windows, hardwood floors and antique furnishings add to the warmth and style. Pennsylvania Dutch surreys arrive and depart from the inn for nostalgic carriage rides.

Rates: $75-$160. Nadine Silnutzer & Carl Glassman.

12 R. 10 PB. 5 FP. Phone available. Continental-plus breakfast. Pool, antiques, arts & craft shops.

Seen in: *National Geographic, Traveller, Women's Day, Inc.*

"The Wedgwood has all the comforts of a highly professional accommodation yet with all the warmth a personal friend would extend."

NORTH WALES ER14/F11

Joseph Ambler Inn
1005 Horsham Rd
North Wales PA 19454
(215) 362-7500

Circa 1734. This beautiful fieldstone-and-wood house was built over a period of three centuries. Originally, it was part of a grant that Joseph Ambler, a Quaker wheelwright, obtained from William Penn in 1688. A large stone bank barn and tenant cottage on 12 acres constitute the remainder of the property. Guests enjoy the cherry wainscoting and walk-in fireplace in the schoolroom.

Rates: $87-$140. Steve & Terry Kratz.

28 R. 28 PB. Beds: QD. Full breakfast. Restaurant. Conference room. CCs: MC VISA AE DC CB DS. Golf, tennis.

Seen in: *Colonial Homes, Country Living.*

"What a wonderful night my husband and I spent. We are already planning to come back to your wonderful getaway."

ORRTANNA EU2/G7

Hickory Bridge Farm
96 Hickory Bridge Rd
Orrtanna PA 17353
(717) 642-5261

Circa 1750. The oldest part of this farmhouse was constructed of mud bricks and straw, on land that once belonged to Charles Carroll, father of

a signer of the Declaration of Independence. Inside there is an attractive stone fireplace for cooking. There are several country cottages in addition to the rooms in the farmhouse. The host family have been innkeepers for nearly 20 years.

Location: Eight miles west of Gettysburg.

Rates: $69-$79. The Hammetts, Robert & Mary Lynn Martin.

7 R. 6 PB. 4 FP. TV available. Beds: Q. B&B. Conference room. CCs: MC VISA. Fishing, golfing, swimming, skiing.

Seen in: *Hanover Times, The Northern Virginia Gazzette.*

"Beautifully decorated and great food!"

PHILADELPHIA ET15/G11

B&B of Valley Forge & Philadelphia
PO Box 562
Philadelphia PA 19481
(215) 783-7838 FAX: (215) 783-7783

Circa 1890. This reservation service features over 100 B&Bs in Valley Forge, Brandywine Valley and Philadelphia. A sample home is a handsome 15-room stone farmhouse near Valley Forge. Its long, white-pillared facade overlooks acres of fields. A tunnel that leads from the keep, a cold storage shed, allowed the owners to escape from the British during the Revolutionary War. Later, it was part of the Underground Railroad for slaves escaping to the North. Tell Carolyn exactly what your dream B&B is and she'll match you up.

Location: Southeast Pennsylvania.

❀Rates: $45-$100.

6 R. 3 PB. 2 FP. Phone in room. TV in room. Beds: KQDTC. Full breakfast. Conference room. FAX. CCs: MC VISA AE DC. Skiing, hunting, horses. One with resident ghost.

Seen in: *Suburban Business Review, Entertainment Magazine, Philadelphia Magazine.*

"I'll never go back to a hotel. This is the way to get a real feel for the people and a chance to really discover the area. You often get the bonus of making lasting friends."

The Independence Park Inn
235 Chestnut St
Philadelphia PA 19106
(215) 922-4443 (800) 624-2988

Circa 1856. This five-story urban inn is listed in the National Register of Historic Places. The high-ceilinged guest rooms feature rich draperies and Chippendale writing tables. In the parlor lobby, guests may enjoy tea and cucumber sandwiches by the fireplace. Breakfast is served on the skylighted court. Conference rooms are available for business travelers.

Rates: $85-$130. Laura Angelore.

36 R. 36 PB. Phone in room. TV in room. Beds: KQT. Continental-plus breakfast. Handicap access. Conference room. CCs: MC VISA AE DC CB. Independence Park, Liberty Bell, Penn's Landing. Afternoon tea.

Seen in: *The Philadelphia Inquirer, The Atlanta Journal and Constitution.*

"Everything possible seems to have been planned for our comfort and needs."

Sea Crest by the Sea
See: Spring Lake, NJ

PITTSBURGH WQ4/E2

The Priory
614 Pressley St
Pittsburgh PA 15212
(412) 231-3338

Circa 1888. The Priory, now a European-style hotel, was built to provide lodging for Benedictine priests traveling through Pittsburgh. It is adjacent to St. Mary's German Catholic Church in historic East Allegheny. The inn's design and maze of rooms and corridors give it a distinctly Old World flavor. All rooms are decorated with Victorian furnishings.

*Rates: $70-$135. Mary Ann Graf.
27 R. 27 PB. Beds: QDTC. Continental-plus breakfast. Handicap access. Conference room. Complimentary wine in sitting room.
Seen in: *The Pittsburgh Press.*
"Although we had been told that the place was elegant, we were hardly prepared for the richness of detail. We felt as though we were guests in a manor."

POTTSTOWN ER12/F10

Coventry Forge Inn
RD 2
Pottstown PA 19464
(215) 469-6222

Circa 1717. The inn is best known for its fine French cuisine served in the 1717 building. The Guest House, built in the 1800s, features simple accommodations with antiques and reproductions. A continental breakfast is served, since the emphasis here is on dinner the night before.
Rates: $65-$75. Wallis & June Callahan.
5 R. 5 PB. Phone in room. TV available. Beds: KDT. Continental breakfast. Restaurant. Conference room. CCs: MC VISA AE DC. Horseback riding, hunting, golf, walking trails.
Seen in: *Philadelphia Inquirer Magazine, New York Times.*

Fairway Farm B&B
Vaughn Rd
Pottstown PA 19464
(215) 326-1315

Circa 1734. This beautiful old fieldstone house is in a parklike setting that includes a spring-fed outdoor pool, a tennis court, a pond, gazebo and flower gardens. The barn contains an internationally-known trumpet museum, and guests are called to breakfast with a trumpet fanfare. (The host was a trumpet soloist with the Freieburg Philharmonic.) European tastes are reflected in a collection of hand-painted Bavarian furnishings and feather beds. Breakfast is served in the gazebo or on the terrace with crystal and china.

Location: Twenty-six miles southwest of Philadelphia.
Rates: $60-$65. Franz & Katherine Streitwieser.
4 R. 4 PB. Phone available. TV available. Beds: KQ. Full breakfast. Spa. Sauna. Swimming pool. Conference room.
Seen in: *Today Show, Philadelphia Magazine.*
"Looks and feels like a touch of Bavaria."

QUAKERTOWN EQ14/E11

Sign of the Sorrel Horse
Box 243, Old Bethlehem Rd
Quakertown PA 18951
(215) 536-4651

Circa 1749. This inn received its tavern license in 1749. Intricately carved French antiques include armoires and four-poster beds and there is a cozy parlor. The dining room atmosphere is created by its stone walls and beamed ceilings. The inn's French and Continental cuisine often features wild boar, Canadian caribou, grouse and quail. (Closed Monday and Tuesday.) In summer, diners enjoy an outdoor terrace with waterfall and flower garden.
Rates: $85-$125. Monique Gaumont-Lanvin & Jon Atkin.
6 R. 6 PB. 1 FP. Phone available. TV available. Beds: D. Continental breakfast. Restaurant. Gourmet meals. Handicap access. CCs: MC VISA. Horseback riding, canoeing, sailing, bicycling, swimming, hiking. Cross-country & downhill skiing nearby. Honeymoon & anniversary specials. Weddings.
Seen in: *The Express, The Inncredible Gourmet.*

READING ER10/F10

The Adamstown Inn B&B
See: Adamstown, PA

The Inn at Centre Park
730 Centre Ave
Reading PA 19601
(215) 374-8557

Circa 1877. This mansion and carriage house preserve the elegance of the Victorian era. The inn features original leaded glass, ornate plaster, and paneled and carved woods. The Inn at Centre Park's large porches and many fireplaces are inviting.

Rates: $130-$190. Andrea & Michael Smith.
4 R. 4 PB. 5 FP. Phone in room. TV available. Beds: KQ. Full breakfast. Gourmet meals. Conference room. FAX. CCs: MC VISA AE. Hiking, golf, cross-country skiing, shopping.
Seen in: *Washington Post, Reading Eagle.*
"The elegance of your house and your warm hospitality was incredible."

Hunter House
118 S Fifth St
Reading PA 19602
(215) 374-6608

Circa 1846. Believed to be the only Greek Revival-style home in town, the inn features many European touches, such as antique furnishings and elaborate 13-foot ceilings topped with ornate plaster moldings. Guests will find shopping here to be some of the best in the nation, with antique shops and world-famous outlet stores within minutes of the inn. Other attractions include the Hawk Mountain Sanctuary and the historic Daniel Boone Homestead.
*Rates: $60-$75. Ray & Norma Staron.
4 R. 2 PB. Phone available. TV in room. Beds: QDT. Full breakfast. CCs: MC VISA. Walking tours, outlet shopping centers.
Seen in: *The Reading Eagle, The Washington Post.*
"The accommodations are lovely, and the hospitality is exceptional."

SOUTH STERLING EK13/C11

Sterling Inn
Rt 191
South Sterling PA 18460
(717) 676-3311

Circa 1857. This inn sits along the Wallenpaupack Creek, surrounded by

forested mountains. The guest house and a string of cottages are stretched out over 103 wood-covered acres. Reproduction country furnishings fill the guest rooms, parlor and sitting room. The Sterling Inn offers complimentary sleigh rides in the winter, weather permitting.
Location: Pocono Mountains.
Rates: $65-$95. Ron & Mary Kay Logan.
56 R. 56 PB. 8 FP. Phone available. TV available. Beds: KQDTC. MAP. Spa. Handicap access. Swimming pool. Conference room. CCs: MC VISA AE. Horseback riding, water sports, downhill skiing, antiquing. Weddings, murder mystery weekends, golf packages.
Seen in: *Philadelphia Inquirer, New Jersey Monthly, The Washington Post.*
"Your 'touch of elegance,' both in service and gourmet food, made all of our guests feel very special."

STARLIGHT EF13/*A11*

The Inn at Starlight Lake
PO Box 27
Starlight PA 18461
(717) 798-2519
Circa 1909. Acres of woodland and meadow surround the last surviving railroad inn on the New York, Ontario and Western lines. Originally a boarding house, the inn had its own store,

church, school, blacksmith shop and creamery. Platforms first erected to accommodate tents for the summer season, were later replaced by individual cottages. The inn is situated on the 45-acre spring-fed Starlight Lake, providing summertime canoeing, swimming, fishing and sailing. (No motor boats are allowed on the lake.)
*Rates: $110-$140. Jack & Judy McMahon.
26 R. 18 PB. 1 FP. Phone available. TV available. Beds: KQDTC. MAP. Restaurant. Gourmet meals. Spa. Game room. CCs: MC VISA. Hiking, biking, cross-country skiing. Golf nearby.
Seen in: *The Philadelphia Inquirer, Newsday.*
"Delicious food and very relaxing."

STRASBURG ET9/*G9*

The King's Cottage
See: Lancaster, PA

Limestone Inn B&B
33 E Main St
Strasburg PA 17579
(717) 687-8392
Circa 1786. The Limestone Inn housed the first Chief Burgess and later became the Headmaster's House for Strasburg Academy. It is a handsome five-bay formal Georgian plan. The Kennell's are sometimes don period costume at breakfast. Located in the Strasburg Historic District, the house is in the National Register. The surrounding scenic Amish farmlands offer sightseeing and antique and craft shopping.
Location: Three miles from route 30.
❀Rates: $65-$80. Jan & Dick Kennell.
6 R. 3 PB. Phone available. Beds: QDT. Full breakfast. Gourmet meals. CCs: AE. Horseback riding, golf, cycling. Amish quilts.
Seen in: *Lancaster New Era, Intelligencer Journal, Strasburg Weekly, Washingtonian Magazine.*
"A beautiful restoration, great innkeepers and a fantasy location."

TOWER CITY EP17/*E9*

The Inn at Elizabethville
See: Elizabethville, PA

WILLIAMSPORT EK4/*C8*

Reighard House
1323 E Third St
Williamsport PA 17701
(717) 326-3593
Circa 1905. This Victorian stone and brick inn is on a hillside overlooking the Susquehanna. The Reighard House offers a formal parlor with a fireplace, a music room with a grand piano, a library, a formal oak-paneled dining room and a breakfast room with a wood-burning stove. Rooms are furnished with four-poster, canopy and brass beds. Each bedroom is decorated with a different color scheme and theme and is identified by a needlepointed sign.
*Rates: $58-$78. Sue & Bill Reighard.
6 R. 6 PB. 1 FP. Phone in room. TV in room. Beds: QDTC. B&B. Conference room. CCs: MC VISA AE DC CB. Hiking, skiing, hunting, fishing, health club membership with pool.
Seen in: *Pennsylvania Business Journal.*
"I know I'm coming back!"

YORK EU6/*G8*

The King's Cottage
See: Lancaster, PA

The Smyser-Bair House
30 S Beaver St
York PA 17401
(717) 854-3411
Circa 1880. This four-story red brick house stands on a corner in downtown York. Its green shutters and Italianate styling add a welcoming touch. The house is decorated in cheerful colors highlighting finely carved moldings, a walnut staircase, high ceilings and parquet floors. It is appointed with crystal chandeliers, floor-to-ceiling gold leaf pier mirrors and Victorian antiques.
Rates: $60-$80. Bob & Hilda King.
4 R. 1 PB. Phone available. Beds: QDT. Full breakfast. Wineries, antique shops.
Seen in: *York Daily Record.*
"We really enjoyed the warmth and hospitality of the innkeepers. They really care about their guests."

RHODE ISLAND

BLOCK ISLAND L22/G6

The Inn at Old Harbour

Water St, PO Box 994
Block Island RI 02807
(401) 466-2212 (401) 466-2933

Circa 1882. This three-story Victorian, with its gingerbread trim and double porch, attracts many photographers.

Recently renovated, all the rooms are appointed with period furnishings and most have views of the Atlantic. Block Island's inviting beaches and seaside cliffs are enjoyed by wind surfers, sailors, cyclists and those just sunning on the sand. A noted wildlife sanctuary at Sandy Point is popular for bird-watchers.

Location: Overlooking the harbor and the Atlantic Ocean.
*Rates: $115-$135. Season: May-October. Kevin & Barbara Butler.
10 R. 5 PB. Phone available. TV available. Beds: KDTC. B&B. FAX. CCs: MC VISA AE. Horseback riding, wind surfing, tennis, fishing & sailing charters, parasailing, jet skiing.
Seen in: *Rhode Island Monthly.*
"The most romantic enchanting inn we have stayed at and what gracious innkeepers!"

NARRAGANSETT I23/F6

Stone Lea

40 Newton Ave
Narragansett RI 02882
(401) 783-9546

Circa 1884. This rambling Victorian estate is situated on two magnificent ocean front acres at the mouth of Narragansett Bay. One of a handful of summer homes built during the peak period of high society in Narragansett, it was designed by McKim, Mead & White of New York. Waves crashing along the rocky shore may be seen

and heard from most guest rooms. English antiques and collections of Victorian china clocks, miniature cars, and ship models are incorporated into the decor. An antique billiard table dominates a large sitting room.

*Rates: $60-$100. Carol & Ernie Cormier.
4 R. 4 PB. 1 FP. Phone available. TV available. Beds: QDT. Full breakfast. Swimming, sailing, boating, fishing, golf, tennis.
"Very beautiful; well prepared food and helpful and concerned hosts."

NEWPORT H24/F7

Admiral Farragut Inn

31 Clarke St
Newport RI 02840
(401) 846-4256

Circa 1702. General Rochambeau, commander of the French forces, quartered his personal staff at the Admiral Farragut house in 1776. It was enlarged to two stories in 1755. Now framed by roses and a white picket fence, this yellow clapboard house showcases colonial cove moldings and 12-over-12 paned windows. In addition to the handcrafted reproduction Shaker four-poster beds, the inn features handpainted armoires and a hand-painted fireplace mantel.

*Rates: $55-$98. Jane Berriman.
10 R. 10 PB. Phone in room. Beds: QD. Continental-plus breakfast. FAX. CCs: MC VISA AE DC. Sailing, swimming, tennis (grass courts).
Seen in: *Country Living, Country Inns.*
"An inspiration in colonial design."

The Brinley Victorian Inn

23 Brinley St
Newport RI 02840
(401) 849-7645

Circa 1850. This is a three-story Victorian with a mansard roof and long porch. A cottage on the property dates from 1850. There are two par-

lors and a library providing a quiet haven from the bustle of the Newport wharfs. Each room is decorated with period wallpapers and furnishings. There are fresh flowers and mints on the pillows. The brick courtyard is planted with bleeding heart, peonies and miniature roses, perennials of the Victorian era.

Location: Newport Historic District.
*Rates: $55-$125. Season: May - October. Peter Carlisle & Claire Boslem.
17 R. 13 PB. 6 FP. Phone available. TV available. Beds: KQD. Continental breakfast. CCs: MC VISA. Sailing, swimming.
Seen in: *New Hampshire Times, Boston Woman, Country Victorian.*
"Ed and I had a wonderful anniversary. The Brinley is as lovely and cozy as ever! The weekend brought back lots of happy memories."

Cliffside Inn

2 Seaview Ave
Newport RI 02840
(401) 847-1811

Circa 1870. The governor of Maryland, Thomas Swann, built this Newport summer house in the style of a Second Empire Victorian. It fea-

tures a mansard roof and many bay windows. The rooms are decorated in a Victorian motif set off by ceiling

moldings painted in pastel colors. The Cliff Walk is located one block from the inn.
Rates: $105-$185. Annette King.
11 R. 11 PB. Beds: KQDT. Full breakfast. Conference room. FAX. CCs: MC VISA AE DC.
Seen in: *Country Inns, The Philadelphia Inquirer.*

Jail House Inn

13 Marlborough St
Newport RI 02840
(401) 847-4638

Circa 1772. The owner of another B&B, the Yankee Peddler, has had a good bit of fun restoring and renovating the old Newport Jail. Prison-

striped bed coverings and tin cups and plates for breakfast express the jailhouse motif. Guests can stay in the Cell Block, Maximum Security or Solitary Confinement, each on a separate level of the inn. Nevertheless, because guests pay for their time here, there are luxuries in abundance.
Rates: $55-$125. Beth Hoban.
22 R. 22 PB. Beds: Q. Continental-plus breakfast. Handicap access. CCs: MC VISA AE. Beaches, centrally located for shopping, plenty of parking.
Seen in: *The Providence Journal.*
"I found this very relaxing and a great pleasure."

The John Banister House

56 Pelham St at Spring
Newport RI 02840
(401) 846-0050

Circa 1751. This Georgian Colonial home, listed in the National Register, was built by a man who ran merchant

ships from the colonies to Europe. He was thought to have been a smuggler. During the Revolutionary War, the house was used by General Prescott as British headquarters. Innkeeper Laurice Shaw restored the home in great detail, including matching original interior paint colors. Genuine antique coverlets top the beds. A full breakfast is served on a table dating back to the 1750s.
*Rates: $60-$125. Laurice Shaw.
9 R. 9 PB. 8 FP. Beds: QD. Full breakfast. Handicap access. CCs: MC VISA AE. Shopping, beaches, restaurants.
Seen in: *The Boston Sunday Globe.*

The Melville House

39 Clarke St
Newport RI 02840
(401) 847-0640

Circa 1750. This attractive, National Register, two-story colonial once housed aides to General Rochambeau during the American Revolution.

Early American furnishings decorate the interior. There is also an unusual collection of old appliances, including a cherry-pitter, mincer, and dough maker collected by innkeeper Sam Rogers, a former household appliance designer. The inn is a pleasant walk from the waterfront and historic sites.
Location: In the heart of Newport's Historic Hill.
Rates: $40-$95. Season: March - January. Rita & Sam Rogers.
7 R. 5 PB. 1 FP. Phone available. Beds: DT. B&B. CCs: MC VISA AE. Swimming, boating, fishing, tennis, golf.
"Comfortable with a quiet elegance."

The Old Dennis House

59 Washington St
Newport RI 02840
(401) 846-1324

Circa 1740. The Dennis House is situated on the oldest residential street in Newport. Its elaborate

pineapple-carved doorway is among the most attractive in Newport. It was built by a sea captain and boasts the city's only flat widow's walk. There are several inviting rooms for those who want to experience historic Newport at its best.
Rates: $50-$150. Rev. Henry G. Turnbull.
5 R. 5 PB. 3 FP. Phone available. TV in room. Continental breakfast.
Seen in: *The New York Times.*
"It was like home away from home."

The Pilgrim House

123 Spring St
Newport RI 02846
(401) 846-0040 (800)525-8373

Circa 1809. Next door to historic Trinity Church, this mansard-roofed Victorian features a third-floor deck to savor expansive views of Newport Harbor, three streets away. The inn is

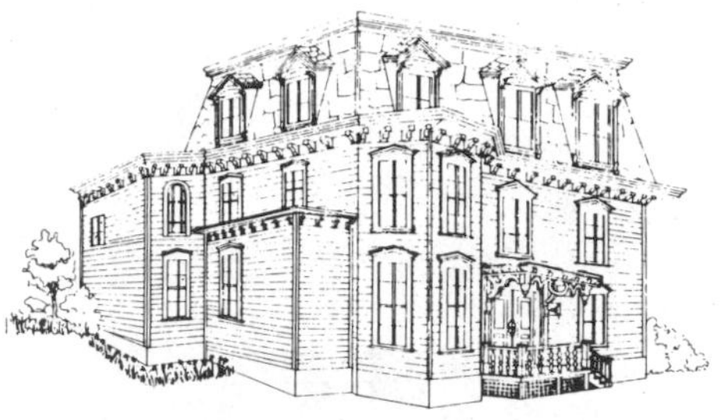

decorated with Victorian period furnishings. A working fireplace in the living room invites a guest to browse through restaurant menus and the inn's library. Eucalyptus wreaths pleasantly scent the air when it's not filled with the fragrance of freshly baked breads and muffins.
Rates: $45-$125. Pam & Bruce Bayuk.
10 R. 8 PB. Phone available. TV available. Beds: D. B&B. CCs: MC VISA. Sailing, tennis, golf. Seen in: *The Times.*

The Victorian Ladies

63 Memorial Blvd
Newport RI 02840
(401) 849-9960

Circa 1841. Guests of this restored three-story Victorian building can stroll to Newport's beaches, the Cliff Walk, the colonial town and the harbor front. At the Victorian Ladies, a charming latticed courtyard connects the main house to the smaller house in back. Reproduction period furniture, crystal and lush floral prints add to the Victorian ambience in the rooms that innkeeper Helene O'Neill decorated.
Rates: $85-$125. Season: Feb. to Dec. Donald & Helene O'Neill.
9 R. 9 PB. Phone available. TV in room. Beds: QDT. Full breakfast. CCs: MC VISA. Golf, beaches, water sports, tennis, shops, restaurants. Seen in: *Country Inns, Glamour, Bride Magazine.*
"We want to move in!"

PROVIDENCE D23/E6

State House Inn

43 Jewett St
Providence RI 02908
(401) 785-1235

Circa 1900. This restored Victorian house is located in a neighborhood of Victorian homes recently nominated as a national historic district. The Rhode Island State Capitol is a five-minute walk away. Guest rooms feature simple furnishings including Shaker, country and colonial reproductions. To accommodate business travelers, the inn provides an office complete with computer, copier and fax machine.

Rates: $85-$105. Frank & Monica Hopton.
10 R. 10 PB. 2 FP. Phone in room. TV in room. Beds: KQT. Full breakfast. FAX. CCs: MC VISA AE. Shopping.
Seen in: *The Phoenix Newspaper.*

WESTERLY J19/F6

Shelter Harbor Inn

10 Wagner Rd, Rt 1
Westerly RI 02891
(401) 322-8883

Circa 1800. This farmhouse at the entrance to the community of Shelter Harbor has been renovated and transformed to create a handsome country inn. Rooms, many with fireplaces, are in the main house, the barn and a carriage house. A third-floor deck provides panoramic views of Block Island Sound. The dining room features local seafood and other traditional New England dishes. Nearby are secluded, barrier beaches, stone fences and salt ponds.

*Rates: $78-$102. Jim & Debbye Dey.
24 R. 24 PB. Full breakfast. Restaurant. Spa. Conference room. CCs: MC VISA DC. Paddle tennis, golf, tennis.
Seen in: *Rhode Island Monthly, The Day.*
"This inn was, on the whole, wonderful."

SOUTH CAROLINA

ANDERSON C4/D2

Evergreen Inn

1109 S Main
Anderson SC 29621
(803) 225-1109

Circa 1830. This gracious Greek Revival house features tall columns rising to the third-story pediment and a wraparound veranda. It is located on two-and-a-half acres, next to another fine National Register mansion, which houses the inn's restaurant. Scarlet's Room features a tall four-poster bed and burgundy velvet drapes. Another guest room boasts an exotic navy satin canopy bed. Antique shops and the downtown area are within walking distance.

Myrna & Peter Ryter.

7 R. 6 PB. 8 FP. Phone available. TV available. Beds: KDT. Continental-plus breakfast. Handicap access. Conference room. CCs: MC VISA AE DC. Lake nearby.

Seen in: *Travel Host Magazine, Greenville News.*

"Fantastic! Very imaginative & fun."

BEAUFORT K10/G5

Bay Street Inn

601 Bay St
Beaufort SC 29902
(803) 524-7720

Circa 1850. Built by one of Beaufort's major cotton planters, the inn is a fine example of Greek Revival architec-

ture. Cracks remain on the front steps where trunks were thrown from the upper gallery when the Union fleet approached during the Civil War. There are 14-foot ceilings, marble fireplaces, and a two-story veranda. All the rooms have unobstructed water views and fireplaces. Joel Pointsett planted the original poinsettia plants while visiting the builder.

Location: On the water in the historic district.

*Rates: $70-$80. Gene & Kathleen Roc.

6 R. 6 PB. 6 FP. Phone available. TV available. Beds: QDW. EP. Conference room. CCs: MC VISA. Golf, tennis, ocean bathing, bikes, fishing, full library.

Seen in: *The New York Times, Southern Living.*

"From the huge piano in the music room to the lush panelling of the library, the old house is an elegant reminder of bygone days of gracious Southern living."

Old Point Inn

212 New St
Beaufort SC 29902
(803) 524-3177

Circa 1898. Built by William Waterhouse as a wedding present to his wife, Isabelle Richmond, this Queen Anne Victorian has wraparound

verandas in the "Beaufort Style." Guests often rock, swing or recline in the hammock while watching boats ply the Intercoastal Waterway. Four pillared fireplaces, pocket doors and eyelash windows are features of the house. The inn is located in the historic district, with a waterfront park, a marina, restaurants and downtown shopping nearby.

Rates: $60-$75. Joe & Joan Carpentiere.

4 R. 4 PB. 1 FP. Phone available. Beds: QDTC. Continental-plus breakfast. Conference room. FAX. CCs: MC VISA. Golf, water sports, tennis, bicycling, beaches. Wedding specials.

Seen in: *A Guide to Historic Beaufort, Islander Magazine.*

"We are still cruising on our memories of a wonderful honeymoon. It certainly had a great start staying at the Old Point Inn. We couldn't have done better."

The Rhett House Inn

1009 Craven St
Beaufort SC 29902
(803) 524-9030

Circa 1820. Most people cannot pass this stunning two-story clapboard house without wanting to step up to the long veranda and try the ham-

mock. Guest rooms are furnished in antiques, with quilts and fresh flowers. Many guest rooms have fireplaces. Handsome gardens feature a fountain and are often the site for romantic weddings. Bicycles are available.

Location: In historic downtown.

*Rates: $80-$125. Steve & Marianne Harrison.

8 R. 8 PB. 2 FP. Phone in room. Beds: QDT. Full breakfast. Handicap access. Game room. Conference room. FAX. CCs: MC VISA. Bicycles, tennis, golf, sailing, swimming, horseback riding, hunting, fishing.

Seen in: *Innsider, Family Business Magazine, The Lowcountry Ledger.*

"A dream come true!"

TwoSuns Inn

1705 Bay St
Beaufort SC 29902
(803) 522-1122

Circa 1917. This neoclassical Revival-style home is on the western side of the Historic Beaufort District. It offers magnificent views of Beaufort Bay, the

surrounding low country islands and the downtown marina. The inn features a wraparound veranda, an oak-beamed dining room, four stairways and an original skylight. Guest rooms are decorated in Victorian, Oriental and country themes. Some rooms have access to a second-floor screened porch or a side veranda.
*Rates: $80-$90. Ron & Carrol Kay.
5 R. 5 PB. 1 FP. Phone in room. TV in room. Beds: KQT. Full breakfast. Handicap access. Conference room. FAX. CCs: MC VISA. Carriage rides, boating, golf, tennis, fishing, hunting. Honeymoon and anniversary specials.
Seen in: *The Beaufort Gazette.*
"One could not wish for a better experience."

CHARLESTON 112/G6

1837 B&B & Tea Room
126 Wentworth St
Charleston SC 29401
(803) 723-7166
Circa 1800. Originally owned by a cot ton planter, this three-story house is centrally located in the historic district. Red cypress wainscoting, cornice molding and heart-of-pine floors adorn the formal parlor, while pine-beamed ceilings and red-brick walls are features of the carriage house. Guest rooms offer antiques and rice beds. Rocking chairs are on several piazzas.
Location: In the historic district.
Rates: $45-$85. Sherri Weaver & Richard Dunn.
8 R. 8 PB. Phone available. TV in room. Beds: QDT. Full breakfast. CCs: MC VISA AE. Beach, water sports, tennis, golf.
Seen in: *The New York Times.*
"This cozy room added that special touch to a much-needed weekend getaway."

Ansonborough Inn
21 Hasell St
Charleston SC 29401
(803) 723-1655 (800)522-2073
Circa 1900. Once a stationer's warehouse, the Ansonborough Inn is an all-suite inn. It features heart-pine beams, locally fired bricks and a striking atrium lobby. Suites have living rooms decorated in classic pine reproductions.
Rates: $89-$168. Allen Johnson.
37 R. 37 PB. Phone in room. TV in room. Beds: KQTC. Continental-plus breakfast. Conference room. CCs: MC VISA AE. Carriage rides, tours. Honeymoon, anniversary specials.
Seen in: *Southern Living, Travel Host, Seabreeze Magazine.*
"Thank you for such charm and hospitality. Elegantly decorated. Warm and friendly staff."

Cannonboro Inn
184 Ashley Ave
Charleston SC 29403
(803) 723-8572
Circa 1840. The city of Charleston considered the Cannonboro irreplaceable because of its semi-circular two-

story, columned piazzas. Shaded by crepe myrtles and palmettos, the inn is also air-conditioned. Rooms are appointed with reproduction antiques such as four-poster and rice beds.
*Rates: $69-$89. Robert Warley, James Hare & Lisa Lemacks.
6 R. 6 PB. Phone available. TV in room. Beds: QDT. Full breakfast. CCs: MC VISA. Water sports, tennis, golf.
Seen in: *Chicago Sun-Times.*
"Thanks for your warm hospitality."

Hayne House
30 King St
Charleston SC 29401
(803) 577-2633
Circa 1755. Located one block from the Battery, this handsome clapboard house is in the National Register of Historic Places. Surrounded by a

wrought-iron garden fence, it has an 1820 addition. It was built three stories tall to capture the harbor breeze. The inn is furnished in antiques, and there is an appealing back porch with rockers and a swing.
Rates: $55-$90. Ben Chapman.
3 R. 3 PB. Phone available. Beds: DT. B&B. Tennis, golf, beach, bicycles, piano, complimentary tea.
"A fantasy realized. What a wonderful gift of hospitality."

Historic Charleston B&B
43 Legare St
Charleston SC 29401
(803) 722-6606
Circa 1713. Listings in this reservation service include flamboyant Victorian mansions, narrow "single houses," pre-Revolutionary carriage houses and rooms overlooking the Battery. The oldest home open to guests was built in 1713. Some hosts are from old Charleston families that go back several generations. Family heirlooms, period antiques and silver tea service are often featured.
Location: Historic district.
Rates: $65-$125. Charlotte Fairey.
65 R. 65 PB. Beds: KQTC. Continental-plus breakfast. Spa. Swimming pool. CCs: MC VISA AE. Swimming, bicycling.
Seen in: *The New York Times, Southern Living.*
"So warm and welcoming."

Indigo Inn
1 Maiden Lane
Charleston SC 29401
(803) 577-5900
Circa 1850. In the heart of the historic district of Charleston is the Indigo Inn. The elegant lobby has a Sheraton sideboard and an Oriental motif. Guest rooms are decorated with 18th-century antiques, reproductions, down pillows and comforters. The inn serves homemade bread. Guests may enjoy breakfast in the lush, tranquil courtyard.
Rates: $110-$125. Larry Deery.
40 R. 40 PB. Phone in room. TV in room. Beds: Q. Continental-plus breakfast. CCs. MC VISA AE. Carriage rides, tours. Honeymoon, anniversary specials.
Seen in: *Charlotte Observer.*
"A warm and friendly staff."

Jasmine House Inn
64 Hasell St
Charleston SC 29401
(803) 577-5900 (800)845-7639
Circa 1840. The Jasmine House Inn is an 1840s Greek Revival mansion. It boasts 14-foot ceilings, cozy fireplaces, gleaming hardwood floors and luxurious Oriental rugs.
Rates: $125-$225. Larry Deery & Martha Ford.
10 R. 10 PB. 10 FP. Phone in room. TV in room. Beds: KQDC. Continental-plus breakfast. Spa. CCs: MC VISA AE. Carriage rides, tours. Honeymoon & special occasion packages.
Seen in: *Southern Living.*

John Rutledge House Inn
116 Broad St
Charleston SC 29401
(803) 723-7999 (800) 476-9741
Circa 1763. John Rutledge, first gover-

nor of South Carolina, Supreme Court Justice, and author and signer of the Constitution of the United States, wrote first drafts of the document in the stately ballroom of his Charleston home. In 1791 George Washington dined in this same room. Both men would be amazed by the house's recent restoration, which includes three lavish suites with elaborately carved Italian marble fireplaces, personal refrigerators, spas, air conditioning and televisions along with fine antiques and reproductions. Exterior ironwork on the house was designed in the 19th century and features palmetto trees and American eagles to honor Mr. Rutledge's service to the state and country.
*Rates: $90-$220. Richard Widman.
19 R. 19 PB. 11 FP. Phone in room. TV in room. Beds: KQD. B&B. Spa. Handicap access. CCs: MC VISA AE. Historic tours, running trail, bicycling, golf, tennis, water sports.
Seen in: *Innsider, Colonial Homes, The New York Times, Southern Living.*
"Two hundred years of American history in two nights; first-class accommodations, great staff. John Rutledge should've had it so good!"

Kings Courtyard Inn
198 King St
Charleston SC 29401
(803) 723-7000 (800) 845-6119
Circa 1853. Architect Francis D. Lee designed this three-story building in the Greek Revival style with unusual touches of Egyptian detail. As

Charleston's oldest structure originally built as an inn, it catered to plantation owners. The atmosphere has been authentically restored and some rooms have fireplaces, canopied beds and views of the two inner courtyards or the garden.
Location: In the historic district.
*Rates: $110-$135. Laura Fox.
34 R. 34 PB. 9 FP. Phone in room. TV in room. Beds: KQT. Continental-plus breakfast. Spa. Handicap access. Conference room. CCs: MC VISA.
Seen in: *Southern Living, USA Today.*

The Kitchen House
126 Tradd St
Charleston SC 29401
(803) 577-6362
Circa 1732. This elegantly restored and refurbished Georgian manor was once the home of Dr. Peter Fayssoux, surgeon-general to the Continental

army during the Revolutionary War. In the double drawing room an Adams-style mantel features molded swags and sunburst patterns. English antiques and flowered chintz draperies are enhanced by finely crafted moldings and exposed interior corner posts. In the walled garden, colonial herbs grow just beyond the shade of an enormous magnolia tree. Guest rooms are in the separate Kitchen House with its four original fireplaces.
*Rates: $75-$135. Lois Evans.
3 R. 3 PB. 4 FP. Phone in room. TV in room. Beds: QT. Full breakfast. CCs: MC VISA AE. Beach nearby.
Seen in: *The New York Times, Colonial Homes.*
"By all comparisons, one of the very best."

Maison Du Pre
317 E Bay St
Charleston SC 29401
(803) 723-8691 (800) 662-4667
Circa 1803. In the downtown Ansonborough Historic District is this inn with its frame and brick buildings. Courtyards, with three fountains, are surrounded by tall garden walls and wrought-iron gates. The inn has a drawing room with a baby grand piano. Guest rooms are furnished with antiques and Oriental carpets. The inn offers "Lowcountry tea" every afternoon.
Rates: $115-$200. Lucille & Robert & Mark Mulholland.
15 R. 15 PB. Phone in room. TV in room. Beds: QTC. Continental breakfast. Conference room. CCs: MC VISA AE. Water sports, golf, tennis, beaches, horseback riding. Catered weddings/receptions, boat tours, honeymoon suite.
Seen in: *Country Inns, Americana.*

Two Meeting Street Inn
2 Meeting St
Charleston SC 29401
(803) 723-7322
Circa 1890. Located directly on the Battery, horses and carriages carry visitors past the inn, perhaps the most

photographed in Charleston. In the Queen Anne style, this Victorian has an unusual veranda graced by several ornate arches. The same family has owned and managed the inn since 1946 with no lapse in gracious Southern hospitality. Among the elegant amenities are original Tiffany stained-glass windows, English oak paneling and exquisite collections of silver and antiques. Continental breakfast is served in the formal dining room or side garden and sherry enjoyed in the rocking chairs on the front piazza every afternoon.
Location: On the Battery.
Rates: $95-$140. Karen B. Spell.
9 R. 9 PB. Phone available. TV available. Beds: QD. Continental breakfast. Water sports, beaches, tennis.
Seen in: *Innsider, Southern Bride.*
"A magnificent Queen Anne mansion," Southern Bride.

Vendue Inn
19 Vendue Range
Charleston SC 29401
(803) 577-7970
Circa 1864. Built as a warehouse in the French Quarter, the inn is one short block from the historic waterfront. The bright lobby features fans and wicker furniture, and latticework screens, leather chairs and writing tables fill the reading room. Afternoon wine and cheese and turndown service are special features.
Location: In the historic district and near city market.
*Rates: $75-$145. Evelyn & Morton Needle.
33 R. 33 PB. 8 FP. Phone in room. TV in room. Beds: KQDC. Continental-plus breakfast. Restaurant. Gourmet meals. Spa. FAX. CCs: MC VISA AE. Bicycles, tennis, golf.
Seen in: *Southern Living, Bon Appetit.*
"Delightful. Excellent service."

COLUMBIA E9/E4

Claussen's Inn

2003 Green St
Columbia SC 29205
(800) 622-3382 (803)745-0440

Circa 1928. The Claussen bakery building, a 25,000-square-foot brick building, has been renovated to accommodate 29 king-size guest rooms. The three-story atrium features skylights and a fountain. All the guest rooms contain traditional furnishings, and some feature four-poster beds.

Location: In Five Points adjacent to the university.

*Rates: $75-$100. Dan Vance.

29 R. 29 PB. Phone in room. Beds: KQD. Continental breakfast. Spa. Handicap access. Conference room. CCs: MC VISA AE.

Seen in: *The State.*

"Rooms are small but nice. We liked it."

MCCLELLANVILLE H14/F6

Laurel Hill Plantation

8913 N Hwy 17, PO Box 190
McClellanville SC 29458
(803) 887-3708

Circa 1850. Laurel Hill, although not an opulent plantation, is a good example of a practical, low country farmhouse. It was originally built by

Richard Morrison a co-founder of the village of McClellanville. Although destroyed by Hurricane Hugo it has been rebuilt by Dr. and Mrs. Richard Leland Morrison III. Its present location overlooks Cape Romain's lush marshes. Country and primitive collections are featured, and there is an antique shop on the lowest level. The good doctor keeps a boat and occasionally takes guests out onto the Intercoastal Waterway to view pelicans.

Location: Thirty minutes north of Charleston on Hwy 17.

*Rates: $65-$75. Jackie and Lee Morrison.

4 R. 4 PB. Phone available. TV in room. Beds: QDTC. Full breakfast. Bird-watching, nature trails, boating, fresh-water fish pond, crabbing in creek.

Seen in: *Country Living Magazine.*

"Southern hospitality at its best plus the charm and dignity of the old republic."

MT PLEASANT I12/G6

Guilds Inn

101 Pitt St
Mt Pleasant SC 29464
(803) 881-0510

Circa 1888. The Guilds Inn is located six miles from Charleston in a building that was purchased by the inn-

keeper's grandfather. The family businesses conducted here have included a hardware store and grocery. The house has been restored and appointed in 18th-century reproduction furnishings. Supper at Seven is the dining room, with gleaming mahogany tables, sterling silver, and gold-rimmed china. Each table has an old-fashioned bell pull.

*Rates: $85-$125. John & Amy Malik.

6 R. 6 PB. Phone in room. TV available. Beds: Q. EP. Restaurant. Spa. Conference room. CCs: MC VISA AE. Bicycles, tennis, both free.

Seen in: *Travelhost, Charleston News and Courier.*

"Supper at Seven is the most outstanding restaurant I have ever visited in South Carolina," Ruth Achermann, *Travelhost.*

PENDLETON C4/D2

Liberty Hall Inn - 1840

621 S Mechanic St
Pendleton SC 29670
(803) 646-7500

Circa 1840. On four acres of woods, lawns and gardens, this house is noted for the two-story columned verandas that stretch across the front.

An elegant foyer with a polished staircase greets guests as they enter the inn. All the rooms are furnished with antiques and original art, and there are wide-pine floorboards throughout. The Pendleton Historic District is one of the largest in the National Register and a short stroll brings guests to the town square.

Location: In the historic district.

*Rates: $57-$67. Tom & Susan Jonas.

10 R. 10 PB. Phone available. Beds: KDT. Continental-plus breakfast. Restaurant. Conference room. CCs: MC VISA AE DC CB DS. Golf, hiking, water sports, historic tours.

Seen in: *Country Home, Anderson Independent-Mail.*

"Elegant surroundings and excellent food! Best job of innkeeping we've seen."

SOUTH DAKOTA

CANOVA F14/D7

B&B at Skoglund Farm

Rt 1 Box 45
Canova SD 57321
(605) 247-3445

Circa 1917. This is a working farm on the South Dakota prairie. Ostriches and peacocks stroll around the farm along with cattle, chickens and horses. Guests can ride horses and enjoy an evening meal with the family. Children under 5 stay for free.

Location: Southeast South Dakota.
*Rates: $50. Alden & Delores.
6 R. Phone available. TV available. Beds: QDT. Full breakfast. Horseback riding.
"Thanks for the down-home hospitality and good food."

CANTON H16/D8

Kennedy Rose Inn

903 N Dakota St
Canton SD 57013
(605) 987-2834

Circa 1913. This 12,000-square-foot mansion of Georgian Revival architecture sits on almost five acres of wooded grounds. The inn features wraparound porches, coffered ceilings, diamond-paned windows, French doors and an ornate fireplace. Guest rooms have four-poster beds with scented sheets. Specialty coffees and a full breakfast are served in the dining room or may be brought to your room.

Rates: $55-$75. Douglas & Irene Koob.
Beds: KQDT. CCs: MC VISA.
Seen in: *Midwest Living, Sioux City Journal, Campus Magazine.*

CUSTER F3/D1

State Game Lodge

HCR 83 Box 74
Custer SD 57730
(605) 255-4541 (800) 658-3530

Circa 1923. The State Game Lodge is listed in the National Register of Historic Places. It served as the summer White House for presidents Coolidge and Eisenhower. Although not a bed and breakfast, the lodge boasts a wonderful setting in the Black Hills. Ask for a room in the historic lodge building. (There are cottages and motel units, as well.) A favorite part of the experience is rocking on the front porch while watching deer graze. Breakfast is paid for separately in the dining room, where you may wish to order a pheasant or buffalo entree in the evening.

Rates: $45-$250. Season: May to Oct. Wayne Saukerson, manager.
67 R. 67 PB. 3 FP. Phone in room. TV in room. Beds: QDT. EP. Restaurant. Gourmet meals. Handicap access. Conference room. CCs: MC VISA AE DS. Horseback riding, swimming, fishing, hiking trails, hayride/cookouts, golf, tennis.
Seen in: *Bon Appetit, Midwest Living, Sunset.*
"Your staff's cheerfulness and can-do attitude added to a most enjoyable stay."

DEADWOOD E3/C1

The Adams House

22 Van Buren
Deadwood SD 57732
(605) 578-3877

Circa 1892. This opulent Victorian mansion once hosted Presidents Teddy Roosevelt, William Howard Taft and Calvin Coolidge. Widow Mary Adams left the house in 1936 when she moved to California, and it remained unoccupied for 51 years. When it was opened as a bed and breakfast inn, all the original bed linens, family photographs, handsome antique furnishings, Oriental rugs, gold bathroom fixtures and candelabra remained. Guests today truly sample another time and place when welcomed to the inn. For the most romantic room ask for the round Taft Room situated in the turret. A full breakfast is served on antique Bavarian china.

Rates: $75-$95. Lynda Clarke.
4 R. 4 PB. 1 FP. Phone available. TV available. Beds: DT. Full breakfast. CCs: MC VISA AE.
Seen in: *Country Inns, Rocky Mountain News, Rapid City Journal.*

HOT SPRINGS G3/D1

Villa Theresa Guest House

801 Almond
Hot Springs SD 57747
(605) 745-4633

This turn-of-the-century guesthouse has a two-story octagonal living room topped off with a lookout room. The living room has a beautiful wooden stenciled ceiling. Guest rooms feature such amenities as hardwood floors, four-poster beds, stenciled floors and pedestal sinks. The Fanny Butler Room has a picture window with a view of the city. When guests arrive, they receive iced tea, lemonade and cookies on the porch or in the parlor.

Rates: $50-$55. Margaret & Dick Hunter.
7 R. 3 PB. Beds: Q. Full breakfast. CCs: MC VISA.

YANKTON I14/E7

The Mulberry Inn

512 Mulberry St
Yankton SD 57078
(605) 665-7116

Circa 1873. In the National Register of Historic Places, this red brick Victorian mansion has an unusual ar-

chitectural style reminiscent of Gothic Revival. In a historic neighborhood, the inn has 18 rooms that feature high ceilings, walnut paneling, marble fireplaces and parquet floors. A Laura Ashley decor prevails. A full breakfast is available by advance arrangement. A walk away is the Missouri River, where visitors enjoy the riverfront parks, boating and fishing. In winter ice fishing and skating are popular.

Rates: $30-$43. Mildred Cameron.
6 R. 2 PB. 1 FP. Beds: KQDT. Continental breakfast. CCs: MC VISA AE.
Seen in: *South Dakota Magazine, Yankton Press and Dakotan.*
"Gorgeous house. Thank you for your hospitality. It made the evening perfect."

TENNESSEE

GATLINBURG E26/*F10*

Buckhorn Inn

Rt 3 Box 393
Gatlinburg TN 37738
(615) 436-4668

Circa 1937. Set high on a hilltop, Buckhorn is surrounded by more than 30 acres of woodlands and green lawns. There are inspiring mountain

views and a spring-fed lake on the grounds. Original paintings enhance the antique-filled guest rooms, most with working fireplaces.

Location: One mile from the Great Smoky Mountains National Park.

Rates: $65-$105. John & Connie Burns.

10 R. 10 PB. 5 FP. Phone available. TV available. Beds: KQDT. B&B. Gourmet meals. Handicap access. Conference room. Ski area nearby.

Seen in: *The Atlanta Journal and Constitution, Country.*

GREENEVILLE N22/*E10*

Big Spring Inn

315 N Main St
Greeneville TN 37743
(615) 638-2917 (800) 245-2155

Circa 1905. This three-story brick manor house has huge porches, leaded and stained-glass windows, a grand entrance hall and an upstairs library. Original wallpaper illustrating a park with willow trees and men, women and children strolling by is still in the dining room. The dining room is also graced with a 1790 Hepplewhite table. The house is in the Main Street Historical District of Greeneville. The smallest state in the United States, Franklin, was formed here when local pioneers seceded from North Carolina. It later became a part of Tennessee, having lasted only three years.

*Rates: $60-$85. Jeanne Driese & Cheryl Van Dyck.

6 R. 5 PB. 2 FP. Phone available. TV available. Beds: KQD. MAP. Gourmet meals. Swimming pool. Conference room. FAX. CCs: MC VISA AE DS. Hiking, whitewater rafting, golf, ballooning, fishing. Honeymoon, golf & hiking packages.

Seen in: *Kingsport Times News, Winston-Salem Journal.*

"We couldn't have chosen any place more perfect."

KNOXVILLE D24/*F9*

Compton Manor

3747 Kingston Pike
Knoxville TN 37919
(615) 523-1204

Circa 1925. This exquisite stone house is reminiscent of the 1485 Compton Wynyates, a Tudor manor in the English countryside. It features a coat of arms, a tower and stone-mullioned windows, all on three acres of green lawns, dogwood, giant oaks and woodland. There is a great hall, a library and a circular staircase. The Duchess is an octagonal room furnished with a mahogany four-poster bed and boasts a fine view of the terrace, garden and pool. Your host family is suitably English.

Rates: $65-$85. Brian & Hala Hunt.

3 R. 3 PB. Phone available. TV available. Beds: KDT. Continental-plus breakfast. Swimming pool. CCs: MC VISA. Water sports, antiquing, Smoky Mountains.

Seen in: *Country Inns.*

"The hospitality was excellent, and the home itself is simply incomparable."

The Graustein Inn

8300 Nubbin Ridge Rd
Knoxville TN 37923
(615) 690-7007

This enchanting European chateau, nestled on 20 wooded acres at the end of a quarter-mile driveway, is a reproduction of an 1870 German inn. Old World craftsmen used historic building methods and materials including 200 tons of limestone to create this gray stone estate. Tongue-and-groove walnut walls and a circular three-story central staircase are features of the inn. The Great Smoky

Mountain National Park is 30 minutes away.

Location: Twenty minutes west of downtown.

*Rates: $55-$125. Darlene & Jim Lara, Vanessa Gwin.

5 R. 3 PB. 1 FP. Phone available. TV available. Beds: QDT. Full breakfast. Gourmet meals. Conference room. CCs: MC VISA AE. Hiking, water skiing.

Seen in: *Knoxville News.*

"Almost overwhelmingly wonderful," Vicki Davis, *Huntsville Times.*

LOUDON E23/*F9*

River Road Inn

River Road, PO Box 372
Loudon TN 37774
(615) 458-4861 (615) 483-9900

Circa 1857. River Road Inn, a Federal-style home, is in the National Register. Furnished with antiques, the inn features a teakwood circular staircase that winds up three floors. Extensive gardens provide additional enjoyment as well as a bushy screen for fishing.

Location: Thirty miles southwest of Knoxville.

*Rates: $65-$85. Kent & Pamela Foster.

5 R. 5 PB. 4 FP. Phone available. TV available. Beds: QDC. Full breakfast. Gourmet meals. Spa. Swimming pool. Conference room. CCs: MC VISA. Boating, fishing, tennis. Weddings, picnics.

Seen in: *Knoxville News Sentinel, News-Herald.*

"Your gracious hospitality and delicious food have ministered to us immensely!"

MEMPHIS H2/G1

Lowenstein-Long House
217 N Waldran-1084 Poplar
Memphis TN 38105
(901) 527-7174

Circa 1900. Department-store owner Abraham Lowenstein built this Victorian mansion, and it later became the Beethoven Music Club. In the For-

ties it was a boarding house, the Elizabeth Club for Girls, in the days before young ladies had their own apartments.

Rates: $50-$70. Samantha & Walter Long.
3 R. 3 PB. 3 FP. Phone available. TV in room. Beds: Q. Continental-plus breakfast. Conference room. CCs: MC VISA AE. Shopping & dining. Wedding facilities.
Seen in: *Commercial Appeal.*
"We found it just lovely and enjoyed our stay very much."

MONTEAGLE H17/G7

Edgeworth Inn
PO Box 340
Monteagle TN 37356
(615) 924-2669 (615) 924-2476

Circa 1896. Edgeworth is a three-story pale yellow Victorian situated on the Monteagle Assembly grounds, formed to provide a 19th-century program of

lectures and entertainment in a resort setting (a chautauqua). Wide verandas are filled with white wicker furnishings and breezy hammocks. Guest rooms are decorated in floral prints with brass and iron beds. The assembly is 96 acres of rolling hills, creeks and Victorian cottages. Waterfalls, natural caves and scenic overlooks are along the trails of nearby South Cumberland State Park.

Rates: $70-$95. Merrily Teasley.
9 R. 8 PB. 1 FP. Phone available. TV available. Beds: KDT. B&B. CCs: MC VISA. Swimming, hiking.
Seen in: *Country Inns.*
"Leaving totally rejuvenated."

ROGERSVILLE M21/E10

Hale Springs Inn
110 W Main St
Rogersville TN 37857
(615) 272-5171

Circa 1824. On the town square, this is the oldest continually operating inn in the state. Presidents Andrew Jack-

son, James Polk and Andrew Johnson stayed here. McKinney Tavern, as it was known then, was Union headquarters during the Civil War. Canopy beds, working fireplaces and an evening meal by candlelight in the elegant dining room all make for a romantic stay. A formal garden with a gazebo has recently been restored.

Location: Near Gatlinburg.
*Rates: $45-$75. Ed Pace & Sue Livesay.
10 R. 10 PB. 9 FP. Phone available. TV in room. Beds: KQT. EP. Restaurant. Game room. Conference room. CCs: MC VISA AE. Swimming, tennis, golf, boating.
Seen in: *The Miami Herald, Southern Living, Travel South.*
"It was truly a step back to a more gracious way of life."

RUGBY C21/E8

Newbury House at Historic Rugby
Hwy 52, PO Box 8
Rugby TN 37733
(615) 628-2430

Circa 1880. Mansard-roofed Newbury House first lodged visitors to this English village when author and social reformer Thomas Hughes, founded Rugby. Filled with authentic Victorian antiques, the inn includes some furnishings that are original to the colony. There is also a restored three-bedroom cottage on the property.

Rates: $50-$60. Historic Rugby Staff.
5 R. 3 PB. 1 FP. Phone available. Beds: DC. Full breakfast. Restaurant. Conference room. CCs: MC VISA. Hiking, white-water rafting, canoeing.
Seen in: *The New York Times, Americana, USA Weekend, The Tennessean.*
"I love the peaceful atmosphere here and the beauty of nature surrounding Rugby."

TEXAS

AMARILLO WE12/*G2*

Parkview House

1311 S Jefferson
Amarillo TX 79101
(806) 373-9464

Circa 1909. This is one of those Grandma's houses filled with friendliness and warmth. There's an eclectic, homey collection of early American

and Victorian country decor. If you plan ahead you may be able to convince Nabil Dia to prepare a Middle Eastern breakfast for you.

*Rates: $50-$75. Carol & Nabil Dia.
5 R. 2 PB. Phone available. TV in room. Beds: QD. Continental-plus breakfast. Spa. CCs: MC VISA. Bicycles, tennis, hiking, fishing, swimming, horseback riding.
Seen in: *Amarillo Globe News, New Orleans Magazine.*

"We have been spoiled and will never want to stay at a dull motel again."

AUSTIN EM7/*D7*

Brook House

609 W 33rd St
Austin TX 78705
(512) 459-0534

Circa 1922. Surrounded by large oaks and lush landscaping, the Brook House is a charming example of period architecture. The large back porch overlooks the backyard and faces the Cottage and Carriage House. Rooms are furnished with antiques. The Rose Room features an antique claw-foot bathtub and a stained-glass window.

Rates: $59-$89. Jan Adaire.
5 R. 5 PB. 1 FP. Phone in room. TV in room. Beds: KQDTC. Full breakfast. Gourmet meals. Water sports, winery tours, shops.
Seen in: *Key Magazine.*

"Your charming warmth and hospitality and attention to every detail made us feel like pampered royalty...and we loved it!"

The McCallum House

613 W 32nd
Austin TX 78705
(512) 451-6744

Circa 1907. This two-story Princess Anne Victorian was built by school superintendent A.N. McCallum and designed by his wife Jane. As Mrs.

McCallum raised her five children she assumed a leadership position in the women's suffrage movement and formed the "Petticoat Lobby" advancing human service reforms in Texas. In 1926 she became secretary of state for Texas. In addition to four rooms in the main house with private porches, all suites with kitchens. It is an eight-block walk to the University of Texas.

Rates: $60-$70. Nancy & Roger Danley.
5 R. 5 PB. Phone in room. TV available. Beds: QDT. Full breakfast. State Capitol Building, LBJ Library.
Seen in: *Austin American Statesman.*

"What a special home and history. It is lucky that you are bringing it back to life!"

Southard House

908 Blanco
Austin TX 78703
(512) 474-4731

Circa 1900. This house, an Austin historic landmark, originally had a single story but was raised to accommodate an additional level at the turn of the century. There is an upper and lower parlor, and 11-foot ceilings provide a background for antiques and paintings. A gazebo, porch and deck are popular spots.

Location: Twelve blocks from the Capitol and within walking distance of the river.
*Rates: $52-$99. The Southards.
5 R. 5 PB. 1 FP. Phone in room. TV available. Beds: QDT. Continental-plus breakfast. CCs: MC VISA AE DC CB DS.

"A memory to be long cherished. We especially enjoyed the home atmosphere and the lovely breakfasts in the garden."

CHAPPELL HILL EM9/*E8*

The Browning Plantation

Rt 1 Box 8
Chappell Hill TX 77426
(409) 836-6144 (713) 661-6761

Circa 1856. Reigning over 170 acres, this graceful white Greek Revival house with dark green shutters has been handsomely reconstructed. It was devastated by a hurricane and abandoned for 22 years before the Ganchans bought it. The restored verandas are a favorite spot. Inside, pastel walls enhance dark wood floors and Victorian furnishings. Each guest room has a half bath, and the third floor holds a "he-man" hunter's bathroom and a Victorian ladies bath.

Rates: $75-$110. Dick & Mildred Ganchan.
6 R. 4 PB. 4 FP. Phone available. TV available. Beds: QDT. Full breakfast. Gourmet meals. Swimming pool. Bicycling, antiquing. Weddings/receptions, special parties & dinners.
Seen in: *The Sunday Express-News, Southern Living, Houston Chronicle, Texas Highways.*

"Thank you for providing this peaceful retreat from what is often a crazy world."

ENNIS EG9/*B8*

Raphael House

500 W Ennis Ave
Ennis TX 75119
(214) 875-1555

Circa 1906. Built and owned by the Raphael family for 82 years, this Greek Revival house is highlighted with a three-story porch. Century-old

pecan trees border a gracious English garden. Inside, the open foyer flows to a parlor, separated only by massive, polished, clear pine Doric columns. There are gleaming heart pine floors throughout and many original furnishings. Spacious bedchambers include handsome antique bedsteads and canopied beds, all with down comforters. A carriage pulled by Belgian horses stops to pick up riders across the street from the inn.

Location: One half hour south of Dallas.
*Rates: $55-$85. Danna K. Cody.
6 R. 6 PB. Phone available. TV available. Beds: KQD. Full breakfast. Gourmet meals. Conference room. FAX. CCs: MC VISA AE. Tennis, golf, fishing, nature trails, antiquing, Super Collider.
Seen in: *Dallas Morning News, Dallas Times-Herald, Ft. Worth Star-Telegram.*
"This house has been refurbished to a truly magnificent standard by a perfectionist."

FORT DAVIS WR8/*D3*

Sutler's Limpia Hotel

PO Box 822
Fort Davis TX 79734
(915) 426-3237

Circa 1912. Located on the town square, this hotel was constructed of pink limestone quarried nearby. It was restored in 1978. The parlor features a fireplace and over-stuffed furniture. All the guest rooms have period oak furnishings. High tin ceilings are found throughout. There is a sun porch and veranda, both with views of the mountains.

Rates: $42-$60. Joan Stocks Nobles.
20 R. 20 PB. Phone available. TV in room. Beds: DT. Restaurant. CCs: MC VISA AE.
Seen in: *San Angelo Standard Times, Texas Monthly.*
"Not many like this one left. Great."

FREDERICKSBURG EM4/*D6*

Country Cottage Inn

405 E Main St
Fredericksburg TX 78624
(512) 997-8549

Circa 1850. This beautifully preserved house was built by blacksmith and cutler Frederick Kiehne. With 2-foot-

thick walls, it was the first two-story limestone house in town. The Country Cottage holds a collection of Texas primitives and German country antiques, accentuated by Laura Ashley linens. Some of the baths include whirlpool tubs.

*Rates: $65-$95. Jeffery Webb, Jean & Mike Sudderth.
5 R. 5 PB. 1 FP. Phone in room. TV available. Beds: KC. Continental-plus breakfast. Spa. CCs: MC. Front-porch swings, water sports.
Seen in: *Weekend Getaway, Dallas Morning News.*
"A step back in time in 1850 style."

GALVESTON EO14/*E9*

Victorian Inn

511 17th St
Galveston TX 77550
(409) 762-3235

Circa 1899. This red brick Italianate-style house is surrounded by the original fences and gates. There is wicker furniture on one side of the wraparound porch. The inn features yellow maple floors, bird's-eye maple wainscoting, five fireplaces of carved oak with Belgian tiles and contemporary furniture. Some guest rooms have fireplaces and private balconies.

Rates: $80-$150. Janice & Bob Hellbusch.
6 R. 2 PB. Phone available. TV available. Beds: KDT. Continental-plus breakfast. Conference room. CCs: MC VISA AE. Water sports, golf, tennis nearby. Honeymoons, retreats.
"The inn was great, and both of you added that little something extra that made my stay truly memorable."

GALVESTON ISLAND EO14/*E9*

Gilded Thistle B&B

1805 Broadway
Galveston Island TX 77550
(409) 763-0194

Circa 1893. The Gilded Thistle is a fanciful Victorian with a double bay and porches overlooking flower gardens. A gracious antique-filled parlor

is dominated by a handsome fireplace and floor-to-ceiling windows. Wine and cheese are served in the evening.

Rates: $100-$135. Season: Jan. - Dec. Helen L. Hanemann.
3 R. 1 PB. Phone available. TV in room. Beds: D. B&B. CCs: MC VISA.
Seen in: *House Beautiful, The New York Times, Texas Monthly, PM Magazine.*
"Best B&B in Texas!"

HOUSTON EN13/*E9*

Durham House

921 Heights Blvd
Houston TX 77008
(713) 868-4654

Circa 1903. Located 10 minutes from downtown Houston, this Victorian house, listed in the National Register of Historic Places, was built by the

area's first fire chief. Antique furniture, a gazebo, player piano, tandem bicycle and tapes of old radio programs create an atmosphere reminiscent of the early 1900s. Breakfast in bed and romantic dining locations are available for guests, and innkeeper Marguerite Swanson offers escorted tours of the city.

*Rates: $60-$75. Marguerite Swanson.
5 R. 4 PB. Phone available. TV in room.

Beds: QD. Full breakfast. CCs: MC VISA AE. Horseback riding, jogging, tennis, swimming, polo. Weddings, receptions, murder-mystery dinner parties.
Seen in: *Victorian Homes, Houston Chronicle.*
"Another comfortable, wonderful stay."

Robin's Nest

4104 Greeley St
Houston TX 77006
(713) 528-5821

Circa 1894. Legend denotes this former dairy farm as one of the oldest homes in Houston. The inn features elegant, tall windows and ceiling fans. Beautiful flowers decorate the front lawn of this home. Guests will appreciate the inn's proximity to downtown Houston, theaters and gourmet restaurants. Located in the Montrose area of the city, the inn is less than an hour from popular attractions such as NASA and Galveston.
Rates: $50-$55. Robin Smith.
4 R. Phone available. TV in room. Beds: D. Full breakfast. CCs: MC VISA. Museums, theater.
Seen in: *Houston Home and Garden.*
"Home away from home at your nest."

Sara's B&B Inn

941 Heights Blvd
Houston TX 77008
(713) 868-1130 (800) 593-1130

Circa 1898. This mauve and white, gingerbread Victorian is located in the Houston Heights, one of the first planned suburbs in Texas. A three-story stairway winds up to a cupola and there are handsome bay windows and a turret. Antiques fill the rooms, named after Texas cities.
Location: Four miles from downtown.
Rates: $46-$96. Donna & Tillman Arledge.
12 R. 3 PB. Phone available. TV available. Beds: KQDTC. Continental breakfast. Spa. CCs: MC VISA AE DC CB. Bicycles, jogging, walking.
Seen in: *Houston Chronicle, Texas Homes, Elle, Travellife.*
"Donna and Tillman Arledge have taken the very best from our British pals and added their own special blend of Texan hospitality and high taste," Elle.

JEFFERSON EF14/B9

McKay House

306 E Delta St
Jefferson TX 75657
(903) 665-7322 (903) 348-1929

Circa 1851. Both Lady Bird Johnson and Alex Haley have enjoyed the gracious Southern hospitality offered at the McKay House. Accented by a Williamsburg-style picket fence, the Greek Revival cottage features a pillared front porch. Heart-of-pine floors, 14-foot ceilings and documented wallpapers complement antique furnishings. Orange and pecan French toast or home-baked muffins and shirred eggs are served on vintage china. Victorian nightshirts and gowns await guests in each of the bedchambers.
*Rates: $70-$125. Peggy & Tom Taylor.
7 R. 7 PB. 7 FP. Phone available. Beds: QD. B&B. CCs: MC VISA. Mule-drawn buggy, trolley, train, museum.
Seen in: *Southern Accents, The Dallas Morning News, Country Home, Southern Bride.*
"The facilities of the McKay House are exceeded only by the service and dedication of the owners."

KARNACK EF15/B10

Mimosa Hall

Rt 1 Box 635
Karnack TX 75661
(903) 679-3632 (214) 938-4982

Circa 1844. Located on 150 acres, Mimosa Hall boasts a Greek Revival portico of hand-hewn cypress. The brick was made in kilns on the plantation. Listed in the National Register of Historic Places, the inn is surrounded by magnolia, cedar, pecan, maple and oak trees and a magnificent American elm. The inn has many antiques and features an 1860s parlor, a library, porches, a balcony and a museum room with information about the house and the area. Homemade biscuits and sweet-potato pie are served at the inn.
Rates: $90-$125. Carter & Virginia Hamilton.
4 R. 2 PB. 4 FP. Phone available. Beds: QDT. Full breakfast. Gourmet meals. Golf, Caddo Lake, historic sites.
Seen in: *Marshall News Messenger, Longview News Journal, The Dallas Morning News.*
"Thanks for making us feel like family."

MARSHALL EF14/B9

Three Oaks

609 N Washington
Marshall TX 75670
(903) 938-6123

Circa 1895. Three towering bur oaks shade the lawn of this Colonial Revival house with a widow's walk atop a sculptured tin roof. A bay window and six-over-six windows attest to Queen Anne accents. Tall columns divide the entrance hall and music rooms highlighting the 13-foot ceilings. Beveled, cut-glass French doors open from the parlor to a conservatory. The house is furnished with period oak and walnut furnishings. Three Oaks is a seven-room suite popular as a "honeymoon retreat" or for two couples traveling together.
Rates: $85. Season: April - December. Sandra & Bob McCoy.
1 R. 1 PB. 1 FP. Phone in room. TV in room. Beds: QD. B&B. Horseback riding, skiing, water sports, golf, tennis, museums, antique shops.
Seen in: *Marshall News Messenger, Longview Morning Journal.*
"The house is magnificent — with hosts to match!!"

Wood Boone Norrell House

215 E Rusk St
Marshall TX 75670
(903) 935-1800 (800) 423-1356

Circa 1884. This Queen Anne house features veranda porches, a large balcony, Eastlake bay windows, ruby red etched glass set in the front door and a grand staircase in the foyer. The subfloors are cypress, and the tongue-and-groove floors are oak and yellow pine. Each room is decorated with turn-of-the-century antiques.
Rates: $65. Mike & Patsy Norrell.
5 R. 5 PB. 4 FP. Phone available. TV available. Beds: QD. Full breakfast. Conference room. CCs: MC VISA AE. Golf, horseback riding, water sports, antiquing. Honeymoon, anniversary & wedding specials. Local tour-guide service.
Seen in: *Marshall News, Dallas Morning News, Plano Profile.*
"Our visit to your house has given us some wonderful memories we will cherish forever."

SAN ANTONIO E05/E7

The Bullis House Inn

621 Pierce St, PO Box 8059
San Antonio TX 78208
(512) 223-9426

Circa 1909. A two-story portico supported by six massive columns accentuates the neo-classical architecture of this home built for General Bullis who was instrumental in the capture of Chief Geronimo. Features include stairways and paneling of tiger's eye oak, marble fireplaces, chandeliers and parquet floors. There are contemporary and antique furnishings.
Rates: $36-$55. Steve & Alma Cross.
8 R. 1 PB. 5 FP. Phone available. TV available. Beds: KQDC. Continental-plus breakfast. Conference room. CCs: MC VISA AE DS. Tennis, golf, horseback riding. Honeymoon, wedding, family reunions.
"Loved your home and your hospitality very much."

SAN AUGUSTINE E15/C10

The Wade House

128 E Columbia St
San Augustine TX 75972
(409) 275-2605 (409) 275-2553

The Wade House is a Mount Vernon-style red brick house located two blocks from the old courthouse square. Guest rooms are decorated in a mixture of contemporary and antique furnishings and are cooled by both ceiling fans and air conditioning.

❀Rates: $40-$80. Julia & Nelsyn Wade.
5 R. 3 PB. Phone available. Beds: KQD. B&B. Handicap access. Conference room. CCs: MC VISA. Golf nearby.
Seen in: *San Augustine Tribune.*
"The house is one of the most beautiful in the area. Each room is decorated to the utmost excellence."

STEPHENVILLE EH6/C7

The Oxford House

563 N Graham
Stephenville TX 76401
(817) 965-6885 (817) 968-8171

Circa 1898. A $3,000 lawyer's fee provided funds for construction of The Oxford House, and the silver was

brought to town in a buckboard by W. J. Oxford, Esq. The house was built of cypress with porches three-quarters of the way around. Hand-turned gingerbread trim and a carved wooden ridgerow are special features.

Rates: $72. Paula & Bill Oxford.
4 R. 4 PB. Phone available. TV available. Beds: QDC. Continental-plus breakfast. Gourmet meals. CCs: MC VISA. Antiquing.
Seen in: *Glamour Magazine.*
"A perfect evening of serenity sitting on the front porch with such kind hosts."

UTAH

MIDWAY E7/B4

The Homestead

700 N Homestead Dr
Midway UT 84049
(801) 654-1102 (800) 327-7220

Circa 1886. Simon Schneitter originally built this two-story brick house for his parents and the family soon began taking in guests when travelers began to appreciate the site's mineral springs. In the Fifties it was redeveloped as the Homestead. The Virginia House is the most historic part of the lodge.

*Rates: $69-$175. Britt Mathwich.

92 R. 92 PB. Phone in room. TV in room. Beds: KQD. Restaurant. Gourmet meals. Spa. Sauna. Handicap access. Swimming pool. Conference room. FAX. CCs: MC VISA AE. Golf, hot air ballooning, tennis, horseback riding, cross-country skiing, sleigh & hay rides, trout fishing, mountain bikes, snowmobiling. Kid camp.

Seen in: *Dallas Morning News, National Geographic, Express-News, Country Inns.*

"The Homestead is the most romantic place Nicole and I have ever been."

PARK CITY D7/C4

The Old Miners' Lodge A B&B Inn

615 Woodside Ave, PO Box 2639
Park City UT 84060-2639
(801) 645-8068 (800) 648-8068

Circa 1893. This originally was established as a miners' boarding house by E. P. Ferry, owner of the Woodside-

Norfolk silver mines. A two-story Victorian with western flavor, the lodge is a significant structure in the Park City National Historic District. Just on the edge of the woods beyond the house is a deck and a steaming hot tub.

Location: In the historic district.

*Rates: $40-$175. Jeff Sadowsky, Susan Wynne & Hugh Daniels.

10 R. 10 PB. 1 FP. Phone available. Beds: KQDTC. B&B. Gourmet meals. Spa. Conference room. CCs: MC VISA AE DS. Downhill & cross-country skiing, golf, tennis, ice skating, hiking. Non-smoking inn.

Seen in: *Boston Herald, Los Angeles Times.*

"This is the creme de la creme. The most wonderful place I have stayed at bar none including ski country in the U.S. and Europe."

Washington School Inn

544 Park Ave, PO Box 536
Park City UT 84060
(801) 649-3800 (800) 824-1672

Circa 1889. Made of local limestone, this inn was the former schoolhouse for Park City children. With its classic

belltower, the four-story building is listed in the National Register. The inn is noted for its luxuriously appointed guest rooms. An inviting spa and sauna are on the property.

Location: Park City Historic District.

*Rates: $75-$225. Nancy Beaufait & Delphine Covington.

15 R. 15 PB. 2 FP. Phone in room. TV available. Beds: KQT. Continental-plus breakfast. Spa. Sauna. Conference room. FAX. CCs: MC VISA AE. Skiing.

Seen in: *San Diego Magazine, The Arizona Daily Star, The Salt Lake Tribune.*

"The end of the rainbow."

SAINT GEORGE M3/G1

Greene Gate Village Historic B&B Inn

76 W Tabernacle
Saint George UT 84770
(801) 628-6999

Circa 1876. This is a cluster of four restored pioneer homes all located within one block. The Bentley House has a comfortable Victorian decor while the Supply Depot is decorated in a style reflective of its origin as a shop for wagoners on their way to California. The Orson Pratt house and the Carriage House are other choices, all carefully restored.

*❀Rates: $35-$75. Mark & Barbara Greene.

15 R. 12 PB. 9 FP. Phone in room. TV in room. Beds: KQDTWC. B&B. Gourmet meals. Spa. Handicap access. Swimming pool. Conference room. CCs: MC VISA AE. Golf, hiking, boating, tennis.

Seen in: *Deseret News, Spectrum.*

"You not only provided me with rest, comfort and wonderful food, but you fed my soul."

Seven Wives Inn

217 N 100 W
Saint George UT 84770
(801) 628-3737 (800) 484-1084 .. 0165

Circa 1873. The inn is named after the innkeeper's great-grandfather Benjamin Johnson who served Joseph Smith, founder of the Mormon Church, as private secretary. Mr. Johnson had seven wives. The Melissa room was named after his first wife and it features a fireplace and American oak antiques. The attic of the house, concealed by a secret door, is thought to have been a refuge for polygamists. It is now the Jane room and has a skylight and stenciling.

*Rates: $35-$70. Donna & Jay Curtis; Alison & Jon Bowcutt.

13 R. 13 PB. 6 FP. Phone available. TV in room. Beds: QTC. Full breakfast. Swimming pool. Conference room. CCs: MC VISA AE DC. Golf, horseback riding. , tennis.

Seen in: *Innsider, Salt Lake Tribune.*

"This was great! We want to return."

SALT LAKE CITY D6/B3

Brigham Street Inn

1135 E South Temple
Salt Lake City UT 84102
(801) 364-4461

Circa 1896. This turreted Victorian is one of many historic mansions that dot South Temple Street (formerly Brigham Street). The formal dining room features golden oak woodwork and a fireplace. With skylights, fireplaces or perhaps a spa, each of the nine rooms was created by a dif-

ferent designer for a showcase benefit for the Utah Heritage Foundation. The American Institute of Architects and several historic associations have presented the inn with architectural awards.
*Rates: $65-$140. Nancy & John Pace.
9 R. 9 PB. 5 FP. Beds: QWC. Continental-plus breakfast. Spa. FAX. CCs: MC VISA AE. 40 minutes from five major ski areas. Seen in: *Innsider.*
"This is a great inn! It's unbelievably elegant and you have a terrific staff."

The Spruces B&B
6151 S 900 E
Salt Lake City UT 84121
(801) 268-8762
Circa 1903. This Gothic Victorian was built as a residence for cabinetmaker Martin Gunnerson and his family. It is

set amidst 16 tall spruce trees transplanted in 1915 from Big Cottonwood Canyon. The house is decorated with folk art and southwestern touches. The Cellar Suite includes a hydrobath and children enjoy its fruit cellar bedroom. A quarter horse breeding farm is adjacent.
*Rates: $50-$100. Jill & Lyle Bates.
7 R. 4 PB. Beds: QDT. Continental-plus breakfast. Spa. Conference room. CCs: MC VISA. Skiing.
"We have never had a more peaceful, serene business trip. Thank you for your hospitality."

VERMONT

ARLINGTON 02/F1

The Arlington Inn

Historic Rt 7A
Arlington VT 05250
(802) 375-6532 (800) 443-9442

Circa 1840. The Arlington Inn is one of Vermont's finest examples of Greek Revival architecture. Set on lushly

landscaped grounds, the inn boasts elegantly appointed guest rooms filled with period antiques. Norman Rockwell once used the carriage house as a studio.

Location: Intersection of Route 313.
*Rates: $70-$150. Paul & Madeline Kruzel.
13 R. 13 PB. 1 FP. Phone available. TV available. Beds: QDT. B&B. Game room. Conference room. CCs: MC VISA AE. Skiing, hiking, biking, canoeing, antiqueing.
Seen in: *New York, Bon Appetit.*
"What a romantic place and such outrageous food!!"

The Inn on Covered Bridge Green

RD 1 Box 3550, River Rd
Arlington VT 05250
(802) 375-9489

Circa 1792. A quaint red covered bridge over the Battenkill River leads to this colonial inn, home to Norman Rockwell for 12 years. The artist was inspired by Arlington's scenes and people and the five guest rooms at the inn are named for the framed Rockwell prints that adorn their walls. The rooms are filled with comfortable chairs, old-fashioned dressers, armoires and desks, Norman Rockwell style. A hearty New England breakfast reinforces your enjoyment of the countryside. The artist's actual two-bedroom studio may be booked by the week. Dinners are available by prior arrangement.

Rates: $100-$160. Anne & Ron Weber.
5 R. 4 PB. Phone available. TV available. Beds: KQDT. B&B. Gourmet meals. Fishing, tubing, canoeing, swimming. Weddings.
Seen in: *Vermont Life, The San Diego Union, The Boston Globe.*
"We find it difficult to leave. Everything is perfect."

Hill Farm Inn

RR 2 Box 2015
Arlington VT 05250
(802) 375-2269 (800) 882-2545

Circa 1790. One of Vermont's original land grant farmsteads, Hill Farm Inn has welcomed guests since 1905 when the widow Mettie Hill opened her

home to summer vacationers. One section of the house was hauled by 40 yoke of oxen to its present location. The farm has recently benefited from a community conservancy group's efforts to save it from subdivision.

Location: One half mile from Historic Route 7A.
**Rates: $65-$90. George & Joanne Hardy.
13 R. 8 PB. Phone available. TV available. Beds: KQTC. MAP. CCs: MC VISA AE DS. Downhill and cross-country skiing, hiking, fishing, bicycles.
Seen in: *Providence Journal, Boston Globe, Innsider.*
"A superb location with lots to do indoors and out. Beautifully kept rooms and excellent home cooking."

The Inn at Sunderland

Historic Rt 7A
Arlington VT 05250
(802) 362-4213

Circa 1840. On the Battenkill River at the foot of Mount Equinox is The Inn at Sunderland. This restored Victorian farmhouse features chestnut trim and doors, 11-foot ceilings, a polished walnut staircase, marble fireplaces and a two-level porch overlooking the back pasture and Green Mountains.

Rates: $65-$95. Season: May - April 10. Tom & Peggy Wall.
10 R. 8 PB. 4 FP. Beds: QDTC. Full breakfast. Handicap access. CCs: MC VISA AE. Fishing, golf, tennis, bicycling, canoeing, hiking.
Seen in: *Yankee, Family Circle, Country Living, Bennington Banner, Boston Globe, Los Angeles Times.*
"We've traveled many inns. This is the best!"

West Mountain Inn

Box 481
Arlington VT 05250
(802) 375-6516

Circa 1849. Goats and llamas graze the hillside of this sprawling New England farmhouse situated on 150

acres of meadows and woodland. The inn overlooks the Battenkill River. Each room boasts amenities such as a lace canopied bed, a balcony or a fireplace. The Rockwell Kent Suite graced with a cathedral ceiling, features a fireplace and king-size bed. Back porches and decks are filled with Adirondack lawn chairs. The innkeepers include a former school principal and a Vermont state senator.

*Rates: $140-$163 MAP. Mary Ann & Wes Carlson.
15 R. 15 PB. 3 FP. Phone available. TV available. Beds: KQD. Full breakfast. Handicap access. Conference room. CCs: MC VISA AE. Hiking, biking, canoeing, cross-country and downhill skiing.
Seen in: *Family Circle, Schenectady Gazette, New York Post, Daily News.*
"Excellent, warm, friendly, relaxing, absolutely the best!"

BARRE H5/C3

Woodruff House

13 East St
Barre VT 05641
(802) 476-7745

Circa 1883. This Queen Anne Victorian with green shutters was built by an area granite manufacturer. (Barre is the Granite Center of the

World and has the world's largest granite quarries.) The Woodruff House has an eclectic atmosphere and friendly family.

Location: Halfway between Boston & Montreal.
Rates: $50-$65. Robert & Terry Somani & Katie.
2 R. Phone available. TV available. Beds: KQ. Full breakfast.
"Friendly and warm. Like going home to Grandma's. The hospitality was wonderful."

BELLOWS FALLS N5/F3

Blue Haven B&B

Rt 5 Box 328
Bellows Falls VT 05101
(802) 463-9008

Circa 1830. Once a schoolhouse, this inn features wide oak-plank flooring, an art library, a wood-warmed country kitchen and a fireplace made from huge stones brought from all over the country and Europe. Guest rooms have period hardwood furniture and goose-down comforters.

*Rates: $58. Helene Champagne.
5 R. 1 FP. Phone available. TV available. Beds: DT. Full breakfast. CCs: MC VISA. Horseback riding, cross-country & downhill skiing, bike trails. Buggy & sleigh rides by arrangement.
Seen in: *Town Crier.*
"Charming, friendly host, homey atmosphere, wonderful breakfast."

BENNINGTON P2/G1

The Arlington Inn

See: Arlington, VT

BETHEL J4/D2

Greenhurst Inn

River St, RD 2 Box 60
Bethel VT 05032
(802) 234-9474

Circa 1890. Greenhurst is a gracious Victorian mansion built for the Harringtons of Philadelphia. Overlooking the White River, the inn's opulent in-

teriors include etched windows once featured on the cover of *Vermont Life.* There are eight masterpiece fireplaces and a north and south parlor.

Location: Route 107, 3 miles west of I-89.
*❀Rates: $50-$95. Lyle & Claire Wolf.
13 R. 7 PB. 8 FP. Phone available. TV available. Beds: QDTC. Continental-plus breakfast. Conference room. CCs: MC VISA DS. Tennis, horseback riding, fishing, hiking, biking, canoeing.
Seen in: *Los Angeles Times, Time Magazine.*
"The inn is magnificent! The hospitality unforgettable."

BRANDON K3/D2

The Arches

53 Park St
Brandon VT 05733
(802) 247-8200

Circa 1910. The facade of this unusual Colonial features five arches at the formal entrance. Built around a courtyard, the house was constructed in a U shape. The guest rooms are spacious and offer selections such as a canopy bed or a room with its own fireplace. Stenciled borders are featured. The breakfast room offers expansive views across manicured green lawns. Middlebury and Rutland are within 20 miles of the inn.

*Rates: $70-$95. Ellen & Jack Scheffey.
7 R. 7 PB. 3 FP. Phone available. TV available. Beds: KDTC. B&B. Restaurant. Conference room. CCs: MC VISA AE. Fishing, golf, horseback riding, tennis, skiing, hiking, biking.
Seen in: *Early American Life.*
"Fantastic. We shall return."

The Churchill House Inn

RD 3 Rt 73 East
Brandon VT 05733
(802) 247-3078

Circa 1871. Caleb Churchill and his son Nathan first built a three-story lumber mill, a grist mill and a distillery here, all water powered. Later, with their milled lumber, they constructed this 20-room house. Because of its location it became a stagecoach stop and has served generations of travelers with comfortable accommodations.

Location: Four miles east of Brandon.
❀Rates: $70-$80 MAP. Roy & Lois Jackson.
9 R. 8 PB. Phone available. Beds: KQT. Full breakfast. Spa. Sauna. Swimming pool. CCs: MC VISA. Hiking, cross-country skiing, fishing, bicycling.
Seen in: *Country Magazine.*
"We felt the warm, welcoming, down-home appeal as we entered the front hall. The food was uncommonly good - home cooking with a gourmet flair!"

Moffett House

69 Park St
Brandon VT 05733
(802) 247-3843 (800)752-5794

Circa 1860. This graceful French Second Empire house has a mansard roof and a Queen Anne Victorian veranda that was added in 1880.

Widow walks top the roof, and gingerbread trim adds to the street-side appeal of Moffett House. The inn was named after Hugh Moffett, Time-Life editor and Vermont legislator. A country breakfast is served in the dining room. The Kellington-Pico ski area is nearby.

Rates: $60-$75. Nancy & Elliot Phillips.
6 R. 2 PB. 1 FP. Phone available. TV available. Beds: KQDTC. Full breakfast. Game room. Horseback riding, canoeing, water sports, fishing, golf, skiing, hiking.
Seen in: *Rutland Business Journal.*
"My mother, aunt, cousin and I were all delighted with the lovely accommodations and the delicious breakfasts."

Old Mill Inn

Rd #2
Brandon VT 05773
(802) 247-8002

Circa 1786. Tucked away on 10 acres of woods, meadows and farmland, this inn overlooks the Green Mountains. The Old Mill Inn was originally a grist mill, then a dairy farm. The guest rooms feature handmade quilts, antique furniture, American folk art,

fresh flowers, mints and juices. Wine and cheese are served in the woodsy sitting room. Breakfast includes fresh eggs from the inn's chickens, homemade breads and jams made from berries grown on the property.
Rates: $75-$85. Annemarie & Karl Schreiber.
6 R. 6 PB. Full breakfast. CCs: MC VISA. Skiing, hiking, golf, fishing.

BRATTLEBORO P5/G3

Blue Haven
See: Bellows Falls, VT

BROOKFIELD I5/D3

Green Trails Country Inn
Pond Village, PO Box 494
Brookfield VT 05036
(802) 276-3412 (800) 243-3412
Circa 1790. Two historic houses join to provide the space for the inn's guest rooms, furnished with quilts and antiques. The Stencil Room features original stencils painted over a century ago on its plaster walls. The inn's spacious lawns and pleasant gardens are popular and just across the road is Sunset Lake with a floating bridge and more scenic views. A Vermont-style dinner is usually available. The inn has 25 miles of cross-country ski trails.
Rates: $68-$85. Season: May - March. Pat & Peter Simpson.
15 R. 9 PB. Phone available. TV available. Beds: DTC. MAP. Conference room. Fishing, swimming, canoeing, biking, hiking, picnicking. Country weddings.
Seen in: *Sunday Republican.*
"The inn is really lovely, the welcome very warm and food is scrumptuous."

CHARLOTTE H2/C1

Green Meadows B&B
PO Box 1300
Charlotte VT 05445
(802) 425-3059
Circa 1864. Built by a pioneer family, this Victorian Italiante country home features nutmeg-toned floors and a variety of beautiful antiques. Guests will enjoy a scrumptious breakfast of mixed fruits, juices and homemade breads. Antique shopping and other attractions including the Church St. Market, Morgan Horse Farm and Shelburne are in proximity to this comfortable inn. A visit to nearby Lake Champlain serves as a relaxing way to spend the day.
Rates: $60-$80. Mary Louise Smith.
4 R. 1 PB. Phone available. Beds: QDT. Spa. CCs: MC VISA. Water sports, skiing, hiking, biking, museum.
"A dream, we will return."

CHELSEA J5/D3

Shire Inn
PO Box 37
Chelsea VT 05038
(802) 685-3031
Circa 1832. This handsome Federal home is highlighted by massive granite lintels over each window and the front door. Accentuated with a

picket fence, the inn is on 17 acres of woods and fields, and a stream from the White River flows on the property. Wide-plank flooring is a fine backdrop for a collection of antiques and fireplaces.
Rates: $70-$95. James & Mary Lee Papa.
6 R. 6 PB. 4 FP. Phone available. Beds: KQD. B&B. Gourmet meals. CCs: MC VISA. Swimming, bicycling, hiking, fishing, cross-country skiing.
Seen in: *Country Inn Review, Vermont Life.*
"Max and I really enjoyed our stay in your wonderful inn and the meals were great."

CHESTER N5/F3

Chester House
Main St, PO Box 708
Chester VT 05143
(802) 875-2205
Circa 1780. This beautifully restored Federal-style clapboard home is listed in the National Registry of Historic

Places. It is situated across from the village green in the quaint and historic village of Chester. The inn is tastefully furnished throughout with early American furniture and appointments.
Rates: $50-$70. Irene & Norm Wright.
4 R. 4 PB. Phone available. TV available. Beds: KQTD. Full breakfast. Spa. Conference room. Downhill & cross-country skiing, bicycling, hiking, antiquing.
"The best hosts and the greatest of inns."

Greenleaf Inn
PO Box 188
Chester VT 05143
(802) 875-3171
Circa 1850. This Victorian has changed ownership only three times in 140 years. Set on a spacious lawn, the inn looks out to ancient apple

trees and a babbling brook. It is furnished with antiques such as a Hepplewhite dining room set, and there is a gallery displaying Vermont artists' paintings of New England life. The innkeeper, Dan Duffield, spent his summers here on the old Newton farm as a boy.
Rates: $70-$80. Elizabeth & Dan Duffield.
5 R. 5 PB. Phone available. Beds: QT. B&B. Game room. CCs: MC VISA. Skiing.
Seen in: *Black River Tribune.*
"We found paradise! Your inn is a piece of heaven on Earth! We'll be back!"

Henry Farm Inn
PO Box 646
Chester VT 05143
(802) 875-2674
Circa 1750. Fifty acres of scenic woodlands provide the setting for this handsomely restored stagecoach stop

in the Green Mountains. There are original wide pine floors, eight fireplaces, and carefully selected early American furnishings. A pond and river are nearby.
Rates: $70-$90. Jean Bowman.
7 R. 7 PB. 8 FP. Phone available. TV available. Beds: TW. Full breakfast. CCs: MC VISA. Skating, antiquing, horseback riding, and skiing.

Hugging Bear Inn & Shoppe
Main St, PO Box 32
Chester VT 05143
(802) 875-2412
Circa 1850. Among the 4,000 teddy

bear inhabitants of this white Victorian inn, several peek out from the third story windows of the octagonal tower. There is a teddy bear shop on the premises and children and adults can borrow a bear to take to bed with them. Rooms are decorated with antiques. A bear puppet show is often staged during breakfast.
Rates: $70-$90. Georgette, Diane & Paul Thomas.
6 R. 6 PB. Phone available. TV available. Beds: DTC. Full breakfast. CCs: MC VISA DS. Tennis, hiking, biking, golf.
Seen in: *Rutland Daily Herald, Exxon Travel Magazine, Teddy Bear Review.*
"Thanks seems to be too small of a word to describe our greatest appreciation toward all of you for all of your warmth and hospitality."

The Inn at Long Last
PO Box 589
Chester VT 05143
(802) 875-2444
Circa 1923. Located on the green, this renovated inn reflects the personality of the owner Jack Coleman, former college president and author. Fulfilling a dream, he has created an inn for all seasons with fine cuisine and civilized surroundings. A library, tennis courts, fishing stream, and personally designed guest rooms contribute to the atmosphere.

*Rates: $160 MAP. Jack Coleman.
30 R. 28 PB. 2 FP. Phone available. TV available. Beds: QDTC. MAP. Restaurant. Gourmet meals. Conference room. CCs: MC VISA. Tennis, skiing, golf, hiking, antiquing.
Seen in: *The New York Times, Philadelphia Inquirer, Gourmet.*
"An inn of character where character has real meaning."

Old Town Farm Inn
See: Gassets, VT

The Stone Hearth Inn
Rt 11 West
Chester VT 05143
(802) 875-2525
Circa 1810. Exposed beams, wide-pine floors and Vermont stone fireplaces are features of this restored country inn near Chester's historic Stone Village. Guests can relax in the parlor, library or attached barn that has been converted into a comfortable common room with a fieldstone fireplace. There is a fully stocked pub on the property.

Location: One mile west of Chester.
*Rates: $60-$90. Janet & Don Strohmeyer.
10 R. 10 PB. Phone available. TV available. Beds: KQTC. Full breakfast. Restaurant. Spa. Conference room. CCs: MC VISA DS. Bicycling, swimming, tennis, golf, fishing, skiing, snowmobiling. Seen in: *The Daily Telegraph, Los Angeles Times.*
"We love coming here and last time we brought the whole family. Good times, memories and friends were made here."

CHITTENDEN K3/*E2*

Tulip Tree Inn
Chittenden Dam Rd
Chittenden VT 05737
(802) 483-6213
Circa 1842. Thomas Edison was a regular guest here when the house was the country home of William Barstow. The inn is surrounded by the Green Mountains on three sides with a stream flowing a few yards away. The guest rooms feature an antique decor.

*Rates: $75-$100. Ed & Rosemary McDowell.
8 R. 8 PB. Phone available. Beds: QT. AP. Spa. CCs: MC VISA. Hiking, bicycling, skiing, horseback riding.
Seen in: *New England Getaways.*
"Tulip Tree Inn is one of the warmest, friendliest and coziest country inns you'll find in New England," New England Getaways.

CRAFTSBURY COMMON F6/*B3*

The Inn on the Common
Main St
Craftsbury Common VT 05827
(802) 586-9619 (800) 521-2233
Circa 1795. The Inn on the Common, built by the Samuel French family, is an integral part of this picturesque classic Vermont village. With its white picket fence and graceful white clapboard exterior, the inn provides a quietly elegant retreat. Pastoral views are framed by the inn's famous perennial gardens.

Rates: $95-$105. Michael & Penny Schmitt.
18 R. 18 PB. Phone available. TV available. Beds: QTC. MAP. Swimming pool. Conference room. CCs: MC VISA. Cross-country skiing, horseback riding, fly fishing school, tennis, hiking, croquet, golf.
Seen in: *The New York Times, Craftsbury Common, Harper's Hideaway Report.*
"The closest my wife and I came to fulfilling our fantasy of a country inn was at The Inn on the Common," Paul Grimes, "In Search of the Perfect Vermont Inn,"*New York Times.*

DANBY M3/*F2*

Silas Griffith Inn
RR 1 Box 66F, S Main St
Danby VT 05739
(802) 293-5567
Circa 1891. Originally on 55,000 acres, this stately Queen Anne Victorian mansion features solid cherry, oak, and bird's eye maple woodwork. Considered an architectural marvel, an eight-foot round solid cherry pocket door separates the original music room from the front parlor.

*❀Rates: $67-$82. Paul & Lois Dansereau.
17 R. 11 PB. Phone available. TV available. Beds: QT. B&B. Restaurant. Swimming pool. Conference room. CCs: MC VISA AE. Hiking, bicycling, skiing.
Seen in: *The Vermont Weathervane, Rutland Business Journal.*
"The warm welcome of antiques and beautiful country surroundings made the inn an ideal place."

DORSET N3/F2

Barrows House

Rt 30

Dorset VT 05251

(802) 867-4455

Circa 1804. The Barrows House is situated on 11 acres of lawns, flowering gardens and back woods in the heart of the village. The oldest section

of the inn once served as the residence of the Minister of Dorset's first minister. A cluster of cottages and other guest quarters date from the 1800s to 1950. The foyer, salon, tavern and parlor feature hand-stenciled borders and comfortable, overstuffed furniture. The old stable on the property now serves as a bike and ski rental shop, depending on the season. Fresh raspberry pancakes are a favorite breakfast of the inn's highly regarded restaurant.

Rates: $155-$200. Sally & Tim Brown.
28 R. 28 PB. 1 FP. Phone available. TV in room. MAP. Restaurant. Gourmet meals. Sauna. Handicap access. Swimming pool. Conference room. CCs: AE. Horseback riding, downhill & cross-country skiing, fishing, hiking, quarry swimming, bicycling.
Seen in: *The Washingtonian, Sunday Times Union, Snow Country, Mirabella.*
"A classic meal, a perfect setting."

EAST MIDDLEBURY J3/D2

Waybury Inn

Rt 125

East Middlebury VT 05740

(802) 388-4015

Circa 1810. This is the famous Bob Newhart inn featured in the TV series. (And yes, Larry, Darryl and his brother Darryl have stayed here.) In continuous operation for more than 150 years, it was originally built as a stagecoach stop and tavern. There remains a fully licensed pub on the premises. Nearby is the local swimming hole, a natural gorge in a rocky river.

Rates: $100-$115. Kimberly Smith.
14 R. 14 PB. Phone available. TV available. Beds: KQD. Full breakfast. CCs: MC VISA AE. Seen in: *Burlington Free Press, New York Times.*

EAST ST JOHNSBURY G7/C4

Echo Ledge Farm Inn

PO Box 77

East St Johnsbury VT 05838

(802) 748-4750 FAX: (802) 748-1640

Circa 1793. Phineas Page settled here on the banks of the Moose River. Later, his son supervised the farm and made it a political meeting place where representatives to Congress were chosen. Today, guests enjoy the stenciled walls, fresh wallpapers and old maple floors polished to a high gloss.

Location: Five miles east of St. Johnsbury on Rt. 2.
Rates: $45-$67. Dorothy & Fred Herman.
6 R. 4 PB. Beds: DT. Full breakfast. CCs: MC VISA. Hay/sleigh rides, skiing, snowmobiling, cycling, fishing, nature trail.
Seen in: *Vermont Country Sampler.*
"Great. We'll come back again!"

FAIRLEE J6/D3

Silver Maple Lodge & Cottages

S Main St, RR1 Box 8

Fairlee VT 05045

(802) 333-4326 (800) 666-1946

Circa 1850. This old Victorian farmhouse became an inn in the Twenties when Elmer & Della Batchelder opened their home to

guests. It became so successful that several cottages, built from lumber on the property, were added and for 60 years the Batchelder family continued the operation. They misnamed the lodge, however, mistaking silver poplar trees on the property for what they thought were silver maples. Guest rooms are decorated with many of the inn's original furnishings and the new innkeepers have carefully restored the rooms and added several bathrooms. A screened-in porch surrounds two sides of the house.

✻❀Rates: $42-$62. Scott & Sharon Wright.
14 R. 12 PB. Phone available. TV available. Beds: KDT. Continental breakfast. CCs: MC VISA AE. Golf, tennis, fishing, hiking, canoeing, hot-air balloon flights, croquet, badminton.
Seen in: *Boston Globe, Vermont Country Sampler.*
"Your gracious hospitality and attractive home all add up to a pleasant experience."

GASSETTS M5/F3

Old Town Farm Inn

Rt 10

Gassetts VT 05143

(802) 875-2346

Circa 1861. This comfortable New England inn with its elegant spiral staircase was called the Town Farm of Chester because anyone who needed

food and lodging were provided for, in return for a day's work on the farm. Fred R. Smith, famous as "Uncle Sam" in the Twenties and Thirties resided here. Artists have been inspired by the scenic views, which include a pond and meadow and woodlands inhabited by deer and wild turkey. Maple syrup from surrounding trees is served, as is the family's popular "Country Inn Spring Water."

✻Rates: $60-$70. Ruth & Dick Lewis.
10 R. 3 PB. Phone available. TV available. Beds: DTC. MAP. Game room. Skiing, hunting, fishing, hiking, golf, swimming, horses.
Seen in: *Yankee Magazine.*
"A warm haven! Very friendly and comfortable."

GAYSVILLE K4/E2

Cobble House Inn

PO Box 49

Gaysville VT 05746

(802) 234-5458

Circa 1864. This Victorian mansion is one of the grandest houses around, and commands a breathtaking view of the Green Mountains. The White

River flows just below the inn, enticing the sporting set to fish for salmon and trout. Canoeing and tubing also are popular.
*❀Rates: $75-$95. Beau, Phil & Sam Benson.
6 R. 6 PB. 1 FP. Phone available. Beds: QD. B&B. Restaurant. Gourmet meals. Conference room. CCs: MC VISA. Cross-country skiing, swimming, fishing, hiking, White River tubing.
Seen in: *Vermont Country Sampler, Syracuse Alumni Magazine.*
"My favorite place!"

GRAFTON N5/F3

The Farmhouse 'Round the Bend

Rt 121 E, Box 57
Grafton VT 05146
(802) 843-2515

Circa 1844. This Early American farmhouse is set amid woods beside a trout stream. It features Vermont made beds with solid foam mattres-

ses, English and American antiques and a large parlor. Breakfast is served in the large country kitchen and dining room in winter and in the glassed-in porch in summer.
Rates: $65-$75. Thomas F. Chiffriller, Jr.
3 R. 3 PB. Phone available. TV available. Beds: QDT. Continental-plus breakfast. Swimming, fishing, hiking, tennis, golf, skiing, ice skating, biking.
Seen in: *Vermont Summer Guide.*
"What a nice time you gave us in your home. Breakfast was a culinary delight!"

KILLINGTON L4/E2

The Inn at Long Trail

Rt 4 Box 267
Killington VT 05751
(802) 775-7181

The inn was the first ski lodge in Vermont. It has an Irish pub with a 22-foot log bar and an enormous boulder incorporated into the decor. The lobby features sofas and tables constructed from tree trunks. Most of the rooms are decorated in a country style and there are several fireplace suites.
Location: Nine miles east of Rutland.
*Rates: $54 & up. Season: July - April. Kyran & Rosemary McGrath.
20 R. 20 PB. 6 FP. Phone available. TV available. Beds: QT. B&B. Restaurant. Spa. Conference room. CCs: MC VISA. Skiing, hiking, golf, tennis, swimming. Irish music on weekends, lovely candlelight dining.
Seen in: *The Mountain Times.*
"We enjoyed our honeymoon for five days at the inn and we loved your Guinness stew after a cold, snowy day."

The Vermont Inn

Rt 4
Killington VT 05751
(802) 775-0708 (800) 541-7795

Circa 1840. Surrounded by mountain views, this rambling red and white farmhouse has provided lodging and superb cuisine for many years. Ex-

posed beams add to the atmosphere in the living and game rooms. The award-winning dining room provides candlelight tables beside a huge fieldstone fireplace.
*Rates: $90-$180. Susan & Judd Levy.
16 R. 12 PB. Phone available. TV available. Beds: QC. Full breakfast. Spa. Sauna. Handicap access. Swimming pool. Game room. CCs: MC VISA. Tennis, shuffleboard. Canoeing and horseback riding nearby. VCR available. The inn is closed April - May.
Seen in: *New York Daily News, New Jersey Star Leader, Rutland Business Journal, Bridgeport Post Telegram.*
"We had a wonderful time. The inn is breathtaking. Hope to be back."

LOWER WATERFORD G7/C4

Rabbit Hill Inn

Pucker St
Lower Waterford VT 05848
(802) 748-5168 (800) 76-BUNNY

Circa 1795. Above the Connecticut River overlooking the White Mountains, Samuel Hodby opened this tavern and provided a general store and inn to travelers. As many as 100 horse teams a day traveled by the inn. The ballroom, constructed in 1855, was supported by bent-wood construction giving the dance floor a spring effect. The classic Greek Revival exterior features solid pine Doric columns.
Location: Historic District.
*Rates: $139-$179.MAP. Season: Closed Nov. 1-15. John & Maureen Magee.
18 R. 18 PB. 5 FP. Phone available. TV available. Beds: KQT. Full breakfast. Restaurant. Gourmet meals. Conference room. CCs: MC VISA. Swimming, fishing, hiking, cross-country skiing, sleigh rides, canoeing, golf.
Seen in: *The New York Times, Los Angeles Herald Examiner, Today Show, Innsider, USA Today.*
"It is not often that one experiences one's vision of a tranquil, beautiful step back in time. This is such an experience. Everyone was so accommodating and gracious."

LUDLOW M4/F2

The Andrie Rose Inn

13 Pleasant St
Ludlow VT 05149
(802) 228-4846

Circa 1829. This village Colonial has been named for Andrie Rose, who operated a guest house here during the Fifties. Recently, the inn has been

polished to a shine and lavishly appointed with antiques, wallpapers, down comforters and whirlpool tubs. A Vermont country breakfast is served buffet style. This is the closest inn to the access road of Okemo Mountain and the ski shuttle stops at the inn.
Location: One block off Main St (Rte. 103).
❀Rates: $100-$110. Rick & Carolyn Bentzinger.
8 R. 8 PB. Phone available. Beds: D. MAP. Gourmet meals. Spa. Game room. CCs: MC VISA AE. Skiing, skating, swimming, golf, tennis, canoeing, horseback riding, hiking, sleigh rides. A Vermont country breakfast is served buffet style. Epicurean fixed five-course dinners are also available.
Seen in: *Upper Valley Magazine, Vermont Magazine.*
"Thank you for a truly relaxing, delicious and romantic getaway."

The Governor's Inn

86 Main St
Ludlow VT 05149
(802) 228-8830

Circa 1890. Governor Stickney built this house for his bride, Elizabeth Lincoln, and it retains the intimate feeling of an elegant country house furnished in the Victorian fashion. The Governor would have been pleased to know that *The Governor's Inn* has been elected to the prestigious Master Chefs Institute of America. It

was also awarded first prize for "Best in American Country Inn Cooking" by Uncle Ben's Rice.
❀Rates: $170 MAP. Charlie & Deedy Marble.
8 R. 8 PB. Phone available. AP. Gourmet meals. CCs: MC VISA. Skiing, golf, tennis, sleigh rides, horses, antiquing.
Seen in: *The Washington Post, Los Angeles Times, Mature Outlook, Gourmet Magazine.*
"As Rolls Royce is to cars... it is the standard by which all other inns can be judged," Ed Oakie.

Old Town Farm Inn
See: Gassets, VT

LYNDONVILLE G7/C4

The Wildflower Inn
Star Rt, Darling Hill Rd
Lyndonville VT 05851
(802) 626-8310 (800) 627-8310
Circa 1796. Would you like to spend a few days at a farm, feed calves and smell hay, where your children will love it too? This B&B on 500 acres in northeast Vermont was designed with the family in mind. In fact this is truly a family operation, with grandparents, sisters, brothers and in-laws all involved in the operation. Even the O'Reilly's children help out, showing guest children the proper attire and manners at meal time. The farm inn pitched high on the hill was a homestead established in the late 1700s. Guests can stay in either the farmhouse or in the carriage barn.
Rates: $64-$125. James & Mary O'Reilly.
20 R. 16 PB. Phone available. TV available. Beds: KQDTC. Full breakfast. Restaurant. Spa. Sauna. Swimming pool. Game room. Conference room. CCs: MC VISA. Skiing, skating, sledding, horse-drawn hay/sleigh rides, horseback riding, children's play area. Honeymoon specials, weekend workshops.
Seen in: *Innsider, The Caledonian-Record.*
"Every aspect of our short stay was absolute perfection."

MANCHESTER N3/F2

The Arlington Inn
See: Arlington, VT

Birch Hill Inn
West Rd, PO Box 346
Manchester VT 05254
(802) 362-2761
Circa 1790. It's rare to meet a Vermont innkeeper actually from Vermont, but at Birch Hill the hostess is the fourth

generation to live in this old farmhouse. The bedrooms are elegantly furnished, and some have mountain views and fireplaces. There are eight miles of groomed, picturesque cross-country trails that lead past a small pond and flowing brook.
Rates: $132-$140. Jim & Pat Lee.
6 R. 6 PB. 1 FP. Phone available. Beds: KQT. AP. Swimming pool. CCs: MC VISA. Downhill and cross-country skiing, hiking, fishing, golf, swimming, biking, private trout pond, walking trails.
Seen in: *The Rye Chronicle.*
"Without a doubt the loveliest country inn it has ever been my pleasure to stay in," I. Pastarnack, *The Rye Chronicle.*

Manchester Highlands Inn
PO Box 1754, Highland Ave
Manchester VT 05255
(802) 362-4565
Circa 1898. This Queen Anne Victorian mansion sits proudly on the crest of a hill overlooking the village. From the three-story turret guests can

look out over Mt. Equinox, the Green Mountains and the valley below. Feather beds and down comforters adorn the beds in the guest rooms. A game room with billiards and a stone fireplace are popular in winter, while summertime guests enjoy the outdoor pool, croquet lawn and veranda. Gourmet country breakfasts and home-baked afternoon snacks are served.
*Rates: $80-$98. Robert & Patricia Eichorn.
15 R. 12 PB. Phone available. TV available. Beds: KQDTC. B&B. Swimming pool. Game room. CCs: MC VISA AE. Downhill and cross-country skiing, golf, tennis, cycling, fishing, horseback riding, canoeing.
Seen in: *Toronto Sun.*
"We couldn't believe such a place existed. Now we can't wait to come again."

The Reluctant Panther Inn
PO Box 678, West Rd
Manchester VT 05254
(802) 362-2568 FAX: (802) 362-2586
Circa 1850. Elm trees line a street of manicured lawns and white clapboard estates. Suddenly, a muted purple clapboard house appears, the Reluc-

tant Panther. Rooms have recently been renovated and some include fireplaces, whirlpool tubs, cable TV and air conditioning.
Rates: $95-$225. Robert & Maye Bachofen.
16 R. 16 PB. Phone in room. Beds: KQT. Full breakfast. Restaurant. Spa. Handicap access. CCs: MC VISA.
Seen in: *Vermont Summer, Sunday Republican.*
"We enjoyed our stay so much that now we want to make it our yearly romantic getaway."

MANCHESTER VILLAGE N3/F2

1811 House
Historic Rt 7A
Manchester Village VT 05254
(802) 362-1811
Circa 1775. Since 1811, the historic Lincoln Home has been operated as an inn, except for one time. It was the private residence of Mary Lincoln Isham, granddaughter of President Lincoln. It has been authentically restored to the Federal period with antiques and canopy beds. The gardens look out over a golf course and it's just a short walk to tennis or swimming.
Location: Center of Manchester Village.
Rates: $100-$170. Bruce & Marnie Duff.
14 R. 14 PB. Phone available. TV available. Beds: KQ. Full breakfast. CCs: MC VISA. Skiing, tennis, golf, hiking.
Seen in: *New York.*

The Inn at Manchester

Box 41, Historic Rt 7A
Manchester Village VT 05254
(802) 362-1793

Circa 1880. This restored Victorian and its carriage house are in the Na-

tional Register. In a setting of beautiful gardens and meadows of wildflowers with a meandering brook, the inn offers an extensive art collection of old prints and paintings. Guest rooms have French doors, bay windows, and antiques. The inn was restored by the innkeepers.

*❀Rates: $70-$105. Harriet & Stan Rosenberg.

14 R. 14 PB. Phone available. TV available. Beds: KQDT. Full breakfast. Swimming pool. Game room. Conference room. CCs: MC VISA AE. Skiing, golf, tennis, swimming, bicycling.

Seen in: *The New York Times, Boston Globe, Travel & Leisure.*

"Spectacular! Bob Newhart - eat your heart out."

Village Country Inn

PO Box 408
Manchester Village VT 05254
(802) 362-1792

Circa 1889. Townsfolk refer to the Village Country Inn as the old summer house of the Kellogg cereal family. A Grecian columned porch spans 100

feet across the front of the house and is filled with chintz-covered rockers and pots of flowers. Decorated in a French Country style, rooms feature French lace and antiques. Dinner is served in a garden dining room which overlooks marble terraces and fountains.

Location: Historic route 7A.

*Rates: $135-$185. Anne & Jay Degen.

30 R. 30 PB. Phone available. TV in room. Beds: KDTW. MAP. Restaurant. Swimming pool. CCs: MC VISA AE. Tennis, golf, skiing, horseback riding.

Seen in: *Country Inn Magazine, Albany Times Union.*

"An inn for choosy guests," Albany Times Union.

Wilburton Inn

PO Box 468, River Rd
Manchester Village VT 05254
(802) 362-2500 (800) 648-4944

Circa 1902. Shaded by tall maples, this three-story brick mansion sits high on a hill overlooking the Battenkill Valley, set against a majestic mountain backdrop. Carved moldings,

mahogany paneling, Oriental carpets, and leaded-glass windows are complemented by carefully chosen antiques. The inn's 17 acres provide three tennis courts, a pool and green lawns and is popular for country weddings.

*Rates: $75-$155. Georgette & Albert Levis, Stanley Holton.

32 R. 32 PB. 3 FP. Phone in room. TV available. Beds: KQDTC. AP. Restaurant. Gourmet meals. Swimming pool. Game room. Conference room. CCs: MC VISA AE. Horseback riding, downhill & cross-country skiing, golf, canoeing, hiking, biking. Specialize in country weddings.

Seen in: *Great Escapes TV, Travelhost, Getaways For Gourmets.*

"I have traveled extensively in Europe and the United States...if there is a more romantic and peaceful setting in the world, then I am not aware of its existence."

MIDDLEBURY I2/D1

Middlebury Inn

14 Courthouse Sq, PO Box 798
Middlebury VT 05753
(802) 388-4961 (800) 842-4666

Circa 1827. For more than 150 years this site has been host to travelers. And for more than 10 years now, the inn, under the watchful eyes of Frank and Jane Emanuel and Aunt Kitty, the inn's 80-some-year-old social hostess, has become a favorite of tens of thousands of satisfied visitors. The inn's specialty is a homey family feeling with parties and semi-buffet dinners, served in what some consider Vermont's most beautiful dining room. During the summer season events include Murder Mystery Weekends, July Festival Week and Tea Time every afternoon.

Rates: $78-$132. Frank & Jane Emanuel.

75 R. 75 PB. Phone in room. TV in room. Beds: DTC. EP. Restaurant. Handicap access. Conference room. CCs: MC VISA. Swimming, golf, boating, hiking, cross-country & downhill skiing. Complimentary afternoon tea for guests.

Seen in: *The Chicago Tribune, Glamour, Burlington Free Press.*

"A wonderful treat, so much nicer than a hotel!"

Swift House Inn

25 Stewart Ln
Middlebury VT 05753
(802) 388-9925 (802) 388-2766

Circa 1815. Former governor of Vermont, John Stewart, bought the elegant Swift House in 1875 from Jonathan Swift. The governor's

daughter, philanthropist Jessica Swift, was born and lived in the mansion there for 110 years, until 1981. Elaborately carved walnut and marble fireplaces and window seats grace the sitting rooms of the inn. The spacious lawns and formal gardens can be enjoyed from terraces and guest rooms.

Location: Corner of Rt. 7 and Stewart Lane.

Rates: $85-$140. John & Andrea Nelson.

20 R. 20 PB. 9 FP. Phone in room. TV in room. Beds: KQDT. B&B. Restaurant. Gourmet meals. Spa. Sauna. Handicap access. Exercise room. Conference room. FAX. CCs: MC VISA AE DC DS. Skiing, bicycling, swimming, golf, tennis, boating, horseback riding, museums.

Seen in: *Valley Voice, Uncommon Lodgings, Boston Magazine.*

"Fabulous wine list, great food, comfortable and relaxing atmosphere, friendly staff."

MIDDLETOWN SPRINGS L3/E2

Middletown Springs Inn

PO Box 1068, On The Green
Middletown Springs VT 05757
(802) 235-2198

Circa 1879. This Italianate Victorian mansion on the green was built when the bubbling springs of Middletown rivaled those of Saratoga. The inn is decorated in middle to late Victorian antiques, with mahogany and cherry furniture, rich wallpapers and lace curtains. A staircase with an ornate newel post sweeps upstairs to the guest rooms. There are additional rooms in the carriage house, once the village blacksmith shop.

Location: Fourteen miles from Rutland on Route 133.

*Rates: $100-$140. Steve & Jane Sax.
10 R. 8 PB. TV available. Beds: QTD. AP. Conference room. CCs: MC VISA. Skiing, hiking, swimming, sailing, golf, bicycles, horses.
Seen in: *National Geographic Traveler, Cleveland Plain Dealer.*
"The charm of the inn, Steve's exquisite cuisine and the ambience you both provide blend wonderfully."

MONTGOMERY VILLAGE D5/B3

Black Lantern Inn
Route 118
Montgomery Village VT 05470
(802) 326-4507

Circa 1803. This brick inn and restaurant originally served as a stagecoach stop. There is a taproom

with beamed ceilings, and two downstairs lounges. A large three-bedroom suite has its own spa. Vermont antiques fill all the guest rooms. A few minutes from the inn, skiers (novice and expert) can ride the tramway to the top of Jay Peak.
*Rates: $60-$75. Rita & Allan Kalsmith.
16 R. 16 PB. 6 FP. Phone available. TV available. Beds: KQDT. MAP. Gourmet meals. Spa. CCs: MC VISA AE. Downhill & cross-country skiing, hiking, biking.
Seen in: *Burlington Free Press, Los Angeles Times, Bon Appetit, Ottawa Citizen.*
"...one of the four or five great meals of your life," Jay Stone, *Ottawa Citizen.*

MONTPELIER H5/C3

The Inn at Montpelier
147 Main St
Montpelier VT 05602
(802) 223-2727 FAX: (802) 223-0722

Circa 1828. Two Federal-style homes compose the Inn at Montpelier. Ten fireplaces, Greek Revival woodwork and glass-fronted china cupboards are original. A favorite guest room is

number two with a lace-canopy bed. A block from the inn are restaurants, business districts, and the 100-acre Hubbard Park. The inn holds a AAA four-diamond award.
Rates: $78-$130. Maureen Russell.
19 R. 19 PB. 6 FP. Phone in room. TV in room. Beds: KQT. B&B. Conference room. CCs: MC VISA AE. Downhill & cross-country skiing nearby, hiking, horseback riding, fishing, swimming.
Seen in: *Glamour Magazine, The Times Argus.*
"My hunch that the Inn at Montpelier would be ideal was well-founded."

NORTH HERO E2/B1

North Hero House
Rt 2 Box 106
North Hero VT 05474
(802) 372-8237

Circa 1891. This three-story inn stands on a slight rise overlooking Lake Champlain and Vermont's highest peak, Mt. Mansfield. Three other houses, including the Wadsworth store located at the City Dock, also provide accommodations for the inn's guests. Rooms hang over the water's edge and feature waterfront porches.
Rates: $50-$95. Season: June - October. Apgar & Sherlock Families.
23 R. 21 PB. Phone available. TV available. Beds: TC. EP. Restaurant. Sauna. Handicap access. Fishing, swimming, tennis, canoeing, sailing, bicycling, boating.
Seen in: *Gourmet.*
"We have visited many inns and this house was by far the best, due mostly to the staff!"

ORWELL K2/D1

Historic Brookside Farms
Rt 22A Box 036
Orwell VT 05760
(802) 948-2727

Circa 1789. Nineteen stately Ionic columns grace the front of this neo-classical Greek Revival farmhouse, designed by James Lamb. This is a working farm with Hereford cattle, Hampshire sheep, maple syrup production and poultry. There are 300 acres of lush country landscape, including a 26-acre pond. Innkeeper Murray Korda is a concert violinist

and speaks seven languages.
*Rates: $100-$200. Joan & Murray Korda & family.
8 R. 3 PB. Phone available. TV available. Beds: DTC. AP. Handicap access. Conference room. Cross-country skiing, fishing, hiking, tennis, golf, horses.
Seen in: *The New York Times, Burlington Free Press, Los Angeles Times.*
"A wonderful piece of living history."

PERKINSVILLE M5/F3

Gwendolyn's B&B
Rt 106 Box 225
Perkinsville VT 05151
(802) 263-5248 (800) 356-5229

Circa 1872. Owned originally by one of the proprietors of a large cotton mill, this elegant mansion comple-

ments the beautiful mountainous surroundings. Breakfasts are served in a large formal dining room with French doors leading out to the veranda. The inn is within walking distance to a village general store and close to antique shops and gourmet restaurants. The surrounding area provides guests the opportunity to take part in both winter and summertime activities, including local traditions such as cider making and maple sugaring.
Rates: $65-$92. Laurie & Win Hathaway & Gwen.
5 R. 3 PB. Phone available. TV available. Beds: DT. Full breakfast. Conference room. FAX. CCs: MC VISA. Horseback riding, skiing, canoeing, hiking, ice skating.
Seen in: *Burlington Free Press, Windsor Chronicle.*
"We've stayed in many B&Bs but never hosted so warmly or in such lovely surroundings."

PITTSFIELD K4/E2

The Inn at Pittsfield

Rt 100 Box 675
Pittsfield VT 05762
(802) 746-8943

Circa 1830. The Inn at Pittsfield stands across from the village green and just

beyond the covered bridge. It was once a stagecoach stop providing both meals and lodging to travelers. A pot-bellied stove warms the common room where guests gather. A country decor is highlighted by old quilts, pull-back curtains, and floral arrangements. A four-course single sitting dinner is served.

*❀Rates: $95-$130. Barbara Morris, Vikki Budasi.

9 R. 9 PB. Phone available. Beds: DT. MAP. CCs: MC VISA AE. Horseback riding, hiking, mountain biking, fishing, golf, tennis, skiing, snowmobiling.

Seen in: *The Discerning Traveler, Country Inns, Toronto Sun, US News and World Report.*

"I am still savoring that great food, hospitality and help that you provided all of us...it was beyond our expectations."

POULTNEY L2/E1

Lake St. Catherine Inn

PO Box 129, Cones Point Rd
Poultney VT 05764
(802) 287-9347

Circa 1932. Towering pine and white birch trees shade this old red country inn situated directly on the lake. There is a player piano, a library and a fireplace in the various common rooms. Decorated in a fresh country style, the inn's guest rooms are comfortable and most have views. An outside deck sits at the water's edge and a small marina features canoes, paddle boats, fishing boats and sailboats. The springfed lake is seven miles. The inn's dining room is waterfront.

Rates: $105-$160. Season: Mid-May - Mid-Oct. Patricia & Raymond Endlich.

35 R. 35 PB. Phone available. TV available. Beds: KDTC. MAP. Restaurant. Handicap access. Game room. Golf, horseback riding, water sports, fishing, swimming, hiking, tennis, biking, free boats.

Seen in: *The Area News, Outdoor Life, The Vermont Sportsman.*

"You have done a marvelous job and epitomize hospitality and service."

Stonebridge Inn

Rt 30
Poultney VT 05764
(802) 287-9849

Circa 1808. The Stonebridge Inn is handsomely situated on a knoll overlooking Main Street. The inn is in a Federal style with a Greek Revival facade. A wing was added in 1841

with a five-foot-thick foundation to accommodate the vault of the First Bank of Poultney. The guest rooms all feature canopy beds, quilts and antiques such as jelly cupboards and pie safes. A taproom, library and parlor are available to guests.

*Rates: $64-$84. Gail R. Turner.

5 R. 2 PB. 3 FP. Phone available. TV available. Beds: QD. Continental-plus breakfast. CCs: MC VISA. Boating, sailing, fishing, cross-country & downhill skiing, tennis, horseback riding, golf.

PROCTORSVILLE M4/F2

Castle Inn

Rt 103 & 131, PO Box 157
Proctorsville VT 05153
(802) 226-7222

Circa 1904. The Fletcher family settled in the Ludlow area in the 1700s. Allen Fletcher grew up in Indiana but returned to Vermont, tearing down a

Victorian house to build this English-style mansion overlooking the Okemo valley. It features an oval dining room, a mahogany-paneled library, and spacious guest accommodations complete with individual sitting areas. In 1911, Mr. Fletcher became governor of Vermont.

Rates: $75-$90. Michael & Sheryl Fratino.

13 R. 9 PB. Phone available. TV available. Beds: QD. MAP. Restaurant. Spa. Sauna. Swimming pool. Game room. Conference room. CCs: MC VISA AE. Bicycling, tennis, swimming, cross-country skiing.

"Castle Inn has to be the very best place in Vermont."

The Golden Stage Inn

Depot St, PO Box 218
Proctorsville VT 05153
(802) 226-7744

Circa 1780. The Golden Stage Inn was a stagecoach stop built shortly after

Vermont's founding. It became a link in the Underground Railroad and the home of Cornelia Otis Skinner. Extensive gardens surround the wraparound porch as well as the swimming pool. The innkeepers were flavor experts for a New York company but now put their tasting skills to work for their guests.

Location: Near Ludlow.

Rates: $135-$145.MAP Kirsten Murphy & Marcel Perret.

10 R. 6 PB. Phone available. Beds: QT. AP. Swimming pool. CCs: VISA. Swimming, golf, bicycling, hiking, cross-country skiing, tennis.

Seen in: *Journal Inquirer, Gourmet Magazine, Los Angeles Times.*

"The essence of a country inn!"

PUTNEY O5/G3

Hickory Ridge House

RFD 3 Box 1410
Putney VT 05346
(802) 387-5709

Circa 1808. This comely brick Federal house was originally built as an elegant farmhouse on a 500-acre

Merino sheep farm. Palladian windows, and six Rumford fireplaces are original features. Rooms are painted in bright Federal colors, such as rose, salmon, blue and yellow. Weddings are popular here and innkeeper Steve Anderson often serves as justice of the peace.

Rates: $42-$75. Jacquie Walker & Steve

Anderson.
7 R. 3 PB. 4 FP. Phone available. TV available. Beds: QDTC. EP. Handicap access. Conference room. CCs: MC VISA. Cross-country skiing; nearby swimming, boating, hiking.
Seen in: *Phildelphia Inquirer, Boston Globe.*
"We love your serene and peaceful house and we thank you for your hospitality and warmth, good food and good company."

RIPTON J3/D2

Chipman Inn
Rt 125
Ripton VT 05766
(802) 388-2390
Circa 1828. This was the home of Daniel Chipman, a prominent legislator and founder of Middlebury College. Chipman also managed the "Center Turnpike" (now Route 125) through the Green Mountains. A replica of the tariff board stands near the inn. The inn's lounge/bar is in the original kitchen, with its old fireplace and bread oven.
Rates: $78-$98. Season: Closed April & Dec. Joyce Henderson & Bill Pierce.
9 R. 9 PB. Phone available. Beds: DT. MAP. Gourmet meals. CCs: MC VISA AE. Hiking trails, downhill & cross-country skiing, swimming, antique shops.
Seen in: *Gourmet, Kirbyville Banner, Addison County Independent.*
"Cozy, warm and friendly."

ROCHESTER J4/D2

Harvey's Mountain View Inn
Rochester VT 05767
(802) 767-4273
Circa 1809. The Harvey family has owned and operated this homestead as a farm for more than 180 years.

During the summer, guests of all ages enjoy gathering eggs and watching the milking when not in the pool. Sunset hayrides are popular, and there are rental horses nearby. A cottage is available for a weekly rate.
Rates: $38-$45. Donald & Maggie Harvey.
9 R. 2 PB. Phone available. TV available. Beds: KQTDC. MAP. Handicap access. Golf, hiking, cross-country skiing, fishing, hunting.
Seen in: *The New York Times.*
"Children are right at home here. They don't fight. They don't fuss. They're too busy. And when the children are happy, the parents are happy."

SAINT JOHNSBURY G7/C4

Rabbit Hill Inn
See: Lower Waterford, VT

SHREWSBURY M4/E2

The Buckmaster Inn
Lincoln Hill Rd, RR 1 Box 118
Shrewsbury VT 05738
(802) 492-3485
Circa 1801. John Buckmaster's tavern was licensed in 1820, and the inn soon became well known on the Woodstock

Road. Standing majestically on a knoll, the Buckmaster overlooks a picturesque red barn and valley scene. Its center hall, grand staircase and wide-pine floors are accentuated with family heirlooms. There are wood-burning fireplaces, a library, and large porches.
Rates: $40-$60. Sam & Grace Husselman.
4 R. 2 PB. Phone available. TV available. Beds: KQTD. B&B. Conference room. Hiking, swimming, fishing, skiing, horseback riding.
Seen in: *The Rutland Business Journal.*
"I've been in many B&Bs but the accommodations and hospitality are best here."

SOUTH LONDONDERRY N4/F2

Londonderry Inn
PO Box 301-57
South Londonderry VT 05155
(802) 824-5226
Circa 1826. For almost 100 years, the Melendy Homestead, overlooking the West River and the village, was a dairy farm. In 1940, it became an inn. A tourist brochure promoting the area in 1881 said, "Are you overworked in the office, counting room or workshop and need invigorating influences? Come ramble over these hills and mountains and try the revivifying effects of Green Mountain oxygen."
Location: Route 100.
*Rates: $31-$75. Jim & Jean Cavanagh.
25 R. 20 PB. Phone available. TV available.

Beds: KQDTC. Full breakfast. Restaurant. Handicap access. Swimming pool. Conference room. Hiking, cross-country skiing.
Seen in: *Ski Magazine.*
"A weekend in a good country inn, such as the Londonderry, is on a par with a weekend on the ocean in Southern Maine, which is to say that it's as good as a full week nearly anyplace else," The Hornet.

SOUTH WOODSTOCK L5/E3

Kedron Valley Inn
Rt 106 Box 145
South Woodstock VT 05071
(802) 457-1473
Circa 1822. This inn has served the traveling public for more than 150 years. One of the guest buildings has

a secret attic passageway and is rumored to have been a stop on the Underground Railway during the Civil War. There is a 45-piece quilt collection that includes 100-year-old quilts made by great-grandmothers of the hostess. Outdoors are a white sand beach and swimming lake. A stable with horses for trail rides or inn-to-inn excursions is nearby.
*Rates: $138-$199. Max & Merrily Comins.
28 R. 28 PB. 7 FP. Phone available. TV in room. Beds: KQDTC. MAP. Restaurant. Handicap access. CCs: MC VISA. Horses, golf, tennis, cross-country & downhill skiing. Private terraces, dining patio.
Seen in: *Oprah Winfrey Show, Good Housekeeping, Country Living.*
"It's what you dream a Vermont country inn should be and the most impressive feature is the innkeepers...outgoing, warm and friendly."

STOWE G4/C2

The 1860 House

School St, PO Box 276
Stowe VT 05672
(802) 253-7351 (800)248-1860

Circa 1860. This charming National Register house is an Italianate style with an intersecting gable. All the

windows are topped with peaked lintel boards, and paired scroll brackets adorn the roof cornices. The interior is beautifully furnished in period antiques or reproductions and Vermont made quilts.

*Rates: $75-$100. Richard M. Hubbard & Rose Marie Matulionis.

5 R. 5 PB. TV available. Beds: KQTC. Full breakfast. Spa. Sauna. Swimming pool. Conference room. CCs: MC VISA. Skiing, skating, hiking, fishing, golf, tennis, horseback riding.

Seen in: *Ski Magazine.*

"A memorable place to visit...You do a great job!"

Green Mountain Inn

PO Box 60
Stowe VT 05672
(802) 253-7301 (800) 445-6629

Circa 1833. This rambling inn consists of several buildings, including the main building and the old depot built

for the Mt. Mansfield Electric Railroad. These two buildings are numbers 13 and 14 in the National Register. Early American reproductions furnish the inn, and there are Walton Blodgett original paintings of Stowe.

*Rates: $69-$175. Darcy Curran.

54 R. 54 PB. 1 FP. Phone in room. TV in room. Beds: QDTC. AP. Restaurant. Gourmet meals. Spa. Sauna. Handicap access. Exercise room. Swimming pool. Game room. Conference room. CCs: MC VISA AE. Tennis, horseback riding, golf, sking, fishing, ice skating.

The Inn at the Brass Lantern

717 Maple St
Stowe VT 05672
(802) 253-2229 (800) 729-2980

Circa 1810. This rambling farmhouse and carriage barn rests at the foot of Mt. Mansfield. A recent renovation has brought a new shine to the inn from the gleaming plank floors to the polished woodwork and crackling fireplaces. Quilts and antiques fill the guest rooms and some, like the Honeymoon Room, have their own fireplace and mountain view. A complimentary evening dessert is provided in the living room and during ski season, an afternoon buffet of breads, soups and beverages is available (extra charge).

Location: One half mile from village center.

Rates: $50-$100. Mindy & Andy Aldrich.

9 R. 9 PB. 3 FP. Phone available. TV available. Beds: QDT. Full breakfast. Conference room. CCs: MC VISA AE. Tennis, sleigh rides, polo, health club/spa, skating, golf, hiking, biking, canoeing, fishing, hot-air balloons. Honeymoons.

Seen in: *Vermont Magazine.*

"The Aldriches remember the little things that made us glad we stopped at their inn."

Ye Olde England Inne

Mountain Rd
Stowe VT 05672
(802) 253-7558 (800) 477-3771

Circa 1890. Originally a farmhouse, Ye Olde England Inne has acquired a Tudor facade, interior beams and stone work. Brass and copper pieces,

Laura Ashley decor and English antiques add to the atmosphere. The inn sponsors polo events and features a polo package. Gliding and golf packages are also available.

*Rates: $80-$190. Christopher & Linda Francis.

20 R. 20 PB. 4 FP. Phone in room. TV in room. Beds: QDT. MAP. Restaurant. Gourmet meals. Spa. Swimming pool. Conference room. FAX. CCs: MC VISA. Horseback riding, skiing, water sports, hiking, climbing, skating, antiquing. Seven rooms with private spas, all rooms are air conditioned.

Seen in: *National Geographic Traveler Magazine.*

"Even more perfect than we anticipated."

WAITSFIELD H4/C2

Knoll Farm Country Inn

Bragg Hill Rd, RFD 179
Waitsfield VT 05673
(802) 496-3939 (802) 496-3527

Circa 1904. This white-frame farmhouse and 150-acre farm sits above the Mad River Valley amid the Green Mountains and offers a spectacular view. The barn is more than 150 years old, and the whole farm has been nominated as a National Historic Site. Farm animals include Scotch Highland beef cattle, horses, dogs, cats and a friendly pig. The inn's vegetables, beef and pork are farm-grown. Guests are served farm-fresh milk, butter and eggs at the large dining-room table. The Knoll Farm Country Inn features antique furniture, bright hooked rugs, original artwork on the walls, a player piano and an ornate 1890 pump organ.

Rates: $100.MAP Ann Day, Harvey & Ethel Horner.

4 R. Phone available. TV available. Beds: QDT. Full breakfast. Conference room. Pond for swimming and skating, hiking, sailing, tennis, golf, canoeing, windsurfing, showshoeing, sledding, cross-country skiing.

Seen in: *Boston Globe, Philadelphia Inquirer, Yankee.*

"Knoll Farm fills my prescription summer after summer."

Lareau Farm Country Inn

Rt 100 Box 563
Waitsfield VT 05673
(802) 496-4949 (800) 833-0766

Circa 1832. This Greek Revival house was built by Simeon Stoddard, the town's first physician. Old-fashioned

roses, lilacs, delphiniums, iris and peonies fill the gardens. The inn sits in a wide meadow next to the crystal-clear Mad River. A canoe trip or a refreshing swim are possibilities here.

Location: Central Vermont, Sugarbush Valley.

*Rates: $60-$90. Dan & Susan Easley.

14 R. 10 PB. Phone available. TV available. Beds: QDT. B&B. Handicap access. CCs: MC VISA. Downhill & cross-country skiing, sleigh rides, hiking. Carriage rides and romantic picnics.

Seen in: *The Pittsburgh Press, The Philadelphia Inquirer, Los Angeles Times.*

"Hospitality is a gift. Thank you for sharing your gift so freely with us."

Mad River Barn

Rt 17 PO Box 88
Waitsfield VT 05673
(802) 496-3310

Circa 1800. The inn consists of two farmhouses and a converted barn. One farmhouse was recently remodeled to include a two-story lounge, game room, bar and restaurant. Guests may stay in the barn or the more luxurious farmhouse. Just beyond the barn is a path to the mountain. Old stone walls and lumber trails run through the property.

*Rates: $50-$75. Betsy Pratt.
16 R. 15 PB. Phone available. Beds: QTC. AP. Restaurant. Swimming pool. Conference room. CCs: MC VISA. Cross-country skiing, golf, tennis, hiking, swimming.
Seen in: *Boston Globe.*

"If I plan a ski trip to Vermont, the Mad River Barn will be where I park myself."

Millbrook

RFD Box 62
Waitsfield VT 05673
(802) 496-2405

Circa 1840. Guests enter Millbrook through the warming room, where an antique Glenwood parlor stove is usually roaring. This classic Cape-

style farmhouse is known for its individually stenciled guest rooms, Green Mountain views, and one of the valley's best dining rooms.

*Rates: $50-$130. Season: Closed May. Joan & Thom Gorman.
7 R. 4 PB. Phone available. Beds: DT. AP. CCs: MC VISA DC. Skiing, horseback riding, golf, hiking, bicycling.
Seen in: *Boston Globe, Travel Today, Gourmet Magazine.*

"A weekend at your place is just what the doctor had in mind."

Newtons' 1824 House Inn

Rt 100 Box 159
Waitsfield VT 05673
(802) 496-7555

Circa 1824. Surrounded by the Green Mountains, Newtons' 1824 House Inn is a white clapboard farmhouse on 52 acres. The Mad River passes through the property. The inn is decorated with Oriental rugs, original art, Victorian wallpaper, crystal and Venetian glass chandeliers and thick European down quilts. Guests may enjoy

homemade breads and muffins and maple syrup tapped from the inn's own maples.

*Rates: $75-$95. Nick & Joyce Newton.
6 R. 6 PB. Phone available. TV available. Beds: KDT. B&B. CCs: MC VISA AE. Horseback riding, hiking, skiing, canoeing, golf, fishing. Tap maple sugar trees.
Seen in: *Los Angeles Times, Miami Herald, Chicago Tribune.*

"Established hospitality - unusual breakfast specialties."

WALLINGFORD M3/E2

White Rocks Inn

RR 1 Box 297, Rt 7
Wallingford VT 05773
(802) 446-2077

Circa 1840. Both the barn and farmhouse are listed in the National Register. The barn is a fine example of Gothic architecture. The house was

built by Israel Munson whose name is still engraved on the front doorbell. Furnished with antiques, Oriental rugs and canopied beds, the inn provides views of White Rocks Mountain.

Location: Eleven miles south of Rutland.
*Rates: $60-$95. Season: Closed November. June & Alfred Matthews.
5 R. 5 PB. Phone available. TV available. Beds: KQTD. Full breakfast. CCs: MC VISA. Horseback riding, hiking, canoeing, skiing.
Seen in: *Rutland Business Journal.*

"Excellent on all counts! We enjoyed every minute. Breakfasts were delightful, as were our hosts."

WARREN I4/D2

Beaver Pond Farm Inn

RD Box 306, Golf Course Rd
Warren VT 05674
(802) 583-2861

Circa 1860. Formerly a working dairy and sheep farm, this Vermont farmhouse is situated in a meadow overlooking several beaver ponds. It has been tastefully and graciously re-

stored by its present owners, with antiques and Laura Ashley wallpapers adding to the decor. Mrs. Hansen holds cooking classes here. The inn is adjacent to the Sugarbush Golf Course and close to the downhill ski trails of Sugarbush and Mad River Glen.

Location: Sugarbush Valley.
*Rates: $32-$45. Betty & Bob Hansen.
6 R. 4 PB. Phone available. TV available. Beds: QT. Full breakfast. Gourmet meals. Conference room. CCs: MC VISA AE. Skiing, golf, tennis, swimming, hiking.
Seen in: *Los Angeles Times, New Woman Magazine.*

"The inn is simply magnificent. I have not been in a nicer one on three continents. Breakfast was outrageous."

WATERBURY H4/C2

The Inn at Blush Hill

Blush Hill Rd, PO Box 1266
Waterbury VT 05676
(802) 244-7529 (800)736-7522

Circa 1790. This shingled Cape-style house was once a stagecoach stop en route to Stowe. A 12-foot-long pine farmhand's table is set near the double fireplace and the kitchen window, revealing views of the Worcester Mountains. A favorite summertime breakfast is pancakes with fresh blueberries.

*❀Rates: $65-$100. Pamela & Gary Gosselin.
6 R. 2 PB. 1 FP. Phone available. TV available. Beds: QD. B&B. CCs: MC VISA. Water sports, golf, cross-country & Alpine skiing, tennis.
Seen in: *Vermont Magazine, Charlotte Observer.*

"Our room was wonderful - especially the fireplace. Everything was so cozy and warm."

The Inn at Thatcher Brook Falls

RD 2 Box 62
Waterbury VT 05676
(802) 244-5911 (800) 292-5911

Circa 1899. Listed in the Vermont Register of Historic Buildings, this restored Victorian mansion features a porch with twin gazebos. A covered walkway leads to the historic Wheeler

House. Guest rooms are decorated in Laura Ashley-style with canopy beds.

The inn specializes in Country French cuisine and Bailey's Fireside Tavern is on the premises.
*Rates: $75-$145. Peter Varty & Kelly Fenton.
24 R. 24 PB. 2 FP. Phone in room. TV available. Beds: KQDT. B&B. Restaurant. Gourmet meals. Spa. Handicap access. Game room. Conference room. CCs: MC VISA AE DS. Skiing, bicycling, hiking, swimming, canoeing, golf, tennis, boating.
"I'd have to put on a black tie in Long Island to find food as good as this and best of all it's in a relaxed country atmosphere. Meals are underpriced."

WATERBURY CENTER G4/C2

The Black Locust Inn

RR 1 Box 715
Waterbury Center VT 05677
(802) 244-7490

Circa 1830. Set on a hill graced with tall black locust trees native to the Southeast is this three-gabled farmhouse. For more than a century the old house presided over a 90-acre dairy farm, looking out to the Green Mountain range and Camel's Hump. Antiques and brass beds decorate guest chambers now, while white wicker chairs are gathered on the front porch. Afternoon snacks are served, with wine and cheese in the evening.
Rates: $70-$95. George & Anita Gajdos.
6 R. 6 PB. Phone available. TV available. Beds: QDT. Full breakfast. Handicap access. CCs: MC VISA DS. All winter & summer activities within five miles.
Seen in: *Hudson Dispatch.*
"Your inn is absolutely beautiful and your breakfast perfect."

WEATHERSFIELD M5/F3

The Inn at Weathersfield

Rt 106 Box 165
Weathersfield VT 05151
(802) 263-9217 (800) 477-4828

Circa 1795. Built by Thomas Prentis, a Revolutionary War veteran, this was originally a four-room farmhouse set on 237 acres of wilderness. Two rooms were added in 1796, and a carriage house in 1830. During the Civil War, the inn served as a station on the Un-

derground Railroad. Six pillars give the inn a Southern colonial look, and there are 12 fireplaces, a beehive oven, wide-plank floors and period antiques throughout.
*Rates: $160-$200. Mary Louise & Ron Thorburn.
12 R. 12 PB. 8 FP. Phone available. TV available. Beds: QDT. AP. Restaurant. Sauna. Handicap access. Conference room. FAX. CCs: MC VISA AE DS. Sleigh rides, cycling, hiking, skiing, horseback riding, canoeing, swimming pond. Thanksgiving in colonial dress, medieval banquets, mystery weekends, High tea. Ski packages and 5-day plans available.
Seen in: *The Boston Herald, Los Angeles Times, Country Inns, Colonial Homes, Better Homes & Gardens, National Geographic Traveler.*
"There isn't one thing we didn't enjoy about our weekend with you and we are constantly reliving it with much happiness."

WEST DOVER P4/G2

Austin Hill Inn

Rt 100 Box 859
West Dover VT 05356
(802) 464-5281 (800)332-RELAX

Situated in a quiet area on the edge of a mountain, this completely renovated inn has walls decorated with old barn board and floral Victorian wallpapers. Old antiques and family heirlooms include family photographs dating from 1845 in antique frames. Most rooms have balconies and four-poster or brass beds. A five-course, home-cooked candlelight dinner is available on weekends.
Location: Two miles from Mount Snow.
Rates: $72-$175. Robbie Sweeney.
12 R. 12 PB. Phone available. TV available. Beds: KQDT. MAP. Restaurant. Gourmet meals. Swimming pool. CCs: MC VISA AE. Horseback riding, skiing, biking, golf.
Seen in: *Garden City Life.*
"A wonderful escape!"

Snow Den Inn

Rt 100 Box 625
West Dover VT 05356
(802) 464-9355

Circa 1885. John Davis built his rambling home from lumber worked in his waterwheel mill. The interior is noted for its original wax-rubbed ash encasements. It was the last home to be built in the town, but it became the first guest inn in the Mt. Snow area in 1952. Several rooms have fireplaces and sitting areas. All have private baths.
*Rates: $85-$140. Season: June 15-April 15. Andrew & Marjorie Trautwein.
8 R. 8 PB. 5 FP. Phone available. TV in room. Beds: QD. EP. CCs: MC VISA AE. Horseback riding, water sports, hiking, golf, skiing, antiquing, music festivals.
Seen in: *Inn Spots & Special Places, Southern Vermont Magazine.*
"No small details are overlooked."

WEST RUTLAND L3/E2

The Silver Fox Inn

Rt 133 Box 1222
West Rutland VT 05777
(802) 438-5555

Circa 1768. One of the first houses built in the area, this was the home of Captain John Smith. It was for Smith's

head the governor of a neighboring state once offered the sum of 40 pounds. The inn is furnished with Queen Anne cherrywood and oak. The Clarendon River runs along the property.
**Rates: $105-$145. Season: May - March. Pam & Gerry Bliss.
7 R. 7 PB. Phone available. TV available. Beds: QD. AP. Restaurant. Gourmet meals. Handicap access. Conference room. CCs: MC VISA. Bicycling, cross-country skiing, golf, tennis, fishing, hiking.
Seen in: *The Rutland Business Journal.*
"We never expected dinner could be so imaginative. We used to stay at a ski condo but breakfast in bed is my idea of a great getaway."

WEST TOWNSEND O4/F2

Windham Hill Inn

RR 1 Box 44
West Townsend VT 05359
(802) 874-4080

Circa 1825. Windham Hill was originally a working dairy farm owned by William Lawrence. It was sold at auction but most of the existing furniture, silverware, rugs, and quilts belonged to the Lawrence family. Surrounded by 175 acres in a

secluded hillside setting, Windham Hill was selected by Uncle Ben's Rice Company and Innsider as one of the top 10 inns for 1988 and 1989.

Rates: $70-$105. Season: May - March. Ken & Linda Busteed.
15 R. 15 PB. Phone available. TV available. Beds: KQTD. AP. Handicap access. CCs: MC VISA. Hiking, cross-country skiing.
Seen in: *Vermont Life, Country Decorating, Boston Magazine.*

"...enhanced. That's how I felt after not very long at all at the end of this particular road. Enhanced by exquisite views, extraordinary food and amiable hosts," James Tabor, Vermont Life.

WESTON N4/F2

1830 Inn on the Green

Rt 100 Box 104
Weston VT 05161
(802) 824-6789

Circa 1830. Originally a wheelwright's shop, the building was later a town hall and an undertaker's parlor. Moved to its present site, it became a private home graced with a beautiful curving staircase from the house of Hetty Green, "The Witch of Wall Street." Situated in the Weston Historic District and tucked in a hollow of the Green Mountains, the inn is across the village green from the oldest summer theater in the state.

Rates: $60-$80. Sandy & Dave Granger.
4 R. 2 PB. Phone available. Beds: KQD. B&B. CCs: MC VISA. Skiing, bicycling, hiking, golf, tennis, fishing, canoeing, horseback riding.
Seen in: *Yankee Homes, Brides Magazine.*

"Your gracious hospitality and delicious breakfasts made our weekend unforgettable."

WILMINGTON P3/G2

The Red Shutter Inn

Box 636, Rt 9
Wilmington VT 05363
(802) 464-3768

Circa 1894. This colonial inn sits on a five-acre hillside amid maples, pin oaks and evergreens. Tucked behind the inn is the renovated carriage house; among its charms is a cozy fireplace suite. In the summer, guests can enjoy alfresco dining on an awning-covered porch. The Red Shutter Inn, with its woodstove in the sitting room, antique furnishings and view of a rushing river, provides a congenial atmosphere. Nearby are antique shops, galleries and craft shops.

Rates: $80-$150. Max & Carolyn Hopkins.
9 R. 9 PB. 2 FP. Phone available. TV in room. Beds: KQD. Full breakfast. Restaurant. Spa. CCs: MC VISA. Golf, downhill & cross-country skiing, hiking, biking, swimming, boating, shopping, antiquing.
Seen in: *USA Weekend.*

"You've made The Red Shutter Inn a cozy and relaxing hideaway."

WOODSTOCK L5/E3

The Charleston House

21 Pleasant St
Woodstock VT 05091
(802) 457-3843

Circa 1835. This authentically restored Greek Revival town house is listed in the National Register. It is furnished

with antiques, an art collection and Oriental rugs. Woodstock has been called one of the most beautiful villages in America by *National Geographic Magazine.*

Rates: $100-$125. Barbara & Bill Hough.
7 R. 7 PB. Phone available. TV available. Beds: QDT. Full breakfast. CCs: MC VISA AE. Cross-country skiing, tennis, fishing, hiking, golf.
Seen in: *The Harbor News, Boston Business Journal.*

"I felt like I was a king, elegant but extremely comfortable."

The Lincoln Inn at the Covered Bridge

RR 2 Box 40
Woodstock VT 05091
(802) 457-3312

Circa 1790. This admirable old farmhouse sits on five acres bordered by the Lincoln Covered Bridge and the Ottauquechee River. Lawns meander to a rise overlooking the water. There's a gazebo here and nearby, a wooden swing on long chains gently sways from a tall maple. A recent renovation has revealed hand-hewn beams in the library and a fireplace in the common room. The inn's continental cuisine provides a memorable dinner.

Rates: $99-$120. Season: May - March. Harry & Pat Francis.
6 R. 6 PB. Phone available. TV available. Beds: KQT. MAP. Restaurant. Gourmet meals. CCs: MC VISA AE. Biking, fishing, hiking, swimming, tennis, skiing, golf, sleigh rides.
Seen in: *Travelhost.*

"Feels like family!"

VIRGINIA

ABINGDON P6/*G3*

Martha Washington Inn

150 W Main St
Abingdon VA 24210
(703) 628-3161

Circa 1832. This historic building has served as Martha Washington College, a Civil War hospital and training barracks for the Washington mounted rifles. The inn features a grand staircase in the entryway, antique furnishings, two lounges and a pub. Some guest suites have fireplaces and spas. Available for banquets, receptions and meetings are the Grand Ballroom with its silk moire wallpaper and satin draperies, and the East Parlor with its original oil paintings and antiques.

Rates: $82. Deborah Bourne.
61 R. 61 PB. 3 FP. Phone in room. TV in room. Beds: KQDTC. Restaurant. Gourmet meals. Spa. Handicap access. Conference room. CCs: MC VISA AE DC CB DS. Horseback riding, boating, fishing, golf, hiking. Weekend packages.
Seen in: *Johnson City Press, Victoria Magazine.*

"A very excellent experience for the entire family."

ALEXANDRIA H21/*D9*

Memory House

See: Arlington, VA

ARLINGTON H2/*C9*

Memory House

6404 N Washington Blvd
Arlington VA 22205
(703) 534-4607

Circa 1899. This vintage Victorian house, built by a former mayor of Falls Church, was restored by the owners over a period of several years. Terra-cotta, cream and green highlight the gingerbread and shingled gables of the house. Inside are stenciled borders, polished hardwood floors, antique furnishings and collectibles. Restaurants are within eight blocks, and the East Falls Church subway station is one block away, making this a convenient base for exploring the nation's capital.

Location: Two blocks from I-66 via exit 22.

*Rates: $65-$70. John & Marlys McGrath.
2 R. 1 PB. Phone in room. TV in room. Beds: DT. Continental-plus breakfast. Tennis, bicycling, sightseeing.
Seen in: *The Washington Post, Northern Virginia Sun.*

"It was a joy to stay in this beautiful home! Marlys and John were perfect hosts."

BOYCE G18/*C8*

River House

Rt 2 Box 135
Boyce VA 22620
(703) 837-1476

Circa 1780. This historic house is located on Shenandoah River frontage and 15 acres of woodlands. Grain from the neighboring mill (now restored) was once shipped from this point to Harpers Ferry, and Stonewall Jackson camped and crossed the river here. Ask to stay in the original 1780 kitchen with its walk-in fireplace or the elegant master bedroom. Cornelia is a former actress and organizes theatrical activities at the inn.

Rates: $70-$85. Cornelia S. Niemann.
5 R. 5 PB. 5 FP. Phone available. TV available. Beds: KDTC. Full breakfast. Handicap access. CCs: MC VISA. Fishing, bicycling, wineries, antiquing. Laughing weekends, family reunions.
Seen in: *The Winchester Star.*

"Not only were we treated with a lovely place to stay but with friends!"

CASTLETON I18/*D8*

Blue Knoll Farm

Rt 1, Box 141
Castleton VA 22716
(703) 937-5234

Circa 1850. The original house of the Blue Knoll Farm is pre-Civil War, and many Civil War battles were fought in the area. The farmhouse is in the scenic valley of Castleton Mountain. Guest rooms feature antiques, family mementos and cozy comforters. Some rooms have fireplaces. Guests may relax on the wicker chairs on the Victorian porch.

Rates: $95-$115. Richard & Joy Cartwright-Brown.
4 R. 4 PB. 1 FP. Phone available. TV available. Beds: KQ. Full breakfast. Gourmet meals. Spa. CCs: MC VISA. Riding, canoeing, hiking. Honeymoon specials.

"The weekend was better than we had hoped. You both are more than partly responsible."

CHARLES CITY N21/*F9*

Edgewood Plantation

Rt 5 Historic Box 490
Charles City VA 23030
(804) 829-2962

Circa 1849. This Carpenter Gothic plantation was built by Spencer Rowland. Romantic guest rooms are furnished with antiques and old-

fashioned country artifacts. There are 10 fireplaces and a winding three-story staircase. A few yards from the inn is a three-story mill with an unusual inside mill wheel built in 1725.

Location: Halfway between Williamsburg and Richmond.
Rates: $88-$135. Dot & Juilian Boulware.
6 R. 2 PB. Phone available. TV available. Beds: KQD. Full breakfast. Spa. Swimming pool. CCs: MC VISA. Hiking, bicycling, golf, fishing, antiquing. Complimentary refreshments at two nearby taverns.
Seen in: *Country Home Magazine, Unique Inns of Virginia.*

"A feast for the eyes."

North Bend Plantation

Rt 1 Box 13A
Charles City VA 23030
(804) 829-5176

Circa 1819. The Copland family lived here for four generations. The present owner is twice great-grandson of noted agriculturist Edmund Ruffin, who is said to have fired the first shot of the Civil War at Fort Sumter. Sheridan headquartered at North Bend. His desk is still here, one of many treasured family heirlooms. Large guest rooms are filled with antiques original to the home. Complimentary refreshments are available at a nearby five-star restaurant.

Location: West of Colonial Williamsburg, 25 minutes.

Rates: $75-$85. George & Ridgely Copland.
4 R. 1 PB. 8 FP. Phone available. TV available. Beds: QD. Full breakfast. Swimming pool. Game room. Swimming, nature walks, croquet, horseshoes, volleyball, badminton.

Seen in: *The Washington Post, Travel Talk.*

"Your hospitality, friendship and history lessons were all priceless. Your love of life embraced us in a warmth I shall never forget."

Piney Grove Southall's Plantation

Rt 615 "Old Main Rd," Rt 1 Box 148
Charles City VA 23030
(804) 829-2480

Circa 1800. The Gordineers welcome you to their two historic homes. Piney Grove is a rare Tidewater log build-

ing, in the National Register of Historic Places, located on the Old Main Road among farms, plantations, country stores and quaint churches. Ladysmith House is a modest antebellum plantation house, (c. 1857). Both homes are furnished with a unique collection of artifacts and antiques that illustrates the history of the property and area. Guests also enjoy meandering among the gardens and grounds.

Location: James River Plantation outside of Williamsburg.

❀Rates: $95-$125. Brian E. Gordineer, Joseph & Joan Gordineer.
6 R. 4 PB. 5 FP. Phone available. TV available. Beds: DT. Full breakfast. Gourmet meals. Swimming pool. Conference room. Historic sightseeing, nature trail, birdwatching, croquet.

Seen in: *Richmond Times-Dispatch, Washington Post.*

"Thanks for all your thoughtfulness and hospitality."

CHARLOTTESVILLE K17/E8

200 South Street Inn

200 South St
Charlottesville VA 22901
(804) 979-0200

Circa 1853. This house was built for Thomas Jefferson Wertenbaker, son of Thomas Jefferson's librarian at the University of Virginia. It is furnished with English and Belgian antiques. Guests may choose rooms with whirlpool baths, fireplaces and canopy beds.

Location: Downtown historic district of Charlottesville.

*Rates: $85-$160. Donna Delbert.
20 R. 20 PB. 11 FP. TV available. Beds: QT. Continental breakfast. Spa. Handicap access. Conference room. CCs: MC VISA. Horseback riding, hiking, golf, skiing, tubing.

Seen in: *The New York Times, Gourmet, Vogue Magazine.*

"True hospitality abounds in this fine inn which is a neatly turned complement to the inspiring history surrounding it."

Guesthouses

PO Box 5737
Charlottesville VA 22905
(804) 979-7264

Circa 1750. Guesthouses, America's first reservation service for bed-and-breakfast accommodations, ap-

propriately originated in an area with a centuries-old tradition of outstanding hospitality. Many of the homes are in the National Register. One, Carrsbrook, circa 1750 was built for Peter Carr who was raised at Monticello and became Thomas Jefferson's secretary. Other homes are located throughout Albermarle County and have been inspected carefully to assure a pleasant stay. Mary Hill Caperton is the director.

Rates: $52-$150. Mary Hill Caperton, director.
CCs: MC VISA AE.

Seen in: *Roanoke Times & World-News, Good Housekeeping.*

"The nicest B&B experience we had on our trip."

Hidden Inn

See: Orange, VA

The Shadows B&B

See: Orange, VA

Silver Thatch Inn

3001 Hollymead Dr
Charlottesville VA 22901
(804) 978-4686

Circa 1780. This white clapboard inn, shaded by tall elms, was built for British officers by Hessian soldiers who were prisoners during the Revolutionary War. Before its current life as a country inn, Silver Thatch was a boys' school, a melon farm and a tobacco plantation. Many additions have been made to the original house, now called the Hessian Room. The inn is filled with antiques. There are three intimate dining rooms featuring fresh American cuisine.

Rates: $110-$130. Joe & Mickey Geller.
7 R. 7 PB. 4 FP. Phone available. TV available. Beds: QD. Continental-plus breakfast. Restaurant. Conference room. CCs: MC VISA. Horseback riding, canoeing, hiking, golf, jogging trails, tennis.

Seen in: *Travel & Leisure, Washington Post, Los Angeles Times, New York Magazine.*

"Everything was absolutely perfect! The room, the food and above all, the people!"

Sunset Hill

See: Nellysford, VA

Woodstock Hall

Rt 3 Box 40
Charlottesville VA 22901
(804) 293-8977 (804) 977-1740

Circa 1757. After leaving Thomas Jefferson's Monticello, a French duke who stayed at Woodstock Hall tavern wrote, "Mr. Woods' Inn is so good and cleanly...I cannot forbear mentioning those circumstances with pleasure." These standards remain at this National Historic Landmark. The two-story clapboard house contains hand-blown windowpanes, a fireplace in each guest room and many period antiques selected from the innkeeper's antique shop.

Location: On Route 637, 1.8 miles off I-64, Ivy exit.

Rates: $95-$130. Jean Wheby & Mary Ann Elder.
4 R. 4 PB. Phone available. TV in room. Beds: KQ. B&B. Gourmet meals. Con-

ference room. Golf, tennis, pool available in summer, walking trail and gazebo.
Seen in: *Colonial Homes.*
"A beautiful inn. Gracious and pleasant."

CHINCOTEAGUE K26/*E12*

The Garden and the Sea Inn
See: New Church, VA

Miss Molly's Inn
113 N Main St
Chincoteague VA 23336
(804) 336-6686

Circa 1886. This Victorian was built by J. T. Rowley, the "Clam King of the World." His daughter Miss Molly lived in it for 84 years. The house has been beautifully restored and furnished in period antiques. Marguerite Henry wrote *Misty of Chincoteague* here while rocking on the front porch with Miss Molly and Captain Jack.
Rates: $55-$105. Season: April - Dec. Dr. & Mrs. James Stam.
7 R. 1 PB. 1 FP. Phone available. TV available. Beds: KDT. B&B. Conference room. Swimming, fishing, clamming, crabbing, hiking, sailing, surfing.
"Your hospitality and warmth exuded with each guest and made all of us feel most at home."

CHRISTIANSBURG N11/*F5*

The Oaks Bed & Breakfast Country Inn
311 E Main St
Christiansburg VA 24073
(703) 381-1500 (800)336-6257

Circa 1889. This Queen Anne Victorian house surrounded by majestic old oak trees is designated a Montgomery County Landmark. The inn features an entry hall with high ceilings, stained-glass windows and a grand staircase. The inn also has tall windows, ornate fireplaces, turrets and a mix of antiques, family heirlooms and modern furniture. Breakfast is served in the formal dining room, on the wraparound porch or on the patio.
Rates: $65-$95. Tom & Margaret Ray.
6 R. 6 PB. 4 FP. Phone available. TV available. Beds: KQD. Full breakfast. Gourmet meals. Spa. Sauna. Conference room. CCs: MC VISA. Hiking, boating, antiquing. Special wedding/birthday/anniversary packages, murder mystery, comedy, romance.
Seen in: *News Messenger, Roanoke Times & World-News.*
"You lovely people have put so much of your personal charm and energy into this beautiful place."

CULPEPER I18/*D8*

Fountain Hall B&B
609 S East St
Culpeper VA 22701
(703) 825-8200 (800) 476-2944

Circa 1859. Culpeper was first surveyed by George Washington. This was Lot No. 3 of a subdivision of 33 acres. Fountain Hall was originally a

Victorian house but in the Twenties was remodeled as a Colonial Revival. Most of the rooms are named after historic families in the community. The Fray Drawing Room displays old prints and a library wall of books from the late 1800s.
*❀Rates: $55-$85. Steve & Kathi Walker.
5 R. 5 PB. 3 FP. Phone in room. TV available. Beds: QDTC. B&B. Handicap access. Conference room. CCs: MC VISA AE DS. Horseback riding, skiing, basketball, tennis, golf.
Seen in: *Culpeper Exponent.*
"Liked the friendly greeting and atmosphere. Food was delicious."

DRAPER O10/*G5*

Claytor Lake Homestead Inn
PO Box 7
Draper VA 24324
(703) 980-6777 (800) 676-LAKE

Circa 1845. This inn was once a two-story log cabin built by slaves for the Ross family. It has been enlarged several times over the past century. The dining room's bay window overlooks Claytor Lake and a private beach. There is also a spectacular view of the lake from the brick-and-stone wraparound porch, which has rocking chairs and a swing. Furnishings include early American and

country antiques, many collected from the historic Hotel Roanoke. Home-ground and seasoned breakfast sausage is a house specialty.
*Rates: $60-$65. Betsey & Bob Thomas.
5 R. 1 FP. Phone in room. TV in room. Beds: KQD. Full breakfast. Conference room. FAX. CCs: MC VISA. Biking, hiking, beach, swimming, boating.
Seen in: *Roanoke Times, Smyth County News, The Southwest Times, Blue Ridge Country Magazine, Blue Ridge Digest.*
"The total environment, including innkeepers, is first class."

DUBLIN N10/*F5*

Bell's B&B
13 Giles Ave, PO Box 405
Dublin VA 24084
(703) 674-6331

Circa 1914. Built by innkeeper David Bell's grandfather, this Victorian home is set off by a large, shady lawn. Fireplaces are found in four of the

guest rooms. A formal dining room seats 12. Made-to-order breakfasts are served. International guests will benefit from innkeeper Helga Bell's fluency in Spanish and German. The historic Newbern community and Claytor Lake State Park are within a few miles.
*Rates: $50-$65. Helga & David Bell.
5 R. 4 FP. TV available. Beds: QDT. Full breakfast. CCs: VISA. Picnics.
Seen in: *The Southwest Times.*
"The house is fascinating and beautiful but not anywhere near as nice as the people in it."

FAIRFAX H20/D9

Bailiwick Inn
4023 Chain Bridge Rd
Fairfax VA 22030
(703) 691-2266 (800) 366-7666

Circa 1800. Located across from the county courthouse where George Washington's will is filed, this distinguished three-story Federal brick house has recently been renovated. The first Civil War casualty occurred on what is now the inn's lawn. The elegant, early-Virginia decor is reminiscent of the state's fine plantation mansions. Ask to stay in the Thomas Jefferson Room, a replica of Mr. Jefferson's bedroom at Monticello.

Rates: $95-$175. Anne & Ray Smith.
14 R. 14 PB. 4 FP. Phone available. Beds: KQT. Full breakfast. Spa. Handicap access. CCs: MC VISA. Civil War battlefields, sightseeing. Weddings & receptions.
Seen in: *The Washington Post, The Journal, The Fairfax Connection.*

"A visit to your establishment clearly transcends any lodging experience that I can recall."

FLINT HILL H18/D8

Caledonia Farm B&B
Rt 1 Box 2080
Flint Hill VA 22627
(703) 675-3693

Circa 1812. This gracious Federal-style stone house is beautifully situated on 52 acres adjacent to Shenandoah National Park. It was built by a Revolutionary War officer, Captain John Dearing and his musket is displayed over the mantel. The house has been restored and the colonial color scheme retained. The inn is a Virginia Historic Landmark and in the National Register of Historic Places. The innkeeper is a retired broadcaster.

Location: Four miles north of Washington, Virginia.
*❀Rates: $70-$100. Phil Irwin.
3 R. 1 PB. 3 FP. Phone available. TV available. Beds: D. Full breakfast. Handicap access. Conference room. CCs: MC VISA. Hiking, golf, tennis, swimming, canoeing, hay rides, lawn games, bicycles.
Seen in: *Country Magazine.*

"We've stayed at many, many B&B's. This is by far the best!"

FREDERICKSBURG J20/D9

La Vista Plantation
4420 Guinea Station Rd
Fredericksburg VA 22401
(703) 898-8444

Circa 1838. La Vista has a long and unusual past rich in Civil War history. Both Confederate and Union armies camped here, and this is where the Ninth Cavalry was sworn in. A Classical Revival structure with high ceilings and pine floors, the house sits on 10 acres of pasture and woods. There is a pond stocked with bass.

Rates: $70. Michele & Edward Schiesser.
2 R. 2 PB. 1 FP. Beds: KQDC. Full breakfast. Conference room. CCs: MC VISA. Fishing, hiking, bicycles, horseback riding.
Seen in: *The Free Lance Star.*

"Thanks for the best weekend we've ever had."

FRONT ROYAL H18/C8

Chester House Inn
43 Chester St
Front Royal VA 22630
(703) 635-3937 (800) 621-0441

Circa 1905. This stately Georgian estate rests on two acres of terraced gardens, which include vast plantings of boxwood, wisteria arbors, a fountain and brick walkways and walls. Elaborately carved marble mantels from London remain, and an original speaker tube extends from the second-floor bedroom to the kitchen. Just down the street is the renovated village commons.

*Rates: $55-$95. Bill & Ann Wilson.
6 R. 1 PB. Phone available. TV available. Beds: KQDT. B&B. Conference room. CCs: MC VISA AE. Boating, hiking, horseback riding, golf, tennis, camping, wineries, antiquing.
Seen in: *Winchester Star, Northern Virginia Daily, Blue Ridge Country Magazine.*

"A home of greater charm would be hard to find."

GORDONSVILLE K18/E8

Sleepy Hollow Farm
Rt 3 Box 43 on VA 231
Gordonsville VA 22942
(703) 832-5555

Circa 1775. Many generations have added on to this brick farmhouse with its 18th-century dining room and bedrooms. The pink and white room was frequently visited by a friendly ghost from Civil War days, according to local stories. She hasn't been seen for several years since the innkeeper, a former missionary, had the house blessed. The grounds include an herb garden, a pond with gazebo, a chestnut slave cabin, terraces and abundant wildlife.

Location: Between Gordonsville & Somerset on Rt 231.
Rates: $55-$85. Beverly Allison.
6 R. 6 PB. 1 FP. Phone available. TV available. Beds: QTC. Full breakfast. Conference room. CCs: MC VISA. Horseback riding, golf, pond swimming, fishing, hiking.
Seen in: *The Orange County Review.*

"This house is truly blessed."

GOSHEN K14/E6

The Rose Hummingbird Inn
Country Lane, PO Box 70
Goshen VA 24439
(703) 997-9065

Circa 1853. This early Victorian mansion is located in the Shenandoah Valley against the backdrop of the Blue Ridge Mountains. Both the first and second floors offer wraparound verandas. Furnished with antiques, the inn features a library and sitting room with fireplaces. Family-style suppers are available by advance reservations. An old barn and babbling creek are on the grounds. Lexington, the Virginia Horse Center, Natural Bridge, the Blue Ridge Parkway and antiquing are all nearby.

*Rates: $50-$60. Bill & Bonnie Saunders.
7 R. 7 PB. Phone available. TV available. Beds: QT. Full breakfast. Gourmet meals. CCs: MC VISA AE DS. Swimming, golf, skiing, fishing, hunting, canoeing, tubing. Honeymoon specials.

"Your hospitality was wonderful and the food was great. You made our sixth anniversary one we'll never forget!"

HARRISONBURG I16/D7

The Widow Kip's Shenandoah Inn

See: Mount Jackson, VA

HILLSBORO G19/C9

Inn Between the Hills

RR 3, Rt 9 PO Box 68A
Hillsboro VA 22132
(703) 668-6162

Circa 1780. Picturesquely set in the gap of the Short Hills, Hillsboro boasts numerous stone houses from the 18th century. Many, like the inn,

saw both Union and Confederate soldiers march to the battles of Bull Run and Manassas. Carefully restored, guest rooms offer feather beds, antiques and fine reproductions. Full gourmet breakfasts and high teas are served.

Rates: $60-$85. Kathy & Josh Margolis.
3 R. 3 FP. Phone available. Beds: QDT. Full breakfast. Canoeing, kayaking, tubing, hiking, biking, antiquing.
Seen in: *Leesburg Today.*
"Finally a B&B that has equally elegant portions of bed and breakfast. It was almost like a fairy tale."

LANCASTER L23/E10

The Inn at Levelfields

State Rt 3 Box 216
Lancaster VA 22503
(804) 435-6887

Circa 1857. This hip-roofed Georgian colonial house stands a quarter of a mile from the road bordered by hedges of 250-year-old English boxwood. Once the center of a large plantation, the mansion has been completely refurbished and filled with family antiques and Oriental rugs, offering the finest in Virginia tradition.

Location: Three hours from Baltimore.
Rates: $75. Warren & Doris Sadler.
4 R. 4 PB. Phone available. TV available. Beds: KQD. Full breakfast. Restaurant. Swimming pool. CCs: MC VISA. Hiking.
Seen in: *Richmond Times-Dispatch, Newport News Daily Press, Woman's Day.*
"Your hospitality far exceeds any we've experienced and truly made our stay one we'll treasure."

LEESBURG G19/C9

Fleetwood Farm

Rt 1 Box 306-A
Leesburg VA 22075
(703) 327-4325

Circa 1745. The Reverend Doctor Charles Green, doctor to George and Martha Washington, built this colonial

manor house. Elegantly furnished rooms include the Sheep Room with its own entrance, a high rope bed, fireplace and spa. Your hostess is knowledgeable about the history of the area and about Dr. Green's relationship with George Washington. A flock of sheep provide bucolic scenery on the inn's acreage.

Rates: $95-$120. Carol & Bill Chamberlin.
2 R. 2 PB. 2 FP. Phone available. TV available. Beds: D. Full breakfast. Canoeing, fishing. Golf, swimming and horseback riding nearby.
Seen in: *Loudoun Times Mirror.*
"Thank you for an absolutely lovely weekend!"

Laurel Brigade Inn

20 W Market St
Leesburg VA 22075
(703) 777-1010

Circa 1759. This handsome Colonial stone house originally opened as an ordinary. Prices were set for lodging by the local parish justices of six shillings "on clean sheets, otherwise nothing." The long ell on the west side of the inn was erected to entertain the Marquis de Lafayette when he visited James Monroe. The inn features marble mantle pieces from France, Swiss door fixtures and a well-known dining room. It has been operated since 1945 by the Flippo family.

Rates: $50-$90. Season: Feb. 14-Dec. 31 Ellen Flippo Wall.
6 R. 6 PB. 2 FP. Phone available. TV available. Beds: KDT. Restaurant. Hiking, horseback riding.
Seen in: *Saturday Evening Post, Southern Living, The New York Times, Washington Post.*

LEXINGTON L14/E6

Fassifern B&B

Rt 5 Box 87- State Rt 39
Lexington VA 24450
(703) 463-1013

Circa 1867. Fassifern, which draws its name from the seat of the Cameron Clan in Scotland, was built on the site

of an older dwelling just after the Civil War. Nestled in the Shenandoah Valley, the inn is on three-and-a-half acres, surrounded by stately trees and graced with a pond.

Location: Route 39, 3/4 miles from I-64, Exit 13.
Rates: $65-$80. Ann Carol & Arthur Perry.
5 R. 5 PB. Phone available. Beds: QDT. Continental-plus breakfast. CCs: MC VISA. Horseback riding, swimming, canoeing, golf, tennis, hiking, fishing.
Seen in: *Mid-Atlantic Country, Geico Direct Spring.*
"A coffee-lover's heaven!"

Llewellyn Lodge at Lexington

603 S Main St
Lexington VA 24450
(703) 463-3235

Circa 1936. This brick colonial shaded by tall trees, features three gables on the third story. It is decorated in an-

tique and traditional furnishings. Nearby historic attractions include the home of Stonewall Jackson, the Natural Bridge and the Robert E. Lee house.

Location: Fifty miles north of Roanoke.
*Rates: $60-$75. Ellen & John Roberts.
6 R. 6 PB. Phone available. TV available. Beds: KQDT. Full breakfast. Handicap access. Conference room. CCs: MC VISA AE. Swimming, golf, tennis, hiking, fishing,

hunting.
Seen in: *The News-Gazette, The New York Times.*
"Like being at home! The breakfast was the best ever."

Oak Spring Farm & Vineyard
See: Raphine, VA

LINCOLN G19/*C9*

Springdale Country Inn
Lincoln VA 22078
(703) 338-1832 (800) 388-1832
Circa 1832. A National Historic Landmark, the Springdale Country Inn was once a schoolhouse, Civil War hospital and traveler's inn. The inn, with its high ceilings and windows, has richly burnished wide-board floors, reproduction wallpaper and antiques. Guest rooms have fresh flowers, stenciled walls and four-poster canopy beds. Guests may relax on a sun and sitting porch.
Rates: $95-$125. Nancy & Roger Fones.
9 R. 6 PB. 4 FP. Phone available. TV available. Beds: DTC. Handicap access. Conference room. CCs: MC VISA. Tennis, bicycling/jogging trail, swimming, golf, horseback riding nearby. Wedding/receptions, business meeting facilities.
Seen in: *The Pamphlet, The Washington Post.*
"Quaint setting and excellent meals."

LURAY I17/*D8*

The Ruffner House
Rt 4 Box 620
Luray VA 22835
(703) 743-7855
Circa 1739. Situated on a farm nestled in the heart of the Shenandoah Valley, this stately manor was built by Peter

Ruffner, the first settler of Page Valley and Luray. Ruffner family members discovered a cavern opposite the entrance to the Luray Caverns, which were found later. Purebred Arabian horses graze in the pasture on this 18-acre estate.
Location: Shenandoah Valley, South of hwys. 211 and 340.
*Rates: $85-$125. Mrs. Merrigan.
7 R. 6 PB. Phone available. TV available. Beds: Q. Full breakfast. Swimming pool. Conference room. CCs: MC VISA. Swimming, golf, canoeing, rafting, horses, tennis, hiking.
Seen in: *Page News and Courier, The Virginian Pilot.*

"This is the loveliest inn we have ever stayed in. We were made to feel very welcome and at ease."

LYNCHBURG M15/*F7*

The Madison House B&B
413 Madison St
Lynchburg VA 24504
(804) 528-1503
Circa 1874. The Madison House B&B is nestled in the foothills of the Blue Ridge Mountains and on the banks of the James River. The house of Italianate and modified Eastlake Victorian architecture is one of the oldest in the Garland Hill Historic District. The inn features a stained-glass peacock window, crystal chandeliers, ornate fireplaces, original woodwork, an ornate wrought iron porch and prize-winning grounds featuring 200 azaleas.
Rates: $60-$90. Irene & Dale Smith.
3 R. 1 PB. 2 FP. Phone available. Beds: QD. Full breakfast. Conference room. FAX. Hiking, biking, shopping. Weddings, business retreat, special activities.
"An excellent facility, very clean, food is outstanding."

MATHEWS M23/*F10*

Ravenswood Inn
PO Box 250
Mathews VA 23109
(804) 725-7272
Circa 1913. This intimate waterfront home is located on five acres along the banks of the East River, where passing boats still harvest crabs and oysters. A long screened porch captures river breezes. Most rooms feature a river view and are decorated in Victorian, country, nautical or wicker. The inn's speciality is its noted French and Mediterranean cuisine. Williamsburg, Jamestown and Yorktown are within an hour.
Rates: $150. Season: Feb. 12-Dec. 12. Marshall & Linda Warner/Peter & Sally Preston.
5 R. 5 PB. Beds: KQT. MAP. Gourmet meals. Spa. Charter fishing, charter sailing, bicycles, sailboats, croquet, badminton.
Seen in: *The Virginian Pilot, Daily Press.*
"While Ravenswood is one of the most beautiful places we've ever been, it is your love, caring and friendship that has made it such a special place for us."

Riverfront House & Cottage
Rt 14 E Box 310
Mathews VA 23109
(804) 725-9975
Circa 1840. This farmhouse and its waterfront cottage are situated on 10 acres along Put In Creek. The main house features a large wraparound veranda. Guests use the dock for crab-

bing, boating and sunbathing. Mathews County is surrounded by the Chesapeake and Mobjack bays and dozens of creeks, harbors and inlets. The landscape includes old sawmills, churches, farmlands and oystering boats. Riverfront House makes a good base for day trips to Williamsburg, Yorktown, Richmond and the James River Plantations.
*Rates: $60-$85. Season: May-November. Annette Waldman Goldreyer.
8 R. 8 PB. Phone available. TV available. Beds: KQT. Full breakfast.
Seen in: *Virginia Pilot.*
"A joyful, relaxing experience."

MIDDLEBURG H19/*C4*

Welbourne
Middleburg VA 22117
(703) 687-3201
Circa 1775. This seventh-generation mansion once presided over 3,000 acres. With family members starting their own estates, Welbourne now

stands at 600 acres. Furnishings were collected during world travels over the past 200 years. Civil War stories fill the family history book, and in the 1930s, F. Scott Fitzgerald and Thomas Wolfe used the house as a setting for their writings.
Location: Fifty miles west of Washington, DC.
*Rates: $80-$100. Mrs. N. H. Morison.
10 R. 10 PB. 7 FP. Phone available. TV available. Beds: QT. Full breakfast. Conference room. Fox hunting.
"Furnishings portray a house and home that's been around for a long, long time. And none of it is held back from guests. Life today at Welbourne is quiet and unobtrusive. It's genteel," Philip Hayward, *Country Magazine.*

MOLLUSK L23/E10

Greenvale Manor

Rt 354 Box 70
Mollusk VA 22517
(804) 462-5995

Circa 1840. Beautifully situated on the Rappahannock River and Greenvale Creek, Greenvale is a classic waterfront plantation. This land was patented to Anthony Stephens in 1651, but in 1607 Captain John Smith said of Virginia's Northern Neck, *"Heaven and earth never agreed better to frame a place for men's habitation... rivers and brooks all running most pleasantly...with fruitful and delightsome land."* The gracious manor lifestyle extends from tastefully furnished guest rooms to a licensed captain available for boat tours from the dock.

Location: Eight miles from Lancaster Courthouse off Route 3.

Rates: $65-$95. Pam & Walt Smith.

9 R. 7 PB. 2 FP. Phone available. TV available. Beds: KQDT. Full breakfast. Swimming pool. Game room. Conference room. Boating, bicycling, golf, tennis, badminton. Private beach.

Seen in: *Rural Living, Conde Nast Traveler, Victoria Magazine, The Washingtonian.*

"The inn and grounds are gorgeous, the water views breathtaking, but it's the innkeepers who make it really special."

MONTEREY J13/D6

Highland Inn

Main Street, PO Box 40
Monterey VA 24465
(703) 468-2143

Circa 1904. Listed in the National Register, this clapboard Victorian hotel has outstanding Eastlake wraparound verandas. Small-town life

may be viewed from rocking chairs and swings. Guest rooms are furnished in country fashion, with iron beds and antiques. Sheep outnumber people in a pastoral setting surrounded by three million acres of National Forest.

Location: Thirty-seven miles west of Staunton.

*Rates: $43-$59. Michael Strand & Cynthia Peel-Strand.

17 R. 17 PB. Phone available. TV available. Beds: KQTWDC. Restaurant. Conference room. CCs: MC VISA. Hiking, cross-country skiing, fishing, golf.

Seen in: *Washington Post, Rural Living Magazine.*

"The most beautiful place I've been."

MONTROSS K22/E10

The Inn at Montross

Courthouse Sq
Montross VA 22520
(804) 493-9097

Circa 1683. Montross was rebuilt in 1800 on the site of a 17th-century tavern. Operating as an "ordinary" since 1683, parts of the structure have

been in continuous use for more than 300 years. It was visited by burgesses and Justices of the Court (Washington, Lee and Jefferson). The guest rooms feature canopy beds and colonial furnishings.

Location: Seven miles from Stratford Hall.

*❀Rates: $115-$125 MAP. Eileen & Michael Longman.

6 R. 6 PB. Phone in room. TV in room. Beds: QDT, Continental-plus breakfast. Restaurant. Gourmet meals. Conference room. CCs: MC VISA DS. Tennis on premises. Brandy & homemade chocolates in room.

Seen in: *The Virginian-Pilot, Travel, Richmond Times-Dispatch.*

"Hospitality is Inn!"

MOUNT JACKSON H16/D7

The Widow Kip's Shenandoah Inn

Rt 1 Box 117
Mount Jackson VA 22842
(703) 477-2400

Circa 1830. This lovingly restored farmhouse with its sweeping view of the Massanutten Mountains is situated on seven acres. It's a stone's

throw from a fork of the Shenandoah River. Locally crafted quilts enhance the four-poster, sleigh and hand-carved Victorian beds. Two restored cottages (the Silk Purse and Sow's Ear) as well as a gift shop, create a Williamsburg-style courtyard. Cows graze unexpectedly a few feet away from the swimming pool.

Location: I-81 to Mt. Jackson. Exit 69 to Route 11, south to 263.

Rates: $65-$80. Rosemary Kip.

7 R. 7 PB. 5 FP. Phone available. TV in room. Beds: QD. Full breakfast. Swimming pool. CCs: VISA DS. Bicycling, skiing, caverns, canoeing.

Seen in: *Country Inns, Mid-Atlantic Country, Americana, Sojourner.*

"Everything sparkled. The rooms were decorated with flair and imagination."

NELLYSFORD L16/E7

Sunset Hill

Rt 1, Box 375
Nellysford VA 22958
(804) 361-1101

Circa 1880. Guests awaken to the smell of freshly baked bread and coffee in this pre-Civil War home, formerly owned by a prominent town

physican. All guest rooms include ceiling fans and antique furniture. The Apricot Lily room boasts a jacuzzi tub and an adjacent sitting room. The Periwinkle, Laurel Blossom and Scarlet Rose rooms are connected by an elegant covered terrace. A full breakfast is served either in the guest rooms, dining room or on a terrace. Guests can take advantage of local horseback riding and golf courses or visit nearby wineries.

*Rates: $95-$115. Karen E. Estey & Elena Woodard.

10 R. 10 PB. Phone available. TV available. Beds: DT. Continental-plus breakfast. Spa. Handicap access. Conference room. Horseback riding, canoeing, tubing, hiking, swimming, golf, fishing, skiing, ice skating, biking. Hiking tours.

Seen in: *Nelson County Times, Charlottesville Observer.*

"Beautiful house! Great romantic spot!"

NEW CHURCH K25/E11

The Garden and the Sea Inn

PO Box 275
New Church VA 23415
(804) 824-0672

Circa 1802. The Garden and the Sea Inn consists of a two-story frame house with guest rooms and a brick building that once served as the first

voting place for northern Accomack County. The brick structure houses a restaurant serving food prepared French-style from local produce and fresh seafood from the farms and waters of the Eastern shore. Rooms are decorated with classic and antique furnishings. Guests may enjoy afternoon tea in the parlor.

Location: Near Chincoteague Island; Virginia's Eastern Shore.
Rates: $75-$95. Season: April to Oct. 31. Victoria Olian & Jack Betz.
6 R. 6 PB. Phone available. Beds: Q. Continental-plus breakfast. Restaurant. Gourmet meals. CCs: MC VISA AE DC CB. Beach, water sports, charter fishing. Wildlife refuge nearby. Receptions, private parties. Seen in: *Eastern Shore News, Salisbury Daily Times.*
"This place is outstanding, really beautiful."

NEW MARKET I16/D7

A Touch of Country B&B

9329 Congress St
New Market VA 22844
(703) 740-8030

Circa 1873. This white clapboard Shenandoah Valley "I"-frame house has a second-story pediment centered above the veranda entrance. It was built by Captain William Rice, commander of the New Market Cavalry, and the house sits on what was once a battleground of the Civil War. Rice's unit was highly praised by General Lee. Guest chambers are in the main house and in the handsome carriage house.

Rates: $55-$65. Jean Schoellig & Dawn M. Kasow.
6 R. 6 PB. Phone available. TV available. Beds: QD. B&B. CCs: MC VISA. Golf, swimming, skiing, hiking, canoeing.
Seen in: *USA Today Weekend.*
"Every morning should start with sunshine, bird song and Dawn's strawberry pancakes."

ORANGE J18/E8

Hidden Inn

249 Caroline St
Orange VA 22960
(703) 672-3625

Circa 1890. Acres of huge old trees can be seen from the wraparound veranda of this Victorian inn nestled

in the Virginia countryside. Meticulous attention has been given to every detail of the inn's restoration, right down to the white lace and fresh cut flowers. Monticello, Blue Ridge, Montpelier and several wineries are located nearby.

Location: Intersection of Rte 15 & Rte 20.
*Rates: $89-$159. Barbara & Ray Lonick.
9 R. 9 PB. 2 FP. Phone available. TV available. Beds: KQDT. EP. Gourmet meals. Spa. FAX. CCs: MC VISA. Fishing, croquet, horseshoes, waterskiing, tennis.
Seen in: *Forbes Magazine.*
"It just doesn't get any better than this!"

Mayhurst Inn

US 15 South, PO Box 707
Orange VA 22960
(703) 672-5597

Circa 1859. An extravagant Italianate Victorian villa, Mayhurst was built by the great-nephew of President James

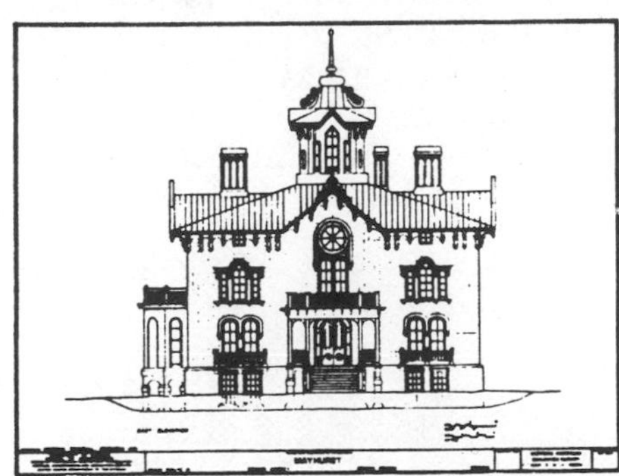

Madison, Col. John Willis. It is noted for its fanciful architecture and oval spiral staircase ascending four floors to a rooftop gazebo. It was once host to General Stonewall Jackson and during the Civil War served as the Northern Virginia army headquarters. Thirty-six acres of old oaks, cedars, and magnolias surround the inn.

Location: One mile south of Orange, 95 miles south of Washington, D.C.
*Rates: $95-$150. Stephen & Shirley Ramsey.
7 R. 7 PB. 5 FP. Phone available. Beds: QDT. Full breakfast. Gourmet meals. Conference room. CCs: MC VISA. Horseback riding, a pond for fishing. Seen in: *Lifestyle.*
"It's Victorian splendor at its highest."

The Shadows B&B Inn

14291 Constitution Hwy
Orange VA 22960
(703) 672-5057

Circa 1913. This vintage farmhouse sits on 44 acres of secluded rolling hills. The inn features fine Victorian and Civil War antiques, lace pillows, claw-foot tubs and pedestal sinks. The Rocking Horse Cabin, one of two cottages, has rocking horses throughout, wicker furniture, natural wood floors and a private porch. Guests of the inn may enjoy a book in front of the library fireplace or sip iced tea or hot cider in the Gathering Room. One may also relax on the porch swing, in the gazebo by the herb garden or by the lily pond.

Rates: $70-$100. Barbara & Pat Loffredo.
6 R. 6 PB. Phone available. TV available. Beds: KQDT. Full breakfast. Conference room. Wineries, museums. Tennis, golf, fishing nearby.
Seen in: *Innsider, Orange County Review, River's Edge.*
"You and your home will leave a lasting impression on my heart and soul."

RAPHINE K14/E7

Oak Spring Farm & Vineyard

Rt 1 Box 356
Raphine VA 24472
(703) 377-2398

Circa 1826. A willow tree droops gracefully over a pond at Oak Spring Farm, a working gentleman's farm

that includes a five-acre vineyard on 40 acres of woods, creeks, lawns and orchards. The historic farmhouse features porch views of the Blue Ridge Mountains and has been pristinely renovated. Filled with fine antiques, the inn offers bouquets of fresh flowers in all the guest rooms. A herd of friendly burros belonging to the

Natural Bridge Petting Zoo live here.
Rates: $55-$65. Jim & Pat Tichenor.
3 R. 3 PB. 2 FP. Phone available. Beds: QDT. Continental-plus breakfast. CCs: MC VISA. Horseback riding, hiking, biking, swimming, skiing.
Seen in: *The News-Gazette, The News and County Press, Mid-Atlantic Country.*
"The good taste, the privacy, the decor and the hosts were unbeatable!"

RICHMOND M20/F9

Abbie Hill B&B
PO Box 4503
Richmond VA 23220
(804) 355-5855

Circa 1909. Situated on a one-acre city lot in the historic district is this Federal-style bed and breakfast. It

once provided a third-story office for realtor John Bagby, while his wife and five children filled the rooms downstairs. The host, an interior designer, has redecorated and furnished guest rooms with antiques such as four-poster beds. Birds and plants fill the bay window in the paneled dining room lighted with a massive crystal chandelier. An afternoon tea and a full Virginia breakfast are house specialties.
Rates: $65-$95. Barbara & Bill Fleming.
3 R. 2 PB. 2 FP. Phone available. TV in room. Beds: QDT. B&B. Walking tours, museums.
"Thanks for the relaxing stay and great breakfast!!"

Bensonhouse — The Emmanuel Hutzler House
2036 Monument Ave
Richmond VA 23220
(804) 353-6900

Circa 1914. This graciously restored Italian Renaissance home is a showcase of mahogany paneling, and a handsome staircase. It's 8,000 square feet includes a stunning parlor with handsome antiques, leaded-glass windows and a marble fireplace. Ask for the largest room with the four-poster mahogany bed, antique sofa and dresser because it has its own spa tucked into an enormous bathroom. Breakfast is served in the formal dining room of this non-smoking inn.
Rates: $89-$125. Lyn M. Benson & John Richardson.
4 R. 4 PB. 2 FP. Phone in room. TV in room. Beds: QT. Full breakfast. CCs: MC VISA AE. Jogging trails, Virginia Museum, St. John's Church. Tours of nearby Civil War battlefields, historic homes, state Capitol.
"I'm glad there are still people like you who painstakingly restore great old houses such as this. A great job of reconstruction and beautifully decorated! Delightful hosts!"

The Catlin-Abbott House
2304 E Broad St
Richmond VA 23223
(804) 780-3746

Circa 1845. This house was built for William Catlin by a slave, William Mitchell, a noted brick mason of the time. During the days of reconstruction, a six-room addition was built to accommodate boarders. It now serves as innkeepers' quarters. This richly appointed inn is one block from St. John's Church, site of Patrick Henry's famous "Liberty or Death" speech.
*Rates: $82-$140. Dr. & Mrs. James L. Abbott.
3 R. 3 PB. Phone available. TV available. Beds: QT. Full breakfast. CCs: MC VISA AE.
Seen in: *Colonial Homes.*
"The accommodations were immaculate."

Mr. Patrick Henry's Inn
2300 E Broad St
Richmond VA 23223
(804) 644-1322

Circa 1858. Elegant Mr. Patrick Henry's is located in Richmond's oldest neighborhood, Church Hill, an area of gas-lit streets and beautifully restored town houses. The Greek Revival inn has an outdoor patio, formal garden, carriage house, and an old bridal path. Most of the guest rooms have a fireplace, kitchenette and private porch.

Rates: $95-$125. Jim & Lynn News.
4 R. 4 PB. 4 FP. Phone in room. TV in room. Beds: KQT. Full breakfast. Restaurant. Conference room. CCs: MC VISA AE DC.
Seen in: *Roanoke Times, Mid-Atlantic Country.*

The West-Bocock House
1107 Grove Ave
Richmond VA 23220
(804) 358-6174

Circa 1871. This Greek Revival home is located in the Fan Area Historic District, found in the National Register. Freshly baked pastries or a

traditional southern breakfast are served every morning either in the dining room or on the veranda. American and English antiques decorate the house, and each guest room contains French linens and fresh flowers. The Virginia Room boasts a four-poster bed, fireplace and sun porch overlooking the garden.
Rates: $65-$75. Mr. & Mrs. James West, Jr.
3 R. 3 PB. 2 FP. Phone in room. TV in room. Beds: QTC. Full breakfast. Conference room. Historic sites, shopping.
"True Southern hospitality."

ROANOKE N12/F6

The Mary Bladon House B&B
381 Washington Ave Old SW
Roanoke VA 24016
(703) 344-5361

Circa 1891. This Elizabethan Victorian, located in Roanoke's historic area once served as a boarding house, operated by "Mother Bladon." There are several ornate fireplaces, and the home is furnished with antiques and local craft items. Spacious porches provide a spot to relax. A charming step back in time for the young and the young at heart.

Location: In the heart of Roanoke's arts and entertainment district.
Rates: $70-$95. Bill & Sheri Bestpitch.
4 R. 2 PB. 2 FP. Phone available. TV available. Beds: D. Full breakfast. CCs: MC VISA. Farmers' Market and "Center in the Square" nearby.
Seen in: *Country Magazine, Roanoke Times.*
"You are doing a fabulous job."

SCOTTSVILLE L17/E8

High Meadows

Rt 4 Box 6
Scottsville VA 24590
(804) 286-2218

Circa 1832. Minutes from Charlottesville on the Constitution Highway (Route 20), High Meadows stands on

22 acres of gardens, forests, ponds, a creek and a vineyard. Listed in the National Register, it is actually two historic homes joined by a breezeway. The inn is furnished in Federal and Victorian styles. Guests are treated to gracious Virginia hospitality in an elegant and peaceful setting.
Rates: $85-$110. Peter Sushka & Mary Jae Abbitt.
7 R. 7 PB. 4 FP. Beds: QDT. Gourmet meals. Conference room. Canoeing, fishing, hiking, croquet, horseshoes, skiing, wineries.
Seen in: *The Washington Times, The Cavalier Daily.*
"We have rarely encountered such a smooth blend of hospitality and expertise in a totally relaxed environment."

SMITH MOUNTAIN LAKE O13/F6

Manor at Taylor's Store

Rt 1 Box 533
Smith Mountain Lake VA 24184
(703) 721-3951

Circa 1820. Situated on 120 acres of rolling countryside, this two-story, columned manor was built on the site of Taylor's Store, a trading post and ordinary just off the old Warwick Road. It served as the plantation house for a prosperous tobacco farmer, Moses Greer Booth. Guest rooms feature a variety of antiques and styles including traditional colonial and English Country. From the solarium, a wildflower trail winds through the inn's green meadows where a canoe awaits those who wish to paddle across one of five ponds on the property.
Rates: $60-$85. Lee & Mary Lynn Tucker.
6 R. 4 PB. 6 FP. Phone available. TV available. Beds: QD. B&B. Gourmet meals. Spa. Handicap access. Exercise room. Swimming pool. Game room. Conference room. CCs: MC VISA. Boating, fishing, golf, tennis, horses, hiking, antiquing, fine dining.
Seen in: *Smith Mountain Eagle, Lake Country, Blue Ridge Country, Franklin News-Post.*
"This B&B experience is a delightful one!"

SPERRYVILLE I17/D8

The Conyers House

Slate Mills Rd, Rt 1 Box 157
Sperryville VA 22740
(703) 987-8025

Circa 1780. Set in Rappahannock County's rolling hunt country in the shadow of Walden Mountain is The Conyers House. The inn has eight cozy fireplaces, Oriental rugs, antique oil paintings, French doors, an antique French tapestry and an 1860 grand piano. Some guest rooms have private porches overlooking the well garden or the mountains. The inn is decorated with antique furniture, heirlooms and collectibles.
Rates: $100-$170. Sandra & Norman Cartwright-Brown.
8 R. 6 PB. 7 FP. Phone available. TV available. Beds: KQD. Full breakfast. Gourmet meals. Spa. Trail rides, mountain climbing, swimming hole, fishing, antiquing. Weddings, family reunions, executive retreats.
Seen in: *Mid-Atlantic Country, The New York Times, The Baltimore Sun, The Washington Post.*
"A delightful place to recharge your spirit and to enjoy the beauty of a Virginia autumn."

STAUNTON K15/E7

Frederick House

Frederick and New Streets
Staunton VA 24401
(703) 885-4220 (800)334-5575(outside VA)

Circa 1810. The five historic town homes that comprise Frederick House have guest rooms or suites and Chumley's Tearoom where full break-

fast is served. The oldest structure is believed to be a copy of a home designed by Thomas Jefferson and built on the campus of the University of Virginia. Original staircases and woodwork are highlighted throughout.
Location: Downtown.
*Rates: $45-$110. Joe & Evy Harman.
14 R. 14 PB. Phone in room. TV in room. Beds: KQTC. Full breakfast. Restaurant. Spa. Sauna. Exercise room. Swimming pool. Conference room. CCs: MC VISA AE DC CB DS. Golf, tennis, skiing, hiking, horseback riding.
Seen in: *Richmond Times-Dispatch, The News Journal.*
"Thanks for making the room so squeaky clean and comfortable! I enjoyed the Virginia hospitality. The furnishings and decor are beautiful."

Oak Spring Farm & Vineyard

See: Raphine, VA

TREVILIANS K18/E8

Prospect Hill

Rt 613, RD 3 Box 430
Trevilians VA 23093
(703) 967-0844

Circa 1732. The Manor House is surround by an English Garden, on a quarter of a mile of green lawn. Rare magnolias shade the inn, and nearby is an old log cabin dating to 1699, now one of the guest accommodations. Guest rooms in the Manor House feature fireplaces, antiques and beds topped with cozy quilts. Other historic outbuildings include a slave kitchen, smoke house and the overseer's house. After the War Between the States, the owners began to take in guests and this hospitality has continued for more than 100 years.
Location: Fifteen miles east of Charlottesville near Zion Crossroads.
*Rates: $110-$160. The Sheehan family.
11 R. 11 PB. 10 FP. Phone available. Beds: QDT. AP. Spa. Swimming pool. Conference room. CCs: MC VISA. Swimming, jogging, walking.
Seen in: *The Washington Post, Americana Magazine, The Daily Progress.*
"We've been to many wonderful inns - this is the nicest!"

WACHAPREAGUE M25/F11

The Burton House

11 Brooklyn St
Wachapreague VA 23480
(804) 787-4560

Circa 1883. Located one block from the waterfront, The Burton House is a good point from which to take day trips to Tangier Island, Chincoteague,

Assateague and the Barrier Islands. Recently restored, the inn has an inviting screened gazebo with gingerbread trim and posts salvaged from the old Wachapreague Hotel. Baskets of red geraniums, wicker furniture and a gentle breeze off the water entice guests to relax awhile.

Location: Midway between Norfolk, Virginia and Salisbury, Maryland.

Rates: $65-$75. Pat, Tom & Mike Hart.

7 R. 1 PB. 1 FP. Phone available. TV available. Beds: QT. Full breakfast. Bicycling, boating, tennis.

Seen in: *Virginia Pilot, Self Magazine.*

"Staying here is like visiting with a favorite cousin."

WARM SPRINGS K13/E6

The Inn at Gristmill Square

PO Box 359
Warm Springs VA 24484
(703) 839-2231

Circa 1800. The inn consists of five restored buildings. The old blacksmith shop and silo, the hardware store, the Steel House and the Miller House all contain guest rooms. (The old mill is now the Waterwheel Restaurant). A few antiques and old prints appear in some rooms while others are furnished in a contemporary style. There are tennis courts and a swimming pool at the inn. A short walk over Warm Springs Mill Stream and down the road brings travelers to historic Warm Springs Pools.

Rates: $85-$127. The McWilliams family.

14 R. 14 PB. 8 FP. Phone in room. TV in room. Beds: KQDTC. MAP. Restaurant. Sauna. Swimming pool. Conference room. CCs: MC VISA. Tennis, golf, skeet, skiing, ice skating, horseback riding, fishing, hunting, chamber music.

Seen in: *The New York Times, Bon Appetit.*

"You have such a wonderful inn - such attention to detail and such a considerate staff."

Meadow Lane Lodge

Star Rt A Box 110
Warm Springs VA 24484
(703) 839-5959

Circa 1920. This lodge, the family home of the present innkeeper's parents, is situated on 1600 acres. It was part of a land grant made by King George III to Charles Lewis, a pioneer settler. Foundations of an old fort and large brick home are still visible, as is an ancient family cemetery. The lodge is decorated with comfortable furnishings and antiques. Two miles of the Jackson River that meanders through the estate are stocked with brown trout for guests. Walking trails pass hay fields, a swimming hole and a beaver bog against Allegheny ridgelines. A limestone spring provides a million gallons of delicious drinking water each day. Deer, fox, herons and osprey are often seen from a nearby cliffside deck.

Rates: $95-$225. Season: April - Jan. Philip & Catherine Hirsh.

11 R. 11 PB. 3 FP. Phone in room. TV in room. Beds: KQDT. Full breakfast. Spa. Handicap access. Swimming pool. Conference room. CCs: MC VISA AE. Horseback riding, skiing, golf, bowling, natural warm springs pools, canoeing, croquet, tennis, mountain biking, farm animals.

Seen in: *The Washingtonian Magazine.*

"This was the cleanest, neatest and best done room we can remember having enjoyed anywhere."

WASHINGTON I18/D8

Caledonia Farm

See: Flint Hill

The Foster-Harris House

PO Box 333
Washington VA 22747
(703) 675-3757 (800) 666-0153

Circa 1901. This Victorian stands on a lot laid out by George Washington and is situated at the edge of the vil-

lage. The streets of the town are exactly as surveyed 225 years ago, and the town is the first of the 28 Washingtons in the United States. The village has galleries and craft shops as well as the Inn at Little Washington, a five-star restaurant. One of the innkeepers is known in the area for her flower beds and floral arrangements.

Location: Fifty miles north of Charlottesville.

*Rates: $85-$125. Camille Harris & Patrick Foster.

3 R. 3 PB. 1 FP. Phone available. TV available. Beds: QDT. Full breakfast. Conference room. CCs: MC VISA. Tennis, canoeing, fishing, cross-country skiing, horseback riding. Seen in: *Culpeper News, Richmond Times-Dispatch.*

"The View Room is charming, as are the hosts."

Heritage House B&B

Main St, PO Box 427
Washington VA 22747
(703) 675-3207

Circa 1837. This two-story columned house is situated in the heart of the historic district of Washington, a town

surveyed by George Washington in 1749. The inn is furnished with antiques. The innkeepers are of Scandinavian heritage and enjoy preparing Swedish country breakfasts. Guests may easily walk to craft and antique shops, an art gallery and a five-star restaurant.

Rates: $95-$115. Polly & Al Erickson.

4 R. 4 PB. Phone available. Beds: KD. Full breakfast. Handicap access. CCs: MC VISA. Hiking, horseback riding, vineyards.

Seen in: *Country Almanac.*

"Having been to a number of bed & breakfasts, yours is No. 1 in its setting, the wonderful food and your hospitality."

WHITE POST G18/C8

L'Auberge Provencale

PO Box 119
White Post VA 22663
(703) 837-1375

Circa 1753. This farmhouse was built with fieldstones gathered from the area. Hessian soldiers crafted the woodwork of the main house, Mt. Airy. It contains three of the inn's dining rooms. Guest rooms are decorated in Victorian antiques.

Location: One mile south of Route 50 on Route 340.

Rates: $110-$175. Season: Feb. - Dec. Alain & Celeste Borel.

10 R. 10 PB. Phone available. Beds: QD. Conference room. CCs: MC VISA DC. Horseback riding, canoeing, golf, fishing, skiing, Skyline Drive.
Seen in: *Washington Dossier, The Washington Post, Richmond Times.*
"Peaceful view and atmosphere, extraordinary food and wines. Honeymoon and heaven all in one!"

WILLIAMSBURG N22/F10

Applewood Colonial B&B
605 Richmond Rd
Williamsburg VA 23185
(804) 229-0205 (800) 899-APLE
Circa 1921. This Flemish-bond brick home was built during the restoration

of Colonial Williamsburg. The inn's parlor is decorated in a colonial style and features dentil crown molding. A crystal chandelier hangs above the dining table where breakfast is served. The Colonel Vaughn suite boasts a private entrance, a fireplace and queen-size canopy bed.
Rates: $65-$100. Fred Strout.
4 R. 4 PB. 1 FP. Phone available. Beds: Q. Continental-plus breakfast. CCs: MC VISA. Pottery factory, outlet stores, shops. Afternoon tea. Seen in: *The Discerning Traveler.*
"Our accommodations were the best, and you were most kind."

Bensonhouse of Williamsburg
Contact Bensonhouse of Richmond
Williamsburg VA 23185
(804) 353-6900
A copy of the 1760 Sheldon's Tavern in Litchfield, Connecticut, this home is located one mile from Colonial Williamsburg and the College of William and Mary in a quiet, wooded area. A Palladian-style window, antique heart-pine, wide-plank floors from Philadelphia, and oak paneling from an old Indiana church are special features. For reservations, contact Bensonhouse, 2036 Monument Avenue, Richmond, VA 23220.
Rates: $85-$95.
1 R. 1 PB. Phone available. Beds: QC. Full breakfast. Handicap access. CCs: MC VISA. Seen in: *Innsider.*
"You certainly chose wisely when you matched us with our hosts!"

Liberty Rose Colonial B&B
1022 Jamestown Rd
Williamsburg VA 23185
(804) 253-1260
Circa 1929. This slate-roofed, two-story clapboard house is tucked among tall trees a mile from Colonial Williamsburg. The inn was con-

structed by the owner of Jamestown. Much of the brick was brought from the Colony before it became a historic landmark. The entry porch is marked with the millstone from one of Williamsburg's old mills. The inn is lavishly decorated with antiques and collectibles.
❀Rates: $75-$125. Brad & Sandra Hirz.
4 R. 4 PB. Phone available. TV in room. Beds: QD. Full breakfast. CCs: MC VISA.
"More delightful than we could possibly have imagined."

Newport House
710 S Henry St
Williamsburg VA 23185
(804) 229-1775
This neo-Palladian house is a 1756 design by Peter Harrison, architect of rebuilt Williamsburg State House. It features wooden rusticated siding. Colonial country dancing is held in the inn's ballroom on Tuesday evenings. Guests are welcome to participate. There are English and American antiques, and reproductions include canopy beds in all the guest

rooms. The host was a museum director and captain of a historic tall ship.
Location: Five-minute walk from Colonial Williamsburg.
*Rates: $85-$110. John & Cathy Millar.
2 R. 2 PB. 1 FP. Phone available. TV available. Beds: QT. B&B. Conference room. Scottish country dancing. Seen in: *Innsider.*
"Host and hostess were charming and warm."

Piney Grove at Southall's Plantation
See: Charles City, VA

WOODSTOCK H17/C8

The Inn at Narrow Passage
PO Box 608
Woodstock VA 22664
(703) 459-8000
Circa 1740. This log inn has been welcoming travelers since the time settlers took refuge here against the Indians. Later, it served as a

stagecoach inn on the old Valley Turnpike, and in 1862, as Stonewall Jackson's headquarters. Many guest rooms feature fireplaces and views of the lawn as it slopes down to the Shenandoah River.
Location: On Shenandoah River and US 11, 2-1/2 miles south of Woodstock.
*Rates: $55-$85. Ellen & Ed Markel.
12 R. 8 PB. Phone available. TV available. Beds: Q. Full breakfast. Conference room. CCs: MC VISA. Horseback riding, fishing, hiking, skiing, boating. Vineyards and historic sites nearby. Seen in: *Capital Entertainment, The Washington Times.*
"Just the setting I needed to unwind from my hectic civilized world."

WASHINGTON

ANACORTES D10/A3

Albatross Bed & Breakfast

5708 Kingsway
Anacortes WA 98221
(206) 293-0677

Circa 1927. This Cape Cod-style house is located on an acre, a block away from Skyline Marina. Most of the guest rooms and the inn's deck have

views of Burrows Bay, islands or the harbor. Each guest room is individually furnished in a traditional-style decor. The innkeepers will pick up guests from the ferry landing (three minutes away) or from the airport.

*Rates: $60-$75. Cecil & Marilyn Short.
4 R. 4 PB. Phone available. TV available. Beds: KQT. Full breakfast. Handicap access. CCs: MC VISA. Boating, fishing, golf, crabbing.
Seen in: *Apropos Magazine, Business Pulse.*
"Our stay with you was a comfortable, enjoyable experience. Such cordiality!"

Channel House

2902 Oakes Ave
Anacortes WA 98221
(206) 293-9382

Circa 1902. Built by an Italian count, the Channel House is designated the

Krebs House by the Historical Home Tour. Guest rooms view Puget Sound and the San Juan Islands, and the ferry is minutes away. The inn has a Victorian flavor, with a library, three fireplaces, and a dining room with French doors leading out to the garden.

Location: 85 miles north of Seattle.
*❀Rates: $65-$85. Dennis & Patricia McIntyre.
6 R. 4 PB. 2 FP. Phone available. Beds: QD. B&B. Spa. CCs: MC VISA. Boating, biking, swimming. Tulip festival.
Seen in: *Skagit Valley Herald.*
"The house is spectacular and your friendly thoughtfulness is the icing on the cake."

ASHFORD K12/D3

Mountain Meadows Inn

28912 SR 706E
Ashford WA 98304
(206) 569-2788

Circa 1910. Originally built for the superintendent of the Pacific National Lumber Company, the house boasts hanging baskets of fushias which accentuate the veranda. Comfortable guest rooms feature a view of the woodland setting, occasionally visited by deer and elk. An unusual collection of railroad artifacts, including museum-quality model trains, is found throughout the inn. Breakfasts are prepared on an 1889 wood cooking stove. The innkeeper also operates the Hobo Inn, six miles away, which features guest rooms in renovated railroad cabooses, one with its own jacuzzi.

*Rates: $65-$75. Chad Darrah.
5 R. 5 PB. 1 FP. Phone available. TV available. Beds: KQ. Full breakfast. CCs: MC VISA. Skiing, hiking, swimming, boating, horseback riding, fishing. Self-guided tours.
Seen in: *Seattle Times, Pacific Northwest Magazine.*
"Our stay here will be one of the nicest memories of our vacation."

BAINBRIDGE ISLAND G10/C3

Bombay House

8490 Beck Rd NE
Bainbridge Island WA 98110
(206) 842-3926

Circa 1907. This Victorian captain's house is set atop Blakely Hill, amidst colorful, unstructured gardens. It boasts a quaint widow's walk and an old-fashioned gazebo overlooking picturesque sailboats and ferries cruising through Rich Passage. Take the scenic Seattle ferry ride six miles to Bainbridge.

Rates: $55-$93. Bunny Cameron & Roger Kanchuk.
5 R. 3 PB. Phone available. TV available. Beds: KT. Continental-plus breakfast. Conference room.
"Your breakfast was marvelous! No lunch today!"

BELLINGHAM C10/A3

The Castle B&B

1103 15th & Knox Sts
Bellingham WA 98225
(206) 676-0974

Circa 1889. All the guest rooms of this Victorian mansion look out to Bellingham Bay and the San Juan Islands. The gables, steeply pitched turret, and bays are highlighted in mauve. The Cupola Room, with its panoramic water view, is the inn's honeymoon suite. Underneath the suite's castle-type furnishings is a red carpet. The Bayview Room opens to a veranda and has its own fireplace. Your hosts have an extensive lamp and clock collection sprinkled throughout the house's 21 rooms.

Location: Historic Fairhaven.
Rates: $45-$75. Gloria & Larry Harriman.
4 R. 1 PB. 1 FP. Phone in room. TV available. Beds: QT. B&B. CCs: MC VISA. Skiing, boating, hiking, golf.
Seen in: *Sunset Magazine, Daughters of the Painted Ladies, West Coast Victorians.*
"Never have I seen a B&B with so many museum-quality pieces of furniture."

North Garden Inn

1014 N Garden

Bellingham WA 98225

(206) 671-7828 (800)922-6414

Circa 1897. Listed in the National Register, this Queen Anne Victorian originally had bars on the basement windows to keep out the bears. Guest rooms feature views of Bellingham Bay and the surrounding islands. A mahogany Steinway piano is often played for guests. The inn is within walking distance to Western Washington University.

*Rates: $44-$54. Frank & Barbara DeFreytas.

10 R. 2 PB. Phone available. Beds: KQD. Full breakfast. Conference room. CCs: MC VISA. Skiing, sailing, golfing.

Seen in: *La Bonne Cuisine, Chocolatier, Victorian Homes.*

"Excellent everything! Room, view, hospitality, breakfast, who could ask for anything more?"

Schnauzer Crossing

4421 Lakeway Dr

Bellingham WA 98226

(206) 733-0055 (206)734-2808

Circa 1938. This contemporary Northwest house, nestled among tall evergreens and overlooking Lake Whatcom, is an outdoor lover's delight, with fishing, boating and swimming a few steps away. Maple, dogwood and birch trees abound, and fresh raspberries and blueberries can be picked from the garden. Guests enjoy lake or garden views from their comfortable rooms, which feature fresh flowers. The family dog is welcome also, as an enclosed outdoor kennel is available.

Location: On Lake Whatcom.

Rates: $75 & up. Vermont & Donna McAllister.

2 R. 2 PB. Phone in room. Beds: KQC. Full breakfast. Spa. CCs: MC VISA. Lake swimming, fishing, canoeing, sailing and tennis. Nearby skiing, hiking, bicycle riding.

Seen in: *Seattle Post-Intelligencer, Oregonian.*

"A lovely retreat. We'll be sure to return."

BREMERTON G10/C3

Willcox House

2390 Tekiu Rd

Bremerton WA 98312

(206) 830-4492

Circa 1936. Colonel Julian Willcox and his family, once members of San Francisco high society, selected Lionel Pries to build this home on a wooded bluff overlooking Hood Canal. Holding court thereafter, the family entertained fashionable Northwest personalities, including Clark Gable. The 7,800 square-foot manse was constructed with a slate tile exterior, copper roofing and vast expanses of

small-paned windows, affording views of the shimmering waters, the Olympic mountains and forested hillsides. There are five marble and copper fireplaces, silk wallpaper, oak floors, fine antiques and period pieces throughout. The Julian Room sports a double whirlpool tub.

*Rates: $90-$150. Cecilia & Phillip Hughes.

5 R. 5 PB. 1 FP. Phone available. Beds: K. Full breakfast. Gourmet meals. Spa. Swimming pool. Game room. CCs: MC VISA. Water sports, hiking, fishing, antiquing, relaxing.

Seen in: *The Olympian, Journal American.*

"Diane & I and Clark love the place and delight in the knowledge that all Californians aren't bad - in fact some are downright wonderful."

CATHLAMET M8/D2

Country Keeper B&B Inn

61 Main St, PO Box 35

Cathlamet WA 98612

(206) 795-3030

Circa 1907. This four-story Eastlake-style house, tucked into a wooded hillside, overlooks the Columbia River and Puget Island. Each guest room is decorated in the theme of an Impressionist painter and filled with period furnishings. Art instructors Terry and Meridith will lend bikes if you'd like to cycle through the national game refuge to look for Canadian geese, bald eagles and deer. Be sure to return in time for the sunsets over the river.

Location: On the Columbia River.

❀Rates: $40-$65. Terry & Meridith Beaston.

5 R. 2 PB. Phone available. TV available. Beds: KDTW. Full breakfast. Conference room. CCs: MC VISA. Golf, tennis, fishing, sailing, canoeing. Mt. St. Helen's visitor's center is a 45-minute drive.

Seen in: *Sunset, Lifestyles.*

"Our vacation was great, but your B&B and more specifically, the evenings spent talking with you, were the best!"

COUPEVILLE E10/B3

The Inn at Penn Cove

702 N Main, PO Box 85

Coupeville WA 98239

(206) 678-8000 (800) 688-COVE

Circa 1887. Two restored historic houses, one a fanciful peach and white Italianate confection in the National Register, comprise the inn. Each

house contains only three guest rooms affording a multitude of small parlors for guests to enjoy. The most romantic accommodation is Desiree's Room with a fireplace, a whirlpool tub for two and mesmerizing views of Puget Sound and Mt. Baker.

*Rates: $75-$125. Jim & Barbara Cinney.

6 R. 6 PB. 3 FP. Phone available. TV available. Beds: KQC. Full breakfast. Spa. Handicap access. Exercise room. Conference room. FAX. CCs: MC VISA DS. Water sports, hiking, day sail.

Seen in: *Whidbey News-Times, Country Inns, Glamour.*

"Our hosts were warm and friendly, but also gave us plenty of space and privacy - a good combination."

The Victorian B&B

PO Box 761, 602 N Main

Coupeville WA 98239

(206) 678-5305

Circa 1889. This graceful Italianate Victorian sits in the heart of one of the nation's few historic reserves. It was built for German immigrant Jacob Jenne, who became the proprietor of the Central Hotel on Front Street. Noted for having the first running water on the island, the house's old wooden water tower stands in the back garden. An old-fashioned storefront, once the local dentist's office, sits demurely behind a picket fence, now a private hideaway for guests.

*❀Rates: $75-$95. Dolores Colton Fresh.

3 R. 3 PB. Phone available. TV available. Beds: Q. Full breakfast. CCs: MC VISA. Hiking, bicycling, sailing, fishing.

Seen in: *The Seattle Times, Country Inns.*

"If kindness and generosity are the precursors to success (and I certainly hope they are!), your success is assured."

DEER PARK F24/B8

B&B With Love's

N 31317 Cedar Rd

Deer Park WA 99006

(509) 276-6939

Set on five acres, this reproduction of a turn-of-the-century home is surrounded by stately pine trees. The inn

features a library with fireplace adjacent to guest rooms, a wrap-around porch with swing and a private hot tub room. In the country kitchen, guests may find a friendly cat curled up by the old cook stove. Guest rooms have country antiques, homemade quilts, old-fashioned beds, lace curtains and plush carpets. Each room opens onto a quiet patio near the garden.
Rates: $53. Bill & Leslie.
2 R. TV available. Bicycles, cross-country skiing, museums, lakes.

EATONVILLE J11/D3

Old Mill House B&B
PO Box 543
Eatonville WA 98328
(206) 832-6506

Circa 1925. Tucked behind huge elm trees, this is a 6,000 square-foot, three-story colonial-style estate. It still

retains its basement speakeasy, with both a bar and a dance floor. Old Mill House was the home of John Galbraith, mill owner and early Eatonville mayor. A Twenties decor prevails, and each room is named for a personality of that era. In the F. Scott Fitzgerald Room, an ongoing novel is being written by a steady stream of guests. Some return just to add to the story.
*Rates: $55-$70. Catharine & Michael Gallagher.
4 R. 1 PB. Phone available. Beds: KQDT. B&B. CCs: MC VISA. Cross-country skiing, water skiing, wildlife reserve.
Seen in: *Seattle Times, Tacoma News Tribune, Dispatch.*

FORKS F5/B1

Miller Tree Inn
PO Box 953
Forks WA 98331
(206) 374-6806 (206) 374-6807

Circa 1917. The Miller Tree Inn is a modernized farmhouse set on three acres adjacent to a favorite grazing spot for local elk. The inn caters to steelhead, salmon and trout fishermen, and will serve breakfast at 4:30 a.m. with advance notice. Comfortable rooms and economical rates make it a popular stopover in this logging town.
Rates: $50. Ted & Prue Miller.
6 R. 2 PB. Phone available. TV in room. Beds: QDT. Full breakfast. Spa. CCs: MC VISA. Hiking, fishing, camping, kayaking.
Seen in: *Peninsula Business Journal, The Walking Magazine.*
"The homey and warm atmosphere was wonderful. You've spoiled us."

FRIDAY HARBOR C9/A2

Tucker House B&B
260 B St
Friday Harbor WA 98250
(206) 378-2783

Circa 1898. Only two blocks from the ferry landing, the white picket fence bordering Tucker House is a welcome sight for guests. The spindled entrance leads to the parlor and the simply furnished five guest rooms in the house. A separate cottage next to the hot tub is popular with honeymooners.
Location: San Juan Island.
Rates: $65-$90. Evelyn & John Lackey & Mitzi Stack.
6 R. 3 PB. 1 FP. Phone available. TV in room. Beds: Q. Full breakfast. Spa. CCs: MC VISA AE. Fishing, whale watching, golf, tennis, bicycling, boating.
Seen in: *Sunset Magazine, Pacific Northwest Magazine, The Western Boatman.*
"A lovely place, the perfect getaway. We'll be back."

GREENBANK E10/B3

Guest House B&B & Cottages
835 E Christenson Rd
Greenbank WA 98253
(206) 678-3115

Circa 1920. This cozy Whidbey Island home is located on 25 acres of forest and meadows, where deer wander by the wildlife pond and storybook cottages. Guest rooms have art deco touches. There is a log house with a free-form spa and a view over the pond to the sound. The Wildflower Suite and the Farm Guest Cottage are the most historic accommodations.
Location: On Whidbey Island.
*❀Rates: $85-$225. Don & Mary Jane Creger.
6 R. 6 PB. 5 FP. Phone available. TV in room. Beds: KQDT. B&B. Spa. Exercise room. Swimming pool. CCs: MC VISA AE DS. Horseback riding, golf, fishing, hiking, clamming, boating. In-room spas, exercise room, bathrobes, complimentary movies.
Seen in: *Los Angeles Times, Woman's Day, Sunset Magazine.*
"Best B&B experience on the West Coast," Lewis Green, *Los Angeles Times.*

KIRKLAND G11/B3

Shumway Mansion
11410 99th Place NE
Kirkland WA 98033
(206) 823-2303

Circa 1909. This resplendent 22-room, 10,000 square-foot mansion is situated on more than two acres overlooking

Juanita Bay. With a large ballroom and veranda with water views, few could guess that a short time ago, the building was hoisted on hydraulic lifts. It was then pulled three miles across town to its present site, near the beach.
Location: West of I-405 at Juanita Bay.
*Rates: $65-$95. Richard & Salli Harris, & daughter Julie.
7 R. 7 PB. Phone available. TV available. Beds: Q. Full breakfast. Spa. Sauna. Exercise room. Swimming pool. Conference room. CCs: MC VISA AE. Skiing, tennis. Athletic club.
Seen in: *Northgate Journal, Journal American, Northwest Living.*
"Guests enjoy the mansion so much they don't want to leave," Northwest Living.

LA CONNER D10/B3

Katy's Inn
PO Box 231, 503 S 3rd
La Conner WA 98257
(206) 466-3366

Circa 1876. This pristinely renovated farmhouse is framed by flower gardens and graceful oak trees. Victorian wallpapers enhance a collection of an-

tique furnishings. Each guest room opens to the veranda or balcony,

providing a view of the countryside. Bicycles and boats can be rented from the village three blocks away.
Rates: $55. Mike Beck, Jeff Nelson.
4 R. Phone available. Beds: DC. B&B. CCs: MC VISA. Boat rentals, bicycles. Victorian playhouse for children.
"The most charming and warmest of the B&Bs in which we stayed."

Rainbow Inn
1075 Chilberg Rd, PO Box 1600
La Conner WA 98257
(206) 466-4578
Circa 1900. This Victorian farmhouse is situated peacefully among fields planted in tulips, daffodils, iris or sweet peas. An enclosed wraparound porch is the site for breakfast. Antiques and artistically arranged country collectibles gathered for several years decorate the inn. Old-fashioned wallpapers, period furnishings and claw-footed tubs add to the atmosphere. The village of La Conner is a half-mile away.
Rates: $70-$90. Marianne & Herb Horen.
8 R. 5 PB. Phone available. Beds: Q. Full breakfast. Spa. CCs: MC VISA.
Seen in: *Sunset, Eddie Bauer Catalog.*
"Lovely and generous service in a gracious country atmosphere. Super hideaway spa."

White Swan Guest House
1388 Moore Rd
La Conner WA 98273
(206) 445-6805
Circa 1898. The turret of this Victorian farmhouse was once used as a lookout for the small ferry that crossed the Skagit River before the

bridge was built. Refurbished by transplanted New York designer Peter Goldfarb, the inn was named after the white swans that flock to the corn fields behind the house. A favorite choice is the Turret Room with its own window seat. There are three sunny rooms in the main house and a private garden cottage in the back meadow. The village of LaConner is six miles away.
Rates: $60-$110. Peter Goldfarb.
3 R. 2 PB. Phone available. Beds: KQ. Continental-plus breakfast. CCs: MC VISA. Tulip field tours, museums. Private, romantic garden cottage. Seen in: *The Spokesman-Review Spokane Chronicle.*
"Guests are encouraged to come in through the back porch, where undoubtedly they'll find fresh-baked cookies and lively conversation." Beverly Hawkins, *Country Home.*

LANGLEY E11/B3

Country Cottage of Langley
215 6th St
Langley WA 98260
(206) 221-8709
Circa 1926. Outstanding views of the Cascades, Saratoga Passage and the village can be seen from the three acres surrounding Country Cottage. Rooms are decorated with Laura Ashley prints and antiques for an elegant country style, and the guest sitting area has a fireplace. A newly-built miniature farmhouse situated for extensive views of the Sound, contains two suites. An old creamery has been converted to another cottage. The garden has decking and a gazebo.
Rates: $75-$85. Trudy & Whitney Martin.
5 R. 5 PB. Phone available. TV available. Beds: Q. Full breakfast. Handicap access. CCs: MC VISA. Sailing, boating, bicycling, hiking, fishing, horseback riding.
"Hospitality plus! Nicely decorated rooms. Beautiful breakfasts."

LEAVENWORTH G15/C5

Haus Lorelei Inn
347 Division St
Leavenworth WA 98826
(509) 548-5726
Circa 1903. This historic Bavarian home is situated on an unparalleled two-acre site overlooking the Wenatchee River and the Cascades. The innkeeper's four children are actively involved in helping out. To make things easy for everyone, all rooms have the same rate. Call early and you may fetch the largest suite! This is a busy family, yet the atmosphere is easy going. If you come a second time, you may feel so much at home that you'll find yourself showing new guests around, answering the phone or organizing a game of tennis. The views are exquisite and the rushing waters of the river soothing.
Rates: $70. Elisabeth Saunders & Bettina, Billy, Kelly, Mike.
6 R. 4 PB. Phone available. Beds: QDT. Full breakfast. Spa.

ORCAS C9/A2

Orcas Hotel
PO Box 155
Orcas WA 98280
(206) 376-4300
Circa 1900. Listed in the National Register, this three-story Victorian inn across from the ferry landing has been a landmark to travelers and boaters

since the early 1900s. An open porch stretches around three sides and is filled with white wicker furniture. From this vantage point, guests enjoy views of terraced lawns and flower beds of peonies, daffodils, iris and roses. A white picket fence and a vista of sea and islands complete the picture.
Location: Overlooking the ferry landing on Orcas Island.
*Rates: $55-$150. Craig Sanders.
12 R. 5 PB. Phone available. TV available. Beds: QTC. Continental breakfast. Restaurant. Gourmet meals. Spa. Handicap access. Conference room. CCs: MC VISA AE. Bicycling, sailing, golfing, horseback riding, fishing, hiking.
Seen in: *Los Angeles Times, Seattle Times, The New York Times.*
"Wonderful hospitality, super-good food, pleasant surroundings, all provided a delightful experience."

ORCAS ISLAND C9/A2

Turtleback Farm Inn
Rt 1 Box 650, Eastsound
Orcas Island WA 98245
(206) 376-4914
Circa 1890. This handsome farmhouse was considered one of the finest homes on Orcas Island in the early 1900s. The inn was restored and expanded from the ground up in 1985,

with particular attention to authenticity and detail, including bathroom fixtures purchased from the old Empress Hotel in Victoria. Cattle graze on the inn's 80 idyllic acres of meadows, pastures and woodlands.
Location: Six miles from ferry landing, 2 miles from Westsound.
*Rates: $65-$135. William & Susan Fletcher.
7 R. 7 PB. Phone available. Beds: KQDT.

B&B. CCs: MC VISA. Golf, kayaking, fishing, sailing, swimming.
Seen in: *Los Angeles Times, USA Today, Travel & Leisure, Contra Costa Sun, The Seattle Times, Northwest Living, Sunset.*
"A peaceful haven for soothing the soul."

PORT ANGELES E8/B2

Tudor Inn
1108 S Oak
Port Angeles WA 98362
(206) 452-3138

Circa 1910. This English Tudor inn has been tastefully restored to display its original woodwork and fir stairway.

Guests enjoy stone fireplaces in the living room and study. A terraced garden with 100-foot oak trees graces the property.
Location: Eleven blocks south of the harbor with water & mountain views.
*Rates: $55-$85. Jane & Jerry Glass.
5 R. 1 PB. Phone available. TV available. Beds: KQTD. Full breakfast. CCs: MC VISA.
Seen in: *Seattle Times, Oregonian, Los Angeles Times, Olympic Magazine.*
"Delicious company and delicious food. Best in hospitality and warmth. Beautiful gardens!"

PORT TOWNSEND E10/B3

Heritage House Inn
305 Pierce St
Port Townsend WA 98368
(206) 385-6800

Circa 1880. This stately Italianate, listed in the National Register, was the home of Francis Pettygrove, a founder of Port Townsend and Portland, Ore. (He flipped a coin to name it Portland or Boston. Portland won.) The innkeepers have collected an array of unusual antiques, including a fold-down bathtub on wheels. Because of the mild climate and low rainfall, half that of Seattle, the town's elegant houses have withstood the ravages of time, and contain the best examples of Victorian architecture north of San Francisco.
Location: Across the street from the water.
*Rates: $55-$89. Pat & Jim Broughton, Bob & Carolyn Ellis.
6 R. 4 PB. Phone available. Beds: QD. B&B. Handicap access. CCs: MC VISA AE. Skiing, fishing, boating.
Seen in: *Country Inns, Japan Airlines Magazine, Oregonian.*
"You two provide the perfect balance between nurturing and unobtrusiveness. Difficult to do!"

James House
1238 Washington
Port Townsend WA 98368
(206) 385-1238

Circa 1889. This Queen Anne mansion built by Francis James overlooks Puget Sound with views of the Cascades and Olympic mountain ranges.

The three-story staircase was constructed of solid wild cherry brought around Cape Horn from Virginia. Parquet floors are composed of oak, cherry, walnut and maple providing a suitable setting for the inn's collection of antiques.
Location: On the bluff overlooking Port Townsend Bay.
Rates: $60-$125. Carol McGough & Anne Tiernan.
12 R. 4 PB. 3 FP. Phone available. TV available. Beds: QD. Continental-plus breakfast. Handicap access. Conference room. CCs: MC VISA. Fishing, tennis, golf, horseback riding, hiking, bicycling, swimming, boat charters.
Seen in: *Washington Magazine, The Seattle Weekly.*
"We were enchanted by Victorian splendor and delicious breakfasts."

Lizzie's
731 Pierce St
Port Townsend WA 98368
(206) 385-4168

Circa 1887. Named for Lizzie Grant, a sea captain's wife, this Italianate Victorian is elegant and airy.

In addition to the gracious interiors, some rooms command an outstanding view of Port Townsend Bay, Puget Sound, and the Olympic and Cascade mountain ranges. Each room is filled with antiques dating from 1840 to the turn-of-the-century. The dog's house in the garden is a one-quarter scale replica of the original house. Lizzie's is known for its elaborate breakfasts, where guests are encouraged to help themselves to seconds.
Location: In uptown Historic District.
Rates: $49-$89. Bill & Patti Wickline.
8 R. 5 PB. Phone available. Beds: KQ. Full breakfast. CCs: MC VISA. Hiking, boating, wind surfing, fishing, golf.
Seen in: *Travel & Leisure.*
"As they say in show biz, you're a hard act to follow."

Old Consulate Inn (F.W. Hastings House)
313 Walker at Washington
Port Townsend WA 98368
(206) 385-6753

Circa 1889. This handsome red Victorian, once the residence of the German consul, commands expansive views of Port Townsend Bay from its

blufftop setting. Fine antiques, a grand piano, elegant stairway and Victorian wallcoverings create a romantic fantasy that is continued in the Tower Suite where five curved turret windows afford majestic water and mountain views.
*Rates: $59-$140. Rob & Joanna Jackson.
8 R. 8 PB. 1 FP. Phone available. TV available. Beds: K. Full breakfast. Gourmet meals. Game room. CCs: MC VISA. Hiking, sport fishing, clamming, tennis, bicycling. Weddings, business retreats, mystery weekends. Afternoon tea & refreshments, evening tea & cocoa.
Seen in: *Pacific Northwest, Best Places to Kiss, Seattle Weekly.*
"Beautiful in every way."

Starrett House Inn
744 Clay St
Port Townsend WA 98368
(206) 385-3205

Circa 1889. George Starrett came from Maine to Port Townsend and became the major residential builder. By 1889, he had constructed one house a week, totaling more than 350 houses. The Smithsonian believes the elaborate free-hung spiral staircase is the only one of its type in the United States. A

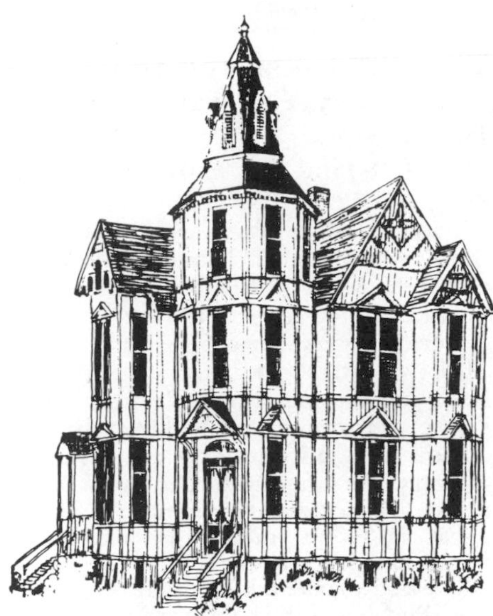

frescoed dome atop the octagonal tower depicts four seasons and four virtues. On the first day of each season, the sun causes a ruby light to point toward the appropriate painting.
Location: Three blocks from the business district.
Rates: $75-$125. Bob & Edel Sokol.
10 R. 8 PB. Phone available. Beds: Q. Full breakfast. CCs: MC VISA. Fishing, wind surfing, golf, cross-country skiing, tennis. Cruises, historic walking tour.
Seen in: *Peninsula Magazine, New York Times, Vancouver Sun, San Francisco Examiner.*
"The Grande Bonbon of them all," Jan Halliday, *Pacific Northwest.*

QUINAULT H7/C1

Lake Quinault Lodge
PO Box 7, S Shore Rd
Quinault WA 98575
(206) 288-2571 (800) 562-6672 (WA only)
Circa 1926. President Franklin Roosevelt stayed here in 1938, and signed the Olympic National Park into law. The lawn of the old lodge slopes to the water's edge. A quaint

gazebo provides views of the wooded slopes beyond. Dominating the lobby, a huge brick fireplace attracts guests who often gather to plan an excursion out to the inn's 20 miles of trails through the rain forest. Under new management, the lodge was refurbished and enlarged in 1989.
Location: Two miles East of US 101, on south shore of Lake Quinault.
*Rates: $34-$95. Tom McFadden.
92 R. 92 PB. 16 FP. Phone available. TV available. Beds: QDTC. EP. Restaurant. Spa. Sauna. Swimming pool. Game room. Conference room. FAX. CCs: MC VISA AE. Hiking, canoeing, paddle boats, fishing.
Seen in: *Seattle Post-Intelligencer.*

SEATTLE G11/C3

Capitol Hill Inn
1713 Belmont Ave
Seattle WA 98122
(206) 323-1955 (206) 726-1984
Circa 1903. This elegant Queen Anne-style home may once have served as a brothel. Recently renovated, the inn features Victorian-era antiques, chandeliers and custom-designed wall coverings. Bedrooms are decorated in the themes of different nations and boast brass beds topped with down comforters. A full breakfast is complemented with an espresso bar. Guests enjoy proximity to popular shops and restaurants.
*Rates: $59-$92. Katherine & Joanne Godmintz.
5 R. 3 PB. 1 FP. Phone available. Beds: QDT. Full breakfast. Conference room. CCs: AE. Bicycle tours.
Seen in: *Capitol Hill Times.*
"Elegant, original, comfortable & memorable. Cooking is fabulous."

Challenger
809 Fairview Place N
Seattle WA 98109
(206) 340-1201 (206) 621-9208
Located at the waterfront on Lake Union and within walking distance of the Seattle Center is this restored army tugboat. It features tongue and groove pine, polished brass fittings and a large salon with a granite fireplace. Rooms are small but the Captain's Cabin has a queen-size bed and view of the Seattle skyline. Seafood omelettes are served in the oak-walled galley and a dinghy is available.
Rates: $65-$110. Jerry Brown.
7 R. 4 PB. Phone in room. TV in room. Beds: QDT. Full breakfast. Conference room. CCs: MC VISA AE. Swimming.
Seen in: *Telegraph-Journal, Sea, Las Vegas Review-Journal, Cosmopolitan.*
"I had a delightful stay on board the Challenger and have been singing your praises since I got home!"

Chambered Nautilus B&B Inn
5005 22nd NE
Seattle WA 98105
(206) 522-2536
Circa 1915. This blue, Georgian Colonial was built by a British missionary, Dr. Herbert Gowen, who founded the Department of Oriental Studies at the University of Washington. Three dormers and Pal-

ladian doors grace the front of the house. Coved ceilings, fireplaces, fully stocked bookcases, Persian rugs, and English and American antiques complement its gracious decor. Many of the guest rooms have French doors and balconies overlooking the gardens.
Location: In the University District.
*Rates: $65-$95. Bunny & Bill Hagemeyer.
6 R. 6 PB. Phone available. Beds: QD. Full breakfast. Conference room. CCs: MC VISA AE DC CB. Boating, skiing, bicycling and jogging trails, tennis, golf.
Seen in: *Innsider Magazine.*
"I think you've spoiled us for any other inn, anyplace. We felt like royalty and family members all at the same time."

Chelsea Station B&B Inn
4915 Linden Ave N
Seattle WA 98103
(206) 547-6077
Circa 1920. This Federal Colonial home is one of Seattle's finest examples of the bricklayer's art. It is located in a tranquil wooded setting in the midst of the city. A secluded hot tub is tucked away in one of the carriage houses. The inn has 29 varieties of its own special roses, including a Mint Julep. The Woodland Park Zoo and Rose Gardens are only a few steps away.
Location: Just north from downtown. Near Greenlake & Seattle's Rose Gardens.
*Rates: $69-$89. Dick & Marylou Jones.
5 R. 5 PB. 2 FP. Phone available. TV available. Beds: K. Full breakfast. Spa. FAX. CCs: MC VISA AE DC CB. Swimming, boating, tennis, biking, golf.
Seen in: *Seattle Post-Intelligencer.*
"What a wonderful fairyland room and hospitable hosts."

The Victorian B&B
See: Coupeville, WA

The Williams House

1505 Fourth Ave N
Seattle WA 98109
(206) 285-0810

Circa 1905. Built by a Midwestern cart builder, the inn features much original woodwork and gaslight fixtures, as well as an ornate gas fireplace. A formal parlor is accentuated with Victorian furnishings. Many of the rooms have commanding views of mountains, lakes, Puget Sound and the downtown Seattle skyline.

Location: Queen Anne Hill.
*❀Rates: $70-$90. Susan & Doug Williams & daughters.
5 R. 3 PB. Phone available. TV available. Beds: KQC. Full breakfast. Swimming pool. Conference room. CCs: MC VISA AE DC CB. Exercise facilities.
"Very comfortable. Excellent food and wonderful people."

SEAVIEW L6/D1

Shelburne Inn

PO Box 250, Pacific Hwy 103 & 45th
Seaview WA 98644
(206) 642-2442

Circa 1896. The Shelburne is known as the oldest continuously operating hotel in the state of Washington. The front desk at the hotel is a former

church altar. Art nouveau stained-glass windows rescued from a church torn down in Morcambe, England now shed light and color on the dining room. The guest rooms are appointed in antiques. In between the Columbia River and the Pacific Ocean, the inn is situated on Long Beach Peninsula, a 28-mile stretch of seacoast that includes bird sanctuaries and lighthouses.

Location: Southwest Washington state.
*Rates: $69-$140. David Campiche & Laurie Anderson.
16 R. 13 PB. Phone available. Beds: QDTC. Full breakfast. Restaurant. Gourmet meals. Handicap access. Conference room. FAX. CCs: MC VISA AE. Horseback riding, fishing, hiking, tennis, bicycling, beach walking, clamming. English-style pub.
Seen in: *Better Homes & Gardens, Bon Appetit, Washington Magazine, Esquire.*
"Homey but elegant atmosphere. Hospitable service, like being a guest in an elegant home."

SOUTH CLE ELUM I14/C4

Moore House B&B Country Inn

PO Box 2861
South Cle Elum WA 98943
(509) 674-5939

Circa 1909. Built by the Chicago, Milwaukee and Pacific railroads, this building was designed to house crew-

men on layover. At the 2,000-foot level of the Cascade Mountains, it is adjacent to Iron Horse State Park, where guests may cross-country ski, take a sleigh ride or ride mountain bikes. In the National Register, the inn has been renovated and guest rooms are decorated with railroad memorabilia. An authentic caboose is available for families. The town of Cle Elum is noted for its old bakery, whose brick oven is said to have been continuously heated since 1906.

*Rates: $41-$95. Monty & Connie Moore.
11 R. 5 PB. Phone available. TV in room. Beds: QDT. B&B. Spa. Conference room. CCs: MC VISA AE. Horse trails, hiking, fishing, boating, mountain bike rentals.
Seen in: *Washington Magazine, Sunset Magazine.*
"Great accommodations and host and hostess who are just plain fun to be with. I am looking forward to my second visit."

TROUT LAKE N13/E4

Mio Amore Pensione

PO Box 208
Trout Lake WA 98650
(509) 395-2264

Circa 1904. This renovated yellow farmhouse is situated on six acres of creek-laced woodland. The inn's eclectic decor includes memorabilia gathered by Tom during the five years he worked in Italy and learned Tuscan cookery. Northern Italian gourmet dinners are served. A deck overlooks the rippling creek, where guests can pause to watch beaver, otter and mink.

Rates: $50-$135. Tom & Jill Westbrook.
4 R. 1 PB. TV available. Beds: QDT. Full breakfast. Restaurant. Gourmet meals. Handicap access. CCs: MC VISA. Cross-country skiing, horseback riding, dog sledding, white water rafting, biking. Mountain climbing, fishing on trout creek, hayrides, German night.
Seen in: *Travel.*
"Couldn't ask for it any better than this."

VASHON ISLAND G10/C3

The Old Tjomsland House

Vashon Hwy & 171st St
PO Box 913
Vashon Island WA 98070
(206) 463-5275

Circa 1890. A.T. Tjomsland, builder of the Methodist church and parsonage, constructed this traditional farmhouse. It reflects the small-town America atmosphere of Vashon Island. The two guest rooms on the upper floor have a separate entrance. They share a common bath, large living room and kitchenette. A hearty country breakfast is served. Your host speaks French and German.

Location: Twenty minutes by ferry from Seattle and Tacoma.
*Rates: $55. Jan & Bill Morosoff.
2 R. Phone available. TV available. Beds: QTC. B&B. CCs: MC VISA. Bicycling, golf, boating, fishing, beach walking. Alcohol-free and smoke-free.
Seen in: *Vashon-Maury Island Beachcomber.*
"Your house is neat as a pin, spotless. We have been at B&Bs all over the world and yours is outstanding."

WASHINGTON DC

WASHINGTON H15/C5

Adams Inn
1744 Lanier Pl NW
Washington DC 20009
(202) 745-3600

Circa 1908. This restored town house has fireplaces, a library and parlor, all furnished home-style, as are the guest rooms. Former residents of this neighborhood include Tallulah Bankhead, Woodrow Wilson and Al Jolson. The Adams-Morgan area is home to diplomats, radio and television personalities and government workers. A notable firehouse across the street holds the record for the fastest response of a horse-drawn fire apparatus.

Location: Two miles from the White House, walking distance to major hotels.
*Rates: $60-$95. Gene & Nancy Thompson.
25 R. 12 PB. Phone available. TV available. Beds: DT. Continental-plus breakfast. CCs: MC VISA AE DC. Sightseeing, antiquing, shops. Seen in: *Travel Host Magazine.*
"We enjoyed your friendly hospitality and the home-like atmosphere. Your suggestions on restaurants and helping plan our visit were appreciated."

The Inn at Buckeystown
See: Buckeystown, MD

Embassy Inn
1627 16 St NW
Washington DC 20009
(202) 234-7800 (800) 423-9111

Circa 1920. A sister inn to Windsor Inn, the Embassy is furnished in a Federalist-style reminiscent of the days of Thomas Jefferson, designer of several of the town houses on 16th Street. The Embassy's philosophy of innkeeping was inspired by the small family hotels of Europe, noted for providing personal attention and cheerful hospitality.
**Rates: $89. Susan Araujo.
39 R. 39 PB. Phone in room. TV in room. Beds: DT. Continental breakfast. CCs: MC VISA AE. Carriage rides, theater, National Zoo, museums. Seen in: *The Business Review.*
"When I return to D.C., I'll be back at the Embassy."

Kalorama Guest House
1854 Mintwood Place NW
Washington DC 20009
(202) 667-6369

Circa 1900. This is a group of six Victorian town houses decorated with period antiques and artwork. The inn features original wainscoting, fireplace mantels and claw-foot tubs. Brass beds, plush comforters, Oriental rugs and sunny bay windows add to the charm. Each house is hosted year-round, and sherry is served by the fireplace each afternoon. The subway is a short walk away, as are the Chinese Embassy, the French Embassy, major hotels and stately Massachusetts Avenue diplomatic residences.
Location: Downtown residential area 10 minutes to the Mall and White House.
*Rates: $45-$95. Tami Wood.
31 R. 12 PB. Phone available. TV available. Beds: QDT. Continental breakfast. Conference room. CCs: MC VISA AE. Horseback riding, hiking, boating.
Seen in: *The Philadelphia Inquirer, The Washington Post.*
"The Kalorama is one of the friendliest and comfortable places that I have stayed in anywhere in the world."

Memory House
See: Arlington, VA

Mount Pleasant House
1760 Park Rd NW
Washington DC 20010
(202) 265-2604

Circa 1908. This urban town house is in the Mount Pleasant National Historic District. The innkeeper, an interior designer, has decorated the inn lavishly. Furnishings of the past mingle with those of the present. The inn features inlaid mahogany floors, beamed ceilings, exposed brick, solid-brass doorknobs, an open stairway with wood panels, fluted columns and ornately turned balusters.

*Rates: $70-$85. Ed Perlman.
5 R. 2 PB. Phone available. TV available. Beds: KQT. Continental-plus breakfast. CCs: MC VISA AE DC DS. Horseback riding, hiking, golfing, biking. Specialty tours. Seen in: *Architectural Digest, The Washington Post.*
"We loved the understated elegance and simplicity of your small inn."

Reeds B&B
PO Box 12011
Washington DC 20005
(202) 328-3510

Circa 1887. This three-story Victorian town house was built by John Shipman, who owned one of the first construction companies in the city. The turn-of-the-century revitalization of Washington began in Logan Circle, considered to be the city's first truly residential area. During the house's restoration, flower gardens, terraces and fountains were

added. Victorian antiques, original wood paneling, stained glass and chandeliers, as well as practical amenities such as air conditioning and laundry facilities make this a comfortable bed-and-breakfast experience.
*Rates: $55-$85. Charles & Jackie Reed.
6 R. 1 PB. Phone in room. TV in room. Beds: QDTC. Continental breakfast. CCs: MC VISA AE DC. Seen in: *Philadelphia Inquirer, Washington Gardner Magazine.*
"This home was the highlight of our stay in Washington!"

Windsor Inn

1842 16th St NW
Washington DC 20009
(202) 667-0300 (800) 423-9111

Circa 1920. Originally operated from 1940 to 1963 by the Dadian family, this large town-house-style inn was closed for over two decades. When the new owners entered, they found everything exactly as it had been 22 years before - including the soap in the bathrooms. Recently renovated, it has been reopened as a bed and breakfast inn. Carved, marble-top antiques are in abundance, and a private club atmosphere prevails. Complimentary cocktails are served each evening.
*❀Rates: $89. Susan Araujo.
49 R. 49 PB. Phone in room. TV in room. Beds: QDT. Continental breakfast. CCs: MC VISA AE. Historical Washington sites and museums.
Seen in: *The InTowner.*
"Being here was like being home."

WEST VIRGINIA

CHARLES TOWN F19/C8

The Cottonwood Inn

Rt 2 Box 61 S
Charles Town WV 25414
(304) 725-3371

Circa 1800. The bucolic six acres of the Cottonwood Inn once belonged to George Washington's 4,000-acre tract, and the land is studded with cotton-

wood and maple trees. Trout are often fished out of Bull Skin Run, a creek that flows across the inn's front lawn. Four-poster beds, porch rockers and pecan griddle cakes are specialties. Children welcome.

Location: Near Harper's Ferry.
Rates: $75-$85. Eleanor & Colin Simpson.
7 R. 7 PB. 1 FP. Phone available. TV in room. Beds: Q. Full breakfast. Gourmet meals. Conference room. CCs: MC VISA. Horse racing, rafting, boating, fishing, auto racing. Seen in: *The Washington Post, Country Inns, Mid-Atlantic Country.*

"The warmth of your home was only a reflection of the personalities you possess."

Gilbert House B&B

PO Box 1104
Charles Town WV 25414
(304) 725-0637

Circa 1760. A magnificent graystone of early Georgian design, the Gilbert House boasts the state's oldest flagstone sidewalk. During restoration, graffiti found on the upstairs bedroom walls included a drawing of President James Polk and a child's growth chart from the 1800s. Elegant appointments include fine Oriental rugs, tasteful art and antique furnishings. The inn is located in the 18th-century village of Middleway, which contains one of the country's most well-preserved collections of log houses.

*Rates: $85-$130. Jean & Bernie Heiler.
3 R. 3 PB. 2 FP. Phone available. TV available. Beds: QD. B&B. Conference room. CCs: MC VISA.

"We have stayed at inns for 15 years, and yours is at the top of the list as best ever!"

GERRARDSTOWN F18/C8

Prospect Hill Farm

PO Box 135
Gerrardstown WV 25420
(304) 229-3346

Circa 1789. An 18th-century gentleman's home, this Georgian mansion belonged to William Wilson, a member of Thomas Jefferson's cabinet. (He outfitted wagon trains going west.) A hand-painted wall mural of colonial scenes winds up the staircase to the third floor. During the Civil War, Mrs. Wilson stood on the landing and Union soldiers shot around her trying to discover where slaves were hidden. Guests enjoy views of 100 acres of woodlands, and an additional 125 acres of pasture, orchards, and vegetable and berry patches. The ponds are stocked for fly fishing.

Location: Three-and-a-half miles west of I-81 on Route 51.
Rates: $75-$85. Hazel & Charles Hudock.
2 R. 2 PB. 2 FP. Phone available. TV in room. Beds: QD. EP. Restaurant. CCs: MC VISA. Hiking, fishing.
Seen in: *The Daily Mail, the Washington Post, West Virginia Magazine.*

"What a wonderful old house, full of history."

HARPERS FERRY F19/C9

Fillmore Street B&B

PO Box 34
Harpers Ferry WV 25425
(301) 377-0070 (304) 535-2619

Circa 1890. This two-story clapboard Victorian was built on the foundation of a Civil War structure on land deeded by Jefferson Davis, secretary

of war. The surrounding acreage was an encampment for both the Union and Confederate soldiers (at different times). Within walking distance to the inn are the national park, museums, shopping, and dining.

Rates: $65-$72. Alden & James Addy.
2 R. 2 PB. 2 FP. Phone available. Beds: Q. Full breakfast. Hiking, rafting, bicycling. Your choice of a full breakfast in the dining room or continental breakfast in guest rooms.

"Delightful! What superb hosts you two are. We enjoyed ourselves luxuriously."

MARTINSBURG F18/C8

Boydville

The Inn at Martinsburg

601 S Queen St
Martinsburg WV 25401
(304) 263-1448

Circa 1812. This Georgian estate was saved from burning by Union troops only by a specific proclamation from President Lincoln dated July 18, 1864.

Tall maples line the long driveway leading up to the house. It is constructed of two-foot-thick stone walls covered with plaster. The entry hall retains the original wallpaper brought from England in 1812 and hand-painted murals, fireplaces, and antiques adorn the spacious guest rooms. Sunlight filters through tree tops onto estate-sized lawns and gardens.
*Rates: $110-$115. Owen Sullivan & Ripley Hotch.
6 R. 6 PB. 2 FP. Phone available. Beds: Q. Full breakfast. Fishing, golf, hiking, skiing.
Seen in: *Washington Post, Mid-Atlantic Country.*
"Your gracious home, hospitality and excellent amenities were enjoyed so much. Such a fine job of innkeeping."

The Dunn Country Inn

Rt 3 Box 33J
Martinsburg WV 25401
(304) 263-8646

Circa 1805. This Federal-style country home was built of native limestone and is surrounded by acres of farmlands and woods. In 1873, a new

addition was constructed with Romanesque and Italianate features, including seven-foot windows and a porch. An ancient 1790 spring house is on the property, a favorite picnic spot. The inn is decorated with period furnishings and country accents.
Location: 90 miles W of Washington, DC & Baltimore.
Rates: $75-$100. Prince & Dianna Dunn.
5 R. 1 PB. 1 FP. Phone available. Beds: KQD. Full breakfast. CCs: MC VISA. White water rafting, hiking, horseback riding, golf, tours of Civil War Battlefield.
Seen in: *Mid-Atlantic Country.*
"It felt like staying with old friends."

ROMNEY F16/C7

Hampshire House 1884

165 N Grafton St
Romney WV 26757
(304) 822-7171

Circa 1884. This inn is located near the south branch of the Potomac River. Its garden has old boxwoods and walnut trees. The inn features ornate brickwork, tall, narrow windows, bay windows, wood-burning fireplaces with handsome period mantels, and period lighting and furniture. The inn has a sitting room with a well-stocked library and a cozy patio. The music room boasts an antique pump organ.
Rates: $60-$65. Jane & Scott Simmons.
4 R. 4 PB. 2 FP. Phone available. TV in room. Beds: QDT. Full breakfast. Gourmet meals. Conference room. CCs: MC VISA AE DC CB. Canoeing, horseback riding, swimming. Therapeutic massage, local wineries.
Seen in: *The Hampshire Review, Mid-Atlantic Country, The Weekend Journal.*
"Your personal attention made us feel at home immediately."

SHEPHERDSTOWN F19/C8

Stonebrake Cottage

Shepherd Grade Rd, PO Box 1612
Shepherdstown WV 25443
(304) 876-6607

Circa 1880. Situated at the edge of a 140-acre farm, Stonebrake Cottage has been refurbished and decorated with

antique country chests and four-poster beds. This completely private Victorian cottage contains three bedrooms, a living room and a kitchen stocked with the makings for a full country breakfast. A 10-acre woodland is nearby for private picnics.
Location: Five minutes from the heart of town.
Rates: $85-$90. Anne & Dennis Small.
3 R. 2 PB. Phone available. TV in room. Beds: QDTC. Full breakfast. CCs: VISA DS. Golf, white-water rafting, canoeing.
Seen in: *The Washington Post, Martinsburg Journal.*
"Absolutely charming...food was wonderful."

Thomas Shepherd Inn

Box 1162, 300 W German St
Shepherdstown WV 25443
(304) 876-3715

Circa 1868. Spreading oaks and towering pines shade this two-story brick

house, once a Lutheran parsonage. It was built on land once owned by Thomas Shepherd, founder of Shepherdstown, West Virginia's oldest town. Furnishings are American antiques.
Location: Eastern panhandle of West Virginia.
Rates: $75-$90. Margaret Perry.
6 R. 4 PB. Phone available. TV available. Beds: QDT. Full breakfast. Conference room. CCs: MC VISA AE. Golf, rafting, canoeing, biking, hiking, shopping.
Seen in: *The Baltimore Sun, Herald Mail, Travel & Leisure, The New York Times.*
"The elegance and tastefulness of the inn, the breakfast and the trip back into time that it affords can only be exceeded by Margaret's hospitality."

WISCONSIN

APPLETON N13/D5

The Queen Anne
837 E College Ave
Appleton WI 54911
(414) 739-7966

Circa 1895. On a tree-lined street, The Queen Anne features polished oak, pine and maple floors, and beveled and stained-glass windows. The dining area has bay windows. Furnishings include Victorian, Louis XV, Eastlake and Empire.

Rates: $65-$75. Susan & Larry Bogenschutz.
3 R. 1 PB. Phone in room. TV available. Beds: Q. Full breakfast. Conference room. Cross-country skiing, nature trails, swimming, museums. Weddings, rehearsal dinners, wedding showers.
Seen in: *The Post Crescent, Valleysun.*
"The Queen Anne is an expression of your warmth & hospitality and a delightful place to be."

BARABOO Q9/E4

The Barrister's House
226 9th Ave
Baraboo WI 53913
(608) 356-3344

Circa 1932. Built by a prominent Baraboo attorney, this stately home was designed by architect Frank Riley (builder of the governor's mansion) to replicate the warmth and grace of colonial New England homes. The fireplaces, crystal chandeliers, library and veranda are favorites with guests.

Rates: $50-$60. Glen & Mary Schulz.
4 R. 4 PB. Beds: QD. Continental-plus breakfast. Skiing, hiking, fishing, swimming, boating.
Seen in: *Country Inns.*
"Your home is simply wonderful, and we've enjoyed every moment. Lovely rooms, gracious hosts, delicious food!"

BAYFIELD E6/A3

Cooper Hill House
33 S Sixth St, PO Box 1288
Bayfield WI 54814
(715) 779-5060

Circa 1888. This inn, built from native hemlock and white pine, offers a view of Lake Superior. Guest rooms are sunny and feature antiques, family heirlooms and quilts. A cozy sitting room offers a place for relaxing, reading and playing games. The inn serves homemade breads, fresh fruit and specially blended coffee.

Rates: $55-$65. Larry & Julie MacDonald.
4 R. 4 PB. Phone available. Beds: QD. Continental-plus breakfast. CCs: MC VISA. Downhill & cross-country skiing, sailing, golf, swimming, fishing, biking, hiking.
Seen in: *Wintertime, Lake Superior Magazine.*
"Thanks for the great time, great food and great company."

Old Rittenhouse Inn
301 Rittenhouse Ave, PO Box 584-1
Bayfield WI 54814
(715) 779-5111

Circa 1890. This rambling Queen Anne Victorian was built by Civil War General Allen Fuller, using cedar shingles and the local brownstone for which Bayfield was famous. Antique furnishings abound throughout the inn, which has 12 working fireplaces. Underneath massive gables, a wraparound veranda is filled with geraniums, petunias and white wicker furnishings. There is a spectacular view of Lake Superior.

Location: On Bayfield's main street, 5 blocks from Lake Superior shore.
Rates: $79-$159. Season: April - Nov. Jerry & Mary Phillips.
11 R. 11 PB. 10 FP. Phone available. TV available. Beds: KQDC. B&B. Restaurant. Gourmet meals. Spa. Handicap access. Conference room. CCs: MC VISA. Cross-country skiing, sailing, swimming, Apostle Island National Lakeshore.
Seen in: *Wisconsin Trails, The Magazine of Good Living.*
"The whole decor, the room, the staff and the food were superb! Your personalities and talents give a great warmth to the inn."

BURLINGTON T13/G5

Hillcrest B&B
540 Storle Ave
Burlington WI 53105
(414) 763-4706

Circa 1908. Boasting what some have called the "most spectacular view in southeast Wisconsin," the inn overlooks two rivers, a lake, rolling farmland and rustic woods. Carved oak woodwork, an open staircase, beveled windows, homemade quilts and wood floors highlight the stately home's antique-filled interior. A cozy breakfast nook offers another breathtaking view of the scenic landscape. Guests also may enjoy the sights from one of the historic estate's two porches while comfortably seated on antique wicker furniture.

Rates: $45-$65. Dick & Karen Granholm.
3 R. 1 PB. Phone available. TV available. Beds: KQ. Full breakfast. CCs: MC VISA. Golf, skiing, water sports, horseback riding, biking.
Seen in: *Racine Journal Times, Burlington Standard Press.*
"We had a delightful time."

CEDARBURG Q14/F5

Stagecoach Inn B&B
W 61 N 520 Washington Ave
Cedarburg WI 53012
(414) 375-0208

Circa 1853. Restored by historian Brook Brown, this stone Greek Revival house was originally used as a stagecoach stop between Milwaukee and Green Bay. Authentically decorated with antiques, all the suites feature king-size whirlpools.

Location: Downtown Cedarburg.

Rates: $55-$95. Brook & Liz Brown.
12 R. 12 PB. Phone available. TV in room. Beds: QTD. Continental-plus breakfast. Spa. Conference room. CCs: MC VISA AE. Cross-country skiing, bicycling, tennis, golf, horseback riding, fishing.
Seen in: *Milwaukee Magazine, Visions, News Graphic Pilot, Midwest Living.*
"I love the Stagecoach Inn and hope to return as often as possible," Jerry Minnich, *Isthmus.*

The Washington House Inn
W 62 N 573 Washington Ave
Cedarburg WI 53012
(414) 375-3550 (800) 369-4088
Circa 1886. Completely renovated, this original Cream-City-brick building is decorated in a light-hearted country Victorian style, featuring antiques, whirlpool baths and fireplaces. The original guest registry, more than 100 years old, is displayed proudly in the lobby.
Location: In the heart of downtown Cedarburg.
*Rates: $59-$139. Wendy Porterfield.
29 R. 29 PB. 9 FP. Phone in room. TV in room. Beds: KQDC. B&B. Spa. Sauna. Handicap access. Conference room. CCs: MC VISA AE DC CB DS. Victorian interlude dinner package.
Seen in: *Country Home, Chicago Sun-Times.*
"A piece of time lost to all but a fortunate few who will experience it. Please save it for my children."

EGG HARBOR K16/C6

Country Gardens B&B
6421 Hwy 42
Egg Harbor WI 54209
(414) 743-7434
Circa 1895. This farm features 160 acres of farmland and orchards. Grain, fruits and vegetables are harvested and sold. Guests enjoy picking strawberries for breakfast and gathering eggs. The house is paneled with wood including the Captain's Quarters guest room, which also features a stone wall, cherry paneling and massive beams.
Location: Door County.
Rates: $55-$65. Jim & Crystal Barnard.
4 R. Phone available. TV available. Beds: QD. Full breakfast. CCs: MC VISA. Hiking, biking, cross-country skiing, tennis, golf, swimming, theater, horses.
Seen in: *The Milwaukee Journal, USA Today.*
"We loved our stay and are only sorry we couldn't stay longer."

ELLISON BAY J16/C6

The Griffin Inn
11976 Mink River Rd
Ellison Bay WI 54210
(414) 854-4306
Circa 1910. This New England-style country inn is situated on five acres of rolling lawns and maple trees with a gazebo. There are verandas with

porch swings, a gracious lobby with a stone fireplace and a cozy library. Guest rooms are furnished with antique beds and dressers and feature handmade quilts. In addition to the main house, there are four cottages.
Location: Two blocks east of Highway 42 on the Door County Peninsula.
Rates: $67 & up. Jim & Laurie Roberts.
10 R. Phone available. Beds: DT. B&B. Gourmet meals. Cross-country skiing, golf, hiking, bicycling, boating, swimming. Weddings, anniversaries, small private luncheons & dinners.
Seen in: *Ladies Circle, Innsider, Country Inns, Green Bay Press Gazette.*
"A classic bed-and-breakfast inn," Travel and Leisure Magazine.

EPHRAIM J16/C6

French Country Inn of Ephraim
3052 Spruce Ln, PO Box 129
Ephraim WI 54211
(414) 854-4001
Circa 1912. Originally the summer home of a Chicago family, this spacious inn features delicate lace curtains and wicker furniture. Just a short distance from Lake Michigan's Green Bay in the state's popular Door County region, the inn also offers a two-bedroom cottage, which is fully equipped for housekeeping. Because of the rugged beauty of the surrounding area, it has come to be known as the "Cape Cod of the Midwest." Repeat guests like to sample the inn's hospitality in various seasons, and Door County is especially noted for its spectacular fall foliage.
Rates: $45-$68. Walt Fisher & Joan Fitzpatrick.
7 R. 2 PB. Phone available. Beds: DT. Continental-plus breakfast. Golf, bicycling, wind surfing, sailing, swimming, cross-country skiing, hiking.
Seen in: *Chicago Tribune.*
"A gracious host in a relaxed, comfortable setting."

FISH CREEK K16/C6

Thorp House Inn & Cottages
4135 Bluff Rd, PO Box 490
Fish Creek WI 54212
(414) 868-2444
Circa 1902. Freeman Thorp picked the site for this home because of its view of Green Bay and the village. Before

his house was finished, however, he perished in the bay when the *Erie L. Hackley* sank. His wife completed it as a guest house. Each room has a view of the harbor, cedar forest or village. A stone fireplace is the focal point of the parlor, and four of the cottages on the property have fireplaces.
Location: Heart of Door County, in the village of Fish Creek.
Rates: $53-$66. Christine & Sverre Falck-Pedersen.
4 R. 4 FP. Phone available. Beds: QD. Continental-plus breakfast. Swimming, fishing, bicycling, hiking, golf, tennis, horseback riding.
Seen in: *Green Bay Press-Gazette.*
"Amazing attention to detail from restoration to the furnishings. A very first-class experience."

HAYWARD G5/B2

Mustard Seed
205 California, PO Box 262
Hayward WI 54843
(715) 634-2908
Circa 1895. Situated in a quiet neighborhood within easy walking distance of downtown Hayward, this inn offers guests a cozy mix of country antique and Scandinavian decor. The inn's enclosed yard helps afford privacy to guests, who may opt for the spacious Governor's Suite (Wisconsin Governor Tommy Thompson was a recent visitor), with its two-sided fireplace, TV and private bath. Breakfasts may be enjoyed in the formal dining area, country-style kitchen or on the patio in summer. Nearby attractions include Historyland, Telemark Ski Area and the National Fresh Water Fishing Hall of Fame.
Rates: $45-$60. James & Betty Teske.
5 R. 1 PB. 1 FP. TV available. Beds: QDT. Full breakfast. CCs: MC VISA. Horseback riding, golf, tennis, water sports, fishing, canoeing, bicycling, hiking, downhill & cross-country skiing.
Seen in: *Sawyer County Record.*
"We cannot believe our good fortune in finding you and your marvelous home."

HAZEL GREEN T7/G3

Wisconsin House Stagecoach Inn

2105 Main
Hazel Green WI 53811
(608) 854-2233

Circa 1846. Located in southwest Wisconsin's historic lead mining region, this one-time stagecoach stop will delight antique-lovers. The innkeepers, who also deal in antiques, enjoy helping guests in their search for that special piece. The spacious two-story inn once hosted Ulysses S. Grant, whose home is just across the border in Illinois. One of the inn's guest rooms bears his name and features a walnut four-poster bed. Don't miss the chance to join the Muellers on a Friday or Saturday evening for one of their famous country-inn dinners. The family-style meals are served, by reservation only, at a handsome 16-foot-long dining table.

Rates: $40-$65. John & Betha Mueller.

9 R. 5 PB. Phone available. TV available. Beds: QDT. Full breakfast. Restaurant. CCs: MC VISA. Cross-country skiing, Mississippi River boat rides.

Seen in: *Chicago Tribune, Milwaukee Journal, Country Living, Midwest Living.*

"Your ears should be burning because we are telling so many about you."

KENOSHA T14/G6

The Manor House

6536 3rd Ave
Kenosha WI 53143
(414) 658-0014

Circa 1928. This stately Georgian mansion overlooking Lake Michigan was built for the daughter of the Nash Motor Company founder. There are Chippendale furnishings and antiques from Rothchild's Mentmore Manor in Buckinghamshire, England. The grounds feature a sunken pool, water fountain and gazebo. Across the street is an 11-acre wooded park with tennis courts, an art gallery and fishing pier.

Rates: $90-$130. Cecil & Janice Nichols.

4 R. 4 PB. 2 FP. Phone in room. TV in room. Beds: KQT. Continental breakfast. Conference room. CCs: MC VISA AE. Tennis, bicycling, skiing nearby, fishing, swimming, golf. Seen in: *Kenosha News.*

"Elegant, magnificent, beautiful beyond words. Absolutely superb."

KEWAUNEE M15/D6

Gables B&B

821 Dodge St
Kewaunee WI 54216
(414) 388-0220

Circa 1883. Milwaukee architect Henry Koch designed this 22-room Queen Anne Victorian three blocks from Lake Michigan. The Windsor

Room features a king-size canopy bed. Penny's garden bursts forth each spring with hundreds of daffodils, tulips and lilacs. Xelda, a Russian Blue cat, and Baron, a handsome dachshund, are the inn's mascots.

Location: The Heartland.

Rates: $55-$65. Earl & Penny Dunbar.

5 R. 1 PB. 2 FP. Phone available. Beds: KQDT. Full breakfast. Spa. Game room. CCs: AE. Beach, parks, fishing, golf, cross-country skiing.

Seen in: *The Kewaunee Star, Green Bay Press-Gazette, Chicago Tribune.*

"You both have a knack for making people feel welcome and at ease. Your home is just beautiful, and the breakfast was delicious."

LA FARGE P7/E3

Trillium

Rt 2 Box 121
La Farge WI 54639
(608) 625-4492

Circa 1929. This little cottage once provided for Grandma when she came to live with her children on the farm. Stones from the banks of nearby Kickapoo River were used to construct the fireplace and the chimney for the old cookstove. Guests reserve the entire cottage, which sleeps six. In spring, a hammock sways beneath blossoming apple trees. A hearty country breakfast is served. Both children and adults enjoy watching deer, wild turkeys and owls or visiting the livestock.

Rates: $63. Rosanne Boyett.

1 PB. 1 FP. Phone available. Beds: DTC. B&B. Private cottage. Horseback riding, canoeing, hiking, biking, fishing, skiing.

Seen in: *Milwaukee Journal.*

"It's a place to unwind, listen to the song birds, putter in the organic garden and orchard, stroll the long country lane, sit by the waterfall or relax in the hammock."

LAKE GENEVA T13/G5

T.C. Smith Inn B&B

865 Main St
Lake Geneva WI 53147
(414) 248-1097

Circa 1845. Listed in the National Register of Historic Places, this High Victorian-style inn blends elements of Greek-Revival and Italianate. The inn has massive carved wooden doors, hand-painted moldings and woodwork, a high-ceilinged foyer, an original parquet floor, Oriental carpets, period antiques and European oil paintings. Guests may enjoy tea in the Grand Parlor by a marble fireplace or enjoy breakfast on an open veranda overlooking Lake Geneva.

Rates: $55-$165. Marks Family.

4 R. Phone available. TV in room. Beds: KQD. Continental-plus breakfast. CCs: MC VISA AE DS. Bike rentals. Honeymoon, anniversary, wedding specials.

Seen in: *Keystone Country Peddler.*

"As much as we wanted to be on the beach, we found it impossible to leave the house. It's so beautiful and relaxing."

MADISON R10/F4

Mansion Hill Inn

424 N Pinckney
Madison WI 53703
(608) 255-3999 (800) 798-9070

Circa 1858. The facade of this Romanesque Revival sandstone mansion boasts magnificent arched windows, Swedish railings, verandas and

a belvedere. There are marble floors, ornate moldings and a magnificent mahogany and walnut staircase that winds up four stories. Recently restored and lavishly decorated, the inn easily rivals rooms at the Ritz for opulence. A special occasion warrants requesting the suite with the secret passageway behind a swinging bookcase.

Rates: $100-$250. Polly Elder.

11 R. 11 PB. 4 FP. Phone in room. TV in room. Beds: KQ. Continental breakfast. Spa. Exercise room. Conference room. CCs: MC VISA AE. Swimming, health club, theaters, shopping. Anniversaries.

Seen in: *Chicago Tribune, The New York Times, Country Inns.*

"The elegance, charm and superb services made it a delightful experience."

Plough Inn B&B

3402 Monroe St

Madison WI 53711

(608) 238-2981

Circa 1853. Originally constructed as a tavern and inn, this Greek Revival building is adjacent to the University

of Wisconsin arboretum. The Arborview Room takes full advantage of this by providing a splendid tree-top view of the landscaped grounds. This room also has its own fireplace, wet bar and whirlpool tub. The original Tap Room is now outfitted as a guest room featuring brass fixtures and plaid decor.

Rates: $55-$89. P. Katherine Naherny & Roger H. Ganser.

3 R. 3 PB. 1 FP. Phone available. TV available. Beds: Q. B&B. CCs: MC VISA. Biking, cross-country skiing, golf, sailing, swimming, tennis.

Seen in: *Chicago Tribune, Milwaukee Journal.*

"This was exactly what we needed."

MAIDEN ROCK M3/D1

Harrisburg Inn

Great River Rd, PO Box 15

Maiden Rock WI 54750

(715) 448-4500

Circa 1892. A breathtakingly beautiful view of Lake Pepin greets guests of this historic country house, which overlooks the Great Mississippi River Valley from its location high on the bluff. All rooms offer handmade quilts, and the Evening Primrose Suite and Morning Glory Room boast private decks to further enjoy the lake view. Country-style breakfasts may be served on the porch, in the kitchen or in the rooms for guests who desire their morning meal in bed. The inn is a pleasant drive from the Twin Cities. Nearby shops will delight those with an eye for the unique.

Rates: $48-$88. Carol Crisp & Bern Paddock.

4 R. 2 PB. Phone available. TV available. Beds: D. Full breakfast. CCs: MC VISA. Hiking, biking, sailing, cross-country skiing, fishing, bird-watching.

Seen in: *Hastings Star Gazette.*

"Thanks for your hospitality and good food!"

MERRILL J9/C4

Candlewick Inn

700 W Main St

Merrill WI 54452

(715) 536-7744

Circa 1883. The graceful beauty of this Italianate Victorian mansion begins at the street. The inn makes a welcoming statement with its colonial blue exterior. Inside, gleaming woodwork and a collection of early American antiques create a pleasant ambience. There are ruffled curtains and wing chairs, and one room features a fireplace.

Rates: $50-$90. Dan & Loretta Zimmerman.

5 R. 3 PB. 1 FP. Phone available. TV available. Beds: KDT. Full breakfast. CCs: MC VISA AE. Water sports, downhill & cross-country skiing, snowmobiling.

Seen in: *Foto News, Wisconsin State Journal.*

"Simply beautiful."

MILWAUKEE R14/F5

Ogden House

2237 N Lake Dr

Milwaukee WI 53202

(414) 272-2740

Circa 1916. Listed in the National Register, this white brick Federal house is located in the North Point-South Historic District. It was built for Miss Ogden, who lived to be 101 years old and was one of the founders of the Milwaukee County Historical Society. Guest rooms feature handmade quilts. There is a sunroom and sundeck with views of the garden.

Location: One block from Lake Michigan, 1 mile north of downtown.

*Rates: $65-$75. Mary Jane & John Moss.

2 R. 2 PB. Phone in room. TV in room. Beds: Q. Continental-plus breakfast. FAX.

Seen in: *The Milwaukee Journal.*

"You made me feel as if I were staying with friends and at the same time added the details desired at a fine hotel. I'm ready to adopt my room."

MONTREAL F8/A3

The Inn

104 Wisconsin Ave, PO Box H

Montreal WI 54550

(715) 561-5180

Circa 1913. The Inn is part of a company-owned town, which is in the National Register of Historic Places. The building once served as the offices of a mining company's superintendent. The innkeepers have filled the third-floor loft with mining paraphernalia and adorned the walls of the inn with old photos of the building's mining past. There is a high-ceilinged entryway, a wood stove in the large open family room, stenciling, antiques and period furniture. All guest accommodations are two-room suites with quilts and lace curtains.

Rates: $70. Doree & Dick Schumacher.

4 R. 4 PB. 1 FP. Phone available. TV available. Beds: DT. Full breakfast. Sauna. Exercise room. Hiking, waterfalls, fishing, hunting, boating, sailing, canoeing, alpine & cross-country skiing, ice fishing. Seminars, retreats, receptions, family reunions.

Seen in: *Midwest Living, The Milwaukee Journal.*

"A delightful change of pace compared to hotel/motel lodging."

OSCEOLA J2/C1

St. Croix River Inn

305 River St

Osceola WI 54020

(715) 294-4248

Circa 1910. This stone house is poised on a bluff overlooking the St. Croix River. The sitting room overlooks the

river. All guest rooms have whirlpool baths. Rooms feature such amenities as four-poster canopy beds, a tile fireplace, a Palladian window that stretches from floor to ceiling, stenciling, bull's-eye moldings and private balconies. Breakfast is served in bed.

Rates: $85-$150. Vickie Farnham.

7 R. 7 PB. 1 FP. Phone available. TV available. Beds: Q. Full breakfast. Spa. CCs: MC VISA AE. Downhill & cross-country skiing, hiking, golf, fishing, boating, antiquing.

Seen in: *Chicago Sun-Times, Skyway News, St. Paul Pioneer Press.*

POYNETTE Q10/F4

Jamieson House

407 N Franklin

Poynette WI 53955

(608) 635-4100 (608)635-2277

Circa 1879. Victorian elegance and proximity to recreational activities and sightseeing attractions help bring enthusiastic guests to this inn, which consists of three air-conditioned structures. A main house, guest house and schoolhouse all are furnished with antiques gathered statewide and from the entire Midwest. Four of the rooms sport whirlpool tubs, and the inn's

breakfast fare is noteworthy as Carl has a restaurant background. Water sports are just a few miles away on Lake Wisconsin, and Baraboo's Circus World Museum, Madison and the Wisconsin Dells are within easy driving distance.
Location: Between Madison & Wisconsin Dells.
Rates: $55-$120. Carl Povlick.
11 R. 11 PB. 1 FP. Phone available. TV available. Beds: KQDT. Full breakfast. Conference room. CCs: MC VISA AE DS. Horseback riding, hiking, skiing, all nearby.
Seen in: *Capital Times, North West News, Poynette Press.*

RACINE S15/F6

Lochnaiar Inn
1121 Lake Ave
Racine WI 53043
(414) 633-3300
Circa 1915. This elegant three-story English Tudor mansion is situated on a bluff overlooking Lake Michigan. It is conveniently located within walk-

ing distance of downtown and the marina, which is well known for its year-round festivals and recreational activities. The finely furnished guest rooms offer visitors European-style comforts, including canopied four-poster beds, empress tubs and fresh-cut flowers. Business travelers will appreciate the many amenities offered for their convenience, while the more casual guests will marvel at the inn's historic grandeur.
Rates: $60-$155. Dawn Weisbrod.
8 R. 8 PB. 6 FP. Phone in room. TV in room. Beds: KQ. Continental-plus breakfast. Handicap access. Conference room. CCs: MC VISA AE. Fishing, tennis, swimming, golf, snowmobiling.
Seen in: *Racine Journal Times.*
"The inn is an absolute gem and you are both a delight."

SOUTH MILWAUKEE S14/F6

Riley House
727 Hawthorne
South Milwaukee WI 53172
(414) 764-3130 (414) 764-2521
Circa 1903. The Riley House boasts antique furniture, stained glass, Victorian reproduction wallpaper, hard-rock maple floors and intricate patterning on the banister of the oak staircase. The front, or ladies', parlor features old photographs, a bird cage and lace curtains. The gentleman's parlor has a fireplace, ceiling fan, upright piano and antique books. The inn offers homemade truffles at bedtime.
Rates: $55-$75. Mark & Bert (Roberta) Tyborski.
4 R. 1 PB. 1 FP. Phone available. TV available. Beds: QDT. Full breakfast. Spa. Swimming, boating, cross-country skiing, hiking, biking, tennis.
Seen in: *Milwaukee Journal.*
"The house is beautiful, the food delicious and the hosts thoughtful and charming."

SPARTA O7/E3

Just-N-Trails B&B
Rt 1 Box 274
Sparta WI 54656
(608) 269-4522
Circa 1920. Nestled in a scenic valley sits the 200-acre dairy farm that grateful guests know better as the Just-N-Trails. Guests are welcome to share in the dairy operations and encouraged to explore the hiking and cross-country ski trails. In addition to delightfully decorated rooms in the farmhouse, there are a Scandinavian log house and plush restored granary for guests desiring more privacy. The well-cared-for grounds and buildings reflect the innkeepers' pride in their home, which was built by Don's grandfather.
Rates: $55 $95. Don & Donna Justin.
6 R. 4 PB. 1 FP. Beds: KQD. Full breakfast. CCs: MC VISA. Cross-country skiing and hiking on groomed trails.
Seen in: *Milwaukee Journal, Country, Wisconsin Woman.*
"Everything was perfect, but our favorite part was calling in the cows."

SPRING GREEN R8/F3

Hill Street B&B
353 W Hill St
Spring Green WI 53588
(608) 588-7751 (608) 546-2951
Circa 1900. A lovely Queen Anne Victorian located in a historic city near the Wisconsin River, the Hill Street Bed & Breakfast is a real traveler's treat. Many buildings in the area bear the mark of renowned architect Frank Lloyd Wright, and one of the inn's rooms is named in his honor. The inn also features a spacious wraparound porch, a turret alcove and beautifully carved antique woodwork. Madison and Wisconsin Dells are within easy driving distance.
Rates: $50. Doris Randall.
7 R. 5 PB. 1 FP. Phone available. TV available. Beds: QT. Full breakfast. Sauna. Conference room. CCs: MC VISA AE. Canoeing, fishing, tennis, golf, cross-country skiing, ice skating, swimming.
Seen in: *Wisconsin Trails, Milwaukee Magazine.*
"The best part of our stay was your wonderful breakfast and your company while we ate."

SPRINGBROOK H4/B2

The Stout Trout
Rt 1 Box 1630
Springbrook WI 54875
(715) 466-2790
Circa 1900. Located on 40 acres of rolling, wooded countryside, The Stout Trout overlooks a lily-ringed bay on Gull Lake. The lake can be viewed from the living room, dining areas and second-floor guest rooms. The inn features wood-plank floors, folk art, classic prints and country-style furniture. The inn serves homemade jams and maple syrup.
Rates: $65. Kathleen Fredricks.
4 R. 4 PB. Phone available. TV available. Beds: QD. Full breakfast. Horseback riding, skiing, fishing, river canoeing, hiking, hunting, bicycling, swimming, birding, wild berry picking.
Seen in: *Chicago Tribune, Wisconsin West Magazine.*
"Thank you again for the comfortable setting, great food and gracious hospitality!"

STURGEON BAY L15/D6

The Barbican
132 N Second Ave
Sturgeon Bay WI 54235
(414) 743-4854
Circa 1870. Located on the beautiful Door County peninsula, The Barbican at Sturgeon Bay boasts two restored English-style estates, originally built for a local lumber baron. Guests enjoy elegant suites, which all feature private baths, whirlpool tubs and air conditioning. The inn is located in Sturgeon Bay's Historic District, just one block from the water. The romantic guest rooms make the inn perfect for honeymoons or anniversaries.
Rates: $85-$120. James, Mike, Cherie, Kirsten Pichette.
8 R. 8 PB. 7 FP. Phone available. TV in room. Beds: Q. Continental-plus breakfast. Spa. CCs: MC VISA. Horseback riding, water sports, charter lake fishing, museums, beaches.
Seen in: *Bon Vivant.*
"The finest place I've stayed."

The Inn at Cedar Crossing
336 Louisiana St
Sturgeon Bay WI 54235
(414) 743-4200
Circa 1884. This historic hotel, in the National Register, is a downtown three-story brick building, which once

housed street-level shops with second-floor apartments for the

tailors, shop keepers and pharmacists who worked below. The upstairs, now guest rooms, is decorated with floral wallpapers, stenciling and antiques. The Anniversary Room, for instance, has a mahogany bed and a whirlpool tub. There are two dining rooms, both with fireplaces, on the lower level. The waterfront is three blocks away.
Rates: $65-$109. Terry Wulf.
9 R. 9 PB. Phone available. TV in room. Beds: KQD. Continental-plus breakfast. Restaurant. Gourmet meals. Spa. Handicap access. CCs: MC VISA DS. Sailing, swimming, tennis, biking, cross-country skiing, fishing, art galleries. Christmas tea, wedding specials, winter/spring packages.
Seen in: *New Month Magazine, Milwaukee Sentinel, Chicago Sun-Times, Green Bay Press Gazette.*
"Your warmth and friendliness is the reason for our returning time and again."

Gray Goose B&B
4258 Bay Shore Dr
Sturgeon Bay WI 54235
(414) 743-9100
Circa 1862. Civil War veteran Alexander Templeton would have been proud of the transformation of his homestead to an intimate country

inn. Surrounded by trees and an apple orchard, the Gray Goose overlooks Green Bay. Jessie, an inveterate antique-collector, has decorated the inn to reflect this passion. All shapes and sizes of old cookie cutters form a unique ceiling border in the Pewter Room, where there is a sunset view of the bay and authentic American pewter on display in the corner cupboard.
Rates: $60-$70. Jack & Jessie Burkhardt.
4 R. Phone available. TV available. Beds: QDT. Full breakfast. Game room. CCs: MC VISA AE. Tennis, fishing, golf, water sports, horseback riding, downhill & cross-country skiing, bicycling, hiking, snowmobiling, ice skating, art galleries.
Seen in: *Door County Advocate, New Month Magazine.*
"Thanks for such charming and comfortable accommodations! It has been a delightful experience. Everything was just great."

The Scofield House B&B
908 Michigan St, PO Box 761
Sturgeon Bay WI 54235
(414) 743-7727
Circa 1902. Mayor Herbert Scofield, prominent locally in the lumber and hardware business, built this late Vic-

torian house with a sturdy square tower and inlaid floors that feature intricate borders patterned in cherry, birch, maple, walnut, and red and white oak. Oak moldings throughout the house boast raised designs of bows, ribbons, swags and flowers. Equally lavish decor is featured in the guest rooms with fluffy flowered comforters and cabbage rose wallpapers highlighting romantic antique bedsteads. Door County cherry muffins are a house specialty.
❀Rates: $60-$110. Bill & Fran Cecil.
5 R. 5 PB. 2 FP. Phone available. TV in room. Beds: QD. B&B. Spa. Horseback riding, hiking, fishing, sailing, biking, cross-country skiing, ice skating, snowmobiling. Gourmet breakfast, double whirlpools.
Seen in: *Innsider, Glamour, Country, Wisconsin Trails, Green Bay Press Gazette.*
"Lovely accommodations and warm hospitality."

White Lace Inn
16 N 5th Ave
Sturgeon Bay WI 54235
(414) 743-1105
Circa 1903. White Lace Inn is three Victorian houses, one an ornate Queen Anne. It is adjacent to two districts listed in the National Register. Often the site for romantic anniversary celebrations, a favorite suite has a two-sided fireplace, magnificent

walnut Eastlake bed, English country fabrics and a two-person whirlpool tub.
Location: Door County, Lake Michigan on one side, Green Bay on the other.
Rates: $62-$130. Dennis & Bonnie Statz.
15 R. 15 PB. Phone available. Beds: Q. B&B. Spa. Handicap access. CCs: MC VISA. Cross-country skiing, beaches.
Seen in: *Milwaukee Sentinel, Brides Magazine, National Geographic Traveller.*
"Each guest room is such an overwhelming visual feast, such a dazzling fusion of colors, textures and beautiful objects. It is one of these rare gems that established a tradition the day it opened," Wisconsin Trails.

VIROQUA P6/E2

Viroqua Heritage Inn
220 E Jefferson St
Viroqua WI 54665
(608) 637-3306
Circa 1890. The three-story turret of this gabled Queen Anne mansion houses the sitting rooms of two guest chambers and the formal first-floor

parlor. Columns, spindles and assorted gingerbread spice the exterior while beveled glass, ornate fireplaces and crystal chandeliers grace the interior. An antique baby grand piano, a violin and Victrola reside in the music room. Breakfast is served on the original carved-oak buffet and dining table.
Rates: $40-$60. Nancy Rhoades.
4 R. Phone available. TV available. Beds: DC. Full breakfast. Conference room. CCs: MC VISA. Canoeing, skiing. Free champagne for honeymooners and anniversary couples.
Seen in: *Milwaukee Magazine, Lax.*
"Wonderful house, great hosts."

WAUPACA M11/D4

Crystal River B&B

E1369 Rural Rd
Waupaca WI 54981
(715) 258-5333

Circa 1853. The stately beauty of this historic Greek Revival farmhouse is rivaled only by its riverside setting.

Each room features a view of the water, garden, woods or all three. Central air conditioning, a Victorian gazebo, down comforters and delicious breakfasts, with pecan sticky buns, a special favorite, add to the guests' enjoyment. Exploring the village of Rural, which is in the National Historic Register will delight those interested in bygone days. Recreational activities abound, with the Chain O'-Lakes and a state park nearby.
Location: Historic district.
Rates: $55-$75. Gene & Lois Sorenson.
5 R. 2 PB. Phone available. TV available. Beds: Q. Full breakfast. CCs: MC VISA. Cross-country skiing, horseback riding, hiking, biking, canoeing. Showers, weddings.
Seen in: *Resorter, Stevens Point Journal, Wisconsin Trail Magazine.*
"It was like being king for a day."

WHITE LAKE K12/C5

Wolf River Lodge

White Lake WI 54491
(715) 882-2182

Circa 1929. This rustic Northwoods lodge is made to order for outdoor-lovers. White-water river rafting, trout fishing, cross-country skiing and

hiking are just a few of the available activities. Hearty homemade fare dominates the menu; crepes suzette, frozen Eskimo jam and American fried potatoes are among the breakfast favorites. Indians, French traders and loggers once populated the area, which now sports the clean, clear Wolf River as its prime attraction.
Rates: $60-$80. Joe & Joan Jesse.
9 R. 2 PB. Phone available. TV available. Beds: QDT. AP. Restaurant. Spa. CCs: MC VISA AE DS. Canoeing, cross-country skiing, horseback riding, hay & sleigh rides.
Seen in: *The New York Times, Better Homes and Gardens, Chicago Tribune, Milwaukee Journal.*
"Thank you for your time, service, smiles and good food."

WHITEWATER S12/F5

Victoria-On-Main B&B

622 W Main St
Whitewater WI 53190
(414) 473-8400

Circa 1895. This Queen Anne Victorian is located in the heart of Whitewater National Historic District, adjacent to the University of Wisconsin. It was built for Edward Engebretson, mayor of Whitewater. Each guest room is named for a Wisconsin hardwood. The Red Oak Room, Cherry Room and Bird's Eye Maple Room all feature antiques, Laura Ashley prints and down comforters. A hearty breakfast is served and there are kitchen facilities available for light meal preparation. Whitewater Lake and Kettle Moraine State Forest are five minutes away.
Location: Between Madison and Milwaukee.
Rates: $55-$65. Nancy S. Wendt.
3 R. 1 PB. Phone available. Beds: D. Full breakfast. CCs: MC VISA. Hiking, biking, golf, fishing, canoeing, cross-country skiing, horseback riding.
"We loved it. Wonderful hospitality."

WISCONSIN DELLS P9/E4

Historic Bennett House

825 Oak St
Wisconsin Dells WI 53965
(608) 254-2500

Circa 1863. This handsomely restored Federal-style home, framed by a white picket fence, housed the Henry Bennetts, whose family still operates the

Bennett photographic studio, the oldest continuously operating studio in the country. Noted for the first stop-action photography, Mr. Bennett's work is displayed in the Smithsonian. Antiques and whimsical collectibles have been gathered to decorate the inn. A Victorian garden is highlighted with a gazebo.
Rates: $45-$89. Gail & Rich Obermeyer.
4 R. 1 PB. Phone available. TV in room. Beds: KQD. B&B. Golf, water sports, skiing, state parks, museums.
Seen in: *Milwaukee Journal.*
"Special people with a very beautiful and special home."

WYOMING

CODY B8/B3

Parson's Pillow

1202 14th St
Cody WY 82414
(307) 587-2382

Circa 1902. This historic building originally served as the Methodist-Episcopal Church. Surrounded by a picket fence and a flower-filled garden, it features a bell tower complete with the original bell donated by a cousin to Buffalo Bill. A baby grand piano sits in the parlor, once the meeting room. Guest rooms feature antiques and quilts. Early breakfasts and box lunches are available for hunters and fishermen. The Buffalo Bill Historical Center and the Cody Historic Walking Tour are nearby.

*Rates: $65. Season: May-Sept., Nov-Dec. Lee & Elly Larabee.
4 R. 4 PB. Phone available. TV available. Beds: Q. Full breakfast. FAX. CCs: MC VISA. Horseback riding, hiking, water skiing, wind surfing, downhill & cross-country skiing, snowmobiling, tennis, racquetball, swimming.

GLENROCK F14/D6

Hotel Higgins

416 W Birch
Glenrock WY 82637
(307) 436-9212

Circa 1916. Elm trees and juniper frame this restored hotel, in the National Register. Located on the Oregon Trail, it is near the home station of the

Pony Express. There are many period furnishings original to the hotel, including brass and iron beds. Polished tile floors and beveled glass doors add to the inn's ambience. Each morning a full gourmet breakfast is served with champagne. The Paisley Shawl is a restaurant on the premises.

Rates: $36-$55. Jack & Margaret Doll.
10 R. 7 PB. Beds: DT. Full breakfast. Restaurant. CCs: MC VISA AE. Tennis, golf, swimming.
Seen in: *Travel & Leisure, Rapid City Journal.*

JACKSON HOLE E5/C1

Big Mountain Inn

PO Box 7453
Jackson Hole WY 83001
(307) 733-1981

Circa 1907. Resembling a Norman Rockwell painting, this picturesque, red and white New England-style house stands in a grove of aspens. Decorated with antiques in a western flavor, there are five guest accommodations, three with mountain views of the Tetons. Two rooms feature Japanese soaking tubs.

Rates: $85-$135. Penny Foster.
5 R. 5 PB. Beds: QD. Full breakfast. CCs: MC VISA.
Seen in: *Travel & Leisure.*

"A special time with a special person to care for us. Your beautiful home is our new getaway!"

RAWLINS H11/E4

Ferris Mansion

607 W Maple St
Rawlins WY 82301
(307) 324-3961

Circa 1903. This Queen Anne Victorian with its gables, steeply pitched turret, gazebo and veranda, was designed by a Knoxville, Tenn. architectural firm, Barber and Klutz. Julia Ferris built it after the death of her husband who was killed by a runaway team of horses when he was returning from his copper mine. An elegant Victorian decor takes full advantage of the house's fanciful design.

Rates: $45-$55. Janice Lubbers.
4 R. 4 PB. 2 FP. Phone available. TV in room. Beds: QDT. Full breakfast.
Seen in: *Daily Times.*

"This has to be the nicest bed and breakfast I've ever experienced!"

SAVERY J11/F4

Savery Creek Thoroughbred Ranch

PO Box 24
Savery WY 82332
(307) 383-7840

Circa 1889. This is a working sheep, cattle and horse ranch that has been taking in guests since the Twenties. In those days, visitors were met with horses at the top of the Continental Divide because the terrain prevented travel by automobile. This popular riding ranch offers both English and Western riding. There is a jumping and cross-country course. The ranch is known for exceptional riding horses and delicious meals. Swimming in the creek is a popular summertime activity.

Location: Nine miles north of Savery (population 25).
*Rates: $55-$200. Joyce B. Saer.
5 R. 1 PB. 1 FP. Phone available. TV available. Beds: QT. AP. Gourmet meals. Cross-country skiing, skating, fishing, tennis on the ranch. Rodeos, picnics, cookouts. An abundant wildlife population includes bald eagles.
Seen in: *Sunset Magazine.*

"Marianne and I had a wonderful stay at your place (too short!)"

PUERTO RICO

CONDADO, SAN JUAN

El Canario Inn

1317 Ashford Ave
Condado, San Juan PR 00907
(809) 722-3861

Circa 1938. This three-story inn is close to white sandy beaches. All

rooms are air-conditioned, and there is a tropical patio with a swimming pool.

*Rates: $80-$85. Judy & Keith Olson
25 R. 25 PB. Phone in room. TV available. Beds: DTC. Continental breakfast. Swimming pool. CCs: MC VISA AE DC DS. Beach, windsurfing, sailing, water skiing, jet ski, casinos, horse races.

DIRECTORY OF AMERICAN BED & BREAKFASTS AND COUNTRY INNS

The following directory contains the names, addresses and phone numbers of more than 6,000 Bed & Breakfasts and Country Inns. Every attempt has been made to be as comprehensive and as accurate as possible; however, changes are to be expected. This list is presented for information purposes only and is offered without warranty of any kind.

Note: Although there are many fine inns in this list, being included does not constitute a recommendation. Nor does the absence of a B&B or inn indicate a non-recommendation.

Listings in **bold type** are described in more detail in the main body of this book.

We suggest that if you are interested in making reservations with any of these that you call or write them requesting brochures and rate sheets. Be sure to mention that you saw them in **The Official Guide to American Historic Inns.**

ALABAMA

ANNISTON G12 / C4
The Noble McCaa Butler House, 1025 Fairmont, 36201 .... (205)236-1791
Victoria, 1604 Quintard Ave, 36201 .... (205)236-0503

DECATUR C7 / A3
Dancy-Polk House, 901 Railroad St NW, 35601 .... (205)353-3579

FAIRHOPE U4 / H1
Mershon Court, 203 Fairhope Ave, 36532 .... (205)928-7398

FRANKLIN P6 / F2
Rutherford Johnson House, PO Box 202, 36444 .... (205)282-4423

LAFAYETTE J13 / D5
Hill-Ware-Dowdell Mansion, 203 2nd Ave SW, 36862 .... (205)864-7861

LEEDS H9 / C3
B&B Birmingham, Rt 2 Box 275, 35094 .... (205)699-9841
Country Sunshine, Rt 2 Box 275, 35094 .... (205)699-9841

MENTONE C12 / A4
Mentone Inn, Highway 117, PO Box 284, 35984 .... (205)634-4836

MILLBROOK L10 / E3
B&B Montgomery, Box 886, 36054 .... (205)285-5421
Federal Colonial, Box 886, 36054 .... (205)285-5421

MOBILE T3 / H1
Malaga Inn, 359 Church St, 36602 .... (205)438-4701
Vincent-Doan Home, 1664 Springhill Ave, 36604 .... (205)433-7121

MONTGOMERY M10 / E4
Red Bluff Cottage Bed and Breakfast, 551 Clay Street, 36101 .... (205)264-0056

ALASKA

ANCHORAGE G6 / C3
A Log Home B&B, 2440 Sprucewood St, 99508 .... (907)276-8527
All The Comforts of Home, 12531 Turk's Turn St, 99516 .... (907)345-4279
Arctic Loon B&B, PO Box 110333, 99511 .... (907)345-4935
Chelsea Inn, 3836 Spenard Rd, 99517 .... (907)276-5002
Green Bough Inn, 3832 Young St, 99508 .... (907)562-4636
McCarthy Wilderness B&B, Box 111241, 99511 .... (907)277-6867

ANGOON I10 / D5
Favorite Bay Inn, PO Box 101, 99820 .... (907)788-3123

BETHEL G3 / C2
Bentley's Porter House B&B, PO Box 529, 99559 .... (907)543-3552

BIG LAKE G6 / C3
Jeanie's on Big Lake, Box 520598, 99652 .... (907)892-7594

DENALI NATIONAL PARK F6 / B3
Camp Denali, 99755 .... (907)683-2290
North Face Lodge, 99755 .... (907)683-2290

FAIRBANKS E6 / B3
Alaska's 7 Gables, 4312 Birch Ln, PO Box 80488, 99708 .... (907)479-0751
Fairbanks B&B, Box 74573, 99707 .... (907)452-4967
The Wild Iris Inn, PO Box 73246, 99707 .... (907)479-4062

GUSTAVUS H10 / C5
Glacier Bay Country Inn, Box 5, Dub-Al-U Ranch, 99826 .... (907)697-2288
Gustavus Inn, PO Box 31, 99826 .... (907)697-3311

HAINES H9 / C5
Fort William Seward B&B, House-1, PO Box 5, 99827 .... (907)766-2856
The Summer Inn B&B, 247 Second Ave, Box 1198, 99827 .... (907)766-2970

HOMER H5 / C3
Brass Ring B&B, 987 Hillfair Ct, 99603 .... (907)235-5450
Driftwood Inn, 135-T W Bunnell Ave, 99603 .... (907)235-8019
Homer B&B/Seekins, Box 1264, 99603 .... (907)235-8996
Seaside Farm B&B, HCR 58335 E End Rd, 99603 .... (907)235-7850

JUNEAU H10 / D5
Dawson's B&B, 1941 Glacier Hwy, 99801 .... (907)586-9708
The Lost Chord, 2200 Fritz Cove Road, 99801 .... (907)789-7296
Mullins House, 526 Seward St, 99802 .... (907)586-2959

KETCHIKAN H1 / D5
Great Alaska Cedar Works Bed & Breakfast, Rt 1, PO Box 813, 99901 .... (907)247-8287

MATANUSKA G6 / C3
Yukon Don's B&B Inn, HC 31, Box 5086, 2221 Macahon, 99687 .... (907)376-7472

PALMER G6 / C3
Hatcher Pass Lodge, Box 2655, 99645 .... (907)745-5897
Russell's B&B, HC01, Box 6229-R, 99645 .... (907)376-7662

PETERSBURG I10 / D5
Scandia House, 110 Nordic Dr, 99833 .... (907)772-4281

SELDOVIA H5 / C3
Annie McKenzie's Boardwalk Hotel, PO Box 72, 99663 .... (907)234-7816

SKAGWAY H10 / C5
Golden North Hotel, PO Box 431, 99840 .... (907)983-2294
Irene's Inn, PO Box 543, 99840 .... (907)983-2520
Skagway Inn, PO Box 292, 99840 .... (907)983-2294

SOLDOTNA G6 / C3
Soldotna Bed & Breakfast, Lover's Lane 399, 99669 .... (907)262-4779

TALKEETNA F6 / C3
Fairview Inn, PO Box 379, 99676 .... (907)733-2423

TENAKEE SPRINGS H10 / D5
Tenakee Inn, 167 S Franklin, 99801 .... (907)586-1000

TOK F7 / B4
1260 Inn, Mi 1260, Ak Hwy, 99780 .... (907)778-2205

VALDEZ G7 / C3
B&B Valdez, Box 442, 99686 .... (907)835-4211

ARIZONA

AJO N5 / F3
The Mine Manager's House, One Greenway Dr, PO Box 486, 85321 .... (602)387-6505

BISBEE P11 / G5
Bisbee Inn, 45 OK St, PO Box 1855, 85603 .... (602)432-5131
The Inn at Castle Rock, Box 1161, 112 Tombstone Canyon, 85603 .... (602)432-7195
The Greenway House, 401 Cole Ave, 85603 .... (602)432-7170
Park Place B&B, 200 E Vista, 85603 .... (602)432-5516

COCHISE N11 / F5
Cochise Hotel, PO Box 27, 85606 .... (602)384-3156

FLAGSTAFF G7 / C4
Arizona Mountain Inn, 685 Lake Mary Rd, 86001 .... (602)774-8959
Birch Tree Inn, 824 W Birch Ave, 86001 .... (602)774-1042
Comfi Cottages, 1612 N Aztec, 86001 .... (602)779-2236
Dierker House B&B, 423 W Cherry, 86001 .... (602)774-3249
Rainbow Ranch, 2860 N Fremont, 86001 .... (602)774-3724
Walking L Ranch, RR 4, Box 721B, 86001 .... (602)774-2219

FOUNTAIN HILLS K7 / E3
Villa Galleria B&B, 16650 E Hawk Dr, 85268 .... (602)837-1400

ORACLE M9 / F5
Villa Cardinale, PO Box 649, 85623 .... (602)896-2516

PEARCE 011 / G6
Grapevine Canyon Ranch, PO Box 302, 85625 .... (602)826-3185

PHOENIX K6 / E3
Maricopa Manor, 15 W Pasadena Ave, 85013 .... (602)274-6302
Westways "Private" Resort Inn, PO Box 41624, 85080 .... (602)582-3868

PRESCOTT I5 / D3
Lynx Creek Farm B&B, Box 4301, 86302 .... (602)778-9573
Marks House Inn, 203 E Union, 86303 .... (602)778-4632
The Prescott Country Inn, 503 S Montezuma, 86303 .... (602)445-7991
Prescott Pines Inn, 901 White Spar Rd, 86303 .... (602)445-7270
Victoria Inn of Prescott B&B, 246 S Cortez St, 86303 .... (602)778-2642

SASABE P7 / G4
Rancho De La Osa, PO Box 1, 85633 .... (602)823-4257

SCOTTSDALE K7 / E3
Valley 'O the Sun B&B, PO Box 2214, 85252 .... (602)941-1281

SEDONA H7 / C4
Briar Patch Inn, Star Rt 3, Box 1002, 86336 .... (602)282-2342
Garland's Oak Creek Lodge, PO Box 152, Hwy 89A, 86336 .. (602)282-3343
Graham's B&B Inn, 150 Canyon Circle Dr, 86336 .... (602)284-1425
Greyfire Farm B&B, 1240 Jacks Canyon Rd, 86336 .... (602)284-2340
Keyes' B&B, Box 1682, 2271 Roadrunner, 86336 .... (602)282-6008
L'Auberge de Sedona Resort, PO Box B, 301 Little Ln, 86336 .... (602)282-7131
Moore's Music Museum B&B, 3085 W Hwy 89A, 86336 .... (602)282-3419
Rose Tree Inn, 376 Cedar St, 86336 .... (602)282-2065
Saddle Rock Ranch, PO Box 10095, 86336 .... (602)282-7640

TEMPE K6 / E3
Mi Casa-Su Casa B&B, PO Box 950, 85281 .... (602)990-0682

TOMBSTONE O10 / G5
The Jeff Milton House, 18 N 3rd St, 85638 .... (602)457-3412

TUCSON N8 / F4
Desert Needlework Ranch, 1645 N Harrison Rd, 85715 .... (602)885-6264
The Desert Yankee, 1615 N Norton Ave, 85719 .... (602)795-8295
Flying V Ranch, 6800 N Flying V Ranch Rd, 85715 .... (602)299-4900
La Posada Del Valle, 1640 N Campbell Ave, 85719 .... (602)795-3840
The Lodge on the Desert, Box 42500, 85733 .... (800)456-5634
The Peppertrees B&B, 724 E University, 85719 .... (602)622-7167
Quail's Nest B&B, 1416 N Richey, 85716 .... (602)325-8938

White Stallion Ranch, 9251 W Twin Peaks Rd, 85743 .... (602)297-0252

WICKENBURG J5 / *D3*
Kay El Bar Ranch, PO Box 2480, 85358 .... (602)684-7593
Rancho De Los Caballeros, Box 1148, 85358 .... (602)684-5484

ARKANSAS

BRINKLEY G9 / *C5*
The Great Southern Hotel, 127 W Cedar, 72021 .... (501)734-4955

CLARKSVILLE E3 / *B2*
May House, 101 Railroad Ave, 72830 .... (501)754-6851

DES ARC F8 / *C5*
The 5-B's, 210 S 2nd St, 72040 .... (501)256-4789

EUREKA SPRINGS B3 / *A2*
Bridgeford Cottage, 263 Spring St, 72632 .... (501)253-7853
Brownstone Inn, 75 Hillside, PO Box 409, 72632 .... (501)253-7505
Coach House Inn, 140A S Main, 72632 .... (501)253-8099
Crescent Cottage Inn, 211 Spring St, 72632 .... (501)253-6022
Crescent Hotel, Prospect St, 72632 .... (501)253-9766
Crescent Moon Townhouse, PO Box 429, 72632 .... (501)253-9463
Dairy Hollow House, 515 Spring St, 72632 .... (501)253-7444
Elmwood House, 110 Spring St #62B, 72632 .... (501)253-7227
Harvest House B&B Inn, 104 Wall St, 72632 .... (501)253-9363
Heart of the Hills Inn, 5 Summit, 72632 .... (501)253-7468
The Heartstone Inn & Cottages, 35 King's Hwy, 72632 .... (501)253-8916
Johnson's Hilltop Cabin, Rt 1, Box 503, 72632 .... (501)253-9537
Lake Lucerne Resort, PO Box 441, 72632 .... (501)253-8085
Lookout Cottage, 12 Lookout Cir, 72632 .... (501)253-9545
Main Street Inn, 217 N Main St, 72632 .... (501)253-6042
Maplewood B&B, 4 Armstrong St, 72632 .... (501)253-8053
New Orleans Hotel, 63 Spring St, 72632 .... (501)253-8630
Oak Crest Cottages, Rt 2, Box 26, 72632 .... (501)253-9493
The Old Homestead, 78-82 Armstrong St, 72632 .... (501)253-7501
Palace Hotel & Bath House, 135 Spring St, 72632 .... (501)253-7474
The Piedmont House, 165 Spring St, 72632 .... (501)253-9258
Red Bud Valley Resort, RR 1, Box 500, 72632 .... (501)253-9028
Redbud Manor, 7 Kings Hwy, 72632 .... (501)253-9649
Riverview Resort, RR 2, Box 475, 72632 .... (501)253-8367
Singleton House B&B, 11 Singleton, 72632 .... (501)253-9111
Sweet Seasons Guest Cottages, 26 Spring St, 72632 .... (501)253-7603
Tatman-Garrett House, Box 171, 72632 .... (501)253-7617
White Flower Cottage, 62 Kings Hwy, 72632 .... (501)253-9636

EVERTON C4 / *A2*
Corn Cob Inn, Rt 1 Box 183, 72633 .... (501)429-6545

FORT SMITH E1 / *B1*
McCartney House, 500 S 19th St, 72901 .... (501)782-9057
Thomas Quinn Guest House, 815 N B St, 72901 .... (501)782-0499

HEBER SPRINGS E7 / *B4*
The Anderson House, PO Box 630, 72543 .... (501)362-5266
Oak Tree Inn, Vinegar Hill & 110 W, 72543 .... (501)362-8870

HELENA H10 / *D6*
Edwardian Inn, 317 S Biscoe, 72342 .... (501)338-9155
Martha's Vineyard, 810 Columbia, 72342 .... (501)338-3814

HOT SPRINGS H4 / *D3*
Stillmeadow Farm Reproduction, Rt 1 Box 434-d, 71913 .... (501)525-9994
Williams House Inn, 420 Quapaw St, 71901 .... (501)624-4275

HOT SPRINGS NATL PK H4 / *D3*
Dogwood Manor B&B, 906 Malvern Ave, 71901 .... (501)624-0896

JASPER C4 / *A3*
Cliff House Inn, Scenic Ark, Hwy 7, 72641 .... (501)446-2292

MORRILTON F5 / *C3*
Tanyard Springs, Rt 3, Box 335, 72110 .... (501)727-5200

MOUNTAIN VIEW D7 / *B4*
The Commercial Hotel-A Vintage Guest House, Washington at Peabody St, PO Box 72, 72560 .... (501)269-4383

PINE BLUFF I7 / *D4*
Margland 11 B&B Inn, 703 W Second, 71611 .... (501)536-6000

ROMANCE F7 / *C4*
Hammons Chapel Farm, 1 Mi off Ark 5, 72136 .... (501)849-2819

SILOAM SPRINGS C1 / *A1*
Washington Street B&B, 1001 S Washington, 72761 .... (501)524-5669

WASHINGTON J3 / *E2*
Old Country Jail, PO Box 157, 71862 .... (501)983-2178

YELLVILLE C5 / *A3*
Red Raven Inn, Box 1217, 72687 .... (501)449-5168

CALIFORNIA

AHWAHNEE NQ14 / *F3*
Ol-Nip Gold Town B&B, 45013 Hwy 49, 93601 .... (209)683-2155

ALAMEDA NP7 / *E1*
Garratt Mansion, 900 Union St, 94501 .... (415)521-4779
Webster House, 1238 Versailles Ave, 94501 .... (415)523-9697

ALBION NK3 / *D1*
Albion River Inn, PO Box 100, 95410 .... (707)937-1919
Fensalden Inn, PO Box 99, 95410 .... (707)937-4042
Wool Loft, 32751 Navarro Ridge Rd, 95410 .... (707)937-0377

ALLEGHANY NJ11 / *D3*
Kenton Mine Lodge, Box 942, 95910 .... (916)287-3212

ALTADENA SK14 / *J4*
Eye Openers, PO Box 694, 91003 .... (818)797-2055

AMADOR CITY NM11 / *E3*
Mine House Inn, PO Box 245, S Hwy 49, 95601 .... (209)267-5900

ANAHEIM SM14 / *J4*
Anaheim Country Inn, 856 S Walnut St, 92802 .... (714)778-0150

ANGELS CAMP NO12 / *F3*
Cooper House, 1184 Church St, PO Box 1388, 95222 .... (209)736-2145
Utica Mansion Inn, 1090 Utica Ln, 95222 .... (209)736-4209

ANGELUS OAKS SL17 / *J5*
Whispering Pines B&B, 5850 Manzanita Ave, 92305 .... (714)794-2962

ANGWIN NM7 / *E2*
Forest Manor, 415 Cold Springs Rd, 94508 .... (707)965-3538

APTOS SB3 / *F2*
Apple Lane Inn, 6265 Soquel Dr, 95003 .... (408)475-6868
Bayview Hotel B&B Inn, 8041 Soquel Dr, 95003 .... (408)688-8654
Mangels House, 570 Aptos Creek Rd, PO Box 302, 95001 .... (408)688-7982

ARCATA NE3 / *B1*
Lady Ann, 902 14th St, 95521 .... (707)822-2797
Plough & the Stars Country Inn, 1800 27th St, 95521 .... (707)822-8236

ARNOLD NN12 / *E3*
Lodge at Manuel Mill Bed and Breakfast, PO Box 998, 95223 .... (209)795-2622

ARROYO GRANDE SH7 / *H2*
Guest House, 120 Hart Ln, 93420 .... (805)481-9304
Rose Victorian Inn, 789 Valley Rd, 93420 .... (805)481-5566
The Village Inn, 407 El Camino Real, 93420 .... (805)489-5926

AUBURN NL10 / *E3*
Dry Creek B&B, 13740 Dry Creek Rd, 95603 .... (916)878-0885
Lincoln House B&B, 191 Lincoln Way, 95603 .... (916)885-8880
Power's Mansion Inn, 164 Cleveland Ave, 95603 .... (916)885-1166
The Victorian Hill House, 195 Park St, 95604 .... (916)885-5879

AVALON SN13 / *K3*
Glenmore Plaza Hotel, 120 Sumner Ave, 90704 .... (213)510-0017
Island Inn, PO Box 467, 125 Metropole, 90704 .... (213)510-1623
The Inn on Mt. Ada, Box 2560, 207 Wrigley Rd, 90704 .... (213)510-2030
The Old Turner Inn, PO Box 97, 90704 .... (213)510-2236
Zane Grey Pueblo Hotel, PO Box 216, 90704 .... (213)510-0966

BALLARD SJ8 / *I2*
Ballard Inn, 2436 Baseline, 93463 .... (805)688-7770

BAYWOOD PARK SH6 / *H2*
Baywood B&B Inn, 1370 2nd St, 93402 .... (805)528-8888

BEN LOMOND SA3 / *F4*
Chateau des Fleurs, 7995 Hwy 9, 95005 .... (408)336-8943
Fairview Manor, 245 Fairview Ave, 95005 .... (408)336-3355

BENICIA NO7 / *E2*
Captain Dillingham's Inn, 145 East D St, 94510 .... (707)746-7164
The Union Hotel, 401 First St, 94510 .... (707)746-0100

BERKELEY NO7 / *E1*
Dolphin B&B, 1007 Leneve Pl, 94530 .... (415)527-9622
Gramma's Inn, 2740 Telegraph, 94705 .... (415)549-2145
Hillegass House, 2834 Hillegass Ave, 94705 .... (415)548-5517

BIG BEAR CITY SK18 / *J5*
Switzerland House, 2194 3rd Ln, 92314 .... (714)585-2455

BIG BEAR LAKE SK17 / *J5*
Cathy's Country Cottage, PO Box 3706, 92314 .... (714)866-7444
Eagle's Nest B&B, Box 1003, 92315 .... (714)866-6465
Knickerbocker Mansion, 869 S Knickerbocker, PO 3661, 92315 .... (714)866-8221

BIG SUR SD3 / *G1*
Deetjen's Big Sur Inn, Highway One, 93920 .... (408)667-2377

BISHOP NQ18 / *G5*
Chalfant House, 213 Academy St, 93514 .... (619)872-1790
The Matlick House, 1313 Rowan Ln, 93514 .... (619)873-3133

BODEGA NN5 / *El*
Estero Vista Inn, 17699 Highway 1, Box 255, 94922 .... (707)876-3300
Schoolhouse Inn, PO Box 136, 94922 .... (707)876-3257

BOLINAS NO6 / *E1*
Blue Heron Inn, 11 Wharf Rd, PO Box 309, 94924 .... (415)868-1102
Garden Pump House, 51 Brighton Ave, PO Box 315, 94924 .... (415)868-0243

BOONVILLE NK4 / *D1*
Anderson Creek Inn, 12050 Anderson Valley Way, 95415 .... (707)895-3091
Bear Wallow Resort, PO Box 533, Manchester Rd, 95415 .... (707)895-3335
Toll House Inn, Box 268, 15301 Hwy 25, 95415 .... (707)895-3630

BRIDGEPORT NN15 / *F4*
The Cain House, 11 Main St, PO Box 454, 93517 .... (619)932-7040

CALISTOGA NM6 / *E2*
Brannan Cottage Inn, 109 Wapoo Ave, 94515 .... (707)942-4200
Calistoga Inn, 1250 Lincoln Ave, 94515 .... (707)942-4101
Calistoga Wayside Inn, 1523 Foothill Blvd, 94515 .... (707)942-0645
Calistoga Wishing Well Inn, 2653 Foothill Blvd, 94515 .... (707)942-5534
Calistoga's Wine Way Inn, 1009 Foothill Blvd, 94515 .... (707)942-0680
The Inn on Cedar Street, 1307 Cedar St, 94515 .... (707)942-9244
Culver's, A Country Inn, 1805 Foothill Blvd, 94515 .... (707)942-4535
The Elms, 1300 Cedar St, 94515 .... (707)942-9476
Foothill House, 3037 Foothill Blvd, 94515 .... (707)942-6933
Larkmead Country Inn, 1103 Larkmead Ln, 94515 .... (707)942-5360
Meadow Lark Country House, 601 Petrified Forest Rd, 94515 .... (707)942-5651
Mount View Hotel, 1457 Lincoln Ave, 94515 .... (707)942-6877
Pine Street Inn, 1202 Pine St, 94515 .... (707)942-6829
The Pink Mansion, 1415 Foothill Blvd, 94515 .... (707)942-0558
Quail Mountain B&B, 4455 N St. Helena Hwy, 94515 .... (707)942-0316
Silver Rose Inn, 351 Rosedale Rd, 94515 .... (707)942-9581
Trailside Inn, 4201 Silverado Tr, 94515 .... (707)942-4106
Wayside Inn, 1523 Foothill Blvd, 94515 .... (707)942-0645
Wine Country Cottage, 400 Meadow Wood Ln, 94515 .... (707)963-0852
Zinfandel House, 1253 Summit Dr, 94515 .... (707)942-0733

CAMBRIA SG5 / *H2*
Beach House, 6432 Charing Ln, 93428 .... (805)927-5865
Blue Whale Inn, 6736 Moonstone Beach Dr, 93428 .... (805)927-4647
J. Patrick House, 2990 Burton Dr, 93428 .... (805)927-3812
Olallieberry Inn, 2476 Main St, 93428 .... (805)927-3222
Pickford House B&B, 2555 MacLeod Way, 93428 .... (805)927-8619

CAMINO NL12 / *E3*
Camino Hotel - Seven Mile House, 4103 Carson Rd, PO Box 1197, 95709 .... (916)644-7740

CAPITOLA-BY-THE-SEA SB3 / *F2*
The Inn at Depot Hill, 250 Monterey Ave, 95010 .... (408)462-3376

CARLSBAD SO16 / *K4*
Pelican Cove Inn, 320 Walnut Ave, 92008 .... (619)434-5995

CARMEL SC3 / *G1*
Carriage House Inn, PO Box 1900, 93921 .... (800)433-4732
The Cobblestone Inn, PO Box 3185, 93921 .... (408)625-5222
Cypress Inn, 7th & Lincoln Streets, PO Box 7, 93921 .... (408)624-3871
Happy Landing Inn, Monte Verde between 5th & 6th, 93921 (408)624-7917
Holiday House, Box 782, Camino Real at 7th Ave, 93921 .... (408)624-6267
Mission Ranch, 26270 Dolores, 93923 .... (408)624-6436
Monte Verde Inn, Box 394, 93921 .... (408)624-6046
Sandpiper Inn-At-the Beach, 2408 Bay View Ave, 93923 .... (408)624-6433
Sea View Inn, Box 4318, 93921 .... (408)624-8778
The Stonehouse Inn, Box 2517, 93921 .... (408)624-4569
Sundial Lodge, PO Box J, 93921 .... (408)624-8578
Vagabond's House Inn, Box 2747, 93921 .... (408)624-7738

CARMEL VALLEY SD4 / *G2*
Robles del Rio Lodge, 200 Punta Del Monte, 93924 .... (408)659-3705
Stonepine, 150 E Carmel Valley Rd, 93921 .... (408)659-2245
Valley Lodge, PO Box 93, 93924 .... (408)659-2261

CAZADERO NM5 / *D1*
Cazanoma Lodge, PO Box 37, 1000 Kidd Creek Rd, 95421 ...... (707)632-5255

CHICO NI8 / *D2*
The O'Flaherty House B&B, 1462 Arcadian Ave, 95926 .... (916)893-5494

CLIO NI12 / *D3*
White Sulphur Springs Ranch, PO Box 136, Hwy 89 S, 96106 .... (916)836-2387

CLOVERDALE NL5 / *D1*
Abrams House Inn, 314 N Main St, 95425 .... (707)894-2412
Vintage Towers Inn, 302 N Main St, 95425 .... (707)894-4535

COLFAX NK11 / *D3*
Bear River Mountain Farm, 21725 Placer Hills Rd, 95713 .... (916)878-8314

COLOMA NL11 / *E3*
Coloma Country Inn, PO Box 502, #2 High St, 95613 .... (916)622-6919
Vineyard House, Cold Spring Rd, PO Box 176, 95613 .... (916)622-2217

COLUMBIA NO12 / *F3*
City Hotel, PO Box 1870, Main St, 95310 .... (209)532-1479
Fallon Hotel, PO Box 1870, Washington St, 95310 .... (209)532-1470

COLUSA NK7 / *D2*
O'Rourke Mansion, 1765 Lurline Rd, 95932 .... (916)458-5625

COULTERVILLE NP13 / *F3*
Hotel Jeffery, PO Box 440, 95311 .... (209)878-3471

CROWLEY LAKE NP17 / *F4*
Rainbow Tarns, PO Box 1097, Rt 1, 93546 .... (619)935-4556

DANA POINT Q17 / *K4*
Blue Lantern Inn, 34343 Street of the Blue Lantern, 92629 .... (800)234-1425

DAVENPORT SB2 / *F1*
New Davenport B&B, 31 Davenport Ave, 95017 .... (408)425-1818

DAVIS NM9 / *E2*
The Partridge Inn, 521 First St, 95616 .... (916)753-1211

DEL MAR SP16 / *K4*
Rock Haus B&B Inn, 410 15th St, 92014 .... (619)481-3764

DESERT HOT SPRINGS SL18 / *K5*
Traveller's Repose, 66920 First St, PO Box 655, 92240 .... (619)329-9584

DINSMORE NF4 / *B1*
Dinsmore Lodge, Hwy 36, 95526 .... (707)574-6466

DORRINGTON NN13 / *E3*
The Dorrington Hotel & Restaurant, 3431 Hwy 4, 95223 .... (209)795-5800

DOWNIEVILLE NJ11 / *D3*
Sierra Shangri-la, PO Box 285, 95936 .... (916)289-3455

DULZURA SQ18 / *L5*
Brookside Farm, 1373 Marron Valley Rd, 92017 .... (619)468-3043

DUNSMUIR ND7 / *B3*
Dunsmuir Inn, 5423 Dunsmuir Ave, 96025 .... (916)235-4543

ELK NK3 / *D1*
Elk Cove Inn, PO Box 367, 95432 .... (707)877-3321
Green Dolphin Inn, PO Box 132, 6145 S Hwy 1, 95432 .... (707)877-3342
Greenwood Lodge, PO Box 172, 5910 S Hwy 1, 95432 .... (707)877-3422
Greenwood Pier Inn, Box 36, 5940 S Hwy 1, 95432 .... (707)877-9997
Harbor House - Inn by the Sea, 5600 S Hwy 1, 95432 .... (707)877-3203
Sandpiper House Inn, 5520 S Hwy 1, 95432 .... (707)877-3587

EUREKA NE2 / *B1*
A. Weaver's Inn, 1440 B St, 95501 .... (707)443-8119
An Elegant Victorian Mansion, 14th & C Sts, 95501 .... (707)444-3144
Carter House, 1033 Third St, 95501 .... (707)445-1390
Craddock Manor, 814 J St, 95501 .... (707)444-8589
Heuer's Victorian Inn, 1302 E St, 95501 .... (707)442-7334
Hotel Carter, 301 L St, 95501 .... (707)444-8062
Old Town B&B Inn, 1521 Third St, 95501 .... (707)445-3951
Steven's House, 917 Third St, 95501 .... (707)445-9080

FALLBROOK SN16 / *K4*
La Estancia Inn, 3135 S Hwy 395, 92028 .... (619)723-2888

FAWNSKIN SK17 / *J5*
The Inn at Fawnskin, PO Box 378, 880 Canyon, 92333 .... (714)866-3200

FERNDALE NF2 / *B1*
Ferndale Inn, PO Box 887, 619 Main St, 95536 .... (707)786-4307
Gingerbread Mansion, 400 Berding St, 95536 .... (707)786-4000
Shaw House Inn, PO Box 1125, 703 Main St, 95536 .... (707)786-9958

FISH CAMP NQ14 / *F4*
Karen's B&B Yosemite Inn, 1144 Railroad Ave, PO Box 8, 93623 .... (209)683-4550
Narrow Gauge Inn, 48571 Hwy 41, 93623 .... (209)683-7720
Yosemite Fish Camp, 1164 Railroad Ave, PO Box 25, 93623 .... (209)683-7426

FOLSOM NM10 / *E3*
Plum Tree Inn, 307 Leidesdorff St, 95630 .... (916)351-1541

FORT BRAGG NJ3 / *C1*
Avalon House, 561 Stewart St, 95437 .... (707)964-5555
Captain Capps, 32980 Gibney Lane, 95437 .... (707)964-1415
Colonial Inn, PO Box 565, 533 E Fir, 95437 .... (707)964-9979
Country Inn, 632 N Main St, 95437 .... (707)964-3737
Glass Beach B&B, 726 N Main St, 95437 .... (707)964-6774
Grey Whale Inn, 615 N Main St, 95437 .... (707)964-0640
Jughandle Beach Country B&B Inn, 32980 Gibney Ln, 95437 .. (707)964-1415
Noyo River Lodge, 500 Casa Del Noyo Dr, 95437 .... (707)964-8045

FREESTONE NN5 / *E1*
Green Apple Inn, 520 Bohemian Hwy, 95472 .... (707)874-2526

FREMONT NP8 / *F2*
Lord Bradley's Inn, 43344 Mission Blvd, 94539 .... (415)490-0520

GARBERVILLE NM3 / *C1*
Benbow Inn, 445 Lake Benbow Dr, 95440 .... (707)923-2125

GEORGETOWN NL11 / *E3*
American River Inn, Orleans St, PO Box 43, 95634 .... (916)333-4499

GEYSERVILLE NL6 / *D1*
Campbell Ranch Inn, 1475 Canyon Rd, 95441 .... (707)857-3476
The Hope-Bosworth & Hope-Merrill House, Box 42, 21253 Geyserville Ave, 95441 .... (707)857-3356

GILROY SB4 / *F2*
Country Rose Inn - A Bed & Breakfast, PO Box 1804, 95021-1804 ....(408)842-0441

GLEN ELLEN NN7 / *E1*
Gaige House, 13540 Arnold Dr, 95442 ....(707)935-0237
Glenelly Inn, 5131 Warm Springs Rd, 95442 ....(707)996-6720
Stone Tree Ranch, PO Box 173, 7910 Sonoma Mtn Rd, 95442 ..(707)996-8173

GOLETA SK9 / *I2*
Circle Bar B Ranch, 1800 Refugio Rd, 93117 ....(805)968-1113

GRASS VALLEY NK10 / *D3*
Annie Horan's, 415 W Main St, 95945 ....(916)272-2418
Domike's Inn, 220 Colfax Ave, 95945 ....(916)273-9010
Golden Ore House B&B, 448 S Auburn, 95945 ....(916)272-6870
Holbrooke Hotel & Purcell House, 212 W Main, 95945 ....(916)273-1353
Murphy's Inn, 318 Neal St, 95945 ....(916)273-6873
Swan-Levine House, 328 S Church St, 95945 ....(916)272-1873

GRIDLEY NJ9 / *D2*
McCracken's Inn, 1835 Sycamore St, 95948 ....(916)846-2108

GROVELAND NP13 / *F3*
The Groveland Hotel, 18767 Main St, PO Box 481, 95321 ....(209)962-4000
Hotel Charlotte, PO Box 884, 95321 ....(209)962-6455

GUALALA NL4 / *D1*
Gualala Hotel, PO Box 675, 95445 ....(707)884-3441
North Coast Country Inn, 34591 S Hwy, 95445 ....(707)884-4537
The Old Milano Hotel & Restaurant, 38300 Hwy 1, 95445 ....(707)884-3256
St. Orres, PO Box 523, 95445 ....(707)884-3303
Whale Watch Inn, 35100 Hwy 1, 95445 ....(707)884-3667

GUERNEVILLE NM5 / *E1*
Creekside Inn, PO Box 2185, 95446 ....(707)869-3623
The Estate Inn, 13555 Hwy 116, 95446 ....(707)869-9093
Ridenhour Ranch, 12850 River Rd, 95446 ....(707)887-1033
Santa Nella House, 12130 Hwy 116, 95466 ....(707)869-9488

HALF MOON BAY NQ7 / *F1*
Cypress Inn on Miramar Beach, 407 Mirada Rd, 94019 ....(415)726-6002
Half Moon Bay B&B, 413 Main St, 94019 ....(415)726-9363
Mill Rose Inn, 615 Mill St, 94019 ....(415)726-9794
Old Thyme Inn, 779 Main St, 94019 ....(415)726-1616
San Benito House, 356 Main St, 94019 ....(415)726-3425
Zaballa House, 324 Main St, 94019 ....(415)726-9123

HANFORD SD10 / *G3*
The Irwin Street Inn, 522 North Irwin St, 93230 ....(209)584-9286

HEALDSBURG NM6 / *D1*
Belle Du Jour Farm, 16276 Healdsburg Ave, 95448 ....(707)433-7892
Calderwood, 25 West Grant St, PO Box 967, 95448 ....(707)431-1110
Camellia Inn, 211 North St, 95448 ....(707)433-8182
Frampton House, 489 Powell Ave, 95448 ....(707)433-5084
Grape Leaf Inn, 539 Johnson St, 95448 ....(707)433-8140
Haydon House, 321 Haydon St, 95448 ....(707)433-5228
Healdsburg Inn On The Plaza, 110-116 Matheson St, PO Box 1196, 95448 ....(707)433-6991
Lytton Springs Inn, 17698 Healdsburg Ave, 95448 ....(707)431-1109
Madrona Manor, A Country Inn, PO Box 818 1001 Westside Rd, 95448 ....(707)433-4231
Raford House, 10630 Wohler Rd, 95448 ....(707)887-9573

HOMEWOOD NK13 / *E4*
Rockwood Lodge, 5295 W Lake Blvd, PO Box 544, 95718 ....(916)525-5273

HOPE VALLEY NL14 / *E4*
Sorensen's Resort, Hwy 88, 96120 ....(916)694-2203

HOPLAND NK5 / *D1*
Hopland House, 12900 S Hwy 101, 95449 ....(707)744-1404

IDYLLWILD SM18 / *K5*
Strawberry Creek Inn, PO Box 1818, 26370 Hwy 243, 92349 ...(714)659-3202
That Special Place, 23481 Hwy 243, Box 2181, 92349 ....(714)659-5033
Wilkum Inn, 26770 Hwy 243, PO Box 1115, 92349 ....(714)659-4087

INDEPENDENCE SB13 / *G5*
Winnedumah Inn, PO Box 209, 211 N Edwards, 93526 ....(619)878-2040

INVERNESS NO6 / *E1*
Alder House, 105 Vision Rd, 94937 ....(415)669-7218
Blackthorne Inn, PO Box 712, 94937 ....(415)663-8621
Dancing Coyote Beach, 12794 Sir Francis Drake Blvd, 94937 ....(415)669-7200
Golden Hinde Inn & Marina, 12938 Sir Francis Drake, 94937 ....(800)339-9398
Manka's Inverness Lodge, PO Box 126, 30 Calendar Way, 94937 ....(415)669-1034
Ten Inverness Way, 10 Inverness Way, 94937 ....(415)669-1648
The Tree House, 73 Drake Summit, 94937 ....(415)663-8720

IONE NN11 / *E3*
The Heirloom, 214 Shakeley Ln, PO Box 322, 95640 ....(209)274-4468

ISLETON NN9 / *E2*
Delta Daze Inn, PO Box 607, 20 Main St, 95641 ....(916)777-7777

JACKSON NN11 / *E3*
Ann Marie's, 410 Stasal St, 95642 ....(209)223-1452
Broadway Hotel, 225 Broadway, 95642 ....(209)223-3503
Court Street Inn, 215 Court St, 95642 ....(209)223-0416
Gate House Inn, 1330 Jackson Gate Rd, 95642 ....(209)223-3500
Wedgewood Inn, 11941 Narcissus Rd, 95642 ....(209)296-4300
Windrose Inn, 1407 Jackson Gate Rd, 95642 ....(209)223-3650

JAMESTOWN NO12 / *F3*
Historic National Hotel B&B, Main Street, PO Box 502, 95327 ....(209)984-3446
Jamestown Hotel, 18153 Main St, 95327 ....(209)984-3902
The Palm Hotel B&B, 10382 Willow St, Box 515, 95327 ....(209)984-5657

JENNER NM5 / *E1*
Murphy's Jenner-by-the-Sea, PO Box 69, Hwy 1, 95450 ....(707)865-2377
Stillwater Cove Ranch, 22555 Coast Hwy 1, 95450 ....(707)847-3227

JULIAN SO18 / *K5*
Julian Gold Rush Hotel, 2032 Main St, PO Box 1856, 92036...(619)765-0201
Julian Lodge, 2720 C St, PO Box 1930, 92036 ....(619)765-1420
Pine Hills Lodge, 2960 La Posada Way, PO Box 2260, 92036 ...(619)765-1100

KELSEY NL11 / *E3*
Mountainside B&B, 5821 Spanish Flat Rd, 95643 ....(916)626-0983

KERNVILLE SF13 / *H4*
Kern River Inn B&B, 119 Kern River Dr, PO Box 1725, 93238 ....(619)376-6750

KLAMATH NC3 / *A1*
The Requa Inn, 451 Requa Rd, 95548 ....(707)482-8205

KNIGHTS FERRY NP12 / *F3*
Knights Ferry Hotel B&B, 17713 Main St, 95361 ....(209)881-3418

KYBURZ NL13 / *E3*
Strawberry Lodge, Hwy 50, 95720 ....(916)659-7030

LA JOLLA SP16 / *L4*
The B&B Inn at La Jolla, 7753 Draper Ave, 92037 ....(619)456-2066
Prospect Park Inn, 1110 Prospect St, 92037 ....(619)454-0133

LAGUNA BEACH SN15 / *K4*
Carriage House, 1322 Catalina St, 92651 ....(714)494-8945
Casa Laguna, 2510 S Coast Hwy, 92651 ....(714)494-2996
Eiler's Inn, 741 S Coast Hwy, 92651 ....(714)494-3004

LAKE ARROWHEAD SK17 / *J5*
Bluebelle House B&B, 263 S State Hwy 173, 92352 ....(714)336-3292
Chateau Du Lac, PO Box 1098, 92352 ....(714)337-6488
Eagles Landing, PO Box 1510, Blue Jay, 92317 ....(714)336-2642
Lakeview Lodge Victorian, Box 128, 92352 ....(714)337-6633

LAKEPORT NK5 / *D1*
Forbestown Inn, 825 Forbes St, 95453 ....(707)263-7858

LEGGETT NH4 / *C1*
Bell Glen Resort, 70400 US 101, 95455 ....(707)925-6425

LITTLE RIVER NJ3 / *D1*
Glendeven, 8221 N Hwy 1, 95456 ....(707)937-0083
Heritage House, 95456 ....(707)937-5885
Little River Inn, 95456 ....(707)937-5942
The Victorian Farmhouse, 7001 N Hwy 1, PO Box 357, 95456 ....(707)937-0697

LODI NN10 / *E2*
Wine & Roses Country Inn, 2505 W Turner Rd, 95242 ....(209)334-6988

LONG BEACH SM14 / *J4*
Appleton Place, 935 Cedar Ave, 90813 ....(213)432-2312
Lord Mayor's B&B Inn, 435 Cedar Ave, 90802 ....(213)436-0324

LOS ALAMOS SJ8 / *I2*
Union Hotel & Victorian Annex, PO Box 616, 362 Bell St, 93440 ....(805)344-2744

LOS ANGELES SL14 / *J4*
Eastlake Victorian Inn, 1442 Kellam Ave, 90026 ....(213)250-1620
Salisbury House, 2273 W 20th St, 90018 ....(213)737-7817
Terrace Manor, 1353 Alvarado Terrace, 90006 ....(213)381-1478
West Adams B&B Inn, 1650 Westmoreland Blvd, 90006 ....(213)737-5041

LOS GATOS SA3 / *F2*
La Hacienda Inn, 18840 Saratoga Rd, 95030 ....(408)354-9230

LOYALTON NI13 / *D4*
Clover Valley Mill House, Box 928, 96118 ....(916)993-4819

MALIBU SL12 / *J3*
Malibu Beach Inn, 22878 Pacific Coast Hwy, 90265 ....(213)456-6444

MAMMOTH LAKES NP16 / *F4*
Jagerhof Lodge, 663 Old Mammoth Rd, PO Box 1648, 93546 ..(619)934-6162
Rivendell Inn, PO Box 3338, 93546 ....(619)934-2873
Snow Goose Inn, PO Box 946, 93546 ....(619)934-2660
White Feather Lodge, PO Box 2849, 93546 ....(619)934-4439

MARIPOSA NQ13 / *F3*
Boulder Creek B&B, 4572 Ben Hur Rd, 95338 ....(209)742-7729

Finch Haven, 4605 Triangle Rd, 95338 ....(209)966-4738
Granny's Garden, 7333 Hwy 49 N, 95338 ....(209)377-8342
Meadow Creek Ranch B&B Inn, 2669 Triangle Rd, 95338 ....(209)966-3843
Oak Meadows, too, 5263 Hwy 140N, Box 619, 95338 ....(209)742-6161
Pelennor-B&B at Bootjack, 3871 Hwy 49 S, 95338 ....(209)966-2832
Rockwood Gardens, 5155 Tip Top Rd, 95338 ....(209)742-6817
Schlageter House, 5038 Bullion St, 95338 ....(209)966-2471

McCloud — ND8 / *B3*
Francois' Grey Squirrel Inn, 417 Lawndale Ct, 96057 ....(916)964-3105
Hogin House, PO Box 550, 96057 ....(916)964-2882
McCloud Guest House, 606 W Colombero Dr, 96057 ....(916)964-3160
Stoney Brook Inn, 309 W Colombero Rd PO Box 1860, 96057. (916)964-2300

Mendocino — NJ4 / *C1*
Agate Cove Inn, PO Box 1150, 95460 ....(707)937-0551
Ames Lodge, PO Box 207, 95460 ....(707)937-0811
B.G. Ranch & Inn, 9601 N Hwy 1, 95460 ....(707)937-5322
Blair House, PO Box 1608, 95460 ....(707)937-1800
Brewery Gulch Inn, 9350 Hwy 1, 95460 ....(707)937-4752
The Headlands Inn, PO Box 132, Howard & Albion Sts, 95460 ....(707)937-4431
Hill House Inn, PO Box 65, 10701 Palette Dr, 95460 ....(707)937-0554
John Dougherty House, 571 Ukiah St, PO Box 817, 95460 ....(707)937-5266
Joshua Grindle Inn, 44800 Little Lake Rd, PO Box 647, 95460 ....(707)937-4143
MacCallum House Inn, 45020 Albion St, 95460 ....(707)937-0289
Main Street Guest House, PO Box 108, 1021 Main St, 95460 ....(707)937-5150
Mendocino Farmhouse, Box 247, 95460 ....(707)937-0241
Mendocino Hotel, PO Box 587, 45080 Main St, 95460 ....(707)937-0511
Mendocino Village Inn, 44860 Main St, PO Box 626, 95460 ....(707)937-0246
Rachel's Inn, Box 134, 8200 N Hwy 1, 94560 ....(707)937-0088
Reed Manor, Little Lake St, 95460 ....(707)937-5446
Sea Gull Inn, PO Box 317, 95460 ....(707)937-5204
Sea Rock B&B, 11101 N Lancing St, 95460 ....(707)937-5517
Sears House Inn, PO Box 844, 95460 ....(707)937-4076
The Stanford Inn by the Sea, PO Box 487, 95460 ....(707)937-5615
Stevens Wood, 82 N Hwy 1, 95456 ....(707)937-2810
Whitegate Inn, PO Box 150, 499 Howard St, 95460 ....(707)937-4892

Mill Valley — NO6 / *E1*
Mountain Home Inn, 810 Panoramic Hwy, 94941 ....(415)381-9000

Mokelumne Hill — NN11 / *E3*
Hotel Leger, PO Box 50, 95245 ....(209)286-1401

Montara — NH18 / *F1*
The Goose & Turrets Bed & Breakfast, PO Box 937, 94037-0937 ....(415)728-5451

Monte Rio — NM5 / *E1*
Huckleberry Springs, PO Box 400, 95462 ....(707)865-2683

Montecito — SK10 / *I3*
San Ysidro Ranch, 900 San Ysidro Ln, 93108 ....(805)969-5046

Monterey — SC3 / *G1*
Del Monte Beach Inn, 1110 Del Monte Ave, 93940 ....(408)649-4410
The Jabberwock, 598 Laine St, 93940 ....(408)372-4777
Merritt House, 386 Pacific St, 93940 ....(408)646-9686
Monterey Hotel, 406 Alvarado St, 93908 ....(408)375-3184
Old Monterey Inn, 500 Martin St, 93940 ....(408)375-8284
The Spindrift Inn, Box 3196, 652 Cannery Row, 93940 ....(408)646-8900

Moss Beach — /
Seal Cove Inn, 221 Cypress Ave, 94038 ....(415)728-7325

Mount Shasta — NC17 / *B3*
Mount Shasta House B&B, 113 S A St, 96067 ....(916)926-5089
Mount Shasta Ranch, 1008 W.A. Barr Rd, 96067 ....(916)926-3870
Ward's "Big Foot" Ranch B&B, PO Box 585, 96067 ....(916)926-5170

Muir Beach — NO6 / *E1*
Butterfly Tree, PO Box T, 94966 ....(415)383-8447
Pelican Inn, 10 Pacific Way, 94965 ....(415)383-6000

Murphys — NN12 / *E3*
Dunbar House, 1880, 271 Jones St, PO Box 1375, 95247 ....(209)728-2897
Murphy's Hotel, 457 Main St, 95247 ....(209)728-3444

Napa — NM7 / *E2*
Arbor Guest House, 1436 G St, 94559 ....(707)252-8144
Beazley House, 1910 First St, 94559 ....(707)257-1649
The Blue Violet Mansion, 443 Brown St, 94559 ....(707)253-2583
Burgundy/Bordeaux House, PO Box 2776, 6600 Washington, 94599 ....(707)944-2855
The Candlelight Inn, 1045 Easum Dr, 94558 ....(707)257-3717
Churchill Manor, 485 Brown St, 94559 ....(707)253-7733
Coombs Residence Inn on the Park, 720 Seminary St, 94559 ....(707)257-0789
Country Garden Inn, 1815 Silverado Trail, 94558 ....(707)255-1197
The Crossroads Inn, 6380 Silverado Tr, 94558 ....(707)944-0646
The Elm House, 800 California St, 94559 ....(707)225-1831
Gallery Osgood B&B Inn, 2230 First St, 94559 ....(707)224-0100
Goodman House, 1225 Division St, 94558 ....(707)257-1166
The Hennessey House B&B, 1727 Main St, 94559 ....(707)226-3774
La Belle Epoque, 1386 Calistoga Ave, 94559 ....(707)257-2161
La Residence Country Inn, 4066 St Helena Hwy, 94558 ....(707)253-0337
Napa Inn, 1137 Warren St, 94559 ....(707)257-1444
Oak Knoll Inn, 2200 E Oak Knoll Ave, 94558 ....(707)255-2200
Old World Inn, 1301 Jefferson, 94559 ....(707)257-0112
Stahlecker House B&B, 1042 Easum Dr, 94558 ....(707)257-1588
Sybron House, 7400 St Helena Hwy, 94559 ....(707)944-2785
Tall Timbers Chalets, 1012 Darms Ln, 94558 ....(707)252-7810

Nevada City — NK11 / *D3*
Downey House, 517 W Broad St, 95959 ....(916)265-2815
Flume's End B&B Inn, 317 S Pine St, 95959 ....(916)265-9665
Grandmere's Inn, 449 Broad St, 95959 ....(916)265-4660
National Hotel, 211 Broad St, 95959 ....(916)265-4551
The Parsonage B&B, 427 Broad St, 95959 ....(916)265-9478
Piety Hill Inn, 523 Sacramento St, 95959 ....(916)265-2245
The Red Castle Inn, 109 Prospect St, 95959 ....(916)265-5135

Newcastle — NL10 / *E3*
Victorian Manor, 482 Main St, 95658 ....(916)663-3009

Newport Beach — SM14 / *K4*
Doryman's Inn, 2102 W Ocean Front, 92663 ....(714)675-7300
Little Inn on the Bay, 617 Lido Park Dr, 92663 ....(714)673-8800

Nice — NK6 / *D1*
Featherbed Railroad Company B&B, 2870 Lakeshore Blvd, 95464 ....(707)274-8378

Nipomo — SI7 / *F2*
The Kaleidoscope Inn, Box 1297, 130 E Dana St, 93444 ....(805)929-5444

Nipton — SG22 / *I7*
Hotel Nipton, HCI, Box 357, 92364 ....(619)856-2335

North Fork — SA10 / *G4*
Ye Old South Fork Inn, 57665 Rd 225, 93643 ....(209)877-7025

North Hollywood — E9 / *J4*
La Maida House, 11154 La Maida St, 91601 ....(818)769-3857

Oakhurst — SA9 / *F4*
Ople's Guest House, 41118 Hwy 41, 93644 ....(209)683-4317

Oakland — NP7 / *E1*
Rockridge B&B, 5428 Thomas Ave, 94618 ....(415)655-1223

Occidental — NM5 / *E1*
Heart's Desire Inn, 3657 Church St, 95465 ....(707)874-1311

Ojai — SK11 / *I3*
Ojai Manor Hotel, 210 E Matilija, 93023 ....(805)646-0961
The Theodore Woolsey House, 1484 E Ojai Ave, 93023 ....(805)646-9779
Wheeler Hot Springs, PO Box 250, 16825 Maricopa, 93023 ....(805)646-8131

Olema — NO6 / *E1*
Bear Valley Inn, PO Box 33, 88 Bear Valley, 94950 ....(415)663-1777
Point Reyes Seashore Lodge, 10021 Coastal Hwy 1, PO Box 39, 94950 ....(415)663-9000
Roundstone Farm, 9940 Sir Francis Drake Blvd, 94950 ....(415)663-1020

Orland — NI8 / *D3*
The Inn at Shallow Creek Farm, Rt 3, Box 3176, 95963 ....(916)865-4093

Orosi — SC11 / *G4*
Valley View Citrus Ranch, 14801 Ave 428, 93647 ....(209)528-2275

Pacific Grove — SC3 / *G1*
Centrella Hotel, PO Box 884, 612 Central, 93950 ....(408)372-3372
Gatehouse Inn, 225 Central Ave, 93950 ....(408)649-8436
Gosby House Inn, 643 Lighthouse Ave, 93950 ....(408)375-1287
Green Gables Inn, 104 5th St, 93950 ....(408)375-2095
Maison Bleu, Box 51371, 93950 ....(408)373-2993
Martine Inn, 255 Ocean View Blvd, 93950 ....(408)373-3388
Old St Angela Inn, 321 Central Ave, 93950 ....(408)372-3246
Roserox Country Inn By-The-Sea, 557 Ocean View Blvd, 93950 ....(408)373-7673
Seven Gables Inn, 555 Ocean View Blvd, 93950 ....(408)372-4341

Palm Springs — SM18 / *K5*
Casa Cody Country Inn, 175 S Cahuilla, 92262 ....(619)320-9346
Ingleside Inn, 200 W Ramon Rd, 92262 ....(619)325-0046
Sakura, Japanese B&B, PO Box 9403, 92263 ....(619)327-0705
Villa Royale Inn, 1620 S Indian Tr, 92264 ....(619)327-2314

Palo Alto — NQ7 / *F1*
Cowper Inn, 705 Cowper St, 94301 ....(415)327-4475
The Victorian On Lytton, 555 Lytton Ave, 94301 ....(415)322-8555

Paso Robles — SG7 / *H2*
Almond View Inn, 912 Walnut Dr, 93446 ....(805)238-4220

Petaluma — NN6 / *E1*
The 7th Street Inn, 525 7th St, 94952 ....(707)769-0480
Cavanagh Inn, 10 Keller St, 94952 ....(707)765-4657

Philo — NK4 / *D1*
Philo Pottery Inn, PO Box 166, 8550 Rt 128, 95466 ....(707)895-3069

PLACERVILLE NL11 / *E3*
Chichester House B&B, 800 Spring St, 95667 ....(916)626-1882
Fleming-Jones Homestead, 3170 Newton Rd, 95667 ....(916)626-5840
Historic Combellack-Blair House, 3059 Cedar Ravine, 95667 ....(916)622-3764
River Rock Inn, PO Box 827, 1756 Georgetown Rd, 95667 ....(916)622-7640

PLEASANTON NP8 / *F2*
Plum Tree Inn, 262 W Angela, 94566 ....(415)426-9588

POINT ARENA NL4 / *D1*
Coast Guard House, 695 Arena Cove, 95468 ....(707)882-2442
Wagner's Windhaven, 46760 Iversen Ln, 95468 ....(707)884-4617

POINT REYES NO5 / *EI*
Holly Tree Inn, Box 642, Pt Reyes St, 94956 ....(415)663-1554

POINT REYES STATION NO6 / *E1*
Carriage House, 325 Mesa Rd, PO Box 1239, 94956 ....(415)663-8627
The Country House, 65 Manana Way, PO Box 98, 94956 ....(415)663-1627
Ferrando's Hideaway, 12010 Hwy 1, 94956 ....(415)663-1966
London House, 11549 State Rt 1, 95956 ....(415)388-2487
Seashore B&B of Marin, PO Box 1239, 94956 ....(415)663-8627
Thirty-nine Cypress, 39 Cypress St, 94956 ....(415)663-1709

POINT RICHMOND NO7 / *E1*
East Brother Light Station Inc, 117 Park Pt, 94801 ....(415)233-2385

PORTOLA NI12 / *D4*
Upper Feather B&B, 256 Commercial St, Box 1528, 96122-1528 ....(916)832-0107

PRINCETON-BY-THE-SEA NQ7 / *F1*
Pillar Point Inn, PO Box 388, El Granada, 94018 ....(415)728-7377

QUINCY NH11 / *D3*
The Feather Bed, 542 Jackson St, PO Box 3200, 95971 ....(916)283-0102

RANCHO CUCAMONGA SL15 / *J4*
Christmas House B&B Inn, 9240 Archibald Ave, 91730 ....(714)980-6450

RED BLUFF NG7 / *C2*
Buttons & Bows B&B Inn, 427 Washington St, 96080 ....(916)527-6405
Faulkner House, 1029 Jefferson St, 96080 ....(916)529-0520
The Jarvis Mansion, 1313 Jackson St, 96080 ....(916)527-6901
The Jeter Victorian Inn, 1107 Jefferson St, 96080 ....(916)527-7574

REDDING NF7 / *C2*
Palisades Paradise B&B, 1200 Palisades Ave, 96003 ....(916)223-5305
Redding's B&B, 1094 Palisades, 96003 ....(916)222-2494

REDLANDS SL17 / *J5*
Georgianna Manor, 816 East High Ave, 92374 ....(714)793-0423
Morey Mansion, 190 Terracina Blvd., 92373 ....(714)793-7970

REEDLEY SC10 / *G3*
Hotel Burgess, 1726 11th St, 93654 ....(209)638-6315

ROMOLAND SM17 / *K5*
The Ozarks, 29011 Watson Rd, 92380 ....(714)679-1001

RUTHERFORD NM7 / *E2*
Rancho Caymus Inn, PO Box 78, 94573 ....(707)963-1777

SACRAMENTO NN10 / *E2*
Amber House, 1315 22nd St, 95816 ....(916)444-8085
Aunt Abigail's, 2120 G St, 95816 ....(916)441-5007
Bear Flag Inn, 2814 I St, 95816 ....(916)448-5417
Driver Mansion Inn, 2019 21st St, 95818 ....(916)455-5243
River Rose, 8201 Freeport Blvd, 95832 ....(916)665-1998
Sterling Hotel, 1300 H St, 95814 ....(916)448-1300

SAINT HELENA NM7 / *E2*
Ambrose Bierce House, 1515 Main St, 94574 ....(707)963-3003
Bartels Ranch & Country Inn, 1200 Conn Valley Rd, 94574 ....(707)963-4001
Bell Creek B&B, 3220 Silverado Trail, 94574 ....(707)963-2383
Chestelson House, 1417 Kearney St, 94574 ....(707)963-2238
Cinnamon Bear B&B, 1407 Kearney St, 94574 ....(707)963-4653
Creekside Inn, 945 Main St, 94574 ....(707)963-7244
Deer Run B&B, 3995 Spring Mtn Rd, 94574 ....(707)963-3794
Elsie's Conn Valley Inn, 726 Rosse Rd, 94574 ....(707)963-4614
Erika's Hillside, 285 Fawn Park, 94574 ....(707)963-2887
Hotel Saint Helena, 1309 Main St, 94574 ....(707)963-4388
Ink House, 1575 St Helena Hwy, 94574 ....(707)963-3890
Judy's Ranch House, 701 Rossi Rd, 94574 ....(707)963-3081
La Fleur B&B, 1475 Inglewood Ave, 94574 ....(707)963-0233
Oliver House B&B Country Inn, 2970 Silverado Tr, 94574 ....(707)963-4089
Prager Winery B&B, 1281 Lewelling Ln, 94574 ....(707)963-3713
Rustridge Ranch, 2910 Lower Chiles Valley Rd, 94574 ....(707)965-9353
Shady Oaks Country Inn, 399 Zinfandel, 94574 ....(707)963-1190
Spanish Villa Inn, 474 Glass Mountain Rd, 94574 ....(707)963-7483
Vigne Del Uomo Felice, 1871 Cabernet Ln, 94574 ....(707)963-2376
Villa St. Helena, 2727 Sulphur Springs Ave, 94574 ....(707)963-2514
White Ranch, 707 White Ln, 94574 ....(707)963-4635
Wine Country Inn, 1152 Lodi Ln, 94574 ....(707)963-7077
Zinfandel Inn, 800 Zinfandel Ln, 94574 ....(707)963-3512

SAN ANDREAS NN12 / *E3*
Black Bart Inn, PO Box 576, 55 St Charles, 95249 ....(209)754-3808
Robin's Nest, PO Box 1408, 247 W St Charles, 95249 ....(209)754-1076

SAN CLEMENTE SN15 / *K4*
Casa de Flores B&B, 184 Ave La Cuesta, 92672 ....(714)498-1344
Casa Tropicana B&B, 610 Avenida Victoria, 92672 ....(714)492-1234

SAN DIEGO SN19 / *L4*
Balboa Park Inn, 3402 Park Blvd, 92130 ....(619)298-0823
Beverly McGahey, 6943 Beagle St, 92111 ....(619)279-5435
Britt House, 406 Maple St, 92103 ....(619)234-2926
Harbor Hill Guest House, 2330 Albatross St, 92101 ....(619)233-0638
Heritage Park B&B Inn, 2470 Heritage Park Row, 92110 ....(619)295-7088
Keating House Inn, 2331 Second Ave, 92101 ....(619)239-8585
The Quince Street Trolley, PO Box 7654, 92107 ....(619)226-8454

SAN FRANCISCO ND21 / *E1*
1818 California, 1818 California St, 94109 ....(415)885-1818
A Country Cottage, 5 Dolores Ter, PO Box 349, 94101 ....(415)931-3083
Albion House, 135 Gough St, 94102 ....(415)621-0896
The Amsterdam Hotel, 749 Taylor St, 94108 ....(415)673-3444
Andrews Hotel, 624 Post St, 94109 ....(415)563-6877
Archbishop's Mansion, 1000 Fulton St, 94117 ....(415)563-7872
Art Center/Wamsley Gallery/B&B, 1902 Filbert St, 94123 ....(415)567-1526
B&B Inn, 4 Charlton Ct, 94123 ....(415)921-9784
B&B Near The Park, 1387 Sixth Ave, 94122 ....(415)753-3574
Bock's B&B, 1448 Willard St, 94117 ....(415)664-6842
Casa Arguello, 225 Arguello Blvd, 94118 ....(415)752-9482
The Chateau Tivoli, 1057 Steiner St, 94115 ....(415)776-5462
Dolores Park Inn, 3641 17th St, 94114 ....(415)621-0482
Edward II Inn, 3155 Scott St, 94123 ....(415)921-9776
El Drisco Hotel, 2901 Pacific Ave, 94115 ....(415)346-2880
Golden Gate Hotel, 775 Bush St, 94108 ....(415)392-3702
Grove Inn, 890 Grove St, 94117 ....(415)929-0780
Hermitage House, 2224 Sacramento St, 94115 ....(415)921-5515
The Inn San Francisco, 943 S Van Ness, 94110 ....(415)641-0188
Jackson Court, 2198 Jackson St, 94115 ....(415)929-7670
Marina Inn B&B, 3110 Octavia St, 94123 ....(415)928-1000
Millefiori Inn, 444 Columbus Ave, 94133 ....(415)433-9111
Moffatt House, 431 Hugo St, 94122 ....(415)661-6210
Monte Cristo, 600 Presidio Ave, 94115 ....(415)931-1875
The No Name B&B, PO Box 349, 94101 ....(415)931-3083
The Nolan House A Bed & Breakfast Inn, 1071 Page St, 94117 ....(415)863-0384
Obrero Hotel & Basque Restaurant, 1208 Stockton St, 94133 ....(415)989-3960
Petite Auberge, 863 Bush St, 94108 ....(415)928-6000
Riley's B&B, 1234 Sixth Ave, 94122 ....(415)731-0788
San Remo Hotel, 2237 Mason St, 94133 ....(415)776-8688
Sherman House, 2160 Green St, 94123 ....(415)563-3600
Spencer House, 1080 Haight St, 94117 ....(415)626-9205
Stanyan Park Hotel, 750 Stanyan St, 94117 ....(415)751-1000
The Inn at Union Square, 440 Post St, 94102 ....(415)397-3510
Union Street Inn, 2229 Union St, 94123 ....(415)345-0424
Victorian Inn On The Park, 301 Lyon St, 94117 ....(415)931-1830
Washington Square Inn, 1660 Stockton St, 94117 ....(415)981-4220
White Swan Inn, 845 Bush St, 94108 ....(415)775-1755
Willows B&B Inn, 710 14th St, 94114 ....(415)431-4770

SAN GREGORIO SA2 / *F1*
Rancho San Gregorio, 5086 San Gregorio Rd, Box 21, 94074 ....(415)747-0722

SAN JOSE NQ8 / *F2*
The Briar Rose B&B Inn, 897 E Jackson St, 95112 ....(408)279-5999
The Hensley House, 456 N Third St, 95112 ....(408)298-3537

SAN JUAN BAUTISTA SB4 / *F2*
B&B San Juan, PO Box 613, 95045 ....(408)623-4101

SAN LEANDRO NP7 / *F2*
Best House, 1315 Clarke St, 94577 ....(415)351-0911

SAN LUIS OBISPO SG8 / *H2*
Apple Farm Inn, 2015 Monterey St, 93401 ....(805)544-2040
Garden Street Inn, 1212 Garden Street, 93401 ....(805)545-9802
Heritage Inn, 978 Olive St, 93401 ....(805)544-7440

SAN MARTIN SB4 / *F2*
Country Rose Inn, 455 Fitzgerald Ave, 95046 ....(408)842-0441

SAN MIGUEL SF7 / *H2*
Victorian Manor B&B, 3200 N Mission, Box 8, 93451 ....(805)467-3306

SAN PEDRO L8 / *J4*
Grand Cottages, 809 S Grand Ave, 90731 ....(213)548-1240

SAN RAFAEL NO6 / *E1*
Casa Soldavini, 531 "C" St, 94901 ....(415)454-3140
Panama Hotel, 4 Bayview St, 94901 ....(415)457-3993

SANTA ANA SM15 / *J4*
The Craftsman, 2900 N Flower St, 92706 ....(714)543-1168

SANTA BARBARA SJ9 / *I3*
The Arlington Inn, 1136 De LaVina St, 93101 ....(805)965-6532
B&B at Valli's View, 340 N Sierra Vista, 93108 ....(805)969-1272
Bath Street Inn, 1720 Bath St, 93101 ....(805)682-9680
Bayberry Inn, 111 W Valerio, 93101 ....(805)682-3199
Blue Quail Inn, 1908 Bath St, 93101 ....(805)687-2300

Cheshire Cat Inn, 36 W Valerio, 93101 .... (805)569-1610
Glenborough Inn, 1327 Bath St, 93101 .... (805)966-0589
Harbour Carriage House, 420 W Montecito St, 93101 .... (805)962-8447
The Old Yacht Club Inn, 431 Corona Del Mar, 93103 .... (805)962-1277
Olive House, 1604 Olive St, 93101 .... (805)962-4902
The Parsonage, 1600 Olive St, 93101 .... (805)962-9336
Simpson House Inn, 121 E Arrellaga St, 93101 .... (805)963-7067
Tiffany Inn, 1323 De La Vina, 93101 .... (805)963-2283
The Upham Hotel & Garden Cottages, 1404 De La Vina St, 93101 .... (805)962-0058
Villa d' Italia, 780 Mission Canyon Rd, 93105 .... (805)687-6933
Villa Rosa, 15 Chapala St, 93101 .... (805)966-0851

SANTA CLARA — NQ9 / *F2*
Madison Street Inn, 1390 Madison St, 95050 .... (408)249-5541

SANTA CRUZ — SA2 / *F1*
Babbling Brook B&B Inn, 1025 Laurel St, 95060 .... (408)427-2437
Chateau Victorian, 118 First St, 95060 .... (408)458-9458
Cliff Crest, 407 Cliff St, 95060 .... (408)427-2609
Darling House, 314 W Cliff Dr, 95060 .... (408)458-1958
Pleasure Point Inn, 2-3665 E Cliff Dr, 95062 .... (408)475-4657

SANTA MONICA — SL13 / *J4*
Channel Road Inn, 219 W Channel Rd, 90402 .... (213)459-1920
Sovereign at Santa Monica Bay, 205 Washington Ave, 90403 .... (800)331-0163

SANTA PAULA — SK11 / *I3*
Glen Tavern Inn, 134 N Mill St, 93060 .... (805)525-6658
The Lemon Tree Inn, 299 W Santa Paula St, 93060 .... (805)525-7747

SANTA ROSA — NM6 / *E1*
The Gables, 4257 Petaluma Hill Rd, 95404 .... (707)585-7777
Gee-Gee's B&B Inn, 7810 Sonoma Hwy, 95405 .... (707)833-6667
Hilltop House B&B, 9550 St Helena Rd, 95404 .... (707)944-0880
Melitta Station Inn, 5850 Melita Rd, 95409 .... (707)538-7712
Pygmalion House, 331 Orange St, 95407 .... (707)526-3407
Sunrise B&B, 1500 Olivet Rd, 95401 .... (707)542-5781
The Inn at the Belvedere, 727 Mendocino Ave, 95401 .... (707)575-1857
Vintners Inn, 4350 Barnes Rd, 95403 .... (707)575-7350

SAUSALITO — NL19 / *E1*
Alta Mira Hotel, 125 Bulkley St, 94965 .... (415)332-1350
Casa Madrona Hotel, 801 Bridgeway, 94965 .... (415)332-0502
Sausalito Hotel, 16 El Portal, 94965 .... (415)332-4155

SCOTIA — NF3 / *B1*
The Scotia Inn, Corner of Mill & Main St, 95565 .... (707)764-5683

SEA RANCH — NL4 / *D1*
Sea Ranch Lodge, PO Box 44, 95497 .... (707)785-2371

SEAL BEACH — L11 / *J4*
The Seal Beach Inn & Gardens, 212 5th St, 90740 .... (213)493-2416

SEBASTOPOL — NM5 / *E1*
The Strout House - Ken & Fran's B&B, 253 Florence Ave, 95472 .... (707)823-5188

SIERRA CITY — NJ12 / *D3*
Busch & Heringlake Country Inn, PO Box 68, 96125 .... (916)862-1501
High Country Inn, Hwy 49 at Bassetts, 96125 .... (916)862-1530

SIERRAVILLE — NI12 / *D4*
Campbell Hot Springs Spiritual Retreat, Box 234 #1 Campbell Hot Springs Rd, 96126 .... (916)994-3737

SKY FOREST — SK17 / *J5*
Storybook Inn, PO Box 362, 28717 Hwy 18, 92385 .... (714)336-1483

SODA SPRINGS — NJ12 / *D3*
Rainbow Lodge, Old Hwy 40, 95728 .... (916)426-3871

SOMIS — SK12 / *J3*
Rancho De Somis, 6441 La Cumbre Rd, 93066 .... (805)987-8455

SONOMA — NM5 / *E2*
Chalet B&B, 18935 5th St W, 95476 .... (707)938-3129
The Hidden Oak, 214 E Napa St, 95476 .... (707)996-9863
Magliulo's Pensione, 681 Broadway, 95476 .... (707)996-1031
Sonoma Hotel, 110 W Spain St, 95476 .... (707)996-2996
Trojan Horse Inn, 19455 Sonoma Hwy, 95476 .... (707)996-2430
Victorian Garden Inn, 316 E Napa St, 95476 .... (707)996-5339

SONORA — NO12 / *F3*
Barretta Gardens Inn, 700 S Barretta St, 95370 .... (209)532-6039
Gunn House, 286 S Washington St, 95370 .... (209)532-3421
Historic Sonora Inn, 160 S Washington, 95370 .... (209)532-7468
Jameson's, 22157 Feather River, 95370 .... (209)532-1248
La Casa Inglesa, 18047 Lime Kiln Rd, 95370 .... (209)532-5822
Lavender Hill B&B, 683 S Barretta St, 95370 .... (209)532-9024
Llamahall Guest Ranch, 18170 Wards Ferry Rd, 95370 .... (209)532-7264
Lulu Belle's, 85 Gold St, 95370 .... (209)533-3455
Oliver's, 56 W Bradford St, 95370 .... (209)532-0275
The Ryan House B&B, 153 S Shepherd St, 95370 .... (209)533-3445
Serenity, 15305 Bear Cub Dr, 95370 .... (209)533-1441
Via Serena Ranch, 18007 Via Serena Dr, 95370 .... (209)532-5307

SOQUEL — SB3 / *F1*
Blue Spruce Inn, 2815 S Main St, 95073 .... (408)464-1137

SOULSBYVILLE — NO13 / *F3*
Willow Springs Country Inn, 20599 Kings Ct., 95372 .... (209)533-2030

SOUTH LAKE TAHOE — NL13 / *E4*
Christiana Inn, PO Box 18298, 95706 .... (916)544-7337
Strawberry Lodge, Hwy 50, 95720 .... (916)659-7030

STANFORD — NJ24 / *F1*
Adella Villa, Box 4528, 94309 .... (415)321-5195

STINSON BEACH — NO6 / *E1*
Casa Del Mar, 37 Belvedere Ave, 94970 .... (415)868-2124

STOCKTON — NO10 / *F2*
The Old Victorian Inn, 207 W Acacia, 95203 .... (209)462-1613

SUMMERLAND — SK10 / *I3*
The Inn on Summer Hill, 2520 Lillie Ave, 93067 .... (805)969-9998

SUNSET BEACH — L12 / *J4*
Sunset B&B Inn, PO Box 1202, 90742 .... (213)592-1666

SUSANVILLE — NG12 / *C4*
The Roseberry House, 609 N St, 96130 .... (916)257-5675

SUTTER CREEK — NN11 / *F3*
The Gold Quartz Inn, 15 Bryson Dr, 95685 .... (209)267-9155
Hanford House, PO Box 847, 95685 .... (209)267-0747
Nancy & Bob's 9 Eureka Street Inn, 55 Eureka St, PO Box 386, 95685 .... (209)267-0342
Sutter Creek Inn, PO Box 385, 7 Main St, 95685 .... (209)267-5606
The Foxes, PO Box 159, 77 Main St, 95685 .... (209)267-5882

TAHOE CITY — NK13 / *E4*
Cedar Tree, PO Box 7106, 95730 .... (916)583-5421
The Cottage Inn, 1690 W Lake Blvd, PO Box 66, 95730 .... (916)581-4073
Mayfield House, 236 Grove St, PO Box 5999, 95730 .... (916)583-1001
River Ranch, PO Box 197, Hwy 89, 95730 .... (916)583-4264

TAHOMA — NK13 / *E4*
The Captain's Alpenhaus, 6941 W Lake Blvd, 95733 .... (916)525-5000

TEMECULA — SN17 / *K5*
Loma Vista B&B, 33350 L Serena Way, 92390 .... (714)676-7047

TEMPLETON — SG6 / *H2*
Country House Inn, 91 Main St, 93465 .... (805)434-1598

THREE RIVERS — SO12 / *G4*
Cort Cottage, PO Box 245, 93271 .... (209)501-4671

TIMBERCOVE — NM5 / *E1*
Timberhill Ranch, 35755 Hauser Bridge Rd, 95421 .... (707)847-3477

TOMALES — NN6 / *E1*
U.S. Hotel, 26985 State Hwy 1, 94971 .... (707)878-2742

TRINIDAD — ND3 / *B1*
Trinidad B&B, PO Box 849, 560 Edwards, 95570 .... (707)677-0840

TRINITY CENTER — NE6 / *B2*
Carrville Inn B&B, Carrville Loop Rd, 96091 .... (916)266-3511

TRUCKEE — NI13 / *D4*
Alta Hotel, PO Box 2118, 95734 .... (916)587-6668
Blue House Inn, 7660 Hwy 89, 95737 .... (916)582-8415
Bradley House, PO Box 2011, 95734 .... (916)587-5388
Richardson House, Spring & High Sts, 95734 .... (916)587-5388

TUOLUMNE — NO14 / *F4*
Oak Hill Ranch, Box 307, 95379 .... (209)928-4717

TWAIN HARTE — NO13 / *F3*
Twain Harte's B&B, PO Box 1718, 95383 .... (209)586-3311

UKIAH — NK5 / *D1*
Oak Knoll B&B, 858 Sanel Dr, 95482 .... (707)468-5646
Sanford House, 306 S Pine, 95482 .... (707)462-1653
Vichy Hot Springs Resort & Inn, 2605 Vichy Springs Rd, 95482 .... (707)462-9515

UNION CITY — NG25 / *F2*
Alexanders Inn-Tenders, PO Box 754, 94587 .... (415)429-0688

VALLEY FORD — NN5 / *E1*
The Inn at Valley Ford, PO Box 439, 14395 Hwy 1, 94972 .... (707)876-3182

VENICE — G6 / *J4*
Venice Beach House, 15 30th Ave, 90291 .... (213)823-1966

VENTURA — SJ11 / *J3*
Bella Maggiore Inn, 67 S California St, 93001 .... (805)652-0277
The Clocktower Inn, 181 E Santa Clara St, 93001 .... (805)652-0141
La Mer, 411 Poli St, 93001 .... (805)643-3600

VOLCANO — NM12 / *E3*
St. George Hotel, 16104 Pine Grove-Volcano Rd, 95689 .... (209)296-4458

WALNUT CREEK — NO8 / *E2*
The Mansion At Lakewood, 1056 Hacienda Dr, 94598 .... (415)946-9075

WATSONVILLE SB4 / *F2*
Dunmovin, 1006 Hecker Pass Rd, 95076 .... (408)728-4154

WEST COVINA F14 / *J4*
Hendrick Inn, 2124 E Merced Ave, 91791 .... (818)919-2125

WESTPORT NI13 / *C1*
Bowen's Pelican Lodge & Inn, PO Box 35, 38921 N Hwy 1, 95488 .... (707)964-5588
Howard Creek Ranch, 40501 N Hwy, PO Box 121, 95488 .... (707)964-6725

WHITTIER SL14 / *J4*
Coleen's California Casa, 11715 S Circle Dr, 90601 .... (213)699-8427

WILLIAMS NK8 / *D2*
Wilbur Hot Springs, 95987 .... (916)473-2306

WILLITS NJ4 / *C1*
The Doll House B&B, 118 School St, 95490 .... (707)459-4055

WINDSOR NM6 / *D1*
Country Meadow Inn, 11360 Old Redwood Hwy, 94492 .... (707)431-1276

WRIGHTWOOD SK15 / *J4*
Albar Country B&B, PO Box 127, 92397 .... (619)249-4755

YOSEMITE, WAWONA NQ14 / *F4*
Telaro's Wawona B&B, 7951 Koon Hollar Rd, PO Box 2215, 95389 .... (209)375-6582

YOUNTVILLE NM7 / *E2*
Burgundy House Inn, 6711 Washington St, 94599 .... (707)944-0889
Magnolia Hotel, PO Box M, 6529 Yount St, 94599 .... (707)944-2056
Napa Valley Railway Inn, Box 2568, 6503 Washington, 94599 .... (707)944-2000
Oleander House, PO Box 2937, 7433 St Helena Hwy, 94599 .... (707)944-8315
The Webber Place, Box 2873, 94599 .... (707)944-8384

YREKA NB7 / *A2*
McFadden's Inn, 418 Third St, 96097 .... (916)842-7712

YUBA CITY NK9 / *D2*
Harkey House B&B, 212 C St, 95991 .... (916)674-1942
The Wicks, 560 Cooper Ave, 95991 .... (916)674-7951

COLORADO

ALAMOSA N11 / *F4*
Cottonwood Inn, 123 San Juan, 81101 .... (719)589-3882

ALLENSPARK E11 / *B4*
Lazy H Ranch, Box 248, 80510 .... (303)747-2532

ARVADA F13 / *C4*
On Golden Pond B&B, 7831 Eldridge, 80005 .... (303)424-2296

ASPEN H8 / *D3*
Alpina Haus, 935 E Durant, 81611 .... (800)242-7736
Ambiance Inn, 66 N 2nd St, PO Box 10932, 81612 .... (303)963-3597
Aspen Ski Lodge, 101 W Main St, 81611 .... (303)925-3434
Brass Bed Inn, 926 E Durant, 81611 .... (303)925-3622
Christmas Inn, 232 W Main St, 81611 .... (303)925-3822
Copper Horse House, 328 W Main St, 81611 .... (303)925-7525
Fireside Inn, 130 W Cooper, 81611 .... (303)925-6000
Hearthstone House, 134 E Hyman St, 81611 .... (303)925-7632
Hotel Lenado, 200 S Aspen St, 81611 .... (303)925-6246
Independence Square Hotel, 404 S Galena St, 81611 .... (303)920-2313
Innsbruck Inn, 233 W Main St, 81611 .... (303)925-2980
Little Red Ski Haus, 118 E Cooper, 81611 .... (303)925-3333
Pomegranate Inn, Box 1368, 81612 .... (800)525-4012
Sardy House, 128 E Main St, 81611 .... (303)920-2525
Snow Queen Lodge, 124 E Cooper, 81611 .... (303)925-8455
Tipple Inn, 747 S Galena St, 81611 .... (800)321-7025
Ullr Lodge, 520 W Main St, 81611 .... (303)925-7696

BAYFIELD D5 / *F2*
Deer Valley Resorts, PO Box 796, 81122 .... (303)884-2600

BOULDER E12 / *C4*
The Inn at Boulder Victoria, 1305 Pine St, 80302 .... (303)938-1305
Briar Rose B&B, 2151 Arapahoe, 80302 .... (303)442-3007
Pearl Street Inn, 1820 Pearl St, 80302 .... (303)444-5584
Sandy Point Inn, 6485 Twin Lakes Rd, 80301 .... (303)530-2939

BRECKENRIDGE G10 / *C4*
Fireside Inn, 212 Wellington, PO Box 2252, 80424 .... (303)453-6456

BUENA VISTA J10 / *D3*
Adobe Inn, Box 1560, 303 N Hwy 24, 81211 .... (719)395-6340
Blue Sky Inn, 719 Arizona St, 81211 .... (719)395-8865

CARBONDALE H7 / *C2*
Crystal River Inn, Hell Roaring Ranch, 12954 Hwy 133, 81657 .... (303)963-3902

CASCADE I13 / *D5*
Eastholme, PO Box 98, 4445 Haggerman, 80809 .... (719)684-9901

CENTRAL CITY F11 / *C4*
Golden Rose Inn, PO Box 157, 80427 .... (303)582-5060
Two Ten Casey, PO Box 154, 80427 .... (303)582-5906

CLARK C7 / *B3*
Home Ranch, Box 822, 80428 .... (303)879-1780

COLORADO SPRINGS J13 / *D5*
Hearthstone Inn, 506 N Cascade Ave, 80903 .... (719)473-4413
Holden House-1902 B&B, 1102 W Pikes Peak Ave, 80904 .... (719)471-3980
Katies Korner, 1304 N El Paso, 80903 .... (719)630-3322

CREEDE M7 / *E3*
4UR Ranch, PO Box 340, 81130 .... (303)658-2202

CRESTED BUTTE I7 / *D3*
Claim Jumper Inn, 704 Whiterock, Box 1181, 81224 .... (303)349-6471
Forest Queen Hotel, Box 127 2nd/Elk Ave, 81224 .... (303)349-5336
Nordic Inn, PO Box 939, 81224 .... (303)349-5542
Purple Mountain Lodge, PO Box 897, 714 Gothic Ave, 81224 .... (303)349-5888

CRIPPLE CREEK J12 / *D4*
Imperial Hotel, 123 N Third St, 80813 .... (719)689-2922

DELORES N3 / *F1*
Rio Grande Southern Hotel, 101 S 5th St, 81323 .... (303)882-7527

DENVER F13 / *C5*
Cambridge Club Hotel, 1560 Sherman, 80203 .... (303)831-1252
Castle Marne, 1572 Race St, 80206 .... (303)331-0621
The Oxford Alexis, 1600 17th St, 80202 .... (800)228-5838
Queen Anne Inn, 2147 Tremont Place, 80205 .... (303)296-6666
Sheets Residence, 577 High St, 80218 .... (303)329-6170
The Merritt House, 941 E 17th Ave, 80218 .... (303)861-5230
Victoria Oaks Inn, 1575 Race St, 80206 .... (303)355-1818

DURANGO O5 / *F2*
B&B Durango, PO Box 544, 81301 .... (303)247-2223
Blue Lake Ranch, 16919 Hwy 140, 81326 .... (303)385-4537
Logwood B&B, 35060 US Hwy 550, 81301 .... (303)259-4396
Penny's Place, 1041 County Rd 307, 81301 .... (303)247-8928
River House B&B, 495 County Rd 203, 81301 .... (303)247-4775
Scrubby Oaks B&B, PO Box 1047, 83102 .... (303)247-2176
Tall Timber, Box 90G, 81301 .... (303)259-4813
Victorian Inn, 2117 W Second Ave, 81301 .... (303)247-2223

EDWARDS F8 / *C3*
The Lodge at Cordillera, PO Box 1110, 81632 .... (303)926-2200

ELDORA F11 / *C4*
Goldminer Hotel, 601 Klondyke Ave, 80466 .... (303)258-7770

ESTES PARK D11 / *B4*
Aspen Lodge, Longs Peak Rte, 80517 .... (303)586-4241
The Baldpate Inn, PO Box 4445RM, 80517 .... (303)586-6151
Emerald Manor, 441 Chiquita Lane, PO Box 3592, 80517 .... (303)586-8050
RiverSong, PO Box 1910, 80517 .... (303)586-4666
Wanek's Lodge at Estes, Box 898, 80517 .... (303)586-5851
Wind River Ranch, PO Box 3410, 80517 .... (303)586-4212

FORT COLLINS C12 / *B4*
Helmshire Inn, 1204 S College, 80524 .... (303)493-4683

FRISCO G10 / *C3*
Frisco Lodge, 321 Main St, 80443 .... (303)668-0195
The Lark B&B, 109 Granite St, PO Box 1646, 80443 .... (303)668-5237

GEORGETOWN F11 / *C4*
The Hardy House, 605 Brownell St, Box 0156, 80444 .... (303)569-3388

GLEN HAVEN C12 / *B4*
The Inn of Glen Haven, 7468 Devils Gulch Rd 43, PO Box 19, 80532 .... (303)586-3897

GLENWOOD SPRINGS G6 / *C2*
Hideout, 1293 County Road 117, 81601 .... (303)945-5621
Kaiser House, 932 Cooper Ave, PO Box 1952, 81602 .... (303)945-8827
Sunlight Inn, 10252 Rd 117, 81601 .... (303)945-5225
Talbott House, 928 Colorado Ave, 81601 .... (303)945-1039

GOLDEN F12 / *C4*
The Dove Inn, 711 14th St, 80401 .... (303)278-2209

GRANBY E10 / *B4*
Drowsy Water Ranch, Box 147A, 80446 .... (303)725-3456

GRAND JUNCTION I3 / *D1*
The Gatehouse, 2502 N 1st St, 81501 .... (303)242-6105

GRANT G11 / *C4*
Tumbling River Ranch, 80448 .... (303)838-5981

GREEN MOUNTAIN FALLS I13 / *D4*
Columbine Lodge, Box 267, 80819 .... (719)684-9062
Outlook Lodge, Box 5, 80819 .... (719)684-2303

GUNNISON K7 / *D3*
The Mary Lawrence Inn, 601 N Taylor, 81230 .... (303)641-3343
Waunita Hot Springs Ranch, 8007 County Rd 877, 81230 .... (303)641-1266

GYPSUM G7 / *C3*
7-W Guest Ranch, 3412 County Rd 151, 81637 .... (303)524-9328
Sweetwater Creek Guest Ranch, 2650 Sweetwater Rd, 81637 .... (303)524-9301

HOTCHKISS J5 / *D2*
Ye Ole Oasis, 3142 J Rd, PO Box 609, 81419 ....(303)872-3794

IGNACIO P5 / *F2*
Ute Creek Ranch, 2192 County Rd 334, 81137 ....(303)563-4464

LA VETA N13 / *F4*
1899 B&B Inn, 314 S Main, 81055 ....(719)742-3576

LAKE CITY M6 / *E2*
Crystal Lodge, 81235 ....(303)944-2201

LEADVILLE H9 / *C3*
Hilltop House, 100 W 9th St, 80461 ....(719)486-2362
The Leadville Country Inn, 127 E Eighth St, 80461 ....(719)486-2354

LIMON H16 / *C6*
Midwest Country Inn, Box X, 795 Main St, 80828 ....(303)775-2373

LOVELAND D12 / *B4*
The Lovelander, 217 W 4th St, 80537 ....(303)669-0798

MANITOU SPRINGS I13 / *D5*
Billy's Cottage, 117 Deer Path, 80829 ....(719)685-1828
Sunnymede, 106 Spencer, 80829 ....(719)685-4619
Two Sisters Inn, 10 Otoe Pl, 80829 ....(719)685-9684

MEREDITH H8 / *C3*
Diamond J Guest Ranch, 26604 Frying Pan Rd, 81642 ....(303)927-3222

MINTURN G9 / *C3*
Eagle River Inn, PO Box 100, 145 N Main St, 81645 ....(303)827-5761

MORRISON G12 / *C4*
Cliff House Lodge, 121 Stone St, 80465 ....(303)697-9732

NATHROP J10 / *D3*
Deer Valley Ranch, Box Y, 81236 ....(303)395-2353

OURAY L5 / *E2*
Baker's Manor, 317 Second St, 81427 ....(303)325-4574
House Of Yesteryear, Box 440, 81427 ....(303)325-4277
The Manor Bed & Breakfast, PO Box 80, 317 Second St, 81427 ....(303)325-4574
St. Elmo Hotel, 426 Main St, PO Box 667, 81427 ....(303)325-4951
Wiesbaden Hot Springs Spa & Lodge, PO Box 349, 625 5th St, 81427 ....(303)325-4347

PAGOSA SPRINGS O7 / *F3*
Davidson's Country Inn B&B, Box 87, Hwy 160, 81147 ....(303)264-5863
Echo Manor Inn, 3366 Hwy 84, 81147 ....(303)264-5646
Royal Pine Inn, 152 CR 337, 81147 ....(303)731-4179

PARSHALL E9 / *B3*
Bar Lazy J Guest Ranch, Box N, 80468 ....(303)725-3437

PUEBLO L14 / *E5*
Abriendo Inn, 300 W Abriendo Ave, 81004 ....(719)544-2703

REDSTONE H6 / *D2*
Avalanche Ranch, 12863 Highway 133, 81623 ....(303)963-2846
Historic Redstone Inn, 82 Redstone Blvd, 81623 ....(303)963-2526
Redstone Castle, 0058 Redstone Blvd, 81623 ....(303)963-3463

RIDGWAY L5 / *E2*
MacTiernan's San Juan Ranch, 2882 Hwy 23, 81432 ....(303)626-5360
Pueblo Hostel & Cantina, PO Box 346, 81432 ....(303)626-5939

RIFLE G5 / *C2*
Coulter Lake Guest Ranch, PO Box 906, 81650 ....(303)625-1473

SALIDA K10 / *D4*
Poor Farm Country Inn, 8495 Co Rd 160, 81201 ....(719)539-3818

SHAWNEE E6 / *B2*
North Fork Ranch, Box B, 80475 ....(303)838-9873

SILVER PLUME F10 / *C4*
Brewery Inn, 246 Main St, PO Box 473, 80476 ....(303)674-5565

SILVERTON M5 / *E2*
Alma House, PO Box 780, 81433 ....(303)387-5336
Fool's Gold, 1069 Snowden, 81433 ....(303)387-5879
Grand Imperial Hotel, 1219 Greene St, 81433 ....(303)387-5527
Teller House Hotel, 1250 Greene St, 81433 ....(303)387-5423
Wingate House B&B, 1045 Snowden St, PO Box 2, 81433 ....(303)387-5423
The Wyman Hotel, 1371 Greene St, 81433 ....(303)387-5372

STEAMBOAT SPRINGS D8 / *B3*
Crawford House, 1184 Crawford Ave, Box 775062, 80477 ....(303)879-1859
Harbor Hotel, PO Box 4109, 80477 ....(800)543-8888
Scandinavian Lodge, PO Box 774484, 80477 ....(800)233-8102
The Inn at Steamboat, 3070 Columbine Dr, 80477 ....(303)879-2600
The House On The Hill, PO Box 770598, 80477 ....(303)879-1650
Vista Verde Guest Ranch, Box 465, 80477 ....(303)879-3858

TELLURIDE M5 / *E2*
Dahl Haus, 122 S Oak St, PO Box 695, 81435 ....(303)728-4158
Johnstone Inn, PO Box 546, 81435 ....(303)728-3316
New Sheridan Hotel, 231 W Colorado Ave, PO Box 980, 81435 ....(303)728-4351
Pennington's Mountain Village Inn, 100 Pennington Ct, PO 2428, 81435 ....(800)543-1437
San Sophia, 330 W Pacific Ave, PO Box 1825, 81435 ....(303)728-3001
Skyline Guest Ranch, 7214 Hwy 145, PO Box 67, 81435 ....(303)728-3757
Victorian Inn, PO Box 217, 81435 ....(303)728-3684

VICTOR J12 / *D4*
The Portland Inn, 412 W Portland Ave, PO Box 32, 80860 ....(719)689-2102

WINTER PARK E11 / *C4*
Engelmann Pines, PO Box 1305, 80482 ....(303)726-4632

WOODLAND PARK I13 / *D4*
Pikes Peak Paradise, PO Box 5760, 236 Pinecrest Rd, 80866 ....(719)687-6656
Woodland Hills Lodge, PO Box 276, 80863 ....(800)621-8386

CONNECTICUT

BOLTON E13 / *E4*
Jared Cone House, 25 Hebron Rd, 06043 ....(203)643-8538

BRIDGEWATER H5 / *F2*
Sanford/Pond House, 20 Main St N, PO Box 306, 06752 ....(203)355-4677

BRISTOL F9 / *E3*
Chimney Crest Manor, 5 Founders Dr, 06010 ....(203)582-4219

BROOKLYN E18 / *E5*
Tannerbrook, 329 Pomfret Rd, 06234 ....(203)774-4822

CLINTON K13 / *G4*
Captain Dibbell House, 21 Commerce St, 06413 ....(203)669-1646

COLCHESTER G14 / *F4*
Hayward House Inn, 35 Hayward Ave, 06415 ....(203)537-5772

COS COB N3 / *H1*
Harbor House Inn, 50 River Rd, 06807 ....(203)661-5845

COVENTRY E15 / *E4*
Maple Hill Farm B&B, 365 Goose Ln, 06238 ....(203)742-0635

DEEP RIVER J13 / *F4*
Riverwind, 209 Main St, 06417 ....(203)526-2014

DURHAM I11 / *F4*
Durham B&B, Carriage Dr, 06422 ....(203)344-2779

EAST HADDAM I13 / *F4*
Bishopsgate Inn, 7 Norwich Rd, PO Box 290, 06423 ....(203)873-1677
Stonecroft Inn, 17 Main St, 06423 ....(203)873-1754
Whispering Winds Inn, 93 River Rd, 06423 ....(203)526-3055

EAST WINDSOR D12 / *E4*
The Stephen Potwine House, 84 Scantic Rd, 06088 ....(203)623-8722

ESSEX J14 / *F4*
Griswold Inn, 36 Main St, 06426 ....(203)767-1776

GLASTONBURY F12 / *E4*
Butternut Farm, 1654 Main St, 06033 ....(203)633-7197

GREENWICH N3 / *H1*
Homestead Inn, 420 Field Point Rd, 06830 ....(203)869-7500
Stanton House Inn, 76 Maple Ave, 06830 ....(203)869-2110

GROTON LONG POINT J17 / *F5*
Shore Inne, 54 East Shore Rd, 06340 ....(203)536-1180

IVORYTON J14 / *F4*
Copper Beech Inn, 46 Main St, 06442 ....(203)767-0330
Ivoryton Inn, 115 Main St, 06442 ....(203)767-0422

KENT F4 / *E1*
1741 Saltbox Inn, PO Box 677, 06757 ....(203)927-4376
Constitution Oak Farm, Beardsley Rd, 06757 ....(203)354-6495
The Sam Matson's B&B, Birch Hill Ln, Box 66, 06757 ....(203)927-3643

KILLINGWORTH J12 / *G4*
Killingworth Inn, 249 Rt 81, 06417 ....(203)663-1103

LAKEVILLE C4 / *D1*
Wake Robin Inn, Rt 41, 06039 ....(203)435-2515

LEDYARD I17 / *F5*
Applewood Farms Inn, 528 Col Ledyard Hwy, 06339 ....(203)536-2022

LITCHFIELD G5 / *E2*
Tollgate Hill Inn, Rt 202 & Tollgate Rd, 06759 ....(203)567-4545

MADISON K12 / *G4*
Dolly Madison Inn, 73 W Wharf Rd, 06443 ....(203)245-7377
Madison Beach Hotel, 94 W Wharf Rd, Box 546, 06443 ....(203)245-1404

MIDDLEBURY H7 / *F2*
Tucker Hill Inn, 96 Tucker Hill Rd, 06762 ....(203)758-8334

MOODUS H13 / *F4*
Fowler House, PO Box 432, 06469 ....(203)873-8906

MYSTIC J18 / *F5*
Comolli's Guest House, 36 Bruggeman Pl, 06355 ....(203)536-8723
The Inn at Mystic, Jct Rt 1 & 27, 06355 ....(203)536-9604

Red Brook Inn, PO Box 237, 06372 .... (203)572-0349
Whalers Inne, PO Box 488t, 06355 .... (203)536-1506

MYSTIC - NOANK J18 / *F5*
Palmer Inn, 25 Church St, 06340 .... (203)572-9000

NEW CANAAN M4 / *G1*
Maples Inn, 179 Oenoke Ridge, 06840 .... (203)966-2927
Roger Sherman Inn, 195 Oenoke Ridge, 06840 .... (203)955-4541

NEW HARTFORD D8 / *D3*
Cobble Hill Farm, Steele Rd, 06057 .... (203)379-0057
Highland Farms B&B, Highland Ave, 06057 .... (203)379-6029

NEW HAVEN K9 / *G3*
The Inn at Chapel West, 1201 Chapel St, 06511 .... (203)777-1201

NEW LONDON J17 / *F5*
Lighthouse Inn, 6 Guthrie Place, 06320 .... (203)443-8411
Queen Anne Inn & Antique Gallery, 265 Williams St, 06320 .... (203)447-2600

NEW MILFORD G4 / *F2*
Homestead Inn, 5 Elm St, 06776 .... (203)354-4080

NEW PRESTON F5 / *E2*
Birches Inn, West Shore Rd, 06777 .... (203)868-0229
Boulders Inn, Rt 45, 06777 .... (203)868-0541
Hopkins Inn, Hopkins Rd, 06777 .... (203)868-7295
The Inn on Lake Waramaug, North Shore Rd, 06777 .... (203)868-0563

NEWTOWN I5 / *F2*
Hawley Manor Inn, 19 Main St, 06470 .... (203)426-4456

NORFOLK B6 / *D2*
Blackberry River Inn, Rt 44, 06058 .... (203)542-5100
Greenwoods Gate, Greenwoods Rd E, 06058 .... (203)542-5439
Manor House, Maple Ave, PO Box 447, 06058 .... (203)542-5690
Mountain View Inn, Rt 272, 06058 .... (203)542-5595
Weaver's House, Rt 44, 06058 .... (203)542-5108

NORTH STONINGTON I19 / *F6*
The Old Tavern Farm, Rt 184, Box 477, 06359 .... (203)599-5264

NORWALK M4 / *G2*
Silvermine Tavern, 194 Perry Aves, 06850 .... (203)847-4558

OLD GREENWICH N3 / *H1*
Harbor House Inn, 165 Shore Rd, 06850 .... (203)637-0145

OLD LYME K14 / *G4*
Bee And Thistle Inn, 100 Lyme St, 06371 .... (203)434-1667
Old Lyme Inn, 85 Lyme St, 06371 .... (203)434-2600

OLD MYSTIC J18 / *F5*
The Old Mystic Inn, 58 Main St, Box 318, 06372 .... (203)572-9422

POMFRET C18 / *D5*
Wintergreen, Rt 44 & 169, 06259 .... (203)928-5741

POMFRET CENTER C18 / *D5*
The Inn at Gwyn Careg, Rt 44, 06230 .... (203)928-9352

PUTMAN HEIGHTS C19 / *D6*
The Felshaw Tavern, Five Mile River Rd, 06260 .... (203)928-3467

PUTNAM C18 / *D5*
Feishaw Tavern, Five Mile River Road, 06260 .... (203)928-3467

RIDGEFIELD K4 / *G1*
The Elms Inn, 500 Main St, 06877 .... (203)438-2541
Epenetus Howe House, 91 N Salem Rd, 06877 .... (203)438-4693
Stonehenge, Rt 7, 06877 .... (203)438-6511
West Lane Inn, 22 West Ln, 06877 .... (203)438-7323

RIVERTON B8 / *D3*
Old Riverton Inn, Rt 20 Box 6, 06065 .... (203)379-8678

SALISBURY B4 / *D2*
Ragamont Inn, Main St, 06068 .... (203)435-2372
Under Mountain Inn, 482 Undermountain Rd, 06068 .... (203)435-0242
White Hart Inn, Village Green, 06068 .... (203)435-2511
Yesterday's Yankee B&B, Rt 44 E, 06068 .... (203)435-9539

SIMSBURY D10 / *E3*
Simsbury 1820 House, 731 Hopmeadow St, 06070 .... (203)658-7658

SOMERSVILLE B12 / *D4*
The Old Mill Inn, 63 Maple St, 06072 .... (203)763-1473

SOUTH WOODSTOCK C18 / *D5*
The Inn at Woodstock Hill, 94 Plaine Hill Rd, PO Box 98, 06267 .... (203)928-0528

SOUTHINGTON J18 / *G5*
Chaffee's B&B, 28 Reussner Rd, 06489 .... (203)628-2750

STAFFORD SPRINGS B15 / *D4*
Winterbrook Farm, Beffa Rd, 06076 .... (203)684-5404

STONINGTON J18 / *G5*
Lasbury's B&B, 24 Orchard St, 06378 .... (203)535-2681

STONY CREEK K11 / *G3*
Cabin in the Woods, 80 Quarry Rd, PO Box 3291, 06405 .... (203)488-5284

STORRS D15 / *E4*
Altnaveigh Inn, 957 Storrs Rd, 06268 .... (203)429-4490
Farmhouse On The Hill, 418 Gurleyville Rd, 06268 .... (203)429-1400

THOMPSON C19 / *D6*
Hedgerow House, 1020 Quaddick Rd, 06277 .... (203)923-9073
Samuel Watson House, Rt 193 Box 86, 06277 .... (203)923-2491

TOLLAND D14 / *E4*
Old Babcock Tavern, 484 Mile Hill Rd, 06084 .... (203)875-1239
Tolland Inn, 63 Tolland Green, PO Box 717, 06084 .... (203)872-0800

UNCASVILLE I16 / *F5*
1851 Guest House, 1851 Norwich-New London Tpke, 06382 .. (203)848-3649

WASHINGTON G5 / *E2*
Mayflower Inn, Rt 47, 06793 .... (203)868-0515

WATERBURY H8 / *F2*
Boulevard B&B, 15 Columbia Blvd, 06710 .... (203)755-0314
The House On The Hill, 92 Woodlawn Terrace, 06710 .... (203)757-9901
The Parsonage, 18 Hewlett St, 06710 .... (203)574-2855

WATERTOWN G7 / *F2*
1849 House B&B, 249 Litchfield Rd, 06795 .... (203)274-1917
The Clark's B&B, 97 Scott Ave, 06795 .... (203)274-4866

WEST WOODSTOCK C18 / *D5*
Ebenezer Stoddard House, Rt 171 & Perrin Rd, 06267 .... (203)974-2552

WESTBROOK K13 / *G4*
Talcott House, 161 Seaside Ave, PO Box 1016, 06498 .... (203)399-5020

WESTPORT M5 / *G2*
Cotswold Inn, 76 Myrtle Ave, 06880 .... (203)226-3766
Longshore Inn, 280 Compo Rd S, 06883 .... (203)226-3316

WETHERSFIELD F11 / *E3*
Chester Bulkley House B&B, 184 Main St, 06109 .... (203)563-4236

WINSTED C8 / *D2*
Provincial House, 151 Main St, 06098 .... (203)879-1631

WOODBURY H6 / *F2*
Curtis House, Main St, 06798 .... (203)263-2101

DELAWARE

BETHANY BEACH J26 / *D8*
166 Ocean View, PO Box 275, 166 Ocean View Pkwy, 19930 ... (302)539-3707
The Addy Sea, Box 275, 19930 .... (302)539-3707
Homestead Guests, 721 Garfield Pkwy, 19930 .... (302)539-7248
Sea-Vista Villas, Box 62, 19930 .... (302)539-3354
The Sandbox, Box 62, 19930 .... (302)539-3354

CAMDEN J23 / *C7*
Jonathan Wallace House, 9 South Main St, 19934 .... (302)697-2921

DOVER F23 / *B7*
The Inn at Meeting House Square, 305 S Governors Ave, 19901 .... (302)678-1242
Nobel Guest House, 33 S Bradford St, 19901 .... (302)674-4048

LAUREL J23 / *D7*
Spring Garden, Rt 1 Box 283-A, 19956 .... (302)875-7015

LEWES I25 / *C8*
Savannah Inn, 330 Savannah Rd, 19958 .... (302)645-5592

NEW CASTLE C23 / *A7*
David Finney Inn, 216 Delaware St, 19720 .... (302)322-6367
The Jefferson House B&B, 5 The Strand at the Wharf, 19720 .... (302)323-0999
William Penn Guest House, 206 Delaware St, 19720 .... (302)328-7736

ODESSA D22 / *B7*
Cantwell House, 107 High St, 19730 .... (302)378-4179

REHOBOTH BEACH I26 / *C8*
Corner Cupboard Inn, 50 Park Ave, 19971 .... (302)227-8553
Gladstone Inn, 3 Olive Ave, 19971 .... (302)227-2641
The Lord and Hamilton Seaside Inn, 20 Brooklyn Ave, 19971 .... (302)227-6960
Lord Baltimore Lodge, 16 Baltimore Ave, 19971 .... (302)227-2855
Tembo Guest House, 100 Laurel St, 19971 .... (302)227-3360

WILMINGTON B23 / *A8*
The Boulevard B&B, 1909 Baynard Blvd, 19802 .... (302)656-9700
The Pink Door, 8 Francis Ln, 19803 .... (302)478-8325
Small Wonder B&B, 213 W Crest Rd, 19803 .... (302)764-0789

FLORIDA

AMELIA ISLAND C12 / *A4*
The 1735 House, 584 S Fletcher Ave, 32034 .... (904)261-4148
Elizabeth Point Lodge, 82 S Fletcher Ave, PO Box 1210, 32034 .... (904)277-4851

Florida House Inn, PO Box 688, 32034 ....(904)261-3300

APALACHICOLA Z9 / *H3*
Gibson Inn, PO Box 221, 32320 ....(904)653-2191
The Pink Camellia Inn, 145 Ave E, 32320 ....(904)653-2107

BIG PINE KEY Y12 / *H4*
The Barnacle, Rt 1, Box 780A, 33043 ....(305)872-3298

BOCA GRANDE R9 / *F3*
Gasparilla Inn, 33921 ....(813)964-2201

BRADENTON O8 / *E3*
Banyan House, 624 Fontana Ln, 33529 ....(813)746-8633

COLEMAN J10 / *C3*
The Son's Shady Brook B&B, PO Box 551, 33521 ....(904)748-7867

CORAL GABLES U16 / *G5*
Hotel Place St. Michel, 162 Alcazar Ave, 33134 ....(305)444-1666

DAYTONA BEACH H13 / *C4*
Captain's Quarters Inn, 3711 S Atlantic Ave, 32019 ....(904)767-3119
Live Oak Inn, 444 S Beach St, 32114 ....(904)252-4667
St. Regis Hotel, 509 Seabreeze Blvd, 32018 ....(904)252-8743

EVERGLADES CITY U12 / *G4*
Rod & Gun Club, PO Box G, 33929 ....(813)695-2101

FERNANDINA BEACH C12 / *A4*
Bailey House, PO Box 805, 32034 ....(904)261-5390
Greyfield Inn, Box 878 Cumberland Isl, 32034 ....(904)261-6408

FLORIDA CITY V15 / *G5*
Grandma Newtons B&B, 40 NW 5th Ave, 30334 ....(305)247-4413

FORT LAUDERDALE T16 / *F5*
The Dolan House, 1401 NE 5 Court, 33301 ....(305)462-8430

FORT MYERS R10 / *F3*
Wind Song Garden, 5570-4 Woodrose Ct, 33907 ....(813)936-6378

FT LAUDERDALE BEACH T16 / *F5*
Casa Alhambra B&B Inn, 3029 Alhambra St, 33304 ....(305)467-2262

HAWTHORNE G10 / *B3*
Yearling Cabins, Rt 3, Box 123, 32640 ....(904)466-3033

HOLMES BEACH O8 / *E3*
Harrington House B&B, 5626 Gulf Dr, 34217 ....(813)778-5444

INDIANTOWN P15 / *E5*
Seminole Country Inn, 15885 Warfield, 33456 ....(305)597-3777

JACKSONVILLE D11 / *B4*
House on Cherry St, 1844 Cherry St, 32205 ....(904)384-1999

KEY LARGO X15 / *H5*
Largo Lodge, 101740 Oversea Hwy, Rt 1, Box 302, 33037 ....(305)451-0424

KEY WEST Z11 / *H4*
Alexander's, 1118 Fleming St, 33040 ....(305)294-9919
Artist House, 534 Eaton St, 33040 ....(305)296-3977
Author's, 725 White At Petronia, 33040 ....(305)294-7381
Coconut Grove Guest House, 817 Fleming St, 33040 ....(305)296-5107
Colours Key West - The Guest Mansion, 410 Fleming St, 33040 ....(305)294-6977
Cypress House, 601 Caroline St, 33040 ....(305)294-6969
Duval House, 815 Duval St, 33040 ....(305)294-1666
Eaton Lodge, 511 Eaton St, 33040 ....(305)294-3800
Eden House, 1015 Fleming, 33040 ....(305)296-6868
Garden House, 329 Elizabeth St, 33040 ....(305)296-5368
Heron House, 512 Simonton St, 33040 ....(305)294-9227
Island City House, 411 William St, 33040 ....(305)294-5702
Island House, 1129 Fleming St, 33040 ....(305)294-6284
Merlinn Guest House, 811 Simonton St, 33040 ....(305)296-3336
Oasis Guest House, 823 Fleming St, 33040 ....(305)296-2131
Palms Of Key West, 820 White St, 33040 ....(305)294-3146
Pines of Key West, 521 United St, 33040 ....(305)296-7467
The Popular House, Key West B&B, 415 William St, 33040 ....(305)296-7274
Simonton Court, 320 Simonton St, 33040 ....(305)294-6386
Sweet Caroline Guest House, 529 Caroline St, 33040 ....(305)296-5173
The Hollinsed House, 609-11 Southard St, 33040 ....(305)296-8031
Walden Guest House, 223 Elizabeth, 33040 ....(305)296-7161
The Watson House, 525 Simonton, 33040 ....(305)294-6712
Whispers B&B Inn at Gideon Lowe House, 409 William St, 33040 ....(305)294-5969
Wicker Guest House, 913 Duval St, 33040 ....(305)296-4275

KISSIMMEE L12 / *D4*
Casa Coppe, 2535 Ridgeway Dr, 34746 ....(407)846-7916
The Unicorn Inn English B&B, 8 S Orlando Ave, 32741 ....(407)846-1200

LAKE WALES M11 / *D4*
Chalet Suzanne, US 27 & 17A, Drawer AC, 33859-9003 ....(813)676-6011

LITTLE TORCH KEY /
Little Palm Island, Rt 4, Box 1036, 33042 ....(305)872-2524

MARATHON Y13 / *H4*
Hopp-Inn Guest House, 5 Man-O-War Dr, 33050 ....(305)743-4118

MAYO E6 / *B2*
Jim Hollis' River Rendezvous, Rt 2, Box 60, 32066 ....(904)294-2510

MIAMI U16 / *G5*
Joann Robert's B&B, 6400 SW 120 Ave, 33183 ....(305)279-9770
Miami River Inn, 118 SW S River Dr, 33130 ....(305)325-0045

MICANOPY G9 / *C3*
Herlong Mansion, Cholakka Blvd, PO Box 667, 32667 ....(904)466-3322

MONTICELLO C4 / *A2*
Peppermill B&B, 625 E Washington St, 32344 ....(904)997-4600

OCALA H10 / *C3*
Doll House B&B, 719 SE 4th St, 32671 ....(904)351-1167
Seven Sisters Inn, 820 SE Fort King St, 32671 ....(904)867-1170

ORANGE PARK 311 / *B4*
Club Continental, 2143 Astor St, 32073 ....(904)264-6070
The Inn at Winterbourne, PO 7059, 32073 ....(904)264-6070

ORANGE SPRINGS G10 / *C3*
Orange Springs, 1 Main St, Box 550, 32682 ....(904)546-2052

ORLANDO K12 / *D4*
Avonelle's, 4755 Anderson Rd, 32806 ....(305)275-8733
The Courtyard at Lake Lucerne, 211 N Lucerne Circle E, 32801 ....(407)648-5188
Fugate House, Box 2009, 32802 ....(305)423-8382
Maggie Hamilton House, PO Box 5411006, 32854-1006 ....(407)894-3820
Meadow Marsh, 940 Tildenville School Rd, 32787 ....(305)656-2064
Spencer Home B&B, 313 Spencer St, 32809 ....(305)855-5603

PENSACOLA X3 / *H1*
Homestead Inn, 7830 Pine Forest Rd, 32506 ....(904)944-4816
Liechty's Homestead Inn, 7830 Pine Forest Rd, 32526 ....(904)944-4816
Sunshine, 508 Decatur Ave, 32507 ....(904)455-6781

SAINT AUGUSTINE F12 / *B4*
Carriage Way B&B, 70 Cuna St, 32084 ....(904)829-2467
Casa de la Paz, 22 Avenida Menendez, 32084 ....(904)829-2915
Casa de Solana, 21 Aviles St, 32084 ....(904)824-3555
Kenwood Inn, 38 Marine St, 32084 ....(904)824-2116
Sailor's Rest, 298 St George St, 32084 ....(904)824-3817
St. Francis Inn, 279 St George St, 32084 ....(904)824-6068
Victorian House B&B, 11 Cadiz St, 32084 ....(904)824-5214
Westcott House, 146 Avenida Menendez, 32084 ....(904)824-4301

SAINT PETERSBURG N8 / *E3*
Bayboro House on Old Tampa Bay, 1719 Beach Dr, SE, 33701 ....(813)823-4955

SANIBEL S10 / *F3*
Kona Kai Motel, 1539 Periwinkle Way, 33957 ....(813)472-1001

SEASIDE X6 / *H2*
Seaside Cottages, PO Box 4730, 32459 ....(904)231-4224

SIESTA KEY, SARASOTA P8 / *E3*
Crescent House, 459 Beach Rd, 34242 ....(813)346-0857

STUART P16 / *E5*
The Homeplace, 501 Akron Ave, 34994 ....(407)220-9148

TALLAHASSEE D3 / *A1*
Governors Inn, 209 S Adams, 32301 ....(904)681-6855
The Riedel House, 1412 Fairway Dr, 32301 ....(904)222-8569

TARPON SPRINGS L8 / *D3*
Spring Bayou Inn, 32 W Tarpon Ave, 34689 ....(813)938-9333

WAKULLA SPRINGS D3 / *B1*
Wakulla Springs Lodge & Conference Ctr, 1 Spring Dr, 32305 ....(904)224-5950

WEST PALM BEACH Q17 / *F5*
Hibiscus House, PO Box 2612, 33402 ....(407)863-5633

GEORGIA

ATLANTA G5 / *C2*
Beverly Hills Inn, 65 Sheridan Dr NE, 30305 ....(404)233-8520
Shellmont B&B Lodge, 821 Piedmont NE, 30308 ....(404)872-9290
The Woodruff B&B Inn, 223 Ponce de Leon Ave, 30302 ....(404)875-9449

AUGUSTA H13 / *C5*
The Clarion Telfair Inn, 326 Greene St, 30901 ....(404)724-3315
Oglethorpe Inn, 836 Greene St, 30901 ....(404)724-9774

BRUNSWICK Q15 / *F6*
Brunswick Manor, 825 Egmont St, 31520 ....(912)265-6889

CHICKAMAUGA C2 / *A1*
Gordon-Lee Mansion B&B, 217 Cove Rd, 30707 ....(404)375-4728

CLARKESVILLE D8 / *A3*
Burns-Sutton House, 124 S Washington St, Box 992, 30523 ....(404)754-5565
Charm House Inn, Box 392, Hwy 441, 30523 ....(404)754-9347
Glen-Ella Springs Hotel, Rt 3, Bear Gap Rd, 30523 ....(404)754-7295
Laprade's, Rt 1, Hwy 197, 30523 ....(404)947-3312

CLEVELAND D7 / *A3*
Ru Sharon, Box 273, 30528 .... (404)865-5173

COLUMBUS L3 / *D1*
De Loffre House, 812 Broadway, 31901 .... (404)324-1146

DAHLONEGA D6 / *B2*
Forest Hills Mt. Resort, Rt 3, 30533 .... (404)864-6456
Mountain Top Lodge, Rt 3, Box 173, 30533 .... (404)864-5257
Smith House, 202 S Chestatee St, 30533 .... (404)864-3566
Worley Homestead Inn, 410 W Main, 30533 .... (404)864-7002

DALTON C3 / *A1*
Amy's Place, 217 W Cuyler, 30720 .... (404)226-2481

DILLARD B8 / *A3*
Dillard House Inn, PO Box 10, 30537 .... (404)746-5349

FORSYTH J7 / *D3*
A Country Place, Rt 3 Box 290, 31019 .... (912)994-2705

FORT OGLETHORPE C2 / *A1*
Captain's Quarters B&B Inn, 13 Barnhardt Circle, 30742 .... (404)858-0624

GAINESVILLE E7 / *B3*
Dunlap House, 635 Green St, 30501 .... (404)536-0200

HARTWELL E10 / *B4*
Hartwell Inn, 504 W Howell St, 30643 .... (404)376-3967

HELEN D7 / *A3*
Derdenhof Inn, PO Box 405, 30545 .... (404)878-2141

LAKEMONT C8 / *A3*
Anapauo Farm, Star Rt, Box 13C, 30522 .... (404)782-6442
The Barn Inn, Rabun Rd, PO Box 192, 30552 .... (404)782-5094
Lake Rabun Hotel, Rt 1 Box 101, 30552 .... (404)782-4946

MACON K8 / *D3*
1842 Inn, 353 College St, 31201 .... (912)741-1842
The Carriage Stop Inn, 1129 Georgia Ave, 31201 .... (912)743-9740
La Petite Maison, 1165 Dures Ln, 31201 .... (912)742-4674
Victorian Village, 1841 Hardeman Ave, 31201 .... (912)743-3333

MARIETTA G4 / *B2*
Arden Hall, 1052 Arden Dr SW, 30060 .... (404)422-0780
The Marlow & Stanley House, 236 Church St, 30060 .... (404)426-1881

MOUNTAIN CITY C8 / *A3*
The York House, PO Box 126, 30562 .... (404)746-2068

NEWNAN I4 / *C1*
Parrott-Camp-Soucy House, 155 Greenville Street, 30263 .... (404)253-4846

PERRY L7 / *D3*
Swift Street Inn B&B, 1204 Swift St, 31069 .... (912)987-3428

PLAINS N5 / *E2*
Plains B&B, 100 W Church St, PO Box 217, 31780 .... (912)824-7252

PLANTATION VILLAGE Q15 / *F6*
Country Hearth Inn, 301 Main St, 31522 .... (912)638-7805

RUTLEDGE H8 / *C3*
Jones Cottage, 1401 Fairplay Rd, 30663 .... (404)557-2516

SAINT MARY'S S15 / *G6*
Riverview Hotel, 105 Osborne St, 31558 .... (912)882-3242

SAINT SIMONS ISLAND Q15 / *F6*
Little St. Simons Island, PO Box 1078 G, 31522 .... (912)638-7472

SAUTEE D7 / *A3*
Stovall House, Rt 1 Box 1476, 30571 .... (404)878-3355
Woodhaven Chalet, Rt 1, Box 39, 30571 .... (404)878-2580

SAVANNAH N16 / *E6*
17 Hundred 90 Inn, 307 E. President, 31401 .... (912)236-7122
Ballastone Inn, 14 E Oglethorpe Ave, 31401 .... (912)236-1484
Bed & Breakfast Inn, 117 W Gordon St at Chatham Sq, 31401 .... (912)238-0518
Charlton Court, 403 E. Charlton St, 31401 .... (912)236-2895
Comer House, 2 East Taylor St, 31401 .... (912)234-2923
East Bay Inn, 225 E Bay St, 31401 .... (912)238-1200
Eliza Thompson House, 5 W Jones St, 31401 .... (912)236-3620
Foley House Inn, 14 W Hull St, 31401 .... (912)232-6622
The Forsyth Park Inn, 102 W Hall St, 31401 .... (912)233-6800
Gastonian, 220 E Gaston St, 31401 .... (912)232-2869
Greystone Inn, 214 E Jones St, 31401 .... (912)236-2442
Haslam-Fort House, 417 E Charlton St, 31401 .... (912)233-6380
Jesse Mount House, 209 W Jones St, 31401 .... (912)236-1774
Liberty Inn 1834, 128 W Liberty St, 31401 .... (912)233-1007
Magnolia Place Inn, 503 Whitaker St, 31401 .... (912)236-7674
Mary Lee's House, PO Box 607, 31402 .... (912)232-0891
Morel House, 117 W Perry St, 31401 .... (912)234-4088
Olde Harbour Inn, 508 E Factors Walk, 31401 .... (912)234-4100
Planters Inn, 29 Abercorn St, 31401 .... (912)232-5678
Presidents' Quarters, 225 E President St, 31401 .... (912)233-1600
Pulaski Square Inn, 203 W Charlton, 31401 .... (800)227-0650
Remshart-Brooks House, 106 W Jones St, 31401 .... (912)234-6928
Royal Colony Inn, 29 Abercorn St, 31401 .... (912)232-5678
RSVP Savannah B&B Reservation Service, 417 E Charlton St, 31401 .... (912)232-7787
Stoddard-Cooper House, 19 W Perry St, 31401 .... (912)233-6809
Timmons House, 407 E Charlton St, 31401 .... (912)233-4456

SENOIA I5 / *C2*
Culpepper House, PO Box 462, 30276 .... (404)599-8182
The Veranda - Hollberg Hotel, 252 Seavy St, Box 177, 30276-0177 .... (404)599-3905

STATESBORO L14 / *D5*
Statesboro Inn B&B, 301 South, 30458 .... (912)489-8628

SWAINSBORO L12 / *D4*
Edenfield House Inn, Box 556, 358 Church St, 30401 .... (912)237-3007

THOMASTON K5 / *D2*
The Guest House, 318 W Main St, 30286 .... (404)647-1203

THOMASVILLE S7 / *G2*
Deer Creek B&B, 1304 Old Monticello Rd, 31792 .... (912)226-7294
Susina Plantation Inn, Rt 3 Box 1010, 31792 .... (912)377-9644

TOCCOA D8 / *A3*
Habersham Manor House, 326 Doyle St, 30577 .... (404)886-6496
Simmons-Bond Inn, 130 W Tugalo St, 30577 .... (404)886-8411

WASHINGTON G10 / *C4*
Liberty Street, 108 W Liberty St, 30673 .... (404)678-3107
Water Oak Cottage, 211 S Jefferson St, 30673 .... (404)678-4645

WINTERVILLE F9 / *B3*
Old Winterville Inn, 108 S Main St, 30683 .... (404)742-7340

HAWAII

AIEA, OAHU H4 / *H2*
Alohaland Guest House, 98-1003 Oliwa St, 96701 .... (808)487-0482

CAPTAIN COOK H10 / *H4*
Adrienne's B&B, RR1 Box 8E, 96704 .... (808)328-9726
Manago Hotel, Box 145, 96704 .... (808)323-2642

HAIKU, MAUI E9 / *F4*
Haikuleana B&B Inn, 69 Haiku Rd, 96708 .... (808)575-2890

HANA, MAUI E10 / *F4*
Heavenly Hana Inn, PO Box 146, 96713 .... (808)248-8442
Kaia Ranch & Co, PO Box 404, Ulaino Rd, 96713 .... (808)248-7725
Volcano Heart Chalet, Box 404, 96713 .... (808)248-7725

HAWI, HAWAII F10 / *G5*
Aha Hui Hawaiian Plantation, PO Box 10, 96719 .... (808)889-5523

HOLUALOA-KONA HAWAII G10 / *H4*
Holualoa Inn, Box 222, 96725 .... (808)324-1121

HONOLULU, OAHU C6 / *H3*
B&B Waikiki Beach, PO Box 89080, 96830 .... (808)923-5459
Hale O Kahala, 4614 Kilauea Ave #565, 96816 .... (808)732-5889
Hawaii Kai, 876 Ka'ahue St, 96825 .... (808)395-8153
The Manoa Valley Inn, 2001 Vancouver Dr, 96822 .... (808)947-6019

KAILUA C6 / *H3*
Sheffield House, 131 Kuulei Rd, 96734 .... (808)262-0721

KALAPANA, HAWAII H12 / *H5*
Kalani Honua, Box 4500, Ocean Hwy 137, 96778 .... (808)965-7828

KANEOHE, OAHU C6 / *H3*
Emma's Guest Rooms, 47-600 Hui Ulili St, 96744 .... (808)239-7248

KAPAA, KAUAI B3 / *E1*
Kay Barker's B&B, PO Box 740, 96746 .... (808)822-3073

KAUNAKAKAI, MOLOKAI D8 / *F3*
Pau Hana Inn, PO Box 546, 96748 .... (800)367-8047

KILAUEA, KAUAI A3 / *E1*
The Mahi Ko Inn, General Delivery, 96754 .... (808)828-1103

KOLOA, KAUAI B2 / *E1*
B&B Hawaiian Style, PO Box 1705, 96756 .... (808)742-7187
Poipu B&B Inn, 2720 Hoonani Rd, Poipu Beach, 96756 .... (808)742-1146
Poipu Plantation, 1792 Pee Rd, 96756 .... (808)742-6757

KULA, MAUI C11 / *F4*
Kula Lodge & Restaurant, Inc., RR1 Box 475, 96790 .... (808)878-1535

LAHAINA, MAUI E8 / *F4*
The Lahaina Hotel, 127 Lahainaluna Rd, 96761 .... (808)661-0577
Plantation Inn, 174 Lahainaluna Rd, 96761 .... (800)433-6815

NAPILI, MAUI B9 / *F4*
Coconut Inn, PO Box 10517, 96791 .... (800)367-8006

POIPU, KAUAI B3 / *E1*
Gloria's Spouting Horn B&B, 4464 Lawai Beach Rd, 96756 .... (808)742-6995

PRINCEVILLE, KAUAI B3 / *E1*
Hale 'Aha Hospitality House, Box 3370, 96722 .... (808)826-6733

VOLCANO H11 / *H5*
Kilauea Lodge, PO Box 116, 96785 .... (808)967-7366

My Island B&B, Box 100, 96785 .... (808)967-7216

IDAHO

BOISE — L4 / F1
Governor's Mansion B&B Inn, 109 W Idaho St, 83702 .... (208)886-2858
Idaho Heritage Inn, 109 W Idaho St, 83702 .... (208)342-8066
Sunrise, 2730 Sunrise Rim Rd, 83705 .... (208)345-5260
Victoria's White House, 10325 W Victory Rd, 83709 .... (208)362-0507

CALDWELL — M2 / F1
Manning House B&B Inn, 1803 S 10th Ave, 83606 .... (208)459-7899

CASCADE — K3 / F2
Triple T Ranch, HC 83 & 85, 83611 .... (208)382-4336
Wapiti Meadow Ranch, HC 72, 83611 .... (208)382-4336

COEUR D'ALENE — D2 / B1
Greenbriar B&B Inn, 315 Wallace, 83814 .... (208)667-9660
Gregory's McFarland House B&B, 601 Foster Ave, 83814 .... (208)667-1232
Inn the First Place, 509 N 15th St, 83814 .... (208)667-3346
Katy's Wild Rose Inn, 1018 Front Ave, 83814 .... (208)756-9474

COUNCIL — K3 / E1
The Old Heartland Inn, PO Box 32, 83612 .... (208)253-NICE

GRANGEVILLE — H3 / D1
Tulip House, 403 S Florence St, 83530 .... (208)983-1034

HAILEY — M6 / G3
Comfort Inn, Box 984, 83333 .... (208)788-2477

HORSESHOE BEND — L3 / F1
Old Riverside Depot, Rt 1 Box 14a, 83629 .... (208)793-2408

IDAHO CITY — M4 / F2
Idaho City Hotel, PO Box 70, 83631 .... (208)392-4290

IDAHO FALLS — M10 / G4
Little Bush Inn, 498 Maple Street, 83402 .... (208)529-0567

IRWIN — N11 / G5
McBride's B&B, PO Box 166, 83428 .... (208)483-4221

KELLOGG — E3 / B1
The Inn at Kellogg, 305 South Division St, 83837 .... (208)786-2311

KETCHUM — M6 / F3
Busterback Ranch, Star Rt, 83340 .... (208)774-2217
Lift Haven Inn, Box 21, 100 Lloyd Dr, 83340 .... (208)726-5601
Lift Tower Lodge, PO Box 185, 83340 .... (208)726-5163

KOOSKIA — G3 / D2
Looking Glass Ranch, HC-75, Box 32, 83539 .... (208)926-0855
Three Rivers Resort, HC75, Box 61, 83539 .... (208)926-4430

LACLEDE — C2 / B1
River Birch Farm B&B, PO Box 608, 83841 .... (208)263-3705

LAVA HOT SPRINGS — O10 / G4
Lava Hot Springs Inn, 5 Portneuf Ave, 83246 .... (208)776-5830

MCCALL — J3 / E2
Hotel McCall, A Mountain Inn, PO Box 1778, 83638 .... (208)634-8105
Northwest Passage B&B Lodge, 201 Rio Vista, PO Box 4208, 83638 .... (208)634-5349

MERIDIAN — M3 / F1
Home Place, 415 W Lake Hazel Rd, 83642 .... (208)888-3857

MOSCOW — F2 / C1
Twin Peaks Inn, 2455 W Twin Rd, 83843 .... (208)882-4651

NEW MEADOWS — J3 / E1
Hartland Inn, PO Box 215, 83654 .... (208)347-2114

NORTHFORK — J6 / E3
Indian Creek Ranch, Rt 2 Box 105, 83466 .... (208)756-0070

POCATELLO — O9 / G4
Holmes Retreat, 178 N Mink Creek Rd, 83204 .... (208)232-5518

RIGGINS — I3 / E1
The Lodge B&B, PO Box 498, 83549 .... (208)628-3863

SAINT MARIES — E3 / C1
Knoll Haus, PO Box 572, 83861 .... (208)245-4137

SANDPOINT — C3 / B1
The Old McFarland Inn, 227 S 1st Ave, 83864 .... (208)265-0260
Whitaker House, 410 Railroad Ave #10, 83864 .... (208)263-0816

STANLEY — L5 / F2
Idaho Rocky Mountain Ranch, HC 64 Box 9934, 83278 .... (208)774-3544
Redfish Lake Lodge, PO Box 9, 83278 .... (208)774-3536
Sawtooth Hotel, West End of Ace of Diamonds, 83278 .... (208)774-9947

SUN VALLEY — M6 / F3
Idaho Country Inn, PO Box 2355, 83353 .... (208)726-1019
River Street Inn, PO Box 182, 83353 .... (208)726-3611

WALLACE — E3 / B2
Jameson B&B, 304 Sixth St, 83873 .... (208)556-1554
Pine Tree Inn, 177 King St, Box 1023, 83873 .... (208)752-4391

ILLINOIS

ALTON — Q7 / F2
Haagen House B&B, 617 State St, 62002 .... (618)462-2419

ARCOLA — N13 / E4
Curly's Corner B&B, RR 2, Box 85B, 61910 .... (217)268-3352

ARTHUR — N12 / E4
Favorite Brother Inn, 106 E Columbia, 61911 .... (217)543-2938

BISHOP HILL — G7 / C2
Holden's Guest House, E Main & Sun-Up Ln, 61419 .... (309)927-3500

BUSHNELL — J6 / C2
The Old Smith Home & Breakfast, 287 W Hail St, 61422 .... (309)772-3908

CARLINVILLE — P8 / E2
Courthouse Inn, 307 E First South St, 62626 .... (217)854-6566

CARLYLE — S9 / F3
Country Haus, 1191 Franklin, 62231 .... (618)594-8313

CARTHAGE — K3 / D1
Wright Farmhouse, RR3, 62321 .... (217)357-2421

CHICAGO — D15 / B5
Bed & Breakfast/Chicago, PO Box 14088, 60614-0088 .... (312)951-0085
Hyde Park House, 5210 S Kenwood Ave, 60615 .... (312)363-4595

CISCO — L12 / D4
Country House, Rt 1 Box 61, 61803 .... (217)669-2291

COLLINSVILLE — R7 / F2
Maggie's B&B, 2102 N Keebler Rd, 62234 .... (618)344-8283

DALLAS CITY — J3 / C1
1850's Guest House, Rt 1, 62330 .... (217)852-3652

DECATUR — M11 / D4
Hamilton House, 500 W Main St, 62522 .... (217)429-1669

DIXON — D9 / B3
Colonial Inn, Rt 3 Grand Detour, 61021 .... (815)652-4422
River View Guest House, 507 E Everett, 61021 .... (815)288-5974

DU QUOIN — U10 / G3
Francie's B&B, 104 S Line St, 62832 .... (618)542-6686

DWIGHT — H13 / C4
La Petite Voyageur, 116 E South St, 60420 .... (815)584-2239

ELSAH — Q6 / F2
Corner Nest B&B, 3 Elm St, PO Box 22, 62028 .... (618)374-1892
Green Tree Inn, 15 Mill St, PO Box 96, 62028 .... (618)374-2821
Maple Leaf Cottage Inn, 12 Selma St, PO Box 156, 62028 .... (618)374-1684

EVANSTON — C15 / A5
Homestead, 1625 Hinman Ave, 60201 .... (708)475-3300
Margarita Inn, 1566 Oak Ave, 60201 .... (708)869-2273

FREEBURG — S8 / F3
The Westerfield House, RR 2, Box 34, 62243 .... (618)539-5643

GALENA — B6 / A2
Aldrich Guest House, 900 Third St, 61036 .... (815)777-3323
Amber Creek Farm, PO Box 5, 61036 .... (815)598-3301
Avery Guest House, 606 S Prospect St, 61036 .... (815)777-3883
Belle Aire Mansion, 11410 Rt 20 W, 61036 .... (815)777-0893
Captain Harris Guest House, 713 S Bench St, 61036 .... (815)777-1611
Chestnut Mountain Resort, 8700 W Chestnut Rd, 61036 .... (800)435-2914
Colonial Guest House, 1004 Park Ave, 61036 .... (815)777-0336
Comfort Guest House, 1000 Third St, 61036 .... (815)777-3062
Country Valley Guest Home, 2690 Blackjack Rd, 61036 .... (815)777-2322
DeSoto House Hotel, 230 S Main St, 61036 .... (815)777-0090
Farmers' Home Hotel, 334 Spring St, 61036 .... (815)777-3456
Farster's Executive Inn, 305 N Main St, 61036 .... (815)777-9125
Felt Manor, 125 S Prospect St, 61036 .... (815)777-9093
Four Oaks Guest House, 6594 Hwy Rt 84 N, 61036 .... (815)777-9567
Gallery Guest Suite, 204 1/2 S Main St, 61036 .... (815)777-1222
The Goldmoor, 9001 Sand Hill Rd, 61036 .... (815)777-3925
Grandview Guest Home, 113 S Prospect St, 61036 .... (815)777-1387
Hellman Guest House, 318 Hill St, 61036 .... (815)777-3638
The Homestead, 1022 Fourth St, 61036 .... (815)777-3536
Log Cabin Guest House, 11661 W Chetlain Ln, 61036 .... (815)777-2845
Mother's Country Inn, 349 Spring St, 61036 .... (815)777-3153
Pat's Country Guest Home, 5148 Hwy 20 W, 61036 .... (815)777-1030
Robert Scribe Harris House, 713 S Bench St, 61036 .... (815)777-1611
Ryan Mansion Inn, Rt 20 W, 61036 .... (815)777-2043
Spring Street Guest House, 418 Spring St, 61036 .... (815)777-0354
Stillman's Country Inn, 513 Bouthillier, 61036 .... (815)777-0557
Stillwater's Country Inn, 7213 W Buckhill Rd, 60613 .... (815)777-0223
Victorian Mansion Guest House, 301 S High St, 61036 .... (815)777-0675
The Wild Turkey, 1048 N Clark Ln, 61036 .... (815)858-3649

GALESBURG — H6 / C2
Seacord House, 624 N Cherry St, 61401 .... (309)342-4107

GALVA — G7 / C2
Country Hills B&B, Rt 1, 61434 .... (309)932-2886

GENEVA D13 / B4
The Oscar Swan Country Inn, 1800 W State St, 60134 .... (708)232-0173

GIBSON CITY J13 / D4
Stolz Home, RR 2, Box 27, 60936 .... (217)784-4502

GOLCONDA X13 / H4
Heritage Haus, Main & Columbus, Box 562, 62938 .... (618)683-3883
Riverview Mansion Hotel, Columbus Ave, PO Box 56, 62938 (618)638-3001
The Mansion Of Golconda, 515 Columbus St, Box 339, 62938 .... (618)683-4400

GOODFIELD J10 / C3
Brick House Inn, Conklin Ct, Box 301, 61742 .... (309)965-2545

GRAND DETOUR D9 / B3
Colonial Inn, Rock & Green Sts, 61021 .... (815)652-4422

GRANT PARK G15 / B5
The Bennett Curtis House, 302 W Taylor, 60940 .... (815)465-6025

GURNEE B14 / A5
Sweet Basil Hill Farm, 15937 W Washington Street, 60031 .... (708)244-3333

HILLSBORO P9 / E3
Hillsboro Hotel's Red Rooster Inn, 123 E Seward, 62049 .... (217)532-6332

JACKSONVILLE N6 / E2
The 258 Inn, 840 W Walnut, 62650 .... (217)245-2588

JOLIET F14 / B4
Stonegate Inn, 619 Cornelia St, 60435 .... (815)723-6548

KEWANEE G8 / B3
Bishop's Inn B&B, 223 W Central Blvd, 61443 .... (309)852-5201

LAKE FOREST B15 / A5
Deer Path Inn, 255 E Illinois Rd, 60045 .... (708)234-2280

LANARK C8 / A3
Standish House, 540 W Carroll St, 61046 .... (815)493-2307

LELAND E11 / B4
Our Country Home, 4359 E 1950th Rd, 60531 .... (815)495-9091
Watseka Farm, 4377 E 2551 Rd, 60531 .... (815)498-9820

LOCKPORT E14 / B4
Hotel President, 933 State St, 60441 .... (815)838-1881

MARSEILLES F12 / B4
Annie Tique's Hotel, 378 Main St, 61341 .... (815)795-5848

MENDOTA F10 / B3
Elizabeth's B&B, 1100 Fifth St, 61432 .... (815)539-5555

MOMENCE G15 / C5
Wikstrom Manor B&B, 304 W Second St, 60954 .... (815)472-3156

MONMOUTH H5 / C2
Carr Mansion Guest House, 416 E Broadway, 61462 .... (309)734-3654

MOSSVILLE I9 / C3
Old Church House Inn B&B, 1416 E Mossville Rd, 61552 .... (309)579-2300

MOUNT CARROLL C7 / A2
Country Palmer House, Rt 3, Box 254, 61053 .... (815)244-2343
The Farm, Rt 1, Box 112, 61053 .... (815)244-9885
Mount Carroll Guest House, 111 N Main, 61053 .... (815)244-9712
Prairie Path Guest House, RR 3, Box 223, 61053 .... (815)244-3462

MOUNT PULASKI L10 / D3
Dorsey's B&B, 318 N Belmont, 62548 .... (217)792-3347

MUNDELEIN C5 / A4
Round-Robin Guesthouse, 231 Maple Ave, 60060 .... (708)566-7664

NAPERVILLE E14 / B4
Die Blaue Gans Guesthaus, 9S 265, Rt 59, 60565 .... (708)355-0835
Harrison House, 26 N Eagle, 60565 .... (708)420-1117

NAUVOO J3 / C1
Hotel Nauvoo, Rt 96 Town Center PO 398, 62354 .... (217)453-2211
Mississippi Memories, Riverview Hgts, Box 291, 62354 .... (217)453-2771

OAK PARK D15 / B5
Toad Hall B&B House, 301 N Scoville, 60302 .... (708)386-8623
Under the Ginkgo Tree, 300 N Kenilworth, 60302 .... (708)310-9010

OAKLAND N14 / E4
The Inn on the Square, 3 Montgomery, 61943 .... (217)346-2289

OBLONG Q15 / F4
Welcome Inn, 506 W Main St, 62449 .... (618)592-3301

OREGON C9 / A3
LynDel Mansion, 400 N 3rd St, 61061 .... (815)732-7313
Pinehill B&B, 400 Mix St, 61061 .... (815)732-2061

PEORIA I9 / C3
Wildlife Prairie Park, RR 2, 61615 .... (309)676-0998

PETERSBURG L8 / D3
Carmody's Clare Inn, 207 S Twelfth St, 62675 .... (217)632-2350
Luthringer House, 122 W Sheridan, 62675 .... (217)893-0469

PLEASANT HILL O4 / E1
Pleasant Haven, 201 E Quincy, PO Box 51, 62366 .... (217)734-9357

POLO D9 / A3
Barber House Inn, 410 W Mason, 61064 .... (815)946-2607

PORT BYRON E6 / B2
The Olde Brick House, 502 N High St, 61275 .... (309)523-3236

QUINCY M2 / D1
The Kaufmann House, 1641 Hampshire, 62301 .... (217)223-2502

ROBINSON Q15 / F5
Bertram Arms B&B, RR#3, Box 243, 62454 .... (618)546-1122

ROCK ISLAND F5 / B2
Potter House B&B, 1906-7 Ave, 61201 .... (309)788-1906
Top O' The Morning, 1505 19th Ave, 61201 .... (309)786-3513

ROCKFORD B10 / A3
The Barn, 6786 Guilford Rd, 61107 .... (815)399-5210
Victoria's B&B, 201 N 6th St, 61107 .... (815)963-3232

SAINT CHARLES D13 / A4
Charleston Guest House, 612 W Main St, 60174 .... (708)377-1277
Stage Coach Inn, 41 W 278 Whitney Rd, 60174 .... (708)584-1263

SAINT JOSEPH /
Home at Last, RR2, Box 273, 61873 .... (217)469-2402

SOMONAUK E12 / B4
Watseka Farm, PO Box 272, 60552 .... (815)498-9820

SPRINGFIELD M8 / D3
Corinne's B&B Inn, 1001 S Sixth St, 62703 .... (217)527-1400
Mischler House, 718 S 8th St, 62703 .... (217)523-5616

STOCKTON B7 / A2
Maple Lane Country Inn, 3115 Rush Creek Rd, 61085 .... (815)947-3773
Memory Lane Lodge, 409 N Canyon Park Rd, 61085 .... (815)947-2726

SYCAMORE D12 / A4
Country Charm B&B, Rt 2 Box 154, Quigley Rd, 60178 .... (815)895-5386
Stratford Inn, 355 W State, 60178 .... (815)895-6789

TOLONO L13 / D4
Aunt Zelma's Country Guest House, RR 1, Box 129, 61880 .... (217)485-5101

WARREN A7 / A2
Noni's B&B, 516 W Main, Hwy 78, 61087 .... (815)745-2045

WEST DUNDEE C13 / A4
Ironhedge Inn, 305 Oregon, 60118 .... (708)426-7777

WEST SALEM S14 / F5
Thelma's B&B, 201 S Broadway, 62476 .... (618)456-8401

WHEATON D14 / B4
Wheaton Inn, Roosevelt Rd & Wheaton Ave, 60187 .... (708)690-2600

WINNETKA C15 / A5
Chateau des Fleurs, 552 Ridge Rd, 60093 .... (708)256-7272

WOODSTOCK B13 / A4
The Bundling Board Inn, 220 E South St, 60098 .... (815)338-7054

INDIANA

AUBURN D15 / A5
Auburn Inn, 225 Touring Dr, 46707 .... (219)925-6363

BATESVILLE P15 / E5
The Beechwood Inn, County Line Rd, 47006 .... (812)934-3426
Sherman House Restaurant & Inn, 35 S Main St, 47006 .... (812)934-2407

BERNE H16 / C5
Schug House Inn, 206 W Main St, 46711 .... (219)589-2303

BEVERLY SHORES B7 / A2
Dunes Shore Inn, Lakeshore County Rd, Box 807, 46301 .... (219)879-9029

BLOOMINGTON Q9 / F3
The Bauer House B&B, 4595 N Maple Grove Rd, 47401 .... (812)336-4383

BRISTOL B12 / A4
Open Hearth B&B, 56782 SR 15, 46507 .... (219)825-2417

CHESTERTON B6 / A2
The Gray Goose, 350 Indian Boundary Road, 46304 .... (219)926-5781
Wingfield's Inn B&B, 526 Indian Oak Mall, 46304 .... (219)348-0766

COLUMBUS Q11 / F4
The Columbus Inn, 445 Fifth St, 47501 .... (812)378-4289
Lafayette Street B&B, 723 Lafayette St, 47201 .... (812)372-7245

CONNERSVILLE N15 / E5
Maple Leaf Inn B&B, 831 N Grand Ave, 47331 .... (317)825-7099

CORYDON W11 / H3
Kintner House Inn, 101 S Capital, 47112 .... (812)738-2020

CRAWFORDSVILLE L7 / D2
Davis House, 1010 W Wabash Ave, 47933 .... (317)364-0461
Yount's Mill Inn, 3729 Old SR 32 W, 47933 .... (317)362-5864

DECATUR P13 / *B5*
Cragwood Inn, 303 N Second St, 46733 .... (219)728-2000

EVANSVILLE X4 / *M1*
Brigadoon B&B Inn, 1201 SE Second St, 47713 .... (812)422-9635

FORT WAYNE F15 / *B5*
The Candlewyck B&B, 331 W Washington Blvd, 46802 .... (219)424-2643
Roebuck Inn, 2727 Canterbury Blvd, 46835 .... (219)485-9619

GOSHEN B12 / *A4*
Checkerberry Inn, 62644 Country Rd 37, 46526 .... (219)642-4445

GRANDVIEW Y6 / *H2*
River Belle B&B, PO Box 669, Hwy 66, 47615 .... (812)649-2500

GREENCASTLE N7 / *E2*
Walden Inn, 2 Seminary Sq, 46135 .... (317)653-2761

HAGERSTOWN M15 / *D5*
Teetor House, 300 W Main St, 47346 .... (317)489-4422

HARTFORD CITY I14 / *C5*
De Coy's B&B, 1546 W 100 N, 47348 .... (317)348-2164

HUNTINGTON G13 / *B4*
Purviance House, 326 S Jefferson, 46750 .... (219)356-4218

INDIANAPOLIS N10 / *E3*
Barn House, 10656 E 63rd St, 46236 .... (317)823-4898
Le Chateau Delaware, 1456 N Delaware St, 46202 .... (317)636-9156
The Nuthatch B&B, 7161 Edgewater Pl, 46240 .... (317)257-2660
Osborne House, 1911 N Delaware, 46202 .... (317)924-1777
Pairadux Inn, 6363 N Guilford Ave, 46220 .... (317)259-8005
Renaissance Tower Historic Inn, 230 E 9th St, 46204 .... (317)631-2328

KNIGHTSTOWN M13 / *D4*
Lavendar Lady, 130 W Main St, 46148 .... (317)345-5400
Old Hoosier House, Rt 2 Box 299-I, 46148 .... (317)345-2969

LAGRANGE R14 / *A4*
The 1886 Inn, PO Box 5, 212 W Factory St, 46761 .... (219)463-4227

LEAVENWORTH W9 / *H3*
Ye Olde Scotts Inn, RR 1, Box 5, 47137 .... (812)739-4747

MADISON T14 / *G5*
Main Street B&B, 739 W Main St, 47250 .... (812)265-3539
The Cliff House, 122 Fairmount Dr, 47250 .... (812)265-5272

METAMORA O15 / *E5*
The Publick House, PO Box 202, 47030 .... (317)647-6729
The Thorpe House, Clayborne St, PO Box 36, 47030 .... (317)647-5425

MICHIGAN CITY B7 / *A2*
Creekwood Inn, Rt 20-35, 46460 .... (219)872-8357
Duneland Beach Inn, 3311 Potawatomi, 46360 .... (219)874-7729
Plantation Inn, RR 2 Box 296-s, 46360 .... (219)874-2418

MIDDLEBURY B12 / *A4*
Bee Hive B&B, PO Box 1191, 46540 .... (219)825-5023
Essenhaus Country Inn, 240 US 20 E, 46540 .... (219)825-9447
Patchwork Quilt Country Inn, 11748 Cr 2, 46540 .... (219)825-2417
Varns Guest House, PO 125, 205 S Main St, 46540 .... (219)825-9666

MISHAWAKA B10 / *A3*
The Beiger Mansion Inn, 317 Lincoln Way E, 46544 .... (219)256-0365

MONTICELLO H8 / *C3*
The Knight House Inn, RR 1, Box 251, 47960 .... (219)253-7794

MORGANTOWN P10 / *E3*
The Rock House, 380 W Washington St, 46160 .... (812)597-5100

MUNCIE K14 / *D5*
Old Franklin House, 704 East Washington St, 47305 .... (317)286-0277

NAPPANEE C11 / *A4*
East 253 Market Guest House, 253 E Market, 46550 .... (219)773-2261
The Victorian Guest House, 302 E Market St, 46550 .... (219)773-4383

NASHVILLE Q10 / *F3*
Allison House, 90 S Jefferson St, 47448 .... (812)988-6664
McGinley's Cabins, Rt 3, Box 332, 47448 .... (812)988-7337
Seasons, PO Box 187, 47448 .... (812)988-2284
Story Inn, PO Box 64, 47448 .... (812)988-2273
Sunset House, RR 3, Box 127, 47448 .... (812)988-6118

NEW HARMONY W2 / *H1*
New Harmony Inn, North St, 47631 .... (812)682-4491

NEWBURGH Y4 / *H2*
Phelps Mansion Inn, 208 N State St, 47630 .... (812)853-7766

PAOLI U9 / *G3*
Braxtan House Inn B&B, 210 N Gospel St, 47454 .... (812)723-4677

PLYMOUTH D10 / *A3*
Driftwood, PO Box 16, 46563 .... (219)546-2274

POLAND P6 / *E2*
Wasatch Lake, 47868 .... (812)986-2227

RICHLAND Y6 / *H2*
Country Homestead, Rt 1, Box 353, 47634 .... (812)359-4870

RISING SUN R17 / *F5*
Jelly House Country Inn, 222 S Walnut St, 47404 .... (812)438-2319

ROCKPORT Y6 / *H2*
The Rockport Inn, Third at Walnut, 47635 .... (812)649-2664

SHIPSHEWANA B13 / *A4*
Green Meadow, Rt 2 Box 592, State Rd 5, 46565 .... (219)768-4221
Old Davis Hotel, 228 W Main St, PO Box 545, 46565 .... (219)768-7300

SOUTH BEND B10 / *A3*
The Book Inn, 508 W Washington, 46601 .... (219)288-1990
Jamison Inn, 1404 N Ivy Rd, 46637 .... (219)277-9682
Queen Anne Inn, 420 W Washington, 46601 .... (219)234-5959

SYRACUSE C12 / *A4*
Anchor Inn B&B, Rt 4, Box 208A, 46567 .... (219)457-4714

WABASH G12 / *C4*
Hilltop House B&B, 88 W Sinclair St, 46992 .... (219)563-7726

WARSAW E12 / *B4*
Candlelight Inn, 503 E Fort Wayne St, 46580 .... (219)267-2906
White Hill Manor, 2513 E Center, 46580 .... (219)269-6933

WASHINGTON T5 / *G2*
Mimi's House, 101 W Maple, 47501 .... (812)254-5562

WESTFIELD L11 / *D3*
Camel Lot, 4512 W 131st St, 46074 .... (317)873-4370

IOWA

ADAIR L9 / *D3*
Farm Pond B&B, RR2, Box 3, 50002 .... (515)742-3606
Stagecoach Inn, 50002 .... (515)742-3658

ADEL K11 / *D4*
Walden Acres B&B, RR 1 Box 30, 50003 .... (515)987-1567

ANAMOSA H21 / *C7*
The Shaw House, 509 S Oak, 52205 .... (319)462-4485

ATLANTIC L7 / *D2*
Chestnut Charm B&B, 1409 Chestnut St, 50022 .... (712)243-5652

AVOCA L6 / *D2*
Victorian B&B Inn, 425 Walnut St, 51521 .... (712)343-6336

BELLEVUE H24 / *C8*
Mont Rest, 300 Spring St, 52031 .... (319)872-4220

BROOKLYN J17 / *C6*
Hotel Brooklyn, 154 Front St, 52211 .... (515)522-9229

BURLINGTON O22 / *E7*
Roads-Gardner House, 521 Court St, 52601 .... (319)689-4222

CALMAR C18 / *A6*
Calmar Guesthouse, RR 1 Box 206, 52132 .... (319)562-3851

CEDAR FALLS G16 / *B6*
Carriage House Inn B&B, 3030 Grand Blvd, 50613 .... (319)277-6724
Townsend Place B&B, 1017 Washington St, 50613 .... (319)266-9455

CLAYTON E21 / *B7*
Claytonian B&B, RR 2, Box 125A, 52049 .... (319)964-2776

CLEAR LAKE C13 / *A4*
Norsk Haus - By The Shore, 3611 N Shore Dr, 50428 .... (515)357-8368

CLERMONT D19 / *A6*
Bushman Cozy Ranch, R #2, Box 100, 52135 .... (319)423-7369

CORNING N8 / *E3*
Pheasants Galore, 616 Davis Ave, 50841 .... (515)322-3749

COUNCIL BLUFFS M4 / *D1*
Robin's Nest Inn B&B, 327 9th Ave, 50501 .... (712)323-1649

DAVENPORT K23 / *D8*
River Oaks Inn, 1234 E River Dr, 52803 .... (319)326-2629
Village B&B, 2017 E 13 St, 52803 .... (319)322-4905

DECORAH C19 / *A6*
Bruvold Farm, RR #1, 52101 .... (319)382-4729
Montgomery Mansion, 812 Maple Ave, 52101 .... (319)382-5088

DES MOINES K12 / *D4*
Carter House Inn, 640 20th St, Sherman Hill, 50314 .... (515)288-7850

DUBUQUE F23 / *B8*
Collier Mansion, 1072 W Third St, 52001 .... (319)588-2130
F.D. Stout House, 1105 Locust St, 52001 .... (800)331-5454
The Hancock House, 1105 Grove Terrace, 52001 .... (319)582-5421
L'Auberge Mandolin, 199 Loras, 52001 .... (319)556-0069
Oak Crest Guest Homes, 9866 Military Rd, 52001 .... (319)582-4207
Redstone Inn, 504 Bluff St, 52001 .... (319)582-1894
The Richards House, 1492 Locust St, 52001 .... (319)557-1492
Stout House, 1105 Locust, 52001 .... (319)582-1890

ELK HORN K7 / *D2*
The Travelling Companion B&B, 4314 Main St, 51531 ....(712)764-8932

ELKADER E20 / *B7*
Little House Vacations, 52043 ....(319)783-7774

ESTHERVILLE B8 / *A3*
Hoffman Guest House, 221 N Eighth St, 51334 ....(712)362-5994

FAIRFIELD N18 / *D6*
Happy Hearth, 400 W Washington, 52556 ....(515)472-9386

FORT ATKINSON C19 / *A6*
Cloverleaf Farm, Rt 2, Box 140A, 52144 ....(319)534-7061

FORT MADISON P21 / *E7*
The Morton House, 7 Highpoint, 52627 ....(319)372-9517

GREENFIELD L9 / *D3*
The Wilson Home, RR1, Box 132, 50849 ....(515)743-2031

HOMESTEAD J19 / *C6*
Die Heimat Country Inn, Main St, Amana Colonies, 52236 ... (319)622-3937

IOWA CITY K20 / *C7*
Haverkamp's Linn St Homestay, 619 N Linn St, 52245 ....(319)337-4363

KEOSAUQUA O18 / *E6*
Hotel Manning, 100 Van Buren St, 52565 ....(319)293-3232
Mason House Inn, RR 2 - Bentonsport, 52565 ....(319)592-3133

KEOTA L18 / *D6*
Elmhurst, RR 1, Box 3, 52248 ....(515)636-3001

LANSING B21 / *A7*
Fitzgerald's Inn, 106 3rd St, 52151 ....(319)538-4872

LE CLAIRE K24 / *C8*
Mohrhaus, 2450 Great River Rd N, 52753 ....(319)289-4503
The Monarch B&B, 303 2nd St, 52753 ....(319)289-3011

LEIGHTON L15 / *D5*
Heritage House, RR 1, 50143 ....(515)626-3092

MAQUOKETA I23 / *C8*
Decker Hotel, 128 N Main, 52060 ....(319)652-6654

MARENGO J18 / *C6*
Loy's B&B, RR 1 Box 82, 52301 ....(319)642-7787

MARION I20 / *C7*
Martin Farm - L-Mar, 1777 Austin Rd, RR #3, 52302 ....(319)377-2055

MASSENA M8 / *D3*
Amdor's Evergreen Inn, RR 1, Box 65, 50853 ....(712)779-3521

MAYNARD E18 / *B6*
Boedeker's Bungalow, 125 7th St N, 50655 ....(319)637-2711

MCGREGOR D21 / *A7*
Little Switzerland Inn, 126 Main St, 52157 ....(319)873-3670
McGregor Riverton Inn, 424 Main St, 52157 ....(319)873-2385
River's Edge B&B, 12 Main St, 52157 ....(319)873-3501

MIDDLE AMANA J19 / *C6*
Dusk to Dawn B & B, Box 124, 52307 ....(319)622-3029

MONTEZUMA K16 / *D5*
English Valley B&B, RR #2, Box 65, 50171 ....(515)623-3663

MONTPELIER K23 / *D8*
Varner's Caboose, 204 E 2nd, Box 10, 52759 ....(319)381-3652

NEVADA I13 / *C4*
Queen Anne B&B, 1110 Ninth St, 50201 ....(515)382-6444

NEWTON K14 / *C5*
La Corsette Maison Inn, 629 First Ave E, 50208 ....(515)792-6833

ONAWA I3 / *C1*
Log Cabin Inn B&B, RR1, Box 116, 51040 ....(712)423-1883

PANORA K10 / *C3*
Hudson House, 300 West Main, 50216 ....(515)755-2797

PELLA L15 / *D5*
Strawtown Inn, 1111 Washington St, 50219 ....(515)628-2681

PRESCOTT N9 / *D3*
Maple Hill Farms, RR #2, Box 83, 50859 ....(515)369-4874

RED OAK N6 / *D2*
Knit & Pearl, 105 Hammond, 51566 ....(712)792-3921

SOUTH AMANA J18 / *C6*
Babi's B&B, Rt 1, 52334 ....(319)662-4381

SPENCER C7 / *A2*
The Hannah Marie Country Inn, Rt 1, Hwy 71 S, 51301 ....(712)262-1286

SPILLVILLE C19 / *A6*
Old World Inn, 331 S Main St, 52168 ....(319)562-3739

STRATFORD H11 / *C4*
Hooks' Point Farmstead B&B, Rt 1, Box 222, 50249 ....(515)838-2781

STUART K10 / *D3*
Summit Grove Inn, 1426 S 7th, 50250 ....(515)523-2147

SWISHER J19 / *C6*
Terra Verde Farm, Rt 1, Box 86, 52338 ....(319)846-2478

THURMAN O4 / *E2*
Plum Creek Inn, RR 1, Box 91, 51654 ....(712)628-2191

TIPTON J21 / *C7*
Victorian House Tipton, 508 E 4th St, 52772 ....(319)886-2633

WALNUT L6 / *D2*
The Wild Rose Inn, 701 Walnut St, PO Box 324, 51577 ....(712)784-3010

WAUKON C20 / *A7*
Allamakee B&B, 700 Allamakee St, 52170 ....(319)568-3103

WEBSTER CITY G12 / *B4*
Centennial Farm, 1091 220th St, 50595 ....(515)832-3050

WILLIAMSBURG K18 / *C6*
Lucille's Country Inn, RR 2, Box 55, 52361 ....(319)668-1185

KANSAS

ABILENE F16 / *C6*
Victorian Reflections B&B Inn, 303 N Cedar, 67410 ....(913)263-7774

ASHLAND L9 / *E3*
Hardesty House, 712 Main St, 67831 ....(316)635-2911

ATWOOD B5 / *A2*
The Flower Patch B&B, 610 Main, 67730 ....(913)626-3780

BERN B20 / *A7*
Lear Acres B&B, Rt 1, Box 31, 66408 ....(913)336-3903

BURLINGTON H21 / *D7*
Victorian Memories, 314 N 4th, 66839 ....(316)364-5752

CASSODAY I18 / *D6*
The Sunbarger Guest House, RR, 66842 ....(316)735-4499

CIMARRON J7 / *D2*
The Cimarron Hotel, 203 N Main, 67835 ....(316)855-2244

COLUMBUS L24 / *E8*
Meriwether House, 322 W Pine, 66725 ....(316)429-2812

CONCORDIA C15 / *B5*
Crystle's B&B, 508 W 7th St, 66901 ....(913)243-2192

COUNCIL GROVE F19 / *C6*
The Cottage House Hotel, 25 N Neosho, 66846 ....(316)767-6828

FORT SCOTT I24 / *D8*
Country Quarters, Rt 5, Box 80, 66701 ....(316)223-2889
Huntington House, 324 S Main, 66701 ....(316)223-3644

GARNETT H22 / *C8*
Kirk House, 145 W 4th Ave, 66032 ....(913)448-5813

GREAT BEND H12 / *C4*
Peaceful Acres B&B, Rt 5, Box 153, 67530 ....(316)793-7527

HALSTEAD I16 / *D5*
Heritage Inn, 300 Main St, 67056 ....(316)835-2118

HAYS F10 / *C3*
Frontier City's Butterfield B&B, Rt 1, Box 200, 67601 ....(913)625-9978

HILL CITY D9 / *B3*
Pomeroy Inn, 224 W Main, 67642 ....(913)674-2098

HOLTON C21 / *B7*
Dodds House B&B, Hwy 75 S, 66436 ....(913)364-3172

HOLYROOD G13 / *C4*
Hollyrood House, Rt 1 Box 47, 67450 ....(913)252-3678

HUTCHINSON I14 / *D5*
Bellmore House B&B, 1500 N Main St, 67501 ....(316)663-5824

LAWRENCE E22 / *C8*
Halcyon House, 1000 Ohio, 66044 ....(913)841-0314

LINCOLN E14 / *B5*
Woody House B&B, Rt 1, Box 156, 67455 ....(913)524-4744

LINDSBORG G15 / *C5*
Swedish Country Inn, 112 W Lincoln, 67456 ....(913)227-2985

MANHATTAN E18 / *B6*
Kimble Cliff, Rt 1 Box 139, 66502 ....(913)539-3816

MELVERN G21 / *C7*
Schoolhouse Inn, 106 E Beck, PO Box 175, 66510 ....(913)549-3473

NEWTON I16 / *D5*
Hawk House B&B, 307 W Broadway, 67062 ....(316)283-2045

PEABODY H17 / *D6*
Jones Sheep Farm B&B, RR 2, 66866 ....(316)983-2815

SALINA F15 / C5
Hunters Leigh B&B, 4109 E North St, 67401 ....(913)823-6750

TONGANOXIE E23 / B8
Almeda's B&B, 220 S Main, 66086 ....(913)845-2295

TOPEKA E21 / B7
Heritage House, 3535 SW 6th St, 66606 ....(913)233-3800

ULYSSES J4 / D1
Fort's Cedar View, 1675 W Patterson Ave, 67880 ....(316)356-2570

VALLEY FALLS D22 / B7
The Barn B&B, RR 2 Box 87, 66088 ....(913)945-3303

WAKEENEY E9 / B3
Thistle Hill B&B, Rt 1, Box 93, 67672 ....(913)743-2644

WAKEFIELD D17 / B6
B&B On Our Farm, Rt 1 Box 132, 67487 ....(913)461-5596

WICHITA J16 / D5
Max Paul Inn, 3910 E Kellogg, 67218 ....(316)689-8101
The Inn at the Park, 3751 E Douglas, 67208 ....(316)652-0500
The Inn at Willowbend, 4130 Tara Circle, 67226 ....(316)636-4227

KENTUCKY

AUBURN O7 / D6
David N. Williams Guest House, 421 W Main St, 42206 ....(502)542-6019

AUGUSTA F18 / A9
Lamplighter Inn, 103 W Second St, 41002 ....(606)756-2603

BARDSTOWN K12 / C7
Bruntwood 1802, 714 N 3 St, 40004 ....(502)348-8218
Jailer's Inn, 111 W Stephen Foster Ave, 40004 ....(502)348-5551
Kenmore Farms, 1050 Bloomfield Rd, US 62E, 40004 ....(502)348-8023
The Mansion, 1003 N Third St, 40004 ....(502)348-2586
Old Talbott Tavern, Court Square, 107 W Stephen Foster, 40004 ....(502)348-3494

BEREA L17 / C9
Boone Tavern Hotel, Main St CPO 2345, 40403 ....(606)986-9358
Holly Tree B&B, 610 Chestnut St, 40403 ....(606)986-2804

BOWLING GREEN O8 / D6
Alpine Lodge, 5310 Morgantown Rd, 42101 ....(502)843-4846
Bowling Green B&B, 659 E 14th Ave, 42101 ....(502)781-3861
Walnut Lawn B&B, 1800 Morgantown Rd, 42101 ....(502)781-7255

BRANDENBURG J9 / C6
Doe Run Inn, Rt 2, 40108 ....(502)422-2982

BURKESVILLE P12 / D7
Cabin Fever, 630 Davidson Rd, 42717 ....(502)737-4980

CARROLLTON F13 / A7
P.T. Baker House, 406 Highland Ave, 41008 ....(502)732-4210

COVINGTON D16 / A8
Amos Shinkle Townhouse, 215 Garrard St, 41011 ....(606)431-2118

CYNTHIANA H17 / B8
Broadwell Acres, Rt 6 Box 58, 41031 ....(606)234-4255

DEATSVILLE J12 / C7
The Deatsville Inn, KY-523 off KY-245, 40016 ....(502)348-6382

ELIZABETHTOWN K10 / C7
Olde Bethlehem Academy Inn, 7051 St John Rd, 42701 ....(502)862-9003

EMINENCE H13 / B7
Eminence Inn B&B, 346 S Main, 40019 ....(502)845-4549

FRANKFORT I14 / B8
Olde Kentucke, 210 E Fourth St, 40601 ....(502)227-7389

GEORGETOWN I15 / B8
Log Cabin B&B, 350 N Broadway, 40324 ....(502)863-3514

GLASGOW O10 / D7
Four Seasons Country Inn, 4107 Scottsville Rd, 42141 ....(502)678-1000
Three O Seven, 307 W Brown St, 42141 ....(502)651-5672

GLENDALE L10 / C7
Petticoat Junction, 223 High St, 42740 ....(502)369-8604

HARRODSBURG K14 / C8
Beaumont Inn, 638 Beaumont Dr, 40330 ....(606)734-3381
Canaan Land Farm B&B, 4355 Lexington Rd, 40330 ....(606)734-3984
Ms. Jesta Bell's B&B, 367 N Main St, 40330 ....(606)734-7834
Shakertown At Pleasant Hill, 3500 Lexington Rd, 40330 ....(606)734-5411

HENDERSON J4 / C5
McCullagh House, 304 S Main St, 42420 ....(502)826-0943

HOPKINSVILLE O4 / D5
Oakland Manor, 9210 Newstead Rd, 42240 ....(502)885-6400

KUTTAWA N2 / D4
Davis House, Rt 2, Box 21A1, 42055 ....(502)388-4468

LEBANON L13 / C7
Myrtledene, 370 N Spaulding Ave, 40033 ....(502)692-2223

LEXINGTON I16 / B8
547 B&B, 547 N Broadway, 40508 ....(606)255-4152
Rokeby Hall, 318 S Mill St, 40508 ....(606)252-2368

LOUISVILLE H11 / B7
Old Louisville B&B, 1454 S Fourth St, 40208 ....(502)636-3661

MARION M2 / D4
Historic Lafayette Heights, Rt 2, Box 174, 42064 ....(502)965-3889

MIDDLESBORO P19 / E9
The Ridge Runner B&B, 208 Arthur Heights, 40965 ....(606)248-4299

MURRAY P1 / E4
The Diuguid House, 603 Main St, 42071 ....(502)753-5470

OWENSBORO B3 / C5
Friendly Farm & Our Tennis House, 5931 KY-56W, 42301 ....(502)771-5590

PADUCAH F5 / D3
Ehrhardts B&B, 285 Springwell Dr, 42001 ....(502)554-0644
Paducah Harbor Plaza B&B, 201 Broadway, 42001 ....(502)442-2698

RAYWICK L12 / C7
Blue Hill Farm B&B, Rt 2, Box 39A, 40060 ....(502)465-4221

RICHMOND K17 / C9
Jordan Hill Farm, 722 Walker Parks Rd, 40475 ....(606)623-8114

RUSSELLVILLE O6 / D6
The Log House, 2139 Franklin Rd, 42276 ....(502)726-8483

SHELBYVILLE I13 / B7
Muir House, Rt 8, Box 423, 40065 ....(502)633-7037

SIMPSONVILLE I12 / B7
The Old Stone Inn, Rt 5, 40065 ....(502)722-8882

SOMERSET N15 / D8
Shadwick House, 411 S Main, 42501 ....(606)678-4675

SPRINGFIELD K13 / C7
Glenmar Plantation B&B, Rt 1, Box 682, 40069 ....(606)284-7791
Maple Hill Manor, Perryville Rd, 40508 ....(606)336-3075
Walton's West Wind, Rt 2, Box 34, 40069 ....(606)336-9283

TAYLORSVILLE I12 / B7
B&B at Taylorsville, Rt 2, Box 218, Hwy 44, 40071 ....(502)477-2473
Bowling's Villa B&B, Rt 4, Box 140, Hwy 44, 40071 ....(502)477-2636

VERSAILLES I15 / B8
Sills Inn B&B, 270 Montgomery Ave, 40383 ....(606)873-4478
Springdale, Rt 1 Box 263, 40383 ....(606)873-3208

LOUISIANA

AMITE H10 / D5
Blythewood Plantation, PO Box 155, 70422 ....(504)748-8183

BATON ROUGE I8 / D4
Mount Hope Plantation, 8151 Highland Rd, 70808 ....(504)766-8600

CLINTON H9 / D5
Brame-Bennet House, 227 S Baton Rouge St, 70722 ....(504)683-5241

COVINGTON I11 / D6
The Guest Cottage, 618 E 7th Ave, 70433 ....(504)893-3767
Plantation Bell Guest House, 204 W 24th Ave, 70433 ....(504)893-7693
Riverside Hills Farm, 96 Gardenia Dr, 70433 ....(504)892-1794

DARROW J9 / E4
Tezcuco Plantation Village, 3138 Hwy 44, 70725 ....(504)562-3929

GLOSTER C2 / B1
Buena Vista Plantation, Rt 2 Box 301, 71030 ....(318)925-2569

JACKSON H8 / D4
Asphodel Plantation, Rt 2 Box 89, 70748 ....(504)654-6868
Milbank, 102 Bank St, 70748 ....(504)634-5901

JEANERETTE J7 / E4
Patout's Guest House, Rt 1, Box 288, 70544 ....(318)364-0644

KENNER J11 / E6
7 Oaks, 2600 Gay Lynn, 70065 ....(504)888-8649

LAFAYETTE I6 / E3
Bois Des Chenes Plantation, 538 N Sterling, 70501 ....(318)233-7816
Mouton Manor Inn, 310 Sidney Martin Rd, 70507 ....(318)237-6996
Ti Frere's House, 1905 Verot School Rd, 70508 ....(318)984-9347

MADISONVILLE I11 / D6
River Run Guest House, 703 Main St, 70447 ....(504)845-4222

MONROE C6 / A3
Boscobel Cottage, 185 Cordell Ln, 71202 ....(318)325-1550

NAPOLEONVILLE J9 / E5
Madewood Plantation, 4250 Hwy 308, 70390 ....(504)369-7151

NEW IBERIA
J7 / *E4*

Masion Marceline, 442 E Main St, 70560 .... (318)364-5922

NEW ORLEANS
J11 / *E6*

A Creole House, 1013 St Ann St, 70116 .... (504)524-8076
A Hotel, the Frenchman, 417 Frenchman St, 70116 .... (504)948-2166
Andrew Jackson Hotel, 919 Royal St, 70166 .... (504)561-5881
B&B at The Chimes, 1360 Moss St, PO Box 52257, 70152-2257 .... (504)525-4640
Burgundy Inn, 911 Burgundy St, 70116 .... (504)524-0141
Columns Hotel, 3811 St Charles Ave, 70115 .... (504)899-9308
Dauzat House, 337 Burgundy St, 70130 .... (504)524-2075
Dusty Mansion, 2231 General Pershing, 70115 .... (504)895-4576
French Quarter Maisons, 1130 Chartres St, 70116 .... (504)524-9918
Grenoble House, 329 Dauphine, 70112 .... (504)522-1331
Hotel Maison De Ville, 727 Rue Toulouse, 70130 .... (504)561-5858
Hotel Ste. Helene, 508 Rue Chartres St, 70130 .... (504)522-5014
Hotel Villa Convento, 616 Ursulines St, 70116 .... (504)522-1793
Jensen's B&B, 1631 Seventh St, 70115 .... (504)897-1895
Josephine Guest House, 1450 Josephine St, 70130 .... (504)524-6361
Lafitte Guest House, 1003 Bourbon St, 70116 .... (504)581-2678
Lamothe House, 621 Esplanade Ave, 70116 .... (504)947-1161
Longpre Garden's Guest House, 1726 Prytania, 70130 .... (504)561-0654
Maison De Ville, 727 Toulouse St, 70130 .... (504)561-5858
Marquette Hostel, 2253 Carondelet St, 70130 .... (504)523-3014
Mazant Street Guest House, 906 Mazant St, 70117 .... (504)944-2662
Melrose, 937 Esplanade Ave, 70116 .... (504)944-2255
Old World Inn, 1330 Prytania, 70130 .... (504)566-1330
P.J. Holbrooks Olde Victorian Inn, 914 N Rampart St, 70116 .... (504)522-2446
Park View, 7004 St Charles St, 70118 .... (504)861-7564
Prince Conti Hotel, 830 Conti St, 70112 .... (504)529-4172
Prytania Inn, 1415 Prytania St, 70130 .... (504)566-1515
The Prytania Park Hotel, 1525 Prytania St, 70130 .... (800)862-1984
Soniat House, 1133 Chartres St, 70116 .... (504)522-0570
St. Charles Guest House, 1748 Prytania St, 70130 .... (504)523-6556
St. Peter House, 1005 St Peter St, 70116 .... (504)524-9232
The Stone Manor Hotel, 3800 St Charles Ave, 70115 .... (504)899-9600
Terrell House Mansion, 1441 Magazine St, 70130 .... (504)524-9859
The Columns Hotel, 3811 St Charles Ave, 70115 .... (504)899-9308
The Victorian Guesthouse, 1021 Moss St, Box 52257, 70152-2257 .... (504)525-4640

NEW ROADS
H8 / *D4*

Pointe Coupee B&B, 605 E Main St, 70760 .... (504)638-6254

OPELOUSAS
H6 / *D3*

Estorge House, 427 N Market St, 70570 .... (318)948-4592

RUSTON
C5 / *A3*

Twin Gables, 711 N Vienna St, 71270 .... (318)255-4452

SAINT FRANCISVILLE
H8 / *D4*

Barrow House, 524 Royal St, PO Box 1461, 70775 .... (504)635-4791
Cottage Plantation, Rt 5 Box 425, 70775 .... (504)635-3674
Myrtles Plantation, US Hwy 61N, PO Box 1100, 70775 .... (504)635-6277

SHREVEPORT
C2 / *A1*

The Columns on Jordan, 615 Jordan, 71101 .... (318)222-5912
Fairfield Place, 2221 Fairfield Ave, 71104 .... (318)222-0048

ST. MARTINVILLE
J7 / *E4*

Evangeline Oak Corner, 215 Evangeline Blvd, 70582 .... (318)394-7675
The Old Castillo Hotel, 220 Evangeline Blvd, PO Box 172, 70582 .... (318)394-4010

VACHERIE
J9 / *E5*

Oak Alley Plantation, Rt 2 Box 10 Hwy 18, 70090 .... (504)265-2151

VINTON
I2 / *E1*

Old Lyons House, 1335 Horridge St, 70668 .... (318)589-2903

WASHINGTON
H6 / *D3*

Camellia Cove, 205 W Hill St, 70589 .... (318)826-7362
La Chaumiere, 217 S Washington St, 70589 .... (318)826-3967

WHITE CASTLE
J8 / *E4*

Nottoway Plantation Inn & Restaurant, Mississippi River Rd, PO Box 160, 70788 .... (504)545-2730

WILSON
G8 / *D4*

Glencoe Plantation, PO Box 178, 70789 .... (504)629-5387

MAINE

ALFRED
K2 / *H1*

The Olde Berry Inn, Kennebunk Rd, 04002 .... (207)324-0603

ASHVILLE
G9 / *F4*

Green Hill Farm, RFD #1, Box 328, 04607 .... (207)422-3273

BAILEY ISLAND
J4 / *G2*

Driftwood Inn, 04003 .... (207)833-5461
Katie's Ketch, Box 105, 04003 .... (207)833-7785
The Lady & The Loon, PO Box 98, 04003 .... (207)833-6871

BAR HARBOR
G9 / *F4*

The Atlantean Inn, 11 Atlantic Ave, 04609 .... (207)288-3270
Bayview Inn & Hotel, 111 Eden St, 04609 .... (207)288-5861
Black Friar Inn, 10 Summer St, 04609 .... (207)288-5091
The Inn at Canoe Point, Rt 3 Box 216R - Hull's Cove, 04644 .... (207)288-9511
Canterbury Cottage, 12 Roberts Ave, 04609 .... (207)288-2112
Cleftstone Manor, 92 Eden St, 04609 .... (207)288-4951
Cottage Inns of Bar Harbor, 16 Roberts Ave, 04609 .... (207)288-3443
Graycote Inn, 40 Holland Ave, 04609 .... (207)288-3044
The Hearthside, 7 High St, 04609 .... (207)288-4533
Holbrook House, 74 Mt Desert St, 04609 .... (207)288-4970
Ledgelawn Inn, 66 Mt Desert, 04609 .... (207)288-4596
Manor House Inn, 104 West St, 04609 .... (207)288-3759
The Maples, 16 Roberts Ave, 04609 .... (207)288-3443
Mira Monte Inn, 69 Mt Desert St, 04609 .... (207)288-4263
Primrose Cottage Inn, 73 Mt Desert St, 04609 .... (207)288-4031
Ridgeway Manor, 11 High St, 04609 .... (207)288-9682
Shady Maples, RD 1 Box 360, 04609 .... (207)288-3793
Stratford House Inn, 45 Mt Desert St, 04609 .... (207)288-5189
The Tides, 119 West St, 04609 .... (207)288-4968
Thornhedge, 47 Mt Desert St, 04609 .... (207)288-5398
Town Guest House, 12 Atlantic Ave, 04609 .... (207)288-5548
Ullikana in the Field, The Field, 04609 .... (207)288-9552

BASS HARBOR
H9 / *F4*

Bass Harbor Inn, Shore Rd, 04653 .... (207)244-5157
Pointy Head Inn, Rt 102A, 04653 .... (207)244-7261

BATH
I4 / *G2*

Elizabeth's B&B, 360 Front St, 04530 .... (207)443-1146
Fairhaven Inn, RR 2 PO Box 85, N Bath Rd, 04530 .... (207)443-4391
Glad II, 60 Pearl St, 04530 .... (207)443-1191
Packard House, 45 Pearl St, 04530 .... (207)443-6069
Pine Hill B&B, HC 31 Box 85, 04530 .... (207)443-2143

BELFAST
G7 / *F3*

Fiddler's Green Farm, RFD #1, Box 656, 04915 .... (207)338-3568
Frost House B&B, 6 Northport Ave, 04915 .... (207)338-4159
Hiram Alden Inn, 19 Church St, 04915 .... (207)338-2151
Horatio Johnson House, 36 Church St, 04915 .... (207)338-5153
The Jeweled Turret Inn, 16 Pearl St, 04915 .... (207)338-2304
Londonderry Inn, Rt 3, Belmont Ave, 04915 .... (207)338-3988
Northport House B&B, City One, Mounted Rt, US Rt 1, 04915 .... (207)338-1422
The Palmer House, 7 Franklin St, 04915 .... (207)338-5790
Penobscot Meadows, Rt 1, 04915 .... (207)338-5320

BETHEL
G2 / *F1*

Bakers B&B, RFD 2 Box 2090, 04217 .... (207)824-2088
Bethel Inn & Court, PO Box 26, 04217 .... (800)654-0125
Chapman Inn, PO Box 206, 04217 .... (207)824-2657
Douglass Place, Rt 2, Box 9, 04217 .... (207)824-2229
Four Seasons Inn, Upper Main St, 04217 .... (207)824-2755
Hammons House, Broad St, 04217 .... (207)824-3170
L'Auberge Country Inn, PO Box 21, 04217 .... (207)824-2774
Norseman Inn, Rt 2 Rumford Rd, 04217 .... (207)824-2002
Sudbury Inn, PO Box 369 Lower Main St, 04217 .... (207)824-2174
Sunday River Inn, Sunday River Rd, 04217 .... (207)824-2410
The Pointed Fir, PO Box 745, 04217 .... (207)824-2251

BIDDEFORD POOL
K3 / *H1*

Lodge, 19 Yates, 04006 .... (207)284-7148

BLUE HILL
G8 / *F4*

Arcady Down East, South St, 04614 .... (207)374-5576
Blue Hill Farm Country Inn, Rt 15 Box 437, 04614 .... (207)374-5126
John Peters Inn, PO Box 916, 04614 .... (207)374-2116

BOOTHBAY
I5 / *G2*

Kenniston Hill Inn, Rt 27, 04537 .... (207)633-2159

BOOTHBAY HARBOR
I5 / *G2*

Admiral's Quarters Inn, 105 Commercial St, 04538 .... (207)633-2474
The Anchor Watch, PO Box, 04538 .... (207)633-2284
The Atlantic Ark Inn, 64 Atlantic Ave, 04538 .... (207)633-5690
Boothbay Harbor Inn, 37 Atlantic Ave, Box 446, 04538 .... (207)633-6302
Captain Sawyer's Place, 87 Commercial St, 04538 .... (207)633-2290
Green Shutters Inn, PO Box 543, 04538 .... (207)633-2646
Harbour Towne Inn, 71 Townsend Ave, 04538 .... (207)633-4300
Hilltop House, 44 Mckown Hill, 04538 .... (207)633-3839
Howard House, Route 27, 04538 .... (207)633-3933
Seafarer Guest House, 38 Union St, 04538 .... (705)633-4441
Thistle Inn, PO Box 176, 04538 .... (207)633-3541
Topside, Mckown Hill, 04538 .... (207)633-5404
Welch House, 36 Mckown St, 04538 .... (207)633-3431
Westgate Guest House, 18 West St, 04538 .... (207)633-3552

BOWDOINHAM
I4 / *G2*

The Maples, RR 1 Box 75, 04008 .... (207)666-3012

BRIDGTON
H2 / *G1*

The 1859 Guest House, 60 S High St, 04009 .... (207)647-2508
Noble House, PO Box 180, 04009 .... (207)647-3733

Tarry-a-While Resort, Box A, Highland Ridge Rd, 04009 ....(207)647-2522

BRISTOL I5 / G2
The Bristol Inn, Upper Round Pond Rd, PO Box 130, 04539 ...(207)563-1125

BRISTOL MILLS I5 / G2
The Old Cape of Bristol Mills B&B, Rt 130, PO Box 129, 04539 ....(207)563-8848

BRUNSWICK I4 / G2
Aaron Dunning House, 76 Federal St, 04011 ....(207)729-4486
Brunswick B&B, 165 Park Row, 04011 ....(207)729-4914
Harborgate B&B, RD 2-2260, 04011 ....(207)725-5894
Harriet Beecher Stowe House, 63 Federal St, 04011 ....(207)725-5543
Samuel Newman House, 7 South St, 04011 ....(207)729-6959

BUCKSPORT F7 / F3
L'ermitage, 219 Main St, 04416 ....(207)469-3361
The Old Parsonage Inn, PO Box 1577, 190 Franklin St, 04416 ....(207)469-6477
The River Inn, 210 Main St, 04416 ....(207)469-3783

CAMDEN H7 / F3
Blackberry Inn, 82 Elm St, 04843 ....(207)236-6060
Blue Harbor House, 67 Elm St, Rt 1, 04843 ....(207)236-3196
The Camden Maine Stay Inn, 22 High St, 04843 ....(207)236-9636
Chestnut House, 69 Chestnut St, 04843 ....(207)236-6137
Edgecombe-Coles House, 64 High St, HCR 60 Box 3010, 04843 ....(207)236-2336
The Elms B&B, 84 Elm St, Rt 1, 04843 ....(207)236-6250
Hartstone Inn, 41 Elm St, 04843 ....(207)236-4259
Hawthorn Inn, 9 High St, 04843 ....(207)236-8842
Hosmer House, Four Pleasant St, 04843 ....(207)236-4012
Lord Camden Inn, 24 Main St, 04843 ....(207)236-4325
Mansard Manor, 5 High St, 04843 ....(207)236-3291
Norumbega Inn, 61 High St, 04843 ....(207)236-4646
Owl And The Turtle, 8 Bay View, 04843 ....(207)235-4769
The Swan House, 49 Mountain St, 04843 ....(207)236-8275
Whitehall Inn, 52 High St, 04843 ....(207)236-3391
Windward House, 6 High St, 04843 ....(207)236-9656

CAPE NEDDICK L2 / H1
Cape Neddick House, Rt 1 Box 70, 03902 ....(207)363-2500
Sea Chimes B&B, Shore Rd, 03902 ....(207)646-5378
Wooden Goose Inn, Rt 1 Box 195, 03902 ....(207)363-5673

CAPE NEWAGEN J5 / G2
Newagen Seaside Inn, Rt 27 S, 04552 ....(207)633-5242

CARRABASSETT VALLEY D4 / E2
Sugarloaf Inn, Carrabasset Vly, 04947 ....(207)237-2701

CASCO I2 / G1
Maplewood Inn, Rt 302 Box 627, 04015 ....(207)655-7586

CASTINE G7 / F3
Castine Inn, PO Box 41, 04421 ....(207)326-4365
The Holiday House, Box 215, Perkins St, 04421 ....(207)326-4335
The Manor, Battle Ave, PO Box 276, 04421 ....(207)326-4861
Pentagoet Inn, PO Box 4, 04421 ....(207)326-8616

CENTER LOVELL H1 / F1
Center Lovell Inn, Rt 5, 04016 ....(207)925-1575
Westways On Kezar Lake, Rt 5, 04016 ....(207)928-2663

CHEBEAGUE ISLAND J3 / G2
Chebeague Inn, 04017 ....(207)967-3118
Chebeague Island Inn, PO Box 492-MBB, 04107 ....(207)846-5155

CHERRYFIELD F10 / F4
Ricker House, Box 256, 04622 ....(207)546-2780

CLARK ISLAND I6 / G3
Craignair Inn, Clark Island Rd, 04859 ....(207)594-7644

COOPERS MILLS H5 / F2
Claryknoll Farm, Rt 215, Box 751, 04341 ....(207)549-5250

CORNISH I1 / G1
Cornish Country Inn, Box 206, 04020 ....(207)625-8673
The Cornish Inn, Rt 25 Box 266, 04020 ....(207)625-8501

CUTLER F12 / F5
Little River Lodge, Rt 191, 04626 ....(207)259-4437

DAMARISCOTTA I5 / G2
Brannon-Bunker Inn, PO Box 045, HCR 64, 04543 ....(207)563-5941
Mill Pond Inn, RFD 1 Box 245, 04553 ....(207)563-8014
Yellow House B&B, Water St, Box 732, 04543 ....(207)563-1388

DEER ISLE H8 / F3
Pilgrim's Inn, Main St, 04627 ....(207)348-6615

DEER ISLE VILLAGE H8 / F3
Laphroaig B&B, Rte 15, PO Box 67, 04627 ....(207)348-6088

DENNYSVILLE E12 / E5
Lincoln House Country Inn, Rts 1 & 86, 04628 ....(207)726-3953

DIXMONT F6 / F3
Ben-Loch Inn, RFD 1 Box 1020, 04932 ....(207)257-4768

DOVER-FOXCROFT D6 / E3
The Foxcroft, 25 W Main St, 04426 ....(207)564-7720

EAST BOOTHBAY I5 / G2
Five Gables Inn, Murray Hill Rd, 04544 ....(207)633-4551
Linekin Village B&B, Ocean Point Rd, Rt 96, 04544 ....(207)633-3681
Ocean Point Inn, Shore Rd, 04544 ....(207)633-4200

EAST MACHIAS F11 / E5
East River B&B, PO Box 205, High St, 04630 ....(207)255-8467

EAST WATERFORD H2 / F1
Waterford Inne, Box 49, 04233 ....(207)583-4037

EASTPORT E13 / E5
Artists Retreat, 29 Washington St, 04631 ....(207)853-4239
Kilby House, 122 Water St, 04631 ....(207)853-4791
The Inn At Eastport, 13 Washington St, 04631 ....(207)853-4307
Todd House, Todd's Head, 04631 ....(207)853-2328
Weston House, 26 Boynton St, 04631 ....(207)853-2907

ELIOT L2 / H1
Ewenicorn Farm B&B, 116 Goodwin Rd, Rt 101, 03903 ....(207)439-1337
High Meadows B&B, Rt 101, 03903 ....(207)439-0590

ELLSWORTH F9 / F4
Victoria's B&B, 58 Pine St, 04605 ....(207)667-5893

FIVE ISLANDS I4 / G2
Coveside, General Delivery, 04546 ....(207)371-2807

FREEPORT I4 / G2
181 Main St, 181 Main St, 04032 ....(207)865-1226
Atlantic Seal B&B, PO Box 146, 25 Main St, 04078 ....(207)865-6112
The Bagley House, RR 3 Box 269C, 04032 ....(207)865-6566
Captain Josiah Mitchell House, 188 Main St, 04032 ....(207)865-3289
Harraseeket Inn, 162 Main St, 04032 ....(207)865-9377
Holbrook Inn, 7 Holbrook St, 04032 ....(207)865-6693
Isaac Randall House, 5 Independence Dr, 04032 ....(207)865-9295
Maple Hill B&B, 18 Maple Ave, 04032 ....(207)865-3730
Nathan Nye Inn, 11 Nathan Nye St, 04032 ....(207)865-9606
Old Red Farm, RR 2 Box 242 Desert Rd, 04032 ....(207)865-4550

FRIENDSHIP I6 / G3
Harbor Hill By-the-Sea, Town Landing Rd, PO Box 35, 04547 ....(207)832-6646

FRYEBURG H1 / G1
The Oxford House Inn, 105 Main St, 04037 ....(207)935-3442

GEORGETOWN I5 / G2
The Grey Havens, Box 308, 04548 ....(207)371-2616
Guilford B&B, Elm & Prospect Sts, 04443 ....(207)876-3477

GORHAM J3 / G1
Country Squire B&B, Box 178 Mighty St Rt1, 04038 ....(207)839-4855

GOULDSBORO G10 / F4
Sunset House, Rt 186, 04607 ....(207)963-7156

GREENVILLE C5 / D2
Evergreen Lodge B&B, HCR 76, Box 58, Rt 15, 04441 ....(207)695-3241
Greenville Inn, Norris St, PO Box 1194, 04441 ....(207)695-2206

GUILFORD D6 / E3
Trebor Inn, PO Box 299, 04443 ....(207)876-4070

HANCOCK G9 / F4
Apple Store B&B, HCR 77 Box 480, 04640 ....(207)422-9959
LeDomaine Restaurant & Inn, US 1, Box 496, 04640 ....(207)422-3395

HARPSWELL J4 / G2
Lookout Point House, 141 Lookout Point Rd, 04079 ....(207)833-5509

HARRISON H2 / F1
Tolman House Inn, PO Box 551, Tolman Rd, 04040 ....(207)583-4445

HARTFORD G3 / F1
Green Acres Inn, RFD #112, Green Acres Rd, 04221 ....(207)597-2333

HOULTON D17 / C4
The Mallard Inn, 48 North St, 04730 ....(207)532-4377

ISLE AU HAUT H8 / G3
The Keeper's House, PO Box 26, 04645 ....(207)367-2261

ISLESBORO G7 / F3
Dark Harbor House Inn, Box 185, 04848 ....(207)734-6669
Islesboro Inn, 04848 ....(207)734-2222

JONESBORO F11 / F5
Chandler River Lodge, Rt 1, 04648 ....(201)679-2778

KENNEBUNK K2 / H1
Alewife House, 1917 Alewive Rd, Rt 35, 04043 ....(207)985-2118
Arundel Meadows Inn, PO Box 1129, 04043 ....(207)985-3770
Kennebunk Inn 1799, 45 Main St, 04043 ....(207)985-3351
The Waldo Emerson Inn, 108 Summer St, 04043 ....(207)985-7854

KENNEBUNK BEACH K2 / H1
Sundial Inn, PO Box 1147, 48 Beach Ave, 04043 ....(207)967-3850

KENNEBUNKPORT K2 / H1

1802 House, Box 646A Locke St, 04046 .... (207)967-5632
Breakwater, PO Box 1160, 04046 .... (207)967-3118
Bufflehead Cove, Box 499, Gornitz Ln, 04046 .... (207)967-3879
Captain Fairfield House, PO Box 202, 04046 .... (207)967-4454
Captain Jefferds Inn, Box 691, 04046 .... (207)967-2311
Captain Lord Mansion, Pleasant & Green, PO Box 800, 04046 .... (207)967-3141
Chetwynd House, PO Box 130, 04046 .... (207)967-2235
Cove House, S Maine St, PO Box 1615, 04046 .... (207)967-3704
Dock Square Inn, PO Box 1123, 04046 .... (207)967-5773
English Robin, Rt 1 Box 194, 04046 .... (207)967-3505
Farm House, RR 1, Box 656, 04046 .... (207)967-4169
Green Heron Inn, Drawer 151, 04046 .... (207)967-3315
The Inn at Harbor Head, Pier Rd, RFD 2 Box 1180, 04046 .... (207)967-5564
Harbor Inn, Ocean Ave, PO Box 538A, 04046 .... (207)967-2074
Kennebunkport Inn, Box 111, Dock Sq, 04046 .... (207)967-2621
Kilburn House, PO Box 1309, 04046 .... (207)967-4762
Kylemere House 1818, South St, PO Box 1333, 04046 .... (207)967-2780
Lake Brook Guest House, RR3, Box 1333, 04046 .... (207)967-4069
Maine Stay Inn & Cottages, Maine St, PO Box 500A, 04046 .... (207)967-9117
Old Fort Inn, Old Fort Ave, PO Box M 24, 04046 .... (207)967-5353
Port Gallery Inn, PO Box 1367, 04046 .... (207)967-3728
Schooners Inn & Restaurant, PO Box 1121 Ocean Ave, 04046 .... (207)967-5333
Seaside Inn, Gooch's Beach, 04046 .... (207)967-4461
The Inn on South Street, PO Box 478A, South St, 04046 .... (207)967-5151
The Green Heron Inn, Ocean Ave, 04046 .... (207)967-3315
Tides Inn By The Sea, Goose Rock Beach, 04046 .... (207)967-3757
Village Cove Inn, PO Box 650, 04046 .... (207)967-3993
The Welby Inn, Ocean Ave, PO Box 774, 04046 .... (207)967-4655
The White Barn Inn, Beach St, RR 3 Box 387, 04046 .... (207)967-2321

KINGFIELD E4 / E2

Herbert Inn, PO Box 67, 04947 .... (800)533-INNS
Three Stanley Avenue, PO Box 169, 04947 .... (207)265-5541
The Inn on Winter's Hill, RR 1 Box 1272, 04947 .... (207)265-5421

KITTERY L2 / H1

Melfair Farm B&B, 11 Wilson Rd, 03904 .... (207)439-0320

KITTERY POINT L2 / H1

Harbor's Watch, RFD 1 Box 42, 03905 .... (207)439-3242
Whaleback Inn, Pepperrell Rd, Box 162, 03905 .... (207)439-9570

LINCOLNVILLE H7 / F3

Cedarholm Cottages, Star Rt, 04849 .... (207)236-3886
Longville, PO Box 75, 04849 .... (207)236-3785
Red House, HC 60, Box 540, 04849 .... (207)236-4621
Sign of the Owl, Rt 1, Box 85, 04849 .... (207)338-4669
Youngtown Inn, Rt 52, 04849 .... (207)763-3037

LINCOLNVILLE BEACH H7 / F3

North House 1792, Box 165, 04849 .... (207)789-5252

LITCHFIELD H4 / F2

Old Tavern Inn, PO Box 445, 04350 .... (207)268-4965

LITTLE DEER ISLE H8 / F4

Eggemoggin Inn, RFD Box 324, 04650 .... (207)348-2540

LUBEC E13 / E5

Bayviews, 6 Monument St, 04652 .... (207)733-2181
Breakers-by-the-Bay, 37 Washington, 04652 .... (207)733-2487
Home Port Inn, 45 Main St, 04652 .... (207)733-2077
Hugel Haus B&B, 55 Main St, 04652 .... (207)733-4965
Overview, RD 2, Box 106, 04652 .... (207)733-2005
Peacock House, 27 Summer St, 04652 .... (207)733-2403

MATINICUS I7 / G3

Tuckanuck Lodge, Shag Hollow Rd, PO Box 217, 04851 .... (207)366-3830

MILBRIDGE G10 / F4

Birch Point Cottage, Wyman Rd, Rte 1, Box 73, 04658 .... (207)546-2955

MONHEGAN J6 / G3

Monhegan House, 04852 .... (207)594-7983

MONHEGAN ISLAND J6 / G3

Island Inn, 10 Ocean Ave, 04852 .... (207)596-0371
Shinning Sails Inc, Box 44, 04852 .... (207)596-0041

MOUNT DESERT G9 / F4

The Collier House, PO Box 198, 04660 .... (207)288-3162

MOUNT VERNON G4 / F2

Feather Bed Inn, Box 65, 04352 .... (207)293-2020

NAPLES I2 / G1

The Augustus Bove House, RR 1 Box 501, 04055 .... (207)693-6365
The Inn at Long Lake, Lake House Rd, PO Box 806, 04055 .... (207)693-6226
Songo B&B, Songon Locks Rd, 04055 .... (207)693-3960
The Epicurean Inn, PO Box Aq, 04055 .... (207)693-3839

NEW HARBOR I5 / G2

Bradley Inn, 361 Pemaquid Pt, 04554 .... (207)677-2105
Gosnold Arms, Northside Rd, Rt 32, 04554 .... (207)677-3727
Southside-By The Harbor, Southside Rd, 04554 .... (207)677-2991

NEWCASTLE I5 / G2

Crown 'N' Anchor Inn, River Rd, PO Box 17, 04553 .... (207)563-8954
Elfinhill, 20 River Rd, PO Box 497, 04553 .... (207)563-1886
Glidden House, Glidden St, RR 1 Box 740, 04553 .... (207)563-1859
Hearthside Inn B&B, 20 River Rd, 04553 .... (207)563-8885
The Newcastle Inn, RR 2 Box 24, River Rd, 04553 .... (207)563-5685
The Captain's House, PO Box 516, 04553 .... (207)563-1482
The Markert House, PO Box 224, Glidden St, 04553 .... (207)563-1309

NEWPORT E6 / E3

Lake Sebasticook B&B, 8 Sebasticook Ave, Box 502, 04953 .... (207)368-5507

NOBLEBORO H5 / G2

Oliver Farm Inn, Old Rt 1, Box 136, 04555 .... (207)563-1527

NORRIDGEWOCK F5 / E2

Norridgewock Colonial Inn, RFD 1 Box 1190, 04957 .... (207)634-3470

NORTH EDGECOMB I5 / G2

Channelridge Farm, 358 Cross Pt Rd, 04556 .... (207)882-7539

NORTH HAVEN H7 / F3

Pulpit Harbor Inn, Crabtree Point Rd, 04853 .... (207)867-2219

NORTH WATERFORD H2 / F1

Olde Rowley Inn, Rt 35 N, 04267 .... (207)583-4143

NORTHEAST HARBOR H9 / F4

Grey Rock Inn, 04662 .... (207)276-9360
Harbourside Inn, 04662 .... (207)276-3272

OGUNQUIT L2 / H1

Blue Shutters, 6 Beachmere Pl, 03907 .... (207)646-2163
Blue Water Inn, Beach St, 03907 .... (207)646-5559
Channing Hall, 3 Pine Hill Rd, 03907 .... (207)646-5222
Gazebo, Rt 1 Box 668, 03907 .... (207)646-3733
Hartwell House, 118 Shore Rd, PO Box 393, 03907 .... (207)646-7210
Hillcrest Inn Resort, Shore Rd, 03907 .... (207)646-7776
Juniper Hill Inn, Rt 1 N, 03907 .... (207)646-4501
Leisure Inn, 6 School St, PO Box 2113, 03907 .... (207)646-2737
Marimor Motor Inn, 66 Shore Rd, 03907 .... (207)646-7397
Morning Dove B&B, 30 Bourne Ln, PO Box 1940, 03907 .... (207)646-3891
Ogunquit House, PO Box 1883, 03907 .... (207)646-2967
Old Village Inn, 30 Main St, 03907 .... (207)646-7088
Sea Chambers-The Sea Bell, 37 Shore Rd, 03907 .... (207)646-9311
Seafair Inn, 24 Shore Rd Box 1221, 03907 .... (207)646-2181
Terrace By the Sea, 11 Wharf Ln, 03907 .... (207)646-3232
Trellis House, Box 2229, 2 Bearhmere Pl, 03907 .... (207)646-7909
Yardarm Village Inn, PO Box 773, 03907 .... (207)646-7006

OQUOSSOC E2 / E1

Oquossoc's Own B&B, PO Box 27, 04964 .... (207)864-5584

OXFORD H2 / F1

Claibern's B&B, Rt 121 PO Box B, 04270 .... (207)539-2352

PEAKS ISLAND /

Kellers B&B, Box 8, Island Ave, 04108 .... (207)766-2441
Moonshell Inn, Island Ave, 04081 .... (207)766-2331

PEMAQUID I5 / G2

Little River Inn, Rt 130, 04558 .... (207)677-2845

PHIPPSBURG I4 / G2

Riverview, Church Ln, Box 29, 04562 .... (207)389-1124

PHIPPSBURG CENTER I4 / G2

The Captain Drummond House, PO Box 72, 04562 .... (207)289-1394

POLAND SPRING I3 / G1

Victorian House, Rt 1 Box 128, Rt 26, 04274 .... (207)998-2169

PORT CLYDE I6 / G3

Copper Light, PO Box 67, 04855 .... (207)372-8510
Ocean House, Box 66, 04855 .... (207)372-6691

PORTLAND J3 / G2

Carleton Gardens, 43 Carleton St, 04102 .... (207)772-3458
Inn on Carleton, 46 Carleton St, 04102 .... (207)775-1910
Pomegranate Inn, 49 Neal St, 04102 .... (207)772-1006
The Inn at Park Spring, 135 Spring St, 04101 .... (207)774-1059

PROSPECT HARBOR G10 / F4

Oceanside Meadows Inn, Box 85, 04669 .... (207)963-5557

RANGELEY E2 / E1

Farmhouse Inn, PO Box 173, 04970 .... (207)864-5805

RAYMOND I3 / G1

North Pines Health Resort, 04071 .... (207)655-7624

ROBINHOOD I4 / G2

Benjamin Riggs House, PO Box 440, 04530 .... (207)371-2256

ROCKPORT H7 / F3

Bread & Roses B&B, 297 Commercial St, Box 606, 04856 .... (207)236-6116
Rosemary Cottage, Russell Ave, 04856 .... (207)236-3513
Sign Of The Unicorn, 191 Beauchamp Ave, 04856 .... (207)236-8789

ROUND POND I5 / G2

The Briar Rose B&B, Rt 32 Box 27, 04564 .... (207)529-5478

SANFORD K2 / *H1*
Oakwood Inn & Motel, 279 Main St, 04073 (207)324-2160

SARGENTVILLE H8 / *F3*
Oakland House, Herricks Rd, 04673 (207)359-8521

SEARSPORT G7 / *F3*
Carriage House Inn, Rt 1 E Main St, 04974 (207)548-2289
Homeport Inn, Rt 1 E Main St, 04974 (207)548-2259
House Of Three Chimneys, Rt 1 Box 397, 04974 (207)548-6117
McGilvery House, PO Box 588, 04974 (207)548-6289
The Hannah Nickels House, Rt 1 Box 38, 04974 (207)548-6691
Thurston House B&B, 8 Elm St, PO Box 686, 04974 (207)548-2213

SEBASCO ESTATES J4 / *G2*
Rock Gardens Inn, 04565 (207)389-1161

SKOWHEGAN F5 / *E2*
Brick Farm B&B, RFD 1, Box 1500, 04976 (207)474-3949

SMALL POINT I4 / *G2*
Edgewater Farm, Small Point Rd, Rt 216, Box 464, 04565 (207)389-1322

SOUTH BERWICK L1 / *H1*
Tatnic B&B, Tatnic Rd, RFD #1, Box 518A, 03908 (207)676-2209

SOUTH BROOKSVILLE G8 / *F3*
Breezemere Farm Inn, PO Box 290, Breezemere Rd, 04617 (207)326-8628
Buck's Harbor Inn, Rt 176 Box 268, 04617 (207)326-8660

SOUTH CASCO I2 / *G1*
Migis Lodge, Rt 302, 04077 (207)655-4524
Thomas Inn & Playhouse, PO Box 128, 04077 (207)655-7728

SOUTH HARPSWELL J4 / *G2*
Alfred M. Senter B&B, Box 830, 04079 (207)833-2874

SOUTH THOMASTON H6 / *G3*
The Weskeag Inn, PO Box 73, 04858 (207)596-6676

SOUTHPORT I5 / *G2*
Albonegon Inn, Capitol Island, 04538 (207)633-2521

SOUTHWEST HARBOR H9 / *F4*
Harbour Woods Lodging, Main St, PO Box 1214, 04679 (207)244-5388
The Island House, PO Box 1006, 04679 (207)244-5180
Island Watch B&B, Box 1359, Freeman Ridge Rd, 04679 (207)244-7229
Kingsleigh Inn, PO Box 1426, 100 Main St, 04679 (207)244-5302
The Lamb's Ear B&B, PO Box 30, 04679 (207)244-9828
Lindenwood Inn, PO Box 1328, 04679 (207)244-5335
The Moorings, Shore Rd, Po Box 744, 04679 (207)244-5523
Penury Hall, Main St Box 68, 04679 (207)244-7102
Two Seasons, PO Box 829, 04679 (207)244-9627

STRATTON D3 / *E1*
Widow's Walk, Box 150, 04982 (207)246-6901

SULLIVAN HARBOR G9 / *F4*
Island View Inn, Rt 1, Box 24, 04689 (207)422-3031
Sullivan Harbor Inn, Rt 1, 04689 (207)422-3591

TENANTS HARBOR I6 / *G3*
Church Hill B&B, Box 126, 04860 (207)372-6256
East Wind Inn & Meeting House, PO Box 149, 04680 (207)372-6366
Mill Pond House, Box 640, 04860 (207)372-6209

THE FORKS C4 / *D2*
Crab Apple Acres, Rt 201, 04985 (207)663-2218

THOMASTON H6 / *G3*
Bedside Manor Guest House, HCR 35, Box 100, 04861 (207)354-8862
Captain Frost's B&B, 241 W Main St, 04861 (207)354-8217
Gracie's B&B, 52 Main St, 04861 (207)354-2326

TOPSHAM I4 / *G2*
Captain Purinton House, 64 Elm St, 04086 (207)729-3603
Middaugh B&B, 36 Elm St, 04086 (207)725-2562
The Walker Wilson House, 2 Melcher Pl, 04086 (207)729-0715

VINALHAVEN H7 / *G3*
Fox Island Inn, Carver St, 04863 (207)863-2122

WALDOBORO H6 / *G3*
Le Vatout, Rt 32, Box 375, 04572 (207)832-4552
Letteney Farm Vacations, RFD 2, Box 166A, 04572 (207)832-5143
Medomark House, PO Box 663, Friendship St, 04572 (207)832-4971
The Roaring Lion, 995 Main St, Box 756, 04572 (207)832-4038
Tide Watch Inn, PO Box 94, Pine St, 04572 (207)832-4987

WALPOLE I5 / *G2*
The Bittersweet Inn, Hcr 64, PO Box 013, 04573 (207)563-5552

WASHINGTON H6 / *F3*
Windward Farm, Young's Hill Rd, 04574 (207)845-2830

WATERFORD H2 / *F1*
Artemus Ward House, 04088 (207)583-4106
Kedarburn Inn, Rt 35 Box 61, 04088 (207)583-6182
Lake House, Rts 35 & 37, 04088 (207)583-4182

WATERVILLE F5 / *F2*
The Inn at Silver Grove, 184 Silver St, 04901 (207)873-7724

WELD F3 / *E1*
Kawanhee Inn Lakeside Lodge, Lake Webb, 04285 (207)778-4306
Weld Inn, Box 8, 04285 (207)585-2429

WELLS K2 / *H1*
Grey Gull Inn, 321 Webhannet Dr, 04090 (207)646-7501
Purple Sandpiper Guest House, RR 3, Box 226, 04090 (207)646-7990

WELLS BEACH L2 / *H1*
The Haven, Church St, 04090 (207)646-4194

WEST BATH I4 / *G2*
Bakke B&B, RD 1, Box 505A, 04530 (207)442-7185
New Meadows Inn, Bath Rd, 04530 (207)443-3921

WEST BOOTHBAY HARBOR I5 / *G2*
Lawnmeer Inn, PO Box 505, 04575 (207)633-2544

WINTER HARBOR G9 / *F4*
Main Stay Inn, PO Box 459, 04693 (207)963-5561

WISCASSET I5 / *G2*
The Squire Tarbox Inn, RR 2 Box 620, 04578 (207)882-7693
The Stacked Arms, RR 2 Box 146, 04578 (207)882-5436

YARMOUTH I3 / *G2*
Homewood Inn, PO Box 196, 04096 (207)846-3351

YORK L2 / *H1*
A Summer Place, D 1 Box 196, 03909 (207)363-5233
Dockside Guest Quarters, PO Box 205, Harris Island, 03909 (207)363-2868
Hannah's Loft, Chases Pond Rd, RFD #2, Box 117, 03909 (207)363-7244
Hutchins House, 173 Organug Rd, 03909 (207)363-3058
Scotland Bridge Inn, PO Box 521, 03909 (207)363-4432
The Wild Rose Of York, 78 Long Sands Rd, 03909 (207)363-2532

YORK BEACH L2 / *H1*
Homestead Inn B&B, PO Box 15, Rt 1A, 03910 (207)363-8952
Jo-Mar B&B on the Ocean, Box 838, 41 Freeman St, 03910 (207)363-4826
The Inn at Katahdin Inn, PO Box 193, 03910 (207)363-2759
Lighthouse Inn, Box 249, Nubble Rd, 03910 (207)363-6072
Lilac Inn, Box 1325 3 Ridge Rd, 03910 (207)363-3930

YORK HARBOR L2 / *H1*
Edwards' Harborside Inn, Stage Neck Rd, 03911 (207)363-3037
Inn at Harmon Park, 415 York St, 03911 (207)363-2031
York Harbor Inn, PO Box 573, Rt 1A, 03911 (207)363-5119

MARYLAND

ANNAPOLIS G18 / *C6*
Annapolis B&B, 235 Prince George St, 21404 (301)269-0669
The Ark & Dove, 149 Prince George St, 21404 (301)268-6277
Charles Inn, 74 Charles St, 21401 (301)268-1451
The College House B&B, One College Ave, 21404 (301)263-6124
Courtyard B&B, 166 Duke of Gloucester St, 21404 (301)263-5593
Gibson's Lodgings, 110 Prince George St, 21401 (301)268-5555
Green Street B&B, 161 Green St, 21401 (301)268-9549
Historic Inns of Annapolis, 16 Church Circle, 21401 (301)263-2641
Hunter House, 154 Prince George St, 21404 (301)626-1268
Jonah Williams House, 101 Severn Ave, 21403 (301)267-7005
Magnolia House B&B, 220 King George St, 21401 (301)269-6232
Maryland Inn, 16 Church Circle, 21401 (301)263-2641
Murphy's B&B, 125 Conduit St, 21401 (301)269-6232
Prince George Inn, 232 Prince George St, 21401 (301)263-6418
The Row House, 28 Fleet St, 21404 (301)263-2187
Shaw's Fancy B&B, 161 Green St, 21401 (301)268-9750
William Page Inn B&B, 8 Martin St, 21401 (301)626-1506

BALTIMORE E17 / *B6*
Admiral Fell Inn, 888 S Broadway, 21231 (301)522-7377
Betsy's B&B, 1428 Park Ave, 21217 (301)383-1274
Bolton Hill B&B, 1534 Bolton St, 21217 (301)669-5356
Celie's Waterfront B&B, 1714 Thames St, 21231 (301)522-2323
Eagles Mere B&B, 102 E Montgomery, 21230 (301)332-1618
Harborview, 112 E Montgomery St, 21230 (301)528-8692
Mulberry House, 111 West Mulberry St, 21201 (301)576-0111
The Shirley-Madison Inn, 205 W Madison St, 21201 (301)728-6550
Society Hill Government House, 1125 N Calvert St, 21202 (301)752-7722
Society Hill Hotel, 58 W Biddle St, 21201 (301)837-3630
Society Hill Hopkins, 3404 St Paul St, 21218 (301)235-8600
Twin Gates, 308 Morris Ave, 21093 (800)635-0370

BETTERTON E20 / *B7*
Lantern Inn, 115 Ericsson Ave, PO Box 29, 21610 (301)348-5809

BUCKEYSTOWN E13 / *B4*
The Inn at Buckeystown, 3521 Buckeystown Pike Gen Del, 21717 (301)874-5755

BURTONSVILLE G15 / *C5*
Upstream at Water's Gift, PO Box 240, 3604 Dustin Rd, 20866 (301)421-9562

CABIN JOHN F5 / *C5*
Winslow Home, 8217 Caraway St, 20818 (301)229-4654

CAMBRIDGE J20 / D7
Commodore's Cottages, 215 Glenburn Ave, 21613 ....(301)228-6938
Glasgow Inn, 1500 Hambrooks Blvd, 21613 ....(301)221-0297
Lodgecliffe on the Choptank, 103 Choptank Ter, 21613 ....(301)228-1760
Sarke Plantation, Rt 3 Box 139, 21613 ....(301)288-7020

CASCADE B12 / A4
Bluebird On The Mountain, 14700 Eyler Ave, 21719 ....(301)241-4161
Inwood Guest House, Box 378, Rt 1, 21719 ....(301)241-3467

CHESTERTOWN F20 / B7
Brampton, RR2, Box 107, 21620 ....(301)778-1860
Flyway Lodge, Rt 1, Box 660, 21620 ....(301)778-5557
Great Oak Manor, Rt 2 Box 608, 21620 ....(301)778-5796
Hill's Inn, 114 Washington Ave, 21620 ....(301)778-4667
Imperial Hotel, 208 High St, 21620 ....(301)778-5000
The Inn at Mitchell House, RD 2 Box 329, Rt 21, 21620 ....(301)778-6500
Radcliffe Cross, Quaker Neck Rd, Rt 3 Box 360, 21620 ....(301)778-5540
White Swan Tavern, 231 High St, 21620 ....(301)778-2300

CUMBERLAND C5 / A2
The Inn at Walnut Bottom, 120 Greene St, 21502 ....(301)777-0003

DENTON H21 / C7
Sophie Kerr House, Rt 3 Box 7-B, Kerr & 5th Aves, 21629 ....(301)479-3421

EASTON I20 / C7
The Bishop's House, 214 Goldsborough St, PO Box 2217, 21601 ....(301)820-7290
Hynson Tourist Home, 804 Dover Rd, 21601 ....(301)822-2777
John S. McDaniel House, 14 N Aurora St, 21601 ....(301)822-3704
Tidewater Inn, Dover & Harrison St, 21601 ....(301)822-1300

ELLICOTT CITY E16 / B5
Hayland Farm, 500 Sheppard Ln, 21043 ....(301)531-5593
Wayside Inn, 4344 Columbia Rd, 21043 ....(301)461-4636

FALLSTON D18 / B6
Broom Hall B&B, 2425 Pocock Rd, 21047 ....(301)557-7321

FREDERICK D13 / B4
Middle Plantation Inn, 9549 Liberty Rd, 21701 ....(301)898-7128
Spring Bank - A B&B Inn, 7945 Worman's Mill Rd, 21701 ....(301)694-0440
Tran Crossing, 9028 Mountainberry Cir, 21701 ....(301)663-8449
Turning Point Inn, 3406 Urbana Pike, 21701 ....(301)874-2421
Tyler-Spite House, 112 W Church St Dr, 21701 ....(301)831-4455

FREELAND B17 / A5
Freeland Farm, 21616 Middletown Rd, 21053 ....(301)357-5364

GAITHERSBURG F14 / B5
Gaithersburg Hospitality B&B, 18908 Chimney Pl, 20879 ....(301)977-7377

GEORGETOWN E21 / B7
Kitty Knight House, Rt 213, 21930 ....(301)648-5305

HAGERSTOWN C11 / A4
Beaver Creek House B&B, Beaver Creek Rd, Rt 9, Box 330, 21740 ....(301)797-4764
Lewrene Farm B&B, RD 3 Box 150, Downsville Pike, 21740 ..(301)582-1735

HARWOOD H17 / C6
Oakwood, 4566 Solomons Island Rd, 20776 ....(301)261-5338

HAVRE DE GRACE C20 / B6
The Spencer Silver Mansion, 200 S Union Ave, 21078 ....(301)939-1097

MANOKIN N22 / E7
Hunters Cove, Box 4, 21836 ....(301)651-9664

MC HENRY C2 / B1
Country Inn, PO Box 397, 21541 ....(301)387-6694

MIDDLETOWN D12 / B4
The Marameade, 2439 Old National Pike, 21769 ....(301)371-4214

MOUNT SAVAGE B5 / A2
The Castle, PO Box 578, Rt 36, 21545 ....(301)759-5946

NEW MARKET E14 / B5
National Pike Inn, 9 W Main St, PO Box 299, 21774 ....(301)865-5055
Strawberry Inn, 17 Main St, PO Box 237, 21774 ....(301)865-3318

OAKLAND D2 / B1
Red Run Inn, Rt 5, Box 268, 21550 ....(301)387-6606

OCEAN CITY L26 / D8
His Honor's Place, 1201 N Baltimore Ave, 21842 ....(301)289-2630

OLNEY F15 / B5
The Thoroughbred B&B, 16410 Batchellors Forest Rd, 20832 ....(301)774-7649

OXFORD J20 / C6
1876 House, 110 N Morris St, 21654 ....(301)226-5496
Oxford Inn/Pope's Tavern, Box 627, 1 S Morris St, 21654 ....(301)226-5220
The Robert Morris Inn, On The Tred Avon, PO Box 70, 21654 ....(301)226-5111

PRINCESS ANNE M22 / D7
Elmwood C. 1770 B&B, Locust Point, PO Box 220, 21853 ....(301)651-1066
Washington Hotel & Inn, Somerset Ave, 21853 ....(301)651-2525

RISING SUN B20 / A7
Chandlee House, 168 Chandlee Rd, 21911 ....(301)658-6958

SAINT LEONARD K18 / D6
Matoaka Cottages, PO Box 124, 20685 ....(301)586-0269

SAINT MICHAELS I19 / C6
The Inn at Christmas Farm, Rt 33, PO Box 39, 21663 ....(301)822-4470
Hambleton Inn/Harbor, 202 Cherry St, Box 299, 21663 ....(301)745-3350
Kemp House Inn, 412 S Talbot St, PO Box 638, 21663 ....(301)745-2243
Parsonage Inn, 210 N Talbot St, 21663 ....(301)745-5519
The Inn at Perry Cabin, 21663 ....(301)745-5178
Two Swan Inn, PO Box 727, 21663 ....(301)745-2929
Wades Point Inn on the Bay, PO Box 7, 21663 ....(301)745-2500

SALISBURY L23 / D7
White Oak Inn, 804 Spring Hill Rd, 21801 ....(301)742-4887

SCOTLAND N19 / E6
St Michael's Manor B&B, 20687 ....(301)872-4025

SHARPSBURG D11 / B4
The Inn at Antietam, PO Box 119, 21782 ....(301)432-6601
Piper House On Antietam Battlefield, Box 100, 21782 ....(301)797-1862

SILVER SPRING G15 / C5
Varborg, 2620 Briggs Chaney Rd, 20904 ....(301)384-2842

SNOW HILL M24 / D8
Snow Hill Inn, 104 E Market St, 21863 ....(301)632-2102

SOLOMONS L18 / D6
Back Creek B&B, Calvert & A St, 20688 ....(301)326-2022
Locust Inn, Box 254, 20688 ....(301)326-9817

SOLOMONS ISLAND L18 / D6
Davis House, PO Box 759, 20688 ....(301)326-4811

STEVENSON L3 / B5
Mensana Inn, 1718 Greenspring Valley Rd, 21153 ....(301)653-2403

SYKESVILLE E15 / B5
Long Way Hill, 7406 Springfield Ave, 21782 ....(301)795-8129

TANEYTOWN C14 / A5
Glenburn, 3515 Runnymede Rd, 21787 ....(301)751-1187

TILGHMAN I19 / C6
"Ida May" Skipjack, Knapps Narrows Marina, 21671 ....(301)822-4470
Black Walnut Point Inn, PO Box 308, 21671 ....(301)886-2452
Harrison's Country Inn, PO Box 310, 21671 ....(301)886-2123

UNIONTOWN C14 / A5
The Newel Post, 3428 Uniontown Rd, 21157 ....(301)775-2655

VIENNA K22 / D7
Governor's Ordinary, Church & Water Box 156, 21869 ....(301)376-3530
Tavern House, 111 Water St, PO Box 98, 21869 ....(301)376-3347

WESTMINSTER C15 / B5
Judge Thomas House, 195 Willis St, 21157 ....(301)876-6686
The Winchester Country Inn, 430 S Bishop St, 21157 ....(301)876-7373

WOODSBORO C13 / B4
Rosebud Inn, 4 N Main St, 21798 ....(301)845-2221

MASSACHUSETTS

ADAMS C4 / B2
Butternut Inn, 6 East St, 01220 ....(413)743-9394

AMHERST F8 / C4
The Amity House, 194 Amity St, 01002 ....(413)549-6446

ASHFIELD D6 / B3
Ashfield Inn, Main St, PO Box 129, 01330 ....(413)628-4571
Bull Frog B&B, Box 210, Star Rt, 01330 ....(413)628-4493
Gold Leaf Inn, Box 477, 01330 ....(413)628-3392

ATTLEBORO J16 / D7
Colonel Blackinton Inn, 203 N Main St, 02703 ....(617)222-6022

AUBURN H12 / C6
Captain Samuel Eddy House Inn, 609 Oxford St S, 01501 ....(508)832-5282

BARNSTABLE L23 / E9
Ashley Manor Inn, 3660 Olde Kings Hwy PO Box 856, 02630(508)362-8044
Cobbs Cove, PO Box 208, Rt 6a, 02630 ....(508)362-9356
Goss House B&B, 61 Pine Ln, 02630 ....(617)362-8559
Thomas Huckins House, 2701 Main St, Rt 6A, 02630 ....(508)362-6379

BARNSTABLE VILLAGE L23 / E9
Beechwood Inn, 2839 Main St, 02630 ....(508)362-6618
Charles Hinckley House, Olde Kings Hwy, PO Box 723, 02630 ....(508)362-9924

BARRE E11 / B5
Olde Jenkins Guest House, Rt 122, 01005 ....(508)355-6444

BASS RIVER L24 / E10
The Anchorage, 122 South Shore Dr, 02664 ....(508)398-8265
Belvedere B&B Inn, 167 Main St, 02664 ....(508)398-6674

Old Cape Inn, 108 Old Main St, 02664 ....(508)398-1068

BECKET F4 / *C2*
Canterbury Farm, Fred Snow Rd, 01223 ....(413)623-8765
Long House B&B, High St, 01223 ....(413)623-8360

BERLIN F14 / *C6*
Stonehedge, 119 Sawyer Hill Rd, 01503 ....(617)838-2574

BERNARDSTON C8 / *B4*
Bernardston Inn, Church St, 01337 ....(413)648-9282

BILLERICA D16 / *B7*
Billerica B&B, 88 Rogers St, 01862 ....(508)667-7317

BOSTON F18 / *C7*
Beacon Hill B&B, 27 Brimmer St, 02108 ....(617)523-7376
The Emma James House, 47 Ocean St, 02124 ....(617)288-8867
The Federal House, 48 Fayette, 02116 ....(617)350-6657
Host Homes of Boston, PO Box 117, Waban Branch, 02168 ....(617)244-1308
The Terrace Townhouse, 60 Chandler St, 02116 ....(617)350-6520
Victorian B&B, 35 Greenwich Park, 02118 ....(617)247-1599

BOYLSTON F13 / *C6*
Frenches' B&B, 5 Scar Hill Rd, 01505 ....(508)869-2666

BREWSTER K25 / *E10*
Bramble Inn, Rt 6a 2019 Main St, 02631 ....(508)896-7644
Captain Freeman Inn, 15 Breakwater Rd, 02631 ....(508)896-7481
Isaiah Clark House, 1187 Old King's Hwy, 02631 ....(508)896-2223
Old Manse Inn, 1861 Main St, PO Box 839, 02631 ....(508)896-3149
Old Sea Pines Inn, 2553 Main St, PO Box 1026, 02631 ....(508)896-6114

BROOKLINE F18 / *C7*
Beacon Inns, 1087 & 1750 Beacon St, 02146 ....(617)566-0088
Beacon Plaza, 1459 Beacon St, 02146 ....(617)232-6550
Beacon Street Guest House, 1047 Beacon St, 02146 ....(800)872-7211
Beech Tree Inn, 83 Longwood Ave, 02146 ....(617)277-1620
Brookline Manor House, 32 Centre St, 02146 ....(617)232-0003
The William Wood House, 71 Perry St, 02146 ....(617)566-2237

BUCKLAND D6 / *B3*
1797 House, Charlemont Rd, 01338 ....(413)625-2975
Scott House, Hawley Rd, 01338 ....(413)625-6624

CAMBRIDGE F18 / *C7*
A Cambridge House B&B Inn, 2218 Massachusetts Ave, 02140 ....(617)491-6300

CENTERVILLE M23 / *E9*
Allen's B&B, 110 Prince Hinckley Rd, 02632-2150 ....(617)428-5702
Carver House, 638 Main St, 02632 ....(617)775-9414
Copper Beech Inn, 497 Main St, 02632 ....(508)771-5488
The Inn at Fernbrook, 481 Main St, 02632 ....(508)775-4334
Old Hundred House, 1211 Craigville Beach Rd, 02632 ....(508)775-6166
Terrace Gardens Inn, 539 Main St, 02632 ....(617)775-4707

CHARLEMONT D6 / *B3*
The Inn at Charlemont, Rt 2, 01339 ....(413)339-5796
Forest Way Farm, Rt 8a (heath), 01339 ....(413)337-8321

CHATHAM L26 / *E10*
Bow Roof House, 59 Queen Anne Rd, 02633 ....(617)945-1346
Bradford Inn, 26 Cross St, 02633 ....(508)945-1030
Captains House Inn of Chatham, 369 Old Harbor Rd, 02633 ..(617)945-0127
Chatham Bars Inn, Shore Rd, 02633 ....(617)945-0096
Chatham Town House Inn, 11 Library Ln, 02633 ....(508)945-2180
Chatham Village Inn, 207 Main St, 02633 ....(508)945-0792
Chatham Wayside Inn, 512 Main St, 02633 ....(508)945-1800
The Cranberry Inn at Chatham, 359 Main St, 02633 ....(508)945-9232
Cyrus Kent House, 63 Cross St, 02633 ....(508)945-9104
Moses Nickerson House, 364 Old Harbor Rd, 02633 ....(508)945-5859
Queen Anne Inn, 70 Queen Anne Rd, 02633 ....(508)945-0394
The Ships Inn at Chatham, 364 Old Harbor Rd, 02633 ....(508)945-5859

CHELMSFORD D16 / *B7*
Westview Landing, Box 4141, 01824 ....(508)256-0074

CHESTNUT HILL I4 / *C7*
The Pleasant Pheasant, 296 Heath St, 02167 ....(617)566-4178

CHILMARK P20 / *F8*
Breakfast at Tiasquam, PO Box 578, 02535 ....(508)645-3685

COLRAIN C6 / *B3*
Grandmother's House, Rt 1 Box 37 Rte 112n, 01340 ....(413)624-3771
Maple Shade Farm B&B, Rt 1, Box 469, 01340 ....(413)624-3931

CONCORD E16 / *B7*
Anderson-Wheeler Homestead, 154 Fitchburg Turnpike, 01742 ....(508)369-3756
Colonel Roger Brown House, 1694 Main St, 01742 ....(508)369-9119
Colonial Inn, 48 Monument Sq, 01742 ....(508)369-9200
Hawthorne Inn, 462 Lexington Rd, 01742 ....(508)369-5610

CONWAY E6 / *B3*
Hilltop B&B, Truce Rd, 01341 ....(413)369-4928

COTUIT M22 / *E9*
Milestones B&B, 90 Piney Rd, PO Box 496, 02635 ....(508)428-6764

Salty Dog B&B, 451 Main St, 02635 ....(617)428-5228

CUMMINGTON E5 / *B3*
Cumworth Farm, Rt 112, RR 1 Box 110, 01026 ....(413)634-5529
Hill Gallery, Cole St, 01026 ....(413)238-5914
Windfields Farm, Rt 1 Box 170 Bush Rd, 01026 ....(413)684-3786

DALTON E3 / *B2*
Dalton House, 955 Main St, 01226 ....(413)684-3854

DANVERS D19 / *B8*
Salem Village B&B, 34 Centre St, 01923 ....(617)774-7851

DEERFIELD D7 / *B4*
Deerfield Inn, The Street, 01342 ....(413)774-5587

DEERFIELD-SOUTH E7 / *B4*
Deerfield B&B - The Yellow Gabled House, 307 N Main St, 01373 ....(413)665-4922

DENNIS L24 / *E10*
Bed & Breakfast, 16 Bay View Rd, Box 789, 02638 ....(508)385-9256
Four Chimneys Inn, 946 Main St, Rt 6A, 02638 ....(508)385-6317
Isaiah Hall B&B Inn, 152 Whig St, 02638 ....(508)385-9928

DENNISPORT L25 / *E10*
By the Sea Guests, 57 Chase Ave, Box 507, 02639 ....(508)398-8685
Rose Petal B&B, 152 Sea St, PO Box 974, 02639 ....(508)398-8470

DUXBURY I21 / *D8*
Black Friar Brook Farm, 636 Union St, 02332 ....(617)834-8528
Campbell's Country B&B, 68 Alden St, 02332 ....(617)934-0862
Winsor House Inn, PO Box 387 Shs 390 Washington St, 02331 ....(617)934-0991

EAST BREWSTER K25 / *E10*
Ocean Gold Cape Cod B&B, 74 Locust Lane Rt 2, 02631 ....(508)255-7045

EAST ORLEANS K26 / *E10*
The Farmhouse At Nauset Beach, 163 Beach Rd, 02653 ....(508)255-6654
The Nauset House Inn, PO Box 774, 02643 ....(508)255-2195
The Parsonage, 202 Main St, PO Box 1016, 02643 ....(508)255-8217
Ships Knee's Inn, 186 Beach Rd, PO Box 756, 02643 ....(508)255-1312

EAST SANDWICH L22 / *E9*
Wingscorton Farm Inn, 11 Wing Blvd, 02537 ....(508)888-0534

EASTHAM K26 / *E10*
Kingsbury House, Rt 6, Box 262, 02642 ....(508)255-6026
Over Look Inn, 3085 County Rd, PO Box 771, 02642 ....(508)255-1886
Whalewalk Inn, 220 Bridge Rd, 02642 ....(508)255-0617

EDGARTOWN O22 / *F9*
The Arbor, 222 Upper Main St, 02539 ....(508)627-8137
Ashley Inn, 129 Main St, 02539 ....(508)627-9655
Captain Dexter House of Edgartown, 35 Pease's Point Way, 02539 ....(508)627-7289
Chadwick Inn, 67 Winter St, 02539 ....(508)627-4435
Charlotte Inn, S Summer St, 02539 ....(508)627-4751
Colonial Inn of Martha's Vineyard, 38 N Water St, PO Box 68, 02539 ....(508)627-4711
Daggett House, PO 1333, 59 N Water St, 02539 ....(508)627-4600
Dr. Shiverick House, Pent Lane, PO Box 640, 02539 ....(508)627-8497
Edgartown Heritage Hotel, 227 Upper Main St, 02539 ....(508)627-5161
Edgartown Inn, 56 N Water, 02539 ....(508)627-4794
Governor Bradford Inn, 128 Main St, 02539 ....(508)627-9510
The Harbor View Hotel, Box 7 N Water St, 02539 ....(508)627-4333
Harborside Inn, Box 67, 02539 ....(617)627-4321
Katama Guest House, RFD 108, 166 Katama Rd, 02539 ....(617)627-5158
Kelly House, PO Box 37, 02539 ....(508)627-4394
Point Way Inn, 104 Main St, PO Box 128, 02539 ....(508)627-8633
Shiretown Inn, N Water St, Box 921, 02539 ....(800)541-0090
The Victorian Inn, 24 S Water St, 02539 ....(508)627-4784

ESSEX C20 / *B8*
George Fuller House, 148 Main St (Rt 133), 01929 ....(508)768-7766

FAIRHAVEN M19 / *E8*
Edgewater B&B, 2 Oxford St, 02719 ....(508)997-5512

FALMOUTH M21 / *F9*
Amherst, 30 Amherst Ave, 02540 ....(617)548-2781
Captain Tom Lawrence House, 75 Locust St, 02540 ....(508)540-1445
Elm Arch Inn, Elm Arch Way, 02540 ....(617)548-0133
Gladstone Inn, 219 Grand Ave S, 02540 ....(617)548-9851
Grafton Inn, 261 Grand Ave S, 02540 ....(508)540-8688
Grandview Guest House, 197 Grand Ave S, 02540 ....(508)548-4025
Hastings By the Sea, 28 Worcester Ave, 02540 ....(617)548-1628
Mostly Hall B&B Inn, 27 Main St, 02540 ....(508)548-3786
Palmer House Inn, 81 Palmer Ave, 02540 ....(508)548-1230
Peacock's "Inn on the Sound", 313 Grand Ave, PO Box 201, 02541 ....(508)457-9666
The Moorings Lodge, 207 Grand Ave, 02540 ....(508)540-2370
Village Green Inn, 40 W Main St, 02540 ....(508)548-5621
Woods Hole Passage, 186 Woods Hole Rd, 02540 ....(508)540-7469
Worcester House, 9 Worcester Ave, 02540 ....(508)540-1592

GARDNER D11 / *B5*
Hawke B&B, 162 Pearl St, 01440 ....(508)632-5909

GLOUCESTER C21 / *B8*
Blue Shutters Inn, 1 Nautilus Rd, 01930 .... (617)281-2706
Gray Manor, 14 Atlantic Rd, 01930 .... (617)283-5409
Williams Guest House, 136 Bass Ave, 01930 .... (617)283-4931

GOSHEN E6 / *B3*
The Whale Inn, Rt 9, Main St, 01032 .... (413)268-7246

GREAT BARRINGTON G2 / *C2*
Bread And Roses, Star Rt 65 Box 50, 01230 .... (413)528-1099
Littlejohn Manor, Newsboy Monument Rt 23, 01230 .... (413)528-2882
Round Hill Farm, 17 Round Hill Rd, 01230 .... (413)528-3366
Seekonk Pines Inn, 142 Seekonk Cross Rd, 01230 .... (413)528-4192
Thornewood, Rt 7 & Rt 183, 01230 .... (413)528-3828
Turning Point Inn, RD 2 Box 140, 3 Lake Buel Rd, 01230 .... (413)528-4777
Windflower Inn, Egremont Star Rt, Box 25 Rt 23, 01230 .... (413)528-2720

GREENFIELD D7 / *B4*
The Hitchcock House, 15 Congress St, 01301 .... (413)774-2964

HARWICH L25 / *E10*
The Shoals Guesthouse, 3 Sea St, 02646 .... (508)432-3837
The Larches, 97 Chatham Rd, 02645 .... (508)432-0150

HARWICH CENTER L25 / *E10*
Victorian Inn At Harwich, Box 340 102 Parallel St, 02645 .... (508)432-8335

HARWICH PORT L25 / *E10*
The Inn on Bank Street, 88 Bank St, 02646 .... (508)432-3206
Bayberry Shores, 255 Lower County Road, 02646 .... (800)272-4343
Captain's Quarters, 85 Bank St, 02646 .... (508)432-0337
Country Inn Acres, 86 Sisson Rd, 02646 .... (508)432-2769
Dunscroft By the Sea, 24 Pilgrim Rd, 02646 .... (508)432-0810
Harbor Breeze, 326 Lower County Rd, 02646 .... (508)432-0337
Harbor Walk, 6 Freeman St, 02646 .... (617)432-1675
The Coach House, 74 Sisson Rd, 02646 .... (508)432-9452

HEATH C6 / *B3*
Pen y Bryn, Jacksonville Stage Rd, 01339 .... (413)376-683

HOLLAND I10 / *D5*
Alpine Haus, Mashapaung Rd, Box 782, 01550 .... (413)245-9082

HOLYOKE G7 / *C4*
Yankee Pedlar Inn, 1866 Northampton St, 01040 .... (413)532-9494

HUNTINGTON G5 / *C3*
Paulson B&B, Allen Coit Rd, 01050 .... (413)667-3208

HYANNIS L24 / *E9*
Acorn House, 240 Sea St, 02601 .... (617)771-4071
Captain Sylvester Baxter House, Park Square Village, 156 Main St, 02601 .... (508)775-5611
Cranberry Cove, Rosetta St, Box 362, 02601 .... (508)775-5049
Elegance By-The-Sea, 162 Sea St, 02601 .... (617)775-3595
Park Square Village, 156 Main St, 02601 .... (617)775-5611
The Inn on Sea Street, 358 Sea St, 02601 .... (508)775-8030

LAKEVILLE K19 / *E8*
Pistachio Cove, 229 County Rd, 02347 .... (617)763-2383

LANESBORO D3 / *B2*
Bascom Lodge, PO Box 686, 01237 .... (413)743-1591
The Tuckered Turkey, 30 Old Cheshire Rd, 01237 .... (413)442-0260

LEE F3 / *C2*
1777 Greylock House, 58 Greylock St, 01238 .... (413)243-1717
Haus Andreas, RR 1 Box 605 B, 01238 .... (413)243-3298
Morgan House, 33 Main St, 01238 .... (413)243-0181
Ramsey House, 203 W Park St, 01238 .... (413)243-1598

LENOX F2 / *C2*
Amity House, 15 Cliffwood St, 01240 .... (413)637-0005
Apple Tree Inn, 224 West St, 01240 .... (413)637-1477
Birchwood Inn, 7 Hubbard St, Box 2020, 01240 .... (413)637-2600
Blantyre, Rt 20, 01240 .... (413)637-3556
Brook Farm Inn, 15 Hawthorne St, 01240 .... (413)637-3013
Candlelight Inn, 53 Walker St, 01240 .... (413)637-1555
Cliffwood Inn, 25 Cliffwood St, 01240 .... (413)637-3330
Cornell House, 197 Main St, 01240 .... (413)637-0562
East Country Berry Farm, 830 East St, 01240 .... (413)442-2057
The Gables Inn, 103 Walker St, Rt 183, 01240 .... (413)637-3416
Garden Gables Inn, 141 Main St, 01240 .... (413)637-0193
Gateways Inn, 71 Walker St, 01240 .... (413)637-2532
Rookwood Inn, 19 Old Stockbridge Rd, 02140 .... (413)637-9750
Strawberry Hill, PO Box 718, 01240 .... (413)637-3381
The Quincy Lodge, 19 Stockbridge Rd, 01240 .... (413)637-9750
Underledge Inn, 76 Cliffwood St, 01240 .... (413)637-0236
Village Inn, 16 Church St, 01240 .... (413)637-0020
Walker House, 74 Walker St, 01240 .... (413)637-1271
Wheatleigh, PO Box 824, 01240 .... (413)637-0610
Whistler's Inn, 5 Greenwood St, 01240 .... (413)637-0975

LEXINGTON E17 / *B7*
Ashley's B&B, 6 Moon Hill Rd, 02173 .... (617)862-6488
Halewood House, 2 Larchmont Ln, 02173 .... (617)862-5404
Red Cape B&B, 61 Williams Rd, 02173 .... (617)862-4913

LOWELL C16 / *B7*
Sherman-Berry House, 163 Dartmouth St, 01851 .... (508)459-4760

LYNN E19 / *B8*
Caron House, 142 Ocean St, 01902 .... (617)599-4470

MANCHESTER D20 / *B8*
Old Corner Inn, 2 Harbor St, 01944 .... (617)526-4996

MARBLEHEAD D20 / *B8*
10 Mugford Street B&B, 10 Mugford St, 01945 .... (508)631-5642
The Garden House, 3 Oak Circle, 01945 .... (508)631-2324
Harbor Light Inn, 58 Washington St, 01945 .... (617)631-2186
Harborside House, 23 Gregory St, 01945 .... (617)631-1032
Lindsey's Garrett, 38 High St, 01945 .... (508)631-2653
Spray Cliff on the Ocean, 25 Spray Ave, 01945 .... (508)741-0680
Ten Mugford Street, 10 Mugford St, 01945 .... (617)639-0343
Tidecrest, Spray Ave, 01945 .... (508)631-4515

MARION L20 / *E8*
Peregrine B&B, 418 Front St, PO Box 302, 02738 .... (508)748-0065

MARTHA'S VINEYARD O21 / *F9*
Captain Dexter House of Vineyard Haven, 100 Main St, PO Box 2457, 02568 .... (508)693-6564
Farmhouse, State Rd, 02568 .... (617)693-5354
Thorncroft Inn, 278 Main St, PO Box 1022, 02568 .... (508)693-3333

MASHPEE M22 / *E9*
The Blackwood's, 11 Weather Crescent, 02649 .... (508)477-9252

MATTAPOISETT M20 / *E8*
Tall Pines B&B, 135 N St, 02739 .... (508)758-2076

MENEMSHA O20 / *F8*
Beach Plum Inn, Box 98, 02552 .... (508)645-9454

MIDDLEFIELD F5 / *C3*
Strawberry Banke Farm, Skyline Tr, 01243 .... (413)623-6481

NANTUCKET P25 / *G10*
1806 Anchor Inn, 66 Centre St, 02554 .... (508)228-0072
76 Main Street, 76 Main St Box E, 02554 .... (508)228-2533
Anchor Inn, 66 Centre St, 02554 .... (508)228-0072
Beachside Resort, 31 N Beach St, 02554 .... (800)322-4433
Beachway Guests, 3 N Beach St, 02554 .... (508)228-1324
Brant Point Inn, 6 North St, 02554 .... (508)228-5442
Brass Lantern Inn, 11 N Water St, 02554 .... (508)228-4064
The Carlisle House Inn, 26 N Water St, 02554 .... (508)228-0720
Centerboard, 8 Chester St, 02584 .... (508)228-9696
Century House, 10 Cliff Rd, PO Box 603, 02554 .... (508)228-0530
Cliff House, 34 Cliff Rd, 02554 .... (508)228-2154
Cliffside Beach Club, PO Box 449, 02554 .... (508)228-0618
Cobblestone Inn, 5 Ash St, 02554 .... (508)228-1987
Corner House, 49 Centre St, PO Box 1828, 02554 .... (508)228-1530
Easton House, 17 N Water St, 02554 .... (508)228-2759
Eighteen Gardner Street, 18 Gardner St, 02554 .... (508)228-1155
Fair Gardens, 27 Fair St, 02554 .... (508)228-4258
Fair Winds, 4 Ash St, 02554 .... (508)228-4899
The Folger Hotel & Cottages, Easton St, 02554 .... (508)228-0313
Four Ash Street, 4 Ash St, 02554 .... (617)228-4899
Four Chimneys, 38 Orange St, 02554 .... (508)228-1912
Great Harbor Inn, 31 India St, 02554 .... (508)228-6609
The Grey Goose, 24 Hussey St, 02554 .... (508)228-6597
Grieder Guest House, 43 Orange St, 02554 .... (508)228-1399
Halliday's Nantucket House, Box 165, 02554 .... (508)228-9450
Hawthorne House, 2 Chestnut St, 02554 .... (508)228-1468
The House At Ten Gay Street, 10 Gay St, 02554 .... (508)228-4425
The House of Orange, 25 Orange St, 02554 .... (508)228-9287
House of the Seven Gables, 32 Cliff Rd, 02554 .... (508)228-4706
Hussey House, 15 N Water St, 02554 .... (508)228-0747
India House, 37 India St, 02554 .... (508)228-9043
The Island Reef, 20 N Water St, 02554 .... (508)228-2156
Ivy Lodge, 2 Chester St, 02554 .... (508)228-0305
Jared Coffin House, 29 Broad St, 02554 .... (508)228-2400
Le Languedoc Inn, 24 Broad St, 02554 .... (508)228-2552
Nantucket Landfall, 4 Harbor View Way, 02554 .... (508)228-0500
The Nantucket Whaler, 8 N Water St, 02554 .... (508)228-6597
The Nesbitt Inn, 21 Broad St, 02554 .... (508)228-0156
Parker Guest House, 4 East Chestnut St, 02554 .... (508)228-4625
Paul West House, 5 Liberty St, 02554 .... (508)228-2495
Periwinkle Guest House, 9 N Water St, 02554 .... (617)228-9267
Phillips House, 54 Fair St, 02554 .... (508)228-9217
Quaker House, 5 Chestnut St, 02554 .... (508)228-0400
Roberts House, 11 India St, 02554 .... (508)228-9009
Ruben Joy Homestead, 107 Main St, 02554 .... (508)228-1703
Ships Inn, 13 Fair St, 02554 .... (508)228-0040
Stumble Inne, 109 Orange St, 02554 .... (508)228-4482
Ten Hussey, 10 Hussey St, 02554 .... (508)228-9552
Ten Lyon Street Inn, 10 Lyon St, 02554 .... (508)228-0072
The White House, 48 Centre St, 02554 .... (508)228-0405
Union Street Inn, 7 Union St, 02554 .... (508)228-9222
The Wauwinet, An Inn by the Sea, PO Box 2580, 02584 .... (800)426-8718

West Moor Inn, Off Cliff Rd, 02554 ....(508)228-0877
The Woodbox Inn, 29 Fair St, 02554 ....(508)228-0587

NANTUCKET ISLAND — P25 / *G10*
Brant Plantation Inn, 6 N Beach St, 02554 ....(508)228-5442
Chestnut House, 3 Chestnut St, 02554 ....(508)228-0049
Martin's Guest House, 61 Centre St, 02554 ....(508)228-0678
Seven Sea Street, 7 Sea St, 02554 ....(508)228-3577
Wharf Cottages, New Whale St, 02554 ....(508)228-4620

NEEDHAM — G17 / *C7*
Brock's B&B, 60 Stevens Rd, 02192 ....(617)444-6573

NEW BEDFORD — M19 / *E8*
Durant Sail Loft Inn, 1 Merrill's Wharf, 02740 ....(508)999-2700
Melville House, 100 Madison St, 02740 ....(508)990-1566
Victorian Mansion, 44 North Water St, 02740 ....(508)993-4944

NEW MARLBOROUGH — H3 / *D2*
Old Inn On The Green, Star Rt 70, 01230 ....(413)229-3131
Red Bird Inn, Rt 57 & Grosby Rd, 01230 ....(413)229-2433

NEWBURYPORT — B19 / *A8*
Essex Street Inn, 7 Essex St, 01950 ....(508)465-3145
Garrison Inn, On Brown Square, 01950 ....(617)465-0910
Morrill Place Inn, 209 High St, 01950 ....(508)462-2808
Windsor House, 38 Federal St, 01950 ....(508)462-3778

NORTH BILLERICA — D16 / *B7*
Ted Barbour, 88 Rogers St, 01862 ....(617)667-7317

NORTH EASTHAM — J26 / *D10*
The Penny House, Rt 6, PO Box 238, 02651 ....(508)255-6632

NORTH FALMOUTH — M21 / *E9*
Wingate Crossing, R 28a/190 N Falmouth Hwy, 02556 ....(508)540-8723

NORTH SCITUATE — G20 / *C8*
Rasberry Ink, 748 Country Way, 02060 ....(617)545-6629

NORTHAMPTON — F7 / *C4*
Autumn Inn, 259 Elm St, 01060 ....(413)584-7660
The Knoll, 230 N Main, 01060 ....(413)584-8164

NORTHFIELD — C8 / *A4*
Centennial House, 94 Main St, 01360 ....(413)498-5921
Northfield Country House, School St, PO Box 617, 01360 ....(413)498-2692

OAK BLUFFS — N22 / *F9*
Arend's Samoset on the Sound, Box 847, 02557 ....(508)693-5148
Attleboro House, 11 Lake Ave Box 1564, 02557 ....(508)693-4346
Circuit House, Box 2422, 150 Circuit Ave, 02557 ....(508)693-5033
The Inn at Dockside, Box 1206, 02557 ....(508)693-2966
Narragansett House, 62 Narragansett Ave, 02557 ....(508)693-3627
Nashua House, 30 Kennebec Ave, PO Box 803, 02557 ....(508)693-0043
The Oak House, PO Box 299AA Seaview Ave, 02557 ....(508)693-4187

ORLEANS — K26 / *E10*
The Captain Doane House, 1 Captain Doane Rd, 02653 ....(508)255-0652

OSTERVILLE — M23 / *E9*
East Bay Lodge, East Bay Rd PO Box N, 02655 ....(508)428-6961
Village B&B, PO Box 785, 02655 ....(508)428-7004

PERU — E4 / *B3*
Chalet d'Alicia, E Windsor Rd, 01235 ....(413)655-8292

PETERSHAM — E10 / *B5*
Winterwood at Petersham, N Main St, 01366 ....(508)724-8885

PITTSFIELD — E3 / *B2*
Country Hearts B&B, 52 Broad St, 01201 ....(413)499-3201
Greer B&B, 193 Wendell Ave, 01201 ....(413)443-3669

PLYMOUTH — J21 / *D8*
Another Place Inn, 240 Sandwich St, 02360 ....(508)746-0126
Colonial House Inn, 207 Sandwich St, 02360 ....(508)747-4274
Morton Park Place, 1 Morton Park Rd, 02360 ....(617)747-1730

PRINCETON — E12 / *B6*
Harrington Farm, 178 Westminster Rd, 01541 ....(617)464-5600
Hill House, PO Box 276, 105 Merriam Rd, 01541 ....(617)464-2061

PROVINCETOWN — I24 / *D10*
1807 House, 54 Commercial St, 02657 ....(508)487-2173
Admiral's Landing Guest House, 158 Bradford St, 02657 ....(508)487-9665
Asheton House, 3 Cook St, 02657 ....(508)487-9966
Bradford Gardens Inn, 178 Bradford St, 02657 ....(508)487-1616
Cape Codder Guest House, 570 Commercial St, 02657 ....(508)487-0131
Captain Lysander Inn, 96 Commercial St, 02657 ....(508)487-2253
Elephant Walk Inn, 156 Bradford St, 02657 ....(508)487-2543
Fairbanks Inn, 90 Bradford St, 02657 ....(508)487-0386
Fiddle Leaf, 186 Commercial St, 02657 ....(508)487-1443
Hargood House, 493 Commercial St, 02657 ....(508)487-1324
Lamplighter Guest House, 26 Bradford St, 02657 ....(508)487-2529
Land's End Inn, 22 Commercial St, 02657 ....(508)487-0706
Ocean's Inn, 386 Commercial St, 02657 ....(508)487-0358
Red Inn, 15 Commercial St, 02657 ....(508)487-0050
Rose And Crown Guest House, 158 Commercial St, 02657 ....(508)487-3332
Somerset House, 378 Commercial St, 02657 ....(508)487-0383
Sunset Inn, 142 Bradford St, 02657 ....(508)487-9810
Twelve Center Guest House, 12 Center St, 02657 ....(508)487-0381
Watership Inn, 7 Winthrop St, 02657 ....(508)487-0094
White Wind Inn, 174 Commercial St, 02657 ....(508)487-1526
Windamar House, 568 Commercial St, 02657 ....(508)487-0599

REHOBOTH — K17 / *E7*
Gilbert's B&B, 30 Spring St, 02769 ....(508)252-6416
Perryville Inn, 157 Perryville Rd, 02769 ....(508)252-9239

RICHMOND — F2 / *C2*
Cogswell Guest House, Rt 41, 01254 ....(413)698-2750
Pierson Place, Rt 41, 01254 ....(617)698-2750
Westgate, Rt 295, 01254 ....(413)698-2657

ROCKPORT — C21 / *B8*
Addison Choate Inn, 49 Broadway, 01966 ....(508)546-7543
Cable House, Norwood Ave, 01966 ....(508)546-6383
Captain's House, 109 Marmion Way, 01966 ....(508)546-3825
The Inn on Cove Hill, 37 Mt Pleasant St, 01966 ....(508)546-2701
Eden Pines Inn, Eden Rd, 01966 ....(508)546-2505
Lantana House, 22 Broadway, 01966 ....(617)546-3535
Linden Tree Inn, 26 King St, 01966 ....(508)546-2494
Mooringstone for Nonsmokers, 12 Norwood Ave, 01966 ....(508)546-2479
Old Farm Inn, 291 Granite St, 01966 ....(508)546-3237
Ralph Waldo Emerson Inn, Phillips Ave, 01966 ....(508)546-6321
Rocky Shores Inn, Eden Rd, 01966 ....(508)546-2823
Sally Webster Inn, 34 Mt Pleasant St, 01966 ....(508)546-9251
Seacrest Manor, 131 Marmion Way, 01966 ....(508)546-2211
Seafarer Inn, 86 Marmion Way, 01966 ....(508)546-6248
Seaward Inn, 62 Marmion Way, 01966 ....(508)546-3471
Seven South Street Inn, 7 S St, 01966 ....(508)546-6708
Tuck Inn, 17 High St, 01966 ....(508)546-6252
Yankee Clipper Inn, Box 2399, 96 Granite St, 01966 ....(508)546-3407

SAGAMORE BEACH — K22 / *E9*
Bed & Breakfast, One Hawes Rd, Box 205, 02562 ....(617)888-1559

SALEM — D19 / *B8*
Amelia Payson Guest House, 16 Winter St, 01970 ....(508)744-8304
Coach House Inn, 284 Lafayette St, 01970 ....(508)744-4092
The Salem Inn, 7 Summer St, 01970 ....(508)741-0680
The Inn at Seven Winter Street, 7 Winter St, 01970 ....(508)745-9520
Stephen Daniels House, 1 Daniels St, 01970 ....(508)744-5709
The Stepping Stone Inn, 19 Washington Square N, 01970 ....(508)741-8900
Suzannah Flint House, 98 Essex St, 01970 ....(508)744-5281

SANDISFIELD — H4 / *D2*
New Boston Inn, Jct Rt 8 & 57, 01255-0120 ....(413)258-4477

SANDWICH — L22 / *E9*
Academy Hill B&B, 4 Academy Rd, 02563 ....(508)888-8083
Bay Beach B&B, 1-3 Bay Beach Ln, 02563 ....(508)888-8813
Captain Ezra Nye House, 152 Main St, 02563 ....(800)388-2278
The Dan'l Webster Inn, 149 Main St, 02563 ....(508)888-3622
Hawthorn Hill, Box 777, 02563 ....(508)888-3333
Isaiah Jones Homestead, 165 Main St, 02563 ....(508)888-9115
Quince Tree, 164 Main St, 02563 ....(508)888-1371
Sandwich B&B, 13 School St, 02563 ....(508)888-4542
Six Water Street, 6 Water St, Rt 130, 02563 ....(508)888-6808
The Summer House, 158 Main St, 02563 ....(508)888-4991

SEEKONK — K16 / *E7*
Simeon's Mansion House, 940 County St, 02771 ....(508)336-6674

SHEFFIELD — H2 / *D2*
Centuryhurst B&B, Box 486 Main St, 01257 ....(413)229-8131
Colonel Ashley Inn, Bow Wow Rd, PO Box 142, 01257 ....(413)229-2929
Ivanhoe Country House, Rt 41, 01257 ....(413)229-2143
Stagecoach Hill Inn, Rt 41, 01257 ....(413)229-8585
Staveleigh House, PO 608, S Main St, 01257 ....(413)229-2129
Unique B&B, Under Mountain Rd, 01257 ....(413)229-3363

SHELBURNE FALLS — D6 / *B3*
Country Comfort, 15 Masonic Ave, 01370 ....(413)625-9877
Parson Hubbard House, Old Village Rd, 01370 ....(413)625-9730
The Elmer House, Bray Rd, RFD #1 Box 224, 01370 ....(413)625-9590

SOUTH DARTMOUTH — M19 / *F8*
Salt Marsh Farm, 322 Smith Neck Rd, 02748 ....(508)992-0980

SOUTH DENNIS — L24 / *E10*
Country Pineapple Inn, 370 Main St, 02660 ....(508)760-3211

SOUTH EGREMONT — H2 / *C2*
Egremont Inn, Old Sheffield Rd, 01258 ....(413)528-2111
Weathervane Inn, Rt 23, Main St, 01258 ....(413)528-9580

SOUTH HARWICH — L25 / *E10*
House on the Hill, PO Box 51, 968 Main St, 02661 ....(617)432-4321

SOUTH LANCASTER — E14 / *B6*
Deershorn Manor B&B, 357 Sterling Rd, PO Box 805, 01561 .(508)365-9022

SOUTH LEE — G3 / *C2*
Federal House Inn, Rt 102 Main St, 01260 ....(413)243-1824
Merrell Tavern Inn, Rt 102 Main St, 01260 ....(413)243-1794

SOUTH ORLEANS K26 / *E10*
Hilbourne House, Rt 28, O Box 190, 02662 .... (508)255-0780

SOUTH SUDBURY F15 / *C6*
Longfellow's Wayside Inn, Wayside Inn Rd, 01776 .... (617)443-8846

SOUTH YARMOUTH L24 / *E10*
Four Winds B&B, 345 High Bank Rd, 02664 .... (508)394-4182
River Street Guest House, 9 River St, 02664 .... (508)398-8946

SOUTHBRIDGE H11 / *D5*
The Prindle House, 71 Prindle Hill Rd, RFD 1, 01550 .... (508)248-3134

SOUTHFIELD H3 / *D2*
Langhaar House, PO Box 191, 01259 .... (413)229-2007

STERLING E13 / *B6*
Sterling Inn, Rt 12 Box 609, 01564 .... (617)422-6592
Sterling Orchards B&B, 60 Kendall Hill Rd, Box 455, 01564 .... (508)422-6595

STOCKBRIDGE G2 / *C2*
Arbor Rose Bed & Breakfast, Box 114 Yale Hill, 01262 .... (413)298-4744
Broad Meadows, N Church St, PO Box 485, 01262 .... (413)298-4972
The Inn at Stockbridge, Rt 7 Box 618, 01262 .... (413)298-3337
Woodside B&B, Box 1096, 01262 .... (413)298-4977

STOW E15 / *B6*
Amerscot House, 61 W Acton Rd, 01775 .... (508)897-0666

STURBRIDGE H11 / *D5*
Bethlehem Inn, 72 Station Hill, Box 451, 01566 .... (508)347-3013
Chamberlain House, PO Box 187, 01566 .... (617)347-3313
Colonel Ebenezer Craft's, PO 187, 01566 .... (508)347-3313
Commonwealth Inn, 11 Summit Ave, 01566 .... (508)347-7603
Publick House Historic Inn, On The Common, 01566 .... (617)347-3313
Sturbridge Country Inn, 530 Main St, 01566 .... (508)347-5503

SUDBURY F15 / *C6*
Checkerberry Corner, 5 Checkerberry Circle, 01776 .... (617)443-8660
Sudbury B&B, 3 Drum Ln, 01776 .... (508)443-2860

SWAMPSCOTT E19 / *B8*
The Maguire's, 43 Hampden St, 01907 .... (617)593-5732
Oak Shores B&B, 64 Fuller Ave, 01907 .... (617)599-7677

TOWNSEND C13 / *B6*
B&B At Wood Farm, 40 Worchester Rd, 01469 .... (617)597-5019
Wood Farm, 40 Worchester Rd, 01469 .... (508)597-5019

TRURO I25 / *D10*
Parker House B&B, Rt 6A, Box 114, 02666 .... (617)349-3358

TYRINGHAM G3 / *C2*
The Golden Goose, Main Rd, PO Box 336, 01264 .... (413)243-3008

UXBRIDGE I14 / *D6*
Capron House, 2 Capron St, 01569 .... (617)278-2214

VINEYARD HAVEN N21 / *F9*
Bayberry, RFD 1 Box 546, 02568 .... (508)693-1984
Gazebo B&B, Edgartown Rd, 02568 .... (617)693-6955
Hanover House, 10 Edgartown Rd, Box 2107, 02568 .... (508)693-1066
High Haven House, Box 289, Summer St, 02568 .... (617)693-9204
Lothrop Merry House, Owen Park, PO Box 1939, 02568 .... (508)693-1646
Ocean Side Inn, Main St, Box 2700, 02568 .... (617)693-1296
Tuckerman House, 45 William St Box 194, 02568 .... (508)693-0417

WARE G10 / *C5*
The 1880 Country Inn, 14 Pleasant St, 01082 .... (413)967-7847
The Wildwood Inn, 121 Church St, 01082 .... (413)967-7798

WAREHAM L20 / *E8*
Little Harbor Guest House, 20 Stockton Shortcut, 02571 .... (508)295-6329
Mulberry B&B, 257 High St, 02571 .... (508)295-0684

WELLFLEET J25 / *D10*
The Inn at Duck Creeke, PO Box 364, 02667 .... (508)349-9333
Holden Inn, Commercial St, PO Box 816, 02667 .... (508)349-3450

WEST BARNSTABLE L23 / *E9*
Honeysuckle Hill, 591 Main St, 02668 .... (508)362-8418

WEST BOYLSTON F13 / *C6*
The Rose Cottage, 24 Worcester St, Rts 12 & 40, 01583 .... (508)835-4034

WEST BROOKFIELD G10 / *C5*
Deer Meadow Farm, Bragg Rd, RFD #1, 01585 .... (413)436-7129

WEST DENNIS L24 / *E10*
The Beach House, 61 Uncle Stephen's Rd, 02670 .... (617)398-8321
The Lighthouse Inn, Lighthouse Rd, 02670 .... (508)398-2244

WEST FALMOUTH M21 / *F9*
Elms, PO 895, 495 W Falmouth Hwy, 02574 .... (508)540-7232
Old Silver Beach B&B, 3 Cliffwood Ln, PO Box 642, 02574 .... (508)540-5446
Sjoholm B&B Inn, 17 Chase Rd Box 430, 02574 .... (508)540-5706
Sunset Hill B&B, 90 Fox Ln, PO Box 539, 02574 .... (508)540-1763

WEST HARWICH L25 / *E10*
Barnaby Inn, PO Box 151, 02671 .... (508)432-6789
Lion's Head Inn, 186 Belmont Rd PO Box 444, 02671 .... (508)432-7766
Sunny Pines B&B Inn, 77 Main St, PO Box 667, 02671 .... (508)432-9628
The Tern Inn, 91 Chase St, 02671 .... (508)432-3714
The Gingerbread House, 141 Division St, Box 226, 02671 .... (508)432-1901

WEST HAWLEY D5 / *B3*
Stump Sprouts Guest Lodge, W Hill Rd, 01339 .... (413)339-4265

WEST HYANNISPORT M23 / *E9*
B&B Cape Cod, PO Box 341, 02672 .... (508)775-2772

WEST NEWTON F17 / *C7*
Sears-Withington House, 274 Otis St, 02165 .... (617)332-8422

WEST STOCKBRIDGE F2 / *C2*
Card Lake Country Inn, Main St, 01266 .... (413)232-7120
Shaker Mill Tavern Inn, Main St, Box 371, 01266 .... (413)232-8565
Westbridge Inn, Main St PO Box 378, 01266 .... (413)232-7120
Williamsville Inn, Rt 41, 01266 .... (413)274-6118

WEST TISBURY O21 / *F8*
Lambert's Cove Country Inn, Lambert's Cove Rd, Box 422, 02568 .... (508)693-2298
Old Parsonage B&B, Box 137 State Rd, 02575 .... (508)693-4289

WEST YARMOUTH L24 / *E9*
Manor House, 57 Maine Ave, 02673 .... (508)771-9211

WESTHAMPTON F6 / *C3*
Outlook Farm, Rt 66, 01027 .... (413)527-0633

WHATELY E7 / *B4*
Sunnyside Farm, 11 River Rd, 01093 .... (413)665-3113

WHITINSVILLE H14 / *C6*
The Victorian, 583 Linwood Ave, 01588 .... (617)234-2500

WILLIAMSBURG F6 / *C3*
Twin Maples B&B, 106 South St, 01096 .... (413)268-7925

WILLIAMSTOWN C3 / *A2*
Le Jardin, 777 Coldspring Rd, 01267 .... (413)458-8032
River Bend Farm, 643 Simonds Rd, 01267 .... (413)458-5504
Steep Acres Farm, 520 White Oaks Rd, 01267 .... (413)458-3774
Upland Meadow House, 1249 Northwest Hill Rd, 01267 .... (413)458-3990

WOODS HOLE N21 / *F8*
Grey Whale Inn, 565 Woods Hole Rd, 02543 .... (508)548-7692
The Marlborough, 320 Woods Hole, 02543 .... (508)548-6218

WORCESTER-RUTLAND F12 / *C5*
The General Rufus Putnam House, 344 Main St, 01543 .... (508)886-4256

WORTHINGTON E5 / *B3*
Country Cricket Village Inn, Huntington Rd, Rt 112, 01098 .... (413)238-5366
Franklin Burrs, Kinne Brook Rd, 01098 .... (413)238-5826
Hill Gallery, HC65, Box 96, 01098 .... (413)238-5914
Inn Yesterday, Rt 112, Huntington Rd, 01098 .... (413)238-5529
Worthington Inn At Four Corners Farm, Rt 143, 01098 .... (413)238-4441

YARMOUTH PORT L24 / *E10*
Colonial House Inn, Rt 6A, 277 Main St, 02675 .... (508)362-4348
Crook' Jaw Inn, 186 Main St, Rt 6A, 02675 .... (508)362-6111
Lane's End Cottage, 268 Main St, 02675 .... (508)362-5298
Liberty Hill Inn, 77 Main St, Rt 6A, 02675 .... (508)362-3976
Old Yarmouth Inn, 223 Main St, 02675 .... (508)362-3191
Olde Captain's Inn, 101 Main St, 02675 .... (508)362-4496
One Centre Street Inn, 1 Centre St, 02675 .... (508)362-8910
Village Inn, 92 Main, Rt 6a, PO Box 1, 02675 .... (508)362-3182
Wedgewood Inn, 83 Main St, 02675 .... (508)362-5157

MICHIGAN

ALDEN L8 / *D3*
Torch Lake B&B, Box 165, 49612 .... (616)331-6424

ALLEGAN V6 / *G2*
DeLano Inn, 302 Cutler St, 49010 .... (616)673-2609
Winchester Inn, 524 Marshall St, 49010 .... (616)673-3621

ALLEN X10 / *H3*
The Olde Bricke House, 231 E Chicago Rd, PO Box 211, 49227 .... (517)869-2349

ALMA R10 / *F3*
Granny's Garret B&B, 910 Vassar St, 48801 .... (517)463-3961

ALPENA K14 / *D4*
Fireside Inn, 18730 Fireside Hwy, 49707 .... (517)595-6369

ANN ARBOR W13 / *G4*
The Urban Retreat, 2759 Canterbury Rd, 48104 .... (313)971-8110

ARCADIA N5 / *D2*
Watervale Inn, Watervale Rd, 49613 .... (616)352-9083

BATTLE CREEK W8 / *G3*
Old Lamplighter's Home, 276 Capital Ave NE, 49017 .... (616)963-2603

BAY CITY Q12 / *F4*
Stonehedge Inn, 924 Center Ave, 48708 .... (517)894-4342

BAY VIEW J9 / C3
Terrace Inn, 216 Fairview Ave, 49770 ....(616)347-2410

BELLAIRE L8 / D3
Bellaire B&B, 212 Park St, 49615 ....(616)533-6077

BENTON HARBOR X4 / H2
Bolins' B&B, 576 Colfax Ave, 49022 ....(616)925-9068

BENZONIA M6 / D2
Crystal B&B, 845 Michigan Ave, 49616 ....(616)882-5741

BEULAH M5 / D2
Brookside Inn, 115 N Michigan, PO Box 506, 49617 ....(616)882-9688
Windermere Inn, 747 Crystal Dr, 49617 ....(616)882-7264

BIG BAY D1 / A1
The Big Bay Point Lighthouse B&B, 3 Lighthouse Rd, 49808 ....(906)345-9957

BLACK RIVER L14 / D5
Silver Creek, 4361 US-23 S, 48721 ....(517)471-2198

BLANEY PARK G6 / B2
Celibeth House, Rt 1 Box 58A, M-77 Blaney Park Rd, 49836 ....(906)283-3409

BLISSFIELD Y13 / H4
Hiram D. Ellis Inn, 415 W Adrian St (US 223), 49228 ....(517)486-3155

BUCKLEY N7 / E2
A Wicklow House, 9270 M-37, 49620 ....(616)269-4212

CADILLAC O8 / E3
Essenmacher's Bed & Breakfast, 204 Locust Lane, 49601 ....(616)775-3828

CALUMET A15 / A5
The Calumet House, 1159 Calumet Ave, 49913 ....(906)337-1936

CARO R14 / F4
Garden Gate B&B, 315 Pearl St, 48723 ....(517)673-2696

CASEVILLE P14 / E5
Country Charm Farm, 5048 Conkey Rd, 48725 ....(517)856-3110

CENTER LINE G9 / G5
The Meares House, 8250 Warren Blvd, 48015 ....(313)756-8250

CENTRAL LAKE K8 / D3
Darmon Street B&B, 7900 Darmon St, PO Box 284, 49622 ....(616)544-3931

CHARLEVOIX J8 / C3
Bay B&B, Rt 1, Box 136-A, 49720 ....(616)599-2570
Belvedere House, 306 Belvedere Ave, 49720 ....(616)547-4501
Bridge Street Inn, 113 Michigan Ave, 49720 ....(616)547-6606

CHASSELL B15 / A5
Palosaari's Rolling Acres B&B, Rt 1, Box 354, 49916 ....(906)523-4947

CLIO S13 / F4
Chandelier Guest House, 1567 Morgan Rd, 48420 ....(313)687-6061

COLDWATER X9 / H3
Chicago Pike Inn, 215 E Chicago St, 49036 ....(517)279-8744

COLUMBIAVILLE S14 / F4
Redwing, 3176 Shady Oak Dr, 48421 ....(313)793-4301

CONKLIN T6 / F2
Miller School Inn, 2959 Roosevelt Rd, 49403 ....(616)677-1026

DAVISON T14 / F5
Oakbrook Inn, 7256 E Court St, 48423 ....(313)653-1744

DE TOUR VILLAGE G12 / C4
Hubbard's Boonevue Lodge, 206 S Huron Box 65, 49725 ....(906)297-2391

DETROIT W15 / G5
The Blanche House Inn, 506 Parkview Dr, 48214 ....(313)822-7090

DIMONDALE V10 / G3
Bannicks B&B, 4608 Michigan Rd (M-99), 48821 ....(517)646-0224

DOUGLAS U5 / G2
Rosemont Inn, 83 Lake Shore Dr, 49406 ....(616)857-2637

EAST LANSING U11 / G3
Coleman Corners B&B, 7733 M-78, 48823 ....(517)339-9360

EASTPORT K8 / D3
Sunrise B&B, PO Box 52, 49627 ....(616)599-2706

EDWARDSBURG Y6 / H2
Glenda's B&B, 68699 M-62, 49112 ....(616)663-7905

ELBERTA M5 / D2
Summer Inn, 809 Frankfort Ave, 49628 ....(616)352-7279

ELK RAPIDS L8 / D3
Cairn House, 8160 Cairn Hwy, 49629 ....(616)264-8994
Widows Walk, 603 River St, 49629 ....(616)264-5767

ELLSWORTH K8 / D3
The House On The Hill, Lake St Box 206, 49729 ....(616)588-6304

EMPIRE L6 / D2
Clipper House Inn, 10085 Front St, PO Box 35, 49630 ....(616)326-5518

ESCANABA H3 / C1
The House of Ludington, 223 Ludington St, 49829 ....(906)786-4000

EVART P8 / E3
B&B at Lynch's Dream, 22177 80th Ave, 49631 ....(616)734-5989

FARMINGTON HILLS V14 / G4
The Botsford Inn, 28000 Grand River, 48024 ....(313)474-4800

FENNVILLE V5 / G2
Crane House, 6051 124th Ave, 49408 ....(616)561-6931
The Fenn Inn, 2254 S 58th St, 49408 ....(616)561-2836
Heritage Manor, 2253 Blue Star Hwy, 49408 ....(616)543-4384
Hidden Pond Farm, 5975 128th Ave, 49408 ....(616)561-2491
The Kingsley House, 626 W Main St, 49408 ....(616)561-6425
The Porches B&B, 2297-70th St, 49408 ....(616)543-4162

FENTON U13 / G4
Pine Ridge, N-10345 Old US-23, 48430 ....(313)629-8911

FLINT T13 / F4
Avon House, 518 Avon St, 48503 ....(313)232-6861

FRANKENMUTH S13 / F4
B&B at the Pines, 327 Ardussi St, 48734 ....(517)652-9019
Bavarian Town B&B, 206 Beyerlein St, 48734 ....(517)652-8057
Frankenmuth Bender Haus, 337 Trinklein St, 48734 ....(517)652-8897
Home Away Lodgings, 176 Parker St, 48734 ....(517)652-6839
Kueffner's Haus, 176 Parker, 48734 ....(517)652-8897
Lewis Haus, 337 Trinklein St, 48734 ....(517)652-3133
Parlberg's Place, 8180 Roedel, 48734 ....(517)652-8134

FRANKFORT M5 / D2
Chimney Corners, 1602 Crystal Dr, 49635 ....(616)352-7522

FRUITPORT S5 / F2
Village Park B&B, 60 W Park St, 49415 ....(616)865-6289

GALESBURG W8 / G3
Old Memories Farm, PO Box 98, 49053 ....(616)665-9516

GAYLORD K10 / D3
Norden Hem, PO Box 623, 49735 ....(517)732-6794

GLADWIN P10 / E3
The Riverside B&B, 66 Lockwood Dr, 48624 ....(517)426-1206

GLEN ARBOR L6 / D2
White Gull Inn, PO Box 351, 49636 ....(616)334-4486

GRAND MARAIS D6 / B2
Lakeview Inn, PO Box 297, 49839 ....(906)494-2612

GRAND RAPIDS T7 / G2
B&B of Grand Rapids, 455 College Ave SE, 49503 ....(616)451-4849
Urban Retreat B&B, 1330 Knapp NE, 49505 ....(616)363-1125

GREENVILLE S8 / F3
The Gibson House, 311 W Washington, 48838 ....(616)754-6691
Winter Inn, 100 N Lafayette, 48838 ....(616)754-7108

HARBOR BEACH P16 / E5
Wellock Inn, 404 S Huron Ave, 48441 ....(517)479-3645

HARBOR SPRINGS J9 / C3
Harbour Inn, Beach Dr, 49740 ....(616)526-2107

HARRISVILLE M14 / D5
Big Paw Resort, 818 N Lake Huron Shore, PO Box 187, 48740 ....(517)724-6326
Red Geranium Inn, 508 E Main St, Box 613, 48740 ....(517)724-6153
Widow's Watch B&B, 401 Lake St, Box 271, 48740 ....(517)724-5465

HOLLAND U5 / G2
The Old Holland Inn, 133 W 11th St, 49423 ....(616)396-6601
The Parsonage, 6 E 24th St, 49423 ....(616)396-1316

HOMER X9 / H3
Grist Mill Inn, 310 E Main, 49245 ....(517)568-4063

HUDSON Y11 / H4
The Sutton-Weed Farm, 18736 Quaker Rd, 49247 ....(517)547-6302

IONIA T9 / G3
The Union Hill Inn, 306 Union, 48846 ....(616)527-0955

ITHACA S10 / F3
Chaffin Farms B&B, 3239 W St Charles Rd, 48847 ....(517)463-4081

JONESVILLE X10 / H3
Munro House B&B, 202 Maumee St, 49250 ....(517)849-9292

KALAMAZOO W7 / G2
Hall House, 106 Thompson St, 49007 ....(616)343-2500
Kalamazoo House, 447 W South St, 49007 ....(616)343-5426
Stuart Avenue Inn, 405 Stuart Ave, 49007 ....(616)342-0230

LAINGSBURG T11 / G4
Seven Oaks Farm, 7891 Hollister Rd, 48848 ....(517)651-5598

LAKESIDE Y4 / *H1*
The Pebble House, 15093 Lakeshore Rd, 49116 .... (616)469-1416

LAMONT T6 / *G2*
The Stagecoach Stop B&B, 4819 Leonard Rd W Box 18, 49430 .... (616)677-3940

LANSING U10 / *G3*
Maplewood, 15945 Wood St, 48906 .... (517)372-7775

LAWRENCE W6 / *H2*
Oak Cove Resort, 58881 46th St, 49064 .... (616)674-8228

LELAND K6 / *D2*
Leland Lodge, 565 Pearl St, PO Box 344, 49654 .... (616)256-9848
Manitou Manor, PO Box 864, 49654 .... (616)256-7712
Riverside Inn, 302 River St, 49654 .... (616)256-9971
Snowbird Inn, PO Box 1021, 49653 .... (616)256-9462
The Highlands, 612 N Lake St, 49654 .... (616)256-7632

LESLIE V11 / *G3*
Hampton's Guest House, 112 Washington St, PO Box 123, 49251 .... (517)589-9929

LEWISTON L11 / *D4*
Lakeview Hills B&B, Lakeview Dr, Fleming Rd, PO Box 365, 49756 .... (517)786-2000

LEXINGTON S17 / *F5*
Governor's Inn, 7277 Simons St, 48450 .... (313)359-5770

LUDINGTON P4 / *E2*
B&B at Ludington, 2458 S Beaune Rd, 49431 .... (616)843-9768
The Doll House Inn, 209 E Ludington Ave, 49431 .... (616)843-2286
The Inn at Ludington, 701 E Ludington Ave, 49431 .... (616)845-7055
White Rose Country Inn, 6036 Barnhart Rd, 49431 .... (616)843-8193

MACKINAC ISLAND H10 / *C3*
Bogan Lake Inn, Box 482, 49757 .... (906)847-3439
Chippewa Hotel, PO Box 250, 49757 .... (906)847-3341
Haan's 1830 Inn, PO Box 123, 49757 .... (906)847-6244
Iroquois Hotel-On-the-Beach, 49757 .... (906)847-3321
Metivier Inn, Box 285, 49757 .... (906)847-6234
Thuya B&B Cottage, Box 459, 49757 .... (906)847-3400

MANISTIQUE G5 / *C2*
Margaret's B&B, 230 Arbutus, PO Box 344, 49854 .... (906)341-5147
Marina Guest House, PO Box 344, 49854 .... (906)341-5147

MAPLE CITY L6 / *D2*
Country Cottage B&B, 135 E Harbor Hwy, 49664 .... (616)228-5328

MARQUETTE E2 / *B1*
Greenwood Estates, 18 Oakridge Dr, 49855 .... (906)249-9246
Michigamme Lake Lodge, 2403 US-41W, 49855 .... (906)225-1393

MARSHALL W9 / *G3*
McCarthy's Bear Creek Inn, 15230 C Drive N, 49068 .... (616)781-8383
The National House Inn, 102 S Parkview, 49068 .... (616)781-7374

MCMILLAN F7 / *B2*
Helmer House Inn, Rt 3 Country Rd 417, 49853 .... (906)586-3204

MEARS Q4 / *F2*
Duneland Inn-Foster's B&B, PO Box 53, 49436 .... (616)873-5128

MECOSTA Q8 / *F3*
Blue Lake Lodge, 9765 Blue Lake Lodge Ln Box 1, 48823 .... (616)972-8391

MENDON X7 / *H3*
The Mendon Country Inn, 440 W Main St, 49072 .... (616)496-8132

MIDLAND Q11 / *F4*
Jay's B&B, 4429 Bay City Rd, 48640 .... (517)496-2498

MIO M11 / *D4*
Kilby House B&B, 405 Morenci Ave, 48647 .... (517)826-3066

MOUNT PLEASANT Q10 / *F3*
Country Chalet, 723 S Meridian Rd, 48858 .... (517)772-9259

NEW BUFFALO Y3 / *H1*
Little Bohemia, 115 S Whittaker, 49117 .... (616)469-1440
Sans Souci B&B, 19265 S Lakeside Rd, 49117 .... (616)756-7206
Tall Oaks Inn B&B, Box 6, Grand Beach, 49117 .... (616)469-0097

NILES Y5 / *H2*
Woods & Hearth B&B, 950 S Third St, 49120 .... (616)683-0876
Yesterday's Inn, 518 N 4th St, 49120 .... (616)683-6079

NORTHPORT K7 / *D2*
Apple Beach Inn, 617 Shabwasung, PO Box 2, 49670 .... (616)386-5022
Hutchinson's Garden, Box 661, 215 N High St, 49670 .... (616)386-5534
North Shore Inn, 12794 Country Rd 640, 49670 .... (616)386-7111
Old Mill Pond Inn, 202 W Third St, 49670 .... (616)386-7341
Vintage House B&B, Box 424, 102 Shabwasung, 49670 .... (616)386-7228

NORTHVILLE V14 / *G4*
The Atchison House, 501 W Dunlap, 48167 .... (313)349-3340

NUNICA T5 / *F2*
Stonegate Inn, 10831 Cleveland, 49448 .... (616)837-9267

OLIVET V9 / *G3*
Ackerman's B&B Inn, 243 Kalamo St, 49076 .... (616)749-9422

OMENA K7 / *D2*
Haus Austrian, 4626 Omena Point Rd, 49674 .... (616)386-7338
Omena B&B, PO Box 75, 49674 .... (616)386-7274

OMER P13 / *E4*
Rifle River B&B, 500 Center Ave, 48749 .... (517)653-2911

OWOSSO T11 / *G4*
Archer's Castle, 203 E King, 48867 .... (517)723-2572
Merkel Manor, 623 N Park St, 48867 .... (517)725-5600
Mulberry House, 1251 N Shiawassee St, 48867 .... (517)723-4890
R & R Farm-ranch, 308 E Hibbard Rd, 48867 .... (517)723-2553
Sylverlynd, 3452 McBride Rd, 48867 .... (517)723-1267

PENTWATER Q5 / *E2*
Pentwater Abbey, PO Box 735, 85 W First St, 49449 .... (616)869-4094
Pentwater Inn, 180 E Lowell Box 98, 49449 .... (616)869-5909

PETOSKEY J9 / *C3*
Apple Tree Inn, 915 Spring St, PO Box 574, 49770 .... (616)347-2900
Bear & The Bay, 421 Charlevoix Ave, 49770 .... (616)347-6077
Bed 'N' Breakfast, 212 Arlington, 49770 .... (616)347-6145
Gull's Way, 118 Boulder Ln, 49770 .... (616)347-9891
Stafford's Bay View Inn, Box 3, 49770 .... (616)347-2771
The Cozy Spot, 1145 Kalamazoo, 49770 .... (616)347-3869

PLYMOUTH V14 / *G4*
Mayflower B&B Hotel, Main & Ann Arbor Tr, 48170 .... (313)453-1620

PORT AUSTIN O15 / *E5*
Garfield Inn, 8544 Lake St, 48467 .... (517)738-5254
Lake Street Manor, 8569 Lake St, 49467 .... (517)738-7720
Questover Inn, 8510 Lake St, 48467 .... (517)738-5253

PORT HURON T17 / *G5*
Victorian Inn, 1229 Seventh St, 48060 .... (313)984-1437

PORT SANILAC R17 / *F5*
Raymond House Inn, M-25, 111 S Ridge St, 48469 .... (313)622-8800

PORTLAND U9 / *G3*
Webber House, 527 James St, 48875 .... (517)647-4671

PRUDENVILLE N10 / *E3*
Spring Brook Inn, PO 390, 565 E West Branch Rd, 48651 .... (517)366-6347

REED CITY P7 / *E3*
Osceola Inn, 110 E Upton, 49677 .... (616)832-5537

ROMEO U15 / *G5*
Country Heritage B&B, 64707 Mound Rd, 48065 .... (313)752-2879

ROSCOMMON N10 / *E3*
Tall Trees, Rt 2, 323 Birch Rd, 48653 .... (517)821-5592

SAGINAW R12 / *F4*
Brockway House, 1631 Brockway, 48602 .... (517)792-0746

SAINT IGNACE H10 / *C3*
Colonial House Inn, 90 N State St, 49781 .... (906)643-6900

SALINE W13 / *H4*
The Homestead B&B, 9279 Macon Rd, 48176 .... (313)429-9625

SAUGATUCK U5 / *G2*
Fairchild House, 606 Butler St, 49453 .... (616)857-5985
Jann's Guest House, 132 Mason St, 49453 .... (616)857-8851
Kemah Guest House, 633 Pleasant St, 49453 .... (616)857-2919
The Kirby House, 294 W Center St, PO Box 1174, 49453 .... (616)857-2904
Maplewood Hotel, 428 Butler St, PO Box 1059, 49453 .... (616)857-1771
Newnham Inn, Box 1106, 131 Griffith St, 49453 .... (800)877-4149
The Park House, 888 Holland St, 49453 .... (616)857-4535
The Red Dog B&B, 132 Mason St, 49453 .... (616)857-8851
Twin Gables Country Inn, Box 881, 49453 .... (616)857-4346
Wickwood Inn, 510 Butler St, 49453 .... (616)857-1097

SEBEWAING Q14 / *F4*
Rummel's Tree Haven, 41 N Beck St, 48759 .... (517)883-2450

SOUTH HAVEN W5 / *G2*
A Country Place B&B, Rt 5, Box 43, 49090 .... (616)637-5523
The Last Resort, 86 N Shore Dr, 49090 .... (616)637-8943
North Beach Inn & Restaurant, 51 North Shore Dr, 49090 .... (616)637-6738
The Ross, 229 Michigan Ave, 49090 .... (616)637-2256
Victoria Resort, 241 Oak, 49090 .... (616)637-6414
Yelton Manor, 140 N Shore Dr, 49090 .... (616)637-5220

SPRING LAKE T5 / *F2*
Alberties Waterfront B&B, 18470 Main St, 49456 .... (616)846-4016
Seascape B&B, 20009 Breton, 49456 .... (616)842-8409
Shifting Sands, 19343 N Shore Dr, 49456 .... (616)842-3594

STANTON S9 / *F3*
Clifford Lake Hotel, 561 Clifford Lake Dr, 48888 .... (517)831-5151

STURGIS Y8 / *H3*
Christmere House, 110 Pleasant, 49091 .... (616)651-8303

SUTTONS BAY L7 / D2
The Cottage B&B, 503 St Joseph Ave, PO Box 653, 49682 (616)271-6348

SWARTZ CREEK T13 / G4
Pink Palace Farms, 6095 Baldwin Rd, 48473 (313)655-4076

TECUMSEH X12 / H4
Boulevard Inn, 904 W Chicago Blvd, 49286 (517)423-5169

TRAVERSE CITY M7 / D2
Bass Lake Inn B&B, 61 Lakeside St, 49684 (616)943-4790
Bowers Harbor B&B, 13972 Peninsula Dr, 49684 (616)223-7869
Cedar Creek, 12666 W Bayshore Dr, 49684 (616)947-5643
Cherry Knoll Farm, 2856 Hammond Rd East, 49684 (616)947-9806
Cider House B&B, 5515 Barney Rd, 49684 (616)947-2833
Linden Lea, 279 S Long Lake Rd, 49684 (616)943-9182
Neahtawanta Inn, 1308 Neahtawanta Rd, 49684 (616)223-7315
Queen Anne's Castle, 500 Webster, 49684 (616)946-1459
Tall Ship Malabar, 13390 W Bay Shore Dr, 49684 (616)941-2000
The Victoriana, 622 Washington St, 49684 (616)929-1009
Warwickshire Inn, 5037 Barney Rd, 49684 (616)946-7176

TRENTON X15 / H5
Bear Haven, 2947 4th St, 48183 (313)675-4844

UNION CITY X8 / H3
Victorian Villa, 601 N Broadway, 49094 (517)741-7383

UNION PIER Y4 / H1
Gordon Beach Inn, 16240 Lakeshore Rd, 49129 (616)469-3344
Pine Garth Inn, 15790 Lakeshore Rd, 49129 (616)469-1642
The Inn at Union Pier, 9708 Berrien, PO Box 222, 49129 (616)469-4700

WAKEFIELD C13 / A4
The Medford House, PO Box 149, 49968 (906)224-5151

WALLOON LAKE VILLAGE J9 / D3
Walloon Lake Inn, PO Box 85, 49796 (616)535-2999

WEST BRANCH O11 / E4
Green Inn, 4045 W M-76, 48661 (517)345-0334
The Rose Brick Inn, 124 East Houghton Ave, 48661 (517)345-3702

WHITE CLOUD R7 / F2
Crow's Nest, 1440 N Luce Ave, 49349 (616)788-2952
Shack Country Inn, 2263 W 14th St, 49349 (616)924-6683

WHITE PIGEON Y7 / H2
River Haven, 9222 St Joseph River Rd, 49099 (616)483-9104

MINNESOTA

AFTON T13 / G4
The Afton House Inn, 3291 St Croix Tr Ave S, 55001 (612)436-8883

ALEXANDRIA P6 / E2
Carrington House, Rt 5, Box 88, 56308 (612)846-7400

ANNANDALE S9 / F3
Thayer Hotel, Highway 55, 55302 (612)274-3371

ASKOV O13 / E4
The Governor's House, Box 252, 55704 (612)838-3296

BAUDETTE E8 / B3
Rainy River Lodge, 56623 (218)634-2730

BRAINERD N9 / E3
Grand View Lodge, Rt 6 Box 22, 56401 (218)763-2234
Woods of Interlachen B&B, 7505 Interlachen Rd, 56401 (218)963-7880

BROOKLYN CENTER S11 / G4
Inn on the Farm, 6150 Summit Dr N, 55430 (612)569-6330

CALEDONIA Y16 / H5
The Inn on the Green, Rt 1, Box 205, 55921 (507)724-2818

CANNON FALLS V12 / G4
Quill & Quilt, 615 W Hoffman St, 55009 (507)263-5507

CHASKA T10 / G3
Bluff Creek Inn, 1161 Bluff Creek Dr, 55318 (612)445-2735

CHATFIELD X14 / H5
Lund's Guest House, 500 Winona St SE, 55923 (507)867-4003

COLD SPRING R8 / F3
Pillow, Pillar & Pine, 419 Main St, 56320 (612)685-3828

COOK I13 / C4
Ludlow's Island Lodge, Box 1146, Lake Vermilion, 55723 (218)666-5407

CROOKSTON I2 / C1
Wilkinson-Thorson B&B, 327 Houston Ave, 56716 (218)281-1601

DEERWOOD N10 / E3
Walden Woods B&B, Rt 1, Box 193, 56444 (612)692-4379

DODGE CENTER W12 / H4
Eden B&B, Rt 1 Box 215, 55927 (507)527-2311

DULUTH M14 / D5
The Ellery House, 28 S 21st Ave E, 55812 (218)724-7639
Fitger's Inn, 600 E Superior St, 55082 (218)722-8826
The Mansion, 3600 London Rd, 55804 (218)724-0739
Stanford Inn, 1415 E Superior St, 55805 (218)724-3044

ELY H15 / C5
Our Mom's B&B Inn, 323 E Sheridan St, 55731 (218)365-6510
Three Deer Haven B&B, Star Rt 2, Box 5086, 55731 (218)365-6464

EXCELSIOR T10 / G3
Christopher Inn, 201 Mill St, 55331 (612)474-6816

FARIBAULT V11 / G4
Hutchinson House B&B, 305 NW Second St, 55021 (507)332-7519

GARVIN W4 / G2
Glenview B&B, RR 1, 56132 (507)629-4808

GLENWOOD Q5 / F2
Peters' Sunset Beach Hotel, Rt 2, Box 118, 56334 (612)634-4501

GOOD THUNDER W9 / H3
Cedar Knoll Farm, Rt 2, Box 147, 56037 (507)524-3813

GRACEVILLE Q3 / F1
Lakeside B&B, 113 W 2nd St, 56240 (612)748-7657

GRAND MARAIS C14 / A5
Cascade Lodge, PO Box 693, 55604 (218)387-1112
East Bay Hotel, 55604 (218)387-2800
Gunflint Lodge, PO 100 Gt, 55604 (218)388-4487
Pincushion Mountain B&B, PO Box 181, 55604 (218)387-1276
Young's Island B&B, Gunflint Trail 67-1, 55604 (218)388-4487

HASTINGS U12 / G4
Hazelwood, 705 Vermillion, 55033 (612)437-3297
The River Rose, 620 Ramsey, 55033 (612)437-3297
Thorwood, 315 Pine St, 55033 (612)437-3297

HENDRICKS U3 / G1
Triple L Farm, Rt 1, Box 141, 56136 (507)275-3740

HERMAN P3 / F1
Lawndale Farm, Rt 2 Box 50, 56248 (612)677-2687

HIBBING J12 / D4
The Adams House, 201 E 23rd St, 55746 (218)263-9742

HINCKLEY P12 / E4
Bed & Breakfast Lodge, Rt 3, Box 84A, 55037 (612)384-6052

KELLOGG V15 / G5
PJ's B&B, 132 Winona Ave, 55945 (507)767-2203

LAKE CITY V14 / G5
Evergreen Knoll Acres, Rt 1 Box 145, 55041 (612)345-2257
Red Gables Inn, 403 N High St, 55041 (612)345-2605
The Victorian B&B, 620 S High St, 55041 (612)345-2167

LANESBORO Y15 / H5
Carrolton Country Inn, RR 2 Box 139, 55949 (507)467-2257
Mrs. B's Historic Lanesboro Inn, 101 Pkwy, 55949 (507)467-2154
Scanlan House, 708 Park Ave S, 55949 (507)467-2158

LE SUEUR V9 / G3
The Cosgrove, 228 S Second St, 56058 (612)665-2763

LITTLE FALLS P8 / E3
Pine Edge Inn, 308 First St SE, 56345 (612)632-6681

LUTSEN D13 / B4
Lindgren's B&B, County Rd 35 W191, 55612 (218)663-7450

MANTORVILLE W13 / H4
Grand Old Mansion, 501 Clay St, 55955 (507)635-3231

MARINE ON ST CROIX S13 / F4
Asa Parker House, 17500 St Croix Tr N, 55047 (612)433-5248

MARSHALL V4 / G2
Blanchford Inn B&B, 600 W Redwood St, 56250 (507)532-5071

MILTONA O6 / E2
The Country House, Rt 3, Box 110, 56354 (218)943-2928

MINNEAPOLIS T11 / G4
Evelo's B&B, 2301 Bryant Ave S, 55405 (612)374-9656
Linn B&B, 2645 Fremont Ave S, 55408 (612)377-4418
Nicollet Island Inn, 95 Merriam, 55401 (612)331-1800

MINNETONKA T11 / G4
Special Places, 4624 Highland Rd, 55345 (612)938-3326

MORRIS Q4 / F1
The American House, 410 E Third St, 56267 (612)589-4054

NEW PRAGUE U10 / G3
Schumacher's New Prague Hotel, 212 W Main St, 56071 (612)758-2133

NORTH BRANCH R12 / F4
Red Pine B&B, 15140 400th St, 55056 (612)583-3326

NORTHFIELD V12 / G4
Archer House, 212 Division St, 55057 (507)645-5661

OLIVIA T6 / *G2*
Sheep Shedde Inn, Hwy 212 & 71 W, 56277 ......(612)523-5000

ORR H12 / *C4*
The Kettle Falls Hotel, Ash River Tr, 55771 ......(218)374-3511

OWATONNA W11 / *H4*
The Northrop House, 358 E Main St, 55060 ......(507)451-4040

PARK RAPIDS L6 / *D2*
Dickson Viking Huss B&B, 202 E Fourth, 56470 ......(218)732-8089
Dorset Schoolhouse, PO Box 201, 56470 ......(218)732-1377

PRINCETON Q10 / *F3*
Rum River Country B&B, RR 6 Box 114, 55371 ......(612)389-2679

RAY F11 / *B4*
Bunt's B&B, Lake Kabetogama, 56669 ......(218)875-3904

RED WING U13 / *G4*
Pratt-Taber Inn, 706 W Fourth, 55066 ......(612)388-5945
St. James Hotel, 406 Main St, 55066 ......(612)388-2846

RUSH CITY Q12 / *F4*
Grant House, Fourth & Bremer (Box 87), 55069 ......(612)358-3661

SAINT JOSEPH Q8 / *F3*
Lamb's B&B, 29738 Island Lake Rd, 56374 ......(612)363-7924

SAINT PAUL T12 / *G4*
Chatsworth B&B, 984 Ashland, 55104 ......(612)227-4288
University Club of St. Paul, 420 Summit Ave, 55102 ......(612)222-1751
Yoerg House, 215 W Isabel, 55107 ......(612)224-9436

SAUK CENTRE Q7 / *F2*
Palmer House Hotel, 500 Sinclair Lewis Ave, 56378 ......(612)352-3431

SHAFER R13 / *F4*
Country B&B, 32030 Ranch Tr., 55074 ......(612)257-4773

SHAKOPEE T10 / *G4*
Sunny Morning Manor, 314 S Scott St, 55379 ......(612)496-1482

SILVER BAY K17 / *D5*
Guest House B&B, 299 Outer Dr, 55614 ......(218)226-4201

SLEEPY EYE V7 / *G2*
The Woodland Inn, Rt 4, Box 68, 56085 ......(507)794-5981

SPICER S7 / *F2*
Spicer Castle, 11600 Indian Beach Rd, 56288 ......(612)796-5870

SPRING GROVE Y16 / *H5*
Touch of the Past, 102 Third Ave SE, 55974 ......(507)498-5146

SPRING LAKE I9 / *C3*
Anchor Inn, Hwy 4, RR, 56680 ......(218)798-2718

SPRING VALLEY Y14 / *H4*
Chase's, 508 N Huron Ave, 55975 ......(507)346-2850

STACY R12 / *F4*
Kings Oakdale Park Guest House, 6933 232nd Ave NE, 55029
......(612)462-5598

STILLWATER S13 / *F4*
Lowell Inn, 102 N Second St, 55082 ......(612)439-1102
Outing Lodge at Pine Point, 11661 Myeron Rd, 55082 ......(612)439-9747
The Overlook Inn, 210 E Laurel, 55082 ......(612)439-3409
Rivertown Inn, 306 W Olive St, 55082 ......(612)430-2955

TAYLORS FALLS R13 / *F4*
The Old Jail Company, 100 Government Rd, 55084 ......(612)465-3112

WABASHA V15 / *G5*
Anderson House, 333 Main St, PO Box 262, 55981 ......(612)565-4524
The Parsonage House, 100 Coulee Way, 55981 ......(612)565-2128

WALKER L8 / *D3*
Chase On The Lake Lodge & Motor Inn, PO Box 206, 56484 (218)547-1531

WEAVER V15 / *G5*
Noble Studio & Galleries, Rt 1 Box 565, 55910 ......(507)767-2244

WINONA W16 / *H5*
Carriage House B&B, 420 Main St, 55987 ......(507)452-8256
The Hotel, 129 W Third St, 55987 ......(507)452-5460

MISSISSIPPI

ABERDEEN E11 / *C5*
Rosemont, 407 S Meridian, 39730 ......(601)369-9434

BROOKHAVEN L6 / *F2*
Edgewood, 412 Storm Ave, 39601 ......(601)833-2001

CHATHAM G5 / *C2*
Mount Holly Plantation House, Box 140, 38731 ......(601)827-2652

COLUMBUS F11 / *C5*
Amzi Love B&B, 305 7th St S, 39701 ......(601)328-5413
Temple Heights, 515 9 St N, 39701 ......(601)329-3533

CORINTH A11 / *A5*
Generals Quarters, 924 Fillmore St, 38834 ......(601)286-3325

FAYETTE K5 / *F2*
Historic Springfield Plantation, Hwy 553, 39069 ......(601)786-3802

HOLLY SPRINGS B9 / *A4*
Hamilton Place, 105 E Mason Ave, 38635 ......(601)252-4368

JACKSON J7 / *E3*
Fairview, 734 Fairview St, 39202 ......(601)948-3429
Millsaps-Buie House, 628 N State St, 39202 ......(601)352-0221

LONG BEACH P10 / *H4*
Red Creek Colonial Inn, 7416 Red Creek Rd, 39560 ......(601)452-3080

LORMAN K5 / *E2*
Rosswood Plantation, Hwy 552, 39096 ......(601)437-4215

MERIDIAN I11 / *E4*
Lincoln, Ltd. B&B, PO Box 3479, 39303 ......(601)482-5483

NATCHEZ L4 / *F1*
The Burn, 712 N Union St, 39120 ......(601)442-1344
Dixie, 211 S Wall St, 39120 ......(601)442-2525
Dunleith, 84 Homochitto, 39120 ......(601)446-8500
Guest House Of Natchez, 210 N Pearl St, 39120 ......(601)445-6000
Hope Farm, 147 Homochitto St, 39120 ......(601)445-4848
Linden, 1 Linden Place, 39120 ......(601)445-5472
Ravennaside, 601 S Union St, 39120 ......(601)442-8015
Silver Street Inn, 1 Silver St, 39120 ......(601)442-4221
Texada, 212 S Wall St, 39120 ......(601)445-4283
Weymouth Hall, One Cemetery Rd, 39120 ......(601)445-2304

OXFORD C9 / *B3*
Oliver-Britt House, 512 Van Buren Ave, 38655 ......(601)234-8043

PORT GIBSON K5 / *E2*
Oak Square Plantation, 1207 Church St, 39150 ......(601)437-4350

VICKSBURG J5 / *E2*
Anchuca Clarion Carriage House Inn, 1010 First E, 39180 ......(601)636-4931
Balfour House, 1002 Crawford St, 39180 ......(601)638-3690
Cedar Grove Mansion Inn, 2300 Washington St, 39180 ......(800)862-1300
The Corners Inn, 601 Klein St, 39180 ......(800)444-7421
The Duff Green Mansion, 1114 First East St, 39180 ......(601)636-6968
Gray Oaks, 4142 Rifle Range Rd, 39180 ......(601)638-4424

MISSOURI

ARROW ROCK G13 / *C3*
Borgman's B&B, Van Buren St, 65320 ......(816)837-3350
Down Over Holdings, 602 Main St, 65320 ......(816)837-3268

BONNE TERRE K20 / *D6*
1909 Depot, Oak & Allen St, 63628 ......(314)731-5003
The Lamplight Inn B&B, 207 E School St, 63628 ......(314)358-4222
Mansion Hill Country Inn, Mansion Hill Dr, 63628 ......(314)358-5311

BRANSON P13 / *F3*
Gaines Landing B&B, 521 W Atlantic St, PO Box 1369, 65616
......(417)334-2280
White Squirrel Hollow Inn, Box 295, 65616 ......(417)334-4720

CARTHAGE N9 / *E2*
Brewer's Maple Lane Farms B&B, RR 1 Box 203, 64836 ......(417)358-6312
Hill House, 1157 S Main, 64836 ......(417)358-6145
The Leggett House, 1106 Grand, 64836 ......(417)358-0683

CONCORDIA G12 / *C3*
Fannie Lee B&B Inn, 902 Main St, 64020 ......(816)463-2730

EMINENCE N18 / *E5*
Eminence Cottages B&B, PO Box 276, 65466 ......(314)226-3642

FULTON H16 / *C4*
Loganberry Inn, 310 W 7th St, 65251 ......(314)642-9229

HANNIBAL E18 / *B5*
Fifth Street Mansion B&B, 213 S Fifth St, 63401 ......(314)221-0445
Garth Woodside Mansion, RR 1, 63401 ......(314)221-2789

HARTVILLE N15 / *E4*
Frisco House, PO Box 118, 65667 ......(417)741-7304

HERMANN H18 / *C5*
Birk's Goethe Street Gasthaus, 700 Goethe St, 65041 ......(314)486-2911
Captain Wohlt Inn, 123 E Third St, 65041 ......(314)486-3357
Seven Sisters B&B Cottage, 108 Schiller St, 65041 ......(314)486-3717
William Klinger Inn, 108 E 2nd St, 65041 ......(314)486-5930

INDEPENDENCE G9 / *C2*
Arthurs' Horse & Carriage House, 601 W Maple, 64050 ......(816)461-6814
Woodstock Inn, 1212 W Lexington, 64050 ......(816)833-2233

JACKSON M23 / *E7*
Trisha's B&B, 203 Bellevue, 63755 ......(314)243-7427

JOPLIN N9 / *E2*
Visages, 327 N Jackson, 64801 ......(417)624-1397

KANSAS CITY G9 / *B2*
Doanleigh Wallagh, 217 E 37th St, 64111 ....(816)753-2667
Dome Ridge, 14360 NW Walker Rd, 64164 ....(816)532-4074
Southmoreland on the Plaza, 116 E 46th St, 64112 ....(816)531-7979

LATHROP E10 / *B2*
Parkview Farm, RR 1, Box 54, 64465 ....(816)664-2744

LESTERVILLE M20 / *E6*
Wilderness Lodge, Box 90, 63654 ....(314)637-2295

MACON E15 / *B4*
Wardell Guest House, 1 Wardell Rd, 63552 ....(816)385-4352

MARSHFIELD M14 / *E3*
The Dickey House B&B Inn, 331 S Clay St, 65706 ....(417)468-3000

MEXICO G16 / *B4*
Hylas House, 811 S Jefferson, 65265 ....(314)581-2011

NEW HAVEN I18 / *C5*
Augustine River Bluff Farm, RR 1, Box 42, 63068 ....(314)237-3198

PARKVILLE F9 / *B2*
Down to Earth Lifestyles, 12500 N Crooked Rd, Rt 22, 64152 ....(816)891-1018

PLATTE CITY F8 / *B2*
Basswood Country Inn B&B, 15880 Interurban Rd, 64079 ....(816)431-5556

ROCHEPORT G15 / *C4*
School House B&B, Third & Clark St, 65279 ....(314)698-2022

SAINT CHARLES H21 / *C6*
Boone's Lick Trail Inn, 1000 S Main St, 63301 ....(314)947-7000
The Saint Charles House, 338 S Main St, 63301 ....(314)946-6221

SAINT JOSEPH D8 / *B2*
Harding House, 219 N 20th St, 64501 ....(816)232-7020

SAINT LOUIS I21 / *C6*
The Coachlight B&B, PO Box 8095, 63156 ....(314)367-5870
Falicon Inn, 1 Grandview Hgts, 63131 ....(314)965-4328
Geandaugh House, 3835-37 S Broadway, 63118 ....(314)771-5447
Lafayette House, 2156 Lafayette Ave, 63104 ....(314)772-4429
Old Convent Guesthouse, 2049 Sidney, 63104 ....(314)772-3531
Seven Gables Inn, 26 N Meramec, 63105 ....(314)863-8400
The Winter House, 3522 Arsenal, 63118 ....(314)664-4399

SAINTE GENEVIEVE K22 / *D6*
Hotel Saint Genevieve, Main & Merchant St, 63670 ....(314)883-2737
The Southern Hotel, 146 S Third St, 63670 ....(314)883-3493
The Inn St. Gemme Beauvais, 78 N Main, PO Box 231, 63670 ....(314)883-5744

SPRINGFIELD N12 / *E3*
The Mansion at Elfindale, 1701 S Fort, 65807 ....(417)831-5400
Walnut Street Inn, 900 E Walnut St, 65806 ....(417)864-3646

VAN BUREN O19 / *E5*
Inn at Park Place, PO Box 268, 63965 ....(314)323-4642

WARRENSBURG H11 / *C3*
Cedarcroft Farm B&B, Rt 3, Box 130, 64093 ....(816)747-5728

WASHINGTON I19 / *C5*
Schwegmann House, 438 West Front Street, 63090 ....(314)239-5025
Washington House B&B Inn, PO Box 527, 63090 ....(314)239-2417

MONTANA

BIG FORK D5 / *B2*
Big Fork Inn, Box 967, 59911 ....(406)837-6680
Flathead Lake Lodge, Rt 35, Box 248, 59911 ....(406)837-4391
O'Duachain Country Inn, 675 Ferndale Dr, 59911 ....(406)837-6851
Schwartz's B&B, 890 McCaffery Rd, 59911 ....(406)837-5463

BIG SKY L11 / *D3*
Lone Mountain Ranch, PO Box 145, 59716 ....(406)995-4644

BIG TIMBER K13 / *D4*
Lazy K Bar Ranch, Box 550 HI, 59011 ....(406)537-4404

BILLINGS K16 / *D5*
PJ's B&B, 722 N 29th St, 59101 ....(406)259-3300

BOZEMAN K11 / *D4*
Hillard's Guest House, 11521 Axtell Gateway Rd, 59715 ....(406)763-4696
Lehrkind Mansion, 719 N Wallace, 59715 ....(406)586-1214
Silver Forest Inn, 15325 Bridger Canyon Rd, 59715 ....(406)586-1882
The Torch & Toes B&B, 309 S Third Ave, 59715 ....(406)586-7285
Voss Inn, 319 S Willson, 59715 ....(406)587-0982

BUTTE J8 / *D3*
Copper King Mansion, 219 West Granite, 59701 ....(406)782-7580

CHOTEAU E9 / *B3*
Pine Butte Guest Ranch, HC 58, Box 34C, 59422 ....(406)466-2158
Seven Lazy P Ranch, Box 178, 59422 ....(406)466-2044

COLUMBIA FALLS C5 / *A2*
Mountain Timbers Wilderness Lodge, 5385 Rabe Rd, 59912 ....(406)387-5830

ESSEX D6 / *B2*
Izaak Walton Inn, PO Box 653, 59916 ....(406)888-5700

EUREKA B4 / *A1*
Grave Creek B&B, PO Box 551, 59917 ....(406)882-4658

GALLATIN GATEWAY L11 / *D3*
Gallatin Gateway, Hwy 191, PO Box 376, 59730 ....(406)763-4672

GREAT FALLS F11 / *B4*
The Chalet B&B Inn, 1204 4th Ave, N, 59401 ....(406)452-9001
Three Pheasant Inn, 626 5th Ave N, 59401 ....(406)453-0519

HELENA I9 / *C3*
The Sanders - Helena's Bed & Breakfast, 328 N Ewing, 59601 ....(406)442-3309

HUSON G5 / *C1*
Whispering Pines, Box 36, 59846 ....(406)626-5664

LIVINGSTON K12 / *D4*
Talcott House, 405 W Lewis, 59047 ....(406)222-7699

POLSON E5 / *B2*
Borchers of Finley Point, 225 Borchers Ln, 59860 ....(406)887-2500

RED LODGE M15 / *E5*
Pitcher Guest House, 2 S Platt PO 1148, 59068 ....(406)446-2859
Willows Inn, 224 S Platt Ave, PO Box 886, 59068 ....(406)446-3913

SHERIDAN L9 / *D3*
King's Rest, 55 Tuke Ln, 59749 ....(406)842-5185

ST IGNATIUS G5 / *B2*
Mission Mountain B&B, RR Box 183-A, 59865 ....(406)745-4331

STEVENSVILLE I5 / *C2*
Bass House Inn, 100 College St, 59870 ....(406)777-5675
Country Caboose, 852 Willoughby Rd, 59870 ....(406)777-3145

TOWNSEND I10 / *C3*
Hidden Hollow Hideaway, Box 233, 59644 ....(406)266-3322

TROY C2 / *A1*
Bull Lake Guest Ranch, 15303 Bull Lake Rd, 59935 ....(406)295-4228

VIRGINIA CITY L9 / *D3*
Nevada City Hotel, PO Box 338, Nevada City, 59755 ....(406)843-5377

WEST YELLOWSTONE N11 / *E4*
Sportsman's High, 750 Deer St, HC66 PO Box 16, 59758 ....(406)646-7865

WHITE SULPHUR SPRING I11 / *C4*
Foxwood Inn, Box 404, 59645 ....(406)547-3918

WHITEFISH C5 / *A2*
Duck Inn, 1305 Columbia Ave, 59937 ....(406)862-3825
Kandahar Lodge, PO Box 1659, 59937 ....(406)862-6098

NEBRASKA

BARTLEY P12 / *D4*
Pheasant Hill, HC 68 Box 12, 69020 ....(308)692-3278

BROWNVILLE O25 / *D8*
Thompson House, Fifth & College Sts, 68321 ....(402)825-6551

DIXON H21 / *B7*
The George's, Rt 1 Box 50, 68732 ....(402)584-2625

ELGIN I18 / *GB6*
Plantation House, Rt 2 Box 17, 68636 ....(402)843-2287

GRAND ISLAND M17 / *D6*
Kirschke House B&B, 1124 W 3rd St, 68801 ....(308)381-6851

HOLDREGE O14 / *D5*
Century B&B, PO Box 13, 68949 ....(308)995-6750

LINCOLN N22 / *D7*
Rogers House, 2145 B St, 68502 ....(402)476-6961

NEBRASKA CITY N24 / *D8*
Whispering Pines, 21st & Sixth Ave, 68410 ....(402)873-5850

NORTH PLATTE L10 / *C3*
Watson Manor Inn, 410 S Sycamore, PO Box 458, 69103 ....(308)532-1124

OMAHA L24 / *C8*
Offutt House, 140 N 39th St, 68131 ....(402)553-0951

OSMOND H19 / *B6*
Willow Way B&B, RR #2, Box H20, 68756 ....(402)748-3593

RED CLOUD P17 / *E6*
The Meadowlark Manor B&B, 241 W 9th Ave, 68970 ....(402)746-3550

NEVADA

CARSON CITY H2 / *D1*
The Edwards House, 204 N Minnesota St, 89703 ....(702)882-4884

GARDNERVILLE H2 / *D1*
The Reid Mansion, 1431 Ezell St, PO Box 758, 89410 .... (702)782-7644
Sierra Spirit Ranch, 3000 Pinenut Rd, 89410 .... (702)782-7011

GENOA H2 / *D1*
Genoa House Inn, PO Box 141, 180 Nixon St, 89411 .... (702)782-7075
Orchard House, Box 77, 89411 .... (702)782-2640
Wally's Hot Springs Resort, 2001 Foothill Rd, Box 26, 89411 .... (702)782-8155
Wild Rose Inn, 2332 Main St, PO Box 256, 89411 .... (702)782-5697

GOLD HILL G2 / *D1*
House on the Hill, Sky Ln, PO Box 625, 89440 .... (702)847-0193

GOLDFIELD K6 / *E3*
Sundog B&B, 211 Sundog Ave, PO Box 486, 89013 .... (702)485-3438

INCLINE VILLAGE H2 / *D1*
Haus Bavaria, PO Box 3308, 89450 .... (702)831-6122

LAMOILLE D9 / *B4*
Breitenstein House, 89828 .... (702)753-6356

RENO G2 / *C1*
Lace & Linen Guest House, 4800 Kietzke Ln, 89502 .... (702)826-3547

SILVER CITY H2 / *D1*
Hardwicke House, Box 96, 89429 .... (702)847-0215

SMITH I3 / *D1*
Windybrush Ranch, Box 85, 89430 .... (702)465-2481

SPARKS G2 / *C1*
Blue Fountain B&B, 1590 B St, 89431 .... (702)359-0359

UNIONVILLE E5 / *B2*
Old Pioneer Garden Guest Ranch, HC-64, Box 79, 89418 .... (702)538-7585

VIRGINIA CITY G2 / *D1*
Chollar Mansion B&B, 565 South D St, PO Box 889, 89440 .... (702)847-9777
Edith Palmer's Country Inn, South B Street, PO Box 756, 89440 .... (702)847-0707
Gold Hill Hotel, Main St, PO Box 304, 89440 .... (702)847-0111

YERINGTON H3 / *D1*
Harbor House, 39 N Center St, 89447 .... (702)463-2991
Robric Ranch, Box 2, 89447 .... (702)463-3515

NEW HAMPSHIRE

ALEXANDRIA L8 / *E4*
Stone Rest B&B, 652 Fowler River Rd, 03222 .... (603)744-6066

ALSTEAD N6 / *F3*
Darby Brook Farm, Hill Rd, 03602 .... (603)835-6624

ANDOVER M8 / *E4*
Andover Arms Guest House, Main St, PO Box 256, 03216 .... (603)735-5953
The English House, PO Box 162, 03216 .... (603)735-5987

ANTRIM O7 / *F4*
Antrim Inn, 155 Main St, 03440 .... (603)588-8000
Breezy Point Inn, RD 1 Box 302, 03440 .... (603)478-5201
Steele Homestead Inn, RR 1 Box 78, Rt 9, 03440 .... (603)588-6772
Uplands Inn, Miltimore Rd, 03440 .... (603)588-6349

ASHLAND K9 / *E4*
Country Options, PO 443, 03217 .... (603)968-7958
Glynn House Victorian Inn, 43 Highland St, PO Box 819, 03217-0819 .... (603)968-3775

BARTLETT I10 / *D5*
The Country Inn at Bartlett, Rt 302 Box 327, 03812 .... (603)374-2353
Notchland Inn, Hart's Location, 03812 .... (603)374-6131

BEDFORD O9 / *G5*
Bedford Village Inn, 2 Old Bedford Rd, 03102 .... (603)472-2001

BENNINGTON O7 / *G4*
David's Inn, Bennington Sq, 03442 .... (603)588-2458

BETHLEHEM H8 / *C4*
The Bells, Strawberry Hill, PO Box 276, 03574 .... (603)869-2647
The Highlands Inn, PO 118 C, 03574 .... (603)869-3978
The Mulburn Inn, Main St, 03574 .... (603)869-3389

BRADFORD N7 / *F4*
The Bradford Inn, RFD 1 Box 40, Main St, 03221 .... (603)938-5309
Mountain Lake Inn, Rt 114, 03221 .... (603)938-2136

BRIDGEWATER L8 / *E4*
Pasquaney Inn On Newfound Lake, Star Rt 1 Box 1066, 03222 .... (603)744-9111

BRISTOL L8 / *E4*
Victorian, 16 Summer St, 03222 .... (603)744-6157

CAMPTON J8 / *D4*
Mountain Fare Inn, Mad River Rd, 03223 .... (603)726-4283
The Campton Inn, Rt 175 N Box 282, 03223 .... (603)726-4449

CANAAN L7 / *E4*
The Inn on Canaan Street, The Kremzners, 03741 .... (603)523-7310
The Towerhouse Inn, 1 Parker St, 03741 .... (603)523-7244

CANTERBURY M9 / *F5*
Sleepy Hollow B&B, RR 1, Baptist Hill Rd, 03223 .... (603)267-6055

CENTER CONWAY J11 / *D5*
Lavender Flower Inn, PO Box 328, 03813 .... (800)729-0381

CENTER HARBOR K9 / *E5*
Dearborn Place, Box 997, 03226 .... (603)253-6711
Kona Mansion Inn, Box 458, 03226 .... (603)253-4900
Red Hill Inn, RD 1 Box 99M, 03226 .... (603)279-7001

CENTER SANDWICH K9 / *D5*
Corner House Inn, Main St PO 204, 03227 .... (603)284-6219

CHARLESTOWN N5 / *F3*
Indian Shutters Inn, Rt 12, 03603 .... (603)826-4445

CHICHESTER N10 / *F5*
Hitching Post B&B, Dover Rd #2, Box 790, 03263 .... (603)798-4951

CHOCORUA J11 / *D5*
Staffords-in-the-Field, PO Box 270, 03817 .... (603)323-7766
The Farmhouse, PO 14 Page Hill Rd, 03817 .... (603)323-8707

CLAREMONT M6 / *F3*
Goddard Mansion B&B, 25 Hillstead Rd, 03743 .... (603)543-0603
The Poplars, 13 Grandview St, 03743 .... (603)543-0858

COLEBROOK D9 / *B5*
Monadnock B&B, 1 Monadnock St, 03576 .... (603)237-8216

CONWAY J11 / *D5*
The Darby Field Inn, Bald Hill, PO Box D, 03818 .... (603)447-2181
Merrill Farm Resort, PO Box 2070, 03818 .... (603)447-3866
Mountain Valley Manner, 148 Washington St, 03818 .... (603)447-3988

CORNISH L6 / *E3*
Chase House B&B, Rt 12 A, RR 2 Box 909, 03745 .... (603)675-5391
Home Hill Country Inn, RFD 23, 03745 .... (603)675-6165

DANBURY L8 / *E4*
The Inn at Danbury, Rt 104, 03230 .... (603)768-3318

DOVER N12 / *F6*
Pinky's Place, 38 Rutland St, 03820 .... (603)742-8789
Silver Street Inn, 03820 .... (603)749-6524

DUBLIN P7 / *G4*
Hidden Brooks B&B, Main St, Box 402, 03444 .... (603)563-8452
Trinitarian Parsonage, Main St, 03444 .... (603)563-8889

DURHAM N12 / *F6*
Hannah House B&B, Packers Falls Rd, 03824 .... (603)659-5500

EAST HEBRON K8 / *E4*
Six Chimneys, Star Rt Box 114, 03232 .... (603)744-2029

EASTON I8 / *D4*
Blanche's B&B, Rt 116, 03580 .... (603)823-7061

EATON CENTER J11 / *D5*
The Inn at Crystal Lake, Rt 153, 03832 .... (603)447-2120
Rockhouse Mountain Farm-Inn, 03832 .... (603)447-2880

ENFIELD L6 / *E4*
Kluge's Sunset Hill Inn, Masacoma Lake, 03748 .... (603)632-4335

EPPING O11 / *F5*
Haley House Farm, N River Rd, 03042 .... (603)679-8713

ETNA K6 / *E3*
Moose Mountain Lodge, Moose Mountain Rd, 03750 .... (603)643-3529

EXETER O11 / *G6*
Exeter Inn, 90 Front St, 03833 .... (603)772-5901

FITZWILLIAM P6 / *G3*
Amos Parker House, PO Box 202, 03447 .... (603)585-6540
Fern Hill, PO Box 13, 03447 .... (603)585-6672
Fitzwilliam Inn, 03447 .... (603)585-9000
The Hannah Davis House, 186 Depot Rd, 03447 .... (603)585-3344

FRANCESTOWN O8 / *G4*
The Inn at Crotched Mountain, Mountain Rd, 03043 .... (603)588-6840
The Francestown B&B, Box 236, 03043 .... (603)547-6333

FRANCONIA H8 / *C4*
Bungay Jar B&B, PO Box 15, 03580 .... (603)823-7775
Cannon Mountain Inn & Cottage, Easton Rd, Rt 116, 03580 .... (603)823-9574
Franconia Inn, Easton Rd, 03580 .... (603)823-5542
Horse and Hound Inn, Wells Rd, 03580 .... (603)823-5501
Lovett's Inn, Rt 18, Profile Rd, 03580 .... (603)823-7761
Pinestead Farm Lodge, Rt 116 RD 1, 03580 .... (603)823-5601
Sugar Hill Inn, Rt 117, 03580 .... (603)823-5621

FRANKLIN M8 / *E4*
Webster Lake Inn, Webster Ave, 03235 .... (603)934-4050

FREEDOM K11 / *D6*
Freedom House, PO Box 478, 1 Maple St, 03836 .... (603)539-4815
Knob Hill B&B, Rt 153, 03836 .... (603)539-6576

GILFORD L9 / *E5*
Cartway House Inn, 83 Old Lake Shore Rd, 03246 .... (603)528-1172
Gunstock Inn, Rt 11A, 03246 .... (603)293-2021
Hall's Hillside B&B, RD #4, BoxGA372, 03246 .... (603)293-7290

GILMONTON M10 / *E5*
The Historic Tavern Inn, Box 365, 03237 .... (603)267-7349

GLEN I11 / *D5*
Bernerhof Inn, Box 240 Rt 302, 03838 .... (603)383-4414

GORHAM G10 / *C5*
The Gables, 139 Main St, 03581 .... (603)466-2875
The Gorham House Inn, 55 Main St, 03581 .... (603)466-2271

GOSHEN M7 / *F3*
Cutter's Loft, Rt 31, 03752 .... (603)863-5306

GREENFIELD O8 / *G4*
The Greenfield B&B Inn, PO Box 400, 03047 .... (603)547-6327

HAMPSTEAD P10 / *G5*
Stillmeadow B&B at Hampstead, 545 Main St, PO Box 565, 03841 .... (603)329-8381

HAMPTON O12 / *G6*
The Curtis Field House, 735 Exeter Rd, 03842 .... (603)929-0082
The Inn at Elmwood Corners, 252 Winnacunnet Rd, 03842 ... (603)929-0443

HAMPTON BEACH P12 / *G6*
Boar's Head, 12 Dumas, 03842 .... (603)926-3911

HANCOCK O7 / *G4*
John Hancock Inn, Main St, 03449 .... (603)525-3318
Westwinds of Hancock, Rt 137, RFD #1, Box 635, 03449 .... (603)525-6600

HANOVER K6 / *E3*
The Trumbull House, PO Box C29, 03755 .... (603)643-1400

HARRISVILLE O7 / *G4*
Harrisville Squire's Inn, Box 19, Keene Rd, 03450 .... (603)827-3925

HAVERHILL I7 / *D4*
Haverhill Inn, Box 95, 03765 .... (603)989-5961
Westgate House, 7 Court St, Box 178A, 03765 .... (603)989-3311

HEBRON K8 / *E4*
Six Chimneys, US Rt 3A, SRB 114 E, 03232 .... (603)744-2029

HENNIKER N8 / *F4*
Colby Hill Inn, Box 778, 03242 .... (603)428-3281
The Meeting House Inn & Restaurant, 35 Flanders Rd, 03242 .... (603)428-3228

HILLSBOROUGH O8 / *F4*
Stonebridge Inn, Rt 9 Box 82, 03244 .... (603)464-3155

HOLDERNESS K9 / *E4*
The Inn on Golden Pond, Rt 3 Box 680, 03245 .... (603)968-7269
Manor On Golden Pond, Rt 3 Box T, 03245 .... (603)968-3348

INTERVALE I11 / *D5*
The Forest-A Country Inn, PO Box 37, 03845 .... (603)356-9772
Mountain Vale Inn, Rt 16A, Box 482, 03845 .... (603)356-9880
New England Inn, Rt 16A Box 428, 03845 .... (603)356-5541
Old Field House, Rt 16A, PO Box I, 03845 .... (603)356-5478
Riverside, An Elegant Country Inn, Rt 16A, 03845 .... (603)356-9060

JACKSON I10 / *D5*
Blake House, Pinkham Notch Rd, PO Box 246, 03846 .... (603)383-9057
Christmas Farm Inn, Rt 16 Box 176, 03846 .... (603)383-4313
Dana Place Inn, Rt 16, Pinkham Notch Rd, 03846 .... (603)383-6822
Ellis River House, Rt 16 Box 656, 03846 .... (603)383-9339
The Inn at Jackson, PO Box H, 03846 .... (603)383-4321
Nestlenook Inn, PO Box Q, Dinsmore Rd, 03846 .... (603)383-9443
The Inn at Thorn Hill, PO Box A, Thorn Hill Rd, 03846 .... (603)383-4242
Village House, Rt 16A Box 359, 03846 .... (603)383-6666
Whitney's Inn, Rt 16B Box W, 03846 .... (603)383-6886
Wildcat Inn, Main St, PO Box T, 03846 .... (603)383-4245

JAFFREY P7 / *G4*
B&B on Board, 247 Old Peterborough Rd, 03452 .... (603)532-8083
The Benjamin Prescott Inn, Rt 124 E, 03452 .... (603)532-6637
Galway House B&B, Old Peterborough Rd, 03452 .... (603)532-8083
Gould Farm, PO Box 27, 03452 .... (603)532-6996
Jaffrey Manor Inn, 13 Stratton Rd, 03452 .... (603)532-8069
Lilac Hill Farm, 5 Ingalls Rd, 03452 .... (603)532-7278
Mill Pond Inn, 50 Prescott Rd, 03452 .... (603)532-7687
Woodbound Inn, Woodbound Rd, 03452 .... (603)532-8341

JAFFREY CENTER P7 / *G4*
Monadnock Inn, Main St Box 103, 03454 .... (603)532-7001

JEFFERSON G9 / *C5*
Davenport Inn, RFD 1 Box 93A, 03583 .... (603)586-4320
Jefferson Inn, Rt 2, 03583 .... (603)586-7998

KEENE P6 / *G3*
289 Court, 289 Court St, 03431 .... (603)357-3195

LACONIA L9 / *E5*
Ferry Point House, Rt 1 Box 335, 03246 .... (603)524-0087
Hickory Stick Farm, RFD 2, 03246 .... (603)524-3333
Kings Grant Inn, 76 Ridgewood Ave, 03246-2224 .... (603)293-4431
Parade Rest Inn, Parade Rd, 03269 .... (603)524-3152
Perry Point House, Lower Bay Rd, 03269 .... (603)524-0087
Tin Whistle Inn, 1047 Union Ave, 03246 .... (603)528-4185

LANCASTER G9 / *C5*
A Touch of Home, 43 N Main St, Rt 3, 03584 .... (603)788-4540

LINCOLN I8 / *D4*
Inn of the White Mountains B&B, PO Box 562, Pollard Rd, 03251 .... (603)745-8517
Red Sleigh Inn B&B, Box 562, 03251 .... (603)745-8517

LISBON H7 / *C4*
Ammonoosuc Inn, Bishops Rd, 03585 .... (603)838-6118

LITTLETON H8 / *C4*
1895 House, 74 Pleasant St, 03561 .... (603)444-5200
Beal House Inn, 247 West Main St, 03561 .... (603)444-2661
Thayers Inn, 136 Main St, 03561 .... (603)444-6469

LYME K6 / *D3*
The Dowds' Country Inn, On the Common, 03768 .... (603)795-4712
Loch Lyme Lodge, Rt 10 RFD 278, 03768 .... (603)795-2141
Lyme Inn, Route 10, 03768 .... (603)795-2222

MARLBOROUGH P6 / *G3*
Peep-Willow Farm, 51 Bixby St, 03455 .... (603)876-3807
Thatcher Hill Inn, Thatcher Hill Rd, 03455 .... (603)876-3361

MEREDITH K9 / *E5*
The Tuckernuck Inn, RFD 4 Box 88 Red Gate Lane, 03253 .... (603)279-5521

MILFORD P9 / *G4*
Ram In The Thicket, Off Rt 101, Maple St, 03055 .... (603)654-6440

MOULTONBORO K10 / *E5*
Olde Orchard Inn, Box 256, 03254 .... (603)476-5004

MOUNT SUNAPEE M7 / *F4*
Blue Goose Inn, Rt 103B Box 117, 03772 .... (603)763-5519

MUNSONVILLE O7 / *G3*
The Old Mill House, Rt 9, Box 224, 03457 .... (603)847-3224

NEW LONDON M7 / *F4*
Maple Hill Farm, RR 1 Box 1620, 03257 .... (603)526-2248
New London Inn, Box 8, Main St, 03257 .... (603)526-2791
Pleasant Lake Inn, PO Box 1030, N Pleasant St, 03257 .... (603)526-6271

NEWMARKET O11 / *F6*
Haley House Farm, Rt 1 N River, 03857 .... (603)679-8713

NEWPORT M4 / *F3*
Backside Inn, RFD 2 Box 213, 03773 .... (603)863-5161
The Inn at Coit Mountain, HCR 63, PO 3 Rt 10, 03773 .... (603)863-3583

NORTH CHARLESTOWN N6 / *F3*
Indian Shutters Inn, Rt 12, 03603 .... (603)826-4445

NORTH CONWAY I11 / *D5*
The 1785 Inn, Rt 16 at The Scenic Vista, 03860 .... (603)356-9025
The Buttonwood Inn, Mt Surprise Rd, PO Box 1817, 03860 ... (603)356-2625
Center Chimney - 1787, PO Box 1220, River Rd, 03860 .... (603)356-6788
Cranmore Inn, Kearsarge St, PO Box 1349, 03860 .... (800)822-5502
Cranmore Mt Lodge, Kearsarge Rd, PO Box 1194, 03860 .... (603)356-2044
Eastman Inn, Main St, Box 882, 03860 .... (603)356-6707
Foothills Farm B&B, PO Box 1904, 03860 .... (207)935-3799
Nereledge Inn & White Horse Pub, River Rd off Main St, PO Box 547, 03860 .... (603)356-2831
Old Red Inn & Cottages, Rt 16 Box 467, 03860 .... (603)356-2642
Peacock Inn, PO Box 1012, 03860 .... (603)356-9041
Scottish Lion Inn, Rt 16, Main St, 03860 .... (603)356-6381
Stonehurst Manor, Rt 16, 03860 .... (603)356-3113
Sunny Side Inn, Seavey St, 03860 .... (603)356-6239
Victorian Harvest Inn, Locust Ln, Box 1763, 03860 .... (603)356-3548

NORTH SUTTON M7 / *F4*
Follansbee Inn, PO Box 92, Keyser St, 03260 .... (603)927-4221

NORTH WOODSTOCK I8 / *D4*
The Birches B&B, Rt 175, PO Box 59, 03262 .... (603)745-6603
Cascade Lodge, 222 Main St, 03262 .... (603)745-2722
Wilderness Inn, RFD1 Box 69, 03262 .... (603)745-3890
Woodstock Inn, Rt 3 Box 118, Main St, 03262 .... (603)745-3951

NORTHWOOD N11 / *F5*
Aviary, Bow Lake, Box 268, 03261 .... (603)942-7755
Lake Shore Farm, Jenness Pond Rd, 03261 .... (603)942-5521
Meadow Farm B&B, Jenness Pond Rd, 03261 .... (603)942-8619

ORFORD J7 / *D3*
White Goose Inn, PO Box 17, 03777 .... (603)353-4812

OSSIPEE K11 / E5
Acorn Lodge, PO Box 144, Duncan Lake, 03864 .... (603)539-2151
Flag Gate Farm B&B, Rt 28, RFD #1, Box 238, 03864 .... (603)539-2231

PITTSFIELD M10 / F5
Appleview Orchard B&B, Upper City Rd, PO Box 104, 03263 (603)435-6867

PLYMOUTH K8 / E4
Colonel Spencer Inn, Rt 3S, RFD 1 Box 206, 03264 .... (603)536-3438
Crab Apple Inn, RR 4 Box 1955, 03264 .... (603)536-4476
Northway House, RFD 1 US Rt 3 North, 03264 .... (603)536-2838

PORTSMOUTH O12 / F6
The Inn at Christian Shore, 335 Maplewood, PO Box 1474, 03801 .... (603)431-6770
Leighton Inn, 69 Richards Ave, 03801 .... (603)433-2188
Martin Hill Inn, 404 Islington St, 03801 .... (603)436-2287
Sheafe Street Inn, 3 Sheafe St, 03801 .... (603)436-9104
Sise Inn, 40 Court St, 03801 .... (603)433-1200
The Inn at Strawbery Banke, 314 Court St, 03801 .... (603)436-7242

RINDGE Q7 / G4
Grassy Pond House, 03461 .... (603)899-5166

RYE O12 / F6
Rock Ledge Manor B&B, 1413 Ocean, 03870 .... (603)431-1413

SHELBURNE G10 / C5
Philbrook Farm Inn, North Rd, 03581 .... (603)466-3831

SNOWVILLE J11 / D5
Snowvillage Inn, Box 176 AAHI, 03849 .... (603)447-2818

SPRINGFIELD L7 / E4
Hide-Away Lodge, PO Box 6, 03257 .... (603)526-4861

STRAFFORD M11 / F5
Province Inn, PO Box 309, Bow Lake, 03884 .... (603)664-2457

STRATHAM O12 / F6
Maple Lodge B&B, 68 Depot Rd, 03885 .... (603)778-9833
Stratham Hill Farm, 273 Portsmouth Ave, 03885 .... (603)772-3999

SUGAR HILL H8 / C4
The Hilltop Inn, Main Street, PO Box 9, 03585 .... (603)823-5695
Ledgeland Inn & Cottages, RR 1, Box 94, 03585 .... (603)823-5341
The Inn at Skunk Hollow, Main St, Rt 117, 03585 .... (603)823-8532
Sunset Hill House, Sunset Rd, 03585 .... (603)823-5522

SUNAPEE M7 / F4
Dexter's Inn & Tennis Club, Stagecoach Rd, Box 703 NS, 03782 .... (603)763-5571
Haus Edelweiss, Box 609, 03782 .... (603)763-2100
Old Governor's House, Lower Main & Myrtle, 03782 .... (603)763-9918
Seven Hearths Inn, Old Rt 11, 03782 .... (603)763-5657
The Inn at Sunapee, Box 336, 03782 .... (603)763-4444
Times Ten Inn, Rt 103b, PO Box 572, 03782 .... (603)763-5120

SUNCOOK N9 / F5
Suncook House, 62 Main St, 03275 .... (603)485-8141

SUTTON MILLS M7 / F4
Village House At Sutton Mills, Box 151, 03221 .... (603)927-4765

TEMPLE P8 / G4
Birchwood Inn, Rt 45, 03084 .... (603)878-3285

TILTON M9 / E5
The Black Swan Inn, 308 W Main St, 03276 .... (603)286-4524
Country Place, RD 2 Box 342, Rt 132 N., 03276 .... (603)286-8551
Tilton Manor, 28 Chestnut St, 03276 .... (603)268-3457

TWIN MOUNTAIN H9 / C5
Partridge House Inn, Profile Rd, PO Box 231, 03595 .... (603)846-2277

WAKEFIELD M11 / E6
Wakefield Inn, Mountain Laurel Rd, Rt 1 Box 2185, 03872 ..... (603)522-8272

WALPOLE O5 / F3
The Josiah Bellows House, N Main St, 03608 .... (603)756-4250

WARREN J7 / D4
The Black Iris B&B, PO Box 83, 03279 .... (603)764-9366

WATERVILLE VALLEY J9 / D5
Silver Squirrel Inn, PO Box 363, Show's Brook Rd, 03223 .... (603)236-8325
Snowy Owl Inn, PO Box 407, Village Rd, 03215 .... (603)236-8383

WENTWORTH J8 / D4
Hilltop Acres, East Side & Buffalo Rd, Box 32, 03282 .... (603)764-5896
Hobson House, Town Common, 03282 .... (603)764-9460
Wentworth Inn, Ellsworth Hill Rd, Off Rt 25, 03282 .... (603)764-9923

WEST CHESTERFIELD P5 / G3
Chesterfield Inn, Rt 9, 03466 .... (603)256-3211

WEST FRANKLIN M8 / F4
Maria Atwood Inn, RFD 2, Rt 3a, 03235 .... (603)934-3666

WEST SPRINGFIELD L7 / E4
Wonderwell, Philbrick Hill Rd, 03284 .... (603)763-5065

WESTMORELAND O5 / G3
Partridge Brook Inn, Hatt Rd, PO Box 151, 03467 .... (603)399-4994

WHITEFIELD G9 / C4
The 1875 Mountain Inn, The Dieterichs, 03598 .... (603)837-2220
Kimball Hill Inn, Kimball Hill Rd, PO Box 03264, 03598 .... (603)837-2284

WILMONT FLAT M7 / F4
Limner Haus, Box 126, 03233 .... (603)526-6451

WILTON CENTER P8 / G4
Stepping Stones, RFD #1, Box 208, 03086 .... (603)654-9048

WOLFEBORO L10 / E5
Tuc'Me Inn, PO 657, 03894 .... (603)569-5702

WOODSVILLE I7 / D4
Green Pastures Farm, RFD #1, Box 42, 03785 .... (603)747-2802

NEW JERSEY

ANDOVER E8 / B3
Hudson Guide Farm, 07821 .... (201)398-2679

AVON-BY-THE-SEA M14 / D5
Cashelmara Inn, 22 Lakeside Ave, 07717 .... (201)776-8727
Sands Of Avon, 42 Sylvania Ave, 07717 .... (201)776-8386

BASKING RIDGE H10 / C3
Old Mill Inn, PO Box 423, 07920 .... (201)221-1100

BAY HEAD N14 / E5
Bay Head Sands, 2 Twilight Rd, 08742 .... (908)899-7016
Conover's Bay Head Inn, 646 Main Ave, 08742 .... (908)892-4664

BEACH HAVEN T12 / F4
Barque, 117 Centre St, 08008 .... (609)492-5539
Green Gables, 212 Centre St, 08008 .... (609)492-3553
Magnolia House, 215 Centre St, 08008 .... (609)492-0398

BELMAR M14 / D5
The Seaflower B&B, 110 9th Ave, 07719 .... (908)681-6006

CAPE MAY Z7 / H2
The Abbey, Columbia Ave & Gurney St, 08204 .... (609)884-4506
Abigail Adams B&B, 12 Jackson St, 08204 .... (609)884-1371
Albert G. Stevens Inn, 127 Myrtle Ave, 08204 .... (609)884-4717
Alexander's Inn, 653 Washington St, 08204 .... (609)884-2555
Angel Of The Sea, 5 Trenton Ave, 08204 .... (800)848-3369
Barnard-Good House, 238 Perry St, 08204 .... (609)884-5381
Bedford Inn, 805 Stockton Ave, 08204 .... (609)884-4158
Bell Shields House, 501 Hughes St, 08204 .... (609)884-8512
Brass Bed Inn, 719 Columbia Ave, 08204 .... (609)884-8075
Captain Mey's Inn, 202 Ocean St, 08204 .... (609)884-7793
The Carroll Villa B&B, 19 Jackson St, 08204 .... (609)884-9619
The Chalfonte, 301 Howard St, 08204 .... (609)884-8409
COLVMNS by the Sea, 1513 Beach Dr, 08204 .... (609)884-2228
Delsea, 621 Columbia Ave, 08204 .... (609)884-8540
Dormer House, International, 800 Columbia Ave, 08204 .... (609)884-7446
Duke of Windsor Inn, 817 Washington St, 08204 .... (609)884-1355
Gingerbread House, 28 Gurney St, 08204 .... (609)884-0211
Hanson House, 111 Ocean St, 08204 .... (609)884-8791
Heirloom B&B, 601 Columbia Ave, 08204 .... (609)884-1666
Holly House, 20 Jackson St, 08204 .... (609)884-7365
Humphrey Hughes House, 29 Ocean St, 08204 .... (609)884-4428
John F. Craig House, 609 Columbia Ave, 08204 .... (609)884-0100
Mainstay Inn & Cottage, 635 Columbia Ave, 08204 .... (609)884-8690
Manse Inn, 510 Hughes St, 08204 .... (609)884-0116
The Mason Cottage, 625 Columbia Ave, 08204 .... (609)884-3358
Mooring, 801 Stockton Ave, 08204 .... (609)884-5425
Perry Street Inn, 29 Perry St, 08204 .... (609)884-4590
Poor Richard's Inn, 17 Jackson St, 08204 .... (609)884-3536
The Prince Edward, 38 Jackson St, 08204 .... (609)884-2131
The Queen Victoria, 102 Ocean St, 08204 .... (609)884-8702
Sand Castle Guest House, 829 Stockton Ave, 08204 .... (609)884-5451
Sea Holly B&B Inn, 815 Stockton Ave, 08204 .... (609)884-6294
Seventh Sister Guesthouse, 10 Jackson St, 08204 .... (609)884-2280
Springside, 18 Jackson St, 08204 .... (609)884-2654
Stetson B&B Inn, 725 Kearney Ave, 08204 .... (609)884-1724
Summer Cottage Inn, 613 Columbia Ave, 08204 .... (609)884-4948
The Manor House, 612 Hughes St, 08204 .... (609)884-4710
Victorian Lace Inn, 901 Stockton Ave, 08204 .... (609)884-1772
Victorian Rose, 719 Columbia Ave, 08204 .... (609)884-2497
White Dove Cottage, 619 Hughes St, 08204 .... (609)884-0613
White House Inn, 831 Beach Dr, 08204 .... (609)884-5329
Windward House, 24 Jackson St, 08204 .... (609)884-3368
The Wooden Rabbit, 609 Hughes St, 08204 .... (609)884-7293
Woodleigh House, 808 Washington St, 08204 .... (609)884-7123

CHATHAM G11 / C4
Parrot Mill Inn, 47 Main St, 07928 .... (201)635-7722

CHESTER G9 / B3
Publick House Inn, 111 Main St, 07930 .... (201)879-6878

DOVER F10 / *B3*
Silver Lining B&B, 467 Rockaway Rd, 07801 .... (201)361-9245

FLEMINGTON J7 / *C3*
The Cabbage Rose Inn, 162 Main St, 08822 .... (908)788-0247
Jerica Hill B&B Inn, 96 Broad St, 08822 .... (908)782-8234

FRENCHTOWN J6 / *C2*
National Hotel, 31 Race St, 08825 .... (201)996-4871
Old Hunterdon House, 12 Bridge St, 08825 .... (201)996-3632

HADDONFIELD P6 / *E3*
Queen Anne Inn, 44 W End Ave, 08033 .... (609)428-2195

HOPE F7 / *B2*
The Inn at Millrace Pond, Rt 159, Box 359, 07844 .... (908)459-4884

ISLAND HEIGHTS P13 / *E4*
Studio of John F. Peto, 102 Cedar Ave, 08732 .... (908)270-6058

LAMBERTVILLE K7 / *D2*
Chimney Hill Farm, 08530 .... (609)397-1516
Coryell House, 44 Coryell St, 08530 .... (609)397-2750

LONGPORT V10 / *G3*
Winchester House, 1 S 24 Ave, 08403 .... (609)822-0623

LYNDHURST G13 / *B4*
The Jeremiah J. Yereance House, 410 Riverside, 07071 .... (201)438-9457

MAYS LANDING U8 / *G3*
The Inn at Sugar Hill, Route 40 & 559, 08330 .... (609)625-2226

MILFORD I6 / *C2*
Chesnut Hill, PO Box N, 63 Church St, 08848 .... (201)995-9761

MONTCLAIR G12 / *B4*
Marboro Inn, 334 Grove St, 07042 .... (201)783-5300

OCEAN CITY V10 / *G3*
BarnaGate B&B, 637 Wesley Ave, 08226 .... (609)391-9366
Bradbury's, 1009 Wesley Ave, 08226 .... (609)398-1008
The Enterprise, 1020 Central Ave, 08226 .... (609)398-1698
Northwood Inn B&B, 401 Wesley Ave, 08226 .... (609)399-6071
Top O'The Waves, 5447 Central Ave, 08226 .... (609)399-0477

OCEAN GROVE M14 / *D5*
The Cordova, 26 Webb Ave, 07756 .... (908)774-3084
Keswick Inn, 32 Embury Ave, 07756 .... (908)877-7506
Pine Tree Inn, 10 Main Ave, 07756 .... (908)775-3264

PRINCETON K9 / *D3*
Peacock Inn, 20 Bayard Ln, 08540 .... (609)924-1707

RED BANK K14 / *D5*
Shaloum Guest House, 119 Tower Hill, 07701 .... (201)530-7759

SALEM S3 / *F1*
Brown's Historic Home B&B, 41-43 Market St, 08079 .... (609)935-8595

SEA GIRT N14 / *E5*
Holly Harbor Guest House, 112 Baltimore Blvd, 08750 .... (908)449-9731

SOUTH BELMAR M14 / *D5*
Hollycroft B&B, 506 N Blvd, 07719 .... (908)681-2254

SPRING LAKE M14 / *D5*
Ashling Cottage, 106 Sussex Ave, 07762 .... (908)449-3553
Chateau, 500 Warren Ave, 07762 .... (908)974-2000
Johnson House, 25 Tuttle Ave, 07762 .... (908)449-1860
Kenilworth, 1505 Ocean Ave, 07762 .... (908)449-5327
The Normandy Inn, 21 Tuttle Ave, 07762 .... (908)449-7172
Sandpiper Hotel, 7 Atlantic Ave, 07762 .... (908)449-6060
Sea Crest by the Sea, 19 Tuttle Ave, 07762 .... (908)449-9031
Stone Post Inn, 115 Washington Ave, 07762 .... (908)449-1212
Victoria House, 214 Monmouth Ave, 07762 .... (908)974-1882
Warren Hotel, 901 Ocean Ave, 07762 .... (908)449-8800

STANHOPE F9 / *B3*
Whistling Swan Inn, Box 791, 110 Main Street, 07874 .... (201)347-6369

STEWARTSVILLE H6 / *C2*
The Stewart Inn, Box 571, RD #1, 08886 .... (908)479-6060

STOCKTON K7 / *D2*
The Stockton Inn, Colligan's, 1 Main St, PO Box C, 08559 .... (609)397-1250
Woolverton Inn, 6 Woolverton Rd, 08559 .... (609)397-0802

WOODBINE W8 / *H3*
Henry Ludlam Inn, 124 S Delsea Dr, RD 3 Box 298, 08270 .... (609)861-5847

NEW MEXICO

ALBUQUERQUE F5 / *C3*
Adobe and Roses B&B, 1011 Ortega NW, 87114 .... (505)898-0654
Casas de Suenos, 310 Rio Grande SW, 87104 .... (505)247-4560
Casita Chamisa, 850 Chamisal Rd NW, 87107 .... (505)897-4644
W.E. Mauger Estate, 701 Roma Ave NW, 87102 .... (505)242-8755

ALTO J7 / *E4*
Sierra Mesa Lodge, Fort Stanton Rd, PO Box 463, 88312 .... (505)336-4515

ANGEL FIRE C8 / *B4*
The Inn at Angel Fire, Hwy 434, PO Box 578, 87710 .... (800)666-1949

CEDAR CREST F6 / *C3*
Elaine's B&B, PO Box 444, 87008 .... (505)281-2467

CHAMA B5 / *A3*
Corkins Lodge, Hwy 512, PO Box 396, 87520 .... (505)588-7261

CHIMAYO D6 / *B4*
Hacienda Rancho De Chimayo, Box 11 State Rd 520, 87522 .... (505)351-2222
La Posada De Chimayo, Box 463, 87522 .... (505)351-4605

CIMARRON C8 / *A5*
Casa del Gavilan, PO Box 518, 87714 .... (505)376-2246
St. James Hotel, RR 1, Box 2, 87714 .... (505)376-2664

CLOUDCROFT K7 / *E4*
The Lodge at Cloudcroft, PO Box 497, 88317 .... (505)682-2566
Pavilion at The Lodge, Corona Place, 88317 .... (505)682-2566

CORRALES F5 / *C3*
Corrales Inn B&B, PO Box 1361, 87048 .... (505)897-4422

EL PRADO C7 / *A4*
Salsa del Salto, Ltd., PO Box 453, 87529 .... (505)776-2422

ESPANOLA D6 / *B3*
La Puebla House, Rt 3, Box 172A, 87532 .... (505)753-3981

GALISTEO F7 / *C4*
Galisteo Inn, Box 4, 87540 .... (505)982-1506

GLENWOOD J1 / *E1*
Los Olmos Guest Ranch, PO Box 127, 88039 .... (505)539-2311

KINGSTON K3 / *E2*
Black Range Lodge, Star Rt 2, Box 119, 88042 .... (505)895 5652

LAS CRUCES L5 / *F3*
Lundeen Inn of the Arts, 618 S Alameda Blvd, 88005 .... (505)526-3327

LAS VEGAS E8 / *B4*
Plaza Hotel, 230 Old Town Plaza, 87701 .... (505)425-3591

LINCOLN J8 / *E4*
Casa de Patron, PO Box 27, 88338 .... (505)653-4676
Wortley Hotel (Country Inn), Box 96, 88338 .... (505)653-4500

LOS ALAMOS E5 / *B3*
Los Alamos B&B, PO Box 1212, 87544 .... (505)662-6041
Walnut Executive Suite, PO Box 777, 87544 .... (505)662-9392

LOS OJOS B5 / *A3*
Casa de Martinez, PO Box 96, 87551 .... (505)588-7858

MESILLA M5 / *F3*
Meson de Mesilla, PO Box 1212, 88046 .... (505)525-9212

MESILLA PARK M5 / *F3*
Elms, PO Box 1176, 88001 .... (505)524-1513

NOGAL J7 / *E4*
Monjeau Shadows Inn, Bonito Rt, 88341 .... (505)336-4191

PLACITAS F6 / *C3*
Hacienda de Las Munecas, PO Box 564, 87043 .... (505)867-3255

RANCHOS DE TAOS C7 / *B4*
Don Pascual Martinez B&B, PO Box 1205, 87557 .... (505)758-7364
Ranchos Ritz B&B, PO Box 669, 87557 .... (505)758-2640
Two Pipes, Box 52, Talpa Rt, 87557 .... (505)758-4770
Whistling Waters, Talpa Rt, Box 9, 87557 .... (505)758-7798

RED RIVER B7 / *A4*
El Western Lodge, Box 301, Gilt Edge Tr, 87558 .... (505)754-2272

SAN JUAN PUEBLO D6 / *B4*
Chinguague Compound, Box 1118, 87566 .... (505)852-2194

SANTA FE E6 / *B4*
Adobe Guest House, PO Box 266, 87504 .... (505)983-9481
Alexander's Inn, 529 E Palace Ave, 87501 .... (505)986-1431
Arius Compound, PO Box 1111, 87504-1111 .... (505)982-8859
Canyon Road Casitas, 652 Canyon Rd, 87501 .... (505)988-5888
Casa De La Cuma B&B, 105 Paseo De La Cuma, 87501 .... (505)983-1717
El Paradero, 220 W Manhattan, 87501 .... (505)988-1177
Grant Corner Inn, 122 Grant Ave, 87501 .... (505)983-6678
Hotel St. Francis, 210 Don Gaspar Ave, 87501 .... (505)983-5700
Inn of the Animal Tracks, 707 Paseo de Peralta, 87501 .... (505)988-1546
La Posada de Santa Fe, 330 E Palace Ave, 87501 .... (800)621-7231
Preston House, 106 Faithway St, 87501 .... (505)982-3465
Pueblo Bonito, 138 W Manhattan, 87501 .... (505)984-8001
Rancho Encantado, Rt 4, Box 57-C, 87501 .... (505)982-3537
Sunrise Springs, Rt 2, Box 203, 87501 .... (505)471-3600
The Inn on the Alameda, 303 E Alameda, 87501 .... (505)984-2121
Water Street Inn, 427 W Water St, 87501 .... (505)984-1193

SILVER CITY K2 / *F1*
Bear Mountain Guest Ranch, PO Box 1163, 88062 .... (505)538-2538

The Carter House, 101 N Cooper St, 88061 ....(505)388-5485

SOCORRO I5 / D3
The Eaton House, 403 Eaton Ave SW, 87801 ....(505)835-1067

TALPA C7 / B4
Blue Door B&B, La Maranda Rd, Box 1168, 87571 ....(505)758-8360

TAOS C7 / B4
American Artists Guest House, PO Box 584, 87571 ....(505)758-4446
Amizette Inn, PO Box 756, 87571 ....(505)265-6777
The Brooks Street Inn, PO Box 4954, 87571 ....(505)898-7027
Casa de las Chimeneas, Box 5303, 87571 ....(505)758-4777
Casa de Milagros, PO Box 2983, 87571 ....(505)758-8001
Casa Europa Inn & Gallery, 157 Upper Ranchitos Rd, 87571 ....(505)758-9798
Casa Feliz, 137 Bent St, 87571 ....(505)758-9790
Dasburg House & Studio, Box 2764, 87571 ....(505)758-9513
Gallery House West, E Kit Carson Rd, PO Box 2983, 87571 ....(505)758-8001
Hacienda del Sol, 109 Mabel Dodge Ln, Box 177, 87571 ....(505)758-0287
Hotel Edelweiss, PO Box 83, 87571 ....(505)776-2301
La Posada De Taos, 309 Juanita Ln, PO Box 1118, 87571 ....(505)758-8164
Las Palomas Conf. Center, Box 6689, 87571 ....(505)758-9456
Mabel Dodge Lujan House, PO Box 3400, 87571 ....(505)758-9456
Plum Tree, Box A-1, Hwy 68, 87571 ....(505)758-4696
Silvertree Inn, PO Box 1528, 87571 ....(505)758-3071
Stewart House, PO Box 2326, 87571 ....(505)776-2913
The Taos Inn, 125 Paseo del Pueblo Norte, 87571 ....(505)758-2233

TRUCHAS D7 / B4
Rancho Arriba B&B, PO Box 338, 87578 ....(505)689-2374

NEW YORK

ADAMS BASIN WC16 / D4
Canalside Inn, 425 Washington St, 14410 ....(716)352-6784

AFTON EQ7 / F7
Jericho Farm Inn, 155 E Main St, 13730 ....(607)639-1842

ALBANY EN15 / E9
Mansion Hill Inn & Restaurant, 115 Philip St at Park Ave, 12202 ....(518)465-2038

ALBION WD15 / D3
Friendship Manor, 349 S Main St, 14411 ....(716)589-7973

ALTAMONT EN13 / E9
Appel Inn, Rte 146, 12009 ....(518)861-6557

AMAGANSETT WM24 / G5
Mill-Garth Country Inn, PO Box 700, Windmill Ln, 11930 ....(516)267-3757

AMENIA ES16 / G9
Troutbeck, Box 26, Leedsville Rd, 12501 ....(914)373-9681

ANGELICA WH16 / F4
Angelica Inn, 64 W Main St, 14709 ....(716)466-3295

AUBURN EM3 / E6
The Irish Rose - A Victorian B&B, 102 South St, 13021 ....(315)255-0196
Springside Inn, Box 520, 13021 ....(315)252-7247

AVERILL PARK EN15 / E9
Ananas Hus B&B, Rt 3 Box 301, 12018 ....(518)766-5035
The Gregory House, PO Box 401, 12018 ....(518)674-3774

AVOCA WH18 / F4
Patchwork Peace B&B, RD 2, Waterbury Hill, 14809 ....(607)566-2443

AVON WE17 / E4
Avon Inn, 55 E Main St, 14414 ....(716)226-8181
Mulligan Farm, 5403 Barber Rd, 14414 ....(716)226-3780

BAINBRIDGE EP8 / F7
Berry Hill Farm, Box 128, RD #1, 13733 ....(607)967-8745

BARRYVILLE EU10 / H8
All Breeze Guest Farm, Haring Rd, 12719 ....(914)557-6485

BATH WH19 / F5
Wheeler B&B, 8876 Rte 53, 14810 ....(607)776-6756

BELLPORT WO18 / H3
The Great South Bay Inn, 160 S County Rd, 11713 ....(516)286-8588
Shell Cottage, 21 Brown's Ln, 11713 ....(516)286-9421

BERLIN EN16 / E10
The Sedgwick Inn, Route 22, Box 250, 12022 ....(518)658-2334

BIG MOOSE LAKE EH10 / C8
Big Moose, 13331 ....(315)357-2042

BOONVILLE EJ8 / D7
Greenmeadow, RD 3, 13309 ....(315)733-0040

BRANCHPORT WG19 / E5
Four Seasons B&B, 470 W Lake Rd, 14418 ....(607)868-4686
Gone With the Wind on Keuka Lake, 453 W Lake Rd, Rt 5A, 14418 ....(607)868-4603

BROCKPORT WC16 / D4
The Portico, 3741 Lake Rd, 14420 ....(716)637-0220

BROOKFIELD EN8 / E7
Bivona Hill Bed and Breakfast, Academy Rd, PO Box 201, 13314 ....(315)899-8921
Gates Hill Homestead, Dugway Rd, Box 96, 13314 ....(315)899-5837

BROOKLYN WP11 / H1
Bed & Breakfast on the Park, 113 Prospect Park W, 11215 ....(718)499-6115

BROOKTONDALE WH22 / F6
Dutch Touch B&B, 2879 Slaterville Rd, 14817 ....(607)539-7091

BUFFALO WE12 / E2
Beau Fleuve B&B Inn, 242 Linwood Ave, 14209 ....(716)882-6116

BURDETT WH21 / F5
The Red House Country Inn, Finger Lks Nat'l Forest, Picnic Rd, 14818 ....(607)546-8566

CADYVILLE EC15 / A9
Martins' B&B, PO Box 84, 12918 ....(518)293-7006

CAMBRIDGE EL16 / D10
Lillybrook Manor, 9 Ave A, 12816 ....(518)677-5028

CANAAN EP16 / F10
The Inn at Shaker Mill Farm, Cherry Ln, 12029 ....(518)794-9345
The Lace House, Rt 22 at Tunnel Hill Rd, 12029 ....(518)781-4669

CANANDAIGUA WE19 / E5
Cricket Club Tearoom, 4510 Bristol Valley Rd, 14424 ....(716)229-5343
J.P. Morgan House B&B, 2920 Smith Rd, 14424 ....(716)394-9232
JP Morgan House Bed and Breakfast, 2920 Smith Rd, 14424 ....(800)233-3252
Nottingham Lodge B&B, 5741 Bristol Valley Rd, 14424 ....(716)374-5355
Oliver Phelps Country Inn, 252 N Main St, 14424 ....(716)396-1650
Wilder Tavern B&B, 5648 N Bloomfield Rd, 14424 ....(716)394-8132

CANASERAGA WH17 / F4
The Country House, 37 Mill St, 14822 ....(607)545-6439

CANDOR EQ4 / F6
Edge Of Thyme, 6 Main St, 13743 ....(607)659-5155

CAZENOVIA EM6 / E6
Brae Loch Inn, 5 Albany St, US Rt 20, 13035 ....(315)655-3431
Lincklaen House, 79 Albany St, Box 36, 13035 ....(315)655-3461

CENTRAL VALLEY EV13 / H9
Gasho Inn, Rt 32, 10917 ....(914)928-2277

CHAUTAUQUA WI10 / F2
Longfellow Inn, 11 Roberts Ave Box Y, 14722 ....(716)357-2285

CHESTERTOWN EI14 / C9
Balsam House Inn, Atateka Dr, RR 1 Box 365, 12817 ....(518)494-2828
The Friends Lake Inn, Friends Lake Rd, 12817 ....(518)494-4251

CHICHESTER EQ13 / F8
Maplewood B&B, 6 Park Rd, PO Box 40, 12416 ....(914)688-5433

CLARENCE WE14 / E3
Asa Ransom House, 10529 Main St, 14031 ....(716)759-2315

CLAYTON EF5 / B6
Thousand Islands Inn, 335 Riverside Dr, 13624 ....(315)686-3030

CLINTON EL8 / D7
Victorian Carriage House, 46 Williams St, 13323 ....(315)733-0040

COBLESKILL EN12 / E8
The Gables, 62 W Main, 12043 ....(315)733-0040

COLD SPRING EU14 / H9
Hudson House, 2 Main St, 10516 ....(914)265-9355
One Market Street, 1 Market St, 10516 ....(914)265-3912
Pig Hill, 73 Main St, 10520 ....(914)265-9247

COLDEN WG13 / E3
Back of the Beyond, 7233 Lower E Hill Rd, 14033 ....(716)652-0427

COOPERSTOWN EN10 / E8
Angelholm, PO Box 705, 14 Elm St, 13326 ....(607)547-2483
The Inn at Brook Willow Farm, Rt 33, RD2, Box 514, 13326 ....(607)547-9700
Cooper Inn, PO Box 311, 13326 ....(607)547-2567
The Inn at Cooperstown, 16 Chestnut St, 13326 ....(607)547-5756
Creekside B&B, RD 1 Box 206, 13326 ....(607)547-8203
Hickory Grove Inn, Rt 80 at Six Mile Pt, 13326 ....(607)547-8100
Hill & Hollow Farm, RD3 Box 70, 13326 ....(607)547-2129
The J. P. Sillhouse, 63 Chestnut St, 13326 ....(607)547-2633

CORINTH EK14 / D9
Agape Farm B&B, 4894 Rt 9N, 12822 ....(518)654-7777

CORNING WI20 / F5
1865 White Birch B&B, 69 E First St, 14830 ....(607)962-6355
Rosewood Inn, 134 E First St, 14830 ....(607)962-3253
Victoria House, 222 Pine St, 14830 ....(607)962-3413
White Birch, 69 E First, 14830 ....(607)962-6355

CRARYVILLE EQ16 / *F9*
The Crary House, Rt 23, Box 209, 12521 .... (518)325-5888

CROTON-ON-HUDSON EV14 / *H9*
Alexander Hamilton House, 49 Van Wyck St, 10520 .... (914)271-6737

CUBA WI15 / *F3*
33 South, 33 South St, 14727 .... (716)968-1387

DAVENPORT EP10 / *F8*
The Davenport Inn, Main St, 13750 .... (607)278-5068

DE BRUCE ES10 / *F8*
De Bruce Country Inn on the Willowemoc, De Bruce Rd, 12758 .... (914)439-3900

DEPOSIT ER8 / *F7*
The White Pillars Inn, 82 Second St, 13754 .... (607)467-4191

DOLGEVILLE EL10 / *F8*
Adrianna B&B, 44 Stewart St, 13329 .... (315)429-3249

DOVER PLAINS ES15 / *G9*
Old Drovers Inn, Old Rt 22, 12522 .... (914)832-9311

DOWNSVILLE ER10 / *F7*
Adams' Farmhouse Inn B&B, Main St, PO Box 18, 13755 .... (607)363-2757
The Victoria Rose B&B, Main St, Box 542, 13755 .... (607)363-7838

DRYDEN EO4 / *F6*
Margaret Thacher's Spruce Haven B&B, 9 James St, PO Box 119, 13053 .... (607)844-8052
Sarah's Dream, 49 W Main St, PO Box 1087, 13053 .... (607)844-4321
Serendipity B&B, 15 North St, PO Box 287, 13053 .... (607)844-9589

DUNDEE WG20 / *E5*
1819 Red Brick Inn, Box 57A, 14837 .... (607)243-8844
Country Manor B&B, 4798 Dundee-Himrod Rd, 14837 .... (607)243-8628
Lakeside Terrace B&B, 660 E Waneta Lake Rd, 14837 .... (607)292-6606
Willow Cove, 77 South Glenora Rd, RD 1 Box 8, 14837 .... (607)243-8482

EAST AURORA WF13 / *E3*
Roycroft Inn, 40 S Grove St, 14052 .... (716)652-9030

EAST HAMPTON WM24 / *G5*
1770 House, 143 Main St, 11937 .... (516)324-1770
Hedges House, 74 James Ln, 11937 .... (516)324-7100
Hunting Inn, 94 Main St, 11937 .... (516)324-0410
Maidstone Arms, 207 Main St, 11937 .... (516)324-5006
Mill House Inn, 33 N Main St, 11937 .... (516)324-9766

EAST WINDHAM EP13 / *F9*
Point Lookout Mountain Inn, Rt 23, PO Box 33, 12439 .... (518)734-3381

ELBRIDGE EL3 / *E6*
Cozy Cottage, 4987 Kingston Rd, 13060 .... (315)689-2082

ELKA PARK EQ14 / *F9*
The Redcoat's Return, Dale Ln, 12427 .... (518)589-9858
Windswept, County Rd 16, 12427 .... (518)589-6275

ELLENBURG DEPOT EB14 / *A9*
The McGregor House B&B, PO Box 91, 12935 .... (518)594-7673

FAIR HAVEN EK2 / *D5*
Brown's Village Inn B&B, Stafford St, PO Box 378, 13064 .... (315)947-5817
Frost Haven B&B Inn, West Bay Rd, PO Box 241, 13064 .... (315)947-5331

FAIRPORT WD18 / *D4*
Woods Edge, 151 Bluhm Rd, 14450 .... (716)223-8877

FLEISCHMANNS EQ12 / *F8*
Runaway Inn, Main St, 12430 .... (914)254-5660

FLY CREEK EN10 / *E7*
Breezy Knoll, RFD #1 Box 18, 13337 .... (607)547-8362
Farm Home at Fly Creek, Valley Rd, PO Box 236, 13337 .... (607)547-5731
Litco Farms, PO Box 148, 13337 .... (607)547-2501

FORESTBURG ET11 / *G8*
The Inn at Lake Joseph, PO Box 81, 12777 .... (914)791-9506

FOSTERDALE ET10 / *G8*
Fosterdale Heights House, Mueller Rd, RD 1, Box 198, 12726 .... (914)482-3369

FRANKFORT EL9 / *E7*
Blueberry Hill, 389 Brockway Rd, 13340 .... (315)733-0040

FREDONIA WH10 / *F2*
The White Inn, 52 E Main St, 14063 .... (716)672-2103

FRIENDSHIP WI15 / *F4*
Merry Maid Inn B&B, 53 W Main St, 14739 .... (716)973-7740

FULTON EK4 / *D6*
Battle Island Inn, RD 1 Box 176, 13069 .... (315)593-3699

GARRISON EV14 / *H9*
Bird & Bottle Inn, Rt 9, Old Post Rd, 10524 .... (914)424-3000
The Golden Eagle Inn, 10524 .... (914)424-3067

GENESEO WF17 / *E4*
American House, 39 Main St, 14454 .... (716)243-5483

GENEVA WE20 / *E5*
The Inn at Belhurst Castle, PO 609, 14456 .... (315)781-0201
The Cobblestones, Rt 2, 14456 .... (315)789-1896
Geneva On The Lake, 1001 Lochland Rd, Rt 14 S, 14456 .... (315)789-7190

GILBERTSVILLE EP9 / *F7*
Leatherstocking Trails, RD 1 Box 40, 13776 .... (607)783-2757

GILBOA EP12 / *F8*
Windy Ridge B&B, S Gilboa Rd, Start Rd, 01276 .... (607)588-6039

GOWANDA WH12 / *F2*
The Teepee, RFD #1 Box 543, 14070 .... (716)532-2168

GREENVILLE F14 / *G2*
Greenville Arms, South St, Box 2 (Greene County), 12083 .... (518)966-5219

GROTON EO4 / *E6*
Benn Conger Inn, 206 W Cortland, 13073 .... (607)898-5817

HADLEY EJ14 / *D9*
Saratoga Rose B&B, 4870 Rockwell St, 12835 .... (518)696-2861

HAGUE EH15 / *C9*
Trout House Village Resort, Lake Shore Dr (Rt 9 N), 12836 .... (518)543-6088

HAINES FALLS EQ13 / *F9*
Huckleberry Hill Inn, Rt 23A, PO Box 398, 12436 .... (518)589-5799

HALCOTTSVILLE EQ11 / *F8*
Lake Wawaka Guest House, Old River Rd, 12438 .... (607)326-4694

HAMLIN WC16 / *D4*
Sandy Creek Manor House, 1960 Redman Rd, 14464-9635 .... (716)964-7528

HAMMONDSPORT WH19 / *F5*
Another Tyme B&B, 7 Church St, 14840 .... (607)569-2747
Blushing Rose B&B, 11 William St, 14840 .... (607)569-3402
The Bowman House, 61 Lake St, PO Box 586, 14840 .... (607)569-2516
Cedar Beach B&B, 642 W Lake Rd, 14840 .... (607)868-3228
Country Barn B&B, 1266 E Lake Rd, 14840 .... (607)292-3559
J.S. Hubbs B&B, 17 Sheather St, PO Box 366, 14840 .... (607)569-2440
Laufersweller, 11 William St, 14840 .... (607)569-3402

HAMPTON BAYS WN21 / *H4*
House on the Water, Box 106, 11946 .... (516)728-3560

HEMPSTEAD WP13 / *H2*
Duvall B&B, 237 Cathedral Ave, 11550 .... (516)292-9219
Tara II B&B, 16 St Pauls Pl, 11550 .... (516)292-0332

HERKIMER EL10 / *E7*
Bellinger Woods, 611 W German St, 13350 .... (315)866-2770

HEUVELTON ED8 / *A7*
Vera's Oswegatchie B&B, Box 322, 13654 .... (315)393-0780

HIGH FALLS ES13 / *G9*
Captain Schoonmaker's House, Rt 2 Box 37, 12440 .... (914)687-7946
House On The Hill, Box 86, 12440 .... (914)687-9627

HILLSDALE EQ16 / *F9*
The Inn at Green River, Green River Rd, 12529 .... (518)325-7248

HOBART EP11 / *F8*
Breezy Acres Farm B&B, RD 1, Box 191, 13788 .... (607)538-9338
Hobart House, Main St, Rt 10, PO Box 38, 13788 .... (607)538-1182

HOMER EO5 / *E6*
David Harum House, 80 S Main St, 13077 .... (607)749-3548

HORSEHEADS WI21 / *F5*
The Muse, 5681 Middle Rd, 14845 .... (607)739-1070

HOWES CAVE EN12 / *E8*
Cavern View, RD #1 Box 23, 12092 .... (315)733-0040

HYDE PARK ES14 / *G9*
Fala B&B, E Market St, 12538 .... (914)229-5937

ILION EL9 / *E7*
Chesham Place, 317 W Main St, 13357 .... (315)894-3552

IRVINGTON-ON-HUDSON WL12 / *G2*
Shadowbrook B&B, 821 N Broadway, 10533 .... (914)591-9291

ITHACA EP3 / *F6*
Buttermilk Falls, 110 E Buttermilk Falls Rd, 14850 .... (607)272-6767
Glendale Farm, 224 Bostwick Rd, 14850 .... (607)272-8756
Hanshaw House, 15 Sapsucker Woods Rd, 14850 .... (607)273-8034
La Tourelle, 1150 Danby Rd, 14850 .... (607)273-2734
The Peirce House B&B, 218 S Albany St, 14850 .... (607)273-0824
Peregrine House, 140 College Ave, 14850 .... (607)272-0919
Rose Inn, Rt 34 N, Box 6576, 14851-6576 .... (607)533-7905

JAMESVILLE EM5 / *E6*
High Meadows B&B, 3740 Eager Rd, 13078 .... (315)492-3517

KEENE EF14 / *B9*
The Bark Eater, Alstead Mill Rd, 12942 .... (518)576-2221

KEESEVILLE ED15 / *B9*
Bosworth Tavern, Rt 9/Mace Chasm Rd Box 177, 12944 .... (518)834-5401

KINGSTON ER14 / *G9*
Rondout B&B, 88 W Chester St, 12401 ... (914)331-2369

LAKE LUZERNE EK14 / *D9*
Lamplight Inn, PO Box 70, 2129 Lake Ave (9N), 12846 ... (518)696-5294

LAKE PLACID EE13 / *B9*
Blackberry Inn, 59 Sentinel Rd, 12946 ... (518)523-3419
Highland House Inn, 3 Highland Pl, 12946 ... (518)523-2377
Interlaken Lodge, 15 Interlaken Ave, 12946 ... (518)523-3180
South Meadow Farm, Cascade Rd, 12946 ... (518)523-9369
Spruce Lodge B&B, 31 Sentinel Rd, 12946 ... (518)523-9350
The Stagecoach Inn, 370 Old Military Rd, 12946 ... (518)523-9474

LANSING EP4 / *F6*
The Bay Horse B&B, 813 Ridge Rd, 14882 ... (607)533-4612

LEWISTON WC12 / *D2*
The Cameo Inn, 4710 Lower River Rd, 14092 ... (716)754-2075
The Peter House, 175 S Fourth St, 14092 ... (716)754-8877

LISLE EP6 / *F6*
Dorchester Farm B&B, RD 1 Keibel Rd, PO Box 6, 13797 ... (607)692-4511

LITTLE VALLEY WI13 / *F3*
Napoli Stagecoach Inn, 14755 ... (716)938-6735

LIVINGSTON MANOR ES10 / *G8*
Lanza's Country Inn, RD 2 Box 446, Shandelee Rd, 12758 ... (914)439-5070

LOCKPORT WD13 / *D3*
Chestnut Ridge Inn, 7205 Chestnut Ridge, 14094 ... (716)439-9124

LOWVILLE EH7 / *C7*
Hill Top B&B, RFD #1, Box 14, 13367 ... (315)376-6364

MACEDON WD19 / *D5*
Iris Farm, 162 Hook Rd, 14502 ... (315)986-4536

MALONE EB12 / *A8*
The Carriage House, 59 Milwaukee St, 12953 ... (518)483-4891

MARGARETVILLE EQ11 / *F8*
Margaretville Mountain Inn, Margaretville Mountain Rd, 12455 ... (914)586-3933

MATTITUCK WM21 / *G4*
Mattituck B&B, 795 Pike St, 11952 ... (516)298-8785

MAYVILLE WI10 / *F2*
Plumbush B&B at Chautauqua, Chautauqua - Stedman Rd, Box 332, 14757 ... (716)789-5309
The Village Inn B&B, 111 S Erie St, 14757 ... (716)753-3583

MEDINA WC14 / *D3*
Crafts B&B, 10283 Ridge Rd at Jeddo, 14103 ... (617)735-7343

MILFORD EO10 / *E8*
The 1860 Spencer House, RD 1, PO Box 65, 13807 ... (607)286-9402

MILLERTON ER16 / *G9*
Simmon's Way Village Inn, Main St, Route 44, 12546 ... (518)789-6235

MONTAUK WM25 / *G5*
Greenhedges Oceanside Villa, Essex St, PO 122, 11954 ... (516)668-5013

MOUNT MORRIS WF16 / *E4*
Allan's Hill B&B, 2446 Sand Hill Rd, 14510 ... (716)658-4591

MOUNT TREMPER ER13 / *F8*
Mt. Tremper Inn, Rt 212 & Wittenberg Rd, 12457 ... (914)688-5329

MUMFORD WE17 / *E4*
Genesee Country Inn, 948 George St, 14511 ... (716)538-2500

NAPLES WG18 / *E4*
The Vagabond Inn, 3300 Sliter Rd, 14512 ... (716)554-6271

NARROWSBURG ET9 / *G7*
Narrowsburg Inn, North Bridge St, PO Box 135, 12764 ... (914)252-3998

NELLISTON EM4 / *E8*
The Historian B&B, Rt 5, Box 224, 13410 ... (518)993-2233

NEW PALTZ ES13 / *G9*
Jingle Bell Farm, 1 Forest Glen Dr, 12561 ... (914)255-6588
Ujjala's B&B, 2 Forest Glen, 12561 ... (914)255-6360

NEW ROCHELLE EX15 / *G2*
Rose Hill, 44 Rose Hill Ave, 10804 ... (914)632-6464

NEW YORK EY14 / *H1*
Chelsea Inn, 46 W 17th St, 10011 ... (212)645-8989
Incentra Village House, 32 8th Ave, 10014 ... (212)206-0007

NEWARK WD20 / *D5*
Twin-Steeples Farm B&B, 4839 Whitbeck Rd, 14513 ... (315)597-2452

NEWFANE WC13 / *D3*
Creekside B&B, 2516 Lockport Olcott Rd, 14108 ... (716)778-9843

NEWFIELD WH22 / *F5*
Decker Pond Inn, 1076 Elmira Rd, 14867 ... (607)273-7133
The Historic Cook House B&B, 167 Main St, 14867 ... (607)564-9926

NICHOLS EJ23 / *G6*
Fawn's Grove B&B, River Rd RR#1, PO Box 285, 13812 ... (607)699-3222
River Tree B&B, RD 2, West River Rd, PO Box 27, 13812 ... (607)699-7484

NICHOLVILLE EC11 / *A8*
Chateau L'Esperance, Hwy 11B, 12965 ... (315)328-4669

NORTH HUDSON EG15 / *C9*
Pine Tree Inn, PO Box 555, 12855 ... (518)532-9255

NORTH RIVER EH13 / *C9*
Garnet Hill Lodge, 13th Lake Rd, 12856 ... (518)251-2821
Highwinds Inn, Barton Mines Rd, 12856 ... (518)251-3760

NUNDA WG16 / *E4*
Butternut B&B, 44 East St, PO Box 728, 14517 ... (716)468-5074

OGDENSBURG EC7 / *A7*
Maple Hill, Riverside Dr Rt 37, 13669 ... (315)393-3961

OLCOTT WC13 / *D3*
Bayside Guest House, 1572 Lockport Olcott Rd, 14126 ... (716)778-7767

OLEAN WJ14 / *F3*
The Old Library Inn, 120 S Union St, 14760 ... (716)373-9804

ONEIDA EL7 / *D7*
The Pollyanna, 302 Main St, 13421 ... (315)363-0524

ONEONTA EP9 / *F7*
Cathedral Farms Country Inn, Rd #1, Box 560, 13820 ... (607)432-7483

ONTARIO WD19 / *D5*
The Tummonds House, 5392 Walworth/Ontario Rd, 14519 ... (315)524-5381

OSWEGO EJ3 / *D6*
King's Inn, 180 E 10th St, 13126 ... (315)342-6200
Thompson Park House, 118 Front St, 13827 ... (607)687-4323

OXFORD EP7 / *F7*
Whitegate B&B in the Country, PO Box 917, 13830 ... (607)843-6965

PAINTED POST WI20 / *F5*
Dannfield, 50 Canada Rd, 14870 ... (607)962-2740

PALENVILLE EQ14 / *F9*
Arlington House B&B, Main St Box 1, 12463 ... (518)678-9081

PALMYRA WD19 / *D5*
Canaltown, 119 Canandaigua St, 14522 ... (315)597-5553

PENN YAN WF20 / *E5*
Finton's Landing, 661 E Lake Rd, 14527 ... (315)536-3146
Fox Run Vineyards B&B, 670 Rte 14 RD 1, 14527 ... (315)536-2507
The Heirlooms, 2756 Coates Rd, 14527 ... (315)536-7682
On the Beach, 191 W Lake Rd, 14527 ... (315)536-4646
The Wagener Estate B&B, 351 Elm St, 14527 ... (315)536-4591

PINE BUSH ET13 / *G8*
Jane Whiteman B&B, RFD #3, Box 455, 12566 ... (914)733-1324

PITTSFORD WD18 / *D4*
Oliver Loud's Inn, 1474 Marsh Rd, 14534 ... (716)248-5200
Richardson's Canal House, 1474 Marsh Rd, 14534 ... (716)248-5000

PLATTSBURGH EC15 / *A9*
Sunny Side Up B&B, Butler Rd, Box 58, 12901 ... (518)563-5677

PORT HENRY EF16 / *B9*
Elk Inn, HCR #1 Box 87, 12974 ... (518)546-7024

PORT JERVIS EV11 / *H8*
Educators Inn East, 23 Hudson St, 12771 ... (914)856-5543

PORTAGEVILLE WG16 / *E4*
Genesee Falls Hotel, Rt 436, 14536 ... (716)493-2484

PT JEFFERSON STATION WM17 / *G3*
Captain Hawkins House, 321 Terryville Rd, 11776 ... (516)473-8211

PULASKI EI5 / *C6*
The Way Inn, 7377 Salina St, 13142 ... (315)298-6073

QUEENSBURG EL14 / *D9*
The Crislip's B&B, RD 1 Box 57, Ridge Rd, 12804 ... (518)793-6869

RED HOOK ER14 / *G9*
The Red Hook Inn, 31 S Broadway, 12571 ... (914)758-8445

RENSSELAER EN15 / *E9*
The Tibbitts House, 100 Columbia Turnpike, 12144 ... (518)472-1348

RENSSELAERVILLE EO13 / *E9*
Sweet Meadow Farm, HC-1 Box 4, 12147 ... (518)797-3158

RHINEBECK ER14 / *G9*
Beekman Arms, Rt 9, 4 Mill St, 12572 ... (914)876-7077
The Jacob Kip River House B&B, Long Dock Rd, 12572 ... (914)876-8330
Village Victorian Inn, 31 Center St, 12572 ... (914)876-8345

RICHFIELD SPRINGS EM9 / *E7*
Country Manor B&B, 50 E Main St, Rt 20, 13439 ... (315)858-2561
Country Spread B&B, 23 Prospect St, PO Box 1863, 13439 ... (315)858-1870
Jonathan House, 39 E Main, 13439 ... (315)858-2870
Summerwood B&B, 72 E Main St, PO Box 388, 13439 ... (315)858-2024

ROCHESTER WD18 / D4
"428 Mt. Vernon"-A B&B Inn, 428 Mt Vernon Ave, 14620........(716)271-0792
Dartmouth House B&B, 215 Dartmouth St, 14607........(716)271-7872
The Rose Mansion & Gardens, 625 Mt Hope Ave, 14620........(716)546-5426
Strawberry Castle B&B, 1883 Penfield Rd, Rt 441, 14526........(716)385-3266
Swan Walk, 189 Stoneridge Dr, 14615........(716)865-7552

ROCK CITY FALLS EL14 / D9
The Mansion, Rt 29 Box 77, 12863........(518)885-1607

ROCK STREAM WH20 / F5
Vintage View B&B, 3975 Rt 14A Box 87, 14878........(607)535-7909

ROME EK8 / D7
Maplecrest B&B, 6480 Williams Rd, 13440........(315)337-0070
Wright Settlement B&B, Wright Settlement Ln, Box 204, 13440 ....(315)337-2417

ROSENDALE ES13 / G9
Astoria Hotel, 25 Main St, 12472........(914)658-8201

ROXBURY EP12 / F8
Scudder Hill House, Scudder Hill Rd, 12474........(607)326-4215

RUSHFORD WH15 / F3
Klartag Farms B&B, West Branch Rd, PO Box 98, 14777-0098 ....(716)437-2946

RUSHVILLE WF19 / E5
Lakeview Farm, 4761 Rt 364, 14544........(716)554-6973

SANDY CREEK WA24 / C6
Pink House Inn, 9125 S Main St, 13145........(315)387-3276

SARANAC LAKE EE13 / B9
The Point, Star Route, 12983........(518)891-5674

SARATOGA SPRINGS EL14 / D9
Adelphi Hotel, 365 Broadway, 12866........(518)587-4688
The Inn on Bacon Hill, 200 Wall St, 12871........(518)695-3693
The Six Sisters B&B, 149 Union Ave, 12866........(518)583-1173
The Westchester House, 102 Lincoln Ave, PO Box 944, 12866 ....(518)587-7613

SAUGERTIES EQ14 / F9
High Woods Inn, 7472 Glasco Turnpike, 12477........(914)246-8655

SCIO WI16 / F4
Scio House Victorian B&B, RD1 Box 280F, 14880........(716)593-1737

SENECA FALLS WE21 / E5
Locustwood Country Inn, 3568 Rt 89, 13148........(315)549-7132

SEVERANCE EG14 / C9
Sawmill B&B, PO Box 125, 12872........(518)532-7734

SHANDAKEN EQ12 / F8
Two Brooks B&B, Rt 42, 12480........(914)688-7101

SHARON SPRINGS EN11 / E8
Roses 'N' Lace, Main St, Rt 10, 13459........(518)284-2335

SHELTER ISLAND WL22 / G5
The Bowditch House, 166 N Ferry Rd, 11965........(516)749-0075
Chequit Inn, 23 Grand Ave, 11965........(516)749-0018

SKANEATELES EM4 / E6
Sherwood Inn, 26 W Genesee St, 13152........(315)685-3405

SODUS WC20 / D5
Maxwell Creek Inn, 7563 Lake Rd, 14551........(315)483-2222

SODUS POINT WC20 / D5
Carriage House Inn, 8375 Wickham Blvd, 14555........(315)483-2100
Silver Waters Guest Home, 8420 Bay St, 14551........(315)483-8098

SOUTH DAYTON WI12 / F2
Town & Country B&B, Pine St, PO Box 208, 14138........(716)988-3340

SOUTHAMPTON WN22 / H4
The Old Post House Inn, 136 Main St, 11968........(516)283-1717
Village Latch, 101 Hill St, 11968........(516)283-2160

SOUTHOLD WL22 / G4
Goose Creek Guesthouse, 1475 Waterview Dr, 11971........(516)765-3356

SPENCER EQ3 / F6
A Slice of Home, 178 N Main St, 14883........(607)589-6073

SPENCERTOWN EP16 / F9
Spencertown Guests, Box 122, Elm St & Rt 203, 12165........(518)392-2358

STANFORDVILLE ES15 / G9
Lakehouse...On Golden Pond, Shelley Hill Rd, 12581........(914)266-8093

STEPHENTOWN EO16 / E10
Kirkmead, Box 169A, 12168........(518)733-5420
Millhof Inn, Rt 43, 12168........(518)733-5606

STONE RIDGE ES13 / G9
Baker's B&B, Rt 2 Box 80, 12484........(914)687-9795
Hasbrouck House Inn, PO Box 76, 12484........(914)687-0055

STONY BROOK WN17 / G3
Three Village Inn, 150 Main St, 11790........(516)751-0555

SYRACUSE EL5 / D6
Russell-Farrenkopf House, 209 Green St, 13203........(315)472-8001

TANNERSVILLE EQ13 / F9
The Kennedy House, Spring & Main St, PO Box 770, 12485........(518)589-6082
The Eggery Inn, County Rd 16, 12485........(518)589-5363

THENDARA EI9 / C7
Moose River House, 12 Birch St, 13472........(315)369-3104

TICONDEROGA EH16 / C9
Bonnie View Acres B&B, Canfield Rd, 12883........(518)585-6098

TROY EN15 / E9
Diane's B&B, 108 Second St, 12180........(518)474-0345

TRUMANSBURG EO3 / E5
Taughannock Farm, Rt 89 & Gorge Rd, 14886........(607)387-7711

TURIN EI8 / C7
Towpath Inn, Box E, 13473........(315)348-8122

WAPPINGERS FALLS ET14 / G9
Castle Hill B&B, Box 325, 12590........(914)298-8000

WARRENSBURG EJ14 / D9
Country Road Lodge, Hickory Hill Rd, Box 227, 12885........(518)623-2207
The Merrill Magee House, 2 Hudson St, 12885........(518)623-2449
White House Lodge, 53 Main St, 12885........(518)623-3640

WATERLOO WE21 / E5
Front Porch B&B, 1248 Rts 5 & 20, 13165........(315)539-8325
The Historic James R. Webster Mansion, 115 E Main St - Rts 5 & 20, 13165 ....(315)539-3032

WATERTOWN EG6 / C6
Starbuck House B&B, 253 Clinton St, 13601........(315)788-7324

WATERVILLE EM8 / E7
B&B of Waterville, 211 White St, 13480........(315)841-8295

WATKINS GLEN WH21 / F5
Shamrock-Thistle Inn, RD 1, Country Line Rd, PO Box 148, 14891 ....(607)535-7526
The Victorian, 216 N Madison Ave, 14891........(607)535-6582

WEBSTER WC18 / D4
Country Schoolhouse, 336 Basket Rd, 14580........(716)265-4720

WESTFIELD WH10 / F1
Westfield House, E Main Rd, PO Box 505, 14787........(716)326-6262
The William Seward Inn, RD 2, S Portage Rd, Rt 394, 14787 ....(716)326-4151

WESTHAMPTON BEACH WO20 / H4
1880 Seafield House, 2 Seafield Ln, 11978........(516)288-1559

WINDHAM WI6 / E0
Albergo Allegria B&B, Rt 296, 12496........(518)734-5560
Country Suite B&B, Rt 23 W, PO Box 700, 12496........(518)734-4079

NORTH CAROLINA

ANDREWS P3 / C1
Walker Inn, 39 Junaluska Rd, 28901........(704)321-5019

ASHEVILLE F1 / C3
Aberdeen Inn, 64 Linden Ave, 28801........(704)254-9336
Albemarle Inn, 86 Edgemont Rd, 28801........(704)255-0027
Applewood Manor, 62 Cumberland Circle, 28801........(704)254-2244
Bridle Path Inn, 30 Lookout Rd, 28804........(704)252-0035
Cairn Brae, 217 Patton Mountain Rd, 28804........(704)252-9219
Carolina B&B, 177 Cumberland Ave, 28801........(704)254-3608
Cedar Crest Victorian Inn, 674 Biltmore Ave, 28803........(704)252-1389
Corner Oak Manor, 53 Saint Dunstans Rd, 28803........(704)253-3525
Cornerstone Inn, 230 Pearson Dr, 28801........(704)253-5644
Flint Street Inn, 100 & 116 Flint St, 28801........(704)253-6723
Heritage Hill, 64 Linden Ave, 28801........(704)254-9336
The Old Reynolds Mansion, 100 Reynolds Hgts, 28804........(704)254-0496
Ray House, 83 Hillside St, 28801........(704)252-0106
Reed House B&B, 119 Dodge St, 28803........(704)274-1604
Richmond Hill Inn & Conference Center, 87 Richmond Hill Dr, 28806 ....(704)252-7313
The Grove Park Inn & Country Club, 290 Macon Ave, 28804.(704)252-2711
The Lion & The Rose, 276 Montford Ave, 28801........(704)255-7673

BALSAM O5 / C2
Balsam Lodge, Box 279, Valley Dr, 28707........(704)456-6528
Balsam Mountain Inn, PO Box 40, 28707........(704)456-9298

BANNER ELK D4 / B4
Archers Inn, Rt 2 Box 56-A, 28604........(704)898-9004
Beech Alpen Inn, 700 Beech Mountain Pkwy, 28604........(704)387-2252
Mountain Chateau, Rt 1, Box 426, 28604........(704)963-6593

BAT CAVE G2 / *C3*
Old Mill Inn, PO Box 252, Hwy 64/74, 28710 .... (701)625-4256
Original Hickory Nut Gap Inn, PO Box 246, 28710 .... (704)625-9108
Stonehearth Inn, PO Box 242, 28710 .... (704)625-4027

BATH F22 / *C9*
Bath Guest House, S Main St, 27808 .... (919)923-6811

BEAUFORT J22 / *D9*
Captains' Quarters Bed & Biscuit, 315 Ann St, 28516 .... (919)728-7711
Cedars at Beaufort, 305 Front St, 28516 .... (919)728-7036
Inlet Inn, 601 Front at Queen St, 28516 .... (919)728-3600
Langdon House, 135 Craven St, 28516 .... (919)728-5499
The Shotgun House, 406 Ann St, Box 833, 28516 .... (919)728-6248

BELHAVEN F22 / *C9*
Pungo River Inn, 526 Riverview St, 27810 .... (919)943-2117
River Forest Manor, 600 E Main St, 28710 .... (919)943-2151

BLACK MOUNTAIN F2 / *C3*
The Blackberry Inn, Box 965, 28711 .... (704)669-8303
Red Rocker Inn, 3888 40 Way S, 28711 .... (704)669-5991

BLOWING ROCK D4 / *B4*
Gideon Ridge Inn, PO Box 1929, 28605 .... (704)295-3644
Hound Ears Lodge & Club, PO Box 188, 28605 .... (704)963-4321
Maple Lodge, PO Box 66, Sunset Drive, 28605 .... (704)295-3331
Meadowbrook Inn, Box 2005, 28605 .... (704)295-9341
Ragged Garden B&B, PO Box 1927, 28605 .... (704)295-9703
Sunshine Inn, Box 528, 28605 .... (704)295-3487

BOONE D4 / *B4*
Overlook Lodge, Box 1327, 28607 .... (704)963-5785

BREVARD P7 / *C2*
Red House Inn, 412 W Probart St, 28712 .... (704)884-9349
The Inn At Brevard, 410 E Main St, 28712 .... (704)884-2105
Womble Inn, 301 W Main St, 28712 .... (704)884-4770

BRYSON CITY O4 / *C2*
Folkestone Inn, 767 W Deep Creek Rd, 28713 .... (704)488-2730
Fryemont Inn, PO Box 459, 28713 .... (704)488-2159
Nantahala Village, PO Drawer J, 28713 .... (704)488-2826
Randolph House, PO Box 816, 28713 .... (704)488-3472

BURNSVILLE E2 / *B3*
Nu-Wray Inn, PO Box 156, 28714 .... (704)682-2329

CHAPEL HILL E13 / *B6*
The Inn at Bingham School, PO Box 267, 27514 .... (919)563-5583
Caroline Inn, Box 1110, 27514 .... (919)933-2001
Hillcrest House, 209 Hillcrest Rd, 27514 .... (919)942-2369
Pineview Inn & Conference Center, Rt 10, Box 265, 27514 .... (919)967-7166

CHARLOTTE H7 / *C5*
Fourth Ward B&B, 523 N Poplar St, 28226 .... (704)334-1485
Hampton Manor, 3327 Carmel Rd, 28211 .... (704)542-6299
The Homeplace B&B, 5901 Sardis Rd, 28226 .... (704)365-1936
Morehead Inn, 1122 E Morehead St, 28204 .... (704)376-3357
The New England Inn, 3726 Providence Rd, 28211 .... (704)362-0008
Overcarsh House, 326 W Eighth St, 28202 .... (704)334-8477
The Inn on Providence, 6700 Providence Rd, 28226 .... (704)366-6700
Still Waters, 6221 Amos Smith Rd, 28214 .... (704)399-6299

CHIMNEY ROCK G2 / *C3*
Esmeralda Inn, Box 57, 28720 .... (704)625-9105
Gingerbread Inn, PO Box 187, Hwy 74, 28720 .... (704)625-4038

CLINTON I16 / *D7*
The Shield House, 216 Sampson St, 28328 .... (919)592-2634

CLYDE N6 / *C2*
Windsong: A Mountain Inn, 120 Ferguson Ridge, 28721 .... (704)627-6111

CULLOWHEE O5 / *C2*
Cullowhee B&B, 150 Ledbetter Rd, 28723 .... (704)293-5447

DILLSBORO O5 / *C2*
Jarrett House, PO Box 219, 28725 .... (704)586-9964

DUCK C25 / *B10*
Sanderling Inn, 1461 Duck Rd, 27949 .... (919)261-4111

DURHAM E14 / *B7*
Arrowhead Inn, 106 Mason Rd, 27712 .... (919)477-8430
The Old North Durham Inn, 922 N Mangum St, 27701 .... (919)683-1885

EAGLE SPRINGS G11 / *C6*
The Inn at Eagle Springs, PO Box 56, Samarcand Rd, 27242 .... (919)673-2722

EDENTON D22 / *B9*
The Lords Proprietors' Inn, 300 N Broad St, 27932 .... (919)482-3641
Mulberry Hill, Box 277, Rt 4, Soundside Rd, 27923 .... (800)348-1405
Trestle House Inn, Rt 4 Box 370, 27932 .... (919)482-2282

ELIZABETH CITY C23 / *B9*
Elizabeth City B&B, 108 E Fearing St, 27909 .... (919)338-2177

EVERETTS F20 / *B8*
Ocean Side, Box 248, 27825 .... (919)792-4548

FLAT ROCK O8 / *C3*
Woodfield Inn, PO Box 98, 28731 .... (704)693-6016

FRANKLIN P4 / *C2*
Buttonwood Inn, 190 Georgia Road, 28734 .... (704)369-8985
Franklin Terrace, 67 Harrison Ave, 28734 .... (704)524-7907
Lullwater Farmhouse Inn, Rt 5, Box 540, 28734 .... (704)524-6532
Poor Richards Summit Inn, PO Box 511, 28734 .... (704)524-2006

GLENDALE SPRINGS C5 / *B4*
Glendale Springs Inn, 28629 .... (919)982-2102
Mountain View Lodge, PO Box 90, 28629 .... (919)982-2233

GLENVILLE P5 / *C2*
Mountain High, Big Ridge Rd, 28736 .... (704)743-3094

GRAHAM D12 / *B6*
Leftwich House, 215 E Harden St, 27253 .... (919)226-5978

GREENSBORO D11 / *B6*
Greenwich Inn, 111 W Washington, 27401 .... (919)272-3474
Greenwood B&B, 205 N Park Dr, 27401 .... (919)274-6350

HAZELWOOD N6 / *C2*
Belle Meade Inn, 804 Balsam Rd, 28738 .... (704)456-3234

HENDERSON C16 / *B7*
La Grange Plantation Inn, Rt 3 Box 610, 27536 .... (919)438-2421

HENDERSONVILLE G1 / *C3*
Claddagh Inn at Hendersonville, 755 N Main St, 28792 .... (800)225-4700
Echo Mountain Inn, 2849 Laurel Park Hwy, 28739 .... (704)693-9626
The Waverly Inn, 783 N Main St, 28792 .... (800)537-8195

HERTFORD C22 / *B9*
Gingerbread Inn, 103 S Church St, 27944 .... (919)426-5809

HIDDENITE E6 / *B4*
Hidden Crystal Inn B&B, School Rd, 28636 .... (704)632-0063

HIGH POINT E10 / *B6*
Premier B&B Inn, 1001 Johnson St, 27262 .... (919)889-8349

HIGHLANDS P5 / *D2*
Colonial Pines Inn, Hickory St, Rt 1, Box 22B, 28741 .... (704)526-2060
Highlands Inn, PO Box 1030, 28741 .... (704)526-9380
Long House B&B, Rt 2, Box 638, 28741 .... (704)526-4394
Old Edwards Inn, 4th & Main St, 28741 .... (704)526-5036
Phelp's House, Main St, Rt 1, Box 55, 28741 .... (704)526-2590

HILLSBOROUGH D13 / *B6*
Colonial Inn, 153 W King St, 27278 .... (919)732-2461
Hillsborough House Inn, 209 E Tryon St, PO Box 880, 27278 .... (919)644-1600
The Inn at Teardrop, 175 W King St, 27278 .... (919)732-1120

KILL DEVIL HILLS D25 / *B10*
The Figurehead B&B, 417 Helga St, 27948 .... (919)441-6929
Ye Olde Cherokee Inn, 500 N Virginia Dare Trail, 27948 .... (919)441-6127

LAKE JUNALUSKA N6 / *C2*
Providence Lodge, 1 Atkins Loop, 28745 .... (704)456-6486
Sunset Inn, 21 N Lakeshore Dr, 28745 .... (704)456-6114

LAKE LURE G2 / *C3*
Fairfield Mountains, Rt 1, Buffalo Rd, 28746 .... (704)625-9111
Lodge On Lake Lure, PO Box 529-A, 28746 .... (704)625-2789

LAKE TOXAWAY P6 / *C2*
Greystone Inn, Greystone Lane, 28747 .... (704)966-4700

LAKE WACCAMAW L15 / *E7*
B&B by the Lake, 404 Lake Shore Dr, 28450 .... (919)646-4744

LEXINGTON E9 / *B5*
Lawrences, Rt 1, Box 641, 27292 .... (704)249-1114

MAGGIE VALLEY N5 / *C2*
Cataloochee Ranch, Rt 1 Box 500, 28751 .... (704)926-1401
Mountainbrook Inn, PO Box 565, Hwy 19, 28751 .... (704)926-3962

MANTEO D25 / *B10*
Scarborough Inn, Box 1310, 27954 .... (919)473-3979
The Tranquil House Inn, Queen Elizabeth St, 27954 .... (919)473-1404

MARS HILL E1 / *B3*
Baird House, 121 S Main St, PO Box 749, 28754 .... (704)689-5722

MARSHALL M7 / *B3*
Marshall House, 5 Hill St, PO Box 865, 28753 .... (704)649-9205

MILTON B13 / *A6*
Woodside Inn, PO Box 197, 28305 .... (919)234-8646

MOORESVILLE F7 / *C5*
Oak Ridge Farm B&B, Rt 5, Box 111, 28115 .... (704)663-7085

MOUNT AIRY B8 / *A5*
Pine Ridge Inn, 2893 W Pine St, 27030 .... (919)789-5034

NAGS HEAD D25 / *B10*
Carefree Cottages, Rt 1 Box 748, 27959 .... (919)441-5340
First Colony Inn, 6720 S Va Dare Tr, 27959 .... (919)441-2343

NEW BERN — H21 / *C9*
The Aerie, 509 Pollock St, 28560 ....(919)636-5553
Harmony House Inn, 215 Pollock St, 28560 ....(919)636-3810
King's Arms Inn, 212 Pollock St, 28560 ....(919)638-4409
New Berne House, 709 Broad St, 28560 ....(800)842-7688

OCRACOKE — H24 / *C10*
The Berkley Center Country Inn, PO Box 220, 27960 ....(919)928-5911
Blackbeard's Lodge, PO Box 37, 27960 ....(919)928-3421
The Lightkeeper's Inn, PO Box 597, 27960 ....(919)928-1821

OCRACOKE ISLAND — H24 / *C10*
Island Inn, Lighthouse Rd, PO Box 9, 27960 ....(919)928-4351
Oscar's House, Box 206, 27960 ....(919)928-1311
Ship's Timbers, PO Box 582, Oyster Shell Ln, 27960 ....(919)928-4061

OLD FORT — F2 / *C3*
The Inn at Old Fort, W Main St, PO Box 1116, 28762 ....(704)668-9384

ORIENTAL — H22 / *C9*
The Tar Heel Inn, 205 Church St, 28571 ....(919)249-1078

PENLAND — E3 / *B3*
Chinquapin Inn, PO Box 145, 28765 ....(704)765-0064

PILOT MOUNTAIN — C8 / *B5*
Pilot Knob-A B&B Inn, PO Box 1280, 27041 ....(919)325-2502

PINEBLUFF — H12 / *C6*
"Finally" The O'Connor House, 145 Peach St, 28373 ....(919)281-5622
Pine Cone Manor, 450 E Philadelphia Ave, 28375 ....(919)281-5307

PINEHURST — H12 / *C6*
Magnolia Inn, Box 266, 28374 ....(919)295-6900
Pine Crest Inn, Dogwood Rd, PO Box 879, 28374 ....(919)295-6121

PITTSBORO — F13 / *C6*
The Fearrington House, 2000 Fearrington Village Ctr, 27312 ....(919)542-2121

POLKVILLE — G4 / *C4*
Patterson's Carriage Shop B&B, PO Box 852, Hwy 10, 28136 ....(704)538-3929

RALEIGH — E15 / *B7*
The Oakwood Inn, 411 N Bloodworth St, 27604 ....(919)832-9712

ROBBINSVILLE — O3 / *C1*
Blue Boar Lodge, 200 Santeetlah Rd, 28771 ....(704)479-8126
Snowbird Mountain Lodge, 275 Santeetlah Rd, 28771 ....(704)479-3433
Wilsons Tourist Home, PO Box 47, 28771 ....(704)479-8679

ROSMAN — P6 / *C2*
Red Lion Inn, Star Rt, Box 47, 28772 ....(704)884-6868

SALISBURY — F8 / *C5*
The 1868 Stewart-Marsh House, 220 S Ellis St, 28144 ....(704)633-6841
Rowan Oak House, 208 S Fulton St, 28144 ....(704)633-2086

SALUDA — H2 / *C3*
Bear Creek Lodge, Rt 1, Box 335, 28773 ....(704)749-2272
The Oaks, PO Box 1008, Greenville St, 28773 ....(704)749-9613
Orchard Inn, PO Box 725, 28773 ....(704)749-5471

SMITHFIELD — G16 / *C7*
Eli Olive's, 3719 US 70 W, 27577 ....(919)934-9823

SOUTHERN PINES — H12 / *C6*
Inn the Pines, 1495 W Connecticut Ave, 28387 ....(919)692-1632
Jefferson Inn, 150 W New Hampshire Ave, 28387 ....(919)692-6400

SPARTA — B6 / *A4*
Turby Villa, E Whitehead St, 28675 ....(919)372-8490

SPRUCE PINE — E3 / *B3*
Ansley Richmond Inn B&B, 101 Pine Ave, 28777 ....(704)765-6993
Fairway Inn, 110 Henry Lane, 28777 ....(704)765-4917

STATESVILLE — F7 / *B5*
Madelyn's B&B, 514 Carroll St, 28677 ....(704)872-3973

SUGAR GROVE — D4 / *B4*
Rivendell Lodge, PO Box 211, 28679 ....(704)297-1685

SYLVA — O5 / *C2*
Mountain Brook, Rt 2 Box 301, 28779 ....(704)586-4329

TARBORO — E19 / *B8*
Little Warren, 304 E Park Ave, 27886 ....(919)823-1314

TRYON — H2 / *C3*
L'Auberge of Tryon, PO Box 1251, 28782 ....(704)859-6992
Mill Farm Inn, PO Box 1251, 28782 ....(704)859-6992
Mimosa Inn, One Mimosa Ln, 28782 ....(704)859-7688
Pine Crest Inn, PO Box 1030, 200 Pine Crest Ln, 28982 ....(704)859-9135
Stone Hedge Inn, Howard Gap Road, PO Box 366, 28782 ....(704)859-9114

VALLE CRUCIS — D4 / *B4*
Mast Farm Inn, PO Box 704, 28691 ....(704)963-5857
The Inn at the Taylor House, PO Box 713, 28691 ....(704)963-5581

WANCHESE — E25 / *B10*
C.W. Pugh's B&B, PO Box 427, 27981 ....(919)473-5466

WARSAW — I17 / *D7*
The Squire's Vintage Inn, Rt 2 Box 130r, 28398 ....(919)473-5466

WASHINGTON — F20 / *C9*
Pamlico House, 400 E Main St, 27889 ....(919)946-7184

WAYNESVILLE — N6 / *C2*
Grandview Lodge, 809 Valley View Cir Rd, 28786 ....(704)456-5212
Hallcrest Inn, 299 Halltop Cir, 28786 ....(704)456-6457
Haywood Street Inn, 409 Haywood St, 28786 ....(704)456-9831
Heath Lodge, 900 Donlan Rd, 28786 ....(704)456-3333
The Palmer House B&B, 108 Pigeon St, 28786 ....(704)456-7521
The Swag, Rt 2 Box 280-A, 28786 ....(704)926-0430

WEAVERVILLE — M7 / *C3*
Dry Ridge Inn, 26 Brown St, 28787 ....(704)658-3899

WILMINGTON — L17 / *E8*
Anderson Guest House, 520 Orange St, 28401 ....(919)343-8128
Catherine's Inn on Orange, N 410 Orange, 28401 ....(919)251-0863
The Dock Street Inn, 522 Dock St, 28401 ....(919)763-7128
Five Star Guest House, 14 N 7th St, 28401 ....(919)763-7581
Historic Stemmerman's 1855 Inn, 138 S Front St, 28401 ....(919)763-7776
James Place B&B, 9 S Fourth St, 28401 ....(919)251-0999
Worth House A Victorian Inn, 412 S Third St, 28401 ....(919)762-8562

WILSON — F17 / *C8*
Miss Betty's B&B Inn, 600 W Nash St, 27893 ....(919)243-4447

WINSTON-SALEM — D9 / *B5*
Brookstown Inn B&B, 200 Brookstown Ave, 27101 ....(919)725-1120
Colonel Ludlow Inn, Summit & W 5th, 27101 ....(919)777-1887
Lowe-Alston House, 204 Cascade Ave, 27127 ....(919)727-1211
Salem Inn, 1168 Burke St, 27101 ....(919)722-8022
Wachovia B&B, 513 Wachovia St, 27101 ....(919)777-0332

NORTH DAKOTA

FESSENDEN — E10 / *C5*
Beiseker Mansion, 1001 Second St NE, 58438 ....(701)547-3313

GRAND FORKS — D15 / *C7*
Lord Bryon, 521 S Fifth, 58201 ....(701)775-0194

KENMARE — B6 / *B3*
Farm Comfort, 58746 ....(701)848-2433

LIDGERWOOD — I15 / *E7*
Kaler B&B, Rt 2, Box 151, 58053 ....(701)538-4848

LUVERNE — F14 / *C7*
Volden Farm, RR2 Box 50, 58056 ....(701)769-2275

MEDORA — G3 / *D1*
The Rough Riders, 58645 ....(701)623-4444

REGENT — H5 / *E2*
The Old West B&B, Box 211, 58650 ....(701)563-4542

STANLEY — C5 / *B2*
Triple T Ranch, Rt 1, Box 93, 58784 ....(701)628-2418

WING — F9 / *D4*
Eva's B&B, HCR 1, Box 10, 58494 ....(701)943-2461

OHIO

AKRON — NI20 / *D7*
Helen's Hospitality House, 1096 Palmetto Ave, 44306 ....(216)724-7151

ALBANY — SG16 / *H5*
Albany House, 9 Clinton St, 45710 ....(614)698-6311

ALLIANCE — NK22 / *D7*
Aleida's B&B, 119 East College, 44601 ....(216)823-1470

ARCHBOLD — NF4 / *C2*
Murbach House, 504 N Defiance St, 43502 ....(419)445-5195

ASHTABULA — ND24 / *B8*
Michael Cahill B&B, PO Box 3024, 1106 Walnut Blvd, 44004 ....(216)964-8449

BELLEFONTAINE — NO7 / *E3*
Whitmore House, 3985 SR 47W, 43311 ....(513)592-4290

BELLVILLE — NM14 / *E5*
Frederick Fitting House, 72 Fitting Ave, 44813 ....(419)886-4283

BELMONT — NQ23 / *F8*
Victorian B&B, 121 West Main St, Box 233, 43718 ....(614)484-4872

BLUE ROCK — SC18 / *F6*
McNutt Farm/Outdoors Lodge, 6120 Cutler Lake Rd, 43720 ....(614)674-4555

CENTERBURG — NO13 / *E4*
Otter Fork Hills, 6642 Bennington Chapel Rd, 43011 ....(614)893-2467

CENTERVILLE — SD5 / *G2*
Yesterday B&B, 39 S Main St, 45458 ....(513)433-0785

CHILLICOTHE SF12 / G4
Chillicothe B&B, 202 S Paint St, 45601 .... (614)772-6848
The Greenhouse B&B, 47 E 5th St, 45601 .... (614)775-5313
Old McDill-Anderson Place, 3656 Polk Hollow Rd, 45601 .... (614)774-1770
Vanmeter B&B, 178 Church St, 45601 .... (614)774-3510

CINCINNATI SH3 / H1
Prospect Hill B&B, 408 Boal St, 45210 .... (513)421-4408

CIRCLEVILLE SD12 / G4
Castle Inn, 610 S Court St, 43113 .... (614)477-3986

CLEVELAND NG19 / C5
Glidden House, 1901 Ford Dr, 44106 .... (216)231-8900
Tudor House, PO Box 18590, 44118 .... (216)321-3213

CLYDE NH12 / C4
Pine Rose Inn, 137 S Main St, 43410 .... (419)547-9707

COLUMBUS SB12 / F4
Fifty Lincoln, 50 E Lincoln St, 43215 .... (614)291-5056
Harrison House B&B, 313 W 5th Ave, 43201 .... (614)421-2202
Victorian B&B, 78 Smith Place, 43201 .... (614)299-1656

CONESVILLE NP18 / F6
Log House B&B, PO Box 30, 43811 .... (614)829-2757

COSHOCTON NP18 / F6
1890 B&B, 663 N Whitewoman St, 43812 .... (614)622-1890
Roscoe Village Inn, 200 N Whitewoman St, 43812 .... (614)622-2222

DANVILLE NN16 / E5
The White Oak Inn, 29683 Walhonding Rd (SR 715), 43014 .... (614)599-6107

DAYTON SC5 / F2
Prices' Steamboat House, 6 Josie St, 45403 .... (513)223-2444

DEGRAFF NO6 / E2
Rollicking Hills B&B, 2 Rollicking Hills Ln, 43318 .... (513)585-5161

DELAWARE NO11 / F4
Olentangy River Valley B&B, 8870 Olentangy River Rd, 43015 .... (614)885-5859

DELLROY NM22 / E7
Litt's Country Inn, 2196 Lodge Rd, Box 41, 44620 .... (216)735-2035
Pleasant Journey Inn, 4247 Roswell Rd SW, 44620 .... (216)735-2987

EAST FULTONHAM SC17 / F5
Hill View Acres B&B, 7320 Old Town Rd, 43735 .... (614)849-2728

GRANVILLE NQ14 / F5
Buxton Inn, 313 E Broadway, 43023 .... (614)587-0001
Granville Inn, 314 E Broadway, 43023 .... (614)587-3333

HANOVERTON NL23 / D8
Crystal Springs B&B, 12471 Bethesda Rd, 44423 .... (216)223-2198

HIRAM NH22 / C7
The Lily Ponds, PO Box 322, 44234 .... (216)569-3222

HURON NG14 / C5
Captain Montague's B&B, 229 Center St, 44839 .... (419)433-4756

JOHNSTOWN NP13 / F5
Pudding House, 60 N Main St, 43031 .... (614)967-6060

KELLEYS ISLAND NF13 / C4
The Beatty House, South Shore Dr, PO Box 402, 43438 .... (419)746-2379
Cricket Lodge, Lakeshore Dr Box 323, 43438 .... (419)746-2263
The Inn on Kelleys Island, Box 11, 43438 .... (419)746-2258
Southaven, PO Box 442, 43438 .... (419)746-2784
Sweet Valley Inn, Division St, PO Box 733, 43438 .... (419)746-2750

KENT NI21 / D7
Eidson House B&B, 141 Columbus St, 44240 .... (216)673-5544

KINSMAN NG25 / C8
Hidden Hollow, 9340 Rt 5 NE, 44428 .... (216)876-8686

LAKESIDE NF13 / C4
Rothenbuler's Guest House, 310 Walnut Ave, 43440 .... (419)798-5404

LAKEVILLE NM16 / E6
Quiet Country B&B, 14758 Tr 453, 44638 .... (216)378-2291

LANCASTER SD14 / G5
Barbara's Country Retreat, 3705 Crumley Rd, 43130 .... (614)687-1689

LEBANON SF5 / G2
Burl Manor, 230 S Mechanic St, 45231 .... (513)932-1266
Golden Lamb, 27 S Broadway, 45036 .... (513)932-5065
White Tor, 1620 Oregonia Rd, 45036 .... (513)932-5892

LEWISVILLE SC22 / F7
Grandma Betty's B&B, 35226 SR 78, 43754 .... (614)567-3456

LEXINGTON NM14 / E5
The White Fence Inn, 8842 Denman Rd, 44904 .... (419)884-2356

LODI NJ17 / D6
Squirrel's Run B&B, 9388 Kennard Rd, 44254 .... (216)948-3026

LOGAN SE15 / G5
B&B of Hocking County, 43138 .... (614)385-4941
Bartholomew, 7657 Twp Rd, 234, 43138 .... (614)385-8363
Bells, Downtown Logan, 43138 .... (614)385-4384
The Inn at Cedar Falls, 21190 State Rt 374, 43138 .... (614)385-7489
Log Cabin, 7657 TWP Rd 234, 43138 .... (614)385-8363
Rainbow's End, 10671 Ellinger Rd, 43138 .... (614)385-2537

LOUDONVILLE NM16 / E5
Blackfork Inn, 303 North Water St, PO Box 149, 44842 .... (419)994-3252

LUCAS NL15 / E5
Pleasant Valley Lodge, 1983 Pleasant Valley Rd, 44843 .... (419)892-2443

MARBLEHEAD NF13 / C4
Old Stone House Inn, 133 Clemons St, 43440 .... (419)798-5922

MARIETTA SF21 / G7
House Of Seven Porches, 331 Fifth St, 45750 .... (614)373-1767
Larchmont B&B, 524 Second St, 45750 .... (614)373-5907

MARION NM11 / E4
Olde Towne Manor, 245 St James St, 43302 .... (614)382-2402

MEDINA NI18 / D6
Oakwood B&B, 226 N Broadway, 44256 .... (216)723-1162

MILAN NH14 / C5
The Coach House Inn B&B, 304 SR 113 W, PO Box 537, 44846 .... (419)499-2435

MILLERSBURG NM18 / E6
Adams Street B&B, 101 W Adams St, 44654 .... (216)674-0766
The Inn at Honey Run, 6920 Country Rd 203, 44654 .... (216)674-0011
Kaufman's B&B, 9905 State Rt 39, R1, 44654 .... (216)674-4123

MORROW SF5 / G2
Country Manor B&B, 6315 Zoar Rd, 45152 .... (513)899-2440

MOUNT GILEAD NN12 / E4
Holiday House, 88 E High St, 43338 .... (419)947-8804

MOUNT VERNON NO14 / E5
Mount Vernon House, 304 Martinsburg Rd, 43050 .... (614)397-1914
Oak Hill B&B, 16720 Park Rd, 43050 .... (614)393-2912
The Russell-Cooper House, 115 E Gambier St, 43050 .... (614)397-8638

NEVADA NL11 / E4
Nevada Comfort B&B, PO Box 399, 203 Hillcrest St, 44849 .... (614)482-2869

NEW RICHMOND SI4 / H2
Hollyhock B&B of New Richmond, 1610 N Altman, 45157 .... (513)553-6585

NEWARK SA15 / F5
Pitzer-Cooper House B&B, 6019 White Chapel Rd SE, 43056 .... (614)323-2680
Wehrle Mansion B&B, 444 Hudson Ave, 43055 .... (614)345-4550

NORWALK NM14 / C5
Old Inn B&B, 1060 Peru Olena Rd, 44857 .... (419)668-6422

OBERLIN NM16 / C5
The Oberlin College Inn, 44074 .... (216)775-1111

ORRVILLE NK18 / D6
Grandma's House B&B, 5598 Chippewa Rd, 44667 .... (216)682-5112

OXFORD SE2 / G1
The Alexander House, 22 N College, 45056 .... (513)523-1200
Duck Pond, 6391 Morning Sun Rd, 45056 .... (513)523-8914

PAINESVILLE NE21 / B7
Rider's 1812 Inn, 792 Mentor Ave, 44077 .... (216)354-8200

PEEBLES SI10 / H3
The Bayberry Inn, 25675 State Rt 41 N, 45660 .... (513)587-2221

PENINSULA NH20 / C7
Centennial House, 5995 Center St, 44264 .... (216)657-2506
Fleder's B&B, 5964 Center St, 44264 .... (216)657-2284

PETTISVILLE NF5 / C2
Tudor Country Inn, Box 113, 43553 .... (419)445-2531

PICKERINGTON SB13 / F4
Central House, 27 W Columbus St, Old Village, 43147 .... (614)837-0932

PIQUA NP4 / F2
Pickwinn B&B, 707 N Downing St, 45356 .... (513)773-8877

POLAND NJ25 / D8
The Inn at the Green, 500 S Main St, 44514 .... (216)758-4688

POMEROY SI17 / H6
Holly Hill Inn, 114 Butternut Ave, 45769 .... (614)992-5657

PORT CLINTON NF12 / C4
Old Island House Inn, Box K, 102 Madison St, 43452 .... (419)734-2166

PUT-IN-BAY NE13 / C4
Bay House B&B, PO Box 631, Catawba Ave, 43456 .... (419)334-9698
Le Vent Passant, 1539 Langram Rd, 43456 .... (419)285-5511
The Vineyard, Box 283, 43456 .... (419)285-6181

RIPLEY — SK7 / *I4*
The Signal House, 234 N Front St, 45167 ....(513)392-1640

SAGAMORE HILLS — NH20 / *C7*
The Inn at Brandywine Falls, 8230 Brandywine Rd, 44067 ....(216)467-1812

SANDUSKY — NG13 / *C4*
Bogart's Corner B&B, 1403 E Bogart, 44870 ....(419)627-2707

The Cottage Rose, 210 W Adams St, 44870 ....(419)625-1285

Pipe Creek, 2719 Columbus Ave, 44870 ....(419)626-2067

The Sanduskian, 232 Jackson St, 44870 ....(419)626-6688

Wagner's 1844 Inn, 230 E Washington St, 44870 ....(419)626-1726

SHARON CENTER — NI19 / *D6*
Hart & Mather B&B, 1343 Sharon-Copley Rd, PO 93, 44274 ....(216)239-2801

SOMERSET — SC16 / *F5*
Somer Tea B&B, 200 S Columbus St, 43783 ....(614)743-2909

SOUTH AMHERST — NH16 / *C5*
Birch Way Villa, 111 White Birch Way, 44001 ....(216)986-2090

SOUTH BLOOMINGVILLE — SF14 / *G5*
Deep Woods, 24830 SR 56, 43152 ....(614)332-6084

THORNVILLE — SB15 / *F5*
Wal-Mec Farm B&B, 5663 SR 204 NW, 43076 ....(614)246-5450

TIFFIN — NI11 / *D4*
Zelkova Inn, 2348 S CR#19, 44883 ....(419)447-4043

TIPP CITY — SB5 / *F2*
Willow Tree Inn, 1900 W State, Rt 571, 45371 ....(513)667-2957

TOLEDO — NE9 / *C3*
Mansion View, 2035 Collingwood Blvd, 43620 ....(419)244-5676

TROY — NQ5 / *F2*
H.W. Allen Villa B&B, 434 S Market St, 45373 ....(513)335-1181

VERMILION — NG15 / *C5*
Village Square Annex B&B, 720 Main St, 44089 ....(216)967-1950

WALNUT CREEK — NN19 / *E6*
Indiantree Farm, PO Box 103, 44687 ....(216)893-2497

WAVERLY — SH12 / *H4*
Governor's Lodge, Lake White, 45690 ....(614)947-2266

WAYNESVILLE — SE6 / *G2*
Waynesville Guest, 117 Main St, PO Box 592, 45068 ....(513)897-3811

WEST MILTON — SB4 / *F2*
Locust Lane Farm, 5590 Kessler Cowlesville Rd, 45383 ....(513)698-4743

WESTERVILLE — NQ12 / *F4*
Cornelia's Corner B&B, 93 W College Ave, 43081 ....(614)882-2678

Priscilla's B&B, 5 S West St, 43081 ....(614)882-3910

Sweet Apple Inn, 61 S Vine St, 43081 ....(614)882-5165

WINCHESTER — SI8 / *H3*
Kitty's Corner B&B, 18877 SR 136, 45697 ....(513)695-0623

WOODSFIELD — SC23 / *F7*
The Black Walnut Inn & Magnolia Manor, 203 W Marietta St, 43793 ....(614)472-0002

WOOSTER — NL17 / *D6*
Howey House, 340 N Bever St, 44691 ....(216)264-8231

The Wooster Inn, 801 E Wayne Ave, 44691 ....(216)264-2341

WORTHINGTON — NQ11 / *F4*
Worthington Inn, 649 High St, 43085 ....(614)885-2600

XENIA — SD7 / *G2*
Hattle House, 502 N King St, 45385 ....(513)372-2315

YELLOW SPRINGS — SC7 / *F2*
Morgan House, 120 W Limestone, 45387 ....(513)767-7509

ZANESFIELD — NO8 / *E3*
Myeerah's Inn B&B, Sandusky St, 43360 ....(513)593-3746

ZOAR — NM20 / *E7*
Cider Mill, PO Box 441, 44697 ....(216)874-3133

Cobbler Shop Inn, Corner of 2nd & Main St, 44697 ....(216)874-2600

Cowger House #9, 9 Fourth St, 44697 ....(216)874-3542

Haven at 4th & Park, PO Box 467, 44697 ....(216)874-4672

Weaving Haus, c/o Zoar Community Assoc Box 621, 44697 ..(216)874-2646

OKLAHOMA

ALINE — D14 / *A5*
Heritage Manor, RR1 Box 33, 73716 ....(405)463-2563

CLAYTON — J23 / *C8*
Clayton Country Inn, Rt 1 Box 8, 74536 ....(918)569-4165

GUTHRIE — F17 / *B6*
Harrison House, 124 W Harrison, 73044 ....(405)282-1000

Stone Lion Inn, 1016 W Warner, 73044 ....(405)282-0012

OKLAHOMA CITY — G17 / *B6*
Chisolm Springs, 824 Evan Hale Rd, 73127 ....(405)942-5193

The Grandison, 1841 NW 15th, 73106 ....(405)521-0011

RAMONA — D21 / *A7*
Jerrett Farm Country Inn, Rt 1, Box 1480, 74061 ....(918)371-9868

TULSA — E21 / *B7*
Holloway House, PO Box 52423, 74152-0423 ....(918)582-8607

OREGON

ALBANY — G5 / *C2*
Farm "Mini Barn" Guest House, 7070 Springhill Dr NW, 97321 ....(503)928-9089

ASHLAND — P6 / *F2*
Ashland Guest Villa, 643 Iowa St, 97520 ....(503)488-1508

Ashland's Main Street Inn, 142 W Main St, 97520 ....(503)488-0969

Auburn Street Cottage, 549 Auburn St, 97520 ....(503)482-3004

Buckhorn Springs, 2200 Buckhorn Springs Rd, 97520 ....(503)488-2200

Chanticleer B&B Inn, 120 Gresham St, 97520 ....(503)482-1919

Coach House Inn, 70 Coolidge St, 97520 ....(503)482-2257

Columbia Hotel, 262 1/2 E Main, 97520 ....(503)482-3726

Country Willows Inn, 1313 Clay St, 97520 ....(503)488-1590

Cowslip's Belle, 159 N Main St, 97520 ....(503)488-2901

Edinburgh Lodge B&B, 586 E Main St, 97520 ....(503)488-1050

Hersey House, 451 N Main St, 97520 ....(503)482-4563

Highland Acres, 1350 E Nevada St, 97520 ....(503)482-2170

Iris Inn, 59 Manzanita St, 97520 ....(503)488-2286

Lithia Rose Lodging, 163 Granite St, 97520 ....(503)482-1882

McCall House, 153 Oak St, 97520 ....(503)482-9296

Morical House, 688 N Main St, 97520 ....(503)482-2254

Neil Creek House, 341 Mowetza Dr, 97520 ....(503)482-1334

Oak Street Station, 239 Oak St, 97520 ....(503)482-1726

Parkside, 171 Granite St, 97520 ....(503)482-2320

Queen Ann, 125 N Main St, 97520 ....(503)482-0220

Romeo Inn, 295 Idaho St, 97520 ....(503)488-0884

RoyAl Carter House, 514 Siskiyou Blvd, 97520 ....(503)482-5623

Scenic View B&B, 467 Scenic Dr, 97520 ....(503)482-2315

Shutes Lazy S, 200 Mowetza Dr, 97520 ....(503)482-5498

Stone House, 80 Hargadine St, 97520 ....(503)482-9233

Treon's Country Homestay, 1819 Colestin Rd, 97520 ....(503)482-0746

Winchester Inn, 35 S 2nd St, 97520 ....(503)488-1113

The Woods House B&B, 333 N Main St, 97520 ....(503)488-1598

ASTORIA — A4 / *A1*
Franklin Street Station, 1140 Franklin, 97103 ....(503)325-4314

Grandview B&B, 1574 Grand Ave, 97103 ....(800)488-3250

BAKER — F20 / *B6*
Powder River B&B, HCR 87, Box 500, 97814 ....(503)523-7143

BANDON — L2 / *D1*
Lighthouse B&B, 650 Jetty Rd, PO Box 24, 97411 ....(503)347-9316

BEND — I10 / *C3*
Lara House B&B, 640 NW Congress, 97701 ....(503)388-4064

Mirror Pond House, 1054 NW Harmon Blvd, 97701 ....(503)389-1680

Mountain View Lodge at Bend, PO Box 7409, 97701 ....(503)388-3855

BROOKINGS — P2 / *F1*
Chetco River Inn, 21202 High Prairie Rd, 97415 ....(503)469-2114

Holmes Sea Cove, 17350 Holmes Dr, 97415 ....(503)469-3025

Ward House B&B Inn, 516 Redwood St, Box 86, 97415 ....(503)469-5557

CANNON BEACH — B3 / *A1*
The Waves, 224 N Larch St, PO Box 3, 97110 ....(503)436-2205

CAVE JUNCTION — P3 / *F1*
Oregon Caves Chateau, PO Box 128, 97523 ....(503)592-3400

CLOVERDALE — E3 / *B1*
The Historic Hudson House, 37700 Hwy 101 S, 97112 ....(503)392-3533

Sandlake Country Inn, 8505 Galloway Rd, 97112 ....(503)965-6745

COBURG — I5 / *C2*
Wheeler's B&B, Box 8201, 404 E McKinzy, 97401 ....(503)344-1366

COOS BAY — K2 / *D1*
Captain's Quarters B&B, PO Box 3231, 97420 ....(503)888-6895

This Olde House B&B, 202 Alder St, 97420 ....(503)267-5224

CORVALLIS — G5 / *C2*
Huntington Manor, 3555 NW Harrison Blvd, 97330 ....(503)753-3735

Madison Inn, 660 SW Madison Ave, 97333 ....(503)757-1274

COTTAGE GROVE — J5 / *D2*
Hillcrest Dairy B&B, 79385 Sears Rd, 97424 ....(503)942-0205

Historic Lea House Inn, 433 Pacific Hwy, 97424 ....(503)942-0933

Ivanoffs' Inn, 3101 Bennett Creek Rd, 97424 ....(503)942-3171

DEPOE BAY — F3 / *B1*
Channel House, 35 Ellingson St, PO Box 56, 97341 ....(503)765-2140

ELMIRA — I4 / *C2*
McGillivray's Log Home B&B, 88680 Evers Rd, 97437 ....(503)935-3564

EUGENE — I5 / *C2*
Backroads B&B, 85269 Lorane Hwy, 97405 ....(503)484-4602

Campus Cottage, 1136 E 19th Ave, 97403 ....(503)342-5346

Country Lane, 31180 Lane's Turn Rd, 97401 .... (503)686-1967
House in the Woods, 814 Lorane Hwy, 97405 .... (503)343-3234
The Lyon & the Lambe, 988 Lawrence at 10th, 97401 .... (503)683-3160
Shelley's Guest House, 1546 Charnelton St, 97401 .... (503)683-2062

FLORENCE — I2 / *C1*
The Johnson House, 216 Maple St, PO Box 1892, 97439 .... (503)997-8000

FRENCHGLEN — N16 / *E5*
Frenchglen Hotel, 97736 .... (503)493-2565

GARDINER — J2 / *D1*
Gardiner by Sea, 401 Front St, Box 222, 97441 .... (503)271-4005

GOLD BEACH — O1 / *E1*
Endicott Gardens, 95768 Jerry's Flat Rd, 97444 .... (503)247-6513
Tu Tu Tun Lodge, 96550 N Bank Rogue, 97444 .... (503)247-6664

GRANTS PASS — O4 / *E2*
Ahlf House, 762 NW 6th St, 97526 .... (503)474-1374
The Clemens House B&B Inn, 612 NW Third St, 97526 .... (503)476-5564
Handmaidens' Inn, 230 Red Spur Dr, 97527 .... (503)476-2932
Lawnridge House, 1304 NW Lawnridge, 97526 .... (503)476-8518
Mt Baldy B&B, 678 Troll View Rd, 97527 .... (503)479-7998
Paradise Ranch Inn, 7000 Monument Dr, 97526 .... (503)479-4333
Riverbanks Inn B&B, 8401 Riverbanks Rd, 97527 .... (503)479-1118
The Washington Inn, 1002 Washington Blvd, 97526 .... (503)476-1131

HALFWAY — F21 / *B7*
Birch Leaf Farm, Route 1 Box 91, 97834 .... (503)742-2990
Clear Creek Farm B&B, Rt 1 Box 138, 97834 .... (503)742-2238

HOOD RIVER — C9 / *A3*
Columbia Gorge Hotel, 4000 Westcliff Dr, 97031 .... (503)386-5566
Hackett House, 922 State St, 97031 .... (503)386-1014
Lake Cliff Estate, 3820 Westcliff Dr, 97031 .... (503)386-7000
State Street Inn, 1005 State St, 97031 .... (503)386-1899

INDEPENDENCE — F5 / *B2*
Davidson House, 887 Monmouth St, 97351 .... (503)838-3280
Out of the Blue B&B, 386 Monmouth St, 97351 .... (503)838-3636

JACKSONVILLE — O5 / *F2*
Jacksonville Inn, 175 E California, 97530 .... (503)899-1900
Livingston Mansion, 4132 Livingston Rd, PO Box 1476, 97530 .... (503)899-7107
McCully House Inn, 240 E California, 97530 .... (503)899-1942
Meadow Lark, 755 E California, 97530 .... (503)899-8963
Reames House, 540 E California St, PO Box 128, 97530 .... (503)899-1868

JOSEPH — D20 / *B7*
Chandler's Bed & Trail Inn, Box 639, 700 E Main, 97846 .... (503)432-9765
Wallowa Lake Lodge, Rt 1 Box 320, 97846 .... (503)432-4082

JUNCTION CITY — H5 / *C2*
Black Bart Bed & Breakfast, 94125 Love Lake Rd, 97448 .... (503)998-1904

KIMBERLY — F14 / *B5*
Land's Inn B&B, Star Rt #1, 97848 .... (503)934-2333

KLAMATH FALLS — P8 / *F3*
Thompsons' B&B by the Lake, 1420 Wild Plum Ct, 97601 .... (503)882-7938

LA GRANDE — D18 / *B6*
Pitcher Inn, 608 "N" Ave, 97850 .... (503)963-9152
Stange Manor, 1612 Walnut, 97850 .... (503)963-2400

LAKESIDE — K2 / *D1*
Country Lane B&B, PO Box Y-177, Country Ln, 97449 .... (503)759-3869

LOWELL — I6 / *C2*
Lakeside Cottage, 234 Pioneer S, Box 263, 97452 .... (503)937-2443

MADRAS — G10 / *C4*
Madras, 343 C Street at Hwy 26, 97741 .... (503)475-2345

MANZANITA — C3 / *A1*
The Inn at Manzanita, PO Box 243, 67 Laneda Ave, 97130 .... (503)368-6754
The Manzanita Inn B&B, Box 117, 97130 .... (503)368-5499

MCMINNVILLE — E5 / *B2*
Mattey House, 10221 NE Mattey Ln, 97128 .... (503)434-5058
Steiger Haus B&B, 360 Wilson, 97128 .... (503)472-0821

MEDFORD — O6 / *E2*
Reuthlinger's B&B, 770 Griffin Creek Rd, 97501 .... (503)535-7423
Under the Greenwood Tree, 3045 Bellinger Ln, 97501 .... (503)776-0000

MERLIN — O4 / *E2*
Morrison's Rogue River Lodge, 8500 Galice Rd, 97532 .... (503)476-3825

MILTON-FREEWATER — B18 / *A6*
Birch Tree Manor, 615 S Main St, 97862 .... (503)938-6455

MILWAUKIE — D6 / *B2*
Historic Broetje House, 3101 SE Courtney, 97222 .... (503)659-8860

MYRTLE CREEK — M5 / *E2*
Sonka's Sheep Station Inn, 901 NW Chadwick, 97457 .... (503)863-5168

NEWPORT — G3 / *C1*
Oar House, 520 SW 2nd St, 97365 .... (503)265-9571
Ocean House B&B, 4920 NW Woody Way, 97365 .... (503)265-6158
Sylvia Beach Hotel, 267 NW Cliff St, 97365 .... (503)265-5428

NORTH BEND — K2 / *D1*
Highlands, 608 Ridge Rd, 97459 .... (503)756-0300
Sherman House B&B, 2380 Sherman Ave, 97459 .... (503)756-3496

OAKLAND — K5 / *D2*
Pringle House, Locust & 7th Sts, PO Box 578, 97462 .... (503)459-5038

OCEANSIDE — D3 / *B1*
Sea Haven Inn, Box 203, 97134 .... (503)842-3151
Three Capes B&B, 1685 Maxwell Mountain Rd, 97134 .... (503)842-6126

OREGON CITY — D7 / *B2*
Ainsworth House B&B, 19131 S Leland Rd, 97045 .... (503)657-7820
Jagger House B&B, 512 Sixth St, 97045 .... (503)657-7820

OTIS — E3 / *B1*
Salmon River Lodge, 5622 Salmon River Hwy, 97368 .... (503)994-2639

PACIFIC CITY — E3 / *B1*
Pacific View B&B, 34930 Hillcrest, PO Box 28, 97135 .... (503)965-6498

PINE CREEK — F21 / *B7*
Pine Creek Guest House, Star Rt, Box 65, 97834 .... (503)785-3320

PORT ORFORD — N1 / *E1*
Gwendolyn's B&B, 735 8th, Box 913, 97465 .... (503)332-4373
Home by the Sea, PO Box 606, 444 Jackson St, 97465 .... (503)332-2855

PORTLAND — D6 / *B2*
Allenhouse B&B, 1918 NW 31st Ave, 97210-1906 .... (503)227-6841
Cape Cod B&B, 5733 SW Dickinson St, 97219 .... (503)246-1839
The Clinkerbrick House, 2311 NE Schuyler, 97212 .... (503)281-2533
Corbett House B&B, 7533 SW Corbett, 97219 .... (503)245-2580
General Hooker's House, 125 SW Hooker, 97201 .... (503)222-4435
Georgian House B&B, 1828 NE Siskiyou, 97212 .... (503)281-2250
Hartman's Hearth, 2937 NE 20th Ave, 97212-3441 .... (503)281-2182
Heron Haus, 2545 NW Westover Rd, 97210 .... (503)274-1846
John Palmer House, 4314 N Mississippi Ave, Ste AA, 97217 .... (503)284-5893
Mumford Manor, 1130 SW King, 97205 .... (503)243-2443
Old Portland Estate, 1870 SE Exeter Dr, 97202 .... (503)236-6533
Portland Guest House, 1720 NE 15th, 97212 .... (503)282-1402
Portland's White House, 1914 NE 22, 97212 .... (503)287-7131

ROCKAWAY BEACH — C3 / *A1*
Beach House B&B, 115 N Miller, 97136 .... (503)355-2411

ROSEBURG — L4 / *D2*
The Woods, 428 Oakview Dr, 97470 .... (503)672-2927

SALEM — F5 / *B2*
Harbison House, 1845 Commercial St, 97302 .... (503)581-8118
State House B&B, 2146 State St, 97301 .... (503)588-1340

SEAL ROCK — G3 / *C1*
Blackberry Inn, 6575 NW Pacific Coast Hwy, 97376 .... (503)563-2259

SEASIDE — B3 / *A1*
The Gilbert Inn, B&B, 341 Beach Dr, 97138 .... (503)738-9770
Riverside Inn, 430 S Holladay Dr, 97138 .... (503)738-8254
The Boarding House, 208 N Holladay Dr, 97138 .... (503)738-9055

SISTERS — H9 / *C3*
Lake Creek Lodge, Star Rt, 97759 .... (503)595-6331

SPRAY — F14 / *B5*
Pioneer B&B, Star Rt, 97874 .... (503)462-3934

STAYTON — F6 / *B2*
Horncroft, 42156 Kingston-Lyons Dr, 97383 .... (503)769-6287

STEAMBOAT — L6 / *D2*
Steamboat Inn, Hwy 138, 97447 .... (503)496-3495

THE DALLES — D10 / *B4*
Bigelow B&B, 606 Washington, 97058 .... (503)298-8239
Williams House Inn, 608 W 6th St, 97058 .... (503)296-2889

TILLAMOOK — D3 / *B1*
Blue Haven Inn, 3025 Gienger Rd, 97141 .... (503)842-2265

VIDA — I6 / *C2*
McKenzie River Inn, 49164 McKenzie Hwy, 97488 .... (503)822-6260

WALDPORT — H3 / *C1*
Cliff House, Adahi St-Yaquina John Pt, Box 436, 97394 .... (503)563-2506

WELCHES — D8 / *B3*
Mountain Shadows B&B, Box 147, 97067 .... (503)622-4746

WESTPORT — A5 / *A2*
King Salmon Lodge, Ferry Rd, 97016 .... (503)455-2400

WILSONVILLE — D6 / *B2*
Key's B&B, 5025 SW Homesteader Rd, 97070 .... (503)638-3722

WOLF CREEK — N4 / *E2*
Wolf Creek Tavern, PO Box 97, 97497 .... (503)866-2474

YACHATS — H3 / *C1*
Adobe, 97498 .... (503)547-3141
Oregon House Inn, 94288 Hwy 101, 97498 .... (503)547-3329

Sea Quest, 95354 Hwy 101, 97498 ....(503)547-3782
Ziggurat, 95330 Hwy 101, 97498 ....(503)547-3925

YAMHILL E5 / *B2*
Flying M Ranch, 23029 NW Flying M Rd, 97148 ....(503)662-3222

PENNSYLVANIA

ADAMSTOWN ER10 / *F10*
The Adamstown Inn B&B, 62 W Main St, PO Box 938, 19501(215)484-0800

ALLENTOWN EP13 / *E11*
Coachaus, 107-111 N 8th St, 18102 ....(215)821-4854

ANNVILLE ER7 / *F10*
Swatara Creek Inn, Box 692, 17003 ....(717)865-3259

ATGLEN EU10 / *G10*
Umble Rest, RD 1 Box 79, 19310 ....(215)593-2274

AVONDALE EU11 / *G10*
Springs Valley Inn, RD 1 Box 532, 19311 ....(215)268-2597

BEACH LAKE EH14 / *B11*
Beach Lake Hotel, PO Box 144, 18405 ....(717)729-8239
East Shore House B&B, Box 12, 18405 ....(717)729-8523

BEAR CREEK EK11 / *C10*
Bischwind, Box 7, One Coach Rd, 18602 ....(717)472-3820

BEDFORD WT12 / *G5*
Bedford House, 203 W Pitt St, 15522 ....(814)623-7171
Jean Bonnet Tavern, Rt 2 Box 188, 15522 ....(814)623-2250

BENDERSVILLE ET3 / *G7*
Historic Paul Sourss Plantation House, PO Box 238, 17306 ....(717)677-6688

BENTON EK8 / *C9*
Grandmaws, Rt 3 Box 239, 17814 ....(717)925-2630

BERLIN WU10 / *G4*
Ogline's B&B, 1001 E Main St, 15530 ....(814)267-3696

BETHLEHEM EO13 / *E11*
The Bethlehem Inn, 476 N New St, 18018 ....(215)867-4985
Salisbury House, 910 East Emmaus Ave, 18103 ....(215)791-4225
Wydnor Hall, Old Bethlehem Pike, RD3, 18015 ....(215)867-6851

BIRD-IN-HAND ET9 / *F9*
Greystone Manor B&B, 2658 Old Philadelphia Pike, 17505 ....(717)393-4233

BLOOMSBURG EM7 / *D9*
Magee's Main Street Inn, 20 W Main St, 17815 ....(717)784-3200
The Inn at Turkey Hill, 991 Central Rd, 17815 ....(717)387-1500

BOILING SPRINGS ES4 / *F7*
The Garmanhaus, 217 Front St, 17007 ....(717)258-3980

BRACKNEY EF10 / *A10*
Indian Mountain Inn B&B, Tripp Lake Rd, RD 1, Box 68, 18812 ....(717)663-2645
Linger Longer at Quaker Lake, RD 1, Box 44, 18812 ....(717)663-2844

BRADFORD WF12 / *A5*
Fisher Homestead B&B, 253 E Main St, 16701 ....(814)368-5759

BUCK HILL FALLS EK14 / *C11*
Buck Hill Inn, 18232 ....(800)233-8113

BUFFALO MILLS WU12 / *G5*
Buffalo Lodge, RD 1, Box 277, 15534 ....(814)623-2207

CANADENSIS EK14 / *C11*
Brookview Manor B&B Inn, RR #1 Box 365, 18325 ....(717)595-2451
Dreamy Acres, PO Box 7, Seese Hill Rd & Rt 44, 18325 ....(717)595-7115
Laurel Grove, Pocono Vacationland, 18325 ....(717)595-7262
Nearbrook, 18325 ....(717)595-3152
Overlook Inn, Dutch Hill Rd, 18325 ....(717)595-7519
Pine Knob, Rt 447, 18325 ....(717)595-2532
Pump House Inn, Sky Top Rd, 18325 ....(717)595-7501

CEDAR RUN EI2 / *C7*
Cedar Run Inn, Rt 414, 17727 ....(717)353-6241

CHALFONT ER14 / *F11*
Simon Butler Mill House B&B, 116 E Butler Ave, 18914 ....(215)822-3582

CHRISTIANA EU10 / *G10*
Winding Glen Farm, PO Box 160, 17509 ....(215)593-5535

CHURCHTOWN ES10 / *F10*
Churchtown Inn, 2100 Main St, 17555 ....(215)445-7794
The Foreman House B&B, 2129 Main St, Rt 23, 17555 ....(215)445-6713
The Inn at Twin Linden, 2092 Main St, 17555 ....(215)445-7619

CLARK WK2 / *C1*
Tara, Box 475, 3665 Valley View, 16113 ....(412)962-3535

COLUMBIA ET7 / *F9*
The Columbian, 360 Chestnut St, 17512 ....(717)684-5869

COOKSBURG WJ9 / *C4*
Clarion River Lodge, River Rd, PO Box 150, 16217 ....(800)648-6743
Gateway Lodge & Cabins, Rt 36 PO Box 125, 16217 ....(814)744-8017

COWANSVILLE WN6 / *D3*
Garrott's B&B, RD 1 Box 73, 16218 ....(412)545-2432

CRANBERRY TOWNSHIP WO4 / *E2*
Cranberry B&B, Box 1009, 16033 ....(412)776-1198

CRESCO EL14 / *C11*
La Anna Guest House, RD 2 Box 1051, 18326 ....(717)676-4225

DANVILLE EM6 / *D8*
The Pine Barn Inn, 1 Pine Barn Place, 17821 ....(717)275-2071

DELAWARE WATER GAP EM14 / *D11*
Mountain House, Mountain Rd, 18327 ....(717)424-2254

DOYLESTOWN ER15 / *F11*
Doylestown Inn, 18 W State St, 18901 ....(215)345-6610
The Inn at Fordhook Farm, 105 New Britain Rd, 18901 ....(215)345-1766
Pear & Partridge Inn, Dept NT, Old Easton Rd, 18901 ....(215)345-7800
Pine Tree Farm, 2155 Lower State Raod, 18901 ....(215)348-0632

DUSHORE EI7 / *C9*
Heritage Guest House B&B, RR 2078, 18614 ....(717)928-7354

EAGLES MERE EJ6 / *C9*
Eagles Mere Inn, PO Box 356, 17731 ....(717)525-3273
Shady Lane Lodge, Allegheny Ave, 17731 ....(717)525-3394

EAST BERLIN EU5 / *G8*
The Bechtel Mansion Inn, 400 W King St, 17316 ....(717)259-7760

EAST STROUDSBURG EM14 / *D11*
The Inn at Meadowbrook, RD 7 Box 7651, 18301 ....(717)629-0296

EBENSBURG WQ11 / *E5*
Noon-Collins Inn, 114 E High St, 15931 ....(814)472-4311

ELIZABETHVILLE EP5 / *F9*
The Inn at Elizabethville, 30 W Main St, 17023 ....(717)362-3476

ELM ES8 / *F9*
Elm Country Inn, Box 37, 17521 ....(717)664-3623

ELVERSON ES11 / *F10*
Rocky Side Farm, RD 1, 19520 ....(215)286-5362

EMIGSVILLE ET6 / *G8*
Emig Mansion, Box 486, 3342 N George St, 17318 ....(717)764-2226

EPHRATA ES9 / *F9*
Covered Bridge Inn, 990 Rettew Mill Rd, 17522 ....(717)733-1592
Gerhart House B&B, 287 Duke St, 17522 ....(717)733-0263
Guesthouse and 1777 House at Doneckers, 318-324 N State St, 17522 ....(717)733-8696
Hackman's Country Inn, 140 Hackman Rd, 17522 ....(717)733-3498
Smithton Inn, 900 W Main St, 17522 ....(717)733-6094

ERIE WE4 / *A2*
Royal Acre Retreat, 5131 Lancaster Rd, 16506 ....(814)838-7928

ERWINNA EP15 / *E12*
Evermay-on-the-Delaware, River Rd, 18920 ....(215)294-9100
Golden Pheasant Inn, River Rd, 18920 ....(215)294-9595
Isaac Stover House, River Rd, PO Box 68, 18920 ....(215)294-8044

EVERETT WT13 / *G5*
Newry Manor, Rt 1 Box 475, 15537 ....(814)623-1250

EXTON ET12 / *F10*
Duling Kurtz House, 146 S Whitford Rd, 19341 ....(215)524-1830

FAIRFIELD EV2 / *G7*
Christiansen Old Barn B&B, 1 Main Tr, 17320 ....(717)642-5711

FAYETTEVILLE EU1 / *G7*
Herb Cottage Inn, Lincoln Hwy E, Rt 30, 17222 ....(717)352-7733

FOGELSVILLE EP12 / *E10*
Glasbern, RD 1 Box 250, 18051-9743 ....(215)285-4723

FRANKLIN WJ5 / *C2*
Quo Vadis House Franklin B&B, 1501 Liberty St, 16232 ....(814)432-4208

GARDENVILLE EQ15 / *F11*
Maplewood Farm B&B, 5090 Durnham Rd, 18926 ....(215)766-0477

GARDNERS ET3 / *G7*
Goose Chase, 200 Blueberry Rd, 17324 ....(717)528-8877

GETTYSBURG EU3 / *G7*
The Brafferton Inn, 44 York St, 17325 ....(717)337-3423
Brierfield B&B, 264 Baltimore St, 17325 ....(717)334-8725
Dobbin House Tavern, 89 Steinwehr Ave, 17325 ....(717)334-2100
The Doubleday Inn, 104 Doubleday Ave, 17325 ....(717)334-9119
Keystone Inn B&B, 231 Hanover St, 17325 ....(717)337-3888
The Old Appleford Inn, 218 Carlisle St, 17325 ....(717)337-1711
Swinn's Lodging, 31 E Lincoln Ave, 17325 ....(717)334-5255

GLEN MILLS EV13 / *G11*
Sweetwater Farm, PO Box 86, Sweetwater Rd, 19342 ....(215)459-4711

GLEN MOORE ES11 / *F10*
Conestoga Horse B&B, Hollow Rd, PO Box 256, 19343 ....(215)458-8535

GORDONVILLE — ET10 / G9
The Osceola Mill House, 313 Osceola Mill Rd, 17529 ... (717)768-3758

HALLSTEAD — EF11 / A10
Log Cabin B&B, Rt 11 Box 393, 18822 ... (717)879-4167

HANOVER — EV5 / G8
Beechmont Inn, 315 Broadway, 17331 ... (717)632-3013
Country View Acres, 676 Beaver Creek Road, 17331 ... (717)637-8992

HAWLEY — EI14 / C11
Academy Street B&B, 528 Academy St, 18428 ... (717)226-3430
Settlers Inn, 4 Main Ave, 18428 ... (717)226-2993

HERSHEY — ER6 / F8
Gibson's B&B, 141 W Caracas Ave, 17033 ... (717)534-1035
Horetsky's Tourist Home, 217 Cocoa Ave, 17033 ... (800)533-5783
Pinehurst Inn B&B, 50 Northeast Dr, 17033 ... (717)533-2603

HICKORY — WR2 / F1
Shady Elms Farm B&B, Rt 1 Box 188, 15340 ... (412)356-7755

HOLICONG — EQ16 / F12
Ash Mill Farm, PO Box 202, 18928 ... (215)794-5373

HOLLIDAYSBURG — WQ13 / E5
Hoenstine's B&B, 418 Montgomery St, 16648 ... (814)695-0632

HONESDALE — EI14 / B11
Hotel Wayne, 1202 Main St, 18431 ... (717)253-3290
Olver's B&B, 1415 N Main St, 18431 ... (717)253-4533
Woodside Mountain House, PO Box 1095, 18431 ... (717)253-5712

HUNTINGDON — WQ15 / E6
Yoder's B&B, RD 1, Box 312, 16652 ... (814)643-3221

JAMESTOWN — WI1 / C1
Das Tannen-Lied, Rt 1, 16134 ... (412)932-5029

JERSEY SHORE — EL3 / C7
Ye Olde Library B&B, 310 S Main St, 17740 ... (717)398-1571

JIM THORPE — EN11 / D10
Harry Packer Mansion, Packer Hill, 18229 ... (717)325-8566

KANE — WH11 / B4
Kane Manor Country Inn, 230 Clay St, 16735 ... (814)837-6522

KENNETT SQUARE — EU12 / G10
Buttonwood Farm, 231 Pemberton Rd, 19348 ... (215)444-0278
Longwood Inn, 815 E Baltimore Pike, 19348 ... (215)444-3515
Meadow Spring Farm, 201 E St Rd, 19348 ... (215)444-3903
Scarlett House, 503 W State St, 19348 ... (215)444-9592

KINTNERSVILLE — EP14 / E11
Bucksville House, Rt 2 Box 146, 18930 ... (215)847-8948

KINZER — ET10 / G10
Bethania Farm, PO Box 228, 17535 ... (717)442-4939
Groff Tourist Farm, RD 1 Box 36, 17353 ... (717)442-8223

LAMPETER — ET9 / G9
Bed & Breakfast - The Manor, PO Box 416, 830 Village Rd, 17537 ... (717)464-9564
Walkabout Inn B&B, 837 Village Rd, 17537 ... (717)464-0707

LANCASTER — ET8 / F9
Buena Kotte B&B, 2020 Marietta Ave, 17603 ... (717)295-2597
Hollinger House, 2336 Hollinger Rd, 17602 ... (717)464-3050
The King's Cottage, 1049 E King St, 17602 ... (717)397-1017
Landyshade Farms, 1801 Colebrook Rd, 17601 ... (717)898-7689
Lincoln Haus Inn B&B, 1687 Lincoln Hwy E, 17602 ... (717)392-9412
New Life Homestead B&B, 1400 E King St, 17602 ... (717)396-8928
O'Flaherty & Dingeldein House B&B, 1105 E King St, 17602 ... (717)293-1723
Patchwork Inn, 2319 Old Philadelphia Pike, 17602 ... (717)293-9078
Witmer's Tavern - Historic 1725 Inn, 2014 Old Philadelphia Pike, 17602 ... (717)299-5305

LANDENBERG — EV11 / G10
Cornerstone B&B Inn, RD 1 Box 155, 19350 ... (215)274-2143

LAUGHLINTOWN — WS9 / F4
Ligonier Country Inn, PO Box 46 Rt 30 E, 15655 ... (412)238-3651

LEESPORT — EQ10 / E10
The Loom Room, RD 1 PO Box 1420, 19533 ... (215)926-3217

LEWISBURG — EM5 / D8
The Inn on Fiddler's Track, PO Box 573A, 17837 ... (717)523-7197
Pineapple Inn, 439 Market St, 17837 ... (717)524-6200

LIGONIER — WR8 / F3
Grant House B&B, 244 W Church St, 15658 ... (412)238-5135

LITITZ — ES8 / F9
The Alden House, 62 E Main St, 17543 ... (717)627-3363
General Sutter Inn, 14 E Main St, 17543 ... (717)626-2115
Swiss Woods B&B, 500 Blantz Rd, 17543 ... (717)627-3358

LOGANVILLE — EU6 / G8
Country Spun Farm B&B, Box 117, 17342 ... (717)428-1162

LUMBERVILLE — EQ15 / E12
1740 House, River Rd, 18933 ... (215)297-5661
Black Bass Hotel, River Rd, 18933 ... (215)297-5770

MALVERN — ET13 / F11
The Great Valley House, 110 Swedesford Rd 3, 19355 ... (215)644-6759
Historic General Warren Inne, Old Lancaster Hwy, 19355 ... (215)296-3637

MANHEIM — ES8 / F9
Herr Farmhouse Inn, 2256 Huber Dr, 17545 ... (717)653-9852
Manheim Manor, 140 S Charlotte St, 17545 ... (717)664-4168
Penn's Valley Farm & Inn, 6182 Metzler Rd, 17545 ... (717)898-7386

MAYTOWN — ET7 / F9
Three Center Square Inn, PO Box 428, 17550 ... (717)653-4338

McKEESPORT — WR5 / F2
Guest Home, 1040 Lincoln Way, 15132 ... (412)751-7143

MCKNIGHTSTOWN — EU2 / G7
New Salem House, 275 Old Rt 30, PO Box 24, 17343 ... (717)337-3520

MERCER — WK3 / C2
The Magoffin Inn, 129 S Pitt St, 16137 ... (412)662-4611
Stranahan House B&B, 117 E Market St, 16137 ... (412)662-4516

MERCERSBURG — WU16 / G6
The Mercersburg Inn, 405 S Main St, 17236 ... (717)328-5231

MERTZTOWN — EP12 / E10
Blair Creek Inn & Lodging, 19539 ... (215)682-6700
Longswamp B&B, RD 2 PO Box 26, 19539 ... (215)682-6197

MILFORD — EJ16 / C12
Black Walnut Inn, 509 Fire Tower Rd, 18337 ... (717)296-6322
Cliff Park Inn, Cliff Park Rd, 18337 ... (717)296-6493
The Vines, 107 E Ann St, 18337 ... (717)296-6775

MILLERSVILLE — ET8 / G9
Walnut Hill B&B, Rt 1 Box 113, 17551 ... (717)872-2283

MONTOURSVILLE — EK5 / C8
The Carriage House at Stonegate, RD 1 Box 11A, 17754 ... (717)433-4340

MONTROSE — EG10 / B10
The Montrose House, 26 S Main St, 18801 ... (717)278-1124

MOUNT BETHEL — EM15 / D11
Elvern Country Lodge, Box 177, 18343 ... (215)588-7922

MOUNT GRETNA — ER7 / F9
Mt Gretna Inn, Kaufman & Pine, 17064 ... (717)964-3234

MOUNT JOY — ES7 / F9
Brenneman Farm B&B, Rt 1, Box 310, 17552 ... (717)653-4213
Cameron Estate Inn, RD 1 Box 305, 17552 ... (717)653-1773
Cedar Hill Farm, 305 Longenecker Rd, 17552 ... (717)653-4655
Green Acres Farm, 1382 Pinkerton Rd, 17552 ... (717)653-4028
Hillside Farm B&B, RD #3 Box 627, 17552 ... (717)653-6697
Nolt Farm Guest Home, S Jacob St Farm, 17552 ... (717)653-4192
Rocky Acre Farm, RD 3, 17552 ... (717)653-4449

MOUNT POCONO — EL13 / D11
Country Road B&B, HCR 1, Box 9A, 18344 ... (813)839-9234
Farmhouse B&B, HCR 1, Box 6B, 18344 ... (717)839-0796

MOUNTVILLE — ET8 / F9
Mountville Antique B&B, 407 E Main St, Rt 462, 17554 ... (717)285-5956

MUNCY — EK5 / C8
The Bodine House B&B, 307 S Main St, 17756 ... (717)546-8949

MYERSTOWN — EQ8 / F9
Tulpehocken Manor Inn & Plantation, 650 W Lincoln Ave, 17067 ... (717)866-4926

NEW ALBANY — EI7 / B9
Waltman's B&B, Rt 1 Box 87, 18833 ... (717)363-2295

NEW HOPE — EQ16 / F12
Backstreet Inn of New Hope, 144 Old York Rd, 18939 ... (215)862-9571
Centre Bridge Inn, Rts 32 & 263, 18938 ... (215)862-9139
Hacienda Inn, 36 W Mechanics St, 18938 ... (215)862-2078
Hotel Du Village, N River Rd, 18938 ... (215)862-9911
Logan Inn, Main & Ferry Sts, 18938 ... (215)862-2300
The Inn at Phillips Mill, N River Rd, 18938 ... (215)862-2984
Pineapple Hill, 1324 River Rd, 18938 ... (215)862-9608
The Wedgwood Inn, 111 W Bridge, 18938 ... (215)862-2570
Whitehall Inn, Pineville Rd, RD 2 Box 250, 18938 ... (215)598-7945

NEW WILMINGTON — WL2 / D1
Tavern, Box 153 On the Square, 16142 ... (412)946-2020

NORTH EAST — WD5 / A2
Brown's Village Inn, 51 E Main St, 16428 ... (814)725-5522

NORTH WALES — ER14 / F11
Joseph Ambler Inn, 1005 Horsham Rd, 19454 ... (215)362-7500

ORBISONIA — WR16 / F6
Salvino's Guest House, PO Box 116, 17243 ... (814)447-5616

ORRTANNA EU2 / *G7*
Hickory Bridge Farm, 96 Hickory Bridge Rd, 17353 ....(717)642-5261

PARADISE ET9 / *F9*
Maple Lane Farm, 505 Paradise Ln, 17562 ....(717)687-7479
Neffdale Farm, 604 Strasburg Rd, 17562 ....(717)687-7837
Pequea Creekside Inn B&B, 44 Leacock Rd, PO Box 435, 17562 ....(717)687-0333
Rayba Acres Farm, 183 Black Horse Rd, 17562 ....(717)687-6729

PEACH BOTTOM EV9 / *G9*
Lofty Acres, RD 1 Box 331, 17563 ....(717)548-3052
Pleasant Grove Farm, Rt 1 Box 132, 17563 ....(717)548-3100

PHILADELPHIA ET15 / *G11*
B&B of Valley Forge & Philadelphia, PO Box 562, 19481 ....(215)783-7838
Germantown B&B, 5925 Wayne Ave, 19144 ....(215)848-1375
The Independence Park Inn, 235 Chestnut St, 19106 ....(215)922-4443
La Reserve, 1804 Pine St, 19103 ....(215)735-0582
The Independence Park Inn, 235 Chestnut St, 19106 ....(215)922-4443
Thomas Bond House, 129 S 2nd St, 19106 ....(215)923-8523

PINE GROVE MILLS WO16 / *E6*
Cedar Hill at Spruce Creek, Box 126, 16868 ....(814)238-1484
Forge B&B Inn, RD#1, Box 438, 17963 ....(717)345-8349

PITTSBURGH WQ4 / *E2*
Oakwood, 235 Johnston Rd, 15241 ....(412)835-9565
The Priory, 614 Pressley St, 15212 ....(412)231-3338

PLUMSTEADVILLE EQ15 / *F12*
Plumsteadville Inn, Box 40, 18949 ....(215)766-7500

POINT PLEASANT EQ15 / *E12*
Tattersall Inn, PO Box 569, 18950 ....(215)297-8233

POTTSTOWN ER12 / *F10*
Coventry Forge Inn, RD 2, 19464 ....(215)469-6222
Fairway Farm B&B, Vaughn Rd, 19464 ....(215)326-1315

QUAKERTOWN EQ14 / *E11*
Sign of the Sorrel Horse, Box 243, Old Bethlehem Rd, 18951 ....(215)536-4651

QUARRYVILLE EU9 / *G9*
Runnymede Farm Guest House B&B, 1030 Robert Fulton Hwy, 17566 ....(717)786-3625

READING ER10 / *F10*
The Inn at Centre Park, 730 Centre Ave, 19601 ....(215)374-8557
Hunter House, 118 S Fifth St, 19602 ....(215)374-6608

RED LION EU7 / *G8*
Red Lion B&B, 101 S Franklin St, 17356 ....(717)244-4739

RIEGELSVILLE EP14 / *E11*
Riegelsville Hotel, 10-12 Delaware Rd, 18077 ....(215)749 2469

RONKS ET9 / *G9*
Candlelite Inn B&B, 2574 Lincoln Hwy E, 17572 ....(717)299-6005

SAYRE EF7 / *A9*
Paetzell Haus B&B, 211 W Lockhart St, 18840 ....(717)888-4748

SCENERY HILL WS4 / *F2*
Century Inn, Rt 40, 15360 ....(412)945-6600

SCHELLSBURG WT12 / *F5*
Millstone Inn, PO Box 279, 15559 ....(814)733-4864

SCOTTDALE WS6 / *F3*
Pine Wood Acres B&B, Rt 1 Box 634, 15683-9567 ....(412)887-5404

SHARTLESVILLE EP9 / *E9*
Haag's Hotel, Main St, 19554 ....(215)488-6692

SHAWNEE-ON-DELAWARE EM15 / *D11*
Eagle Rock Lodge, River Rd, Box 265, 18354 ....(717)421-2139

SHIPPENSBURG ET1 / *F7*
Field & Pine B&B, 2155 Ritner Hwy, 17257 ....(717)776-7179

SIEGEL WK9 / *C4*
Discoveries B&B, RD #1, Box 42, 15680 ....(814)752-2632

SLIPPERY ROCK WL4 / *D2*
Applebutter Inn, 152 Applewood Ln, 16057 ....(412)794-1844

SMETHPORT WG13 / *B5*
Blackberry Inn B&B, 820 West Main St, 16749 ....(814)887-7777

SMOKETOWN ET9 / *F9*
Homestead Lodging, 17576 ....(717)393-6927
Smoketown Village Tourist Home, 2495 Old Phila. Pike, 17576 ....(717)393-5975

SOLEBURY EQ15 / *F12*
Holly Hedge Estate, PO Box 213, 18963 ....(215)862-3136
Rambouillet at Hollyhedge Estate, Box 213, 6987 Upper York Rd, 18963 ....(215)862-3136

SOUTH STERLING EK13 / *C11*
Sterling Inn, Rt 191, 18460 ....(717)676-3311
The French Manor Inn, PO Box 39, 18460 ....(717)676-3244

STARLIGHT EF13 / *A11*
The Inn at Starlight Lake, PO Box 27, 18461 ....(717)798-2519

STRASBURG ET9 / *G9*
Limestone Inn B&B, 33 E Main St, 17579 ....(717)687-8392
Siloan, Village Rd Box 82, 17579 ....(717)687-6231
Strasburg Village Inn, 1 W Main St, 17579 ....(717)687-0900
The Decoy, 958 Eisenberger Rd, 17579 ....(717)687-8585

SUMNEYTOWN ER13 / *F11*
Kaufman House, Box 183, Rt 63, 18084 ....(215)234-4181

THOMPSON EG12 / *B11*
Jefferson Inn, Rt 2 Box 36, 18465 ....(717)727-2625

THORNDALE ET11 / *G10*
Pheasant Hollow Farm B&B, PO Box 356, S Bailey Rd, 19372 ....(215)384-4694

TOWANDA EG7 / *B9*
Victorian Guest House, 118 York Ave, 18848 ....(717)265-6972

TYLER HILL EH14 / *B11*
Tyler Hill B&B, Rt 371, PO Box 62, 18469 ....(717)224-6418

UPPER BLACK EDDY EP15 / *E11*
Bridgeton House, PO Box 167, 18972 ....(215)982-5856
Tara, 1 Bridgeton Hill, 18972 ....(215)982-5457

WASHINGTON CROSSING ER16 / *F12*
Woodhill Farms Inn, 150 Glenwood Dr, 18977 ....(215)493-1974

WATERVILLE EK2 / *C7*
The Point House, Church St, 17776 ....(717)299-5305

WELLSBORO EH3 / *B7*
Kaltenbach's B&B, RR #6 Box 106A, 16901 ....(717)724-4954

WEST CHESTER ET12 / *G11*
The Barn, 1131 Grove Rd, 19380 ....(215)436-4544
Crooked Windsor, 409 S Church St, 19382 ....(215)692-4896
Highland Manor B&B, 855 Hillsdale Rd, 19382 ....(215)686-6251
Quarry House, RD 5, Street Rd, 19382 ....(215)793-1725

WILLIAMSPORT EK4 / *C8*
Reighard House, 1323 E Third St, 17701 ....(717)326-3593

WILLOW STREET ET8 / *G9*
The Apple Bin Inn, 2835 Willow St Pike, 17584 ....(717)464-5881
Green Gables B&B, 2532 Willow St Pike, 17584 ....(717)464-5546

WOODWARD EN2 / *D7*
Woodward Inn, Box 177, 16882 ....(814)349 8118

WRIGHTSTOWN ER16 / *F12*
Aberdare B&B, 201 Pineville Rd, 18940 ....(215)598-3896
Hollileif, 677 Durham Road (Rt 413), 18940 ....(215)598-3100

WRIGHTSVILLE ET7 / *F9*
Roundtop B&B, RD #2, Box 258, 17368 ....(717)252-3169

YORK EU6 / *G8*
The Inn at Mundis Mill, Rt 1 Box 15, Mundis Race Rd, 17402 ....(717)755-2002
The Smyser-Bair House, 30 S Beaver St, 17401 ....(717)854-3411

RHODE ISLAND

BLOCK ISLAND L22 / *G6*
1661 Inn, PO Box 1, 02807 ....(401)466-2421
Atlantic Inn, Box 188, 02807 ....(401)466-2005
The Barrington Inn, Beach & Queen Ave, PO Box 397Y, 02807 ....(401)466-5510
Bellevue, High St, 02807 ....(401)466-2389
Blue Dory Inn, Box 488, Dodge St, 02807 ....(401)466-5891
Driftwind Guests, High St, 02807 ....(401)466-5548
Gables Inn, PO Box 516, 02807 ....(401)466-2213
The Gothic Inn, Dodge St, PO Box 537, 02807 ....(401)466-2918
Guest House, PO Box 24, Center Rd, 02807 ....(401)466-2676
Hotel Manisses, PO Box 1, 02807 ....(401)466-2836
Island Manor Resort, Chapel St, 02807 ....(401)466-5567
Mill Pond Cottages, Old Town Rd, 02807 ....(401)466-2423
New Shoreham House, PO Box 356, Water St, 02807 ....(401)466-2651
The Inn at Old Harbour, Water St, PO Box 994, 02807 ....(401)466-2212
Old Town Inn, Old Town Rd, Box 35, 02807 ....(401)466-5958
Rose Farm Inn, Roselyn Rd, 02807 ....(401)466-2021
Sea Breeze Inn, Spring St, Box 141, 02807 ....(401)466-2275
Seacrest Inn, 207 High St, 02807 ....(401)466-2882
Sheffield House, High St, Box C-2, 02807 ....(401)466-2494
The White House, Box 447, 02807 ....(401)466-2653
Willow Grove, Corn Neck Rd PO Box 156, 02807 ....(401)466-2896

BRISTOL F24 / *E7*
The Joseph Reynolds House, 956 Hope St, PO Box 5, 02809 ....(401)254-0230

CHARLESTOWN J21 / *F6*
General Stanton Inn, Rt 1 Box 222, 02813 ....(401)364-8888

Inn the Meadow, 1045 Shannock Rd, 02813 ....(401)789-1473

EAST PROVIDENCE D23 / *E7*
The Last Resort, 330 Sea View Ave, 02915 ....(401)433-1577

GREEN HILL J21 / *F6*
Fairfield-by-the-Sea, 527 Green Hill Beach Rd, 02879 ....(401)789-4717

JAMESTOWN H23 / *F7*
Calico Cat Guest House, 14 Union St, 02835 ....(401)423-2641

LITTLE COMPTON H25 / *F7*
Ballyvoreen, Stone Church Rd, 02837 ....(401)635-4396

MIDDLETOWN H24 / *F7*
Finnegan's Inn, 120 Miantonomi Ave, 02840 ....(401)847-0902
Lindsey's Guest House, 6 James St, 02840 ....(401)846-9386
Peckham's Guest Home, 272 Paradise Ave, 02840 ....(401)846-2382
Stone Towers, 152 Tuckerman Ave, 02840 ....(401)846-3227
Whimsey Cottage, 42 Briarwood Ave, 02840 ....(401)841-5824

MISQUAMICUT J19 / *G6*
Andrea Hotel, 89 Atlantic Ave, 02891 ....(401)348-8788
Atlantic Inn, Crandall Ave, 02891 ....(401)596-7737

MISQUAMICUT BEACH J19 / *G6*
Ocean View, Atlantic Ave, 02891 ....(401)596-7170

NARRAGANSETT I23 / *F6*
Chestnut House, 11 Chestnut St, 02882 ....(401)789-5335
Four Gables, 12 S Pier Rd, 02882 ....(401)789-6948
Ilverthorpe Cottage, 41 Robinson St, 02882 ....(401)789-2392
Kenyon Farms, PO Box 648, 02882 ....(401)783-7123
Louis Sherry Cottage, 59 Gibson Ave, 02882 ....(401)783-8626
Mon Reve, 41 Gibson Ave, 02882 ....(401)783-2846
Murphy's B&B, 43 S Pier Rd, 02882 ....(401)789-1824
Narragansett Pier Inn, 7 Prospect Ave, 02882 ....(401)783-8090
Phoenix House, 29 Gibson Ave, 02882 ....(401)783-2846
Sea Gull Guest House, 50 Narragansett Ave, 02882 ....(401)783-4636
Southwest Wind Acres, 8 Lindsley Rd, 02882 ....(401)783-5860
Starr Cottage, 68 Caswell St, 02882 ....(401)783-2411
Stone Lea, 40 Newton Ave, 02882 ....(401)783-9546
Summer House Inn, 87 Narragansett Ave, 02882 ....(401)783-0123
The House Of Snee, 191 Ocean Rd, 02882 ....(401)783-9494

NEWPORT H24 / *F7*
Admiral Benbow Inn, 93 Pelham St, 02840 ....(401)846-4256
Admiral Farragut Inn, 31 Clarke St, 02840 ....(401)846-4256
The Admiral Fitzroy, 398 Thames St, 02840 ....(401)846-4256
Beachstone, 14 Kay Blvd, 02840 ....(401)849-3839
Bellevue House, 14 Catherine St, 02840 ....(401)847-1355
Blue Stone, 33 Russell Ave, 02840 ....(401)846-5408
The Brinley Victorian Inn, 23 Brinley St, 02840 ....(401)849-7645
The Inn at Castle Hill, Ocean Dr, 02840 ....(401)849-3800
Cliff Walk Manor, 82 Memorial Blvd, 02840 ....(401)847-1300
Cliffside Inn, 2 Seaview Ave, 02840 ....(401)847-1811
Covell Guest House, 43 Farewell St, 02840 ....(401)847-8872
Easton's Inn On The Beach, 30 Wave Ave, 02840 ....(401)846-0310
Ellery Park House, 44 Farewell St, 02840 ....(401)847-6320
The Elliott Boss House, 20 Second St, 02840 ....(401)849-9425
Flower Garden Guests, 1 Kyle Terrace, 02840 ....(401)846-3119
Francis Malbone House, 392 Thames St, 02840 ....(401)846-0392
Gingerbread B&B, 16 Park St, 02840-2104 ....(401)846-3037
Hammett House Inn, 505 Thames St, 02840 ....(401)848-0593
Harborside Inn, Christie's Landing, 02840 ....(401)846-6600
Inn of Jonathan Bowen, 29 Pelham St, 02840 ....(401)846-3324
Inntowne, 6 Mary St, 02840 ....(401)846-9200
Ivy Lodge, 12 Clay St, 02840 ....(401)849-6865
Jail House Inn, 13 Marlborough St, 02840 ....(401)847-4638
The John Banister House, 56 Pelham St at Spring, 02840 ....(401)846-0050
La Forge Cottage, 96 Pelham St, 02840 ....(401)847-4400
Ma Gallagher's, 348 Thames St, 02840 ....(401)849-3975
The Melville House, 39 Clarke St, 02840 ....(401)847-0640
Merritt House Guest, 57 2nd St, 02840 ....(401)847-4289
Mill Street Inn, 75 Mill St, 02840 ....(401)849-9500
Moulton-Weaver House, 4 Training Station Rd, 02840 ....(401)847-0133
Oceancliff, Ocean Dr, 02840 ....(401)847-7777
The Old Dennis House, 59 Washington St, 02840 ....(401)846-1324
The Pilgrim House, 123 Spring St, 02846 ....(401)846-0040
Queen Anne Inn, 16 Clarke St, 02840 ....(401)846-5676
Serendipity Cottage, 35 Carey St, 02840 ....(401)847-7080
Spring Street Inn, 353 Spring St, 02840 ....(401)847-4767
Sunnyside Mansion, 25 Old Beach Rd, 02840 ....(401)849-3114
Tripp Southwick B&B, 71 Washington St, 02840 ....(401)849-2862
The Victorian Ladies, 63 Memorial Blvd, 02840 ....(401)849-9960
Wayside, Bellevue Ave, 02840 ....(401)847-0302
William Fludder House, 30 Bellevue Ave, 02840 ....(401)849-4220
Willows of Newport, 8-10 Willow St, 02840 ....(401)846-5486
Yankee Peddler Inn, 113 Touro St, 02840 ....(401)846-1323
Yellow Cottage, 82 Gibbs Ave, 02840 ....(401)847-6568

NORTH KINGSTOWN G22 / *F6*
Meadowland, 765 Old Baptist Rd, 02852 ....(401)294-4168
The John Updike House, 19 Pleasant St, 02852 ....(401)294-4905

PORTSMOUTH G24 / *F7*
Sunset Cabins, 1172 W Main Rd, 02871 ....(401)683-1874

PROVIDENCE D23 / *E6*
Charles Hodges House, 19 Pratt St, PO Box 2591, 02906 ....(401)861-7244
Old Court B&B, 144 Benefit St, 02903 ....(401)751-2002
State House Inn, 43 Jewett St, 02908 ....(401)785-1235

SNUG HARBOR I22 / *F6*
Gooseberry Marina B&B, 500 Gooseberry Rd, 02879 ....(401)789-5431

SOUTH KINGSTON H22 / *F6*
Admiral Dewey Inn, 668 Matunuck Beach Rd, 02879 ....(401)783-2090

WAKEFIELD I22 / *F6*
B&B At Highland Farm, 4145 Tower Hill Rd, 02879 ....(401)783-2408
Blueberry Bush B&B, 128 South Rd, 02879 ....(401)783-0907
Highland Farm, 4145 Tower Hill Rd, Rt 1, 02879 ....(401)783-2408
Larchwood Inn, 176 Main St, 02879 ....(401)783-1709

WARREN E24 / *E7*
Weatherside B&B, 12 Leonard St, 02885 ....(401)245-6665

WARWICK F23 / *E7*
Ope Gat Motel, 840 Quaker Ln, 02886 ....(401)884-4490

WATCH HILL J19 / *G6*
Watch Hill Inn, 50 Bay St, 02891 ....(401)348-8912

WEEKAPAUG J20 / *G6*
J. Livingston's Guest House By The Sea, 39 Weekapaug Rd, 02891 ....(401)322-0249
Weekapaug Inn, 02891 ....(401)322-0301

WESTERLY J19 / *F6*
Grandview B&B, 212 Shore Rd, 02891 ....(401)596-6384
Longvue Guest House, 311 Shore Rt 1, 02891 ....(401)322-0465
Shelter Harbor Inn, 10 Wagner Rd, Rt 1, 02891 ....(401)322-8883
The Shore Inn at Misquamicut, Shore Rd, 02891 ....(401)348-8637
The Inn on the Hill, 29 Summer St, 02891 ....(401)596-3791
Woody Hill Guest House, 330 Woody Hill Rd, 02891 ....(401)322-0452

WICKFORD G22 / *F6*
Sparrow's Nest, 470 Annaquatucket Rd, 02852 ....(401)295-1142

SOUTH CAROLINA

ABBEVILLE D5 / *E3*
Belmont Inn, 106 E Pickens St, 29620 ....(803)459-9625

AIKEN G7 / *F4*
Holley Inn, 235 Richland Ave, 29801 ....(803)648-4265
Pine Knoll Inn, 305 Lancaster St, 29801 ....(803)649-5939
The Brodie Residence, 422 York St, 29801 ....(803)648-1445

ANDERSON C4 / *D2*
Evergreen Inn, 1109 S Main, 29621 ....(803)225-1109

BEAUFORT K10 / *G5*
Bay Street Inn, 601 Bay St, 29902 ....(803)524-7720
Old Point Inn, 212 New St, 29902 ....(803)524-3177
The Rhett House Inn, 1009 Craven St, 29902 ....(803)524-9030
Trescot Inn, 500 Washington, 29902 ....(803)522-8552
Twelve Oaks Inn, PO Box 4126, Rt 2 Box 293, 29902 ....(803)525-1371
TwoSuns Inn, 1705 Bay St, 29902 ....(803)522-1122

BEECH ISLAND G6 / *F3*
The Cedars B&B Inn, Box 117, 1325 Williston Rd, 29841 ....(803)827-0248

BLUFFTON K9 / *H4*
Fripp House Inn, Bridge & Boundary, PO Box 857, 29910 ....(803)757-2139

CAMDEN D10 / *E5*
Aberdeen, 1409 Broad St, 29020 ....(803)432-2524
The Carriage House, 1413 Lyttleton St, 29020 ....(803)432-2430
Greenleaf Inn, 1310 Broad St, 29020 ....(803)425-1806

CHARLESTON I12 / *G6*
1837 B&B & Tea Room, 126 Wentworth St, 29401 ....(803)723-7166
Ann Harper's B&B, 56 Smith St, 29401 ....(803)723-3947
Ansonborough Inn, 21 Hasell St, 29401 ....(803)723-1655
B&B, 36 Meeting St, 29401 ....(803)722-1034
Barksdale House Inn, 27 George St, 29401 ....(803)577-4800
Battery Carriage House, 20 S Battery St, 29401 ....(803)723-9881
Belvedere B&B, 40 Rutledge Ave, 29401 ....(803)722-0973
Cannonboro Inn, 184 Ashley Ave, 29403 ....(803)723-8572
Capers-Motte House, 69 Church St, 29401 ....(803)722-2263
Church Street Inn, 177 Church St, 29401 ....(800)845-7638
Coach House, 39 E Battery Pl, 29401 ....(803)722-8145
Elliott House Inn, 78 Queen St, 29401 ....(803)723-1855
Hayne House, 30 King St, 29401 ....(803)577-2633
Historic Charleston B&B, 43 Legare St, 29401 ....(803)722-6606
Indigo Inn, 1 Maiden Lane, 29401 ....(803)577-5900
Jasmine House Inn, 64 Hasell St, 29401 ....(803)577-5900
John Rutledge House Inn, 116 Broad St, 29401 ....(803)723-7999
Kings Courtyard Inn, 198 King St, 29401 ....(803)723-7000
The Kitchen House, 126 Tradd St, 29401 ....(803)577-6362
Maison Du Pre, 317 E Bay St, 29401 ....(803)723-8691

Meeting Street Inn, 173 Meeting St, 29401 ....(803)723-9881
Middleton Inn, Ashley River Rd, 29407 ....(803)556-0500
Palmer Home, 5 East Battery, 29401 ....(803)723-1574
Planters Inn, 112 N Market St, 29401 ....(803)722-2345
Sweet Grass Inn, 23 Vendue Range, 29401 ....(803)723-9980
Sword Gate Inn, 111 Tradd St, 29401 ....(803)723-8518
The Lodge Alley Inn, 195 E Bay St, 29401 ....(803)722-1611
Two Meeting Street Inn, 2 Meeting St, 29401 ....(803)723-7322
Vendue Inn, 19 Vendue Range, 29401 ....(803)577-7970
Villa de La Fontaine B&B, 138 Wentworth St, 29401 ....(803)577-7709

CHERAW C12 / *D6*
Spears B&B, 501 Kershaw St, 29520 ....(803)537-7733

CLEMSON C3 / *D2*
Nord-Lac, Box 1111, 29633 ....(803)639-2939

COLUMBIA E9 / *E4*
Claussen's Inn, 2003 Green St, 29205 ....(800)622-3382

DALE J10 / *G5*
Coosaw Plantation, 29401 ....(803)846-8225

DILLON D14 / *E6*
Magnolia Inn B&B, 601 E Main St, 29536 ....(803)774-0679

EDGEFIELD F6 / *E3*
The Village Inn, Court House Sq, 29824 ....(803)637-3789

ESTILL J8 / *G4*
The John Lawton House, 159 Third St E, 29918 ....(803)625-3240

FORT MILL A9 / *D4*
Pleasant Valley B&B, 160 East At Blackweider, 29715 ....(803)548-5671

GEORGETOWN G14 / *F6*
1790 House, 630 Highmarket St, 29440 ....(803)546-4821
Five Thirty Prince Street B&B, 530 Prince St, 29440 ....(803)527-1114
Shaw House, 8 Cypress Ct, 29440 ....(803)546-9663
Walton House, 530 Prince St, 29440 ....(803)527-4330

HILTON HEAD ISLAND L10 / *H5*
Halcyon, Harbormaster 604, 29928 ....(803)785-7912

JOHNSTON F6 / *E4*
The Cox House Inn, 602 Lee St, PO Box 486, 29832 ....(803)275-3234

LANCASTER B10 / *D5*
Wade-Beckham House, Rt 7 Box 348, 29720 ....(803)285-1105

LANDRUM A5 / *C3*
Holly Hill, Rt 1, Box 223, 29356 ....(803)457-4010

LEESVILLE E7 / *E4*
The Able House Inn, 244 W Church St, 29070 ....(803)532-2763

LITTLE RIVER E16 / *E7*
Stella's Guest House, PO Box 564, 29566 ....(803)249-1871

LONG CREEK B2 / *D2*
Chauga River House Inn, Box 100, 29658 ....(803)647-9587

MAYESVILLE E11 / *E5*
Windsong, Rt 1 Box 300, 29104 ....(803)453-5004

MCCLELLANVILLE H14 / *F6*
Laurel Hill Plantation, 8913 N Hwy 17, PO Box 190, 29458 ....(803)887-3708

MONCKS CORNER H12 / *F6*
Rice Hope Plantation Inn, Box 355, 29461 ....(803)761-4832

MONTMORENCI G7 / *F4*
Annie's Inn, PO Box 311, 29839 ....(803)649-6836

MT PLEASANT I12 / *G6*
Guilds Inn, 101 Pitt St, 29464 ....(803)881-0510

MULLINS D14 / *E6*
Webster Manor, 115 E James St, 29574 ....(803)464-9632

MYRTLE BEACH F15 / *F7*
Serendipity Inn, 407 71st Ave N, 29577 ....(803)449-5268

PENDLETON C4 / *D2*
Liberty Hall Inn - 1840, 621 S Mechanic St, 29670 ....(803)646-7500

PICKENS B4 / *D2*
The Schell Haus, 4913 Hwy 11, 29671 ....(803)878-0078

SALEM B3 / *D2*
Sunrise Farm B&B, PO Box 164, 29676 ....(803)944-0121

SPARTANBURG B6 / *D3*
Nicholls-Crook Plantation House, PO Box 5812, 29388 ....(803)583-7337

SULLIVAN'S ISLAND I13 / *G6*
The Palmettos, 2014 Middle St, PO Box 706, 29482 ....(803)883-3389

SUMMERVILLE I11 / *G5*
B&B of Summerville, 304 S Hamilton St, 29483 ....(803)871-5275

UNION C7 / *D4*
Forest Hill Manor, Rt 2 Box 725, 29379 ....(803)427-4525
The Inn at Merridun, 100 Merridun Pl, 29379 ....(803)427-7052

WOODRUFF B6 / *D3*
The Nicholls-Crook Plantation House, 120 Plantation Dr, 29388 ....(803)583-7337

YORK B8 / *D4*
Kings Mountain Street Inn, 225 Kings Mountain St, 29745 ....(803)684-7013

SOUTH DAKOTA

BUFFALO B3 / *A1*
Real Ranch Living, HCR 2, Box 112, 57720 ....(605)375-3306

CANOVA F14 / *D7*
B&B at Skoglund Farm, Rt 1 Box 45, 57321 ....(605)247-3445

CANTON H16 / *D8*
Kennedy Rose Inn, 903 N Dakota St, 57013 ....(605)987-2834
Ryger Union House, 903 N Dakota St, 57013 ....(605)987-2834
South Dakota B&B, 903 N Dakota St, 57013 ....(605)987-2834
Welcome Inn, 903 N Dakota St, 57013 ....(605)987-2834

CHAMBERLAIN F11 / *D5*
B&B Riverview Ridge, HC 69, Box 82A, 57325 ....(605)734-6084

CUSTER F3 / *D1*
Hidden Fortune B&B, Box 748, 57730 ....(605)666-4744
State Game Lodge, HCR 83 Box 74, 57730 ....(605)255-4541
Sylvan Lake Resort, PO Box 752, 57730 ....(605)574-2561

DEADWOOD E3 / *C1*
The Adams House, 22 Van Buren, 57732 ....(605)578-3877
Maison on Lincoln B&B, 21 Lincoln, 57732 ....(605)578-3316

HILL CITY F3 / *C1*
Heart of the Hills B&B, 517 Main St, 57745 ....(605)574-2704

HOT SPRINGS G3 / *D1*
Cascade Ranch, PO Box 461, 57747 ....(605)745-3397
Villa Theresa Guest House, 801 Almond, 57747 ....(605)745-4633

LEAD E3 / *C1*
Cheyenne Crossing B&B, HC 37, Box 1220, 57754 ....(605)584-3510

MILESVILLE E6 / *C3*
Fitch Farms, Box 8, 57553 ....(605)544-3227

MITCHELL G13 / *D7*
Riverview B&B, Box 318, Rt 1, 57301 ....(605)996-2332

RAPID CITY F4 / *C2*
Audrie's Cranbury Corner B&B, RR 8 Box 2400, 57702 ....(605)342-7788
Black Forest Inn B&B Lodge, HC 33, Box 3123, 57702 ....(605)574-2000
H-D Lodge, Rt 8, Box 3310, 57702 ....(605)341-7580
Willow Springs Cabin, HCR 39, Box 108, 57702 ....(605)342-3665

SCENIC G5 / *D2*
Circle View Ranch, Box 10, 57780 ....(605)433-5355

WATERTOWN D15 / *B8*
Blue Fountain Inn B&B, 18 Fourth St SE, 57201 ....(605)886-9309

YANKTON I14 / *E7*
The Mulberry Inn, 512 Mulberry St, 57078 ....(605)665-7116

TENNESSEE

ALLARDT B21 / *E8*
Charlo B&B, Box 69, 38504 ....(615)879-8056

BOLIVAR G6 / *G3*
Magnolia Manor, 418 N Main St, 38008 ....(901)658-6700

BRENTWOOD D14 / *F5*
Herbert's B&B, Box 2166, Old Smyrna, 37027 ....(615)373-9300
Sunny Hill Farm B&B, 6112 Murray Ln, 37027 ....(615)373-1514

BROWNSVILLE F5 / *F2*
Abbey Road - A Country Retreat, PO Box 27, 1551 Abbey Rd, 38012 ....(901)772-5680

BUTLER M25 / *E12*
Doe Mountain Inn, Rt 3, Box 3010, 37640 ....(615)727-9447

CHATTANOOGA H19 / *G7*
Alford House, 2501 Lookout Mtn Pkwy, 37419 ....(615)821-7625
The Chattanooga Choo-Choo Inn, 1400 Market St, 37402 ....(615)266-5000
Lookout Mountain Guest House, 4415 Guild Tr, 37409 ....(615)821-8307

CLARKSVILLE B12 / *E5*
Hachland Hill Inn, 1601 Madison St, 37040 ....(615)255-1727

CLIFTON G10 / *G4*
Hidden Hollow Farm-Log Cabin, Beech Creek Rd, Hwy 228, 38424 ....(615)676-5295

COOKEVILLE C19 / *E7*
Scarecrow Country Inn, 1720 E Spring St, 38501 ....(615)526-3431

COWAN H17 / *G7*
Cumberland Place B&B, 411 E Cumberland St, Rt 1, Box 29B, 37318 ....(615)967-0908

DANDRIDGE D26 / *F10*
Mill Dale Farm, 140 Mill Dale Rd, 37725 .... (615)397-3470
Sugar Fork Lodge, 743 Garrett Rd, 37725 .... (615)397-7327

FAYETTEVILLE H15 / *G6*
Old Cowan Plantation B&B, Box 17, Rt 2, 37334 .... (615)433-0225
The Magnolias, Box 806, 37334 .... (615)433-3351

FRANKLIN E14 / *F5*
Windsong Farm, Rt 3, Sweeney Hollow Rd, 37064 .... (615)794-6162

GATLINBURG E26 / *F10*
Buckhorn Inn, Rt 3 Box 393, 37738 .... (615)436-4668
Butcher House B&B, Rt 2 Box 750, 37738 .... (615)436-9457
The Colonel's Lady, Rt 1 Box 273, 37738 .... (615)436-5432
Eight Gables Inn, Rt 4, Box 109, 37738 .... (615)430-3344
Leconte Lodge, PO Box 350, 37738 .... (615)436-4473
Mountainbrook Inn, Rt 3, Box 603, Hwy 321, 37738 .... (800)251-2811
T.G. Sheppard's Moon Mountain Lodge, PO Box 871, 37738 .. (615)436-2131
Windhover, Rt 4, Box 371, 37738 .... (615)436-4068
Wonderland Hotel, Rt 2, 37738 .... (615)436-5490

GORDONSVILLE C17 / *E7*
Pride Hollow B&B, Rt 1, Box 86, 38563 .... (615)683-6396

GREENEVILLE N22 / *E10*
Big Spring Inn, 315 N Main St, 37743 .... (615)638-2917
Hilltop House B&B, Rt 7, Box 180, 37743 .... (615)639-8202
The Inn at Pigeon Creek Farm, Pigeon Creek Rd, PO 816, 37744 .... (615)638-7990

HENDERSONVILLE C15 / *E6*
Monthaven, 1154 W Main, 37075 .... (615)824-6319

JEFFERSON CITY D26 / *E10*
Branner-Hicks House, 1169 N Chucky Pk, 37760 .... (615)475-2302

JOHNSON CITY M23 / *E11*
A Touch of Thyme B&B, 501 E Watauga Ave, 37601 .... (615)926-7570

JONESBOROUGH M23 / *E11*
Aiken-Brow House, 104 3rd Ave S, 37659 .... (615)753-9440
Hawley House B&B, 114 E Woodrow Ave, 37659 .... (615)753-8869
Jonesborough, 100 Woodrow Ave, 37659 .... (615)753-9223
Robertson House B&B, 212 E Main St, 37659 .... (615)753-3039

KNOXVILLE D24 / *F9*
Compton Manor, 3747 Kingston Pike, 37919 .... (615)523-1204
The Graustein Inn, 8300 Nubbin Ridge Rd, 37923 .... (615)690-7007
The Middleton, 800 W Hill Ave, 37902 .... (615)524-8100
Mountain Breeze B&B, 501 Mtn Breeze Ln, 37922 .... (615)966-3917
Three Chimneys, 1302 White Ave, 37916 .... (615)521-4970
Windy Hill B&B, 1031 W Park Dr, 37909 .... (615)690-1488

KODAK E25 / *F9*
Grandma's House, 734 Pollard Rd, 37764 .... (615)933-3512

LAWRENCEBURG H12 / *G5*
The Granville House, 229 Pulaski St, 38464 .... (615)762-3129

LIMESTONE M23 / *E11*
Snapp Inn B&B, Rt 3 Box 102, 37681 .... (615)257-2482

LOOKOUT MOUNTAIN M1 / *G7*
Chanticleer Inn, 1300 Mockingbird Ln, 37350 .... (404)820-2015

LOUDON E23 / *F9*
The Mason Place - B&B Inn, 600 Commerce St, 37774 .... (615)458-3921
River Road Inn, River Road, PO Box 372, 37774 .... (615)458-4861

LYLES E12 / *F5*
Silver Leaf 1815-Country Inn, Rt 1 Box 122, 37098 .... (615)670-3048

LYNCHBURG G16 / *G6*
Lynchburg B&B, PO Box 34, 37532 .... (615)759-7158

MARTIN C7 / *E3*
Wren's Nest Inn, 109 Park St, 38237 .... (901)587-6563

MEMPHIS H2 / *G1*
April House, 1320 Central/Lamar, 38104 .... (901)726-6970
Lowenstein-Long House, 217 N Waldran-1084 Poplar, 38105. (901)527-7174

MONTEAGLE H17 / *G7*
Edgeworth Inn, PO Box 340, 37356 .... (615)924-2669
North Gate Lodge, PO Box 858, 37356 .... (615)924-2799

MOUNTAIN CITY L25 / *E12*
Hidden Acres Farm B&B, Rt 3, Box 39, 37683 .... (615)727-6564
Newcomb Place B&B, Rt 4, Box 39A, 37683 .... (615)727-5392

MURFREESBORO E15 / *F6*
Clardy's Guest House, 435 E Main St, 37130 .... (615)893-6030

NASHVILLE D14 / *E6*
B&B Host Homes of Tennessee, PO Box 110227, 37222-0227 ... (615)331-5244
Host Homes Of Tennessee, Box 110227, 37222-0227 .... (615)331-5244
Miss Anne's B&B, 3033 Windemere Cir, 37214 .... (615)885-1899

NORMANDY G16 / *G7*
Parish Patch Farm & Inn, PO Box 27, 37360 .... (615)857-3441

PICKWICK DAM H9 / *G4*
Homestead House Inn, Box 76, 38365 .... (901)689-5500

PIGEON FORGE E26 / *E10*
Day Dreams Country Inn, 915 Colonial Dr, 37863 .... (615)428-0370
Mountain Home Inn & Cottage, 200 Two View Rd, PO Box 10, 37863 .... (615)453-6465
Town Villas Luxury Suites, 102 Carlstown Dr, 37863 .... (615)428-3333

RED BOILING SPRINGS B17 / *E7*
Donoho Hotel, Box 36, 37150 .... (615)699-3141
Red Boiling Inn, Box 40, 37150 .... (615)699-2180

ROGERSVILLE M21 / *E10*
Hale Springs Inn, 110 W Main St, 37857 .... (615)272-5171

RUGBY C21 / *E8*
Grey Gables B&B, PO Box 5252, Hwy 52, 37733 .... (615)628-5252
Newbury House at Historic Rugby, Hwy 52, PO Box 8, 37733 .... (615)628-2430

SEVIERVILLE E26 / *F10*
Blue Mountain Mist Country Inn, Rt 3 Box 490, 37862 .... (615)428-2335
Cove Country Inn, Rt 6, Box 197, 37862 .... (615)453-3997
The Gallery House, PO Box 5274, 37864 .... (615)428-6937
Hannah's House, Rt 3, Box 674, 37862 .... (615)428-2192
Kero Mountain Resort, Rt 11, Box 380, 37862 .... (615)453-7514
Milk & Honey Country Hideaway, PO Box 4972, 37864 .... (615)428-4858
Von-Bryan Inn, 2402 Hatcher Mountain Rd, 37862 .... (615)453-9832

SEYMOUR E25 / *F9*
Country Inn, Rt 3, Chris Haven Dr, 37865 .... (615)573-7170

SHILOH C26 / *E10*
Leawood-Williams Estate, PO Box 24, 38376 .... (901)689-5106

SOMERVILLE G5 / *GG2*
Magnolia Place, 408 S Main St, 38068 .... (901)465-3906

SWEETWATER F22 / *F8*
Flow Blue Inn, PO Box 495, 37874 .... (615)442-2964
The Fox Trot Inn, 402 May St, 37874 .... (615)337-4236

TOWNSEND F25 / *F9*
Smoky Bear Lodge, 160 Bear Lodge Dr, 37882 .... (615)448-6442

TULLAHOMA G16 / *G6*
Jenny's B&B, 2303 Ovoca Rd, 37388 .... (615)455-9496
The Tullahoma B&B, 308 N Atlantic St, 37388 .... (615)455-8876

VONORE F23 / *F9*
Edna's B&B Home, Rt 1, Box 353A, 37885 .... (615)295-2354

WARTRACE F16 / *G6*
Ledford Mill & Museum, Rt 2 Box 152, 37183 .... (615)298-5674
Walking Horse Hotel & Restaurant, PO Box 266, 37183 .... (615)389-6407

WAVERLY D10 / *F4*
Nolan House Inn, Rt 4 Box 164, 37185 .... (615)296-2511

TEXAS

AMARILLO WE12 / *G2*
Galbraith House B&B Inn, 1710 S Polk St, 79102 .... (806)374-0237
Parkview House, 1311 S Jefferson, 79101 .... (806)373-9464

AUSTIN EM7 / *D7*
Brook House, 609 W 33rd St, 78705 .... (512)459-0534
Carrington's Bluff, 1900 David, 78705 .... (512)479-0638
LaPrelle Place, 2204 Lindell Ave, 78704 .... (512)441-2204
The McCallum House, 613 W 32nd, 78705 .... (512)451-6744
Southard House, 908 Blanco, 78703 .... (512)474-4731

BANDERA EN4 / *E6*
Mayan Dude Ranch, PO Box 577, 78003 .... (512)796-3312

BASTROP EM8 / *D7*
Pfeiffer House, 1802 Main St, 78602 .... (512)321-2100

BELLVILLE EN11 / *E8*
High Cotton Inn, 214 S Live Oak, 77419 .... (409)865-9796

BEN WHEELER EG11 / *B9*
Wild Briar, PO Box 21, 75754 .... (214)852-3975

BIG SANDY EF13 / *B9*
Annie's B&B, 106 N Tyler, PO Box 928, 75755 .... (903)636-4355

BOERNE EN5 / *E6*
Ye Kendall Inn, 128 W Blanco, 78006 .... (512)249-8548

BROWNWOOD EI4 / *C6*
Troxler House, 701 Main, 76801 .... (915)646-0889

BUCHANAN DAM EL5 / *D7*
Knittel House, PO Box 261, 78639 .... (512)793-6408

CALVERT EK9 / *D7*
Our House, 406 E Texas, PO Box 113, 77837 .... (409)364-2909

CANYON WF12 / *G2*
Hudspeth House, 1905 Fourth Ave, 79015 .... (806)655-9800

CENTER — EH15 / *C10*
- Pine Colony Inn, 500 Shelbyville St, 75935 ... (409)598-7700

CHAPPELL HILL — EM9 / *E8*
- **The Browning Plantation**, Rt 1 Box 8, 77426 ... (409)836-6144

CHIRENO — EI15 / *C9*
- Gingerbread House, Gingerbread St, Box 94, 75937 ... (409)362-2365

CLEBURNE — EG8 / *B7*
- Cleburne House, 201 N Anglin, 76031 ... (817)641-0085

COMFORT — EN4 / *E6*
- **Gast Haus Lodge**, 944 High St, PO Box 514, 78013 ... (512)995-2304

CROSBYTON — WI14 / *A5*
- Smith House, 306 W Aspen Street, 79322 ... (806)675-2178

CUERO — EP8 / *E7*
- Reiffert-Mugge Inn, 304 W Prairie, 77954 ... (512)275-2626

DALLAS — EF9 / *B8*
- B&B Texas Style, 4224 W Red Bird Ln, 75237 ... (214)298-8586

EAGLE LAKE — EO10 / *E8*
- Farris 1912, 201 N McCarty, 77434 ... (409)234-2546

EDOM — EG11 / *B9*
- Red Rooster Square, Rt 3, Box 3387, 75756 ... (214)852-6774

EL PASO — WN2 / *C1*
- Gardner Hotel, 311 E Franklin Ave, 79901 ... (915)532-3661
- Room with a View, 821 Rim Rd, 79902 ... (915)534-4400

ENNIS — EG9 / *B8*
- **Raphael House**, 500 W Ennis Ave, 75119 ... (214)875-1555

FORT DAVIS — WR8 / *D3*
- Indian Lodge, PO Box 786, 79734 ... (915)426-3254
- **Sutler's Limpia Hotel**, PO Box 822, 79734 ... (915)426-3237

FORT WORTH — EF8 / *B7*
- Medford House, 2344 Medford Court East, 76109 ... (817)924-2765
- Miss Molly's Hotel, 109 1/2 W Exchange St, 76106 ... (817)626-1522
- Stockyards Hotel, Main & Exchange St, 76106 ... (817)625-6427

FREDERICKSBURG — EM4 / *D6*
- B&B Fredericksburg, 407 S Cherry, 78624 ... (512)997-4712
- Baron's Creek Inn, 110 E Creek St, 78624 ... (512)997-9398
- Chemist Loft B&B, 310 E Main, 78624 ... (512)997-8615
- Claus Haus, 501 W Main, 78624 ... (512)997-5612
- **Country Cottage Inn**, 405 E Main St, 78624 ... (512)997-8549
- Dás College Haus, 106 W College, 78624 ... (512)997-9047
- Delforge Place, 501 W Main, 78624 ... (512)997-5612
- Gastehaus Schmidt, 501 W Main St, 78624 ... (512)997-5612
- Historic Properties, 107 N Washington, 78624 ... (512)997-9585
- J Bar K Ranch B&B, Mason Rt Box 53-A, 78624 ... (512)669-2471
- John Jakob Peter Haus, 501 W Main, 78624 ... (512)667-5612
- Krieger Geyer House, 501 W Main, 78624 ... (512)997-5612
- Palo Alto Log Cabin, 501 W Main, 78624 ... (512)997-5612
- Schmidt Barn, 501 West Main, 78624 ... (512)997-5612
- Town Creek Log Cabin, 501 W Main, 78624 ... (512)997-5612
- Victorian Lace Gastehaus, 501 W Main, 78624 ... (512)997-5612
- Wunderlich Home, Cabin & Barn, 501 W Main, 78624 ... (512)997-5612

GALVESTON — EO14 / *E9*
- Hazelwood House, 1127 Church, 77550 ... (713)762-1668
- Key Largo, 5400 Seawall Blvd, 77550 ... (800)833-0120
- La Quinta Inn, 1402 Seawall Blvd, 77550 ... (800)531-5900
- Mather-Root Home, 1816 Winnie, 77550 ... (713)439-6253
- Michael's B&B Inn, 1715-35th St, 77550 ... (409)763-3760
- Tremont House, 2300 Ship's Mechanic Row, 77550 ... (409)763-0300
- **Victorian Inn**, 511 17th St, 77550 ... (409)762-3235
- Virginia Point Inn, 2327 Ave K, 77550 ... (409)763-2450
- The White Horse Inn, 2217 Broadway, 77550 ... (800)762-2632

GALVESTON ISLAND — EO14 / *E9*
- **Gilded Thistle B&B**, 1805 Broadway, 77550 ... (409)763-0194
- Matali B&B Inn, 1727 Sealy, 77550 ... (409)763-4526

GLEN ROSE — EH7 / *C7*
- The Inn on the River, PO Box 1417, 76043 ... (817)897-2101

GOLIAD — EQ8 / *F7*
- White House Inn, PO Box 922, 77963 ... (512)645-2701

GONZALES — EO8 / *E7*
- Saint James Inn, 723 St James, 78629 ... (512)672-7006

GRANBURY — EG7 / *B7*
- Nutt House, Town Square, 76048 ... (817)573-5612

HILLSBORO — EH8 / *C7*
- Tarlton House of 1895, 211 N Pleasant St, 76645 ... (817)582-7216

HOUSTON — EN13 / *E9*
- **Durham House**, 921 Heights Blvd, 77008 ... (713)868-4654
- The Highlander, 607 Highland St, 77009 ... (713)861-7545
- La Colombe D'or, 3410 Montrose Blvd, 77006 ... (713)524-7999
- **Robin's Nest**, 4104 Greeley St, 77006 ... (713)528-5821
- **Sara's B&B Inn**, 941 Heights Blvd, 77008 ... (713)868-1130

HUNTSVILLE — EK12 / *D9*
- The Whistler B&B, 906 Ave M, 77340 ... (409)295-2834

JEFFERSON — EF14 / *B9*
- Austin Cottage, 402 W Austin St, 75657 ... (903)938-5941
- Excelsior House, 211 W Austin, 75657 ... (903)665-2513
- Hale House, 702 S Lee, 75657 ... (903)665-8877
- Hotel Jefferson, 124 Austin St, 75657 ... (903)665-2631
- The Magnolias, 209 Broadway, 75657 ... (903)665-2754
- **McKay House**, 306 E Delta St, 75657 ... (903)665-7322
- **Pride House**, 409 Broadway, 75657 ... (903)665-2675
- Queen Anne's Lace, 304 N Alley, 75657 ... (903)665-2483
- Roseville Manor, PO Box 549, 217 Lafayette St, 75657 ... (800)336-7736
- Stillwater Inn, 203 E Broadway, 75657 ... (903)665-8415
- The Cottage in Jefferson, 307 Soda, 75657 ... (903)665-8572
- William Clark House, 201 W Henderson, 75657 ... (903)665-8880
- Wise Manor, 312 Houston St, 75657 ... (903)665-2386

KARNACK — EF15 / *B10*
- **Mimosa Hall**, Rt 1 Box 635, 75661 ... (903)679-3632

LAJITAS — WU8 / *E3*
- Lajitas on Rio Grande, Box 400, 79852 ... (915)424-3471

LEDBETTER — EM9 / *D8*
- Ledbetter Hotel, PO Box 212, 78946 ... (409)249-3066

LLANO — EL5 / *D6*
- Badu House, 601 Bessemer, 78643 ... (915)247-4304

MARATHON — WS9 / *D3*
- The Gage Hotel, W Hwy 90, PO Box 46, 79842 ... (915)386-4205

MARBLE FALLS — EL6 / *D7*
- La Casita B&B, 1908 Redwood Dr, 78654 ... (512)598-6443

MARSHALL — EF14 / *B9*
- Cotten's Patch, 703 E Rusk, 75670 ... (903)938-8756
- Ginocchio Hotel, 707 N Washington, 75670 ... (903)935-7635
- La Maison Malfacon, 70 E Rusk, 75670 ... (903)935-6039
- Meredith House, 410 E Meredith St, 75670 ... (903)935-7147
- **Three Oaks**, 609 N Washington, 75670 ... (903)938-6123
- Weisman-Hirsch-Beil Home, 313 S Washington, 75670 ... (903)938-5504
- **Wood Boone Norrell House**, 215 E Rusk St, 75670 ... (903)935-1800

MINEOLA — EF12 / *B9*
- Munzesheimer Manor, 202 N Newsom, 75773 ... (903)569-6634
- Sellers' Corner, 411 E Kilpatrick, 75773 ... (214)569-6560

MOUNT VERNON — EE12 / *B9*
- Dutton-Teague B&B Inn, 110 Roach St, 75457 ... (214)537-2603

NACOGDOCHES — EI14 / *C9*
- Haden Edwards Inn, 106 N Nanana, 75961 ... (409)564-9999
- Tol Barret House, Rt 4, Box 9400, 75961 ... (409)569-1249

NAVASOTA — EL11 / *D8*
- The Castle, 1403 E Washington, 77868 ... (409)825-8051

NEW BRAUNFELS — EN6 / *E7*
- Comfort Common, 240 S Seguin Ave, 78130 ... (512)995-3030
- Prince Solms Inn, 295 E San Antonio, 78130 ... (512)625-9169

RIO GRANDE CITY — EW5 / *H6*
- La Borde House, 601 E Main St, 78582 ... (512)487-5101

SALADO — EK7 / *D7*
- The Inn on Creek, Center Circle, PO Box 261, 76571 ... (817)947-5554
- Rose Mansion, PO Box 500, 76571 ... (817)947-5999
- The Inn at Salado, N Main at Pace Park, 76571 ... (817)947-8200

SAN ANTONIO — EO5 / *E7*
- Belle Of Monte Vista, 505 Belknap Pl, 78212 ... (512)732-4006
- Bonner Garden, 145 E Agarita, 78212 ... (512)733-4222
- **The Bullis House Inn**, 621 Pierce St, PO Box 8059, 78208 ... (512)223-9426
- The Fairmount Hotel, 401 S Alamo, 78208 ... (512)224-8800
- Menger Hotel, 204 Alamo Plaza, 78205 ... (512)223-4361
- Norton Brackenridge House, 230 Madison, 78204 ... (512)271-3442
- Terrell Castle, 950 E Grayson St, 78208 ... (512)271-9145

SAN AUGUSTINE — EI5 / *C10*
- Captain E.D. Downs House, 301 Main St, 75972 ... (409)275-5305
- **The Wade House**, 128 E Columbia St, 75972 ... (409)275-2605

SAN MARCOS — EN7 / *E7*
- Aquarena Springs Inn, 1 Aquarena Dr, 78666 ... (512)396-8901
- Crystal River Inn, 326 W Hopkins, 78666 ... (512)396-3739

STEPHENVILLE — EH6 / *C7*
- **The Oxford House**, 563 N Graham, 76401 ... (817)965-6885

TURKEY — WG14 / *A5*
- Hotel Turkey Living Museum, 3rd & Alexander, PO Box 37, 79261 ... (806)423-1151

TYLER — EG12 / *B9*
- Rosevine Inn B&B, 415 S Vine, 75702 ... (903)592-2221

UTOPIA — EO3 / *E6*
- Utopia on the River, Hwy 187, PO Box 14, 78884 ... (512)966-2444

UVALDE
EP2 / *E6*

Casa de Leona, 1149 Pearsall Rd, PO Box 1829, 78802 ....(512)278-8550

VICTORIA
EQ9 / *F8*

Santa Rosa Oaks B&B, 601 E Santa Rosa, 77902 ....(512)578-1605

WAXAHACHIE
EG9 / *E8*

Bonnynook B&B, 414 W Main, 75165 ....(214)937-7207

WEIMAR
EN9 / *E8*

Weimar Country Inn, Jackson Sq, 78962 ....(409)725-8888

WESLACO
EX7 / *H7*

Rio Grande B&B, PO Box 16, 78596 ....(512)968-9646

WIMBERLEY
EN6 / *E7*

B&B of Wimberley, Box 589, 78676 ....(512)847-9666
Southwind B&B, Rt 2, Box 15, 78676 ....(512)847-5277

WINNSBORO
EE12 / *B9*

Thee Hubbell House, 307 W Elm, 75494 ....(903)342-5629
Yesteryear B&B, 208 N Myrtle, 75494 ....(903)342-3024

YORKTOWN
EP8 / *E7*

Hygeia Health Retreat, 439 Main St, 78164 ....(512)564-3670

UTAH

BLANDING
L11 / *F6*

The Old Hotel B&B, 118 E 300 S, 84511 ....(801)678-2388

BLUFF
M11 / *G6*

Bluff B&B, PO Box 158, 84512 ....(801)672-2220
Recapture Lodge, Box 36, 84512 ....(801)672-2281
The Scorup House, PO Box 127, 84512 ....(801)672-2272

CASTLE VALLEY
I11 / *E6*

Sistelita, Box 1905 CVSR, 84532 ....(801)259-6012

CEDAR CITY
L4 / *F2*

Meadeau View Lodge, Box 356, 84720 ....(801)682-2495
Paxman's Summer House, 170 N 400 W, 84720 ....(801)586-3755
Woodbury Guest House, 237 S 300 W, 84720 ....(801)586-6696

EPHRAIM
H7 / *D3*

Our House Lodging, 135 W 100 N, 84627 ....(801)283-6367

HEBER CITY
E7 / *C4*

The Cottage B&B, 830 S Main St, 84032 ....(801)654-2236

HENEFER
C7 / *B3*

Dearden B&B Inn, 20 W 100 N, 84033 ....(801)336-5698

HUNTSVILLE
C6 / *B3*

Jackson Fork Inn, Hwy 39, 7345 E 900 S, 84317 ....(801)745-0051

HURRICANE
M3 / *G2*

Pah Tempe Hot Springs B&B, 34-4, 84737 ....(801)635-2879

KANAB
N5 / *G2*

Miss Sophie's B&B, 30 N 200 W, 84741 ....(801)644-5952
Nine Gables Inn, 106 W 100 N, 84741 ....(801)644-5079

MANTI
H7 / *D3*

Manti House Inn, 401 N Main St, 84642 ....(801)835-0161
Yardley's Inn, 190 W 200 S, 84642 ....(801)835-1861

MIDWAY
E7 / *B4*

The Homestead, 700 N Homestead Dr, 84049 ....(801)654-1102
Schneitter Family Hotel B&B, 700 N Homestead Dr, 84049 ....(800)327-7220

MOAB
I11 / *E6*

Canyon Country B&B, 590 N 500 W, 84532 ....(801)259-7882
Pack Creek Ranch, A Country Inn, PO Box 1270, 84532 ....(801)259-5505
Shiloh B&B, 2390 Old City Park Rd, 84532 ....(801)259-8684
Village Townhouses, 450 Emma Blvd, 84532 ....(801)259-6166
Westwood Guesthouse, 81 E 100 S #4, 84532 ....(801)259-7283

MONROE
J6 / *E3*

Peterson's B&B, 95 N 300 W, PO Box 142, 84754 ....(801)527-4830

MONTICELLO
K11 / *F6*

The Grist Mill Inn B&B, 64 S 300 E, 84535 ....(801)587-2597

MOUNT PLEASANT
G7 / *D4*

Mansion House B&B, 298 S State St, 84647 ....(801)462-3031

NEPHI
G6 / *D3*

The Whitmore Mansion B&B, 110 S Main St, 84648 ....(801)623-2047

PARK CITY
D7 / *C4*

The Blue Church Lodge, 424 Park Ave, 84060 ....(801)649-8009
Claimjumper Hotel, 573 Main St, 84060 ....(801)649-8051
The Old Miners' Lodge A B&B Inn, 615 Woodside Ave, PO Box 2639, 84060-2639 ....(801)645-8068
The Snowed Inn, 3770 N Hwy 224, PO Box 1846, 84060 ....(801)649-5713
Star Hotel, 227 Main St, 84060 ....(801)649-8333
The Imperial Hotel, 221 Main St, PO Box 1628, 84060 ....(801)649-1904
Washington School Inn, 544 Park Ave, PO Box 536, 84060 ....(801)649-3800

SAINT GEORGE
M3 / *G1*

Greene Gate Village Historic B&B Inn, 76 W Tabernacle, 84770 ....(801)628-6999
Seven Wives Inn, 217 N 100 W, 84770 ....(801)628-3737

SALT LAKE CITY
D6 / *B3*

The Anton Boxrud B&B, 57 S 600 E, 84102 ....(801)363-8035
Brigham Street Inn, 1135 E South Temple, 84102 ....(801)364-4461
Dave's Cozy Cabin Inn, 2293 E 6200 S, 84102 ....(801)278-6136
Pinecrest B&B Inn, 6211 Emigration Canyon Rd, 84108 ....(801)583-6663
Saltair B&B, 164 S 9th E, 84102 ....(801)533-8184
The Spruces B&B, 6151 S 900 E, 84121 ....(801)268-8762
Westminster B&B, 1156 Blain Ave, 84105 ....(801)467-4114

SANDY
E6 / *B3*

Mountain Hollow B&B Inn, 10209 S Dimple Dell Rd, 84092 ....(801)942-3428
Quail Hills B&B, 3744 E N Little Cottonwood, 84092 ....(801)942-2858

SPRINGDALE
M4 / *G2*

Under The Eaves Guest House, 980 Zion Park Blvd, PO Box 29, 84767 ....(801)772-3457
Zion House B&B, 801 Zion Park Blvd, PO Box 323, 84767 ....(801)772-3281

VERMONT

ALBURG
D2 / *A1*

Auberge Alburg, RD 1, Box 3, 05440 ....(802)796-3169
Thomas Mott Homestead, RFD 2, Box 149B, 05440 ....(802)796-3736

ANDOVER
N4 / *F2*

Hillside B&B, Box 196, Cobb Rd, 05143 ....(802)875-3844

ARLINGTON
O2 / *F1*

The Arlington Inn, Historic Rt 7A, 05250 ....(802)375-6532
Arlington's West Mountain Inn, PO Box 481, 05250 ....(802)375-6516
The Inn on Covered Bridge Green, RD 1 Box 3550, River Rd, 05250 ....(802)375-9489
Evergreen, Sandgate, Box 2480, 05250 ....(802)375-2272
Four Winds Country Inn, River Rd, 05250 ....(802)375-6734
Hill Farm Inn, RR 2 Box 2015, 05250 ....(802)375-2269
Shenandoah Farm, Rt 313, Battenkill Rd, 05250 ....(802)375-6372
The Inn at Sunderland, Historic Rt 7A, 05250 ....(802)362-4213
Sycamore Inn, Rt 7 Box 2485, 05250 ....(802)362-2284
The Evergreen, Sandgate Rd, 05250 ....(802)375-2272
West Mountain Inn, Box 481, 05250 ....(802)375-6516

BARNARD
K5 / *E3*

The Silver Lake House, PO Box 13, North Rd, 05081 ....(802)234-9957

BARNET
H7 / *C4*

Innwood Manor, Lower Waterford Rd, 05821 ....(802)633-4047
Old Homestead Inn, PO Box 35, 05821 ....(802)633-4100

BARRE
H5 / *C3*

Woodruff House, 13 East St, 05641 ....(802)476-7745

BARTON
E6 / *B3*

The Barton Inn, PO Box 67, Main St, 05822 ....(802)525-4721
Fox Hall B&B, Willoughby Lake Rd, 05822 ....(802)525-6930
Lafont's B&B, RFD #3, Box 86, 05822 ....(802)755-6127
Paupers Manse B&B, Willoughby Lake Rd, 96A, 05822 ....(802)525-3222

BELLOWS FALLS
N5 / *F3*

Blue Haven B&B, Rt 5 Box 328, 05101 ....(802)463-9008
Horsefeathers B&B, 16 Webb Terr, 05101 ....(802)463-9776

BELMONT
M4 / *E2*

The Parmenter House, Church St, 05730 ....(802)259-2009

BENNINGTON
P2 / *G1*

Bennington Haus, 208 Washington Ave, 05201 ....(802)447-7972
Four Chimneys Inn, 21 West Rd, 05201 ....(802)447-3500
Mt. Anthony Guest House, 226 Main St, 05201 ....(802)447-7396
Safford Manor B&B, 722 Main St, 05201 ....(802)442-5934
South Shire Inn, 124 Elm St, 05201 ....(802)447-3839

BETHEL
J4 / *D2*

Eastwood House, Rt 2 Rt 107, 05032 ....(802)234-9686
Greenhurst Inn, River St, RD 2 Box 60, 05032 ....(802)234-9474
Poplar Manor, Rt 2, 05032 ....(802)234-5426

BOLTON VALLEY
G4 / *C2*

The Black Bear Inn, Mountain Rd, 05477 ....(802)434-2126

BONDVILLE
N3 / *F2*

Alpenrose Inn, Winhall Hollow Rd, 05340 ....(802)297-2750

BRADFORD
J7 / *D3*

Merry Meadow Farm, Lower Plain, Rt 5, 05033 ....(802)222-4412
The Village Inn of Bradford, PO Box 354, 05033 ....(802)222-9303

BRANDON
K3 / *D2*

The Arches, 53 Park St, 05733 ....(802)247-8200
Brandon Inn, 20 Park Green, 05733 ....(802)247-5766
The Churchill House Inn, RD 3 Rt 73 East, 05733 ....(802)247-3078
Fort Vengeance, Rt 7, RFD #1, 05733 ....(802)483-2136
Moffett House, 69 Park St, 05733 ....(802)247-3843
Old Mill Inn, Rd #2, 05773 ....(802)247-8002

BRATTLEBORO P5 / *G3*
Green River Homespun, Jacksonville Stage Rd, 05301 ....(802)257-7275

BRIDGEWATER CORNERS L4 / *E2*
October Country Inn, PO Box 66, 05035 ....(802)672-3412

BRISTOL I3 / *D2*
Long Run Inn, RD 1, Box 560, 05443 ....(802)453-3233
Maplewood Farm B&B, Rt 17, RD2, Box 520, 05443 ....(802)453-2992

BROOKFIELD I5 / *D3*
Green Trails Country Inn, Pond Village, PO Box 494, 05036 ....(802)276-3412

BROOKLINE O4 / *G2*
Massey Farm, 340 Grassy Brook Rd, 05345 ....(802)365-4716

BROWNSVILLE M5 / *E3*
Mill Brook B&B, PO Box 410, Rt 44, 05037 ....(802)484-7283
The Inn at Mt. Ascutney, Brook Rd, 05037 ....(802)484-7725

BURLINGTON G2 / *C1*
Howden Cottage B&B, 32 N Champlain St, 05401 ....(802)864-7198

CALAIS G5 / *C3*
Evergreen's Chalet, HC 32, Box 41, 05648 ....(802)223-5156

CHARLOTTE H2 / *C1*
Green Meadows B&B, PO Box 1300, 05445 ....(802)425-3059

CHELSEA J5 / *D3*
Shire Inn, PO Box 37, 05038 ....(802)685-3031

CHESTER N5 / *F3*
Chester House, Main St, PO Box 708, 05143 ....(802)875-2205
Greenleaf Inn, PO Box 188, 05143 ....(802)875-3171
Henry Farm Inn, PO Box 646, 05143 ....(802)875-2674
Hugging Bear Inn & Shoppe, Main St, PO Box 32, 05143 ....(802)875-2412
The Inn at Long Last, PO Box 589, 05143 ....(802)875-2444
Old Town Farm Inn, RD 4, Box 383B, 05143 ....(802)875-2346
Rowell's Inn, RR 1, Box 269, 05143 ....(802)875-3658
The Stone Hearth Inn, Rt 11 West, 05143 ....(802)875-2525

CHITTENDEN K3 / *E2*
Mountain Top Inn, Box 493, Mountain Top Rd, 05737 ....(800)445-2100
Tulip Tree Inn, Chittenden Dam Rd, 05737 ....(802)483-6213

COLCHESTER F2 / *C2*
On the Lamb B&B, 60 Depot Rd, 05446 ....(802)862-2144

CRAFTSBURY F6 / *B3*
Craftsbury Inn, Main St, Box 36, 05826 ....(802)586-2848
Gary Meadow Dairy Farm, RR 1 Box 11, 05826 ....(802)586-2536

CRAFTSBURY COMMON F6 / *B3*
The Inn on the Common, Main St, 05827 ....(802)586-9619

CUTTINGSVILLE M4 / *E2*
Maple Crest Farm, Box 120, 05738 ....(802)492-3367

DANBY M3 / *F2*
Quail's Nest B&B, PO Box 221, Main St, 05739 ....(802)293-5099
Silas Griffith Inn, RR 1 Box 66F, S Main St, 05739 ....(802)293-5567

DERBY LINE D7 / *A4*
Derby Village Inn, 46 Main St, 05830 ....(802)873-3604

DORSET N3 / *F2*
Barrows House, Rt 30, 05251 ....(802)867-4455
Cornucopia Of Dorset, Rt 30 Box 307, 05251 ....(802)867-5751
Dorset Hollow B&B, Dorset Hollow Rd, Box 655, 05251 ....(802)867-5993
Dorset Inn, 05251 ....(802)867-5500
Dovetail Inn, Rt 30 Box 976, 05251 ....(802)867-5747
The Little Lodge at Dorset, Rt 30 Box 673, 05251 ....(802)867-4040
Maplewood Colonial Inn, Rt 30 Box 1019, 05251 ....(802)867-4470
Marble West Inn, PO Box 847, Dorset West Rd, 05251 ....(802)867-4155
The Inn at West View Farm, Rt 30, 05251 ....(802)867-5715

EAST BARNET H7 / *C4*
Inwood Manor, Lower Waterford Rd, 05821 ....(802)633-4047

EAST BURKE F7 / *B4*
Burke Green, RR 1 Box 81, 05832 ....(802)467-3472
Garrison Inn, Burke Hollow Rd, 05832 ....(802)626-8329
Nutmegger, Box 73, Mountain Rd, 05832 ....(802)626-5205
Old Cutter Inn, Burke Mt Access Rd, 05832 ....(802)626-5152

EAST CALAIS G5 / *C3*
Lake House B&B, RFD #1, Box 142, 05650 ....(802)456-8186

EAST DOVER P4 / *G2*
Cooper Hill Inn, PO Box 146, Cooper Hill Rd, 05341 ....(802)348-6333

EAST HARDWICK G6 / *C3*
Brick House, Box 128, Brick House Rd, 05836 ....(802)472-5512

EAST MIDDLEBURY J3 / *D2*
Robert Frost B&B, Box 246, 05740 ....(802)388-6042
Waybury Inn, Rt 125, 05740 ....(802)388-4015

EAST POULTNEY L2 / *E1*
Eagle Tavern, PO Box 587, 05741 ....(802)287-9498

EAST ST JOHNSBURY G7 / *C4*
Echo Ledge Farm Inn, PO Box 77, 05838 ....(802)748-4750

EAST WALLINGTON L3 / *E2*
White Rocks Inn, 05733 ....(802)446-2077

EAST WARREN I4 / *D2*
The Soft Landing, Airport Rd, Box 116-G, 05674 ....(802)496-6531

ESSEX JUNCTION G3 / *C2*
Varnum's, 143 Weed Rd, 05452 ....(802)899-4577

FAIR HAVEN L2 / *E1*
Fair Haven Inn, 5 Adams St, 05743 ....(802)254-4907
Maplewood Inn, Rt 22A, South, 05743 ....(802)265-8039
Vermont Marble Inn, 12 W Park Dr, 05743 ....(802)265-8383

FAIRFIELD E3 / *B2*
Hillside View Farm, South Rd, 05455 ....(802)827-4480

FAIRLEE J6 / *D3*
Aloha Manor, Lake Morey, 05045 ....(802)333-4478
Silver Maple Lodge & Cottages, S Main St, RR1 Box 8, 05045 ....(802)333-4326

FRANKLIN D3 / *A2*
Fair Meadows Farm, Rt 235 Box 430, 05457 ....(802)285-2132

GASSETTS M5 / *F3*
Old Town Farm Inn, Rt 10, 05143 ....(802)875-2346

GAYSVILLE K4 / *E2*
Cobble House Inn, PO Box 49, 05746 ....(802)234-5458
Laolke Lodge, PO Box 107, 05746 ....(802)234-9205

GRAFTON N5 / *F3*
The Farmhouse 'Round the Bend, Rt 121 E, Box 57, 05146 ....(802)843-2515
Old Tavern at Grafton, Main St, 05146 ....(802)843-2231
The Hayes House, 05146 ....(802)843-2461
Woodchuck Hill Farm, Middletown Rd, 05146 ....(802)843-2398

GREENSBORO F6 / *C3*
Highland Lodge, Caspian Lake, 05841 ....(802)533-2647

GUILDHALL F9 / *C4*
Guildhall Inn, Box 129, 05905 ....(802)676-3720

HANCOCK J4 / *D2*
Kincraft Inn, Rt 100 Box 96, 05748 ....(802)767-3734

HARDWICK G6 / *C3*
Carolyn's B&B, 15 Church St, 05843 ....(802)472-6338
Kahagon At Nichols Pond, Box 728, Nichols Pond, 05843 ....(802)472-6446

HARTFORD K6 / *E3*
House of Seven Gables, 221 Main St, Box 526, 05047 ....(802)295-1200

HIGHGATE SPRINGS D2 / *A2*
Tyler Place, 05460 ....(802)868-3301

HYDE PARK F5 / *B3*
Fitch Hill Inn, RFD 1 Box 1879, 05655 ....(802)888-5941

JAMAICA O4 / *F2*
Three Mountain Inn, Box 180 Bbi, 05343 ....(802)874-4140

JAY D5 / *B3*
Jay Village Inn, Rt 242, 05859 ....(802)988-2643
Woodshed Lodge, 05859 ....(802)988-4444

JEFFERSONVILLE F4 / *B2*
Jefferson House, PO Box 288, Main St, 05464 ....(802)644-2030
Smugglers' Notch Inn, PO Box 280, 05464 ....(802)644-2412
Windridge Inn, Main St, 05464 ....(802)644-8281

JERICHO G3 / *C2*
Homeplace B&B, RR2, Box 367, Old Pump Rd, 05465 ....(802)899-4694
Milliken's, RD 2 Box 397, 05465 ....(802)899-3993

KILLINGTON L4 / *E2*
Cortina Inn, Box CIB, HCR-34, 05751 ....(800)451-6108
Grey Bonnet Inn, 05751 ....(800)342-2086
The Inn at Long Trail, Rt 4 Box 267, 05751 ....(802)775-7181
Mountain Meadows Lodge, Rt 1 Box 3, 05751 ....(802)775-1010
Mountain Morgans, RFD #1, Box 138-A, 05751 ....(802)422-3096
Sherburne Valley Inn, Rt 4, 05751 ....(802)422-9888
The Vermont Inn, Rt 4, 05751 ....(802)775-0708

LANDGROVE N4 / *F2*
Nordic Inn, Rt 11, PO Box 96, 05148 ....(802)824-6444

LONDONDERRY N4 / *F2*
Blue Gentian Lodge, Box 29, RR #1, 05148 ....(802)824-5908
Country Hare, Rt 11 & Magic Mtn Rd, 05148 ....(802)824-3131
The Highland House, RR 1 Box 107, 05148 ....(802)842-3019
The Village Inn At Landgrove, RD Box 215, Landgrove, 05148 ....(802)824-6673

LOWER WATERFORD G7 / *C4*
Rabbit Hill Inn, Pucker St, 05848 ....(802)748-5168
Yankee Woods B&B, White Village, 05848 ....(802)748-5420

LUDLOW M4 / *F2*
The Andrie Rose Inn, 13 Pleasant St, 05149 ....(802)228-4846
Black River Inn, 100 Main St, 05149 ....(802)228-5585
Combes Family Inn, RFD 1 Box 275, 05149 ....(802)228-8799
Echo Lake, PO Box 142, 05149 ....(802)228-8602
The Governor's Inn, 86 Main St, 05149 ....(802)228-8830
Jewell Brook Inn, 82 Andover St, Rt 100, 05149 ....(802)228-8926
Okemo Inn, RFD 1 Box 133, 05149 ....(802)228-8834

LYNDONVILLE G7 / *C4*
The Wildflower Inn, Star Rt, Darling Hill Rd, 05851 ....(802)626-8310

MANCHESTER N3 / *F2*
Birch Hill Inn, West Rd, PO Box 346, 05254 ....(802)362-2761
Brook-N-Hearth, Rts 11 & 30, PO Box 508, 05255 ....(802)362-3604
Butternut Country House, Butternut Ln, PO Box 2043, 05255 ....(802)362-3371
Equinox Sky Line Inn, Box 325, 05254 ....(802)362-1113
Manchester Highlands Inn, PO Box 1754, Highland Ave, 05255 ....(802)362-4565
The Reluctant Panther Inn, PO Box 678, West Rd, 05254 ....(802)362-2568
River Meadow Farm, PO Box 822, 05255 ....(802)362-3700
Sky Line Inn, Box 325, 05254 ....(802)362-1113
The Inn at Willow Pond, Rt 7 Box 1429, 05255 ....(802)362-4733

MANCHESTER VILLAGE N3 / *F2*
1811 House, Historic Rt 7A, 05254 ....(802)362-1811
The Inn at Manchester, Box 41, Historic Rt 7A, 05254 ....(802)362-1793
Village Country Inn, PO Box 408, 05254 ....(802)362-1792
Wilburton Inn, PO Box 468, River Rd, 05254 ....(802)362-2500

MENDON L3 / *E2*
Red Clover Inn, Woodward Rd, 05701 ....(802)775-2290

MIDDLEBURY I2 / *D1*
Brookside Meadows, RD 3, Box 2460, 05753 ....(802)388-6429
Middlebury Inn, 14 Courthouse Sq, PO Box 798, 05753 ....(802)388-4961
Stevenson House, RFD #4, Box 300, 05753 ....(802)462-2866
Swift House Inn, 25 Stewart Ln, 05753 ....(802)388-9925

MIDDLETOWN SPRINGS L3 / *E2*
Middletown Springs Inn, PO Box 1068, On The Green, 05757 ....(802)235-2198

MONTGOMERY D5 / *B3*
Eagle Lodge, Box 900, 05471 ....(802)326-4518

MONTGOMERY CENTER E5 / *B3*
The Inn on Trout River, The Main St, PO Box 76, 05471 ....(802)326-4391

MONTGOMERY VILLAGE D5 / *B3*
Black Lantern Inn, Route 118, 05470 ....(802)326-4507

MONTPELIER H5 / *C3*
The Inn at Montpelier, 147 Main St, 05602 ....(802)223-2727

MORETOWN H4 / *C2*
Camel's Hump View Farm, Rt 100B, 05660 ....(802)496-3614
Schultzes' Village Inn, PO Box 465, 05660 ....(802)496-2366

MORGAN D7 / *B4*
Seymour Lake Lodge, Rt 111, 05853 ....(802)895-2752

MOUNT HOLLY M4 / *E2*
Austria Haus, Box 2 Austria Haus Rd, 05758 ....(802)259-2441
Hortonville Inn, RD 1 Box 14, 05758 ....(802)259-2587
Hound's Folly, Box 591, 05758 ....(802)259-2718

NEW HAVEN I2 / *D1*
Horn Farnsworth B&B, Rt 7 & River Rd, Box 170A, 05472 ....(802)388-2300

NEWBURY I7 / *D4*
A Century Past, Rt 5 Box 186, 05051 ....(802)866-3358

NEWFANE O4 / *G2*
Four Columns Inn, 05345 ....(802)365-7713
Old Newfane Inn, PO Box 101, 05345 ....(802)365-4427
West River Lodge, RR 1 Box 693, 05354 ....(802)365-7745

NORTH FERRISBURG H2 / *C1*
Dunn-Inn, Box 922, 05473 ....(802)425-2902

NORTH HERO E2 / *B1*
Charlie's Northland Lodge, Box 88, 05474 ....(802)372-8822
North Hero House, Rt 2 Box 106, 05474 ....(802)372-8237

NORTH THETFORD J6 / *D3*
Stone House Inn, Rt 5 Box 47, 05054 ....(802)333-9124

NORTH TROY D5 / *A3*
Rose Apple Acres Farm, Box 300, E Hill Rd, 05859 ....(802)988-4300

NORTHFIELD I4 / *D2*
Northfield Inn, 27 Highland Ave, 05663 ....(802)485-8558

NORWICH K6 / *E3*
The Inn at Norwich, 225 Main St, 05055 ....(802)649-1143

ORLEANS E6 / *B3*
Valley House Inn, 4 Memorial Sq, 05860 ....(802)754-6665

ORWELL K2 / *D1*
Historic Brookside Farms, Rt 22A Box 036, 05760 ....(802)948-2727

PERKINSVILLE M5 / *F3*
Gwendolyn's B&B, Rt 106 Box 225, 05151 ....(802)263-5248
Peregrine's Rest, Upper Falls Rd, 05151 ....(802)263-5784

PERU N3 / *F2*
Johnny Seesaw's, PO Box 68, 05152 ....(802)824-5533
Russell Inn, 05152 ....(802)824-6631
Wiley Inn, PO Box 37, 05152 ....(802)842-6600

PITTSFIELD K4 / *E2*
The Inn at Pittsfield, Rt 100 Box 675, 05762 ....(802)746-8943
Swiss Farm Lodge, Rt 100N, 05762 ....(802)746-8341

PITTSFORD K3 / *E2*
Fox Brothers Farm, Corn Hill Rd, 05763 ....(802)483-2870
Ironmasters Inn, Furnace Rd, RFD #1, Box 101, 05763 ....(802)483-2318

PLAINFIELD H5 / *C3*
Northview, RD #2, 05667 ....(802)454-7191
Yankees' Northview B&B, RD 2 Box 1000, 05667 ....(802)454-7191

PLYMOUTH L4 / *E2*
The Hawk Inn, Rt 100, 05056 ....(802)672-3811

POST MILLS J6 / *D3*
Lake House Inn, Rt 244, PO Box 65, 05058 ....(802)333-4025

POULTNEY L2 / *E1*
Lake St. Catherine Inn, PO Box 129, Cones Point Rd, 05764 ....(802)287-9347
Stonebridge Inn, Rt 30, 05764 ....(802)287-9849
Tower Hall B&B, 2 Bentley Ave, 05764 ....(802)287-4004

PROCTORSVILLE M4 / *F2*
Allens' Inn of Proctorsville, Depot St, PO Box 78, 05153 ....(802)226-7970
Castle Inn, Rt 103 & 131, PO Box 157, 05153 ....(802)226-7222
The Golden Stage Inn, Depot St, PO Box 218, 05153 ....(802)226-7744
Okemo Lantern Lodge, PO Box 247, 05153 ....(802)226-7770

PUTNEY O5 / *G3*
Hickory Ridge House, RFD 3 Box 1410, 05346 ....(802)387-5709
Mapleton Farm B&B, RD 2, Box 510, 05346 ....(802)257-5252
Misty Meadows, RD 1, Box 458, 05346 ....(802)722-9517
Putney Inn, Depot Rd, 05346 ....(802)387-5517

QUECHEE L5 / *E3*
Parker House, 16 Main St, Box 0780, 05059 ....(802)295-6077
Quechee B&B, Rt 4 Box 0080, 05059 ....(802)295-1776
Quechee Inn At Marshland Farm, Clubhouse Rd, Box 104, 05059 ....(802)295-3133

RANDOLPH J4 / *D2*
The Three Stallion Inn, RD 2, Stock Farm Rd, 05060 ....(802)728-5575

READING M5 / *E3*
Hapgood Cottage, Bailey's Mills Rd, 05062 ....(802)484-5540
The Peeping Cow B&B, Rt 106 Box 47, 05062 ....(802)484-5036

READSBORO P3 / *G2*
Old Coach Inn, RR 1 Box 260, 05350 ....(802)423-5394

RICHMOND G3 / *C2*
Rich Mound Acres B&B, Williams Hill Rd, Box 272, 05477 ....(802)434-2454

RIPTON J3 / *D2*
Chipman Inn, Rt 125, 05766 ....(802)388-2390

ROCHESTER J4 / *D2*
Harvey's Mountain View Inn, 05767 ....(802)767-4273
Liberty Hill Farm, Liberty Hill Rd, 05767 ....(802)767-3926
The New Homestead, PO Box 25, 05767 ....(802)767-4751
Tupper Farm Lodge, RR 1 Box 149, 05767 ....(802)767-4243

ROYALTON K5 / *D3*
Fox Stand Inn & Restaurant, Rt 14, 05068 ....(802)763-8437

RUTLAND L3 / *E2*
Hillcrest Guest House, RR 1 Box 4459, 05701 ....(802)775-1670

SAINT ALBANS E3 / *B2*
Bellevue, 9 Parsons Ln, 05478 ....(802)527-1115

SAINT JOHNSBURY G7 / *C4*
Broadview Farm B&B, RFD #2, Box 153, 05819 ....(802)748-9902
Looking Glass Inn, Rt 18 Box 199, 05819 ....(802)748-3052

SAXTONS RIVER N5 / *F3*
Red Barn Guest House, Hatfield Ln, 05154 ....(802)869-2566
Saxtons River Inn, Main St, 05154 ....(802)869-2110

SHAFTSBURY O2 / *G1*
Munro Hawkins House, Historic Rt 7A, 05262 ....(802)447-2286

SHOREHAM VILLAGE J2 / *D1*
Shoreham Inn & Country Store, On The Green, Main St, 05770 ....(802)897-5081

SHREWSBURY M4 / *E2*
The Buckmaster Inn, Lincoln Hill Rd, RR 1 Box 118, 05738 ....(802)492-3485

SOUTH BURLINGTON G2 / *C1*
Lindenwood, 916 Shelburne Rd, 05404 ....(802)862-2144

SOUTH LONDONDERRY N4 / *F2*
Londonderry Inn, PO Box 301-57, 05155 ....(802)824-5226

SOUTH NEWFANE P4 / *G2*
The Inn at South Newfane, Dover Rd, 05351 ....(802)348-7191

SOUTH STRAFFORD K6 / *D3*
Watercourse Way B&B, Rt 132 Box 101, 05070 ....(802)765-4314

SOUTH WALLINGFORD M3 / *E2*
Green Mountain Tea Room, Rt 7 RR 1 Box 400, 05773 ....(802)446-2611

SOUTH WOODSTOCK L5 / *E3*
Kedron Valley Inn, Rt 106 Box 145, 05071 ....(802)457-1473

SPRINGFIELD M5 / *F3*
Hartness House Inn, 30 Orchard St, 05156 ....(802)885-2115

STARKSBORO H3 / *C2*
North Country B&B, Rt 116, PO Box 1, 05487 ....(802)453-3911

STOCKBRIDGE K4 / *E2*
Scarborough Inn, Rt 100 HC65 #23, 05772 ....(802)746-8141
Stockbridge Inn B&B, PO Box 45, Rt 100 N, 05772 ....(802)746-8165

STOWE G4 / *C2*
The 1860 House, School St, PO Box 276, 05672 ....(802)253-7351
Andersen Lodge, RR1 Box 1450, 05672 ....(802)253-7336
Baas' Gastehaus, 180 Edson Hill, 05672 ....(802)253-8376
Bittersweet Inn, Rt 100 S, 05672 ....(802)253-7787
Butternut Inn, Mountain Rd, RD1, Box 950, 05672 ....(802)253-4277
Fiddler's Green Inn, Mountain Rd Rt 108, 05672 ....(802)253 8124
Fountain House, RR2, Box 2480, 05672 ....(802)253-9285
Foxfire Inn, RD 2 Rt 100, 05672 ....(802)253-4887
Gables Inn, 1457 Mountain Rd, 05672 ....(802)253-7730
Green Mountain Inn, PO Box 60, 05672 ....(802)253-7301
Grey Fox Inn, Route 108, 05672 ....(802)253-8921
Guest House Horman, RR1, Box 1635, Mountain Rd, 05672 ....(802)253-4846
Innsbruck Inn, RR1, Box 1570, 05672 ....(802)253-8582
Logwood Inn, Rt 1, Box 2290, 05672 ....(802)253-7354
Mountain Brook Inn, PO Box 1152, 05672 ....(800)553-3035
Nichols Lodge, Box 1098, 05672 ....(802)253-7683
Scandinavia Inn, RR1, Box 1470CI, 05672 ....(802)253-8555
Ski Inn, Rt 108, Mountain Rd, 05672 ....(802)253-4050
Spruce Pond Inn, 05672 ....(802)253-4828
Stowe-Away Lodge, RR 1 Box 1360, 05672 ....(802)253-7574
Stowe-Bound Lodge, RR 2 Box 2890, 05672 ....(802)253-4515
Stowehof Inn, PO Box 1108, Edson Hill Rd, 05672 ....(802)253-9722
Ten Acres Lodge, 14 Barrows Rd, 05672 ....(800)327-7357
The Inn at the Brass Lantern, 717 Maple St, 05672 ....(802)253-2229
The Siebeness, Mountain Rd, Box 1490, 05672 ....(802)253-8942
The Yodler, Rt 1 Box 10, 05672 ....(802)253-4836
Timberholm Inn, 452 Cottage Club Rd, 05672 ....(802)253-7603
Topnotch at Stowe, PO Box 1458, 05672 ....(802)253-8585
Trapp Family Lodge, 42 Trapp Hill Rd, 05672 ....(802)253-8511
Wood Chip Inn, RR 1, Box 1618, 05672 ....(802)253-9080
Ye Olde England Inne, Mountain Rd, 05672 ....(802)253-7558

SUNDERLAND N3 / *F2*
Eastbrook B&B, River Rd, 05250 ....(802)375-6509

TOWNSHEND O4 / *F2*
Boardman House, Box 112, 05353 ....(802)365-4086
Townshend Country Inn, RR 1, Box 3100, 05353 ....(802)365-4141

TUNBRIDGE J5 / *D3*
Mill Pond B&B, Rt 110 Spring Rd, Box 1, 05077 ....(802)889-9441

TYSON M4 / *E2*
Echo Lake Inn, Rt 100, 05056 ....(802)228-8602

UNDERHILL CENTER G3 / *C2*
Haus Kelley B&B, Old W Bolton Rd, 05490 ....(802)899-3905

VERGENNES I2 / *D1*
Basin Harbor Club, Basin Harbor Rd, 05491 ....(802)475-2311
Emersons' Guest House, 82 Main St, 05491 ....(802)877-3293
Strong House Inn, RD 1 Box 9, Rt 22A, 05491 ....(802)877-3337

WAITSFIELD H4 / *C2*
Honeysuckle Inn, PO Box 828, 05673 ....(802)496-6200
Hyde Away, Rt 17, 05673 ....(802)496-2322
Knoll Farm Country Inn, Bragg Hill Rd, RFD 179, 05673 ....(802)496-3939
Lareau Farm Country Inn, Rt 100 Box 563, 05673 ....(802)496-4949
Mad River Barn, Rt 17 PO Box 88, 05673 ....(802)496-3310
Mad River Inn, PO Box 75, 05673 ....(802)496-7900
Millbrook, RFD Box 62, 05673 ....(802)496-2405
Mountain View Inn, Rt 17 RFD Box 69, 05673 ....(802)496-2426
Newtons' 1824 House Inn, Rt 100 Box 159, 05673 ....(802)496-7555
Olde Tymes Inn, Rt 100, PO Box 165, 05673 ....(802)496-3875
Plum Creek, PO Box 771, 05673 ....(802)496-6886
Round Barn Farm, RR Box 247, 05673 ....(802)496-2276
Snuggery Inn, Box 65, RR #1, 05673 ....(802)496-2322
The Valley Inn, Rt 100 Box 8, 05673 ....(802)496-3450
Tucker Hill Lodge, RFD1, Box 147, Rt 17, 05673 ....(802)496-3983
Waitsfield Inn, Rt 100, Box 969, 05673 ....(802)496-3979
Weathertop Lodge, Rt 17, Box 151, 05673 ....(802)496-4909

WALLINGFORD M3 / *E2*
Dunham House, 7 S Main St, 05773 ....(802)446-2600
Wallingford Inn, Box 404, 05773 ....(802)446-2849
White Rocks Inn, RR 1 Box 297, Rt 7, 05773 ....(802)446-2077

WARREN I4 / *D2*
Beaver Pond Farm Inn, RD Box 306, Golf Course Rd, 05674 ....(802)583-2861
Pitcher Inn, PO Box 408, 05674 ....(802)496-3831
South Hollow Farm, RR1, Box 287, 05674 ....(802)496-5627
Sugartree Inn, RR Box 38, Sugarbush Access Rd, 05674 ....(802)583-3211
The Sugarbush Inn, Access Rd, 05674 ....(802)583-2301

WATERBURY H4 / *C2*
The Inn at Blush Hill, Blush Hill Rd, PO Box 1266, 05676 ....(802)244-7529
Grunberg Haus B&B, RR2 Box 1595, 05676 ....(802)244-7726
The Inn at Thatcher Brook Falls, RD 2 Box 62, 05676 ....(802)244-5911

WATERBURY CENTER G4 / *C2*
The Black Locust Inn, RR 1 Box 715, 05677 ....(802)244-7490

WEATHERSFIELD M5 / *F3*
The Inn at Weathersfield, Rt 106 Box 165, 05151 ....(802)263-9217

WEST CHARLESTON D7 / *B4*
Hunt's Hideaway, RR1, Box 570, 05872 ....(802)895-4432

WEST DOVER P4 / *G2*
Austin Hill Inn, Rt 100 Box 859, 05356 ....(802)464-5281
Deerhill Inn, PO Box 397, 05356 ....(802)464-3100
Doveberry Inn, Rt 100, 05356 ....(802)464-5652
The Inn at Sawmill Farm, Box 8, 05356 ....(802)464-8131
Shield Inn, Rt 100, Box 366, 05356 ....(802)464-3984
Snow Den Inn, Rt 100 Box 625, 05356 ....(802)464-9355
Weathervane Lodge, Box 57, Dorr Fitch Rd, 05356 ....(802)464-5426
West Dover Inn, Rt 100 Box 506, 05356 ....(802)464-5207

WEST RUTLAND L3 / *E2*
The Silver Fox Inn, Rt 133 Box 1222, 05777 ....(802)438-5555

WEST TOWNSEND O4 / *F2*
Windham Hill Inn, RR 1 Box 44, 05359 ....(802)874-4080

WESTON N4 / *F2*
1830 Inn on the Green, Rt 100 Box 104, 05161 ....(802)824-6789
Darling Family Inn, Rt 100, 05161 ....(802)824-6286
The Colonial House, Rt 100 Box 138, 05161 ....(802)824-6286
The Inn at Weston, Rt 100 Box 56, 05161 ....(802)824-5804
Wilder Homestead Inn, RR 1 Box 106D, 05161 ....(802)842-8172

WHITE RIVER JUNCTION K6 / *E3*
Serenity Hill Farm, Center of Town Rd, 05001 ....(802)295-9075

WILLIAMSTOWN I5 / *D3*
Autumn Crest Inn, Clark Rd, 05679 ....(802)433-6627
Rosewood Inn, Rt 14 Box 31, 05679 ....(802)433-5822

WILLIAMSVILLE O5 / *G2*
The Country Inn Williamsville, Grimes Hill Rd, Box 166, 05362 ....(802)348-7148

WILLISTON G3 / *C2*
Partridge Hill B&B, 102 Partridge Hill, 05495 ....(802)878-4741

WILMINGTON P3 / *G2*
Brook Bound Bldg/Hermitage, Coldbrook Rd, 05363 ....(802)464-3511
Darcroft's Schoolhouse, Rt 100, 05363 ....(802)464-2631
Fjord Gate Inn & Farm, RR1, Box 138F, Higley Hill Rd, 05363 ....(802)464-2783
Hermitage Inn, Coldbrook Rd, 05363 ....(802)464-3511
Misty Mountain Lodge, Stowe Hill Rd, Box 114, 05363 ....(802)464-3961
Nordic Hills Lodge, 179 Coldbrook Rd, 05363 ....(802)464-5130
Nutmeg Inn, Rt 9W, Molly Starke Tr, 05363 ....(802)464-3351
On the Rocks Lodge, 05363 ....(802)464-8364
The Red Shutter Inn, Box 636, Rt 9, 05363 ....(802)464-3768
Schroder Haus, Higley Hill Rd, 05363 ....(802)464-2783
Slalom Lodge, Shafter St, 05363 ....(802)464-3783
The White House, Rt 9, 05363 ....(802)464-2136
Trail's End, Smith Rd, 05363 ....(802)464-2727

WINDSOR M5 / *E3*
Juniper Hill Inn, Juniper Hill Rd, RR 1 Box 79, 05089 ....(802)464-2135

WOODSTOCK L5 / *E3*
The Canterbury House, 43 Pleasant St, 05091 ....(802)457-3077
Carriage House of Woodstock, Rt 4 W, 05091 ....(802)457-4322
The Charleston House, 21 Pleasant St, 05091 ....(802)457-3843
Deer Brook Inn, HCR 35, Box 189, 05091 ....(802)672-3713
The Lincoln Inn at the Covered Bridge, RR 2 Box 40, 05091 ....(802)457-3312
Riverside Guest House, 61 River St, 05091 ....(802)457-3896
The Winslow House, #38, Rt 4 W, 05091 ....(802)457-1820

Three Church Street, 3 Church St, 05091 .... (802)457-1925
Village Inn Of Woodstock, 41 Pleasant St, 05091 .... (802)457-1255
Woodstock Inn & Resort, 14 the Green, 05091 .... (802)457-1100
Woodstocker B&B, 61 River St, 05091 .... (802)457-3896

VIRGINIA

ABINGDON P6 / *G3*
Litchfield Hall, 247 E Valley St, 24210 .... (703)628-9317
Martha Washington Inn, 150 W Main St, 24210 .... (703)628-3161
Mason Place B&B, 243 Mason Place, NW, 24210 .... (703)628-2887
Summerfield Inn, 101 W Valley St, 24210 .... (703)628-5905

ALDIE G19 / *C9*
Little River Inn, PO Box 116, 22001 .... (703)327-6742

ALEXANDRIA H21 / *D9*
Alexandria Lodgings, PO Box 416, 22313 .... (703)836-5575
Morrison House, 116 S Alfred St, 22314 .... (703)838-8000

AMHERST M15 / *F7*
Dulwich Manor B&B, Rt 5, Box 173A, Rt 60E, 24521 .... (804)946-7207

ARLINGTON H2 / *C9*
Crystal B&B, 2620 S Fern St, 22202 .... (703)548-7652
Memory House, 6404 N Washington Blvd, 22205 .... (703)534-4607
Oak Grove Plantation, 3316 N 21st Ave, 22207 .... (703)827-0511
Swedish Inn, C/O3623 N 37th St, 22207 .... (703)524-4682

BANCO I18 / *D8*
Olive Mill B&B, Rt 231, 22711 .... (703)923-4664

BASSETT P12 / *G6*
Annie's Country Inn, Rt 5 Box 562, 24055 .... (703)629-1517

BEDFORD N14 / *F6*
Elmo's Rest, Rt 2 Box 198, 24523 .... (703)586-3707
The Longwood Inn, 517 Longwood Ave, 24523 .... (703)586-2282
Peaks of Otter Lodge, PO Box 489, 24523 .... (703)586-1081

BOSTON I18 / *D8*
Thistle Hill B&B, Rt 1, Box 291, 22713 .... (703)987-9142

BOYCE G18 / *C8*
River House, Rt 2 Box 135, 22620 .... (703)837-1476

BRIDGEWATER J15 / *D7*
Bear & Dragon B&B, 401 N Main St, 22812 .... (703)828-2807

BUMPASS K19 / *E8*
Rockland Farm Retreat, Rt 1, Box 1120, 23024 .... (703)895-5098

BURKEVILLE N18 / *F8*
Hyde Park Farm, Rt 2 Box 38, 23922 .... (804)645-8431

CAPE CHARLES N24 / *F11*
Nottingham Ridge B&B, Box 97-B, 23310 .... (804)331-1010
Pickett's Harbor, Box 97AA, 23310 .... (804)331-2212
Sea Gate, 9 Tazewell Ave, 23310 .... (804)331-2206

CASTLETON I18 / *D8*
Blue Knoll Farm, Rt 1, Box 141, 22716 .... (703)937-5234

CHARLES CITY N21 / *F9*
Edgewood Plantation, Rt 5 Historic Box 490, 23030 .... (804)829-2962
North Bend Plantation, Rt 1 Box 13A, 23030 .... (804)829-5176
Piney Grove Southall's Plantation, Rt 615 "Old Main Rd," Rt 1 Box 148, 23030
.... (804)829-2480

CHARLOTTESVILLE K17 / *E8*
200 South Street Inn, 200 South St, 22901 .... (804)979-0200
Carrsbrook, Guesthouses, PO Box 5737, 22905 .... (804)979-7264
Clifton Country Inn, Rt 9, Box 412, 22901 .... (804)971-1800
English Inn, 316 14th St NW, 22903 .... (804)295-7707
Guesthouses, PO Box 5737, 22905 .... (804)979-7264
Silver Thatch Inn, 3001 Hollymead Dr, 22901 .... (804)978-4686
Westbury, Guesthouses, PO Box 5737, 22905 .... (804)979-8327
Woodstock Hall, Rt 3 Box 40, 22901 .... (804)293-8977

CHATHAM P14 / *G6*
Sims-Mitchell House, Box 846, 242 Whittle St SW, 24531 .... (804)432-0595

CHINCOTEAGUE K26 / *E12*
Channel Bass Inn, 100 Church St, 23336 .... (804)336-6148
Miss Molly's Inn, 113 N Main St, 23336 .... (804)336-6686
Year Of The Horse Inn, 600 S Main St, 22336 .... (804)336-3221

CHRISTIANSBURG N11 / *F5*
The Oaks Bed & Breakfast Country Inn, 311 E Main St, 24073
.... (703)381-1500

CHURCHVILLE J15 / *E7*
Buckhorn Inn, Star Rt Box 139, 24421 .... (703)337-6900

CLARKSVILLE P16 / *G7*
Needmoor Inn, 801 Virginia Ave, PO Box 629, 23927 .... (804)374-2866

CLUSTER SPRINGS P15 / *G7*
Oak Grove Plantation B&B, PO Box 45, Hwy 658, 24535 .... (804)575-7613

CULPEPER I18 / *D8*
Fountain Hall B&B, 609 S East St, 22701 .... (703)825-8200

DILLWYN M17 / *F8*
Buckingham Springs Plantation, Rt 3, Box 176, 23936 .... (804)392-8770

DRAPER O10 / *G5*
Claytor Lake Homestead Inn, PO Box 7, 24324 .... (703)980-6777

DUBLIN N10 / *F5*
Bell's B&B, 13 Giles Ave, PO Box 405, 24084 .... (703)674-6331

FAIRFAX H20 / *D9*
Bailiwick Inn, 4023 Chain Bridge Rd, 22030 .... (703)691-2266

FLINT HILL H18 / *D8*
Caledonia Farm B&B, Rt 1 Box 2080, 22627 .... (703)675-3693
The School House, PO Box 31, 22627 .... (703)675-3030
Stone House Hollow, PO Box 2090, 22627 .... (703)675-3279

FLOYD O11 / *G5*
Brookfield Inn B&B, PO Box 341, 24091 .... (703)763-3363

FREDERICKSBURG J20 / *D9*
Fredericksburg Colonial Inn, 1707 Princess Anne St, 22401
.... (703)371-5666
Kenmore Inn, 1200 Princess Anne St, 22401 .... (703)371-7622
La Vista Plantation, 4420 Guinea Station Rd, 22401 .... (703)898-8444
The Richard Johnston Inn, 711 Caroline St, 22401 .... (703)899-7606
The McGrath House, 225 Princess Anne St, 22401 .... (703)371-4363

FRONT ROYAL H18 / *C8*
Chester House Inn, 43 Chester St, 22630 .... (703)635-3937

GORDONSVILLE K18 / *E8*
Sleepy Hollow Farm, Rt 3 Box 43 on VA 231, 22942 .... (703)832-5555

GOSHEN K14 / *E6*
The Rose Hummingbird Inn, Country Lane, PO Box 70, 24439
.... (703)997-9065

HAMILTON G19 / *C9*
Hamilton Garden Inn, 353 W Colonial Hwy, 22068 .... (703)338-3693
Stonegate, 325 W Colonial Hwy, 22068 .... (703)338-9519

HARRISONBURG I16 / *D7*
Joshua Wilton House, 412 S Main St, 22801 .... (703)434-4464
Kingsway B&B, 3581 Singers Glen Rd, 22801 .... (703)867-9696

HAYWOOD J17 / *D8*
Shenandoah Springs Country Inn, 22722 .... (703)923-4300

HILLSBORO G19 / *C9*
Inn Between the Hills, RR 3, Rt 9 PO Box 68A, 22132 .... (703)668-6162

HOT SPRINGS K13 / *E6*
The Carriage Court, Rt 220, Box 620, 24445 .... (703)839-2345

IRVINGTON L23 / *E10*
Kendall Hall Inn, PO Box 337, Rt 200, 22480 .... (804)438-6927
King Carter Inn, PO Box 425, 22480 .... (804)438-6053

LANCASTER L23 / *E10*
The Inn at Levelfields, State Rt 3 Box 216, 22503 .... (804)435-6887

LEESBURG G19 / *C9*
Colonial Inn, 19 S King St, 22075 .... (703)777-5000
Fleetwood Farm, Rt 1 Box 306-A, 22075 .... (703)327-4325
Laurel Brigade Inn, 20 W Market St, 22075 .... (703)777-1010

LEXINGTON L14 / *E6*
Alexander-Winthrow House, 11 N Main St, 24450 .... (703)463-2044
Fassifern B&B, Rt 5 Box 87- State Rt 39, 24450 .... (703)463-1013
Historic Country Inns, 11 N Main St, 24450 .... (703)463-2044
Llewellyn Lodge at Lexington, 603 S Main St, 24450 .... (703)463-3235
Maple Hall, 11 N Main St, 24450 .... (703)463-2044
McCampbell Inn, 11 N Main St, 24450 .... (703)463-2044

LINCOLN G19 / *C9*
Springdale Country Inn, 22078 .... (703)338-1832

LURAY I17 / *D8*
Mountain View House B&B, 151 S Court St, 22835 .... (703)743-3723
The Ruffner House, Rt 4 Box 620, 22835 .... (703)743-7855
Shenandoah Countryside B&B, Rt 2 Box 377, 22835 .... (703)743-6434

LYNCHBURG M15 / *F7*
The Madison House B&B, 413 Madison St, 24504 .... (804)528-1503

MADISON HEIGHTS M15 / *F7*
Winridge, Rt 1, Box 362, 24572 .... (804)384-7220

MATHEWS M23 / *F10*
Ravenswood Inn, PO Box 250, 23109 .... (804)725-7272
Riverfront House & Cottage, Rt 14 E Box 310, 23109 .... (804)725-9975

MCGAHEYSVILLE J16 / *D7*
Shenandoah Valley Farm & Inn, Rt 1 Box 142, 22840 .... (703)289-5402

MIDDLEBURG H19 / *C4*
Briar Patch At Middleburg, PO Box 803, 22117 .... (703)327-4455
Red Fox Inn & Mosby's Tavern, PO Box 385, 2 E Washington St, 22117
.... (703)687-6301

Welbourne, 22117 .... (703)687-3201
Windsor House, 2 W Washington St, 22117 .... (703)687-6800

MIDDLETOWN G17 / C8
Wayside Inn Since 1797, 7783 Main St, 22645 .... (703)869-1797

MILLWOOD G18 / C8
Brookside, 22646 .... (703)837-1780

MITCHELLS J18 / D8
Stuartfield Hearth, Rt 1, Box 199, 22729 .... (703)825-8132

MOLLUSK L23 / E10
Greenvale Manor, Rt 354 Box 70, 22517 .... (804)462-5995

MONTEREY J13 / D6
Highland Inn, Main Street, PO Box 40, 24465 .... (703)468-2143

MONTROSS K22 / E10
The Inn at Montross, Courthouse Sq, 22520 .... (804)493-9097

MORATTICO L22 / E10
Holly Point, Box 64, 22523 .... (804)462-7759

MOUNT JACKSON H16 / D7
Sky Chalet, Star Rd, Box 28, 22842 .... (703)856-2147
The Widow Kip's Shenandoah Inn, Rt 1 Box 117, 22842 .... (703)477-2400

NATURAL BRIDGE M14 / F6
Burger's County Inn B&B, Rt 1 Box 564, 24578 .... (703)291-2464

NELLYSFORD L16 / E7
The Meander Inn at Penny Lane Farm, Rts 612 & 613 Box 443, 22958 .... (804)361-1121
Sunset Hill, Rt 1, Box 375, 22958 .... (804)361-1101

NEW CHURCH K25 / E11
The Garden and the Sea Inn, PO Box 275, 23415 .... (804)824-0672

NEW MARKET I16 / D7
A Touch of Country B&B, 9329 Congress St, 22844 .... (703)740-8030

NORTH M23 / F10
Cedar Point Country Inn, PO Box 369, 23128 .... (804)725-9535

NORTH GARDEN L17 / E8
The Inn at the Crossroads, Rt 2, Box 6, 22959 .... (804)979-6452

OCCOQUAN I20 / D9
Rockledge B&B, 410 Mill St, 22125 .... (703)690-3377

ONANCOCK L25 / E11
Colonial Manor Inn, PO Box 94; 84 Market St, 23417 .... (804)787-3521

ORANGE J18 / E8
Hidden Inn, 249 Caroline St, 22960 .... (703)672-3625
Mayhurst Inn, US 15 South, PO Box 707, 22960 .... (703)672-5597
The Shadows B&B Inn, 14291 Constitution Hwy, 22960 .... (703)672-5057

PARIS G18 / C8
The Ashby Inn, Rt 1 Box 2A, 22130 .... (703)592-3900

PETERSBURG N20 / F9
The High Street Inn, 405 High St, 23803 .... (804)733-0505
Mayfield Inn, W Washington PO Box 2265, 23803 .... (804)733-0866

RAPHINE K14 / E7
Oak Spring Farm & Vineyard, Rt 1 Box 356, 24472 .... (703)377-2398

RAPPAHANNOCK H18 / C8
Bunree, PO Box 53, 22002 .... (703)937-4133

REEDVILLE L23 / E10
Cedar Grove, Rt 1 Box 2535, 22539 .... (804)453-3915
Elizabeth House, PO Box 163, 22539 .... (804)453-7016

RICHMOND M20 / F9
Abbie Hill B&B, PO Box 4503, 23220 .... (804)355-5855
B&B On The Hill, 2304 E Broad St, 23223 .... (804)780-3746
Bensonhouse, The Emmanuel Hutzler House, 2036 Monument Ave, 23220 .... (804)353-6900
Carrington Row Inn, 2309 E Broad St, 23223 .... (804)343-7005
The Catlin-Abbott House, 2304 E Broad St, 23223 .... (804)780-3746
Duncan Lee House, PO Box 15131, 22314 .... (804)321-6277
Hanover Hosts in the Fun, Box 25145, 23260 .... (804)355-5855
Linden Row, First & Franklin Sts, 23219 .... (804)783-7000
Mr. Patrick Henry's Inn, 2300 E Broad St, 23223 .... (804)644-1322
The Leonine Experience, PO Box 4772, 23220 .... (804)349-1952
The West-Bocock House, 1107 Grove Ave, 23220 .... (804)358-6174

ROANOKE N12 / F6
Lone Oaks B&B, 3348 Grandin Rd, 24018 .... (703)989-9599
The Mary Bladon House B&B, 381 Washington Ave Old SW, 24016 .... (703)344-5361

SCOTTSVILLE L17 / E8
Chester, Rt 4, PO Box 57, 24590 .... (804)286-3960
High Meadows, Rt 4 Box 6, 24590 .... (804)286-2218

SMITH MOUNTAIN LAKE O13 / F6
Holland-Duncan House, Rt 3 Box 681, 24121 .... (703)721-8510
Manor at Taylor's Store, Rt 1 Box 533, 24184 .... (703)721-3951

SMITHFIELD O22 / G10
Isle of Wight Inn, 1607 S Church St, 23430 .... (804)357-3176

SPERRYVILLE I17 / D8
The Conyers House, Slate Mills Rd, Rt 1 Box 157, 22740 .... (703)987-8025
Nethers Mill, Rt 1, Box 62, 22740 .... (703)987-8625

STAUNTON K15 / E7
Belle Grae Inn, 515 W Frederick St, 24401 .... (703)886-5151
Frederick House, Frederick and New Streets, 24401 .... (703)885-4220
Thornrose House At Gypsy Hill, 531 Thornrose Ave, 24401 .... (703)885-7026

STEELE'S TAVERN K15 / E7
The Osceola Mill Country Inn, 24476 .... (703)377-6455

STRASBURG G17 / C8
Hotel Strasburg, 201 Holliday St, 22657 .... (703)465-9191

SURRY N22 / F10
Surrey House, 23883 .... (804)294-3191

SWOOPE K14 / E7
Lambsgate B&B, Rt 1 Box 63, 24479 .... (703)337-6929

SYRIA J17 / D8
Grave's Mountain Lodge, 22743 .... (703)923-4231

TANGIER L24 / E11
Sunset Inn, Box 156, 23440 .... (804)891-2535

TOANO N22 / F10
Blue Bird Haven, 8691 Barhamsville Rd, 23168 .... (804)566-0177

TREVILIANS K18 / E8
Prospect Hill, Rt 613, RD 3 Box 430, 23093 .... (703)967-0844

UPPERVILLE G18 / C8
1763 Inn, Rt 1 Box 19, 22176 .... (703)592-3848

URBANNA L22 / F10
The Town House, 1880 Prince George St, Box 757, 23175 .... (804)758-3521

VESUVIUS L15 / E7
Irish Gap Inns, Rt 1 Box 40, 24483 .... (804)922-7701

VIRGINIA BEACH O24 / G11
The Picket Fence, 209 43rd St, 23451 .... (804)428-8861

WACHAPREAGUE M25 / F11
The Burton House, 11 Brooklyn St, 23480 .... (804)787-4560

WARM SPRINGS K13 / E6
The Inn at Gristmill Square, PO Box 359, 24484 .... (703)839-2231
Meadow Lane Lodge, Star Rt A Box 110, 24484 .... (703)839-5959
Three Hills Inn, PO Box 99, 24484 .... (703)839-5381

WARRENTON I19 / D8
Rosemont Farm Inn, Rt 3 Box 240, 22186 .... (703)347-5422

WASHINGTON I18 / D8
The Foster-Harris House, PO Box 333, 22747 .... (703)675-3757
Gay Street Inn, Po Box 237, 22747 .... (703)675-3288
Heritage House B&B, Main St, PO Box 427, 22747 .... (703)675-3207
The Inn at Little Washington, PO Box 300, Middle & Main Sts, 22747 .... (703)675-3800
Sycamore Hill House, Rt 1 Box 978, 227547 .... (703)675-3046

WATERFORD G20 / C9
The Pink House, 22190 .... (703)882-3453

WHITE POST G18 / C8
L'Auberge Provencale, PO Box 119, 22663 .... (703)837-1375

WILLIAMSBURG N22 / F10
Applewood Colonial B&B, 605 Richmond Rd, 23185 .... (804)229-0205
Bensonhouse of Williamsburg, Contact Bensonhouse of Richmond, 23185 .... (804)353-6900
Brass Lantern Lodge, 1782 Jamestown Rd, 23185 .... (804)229-4320
The Cedars, 616 Jamestown Rd, 23185 .... (804)229-3591
Fox Grape Of Williamsburg, 701 Monumental Ave, 23185 .... (804)229-6914
Governor's Trace, 303 Capitol Landing Rd, 23185 .... (804)229-7552
Himmel-B&B, 706 Richmond Rd, 23185 .... (804)229-6421
Liberty Rose Colonial B&B, 1022 Jamestown Rd, 23185 .... (804)253-1260
Newport House, 710 S Henry St, 23185 .... (804)229-1775
War Hill Inn, 4560 Long Hill Rd, 23185 .... (804)565-0248
Wood's Guest Home, 1208 Stewart Dr, 23185 .... (804)229-3376

WINTERGREEN K16 / E7
Trillium House, PO Box 280, 22958 .... (804)325-9126

WOODSTOCK H17 / C8
Azalea House B&B, 551 S Main St, 22664 .... (703)459-3500
The Candlewick Inn, 127 N Church St, 22664 .... (703)459-8008
Country Fare, 402 N Main St, Rt 11, 22664 .... (703)459-4828
The Inn at Narrow Passage, PO Box 608, 22664 .... (703)459-8000
River'd Inn, Rt 1, Box 217A1, 22664 .... (703)459-5369

WASHINGTON

ACME C11 / A3
River Valley B&B, Box 158, 98220 .... (206)595-2686

ANACORTES D10 / A3
Albatross Bed & Breakfast, 5708 Kingsway, 98221 .... (206)293-0677
Campbell House, 917 36th, 98221 .... (206)293-4910
Channel House, 2902 Oakes Ave, 98221 .... (206)293-9382
Dutch Treat House, 1220 31st St, 98221 .... (206)293-8154
Hasty Pudding House, 1312 8th Street, 98221 .... (206)293-5773
Lowman House, 701 "K" Ave, 98221 .... (206)293-0590
Nantucket Inn, 3402 Commercial Ave, 98221 .... (206)293-6007

ANDERSON ISLAND I10 / C3
The Inn at Burg's Landing, 8808 Villa Beach Rd, 98303 .... (206)884-9185

ASHFORD K12 / D3
Alexander's Country Inn, Hwy 706, 98304 .... (206)569-2300
Ashford Mansion, Box G, 98304 .... (206)569-2739
Growly Bear, PO Box 103, 98304 .... (206)569-2339
Mountain Meadows Inn, 28912 SR 706E, 98304 .... (206)569-2788
National Park Inn, Mt Rainier Guest Services, Star Rt, 98304 .... (206)569-2563

BAINBRIDGE ISLAND G10 / C3
Beach Cottage, 5831 Ward Ave NE, 98110 .... (206)842-6081
Bombay House, 8490 Beck Rd NE, 98110 .... (206)842-3926
Olympic View B&B, 15415 Harvey Rd NE, 98110 .... (206)842-4671

BELLINGHAM C10 / A3
Bellingham's De Cann House B&B, 2610 Eldridge Ave, 98225 .... (206)734-9172
The Castle B&B, 1103 15th & Knox Sts, 98225 .... (206)676-0974
North Garden Inn, 1014 N Garden, 98225 .... (206)671-7828
Schnauzer Crossing, 4421 Lakeway Dr, 98226 .... (206)733-0055

BINGEN D13 / E4
The Grand Old House, Hwy 14 PO Box 667, 98605 .... (509)493-2838

BREMERTON G10 / C3
Willcox House, 2390 Tekiu Rd, 98312 .... (206)830-4492

CARSON D12 / E3
Carson Hot Springs Hotel, PO Box 370, 98610 .... (509)427-8292

CATHLAMET M8 / D2
Cathlamet Hotel, 69 Main St, PO Box 62, 98612 .... (800)446-0454
Country Keeper B&B Inn, 61 Main St, PO Box 35, 98612 .... (206)795-3030

CHELAN F15 / B5
Em's B&B, PO Box 206, 304 Wapato, 98816 .... (509)682-4149
Mary Kay's Whaley Mansion, Rt 1, Box 693, 98816 .... (509)682-5735
North Cascades Lodge, PO Box W, 98816 .... (509)682-4711

CHIMACUM E10 / B3
Summer House, 2603 Center Rd, 98325 .... (206)732-4017

CLINTON F11 / B3
Home by the Sea, 2388 E Sunlight Beach Rd, 98236 .... (206)221-2964

COLVILLE C23 / A7
Lake Side Manor, Tiger Star Rt, Box 194, 99114 .... (509)684-8741

CONCRETE C12 / A4
Cascade Mountain Inn, 3840 Pioneer Ln, Birdsview, 98237 .... (206)826-4333

COSMOPOLIS J7 / C2
Cooney Mansion B&B, 802 E Fifth St, PO Box 54, 98537 .... (206)533-0602

COUPEVILLE E10 / B3
Captain Whidbey, 2072 W Captain Whidbey Inn Rd, 98239 .... (206)678-4097
Colonel Crockett Farm, 1012 S Ft. Casey Rd, 98239 .... (206)466-3207
The Inn at Penn Cove, 702 N Main, PO Box 85, 98239 .... (206)678-8000
The Victorian B&B, PO Box 761, 602 N Main, 98239 .... (206)678-5305

DEER PARK F24 / B8
B&B With Love's, N 31317 Cedar Rd, 99006 .... (509)276-6939

EASTSOUND C9 / A2
Kangaroo House, 5 North Beach Rd, Orcas Island, 98245 .... (206)376-2175
Outlook Inn, Box 210 Main St, 98245 .... (206)376-2200
Rosario Resort Hotel, 98245 .... (206)376-2222

EATONVILLE J11 / D3
Old Mill House B&B, PO Box 543, 98328 .... (206)832-6506

EDMONDS F11 / B3
Heather House, 1011 "B" Ave, 98020 .... (206)778-7233
Hudgens Haven, 9313 190th SW, 98020 .... (206)776-2202
Maple Tree B&B, 18313 Olympic View Dr, 98020 .... (206)774-8420
Pinkham's Pillow, Dayton St & 3rd Ave, 98020 .... (206)774-3406

FERNDALE B10 / A3
Anderson House B&B, 2140 Main St, 98248 .... (206)384-3450
Hill Top B&B, 5832 Church Rd, 98248 .... (206)384-3619

FORKS F5 / B1
Miller Tree Inn, PO Box 953, 98331 .... (206)374-6806

FOX ISLAND H10 / C3
The Beach Place, 158 Brick Kiln Rd, 98333 .... (206)549-2555

FREELAND F10 / B3
Cliff House & Seacliff Cottage, 5440 Windmill Rd, 98249 .... (206)321-1566
Pillars By The Sea, 1367 E Bayview, 98249 .... (205)221-7736

FRIDAY HARBOR C9 / A2
Blair House B&B, 345 Blair Ave, 98250 .... (206)378-5907
Collins House, 225 A St, 98250 .... (206)378-5834
Hillside House, 365 Carter Ave, 98250 .... (206)378-4730
Moon and Sixpence, 3021 Beverton Valley Rd, 98250 .... (206)378-4138
Olympic Lights, 4531A Cattle Point Rd, 98250 .... (206)378-3186
San Juan Inn, PO Box 776, 98250 .... (206)378-2070
Tucker House B&B, 260 B St, 98250 .... (206)378-2783
Wharfside B&B Aboard the Jacquelyn, PO Box 1212, 98250 .... (206)378-5661

GIG HARBOR H10 / C2
Olde Glencove Hotel, 9418 Glencove Rd, 98335 .... (206)884-2835

GLENWOOD N13 / E4
Flying L Ranch, 25 Flying L Ln, 98619 .... (509)364-3488

GOLDENDALE N15 / E4
Three Creeks Lodge, 2120 Hwy 97 Satus Pass, 98620 .... (509)773-4026

GOOSE PRAIRIE J14 / D4
Hopkinson House, 862 Bumping River Rd, 98929 .... (509)248-2264

GRAPEVIEW H9 / C2
Llewop B&B, Box 97, 98546 .... (206)275-2287

GREENBANK E10 / B3
Guest House B&B & Cottages, 835 E Christenson Rd, 98253 (206)678-3115

ILWACO L6 / D1
The Inn at Ilwaco, 120 Williams St, NE, 98624 .... (206)642-8686

INDEX F13 / B4
Bush House, PO Box 58, 98256 .... (206)793-2312

ISSAQUAH H12 / C3
Wildflower Inn, 25237 Issaquah-Fall City Rd, 98027 .... (206)392-1196

KIRKLAND G11 / B3
Shumway Mansion, 11410 99th Place NE, 98033 .... (206)823-2303

LA CONNER D10 / D3
Downey House, 1880 Chilberg Rd, 98257 .... (206)678-3115
Heron in La Conner, Box 716, 117 Maple St, 98257 .... (206)466-4626
Katy's Inn, PO Box 231, 503 S 3rd, 98257 .... (206)466-3366
La Conner Country Inn, PO Box 573, 98257 .... (206)466-3101
Rainbow Inn, 1075 Chilberg Rd, PO Box 1600, 98257 .... (206)466-4578
White Swan Guest House, 1388 Moore Rd, 98273 .... (206)445-6805

LANGLEY E11 / B3
Country Cottage of Langley, 215 6th St, 98260 .... (206)221-8709
Eagles Nest Inn, 3236 E Saratoga Rd, 98260 .... (206)321-5331
The Inn at Langley, 400 First St, 98260 .... (206)221-3033
Log Castle B&B, 3273 E Saratoga Rd, 98260 .... (206)321-5483
Lone Lake B&B, 5206 S Bayview, 98260 .... (206)321-5325
Saratoga Inn, 4850 South Coles Rd, 98260 .... (206)221-7526
The Orchard, 619 3rd St, 98260 .... (206)221-7880
Whidbey House, PO Box 156, 106 First St, 98260 .... (206)221-7115

LEAVENWORTH G15 / C5
Bavarian Meadows B&B, 11099 Eagle Creek Rd, 98826 .... (509)548-4449
Brown's Farm B&B, 11150 Hwy 209, 98826 .... (509)548-7863
Edel Haus B&B, 320 Ninth St, 98826 .... (509)548-4412
Haus Lorelei Inn, 347 Division St, 98826 .... (509)548-5726
Haus Rohrback, 12882 Ranger Rd, 98826 .... (206)548-7024
Hotel Europa, 833 Front St, 98826 .... (509)548-5221
Mountain Home Lodge, PO Box 687, 98826 .... (509)548-7077
Old Blewett Pass B&B, 3470 Hwy 97, 98826 .... (509)548-4475
Run of the River B&B, PO Box 285, 98826 .... (509)548-7171

LONGMIRE K12 / D3
National Park Inn, 98398 .... (206)569-2565

LOPEZ ISLAND C9 / A2
MacKaye Harbor Inn, Rt 1, Box 1940, 98261 .... (206)468-2253
The Inn at Swifts Bay, Rt 2 Box 3402, 98261 .... (206)468-3636

LUMMI ISLAND C10 / A3
The Willows, 2579 W Shore Dr, 98262 .... (206)758-2620
West Shore Farm, 2781 W Shore Dr, 98262 .... (206)758-2600

LYNDEN B11 / A3
Le Cocq House, 719 W Edson, 98264 .... (206)354-3032

MAPLE VALLEY H11 / C3
Maple Valley B&B, 20020 SE 228th, 98038 .... (206)432-1409

MAZAMA C16 / A5
Mazama Country Inn, PO Box 215, 98833 .... (509)996-2681

MERCER ISLAND K4 / C3
Mole House B&B, 3308 W Mercer Way, 98040 .... (206)232-1611

MONTESANO J7 / C2
Sylvan Haus, Box 416, 417 Wilder Hill Rd, 98563 .... (206)249-3453

MOUNT VERNON D11 / A3
Downey House, 1880 Chilberg Rd, 98272 .... (206)466-3207

NORDLAND E10 / B3
Ecologic Place, 10 Beach Dr, 98358 .... (206)385-3077

NORTH BEND H12 / C4
Apple Tree Inn, 43317 S North Bend Way, 98045 ....(206)888-3672
Hillwood Gardens, 41812 SE 142nd St, 98045 ....(206)888-0799

OLYMPIA I9 / C2
Harbinger Inn, 1136 E Bay Dr, 98506 ....(206)754-0389
Puget View Guesthouse, 7924 61st NE, 98506 ....(206)459-1676

ORCAS C9 / A2
Orcas Hotel, PO Box 155, 98280 ....(206)376-4300
Woodsong B&B, PO Box 32, 98280 ....(206)376-2340

ORCAS ISLAND C9 / A2
Turtleback Farm Inn, Rt 1 Box 650, Eastsound, 98245 ....(206)376-4914

PACKWOOD K12 / D3
Packwood Hotel, Rt 256, 98361 ....(206)494-5431

PATEROS E17 / B5
Amy's Manor B&B, PO Box 411, 98846 ....(509)923-2334
French House B&B, 206 W Warren, 98846 ....(509)923-2626

PORT ANGELES E8 / B2
Bennett House B&B, 325 E 6th, 98362 ....(206)457-0870
Glen Mar By the Sea, 318 N Eunice, 98362 ....(206)457-3424
Lake Crescent Lodge, Star Rt 1, 98362 ....(206)928-3211

PORT HADLOCK E10 / B3
Port Hadlock Inn & Marina, PO Box 29, 98339 ....(800)395-1595

PORT ORCHARD G10 / C3
Ogle's B&B, 1307 Dogwood Hills SW, 98366 ....(206)876-9170

PORT TOWNSEND E10 / B3
Arcadia Country Inn, 1891 S Jacob Miller Rd, 98368 ....(206)385-5245
Bishop Victorian Suites, 714 Washington St, 98368 ....(206)385-6122
Heritage House Inn, 305 Pierce St, 98368 ....(206)385-6800
Holly Hill House B&B, 611 Polk, 98368 ....(206)385-5619
James House, 1238 Washington, 98368 ....(206)385-1238
Lincoln Inn, 538 Lincoln, 98368 ....(206)385-6677
Lizzie's, 731 Pierce St, 98368 ....(206)385-4168
Manresa Castle, PO Box 564, 7th & Sheridan, 98368 ....(206)385-5750
Old Consulate Inn F.W. Hastings House, 313 Walker at Washington, 98368 ....(206)385-6753
Palace Hotel, 1004 Water St, 98368 ....(206)385-0773
Ravenscroft Inn, 533 Quincy St, 98368 ....(206)385-2784
Starrett House Inn, 744 Clay St, 98368 ....(206)385-3205

POULSBO G10 / C3
Manor Farm Inn, 26069 Big Valley Rd, 98370 ....(206)779-4628

QUINAULT H7 / C1
Lake Quinault Lodge, PO Box 7, S Shore Rd, 98575 ....(206)288-2571

RANDLE K12 / D3
Hampton House B&B, 409 Silverboork Rd, 98377 ....(206)497-2907

REDMOND G11 / B3
A Colonial B&B, 1011-240th Ave NE, 98053 ....(206)868-4159

ROCHE HARBOR C9 / A2
Hotel De Haro, PO Box 1, 98250 ....(206)378-2155
Roche Harbor Resort, 98250 ....(206)378-2155

SEATTLE G11 / C3
Beech Tree Manor, 1405 Queen Anne Ave N, 98109 ....(206)281-7037
Capitol Hill Inn, 1713 Belmont Ave, 98122 ....(206)323-1955
Challenger, 809 Fairview Place N, 98109 ....(206)340-1201
Chambered Nautilus B&B Inn, 5005 22nd NE, 98105 ....(206)522-2536
Chelsea Station B&B Inn, 4915 Linden Ave N, 98103 ....(206)547-6077
College Inn Guest House, 4000 University Way NE, 98105 ....(206)633-4441
Emerald City Inn, 1520 Bellevue Ave, 98122 ....(206)587-6565
Galer Place, 318 W Galer St, 98119 ....(206)282-5339
Hanson House, 1526 Palm Ave SW, 98116 ....(206)937-4157
Marit's B&B, 6208 Palatine Ave N, 98103 ....(206)782-7900
Mildred's B&B, 1202 15th Ave E, 98112 ....(206)325-6072
Prince of Wales, 133 Thirteenth Ave E, 98102 ....(206)325-9692
Roberta's B&B, 1147 16th Ave E, 98112 ....(206)329-3326
Salisbury House, 750 16th Ave E, 98112 ....(206)328-8682
Shafer Mansion, 907 14th Ave, 98112 ....(206)823-2303
The Williams House, 1505 Fourth Ave N, 98109 ....(206)285-0810

SEAVIEW L6 / D1
Shelburne Inn, PO Box 250, Pacific Hwy 103 & 45th, 98644 ....(206)642-2442

SEQUIM E9 / B2
Brigadoon B&B, 105 Brigadoon Blvd, 98382 ....(206)683-2255
Margie's B&B, 120 Forrest Rd, 98382 ....(206)683-7011

SHELTON H9 / C2
Twin River Ranch, E 5730 Hwy 3, 98584 ....(206)426-1023

SNOHOMISH F12 / B3
Country Manner B&B, 1120 First St, 98290 ....(206)568-8254
Countryman's B&B, 119 Cedar St, 98290 ....(206)568-9622

SNOQUALMIE H13 / C4
Old Honey Farm, 8910-384th Ave SE, 98065 ....(206)329-4628

SOUTH CLE ELUM I14 / C4
Moore House Country Inn, PO Box 2861, 98943 ....(509)674-5939

SPOKANE G24 / B8
Blakely Estate B&B, E 7710 Hodin Dr, 99212 ....(509)926-9426
Durocher House B&B, W 4000 Randolph Rd, 99204 ....(509)325-4739
Fotheringham House, 2128 W 2nd Ave, 99204 ....(509)838-4363
Marianna Stoltz House, E 427 Indiana, 99207 ....(509)483-4316

SUNNYSIDE L17 / D5
Sunnyside Inn B&B, 800 E Edison, 98944 ....(509)839-5557

TACOMA I10 / C3
Keenan House, 2610 N Warner, 98407 ....(206)752-0702

TOKELAND K6 / D1
Tokeland Hotel, 100 Hotel Rd, 98590 ....(206)292-9198

TROUT LAKE N13 / E4
Mio Amore Pensione, PO Box 208, 98650 ....(509)395-2264

USK D24 / B8
River Bend Inn, Rt 2 Box 943, 99180 ....(509)445-1476

VASHON ISLAND G10 / C3
Island Inn B&B, Rt 1, Box 950, 98070 ....(206)567-4832
The Old Tjomsland House, Vashon Hwy & 171st St, PO Box 913, 98070 ....(206)463-5275
Swallow's Nest, Rt 3, Box 221, 98070 ....(206)463-2646

WALLA WALLA M22 / E7
Rees Mansion Inn, 260 E Birch St, 99362 ....(509)529-7845

WENATCHEE H16 / C5
Forget-Me-Not B&B, 1133 Washington St, 98801 ....(800)843-7552

WHITE SALMON O13 / E4
Inn of the White Salmon, PO 1446, 172 SE Jewett, 98672 ....(509)493-2335
Orchard Hill Inn, Rt 2 Box 130, 98672 ....(509)493-3024

WASHINGTON DC

WASHINGTON H15 / C5
Adams Inn, 1744 Lanier Pl NW, 20009 ....(202)745-3600
Connecticut-Woodley, 2647 Woodley Rd NW, 20008 ....(202)667-0218
Embassy Inn, 1627 16 St NW, 20009 ....(202)234-7800
Kalorama Guest House, 1854 Mintwood Place NW, 20009 ....(202)667-6369
Kalorama Guest House at Woodley Park, 2700 Cathedral Ave NW, 20008 ....(202)328-0860
Meg's International Guest House, 1315 Euclid St NW, 20009 ....(202)232-5837
Morrison-Clark Inn, Massachusetts & 11 St NW, 20001 ....(202)898-1200
Mount Pleasant House, 1760 Park Rd NW, 20010 ....(202)265-2604
Reeds B&B, PO Box 12011, 20005 ....(202)328-3510
Swiss Inn, 1204 Massachusetts Ave NW, 20005 ....(202)371-1816
Tabard Inn, 1739 N St NW, 20036 ....(202)785-1277
Victorian Accommodations, 1309 Rhode Island Ave NW, 20005 ....(202)234-6292
Windsor Inn, 1842 16th St NW, 20009 ....(202)667-0300

WEST VIRGINIA

ATHENS M9 / F5
Concord Church Inn, 304 Vermillion St, 24712 ....(304)384-5084

AURORA F14 / C6
Cabin Lodge, Box 355, Rt 50, 26705 ....(304)735-3563

BERKELEY SPRINGS E17 / B8
Country Inn, 207 S Washington St, 25411 ....(304)258-2210
Folkestone B&B, Rt 2 Box 404, 25411 ....(304)258-3743
Highlawn Inn, 304 Market St, 25411 ....(304)258-5700
Maria's Garden & Inn, 201 Independence St, 25411 ....(304)258-2021
The Manor, 415 Fairfax St, 25411 ....(304)258-1552

BRAMWELL N8 / F4
The Bluestone Inn, 1 Main St, 24715 ....(304)248-7402
Three Oaks & A Quilt, Duhring St, 24715 ....(304)248-8316

BURLINGTON F16 / C7
Shelly's Homestead, Rt 1, Box 1-A, 26710 ....(304)289-3941

CASS J12 / D6
Shay Inn, General Delivery, 24927 ....(304)456-4652

CHARLES TOWN F19 / C8
The Cottonwood Inn, Rt 2 Box 61 S, 25414 ....(304)725-3371
Gilbert House B&B, PO Box 1104, 25414 ....(304)725-0637
Hillbrook Inn, Rt 2 Box 152, 25414 ....(304)725-4223
Magnus Tate's Kitchen, 201 E Washington St, 25414 ....(304)725-8052

CHLOE I9 / D4
Pennbrooke Farm B&B, Granny-she Run, 25235 ....(304)655-7367

CRAWLEY K10 / E5
Oak Knoll B&B, General Delivery, 24931 ....(304)392-6903

DAVIS G14 / C6
Bright Morning, William Ave, Rt 32, 26260 ....(304)259-5119

Twisted Thistle B&B, Box 480, 26260 ....(304)259-5389

ELKINS H13 / C6
Cheat River Lodge, Rt 1, Box 116, 26241 ....(304)636-2301
Lincoln Crest B&B, Box 408, 26241 ....(304)636-8460
Marian's Guest House, 731 Harrison Ave, 26241 ....(304)636-9883
The Retreat at Buffalo Run, 214 Harpertown Rd, 26241 ....(304)636-2960
The Wayside Inn, 201 Sycamore St, 26241 ....(304)636-1985

FAIRMONT E12 / B6
Tichnell's Tourist Home, 1367 Locust Ave, 26554 ....(304)366-3811

GAULEY BRIDGE J9 / E4
Three Rivers Inn, PO Box 231, 25085 ....(304)632-2121

GERRARDSTOWN F18 / C8
Prospect Hill Farm, PO Box 135, 25420 ....(304)229-3346

GLEN FERRIS J9 / E4
Glen Ferris Inn, 25090 ....(304)632-1111

GREENBRIER COUNTY K11 / E5
Oak Knoll B&B, Crawley, 24931 ....(304)392-6903

HARPERS FERRY F19 / C9
Fillmore Street B&B, PO Box 34, 25425 ....(301)377-0070
The View B&B, Box 286, 25425 ....(304)535-2688

HELVETIA H11 / D6
Beekeeper Inn, 26224 ....(304)924-6435

HILLSBORO K12 / E6
The Current, Box 135, 25945 ....(304)653-4722

HUNTINGTON I5 / D3
Heritage Station, 11th St & Veterans Mem Blvd, 25701 ....(304)523-6373

HUTTONSVILLE I12 / D6
The Cardinal Inn, Rt 1 Box 1, 26273 ....(304)335-6149

JANE LEW G11 / C5
West Fork Inn, Rt 2 Box 212, 26378 ....(304)745-4893

LEWISBURG L11 / E5
Lynn's Inn B&B, Rt 4 Box 40, 24901 ....(304)645-2003
Minnie Manor, 403 E Washington St, 24901 ....(304)647-4096

LOST CREEK G11 / C5
Country Corner, Box 112, 26385 ....(304)745-3017

LOST RIVER G16 / C7
Guest House, Low-Gap, 26811 ....(304)897-5707

MARTINSBURG F18 / C8
Aspen Hall Inn, 405 Boyd Ave, 25401 ....(304)263-4385
Boydville The Inn at Martinsburg, 601 S Queen St, 25401 ....(304)263-1448
The Dunn Country Inn, Rt 3 Box 33J, 25401 ....(304)263-8646

MATHIAS H16 / D7
Valley View Farm, PO Box 467, 26812 ....(304)897-5229

MOOREFIELD G15 / C7
McMechen House Inn, 109 N Main St, 26836 ....(304)538-2417

MORGANTOWN E12 / B6
Chestnut Ridge School, 1000 Stewartstown Rd, 26505 ....(304)598-2262
Maxwell B&B, Rt 12, Box 197, 26505 ....(304)594-3041

ORLANDO H10 / C5
Kilmarnock Farms, Rt 1 Box 91, 26412 ....(304)452-8319

PARKERSBURG F8 / C4
Harmony House B&B Inn, 710 Ann St, 26101 ....(304)485-1458

PENCE SPRINGS L10 / E5
The Pence Springs Hotel, Rt 3, 24962 ....(304)445-2606

PETERSBURG G15 / C7
Smoke Hole Lodge, PO Box 953, 26059 ....(304)242-8377

PROSPERITY L9 / E4
Prosperity Farmhouse, Box 393, 25909 ....(304)255-4245

ROMNEY F16 / C7
Hampshire House 1884, 165 N Grafton St, 26757 ....(304)822-7171

SHEPHERDSTOWN F19 / C8
Bavarian Inn & Lodge, Rt 1 Box 30, 25443 ....(304)876-2551
Fuss 'N Feathers, Box 1088, 210 W German, 25443 ....(304)876-6469
The Little Inn, PO 219, Princess at German St, 25443 ....(304)876-2208
Mecklenburg Inn, 128 E German St, 25443 ....(304)876-2126
Shang-Ra-La B&B, Rt 1, Box 156, 25443 ....(304)876-2391
Stonebrake Cottage, Shepherd Grade Rd, PO Box 1612, 25443 ....(304)876-6607
Thomas Shepherd Inn, Box 1162, 300 W German St, 25443 ....(304)876-3715

SINKS GROVE M10 / F5
Morgan Orchard, Rt 2 Box 114, 24976 ....(304)772-3638

SISTERSVILLE F19 / C8
Cobblestone Inn B&B, 103 Charles St, 25175 ....(304)652-1206
Wells Inn, 316 Charles St, 26175 ....(304)652-1312

SLATYFORK J12 / D6
Elk River Touring Center, 26291 ....(304)572-3771
Fassiferns Farms, Rt 219 N, 26291 ....(304)572-4645
Willis Farm, Rt 219, 26291 ....(304)572-3771

SNOWSHOE I12 / D6
Whistlepunk Inn, PO Box 70, 26209 ....(304)572-1126

SUMMERSVILLE J10 / D5
Old Wilderness Inn, 1 Old Wilderness Rd, 26651 ....(304)872-3481

SUMMIT POINT F19 / C8
Countryside, PO Box 57, 25446 ....(304)725-2614

VALLEY CHAPEL G11 / C5
Ingeberg Acres, PO Box 199, 26446 ....(304)269-2834

WELLSBURG G15 / C7
Dovers Inn, 1001 Washington Pike, 26070 ....(304)737-0188

WHEELING C10 / A5
Yesterdays, Ltd., 614 Main St, 26003 ....(304)232-0864

WHITE SULPHUR SPRING L11 / E5
The Greenbrier, 24986 ....(304)536-1110

WINONA J12 / E6
Garvey House, Box 98, 25942 ....(304)574-3235

WISCONSIN

ALBANY S10 / G4
Albany Guest House, 405 S Mill St, 53502 ....(608)862-3636

ALGOMA L15 / D6
Amberwood Inn, N7136 Hwy 42, 54201 ....(414)487-3471
B&B Guesthomes, 698 County Rt 2, 54201 ....(414)743-9742
King Olaf's Pub & Inn, PO Box 83, 54201 ....(414)487-2090

ALMA N4 / D1
The Gallery House, 215 N Main St, 54610 ....(608)685-4975
Laue House, 1111 S Main, 54610 ....(608)685-4923

APPLETON N13 / D5
The Queen Anne, 837 E College Ave, 54911 ....(414)739-7966

ASHLAND E6 / A3
Hotel Chequamegon, 101 W Front St, 54806 ....(715)682-9095

BALDWIN K2 / C1
Kaleidoscope Inn, 800 11th Ave, 54002 ....(715)684-4575

BARABOO Q9 / E4
The Barrister's House, 226 9th Ave, 53913 ....(608)356-3344
Frantiques Showplace, 704 Ash St, 53913 ....(608)356-5273
House Of Seven Gables, PO 204, 215 6th St, 53913 ....(608)356-8387
Pinehaven B&B, E13083 Hwy 33, 53913 ....(608)356-3489

BAYFIELD E6 / A3
Chez Joliet, PO Box 768, Bayfield, 54814 ....(715)779-5480
Cooper Hill House, 33 S Sixth St, PO Box 1288, 54814 ....(715)779-5060
Greunke's Inn, 17 Rittenhouse, 54184 ....(715)779-5480
Grey Oak Guest House, 7th & Manypenny, 54814 ....(715)779-5111
Le Chateau Boutin, PO Box 584, 54814 ....(715)779-5111
Old Rittenhouse Inn, 301 Rittenhouse Ave, PO Box 584-1, 54814 ....(715)779-5111
Pinehurst Inn, Hwy 13, PO Box 222, 54814 ....(715)779-3676

BELLEVILLE S10 / F4
Abendruh B&B Swiss Style, 7019 Gehin Rd, 53508 ....(608)424-3808

BELOIT T11 / G4
Richardson House, 829 Church St, 53511 ....(608)365-1627

BRANTWOOD I8 / C3
Palmquist Farm, River Rd, Rt 1, Box 134, 54513 ....(715)564-2558

BURLINGTON T13 / G5
Hillcrest B&B, 540 Storle Ave, 53105 ....(414)763-4706

CAMPBELLSPORT P13 / E5
Mielke-Mauk House, 994 County Hwy F, 53010 ....(414)533-8602

CASHTON P7 / E3
The Convent House, Rt 1, Box 160, 54619 ....(608)823-7906

CASSVILLE S6 / F2
The Geiger House, 401 Denniston, 53806 ....(608)725-5419

CEDARBURG Q14 / F5
Stagecoach Inn B&B, W 61 N 520 Washington Ave, 53012 ....(414)375-0208
The Washington House Inn, W 62 N 573 Washington Ave, 53012 ....(414)375-3550

CHIPPEWA FALLS K5 / C2
Wilson House, 320 Superior St, 54729 ....(715)723-0055

COLFAX K4 / C2
ClearView Hills B&B, Rt 2, Box 87, 54730 ....(608)255-4230
Son-ne-vale Farm B&B, Rt 1, Box 132, 54730 ....(715)962-4342

COLUMBUS Q11 / F4
By the Okeag, 446 Wisconsin St, 53925 ....(414)623-3007

CURTISS K7 / C3
Thompson's Inn, PO Box 128, County Hwy E, 54422 ....(715)223-6041

DANE R10 / *F4*
Dunroven House, 7809 Dunroven Rd, 53529 ....(608)592-4560

DE PERE M14 / *D5*
Birch Creek Inn, 2263 Birch Creek Rd, 54415 ....(414)336-7575
R&R Homestead, 803 Morning Glory Ln, 54115 ....(414)336-8244

DEFOREST R10 / *F4*
Circle B B&B, 3804 Vinburn Rd, 53532 ....(608)846-3481

DELAVAN T12 / *G5*
Jeremiah Mabie House B&B, 711 Walworth St, 53115 ....(414)728-1876

DOWNSVILLE L4 / *D1*
Creamery, Box 22, 54735 ....(715)664-8354

EAGLE RIVER H11 / *B4*
Brennan Manor, 1079 Everett Rd, 54521 ....(715)479-7353

EAST TROY S13 / *F5*
Pine Ridge B&B, 1152 Scout Rd, 53120 ....(414)594-3269

EAU CLAIRE L5 / *D2*
Fanny Hill Inn, 3919 Crescent Ave, 54703 ....(715)836-8184
Otter Creek Inn, 2536 Hwy 12, 54701 ....(715)832-2945
Westlin Winds, 3508 Halsey St, 54701 ....(715)832-1110

EGG HARBOR K16 / *C6*
Country Gardens B&B, 6421 Hwy 42, 54209 ....(414)743-7434

ELKHART LAKE O14 / *E5*
Siebken's, 284 S Lake St, 53020 ....(414)876-2600

ELLISON BAY J16 / *C6*
The Griffin Inn, 11976 Mink River Rd, 54210 ....(414)854-4306
Haus Zur Gemutlichkeit, 1052 Berry Ln N, 54210 ....(414)854-4848
The Nelson Farm, 1526 Ranch Ln, 54210 ....(414)854-5224

ELM GROVE X2 / *F5*
The Krupp Farm Homestead, 1030 Terrace Dr, 53122 ....(414)894-3216

ELROY P8 / *E3*
Waarvik Century Farm B&B, N4621 County H, 53929 ....(608)462-8595

ELTON K12 / *C4*
DeHart's Section House & Evergreen Inn, Hwy 64, PO Box 12, 54430 ....(715)882-4781

EPHRAIM J16 / *C6*
Eagle Harbor Inn, PO Box 72 B, 54211 ....(414)854-2121
The Ephraim Inn, Rt 42, PO Box 247, 54211 ....(414)854-4515
French Country Inn of Ephraim, 3052 Spruce Ln, PO Box 129, 54211 ....(414)854-4001
Hillside Hotel, PO Box 17, 54211 ....(414)854-2417

FERRYVILLE Q6 / *E2*
Mississippi Humble Bush, Box 297, 54628 ....(608)734-3930

FISH CREEK K16 / *C6*
Thorp House Inn & Cottages, 4135 Bluff Rd, PO Box 490, 54212 ....(414)868-2444
Whistling Swan Inn, Main St Box 193, 54212 ....(414)868-3442
White Gull Inn, PO Box 175, 54212 ....(414)868-3517

FONTANA-GENEVA LAKE /
Emerald View House, PO Box 322, 53125 ....(414)275-2266

FORT ATKINSON S12 / *F5*
The Lamp Post Inn, 408 S Main St, 53538 ....(414)563-6561

FRIENDSHIP O9 / *E4*
Silver Maples B&B, 1602 16th Court, 53934 ....(608)564-2388

GILLS ROCK J16 / *C6*
Harbor House Inn, 12666 Hwy 42, 54210 ....(414)854-5196

GREEN BAY M14 / *D5*
Stonewood Haus, PO Box 10201, 54307 ....(414)499-3786

GREEN LAKE O11 / *E4*
McConnell Inn, 497 S Lawson Dr, Box 639, 54941 ....(414)294-6430
Oakwood Lodge, 365 Lake St, 54941 ....(414)294-6580
Strawberry Hill B&B, Rt 1 Box 524-d, 54941 ....(414)294-3450

HARTFORD Q13 / *F5*
Jordan House, 81 S Main St, 53027 ....(414)673-5643

HARTLAND R13 / *F5*
Monches Mill House, W 301 N 9430 Hwy E, 53029 ....(414)966-7546

HAYWARD G5 / *B2*
Edgewater Inn, Rt 1, Box 1293, 54843 ....(715)462-9412
Mustard Seed, 205 California, PO Box 262, 54843 ....(715)634-2908
Ross' Teal Lake Lodge, Rt 7L, 54843 ....(715)462-3631

HAZEL GREEN T7 / *G3*
De Winters of Hazel Green, 22nd at Main St, 53811 ....(608)854-2768
Wisconsin House Stagecoach Inn, 2105 Main, 53811 ....(608)854-2233

HAZELHURST H9 / *B4*
Hazelhurst Inn, 6941 Hwy 51, 54531 ....(715)356-6571

HILLSBORO P8 / *E3*
Mascione's Hidden Valley, Rt 2, Box 74, 54634 ....(608)489-3443

HOLLANDALE S9 / *F3*
The Old Granary Inn, Rt 1, Box 70-A, 53544 ....(608)967-2140

HORICON Q12 / *E5*
The Charly House, 111 N Cedar St, 53032 ....(414)485-3144

HOULTON K2 / *C1*
Shady Ridge Farm B&B, 410 Highland View, 54082 ....(715)549-6255

HUDSON K2 / *C1*
Jefferson-Day House, 1109 Third St, 54016 ....(715)386-7111

IOLA M11 / *D4*
Taylor House B&B, 210 E Iola St, 54945 ....(715)445-2204

JANESVILLE T11 / *G4*
Jackson Street Inn, 210 S Jackson St, 53545 ....(608)754-7250

KENDALL P8 / *E3*
Dusk to Dawn B&B, Rt 1, Box 191, 54638 ....(608)463-7547

KENOSHA T14 / *G6*
Library Square B&B, 6003-7th Ave, 53140 ....(414)656-0207
The Manor House, 6536 3rd Ave, 53143 ....(414)658-0014

KEWAUNEE M15 / *D6*
Duvall House, 815 Milwaukee St, 54216 ....(414)388-0501
Gables B&B, 821 Dodge St, 54216 ....(414)388-0220

KIEL O14 / *E5*
River Terrace B&B, 521 River Terrace, 53042-1343 ....(414)894-2032

KOHLER P15 / *E6*
The American Club, Highland Dr, 53044 ....(414)457-8000

LA FARGE P7 / *E3*
Trillium, Rt 2 Box 121, 54639 ....(608)625-4492

LA POINTE D7 / *A3*
Woods Manor, 165 Front St, PO Box 7, 54850 ....(715)747-3102

LAC DU FLAMBEAU H9 / *B3*
Ty-Bach, 3104 Simpson Ln, 54538 ....(715)588-7851

LACROSSE P5 / *E2*
The Martindale House, 237 S 10th St, 54601 ....(608)782-4224

LAKE DELTON P9 / *E4*
OJ's Victorian Village, Box 98, Hwy 12, 53940 ....(608)254-6568
The Swallow's Nest, 141 Sarrington, PO Box 418, 53940 ....(608)254-6900

LAKE GENEVA T13 / *G5*
Eleven Gables Inn, 493 Wrigley Dr, 53147 ....(414)248-8393
Elizabethian Inn, 463 Wrigley Dr, 53147 ....(414)248-9131
The Geneva Inn on the Lake, 804 S Lake Shore Dr, 53147 ....(414)248-5680
T.C. Smith Inn B&B, 865 Main St, 53147 ....(414)248-1097
Two Akers of England, 306 Center St, 53147 ....(414)248-4826

LAKE MILLS R12 / *F4*
The Bayberry Inn, 265 S Main St, 53551 ....(414)648-3654
Fargo Mansion Inn, 406 Mulberry St, 53551 ....(414)648-3654

LEWIS I2 / *B1*
Seven Pines Lodge, 54851 ....(715)653-2323

LIVINGSTON S8 / *F3*
Oak Hill Farm, 9850 Hwy 80, 53554 ....(608)943-6006

LODI Q10 / *F4*
Victorian Treasure B&B, 115 Prairie St, 53555 ....(608)592-5199

MADISON R10 / *F4*
Annie's Hill House B&B, 2117 Sheridan Dr, 53704 ....(608)244-2224
The Collins House, 704 E Gorham, 53703 ....(608)255-4230
Mansion Hill Inn, 424 N Pinckney, 53703 ....(608)255-3999
Plough Inn B&B, 3402 Monroe St, 53711 ....(608)238-2981

MAIDEN ROCK M3 / *D1*
Harrisburg Inn, Great River Rd, PO Box 15, 54750 ....(715)448-4500

MANITOWOC N15 / *E6*
Mahloch's Cozy B&B, 2104 Madson Rd, 54220 ....(414)775-4404

MAUSTON P8 / *E3*
Edward's Estates, N4775 22nd Ave, 53948 ....(608)847-5246

MAYVILLE Q13 / *E5*
The Audubon Inn, 45 N Main, 53050 ....(414)387-5858

MENOMONEE FALLS R14 / *F5*
Dorshel's B&B Guest House, N7616 Lilly Rd, 53051 ....(414)255-7866

MENOMONIE L4 / *D1*
Cedar Trail Guesthouse, Rt 4, Box 175, 54751 ....(715)664-8828
Katy May House, 2013 Wilson St, 54751 ....(715)235-1792

MEQUON R14 / *F5*
American Country Farm, 12112 N Wauwatosa Rd, 53092 ....(414)242-0194
The Homestead of Mequon, 1916 W Donges Bay Rd, 53092 ....(414)242-4174
Sonnenhof Inn, 13907 N Port Washington, 53092 ....(414)375-4294

MERRILL J9 / *C4*
The Brick House, 108 S Cleveland St, 54452 ....(715)536-3230
Candlewick Inn, 700 W Main St, 54452 ....(715)536-7744

MERRIMAC Q9 / *F4*
Grandpa's Gate, E13841 Lower DL, PO Box 101, 53561 .... (608)493-2755

MILWAUKEE R14 / *F5*
Guest House of 819, 819 N Cass St, 53202 .... (414)271-1979
Marie's, 346 E Wilson St, 53207 .... (414)483-1512
Ogden House, 2237 N Lake Dr, 53202 .... (414)272-2740
Pfister Hotel, 424 E Wisconsin Ave, 53202 .... (414)273-8222

MINERAL POINT S8 / *F3*
Duke Guest House B&B, 618 Maiden St, 53565 .... (608)987-2821
General Store, 262 High St, 53565 .... (608)987-2799
Jones House, 215 Ridge St, Hwy 151, 53565 .... (608)987-2337
Knudson's Guest House, 415 Ridge St, 53565 .... (608)987-2733
Wilson House Inn, 110 Dodge St Hwy 151, 53565 .... (608)987-3600

MINOCQUA H9 / *B4*
Phoenix House B&B, 1075 Hwy F, 54548 .... (715)356-3535

MISHICOT N15 / *D6*
Victorian Blue B&B, 314 Jackson St, 54228 .... (414)755-4907

MONONA R10 / *F4*
The Lake House on Monona, 4027 Monona Dr, 53716 .... (608)222-4601

MONROE T10 / *G4*
The Nathaniel Treat House, 1222 11th St, 53566 .... (608)325-5656
Victorian Garden B&B, 1720 16th St, 53566 .... (608)328-1720

MONTELLO P10 / *E4*
Country Peddler Guest House, Rt 2 Box 188, 53949 .... (414)295-0100
Westmont Farms, Rt 3, Box 556, 53959 .... (414)293-4456

MONTREAL F8 / *A3*
The Inn, 104 Wisconsin Ave, PO Box H, 54550 .... (715)561-5180

MOUNT HOREB R9 / *F4*
The H.B. Dahle House B&B Inn, 200 N 2nd St, 53572 .... (608)437-8894

NEILLSVILLE M7 / *D3*
Bluebell Inn, 122 Hewett St, 54456 .... (715)743-2929

NEW HOLSTEIN O14 / *E5*
The Farm Homestead, W1982 Kiel Rd, Rt 2, 53061 .... (414)782-5421

NEWTON N15 / *E6*
Rambling Hills Tree Farm, 8825 Willever Ln, 53063 .... (414)726-4388

NORWALK O7 / *E3*
Lonesome Jake's Devil's Hole Ranch, Rt 1, 104, 54648 .... (608)823-7585

OCONOMOWOC R13 / *F5*
The Inn at Pine Terrace, 351 Lisbon Rd, 53066 .... (414)567-7463

ONTARIO P7 / *E3*
Downings' B&B, Hwy 33, 54651 .... (608)337-4352
The Inn at Wildcat Mountain - B&B, Hwy 33, PO Box 112, 54651 .... (608)337-4352

OSCEOLA J2 / *C1*
St. Croix River Inn, 305 River St, 54020 .... (715)294-4248

OSHKOSH O12 / *E5*
Tiffany Inn, 206 Algoma Blvd, 54901 .... (414)426-1000

OXFORD P10 / *E4*
Halfway House, Rt 2 Box 80, 53952 .... (608)586-5489

PHELPS G11 / *B4*
Limberlost Inn, 2483 Hwy 17, 54554 .... (715)545-2685

PLAIN Q9 / *F3*
Attic Treasures Country Estate B&B, S8711 State Hwy 23, 53577 .... (608)546-4371
Bettinger House B&B, Hwy 23, 53577 .... (608)546-2951
The Kraemer House, 1190 Spruce St, 53577 .... (608)546-3161

PLATTEVILLE S7 / *F3*
The Cunningham House, 110 Market St, 53818 .... (608)348-5532

PLYMOUTH P14 / *E5*
52 Stafford, An Irish Guest House, 52 Stafford St, 53073 .... (414)893-0552
Yankee Hill B&B, 315 Collins St, 53073 .... (414)892-2222

PORT WASHINGTON Q14 / *F6*
Grand Inn, 832 W Grand Ave, 53074 .... (414)284-6719
Washington's Inn, 308 W Washington St, 53074 .... (414)284-5583

PORTAGE P10 / *E4*
Breese Waye B&B, 816 Macfarlane Rd, 53901 .... (608)742-5281
Country Aire, Rt 2, Box 175, 53901 .... (608)742-5716

POTOSI T7 / *G3*
O'Reilly House, 7509 Stiger Rd, 53820 .... (608)763-2386

POYNETTE Q10 / *F4*
Jamieson House, 407 N Franklin, 53955 .... (608)635-4100

PRAIRIE DU CHIEN R6 / *F2*
Neumann House B&B, 121 N Michigan St, 53821 .... (608)326-8104

PRESCOTT L1 / *D1*
The Oak Street Inn B&B, 506 Oak St, 54021 .... (715)262-4110
Yankee Bugler Inn, 506 Oak St, 54021 .... (715)262-3019

PRINCETON O11 / *E4*
The Gray Lion Inn, 115 Harvard, 54968 .... (414)295-4101

RACINE S15 / *F6*
Lochnaiar Inn, 1121 Lake Ave, 53043 .... (414)633-3300
The Mansards-on-the-Lake, 827 Lake Ave, #3, 53403 .... (414)632-1135

REEDSBURG P9 / *E3*
Parkview B&B, 211 N Park St, 53959 .... (608)524-4333

RHINELANDER I10 / *B4*
Cranberry Hill B&B, 209 E Frederick St, 54501 .... (715)369-3504

RICHLAND CENTER Q8 / *F3*
Mansion, 323 S Central, 53581 .... (608)647-2808

RIPON O12 / *E5*
The Farmer's Daughter Inn, Rt 1, Box 37, 54971 .... (414)748-2146

RIVER FALLS L2 / *D1*
Knollwood House, Rt 1, Box 4 Knollwood Dr, 54022 .... (715)425-1040

SAINT GERMAIN H10 / *B4*
Stonehouse B&B, 7855 Lost Lake Dr N, 54558 .... (715)542-3733

SHEBOYGAN FALLS P14 / *E6*
The Rochester Inn, 504 Water St, 53085 .... (414)467-3123

SISTER BAY J16 / *C6*
Church Hill Inn, 425 Gateway Dr, 54234 .... (414)854-4885
Renaissance Inn, 414 Maple Dr, 54234 .... (414)854-5107

SOLDIERS GROVE Q7 / *F3*
Page's Old Oak Inn, Hwy 131 S, 54655 .... (608)624-5217

SOUTH MILWAUKEE S14 / *F6*
Riley House, 727 Hawthorne, 53172 .... (414)764-3130

SPARTA O7 / *E3*
The Franklin Victorian, 220 E Franklin St, 54656 .... (608)269-3894
Just-N-Trails B&B, Rt 1 Box 274, 54656 .... (608)269-4522

SPRING GREEN R8 / *F3*
Hardyns House, 250 N Winstead, 53588 .... (608)588-7007
Hill Street B&B, 353 W Hill St, 53588 .... (608)588-7751
Spring Green, Box ML3, 53588 .... (608)588-2042

SPRINGBROOK H4 / *B2*
The Stout Trout, Rt 1 Box 1630, 54875 .... (715)466-2790

STAR LAKE G10 / *B4*
The Whip-Poor-Will Inn, PO Box 64, 54561 .... (715)542-3600

STEVENS POINT M10 / *D4*
Dreams of Yesteryear, 1100 Brawley St, 54481 .... (715)341-4525

STOCKHOLM M3 / *D1*
Great River Farm, General Delivery, 54769 .... (715)442-5656

STOUGHTON S11 / *F4*
Stokstad's Century Farm B&B, 305 Hwy 51, 53589 .... (608)884-4941

STRUM M5 / *D2*
Lake House, RR 2 Box 217, 54770 .... (715)693-3519

STURGEON BAY L15 / *D6*
The Barbican, 132 N Second Ave, 54235 .... (414)743-4854
Bay Shore Inn, 4205 Bay Shore Dr, 54235 .... (414)743-4551
The Inn at Cedar Crossing, 336 Louisiana St, 54235 .... (414)743-4200
Country Comforts, 5031 County TT, 54235 .... (414)743-6317
Gandt's Haus, 2962 Lake Forest Park Rd, 54235 .... (414)743-1238
Gray Goose B&B, 4258 Bay Shore Dr, 54235 .... (414)743-9100
The Scofield House B&B, 908 Michigan St, PO Box 761, 54235 .... (414)743-7727
White Lace Inn, 16 N 5th Ave, 54235 .... (414)743-1105

THREE LAKES H11 / *B4*
Three Lakes Haven Country House, 7265 Chicken-In-The-Woods Rd, 54562 .... (715)546-2012

TOMAHAWK I9 / *C4*
Frenchtown B&B Inn, 822 S Tomahawk Ave, 54487 .... (715)453-3499
Prides English Manor, 204 S Second, 54487 .... (715)453-7670

TWO RIVERS N15 / *E6*
The Red Forest B&B, 1421 25th St, 54241 .... (414)793-1794

VERONA R10 / *F4*
Riley Tavern B&B, 8205 Klevenville-Riley Rd, 53593 .... (608)845-9150

VIROQUA P6 / *E2*
Serendipity Farm, Rt 3, Box 162, 54665 .... (608)637-7708
Viroqua Heritage Inn, 220 E Jefferson St, 54665 .... (608)637-3306

WAUPACA M11 / *D4*
Crystal River B&B, E1369 Rural Rd, 54981 .... (715)258-5333

WAUSAU K10 / *C4*
Rosenberry Inn, 511 Franklin St, 54401 .... (715)842-5733

WAUTOMA O10 / *E4*
Kristine Ann's Inn, Rt 1, Box 10, 303 E Main, 54982 .... (414)787-4901

WEST SALEM
O6 / *E2*

Wolfway Farm, RR 1, Box 18, 54669 ....(608)486-2686

WESTBY
P6 / *E2*

Westby House, State St, 54667 ....(608)634-4112

WESTFIELD
O10 / *E4*

Martha's Ethnic B&B, 226-2nd St, 53964 ....(608)296-3361

WHITE LAKE
K12 / *C5*

Wolf River Lodge, 54491 ....(715)882-2182

WHITEWATER
S12 / *F5*

The Greene House B&B, Rt 2, Box 214, Hwy 12, 53190 ....(414)495-8771
Victoria-On-Main B&B, 622 W Main St, 53190 ....(414)473-8400

WILTON
O7 / *E3*

Foothills, Rt 1, Box 261, 54670-9732 ....(608)435-6877
Pahl's B&B, 608 Railroad St, 54670 ....(608)435-6434

WISCONSIN DELLS
P9 / *E4*

Historic Bennett House, 825 Oak St, 53965 ....(608)254-2500
Sherman House, 930 River Rd, Box 397, 53965 ....(608)253-2721
Thomson House, 922 River Rd, 53965 ....(608)253-7299
Thunder Valley B&B, W15344 Waubeek Rd, 53965 ....(608)254-4145

WISCONSIN RAPIDS
M9 / *D4*

Nash House, 1020 Oak St, 54494 ....(715)424-2001

WYOMING

BUFFALO
C12 / *B5*

Paradise Guest Ranch, PO Box 790, 82834 ....(307)684-7876
South Fork Inn, Box 854, 82834 ....(307)684-9609

CODY
B8 / *B3*

Goff Creek Lodge, 995 Yellowstone Hwy, PO Box 155, 82414 ....(307)587-3753
Hidden Valley Ranch, 153 Rd, 6MF, S Fork Rd, 82414 ....(307)587-5090
Hunter Peak Ranch, Box 1731, Painter Rd, 82414 ....(307)587-3711
The Lockhart Inn, 109 W Yellowstone Ave, 82414 ....(307)587-6074
Parson's Pillow, 1202 14th St, 82414 ....(307)587-2382
Rimrock Dude Ranch, 2728 N Fork Rt, 82414 ....(307)587-3970
Seven D Ranch, PO Box 100, 82414 ....(307)587-3997
Shoshone Lodge Resort, PO Box 790bb, 82414 ....(307)587-4044
Trout Creek Inn, Yellowstone Pk Hwy 14,16,20, 82414 ....(307)587-6288
Valley Ranch, 100 Valley Ranch Rd, 82414 ....(307)587-4661

DOUGLAS
F14 / *D6*

Akers Ranch, 81 Inez Rd, Rt 1, 82633 ....(307)358-3741
Deer Forks Ranch, 1200 Poison Lake Rd, 82633 ....(307)358-2033

ENCAMPMENT
J12 / *F5*

Lorraine's B&B, 1016 Lomax, Box 312, 82325 ....(307)327-5200
Platt's Rustic Mountain Lodge, Star Rt 49, 82325 ....(307)327-5539

EVANSTON
J5 / *F1*

Pine Gables B&B, 1049 Center St, 82930 ....(307)789-2069

GLENROCK
F14 / *D6*

Hotel Higgins, 416 W Birch, 82637 ....(307)436-9212

JACKSON
E5 / *C1*

Sundance Inn, 135 W Broadway, 83001 ....(307)733-3444

JACKSON HOLE
E5 / *C1*

Big Mountain Inn, PO Box 7453, 83001 ....(307)733-1981
Buckrail Lodge, Box 23, 110 E Karns Ave, 83001 ....(307)733-2079
Powderhorn Ranch, PO Box 7400, 83001 ....(307)733-3845
Spring Creek Ranch, Box 3154, 83001 ....(307)733-8833

KELLY
D6 / *C1*

Red Rock Ranch, PO Box 38, 83011 ....(307)733-6288

LANDER
F9 / *D3*

Black Mountain Ranch, 548 N Fork Rd, 82520 ....(307)332-6442
Country Fare B&B, 904 Main St, 82520 ....(307)332-9604
Miner's Delight Inn, Atlantic City Rt, PO Box 205, 82520 ....(307)332-3513

LARAMIE
I14 / *F6*

Annie Moore's Guest House, 819 University, 82070 ....(307)721-4177

MOOSE
D5 / *C1*

Bunkhouse, PO Box 384, 83012 ....(307)733-7283
Triangle X Ranch, Hwy 187-26-89, 83012 ....(307)733-2183

MORAN
D6 / *C1*

Box K Ranch B&B, Box 110, 83013 ....(307)543-2407
Fir Creek Ranch, PO Box 190, 83013 ....(307)543-2416
Jenny Lake Lodge, PO Box 240, 83013 ....(307)733-4677

RAWLINS
H11 / *E4*

Ferris Mansion, 607 W Maple St, 82301 ....(307)324-3961

SARATOGA
I12 / *F5*

Wolf Hotel, PO Box 1298, 101 E Bridge, 82331 ....(307)326-5525

SAVERY
J11 / *F4*

Savery Creek Thoroughbred Ranch, PO Box 24, 82332 ....(307)383-7840

SHERIDAN
B12 / *B5*

Kilbourne Kastle, 320 S Main, 82801 ....(307)674-8716

WAPITI
B8 / *B2*

Elephant Head Lodge, 1170 Yellowstone Hwy, 82450 ....(307)587-3980
Mountain Shadows Ranch, Box 110BB, 82450 ....(307)587-2143

WILSON
E5 / *C1*

Heck Of A Hill Homestead, PO Box 105, 83014 ....(307)733-8023
Snow Job, PO Box 371, 83014 ....(307)739-9695
Teton Tree House, Box 550 (Jackson Hole), 83014 ....(307)733-3233
Teton View B&B, PO Box 652, 2136 Coyote Loop, 83014 ....(307)733-7954

U.S. TERRITORIES

PUERTO RICO

CONDADO, SAN JUAN
El Canario Inn, 1317 Ashford Ave, 00907 ....(809)722-3861

CULEBRA
Posada La Hamaca, 68 Castelar St, 00645 ....(809)742-3516

CULEBRA ISLAND
Villa Boheme, PO Box 218, 00645 ....(809)742-3508

ISLAND VERDE
La Casa Mathlesen, 14 Calle Uno Villamar, 00913 ....(809)727-3223
La Playa, 6 Amapola, 00630 ....(809)791-1115

LUQUILLO
Parador Martorell, PO Box 384, 00673 ....(809)889-2710

MARICAO
Parador Hacienda Juanita, PO Box 838, 00706 ....(809)838-2550

OCEAN PARK
Beach House, 1957 Italia, 00913 ....(809)727-5482
Buena Vista by-Sea, 2218 Gen Del Valle, 00913 ....(809)726-2796

OCEAN PARK, SANTURCE
La Condesa Inn, Cacique 2071, 00911 ....(809)727-3698

SAN GERMAN
Parador Oasis, PO Box 144, 00753 ....(809)892-1175

SAN JUAN
Arcade Inn-Guest House, Taft St #8, 00911 ....(809)725-0668
El Prado Inn, 1350 Luchetti St. Condado, 00907 ....(809)728-5526
Green Isle Inn, 36 Calle Uno-Villamar, 00913 ....(809)726-4330
Jewel's by the Sea, Seaview 1125-Condado, 00907 ....(809)725-5313
Tres Palmas Guest House, 2212 Park Blvd, 00913 ....(809)727-4617
Wind Chimer, 53 Calle Taft, 00911 ....(809)727-4153

VIEQUES
La Casa Del Frances, PO Box 458, Esperanza, 00765 ....(809)741-3751
Sea Gate Guest House, Barriada Fuerts, 00765 ....(809)741-4661

VIRGIN ISLANDS

SAINT CROIX
Pink Fancy, 27 Prince St, Christiansted, 00820 ....(809)773-8460

SAINT JOHN
Cruz Inn, Box 566, Cruz Bay, 00830 ....(809)776-7688
Estate Zootenvaal, Hurricane Hole, 00830 ....(809)776-6321
Gallows Point, Box 58, 00830 ....(809)776-6434
Intimate Inn of St. John, POB 432, Cruz Bay, 00830 ....(809)776-6133
Raintree Inn, Box 566, 00830 ....(809)776-7449
Selene's, PO Box 30, Cruz Bay, 00830 ....(809)776-7850

SAINT THOMAS
Danish Chalet Inn, PO Box 4319, 00801 ....(809)774-5764
Galleon House, PO Box 6577, 00801 ....(809)774-6952
Hotel 1829, PO Box 1567, 00804-1567 ....(809)776-1829
Island View Guest House, PO Box 1903, 00901 ....(809)774-4270
Mafolie Hotel, PO Box 1506, 00801 ....(809)774-2790
Maison Greaux Guest House, PO Box 1856, 00801 ....(809)774-0063
The Inn at Mandahl, PO Box 2483, 00801 ....(809)775-2100
Pavillions & Pools Hotel, Rt 6, 00802 ....(800)524-2001
Pelican Beach Club, Box 8387, 00801 ....(809)775-6855
Twins Guest House, 5 Garden St, Charlotte Ama, 00801 ....(809)776-0131
Villa Elaine, 66 Water Island, 00802 ....(809)774-0290

RESERVATION SERVICES

ALABAMA

Bed and Breakfast Montgomery, 1026 Montgomery
Milbrook AL 36054 .... (205)264-0056

ALASKA

Stay With a Friend, 3605 Arctic Blvd #173
Anchorage AK 99503 .... (907)344-4006
B&B by the Sea, PO Box 470
Homer AK 99603 .... (907)235-7886
Alaska Bed and Breakfast, 526 Seward St
Juneau AK 99801 .... (907)586-2959
Kodiak B&B, 308 Cope St
Kodiak AK 99615 .... (907)486-5367
Mat-su Valley B&B, HCOI Box 6229-R
Palmer AK 99645 .... (907)376-7662

ARIZONA

B&B Scottsdale and the West, PO Box 3999
Prescott AZ 86302 .... (602)776-1102
Bed and Breakfast in Arizona, PO Box 8628
Scottsdale AZ 85252 .... (602)995-2831
Mi Casa Su Casa, Bed & Breakfast, 1456 N Scottsdale Rd, Ste 110
Tempe AZ 85281 .... (602)990-0682
Old Pueblo Homestays, PO Box 13603
Tucson AZ 85732 .... (602)790-2399

ARKANSAS

Bed & Breakfast in the Arkansas Ozarks, Rt 1, PO Box 188
Calico Rock AR 72519 .... (501)297-8764
Assoc. of B&Bs, Cabins & Cottages, PO Box 27
Eureka Springs AR 72632 .... (501)253-6767
Bed & Breakfast Reservations, 11 Singleton
Eureka Springs AR 72632 .... (501)253-9111

CALIFORNIA

Eye Openers B&B, Box 694
Altadena CA 91001 .... (818)797-2055
B&B Exchange, 1458 Lincoln Ave
Calistoga CA 94515 .... (707)942-5900
B&B Homestay, Box 326
Cambria CA 93428 .... (805)927-4613
Carmel Tourist Valley, PO Box 7430
Carmel CA 93921 .... (408)624-1711
B&B of Southern California, Box 218
Fullerton CA 92632 .... (714)738-8361
Rent-A-Room International, 11531 Varna St
Garden Grove CA 92640 .... (714)638-1406
California Riviera 800, 31655 Pacific Coast Hwy, Suite C
Laguna Beach CA 92677 .... (800)621-0500
Napa Valley's Finest Lodging, 1557 Madrid Ct
Napa CA 94559 .... (707)224-4667
America Family Inn B&B, Box 349
San Francisco CA 94101 .... (415)931-3083
B&B International, PO Box 282910
San Francisco CA 94128-2910 .... (415)696-1690
Megan's Friends B&B Reservations, 1776 Royal Way
San Luis Obispo CA 93405 .... (805)544-4406
California Houseguests International, 6051 Lindley Ave #6
Tarzana CA 91356 .... (818)344-7878
B&B of Los Angeles, 32127 Harborview Ln
Westlake Village CA 91361 .... (818)889-7325
Co-Host, America's B&B, 11715 S Circle Dr
Whittier CA 90601 .... (213)699-8427

COLORADO

B&B Rocky Mountains, PO Box 804
Colorado Springs CO 80901 .... (719)630-3433
Vail B&B, Box 491
Vail CO 81658 .... (303)949-1212

CONNECTICUT

Nutmeg B&B, 222 Girard Ave
Hartford CT 06105 .... (203)236-6698
Bed & Breakfast, Ltd in New Haven, PO Box 216
New Haven CT 06518 .... (203)469-3260
Covered Bridge B&B, Box 447
Norfolk CT 06058 .... (203)542-5944

DELAWARE

Bed & Breakfast of Delaware, 1804 Breen Ln
Wilmington DE 19810 .... (302)479-9500

FLORIDA

B&B of the Keys & the Palm Beaches, 5 Man-O-War Dr
Marathon FL 33050 .... (305)743-4118
B&B Company, Box 262
S Miami FL 33243 .... (305)661-3270
B&B Suncoast Accommodations, 8690 Gulf Blvd
St Petersburg Beach FL 33706 .... (813)360-1753

GEORGIA

Atlanta Home Hospitality, 2472 Lauderdale Dr NE
Atlanta GA 30345 .... (404)493-1930
B&B Atlanta, 1801 Piedmont Ave NE #208
Atlanta GA 30324 .... (404)875-0525
Savannah Historic Inns & Guesthouses, 1900 Lincoln St
Savannah GA 31401 .... (912)226-7218
Quail Country Bed & Breakfast Ltd, 1104 Old Monticello Rd
Thomasville GA 31792 .... (912)226-6882

HAWAII

B&B Honolulu, 3242 Kaohinani Dr
Honolulu, Oahu HI 96817 .... (808)595-7533
Pacific-Hawaii B&B, 970 N Kaleheo Ave, Ste A-218
Kailua, Oahu HI 96734 .... (808)262-6026
B&B Hawaii, Box 449
Kapaa HI 96746 .... (808)822-7771

IDAHO

B&B of Idaho, 109 West Idaho
Boise ID 83702 .... (208)342-8066
Central Resort Reservations, PO Box 20
Sun Valley ID 83353 .... (800)635-4156

ILLINOIS

Heritage B&B, PO Box 409218
Chicago IL 60640 .... (312)728-7935
B&B Northwest Suburban Homestays-Chicago, PO Box 95503
Hoffman Estates IL 60195 .... (708)310-9010

INDIANA

Indiana Amish Country B&B, 1660 W Market St
Nappanee IN 46550 .... (219)773-4188
B&B Indiana, PO Box 481
Nashville IN 47448 .... (812)988-0733

IOWA

Bed & Breakfast in Iowa, Box 430
Preston IA 52069 .... (319)689-4222

KANSAS

B&B Kansas City, Box 14781
Lenexa KS 66215 .... (913)888-3636

KENTUCKY

Ohio Valley B&B, 6876 Taylor Mill Rd
Independence KY 41051 .... (606)356-7865
Kentucky Homes B&B, 508 Belgravia Ct
Louisville KY 40208 .... (502)635-7341

Bluegrass B&B, Rt 1, Box 263
Versailles KY 40383 .... (606)873-3208

LOUISIANA

Southern Comfort B&B Reservation Service, 2856 Hundred Oaks
Baton Rouge LA 70808 .... (504)346-1928
B&B Inc, 1360 Moss St
New Orleans LA 70152-2257 .... (504)525-4640
New Orleans B&B, PO Box 8128
New Orleans LA 70182 .... (504)838-0071
Peggy Lindsay B&B, PO Box 52466
New Orleans LA 70152 .... (504)897-3867

MAINE

B&B Down East, Box 547
Eastbrook ME 04634 .... (207)565-3517
B&B of Maine, 32 Colonial Village
Falmouth ME 04105 .... (207)781-4528

MARYLAND

Traveller in Maryland, 33 West St
Annapolis MD 21401 .... (301)269-6232
Armanda's B&B, 1428 Park Ave
Baltimore MD 21217-4230 .... (301)225-0001

MASSACHUSETTS

B&B Agency of Boston, 47 Commercial Wharf
Boston MA 02110 .... (617)720-3540
B&B Associates Bay Colony Ltd, Box 166 Babson Park
Boston MA 02157 .... (617)449-5302
Folkstone B&B, PO Box 931
Boylston MA 01505 .... (508)943-7118
A B&B Above the Rest, Box 732
Brookline MA 02146 .... (617)277-2292
Greater Boston Hospitality, Box 1142
Brookline MA 02146 .... (617)277-5430
B&B Cambridge & Greater Boston, Box 665 Kirkland St
Cambridge MA 02140 .... (617)576-1492
B&B in Minuteman Country, Box 665
Cambridge MA 02140 .... (617)576-2112
Christian Hospitality, 636 Union St
Duxbury MA 02332 .... (617)834-8528
Pineapple Hospitality Inc, 47 N Second St, Ste 3A
New Bedford MA 02740 .... (508)990-1696
Host Homes of Boston, Box 117
Newton MA 02158 .... (617)244-1308
New England B&B, 1045 Centre St
Newton Centre MA 02159 .... (617)244-2112
Orleans B&B Associates, Box 1312
Orleans MA 02653 .... (508)255-3824
Be Our Guest B&B, Box 1333
Plymouth MA 02360 .... (617)837-9867
B&B Cape Cod, Box 341
West Hyannisport MA 02672 .... (508)775-2772
B&B Folks, 73 Providence Rd
Westford MA 01886 .... (508)692-3232
Berkshire Bed & Breakfast, PO Box 211, Main St
Williamsburg MA 01096-0211 .... (413)268-7244

MICHIGAN

Betsy Ross B&B in Michigan, PO Box 1731
Dearborn MI 48121 .... (313)561-6041
Frankenmuth Area B&B, 337 Trinklein St
Frankenmuth MI 48734 .... (517)652-8897
Go Native...Hawaii, Box 13115
Lansing MI 48901 .... (517)349-9598
B&B Connection, PO Box 2201
Traverse City MI 49685 .... (616)943-9182
B&B of Grand Traverse, PO Box 5112
Traverse City MI 49685-5112 .... (616)929-1009

MISSISSIPPI

Lincoln, Ltd, Bed & Breakfast, PO Box 3479
Meridian MS 39303 .... (601)482-5483
Natchez Pilgrimage Tours, Box 347
Natchez MS 39120 .... (601)446-6631

MISSOURI

River Country B&B of St Louis, 1900 Wyoming
St Louis MO 63118 .... (314)965-4328

MONTANA

B&B Western Adventure, PO Box 20972
Billings MT 59104 .... (406)259-7993

NEBRASKA

Swede Hospitality B&B, 1617 Ave A
Gothenburg NE 69138 .... (308)537-2680
B&B of the Great Plains, PO Box 2333
Lincoln NE 68502 .... (402)423-3480

NEVADA

Nevada Commission on Tourism, Capitol Complex
Carson City NV 89710 .... (702)687-4322

NEW HAMPSHIRE

New Hampshire Bed & Breakfast, RFD 4, Box 88
Meredith NH 03253 .... (603)279-8348

NEW JERSEY

Northern NJ Bed & Breakfast, 11 Sunset Trail
Denville NJ 07834 .... (201)625-5129
Bed and Breakfast of New Jersey, Suite 132, 103 Godwin Ave
Midland Park NJ 07432 .... (201)444-7409
B&B of Princeton, PO Box 571
Princeton NJ 08540 .... (609)924-3189

NEW MEXICO

New Mexico B&B, Box 2805
Santa Fe NM 87504 .... (505)982-3332

NEW YORK

Bed & Breakfast, USA Ltd, PO Box 606
Croton-on-Hudson NY 10520 .... (914)271-6228
Alternate Lodgings, Inc, PO Box 1782
East Hampton NY 11937 .... (516)324-9449
Hampton Bed & Breakfast, PO Box 378
East Moriches NY 11940 .... (516)928-4034
Bed & Breakfast Rochester, Box 444
Fairport NY 14450 .... (716)223-8510
Leatherstocking B&B, 389 Brockway Rd
Frankfort NY 13340 .... (315)733-0040
Blue Heron B&B, 384 Pleasant Valley Rd
Groton NY 13073 .... (607)898-3814
Cherry Valley Ventures, 6119 Cherry Valley Turnpike
Lafayette NY 13084 .... (315)677-9723
New World Bed & Breakfast, Ltd, 150 Fifth Ave, Ste 711
New York NY 10011 .... (212)675-5600
Urban Ventures, PO Box 426
New York NY 10024 .... (212)594-5650
Rainbow Hospitality Bed & Breakfast, 9348 Hennepin Ave
Niagara Falls NY 14304 .... (716)283-4794
Elaine's B&B & Inns, PO Box 392
Old Westbury NY 11568 .... (516)334-6231
A Reasonable Alternative, 117 Spring St
Port Jefferson NY 11777 .... (516)928-4034
American Country Collection of B&B Homes, 984 Gloucester Place
Schenectady NY 12309 .... (518)370-4948
B&B of Greater Syracuse, 143 Didama St
Syracuse NY 13224 .... (315)446-4199
Bed & Breakfast Connection NY, RD#1, Box 325
Vernon NY 13476 .... (315)829-4888

NORTH CAROLINA

B&B in the Albemarle, PO Box 248
Everetts NC 27825 .... (919)335-3491

NORTH DAKOTA

Old West B&B Association, Box 211
Regent ND 58650 .... (701)563-4542

OHIO

Ohio Valley B&B, 1 w 4th St, #111
Cincinnati OH 45243 .... (606)356-7865
Private Lodging, PO Box 18590
Cleveland OH 44118 .... (216)321-3213
Columbus Bed & Breakfast Group, 769 S Third St
Columbus OH 43206 .... (614)443-3680
Buckeye Bed & Breakfast, PO Box 130
Powell OH 43065 .... (614)548-4555

OREGON

B&B Oregon, 2321 NE 28th Ave
Portland OR 97212 .... (503)245-0642
Bed & Breakfast Accommodations -, 2321 NE 28th Ave
Portland OR 97212 .... (503)287-4704
Northwest Bed and Breakfast Travel, 610 SW Broadway
Portland OR 97205 .... (503)243-7616

PENNSYLVANIA

Bed & Breakfast of Philadelphia, PO Box 630
Chester Springs PA 19425 .... (215)783-7838
B&B Traveler, PO Box 21
Devon PA 19333 .... (215)687-3565
Hershey B&B, PO Box 208
Hershey PA 17033-0208 .... (717)533-2928
Bed & Breakfast of Chester County, PO Box 825
Kennett Square PA 19348 .... (215)444-1367
Bed & Breakfast of Lancaster County, PO Box 19
Mountville PA .... (717)285-5956
Bed & Breakfast Center City, 1804 Pine St
Philadelphia PA 19103 .... (215)735-1137
Rest & Repast, PO Box 126
Pine Grove Mills PA 16868 .... (814)238-1484
Pittsburgh Bed & Breakfast
Pittsburgh PA .... (412)934-1212
All About Town, PO Box 562
Valley Forge PA 19481 .... (215)783-7838
B&B of Valley Forge
Valley Forge PA 19481-0562 .... (215)783-7838
Brandywine Valley, PO Box 562
Valley Forge PA 19481 .... (215)783-7838
Guesthouses B&B Reservations, RD 9
West Chester PA 19380 .... (215)692-4575

RHODE ISLAND

Bed & Breakfast of Rhode Island, Inc, PO Box 3291
Newport RI 02840 .... (401)849-1298
Castle Keep Bed & Breakfast, 44 Everett St
Newport RI 02804 .... (401)846-0362
Guest House Association of Newport, 23 Brinley St
Newport RI 02840 .... (401)849-7645

SOUTH CAROLINA

Bay Street Accommodations, 601 Bay St
Beaufort SC 29902 .... (803)524-7720
Charleston Society Bed & Breakfast, 84 Murray Blvd
Charleston SC 29401 .... (803)723-4948
Historic Charleston Bed & Breakfast, 43 Legare St
Charleston SC 29401 .... (803)722-6606

SOUTH DAKOTA

South Dakota Bed & Breakfast, PO Box 80137
Sioux Falls SD 57116 .... (605)987-2834

TENNESSEE

Bed & Breakfast in Memphis, PO Box 41621
Memphis TN 38174 .... (901)726-5920

TEXAS

Sand Dollar Hospitality B&B, 3605 Mendenhall
Corpus Christi TX 78415 .... (512)853-1222
Bed & Breakfast Texas Style, 4224 W Red Bird Ln
Dallas TX 75237 .... (214)298-5433
Bed & Breakfast Hosts of San Antonio, 166 Rockhill
San Antonio TX 78209 .... (512)824-8036

VERMONT

Vermont Bed & Breakfast, Box 1
East Fairfield VT 05448 .... (802)827-3827
American Bed & Breakfast in New England, Box 983
St Albans VT 05478 .... (802)524-4731

VIRGINIA

Princely B&B, Ltd, 819 Prince St
Alexandria VA 22314 .... (703)683-2159
Blue Ridge B&B, Rocks & Rills, R 2, Box 3895
Berryville VA 22611 .... (703)955-1246
Rockbridge Reservations, PO Box 76
Brownsburg VA 24415 .... (703)348-5698
Guesthouses - B&B, Inc., PO Box 5737
Charlottesville VA 22905 .... (804)979-7264
Bed & Breakfast of Tidewater, PO Box 3343
Norfolk VA 23514 .... (804)627-1983
Bensonhouse of Richmond and Williamsburg, 2036 Monument Ave
Richmond VA 23220 .... (804)648-7560
Travel Tree, PO Box 838
Williamsburg VA 23187 .... (804)253-1571

WASHINGTON

(BABS) Bed & Breakfast Service, PO Box 5025
Bellingham WA 98227 .... (206)733-8642
Travellers' Bed & Breakfast, PO Box 492
Mercer Island WA 98040 .... (206)232-2345
Pacific Bed & Breakfast, 701 NW 60th St
Seattle WA 98107 .... (206)784-0539
INNterlodging Co-op, PO Box 7044
Tacoma WA 98407 .... (206)756-0343

WASHINGTON DC

Bed 'n Breakfast Ltd, PO Box 12011
Washington DC 20005 .... (202)328-3510

WISCONSIN

Wisconsin Southern Lakes B&B Reservation, PO Box 322
Fontana WI 53125 .... (414)275-2266
B&B of Milwaukee, 1916 W Donges Bay Rd
Mequon WI 53092 .... (414)242-9680
Bed & Breakfast of Milwaukee, 320 E Buffalo St
Milwaukee WI 53202 .... (414)242-9680

STATE TOURISM OFFICES

ALABAMA
Alabama Bureau of Tourism & Travel, 532 S Perry St
Montgomery AL 36104 .... (800)252-2262

ALASKA
Alaska Division of Tourism, PO Box E-445
Juneau AK 99811 .... (907)465-2010

ARIZONA
Arizona Office of Tourism, 1100 W Washington St
Phoenix AZ 85007 .... (602)542-8687

ARKANSAS
Arkansas Dept of Parks & Tourism, 1 Capitol Mall
Little Rock AR 72201 .... (501)682-1511

CALIFORNIA
California Office of Tourism, 1121 L St, Ste 103
Sacramento CA 95814 .... (800)862-2543

COLORADO
Colorado Board of Tourism, 1625 Broadway, Ste 1700
Denver CO 80202 .... (800)255-5550

CONNECTICUT
Connecticut Tourism, 865 Brooks St
Rocky Hills CT .... (203)258-4300

DELAWARE
Delaware Tourism Office, 99 Kings Hwy, PO Box 1401
Dover DE 19903 .... (800)441-8846

FLORIDA
Florida Dept of Commerce, 107 W Gaines St, Ste 530
Tallahassee FL 32399 .... (904)488-4141

GEORGIA
Georgia Dept of Industry, PO Box 1776
Atlanta GA 30301 .... (404)656-3590

HAWAII
Hawaii Visitors Bureau, 3440 Wilshire Blvd, Ste 502
Los Angeles CA 90010 .... (213)385-5301

IDAHO
Dept of Commerce, 700 W State St
Boise ID 83720 .... (208)635-7820

ILLINOIS
Illinois Office of Tourism, 100 W Randolph St, Ste 3-400
Chicago IL 60601 .... (312)814-4732

INDIANA
Indiana Dept of Commerce, 1 N Capitol Ave, Ste 700
Indianapolis IN 46204 .... (317)232-8860

IOWA
Iowa Tourism, 200 E Grand Ave, Ste A
Des Moines IA 50309 .... (800)345-4692

KANSAS
Kansas Dept of Commerce, 400 SW 8th St, 5th Floor
Topeka KS 66603 .... (913)296-2009

KENTUCKY
Kentucky Dept of Travel, Capitol Plaza Tower, 22nd Floor
Frankfort KY 40601 .... (800)225-8747

LOUISIANA
Louisiana Office of Tourism, PO Box 94291
Baton Rouge LA 70804-9291 .... (800)334-8626

MAINE
Maine Publicity Bureau, 97 Winthrop St
Hallowell ME 04347 .... (207)289-2423

MARYLAND
Maryland Office of Tourism, 217 E Redwood St
Baltimore MD 21202 .... (800)543-1036

MASSACHUSETTS
Massachusetts Office of Travel & Tourism, 100 Cambridge St, 13th Floor
Boston MA 02202 .... (617)727-3201

MICHIGAN
Michigan Travel Bureau, Box 30226
Lansing MI 48909 .... (800)543-2937

MINNESOTA
Minnesota Office of Tourism, 250 Skyway Level, 375 Jackson St
St Paul MN 55101 .... (800)328-1461

MISSISSIPPI
Mississippi Dept of Tourist Development, PO Box 2285
Jackson MS 39205-0849 .... (800)647-2290

MISSOURI
Missouri Division of Tourism, PO Box 1055
Jefferson City MO 65102 .... (314)751-4133

MONTANA
Travel Montana, 1424 9th Ave
Helena MT 59620 .... (800)548-3390

NEBRASKA
Travel & Tourism, State Dept of, PO Box 94666
Lincoln NE 68509 .... (800)228-4307

NEVADA
Nevada Commission on Tourism, Capitol Complex
Carson City NV 89710 .... (702)687-4322

NEW HAMPSHIRE
Office of Vacation Travel, PO Box 856
Concord NH 03301 .... (603)271-2666

NEW JERSEY
Dept of Commerce & Economic Development, CN 826, 20 W State St
Trenton NJ 08625 .... (609)292-2470

NEW MEXICO
New Mexico Tourism & Travel, 1100 St Francis Dr, Joe Montoya Bld
Santa Fe NM 87503 .... (800)545-2040

NEW YORK
Division of Tourism, 1 Commerce Plaza
Albany NY 12245 .... (800)225-5697

NORTH CAROLINA
North Carolina Division of Travel, 430 N Salisbury St, 6th Floor
Raleigh NC 27611 .... (800)847-4762

NORTH DAKOTA
Tourism Promotion Division, State Capitol Grounds
Bismarck ND 58505 .... (800)437-2077

OHIO
Ohio Division of Travel & Trouism, PO Box 1001
Columbus OH 43215 .... (800)282-5393

OKLAHOMA
Tourism & Recreation Dept, 500 Will Rogers Bldg
Oklahoma City OK 73105 .... (405)521-2406

OREGON
Tourism Division, Oregon Economic, 775 Summer St, NE
Salem OR 97310 .... (800)547-7842

PENNSYLVANIA
Travel Development Bureau, 416 Forum Bldg
Harrisburg PA 17120 .... (800)847-4872

RHODE ISLAND
Rhode Island Dept of Economic Develop, 7 Jackson Walkway
Providence RI 02903 .... (800)556-2484

SOUTH CAROLINA
South Carolina Department of, PO Box 71, Inquiry Sections
Columbia SC 29202 .... (803)734-0235

SOUTH DAKOTA

South Dakota Dept of Tourism, 711 Wells Ave
Pierre SD 57501-3335 .... (800)843-8000

TENNESSEE

Tennessee Tourist Development, PO Box 23170
Nashville TN 37202 .... (615)741-2158

TEXAS

Texas Dept of Commerce, PO Box 12008
Austin TX 78711 .... (512)462-9191

UTAH

Utah Travel Council, Capitol Hill
Salt Lake City UT 84114 .... (801)538-1030

VERMONT

Travel Division, Agency of Development, 134 State St
Montpelier VT 05602 .... (800)828-3236

VIRGINIA

Virginia Division of Tourism, 1021 E Cary St
Richmond VA 23219 .... (800)847-4882

WASHINGTON

Washington State Tourism, 101 General Admin Bldg
Olympia WA 98504 .... (206)586-2088

WASHINGTON DC

Washington Convention & Visitors Assn, 1212 New York Ave NW, 6th Floor
Washington DC 20005 .... (202)789-7000

WEST VIRGINIA

West Virginia Travel, 1900 Washington St E, Bldg 6
Charleston WV 25305 .... (800)225-5982

WISCONSIN

Wisconsin Division of Tourism, PO Box 7606
Madison WI 53707 .... (608)266-2161

WYOMING

Wyoming Travel Commission, I-25 & College Dr
Cheyenne WY 82002 .... (800)225-5996

INNS OF INTEREST

LIGHTHOUSES

East Brother Light Station .... Point Richmond, CA
The Keeper's House .... Isle Au Haut, ME
Lighthouse Inn .... West Dennis, MA
Big Bay Point Lighthouse B&B .... Big Bay, MI

SCHOOLHOUSES

Ojai Manor Hotel .... Ojai, CA
The Bagley House .... Freeport, ME
Old Sea Pines Inn .... Brewster, MA
1797 House .... Buckland, MA
Dorset Schoolhouse .... Park Rapids, MN
School House B&B .... Rocheport, MO
The Mansion at Elfindale .... Springfield, MO
Washington School Inn .... Park City, UT

STAGE COACH STOPS

Fensalden B&B .... Albion, CA
Hotel Jeffery .... Coulterville, CA
Green Apple Inn .... Freestone, CA
Anderson-Wheeler Homestead .... Concord, MA
Six Chimneys .... East Hebron, NH
John Hancock Inn .... Hancock, NH
Tamworth Inn .... Tamworth, NH
Wakefield Inn .... Wakefield, NH
The Inn at Pittsfield .... Pittsfield, VT
Inn at Blush Hill .... Waterbury, VT

JAIL HOUSES

Jailer's Inn .... Bardstown, KY
Jail House Inn .... Newport, RI

ARCHEOLOGICAL SITES

White Oak Inn .... Danville, OH
Casita Chamisa .... Albuquerque, NM

OLD MILLS

Old Mill Inn .... Somersville, CT
Osceola Mill House .... Gordonville, PA
Edgewood Plantation .... Charles City, VA
The Inn at Gristmill Square .... Warm Springs, VA

OLD TAVERNS

Red Brook Inn .... Mystic, CT
Silvermine Tavern .... Norwalk, CT
White Swan Tavern .... Chestertown, MD
Historic Inns of Annapolis .... Annapolis, MD
The Dan'l Webster Inn .... Sandwich, MA
Merrell Tavern Inn .... South Lee, MA
Bird & Bottle Inn .... Garrison, NY
American House .... Geneseo, NY
Rider's 1812 Inn .... Painesville, OH
Smithton Inn .... Ephrata, PA
Rabbit Hill Inn .... Lower Waterford, VT
Laurel Brigade .... Leesburg, VA
Plough Inn .... Madison, WI

TUNNELS, SECRET PASSAGEWAYS & CAVES

Historic Inns of Annapolis .... Annapolis, MD
Ashley Manor .... Barnstable, MA
Wingscorton Farm .... East Sandwich, MA
Sterling Orchards .... Sterling, MA
Kemah Guest House .... Saugatuck, MI
Backstreet Inn B&B .... New Hope, PA
B&B of Valley Forge
& Philadelphia .... Philadelphia, PA
Seven Wives Inn .... St. George, UT
Kedron Valley Inn .... South Woodstock, VT

COBBLER SHOP

Cobbler Shop Inn .... Zoar Village, OH

CHURCH

Old Church House Inn .... Mossville, IL

TRAIN STATIONS

Melitta Station .... Santa Rosa, CA
1909 Depot .... Bonne Terre, MO
Green Mountain Inn .... Stowe, VT
Moore House .... South Cle Elum, WA

UNUSUAL SLEEPING SPACES

Atop a gold mine
American River Inn .... Georgetown, CA

In a '50s Cadillac Convertible
Union Hotel .... Los Alamos, CA

In a water tower
John Dougherty House .... Mendocino, CA

Atop an Indian Village
Casita Chamisa .... Albuquerque, NM

UNUSUAL ARCHITECTURE

La Corsette Maison Inn .... Newton, IA

Haan's 1830 Inn .... Mackinac Island, MI
Castle Inn .... Circleville, OH

LIVING MUSEUMS

Shakertown at Pleasant Hill .... Harrodsburg, KY

REVOLUTIONARY WAR

Lincoln House Country Inn ....Dennysville, ME
The Robert Morris Inn ....Oxford, MD
Ashley Manor Inn .... Barnstable, MA
Colonel Roger Brown House ....Concord, MA
Village Green Inn ....Falmouth, MA
The Dan'l Webster Inn ....Sandwich, MA
Churchtown Inn .... Churchtown, PA
B&B of Valley Forge & Philadelphia ..... Philadelphia, PA
The Melville House ....Newport, RI
John Rutledge House Inn ....Charleston, SC
The Inn at Weathersfield .... Weathersfield, VT
Silver Thatch Inn .... Charlottesville, VA
Caledonia Farm B&B .... Flint Hill, VA

CIVIL WAR

The Sedgwick Inn ....Berlin, NY
The Russell-Cooper House .... Mount Vernon, OH
Churchtown Inn .... Churchtown, PA
Beechmont Inn ....Hanover, PA
Culpepper House .... Senoia, GA
Rosswood Plantation ....Lorman, MS
Oak Square Plantation ....Port Gibson, MS
Cedar Grove Mansion Inn .... Vicksburg, MS
Dry Ridge Inn ....Weaverville, NC
The Doubleday Inn ....Gettysburg, PA
Kane Manor Country Inn ....Kane, PA
Bay Street Inn .... Beaufort, SC
Hale Springs Inn .... Rogersville, TN
La Vista Plantation ....Fredericksburg, VA
Welbourne .... Middleburg, VA
The Widow Kip's Shenandoah Inn ...Mount Jackson, VA
Mayhurst Inn..Orange, VA
Prospect Hill .... Trevilians, VA
Old Rittenhouse Inn .... Bayfield, WI
Prospect Hill Farm ....Gerrardstown, WV
Fillmore Street B&B .... Harpers Ferry, WV
Boydville - The Inn at Martinsburg......Martinsburg, WV

ASSOCIATED WITH LITERARY FIGURES

Robert Louis Stevenson
Brannan Cottage Inn....................................Calistoga, CA

Jack London, Mark Twain
Vichy Hot Springs Resort & Inn ....Ukiah, CA

Arthur Miller
Homestead Inn ....New Milford, CT

Margaret Mitchell (Gone With the Wind)
The Veranda - Hollberg Hotel .... Senoia, GA

Longfellow's The Courtship of Miles Standish
Isaac Randall House ....Freeport, ME

Ralph Waldo Emerson
The Island House ....Southwest Harbor, ME

Ralph Waldo Emerson, Louisa May Alcott, Nathaniel Hawthorne
Hawthorne Inn ....Concord, MA

Edith Wharton
The Gables Inn..Lenox, MA

The Yankee Bodleys Naomi Babson
Old Farm Inn ....Rockport, MA

F. Scott Fitzgerald
University Club of St. Paul .... Saint Paul, MN

Mark Twain
Fifth Street Mansion B&B ....Hannibal, MO
Garth Woodside Mansion.............................Hannibal, MO

Becky Thatcher
Fifth Street Mansion B&B ....Hannibal, MO

D.H. Lawrence
Hacienda del Sol ....Taos, NM

Marguerite Henry's Misty of Chincoteague
Miss Molly's Inn .... Chincoteague, VA

F. Scott Fitzgerald, Thomas Wolfe
Welbourne...Middleburg, VA

Jonathan Swift
Swift House Inn...Middlebury, VT

BLACK HISTORY

Dauzat House ....New Orleans, LA
Isaac Randall House ....Freeport, ME
Twin Gates .... Baltimore, MD
Old Manse Inn ....Brewster, MA
Wingscorton Farm Inn .... East Sandwich, MA
Rosswood Plantation .... Lorman, MS
The Wooden Rabbit ....Cape May, NJ
Troutbeck .... Amenia, NY
B&B Valley Forge & Philadelphia ....Philadelphia, PA
The Inn at Weathersfield .... Weathersfield, VT
Kedron Valley Inn ....South Woodstock, VT
Sleepy Hollow Farm ....Gordonsville, VA
Prospect Hill ....Trevilians, VA

GOLD MINES/GOLD PANNING

Power's Mansion Inn ....Auburn, CA
City Hotel ....Columbia, CA
Julian Gold Rush Hotel..Julian, CA
Hotel Nipton ....Nipton, CA
The Ryan House B&B ....Sonora, CA
Livingston Mansion ....Jacksonville, OR

LOG HOUSES

Belle Aire Mansion ....Galena, IL
Log Cabin B&B ....Georgetown, KY
Inn at Cedar Falls ....Logan, OH

INNS ON ISLANDS

The Manoa Valley Inn .... Honolulu, HI
Poipu B&B Inn .... Koloa,Kauai, HI
The Lahaina Hotel .... Lahaina, Maui, HI
Haan's 1830 Inn .... Mackinac Island, MI
The Beatty House .... Kelleys Island, OH
Bombay House .... Bainbridge Island, WA
The Inn at Penn Cove .... Coupeville, WA
The Victorian B&B .... Coupeville, WA
Guest House B&B & Cottages .... Greenbank, WA
Turtleback Farm Inn .... Orcas Island, WA
The Old Tjomsland House .... Vashon Island, WA

NATURAL HOT SPRINGS

Palace Hotel & Bath House .... Eureka Springs, AR
Rainbow Tarns .... Crowley Lake, CA
Vichy Hot Springs Resort & Inn .... Ukiah, CA
Glen-Ella Springs Hotel .... Clarkesville, GA
Idaho Rocky Mountain Ranch .... Stanley, ID

OLDEST CONTINUOUSLY OPERATED INNS

The York House .... Mountain City, GA
The Cranberry Inn at Chatham .... Chatham, MA
Village Inn .... Lenox, MA
Century House .... Nantucket, MA
Fitzwilliam Inn .... Fitzwilliam, NH
Wakefield Inn .... Wakefield, NH
The Stockton Inn, Colligan's .... Stockton, NJ
Hale Springs Inn .... Rogersville, TN
The Inn at Montross .... Montross, VA
The Inn at Gristmill Square .... Warm Springs, VA

STILL IN THE FAMILY

Standish House .... Lanark, IL
Salt Marsh Farm .... South Dartmouth, MA
Sterling Orchards B&B .... Sterling, MA
The Old Holland Inn .... Holland, MI
The Sutton-Weed Farm .... Hudson, MI
Lowell Inn .... Stillwater, MN
Millsaps-Buie House .... Jackson, MS
Rockhouse Mountain Farm-Inn .... Eaton Center, NH
Chalfonte .... Cape May, NJ
The Inn at Fordhook Farm .... Doylestown, PA
Historic Charleston B&B .... Charleston, SC
Birch Hill Inn .... Manchester, VT
North Bend Plantation .... Charles City, VA
Welbourne .... Middleburg, VA

WHO SLEPT HERE

Lillian Russell
Bayview Hotel B&B Inn .... Aptos, CA

John Phillip Souza
The B&B Inn at La Jolla .... La Jolla, CA

Herbert Hoover, Hearst family
McCloud Guest House .... McCloud, CA

Scripps family
Britt House .... San Diego, CA

Teddy Roosevelt
Vichy Hot Springs Resort & Inn .... Ukiah, CA

President Hoover, Will Rogers, Greta Garbo
Wake Robin Inn .... Lakeville, CT

Marilyn Monroe
Homestead Inn .... New Milford, CT

William Penn
William Penn Guest House .... New Castle, DE

Judy Garland, Pancho Villa, Clark Gable

Ulysses S. Grant
Stillman's Country Inn .... Galena, IL

Lowell Thomas, Wendell Wilkie, Charles Kittering
Teetor House .... Hagerstown, IN

Martin Van Buren
Old Hoosier House .... Knightstown, IN

Karl Menninger
Heritage House .... Topeka, KS

Bette Davis
Blackberry Inn .... Camden, ME

John James Audubon
Lincoln House Country Inn .... Dennysville, ME
Weston House .... Eastport, ME

Gloria Swanson, Cecile B. DeMille
The Inn at Fernbrook .... Centerville, MA

Susan B. Anthony
The Park House .... Saugatuck, MI

Woolworth family, Barbara Hutton, Cary Grant
The Mulburn Inn .... Bethlehem, NH

Bob & Dolores Hope
The Greenfield B&B Inn .... Greenfield, NH

Stanford White, architect
The Inn at Jackson .... Jackson, NH

Babe Ruth
Cranmore Mt Lodge .... North Conway, NH

Bigelow family
Stonehurst Manor .... North Conway, NH
The Lodge at Cloudcroft .... Cloudcroft, NM

Billy the Kid
Casa de Patron .... Lincoln, NM

Georgia O'Keefe
Hacienda del Sol .... Taos, NM

Robert E. Lee
The Wooden Rabbit .... Cape May, NJ

Presidents Wilson, Cleveland and Roosevelt
The Cordova .... Ocean Grove, NJ

Teddy Roosevelt
Troutbeck .... Amenia, NY

William Rockefeller
The Point .... Saranac Lake, NY

William Seward
The William Seward Inn .... Westfield, NY

Barrymore family
Evermay-on-the-Delaware .... Erwinna, PA

Burpee family
The Inn at Fordhook Farm .... Doylestown, PA

President John Adams
Witmer's Tavern-Historic 1725 Inn .... Lancaster, PA

President Herbert Hoover
The Carriage House at Stonegate .... Montoursville, PA

Charles Carroll
Hickory Bridge Farm .... Orrtanna, PA

Kellogg family
Village Country Inn .... Manchester Village, VT

Norman Rockwell
The Inn on Covered Bridge Green .... Arlington, VT

Thomas Edison
Tulip Tree Inn .... Chittenden, VT

General Stonewall Jackson
Mayhurst Inn .... Orange, VA
The Inn at Narrow Passage .... Woodstock, VA

Clark Gable
Willcox House .... Bremerton, WA

Henry Bennett, photographer
Historic Bennett House .... Wisconsin Dells, WI

INNS PRIOR TO 1800

1637 York Harbor Inn .... York Harbor ME
1660 The Taos Inn .... Taos NM
1667 Stephen Daniels House .... Salem MA
1682 William Penn Guest House .... New Castle DE
1683 The Inn at Montross .... Montross VA
1692 The Dan'l Webster Inn .... Sandwich MA
1699 Ashley Manor Inn .... Barnstable MA
1700 Historic Inns of Annapolis .... Annapolis MD
1700 Tulpehocken Manor Inn & PlantatioMyerstown PA
1702 Admiral Farragut Inn .... Newport RI
1704 Stumble Inne .... Nantucket MA
1705 Thomas Huckins House .... Barnstable MA
1708 Black Friar Brook Farm .... Duxbury MA
1708 The Jacob Kip River House B&B .... Rhinebeck NY
1709 B&B Cape Cod .... West Hyannisport MA
1709 The Woodbox Inn .... Nantucket MA
1710 The Robert Morris Inn .... Oxford MD
1710 The Stockton Inn, Colligan's .... Stockton NJ
1712 Harbor Light Inn .... Marblehead MA
1713 Historic Charleston B&B .... Charleston SC
1714 Hartwell House .... Ogunquit ME
1717 Coventry Forge Inn .... Pottstown PA
1720 Butternut Farm .... Glastonbury CT
1722 Logan Inn .... New Hope PA
1723 Corner House .... Nantucket MA
1725 Cobblestone Inn .... Nantucket MA
1725 Witmer's Tavern - Historic 1725 Inn... Lancaster PA
1730 Colonial House Inn .... Yarmouth Port MA
1730 White Swan Tavern .... Chestertown MD
1731 Maple Hill Farm B&B .... Coventry CT
1732 The Kitchen House .... Charleston SC
1732 Prospect Hill .... Trevilians VA
1734 Fairway Farm B&B .... Pottstown PA
1734 Joseph Ambler Inn .... North Wales PA
1735 Churchtown Inn .... Churchtown PA
1736 High Meadows B&B .... Eliot ME
1737 New Boston Inn .... Sandisfield MA
1738 Brown's Historic Home B&B .... Salem NJ
1738 Herr Farmhouse Inn .... Manheim PA
1739 The Ruffner House .... Luray VA
1740 Evermay-on-the-Delaware .... Erwinna PA
1740 The Inn at Narrow Passage .... Woodstock VA
1740 The Old Dennis House .... Newport RI
1740 Red Brook Inn .... Mystic CT
1740 Sterling Orchards B&B .... Sterling MA
1740 Under Mountain Inn .... Salisbury CT
1743 Hotel Maison de Ville .... New Orleans LA
1744 Yesterday's Yankee B&B .... Salisbury CT
1745 Black Bass Hotel .... Lumberville PA
1745 Fleetwood Farm .... Leesburg VA
1745 Tollgate Hill Inn .... Litchfield CT
1749 Sign of the Sorrel Horse .... Quakertown PA
1750 Backstreet Inn of New Hope .... New Hope PA
1750 Galisteo Inn .... Galisteo NM
1750 The General Rufus Putnam House .... Worcester-Rutland MA
1750 Golden Plough Inn .... Lahaska PA
1750 Guesthouses .... Charlottesville VA
1750 Henry Farm Inn .... Chester VT
1750 Hickory Bridge Farm .... Orrtanna PA
1750 The Melville House .... Newport RI
1750 Tannerbrook .... Brooklyn CT
1751 The John Banister House .... Newport RI
1751 The Penny House .... North Eastham MA
1751 Three Village Inn .... Stony Brook NY
1753 L'Auberge Provencale .... White Post VA
1755 Hayne House .... Charleston SC
1757 Wingscorton Farm Inn .... East Sandwich MA
1757 Woodstock Hall .... Charlottesville VA
1759 Laurel Brigade Inn .... Leesburg VA
1760 Edgewater B&B .... Fairhaven MA
1760 The Inn at Fordhook Farm .... Doylestown PA
1760 Gilbert House B&B .... Charles Town WV
1760 Glasgow Inn .... Cambridge MD
1760 Henry Ludlam Inn .... Woodbine NJ
1760 Mountain Lake Inn .... Bradford NH
1760 The Winchester Country Inn .... Westminster MD
1761 Bird & Bottle Inn .... Garrison NY
1762 Goose Chase .... Gardners PA
1763 Blackberry River Inn .... Norfolk CT
1763 John Rutledge House Inn .... Charleston SC
1763 Smithton Inn .... Ephrata PA
1764 Colonel Spencer Inn .... Plymouth NH
1765 Captain Samuel Eddy House Inn .... Auburn MA
1765 The Carlisle House Inn .... Nantucket MA
1766 The Osceola Mill House .... Gordonville PA
1768 Cedars at Beaufort .... Beaufort NC
1768 The Silver Fox Inn .... West Rutland VT
1768 The Inn at Teardrop .... Hillsborough NC
1770 Garden Gables Inn .... Lenox MA
1770 La Grange Plantation Inn .... Henderson NC

1770 The Parsonage .... East Orleans MA
1771 Village Inn .... Lenox MA
1772 The Bagley House .... Freeport ME
1772 Jail House Inn .... Newport RI
1773 Peacock Inn .... North Conway NH
1775 1811 House .... Manchester Village VT
1775 Arrowhead Inn .... Durham NC
1775 Colonel Roger Brown House .... Concord MA
1775 Jared Cone House .... Bolton CT
1775 Salt Marsh Farm .... South Dartmouth MA
1775 Sleepy Hollow Farm .... Gordonsville VA
1775 Todd House .... Eastport ME
1775 Welbourne .... Middleburg VA
1776 Griswold Inn .... Essex CT
1778 Staffords-in-the-Field .... Chocorua NH
1779 Captain Josiah Mitchell House .... Freeport ME
1780 Amos Parker House .... Fitzwilliam NH
1780 Chester House .... Chester VT
1780 The Conyers House .... Sperryville VA
1780 Egremont Inn .... South Egremont MA
1780 The Golden Stage Inn .... Proctorsville VT
1780 Inn Between the Hills .... Hillsboro VA
1780 Isaiah Clark House .... Brewster MA
1780 Ivanhoe Country House .... Sheffield MA
1780 River House .... Boyce VA
1780 Silver Thatch Inn .... Charlottesville VA
1780 Spring Garden .... Laurel DE
1784 Lovett's Inn .... Franconia NH
1785 The 1785 Inn .... North Conway NH
1785 Weathervane Inn .... South Egremont MA
1786 The Brafferton Inn .... Gettysburg PA
1786 Gibson's Lodgings .... Annapolis MD
1786 Kenniston Hill Inn .... Boothbay ME
1786 Limestone Inn B&B .... Strasburg PA
1786 Old Mill Inn .... Brandon VT
1786 Silvermine Tavern .... Norwalk CT
1786 Windsor House .... Newburyport MA
1787 Lincoln House Country Inn .... Dennysville ME
1787 The Lords Proprietors' Inn .... Edenton NC
1787 Nereledge Inn & White Horse Pub .... North Conway NH
1787 Rose And Crown Guest House .. Provincetown MA
1788 Dauzat House .... New Orleans LA
1789 Historic Brookside Farms .... Orwell VT
1789 John Hancock Inn .... Hancock NH
1789 Longswamp B&B .... Mertztown PA
1789 Prospect Hill Farm .... Gerrardstown WV
1790 Admiral Fell Inn .... Baltimore MD
1790 Ash Mill Farm .... Holicong PA
1790 Birch Hill Inn .... Manchester VT
1790 The Inn at Blush Hill .... Waterbury VT
1790 The Inn at Coit Mountain .... Newport NH
1790 Crook' Jaw Inn .... Yarmouth Port MA
1790 Crown 'N' Anchor Inn .... Newcastle ME
1790 Fairhaven Inn .... Bath ME
1790 Geandaugh House .... Saint Louis MO
1790 Green Trails Country Inn .... Brookfield VT
1790 Hill Farm Inn .... Arlington VT
1790 Hillsborough House Inn .... Hillsborough NC
1790 The Lincoln Inn at the Covered Bridge .... Woodstock VT
1790 Lothrop Merry House .... Vineyard Haven MA
1790 Olde Rowley Inn .... North Waterford ME
1790 Packard House .... Bath ME
1791 The Inn on Cove Hill .... Rockport MA
1791 Historic Springfield Plantation .... Fayette MS
1791 The Sedgwick Inn .... Berlin NY
1791 Six Chimneys .... East Hebron NH
1791 St. Francis Inn .... Saint Augustine FL
1792 The Inn on Covered Bridge Green ...... Arlington VT
1792 New London Inn .... New London NH
1793 Echo Ledge Farm Inn .... East St Johnsbury VT
1793 Woolverton Inn .... Stockton NJ
1794 Merrell Tavern Inn .... South Lee MA
1795 Canaan Land Farm B&B .... Harrodsburg KY
1795 Rabbit Hill Inn .... Lower Waterford VT
1795 The Inn on the Common ... Craftsbury Common VT
1795 The Inn at Weathersfield .... Weathersfield VT
1796 Cobble Hill Farm .... New Hartford CT
1796 Fitzwilliam Inn .... Fitzwilliam NH
1796 Myrtles Plantation .... Saint Francisville LA
1796 National Pike Inn .... New Market MD
1796 The Wildflower Inn .... Lyndonville VT
1797 1797 House .... Buckland MA
1797 Lake House .... Waterford ME
1798 East Country Berry Farm .... Lenox MA
1798 Edgartown Inn .... Edgartown MA
1799 Old Farm Inn .... Rockport MA

OUTSTANDING ACHIEVEMENT AWARD

Each year the Association of American Historic Inns presents an Outstanding Achievement Award to an innkeeper who has made significant contributions to the preservation of historic properties. These individuals go beyond the confines of their own inn and reach out to the community encouraging historic preservation and restoration locally, state-wide and even nationally.

Nominations for future awards should be sent to **The Association of American Historic Inns, PO Box 336, Dana Point, CA 92629.**

We congratulate the winner and are pleased to honor him with this award.

ASSOCIATION OF AMERICAN HISTORIC INNS

Outstanding Achievement Award

Ned Shank

Dairy Hollow House

Eureka Springs, Arkansas

"To me, preservation's not embalming historic structures. It's active and interactive — vital, and people-connected. We are challenged to think and feel in new ways, and to consider old ways — how those before us thought and felt. By this contact we are more rooted; with strong roots, we grow. Preservation is as much about people — how they live in and use buildings, how they understand themselves and their communities, why they build the environment they do — as it is about the structures themselves." Ned Shank.

Ned Shank is a historic preservationist, and innkeeper at Dairy Hollow House, a country inn in the Ozark Mountain resort community of Eureka Springs, Arkansas. There, in addition to restoring the inn's 1888 farmhouse, he volunteers hundreds of hours annually as chairman of the Eureka Springs Historic District Commission, the Eureka Springs Historical Museum and the state-wide Historic Preservation Alliance of Arkansas (which he helped found in 1981).

"Arkansas is great," he says. "The huge diversity of the built and natural environments make it highly interesting. And the fact that its population is so small means each person can still make a difference."

Dairy Hollow House was the first bed-and-breakfast inn in the town, and one of the first in the state. "My wife and I wanted to show that tourism and preservation could go hand in hand," says Shank. "Historic accommodations, like any taste of truly regional culture — be it local music, crafts, even cuisine — enrich the travel experience."

As a boy, Ned spent several summers with his father, Wesley Shank, a professor of architectural history, as he worked on Historic American Buildings Survey projects in such diverse locations as the Delaware Water Gap, New Jersey, and San Antonio, Texas. "It gave me an appreciation for the richness and variety of American regional architecture," he says.

While still in college, Ned nominated a carriage manufacturing plant to the National Register of Historic Places. Upon graduation from Grinnell College he interned with the National Trust for Historic Preservation, which subsequently found him his first job, in Arkansas: writing a history of the 1836 Greek Revival First State Capitol. There, he met his wife, author Crescent Dragonwagon, at a potluck dinner, given in a Victorian Steamboat Gothic mansion. Crescent introduced Ned to her home in northwest Arkansas, in Eureka Springs.

Ned fell in love with the quirky Victorian community, a settlement, rich in mineral springs, that had grown up as a health spa in the 1880s. Soon the city became known not only as a health resort, but as a mecca for artists, writers and craftspeople, a reputation it has maintained to this day. "The unusual topography of the city, steep hills, cliffs and ridges, forced the indigenous architecture to take unusual forms. That, with the bizarre collection of personalities and characters who have been attracted to the town, straight through from its founding to the present day, have produced a place of never-ending visual, architectural, and gossipy-historical interest," says Shank. "It's a feast."

Ned and Crescent's personal warmth and hospitality have enriched the lives of those who stayed or dined at their Dairy Hollow House.

PAST RECIPIENTS OF THE AWARD

Kit Sargent
Casita Chamisa, Albuquerque, New Mexico

Tom Carroll
Mainstay Inn, Cape May, New Jersey

Tim Tyler
Russell-Cooper House B&B, Mount Vernon, Ohio

Ruth Keyes
Red Brook Inn, Old Mystic, Connecticut

Chuck & Ann Hillestad
Queen Anne Inn, Denver, Colorado

INNS BY NAME

The following alphabetical listing includes only those inns listed in the main part of this book.

The 1735 House .... Amelia Island, FL
The 1785 Inn .... North Conway, NH
1797 House .... Buckland, MA
1802 House .... Kennebunkport, ME
1811 House .... Manchester Village, VT
1830 Inn on the Green .... Weston, VT
1837 B&B & Tea Room .... Charleston, SC
1842 Inn .... Macon, GA
The 1860 House .... Stowe, VT
The 1868 Stewart-Marsh House .... Salisbury, NC
1876 House .... Oxford, MD
1880 Seafield House .... Westhampton Beach, NY
1890 B&B .... Coshocton, OH
1909 Depot .... Bonne Terre, MO
200 South Street Inn .... Charlottesville, VA
417 The Haslam-Fort House .... Savannah, GA
A Cambridge House B&B Inn .... Cambridge, MA
A Touch of Country B&B .... New Market, VA
The Abbey .... Cape May, NJ
Abbie Hill B&B .... Richmond, VA
Aberdeen Inn .... Asheville, NC
Abigail Adams B&B .... Cape May, NJ
Abriendo Inn .... Pueblo, CO
Academy Street B&B .... Hawley, PA
The Adams House .... Deadwood, SD
Adams Inn .... Washington, DC
The Adamstown Inn B&B .... Adamstown, PA
Addison Choate Inn .... Rockport, MA
Adelphi Hotel .... Saratoga Springs, NY
Admiral Farragut Inn .... Newport, RI
Admiral Fell Inn .... Baltimore, MD
Admiral's Quarters Inn .... Boothbay Harbor, ME
The Aerie .... New Bern, NC
Agate Cove Inn .... Mendocino, CA
Ahlf House .... Grants Pass, OR
Alaska's 7 Gables .... Fairbanks, AK
Albatross Bed & Breakfast .... Anacortes, WA
Albemarle Inn .... Asheville, NC
Albert G. Stevens Inn .... Cape May, NJ
Albion River Inn .... Albion, CA
Albonegon Inn .... Southport, ME
The Alden House .... Lititz, PA
Aldrich Guest House .... Galena, IL
Alexander Hamilton House .... Croton-on-Hudson, NY
Alexander's Inn .... Santa Fe, NM
Amber House .... Sacramento, CA
Amelia Payson Guest House .... Salem, MA
American House .... Geneseo, NY
American River Inn .... Georgetown, CA
Amos Parker House .... Fitzwilliam, NH
Amos Shinkle Townhouse .... Covington, KY
An Elegant Victorian Mansion .... Eureka, CA
Anaheim Country Inn .... Anaheim, CA
Anchuca Clarion Carriage House Inn .... Vicksburg, MS
Anderson Guest House .... Wilmington, NC
Anderson-Wheeler Homestead .... Concord, MA
The Andrie Rose Inn .... Ludlow, VT
Angel Of The Sea .... Cape May, NJ
Angelica Inn .... Angelica, NY
Ansonborough Inn .... Charleston, SC
The Inn at Antietam .... Sharpsburg, MD
Apple Lane Inn .... Aptos, CA
Applewood Colonial B&B .... Williamsburg, VA
Applewood Farms Inn .... Ledyard, CT
Applewood Manor .... Asheville, NC
The Arbor .... Edgartown, MA
Archbishop's Mansion .... San Francisco, CA
Archers Inn .... Banner Elk, NC
The Arches .... Brandon, VT
The Arlington Inn .... Arlington, VT
Arrowhead Inn .... Durham, NC
Art Center/Wamsley Gallery/B&B .... San Francisco, CA
Asa Ransom House .... Clarence, NY
Ash Mill Farm .... Holicong, PA
Ashfield Inn .... Ashfield, MA
Ashley Manor Inn .... Barnstable, MA
The Atchison House .... Northville, MI
The Augustus Bove House .... Naples, ME
Austin Hill Inn .... West Dover, VT
Avalon House .... Fort Bragg, CA
Avery Guest House .... Galena, IL
B&B at Skoglund Farm .... Canova, SD
B&B at The Chimes .... New Orleans, LA
B&B Cape Cod .... West Hyannisport, MA
The B&B Inn at La Jolla .... La Jolla, CA
B&B of Valley Forge & Philadelphia .... Philadelphia, PA
B&B With Love's .... Deer Park, WA
Babbling Brook B&B Inn .... Santa Cruz, CA
Backstreet Inn of New Hope .... New Hope, PA
The Inn on Bacon Hill .... Saratoga Springs, NY
The Bagley House .... Freeport, ME
Bailey House .... Fernandina Beach, FL
Bailiwick Inn .... Fairfax, VA
The Baldpate Inn .... Estes Park, CO
Ballastone Inn .... Savannah, GA
Balsam Mountain Inn .... Balsam, NC
The Barbican .... Sturgeon Bay, WI
The Bark Eater .... Keene, NY
BarnaGate B&B .... Ocean City, NJ
Barnard-Good House .... Cape May, NJ
The Barrister's House .... Baraboo, WI
Barrow House .... Saint Francisville, LA
Barrows House .... Dorset, VT
Bath Street Inn .... Santa Barbara, CA
Battle Island Inn .... Fulton, NY
Bay Street Inn .... Beaufort, SC
Bayboro House on Old Tampa Bay .... Saint Petersburg, FL
Bayview Hotel B&B Inn .... Aptos, CA
Beacon Hill B&B .... Boston, MA
Beal House Inn .... Littleton, NH
Bear & The Bay .... Petoskey, MI
The Beatty House .... Kelleys Island, OH
Beaumont Inn .... Harrodsburg, KY
Beaver Pond Farm Inn .... Warren, VT

Edgecombe-Coles House ... Camden, ME
Edgewater B&B ... Fairhaven, MA
Edgewood Plantation ... Charles City, VA
Edgeworth Inn ... Monteagle, TN
Edinburgh Lodge B&B ... Ashland, OR
Edith Palmer's Country Inn ... Virginia City, NV
Edwardian Inn ... Helena, AR
Egremont Inn ... South Egremont, MA
Eiler's Inn ... Laguna Beach, CA
El Canario Inn ... Condado, San Juan, PR
El Paradero ... Santa Fe, NM
Elizabeth's B&B ... Bath, ME
The Inn at Elizabethville ... Elizabethville, PA
Elk Cove Inn ... Elk, CA
Ellis River House ... Jackson, NH
The Elms B&B ... Camden, ME
The Inn at Elmwood Corners ... Hampton, NH
Embassy Inn ... Washington, DC
The Emma James House ... Boston, MA
The English House ... Andover, NH
Evergreen Inn ... Anderson, SC
Evermay-on-the-Delaware ... Erwinna, PA
Exeter Inn ... Exeter, NH
Eye Openers ... Altadena, CA
Fairfield Place ... Shreveport, LA
Fairhaven Inn ... Bath, ME
Fairway Farm B&B ... Pottstown, PA
Fallon Hotel ... Columbia, CA
The Farmhouse 'Round the Bend ... Grafton, VT
Fassifern B&B ... Lexington, VA
Faulkner House ... Red Bluff, CA
The Fearrington House ... Pittsboro, NC
The Feather Bed ... Quincy, CA
Featherbed Railroad Company B&B ... Nice, CA
Fensalden Inn ... Albion, CA
The Inn at Fernbrook ... Centerville, MA
Ferris Mansion ... Rawlins, WY
Fifth Street Mansion B&B ... Hannibal, MO
Fillmore Street B&B ... Harpers Ferry, WV
Fitzwilliam Inn ... Fitzwilliam, NH
Fleetwood Farm ... Leesburg, VA
Flint Street Inn ... Asheville, NC
Florida House Inn ... Amelia Island, FL
Foley House Inn ... Savannah, GA
The Folger Hotel & Cottages ... Nantucket, MA
Folkestone Inn ... Bryson City, NC
Follansbee Inn ... North Sutton, NH
Foothill House ... Calistoga, CA
The Inn at Fordhook Farm ... Doylestown, PA
The Foreman House B&B ... Churchtown, PA
The Forsyth Park Inn ... Savannah, GA
The Foster-Harris House ... Washington, VA
Fountain Hall B&B ... Culpeper, VA
Four Chimneys ... Nantucket, MA
Four Chimneys Inn ... Dennis, MA
Franconia Inn ... Franconia, NH
Frederick House ... Staunton, VA
French Country Inn of Ephraim ... Ephraim, WI
Fryemont Inn ... Bryson City, NC
The Gables ... Santa Rosa, CA
Gables B&B ... Kewaunee, WI
The Gables Inn ... Lenox, MA
Galisteo Inn ... Galisteo, NM
Gallatin Gateway ... Gallatin Gateway, MT
The Garden and the Sea Inn ... New Church, VA
Garden Gables Inn ... Lenox, MA
Garden Street Inn ... San Luis Obispo, CA
Garland's Oak Creek Lodge ... Sedona, AZ
Garratt Mansion ... Alameda, CA
Garrison Inn ... Newburyport, MA
Garth Woodside Mansion ... Hannibal, MO
Gatehouse Inn ... Pacific Grove, CA
Geandaugh House ... Saint Louis, MO
The General Rufus Putnam House ... Worcester-Rutland, MA
Geneva On The Lake ... Geneva, NY
George Fuller House ... Essex, MA
Georgianna Manor ... Redlands, CA
Gerhart House B&B ... Ephrata, PA
Gibson's Lodgings ... Annapolis, MD
Gilbert House B&B ... Charles Town, WV
The Gilbert Inn, B&B ... Seaside, OR
Gilded Thistle B&B ... Galveston Island, TX
Gingerbread House ... Cape May, NJ
Gingerbread Inn ... Hertford, NC
Glasgow Inn ... Cambridge, MD
Glen-Ella Springs Hotel ... Clarkesville, GA
Glendeven ... Little River, CA
Glidden House ... Cleveland, OH
Glynn House Victorian Inn ... Ashland, NH
Goddard Mansion B&B ... Claremont, NH
Golden Gate Hotel ... San Francisco, CA
The Golden Goose ... Tyringham, MA
Golden Lamb ... Lebanon, OH
Golden Pheasant Inn ... Erwinna, PA
Golden Plough Inn ... Lahaska, PA
The Inn on Golden Pond ... Holderness, NH
The Golden Stage Inn ... Proctorsville, VT
Goldminer Hotel ... Eldora, CO
Goose Chase ... Gardners, PA
Goose Creek Guesthouse ... Southold, NY
Gosby House Inn ... Pacific Grove, CA
Gosnold Arms ... New Harbor, ME
The Governor's Inn ... Ludlow, VT
Grafton Inn ... Falmouth, MA
Gramma's Inn ... Berkeley, CA
The Grandison ... Oklahoma City, OK
Grandmere's Inn ... Nevada City, CA
Grandview B&B ... Astoria, OR
Grandview Lodge ... Waynesville, NC
Grant Corner Inn ... Santa Fe, NM
The Graustein Inn ... Knoxville, TN
The Gray Goose ... Chesterton, IN
Gray Goose B&B ... Sturgeon Bay, WI
Graycote Inn ... Bar Harbor, ME
The Great Southern Hotel ... Brinkley, AR
Green Apple Inn ... Freestone, CA
Green Gables Inn ... Pacific Grove, CA
Green Meadows B&B ... Charlotte, VT
Green Mountain Inn ... Stowe, VT
Green Trails Country Inn ... Brookfield, VT
Green Tree Inn ... Elsah, IL
Greenbriar B&B Inn ... Coeur d'Alene, ID
Greene Gate Village Historic B&B Inn ... Saint George, UT
The Greenfield B&B Inn ... Greenfield, NH
Greenhurst Inn ... Bethel, VT
Greenleaf Inn ... Chester, VT
Greenvale Manor ... Mollusk, VA
Greenville Arms ... Greenville, NY
Greenville Inn ... Greenville, ME
Greenwood B&B ... Greensboro, NC
The Gregory House ... Averill Park, NY
Grenoble House ... New Orleans, LA
Grey Whale Inn ... Fort Bragg, CA
Greystone Manor B&B ... Bird-in-hand, PA
The Griffin Inn ... Ellison Bay, WI
The Inn at Gristmill Square ... Warm Springs, VA
Griswold Inn ... Essex, CT
The Groveland Hotel ... Groveland, CA
Guest House ... Arroyo Grande, CA
Guest House B&B & Cottages ... Greenbank, WA
Guesthouses ... Charlottesville, VA
Guilds Inn ... Mt Pleasant, SC
Gustavus Inn ... Gustavus, AK
Gwendolyn's B&B ... Perkinsville, VT
H.W. Allen Villa B&B ... Troy, OH
Haan's 1830 Inn ... Mackinac Island, MI
Hacienda del Sol ... Taos, NM
Haikuleana B&B Inn ... Haiku, Maui, HI

The Mercersburg Inn ... Mercersburg, PA
Merrell Tavern Inn ... South Lee, MA
Mershon Court ... Fairhope, AL
Michigamme Lake Lodge ... Marquette, MI
Middlebury Inn ... Middlebury, VT
Middletown Springs Inn ... Middletown Springs, VT
Mill Rose Inn ... Half Moon Bay, CA
Millbrook ... Waitsfield, VT
Miller Tree Inn ... Forks, WA
Millsaps-Buie House ... Jackson, MS
Mimi's House ... Washington, IN
Mimosa Hall ... Karnack, TX
The Mine Manager's House ... Ajo, AZ
Mio Amore Pensione ... Trout Lake, WA
Mira Monte Inn ... Bar Harbor, ME
Miss Betty's B&B Inn ... Wilson, NC
Miss Molly's Inn ... Chincoteague, VA
Moffatt House ... San Francisco, CA
Moffett House ... Brandon, VT
The Inn at Montpelier ... Montpelier, VT
The Montrose House ... Montrose, PA
The Inn at Montross ... Montross, VA
Moore House Country Inn ... South Cle Elum, WA
Moose Mountain Lodge ... Etna, NH
Morehead Inn ... Charlotte, NC
Morical House ... Ashland, OR
Morning Dove B&B ... Ogunquit, ME
Moses Nickerson House ... Chatham, MA
Mostly Hall B&B Inn ... Falmouth, MA
Mount Pleasant House ... Washington, DC
Mountain Brook ... Sylva, NC
Mountain Fare Inn ... Campton, NH
Mountain Home Inn ... Mill Valley, CA
Mountain Lake Inn ... Bradford, NH
Mountain Valley Manner ... Conway, NH
Mr. Patrick Henry's Inn ... Richmond, VA
Mrs. B's Historic Lanesboro Inn ... Lanesboro, MN
The Inn on Mt. Ada ... Avalon, CA
Mt. Tremper Inn ... Mount Tremper, NY
The Mulberry Inn ... Yankton, SD
The Mulburn Inn ... Bethlehem, NH
Mumford Manor ... Portland, OR
Mustard Seed ... Hayward, WI
My Island B&B ... Volcano, HI
Myrtles Plantation ... Saint Francisville, LA
The Inn at Mystic ... Mystic, CT
Napa Inn ... Napa, CA
The Inn at Narrow Passage ... Woodstock, VA
National Hotel ... Nevada City, CA
National Pike Inn ... New Market, MD
The Nauset House Inn ... East Orleans, MA
Nereledge Inn & White Horse Pub ... North Conway, NH
New Boston Inn ... Sandisfield, MA
New Davenport B&B ... Davenport, CA
New England Inn ... Intervale, NH
New London Inn ... New London, NH
Newbury House at Historic Rugby ... Rugby, TN
The Newcastle Inn ... Newcastle, ME
Newport House ... Williamsburg, VA
Newry Manor ... Everett, PA
Newtons' 1824 House Inn ... Waitsfield, VT
Noble House ... Bridgton, ME
The Noble McCaa Butler House ... Anniston, AL
The Nolan House A Bed & Breakfast Inn ... San Francisco, CA
The Normandy Inn ... Spring Lake, NJ
North Bend Plantation ... Charles City, VA
North Garden Inn ... Bellingham, WA
North Hero House ... North Hero, VT
Nottoway Plantation Inn & Restaurant ... White Castle, LA
Noyo River Lodge ... Fort Bragg, CA
The Oak House ... Oak Bluffs, MA
Oak Spring Farm & Vineyard ... Raphine, VA
Oak Square Plantation ... Port Gibson, MS
The Oaks Bed & Breakfast Country Inn ... Christiansburg, VA
The Oakwood Inn ... Raleigh, NC
Offutt House ... Omaha, NE
Ogden House ... Milwaukee, WI
Oglethorpe Inn ... Augusta, GA
Ojai Manor Hotel ... Ojai, CA
Olallieberry Inn ... Cambria, CA
The Old Appleford Inn ... Gettysburg, PA
Old Church House Inn B&B ... Mossville, IL
Old Consulate Inn F.W. Hastings House ... Port Townsend, WA
The Old Dennis House ... Newport, RI
Old Farm Inn ... Rockport, MA
Old Fort Inn ... Kennebunkport, ME
The Inn at Old Harbour ... Block Island, RI
The Old Holland Inn ... Holland, MI
Old Hoosier House ... Knightstown, IN
Old Hunterdon House ... Frenchtown, NJ
The Old Library Inn ... Olean, NY
Old Lyme Inn ... Old Lyme, CT
Old Manse Inn ... Brewster, MA
The Old Milano Hotel & Restaurant ... Gualala, CA
Old Mill House B&B ... Eatonville, WA
The Old Mill Inn ... Somersville, CT
Old Mill Inn ... Brandon, VT
Old Mill Pond Inn ... Northport, MI
The Old Miners' Lodge A B&B Inn ... Park City, UT
Old Monterey Inn ... Monterey, CA
The Old Parsonage Inn ... Bucksport, ME
Old Pioneer Garden Guest Ranch ... Unionville, NV
Old Point Inn ... Beaufort, SC
The Old Reynolds Mansion ... Asheville, NC
Old Rittenhouse Inn ... Bayfield, WI
Old Sea Pines Inn ... Brewster, MA
Old Stone House Inn ... Marblehead, OH
Old Thyme Inn ... Half Moon Bay, CA
The Old Tjomsland House ... Vashon Island, WA
Old Town B&B Inn ... Eureka, CA
Old Town Farm Inn ... Gassetts, VT
The Old West B&B ... Regent, ND
Old World Inn ... Napa, CA
The Old Yacht Club Inn ... Santa Barbara, CA
Olde Harbour Inn ... Savannah, GA
Olde Rowley Inn ... North Waterford, ME
Oliver Loud's Inn ... Pittsford, NY
Orcas Hotel ... Orcas, WA
The Osceola Mill House ... Gordonville, PA
Outlook Lodge ... Green Mountain Falls, CO
Over Look Inn ... Eastham, MA
The Oxford House ... Stephenville, TX
Packard House ... Bath, ME
Palace Hotel & Bath House ... Eureka Springs, AR
The Palmer House B&B ... Waynesville, NC
Palmer House Inn ... Falmouth, MA
Pamlico House ... Washington, NC
The Park House ... Saugatuck, MI
Park Place B&B ... Bisbee, AZ
Parkview House ... Amarillo, TX
Parson's Pillow ... Cody, WY
The Parsonage ... East Orleans, MA
Parsonage Inn ... Saint Michaels, MD
Peacock House ... Lubec, ME
Peacock Inn ... North Conway, NH
Peacock's "Inn on the Sound" ... Falmouth, MA
Pearl Street Inn ... Boulder, CO
The Pebble House ... Lakeside, MI
The Inn at Penn Cove ... Coupeville, WA
The Penny House ... North Eastham, MA
Penobscot Meadows ... Belfast, ME
Peppermill B&B ... Monticello, FL
The Peppertrees B&B ... Tucson, AZ
Peregrine House ... Ithaca, NY
Perryville Inn ... Rehoboth, MA
Petite Auberge ... San Francisco, CA
Pickwinn B&B ... Piqua, OH
The Piedmont House ... Eureka Springs, AR

25% discount off one night's stay during off-season (October - April).

Alaska's 7 Gables
4312 Birch Ln, PO Box 80488
Fairbanks AK 99708
(907)479-0751

Valid thru 12/92. Void if detached.

Third night is free. Must be requested at time of reservation.

Westways "Private" Resort Inn
PO Box 41624
Phoenix AZ 85080
(602)582 3868

Valid thru 12/92. Void if detached.

A free inn mug and 10% off regular rates for your first visit. Must mention discount at time of reservation.

Prescott Pines Inn
901 White Spar Rd
Prescott AZ 86303
(602)445-7270

Valid thru 12/92. Void if detached.

10% discount Sunday through Thursday. Excludes holidays.

Saddle Rock Ranch
PO Box 10095
Sedona AZ 86336
(602)282 7640

Valid thru 12/92. Void if detached.

"Take a friend to breakfast." Coupon good for one free breakfast for a friend while staying here. Business people bring a local associate. University of Arizona parents bring your son or daughter along to share the goodies.

The Peppertrees B&B
724 E University
Tucson AZ 85719
(602)622-7167

Valid thru 12/92. Void if detached.

Present this certificate and receive a free copy of "The Heartstone Inn Breakfast Cookbook" with any stay of three or more nights.

The Heartstone Inn & Cottages
35 King's Hwy
Eureka Springs AR 72632
(501)253-8916

Valid thru 12/92. Void if detached.

10% off one night's stay. Sunday - Thursday only.

The Commercial Hotel-A Vintage Guest House
Washington at Peabody St, PO Box 72
Mountain View AR 72560
(501)269-4383

Valid thru 12/92. Void if detached.

Receive a 15% discount (Sunday - Thursday) on our regular room rate. Excludes weekends and holiday seasons.

Fensalden Inn
PO Box 99
Albion CA 95410
(707)937 4042

Valid thru 12/92. Void if detached.

Three nights for the price of 2! Stay with us 3 weekday nights (Sunday - Thursday) and pay for only 2. Excluding holidays.

Bayview Hotel B&B Inn
8041 Soquel Dr
Aptos CA 95003
(408)688-8654

Valid thru 12/92. Void if detached.

Stay 2 nights and the 3rd night is free. Valid anytime with advance reservation.

Power's Mansion Inn
164 Cleveland Ave
Auburn CA 95603
(916)885 1166

Valid thru 12/92. Void if detached.

10% discount anytime (excluding holidays) plus personal photo taken in Victorian Charm and sent to you.

Chalfant House
213 Academy St
Bishop CA 93514
(619)872-1790

Valid thru 12/92. Void if detached.

Senior Citizen rates: 10% discount on any room midweek (Sunday - Thursday).

Foothill House
3037 Foothill Blvd
Calistoga CA 94515
(707)942-6933

Valid thru 12/92. Void if detached.

Mid-winter-midweek special. From December - March, Sunday - Thursday, stay 2 nights and the 2nd night is $20 off.

Scarlett's Country Inn
3918 Silverado Trail N
Calistoga CA 94515
(707)942 6669

Valid thru 12/92. Void if detached.

Eureka's most opulent lodging will give a 10% discount Monday through Thursday. Not valid June through September. Or complimentary ride in horse-drawn carriage included in normal room rate, when this certificate is presented.

An Elegant Victorian Mansion
14th & C Sts
Eureka CA 95501
(707)444-3144

Valid thru 12/92. Void if detached.

Present this coupon, when checking in, to receive 2 Sunday brunches for the price of one. Enjoy your brunch on our multi-leveled dining deck, overlooking the Noyo Yacht Harbor, and enjoy the best view and weather on the Mendocino Coast.

Noyo River Lodge
500 Casa Del Noyo Dr
Fort Bragg CA 95437
(707)964-8045

Valid thru 12/92. Void if detached.

Midweek special, Monday through Thursday. Present this certificate and you will be given $5.00 off from our already low midweek rates.

Old Thyme Inn
779 Main St
Half Moon Bay CA 94019
(415)726-1616

Valid thru 12/92. Void if detached.

Receive $10.00 off our low midweek rate when you see the ghost. (Usually seen on the stairs.)

Zaballa House
324 Main St
Half Moon Bay CA 94019
(415)726-9123

Valid thru 12/92. Void if detached.

Present this certificate for a bottle of the county's finest white wine and a 5% discount if you stay the next night at Cinnamon Bear in St. Helena.

Healdsburg Inn On The Plaza
110-116 Matheson St, PO Box 1196
Healdsburg CA 95448
(707)433-6991

Valid thru 12/92. Void if detached.

A bottle of our house champagne will be placed in your room with two glasses to begin the celebration of your "great getaway" vacation.

Madrona Manor, A Country Inn
PO Box 818 1001 Westside Rd
Healdsburg CA 95448
(707)433 4231

Valid thru 12/92. Void if detached.

Our wishes for you on your birthday. Health and happiness. Our gift to you - 10% discount. Patricia and Melisande.

The Heirloom
214 Shakeley Ln, PO Box 322
Ione CA 95640
(209)274 4468

Valid thru 12/92. Void if detached.

25% off second-night visit.

Court Street Inn
215 Court St
Jackson CA 95642
(209)223-0416

Valid thru 12/92. Void if detached.

Midweek, non-holiday discounts of $10-$30 per night. Available upon request.

Historic National Hotel B&B
Main Street, PO Box 502
Jamestown CA 95327
(209)984 3446

Valid thru 12/92. Void if detached.

15% discount valid Monday through Thursday. Holidays excluded.

Julian Gold Rush Hotel
2032 Main St, PO Box 1856
Julian CA 92036
(619)765-0201

Valid thru 12/92. Void if detached.

Save $5.00 on any room.

Casa Laguna
2510 S Coast Hwy
Laguna Beach CA 92651
(714)494 2996

Valid thru 12/92. Void if detached.

For guests staying four nights or longer we offer a full case of wine with our compliments.

Eastlake Victorian Inn
1442 Kellam Ave
Los Angeles CA 90026
(213)250 1620

Valid thru 12/92. Void if detached.

10% off any room Monday through Thursday, excluding August.

John Dougherty House
571 Ukiah St, PO Box 817
Mendocino CA 95460
(707)937-5266

Valid thru 12/92. Void if detached.

Ask about our mid-week (Sunday through Thursday) discount rates.

Napa Inn
1137 Warren St
Napa CA 94559
(707)257 1444

Valid thru 12/92. Void if detached.

10% off room price Sunday through Thursday.

The Kaleidoscope Inn
Box 1297, 130 E Dana St
Nipomo CA 93444
(805)929 5444

Valid thru 12/92. Void if detached.

Purchase a Georgianna Manor gift certificate for Honeymoons, Anniversaries, Birthdays, etc. 15% discount good anytime.

Georgianna Manor
816 East High Ave
Redlands CA 92374
(714)793-0423

Valid thru 12/92. Void if detached.

Present this certificate for a souvenir teddy bear and a 5% discount if you stay the next night at Healdsburg Inn on the Plaza.

Cinnamon Bear B&B
1407 Kearney St
Saint Helena CA 94574
(707)963-4653

Valid thru 12/92. Void if detached.

Senior citizens are welcome free, with the reservation of the family as are children under 5, with no additional charge. Ask about art lessons.

Art Center/Wamsley Gallery/B&B
1902 Filbert St
San Francisco CA 94123
(415)567 1526

Valid thru 12/92. Void if detached.

San Francisco Holiday: Two-night accommodations (including tax), bottle of California wine, afternoon tea, deluxe city tour and bay cruise, tour of Muir Woods and Sausalito, Sausalito ferry ticket, cable-car ticket. $200 single, $250 for two (advance reservations, please).

Golden Gate Hotel
775 Bush St
San Francisco CA 94108
(415)392-3702

Valid thru 12/92. Void if detached.

With this certificate, save 10% off our standard rates and we won't require a 2-night weekend minimum stay! Phone ahead for availability and mention this certificate.

The Nolan House
A Bed & Breakfast Inn
1071 Page St
San Francisco CA 94117
(415)863-0384

Valid thru 12/92. Void if detached.

Present this certificate and you will receive a 10% discount on the first night of your stay and a bottle of champagne.

Victorian Inn On The Park
301 Lyon St
San Francisco CA 94117
(415)931-1830

Valid thru 12/92. Void if detached.

20% discount Monday - Thursday Oct. 15, 1991 - April 30, 1992 and Oct. 15 - Dec. 31, 1992. Holiday seasons excluded.

Simpson House Inn
121 E Arrellaga St
Santa Barbara CA 93101
(805)963 7067

Valid thru 12/92. Void if detached.

15% discount on room rates any night all year if you mention "The Official Guide to American Historic Inns."

Madison Street Inn
1390 Madison St
Santa Clara CA 95050
(408)249-5541

Valid thru 12/92. Void if detached.

Stay any one night at full price, and stay the next night for 1/2 price. Midweek only.

Melitta Station Inn
5850 Melita Rd
Santa Rosa CA 95409
(707)538-7712

Valid thru 12/92. Void if detached.

Alpine winter and spring escape. 25% off or two nights for the price of one Monday through Thursday, January through June.

Storybook Inn
PO Box 362, 28717 Hwy 18
Sky Forest CA 92385
(714)336-1483

Valid thru 12/92. Void if detached.

Stay 2 nights and the 3rd night is on us any Sunday through Thursday (excluding holidays).

Mayfield House
236 Grove St, PO Box 5999
Tahoe City CA 95730
(916)583 1001

Valid thru 12/92. Void if detached.

A complimentary one-hour massage awaits you on your birthday with a 2-day stay (1 massage per room). Please bring documentation. With a 3-day stay 1 massage, with a 4-day stay 2 massages regardless of birthday.

Vichy Hot Springs Resort & Inn
2605 Vichy Springs Rd
Ukiah CA 95482
(707)462-9515

Valid thru 12/92. Void if detached.

Romantic weekend (or weekday): We will include a free mini-bottle of champagne and fresh-cut flowers for any honeymoons or anniversaries.

Cottonwood Inn
123 San Juan
Alamosa CO 81101
(719)589-3882

Valid thru 12/92. Void if detached.

Complimentary welcome cocktail in Jack's Bar with your first night's stay.

Sardy House
128 E Main St
Aspen CO 81611
(303)920-2525

Valid thru 12/92. Void if detached.

Victorian Winter Getaway from November 1992 - March 1993 (our 90th year) receive a 10% discount off any room.

Holden House-1902 B&B
1102 W Pikes Peak Ave
Colorado Springs CO 80904
(719)471-3980

Valid thru 12/92. Void if detached.

10% discount anytime.

Queen Anne Inn
2147 Tremont Place
Denver CO 80205
(303)296-6666

Valid thru 12/92. Void if detached.

Free backcountry and goldmine area tour by jeep (May - November) or by Snowcat (November - April) with Sunday - Thursday stay.

Goldminer Hotel
601 Klondyke Ave
Eldora CO 80466
(303)258-7770

Valid thru 12/92. Void if detached.

Honeymoon Couples - Free bottle of champagne served in the San Sophia Observatory.

San Sophia
330 W Pacific Ave, PO Box 1825
Telluride CO 81435
(303)728-3001

Valid thru 12/92. Void if detached.

"A warm experience to be tucked away and savored." Save 15% on a Sunday through Thursday stay anytime.

Captain Dibbell House
21 Commerce St
Clinton CT 06413
(203)669 1646

Valid thru 12/92. Void if detached.

One night free after 3-night stay.

Wake Robin Inn
Rt 41
Lakeville CT 06039
(203)435 2515

Valid thru 12/92. Void if detached.

10% discount on midweek stays and a romantic carriage or sleigh ride (excluding foliage and holidays).

Manor House
Maple Ave, PO Box 447
Norfolk CT 06058
(203)542-5690

Valid thru 12/92. Void if detached.

Let us serve you from our new Sunday brunch menu. Bring this certificate for a complimentary Bloody Mary.

Old Lyme Inn
85 Lyme St
Old Lyme CT 06371
(203)434-2600

Valid thru 12/92. Void if detached.

A complimentary bottle of Samuel Smith ale, imported from England, on presentation of coupon by anyone staying with us.

Under Mountain Inn
482 Undermountain Rd
Salisbury CT 06068
(203)435-0242

Valid thru 12/92. Void if detached.

15% discount midweek Monday through Thursday.

Yesterday's Yankee B&B
Rt 44 E
Salisbury CT 06068
(203)435-9539

Valid thru 12/92. Void if detached.

We are making a Federal Case (for you to stay at our B&B): Stay in our Federal-style B&B for two nights and get the third night free.

The Jefferson House B&B
5 The Strand at the Wharf
New Castle DE 19720
(302)323 0999

Valid thru 12/92. Void if detached.

Sunday through Thursday (except Thanksgiving week, Christmas week and Easter week): $10.00 off midweek rates.

Carriage Way B&B
70 Cuna St
Saint Augustine FL 32084
(904)829-2467

Valid thru 12/92. Void if detached.

Nostalgia Bonus: 5% off your room rate and take home a keepsake as well.

Bayboro House on Old Tampa Bay
1719 Beach Dr, SE
Saint Petersburg FL 33701
(813)823-4955

Valid thru 12/92. Void if detached.

Double room for the price of a single - Regular rates $74.00 - with coupon $59.00 (+ tax).

Beverly Hills Inn
65 Sheridan Dr NE
Atlanta GA 30305
(404)233 8520

Valid thru 12/92. Void if detached.

Present this certificate upon arrival and receive two free passes for a historic carriage tour.

Olde Harbour Inn
508 E Factors Walk
Savannah GA 31401
(912)234-4100

Valid thru 12/92. Void if detached.

10% off any two-night stay, or free champagne and breakfast in bed with two-night stay.

Greenbriar B&B Inn
315 Wallace
Coeur d'Alene ID 83814
(208)667-9660

Valid thru 12/92. Void if detached.

Spend a night or two in our Canopy Suite and have breakfast delivered to your room!

Belle Aire Mansion
11410 Rt 20 W
Galena IL 61036
(815)777-0893

Valid thru 12/92. Void if detached.

Free Sunday Brunch for two at Norman's Restaurant in Historic Union Station. (Beverages not included). Coupon valid with a Friday and Saturday night stay at the Inn.

Renaissance Tower Historic Inn
230 E 9th St
Indianapolis IN 46204
(317)631-2328

Valid thru 12/92. Void if detached.

40% off Friday and Saturday rates on Sunday through Thursday stays (excluding holidays), full breakfast included.

The Richards House
1492 Locust St
Dubuque IA 52001
(319)557-1492

Valid thru 12/92. Void if detached.

Upon arrival present this certificate and you will receive a complimentary glass of wine.

Die Heimat Country Inn
Main St, Amana Colonies
Homestead IA 52236
(319)622-3937

Valid thru 12/92. Void if detached.

Enjoy our hospitality Sunday through Thursday and we'll take $10.00 off your guest-room rate. You'll experience our wonderful service of afternoon tea, hearty breakfast with dessert and chocolate truffles on your bed pillow.

The Hannah Marie Country Inn
Rt 1, Hwy 71 S
Spencer IA 51301
(712)262 1286

Valid thru 12/92. Void if detached.

10% discount for one-week stay.

Prytania Inn
1415 Prytania St
New Orleans LA 70130
(504)566-1515

Valid thru 12/92. Void if detached.

Stay two nights November through May and we will guarantee the off-season rate for one night's stay during the summer months of June through October. This offer never expires!

Blue Harbor House
67 Elm St, Rt 1
Camden ME 04843
(207)236-3196

Valid thru 12/92. Void if detached.

1854 rates on your birthday! Present this coupon on your birthday and you'll be charged $2.00 for that night. (The person sharing your suite will be charged the current single rate.)

Laphroaig B&B
Rte 15, PO Box 67
Deer Isle Village ME 04627
(207)348-6088

Valid thru 12/92. Void if detached.

An additional 10% off all regular off-season room rates, Sunday - Thursday, between Nov. 1 and May 20. Honeymoon specials: June and September $5 discount for newlyweds.

Isaac Randall House
5 Independence Dr
Freeport ME 04032
(207)865-9295

Valid thru 12/92. Void if detached.

Spring Bride Special. 25% discount to honeymooners during the months of May and June.

The Keeper's House
PO Box 26
Isle Au Haut ME 04645
(207)367-2261

Valid thru 12/92. Void if detached.

Enjoy our cozy, warm atmosphere between Nov. 1 and June 1 and also enjoy $10 off per night.

1802 House
Box 646A Locke St
Kennebunkport ME 04046
(207)967-5632

Valid thru 12/92. Void if detached.

10% discount off regular room rates when this coupon is presented.

York Harbor Inn
PO Box 573, Rt 1A
York Harbor ME 03911
(207)363-5119

Valid thru 12/92. Void if detached.

The Perfect "Getaway" weekend! Enjoy 3 nights for the price of 2 Thursday through Sunday, November 15 to April 15.

Shaw's Fancy B&B
161 Green St
Annapolis MD 21401
(301)268-9750

Valid thru 12/92. Void if detached.

Business Travelers Discount. Present this certificate for 20% discount Monday through Thursday. Located within an hour drive of Washington, D.C. and Baltimore, Maryland.

Spring Bank - A B&B Inn
7945 Worman's Mill Rd
Frederick MD 21701
(301)694 0440

Valid thru 12/92. Void if detached.

Anniversary Special: Guests staying on their anniversary will receive a discount from the regular room rate equal to the number of years the guests have been married. (Married 5 years? Save $5.)

The Spencer Silver Mansion
200 S Union Ave
Havre De Grace MD 21078
(301)939-1097

Valid thru 12/92. Void if detached.

10% discount Monday through Thursday, except holidays, or champagne and flowers for two anytime.

Kemp House Inn
412 S Talbot St, PO Box 638
Saint Michaels MD 21663
(301)745 2243

Valid thru 12/92. Void if detached.

Midweek Special: Join us for two or three nights (Sunday through Thursday) and take 20% off our regular rates!

Parsonage Inn
210 N Talbot St
Saint Michaels MD 21663
(301)745-5519

Valid thru 12/92. Void if detached.

10% off midweek rates, Sunday through Thursday. Two-night minimum. Off-season only (February 1-June 13).

Captain Tom Lawrence House
75 Locust St
Falmouth MA 02540
(508)540-1445

Valid thru 12/92. Void if detached.

For anyone staying at least 4 days, just ask for our 30% Wednesday night discount. An extra 30% off on a Wednesday as part of the time stayed.

The Oak House
PO Box 299AA Seaview Ave
Oak Bluffs MA 02557
(508)693-4187

Valid thru 12/92. Void if detached.

The off-season deal! Present this certificate anytime October 15 through May 15 and get the second consecutive night free.

Watership Inn
7 Winthrop St
Provincetown MA 02657
(508)487-0094

Valid thru 12/92. Void if detached.

Extend your stay and save 15%. (Applies after first night is paid at full rate.)

Amelia Payson Guest House
16 Winter St
Salem MA 01970
(508)744-8304

Valid thru 12/92. Void if detached.

Receive 20% discount on second night's stay. Good for any Sunday through Thursday stay.

Isaiah Jones Homestead
165 Main St
Sandwich MA 02563
(508)888-9115

Valid thru 12/92. Void if detached.

One free admission per room to the world-famous Sandwich Glass Museum.

The Summer House
158 Main St
Sandwich MA 02563
(508)888-4991

Valid thru 12/92. Void if detached.

15% discount midweek.

Staveleigh House
PO 608, S Main St
Sheffield MA 01257
(413)229-2129

Valid thru 12/92. Void if detached.

Come and visit one of New England's most authentic stagecoach inns and receive a 10% discount for any Sunday through Thursday inclusive.

Merrell Tavern Inn
Rt 102 Main St
South Lee MA 01260
(413)243-1794

Valid thru 12/92. Void if detached.

FREE! One night's accommodation with any paid reservation. Only valid Sunday through Thursday. January through April. Not valid with other discounts.

Sturbridge Country Inn
530 Main St
Sturbridge MA 01566
(508)347-5503

Valid thru 12/92. Void if detached.

Free Monday night with Friday, Saturday & Sunday inclusive. Reservation directly preceding 50% discount for Monday night directly following combination Saturday & Sunday night reservation. Some holidays excluded. Subject to availability. Book early for best selection.

The Wildwood Inn
121 Church St
Ware MA 01082
(413)967-7798

Valid thru 12/92. Void if detached.

American or Continental picnic basket one-half price.

Crook' Jaw Inn
186 Main St, Rt 6A
Yarmouth Port MA 02675
(508)362-6111

Valid thru 12/92. Void if detached.

20% discount on second-night stay (January 7 to April 30) excluding Valentine's weekend.

Yesterday's Inn
518 N 4th St
Niles MI 49120
(616)683-6079

Valid thru 12/92. Void if detached.

Happy Birthday To You! Stay with us on your birthday and receive a discount for that date equal to your age. (Certificate must be used on actual birthdate). Minimum-stay requirements from May through October may still apply. OR Save some time for browsing in our gift corner where you'll find select guide books and take home gifts. You pick your favorite and we'll pick up the tab...our souvenir gift to you!

The Park House
888 Holland St
Saugatuck MI 49453
(616)857-4535

Valid thru 12/92. Void if detached.

Second night free in main lodge October 25-December 20 and March 1-June 20.

Cascade Lodge
PO Box 693
Grand Marais MN 55604
(218)387-1112

Valid thru 12/92. Void if detached.

Receive $15.00 off any of our whirlpool rooms for a weekday night stay.

Rivertown Inn
306 W Olive St
Stillwater MN 55082
(612)430-2955

Valid thru 12/92. Void if detached.

BET & BREAKFAST: That's right...$6.00 discount on day or evening casino-style cruise ticket for each guest interested. OR we "bet" you'll accept our offer of a single rate for any couple staying three or more nights.

Red Creek Colonial Inn
7416 Red Creek Rd
Long Beach MS 39560
(601)452-3080

Valid thru 12/92. Void if detached.

Stay two nights and get third night at half price (not valid with other discounts.)

Anchuca Clarion
Carriage House Inn
1010 First E
Vicksburg MS 39180
(601)636-4931

Valid thru 12/92. Void if detached.

Enhance your wedding or anniversary experience with a romantic night at The Corners. Let us know the occasion and we will have flowers and a sparkling beverage in your room.

The Corners Inn
601 Klein St
Vicksburg MS 39180
(800)444-7421

Valid thru 12/92. Void if detached.

Nightshirts to wear, plus $10 off two-night stay (Monday through Thursday).

Garth Woodside Mansion
RR 1
Hannibal MO 63401
(314)221 2789

Valid thru 12/92. Void if detached.

Stay at The Coachlight B&B on your honeymoon. Notify us that it is your honeymoon at the time of reservations, present this certificate at check-in and you will receive a sparkling treat complimentary.

The Coachlight B&B
PO Box 8095
Saint Louis MO 63156
(314)367-5870

Valid thru 12/92. Void if detached.

10% discount Monday through Thursday.

Geandaugh House
3835-37 S Broadway
Saint Louis MO 63118
(314)771-5447

Valid thru 12/92. Void if detached.

We would like to offer all railroad enthusiasts some rates from the past! Bring in this certificate and receive a 20% discount off our rack rates between Oct. 1 to Dec. 15 (not including Thanksgiving) or between April 1 and June 1.

Izaak Walton Inn
PO Box 653
Essex MT 59916
(406)888 5700

Valid thru 12/92. Void if detached.

15% discount on a one or two-night stay. Based on room availability. Not good with any other discount.

The Chalet B&B Inn
1204 4th Ave, N
Great Falls MT 59401
(406)452-9001

Valid thru 12/92. Void if detached.

"Special Weekday Discount". Enjoy a 15% discount when you spend any weekday evening (Monday through Thursday). Discount applies October through May. Must book direct.

Willows Inn
224 S Platt Ave, PO Box 886
Red Lodge MT 59068
(406)446-3913

Valid thru 12/92. Void if detached.

Hiker and Skier Special! Stay 3 nights and the 4th night is free. Plus free hiking advice and trail map. We welcome you!

The Country Inn at Bartlett
Rt 302 Box 327
Bartlett NH 03812
(603)374-2353

Valid thru 12/92. Void if detached.

10% discount on our MAP rate valid year-round, Sunday through Thursday.

The Bradford Inn
RFD 1 Box 40, Main St
Bradford NH 03221
(603)938-5309

Valid thru 12/92. Void if detached.

Midweek "peace" pass. Come to hike, bike or ski during the lovely, peaceful midweek, non-holiday periods and pay only $15.00 per person for your room. Please bring the pass! Welcome.

Mountain Fare Inn
Mad River Rd
Campton NH 03223
(603)726-4283

Valid thru 12/92. Void if detached.

What is a Bungay Jar? Correctly guess and stay for free (the person sharing your room will be charged the current single rate).

Bungay Jar B&B
PO Box 15
Franconia NH 03580
(603)823-7775

Valid thru 12/92. Void if detached.

"A toast to celebrate your special event." Present this certificate on either your birthday, honeymoon or anniversary and we will have a chilled bottle of spirits to help celebrate your day.

Ellis River House
Rt 16 Box 656
Jackson NH 03846
(603)383-9339

Valid thru 12/92. Void if detached.

A 10% discount for any room during the summer midweek (Sunday through Thursday) and 20% discount in May, June and March. Holidays and food excluded in discount.

Jefferson Inn
Rt 2
Jefferson NH 03583
(603)586-7998

Valid thru 12/92. Void if detached.

"Five Nights for the Price of Four." Sunday through Thursday (midweek special) excluding holiday weeks.

Cranmore Mt Lodge
Kearsarge Rd, PO Box 1194
North Conway NH 03860
(603)356-2044

Valid thru 12/92. Void if detached.

Champagne for you, 10% off for two. Complimentary champagne first night, 10% off second night (regular rates). Excludes holiday season.

Peacock Inn
PO Box 1012
North Conway NH 03860
(603)356-9041

Valid thru 12/92. Void if detached.

Your sweet tooth will be pampered with a delightful dessert during your stay at the Follansbee Inn.

Follansbee Inn
PO Box 92, Keyser St
North Sutton NH 03260
(603)927-4221

Valid thru 12/92. Void if detached.

10% discount good anytime.

Martin Hill Inn
404 Islington St
Portsmouth NH 03801
(603)436-2287

Valid thru 12/92. Void if detached.

Receive a 10% discount, Sunday through Thursday. A full hearty breakfast and complimentary snacks are included. Not valid during holidays and foliage season.

Maria Atwood Inn
RFD 2, Rt 3a
West Franklin NH 03235
(603)934-3666

Valid thru 12/92. Void if detached.

Breakfast by candlelight and classical music. 10% discount subject to availability.

Captain Mey's Inn
202 Ocean St
Cape May NJ 08204
(609)884-7793

Valid thru 12/92. Void if detached.

Take a little bit of the Mainstay home. Present this certificate at check-out for a free copy of the famous cookbook, Breakfast at Nine, Tea at Four.

Mainstay Inn & Cottage
635 Columbia Ave
Cape May NJ 08204
(609)884-8690

Valid thru 12/92. Void if detached.

$10.00 off regular rate, November through April.

Sand Castle Guest House
829 Stockton Ave
Cape May NJ 08204
(609)884-5451

Valid thru 12/92. Void if detached.

Bring a friend(s) and the second room is free! Or stay 2 nights and the second night is free! Valid September through June, Sunday through Thursday, excluding holidays.

The Normandy Inn
21 Tuttle Ave
Spring Lake NJ 07762
(908)449-7172

Valid thru 12/92. Void if detached.

10% discount with this certificate.

Alexander's Inn
529 E Palace Ave
Santa Fe NM 87501
(505)986-1431

Valid thru 12/92. Void if detached.

Present this certificate for a COMPLIMENTARY bottle of Domaine Cheurlin Methode Champagne. Winner of New Mexico State Fair Best of State. Minimum two-day stay required.

Canyon Road Casitas
652 Canyon Rd
Santa Fe NM 87501
(505)988-5888

Valid thru 12/92. Void if detached.

Celebration Bonus: Upon presentation of this certificate on your birthday, anniversary, honeymoon or if you are 50 years old or older, $10.00 will be deducted from your final bill...our way of saying congratulations and best wishes.

The Red House Country Inn
Finger Lks Nat'l Forest, Picnic Rd
Burdett NY 14818
(607)546-8566

Valid thru 12/92. Void if detached.

You receive 20% off the price of your room when you bring another couple along to share the fun of country living. (Second couple pays full price.)

Battle Island Inn
RD 1 Box 176
Fulton NY 13069
(315)593-3699

Valid thru 12/92. Void if detached.

Stay three nights and one midweek night is half price. Not valid during racing season and special weekends.

The Westchester House
102 Lincoln Ave, PO Box 944
Saratoga Springs NY 12866
(518)587-7613

Valid thru 12/92. Void if detached.

Victorian rates $5.00 on your birthday. Present this certificate on your birthday and you will be charged only $5.00. (The person sharing your room will be charged the current single rate.)

Carriage House Inn
8375 Wickham Blvd
Sodus Point, NY 14555
(315)483-2100

Valid thru 12/92. Void if detached.

Second night 1/2 price, Monday through Thursday except July and August.

Westfield House
E Main Rd, PO Box 505
Westfield NY 14787
(716)326-6262

Valid thru 12/92. Void if detached.

Cozy Winter Rates: 10% discount during the months of January and February (Monday-Thursday) excluding holidays.

Applewood Manor
62 Cumberland Circle
Asheville NC 28801
(704)254-2244

Valid thru 12/92. Void if detached.

This entitles you to a discount of 10% on your room, during your entire stay at beautiful Ragged Garden.

Ragged Garden B&B
PO Box 1927
Blowing Rock NC 28605
(704)295-9703

Valid thru 12/92. Void if detached.

"It's Inn-Credible!" This certificate entitles the bearer to a $25.00 savings on a two-night stay when you visit the Folkestone Inn between December 1 and March 31.

Folkestone Inn
767 W Deep Creek Rd
Bryson City NC 28713
(704)488-2730

Valid thru 12/92. Void if detached.

10% discount any Monday through Thursday stay with advance reservations.

Fryemont Inn
PO Box 459
Bryson City NC 28713
(704)488-2159

Valid thru 12/92. Void if detached.

Half price on the real holidays, February 12 & 22, May 30, September 1, and November 11 & 21.

Greenwood B&B
205 N Park Dr
Greensboro NC 27401
(919)274 6350

Valid thru 12/92. Void if detached.

25% off any room rental from November through May. Not good for holiday visits. Additional 5% off on second or subsequent night's stay (must be consecutive).

Claddagh Inn at Hendersonville
755 N Main St
Hendersonville NC 28792
(800)225-4700

Valid thru 12/92. Void if detached.

Anniversary Special! Two for the price of one! Spend your anniversary with us and you will be charged our single-room rate. Advance reservations required. Coupon must be presented at check-in.

Grandview Lodge
809 Valley View Cir Rd
Waynesville NC 28786
(704)456-5212

Valid thru 12/92. Void if detached.

Stay with us at our regular rate the night before or after your birthday or anniversary and we will give you that special night at half-price, plus an invitation rate for this to become an annual tradition for you!

Old McDill-Anderson Place
3656 Polk Hollow Rd
Chillicothe OH 45601
(614)774-1770

Valid thru 12/92. Void if detached.

10% discount Monday through Thursday.

Wagner's 1844 Inn
230 E Washington St
Sandusky OH 44870
(419)626-1726

Valid thru 12/92. Void if detached.

$10 off room price Sunday through Thursday.

Willow Tree Inn
1900 W State, Rt 571
Tipp City OH 45371
(513)667-2957

Valid thru 12/92. Void if detached.

10% discount weeknights upon availability - Sunday through Wednesday.

Harrison House
124 W Harrison
Guthrie OK 73044
(405)282-1000

Valid thru 12/92. Void if detached.

10% discount on any dinner menu items.

McCully House Inn
240 E California
Jacksonville OR 97530
(503)899-1942

Valid thru 12/92. Void if detached.

Half price on the week of your birthday. Present this certificate with proof of age (person sharing room will be charged regular rate for single occupancy).

Black Bart Bed & Breakfast
94125 Love Lake Rd
Junction City OR 97448
(503)998-1904

Valid thru 12/92. Void if detached.

If your birthday falls on a weekday this year, treat yourself to a night at The Brafferton Inn for 1/2 price. (Weekdays only).

The Brafferton Inn
44 York St
Gettysburg PA 17325
(717)337-3423

Valid thru 12/92. Void if detached.

Stay two nights and receive your third night free! Advance reservations only. Not valid in conjunction with any other discounts, for special events or holidays.

The Doubleday Inn
104 Doubleday Ave
Gettysburg PA 17325
(717)334-9119

Valid thru 12/92. Void if detached.

Beat the crowds and take advantage of our weekday special. Four nights for the price of three!! Sunday through Thursday.

Keystone Inn B&B
231 Hanover St
Gettysburg PA 17325
(717)337-3888

Valid thru 12/92. Void if detached.

20% discount Sunday through Thursday (excluding holidays).

Beechmont Inn
315 Broadway
Hanover PA 17331
(717)632-3013

Valid thru 12/92. Void if detached.

Australian Walkabout Rates: Going walkabout? Stay with us any Sunday through Thursday night and receive $5.00 off the current room rate or Amish dinner. (Not valid with any other Walkabout Specials or on holidays.)

Walkabout Inn B&B
837 Village Rd
Lampeter PA 17537
(717)464-0707

Valid thru 12/92. Void if detached.

Discover who the original architect of The King's Cottage was for a free night's stay. You must be able to give evidence of who this is. OR 10% discount upon presentation of this certificate. Not valid holidays or with any other discounts or packages.

The King's Cottage
1049 E King St
Lancaster PA 17602
(717)397-1017

Valid thru 12/92. Void if detached.

Deduct $5.00 nightly - single or double.

B&B of Valley Forge & Philadelphia
PO Box 562
Philadelphia PA 19481
(215)783-7838

Valid thru 12/92. Void if detached.

$10.00 off midweek rates, Sunday through Thursday, except holidays. Two-night minimum, January 15 to May 15.

Limestone Inn B&B
33 E Main St
Strasburg PA 17579
(717)687-8392

Valid thru 12/92. Void if detached.

Free. Guided historical tour of City of San Augustine. The Wade House is along the marked "Heritage Trail."

The Wade House
128 E Columbia St
San Augustine TX 75972
(409)275-2605

Valid thru 12/92. Void if detached.

Third Night Free!! Listed as the "best place in the West to retire" by Rand McNally. Come and see for yourself and enjoy your third night free.

Greene Gate Village Historic B&B Inn
76 W Tabernacle
Saint George UT 84770
(801)628-6999

Valid thru 12/92. Void if detached.

Complimentary copy of recipes from the kitchen of Hill Farm Inn.

Hill Farm Inn
RR 2 Box 2015
Arlington VT 05250
(802)375-2269

Valid thru 12/92. Void if detached.

Stay two nights, your third night is free. (Not valid September and October.)

Greenhurst Inn
River St, RD 2 Box 60
Bethel VT 05032
(802)234-9474

Valid thru 12/92. Void if detached.

$25 off 2-night stay, double occupancy. Not valid foliage weekends.

The Churchill House Inn
RD 3 Rt 73 East
Brandon VT 05733
(802)247-3078

Valid thru 12/92. Void if detached.

Wine, cheese and flowers, and a romantic stay in the Silas Griffith Room.

Silas Griffith Inn
RR 1 Box 66F, S Main St
Danby VT 05739
(802)293-5567

Valid thru 12/92. Void if detached.

Third night free. Stay any two nights, third consecutive night is free. Valid November through May.

Silver Maple Lodge & Cottages
S Main St, RR1 Box 8
Fairlee VT 05045
(802)333-4326

Valid thru 12/92. Void if detached.

Birthday or anniversary treat from our chef. On this special occasion, present this certificate and dessert is on us.

Cobble House Inn
PO Box 49
Gaysville VT 05746
(802)234-5458

Valid thru 12/92. Void if detached.

Stay 2 nights at our elegant circa 1829 country village inn and receive 1/2 off your third-night stay. Valid May through August during non-holidays.

The Andrie Rose Inn
13 Pleasant St
Ludlow VT 05149
(802)228-4846

Valid thru 12/92. Void if detached.

SKI FREE: Guests who have come to Ski Okemo, stay with us any four nights, purchase a four-day Okemo pass and we'll pay for one of those days. SUMMER VISITORS: June 1 to September 1, receive a $30 credit on your final bill.

The Governor's Inn
86 Main St
Ludlow VT 05149
(802)228-8830

Valid thru 12/92. Void if detached.

Celebrate your romantic anniversary at the inn with a complimentary bottle of champagne and this $10.00 gift certificate toward your second night's stay!

The Inn at Manchester
Box 41, Historic Rt 7A
Manchester Village VT 05254
(802)362-1793

Valid thru 12/92. Void if detached.

Complimentary bottle of wine with first night's dinner.

The Inn at Pittsfield
Rt 100 Box 675
Pittsfield VT 05762
(802)746-8943

Valid thru 12/92. Void if detached.

Stay two nights and the third night is free. Not valid holidays or foliage season.

The Inn at Blush Hill
Blush Hill Rd, PO Box 1266
Waterbury VT 05676
(802)244-7529

Valid thru 12/92. Void if detached.

20% discount Sunday through Thursday. 10% discount weekends. Not valid foliage season.

The Silver Fox Inn
Rt 133 Box 1222
West Rutland VT 05777
(802)438-5555

Valid thru 12/92. Void if detached.

Second night half price. Advance reservations required.

Piney Grove
Southall's Plantation
Rt 615 "Old Main Rd," Rt 1 Box 148
Charles City VA 23030
(804)829 2480

Valid thru 12/92. Void if detached.

1/2 price discount on second consecutive night stay from November 1 to March 31. Receive a 10% discount, Monday through Thursday from April 1 to September 30.

Fountain Hall B&B
609 S East St
Culpeper VA 22701
(703)825-8200

Valid thru 12/92. Void if detached.

Splendor for all seasons and a 10% discount for a two-night visit any Sunday through Thursday.

Caledonia Farm B&B
Rt 1 Box 2080
Flint Hill VA 22627
(703)675-3693

Valid thru 12/92. Void if detached.

$10 off two-night stay (Sunday through Thursday).

The Inn at Montross
Courthouse Sq
Montross VA 22520
(804)493-9097

Valid thru 12/92. Void if detached.

Honeymooners! Mention this certificate to "Williamsburg's most romantic" B&B when making your reservation. A charming gift ($20.00 value) will be waiting for you in your choice of our delightful rooms.

Liberty Rose Colonial B&B
1022 Jamestown Rd
Williamsburg VA 23185
(804)253-1260

Valid thru 12/92. Void if detached.

Free copy of Channel House Cookbook.

Channel House
2902 Oakes Ave
Anacortes WA 98221
(206)293-9382

Valid thru 12/92. Void if detached.

Explore the unique lower Columbia River during the beautiful winter months and visit the national game refuge nearby, with free entry to see deer, elk, bald eagles, wild geese and ducks and save 10% off our room rates from November to March, Sunday - Thursday inclusive.

Country Keeper B&B Inn
61 Main St, PO Box 35
Cathlamet WA 98612
(206)795-3030

Valid thru 12/92. Void if detached.

Take advantage of the off-season. 10% discount Sunday-Thursday, October-May. 10% discount two-night weekend, October-May.

The Victorian B&B
PO Box 761, 602 N Main
Coupeville WA 98239
(206)678-5305

Valid thru 12/92. Void if detached.

Privacy, Peace, Pampering. Present this certificate for a 10% discount on any stay for a romantic holiday. (Rates are seasonal and subject to change. Only one discount applies.)

Guest House B&B & Cottages
835 E Christenson Rd
Greenbank WA 98253
(206)678-3115

Valid thru 12/92. Void if detached.

Plan a great family or business party in Seattle! Take the whole mansion (6 bedrooms) for two or more consecutive weekdays from Nov. 1 - April 1, and enjoy an additional 10% discount (below our off-season rates!) on all rooms. Special-function amenities included. (Sunday - Thursday)

Chambered Nautilus B&B Inn
5005 22nd NE
Seattle WA 98105
(206)522-2536

Valid thru 12/92. Void if detached.

10% off regular rates for weekdays (Sunday through Thursday) stay of 2 or more days (excludes holiday periods October through April).

The Williams House
1505 Fourth Ave N
Seattle WA 98109
(206)285-0810

Valid thru 12/92. Void if detached.

European hospitality in the nation's capital: Receive a 25% discount off rack rates with this certificate and also receive a complimentary bottle of chilled champagne at either the Embassy Inn or Windsor Inn.

Embassy Inn
1627 16 St NW
Washington DC 20009
(202)234-7800

Valid thru 12/92. Void if detached.

European hospitality in the nation's capital: Receive a 25% discount off rack rates with this certificate and also receive a complimentary bottle of chilled champagne at either the Embassy Inn or Windsor Inn.

Windsor Inn
1842 16th St NW
Washington DC 20009
(202)667-0300

Valid thru 12/92. Void if detached.

$5.00 additional off low midweek rates. Room of your choice. Offer good Sunday through Thursday evenings anytime before July 4 or after Labor Day through October.

Harbor House Inn
12666 Hwy 42
Gills Rock WI 54210
(414)854-5196

Valid thru 12/92. Void if detached.

10% discount on midweek stays Monday through Thursday - when staying more than one night. Complimentary cookies, tea and cocoa nightly.

The Scofield House B&B
908 Michigan St, PO Box 761
Sturgeon Bay WI 54235
(414)743-7727

Valid thru 12/92. Void if detached.

Note: Please be sure to mention that you wish to use the Discount Certificate when making reservations. All offers are subject to availability. Discount offers may not apply at all times.

Always mention *The Offcial Guide to American Historic Inns* when making inquiries or reservations.

Certificates are not valid if removed from this book.

Innkeeper: Please sign the Discount Certificate when used.

Association of American Historic Inns

PO Box 336 Dana Point CA 92693 (714) 496-6953

Inn Evaluation Form

The Inn we visited: ______________________________

	A	B	C	D	F
Location for our needs					
Cleanliness					
Bathroom facilities					
Beds					
Attitude & Friendliness of host					
Food & Presentation					
Worth the price					

A = Outstanding
B = Good
C = Average
D = Needs to be improved
F = Disaster

Any comments on the above: ______________________________

____

I especially appreciated: ______________________________

____

Suggestions for improvement: ______________________________

____

Name (optional): ______________________________

Date of stay: ______________________________

Please COPY and complete this form for each stay and mail to the address above. Since 1981 we have maintained files that include thousands of evaluations by inn goers. We value your comments which help us to keep abreast of the hundreds of new inns that open each year and to follow the changes in established inns.

Thank you.

BOOKS ABOUT BED & BREAKFASTS AND COUNTRY INNS

To help you find the very best bed and breakfast and country inns, order one or more of these NEW bed and breakfast books, published by American Historic Inns, Inc.

The following titles are available from book stores everywhere.

THE BEST BED & BREAKFAST AND COUNTRY INNS SERIES

Produced by American Historic Inns, Inc. and Rand McNally Company.
Authors: Tim and Deborah Sakach

The four beautiful books in this series include the location of each inn marked on Rand McNally state road maps. Each Bed & Breakfast and Country Inn was carefully selected by the authors, Tim and Deborah Sakach, who have been visiting and photographing inns since 1981. Each of the four books is designed to fit easily into your glove compartment or travel bag. The four books are the most comprehensive regional guides available. Each book is $6.95.

The Best Bed & Breakfast and Country Inns — Northeast

Features 482 B&Bs, 250 illustrations and travel discount coupons worth more than $1,200. Rand McNally road maps pinpoint inn locations for Connecticut, Maine, Massachusetts, New Hampshire, New Jersey, New York, Pennsylvania, Rhode Island and Vermont. ISBN 0-528-90919-3 $6.95.

The Best Bed & Breakfast and Country Inns — South

Features 300 B&Bs, 150 illustrations, 32 pages of full-color maps, a comprehensive directory and FREE travel coupons worth more than $700. Rand McNally road maps pinpoint inns for Alabama, Arkansas, Delaware, Florida, Georgia, Kentucky, Louisiana, Maryland, Mississippi, North Carolina, Oklahoma, South Carolina, Tennessee, Texas, Virginia and West Virginia. ISBN 0-528-90921-5 $6.95.

The Best Bed & Breakfast and Country Inns — Midwest

Features 299 B&Bs, 150 illustrations, 30 pages of full-color maps, a comprehensive directory and FREE travel coupons worth more than $300. Rand McNally road maps pinpoint inns in Illinois, Indiana, Iowa, Kansas, Kentucky, Michigan, Minnesota, Missouri, Nebraska, North Dakota, Ohio, South Dakota and Wisconsin. ISBN 0-528-90920-7 $6.95.

The Best Bed & Breakfast and Country Inns — West

Features 321 B&Bs, 135 illustrations and a comprehensive directory to 1,200 inns and B&Bs with discount coupons worth more than $1,000. Rand McNally road maps pinpoint inns for Alaska, Arizona, California, Colorado, Hawaii, Idaho, Montana, Nevada, New Mexico, Oregon, Utah, Washington and Wyoming. ISBN 0-528-90922-3 $6.95.

THE OFFICIAL GUIDE TO AMERICAN HISTORIC INNS

by Tim and Deborah Sakach

This handsome book lists more than 6,000 historic inns & B&Bs with complete descriptions of more than 1,400. It contains more than 800 illustrations. All establishments are in buildings built in the 17th through early 20th centuries. The book contains travel discount coupons worth more than $2,000.

Twice awarded the Benjamin Franklin award:"Best Travel Guide," "Best Directory". Awarded "Best Travel Reference" by Travel Publishing News.

Recommended by ***McCalls, Changing Times, Woman's Day, Country Living, Library Journal, Los Angeles Times, Publisher's Weekly, USA Today, Washington Post*** and more.

The Official Guide to American Historic Inns has been selected for three years by Book-of-the-Month Club. Rated "Outstanding" by Morgan Rand ***Directory Reviews.***

ISBN 0-9615481-4-2

368 pages, Paperback, Full-color cover. $14.95

How to Start and Operate a Bed & Breakfast Inn

by Association of American Historic Inns

AVAILABLE ONLY FROM:
AMERICAN HISTORIC INNS, INC.
PO BOX 336
DANA POINT CA 92629

From the highly acclaimed seminar this book includes: How to find the right location. Pros and cons of buying, building or renovating. Marketing and managing your inn as a business. Includes day-to-day operating forms for reservations, daily, weekly and monthly duties, budget planning, registration. Includes appraisal forms and checklists for evaluating potential inns and includes sources of supplies and information on innkeeping. **$25.**